…c'est la vie!

An Autobiogra

By

Roy Robinson

A story of a young boy's experiences during World War II

Foster Care, Institutions and Adolescence

c'est la vie!

That's Life

c'est la vie

The true and moving story of the life of a boy, born into care.

****

1st Edition Printed and Published January 2012

ISBN no 978-0-9569275-3-8

****

Edited by Terry Roberts Nov 2011

Printed and Published

By

JTM Nuneaton

21 Thornhill Drive

Whitestone

Nuneaton CV11 6TD

Phone 02476 346545

Email: jtmnuneaton@hotmail.co.uk

****

Contents

Part One - Childhood

Part Two - The Later Years

By Terry Roberts
Adapted from an original manuscript

Part Three

Footnote to the Narrative by Roy Robinson - 2010

Appendices

c'est la vie

The Story of Roy Robinson

29th December 1931 to 6th August 2011

Dedication

This book is dedicated to The Children's Society in appreciation for the help and understanding given to myself and thousands of others in the search of their biological families.

****

The Children's Society

A short history since 1881.

The Children's Society has been a pioneer in the field of child care, offering professional support and a renewed sense of hope for thousands of children every year since it was founded in 1881 by ***Edward De Montjoie Rudolph,*** *a young Sunday School teacher and Civil Servant. It was while working at his Sunday School in South London that Rudolph formed the Children's Society.*

Worried when two young people failed to turn up for lessons, he set out to look for them and found them begging in the streets, He learned that their father had died and left their mother struggling to support seven children under the age of eleven. Social Security did not exist in Victorian England and Wales, and lest they could find some other way of supporting themselves, there was a danger the family would have to go into the workhouse, these places were squalid and over crowded, and families entering them were often split up.

Rudolph saw there was a need to help destitute children such as his pupils and he felt that the Church of England should lead the way, with this in mind he led a deputation to the |Archbishop of Canterbury to put forward a plan for a Church of England children's home. Archbishop Tait warmed to the idea, saying ***"If this thing is to be done, this man Rudolph is the man to do it. I have never heard a plan more admirably urged".***

Shortly afterwards, Rudolph's new organisation was registered as the ***Church of England Central Home for Waifs and Strays.*** *In 1893, it became the* ***Church of England Incorporated Society*** *for providing homes for Waifs and Strays.* *This changed again in 1946 to the* ***Church of England Children's Society,*** *and in 1982 it adopted the informal title of the* ***Children's Society****.*

Foreword

By Terry Roberts

Roy Robinson was born on 29th December 1931, the illegitimate child of a partially paralysed and highly strung mother, suffering from fits of mental depression, deserted by her husband and unable to cope with the responsibilities of raising a child. She was admitted into the County Institution at Sleaford, Lincolnshire following his birth, where she was maintained until her death in 1955.

Roy was taken into care from birth by Kesteven Local Authorities and adopted by Lincolnshire County Council on 10th April 1933 under the Poor Law Act of 1930. He was fostered out to the care of Mr and Mrs Barber of West St. Folkingham, having a happy and contented upbringing, attending the local C of E village school with average to good reports.

All this was to change. Mrs Barber died suddenly on 7th April 1944 and Roy was moved by the Council on 19th June to the Stamford Boys Home, a move which was to affect Roy for the rest of his life. Stamford Boys Home was an institute with a hard and dictatorial regime, run and directed by an ungiving and uncompassionate Matron and Superintendent. Roy could not settle, missing his village friends and his dog Rex, absconding from the home on several occasions to find his way back to Folkingham, only to be returned by the authorities back to Stamford. On 19th August 1944, after absconding for the 6th time, he was found by local Police, when, on being returned to Stamford, he ran away from under the noses of the compassionate policemen whilst on the doorstep of the Boys Home, sleeping rough before giving himself up to the care authorities, and was admitted into the Sleaford Public Institution Workhouse for Adults for temporary care, residing there until 30th October, when he was taken to St Michael's Boys Home at Guy's Cliffe. This proved to be the turning point in Roy's life. At Guy's Cliffe Roy found Friendship, Guidance, Respect and an acceptance of responsibilities. He became involved in All Saints Parish Church under the guidance of Rev Delanoy Saberton

After Guy's Cliffe closed in 1945 he was fostered, after a short stay in Emscote, to the Robin's family in Albert St. Leamington Spa. It took time for him to adjust, desperately missing the atmosphere and camaraderie of Guy's Cliffe. After leaving school, Roy started work as an apprentice painter & decorator. He became interested in music, took piano lessons, bought an accordion and sang solo with All Saints Church choir. National Service saw Roy conscripted into the RAF in 1951, serving at Cosford, Innsworth, St. Athan and Gibraltar. He trained & became a Culinary Technician until his return to Civvy Street in 1953. After taking a number of jobs, he qualified as a teacher for the Mentally Handicapped, obtaining a diploma after training at Bournemouth College. After practical experience at Chelmsley Hospital, followed by 9 years at Stratford on Avon, Roy was placed in charge of Speech Therapy in Warwick, becoming Deputy Officer at a residential home, serving 5 years prior to taking early retirement.

He became involved in voluntary work, starting a Youth Club and Drama group at All Saints church in Emscote, and a table tennis coach, running four teams at Lillington for 17 years, and personally reaching National coaching level.

Roy was extremely thankful for the assistance given to him by the Children's Society in London, in tracing his parentage & providing documentary evidence.

Sadly Roy died Saturday 6th August this year without family or next of kin.

Terry Roberts

November 2011

One

Introduction

Memory is not always the truest of friends, just when we think we have remembered about some special day, we forget some small detail that means so much when we are reminded of it. Likewise, we often remember events that happened to us as children, as if they took place only yesterday, while completely overlooking events in the news, or things that were said only a month ago. Our earliest memories tend to be strange, abstract images, coloured by the simplicity of our infancy, and almost impenetrable to us as adults. Mine happen to be just that.

Roy Robinson - 2007

Two

The Early Years

Enter Me and Miss Shee. BEM

The very first image I can recall is of a very small hole in the floor of the car in which I was travelling. I watched the hole, fascinated by the blur of the tarmac below as we sped along. Thankfully the hole was not growing any larger, if it was I would have been too young at the age of four to be alarmed. I kept looking down towards it as if it held me in a kind of spell. As I watched the ground beneath rushing by, I felt borne aloft, urged onwards by beautiful breath-taking speed. To where, I could not say.

As the car slowed down to a walking pace I looked down again, and was surprised to find I could pick out all the different patterns on the road large and small stones, and some appeared to glisten. Then, in places, the road seemed to be dark, and less bumpy. Now and again I could just make out small patches of white through the hole as the car moved regally from side to side. The road surface would pass by much faster, and become blurred again as the car accelerated. When the car came to a complete halt, I was able to see small drops of liquid, oval in shape on the ground. Onwards we moved and I began to feel drowsy. Suddenly, my slumber was halted as we swerved round an object in the road. Again I came to regard this small hole but could find nothing different or exceptional therein.

As a handy alternative, I turned to look at the lady sat beside me. She would have been in her thirties though of course I had no concept of this at the time. She was slim, and wore a dark coloured fur coat, her hair, or what could be seen of it beneath her hat was almost black, cut short, and clung in tight curls to the sides of her slim face. She wore very little make-up. With brown-kid-gloved-hands she held the steering wheel. She looked straight-ahead not saying a word to me though occasionally she would glance towards me, and her face would light up with a little smile. Eventually the car stopped outside a row of ten, very old, semi-detached cottages. The lady stepped smartly out of the car, and took out a small suitcase from the boot. Then, having opened the door on my side of the car, she took my little hand in hers. I was surprised how tall she looked. It was then that she spoke to me for the first time.

"We're here now; this is your new home," she said before leading me round to the rear of the house to find its only door. The lady who opened the door was much older than the lady holding my hand. She wore a very pretty apron with a flowery pattern. She beamed down at me, and then turned to the lady still holding my hand. "Come in she said," still smiling. "I've got the kettle on. Would you like a cup of tea? "That's nice, thank you very much Mrs. Barber," she answered. As she handed over my suitcase she continued. "I am sorry I can't stay too long, as I have to get back to my office."

My escort, Miss Shee was the children's officer, for Kesteven in South Lincolnshire. Apparently she was a very busy person, and had responsibility for all the children assigned to her care. Her brief included the fostering and supervision of children in the county and private foster homes. Having finished her cup of tea and the formalities of the fostering procedure were over, she promptly rose to her feet, and smiling at Mrs. Barber she said, "I must take my leave now, thank you very much for the tea. It was very nice."
Miss Shee retired in the 1960 she was awarded the OBE and BEM for her work with children. She died at Portsmouth in the 1980s.

Strangely enough she is the first person that I can recall before I was fostered with the Barber's. Being four years old I had no recollection of where I had been or if I had been fostered before this particular day. All I do know is that I was born in the hospital wing of the Grantham workhouse which was situated in the Dysart Road. Prior to this foster home, this is one part of my early life that I would love to have more knowledge, for example was I fostered with aunts, uncles or with my grandmother? (I will write of this later). Mrs. Barber, holding the teapot aloft added. *" Would you like another cup of tea before you leave"?*

Grantham's old workhouse ...

ABOVE and BELOW: Hill View Hospital, and former work house, demolished in 1970.
Photograph courtesy of Malcolm G. Knapp.

HILL View Hospital, originally the town's workhouse, was built in the 1890s.

It was the place where vagrants and wayward girls were sent and had to work by scrubbing floors or chopping wood to earn their keep.

It became a maternity hospital and later an overflow for Grantham Hospital maternity unit, where mums went to convalesce after giving birth.

It was demolished in 1971 to make way for Harrison House.

The Old Grantham Workhouse, Dysart Road where I was born.

"No thank you all the same." She then checked her wrist watch by the ornate wooden clock hanging above the mantel shelf. "*It's getting late. I really must be off I have an important meeting to attend when I get back to my office."* Checking to see that she had not left behind she looked down at me, smiled, then shook Mrs. Barber's hand, and said. *"Goodbye, I will call very soon to see how Roy is settling in.*" She swept through the kitchen door and was on her way to her urgent engagement.

I gazed around me in amazement, and I saw a door that was partly open which led to another room. I could just see the end of an oval shaped table. It was made of lightly coloured wood, and was very highly polished. It had a flowery pattern with golden lines running around the top surface.

Mrs. Barber smiled at me and said. "*You can call me Aunt Nin and when my husband comes home from work you can call him Uncle Alf."*

She could see I was curious about the other room so she took me by my hand, and led me through the door. Quietly she spoke. *"This is our front room. In here you will be able to have your friends come, and play with you. You would like that wouldn't you?"*

The room was quite small. The oval shaped table stood in the centre. There was an open fireplace, and on the mantelshelf stood two matching small ornate brass cannon shell cases. No doubt these were relics from the First World War they were of highly polished brass, and had serrated tops.

There was a large aspidistra plant in an equally large ornate vase on the windowsill. The windows had small square panes, and were draped with green curtains matching the thick carpet. Two highly polished chairs stood either side of the fireplace.

She took me back into the kitchen that she called the parlour. Here, the open fire had an oven at each side, and a kettle hanging on a hook that was suspended from the chimney breast. A table stood in the centre of the kitchen surrounded by four farmhouse chairs. A little wooden stool nestled by the fire. Pots, and pans hung from the tall mantel shelf above the range, and in the hearth stood a copper coal scuttle complete with hand brush, and shovel. The range was of solid iron, shiny black, no doubt due to plenty of elbow grease with black lead polish. The oven doors were engraved with embossed floral patterns, and had large highly polished brass handles. Sepia coloured photographs in dark wooden frames adorned the walls, and one very large coloured photograph, in an equally large frame was a portrait of a sailor, wearing a broad smile, with arms folded in a candid confident manner. Brass horse badges hung on leather straps by the side of the fireplace, and sparkled in the summer sunlight streaming through the parlour window.

Aunt Nin was nearly fifty years old. She was about five, and a half feet tall, fairly slim, and had a very fair complexion, and an attractive face. She spoke with a quite husky voice and she only required the use of spectacles for reading purposes.

Aunt Nin 1920

No. 3 West Street, My first foster home in Folkingham

Leading off from the parlour door gave access to the stairs, and the three bedrooms above. There was no bathroom, inside toilet or running water. She took me outside to have a look around the garden. Outside an earth toilet was situated with two holes in the wooden plank that served as the seat. One hole larger than the other; the smaller opening no doubt was for the use of little children, who had to be very careful to select the correct orifice, lest they were to vanish out of sight with dire consequences. On the inside of the toilet door, and threaded through a length of string hung squares of newspaper. Adjacent to the toilet was the wash house; a hand pump was situated here where rainwater could be drawn from a well located in the backyard.

"Now you will be very careful when you go to the toilet, we don't want to be fishing you out of there in a hurry." Aunt Nin advised. Like all the other nine cottages in the street there was a long garden complete with a shed. Leaning here against the shed was a motley set of garden tools. "Don't put your fingers through the gaps in the wood." Aunt Nin anxiously warned me as with wide eyes. I eagerly, but timidly approached the pig sty. One enormous snorting resident occupied the sty, and completing this outdoor ambience was a chicken run with many bantams scuttling about, closely guarded by a strutting cock bird.

For me, not quite four years old, this was to be my home. At first I was quite bewildered by the surroundings, and circumstances. How could I, with a four year-old mind, and emotions interpret all the happenings? It was all very odd. The travelling had a wearying effect on me and I soon dozed off to sleep in one of the farmhouse chairs. I was woken up to the sounds of Mr. Barber entering the house. The first thing I noticed was that he had a slight limp. He was a portly little man, standing about five, and- a- half- feet tall, with a ruddy outdoor complexion. He would be about fifty years old, and had short-cropped grey hair. A silver watch chain hung from his waistcoat pocket. Specks of mud splattered his puttees, and his hob-nailed boots. He peered down at me with a curious squint, I was still only half-awake, and then a large smile spread across his face. *"Hello, so you're Roy, and you've come to live with us?"*

Very nervously I replied. *"Yes."* I thought this must be Mr. Barber.

"Have you had anything to eat?" He asked me.

"Yes, plenty of homemade jam tarts, and cakes." Aunt Nin cut in, and then she decided it was time for me to go to bed. The bedroom was quite small, and was situated at the side of the house. On the walls hung floral patterned wallpaper a small single bed was draped with a blue counterpane, and a chest of drawers stood close to the small window which overlooked the next block of semi-detached cottages. Looking out of the window, the raucous sound of rooks could be heard in the tall poplar trees in the vicarage grounds. From the chest of drawers she took out a pair of pajamas, while I was putting them on, she brought me a mug of milk. Then having tucked me up in bed she gave me a kiss, and said. *"Goodnight, sleep well, and I'll see you in the morning."*

This was my first foster home that I recall, living with the Barbers in the village of Folkingham, and in the county of Lincoln. I did not need any rocking, and within seconds of my head touching the pillow, I was fast asleep.

This village of Folkingham with its row of ten small semi-detached cottages that occupied only one side of the main road, the other side being free of buildings, composed entirely of grassy fields, and open spaces. In the distance, small hills rose to greet the sunrise. Below them, green banks of hedges, and vegetation thrived, and tall trees with mighty branches swayed in the breeze. As if a traveller, you were passing through this scenic backdrop to my early life, and chose to travel north along the road out of the village, you would soon come across isolated farms, and winding lanes leading to other outposts of human life. Heaven knows how long they had been there; there was a real sense of walking along paths travelled many times by lives that had passed before. Around us were other similarly scenic undisturbed villages.

The Village at Folkingham

To the North of Folkingham lay Pickworth and Walcot with Lenton and Aslackby to the south. Folkingham lies on the A15 main road between Bourne, and Sleaford. At the brow of the hill in the village, there is a large Market Square that witnessed many trade fairs, during the eighteenth century. Just north of the Market Square stands the eighteenth century Greyhound Inn, once a busy staging post in the days of the horse-drawn stagecoaches, and is reputed to be haunted. The Inn looks down the hill towards a fine seventeenth century manor house. The fifteenth century church of St Andrew, with its very a large tower stands majestically to the north west of the Market Square and dominates the skyline for miles around. The church housed prisoners of war captured by Marshall Schomberg in 1689. The church suffered the collapse of two pinnacles during the 2007 storms.

The Rev Edward Bradley, one time priest in the village, wrote 'Verdant Green', under the pen name of Cuthbert Bede.

Along the Billingborough Road, leading out of the village, the facade of the original House of Correction still stands on the site of an ancient castle. When the main part of the building was demolished residential dwellings were erected behind the facade.

Lincolnshire boasts some notable personages. John Wesley, founder of Methodism, was born at Epworth in 1703. Alfred Lord Tennyson in 1809 was born at Somerby. In 1895 the musician Sir Malcolm Sergeant was born in the south of the county at Stamford, and in more recent times, Lady Margaret Thatcher was born at Grantham. This incidentally was my birthplace. In 1643 Sir Isaac Newton was born at Woolsthorpe-by-Colsterworth, and died in 1727 at Kensington, London. Probably one of the finest examples of early Gothic architecture in England is the magnificent Lincoln Cathedral. The twelfth-century bridge in Lincoln is the oldest of its kind to still have buildings standing upon its foundations. In the middle Ages, Lincoln, standing by the river Witham, was a busy industrial city at the height of the wool trade.

The very fine, and interesting town of Boston, and the parish church of Saint Botolph with its magnificent tower, nicknamed Boston Stump, can be seen for miles around in the fen country side, and acts as a beacon for sailors out in the Wash. Among the towns of Stamford, Louth, and the city of Lincoln, the town of Grantham is one of the few to be mentioned in the Doomsday Book. In Nicolas Nickleby, Dickens said of the George Inn at Grantham "it being one of the best in England." The George Inn stands in the High Street, and boasts a fine facade. Grantham was a busy coaching stop in the height of the horse-drawn coaching era. At a staging point at the bottom of Great Gonnerby hill, about a mile from Grantham, the horses struggled, and discovered the going very difficult to maintain momentum. To reach the top an extra team of horses would be added. Harlexton Manor near Grantham is one of the largest in the country.

Stamford is a very picturesque town, and has a similarity to Cotswold stonework. At one time it boasted as many as sixteen churches. One of these places of worship now houses a supermarket. Until recent times Stamford stood on the great North Road, now the town has a bypass. It was a very important place in the coaching period. It is alleged that in those days there were no fewer than sixty-five public houses in the town, no doubt keeping the wayfarers very happy.

Probably, one of the oldest publications of its kind originated in Stamford was called The Stamford Mercury. The publisher was a Richard Newcomb. Richard Newcomb hailed from Billingborough, which is three miles from Folkingham.

****

"Hello, who have we here?" I looked up, and saw that a large fellow had put this question to me. It was the bright shiny buckle on his belt that first caught my interest. Standing there, this large man in a similarly large black uniform beamed down at me, merriment turning up the corners of his mouth, and dancing all over his generous features. On his uniform he sported a series of silvery buttons which gleamed in the sunlight. He towered over me, and scrutinised my little form, maintaining a cheerful expression on his weathered face. I think you must be lost young man," he chuckled. I was not able to utter a word as the large form that towered over me, took me by my hand, and led me off bemused.

Aunt Nin stood on the doorstep with a relieved expression abounding over her face. *"I hadn't any idea that he had gone, Mr. Holland. I only turned my back for a second or two, and he had vanished. Where did you find him?"*

"Only a little way down the road, sitting by the first gate along the lane; he didn't seem frightened at all." He

looked down at me. *"We'll have to keep an eye on you young fellow."* He smiled at Aunt Nin. *"You appear to have your hands full Mrs. Barber.*

With a tone of relief ringing in her voice, she said, *"Mr Holland I am most grateful to you,"*

With a cheerful wave and whistling, the village policeman strode off down the road. In a childlike dream no doubt, I had wandered away from my first foster home. It seemed to be worth the exertion because everyone was pleased to see me returned back safely. Was this action on my part the harbinger of things to come?

****

"Now you sit as still as possible!" Lucy the village milkmaid cried as she struggled to pedal her cycle, with its squeaking cart loaded with milk churns. She was on her daily door to door delivery of milk. *"If you keep shunting around like that you have me off, and milk all over the road!"*

Wedged between the rattling milk churns, I held on, I was determined not to be tipped out. "*I am sitting as still as I can but you wobble too much. I can't help shifting about,"* I shouted back.

Not yet old enough to start school, Lucy would take me round in her milk cart. When not engaged on these excursions I would amuse myself, with bucket in hand, knocking on neighbouring doors crying out *" Any milk today Madam" "No thank you. I have enough for today. Tomorrow perhaps,"* was the usual reply I received.

Sometimes, to humour me, people would say. "*Yes I'll have just half a pint today.*" Then with ladle in hand I would scoop out water from my bucket, and pour it into a jug that she had brought to the door. Having proffered my wares, she would then offer me a farthing, and if I was fortunate, sometimes a halfpenny.

Amusing myself by painting Uncle Alf's garden shed with water, was another way of passing the hours away before starting school life at the age of five.

When the day arrived, Aunt Nin escorted me to the village school that was quite close to our house. Although at the time it seemed a very long trek indeed. Lucy would sometimes take me to the school in her milk cart. Eventually, I grew confident, and would trundle on with the other children. Our little world of Folkingham was perfectly self-contained. No one had any reason to suspect it would ever be different. Sometimes we very young children would play with a whip and top as we wandered on our way to school each morning. Occasionally we would be responsible for breaking the odd window in the process. There were mainly two classifications of these spinning-tops, both being made of wood with a metal insert at the bottom to lessen the wear. Of course the design of the top made a big difference to the individual performance, and owning the smartest one was the subject of much competition, and rivalry. One was shaped like a mushroom, and never traveled as far or as fast as the other model. This superior design was modeled like a very thick stumpy carrot, and could be lethal to any unsuspecting being, or as it usually turned out, a window. To own one of these monsters was a matter of great prestige. While your top-spinning peers held you in respect, the adult population took a more cynical view of the proceedings.

Another mundane piece of school-journey accompaniment was a large metal hoop that was propelled along by holding a metal version of a shepherd's crook connected to the hoop as you pushed it along. These metal-wheeled monsters were almost the height of a small child, and sometimes they would get out of control, and be very difficult to handle.

"You go and get it," John shouted at me, as we watched his hoop careering down the hill, and finally coming to rest inside the doorway of the butcher's shop.

I protested, "*I'm not going in there again. I always upset the butcher whenever I go near him, just because one day I told him I didn't like his meat."*

"You know I don't like going in there no more than you do," John moaned.

"*Oh, alright then; I suppose I'd better,"* I replied reluctantly.

"Thanks, I knew you would Roy," John replied, thankful he would not have to endure the wrath of the butcher. John was about my age, and lived two doors away from my house. He was a nephew of my foster parents. This was a regular occurrence when we bowled our hoops to school. This practice soon came to a halt when the butcher protested strongly to the school's head teacher.

The scooter, which was propelled along by one foot, was another means of traversing to school, this mode of transport was not very popular with some parents due to one shoe wearing out long before the other. Hopscotch was another game we toyed with on the way to school, and skipping from one paving slab to another, without landing on a crack, because if you managed to put a foot on a joint in the slabs, it was considered very unlucky indeed. This game never failed to please us. Empty golden syrup tins (that is if one could require golden syrup in those days) or some similar tin, could be used as miniature stilts. By turning the tin upside down, and piercing holes in the bottom, then threading a long piece of string through the holes in each tin, and making a loop longing enough to reach each hand. One would step on each tin, and holding the lengths of string in each hand, could merrily walk along by pulling on the two strings in turn, lifting up each foot to proceed onwards to school. The village infant school teacher was very tolerant; she would find lodging space for our play paraphernalia somewhere on the school premises. Nevertheless, if we were late arriving at school, this privilege would be withdrawn, and our playthings would have to remain at home. The school had only two classrooms. One for infants, the other for seniors.

My infant school days were very exciting down to the enormous imagination on the part of our infant class teacher. She would organise nature walks in the afternoon. Exhausted, when we arrived back at the school, we were allowed to put our heads down on our desk, and nod off to sleep. I loved those innocent sleepy days of green fields, fresh air, classroom tales, and toys, and soon came to miss them. The school still stands at the bottom of the hill in the village. In the last few decades it has taken on housing varying business ventures. A craft centre, offices for social services organisations, and the like.

There was no resident dentist in the village so periodically a large mobile dental clinic would arrive, it would park in the middle of the Market Square and stay there until the dentist had inspected, and treated all the children. The drill that the dentist employed was a very antiquated piece of equipment that was driven via a foot treadle. As ancient as this drill may have been, plus the quality of workmanship in those days, I had still one tooth filling intact thirty years after I had visited this dentist. All too quickly, I outgrew these joyful infant school days, and was put into the senior class. Not being practically minded towards schoolwork, and academic pursuits I soon fell behind, and was derided for it.

The simple happiness of yesterday was slowly eroded. I was not at all happy and began to feel out of my depth, swimming against a strong current that I could not master. I had not been asked to sit any exams to move up into the senior class, I was simply transferred when I was deemed old enough, regardless of my ability-or lack of it-in class. Above all else I missed our delightful infant school mistress. I suppose in a small uninformed and utterly boyish way, I had developed a silly crush on her. For all my misgivings there is no doubt that the headmaster of the senior school was a good, and conscientious teacher, he succeeded in getting many children scholarships into Sleaford Grammar School. There was a local bus service based in the village the proprietor being a Mr. King. The service would take pupils from the village to the grammar school. On most days the vehicle would complete many trips to, and from the village to places like Grantham, and Boston, collecting passengers en route. One bizarre quirk of the times was that the proprietor of the local bus service was not allowed to depart for Grantham or other destinations until the more important 'Lincolnshire Green' bus had first passed through the village. To this day I believe there is still this service based in the village. There was one trip taken by Mr. King's transport that I shall never forget. It was to the Royal Estate at Sandringham House in Norfolk. Aunt Nin had a relative employed there, and she had been invited to a function. What the function was all about at that time I am not clear? I remember standing in the driveway as if on parade awaiting inspection, as a processing of grand looking, elegant dressed people passed by. One man in particular caught my eye, he was very imposing, he wore a homburg hat, and he had an immaculate cut beard plus a similarly magnificent drooping moustache. I believe it was no less a personage than King George V. Aunt Nin had other relatives in the surrounding villages, and she would take me on this mode transport when she ventured a visit. One relative lived in a large white roundhouse with Gothic windows, and a thatched roof. This was the Tollhouse near Sutterton roughly about twelve miles from Folkingham.

One very windy day she decided to take me to Sleaford. We sat in the rear of the bus, giving us a panoramic view out of the rear window. Having just overtaken the village postman, who cycling with his head well tucked down over the handlebars, pedaling hard against the strong wind. A little further on, the bus had to make a stop to pick up some more passengers. This gave time for the postman to catch up, and because his head was still stooped over the handlebars, and bracing himself against the elements, he had failed to notice that the bus had stopped, and ran straight into the rear, causing the peak of his cap to crunch, and get wedged tightly into the top of his coat. I witnessed this incident with great excitement though I was happy to find out later that he eventually recovered from his rather embarrassing ordeal. As I grew older the activities at school began to make more sense to me. Like in any other school there were times when a certain amount of bullying occurred, fortunately it was never anything serious. One group of boys found it amusing to pull a jacket tightly over the heads of other boys. I hated it when it was my unfortunate turn to fall victim to this rather silly practice, because it was very claustrophobic, and one had difficulty breathing. This bullying did not occur very often, and was never allowed to get out of hand. The day arrived when our present schoolmaster retired. During his time at Folkingham he had done an excellent job with the pupils.

Canon Valentine Heath vicar of the parish, who was wheelchair-bound, was a very handsome man in his sixties, with a flock of silver curly hair, and was always smartly dressed in a grey pinstriped suit. Normally wearing a grey trilby hat, but on warm summer days he could be seen sporting a Panama hat, he would give a cheery wave with his walking stick as he propelled himself along in his wheelchair.

At the headmaster's retirement function, Canon Heath addressed the gathering with a lengthy speech as long as his habitual sermons in church on Sundays. Other dignitaries spoke of the headmaster's, good and faithful service during his period at the school. The proceedings then moved to the presentation of a very large clock, and the evening closed, with what we children in anticipation had been waiting for, the bun-fight. The Second World War, still in its cold period, and not yet loomed upon us so there was plenty to eat for all. When the official proceedings were over, and the faithful ladies catering band, were busy serving the refreshments there was much small talk amongst the gathered assembly. Scrutinising all the proceedings from a discreet distance in the hall, the newly appointed head of the school was eyeing us children with an air of great suspicion We made sure that she didn't catch our eyes. Little did she know she was also being closely observed, be it somewhat with downcast instruments of vision by us children?

We speculated what she would be like as we chatted amongst ourselves. She looked very stern and very old-fashioned. Her keen eyes darted all around the hall, not resting for many seconds on any particular person or object. It was a little disturbing to say the least, and we were going to miss out retiring headmaster.

Three

Village School

Enter Mrs. Lees

It was a distinctive facial tic that was the course of much fascination, and hilarity for all of us children, until we became accustomed to it. This twitch could be so pronounced it often caused the chains the spectacles to audibly rattle. The owner of this undesirable affliction was the new head of school, Mrs. Lees. This lady was in her fifties, and was married to the village carpenter. She was stout in build, and dressed in rather old-fashioned clothes, and was always seen sporting a brown, pork-pie style hat and thick brogue shoes. She appeared to be the do-it-yourself type of person, and apparently made all her own, and husband's clothes.

Her first meeting with the parents, her businesslike manner manifested itself, and there was no doubt, that she would instill this straight into us unsuspecting scholars, once she took command of the helm. From the onset, it was apparent she was very determined to be involved in the village way of life and it wasn't long before she managed to cajole the parents into purchasing a wireless set for the school. Some characters in the village eyed her with resolute suspicion. But like most newcomers to village life she was not deemed popular with some of the natives. Later on, people postulated that she was well below par, and nowhere near the standard of the previous head master.

Mrs. Lees was always abreast of current affairs, and one day, before the new wireless set arrived at the school, she took the entire class to her house which was east of the Market Square, and listen to the launching of the Queen Elizabeth 1st ocean liner. Those of us, whom were powerless to get into her living room, where the wireless set was situated, were crammed into the hall. We strained out ears to listen what was being said but all we could hear was a lot of cheering, obviously from the crowd witnessing the spectacle of the launch.

When, eventually the new wireless set arrived it was a proud moment for all and it opened up a whole new meaning to our very basic school curriculum with many fascinating programmes for us to listen to. One interesting project was called, 'Exploring your own village history'. There were programmes, and current affairs, social history, life in the Stone Age and the like. Having an artistic intellect, Mrs. Lees soon got to grips by writing, and producing plays for the class. We launched ourselves into these sagas with verve and gusto. One day a very smart gentleman arrived at the school. Mrs. Lees introduced him to the class, and it was none other than, Ted Kavanagh who was involved with the popular radio comedy show of the day, 'ITMA', 'It's That Man Again', the half-hour radio comedy series. Tommy Handly the radio comedian was 'That Man Again', aided by Jack Train playing 'Colonel Chinstrap' Dorothy Summers as 'Mrs. Mop', and Derek Guyler who played many more of the characters in this amusing production.

The school had its own gardens, just a little way outside of the village. A half-day would be spent working on the plot. The produce was sold to the local stores. Some of this harvest would find its way to the Sleaford market. The local residents also had the opportunity to purchase the results of our hard-won efforts.

Folkingham Village School

****

A particular Sunday will be marked forever in other people's minds, and mine. It was September the third 1939 the day Britain declared war on Germany. We didn't possess a wireless set at home so the first we heard about the war, was when our next-door neighbour came rushing in to expound the news. There was excitement followed by worried expressions especially by the adults. Of course, 1940 embroiled Britain in the war. Goering's Luftwaffe did their best to curtail merchant shipping to England's seaports, and consequently food became very scarce. With rationing now considered being a normal spoke in the wheel of everyday life, everyone was encouraged to start digging for victory, and sure enough Mrs. Lees with an air of national obsequiousness, accelerated us all into action, and thus our school played its part.

An amusing incident took place one Sunday afternoon when a gang of us boys, with nothing better to do, decided to wander around the school allotment. As we joked about, one lad pretended to cut off a prized-sized marrow at its roots. Not realising he was simply pretending, I took out my pocket knife, and cut one off for real. The other boys had no intention of damaging the crop and looked at me in horror, as I held aloft my trophy. The wrath of the headmistress suddenly seemed very real, and very near. I was terrified she would find out what I had done, probably from one of the other lads, and I stayed away from school the next day pretending to be ill. Sadly and not realising the full implications of my actions, this was just the first in a series of crop vandalism actions on my part. On another Sunday afternoon our gang came upon a plot of land this time belonging to a local pig farmer. This particular acreage was used to grow beans, which the farmer fed to his pigs. To us it looked as if the crop had been left to go to seed, unwanted, abandoned, and sadly forgotten. With that in mind we took especial pleasure in flattening the entire site. My activities did not go unreported. The very next day, when I came home from school for lunch, the village policeman was standing on our doorstep with a very severe expression on his face. The punishment, besides loss of pocket money, which was bad enough, was to labour on this poor man's plot until the damage was made good. The erecting upright of the depleted crop took us one entire evening, and was no easy assignment, nor was the task of erecting the crop possible. We were also administered six of the best from Mrs. Lees with her trusty rod when next we returned to school.

Indirectly tramping of the allotment led to our next fiendish scheme. And we received a fair pasting from headmistresses again. We concluded that she was over enthusiastic when it came to doling out this type of retribution. Immediately we resolved to do something about it. After a lunch break and nipping back early to school our golden opportunity arose. She had left the cupboard unlocked that housed her terrifying arsenal of canes. These implements of terror were of varying lengths, and thickness, and of pain rendering capability, in order to match the punishment to the crime. We grabbed all six of them, and racked our brains for an imaginative way to dispose of them. We opted to bend then up, small enough to conceal them under our jackets, sneak them out before she returned from lunch, and then bury them beneath the village hut. Upon discovering the grievous crime, she was predictably furious, and lined everyone up in front of her desk. The bid was to shame the culprits into submission. After a few moments of stalemate to our utter amazement, she rested her head on her desk, and began to cry. This apparently ludicrous situation began to strike me as funny. I began smirking, and tittering. Needless to say, this irreverent attitude stung the lady into further fury. On observing my reckless frivolity, she pounced on me with the startling immediacy of a caged tiger. Grabbing me by the stuff of my neck she frog-marched me home. Once home, I received a jolly good hiding, and worse was to come. Having replaced the purloined canes with another devilish set, she set about us with a vengeance.

After this incident I made the mistake of adding slander to my growing list of sins. In the local confectionery shop I was overheard calling Mrs. Lees a series of uncomplimentary names. This slur was duly disclosed to the lady in question, and before I knew it I was in close arrest in class, and writing out the following lines five hundred times. 'Thou shalt keep thy tongue from speaking evil, and thy lips shall speak no guile.' Needless to say, the only profitable step as far as I was concerned to benefit me from this punishment, was I never had trouble spelling the words ' tongue ,' and 'guile' ever again. I was, beyond any doubt, a mischief-maker, or as it was said in those times, a 'marked boy'.

A coal-fired stove that stood close by our head teacher's desk provided the school heating in those days. On the top of the stove stood a container holding water, and modelled something like an upturned tortoise. The water in this reservoir was to supply a certain amount of humidity to the classroom. The fuel for the stove was kept outside in the coalhouse situated in a corner of the playground. Until now, I had never been aware that the coalhouse ever needed to be cleaned out. Suddenly, now the job had to be undertaken, post haste. Being a 'marked boy' the task of cleaning out this filthy place fell upon me. With choking black clouds of dust flying all around this was a singularly unpleasant job, and some would say "deservedly so."

In order to ease the burden of the housekeeping, Aunt Nin undertook, on a part-time basis, domestic work for Mrs. Lees. In an amazing act of courage, I threatened the teacher that my aunt would not be doing any more work for her if she continued to make me clean out the bloody school coalhouse. This certainly was not a wise move. I was in trouble again, this time for having the assertiveness to speak in such a manner to the teacher. The next day I conveniently fell ill again.

In those days, the vicar, the village squire and the head teacher were highly respected figures of society, and actually wielded a great amount of influence in how the village affairs were conducted. By falling foul of Mrs. Lees, I had clearly not got off to the best of starts in life. Occasionally we would have a sports afternoon, and it was amusing to note the extent our school head would get involved. As we attempted to play football in one of the farmer's fields close by, dodging the cowpats in the process, it was an astonishing, and ultimately hilarious sight to see her charging down the field shouting extremely vague instructions. Wearing her porkpie style hat and with her overcoat bellowing in the wind she would yell. "Kick the ball harder!" She didn't appear to have any concept in which direction the ball should traverse so long as it flew in the general direction, and was kicked, and kicked hard. As a consequence we all tended to descend on the ball in one unruly kicking mob. It was muddy madness, and cowpats would fly in all directions.

Cricket was also played in the same farmer's field. Being a 'marked boy', and according to Mrs. Lees, I was not allowed to bat. I felt pretty aggrieved, this being the most accelerating part of the game in my boy's opinion, and most cricket-loving lads probably would agree. However, I did have one consolation, on one occasion I managed to clean bowl Mrs. Lees. I was delighted to see the bails flying high through the air. She always demanded to bat first, and strangely enough, she always won the toss, and her team always batted first. She herself always opened the batting. It was not long before some of the boys caught on to her ploy, and thought up a devilishly mean scheme to play a trick on her whenever possible. On one such occasion, when she was due to take the bat, some of the boys took great efforts to make sure they placed the cricket stumps adjacent to an offending cowpat. There was little chance of anyone else falling into the devilish plot since only one person batted at a time. All was set. The bowler had been instructed to pitch the ball quite short, and as close as possible to the cowpat. Knowing that Mrs. Lees would have to move down the wicket to reach the ball, It was very unlikely, that in the urgency, to encounter the ball, all her concentration would be focused on the oncoming projectile; she would fail to notice the offending object just in front of her. With a great swipe at the ball showered fragments of the cowpat in all directions, splattering any unfortunate player who had not had the foresight to take the precaution to widen his fielding positions. This particular stratagem didn't last for very long. She soon caught on that something was wrong but never disclosed her hypothesis, and eventually she gave up batting altogether. This meant that cricket wasn't so popular a recreation, and rarely appeared on the school curriculum.

There came a time when I actually had a very good reason to be most grateful to my nemesis. A war aid drive had been organised by the school. It was early November, and we were picking rosehips. The collection of these berries would be sent away, and turned into the well-known seller, Rosehip Syrup. On one of these occasions, I had scratched the palm of my right hand on a particular vicious looking thorn that had clearly evaded capture. This wound turned out to be very nasty indeed, and eventually became severely septic. I had it dressed in the usual manner but it throbbed consistently, was very stubborn to heal. It was a very long time before I gained the use of my right hand. I remember the headmistress checking the wound daily placing more kaolin poultices over it and using suspiciously generous amounts of Dettol. Alas, the very best efforts of Reichsmarshal Goring to curtail our essential supplies of Dettol had failed. Despite the pain she was resolute I kept my hand as mobile as possible. She would constantly harass me on this subject, her main ruse being that if I failed to exercise the injured hand frequently, I could expect the poison to infiltrate other parts of my anatomy starting with my right arm. This, she said, this would be the first sign that I would have to have the rotten hand amputated. For all I know she may have been correct.

At the very trough of my misery I had no feeling in my hand at all. I knew her methods had succeeded when my palm began to itch, and I started to regain some feeling. Soon there came alleviation from the pain, and I knew I was on the mend. Mrs. Lees would expose us to good music, and she gave us lessons in the art and craft of the beauty of music. But before we were let loose on any songs she demanded the best, and was not to be the subject of crude renderings, we were at first obliged to go through the ritual of breath control exercises. She would display the music score on a very large sheet of paper, this she would drape over the black board. On this sheet there was the musical staff, with the various notes displayed. For rhythm practice, we would have to sing taffy tar tar taffy tar tar as she pointed to the notes on the sheet. When she was fully satisfied that we had accomplished to her satisfaction, a reasonable degree of tone, rhythm, and theory competence. Then, finally we would be allowed to sing songs that were mainly of a patriotic nature including selections from Edward German's *'Merrie England'*. One aria from his Operetta, *'The Yeomen of England'*, gave us ample opportunity to sing out loud in a very raucous vogue, hopelessly out of tune. One favourite song of our musical educator was, Ivor Novello's *'Rose of England'*. Usually on Friday afternoons we were occasionally allowed to take in our favourite toys, or we could construct models out of bits, and pieces of junk we took to school. One lesson we all favoured on these afternoons was, when Mrs. Lees read chapters from the classic stories. One particular great favourite was, 'Black Beauty' By Anna Sewell.

The war loomed on, and at school we children were having drummed into us the fact that there was still a war going on, and there was to be no let-up in security. All the time new propaganda posters were being displayed in the school, and around the village. They spelt out the message that it was imperative that everyone should know the rules and obey them. To remind us that we should always be on our guard to whom we talked, there was a poster that read *'Mums the Word'*, which depicted a portrait of a very ravishing lady slouched on a settee, with elegantly dressed gentlemen in the background, holding drinks, and smoking cigarettes. The caption read. *'Keep Mum, She's Not So Dumb*!' At the bottom of the poster was the slogan *'Careless Talk Costs Lives'*. The Ministry of information created many characters depicting the careless public. To name a few strange oddities, included such delights as ' *Mr. Pride in Prophecy', 'Miss Leaky Mouth'*, and *'Miss Teacup Whisper'*. Mrs. Lees had a tendency to arrange artistic competitions; she would expect the class individuals to select some episode and aspect of the war. Of course the lads opted for exciting, and thrilling action that we considered our own little war effort. There was to be a prize for the best picture, and the winning poster would go alongside the professional posters in the village, hopefully attracting plenty of attention, and at the same time pushing home the message for which they were intended. Not only were there propaganda posters regarding careless talk, and the like displayed around the village, and school, there were also the campaign, and moral boosting types. One old chestnut *'Dig for Victory'*, which we felt, we had been doing for quite some time! Another poster was *'Wings for Victory'*. This dramatic poster was a romantic picture of an allied fighter aircraft diving through the clouds, cannon shells bursting, and tracer bullets darting at an unseen enemy. As painting was one of the few subjects that I excelled in, and it was this topic that I thoroughly enjoyed, I would throw myself into this project with more gusto than any other item on the curricula. This time perhaps inspired by the *'Wings for Victory'*, poster. My subject was a stricken airman leaping from his crippled fighter plane. His parachute cords were hopelessly tangled, his chances of survival very remote indeed, and the look on his face was one of extreme horror, and understandable concern. My slogan was, *'Collect A Hundred Pounds, and Buy a Proper Parachute'*. In those days parachutes were made of silk, and required the sum of about forty pounds to purchase just one. Forty pounds in those days was a considerable amount of money. I was very pleased when a gentleman paid a visit to our school, and awarded me first prize for my effort. Many more posters were painted in the school art lessons and other children joined me in the ranks of prizewinners.

While at school we were kept on our toes regarding air raid drill, and Mrs. Lees would enlist the services of the local air raid warden. He took great pride in organising mock air raid warnings. Standing in the centre of the main road, just outside of the school, he would stop any traffic that happened to be passing at the time. With chest thrown out, and with an air of national pomp, and pride, he would sound a long ear-piercing blast on his war ministry issued whistle. With as many blasts on his whistle he could maintain, his red cheeks puffed out, before we all entered the air raid shelter. On hearing this arresting warning we would race out of the school into a disorganised rabble across the road clutching our gas masks, and take refuge in the shelter. Our enthusiasm for air raid drill was high as it meant missing part of the school day curriculum. Returning to the classroom after these activities was never anything like as urgent or as expeditious as was the outward journey. The last thing we wanted to do after that sort of excitement was to return to our lessons. Wherever we went we had to carry our gas masks. They were housed in a cardboard box, and were slung over our shoulders with a length of string. This became second nature, if we were ever caught without this vital piece of safety apparatus, the air raid warden would chastise us very severely indeed.

Four

Start of World War II

Enter Rationing

Having little thought regarding our nation's predicament, and with the acute shortage of sweets, and sugar, it being brought home to me sometime later that this war was still with us. One was not allowed to take much sugar in ones tea, and unfortunately I had a sweet tooth. The shelves in the village shops began to look very sparse indeed. Living in the country we were relatively lucky to obtain easy access to vegetables, because nearly every household owned their own allotment. Eggs were rarely a problem as most families kept chickens, bantam, ducks or geese. Ration books containing coupons for various commodities required in everyday use, issued to each member of the family; we needed coupons for food, clothing, and just about everything else in life. It quickly became an orthodox scheme of life to take your ration book with you whenever you went shopping. Typically one person being allowed for one week, 4oz of bacon, 8oz of sugar, 2oz of butter, 8oz of cooking fats, a shilling's worth of meat, 2oz of tea, 1oz of cheese, and 2oz of jam.

Rabbits were never in scarce supply, and the people would keep them to supplement their meat ration. In some areas, there were Pig Clubs, and people would pool money to purchase a pig, and share out the produce. My foster parents kept a pig, and it was saddening when the local butcher came to dispatch the poor beast. To me at this tragic moment it seemed that the all pig population of the village was aware of what was going on, and squealing could be heard for miles around, and no sooner had the porker been slaughtered, neighbour would assist neighbour in the cleansing process of the carcass. This was part of the community spirit that would persist throughout the war years. Sides of bacon would be hung up in the outhouses, and salted. When required, portions would be sliced off, and shared with the neighbours, and greatly enjoyed by all. Some folk would have two pigs. If this being the case, they were allowed to own one for their personal consumption, and the other, by law had to be sold to the Food Ministry.

The Music Hall entertainers of the day, Elsie, and Doris Waters, known as Gert, and Daisy, would jump on the Band Wagon, giving their unique views on culinary matters in their book, 'Gert, and Daisy's Wartime Cookery Book'. It is astonishing what we ate in those far away days. Just to state a few almost unbelievable culinary examples, roast sparrow, squirrel tail soup, hedgehog soup, whale shark steak, were just a snippet of items on the menu. Bananas, lemons, oranges, and grapefruit seem to have completely vanished from off the face of the earth. When the banana finally put in an appearance some children who had never set eyes on one before, had no idea how to go about consuming it, and were seen to bite straight into the skin not realising it had to be peeled first. A packet of lemon flavoured powder, which was known as Kali, and a licorice tube-stick, with which to draw up the powder from out of the bag, seemed always to be a favourite and only cost about a farthing.

One method to make your chocolate rations spin out was to cut a Mars Bar into very thin slivers and strive to make it last for a few days. This strategy did not succeed with us children. Being obese in those days was extremely rare. One good thing to emerge from food rationing, people weren't in a position to eat to excess, and no doubt this was considered to remain a reasonable thing, due to this deprivation in their diet. Luxuries, which today we take for granted, in those days commodities were extremely expensive, and difficult to procure, unless you knew someone involved in the black market. It was amazing what marvels could be achieved with batter, and Spam. In some circles, when cooked in batter, it was known as Ballotine de Jambon Valentinoise. You would get a very suspicious look from the proprietor of our butcher store if you requested your Spam in batter, in this terminology. Not only was food rationed, clothing also came under the rationing umbrella. Sixty-six clothing coupons a year was the personal allowance, and this form of rationing for the ladies was very grave indeed, considering a pair of stockings cost two coupons.

To supplement our pocket money, on weekends, and in the school holidays, we would do casual jobs around on the nearby farms in the area. One project involved a reasonable number of boys; this was during the bush-beating season, in the autumn. Trampling across the fields during the annual shoot organised by the regional farmers, meant we had to start at one end of the farmland, and tread the entire beat, driving the game towards the guns. Shouting, and creating a hullabaloo bashing hedgerows with sticks, and creating as much cacophony as humanly possible. The latter presented little problem to us, as we considered it prudent to let the gun hands know we were still about, although out of sight. Some marksmen could get inordinately excited at the sight of a pheasant or rabbit. The last thing we wished was to be peppered by stray buckshot emanating from the oncoming shotguns. However, at the end of a long and tiring day, we were never offered any of the spoils, and would rarely get paid for our arduous efforts. In fact we were treated with utter contempt by some of the farmer's guests, which we considered were arrogant snobs. By late autumn when some of these activities normally took place, Lincolnshire could be a very cold county, and to get home to a hot meal, and thaw out by a roaring fire was complete utter bliss.

Foxhunting would take place about this time of year, and we would be expected by the huntsman to open any gates as the hunt chased across the fields. Also, we had to warn them of any impending, menacing barbed wire that happened to be lurking in the vicinity. This warning was usually signified by a board with letters painted in red, warning of barbed wire. Opening the gates as the horses approached, we would point, and shout *'Barbed wire'*. After the huntsman had passed through they would nonchalantly throw down the odd coin. More often than not, they would shout. *"Haven't any loose change now sonny, see you later."* We knew they didn't mean this is so we would look for some alternative means of raising our pocket money.

In the summer the jobs on the farmlands were more enjoyable, and especially sheep tending. The general idea of this task, was to keep one farmer's sheep from straying into the fields belonging to a neighbouring farmer, or wandering onto the roads. Considering the number of gaps that appeared in the hedgerows, keeping an eye on a large flock was no small task. This problem became a thorny issue for us sheep watchers. We decided to make the job a little easier, by blocking off gaps in the hedgerow with bits of corrugated sheet, or anything else, we could lay our hands on. We soon perfected this scheme, and one of the benefits was, that it freed time to let us get down to some more serious business of dozing in the tranquil shade.

At the end of the week we would have to wait a long time at the farmer's house for our wages to be handed over. We were always forced to wait outside the back door of the farmhouse for the money to be proffered We'd often still be waiting an hour after arriving. We imagined that the farmer was hoping we would get tired of waiting, and evaporate. We never did.

Pea picking was another means of raising cash. For this task we were paid by the weight of the sack that was filled; of course, the peas were still in their pods. We considered we were helping the war effort. Each picker would bring along a galvanised bucket, and fill it with peas. When the bucket or whatever container was used was full, the contents would be tipped into the sack. We would continue in this manner until the sack appeared to be about the correct weight which was approximately a hundredweight. The farmhand would appear with a trailer, and weighing scales. Then if satisfied with our efforts would hand over the cash. If the picking conditions were extremely bad, with many thistles, and weeds amongst the crop, the rate paid per sack would be higher. Working in very poor conditions, and perhaps for the best part of the day, one would probably have only picked one sack then you considered yourself lucky if you received about five old shillings. We knew the weight of the sack was calculated in stones, so many per sack. Before long, this led to another of our devious schemes. Speaking of stones, one might like to consider the other type of stone, the geological kind. To amplify on this subject of the stone, the following tale will explain.

During the summer pea-picking season there was ample opportunity for gypsies, and tinkers to find casual labour. We were not averse to gypsies and tinkers in general, but there was one occasion when we had a very good reason to resent their presence on the field. They had established a nasty habit of stealing partially filled sacks of peas. As you worked, sometimes your sack was left a short distance behind you while you were filling your bucket. Another ploy these people enjoyed was to place stones at the bottom of their sacks to add weight, thus cheating the farmer at the same time. We decided we had had enough of their habitual cheating, and of course we resolved to take them on at their own game. Between as we produced an extra sack of peas, and loaded it with a generous amount of stone's. When nearly full we left it near where they were working, giving them ample opportunity to steal it if they so desired. Sure enough they took the bait, and all we had to do was be patient and hear what the farmhand had to say when they claimed the sack of peas was theirs. There were so many stone's in the bottom of the sack that it nearly shot the hand off the weighing scales because of phenomenal weight. The farmhand immediately suspected something was wrong, and instantly chased them off the field, we never saw that gang again.

At home about once a year we had a lady Romany wanderer call to sell her ribbons, clothes pegs, and her lucky charms, and providing we placed a silver sixpenny piece across her palm, she would tell us our fortunes. On one occasion she pointed out that Aunt Nin had a tear in the linoleum covering on the pantry shelf. She was not in view of the said item, if she hadn't found out this fact from a neighbour, it is extraordinary how she could have possibly known.

Potato picking was the job that kept us occupied when the time arrived for the lifting. This was much harder work than the pea picking. The potatoes were either ploughed or spun out of the ground. Both ways of retrieving the potatoes we considered very grueling indeed. If the ground was wet and soggy lifting the tubers from the furrows was painful in the lower region of your back. Having been spun out of the ground, the potatoes were strewn all over the ground, one had to work very fast to pick them up, throw them in the bucket then into the cart, which was pulled by a Suffolk Punch shire horse. The faster the spinner went, the faster we had to work. When one considers the work we did in the fields at that time it is hard to imagine if children in their early years would be able to cope with this type of work today. By the end of the working day my back ached mirthlessly, and whichever method was employed, I was pleased to see the end of this task. The beauty of the pea picking, and potato picking was you were paid piece-time rates. But with sheep tending, and other farmyard duties there was always that nagging feeling that you wouldn't be paid at the end of the week for all your hard labour. Potato picking at times was an unpleasant task, but the toughest job of all was to me, the dreaded sugar beet lifting. It was on Bert and Dick Wadsley's farm where I would perform this back-aching work. For some unknown reason I appeared to be the only one that took on this job. This could have been due to the fact that my foster parents were friends of the Wadsley's. At the time I considered it some kind of punishment. To make matters much worse, the weather always seemed to be bitterly cold with a biting east wind, and the work was unremittingly heavy. The sugar beet had to be ploughed out, being too heavy for the spinner to move. When the beet had been ploughed up, it would then be laid in such a manner so that the farmer could go along the furrows chopping off the green tops with his billhook. A wagon drawn by a muscular Shire horse was brought into the field, and it was my job to lift the beet throw it into galvanised tubs, and then heave it into the wagon. The Shire horse that pulled the wagon was called Boxer a Suffolk Punch, a lovable creature; he was a very clever animal. He would obey a variety of commands, and appear to know exactly where, and when to stop with very little prompting. When the wagon was full it would be taken out of the field by this sturdy helper and the contents stacked along the grass verge by the side of the road ready for collection. These stacks looked very much like ancient long burial barrows, about forty feet long, and roughly ten feet in length. Here the beet would await the arrival of a lorry, which would transport it to a refining factory, at that time near Peterborough. It was always a relief to see the end of the sugar beet season, and I hoped silently that it would never come round again. My reward was little pay, aching back, and plenty of chilblains.

However, I did get the chance to ride, with little legs straggled across Boxer's broad bulked back to his stable, and groom him at the end of each working day. This riding on Boxer's back helped to make the hard labour of the working day seem more worthwhile. There were times when I would assist with the cutting of the cow cake. The cake was a source of nutrition for these bovine creatures. Large pieces of this cake would be sliced by hand, with a vicious looking circular blade that could cut the cake, and unwary fingers, if one did not treat this piece of farm machinery with plenty of respect. I would sample chunks of this cake, and I discovered that it did not taste at all unsavoury, and I didn't suffer any ill effects. Then to swill the cake down, I would squeeze the teat of a cow to sample the warm milk, that is, if no one was around. I was never very adept at this teat-squeezing and often I would find myself sprawled flat out on the cowshed floor, having failed to maintain a close eye on the beast's rear legs.

Thankfully, it wasn't all work in the school holidays, and at weekends, there were plenty of opportunities for boyish adventures. Just beyond the outskirts of the village there was a brook where we could catch fish in a butterfly net, mostly minnows and sticklebacks. When we caught them, we would put water from the brook into a two-pound jam jar, and then take them home. The poor things did not live to see the end of the day in these conditions. When tired of fishing or the fish did not appear to be interested in our nets, we would splash about in the water, and create a lot of noise. An old ruined mansion house a little way out of the village gave us the opportunity for plenty of amusement. It was a very dangerous place to be. What attracted us to the ruins, it was said to be haunted, and this haunting prospect fascinated us somewhat. Had an apparition appeared, we would have swiftly dispatched our bodies from this eerie ambience. The village policeman was always chasing us off whenever he caught us near the house. The place was extremely spooky, and we would take torches or candles to explore. The fascination of the building would keep us occupied, and by telling tales to our peers, saying that we had seen a ghost, and we had heard weird noises like the squealing voices of demented demons. The banging of doors, and the rattling of windows, and how the tattered curtains clung to the window frames as if it was a matter of life and death if they were ever blown away. This was all good fun, and at every opportunity we elaborated on the story with even more explicit visions in the ruin. Then later we would pay a visit to the old mansion once again, in a strange way we had become to love the old place.

Another ancient relic of time past was situated in the village along the Billingborough Road. This was The House of Correction that occupied the site of the old castle of Folkingham. All that remains now is the facade gatehouse. During the time that I lived in the village the building had been turned into residential dwellings. Amongst other families living in this domain there was a strange old man who, for no reason long forgotten, we called Old Minty. He used to frighten the life out of me. He always carried a large stick, and shouted "clear off," with a very loud bellowing voice, his beard bobbing up and down in unison with his call like a yo-yo. Brandishing his walking stick above his head, and charging down his footpath he looked something akin to a Zulu warrior. I was never happy when some of the lads said. "Let's go and visit our friends at The House of Correction."

There was an artist living in the village a Mr. Bradley, who specialised in water paintings of horses, and hunting scenes. We often used to come across him at his work in his studio, which reminded me of a large greenhouse. I was very fascinated to see how he brought his pictures to life. If there happened to be a large group of us spying on him he would chase us off. I always harboured a secret wish to go inside, and watch him at work more closely. Probably, had I not been with the other lads, and approached him in a different manner he might have let me watch him at his work. Occasionally when he did manage to speak to us in a civil tongue he would ask us to search, and bring him pictures depicting horses, which he loved to copy. The pictures we gave him never appeared to be satisfactory, as he would never accept them, especially on one occasion when one cheeky beggar took him a copy of a rocking horse. Some years later when on a canoeing trip on the River Wye, and during a break in the paddling our group decided liquid refreshment was called for. Having a perusal around the public bar, in Hay on Wye, I spotted one of Mr. Bradley's water colours hanging on a wall. The barman was not at all interested in selling it to me, what a pity! Inspired by having watched him at work, and perhaps with all that was going on around us, three of us decided to construct a battleship, with bits, and pieces of wood, and any scrap metal that we could scrounge. After spending a week or so working on it, we faced the predicament of deciding what to do with it. A suggestion that it be put on water was quickly squashed when we had a trial launch in a neighbour's tin bath. It promptly sank to the bottom. We should have known better, the thing was about six feet long and fairly heavy. After letting the vessel dry out, and sneaking back the unsuspecting neighbour's tin bath, we forgot it for a while, or at least for as long as you can forget about something that is about six feet long, fairly heavy, sinkable, and battleship shape. One of us had a bright notion. We would build a trolley, and cart it around the village, and collect money for the Red Cross. This scheme proved very popular, and when we had bled the villagers dry it appeared that the model would be rendered obsolete. But all was not lost. We had yet another brainwave, and realised by strategic positioning the boat could attract a lot more in the way of donations. We placed it outside The New Inn public house, and also a friend's house; we positioned it on the grass verge at the roadside for a very good reason. The building contractors, Bovis Ltd, were constructing an American air base to the north of the village. There would be C - 47 - Dakota aircraft based there, which would tow the troop-carrying gliders in preparation for the eventual D - Day landings in Northern France. The labour force working on this site was mainly Irish personnel, who always seemed to be extremely well paid, and generous to a fault. In Folkingham there were four public houses, and when work was finished for the day, the labourers would flock their way into the village, and swamp the taverns in search of liquid refreshment. En route they would have to pass our battleship. Night-after night the labourer's generosity shone like a beacon. They seemed to view it as their duty to make a small donation every time they passed and of course we cashed in on their act of generosity. Their contributions helped swell our charity course beyond our imagination. Our headmistress saw to it that we received a good report in the Grantham Journal. This made me feel very proud of myself. Best of all, Mrs. Lees began to view my activities in a slightly more positive light.

For the children in our community, life was to take on a slightly different perspective with the influx of evacuees. There were already plenty of youngsters living in the area. There was one family in our row of cottages with no less than seven children. They lived in the same type of cottage as mine, with one small rear, and front parlour, three bedrooms, no bathroom, or inside toilet, no running water or electricity. There were other families in much the same circumstances, yet managed to survive quite happily.

My foster parents took in another foster child, a girl named Kathleen; she was older than me. The Barbers already had one foster son who was named Bob, and he was in the Royal Navy, serving on the flagship H.M.S.Nelson It was his portrait that hung on our parlour wall. When not engaged in working activities we would amuse ourselves by utilising the village air-raid shelters as handy play areas. The shelters stood in the Market Square, and were built of red brick, and always looked pretty ineffectual to me. I could see no reason why a strategically placed bomb could not fail to blow such a fragile looking form of protection into a thousand pieces. It was always dank and dark inside, and we would take in candles or torches to see our way around. In the interior at one end of each shelter you would find a very large iron handle much like a car-starting handle of the day, (the latter not being required anymore with the appearance of the modern automobile), that was imbedded into the brickwork. The idea was, if the entrance became blocked with rubble you could heave on the handle, and hopefully part of the wall would collapse allowing you to escape. We often used to wonder if such an escape strategy was viable, but dare not test the mechanism, and hoped that the Luftwaffe would never call on us to find out. There were other brick built shelters dotted around the area. Some of the inhabitants built their own corrugated Anderson shelters that were delivered in kit form. The shelter would be sunk into the garden, and earthed over, and could be erected in a very short time with little difficulty for anyone having DIY experience. The shelter acquired its name after its inventor Sir John Anderson, Home Secretary (1939-40).

In the winter, when it grew dark quite early, we were often the bane of the local ARP Warden. I have lost count the number of times he screamed at us *"Put out them there lights you lot, or I'll get Mr. Holland the policeman to see to you lot! So there you are you 'orrible mob, I shan't tell you again, so bloody well clear off, you bloody 'ooligans!"* was the cry of the Air Raid Warden, when he caught us misbehaving. To have annoyed this man in some way seemed the epitome of a decent night's work. Existing past times was easy to come by in the dark evenings. In the grounds of the vicarage, we came across some disused stables. In one stable, was an old a redundant wicker-basket wheel chair that belonged to the vicar, which he no longer used. He appeared to have discarded the wicker-basket chair, having purchased the latest model. The fact that the old contraption was on wheels presented new and exciting possibilities to us for its use. When dusk had fallen, we would sneak into the stable where the chair was housed, and drag it out at the top of the hill that ran through the village, taking it in turns to pilot the chair as it careered with ever increasing speed down the hill. Once it had achieved rapid acceleration, it was very difficult to bring it to a halt as no efficient braking system had been designed, and the chair's manufactures had clearly not had envisaged this particular usage. It was, in fact, highly dangerous, as the steering was by means of just one handle connected to a small front wheel. Thankfully, road traffic was virtually non-existent in the dark hours of wartime Folkingham. No one ever found out about our nocturnal pranks, which seemed odd, and amazingly no one was ever seriously hurt as a consequence. The chair must have been very well made; it never sustained any serious damage considering all the abuse that it suffered at our hands. We were in trouble again when we were summoned into the schoolmistress presence; we imagined that it concerned our escapades with the wheelchair.

She demanded. *"Who has created a large swastika on the vicar's lawn?"*

"Not me!" Was the predictable chorus, as we stood there in front of her desk, and recalling the previous episode of the cane-mutilating saga, and expecting an explosive rage from the teacher? I thought it prudent to keep a very low profile. We had discovered a large pile of grass cuttings in a corner of the vicarage large garden. In madness we threw the grass cuttings in the form of a large swastika in the middle of the lawn. Somehow this act of treason had got to the ears of our schoolmistress, and this is why we were having this confrontation with her. In view of the fact that in the past we had been of reasonably good behaviour, and she obviously remembered our Red Cross fund-raising effort, she let us off with a very stern warning, and promising, that if we stood in front of her again, there would be very dire consequences for us all. We considered the fact, and marvelled that we had been very fortunate that we had not been found out about the bath chair escapades. Or if she had discovered our silly prank she had decided to let the matter rest. Possibly hoping someone else would deal with the matter if it ever came to light.

Our mischievous activities were not limited to reckless wheelchair runs. Under the cover of darkness, we would take a long piece of black thread, and carefully tie one end to some unsuspecting neighbour's front doorknocker, and then conceal the rest of the thread out of sight. Unwinding the thread, and secreting ourselves some little way from the house to make sure we were out of view of anyone answering the door, we would pull hard on the thread. Usually the knocking was answered, and after observing quizzical looks, and the opening, and closing of the door, we would repeat the dastardly deed all over again. This would continue until the victim tired of answering the door, or more often that we tired of the very silly activity that we were committing. I often wondered how many genuine callers were ignored, due to this silly prank. It was simply another of our inventive activities, designed to relieve some of the boredom we experienced. Considering today the vandalism that goes on, our pranks were nothing in comparison. They never really harmed anyone, and some people who encountered some of the trickery that we played on people, privately were amused about our inventiveness.

One day, I was aimlessly wandering through the fields, when a brown, and white cocker spaniel darted from out of nowhere, and began to trot beside me. To my delight it followed me all the way home, nevertheless, with some encouragement from me.

When I arrived home I excitedly asked my foster mother. "Can I keep the dog?"

"You will have to wait, and see what Uncle Alf has to say when he comes home from work, and we have to find the rightful owner. Do you know the dog belongs to?" "No I don't, it just followed me, and can I keep it anyway?" I pleaded.

"No! I told you, we must find out whom the dog belongs to. We can't keep it just because it followed you home." I knew it was no use protesting any more so I let the matter drop, and went into the garden. The dog followed me. It was not long before uncle Alf came home from work. He was a little earlier than usual. I ran to him excitedly, calling. *"Can I keep the dog?"*

"What dog?" He enquired with a rather bewildered look on his face. *"Hello little dog, you're the cause of all the excitement are you?"* He said, giving the dog a friendly pat. Later on he notified the village policeman. I was somewhat apprehensive about the outcome because it was the same constable that had dealt with our bean-trampling incident earlier. The constable might well presume I had stolen the dog. To my great relief, he told my foster father that I could keep the dog providing no one reported it missing within a month, and also providing I had my foster parent's permission. For a whole month I was intensely anxious, and kept badgering my foster parents about the dog. I quickly had grown fond of this new addition to the family, and every morning I would wake up dreading the prospect of someone claiming him as theirs, after all dogs just don't materialise out of thin air. Then, one morning long before I was up, there was a knock on the door. Aunt Nin called me to get up. I rushed downstairs to see what was going on, and standing on the doorstep was Mr. Holland the village constable my heart sank!

"I have spoken to your foster parents, and they say they are quite happy for you to keep the dog, so the dog is yours son, take good care of it," he stated. He winked, then smiled, and was off down the road.

I was ecstatic of course, though deep inside I always suspected the little chap had strayed from some farm nearby, and the owner, being informed of my attachment to the animal, had spoken to the policeman, and told him to let me keep it. There was a feeling of euphoria, and having a dog (I now christened him Rex) to look after gave me an injection of responsibility. I would go with Uncle Alf for long walks on Sunday mornings, and we would take Rex with us. He was incredibly energetic, and could usually spot a rabbit long before they saw him. Any rabbits that did put in an appearance, he would give them chase although he was never quite quick enough to catch one. He would frantically scratch at the rabbit burrow, and when he was finally dragged away, he would look really disdainfully at me with appealing eyes, and a very grubby nose. Uncle Alf would stride out very quickly, and I would be exhausted trying to keep pace with him as we made for home. Then he would pop into one of the local taverns for a refreshing drink before lunch.

Uncle Alf was employed as a steam traction engine driver. During harvest time, I would accompany him to where his engine was located; there he would perform the ritual of preparing the machine for the next day's threshing of the crop. At the end of each working day he would check that the fire beneath the boiler was lit. If it was going well he would dampen it down, so that first thing in the morning all he would have to do was open the door of the firebox, give the contents a good poke, and in no time he would have steam up, ready for another day's work. This would be a regular occurrence during the harvest time, and the steam engine was the heart of the threshing process. A large flywheel on the engine had a wide belt that in turn was connected to another drive wheel on the side of the large threshing drum.

This drum is where sheaves of wheat, barley or oats were deposited, being hurled inside by men standing on top of the drum, and in turn received the sheaves from other farmhands as they unloaded the wagons by the side of the drum. The harvest binder that was towed around the field by Shire horses or tractor had previously harvested the crop. As the binder revolved it cut the crop at ground level before spewing out the sheaves that it had already bound with twine. The job we children like doing was leaning the sheaves together in-groups of about six, so that when finished they looked like small wigwams. This was to let the seed dry out before the threshing process. While the cutting was going on the farmer and some of his guests, probably other farmers, would be waiting guns in arms for any terrified rabbits that might dart out from the crop. After the guns had spoken, dogs would be dispatched to collect the spoils.

Once the field was almost stripped of the crop the rabbits would have very little cover. On some occasions they would be too terrified to move, and would be swept up by the binder blades, not a pleasant sight. When the time came to collect the sheaves, horse and wagon would take them to where the threshing process would begin. We knew the threshing had started when the fields became engulfed in clouds of dust and debris. Working in these conditions, the lunch break was always very welcome. Our throats were very parched and dry indeed, Jam turnovers and apple pies, washed down with cold sweet tea, minus milk-was heaven. This beverage was drunk from Corona bottles, with porcelain spring stoppers, unique to the age. In the war years farmhands worked hard and very long hours from daylight until dusk, this arduous labour played a very important role in the economy of the country.

I used to lend a hand with the annual sheep dipping. With great enthusiasm, and vigor I would drive the sheep into the dip that was usually positioned at the corner of the field. The dip was very large, and was sunk into the ground allowing the sheep reasonably easy access. With all the enthusiasm I had to be cautious not to join my charges into the disinfecting trough. There was no guarantee that I wouldn't. Falling into this powerful foul smelling yellow goo was not advisable but I nevertheless managed to get a thorough soaking on more than one occasion as the sheep dashed out of the dip shaking their woolly bodies. My aunt quickly grew exasperated by my tentative returns to the house with clothes tinged yellow, and smelling to high heaven.

My foster sister Kathleen made friends with an airman who was stationed on an airfield somewhere near Sleaford. He would often come to our house on Sunday afternoons, and stay for tea. There were times, when going for walks I would quiz the airman about a dummy airfield which was quite close to our village, replete with full sized replicas of Spitfires, and Hurricane aircraft. The airfield had been created to fool the Luftwaffe, the hope being that they would repeatedly bomb this mock-up airfield thus leaving us alone. It may have been a decoy regarding the armaments factory at Grantham, and the new air base being constructed by Bovis Ltd, a few miles away from our village. There were several airmen stationed on this intriguing set-up, and they would regularly move the aircraft around to create the impression of an authentic operational, active station. I would continue to quiz Kathleen's boyfriend about the aerodrome but he would never talk about it, and would swiftly change the topic of conversation, avoiding any embarrassing encounters regarding military operations. I had grown to like the airman; he was friendly, and gallant, and always supplied a gentle antidote to entertain us. I was sorry when he was posted further away, and couldn't see him again. I was inspired somewhat at that time to join the Royal Air Force by this young man's disposition.

Wherever we went we always had to carry our gas masks, and the ARP Warden would keep a close eye on us all to make certain we were doing so. He would chastise us had we not been carrying them. The fear of another type of lethal gas that might be deposited upon us by the Germans prompted the War Ministry to add an additional filter to the end of our current mask. The babies at that time had to be literally deposited inside their large baby carrier type gas masks, and there would be much screaming from these poor little creatures, as their parents struggled with the task of getting them into this mask of protection.

At school most of the children, including myself, were very apprehensive when first told to put the gas mask on. We soon got used to the drill, and would laugh at each other seeing how comical we must have looked. It was amazing how many different types of gas mask there were. Some with large round eyepieces acquired the nickname, the Mickey Mouse gas mask, and others had very long breathing tubes, even more comical to look at. The odour of the rubber of which these masks were manufactured would linger in my nostrils for hours after removing this safety device. My foster brother Bob, whom I didn't see very often, due to the fact that he was serving in the Royal Navy. His success was much pride in the family. News that he was coming home on leave was the perfect excuse for great excitement.

As mentioned earlier, a large framed photograph of him, confident, and immaculate in his uniform took pride of place in our front parlour. When he was present he would always ensure that I looked smart before I left the house, and especially so if I was going somewhere very important. He would tie astonishingly delicate knots in my necktie, and his deft fingers always had the odour of strong tobacco. This fascinated me, and I came to regard him as a hero, and constantly sung its praises to my friends.

Bob owned a racing cycle, which was suspended from the roof in our outhouse while he was away at sea. I would look at it lovingly, and occasionally pinched the tyres to ensure they weren't flat. Time, and time again I could be found in the outhouse gazing at this two-wheeled beauty.

I would fantasise that I would one day be able to ride it to school making every other boy in the class jealous. Uncle Alf once noticed me staring at the cycle but considered it too large, and unwieldy for me to ride. Then, not long after, a second bicycle appeared. It wasn't a new one or as flashy as Bob's racer. It was smaller but above all else it was mine. That was all that mattered. With the help of my uncle I made my first tentative journey on two wheels, wobbling, and falling off a few times. I didn't take too long to master the skills of balance, because unknown to Uncle Alf I already had experience in piloting three-wheeled chairs downhill. This bicycle however, gave me a feeling of freedom, and I enjoyed its use immensely. Touring around the village was accelerating, and I quickly became the envy of my pals, few of whom had a bike. My enthusiasm did not go unnoticed, and I eventually inherited Bob's racer.

As children, we still found the war exciting, even with the rationing and were blind to the potential dangers. American airman had arrived at the new airbase, and we often would chat to them whenever they came into the village. They seemed to have one particle interest, they would ask. *"Do you have an older sister?"* Despite this obsession with the opposite sex, they appear to have limitless supply of chewing gum, and were always generous when it came to sharing it. We soon learned how to handle these exuberant young men. When they asked us if we had an older sister, we replied cheekily. *"Got any gum chum?"* When they had handed over the bribe we would inform them that our elder sisters already had boyfriends. We concluded that these airmen were very brash, and loud mouthed. We began to resent them at times. We also considered it a good thing that the Irish labourers had completed the work on the airfield, and that they had returned home to Ireland, otherwise there would probably have been much rivalry between the two parties, calumniating in fisticuffs no doubt.

After closing time in the local pub, we adopted the well-known phrase *'The Yanks are over paid, over sexed, and over here'.* They certainly thought they were God's gift to women.

It is with the exception of the war; life in the village carried on much the same as it always had done. For us children it meant going to school, doing odd jobs in the holidays, and generally making a nuisance of ourselves when bored.

My pocket money was two old pence per week, plus anything I received from the farm labouring jobs. However, life was about to change. The village was to succumb to a very considerable change, like it had never seen before or unlikely again in the future.

Five

Wartime Experiences

Enter Evacuees and Propaganda

By the time the school holidays, four weeks in the summer, a week at Christmas, and a week at Easter, were finished I had spent everything I had earned. With each passing season my duties varied, and I dreaded the onset of the sugar beet lifting season coming round again. All the time the spectre of Hitler loomed over us yet somehow, in our small, tidy world, the spirit, and fraternities of our community made us feel safe, and detached from the horrors of Europe. When the children began to arrive in our midst we found ourselves out numbered about two to one. These sad looking children were the evacuees from Kingston upon Hull, and their city was taking a pounding, because of its status as an important seaport. We had to take a boy, and his sister into our home bringing the total occupants in the house to six, not counting Bob who was still at sea.

Needless to say, our school was swamped with children. To our eyes the newcomers seemed rough, and tough, and we were not used to this town-type attitude in our village. At first they were determined to give us a hard time. This was quite understandable, after all they had had to leave their home, their parents, families, and friends. They knew nothing of life in a rural village, and we knew nothing of life in a busy city. Eventually, we found some common ground, and friendships began to blossom. Even some time after I'd left the village, I maintained a correspondence with one girl I had become particularly attached to long after she returned home to Kingston upon Hull.

One evacuee boy, about the age of eight could play the piano accordion with considerable dexterity for his age. I would have loved to have played his instrument in the manner he played it, but I never could pick up the courage to ask him to give me some lessons. I am sure it would have come natural to him, to teach me how to play the instrument. Nevertheless, I spent many lazy summer evenings listening to his skilful playing. And this lad inspired me to take up the instrument later in life.

A little further down the road Uncle Alf's sister, whom I called Aunt Mary, lived with her husband Uncle Joe, and their grown-up son Alfred. Their house was even smaller than ours. Alfred on a Sunday morning would sit in our front parlour, and peruse the war's progress in the newspapers. After finishing a cup of cocoa or tea Alfred used to tease Aunt Nin, and would say to me, laughing at the same time. "*Coming down to the pub Rob?*"

"Yes, why not, I could do with a drink," I joked.

I couldn't go of course. It was just his way of pulling my aunt's leg.

We didn't have the extravagance of a wireless set in our home so I would often make excursions to Aunt Mary's to listen to hers. The programmes I liked were *'Variety Bandbox,'* and *'Happidrome'*. The three comedians in 'Happidrome were Mr. Lovejoy, Ramsbottom, and Enoch. Frankie Howard made his debut in Happidrome, produced by Betty Fox.. During the war years we soon familiarised ourselves with the newsreaders. Among the many announces there were John Snagge, Robert Robinson, and Bruce Belfridge, just to mention a few. Evidently, Bruce Bellfridge, being a real professional, carried on reading the news bulletin as a bomb from the Luftwaffe was deposited on broadcasting house. In those days the newsreaders always identified themselves on the account that the public would distinguish the bulletin as the genuine article. Whenever I happened to be at Aunt Mary's house, and Robert Robinson was reading the news; Uncle Joe would pull my leg because this particular newsreader had the same surname as mine. Robinson chaired many quizzes later on Radio, and Television.

Occasionally Aunt Mary would offer me a cigarette. She did this for pure devilment, although I never took one. Another one of her tricks to launch me into the noble art of smoking was to buy me a copy of the 'Dandy' comic and insert a loose cigarette into the centre pages. Uncle Joe used to appear at our house on Christmas day dressed as Father Christmas. This gesture of goodwill initially scared the living day lights out of me, but later I came to look forward to these festive frolics. I always treasured one Christmas present.

Eagerly, unwrapping a very large parcel I saw a box, and written in bright coloured letters on the lid, were the words 'Meccano Set'. I was ecstatic when I opened the box, and saw all the brightly coloured metal pieces. In the separate compartments were screws, nuts, bolts, pulleys, chains, strong rubber bands, and all manner of little tools that would be required to assemble the models. There was a very large book with all the plans for creating various models. I was impatient to get started, and the first thing I wanted to make was a steam traction engine like Uncle Alf's. This project was one of the most difficult in the set. There were pulley wheels, and chains to be assembled. Bob had come home on leave, and he was eager to help me assemble the pieces. It was well into the New Year before I completed this particular model, and when it was finished I looked at it in amazement, and would show it off to any of my friends that called at our house.

Christmas Day was the only day I didn't have to attend church, that is, until I joined the church choir. An evacuee friend of mine, who had a very good singing voice, joined the church choir. Canon Heath recruited us one day, when he spotted us playing hopscotch in the street. He called us over to him, and said "*You boys ought to be doing something more constructive with your lives, how about joining the church choir?*"

We both got on very well together, this may have something to do with the fact we both had the same Christian names. There already was a substantial ladies choir in the church. We were the only boys involved. To be honest I rather savoured this unbalanced situation. Indeed church life began to take on an all-new meaning for me once I began to get involved in the singing. We didn't have any choir practices as such, and most of the music we sang off-the-cuff. Prior to this, I had been forced to trot along to church every Sunday evening with my foster parents, and I sat through the sermons as if the subject was of eternal purgatory. I would usually be given a sweet just before the sermon began, this was a blessing in disguise as it was extremely difficult to remove the wrapper with subtlety in such a deadly silence, and reverential environment, and I would spend several minutes working on this delicate operation. This exercise swallowed up much time, and when I'd finished, thankfully the sermon was well on its way to its conclusion. This operation was akin to defusing a bomb. Sitting just below the pulpit, I was a prime target for the vicar's beady eyes, and dreaded looking up to find him peering down at me. Trusting to superstition, I decided that I would be safe providing I kept my eyes on the unwrapping operation, and didn't look up. My theory was that if I didn't look up he wouldn't look down. This seemed a wise maneuver as the vicar's wroth never did fall upon me.

A very tall lady in the choir, who had a singularly strident soprano voice, and seemed to sing everything con brio, had clearly gathered the rest of the ladies under her wing in a subservient huddle, and would look down her nose in a disapproving manner at us new recruits. Unlike the vicar, she constantly suspected us of misbehaving, something I would never do in church because my foster parents would be present sitting in the front row of the pews. The sweet unwrapping struggle was deemed acceptable. As I got used to my new role in the choir, the routine seemed less mundane. There was always the consolation that if ever I got bored with my life as a chorister, my good evacuee friend, and previously a city dweller, and used to a faster pace of life, was probably just as bored.

The village church of St. Andrew had a very fine large tower that could be seen for miles around. Just as in the 'Dads Army' television programme, the local home guard made use of the tower, and found it an excellent observation point for spotting any advancing Luftwaffe aircraft. They would always place someone on duty to occupy it by night, in search of enemy aircraft, and parachutes no doubt. They had created another lookout point opposite the Village Square by removing a brick from the corner of a house utilising it as a lookout point. The positioning of this look-out point gave a panoramic view of this particular are, and was a great advantage, had any invading enemy approached the village. As a child, I never gave many notions to the possibility of invasion. But with all this activity going on it was inevitable that the gentlemen of the home guard became a comforting presence, I simply took it for granted. This building was the corner store, and had a very low windowsill. In a bid to prevent us village urchins from placing our bottoms on the sill, broken glass.

From the chapel in the village on a Sunday morning, robust singing voices could be heard serenading the air at a considerable distance away. Ironically, the chapel began to accumulate a larger congregation than the church. This was probably due to the more boisterous type of hymn singing, and that a congregation discovered it could really be involved.

St Andrew's Church Folkingham

The Nave of St Andrew's Church

My namesake evacuee friend would accompany me to the Sunday school classes in the church vestry. This was something we did not relish one iota. Our teacher, Miss Lavat was very severe, and she expected much of us in the art of learning the collect for that particular day, and of course, by memory. Hatred of this discipline was made ten times worse by the knowledge that our friends would be playing out in the fields, and enjoying themselves. There was no point in us devising schemes to skive off, because an attendant stamp was given each time we were present. These stamps accumulated in an album, and were the evidence of one's attendance, so everyone would know if one were skipping the classes. If all was well, the Sunday school pupils would collect enough attendance stamps to be illegible for a special Sunday school outing to Skegness. One year I felt cruelly cheated, for despite having the requisite number of stamps, I had managed to facture my right leg, and was wheelchair-bound during the trip. I couldn't go paddling or running about feverishly along the beach as I wished, but at least I went. In a display, that now seems freakish, there was a man with only one arm who would dive off the pier to make money, and added entertainment for the holidaymakers. Later, we would go round the Woolworth's store, and noticed that every counter displayed a sign quoting 'Nothing over Sixpence'. As I grew older my visits to Sunday school became more sporadic. My attendance album became a thing of shame, and eventually I stopped going altogether.

It was not all doom, and gloom during those dark war years. The parish councilors would do all they could to help relieve the trauma of war by organising dances in the village hut. These functions proved very popular, and at times it seemed that the whole village population was in attendance. When I was allowed to go to these really memorable events, these hops were some of the happiest times for me whilst living in the village. The dances were held about once a month, and waiting in anticipation for the next event was sometimes as much as I could endure. For this, there was a very good reason, and the reason being was an evacuee girl-Valerie. The very first dance I was allowed to attend I took the best part of an hour grooming myself. I would do something that was not natural for me; I would scrub my face and neck until they were almost bright red. I would douse gallons of Brilliantine on my hair, failing that; I would procure some of Bob's Brylcreem, thus flattening down my curls. This was my debut so I was extremely anxious that I should look good, because I hoped Valerie would be there. I had a strong crush on this unsuspecting girl ever since she arrived from Kingston-upon-Hull. I had been too nervous to say anything to her about the dance while at school. One major problem was my complete inability to dance or do anything resembling a waltz or quickstep. In this respect I was no worse off than any of the other lads; it was a stumbling block all the same. Nearly all the evacuee girls were surprisingly adept when dancing, and they would get extremely annoyed with the lads they were dancing with who happened to have two left feet, or worse, if they started messing about. Being townies, they no doubt were very conversant with the dance halls, and had ample opportunities to refine their ballroom skills. Most of the time the unfortunate girls had to dance with each other; this sad state of affairs showed how far behind we lads were in the finer points of the social graces. Also it probably appeared to them that we weren't interested in dancing properly, and only wanted to cause a fracas. Frustration would set in, and we would make ourselves a positive nuisance.

The adults would dance the foxtrot the waltzes, and tangos, all we could do was to get in their way. We would make ourselves very unpopular when we tried to join in the Palais de Glide. It was not long before we received an ultimatum-either stop messing about or stay away. We soon got the message, and things began to improve. In our own interests we made great efforts to join in the Lambeth Walk, and the like, and gradually we became accepted. A trio of musicians provided the music for the dancing, the piano being played by the church organist. The Lady with the strident soprano voice was always there. We hoped that she would not attempt to sing, and wreck the evening. She was never without a partner, her energy was boundless, and she appeared to dance all night long. We lads were always wary of her; her eyes seemed to be everywhere. There was one particular number we lads would muscle in on, and it went something like this:

'Horsy Horsy, don't you stop, just let your feet ago clickety clop. Your tail go swish your wheels go round. Giddy up, we're homeward bound'.

This was an example of a community dance, and everyone had to be particularly careful not to slip because the floor had been dusted with talcum powder to enhance the sliding characteristics of the dance locality. This enhancement of the dance floor gave me the perfect excuse, and opportunity to slide towards, and get my arms around Valerie. I would blush, and my legs would turn to jelly. I wanted to ask her if I could walk her home. I'm afraid the words were not there, I was too bashful. The night would fly past much too quickly, if I weren't engaged in trying to dance, I would sit, and watch Valerie, hoping she would ask me to dance with her. Obviously I should have put the question but I was too shy and couldn't spurt out the words. These carefree hours were limited, and I had to be in by midnight. I had no intention of losing this privilege so I adhered to the rules. I knew my foster parents would be waiting up for me so there would little opportunity for me to sneak in late. Secretly, if only I could have plucked up enough courage, I would have very much loved to have escorted Valerie home. The village hut was in easy walking distance of the residential areas of the village where most of the children lived. Nearly all the parents and guardians would meet their offspring from the dances, assuming they weren't there, and dancing themselves. There were always plenty of responsible adults around to see the young one's home safely, and we never felt threatened or in any kind of peril. I would get home very tired, have a hot drink, then to bed, and would soon be asleep, and dreaming of whisking Valerie around the dance floor, to the strains of an impassioned tango.

There were two occasions I had cause to spend time in Grantham General Hospital. The first time was when I had to have a visit from the village doctor because I was feeling ill. It transpired that I had the mumps. The doctor said that as soon as I had recovered from the mumps I must be taken straight into hospital, where I would have to have my tonsils extracted. I was taken to the hospital for the removal of the offending oral organs. I recall how strong the ether smelt, and how sore my throat was after this operation. My second visit was after breaking my right leg. This fracture did not arise as a result of tobogganing, cycling or steering wheel chairs in free-fall down hillsides, but from of all things, skipping. On both occasions I only had to stay in for a few days. Every evening the children's ward would be vacated, and we were taken down into the hospital's shelter outside; this was simply a precautionary measure in case the Luftwaffe was to mistake our hospital for an industrial centre. Once in the shelter, Nurse Hunter a delightful lady, whom all the children adored would read to us until we fell asleep. We did suffer the occasional air raid but there was no direct hit on the hospital during my time there. However, we did hear the frightening crumbling, and thumping sound of bombs exploding in Grantham. Goering's Luftwaffe target was presumably the ordinance factory, which was installed in the old railway construction sheds. There were children in the hospital with such common unpleasant ailments as scarlet fever, German measles, whooping cough, and chickenpox. I managed to contact German measles but never succumbed to anything worse.

Some of the children in our village suffered from ringworms, and sported nasty red splotches round their necks. Headlice was another persistent problem. The district nurse would arrive on her cycle to the school, accompanied by her special comb, and any hapless child that was suspected of harbouring miniature livestock could expect a good grilling with her comb. She would make us stand on a piece of newspaper to see if any of the offending creatures were lurking in our hair. The children, for the fun of it would aggressively stamp on the newspaper as if crushing any offending inhabitants that may have been evicted from their scalps. All the infected children were doused with D.D.T.Powder, and had to endure the taunts of the other children. They were unceremoniously dubbed ' flea heads'. This was plainly a traumatic experience for these unhappy children. I was very fortunate indeed to escape the Headlice saga.

The only thing I suffered from on a regular basis at that time was recurring nightmares. At its worst, this resulted in sleepwalking. On one occasion I was discovered on the doorstep of the village post office, bleary eyed and confused. On another occasion I somehow had wandered downstairs into our rear parlour where I proceeded to fill the kettle with water, and was about to make a pot of tea. I was shocked into reality when a torch was shone into my face. It was Uncle Alf, who no doubt suspected a burglar was at large in the house. I remembered him talking to me then turning me round, and walking me back upstairs while I was still asleep. Eventually, I had to have chairs tied around my bed in a bid to stop me from climbing out but this was to no avail. Thankfully, after some months the bouts passed.

The war still continued to drag on. Despite our apparently secluded location, there was never any shortage of exciting activity in our area. One night I woke with a start, hearing a loud rumbling sound coming from the direction of the fields across the road. Suddenly, and to my astonishment, flares brilliantly illuminated my bedroom. I leapt out of bed, and dashed to the window. As I peered out from behind the curtains I could see the area of the field where the noise was coming from. I had to crane my neck to see clearly because my bedroom was at side of the house, facing the house next door, and the vicarage grounds, with its poplar trees glistening in the pale moonlight night. Opening my window wide, and leaning out, I obtained a better view. A number of flares were lighting up the night sky as they floated serenely down-to-earth. I could just make out a Westland Lysander plane settling in to the grass. This type of aircraft could land and take off in a very small area, and they were considered the perfect plane for dropping and picking up agents in foreign regions. The pilot of the single engined plane had suffered a problem with the Bristol Mercury engine, and had performed an emergency landing. He had used the flares to illuminate the night sky to see where he was heading. The sudden, and unexpected arrival of the Lysander naturally caused great excitement. The home guard gave this interloper their full attention with rifles at the ready. The ARP warden inevitably put in an appearance, and so did the police constable, who acted as if this harmless monoplane was an enemy fighter with an unexploded bomb in its belly. The next morning after some hasty repairs, and a good breakfast at the army headquarters at the Greyhound Inn, the pilot managed to aviate safely.

There was a similar incident one Sunday afternoon; it appeared that the entire population of Folkingham had dashed out to another field, just a little way out of the village, where a single engined biplane had put down with a fuel problem. It had come to a halt just a few yards from a water tower. (Now there is a new water tower in place). When we arrived at the scene the pilot was in conversation with the village constable who had satisfied himself that both aircraft and pilot were of British origin. The biplane had obviously leaking fuel, and a worried murmur spread among the assembled crowd of onlookers, who promptly moved away without any encouragement from the constable. Amazingly the pilot solved this problem by scrounging a piece of chewing gum, and some tape to plug the offending leak in the aircraft's fuel-pipe system. After completing this task he simply turned his aircraft into the wind, and took off without any further difficulty. It was an astonishing piece of flying, and it was the focus of much banter for quite some time. Later, many people pondered whether the pilot would be able to complete his trip without another mishap. The Aviation Authority evidently were not aware of this incident, that is, if this organisation existed during the war years.

We lads of the village, and the evacuees would play mock war games, and were quite proficient in aircraft recognition. Not seeing too many German planes in the daylight hours made this exercise much more difficult. The aircraft we were reasonably adept in recognizing were the Junkers 88, Dorniers, the Heinkel's, Stukas, and Messerchmitts. We had religiously studied pictures of these aircraft in newspapers and magazines of the day. Allied aircraft were much easier a proposition because they were nearly always on our view in our skies in daylight hours. Nevertheless, there was a clue, and the way of recognizing German aircraft was very often by sound. We had become accustomed to this fact, and here lies the clue. Some of the twin-engine German planes had a distinct sibilant sound due to their non--synchronised engines. We soon latched on to this method of aircraft recognition, and could supply our acquired knowledge to the adults, be it only a snippet of information. Nevertheless, they were quite impressed by our acute childlike observations. This ability in enabling us to be familiar with different aircraft types made it easy to recognize the American P-38. One incident will forever remain fresh in my memory. The Americans had started to operate P-38 Lightning's, long-range fighters with two engines, and distinctive twin-boom tails.

On one very hot Saturday morning a group of us were playing in one of the nearby fields when a terrible shrieking noise stopped us in our tracks. We looked up to the source of the sound, and to our amazement, and horror saw a P-38 American Lightening fighter bomber spiraling towards the ground, twisting, and swirling, getting closer to the ground dropping like a stone, completely beyond control. Then, with only a few hundred feet to fall, a parachute emerged from the aircraft, twisted and only partly open, spiraling and twirling. The cracking sound of the chute's material haunted the sky, ever increasing in acceleration as it sped hopelessly to earth. It vanished out of sight for a brief while, and then, came to rest behind some very tall poplar trees. A sudden horrendous boom engulfed the air as the stricken aircraft impacted into the hard solid ground. We were traumatised by what we saw, and the sight is just as fresh in my mind today as it was then. The pilot had clearly bailed out too late. He obviously had little time, and his parachute had not time to open properly before it struck the ground. That summer had been extremely hot. The ground was dry, and hard, and totally unforgiving to anything that plummeted at it with speed. The aircraft had crashed about a half a mile away, but its pilot lay before us-motionless-and quite dead. His face charred, his useless parachute twisted around his body like a shroud, and partly entangled on a large role of barbed wire only a few feet away. Thankfully, we were only there at the scene for a short while before the village constable moved us on. We sensed that each of us had said a silent prayer before leaving. It was a very horrific weekend but further south there must have been scenes like this every day.

My impression of the P38 American fighter bomber which crashed near Folkingham

In those heady summer evenings when it never seemed to get truly dark, we would gaze in awe at the aircraft flying overhead, and forming into defensive squadrons in the skies over the village. They came from air bases at Scampton, Waddington, Cranwell, and other satellite airfields around. Guy Gibson and the legendary Dam Busters Squadron were based at nearby Scampton. These brave men flew their lumbering, Avro Lancaster's into the heart of Germany where at low level; they would deliver Barns Wallis's famous bouncing bombs in a bid to knock out the dams of the Ruhr, on the nights of the 16/17th of May 1943. On returning, Lincoln Cathedral would, for the crews, be a welcome sight for sore eyes, and they would use the cathedral as a landmark.

It wasn't an uncommon sight in the winter months to witnessed very deep snow with telegraph poles peeping out the tops of the snowdrifts. We made the best of these severe winters. Tobogganing was a favourite pastime. Canon Heath's grown-up son Edward (which, with his father's surname, we nicknamed him Ted after the famous bandleader, Ted Heath) was at college, and he possessed a very large, and well-constructed sledge. It could seek six comfortably, and at a pinch, eight small bodies. We eventually persuaded Canon Heath to give us a loan of this monster for which in return we collected firewood for him. Just outside of the village there was a steep hill that proved excellent runs, and we would be fully occupied with this sport for days on end during the Christmas break. Many ponds were scattered around the area, and we enjoyed sliding on the ice. Several adults in the village owned ice skates, and we would watch them gliding regally across the pond with their air of loose limber languor. In complete contrast we would simply career widely across, wearing our normal footwear for the season. As we grew more reckless, we took running jumps at the pond, launching ourselves from the bank, and skidding across the ice. So much force was employed in this enterprise that large cracks would appear in the ice, much to the alarm of anybody else happening to be skating. Fortunately the ponds were not deep but if you did happen to fall in, the water was exceedingly cold.

Later on, film shows were presented in the evenings at the school. We children were not allowed to attend as they contained footage of war atrocities, so we were told. This statement made us the more curious so, consequently, we took it in turns to stand on a dustbin, and sneak a peek through one of the windows that had a gap in the blackout curtains. Once we were caught getting a free view, by the ARP warden whom bawled at us, with his usual habitual call. *"Clear off you lot!* Or *I'll get the policeman to see to you. "You horrid mob!"*

After giving him plenty of cheek we would dash off not particularly perturbed. There were films that we were allowed to watch, and these films came to the village by courtesy of travelling nuns. Parking their very large van awkwardly in the Village Square, they would then invite the public to watch the movies. People would stand at the rear of the van, hoping it wouldn't snow or rain. Of course these films were of a religious nature, and we children found them extremely boring. They were screened for two or three nights a week, and there was usually a good attendance. These films were of scant interest to the children who wanted action but they did serve to relieve some of the occasional boredom of village life. Although we didn't find the films as exciting as we would have liked, they did however, give us a talking point for some time after. The nuns would distribute colour picture cards containing religious text. William Holman Hunt's famous painting' The Light of The World' was one such card. While the nuns were staying in the village, the locals would take it in turn to offer them hospitality.

One day there was a buzz of excitement among the villagers. Parked in the square was a very long trailer, and on the trailer and equally large-scale model of a Corvette. This flush-decked war vessel, with its one tier of guns, was a very fast naval-escort ship. It being such a large, and well-detailed model, at first some people thought it was the real thing, and it was the topic of conversation for sometime in, and around the village.

During one long spell of bitterly cold weather there was a very large convoy of armoured vehicles, and troops passing through Folkingham. The convoy took the best part of a week to journey through the village. Vehicle after vehicle, gun-carrier after gun-carrier, and all the paraphernalia of warfare passed through. When we saw an armoured car displaying a green flag mounted on the rear of the vehicle, we assumed that the convoy had passed through. Not so, more vehicles would appear. In the main road running through the village there was a very dangerous bend, this road led to Sleaford, and in the past many accidents had happened at this point. The military, no doubt, felt it prudent to post a traffic control at this danger spot. We would watch the two soldiers as they took it in turn to direct the traffic safely. They would continually stamp their feet in the cold winter air in a bid to keep warm. People in the village would supply them with mugs of steaming hot tea, and soup. Women knitted squares of thick wool. These squares they sewed together to make a scarf for each controller. No doubt the soldiers were very grateful to the ladies for their generosity, and goodwill. The garments would help to soften the icy blast coming in from the Wash, across the Fen Country into our part of the world.

When we had some money to spare, we would frequent the local fish, and chip shop in the village. There was little in the way of fish but chips were generally plentiful. On winter evenings we would make this establishment a regular rendezvous, making our purchases spin out as long as possible. A steamy, warm, and cosy atmosphere lingered in the chip shop and we would be very reluctant to leave. In the background the popular songs of the day could be heard emanating from a radio. We would join in with some of the numbers, for example, *'Don't Fence Me In'*, *'Maitzy Doats, and Dozy Doats'*, *'Knees up Mother Brown'*, *'Bless' em All'*, *'Run Rabbit Run'*, *'Lili Marlene'* and many more. No doubt this robust singing could be heard all over the village. As the evening drew on, with heavy blinds drawn the chip shop would be heaving in steam. This created a congenial atmosphere, and we were always reluctant to leave. Somehow, being in this greasy atmosphere, we were not aware of it at the time, inhaling these fatty fumes probably helped lubricate the larynx. The adult population would turn a blind eye to these musical frolics because while in the chip shop we were not getting up to any mischief out of doors. Of course the proprietor had a monetary interest in the proceedings also. When we had to depart from this cosy warm atmosphere, and step outside into the cold night air, it came as an immense shock, and we didn't hang around outside a very long. We would soon be at home beside a large roaring fire.

Some evenings, the strains of *'Somewhere over the Rainbow'*, made famous by Judy Garland in the film' The Wizard of Oz', could be heard being played on a trumpet. Probably the person was practicing for one of the concerts that were produced by the local talent in the village hall. I was taken to these amateur concerts, where the locals would show off their artistic skills. There were jugglers, conjurers, singers, comedians, and comedy sketches, which were all part of the show. One comedy sketch scared the living daylights out of me. A figure suddenly appeared from behind the curtains. Completely covered in a white bed sheet, and stupidly cavorted about the stage. In the past, the village tailor we nicknamed Old Humpty because of his unfortunate deformity, told me that if I didn't behave myself the bogeyman would get me. At this juncture in the concert it struck me that the Demon really had arrived. For many nights after this experience I had very bad dreams about the bogeyman. He would take on the guise of an enormous spider, and another appearance would be of a very gruesome looking man with a bluish face. I would lie in bed, and stare at the corners of the ceiling expecting some spectre to appear, and then the corners of the ceiling would retreat into infinity. This experience lasted several minutes until I closed my eyes. When I opened them again everything would be back to normal. These nocturnal experiences could well have triggered the nightmares I later experienced and also the sleepwalking episodes.

****

Out bird-nesting one day I stupidly succeeded in tearing my trousers on barbed wire, and I cut my leg just above the knee. As it turned out the tearing of the trousers, and the cutting of my leg, meant I had close encounters with two persons in the village that I would normally have avoided like the plague.

I timidly rang the surgery doorbell. The doctor flung open the door. *"Yes, what have you come for?"* He snapped sharply. *"I have cut my knee Dr Stanton."* I replied timidly.

"Well you had better go, and wait in my awaiting room." He aggressively replied.

I sat down nervously on the bench in the waiting room. I was afraid to tell the doctor that I had been bird nesting. I realised how irate he could be had he known the truth. Another notion struck me, he could easily have worked it out of me, and in any case he would probably guess. The waiting room door was flung open *"This way!"* He waved me into his consulting room. I noticed how melancholy he was looking, perhaps the current news bulletin of the war was not too good. *"Sit down here!"* He motioned me to a chair by his desk. He continued. *"Now let me have a look at your leg. Well it doesn't look too bad to me, just as well you came, and it won't need stitches."*

At this last statement, I was relieved. He looked at me hard. Then came the question I was dreading I held my breath, and waited. *"How did you manage to get this nasty gash?"* He snapped.

"On barbed wire Dr Stanton," I said meekly. *"What were you doing on barbed wire?"*

"Getting through it"

He obviously had guessed what I had been doing, because his following remark confirmed that his assumption was correct. He sniggered. *"That will teach you to go stealing bird's eggs,"* and then promptly slapped on a fresh dressing, and quickly ushered me out of the surgery he said. *"Come, and see me again if it hasn't healed properly within a week!"* Promptly slamming the door, he then vanished out of sight.

This bird-nesting caper not only made it imperative for me to visit the doctor. It also meant that sooner or later I would have to have a confrontation with the village tailor. He would regularly visit our home on a Thursday evening, and in return for a minimal amount of sowing, Aunt Nin would give him his supper, cocoa, and anything else that was available, and was going free at the time. She had warned me of the impending visit by the village couturier, and she had already asked him to repair the trousers. The following Thursday evening he arrived, and when Aunt Nin opened the door to him, I attempted to make myself very scarce indeed. I always did so on these occasions, but this time I was more determined than ever he shouldn't see me. I darted for the front parlour, I was too late, and he had spotted me, as he closed the door behind him. *"Don't run away sonny, what have you been up to?"* He croaked.

"Nothing," I replied *"Bet you have,"* he gave me a quizzical stare. *"I know all the tricks, and things you naughty boys do. Your aunt tells me you have been up to mischief again!"* I eyed him suspiciously, and looked for an escape route. I thought I will dash for the front parlour, but before I could move, he then stunned me with a hypnotic glare. *"You're a naughty, naughty, naughty boy!"* He shouted.
Gosh! He's in a bloody bad mood tonight I thought. I knew it was hopeless trying to escape, so I decided to stay in the kitchen. I thought, you wouldn't have shouted like that at me if Uncle Alf had been around. Uncle had gone to see a farmer about the next day's work undertaking. In submission, I shrank further back into the room, but I didn't wish to get any closer to Old Humpty than necessary. As he agitatedly twitched about, I noticed the needles, and dolly pins in his jacket lapels glinting in the light of the oil lamp that stood on the kitchen table. His wizard form cast grotesque shadows on the walls as he hovered, and hesitated like a bewildered moth. I thought he's going to sit down. I could see he was eyeing the seat near the fire. I had considered if you were claiming it mate I will beat you to it. This chair was the only one I usually sat in on cold winter nights. Anyone else sitting in it I wouldn't mind, but I had serious reservations regarding the village tailor more so now, being as he had chastised me. He watched me very closely, and with uncanny foresight, beat me to the chair. Across his wizened face a malicious smile crept as he nestled down, and made himself comfortable. I had lost another battle.

"He ought to be in bed" he said, looking at Aunt Nin, *Naughty, Naughty boy"*. I mumbled. *"He never gives up."*

"What's that you say sonny?" I promptly replied. *"I said you like a big cup!"*

"Oh, yes, yes. I will, yes. I will have a big cup."

There was little chance of him saying please or thank you. I thought I had got one over him, as he hadn't heard properly what I had said. I was glad that I had not had to take my torn trousers to his house. Previously I had to collect some repair work he had done for my aunt. I didn't relish another errand to his house one bit. His dwelling was halfway down a very narrow dark alley in the village. The outside of the house was extremely dismal. It had two very large front windows. Before ringing the front door bell, I became inquisitive, and peered through one of the windows. The house inside looked cold, and lifeless, extremely dingy, untidy, and much more depressing than the outside. I shuddered. Suddenly I was shook out of my senses by a high-pitched snapping voice. *"What do you think you are playing at boy?"* The voice rasped.

I staggered back at the sight of this hideously deformed creature, and in my fright I stumbled over a very large flowerpot, the contents being unceremoniously strewn over the footpath. Of course it was Old Humpty himself. He had sneaked from the rear of the house. This was my first close-up encounter I had with the village tailor. When he witnessed my obvious fright, he hopped from one foot to the other. His twisted form rocked from side to side, and with cynical glee he croaked.

"Come for Mrs. Barber sewing have you?" His eyes pierced through me, and then pointing with a determined look at the doorstep, said. *"Wait there."* He then vanished inside the house. He came shuffling back with the repaired garments in a brown paper package tied roughly with string. *"Mind you get it home in one piece. Now be off with you! Go straight home!"* He shouted which caused me to trip over the upturned flowerpot as he slammed the front door in my face. From that day on, I vowed I would not go to his house again. I mused over these thoughts as I squatted on the stool close by the fire.

The tailor caught my suspicious glance towards him. He gave me a fiendish grin in return. "*Where are the torn trousers?"* He asked my aunt.

I noticed he spoke to her in more dulcet tone than he ever did to me. "*I'll get them for you. They are in the front parlour."* The tailor grinned at me as my aunt left the kitchen. She returned with the trousers, and handed them to him, saying in a contrite manner. "*Here they are I do hope they are not passed redemption."*

"What a bloody mess" screamed Humpty the he scrutenised them more closely, and holding them aloft, as if venerating the gods as a piece offering, continued. *"What the heck am I supposed to do with these?"*

This sudden outburst shook Aunt Nin; nevertheless she managed to compose herself saying she would now make the drinks. The suggestion of a beverage break mellowed the tailor's manner somewhat. He quietly said he would try, and do its best to repair the trousers. I thought a blooming good sized patch should do the trick. Aunt Nin offered Old Humpty homemade jam tarts, and biscuits, and then she prodded the fire with the poker. There was whoosh as the fire roared back into life. Old Humpty always treated us to his ritual of pouring out the last drops of cocoa into his saucer, and then, with what appeared great delight to him, slurped up the remains to the accompaniment of a long drawn-out, 'ahaaa'. When he had finished eating, and drinking his cocoa, he would carefully scrutinised his plate for any leftover morsels, following this ceremonial he would then lick his forefinger, and swoop down on any unsuspecting crumbs, and swiftly deposit them into his mouth. He carefully selected a needle from the lapel of his jacket. After close inspection of the needle, he stuck it back again.

"Too small," he muttered, and then selected another. This one being to his satisfaction, he then proceeded to unwind some thread from a cotton reel he produced from his jacket pocket. I watched, fascinated by his wizened face, illuminated by the glow of the oil lamp, as his scrawny fingers deftly threaded the needle. When this task was completed, he immediately swung round at me, pointing the threaded needle at my face, and in a gyrating manner zoomed the needle point close to my face, and at the very last millisecond, diverted it towards the trousers. "*Ha, ha, nearly got you!"* He grimaced, and had clearly gained satisfaction by almost frightening me to death.

When listening to the wireless set at Aunt Mary's house, I sometimes would hear the familiar nasal tones of William Joyce (Lord Haw, Haw) the British public were not encouraged to listen to his propaganda speeches from Germany. William Joyce was of Irish descent. He joined the regular army but was discharged when he was only sixteen years old. The reason, he was too young, and from then onwards he felt intensely bitter towards the authorities. To us youngsters he was fascinating to listen to, with the familiar 'This Is Germany Calling. This Is Germany Calling'. The adult population took a more cynical view to these broadcasts from Germany. It was very disturbing indeed what he had to say in one of his propaganda speeches, he stated that he knew all about the dummy aerodrome near our village. Far more disturbing was what he had to say about, of all things, the bench outside our parish church. He referred to the fact that it had just been renovated, and painted. Without specific information from an informant, how could he have possibly known this fact? Consequently, the village became the focus of military search for informants. Shadowy figures racing around the village, like us boys, were the immediate suspects. Evidently, the nasal tones of William Joyce were the result of a fight when he was a youngster. When he eventually was arrested, and it apparently appeared that he wanted to be taken into custody as he did little to conceal the fact of his true identity. After the war he was seen wandering along a footpath collecting firewood in the German countryside, by two very observant British soldiers, and evidently he made no attempt to escape, in fact he was most cooperative when questioned about his identity. He was executed at Wandsworth prison on January 3rd 1946.

My impression of Old Humpty, the village tailor

There were other strange happenings in the village during the war. We became increasingly interested in the comings, and goings of trucks destined for the American airbase near the village. They were, in fact, transporting gravel from the quarries near Stamford. A number of different contractors were seconded for this work, and lorries always had to pass through our village. The adults did their best to ignore them, but they soon attracted the children's interest. During the summer holidays when we weren't labouring on the farmer's field, for sheer fun, and with nothing better to occupy our child-like minds, we discovered we were able to flag down these lorries, and could hitch rides, to and from Stamford, and the airbase. These days one can identify a lorry, and the company it belongs to by the name, telephone number, and website address. During the war years these identification indicators were strictly prohibited for security reasons. There was, however, a name on a Bedford tip-up truck that I will never forget. This vehicle was painted bright green except for the bar across the radiator, which was painted bright red. On the bar were the words 'Spriggy King of the Road', displayed in bold yellow handwriting. Spriggy undoubtedly was our favourite driver, and he would always pick us up when we flagged him down. On one occasion, Spriggy, and his unmistakable truck rumbled through the village, but to our surprise, and disappointment, the lorry failed to stop. This odd behaviour seemed out of character to say the least. We continued to wait for his return from the base. We attempted to flag him down again. This time the vehicle stopped. We jumped in, said hello, and off we moved. Not until we had been in the lorry's cab for a few seconds did we realise that it wasn't Spriggy driving. This driver, like the real King of the Road, did not reply to our questions properly when we spoke to him, nor did he utter a word on the way to the quarry, which was some twenty miles from the village. Very concerned at this strange development in the saga we indicated that we wanted to alight when next arriving back in the village. He mumbled something inaudible under his breath. We eventually came very suspicious about this character realising that he had fair hair, and he didn't appear to understand or speak English. We never saw Spriggy again. Who knows, maybe this was the informant the army was searching for? If he was, he had the ideal opportunity for gleaning information about the development of the airbase.

On long summer evenings, before darkness set in, we would play the game of tag in the square, and would chase each other around these shelters. Because the evenings were pleasantly cool at that time of the year, there were always lots of people milling around including the Irish labourers who only recently had given so generously to our battleship Red Cross fund. During one of these tag-playing sessions, I had called out to one of my friends, whom happened to be on my side of the game, to warn him of an impending tag *"Look Out he's coming!"* I screamed at the top of my voice. *"Where*"? He shouted back.

"*There, just coming round the corner, quick! Or he'll get you.*" I replied. "*I can't see him*" Bellowed my team mate. I took no more notice of my friend's reply; I only wanted to get out of the way of the impending tag from the other side. I diverted my course to behind one of the shelters. As I rounded the corner of the red brick refuge, I reeled back in horror. I had narrowly avoided being impaled on a bayonet attached to the business end of a 303 Lee Enfield rifle. I came to a sudden halt, and reeled back further as the sharp end of the bayonet, was pushed sickeningly close to my stomach. On the other end of this rifle was a soldier. He glared at me. *"Shut up and be quiet; Don't move; Stay where you are!* " He screamed as he pinned me against the air raid shelter wall. I pissed myself, and for several seconds I was petrified not knowing what to expect next. My legs began to crumble under me. I felt myself beginning to slide down the wall of the shelter. The terrifying closeness and pressure of the weapon at my stomach gave me the presence of mind to freeze on the spot.

"I said don't move!" The soldier insisted with much menace in his voice. Shuddering, not uttering a syllable I was terrified of what the soldier was about to do. We as lads played at war games, and the shock of this realistic, nasty, terrifying experience suddenly brought home to me the horrors of this war. It wasn't a game anymore. The first sober thought to enter my head was that from now on I should be a good boy, and everything would work out alright. I began to collect some composure, and the horrific, menacing form of this soldier towering over me, now seemed a little less frightening. Trembling I replied "*I was only calling my friends over there."*

"Never mind who you were calling you will come with me!" He commanded as he motioned me with the butt of his rifle, indicating the direction that I should go. I looked around; all the children I had been playing with a few seconds earlier had completely vanished. Unknown to me at that time, the army had been keeping a close watch on one of the workers from the American airbase. One man in particular was suspected of being a fifth columnist, or spy. The army let me go when it was clearly apparent that I was not in league with the Third Reich, and a recruit of the Hitler Jugend, although, at eleven years, I was certainly old enough.

Six

Stamford Boys Home

Enter the Dragons

Early one summer morning my foster father woke me up, and then took the extraordinary step of giving me a haircut. Never before had he cut my hair this early in the day. Indeed it was very strange; he also had forgotten to put the pudding basin on my head, which he always had done before. This was the day when Aunt Nin died in the early hours on the morning of June7th. At the funeral, and looking down into the grave at her coffin, and seeing her age, only sixty-one, I was racked with pangs of guilt. I thought of all the times I knowingly played her up.

Only a few days after the funeral, Miss Shee, who had brought me first to this house in Folkingham, again visited me. She was no stranger to the family. I had become rather afraid of her because of the commanding and authoritative manner that she adopted. Whenever she paid us a visit she seemed to look at me in a calculating detached manner, as if appraising my development on the scale of one to ten. I would try, and sneak away when she appeared. I always associated Aunt Nin's threats to send me away with the visit of this lady. My heart was a desert, my body, and spirit contorted with desolation. I was to lose everything familiar to me. Now I was to embrace strangers, and adventure, trembling with fear, and sadness, into the darkness. An uncertain future waited, beckoning me on with cold, pale fingers.

At the conclusion of the journey we pulled up outside a very austere looking building built of yellow brick, and sporting a large number of huge windows. It could hardly have been more different to my own little house in Folkingham. Feeling dwarfed, and cowed, I was ushered through a tall wrought iron gate. My heart was a mangle of uncertainty as I stared at the tubby gentleman who opened the gate as we approached. He was wearing a light grey trilby hat, with the brim tilted down, partly obscuring its pale, chubby face. When he looked up his eyes were small, and slate-coloured, his stare fast. A bulbous nose protruded from his face looking somewhat out of place, as if it had been placed there for safekeeping. As we passed I noticed that now, and again, his face would twitch, and there would be a flicker in those cold slate-coloured eyes. He wore a thinly striped blue and white shirt with collar two or three sizes too small, causing red chafed marks to appear on his neck as he moved his head. Shiny black shoes were just visible peeping out from the bottom of his grey flannel trousers that were clearly much too long for him. He stood upright, as if in a constant state of indignation, with his stomach protruding forward like an overgrown pumpkin. The trilby hat was raised to Miss Shee as we passed through the gates. His head pitched back and forth like a chicken scratching for daylight, as he spoke.

"*Have you had a pleasant journey*?" He enquired.

"*Quite So, This is Roy"* Miss Shee replied, and then with an index finger pointing to the subject in question, with nothing more to add to the introduction, she gripped my hand tightly, and began to stride purposefully towards the house. The fat man hurriedly closed the main gate as if to keep us incarcerated, and with a rushed waddle to catch us up before we reached a very large and oppressive looking front door. It was a rather ominous looking thing, more of a warning than a welcome. It didn't look as if it had seen a coat of paint in the last fifty years. There was a large round tarnished brass knob in the centre of the door, appearing as it had be assigned the task of holding together what little paint still remained on the woodwork. With an ungainly spurt of speed, he overtook us, and with a slightly ludicrous bow, with chubby fingers grabbed the doorknob, pushed the door open, and asked us to enter. I was swallowed up in the darkness of the hallway. The upper half was painted a yellowish cream. Some of the paint was flaking off in places, and there were scuffmarks all around the lower half, evidence of careless people catching parts of the wall with their ungainly hefty fat feet. In the dismal shadow, the ceiling could just about be discerned, a murky whiteness. Suspending from the centre of this ceiling there hung a tatty, sepia coloured lampshade dangling from a well-worn length of electric flex. The electric light bulb provided a miserable excuse for any semblance of illumination, and was barely enough to disburse the shade, simply creating an abundance of twisted jumping shadows. Eerie shapes appeared to creep across the ceiling, and the light was cast brilliantly this time onto cobwebs clinging between the flex, and shade. Outside, and far away, was warmth, and everything I had come to know as safe, and regular. In here there was only gaunt quiet. Perhaps I would continue on, and on until I became nothing. Little could raise my dwarfed spirits.

From a door at the far end of the hallway there now appeared a little tubby woman. I could not help but think of a spider scuttling across its web having been alerted by the vibrations of prey thrashing, and rising within its silky folds. The woman who came scurrying towards us was dressed in a white coat similar to the man, although hers was a superior fit. Her face was chubby, and pallid her colourless cheeks drawn tightly around the curves of her jaw. Small dark eyes peered at me over a long nose. Her hair was steely grey, and held together on her crown by way of a massive curled comb. I imagined if the comb fell out, her hair would collapse around her head, and shoulders, she would then appear akin to a storybook crone. She wore flat black shoes. She scurried closer, greeting us with a half smile, and a meagre courtesy. When she spoke, her voice was thin, and brittle. I thought she sounded very much like an alarmed curlew. She said "*Warm day, 'ain't it. I 'ope you had a good journey,"* she continued, as if we were visitors from some sunny, far-off land.

My Impression of the Master and Matron at Stamford Boy's Home

Abruptly, Miss Shee let go of my hand. In that very moment it seemed as if she had passed over complete responsibility for my well being to these strange people. She clearly had no intention of staying within these four walls any longer than necessary. With a series of curt exchanges, and the handing over of the certified documents, I was now deemed a resident of this institution. Miss Shee wasted no time in making her exit. She wheeled round her dress swirling in the wake. She said she would see herself out, and waved good bye. Carrying the look of someone enduring a revolting smell, she walked briskly through the front door, and out of my life. The slam of the door resonated in my consciousness like the closing of a sarcophagus lid. I could think of little more final as I was engulfed in the solitude with only these strange people with me. On hearing her car pull away, I felt out of place, and utterly rejected.

"We'll put your suitcase with the others," said the little bulky woman, as she ushered the suitcase, and me into a small cluttered storeroom. On entering this room, I immediately noticed that the shelves therein were stacked high with bed linen, towels, and a motley collection of items required to run an institution for a large contingent of children. Rays of sunshine managed to pierce the storeroom through its only small window and below it on the table stood a sewing machine with a bed sheet in the process of repair. The woman's swept aside the sheet revealing the table.

"Put that 'ere!" She said, pointing to my suitcase. No sooner had I done so, her stumpy finger set to work on the lid.

"It don't seem to open very easily" she snapped, struggling with the suitcase catches, her face taking on a curious hue. "*Is the case still locked*?" She enquired savagely.

"No, it isn't. It's not being very easy to open ever since I first had it," I nervously replied.

"*Oh well, never mind,"* she puffed, as the catches finally succumbed to her meddling.

My senses of unhappiness, and dread began to deepen as I stood there watching this bizarre woman clawing her way through my few possessions. These consisted simply of two shirts, two neckties, two pairs of short trousers, some socks, three handkerchiefs, a woolen scarf, two pairs of shoes, my navy blue blazer, overcoat, and underwear.

"Err, not much 'ere 'ave you?" She grumbled. I felt numb, too frightened to respond to her griping about my suitcase its catches, and the contents.

"*We'll 'ave to do something about it then, won't we?"* She stated flatly. It was just then that the man came into the storeroom "*All done then*?" He asked the woman.

"*Well, I opened this 'ere suitcase but there ain't got a lot in it.*" She continued, "*no doubt we'll 'ave to try, and get some extra clothes for the boy."*

"*You know that's impossible,"* exclaimed the man. "*You know we are strapped for the money since the county won't supply any more cash.*" He then looked at me, his face rigid, and unfeeling. "*This is matron, you will call her Miss.*" He stated firmly, he continued, *I'm the superintendent, and you will be calling me Sir. Is that understood?"*

"*Yes sir,*" I meekly answered. Treacherous tears were beginning to well up in my eyes.

"This is your home now so behave yourself, and don't fall out with the other boys," he stated forcefully.

"*You'll be wanting some more new socks before very long."* The matron interrupted, picking up the ration book out of my suitcase, and scoured through it. She groaned. *"Not many clothes coupons left. I'll be 'aving to 'ave a go at darning these socks the best I can."* Continuing to grumble, she struck an index finger through a gaping hole in one of the socks. Completely changing tack, she continued. *"We'll be 'aving boiled fish, and parsley sauce for dinner when the other boys get 'ome from school,"* she said, poking a curled finger at me through the hole in the sock. "*There'll be 'ere at about a quarter past twelve. Don't you go falling out with any of em? You mark my words!"*

Again my body shuddered as I fought back the rising tide of tears. I was convinced that living here would be like purgatory that's if I understood what purgatory meant. I had a bleak, half formed desire to dash from the storeroom, out of the front gate, and run all the way home. But what welcome would I have found there? I was going to hate living here, I knew it for certain. The thought of all the other boys who lived here filled my being. I wondered how many there would be, and what would they be like, would they like me, or bully me? I stared disconsolately at the grubby ceiling. Through the little window, I caught a glimpse of a blue-tit fluttering about in the branches of a tree. My stomach churned, and my heart was heavy. I remembered the poor little bird I had caught last winter. Devising methods of catching blue tits was another misdemeanor of mine. My friends and I would place some bread beneath a garden sieve that was propped up by a stick. Having tied a long piece of string to the stick, we would hide in wait for a poor unfortunate bird to come along, and take the bait. Once inside, we would snatch on the string, trapping the unfortunate prey inside the sieve. Now the tables are turned, and it was my time to be imprisoned. I felt the black walls of the sieve coming tumbling down around me. If I could have only turned back the clock to that moment, and release the bird from the cage I had created for it. If only to I could spread my wings, and fly far, far from this horrible place with its musty smell, the dingy walls, and these frightening ugly people. What had Miss Shee done bringing me here? What had I done to earn this sorrow? If only she would return back, I would hug her, and plead with it to take me away from this loathsome place. I would actually be pleased to see Old Humpty again, and would not mind going to his house, if it meant I could leave here, and go back home. Would I ever leave, would I? I prayed to be set free. The matron jerked me from my inner turmoil with a jolt. She announced she would take me to see the dining room. Back through the hall we went before turning left and entering a large room with a long table positioned in the centre. I mentally counted fifteen kitchen chairs positioned around it. The table was completely bare, and scrubbed white.

The matron ambled across the room, and pulled out a very large tablecloth from an ancient looking sideboard. *"I suppose I don't 'ave to tell you 'ow to lay the table?"* She snorted, dropping the cloth into my arms. I was just about to tell that I did, but she broke in before I could begin. *"When you've done that, you can put out the knives, and forks.*" She paused. *"Oh, I almost forgot the spoons for pudding. It's sago today."*

Although, always hungry I hated sago, and boiled fish. The thought of having both for in one meal was as much as I could take, also, assisting with its preparation did nothing to raise my spirits. I felt more, and more that I wanted to run away from this place. No depth of feeling could be reached though, without her sharp voice interrupting my thoughts. *"Mind you put the knives on the right, and forks on the left, the spoons along the top with the 'andles's nearest the knives, got that?"* She said sharply. She told me all the boys had certain jobs to do around the place. By giving me this one was one way of me getting used to the way things were run. "*You'll soon fit in.*" She barked as she hurried out of the room.

I thought, no, I bleeding well won't. When the ringing of her voice in my ears had subsided, I collected my thoughts, and as soon as she out of the way, I realised I had time to examine the room properly. Opposite the long dining table, there was a very large window commanding a prospect of the major road, which I'd travelled along in the car. In the other wall was another window. This window was much smaller, and looked out to the side of the house. Peering through it, I could see the Iron Gate, and the route we took to the front door. On the opposite wall there was a third window, and looking through this one gave me a view of a yard. At the opposite side of this yard was a long open ramshackle shed. Stacked underneath its roof, were metal barrels about three feet in diameter, and about two and a half feet high. There were also large brooms, and shovels lying about, a heavy looking wooden wheelbarrow, and what appeared to be vegetables with large green leaves drooping over its sides. Strewn all around were vegetable boxes in untidy heaps. A stirrup pump and a rubber hosepipe littered the yard. A water tap dripped persistently into a strategically positioned bucket. To the left of the yard I could see a group of terraced cottages built of grey stone. All had tiny windows adorned with the familiar crosses of gummed paper stuck to the window panes. This paper would reduce the severity of shattering glass in an air raid. Railings and a strip of russet coloured glass separated the yard from the cottages. A column of smoke drifted surreally from one of the houses. I could hear a low humming sound, which appeared to emerge from across the other side of the main road. Straining myself against the window overlooking the road, I could see tall evergreen trees, a large building with a corrugated roof, and having many small windows, the humming sound apparently was coming from this building. The sounds of industry at work no doubt.

Stamford Boy's Home in 2000 (very little altered)

The image of life going on around me began to stir memories. I hoped there would be peas for dinner to cushion the shock of having to eat boiled fish. The thought of the peas led me to daydream of great days in the garden at home where I would help to shell peas that Uncle Alf had grown. Even dear Rex liked to eat garden peas. I was immediately transfixed by the image of his head snuggled on my knee, the soft brown eyes fastened on mine, hoping to catch a pea thrown his way. I would flick one into his mouth; he would then beg, and issue a muffled bark for another. So I would repeat the process all over again. I felt tears beginning to stream down my cheeks. I wiped them away quickly, and continued to put out the cutlery. I noticed how heavy, and stained the rough ivory handles were. A shrill ten-second-blast brought me back to reality. It startled me, not knowing what it was. I was quickly to find out where the sound had originated when matron came dashing back into the dining room. Rubbing her hands on a scruffy apron she shouted at me.

"Come on now, that's the dinnertime 'ooter from the factory over the road you just 'eard. Move yourself! All the boys will be charging in 'ere for their dinners in a minute."

"I finished laying the table," I said.

"*Not very good,"* she sniffed unkindly. She adjusted some of the cutlery arrangements, and smoothed out the tablecloth. She continued in knowing voice. "*That 'ooter you just 'eard was from the factory over the road. When it goes off I knows the lads won't be long getting in 'ere for their dinners. So we 'as to be sharp like, because they 'ave a long trek back to school after."* She moved over to the sideboard, and picked up huge aluminum jug, which she thumped down heavily onto the dining table. "*There, that's their water,*" she indicated, with a flabby hand. She had her sleeves rolled up, and I noticed her arms were fat, and bulb-shaped, and covered in unpleasant red blotches. "*Get the glasses for water in the cupboard there* the!" She instructed, pointing to a derelict piece of old furniture in the corner of the room. I scrambled up to the highest shelf when, looking completely out of place, I noticed a large bamboo cane resting on the middle shelf. It was an all too familiar sight, and for a second, I froze. Perhaps the matron sensed I had spotted the apparatus of torture because she immediately began to force me along. I put out fifteen glasses one by each set of cutlery. *"Now we want salt, and pepper. It's there, on the middle shelf,"* she said impatiently, directing me back to the cupboard. "*There's three salt, and three pepper pots*." Once again, my gaze came to rest upon the cane from a position just behind the condiment pots. It almost appeared as a warning of the consequences of misbehaving. Here was evidence of what I could expect if I stepped out of line. I wondered how often matron had reason to operate this device, and whether the boys existed in a climate of fear. As I set out the condiments, and placed them at frequent intervals along the table, I could feel the matron's icy stare boring into me.

"*That's good, so now you know*!" This assurance was not uplifting. She seemed to be reminding me that good behaviour here was mandatory. The heartless woman stilted speech was the new law. She continued bustling around the dining room, and when she appeared to have exhausted herself, she looked intently at me with cold icy eyes, saying. "*You can sit 'ere for your dinner, when the time comes,"* which she indicated by slapping the back of a chair. She continued her instructions *"This one and only this one*." Glaring at my hands she grated. *"When you've washed those filthy 'ands, I'll show you where you can do that, come with me."* She took me through another tiny door that led from the dining area, and into the kitchen. It was quite a large place.

There was a coal-burning stove in the centre, with ovens each side, a large deep sink beneath the window, wooden trays containing vegetables were stacked against the end wall by another door which was partly open allowing me a view of the interior. There were many loaves of bread stacked upon a shelf. A dirty looking mop lent lazily in a bucket by the sink. Scrubbing brushes were lined up along the window sill on each brush were a rectangular slab of washing soap resting on the bristles. As my eyes rested on this scene the matron barked "*Wash your 'ands in 'ere,*" she snapped pointing to the deep sink. *"Use the soap, and scrubbing brush, put some water in a bowl, and get on with it, now!"* I turned on the tap, and half-filled the bowl with water. I grabbed a bar of soap, which obviously had been cut from a larger slab of soap.

"No hot water?" I asked nervously.

"Make do with that! What do you need 'ot water for?" She bellowed. I began to wash my hands, scrubbing with little gusto, and employing this timid method I realised I was already disobeying this horrible woman. I thought I hate you and this dreadful place as I continued to wash my hands.

She spied me closely, and then she barked. *"There's a towel there,"* pointing to a soggy looking roller towel hanging on the back of the kitchen door.

As I grabbed hold of the clammy towel, I noticed a barrel, similar to the ones I'd seen outside which contained peeled potatoes, residing in the murky water. As I continued to wipe my hands there was a commotion, evidently coming from the vicinity of the hall. Matron at once ran out of the kitchen, and seconds later I heard her admonishing the boys that had arrived home from school for their dinner. *"Be quiet! Get on, and wash your 'ands!"* She screamed at the boys.

There was a frantic dash for the kitchen sink with bodies scrambling everywhere. On went the tap not bothering to fill the bowl; the boys dived into the sink with their hands, fountains of water showering high, and low. No one had noticed me in the melee until a tall fair-haired boy with eyes half closed, was searching for the towel, he was suddenly stopped in his tracks when he spotted me.

"Oh, you got it," he said in a manner that suggested that he might have known me all my life. He snatched the towel from my hands. *"Ta,"* he then began drying his hands. He rushed off towards the dining room; I stood dumbfounded, with the splashing of the water still going on in the kitchen sink. Events were beginning to overwhelm me, I pondered, what would happen next?

Matron returned to the kitchen, and bungled us into the dining room. *"Sit down and be quiet,"* someone, say grace." Before anyone had the chance to open his mouth to give thanks of what we were about to receive. She shouted. *"Jenkins, you'll do*!" Without any more ado, a small dark-haired boy stood up, and in an extremely knowledgeable manner did the honors; I was only too relieved she hadn't picked on me. She went back into the kitchen taking the tall fair-haired boy with her. When they returned with the fish, mashed potatoes, and turnips, the superintendent strutted in with a large tureen containing the parsley sauce, carrying it as if he was parading a haggis. Having dispatched the first course with much speed, the other boys sat waiting for another boy to collect the dirty plates. By the time he reached me I had not finished my first course, and I was the cause of much embarrassment, until I had. They were all waiting for the second course, which I was told earlier by matron, sago pudding, something I found difficult to stomach, even though it was wartime, and I was always hungry, when I looked down at my plate at the glutinous globules, I thought if I half close my eyes, and say a silent prayer, then, not lingering too long, I can then gulp this lot down as fast as possible. To my delight, I saw my dish was empty. The husband, and wife team, didn't dine with us, they ate in their own private quarters.

On a wireless set in the distance I could hear the strains of Henry Purcell's 'Lilibullero', the signature tune of the BBC World Service programme, echoing from their living room. When the meal was over, we all had to take our pudding dishes into the kitchen to be washed up. This day the washing-up fell to me. Since I wasn't starting school until the following day, to keep me occupied I was allotted jobs about the home. After helping matron with the washing-up, the other boys having gone back to school, she told me. "*You can put the knives, and forks back where you found 'em, and make sure you put 'em back in the right place, then when you've done that, come to me in the linen store."* I knocked timidly on the linen room door.

Come in!" She shouted. As I reluctantly entered she glared at me standing in the doorway. "*Come in! Don't stand there like a pregnant earwig! Sit down there!"* She demanded, pointing with a dumpling hand to a rather rickety looking chair. She glared at me again with those cold eyes, which were dancing all over me. *"Now, let me tell you this, we 'ave to look after our clothes 'ere,"* and, fondling the contents of my suitcase she continued, *"you ain't got much in the way of clothes 'ave you?"*

"*That's all I brought with me, I've got more things at home."* "*Ome! Ome! This is your ome now."* Screaming, and modulating the pitch of her voice an octave higher, she continued. *"Ome, 'ome, this is your 'ome, and don't you be forgetting it!"*

When the tirade was over I was paralysed. I couldn't comprehend what was going on, it must be a nightmare. Yes that's what it was, a nightmare. As my trembling subsided I looked at this slob of a female. She continued glaring. Seconds ticked by, then plucking up courage, and with a halted voice I calmly responded, hoping my tone will assuage her rage. "*Probably the lady will bring some more things*."

Realising that she had made her point, her voice mellowed a little. *"You have to realise that this is your 'ome now, and that's that, there's nothing you can do about it, so you 'ave to make the best of it."* She carried on. "*And you 'ave to get on with the other boys."* Smirking, she remarked," *I love 'em."*

I thought, bloody hell what a strange thing to say after all the shouting, and ranting. Probably the boys were scared into submission? I felt that the statement she had just made regarding I love them, had a sinister ring about it. The interrogation continued, "*'ave you got another coat, do you 'ave another jacket, and what about Wellington boots?"* She droned on, and on. For a brief second or two I switched off, and drifted into a paradise of my own making. The matron scrambled onto a chair, and reaching to the top shelf of the storeroom jerked me back into reality of this strange and weird world about me. Lifting down a battered cardboard box, and blowing the dust from off the lid, she then scattered the contents on the table. Rummaging through the motley assortment of clothing she held up a black pair of swimming trunks, put her hand inside stretching them, confirming that they were wholesome, and intact, she then winged them around in the air, creating clouds of dust, then barked. *"They'll have to do."* She acknowledged my puzzled look by saying in a forthright manner. *"When the boys get 'ome from school in the afternoon, they change into their swimming trunks, this saves wear, and tear on their clothes, especially their school uniforms. So you will do the same."* I could not follow the rationale behind this. I could understand having to change from a school uniform; I had never encountered such apparel before. I thought why all the fuss about me not having much in the way of clothes if I was to wear these bloody bathers all the time. I could not understand the logic one bit. She again thrust me out of my pondering, by instructing me to take the bathers with me, and she would show me where I could change. She took me upstairs to the dormitory at the top of a lengthy flight of stairs which had a small landing halfway, here there was a big window draped with dark green curtains looking out towards the main road. From this vantage point, I had a much better perspective of the factory in the main road. Workers were scurrying through the main gates. The humming sound of the factory was much louder from where I stood gazing, longing to go anywhere back along the main road, to be free from this dreadful place, and this hateful woman.

"Don't stand there gawking boy, we've got things to do!" She yapped. We reached the head of the second flight of stairs. She opened the door on our left, and pointed to another door on the right. She rasped. *"That there door is another storeroom, so there's no need for you to go poking around in there, got that?"* She continued. "*This is your dormitory; your bed is the second on the left."* All the beds were covered with blue counterpanes, at the side of each bed stood a small wardrobe and a small chair. There was a distinct smell of beeswax, and shafts of sunlight pouring through the windows created a pool of dancing light on the highly polished linoleum floor. This faintly lifted my spirits. It was a brighter place that I had already witnessed in this dreadful place. A large clock with a very pronounced tick hung precariously on the far wall, two large windows on either side of the dormitory with long navy blue curtains almost touching the floor. The brick walls were decorated a buff colour, from floor-to-ceiling, and this was like the dingy off-white of the hallway. The dormitory was a melancholy sight as the clouds obscured the sun, causing the dancing reflection on the floor to scurry, and take cover. Matron did not give up on her repeated demands, and instructions. "*You change into your bathing trunks now, and when you 'ave done that, put your clothes you are wearing now in your wardrobe, get on with it!"* I thought aggressively, doesn't this woman ever stop nagging? I felt too shy to change into the bathers in front of her, so I just stood staring at her, then after a few seconds she stormed out of the dormitory shouting loudly as she went clattering down the stairs. *"Don't be long about it, and come down to me in the kitchen when you've changed!"* When she saw that the swim trunks were too small, and were tightly grasping my lower anatomy, causing me much embarrassment she then equipped me with another pair of trunks, which were, if anything, rather on the huge size. The swimming trunks were already beginning to slip down my legs as I struggled with more embarrassment to keep them up. *"You're going to grow into 'em,"* she muttered, then told me to follow her into the linen store. *"You can tidy up in 'ere,"* she said, pointing to a very large untidy heap of clothes. She continued. *"Fold 'em up, and put 'em in the basket,"* she then *added* firmly. *"You call me Miss, don't forget that!"* By the time I had reached the linen store the trunks had wrapped themselves unceremoniously round my ankles. With extreme urgency, I pulled them up, and held onto them tightly fearing the worst if this embarrassing occurrence should befall me once more. I had hardly finished struggling with this task when the superintendent came into the linen store. He looked intently at me, saw the predicament I was in, he handed me a belt, saying he would get me a better fitting pair Then with a curved forefinger he beckoned me saying. *"Come with me, I've got a job for you."* I followed him out of the store wondering what the job would be. I was soon to find out. As we passed through the kitchen, he picked up two metal bowls, and carried them out into the yard. *"Come on, this way!"* He called as he turned around to see me follow him in the same brisk manner he had adopted. When we arrived at the long shed outside, he pointed to one of the barrels that I'd spotted earlier. *"In that bowl you will find some potatoes, take some out, and put them in this bowl."* He handed me one of the bowls he was carrying. *"Put some potatoes in it, and some water from that tap,"* pointing to it with a fat flabby hand. *"Then scrape them."* He continued. *"You only scrape them, don't peel them, we can't afford to waste anything, sit on that stool."* He took a potato peeler from his coat pocket telling me to get on with the job, saying, the more I do now, the less there was for the other boys to do when they arrive home from school. Before he reached the kitchen door on his way back, he added. *"When you've finished the first bowl, get another one from the kitchen."* I couldn't see my way to finishing the first let alone another. I sat down, and began to scrape away. There seemed to be thousands of potatoes. I resorted to peeling them; they were much too hard to scrape, the outcome resembling cubes of varying sizes. The potatoes were big with massive eyes in them. I must have been struggling for about twenty minutes, congratulating myself on doing so well, and counting what I had accomplished - mainly peeled. I had done twelve. By the time I had finished the first bowl the boys were already arriving home from school. On arrival, they change into their bathing trunks and got on with their allotted tasks. Six of the boys came over to me, still struggling with the potatoes. At lunchtime I had not got to know any of them,

in fact I could not recall any of their faces except the boy who had snatched the hand towel from me. Then a small dark-haired boy with tight curls and a chubby cheeky face asked. "*What's your name*?"

"*It's Roy*," I replied. "*Oh*," came is rather vague response that halted any enquiry on my part requesting his name. I was about to do so when he asked. "*Did matron tell you to change into bathers?*"

"Yes, she did, I had to change the first pair, they were too small, and these seem too big."

Scanning all of my body, his eyes eventually settling on my trunks, he quipped, *"No they're not, anyway you'll grow into them," "She said that!"* I informed him.

"I thought she would, she says that every time. "By the way, my name is Dave," he quickly added. He then continued. "*That first skimpy pair of bathers she gave you, she always gives the identical pair to any new boy here. They've seen more legs than on a centipede. They would be too tight on a three-year old. She does it purposely to get a kick out of seeing the boy's embarrassment."*

I was the source of much interest from the group standing around I referred to the potatoes as taties, and the cold water as code water. This strange dialect was amusing to the group of boys. The towel-snatching boy came sauntering across from the area of the kitchen. I could see as he drew closer that he had an abundance of freckles on his face, forearms, and the upper part of his body. He leant nonchalantly against one of the pillows supporting the roof of the shed, he scrutinised me closely then said. *"You ain't done many spuds have you?"*

From where I was sitting on the stool he appeared enormous as he towered over me. A thought ran through my mind wondering if he was a bully. He appeared to be in charge of the boys here, so no doubt he probably was. I hesitated for a second before opening my mouth. *"The taties have got a lot of eyes in them, and the skins are too tough to scrape."* I nervously replied.

"Shit! You don't want to worry about scraping them; we all do the same thing, peel 'em" He chuckled.

I felt a little bit easier now. As he appeared to support my predicament, he noticed my little smile, and volunteered his name informing me it was Peter.

Looking around at the rest of the lads he quickly introduced me, and before very long I'd forgotten most of their names. This, apparently, broke some of the ice. The group began to question me, and made remarks about my strange accent. As if on cue, the boys began to close in around me. I felt like a peep show as they eyed my skinny body. As I gazed at them one by one, I was struck by the sadness in their faces. Even the chubby-faced little boy had a hungry appearance, most had pale cheeks and showed no glimmer of a twinkle in their sad eyes. For a brief moment all my own sadness melted away with this sorrowful countenances peering sadly, and searching for some form of condolence, and strangely, for a second, I thought, from me. I was too inadequate to offer any solace to these woeful boys. Once again my innermost, sacrosanct thoughts were startled by the screaming of matron resounding from the vicinity of the kitchen. *"Get on with yer work you lazy lot!"* Making sure we understood she repeated her command in a much louder voice. There was no more talking for a short while. The other boys seem to remain locked in to their respective places as if computer programmed robots. It was not long before like all lads, the reprimand, and stinging tones were soon forgotten, and they began to start chatting in muted tones to each other. Then a small boy with auburn coloured hair and a tooth brace cluttering up his mouth, and was called Ginger by the others, shuffled up to me, and asked me where I had lived. At great length I explained it was a village called Folkingham. *"Where's that?"*

"On the A15, near Sleaford," I told him. He looked bemused, and I gathered there was little point in trying to describe the precise geographical location, and I emphasised the point with a shrug of my shoulders. No doubt he gathered from my gesture that there was little mileage in pursuing the matter any further. One lad appeared to be knowledgeable about the area when I mentioned the town of Grantham during the conversation. The place name wasn't familiar to me, but Grantham was. The knowledgeable boy's name was Richard. He was average height for a boy about ten years. He looked healthy enough, and had a strapping physique, but like all the others; there was this lonely and sorrowful expression on his face. His hair was golden and shiny and what was striking about him, were the blue grey eyes, with a passionate appeal about them. He spoke in a hushed voice, appearing to be miles away, deep in his private thoughts. As the discussion progressed in a more animated fashion, the other boys began

to relax, and raised voices were the norm. I did not realise it then, but later I was to have a closer relationship with this boy Richard. There was another admonition vocalised by matron to get on with our work. We laboured on until the superintendent appeared, calling us in for tea. As part of the institution's regime, we could not sit down to tea in our bathing trunks until we had changed into our indoor clothes. I asked Richard why we had to go through all this rigmarole. "It's one of the ways they can save on money I suppose, it's a blooming nuisance though," came is rather despondent reply.

As we were changing, I discovered that the rest of the inmates had been doing various jobs about the institution while we were scraping potatoes. The tall fair-haired boy Peter had been cleaning out the kitchen range, and chopping wood for the following day, when he would light the fire at about six thirty in the morning. *"Does he do this every day?"* I asked. Before Richard could give me an answer another boy named Alan, from the distant end of the dormitory quickly answered my question.

"Most times he does, he seems to be the best at it, and so they let him get on with it."

"Do we always have to scrape taties?" I wearily asked.

"Yes every day except Sundays." Called out a fat little lad, who strangely, up to now I had not noticed? He had a very scruffy look about him, his mousy coloured hair was untidy, and his face entertained many spots. His voice had a gruff edged as he spoke in staccato bursts. I was to discover that he was quite intelligent, and a wealth of information, and considered the MI5 of the institution. I was told if you wanted to know anything regarding the home you only had to ask this lad, whose name was Graham. Nevertheless, I was warned at times he would make up stories; this was probably attention seeking, and also loneliness manifesting itself.

"Why not Sundays?" I asked Graham, and at the selfsame time bearing in mind that he might come in handy to me if ever I wanted to get out of this horrid place in a hurry.

"We have to go to St George's church on Sundays, and some of us are in the choir," he put in knowingly. *"I expect you might have to sing in the choir can you sing?"* He added.

I told him that I had sung at home in the church choir for some time, however, I was not keen on singing here. I thought, again everything is moving so fast, is this how things develop in the towns, everything seems to be racing mad. I'd only been in this hateful place for a few hours. Little could I comprehend all that was going on, or absorb the events, and at this instant I was not in the shape of mind to indulge in the subtle arts, certainly not here. At home affairs were taken in a relaxed pace; well they seemed to be compared with this place. I knew deep down in my soul I did not fit in here I did not have the desire to join in. The chatty boys were all the consolation I had at this sad moment in my life. I felt I had no intentions of staying around for the duration. I was jerked out of my daydreaming once again when another tall boy called Greg spoke to me.

"You will find out soon enough about this place," he said, seeming to read my innermost thoughts, which appeared rather uncanny at the time. This boy was well built, and had a distinct North Country accent. He spoke quietly, and seemed to be the oldest of the company assembled in the dormitory. Just then Peter came rushing in, perspiring, and panting-gasping for breath in-between the narration he was trying to convey to the rest of us. "*The...Master.....says.... you're.....all...to...get....a...move....on.*" He took a very deep breath, and then continued. "*Come on... He means it!*"

There was much speculation from some of the boys who had not been in the home for very long. I was beginning to think it was another ruse just to keep everyone on their toes. As it turned out, I was justified in my assumption. Evidently, matron was a stickler for punctuality, and the tea was ready so everybody had to be at the meal table as, and when required. Richard quickly installed this rule into me he also pointed out to me in a whisper.

"Don't worry; you'll become used to all these rules, we all do sooner or later." Looking at my bed he said. *"Don't leave your bathers lying on your bed like that, or leave your clothes lying about, or you'll be in trouble with matron."*

"Thanks, I'll try, and remember." I dreamily replied. When the mother-hen tending had subsided, there was much speculation of what was for tea.

"I bet it's those horrible fish paste sandwiches again," I hate 'em," cried out Richard.

"No, *I bet it's something left over from dinner. You should know Peter being as you work in the kitchen,*" shouted another boy, whose name I never did manage to know.

"All I know, its sandwiches." Peter replied calmly. Given his stature, and superior looks, Peter had a calm disposition, and probably this was the reason that he was given some of the more demeaning task about the institution. Having finished our fish paste sandwiches, and some rather granular-dry biscuits, and very weak tea, I asked Peter, hopefully. *"What do we do now?"* Any perceptions I had of freedom were quickly dashed by his reply.

"We have to stay indoors, we are not allowed out on our own, and when we do go out we all have to go together in one group." His reply came in a tone of pathetic obedience. I could not help feeling sorry for these boys, they were subjected, and stripped of any individuality, and I was going to be like this very soon.

"Why can't we go out by ourselves?"

"We never have been allowed to as long as I can remember," answered Peter.

"How long have you been here?" I enquired.

"Four years next month." He looked up, and deep in thought then continued. *"Some of the boys have been around five years, and some even longer than that."* He pondered before continuing, his eyes in a faraway look unsmilingly said. "*I don't bother much about it, I like the boys here. It wouldn't be so bad if matron wasn't so hard. This super's is not too bad but he has to do what she says, after all she is his wife."* As he finished speaking it appeared that he had almost fallen into a trance, and I wondered what was going through is tormented mind. One vague source of reassurance soon manifested itself. The other boys were just ordinary boys like me, some lost, and some slightly hardened, but all hard-working, slightly sad souls with a story to tell. I had shared a meal with them that day like it was the Last Supper. There was little jollity in the dining room where we all had to play games, mainly jigsaw puzzles, there were some tatty boy's annuals, and magazines lying around that appeared to have seen better days.

Very timidly entering the room, I didn't know quite what to say or do. It seemed an eternity as I stood in the doorway, hesitating, apprehensive and feeling rather desolate. I wondered what the lads at Folkingham would be doing right now. A little smile ventured over my face. No doubt, in June they would be out playing in the fields, probably still having rides on the gravel lorries. Then a pang hit my stomach. I had thought of Rex, he would be missing me. I again found it difficult to dam the tears welling up in my eyes. Then I saw a vision of Valerie, and my sorrows began to fade as I delved deeper and deeper into my ruminations about her. I thought, there might be a village dance this weekend, if only I could be there! This place, it is only a nightmare, and a very bad dream. Reality struck me again; I knew it wasn't a dream. I wished Valerie, and my village friends were here with me. Would they understand what aches were crushing me, sapping my individuality that was mine? One thing I knew, nothing could take away my emotions, my thoughts of Valerie. She was there in my being, and to me that's all that mattered at this moment. The institution or not, I was not going to be submerged in its morass, and lay waste, and then a non-entity. The rattling of the dice the clatter of the dominoes brought me back again to this small world around me.

"Come and help with this," called Dave, who was leaning over the dining room table, with pieces of a jigsaw puzzle clutched in his hand, and was in an argument with Peter as to where the piece should go. *"I think there must be some pieces missing,"* moaned Dave, and glancing below the table he said. *"Let's have a look."*

I was invited to assist in the search of the elusive piece of the jigsaw. Having yet only been scrambling under the table for a few seconds, and creating a big commotion, I spied a pair of grey flannel trousers hovering around the table. The all-too-familiar trousers were drooping over the all-too-familiar black shoes, and I thought they could only belong to one person-the superintendent. I looked at Peter, hoping for advice on how to behave in such a precarious situation as this. Dave was not knowledgeable of our predicament, but a nudge from Peter was enough for him to freeze at the sight of those grey flannel trousers. *"What are you doing under there?"* Bellowed the superintendent, as he leaned down with his portly figure, his piggish eyes inverted in their sockets, horribly close to mine, and his lips adopted a contorted fashion, as he spurted out. *"Come out at once!"*

Meekly, and in unison we responded. "*We're looking for the last piece of jigsaw sir."*

"Well, it's now time for supper, and then off to bed!" He turned, and was gone out of the room in seconds.

We shuffled from underneath the table, and squatted on the floor feeling extremely lucky not to being furnished with any more wrath from the superintendent. This fact I discussed with my jigsaw comrades.

"Have you seen your knees lately?" Dave laughed, poking my knees with grubby fingers.

As I looked at them I realised I could be in trouble for they were black. I spat on my hands, and rubbed furiously at each kneecap to no avail. It was no good, they stayed a black, grimy mess, and stubborn, unyielding no matter how hard I rubbed. I was stuck with these black sullied knees. The boys told me it was because of all the polish they had piled on top of the dirt when they polished, and buffed the floor. They suggested I go, and scrub my knees in the washroom.

"Not with those hard scrubbing brushes, used on the kitchen floor?" I cried.

"No, the ones in the washroom, they're much softer," replied Peter. We trundled into the washroom. We had to move quickly because it was time for our bedtime drink, and biscuits. The washroom was adjacent to the kitchen. There were five hand basins with stained mirrors above each one. Slimy pieces of soap clung to the sides of the hand basins; grubby hand towels ornamented the end wall.

"A quick scrub in here then we'll have to get back into the dining room, so now you know where the washroom is. You want to get in here as quick as you can or you'll have to wait your turn, and all the hot water will be gone. I can tell you it's pretty cold here first thing in the morning." Peter informed me, with an air of authority.

I asked. "*What time do you have to get up in the morning*?"

Giving a whimsical smile Peter replied "*Depends on what work you have to do before breakfast, I am up at about ten minutes to six, I usually have to light the kitchen stove, ready for breakfast."*

"What time shall I have to get up?" I tentatively enquired.

"*When all the others do*," he mused for a few seconds, and then added. *"You will know soon enough, there's always a din first thing in the morning, anyway the superintendent goes round the dormitory shouting his mouth off and getting everybody up and that's usually about a quarter past six."*

I wasn't ecstatic with this idea one bit. At home in the late summer I would be up quite early but that was different. I would be looking forward to helping in the harvest fields. The winter months were another proposition. I enquired if we all had to get up that early in the winter.

"Yeah, it makes no difference, and I can tell you it's freezing in the washroom then, cold enough to freeze the balls off a brass monkey."

Although not too cold now, I shivered with this perishing thought. I certainly had no designs on still being here during the coming winter months. I couldn't visualise anything so fearful. It seemed unthinkable that I could still be here. I wasn't to know it but the seeds of absconding were already been sown in my psyche. It was just a cursory scrub with soap, and brush, and then into the dining room for our bedtime meal which consisted of cocoa, and a meagre splash of milk, and very little sugar. The cocoa was strong, and tasted very bitter. The homemade cakes were dry, and lifeless, and very resistant to the teeth. It was then, that Ginger began to question me about my life before arriving here.

"Is your mum dead then?" He asked.

"I don't remember my mum; I lived with my Aunt Nin." I embarrassingly replied.

He still probed but he could see that with more questioning, I wouldn't be forthcoming with any answers, so he left me alone immersed in my own thoughts. The superintendent appeared in the room, and began to announce the following day's sequence of events, which amounted to very little that I already, didn't know. The only item I was not sure about was school. He told me that I would be attending St. Michael's secondary school in Stamford, and that Peter would take a note to the headmaster which would be some form of introduction. I was to wear the clothes I arrived in for school the next day. He told me he hoped to get a school uniform for me by next week. These, I discovered later were a second-hand-me-down livery. He then told us to get to bed, and not to make any noise. I was very disappointed; it was only eight thirty. Before we retired matron spotted my filthy knees I failed miserably to eradicate the grime. Not only was I chastised, so were Peter, and Dave, she chased us towards the washroom in a threatening manner.

"Get in the washroom, and scrub your knees, now!" She bellowed.

As we scrubbed, I noticed Peter, and David chuckling. We emerge rather sheepishly from the washroom. Matron was waiting outside, arms folded, in Gestapo fashion. She glared at as with wild eyes, she wasn't satisfied with our pathetic efforts, and she told us to go back and, wash them again, properly this time. Then, with hard bony fingers, she prodded the small of our backs, and steered us back into the washroom. We finally passed the test, and were allowed to go upstairs to bed. As tired as I was, I knew I would not sleep well that night. I realised as I slipped in between the rough sheets; the bed was not as soft as mine at Folkingham. My bed, being next to Richards, I saw he had already settled down, he whispered to me.

"Goodnight Roy."

"*Goodnight Richard.*" As I lie there, quite wide-awake, I worried what was in store for me the next day when I would arrive at school and what would it be like? How would I get on with the other children, would they bully me? I thought, so far the boys here haven't done so. How long will I have to stay here, in this horrible place with its nasty matron, and strange superintendent? I mused perhaps she won't be so bad tomorrow? I succumbed to tears; all day long I had resisted the temptation of weeping. Now that I was immersed in my quiet world of wretchedness I could let my emotions accept my fate. If bereft of love, and nurturing I would drop into the depths of utter despair. A voice inside of me declared that this was not to happen, I was not to give up I sank into sporadic sleep each time I woke, I heard the humming sound emanating from the factory across the road. Then I heard sobbing; it was Richard. I felt so powerless to comfort him. He told me he was very homesick, and he didn't like this place and would like to run away. Good God! Had he read my mind? Was this to be? I dropped off to sleep. I woke up after more sporadic sleep. Sorrow for Richard emerged from my body. I felt guilt as I began to sob at my own pity I found that my compassion for Richard had evaporated by my own selfish thoughts. Eventually, the sobbing lulled me to sleep much deeper this time. Then, as I opened my eyes, my heart sank, realising that I was still here in this horrible place, and it was dawn. Heavy pangs continued to torture me, my heart leapt, and shock overtook me. I began to quietly cry. I looked at Richard; he was lying quiet still. I reflected, he must be tired out poor boy, probably been crying most of the night. The continual humming from the factory was still in the air, would it never go away? Bellowing from the superintendent broke the comparative quiet solitude of the dormitory.

Come on! Out of bed! Hands off cocks pull on socks, move yourselves!" He was a man that was obviously under great influence from his wife, and his manner that he manifested towards us was one way of showing is manhood, pathetic as it was. His tirade of instructions awoke Richard. He slowly heaved his body up, yawned, stretched, and rubbed his bleary blue eyes, and then he looked at me vacantly, and said, *"I'm sorry."*

"*Sorry for what?"*

"For keeping you awake last night, I didn't mean to," he replied in a husky half-awake voice. He tugged at his fair hair involuntary, in an effort to rouse himself.

"*Come on, out of your beds! I won't tell you a lot again, if you're not downstairs, and in the washroom in five minutes, you'll be in severe trouble*," stormed the superintendent, shattering any solitude that Richard and I longed for.

Dressing in a hurry not wishing to induce any more wrath from the superintendent, knowing full well that matron would be on the warpath if she perceived the slightest insubordination towards her husband.

I noticed on the other side of the dormitory, a vacant bed. This must be Peter's. I had not been mindful of his rising; he obviously must have been very considerate, and extremely quiet. My heart missed a few beats by Peter's early rising; reminding me of the time I'd helped Uncle Alf to start the traction engine boiler fire. When the fire was roaring away, he would slam the fire door shut, rub his hands, and a gleeful gleam would appear in his eyes, and joy would spread across his face from cheek to cheek. Having to go via the kitchen to get to the washroom, I was amused by Peter's attitude to towards his fire lighting chore. I stopped to watch him attending his duty. He was piling wood into the stove leaving a small margin at the top to accommodate the coal. From a box of safety matches he ignited a match, and flicked it onto the paper. When the flames reached what he considered a desirable torridness, and engulfed the timber completely, he then tipped in some coal, and dashing outside, and returning with a bucket of anthracite. He tipped the anthracite into the stove, filling it to the brim. It wasn't long before the kitchen was engulfed in choking black smoke. With a nonchalant gesture he slammed the lid down on the stove, brought his foot hard down on the bottom flu door, gave it a hard kick, and said in a satisfied tone. "*That should take care of that!*" Rubbing his hands together a few times, and then adding. *"That should do for the old bat!"*

We had to dress in our swimming trunks, and I was informed earlier by Peter that it was quite chilly at that time of the morning in the washroom even though it was still summertime. I now had another better fitting pair of trunks just given me. I dreaded to think what it would be like here in the winter. Not wishing to prolong the agony of the chilly surroundings any longer, I dashed upstairs to change into my day clothes. I wandered into the dining room, with much trepidation for my first breakfast here at this horrible place. I only wished that my evacuee friends were here with me. I would give anything just to see one face, just one, especially Valerie's. I knew how bewildered the evacuees would have been on their first day at Folkingham School; apprehensive no doubt like I was now. But this was all different; I was on my own, very much on my own. As I struggled through my breakfast of solid porridge, and soggy toast, more trepidation entered my being with the thought of going to a new school, facing more strangers, and I thought once again, would I be bullied?

Having a sweet tooth I grimaced at the lack of sugar in the tea, I was reminded by the screaming tones of matron" There's a war on you knows!"

Eventually, being worn down with hunger I would stomach the stodgy porridge, the soggy toast, and marmalade, and occasionally we would have sausages, bacon or an egg. I never did manage to overcome the bitterness of the tea, due to the meagre amount of sugar that we were allowed. After helping ginger with washing-up the breakfast crockery, and having completed this task to the dissatisfaction of matron, we were then lined up in front of the superintendent to be glared at, inspected, scrutinised, and prodded into line before venturing out in crocodile form to school. This jaunt was about three-quarters of a mile along the main Ryhall Road. On this particular morning as we passed through that horrible gaunt iron front gate of the institution, I only wished it would be for good. The factory opposite was spewing out clouds of acrid yellow smoke accompanied by the persistent humming. What struck me as being very strange, as we wandered along the main road, was the bustle of traffic, nothing like the solitude of Folkingham. Apart from the gravel lorries passing through the village, there would be little or no traffic to speak of. On this morning I stared very hard at every lorry that past hoping I might catch a sight of Spriggy again.

Close by the factory, and on the same side of the road there were terraced houses, about forty in all, with well maintained front gardens, and that this time of year the flowers were pleasant, and in full bloom. Perfume wafted on a slight breeze of the morning air created enough refreshing interludes from the decay of the institution. For a few fleeting precious moments I was free, if only I could keep walking in this beautiful fresh morning air, but, knowing only too well, later I will be back again inside those walls of gloom. The main road joined another road as we neared the town centre. The school I was to attend was down a narrow lane, leading off from the main street. As we approached the foreboding looking grey-stone building, which stood gaunt-like on high ground, and a little way in from the lane. It had a large playground elevated from the footpath, and surrounded by very tall railings. This vista caused my heart to miss many beats. I began to tremble at the thought of entering those very hefty front gates of the school. All the kids screaming and charging about in the playground manufactured anxiety in me, and only filled me with more trepidation as I watched them milling about. This scene being performed in front of my eyes reminded me once again about the evacuees at Folkingham, and their first day at a strange school, but they had comfort in numbers, not me, looking bewildered, and not daring to put one foot in front of the other to enter the gates. It was then that Peter thrust a friendly hand on my shoulder, and guided me through the gates, and at the front door of the school. He told me there was no need to get worried; he spoke of how nervous he was the first day at the school. And he told me I would be all right. He then led me into the front office just inside the main hall, and knocked on the door.

It was answered by a bellowing basso profundo voice. *"Come!"* A very large man sat behind a desk, wearing a tweed jacket with a red spotted handkerchief dangling from his breast pocket, which matched his bow tie. He was completely bald. When he stood up he appeared enormous. He stared at me, then at Peter taking the letter from Peter he told him to take me to my form master, Mr. Stuart. Where, after more brief formalities, and with little more ado I was fully initiated into the Stamford Boy's St Michael's Secondary School. Mr. Stuart told us to go back into the playground.

I was pleased that Peter had stayed with me during this awkward interval before the lessons commenced. Fear was beginning to creep up on me as I dreaded what would be expected of me, in this huge place. At last the lesson's bell rang, and pupils scrambled to their allotted classrooms. Peter was in a different form to me, and when it was time for us to part he held my hand reassuringly, and said he would see me later. When he left me I felt very exposed. I dawdled nervously to my classroom, and stood in the open doorway, not sure what to do.

In clipped tone's Mr. Stuart said. *"Come in boy! Don't stand there! We won't eat you!"* His opening speech was interjected by faint tittering from the rest of the class. He continued. *"Sit there, by Perkins,"* indicating the locality of Perkins with a wave of the black board eraser that he held loosely in his hand. For a brief moment I thought he was about to propel it in the direction of Perkins. Observing the boy in question, I noticed he looked in a state of stupor. This boy I sat next to had a mop of unruly ginger hair. He slumped over the desk, torso limiting the quantity of space allotted for me. Glancing sideways I noted how spotty and unclean his face was, and that he had an irritating habit of wriggling his legs from side to side. I was not at all enamoured by having him as a desk associate. When the first lesson commenced, I had not the slightest idea of what it concerned. To the best of my knowledge I had never heard of the word science, and to study the subject was a complete mystery to me. How I managed to get through this first lesson was a sheer miracle. Had I been there at the beginning of term, I may have had a remote chance, and probably being capable of coping with the subject. The mid-morning break came as a great relief but having stepped outside into the playground and to see all those strange faces, I wished for a brief moment that I was back in the security of the science room, although not understanding the topic, at least there I felt safe. The first boy to approach me on the playground that morning proved very hostile towards me. He, for some reason unbeknown to me resented the fact that my Christian name, and surname were the same as his, and he asked me in a bullying tone. "What was I going to do about it?" This statement appeared very bizarre by his tone of voice that for some obscure motive he had the sole right on our particular identities. It was just then that Peter came to my rescue, and we caught up with Ginger and Dave, and then we sauntered off to another area of the playground. Whether it was anything to do with Peter's glare at my namesake, I never did find out, there were no more unpleasant incidents about my name, or any attempts of bullying me from this boy. I did however wonder why a person could get so irate regarding sameness of names. Normally I would have thought a more positive reaction would manifest itself, regarding our names.

Worse was to come. The curriculum for the second half of the morning was mathematics. Again, I was completely out of my depth. I don't believe I had ever heard sums called mathematics, certainly not in the village school at Folkingham. On this topic Mr. Stuart was a little less forgiving. He realised I couldn't understand the way that science worked but he was aghast that I was bereft in mathematics. In fact, he was very perturbed by the sheer inadequate manner I approached the subject. To put it bluntly, he declared I was useless, and needed to pay more attention to the numbers game. I thought he might have thought it a game. I certainly didn't! For the remainder of the morning I was in a complete daze. I felt so wretched, and alone. What had I done to deserve this turmoil, this galling situation? I found myself fretting, and the thought of returning to the boy's home heaped upon me more distress, as I knew I couldn't endure this for much longer. My anxieties were beginning to heighten with each step I took getting nearer, and nearer to the home. The thought of consuming food at lunch-time this day heralded sheer panic, and an attack of nausea, fortunately lasting only briefly, and soon Peter, Ginger, and I were passing through the depressing iron gate. After washing our hands we were soon sat down at the dining table. Boiled potatoes, cabbage, and the fatty ham, followed by semolina pudding, again accompanied by the strain top 'Lilibullero'.

The first lesson in the afternoon was English, and I had to read a passage from one of the classics. As I read, I could not understand why there was so much *sotto voce* tittering in the classroom. It finally dawned on me; it was no doubt due to my very extraordinarily broad accent. Before the mid-afternoon break, and for a brief period, I had another unpleasant incident. I needed urgently to pay the toilet a visit. I discovered that there was an attenuated procedure to go through before one could continue with an urgent appointment. I was told, at first that I must knock on the headmaster's study door, and request a toilet roll, and when finished to take it back. After knocking on his door I was kept waiting for what seemed an eternity before my knock was acknowledged. The anguish words *"Come boy!"* were utter bliss. My emergency at this time was very apparent to the head. His face gleamed with a touch of sadistic pleasure he handed me the toilet roll as I turned to leave his study he bellowed. *"Don't run boy."*

To add to my frustration the toilets were outside, and I wasn't sure where they were, nevertheless my urgency guided me to the exact location.

Matron made sure we changed into our swimming trunks as soon as we arrived home at tea time. It was potato scraping for me again. Some boys had to clean out the toilets, some had to polish the hall, and dining room floor, and dust anything that didn't move. Carpets had to be taken outside, slung onto the washing line, and given a good beating with the business end of a yard broom. After laying down generous amounts of floor wax, the area would be polished with a bumper. This was a heavy wooden block attached to a handle by means of a swiveled joint. This pivot enabled the bumper to be swung backwards, and forwards. Felt pads on the underside of the wooden block eventually created, with copious amounts of sweat, highly polished, and slippery floors. The scuffed marks on the skirting board in the hallway that I initially saw when entering the building, were in no doubt due to the boys losing control of this very large piece of house-work equipment. The rewards for this toil were big biceps, and aching backs. The stairways had to be swept the banister rails polished, and of course the dormitory, plus any other nooks, and crannies matron thought fit. She saw to it that we did not skimp the jobs, and if our labouring was not to her satisfaction, we would have the go through the entire procedure once again. Very often we were extremely tired to appreciate the evening recreational games in the dining room later. The evening was pretty much the same as the preceding day. I came to the conclusion that this was the usual course of things as each day dawned in this horrid place. I was awoken early the following morning by the noise from the factory. I had little sleep down to Richard's crying again. One blessing, I had not got to go to school this day, it being a Saturday, no doubt we would be kept fully occupied by the master, and matron, who would devise innovate methods of finding us plenty of jobs to do about the institution. When we had completed our duties in the morning, and had a slightly better lunch than the preceding day, Ginger informed me that we were going to the cinema in Stamford that afternoon. He told me that we had all got to go together. We had to behave ourselves when out with the master. He told me that we went almost every Saturday; he said he did not care for it very much, when it was stifling hot like it was today. I could easily see his point; the day was very sultry indeed. The last, and only time I'd been to a cinema was on one of the visits to Grantham with Uncle Alf. The film showing was called 'Gas Bags', or some such title, a slapstick comedy. I did not recall much about the plot, only that one of the characters, sitting on a large barrage balloon, managed to rip a hole in the material with his pocketknife, causing mayhem. There was a routine to go through before anyone could step outside that inhospitable front iron gate. No sooner had we washed the lunch dishes, made certain there were enough potatoes scraped for the following day, and dealt with our own ablutions we were then marched outside. Once outside in the yard, we were lined up facing the house, and matron commenced again with a thorough inspection from top toe, starting with our ears, checking for any traces of tide marks round our necks. Finger nails came in for very close scrutiny. She took a swift glance down to our black shoes, and then checked the finger nails again, making sure they didn't match the shoes. By the time she arrived at the end of the line of fifteen boys, standing like the 'Parade of the Tin Soldiers', the superintendent had started his own inspection. He would be delighted if he had discovered a misdemeanour on matron's part in missing any unsightly appearance on our person. He would gleefully point out what he had discovered. There obviously was much rivalry between the two at our expense regarding our appearance. Having inspected the front of the line, matron then would walk round the back checking the length of our hair. She then produced a bottle of Brilliantine, slapping some of the contents in the palms of her hands; she would commence to roughly rub the oily substance into our scalps, immediately followed by the superintendent waddling along the line, combing our hair, with the obligatory institution hairstyle.

One Saturday, there was a break from this routine to the cinema. We were to go swimming. At the thought of swimming I took a renewed interest in the Saturday afternoon leisure pursuits. The thought of being taught to swim thrilled me. I asked Peter where the swimming baths were in Stamford. He told me rather grimly that we didn't go to the swimming baths, we went to the river. My heart sank- the river! This did not appear very appealing, as the day was decidedly chilly for this time of year. Suddenly, all enthusiasm for any real watery exploits vanished, and the cinema took on a more enticing role. With bathers, and towels tucked under our arms, in rigid crocodiles form of we arrived at the riverbank. The sight of the dark river water shocked me. I thought it must be bloody deep. The superintendent told us to change. I looked hard at the dark chilly waters. I could not see the bottom. I wondered how deep it could it be? The thought of getting into that river struck me with horror, as the bank was very steep. After what seemed an eternity, one boy slid gingerly down the bank, and with a plop, launched his body into the water. After surfacing from the deep, he looked around with appealing eyes at the audience on the bank, shivered;

then stating how very cold it was, scrambled out and, laid face down on the grass. I shivered with him. One or two of the boys made valiant attempts to remain in the water and after making a few desultory strokes at the water, wasted no time in scrambling out, and vigorously rubbed their blue bodies with the institution towels.

"Aren't you going to get in?" The superintendent said to me as I squatted on the riverbank. I did not answer; I tucked my head in between my knees with indifference, and stayed like this, shivering, just like all the other boys. I also thought what a bloody stupid man; he had not checked if I could swim, and expecting me to get into the deep water. The idea of absconding once again lurked in the recesses of my mind. After tea-time one Friday the superintendent began fussing over our appearance which I did not understand at the time. It transpired that we were going to assist in the preparations for a church garden party in Stamford the following day.

The master was spruced up, and wearing his best blue-grey suit. I could never make up my mind about this suit. Had it been dyed blue at some time, probably from the original colour of grey, or had it succumbed with age? Today, he wore a different trilby hat. This one was dark brown that clashed with this suit. There were spots of grease marks on the crown. He was wearing what appeared to me the obligatory shirt with a tight-fitting collar. It appeared matron was not going to the fate preparations, so with little more ado she duly inspected as for clean faces, and fingernails and we had to endure the dreaded hair grooming from the husband, and wife team once again.

After humping tables, and chairs about, and alternative jobs, we were given a glass of insipid fruit juice, and then marched back to the institution. The following day we were promenaded in the proverbial crocodile manner to the church garden fete. Considering there was a war raging on, there were plenty of garden party attractions. It was amazing what goodies turned up on the various stalls. One was invited to guess how many sweets they were in a very large glass jar. Guess the weight of a big fruitcake. For sale there were homemade sausage rolls, cakes, sponges, cheese, and a variety of drinks. A juggler created magic patterns through the air with tennis balls. Various groups of persons dressed in period costumes, and standing inside large wooden frames were depicting scenes from great masterpieces by renowned artists. There was a dog show, which eventually created trepidation among the organisers, when two of these canine brutes broke loose from their owners. Then began to fight, and caused much merriment, and excitement to all present, with the exception of the luckless dog owners. Most of the clearing up at the event was laid at our door. Picking up the debris that was strewn around the lawn, clearing away the tables, and chairs; by the time we were finished we were hot and tired. With all this activity, my mind had wandered away to my village life for a brief while. On the way back from the garden fete the superintendent told me I would be joining the St George's Church choir in Stamford. This piece of news gave me something to ponder over, I thought, I have not been here very long, and I am to join another church choir. Once again my stomach sank. Thoughts took flight through my head, recalling the church choir in the village, and I thought also my evacuee friend. I indulged in an inward sweet little smile, and thought he would manage without me. Having a good strong voice, he could certainly hold his own with the tall lady, and her strident voice.

A number of boys from the home were in the choir that I was soon to become a member. The choir I discovered was quite large, and had a good reputation. I thought if I was to join, the choir's reputation could be forfeit. The music they sang was more difficult than I was imagined. At Folkingham we never attempted difficult anthems or motets. I worried about the singing. I need not have done so, as it happened I managed quite well, and I discovered that I had a flair for music. Although, not so happy singing in this choir, as in the village choir, it did have an advantage by alleviating the tedious routine of being taken to church in crocodile fashion, and always the superintendent bringing up the rear. Being members of the choir we had to be at the church much earlier than the rest of the congregation, as the music for the oncoming service had to be rehearsed. Thankfully we were allowed to go to church in a smaller group with Peter in charge. We wore cassocks of royal blue accompanied by brilliant white surplices. The stiff Eton School style collars held the head in a stiff forward-looking position, and gave one a very limited lateral movement.

One day on my return from school at lunchtime, for some strange reason I held back from the main body of boys and slipped into the front garden of one of the terraced houses in the Ryhall Road. This house was not a considerable distance from the institution, so I knew if I ran I could soon catch up with the other boys. I skipped with excitement up to the front door of the house and knocked. A tall lady answered the door I took a deep breath, and felt a pang of guilt. I noticed there was no hall, and I could see directly into the living room, and there I saw a piano. I looked up at the lady, and pathetically blurted out. "*Can I come, and live with you lady?"*

This outburst took the lady by complete surprise. She looked startled, and astonished, at this unwarranted and sudden unexpected remark. When having finally recovered her composure, blinking, and smiling, she said. *"You had better come inside."*

I stood motionless in the living room, and more guilt entrapped me. I felt how nice it was to be in a typical home again. I perceived the living room was much larger than our parlour in my home in Folkingham. There were many pictures on the walls. This is what I missed in the institution, it being bereft of illustrations or ornaments of any kind. My eyes wandered in amazement around the room, and finally settling on the piano that held an array of photographs in a line along the top.

"Can you play the piano?" asked the lady.

"No," I timidly replied.

"I have noticed you looking into my garden as you pass by on your way to school with the other boys from the home. I don't mind one bit you looking at my garden. You mustn't stay around too long or you'll be late for your dinner." She had advised.

I felt rather saddened. I was hoping that the lady would say I could live with her. When I saw her again, she told me I could live with her when I had grown up, and had left school. Somehow I knew this would not transpire, and some years afterwards I came to the conclusion that her last statement was saying, that there was very little reimbursement for fostering children in those days. Remorselessly, the days dragged. Sometimes I would shiver just wearing swimming trunks in the shade of the ramshackle shed on late chilly afternoons endlessly scraping spuds. How I loathed all this! There were times when I would gaze out of the dining room window, in the hope of seeing Miss Shee's car come trundling along the main road to whisk me away. I gazed, and gazed; the car never came for me. When she did make the occasional scanned visits to the home, I don't ever recall her speaking to me which, at the time hurt. She only stayed very briefly, just routine visits to see that all was well.

I was a prisoner in this place, never to be freed. It would have been more bearable had I been allowed out on my own occasionally, or with one or two of the other boys, to meander about the town. I was a prisoner: this fact, there was no doubt in my mind. And with my previous history of absconding, this wish of ever leaving here, I guessed would never come to fruition. The endless routine of scraping potatoes, polishing floors, dusting, and beating of the threadbare carpets, matron always chastised us. The monotonous routine of everyday life in this institution was beginning to bear me down. I was so distressed with this world, and all that had suddenly happened to be my way of life. I was in the uttermost depths of despair. In a boyish way I was desperately trying to come to terms with the situation but every day was purgatory, and I was missing Valerie, Aunt Nin, Uncle Alf, and all my other friends at Folkingham. I was desperate to see them all again, and I would sacrifice anything to be with them now. Kathleen and her boyfriend visited me one Sunday afternoon, and treated me to tea, and biscuits, in a café situated in Red Lion Square in the town. When they departed I collapsed in a flood of tears, I was left isolated in this loathsome place.

We were about to have tea on this memorable Friday afternoon. I had completed scraping an enormous pile of potatoes, and feeling utterly wretched, and devoid of any kind of uplifting spirit as I meandered aimlessly towards the washroom. Suddenly, my thoughts employed more positive thinking. I again thought I must not give in to this melancholy state I had adopted. My incarceration had fuelled my powers of perception. I had become more alert to all that was going on around me in this place. I perceived the habitual routine here each day, how the master, matron, and inmates had let themselves be governed by each other's institutionalised behaviour, acting almost like robots with no individuality whatsoever. It didn't take me long to realise at this time of the day on a Friday, the boys paid much more attention to their ablutions once they had finished their tasks. The extra time spent in the washroom, was, because on Friday evenings we would, without fail, always be marched out in crocodile fashion with the master, to some meaningless event, and it was imperative our appearance was smart on these occasions. Matron and the superintendent would, with some of the other inmates, busy themselves preparing the tea. There would be no boys in the dormitory for some time yet. Instinct prompted me to halt my steps towards the washroom, and an inner voice told me, it's now or never. I dashed upstairs to the dormitory, changed out of my bathers into my short trousers, and summer shirt. I rushed down the stairs, out through the front door, through that austere Iron Gate. This only took about a minute, and unless someone had seen me, for the moment, I was free.

I took a deep breath of fresh air surrounding me in sharp contrast to the stale environment inside these institutional walls. I stood for a few seconds outside the home. I trembled with pent-up emotion, and for many seconds I froze on the spot, paralysed with my own won freedom. People passed by, I didn't perceive if they realised as I stood there, that I had just run away from the Boy's Home in Ryhall Road. I didn't care, my next thought was, where do I go now? I decided to go towards the town. I could probably get a bus going towards my village. Suddenly, I realised I haven't any money. I had made such a swift exit out of the house the thought of cash never occurred to me. I felt exhilarated. My heart throbbed with the excitement of freedom. I didn't think it was wise to loiter too close to the gate. I began to head towards Stamford. I thought it wise to put as much distance between the home, and myself as quickly as possible so I quickened my pace towards the town. As I neared the centre of Stamford, I thought how was I to get to Folkingham without money? It was twenty miles away, too far to walk. Probably I could hitch a lift with some poor unsuspecting lorry driver? I hung around one of the cafes in the town and finally plucked up enough courage to scrounge a lift in a lorry going most of the way to Folkingham. The driver said he would be turning off at Aslackby about three miles before he reached my village. When he finally dropped me off, I had almost three, and a half miles to walk before I reached the outskirts of Folkingham. The evening was warm and sunny as I trekked along the country lanes. I was beginning to feel in the best of spirits now with my new-found freedom, and I accompanied the birds by singing, and whistling. Within no time at all in the distance I saw the familiar outline of St Andrew's church tower proudly prodding the skyline. I'd only had just about a mile to go before I reached the farms that straddled the outskirts of the village. Tall hedges lined the meadows with lush vegetation. The ditches were filled with an abundance of brightly coloured wild flowers. On this balmy summer evening, fragrant breezes wafting over this vista of the peaceful tranquil countryside. I immersed myself in its beauty as I moved nearer to the village.

I jumped over a gate leading into a meadow, which had an elevated view of the village. Keeping as close to the hedgerows as possible until I got close enough to see clearly the rear of the row of semi-detached cottages, and especially number three that was my home. I lay down, and peeked above the long grass to survey the view in front of me. I could clearly see people working in their gardens. Bonfire smoke drifted serenely upwards into the warm evening air. I heard the church clock toll eight times. I lay there watching for some while, not daring to sit up straight, or even move any closer. Suddenly, I acquired a feeling of guilt once again, knowing only too well that I shouldn't be here, and I couldn't expect congratulations from anyone for the predicament I was in at this time. From a distance in the still evening air I could hear familiar voices that carried across the fields; this caused my heart to race. The deep barking of a dog that appeared to be quite close startled me. Could it be Rex? It certainly sounded very much like his bark, for all I know he may have sensed that I was here in the vicinity. I lay quite still, peeping through the long blades of grass, I could see people pottering about in their gardens. Some were hoeing, some were watering their plants, and some were lazing in their garden chairs making the most of this very beautiful balmy summer evening. The urge for me to move on into the village was great, but I thought I must wait a little longer. The truth being, I was frightened to meet anyone that knew me, so I sat tight. The dog barked again. I caught the sound of children's voices, I wondered if any of them had already spotted me. I gazed down at the lush grass, and recalled happier days when, how we would diligently search for that elusive four-leaf-clover which we never did find. Perhaps I would find one now. It was supposed to be lucky so I began to search.

Suddenly, the sound of rustling in the grass, and excited yelping caused me to stand up. I spied a brown, and white cocker spaniel pounding towards me. It was Rex, he had found me. With his body twisted, and contorted, and wagging his tail violently he thrust his writhing torso against my thighs. His yelping, and deep barking echoed throughout the entire neighbourhood, shattering the serenity of the evening. There seemed to be little choice for me now but to head for home. His tail wagging even faster, Rex seemed perplexed at my hesitant strides toward the garden gate. As I closed my hand around the latch my heart thumped hard with the loud creaking of the gate as I pushed it open. I strode quietly up the garden path towards the house; I wondered what Uncle Alf would say when he saw me. I thought he might have come out into the garden when he heard Rex barking, probably he took it for granted since Rex did a lot of barking if I recall correctly. It was a peculiar feeling knocking my own back door. Uncle Alf began to shed a few tears as he saw me standing on the doorstep looking disheveled, and tired. "*Come on in,*" he said, struggling to hold back more tears, *"I'll go and get Aunt Edie, I won't be a minute."*

Sitting on my little stool, Rex snuggled up to me. I felt more relaxed as my eyes wandered around the parlour. Then, an icy shiver shot through my body. For some inexplicable reason I hadn't realised that Aunt Nin was not here anymore. I began to cry, I felt utterly desolate, and vulnerable to the whole world. I knew I would not see her again, and I was still sobbing when Aunt Edie entered the parlour with Uncle Alf. Aunt Edie was Uncle Alf's sister in law, and no doubt since Aunt Nin had departed from out of his life, he had called her for help and solace many a time.

"Hello, are you all right, and what are we going to do about you?" Aunt Edie said wonderingly. They both were suddenly presented with an unforeseen dilemma. I thought when they got over the initial shock of my untimely appearance, that they would know what to do. I naively thought, they would get me something to eat, and make my bed, and all would be well. After a welcome cold drink, and portions of cake, I began to feel once again at home. I detected an anxious look on Uncle Alf's face. The problem I had set before him appeared insurmountable! Aunt Edie told me to run outside, and play for a while with the other boys who, by now, with much curiosity had gathered outside the house. She evidently needed some breathing space while she and Uncle Alf contemplated what to do about me, a naughty boy who had run away from the Boy's Home.

As we wandered outside, and sat on the familiar grass verge by the roadside where we would sit, and wait for Spriggy to come along in his lorry, I thought, would I ever be free of that place? I tried to dismiss all thoughts of the institution as I gazed down at the grass verge in the hope of finding a four-leaf-clover. I noticed how parched the grass appeared after not seeing it for some weeks. I was in a complete turmoil; I needed someone to cuddle me. Why was this happening to me? What had I done that caused me to leave my friends, and my loving village life? Everything seemed very matter-of-fact that Friday evening as my friends, and I talked about our village life. No one questioned what I'd been doing for the last few weeks. This was strange. It was as if I had never been away from the village. We talked, and laughed, and watched the labourers coming into the village for their habitual relaxation, and liquid sustenance. We would hear, and witness the Lancaster aircraft overhead. There were many army vehicles cruising about in the village, and a strange air of alertness hung around the area. The odour of fish, and chips wafted through the calm air as we chatted. The chip shop proprietor managed to acquire some fish to fry on Friday evenings. It was just then that I saw her. My heart leapt with excitement. It was Valerie. She was coming towards us, and then she stopped at a door further down the road, knocked, and entered. She obviously hadn't noticed me. If she had, I felt she didn't want anything to do with me. I had not had the opportunity to say goodbye to her before I left for Stamford, and she probably thought I wasn't interested in her any more. If this was the case, I could forgive her if she had ignored me. I doubted if she was aware, that I'd thought about every hour of the day since I left, which at the time these sweet thoughts of mine had lifted my spirits in the institution.

The lads in the village told me there was to be a dance in the village the following evening. I made a mental note, that there, and then I would ask Valerie if I could accompany her to the dance. I would not be shy, as I had been in the past. I would ask her this time for sure. I felt very elated at the prospect of taking her to the dance tomorrow evening. All thoughts of the institution I banished from my mind. Yes, I was at home at last! Unbeknown to me there was frantic business going on between Stamford, and Sleaford.

Sleaford; The home and business premises of Miss Shea.. It was obvious that sooner or later I would be missed, and I naively had forgotten this. Not having put in an appearance for tea at the institution the superintendent would have notified the Police and Miss Shee about my sudden disappearance. The superintendent would have pitched in with all his might in a bid to retrieve me, and confine me in custody. I was made aware of this when Miss Shee finally arrived in her black Ford saloon to collect me, at about 9 p.m. I was still sitting on the grass verge chatting to my friends when the car pulled up outside of the house. She seemed to signal danger amongst the children, and they all scattered like terrified rabbits no sooner had she stepped out of her car. Again I was isolated. She stood for a second or two eyeing me reproachfully, then sternly said. "*Come into the house with me*!" Her angry countenance heralded trouble for me so obediently, I swiftly obeyed her command, trembling with every step towards the house, and sheepishly following her like a lamb to the rear parlour. After admonishing me, and exchanging information with Uncle Alf, she put me into the car, and swung the starting handle, the motor immediately sprung into life, and then stepping into the car, and after a quick glance at the water temperature gauge, she switched off the engine. She peered at me very sternly once again, and then said. *"I need some water for the radiator so I will go, and ask Mr. Barber to let me have some. Now I'm going to leave you here so you won't run away will you?"*

I sat there motionless, and feeling utterly despondent. When I collected my thoughts I realised I would not be seeing Valerie again, or taking her to the dance tomorrow night. The terrible notion of my returning to that dismal home again crossed my mind. I thought now I was in a position to do something about it. I would jump out of the car, and race across the fields, and then come back later. I let my eyes aimlessly wander around the car's dashboard, and towards the instruments. If only I could drive this car, it would be so easy to get away. I looked at the small clock; the hands were at ten minutes past nine. I calculated I would be back at the home by about ten o'clock. The last statement Miss Shee had said to me before she went into the house for the water, I was not to run away again. I realised that her tone was a little less severe than normal. I was tormented again, and confused to by all that was going on around me, but I hadn't the wisdom to know that it was all my own doing, and that I had brought this trauma upon myself.

Reflecting again on my predicament, and the fact that I was trusted to be alone meant that Miss Shee trusted me. I felt a pang of remorse, and was sorry for her. She had trusted me not to run off again, and I must not fail her. I had got to let her take me back to the institution, and face the wrath of the superintendent, and matron. I cogitated, when I get back to the institution I might then be a hero with the other inmates. Selfishly I felt a little happier by this belief but this fantasy quickly evaporated as I visualised the grossness of the place; I could never feel happy living there. I could not come to terms with the situation that I found myself. I had done wrong by running away from the gruesome dwelling. I comforted myself with the thought it I wasn't my fault that I had to go to the Boy's Home in the first place. I must have been looking very perplexed when Miss Shee returned to the car with a jug of water, and she no doubt was singularly perplexed, seeing me still seated in her car. Suddenly, she brought me back to reality by asking me, if all was well. She then commenced to pour the water into the car's radiator. Uncle Alf and Auntie Edie came out to see us off. My guardian handed the empty jug back to Uncle Alf, said goodbye, and without any more procrastination, we were on our way back to Stamford. The journey was all too swift, and as we drew near the institution I was apprehensive of what was in store for me. It was with considerable trepidation that I stepped out of the car. I knew I would not be treated like the prodigal son, and this abundantly was a certainty! I was very frightened, and for some crumbs of comfort, I looked up at Miss Shee. Would there be a policeman waiting for me? She didn't appear to sense my anxiety. I thought it would have been considerably better had she told me off. Naively I considered it would have got it all over in one fell swoop. What would master and matron do? Would they give me a caning? Or would I have a lot more work to do? I was no doubt that I would not receive any more pocket money for some considerable time. Perhaps I would not be allowed to go to the cinema with the other boys? I expect I shall have to scrub the kitchen floor on my hands, and knees? I thought that would not be an additional hardship since we had to do that anyway, even if we hadn't put a foot wrong. It was just after ten o'clock when we arrived at the home, and it was still light, and all the boys were in bed. I doubted if any of them were asleep. They would have been aware of my absconding, and the buzz of excitement going on all around them would keep them awake. No doubt there would be much gossip about my impending outcome. I dare not look up to the dormitory window, but I guessed that there were many small wide eyes peering out from the slightly drawn curtains.

No sooner had the car arrived outside the home. Little ears would be straining for any snippets of information they could glean. A boy brave enough to post his head out of the window would relay any news of interest. If a boy was caught looking out of a window when he should have been in bed, he would be severely reprimanded, and lose his pocket money. Talking in the dormitory was very seriously frowned upon, and any boy caught in conversation was awarded additional work. Any nocturnal misdemeanors whilst in the dormitory were also considered punishable offences, and were severely dealt with at the time. A boy brave enough to run the gauntlet by leaning out of the dormitory window was considered by his peers very courageous indeed. A whole week's sweet ration was a fitting reward for any gallant deeds performed on behalf of the boy inmates in this institution. I was not intending to linger in thought any longer that deemed feasible, so my interest in the intrigues of these poor unfortunate beings soon waned. The thought of being incarcerated again in this dreadful place sent a shudder through my entire body as we neared the horrible front gate, and the dour looking front door, which was suddenly flung open by the superintendent, and tripping behind him was matron. I thought how severe they both looked. It was obvious I was at the very least, due for a very severe drubbing.

It was then I heard the familiar cry of Miss Shee. *"Here we are."* For a brief moment, her voice broke the tension. How many more times was I to hear this cry? 'This is your new home now'. Although, this on this occasion she did not add, 'this is your new home!'

The two ogres glared down at me. If only the confrontation could be delayed, I could shoot off down the road again, but I remembered I had told Miss Shee I would not run away again, but that was when I was sitting in her car! The superintendent was displaying the chicken-like motions, his head twitching back, and forth, his agitated flabby face conjuring up gross malice, and figuring out the sentence that would fit the crime. Matron persistently shook her head with rage as I stood there waiting for the sentence to be passed thereupon. I fretted as I tried to guess which one would pronounce the castigation. It appeared that at any second, they would pounce on me, and then I realised they probably would make no decisive move until Miss Shee had departed. These were agonising moments, and I waited anxiously for their next move. The tension increased as I watched matron's mouth opening, and closing in the manner of a goldfish, and her face turning a bright red. It was not long before she regained her composure.

Looking at me, and with a cynical smile she said. "*There is nothing to eat for you at this time of night!*" She taunted, putting on her posh accent for the benefit of Miss Shee. I was entirely aware that Miss Shee was a lady of breeding, and would not be fooled by matron's stupidity, and if she continued her nagging much longer, it would not be long before she committed a faux pas in front of my escort. I do believe matron read my thoughts as she realised that her attitude and negative statement had fallen upon stony ground by the unmistakable air of nonchalance, and lack of interest manifested by me.

Matron contemplated another strategy, and called on me to go to bed immediately. The superintendent with a nervous twitch of his head, agreed with much approval, and supported her command. He appeared relieved at the speedy disposal of me as I shot past him, and up the stairs, and sought refuge in the dormitory with the other boys. I quickly undressed, and put on my pajamas, and slipped into bed. There was not a murmur from anyone in the dormitory. I was expecting some remarks either from Peter or Dave. All was silent. No doubt the boys were awake. They would not dare stir in any fashion in case the superintendent and matron were to appear suddenly, hoping to catch an unfortunate boy committing some misconduct, and then award him extra fatigues the following day. I did not care about having to go to bed without anything to eat, after all, I'd had cake, and biscuits at Folkingham, so far as I was concerned matron could keep her lousy food. I made up my mind that nothing mattered any more, all I wanted to do was to leave this institution. It was not the company of the boys I detested; it was the regime, and proprietors of this place that I loathed. I however could not comprehend how severe they were towards these boys who after all, did not warrant this very harsh treatment.

Tiredness soon overtook me, my eyes closed, and I was soon immersed in deep sleep. Matrons bellowing voice suddenly aroused me. Evidently some boys had been talking whilst I was asleep, and her chastising had awoken me. No sooner had she disappeared, faint whisperings could be heard floating around the dormitory, and then, about some minutes later all was silent again. I struggled to get back to sleep, but before I could I heard Richard quietly crying. My final thoughts before I drifted off into slender sleep, I wished that I was back in my own little bed once more. It was nearly to be, but not quite. Sometime! Sometime! I had made up my mind I would not be around very long. I heard Richard's plaintive crying again as I drifted slowly into sleep. The bellowing of matron to all, and sundry in the dormitory to get out of bed shook me from my sporadic sleep, and for a moment or two; I was at a loss to understand where I was. The shock of the surroundings quickly dispelled any sweet thoughts of home, and again I was despondent with the notion of having to dwell another day in this dreadful house. Richard looked at me pathetically, and I could see in his swollen eyes, a petition reaching out for some comfort from me. He probably knew I might have heard him crying, and by his appearance I could see he was beseeching me not to talk to anyone about his dilemma, so I didn't question him, and I knew if he wanted, he would tell me why he was so upset. My hypothesis was, like me he was homesick. We were both unaware at the time that this morning's temporal interlude had bound us closer together, more than we could possibly imagine.

I smartly jumped out of bed, because I did not wish to add to my already ignominious state of affairs. Dressing quickly, and scampering down the stairs to the ablutions, and splashing my face with cold water, I was prepared to brave the fury of master, and matron. I had forgotten what my pre-breakfast duties were, so I grabbed a broom, and commenced nonchalantly to sweep the hallway. The directors in charge must have been aware of my feigned activities, but nothing was said to me so, when I considered it prudent, I sauntered into the dining room for breakfast. The isolation towards me by the master, and matron was disconcerting. No doubt it was a ploy on their part to keep me in suspense, knowing my fretting regarding any punishment that was due would make me suffer all the more. For their part, they had succeeded, for I was upon flimsy ground. Had I already known my impending punishment it would no doubt have been easier for me to accept? With this in mind I did not enjoy my breakfast, although I was fairly hungry. It was not long before I learned the outcome of my fate. No sooner had I finished eating, I was summoned by the master to his pokey little office adjacent to the kitchen. When I entered matron was also there, standing upright with her arms folded pounding against her stomach. Her face betrayed an expression of sadistic delight; her lips pursed, and primed for the verbal onslaught that was pending.

"*You 'ave been a very, very wicked boy!*" She shouted, and then with the urgency to take more breath she continued with her discourse regarding my absconding. "*You 'ave to be punished, for all the trouble you 'ave caused us by running away.*"

She was about to continue when her husband bravely interrupted her, who fearing his status might be eroded. He interjected swiftly. "*And why did you run away?*"

A reasonable question, but on subsequent thought, I considered it rather stupid, although with some trepidation I replied, *"I don't know."* As I uttered my answer I knew full well, but being afraid of the consequences I did not disclose my feelings at this time. I kept my own counsel.

"This nonsense will 'ave to stop" Matron cut in sharply.

Not to be out done again, the superintendent wormed his way back into the interrogation. "*We were put to a great deal of trouble yesterday evening, your pocket money will have to be stopped until we feel it fit to restore it."*

Before he could say any more on the matter, she seized on the fiscal aspect, and demanding in a very high voice. *"Where do you get the money from for the journey, surely you didn't walk!"*

"I didn't have any money, and I didn't walk. I cadged a lift in a lorry most of the way."

"I don't believe it!" She shouted thumping the desk to emphasise her point. She carried on in frenzy. *"You must 'ave 'ad some money, I expect you pinched it from the cash box 'ere!"* She pointed to a black metal box, and shook it menacingly close to my face, no doubt with the ploy of extracting a confession from me.

"I didn't have any money, and I didn't take any money from the cash box. I have never seen the box before."

It was quite apparent she did not believe me. She carried on with the inquisition. "You must 'ave 'ad money for the bus fare to Folkingham!"

I protested, and in a more assertive manner, as with her accusations, she was beginning to irritate me. "I told you, I got a lift home in a lorry!"

"'Ome....Ome....Ome.....Did you say ome? This is your ome now, and don't you forget it!" She bellowed.

Gosh, I thought, can't this woman shout, and she never gives up. I bestowed upon them both a minor degree of intellect, for they could see it was futile continuing any further the grilling, and with exasperated sighs they bundled me out of the office. They told me the matter was by no means closed, and I would be hearing more about it later. The following day I was duly summoned to appear before them again to explain how I had obtained the money to go to Folkingham. The interrogation was a repeat of the previous day. They flatly refused to believe me, and continued to harass me on the matter. There was no way I could convince them of my innocence. They did not want to believe me, how much I pleaded my freedom of guilt. I had to grin, and bear the suspicion that was heaped upon me. To make matters worse this saga had leaked out to the boys, and I was being branded the home-boy-thief. It was very distressing. I had never stolen before, never. The interrogators never did disclose how much money was missing from the money box. For many days the other boys shunned me causing me to be extremely withdrawn, and this was not typical behaviour for me. One evening, Richard noticed my grieving came to me as I sat moping. Realising I was distressed by the accusation leveled against me, placed a comforting hand on my shoulder. For a second, I was startled. I looked round, and saw a reassuring smile, and then he said quietly.

"I believe you Roy; I don't think you could have taken the money, from what you have told me, and how quickly you left the house you wouldn't have had time to search for a stupid money box." He gave my shoulder a squeeze then said with conviction. "*I can't believe it, those two saying that you are a thief, it's not like you, and even the little I know of you. They would make up a story like that just to get back at you for the trouble you caused them. I could trust you I know that much!"*

There was silence for a few seconds then I felt a warm glow overwhelmingly me. I knew at least that I had one true friend here. I began to feel much better. If only one person believed me, that is all that mattered at this time. Richard did his best to instill his belief in my innocence. At this time, this was a huge comfort. I was greatly indebted to him for his faith in me. It was some time later that I discovered via the boys, who told me that, the alleged theft of the money never happened. Richard was correct that it was a manifestation in vengeance on the part of the proprietors to put me in so such misery. They obviously had meant that I should suffer for running off, and giving them so much hassle. They had no intention of apologising or making any attempt to rectify the situation with me. With the hostility from the other boys rapidly waning, I focused my thoughts again on another attempt to abscond. Knowing that I was completely innocent of the alleged theft, now my spirit was no longer dampened.

I was more and more determined to quit this place. There were many unjust practices that the boys had to endure in this establishment. I had made up my mind I was not going to become prey to the organisation any longer than necessary. I considered that next time I would make certain I did not come back. If I did, I was prepared to tolerate any punishment awarded me, but I was not happy by the thought of being accused of stealing. I felt a little proud of myself having been vindicated. As, the days dragged on mercilessly it was imperative now that I behave myself, because the superintendent, and matron would be scrutinising my every move.

The following Saturday again we were in crocodile fashion hassled by the superintendent to the cinema. The feature film after the interval was a Western. Because my mind was in a whirl, I did not follow the plot very closely. All I remember that it was in colour, and there was much shooting, and fighting. During this performance, I attempted to hatch a plot to run away again. Many ideas had been formulating in my mind. The first was to challenge the master, and matron, and say I was going to leave, then just leave. No! This theory was out of the question. There was just one boy I could trust if I required a confederate in my plans, and this of course was Richard. I had not formulated any plan that would involve anyone else because the idea had never occurred to me until now. I could not envisage anyone else, or even Richard, whom I trusted, needed to be involved. The sole reason I would need an ally would be purely the company. I thought long, and hard.

The film moved on with more fighting, and shooting, and the capture of cowboys by the Red Indians. Horses swept across the screen that is what I needed, a horse. All sorts of ideas whirled through my mind, and these notions were beginning to feel a little silly. Of course, a horse would definitely speed up any escape attempt from the institution. Many crazed plans percolated in my head, would they ever come to fruition?

My thoughts wandered back to Richard, he was sitting only a few seats away, and it was impossible for me to converse with him without disturbing everyone. Also, the superintendent was sitting between us, no doubt keeping a beady eye on me, lest I should attempt to disappear once again. The flickering gleam of the projector's beam highlighted his trilby, and tobacco smoke. My eyes were drawn back to the screen, and another Red Indian fell into the prairie dust. The day was stifling, and the cinema by now was becoming most unbearable, almost to the point of asphyxiation. An usherette moved round the emptying auditorium with a flit spray, sending a waft of freshness into my nostrils. It was with considerable relief when the show ended, and the atmosphere outside, although still warm, was unbelievably fresh in comparison with the airless atmosphere of the cinema auditorium. I was confident in my mind that the ideal time to leave the house was during the night. Many aspects had to be considered, and for some of these, I would need an associate, and again I thought of Richard. I knew, as a friend I could trust him, if I was to include him in my plan. Selfishly, I thought we could probably go together; he would be company for me. I would convey the proposal to him when we had some privacy. My suitcase and clothes were kept in the linen store that was usually locked. If I ran away now before reaching the institution, I would already be wearing some decent clothes so I would not have the problem of acquiring my attire from the linen store. A sudden idea struck me; I wanted to take my suitcase, because this time I would not be returning. All of these speculations rushed through my head as I sauntered back in crocodile formation to the institution with the superintendent bringing up the rear, and always keeping a vigilant eye on all, and especially me.

Not able to talk to Richard in the cinema because I'm convinced someone would have been eavesdropping, I felt I must try, and whisper to him my notions tonight in the dormitory. There would be an opportunity when the others were asleep. My heart was heavy, and I was hoping that I could trust Richard. This negative thought I considered, I must banish from my head because I knew I could trust him. After the chores for that day were completed, and we were playing games in the dining room, the superintendent entered, and told us it was time for bed. This was much earlier than most Saturday evenings. If we had not committed a misdemeanour during the week, we were allowed to stay up until nine o'clock on Saturdays. It was now only twenty five minutes past eight, unfortunately the rest of the boys were punished for my absconding. I felt this was so unfair on the part of the ogres to make the rest forfeit their privileges. I was very upset, and remorseful on this account, and I wished to make amends. I had been given extra chores to do, and would have to expect to be packed off to bed earlier than the others. This punishment I would have to endure, but to chastise the other boys, except me was wrong. I deliberated for some time whether to abandon my plan, since it only meant that more suffering for my peers. I lay awake for a prolonged time that night agonising, should I talk to Richard?

In the dimness of the dormitory, I could make out his form, and he was fast asleep. Should I wake him? No! That would be unfair; I had caused too much heartache already. I tried to go to sleep. This intrinsic function eluded me for several hours. Then sometime during the night, after falling into a shallow sleep, I was aroused by what I thought was crying coming from the bed nearest to mine. When fully awake in the morning I remembered, but was not fully sure if it could have been Richard. He looked extremely tired, and drained as his limp body crawled out of his bed. I felt a pang in the pit of my stomach, realising that I was not the only one here feeling very homesick, and lonely. I presumed the crying came from Richard, and I felt I must do what I could to comfort him if he so desired. The following few days were uneventful, and another weekend came around again, and the perpetual visits to the cinema still continued. The routine of having to change into swim trunks after school, the continual scraping of potatoes, the endless floor polishing, the carpet beating plus other demanding tasks, were now really beginning to get me down. The time I thought was now. I would confide in Richard. I desperately needed to talk to someone. No matter what the outcome, I was determined to moot the matter about absconding, hoping he would collaborate.

That day he was confined to bed with a heavy cold, this caused by chilly late afternoons wearing only skimpy swimming trunks, and shivering, scraping potatoes in the yard outside. I was hoping he was not too ill to listen to my proposed plan. He was fast asleep when we all turned in, so I slipped into bed not having the heart to wake him. I lay awake hoping that he might rouse then I could talk to him. I had almost dozed off when I heard faint sobbing emanating from the vicinity of Richard's bed. It was then that I heard him, and just above a whisper he murmured.

"I want my mum," he continued to sob.

"*Shush, shush, or you will wake up the others*," I whispered. He continued in this manner for a little while, I then realised he probably had not heard me so I slipped out of my bed, and moved nearer to him, repeating my instructions not to wake the rest of the boys. He continued to sob, and in a distressing way he told me his mother had died recently, and he missed her very much. I desperately wanted to console him but had no idea how to go about it. Then, while I was deep in thought, he whispered through his tears, words I could not quite catch. I leaned nearer to him, my ear close to his face, straining to catch every word.

"*My grandmother lives near where you came from*," he mumbled.

"Whisper a little louder but don't wake up the rest of the boys," I beseeched him. Although the heavy curtains were drawn over the four windows in the dormitory, and not being completely dark, my eyes had become accustomed to the dim light. I could see Richard clearly as he sat up in bed. Then he leaned towards me, and whispered in my ear.

"I said my grandmother lives near where you came from. "Excitedly I asked. "*Where is that*?" At the same time realising that I had raised my voice.

"Shush!" He mouthed quietly. Again I asked him, "*Where is it?"*

"Not far from where you told me you were born."

Again I asked him, *"Where is it?"* Infuriating, he said. *"I'm sweating; it's too hot in here."*

*"Don't forget you've got a cold, I think you should get back under the she*ets." I told him.

"I'll sweat like mad?" He protested as he partly vanished in between the bedclothes.

"Come on, you were going to tell me where your grandma lives, where is it?" I pleaded.

"Did we have a thunderstorm while I was asleep?" He asked.

"*No we didn't*," I was beginning to get a little exasperated, and was about to quiz him again then I noticed his eyes were closed he was dropping off to sleep. I lay back in bed. At least he was right about the heat; it was getting very humid. I hoped we were not going to have a storm. While still gazing at Richard, I recalled seeing the results of a thunderstorm in my village. Cattle had been sheltering under a tree from the torrential rain, the tree being close to a barbed wire fence. In one terrific crash; all three were killed outright. The sight of those poor creatures lingered in my mind as sleep began to overtake me. For a very long time after that incident I was not well pleased by thunderstorms. The shaking of my shoulder aroused me from my slumber.

"Are you awake?" Richard whispered. *"I am now!"*

"*Can we talk*?" "*Yes, I would like to,*" I replied wearily, hoping to glean information to the whereabouts of his grandma's residence. *"We will have to talk quietly or we'll wake the others."*

Richard was well awake by now, and began to get excited. I had to remind him again to whisper I asked him. *"What do you want to talk about, your mum?"* My conscience pricked, plus no sooner had I commented about his mother, he began to cry again. I felt so sorry for him, and I was tormented by his grief. How could I, at my age, find the words of comfort other than an apathetic sorry I could not hold back the tears welling up in my eyes, and for some time; we both wept, with hands locked together.

Having sweated with my extra tasks as punishment for my absconding, I was still contemplating yet another escape from this place. The following Friday night I found myself whispering to Richard in the dormitory once again. *"Last week do you remember you were going to tell me where your grandma lived?"*

"Great Gonerby" He whispered. *"What! You mean Grantham?"* *"Yes."*

"*Well, how far is Great Gonerby from Grantham?"* I asked him.

"It's about a mile north of Grantham, there is a big hill," he knowingly replied.

I was well aware that Grantham was about twelve miles from my village of Folkingham and from here that would make it about thirty-six miles. *"It's a long way from here*." I told him.

"I know, I just thought I would tell you, I thought you might like to know."

I lay back in bed again to think. I desperately wanted Richard to go with me.

"Richard," I whispered. There was no reply. I gazed across at him, I could see in the dimness that his eyes were closed, and he was asleep. Well, it could wait until tomorrow. The following evening, after we were bundled off to bed, I again wished to raise the topic of running away, but had not directly asked Richard to come with me.

""Richard, are you awake, I want to talk to you?" I whispered close to his ear. *"Yes, what do you want?"*

"I am planning to run away again. I know that you're not happy here so I thought that we might run away together. Will you come with me?"

There was a lengthy pause implying that he was apprehensive about the idea. I waited for his answer. It wasn't forthcoming. After all, perhaps he would need more time to think about it. He had seen the extra work I'd been given also the cold shoulder I had receive from the other boys. There was the chance that he might be accused of stealing, like I had been. All these thoughts passed through my mind. I then confessed to him that I was frightened to run away on my own especially at night. After a long pause, eventually came his answer.

"*Okay but I'll be scared,"* he replied.

I felt much happier now that there was a positive response from Richard; nevertheless I still needed the reassurance of his loyalty.

"Richard, .You won't tell anyone else about this will you?" *"Of course not"* He replied.

By his ordinary but positive reply I knew I could trust him.

He continued. *"Why should I want to tell anybody, I'm going with you aren't I?"*

With hindsight, my remark was rather silly. There would be no reason to talk to anyone else. I apologise to him for my blunder. We talked more about running away. I then considered the situation of my clothes. "Will we be able to get our things from the linen store?" I asked him, knowing it wasn't always locked but it was possible it might be.

"It should be all right, we'll find a way of getting into the linen store," he told me.

"But don't they lock it at night?" I asked in a doubtful tone.

"*Most nights I expect they do but not always, they sometimes forget."*

"If the door is locked, probably we had better forget the idea altogether," I said.

Winking at me he replied. "*No, I still want to get away the same as you do, the more I think about it the more I want to leave."* He continued *"They don't lock the store until late, well after we have gone to bed, so let's hope for the best. We'll think of something, won't we?"*

With this added confident attitude from Richard, and knowing I wouldn't be on my own, I thought the planned following Saturday night couldn't come fast enough for me, and I sensed my whole body overflowing with excitement, and apprehension at the same time. The thought of getting away from this place, hopefully for ever and accompanied with my good companion Richard gave me the good-feel-factor. By now I was getting accustomed to the extra work given me, and I dealt with these jobs with an air of arrogance. After all, I had earned the fatigues by trying to beat the system by way of protesting the only way I knew. I mistakenly thought that the boys hoped I might run away again, and when caught, I would do all the extra work, thus less work for them to undertake. This was not the case at all; the boys were punished for any wrongdoing committed by me. Selfishly I thought I would have Richard with me this time, and I knew if we were caught, we would share the punishment. At that time I didn't realise the meaning of the word mutiny, and naively, one time I actually thought of inciting all the boys to abscond en mass. It seemed a lifetime for Saturday to arrive, and when the waiting was over, and the evening finally did arrive, I had the duty of polishing the hallway floor. The linen store was adjacent to the hallway. While polishing, I had an opportunity to check if the door was unlocked in the hope of seeing where my clothes and suitcase were. Although it was still early evening, it could be locked. Richard had said it was never locked until late. I thought you'd never know with these people they would lock up everything including us if they could.

"Make a good job of it or you won't be going to Wicksteed Park with us next weekend," the superintendent said, leering at me as beads of perspiration ran down my body as I laboured on the hallway floor.

Sod it! I thought, I will, and hopefully, it will be the last time I polish it. When he moved away I negotiated myself near the door of the linen store. I thought I'd try, and see if it was unlocked if it is, I will have to take the risk of being caught with it open. If I am caught I will say I opened it so that I wouldn't damage the door with the polishing bumper. To my great delight I discovered it wasn't locked. I brazenly opened it, and continued to polish the floor just inside the doorway. At the same time I took the opportunity to take a swift look round the store. I could see my suitcase; it was on the table. I also noticed that there were some of my clothes Miss Shee had recently brought. Like lightning, I bundled all my attire that was in sight into the suitcase, snapped the lid shut, and shot back to the door, closed it quietly behind me then carried on with polishing the hallway as if nothing untoward had happened. I polished with more vigour than I had ever done before. Richard strolled past; I gestured with a thumb-up sign. I assumed he understood what I'd been up to. Then jokingly I reprimanded him for walking on my highly polished slippery floor. Not long after my drudgery in the hallway was over, we were all in bed, and I was much too worked-up to sleep.

"How much longer are we going to wait?" Richard asked.

"Not too long," I assured him. I lay down on my bed but I was determined not to drop off to sleep. I had waited too long for this Saturday night, and I didn't want to miss the opportunity of getting away again. It must have been about an hour later when in the distance I've heard a church clock strike ten o'clock. The dormitory was still slightly illuminated by the dwindling light outside. Richard had gone off to sleep. I thought I should wait a little longer to make sure it was fully dark. All the time I was thinking about the event which was soon to happen and I was struggling very hard to stay awake. Then I heard the church clock strike again which must have been about half past ten. I now decided to wake Richard. Then I thought what about his clothes? I remembered he said he would wear his school uniform so I need not have panicked about it. *"Richard, Richard Wake u*p!" I nudged his shoulder. It was a little while before he roused and said *"What's the matter?"*

"Richard, come on, let's go!"

"Go where?" He said. I could just about see him rubbing his eyes.

"It's time we were off!" He obviously needed a little more time to come round; after all he had been fast asleep for least two hours so I patiently waited for him to become fully awake before I said anything else.

He sat up in bed, and croaked, *"I'm not going."*

"What! Oh shit! What do you mean Richard?" I cried in amazement, and forgetting for a moment that I had raised my voice. There was groaning coming from the other side of the dormitory. I thought sod it! That's done it!

"I'm frightened, I'm sorry," Richard sobbed.

"So am I but we'll be together, so there's no need to be frightened, when we get going it will be all right, you'll see," I said reassuringly.

"But where are we going?" He implored.

Suddenly I thought I knew where I was going but nothing had been decided as to where Richard's destination was to be.

Then I suddenly blurted out, "*You could stay with me until we sort something out, you'll be all right with me Richard, honest, you will,*" I promised.

He began to cry again, and I thought before long the whole of dormitory would be awake. I was getting desperate now, "*please doesn't cry or you'll wake up the others,*" I whispered. I could see it was futile entreating him any further. Now, I quickly had to make up my own mind. The problem was that we might have woken up the others in the dormitory I quickly got dressed in my short trousers, summer shirt, and sandals. I knew where I was heading, for-Folkingham. Again, it was now or never. I hoped there wasn't going to be a thunderstorm, the night was very humid. I began to have second thoughts, and started to panic about running away at this point, and not having my dear friend Richard for company saddened me. I mused, should I have waited for another opportunity, and then probably Richard would have come with me? It was too late now; I can't go back, and let Richard see I'm scared stiff. I crept down the stairway, tightly holding the banister rail careful trying not to trip.

In the semi-darkness I finally reached the linen store door. Holding my breath I turned the handle, and gently pushed, it didn't budge. I tried pushing a little harder, still it stubbornly held fast. I panicked; I thought blast! It must be locked. I put my shoulder against a door panel for extra leverage, and pushed, and with a deafening creek, and to my great relief it flew open. I groped around in the darkness of the gloomy interior, and after a few seconds my eyes adjusted to the light. To my relief, the suitcase was still where it was when I entered earlier in the evening. I fumbled about inside making sure the clothes were still inside-they were. I wasted little time in leaving the store, and after quietly closing the door behind me; I groped my way to the front door. All the time trying to avoid any obstacles that might impede my progress. I could see a faint glimmer of light coming through the grimy glass panels above the front door as I approached it. Within seconds my hands had grabbed the top bolt, it protested under pressure to slide open, the bottom one was just as stubborn, not wanting to move easily. Turning the latch on the lock, and silently opening the door, then tip-toeing through and quietly closing it behind me. I felt very vulnerable as I stood on the doorstep, and stepped into the unknown and darkness of the night.

Mid-summer was upon us, the night air felt oppressive, and humid. Maybe it was just the tension I felt as I slipped away from the big house into the forest of uncertainty. I held my suitcase close to me as if its familiarity might protect me from whatsoever might be lurking out there. The only way forward was to take the first step and I considered that I had already taken far too many already in my young life. As the semi-darkness swallowed me, I could sense all my fears and all my hopes colliding in one great, strange moment of union. Behind, stood everything that was wrong with my world, In front of me stood nothing but an invisible, and beckoning question mark. What was meant to be could not be reversed. I had come too far to turn back I moved forward away from the gate and high walls. Who knew what horrors lurked there in this shadowy world I now embraced? What vampire or foul gobbling waited there, twisted face mottled, and disguised by shadow? I was aware of the air's thickness scented with the rich summer smell of vegetation. As I moved onward further and further away from the light, no terrible monstrosity reached down to pluck at my eyes. No demon waited for me save my own fears. I tried to think of mundane things. I forced myself to make a mental note of all the items in my suitcase. One item that I treasured very much was my navy blue blazer, with the Ovaltineys badge on the breast pocket. I had been very proud when Aunt Nin had stitched the badge onto the blazer for me. I thought over the items - shoes, clothes, anything. On and on I struggled, I walked for what seemed to be a very long way and a very long time. By now I had passed all the roads leading off from the main Ryhall Road, and was well into the countryside, and on my way to Bourne, which I knew, was about ten miles from Stamford. I guessed that when I arrived at Bourne, I would be roughly halfway home.

The night seemed to be getting more hellishly humid as I laboured one foot in front of the other. There were fields popping up along the roadside, and I thought I would soon be seeing the outskirts of Bourne. There was a narrow road leading to the hamlet of Ryhall, I knew by this navigational point that I had covered about three miles. There were still seven more to trudge before I reached the town. I began to sweat profusely so I stripped off my shirt, and with its sleeves tied it round my waist I carried on. Although the night was heavy, and breathless, what bit of life was left in the air, wafted spasmodically over my body bringing cooling relief for some brief moments? The perspiration with its salty flavour moistened my lips as I struggled on. The suitcase at my side was weighing me down. Every step I took, it seemed to acknowledge by becoming heavier. Eventually, I came across a wide grass verge, and sat down to rest my exhausted body I stretched out on my back, and the coolness of the velvety vegetation soothed my torso. I ran my hands down my chest to my waistband of my shorts flicking off droplets of sweat. I realised that up to this point in time, no cars had met or passed by me. I thought it must have been getting very late. Then I heard the rumble of a vehicle coming from the opposite direction, I lay as flat as I could hoping not to be spotted because the car would be going towards Stamford, and that is the last place that at this moment wished to go. When it had passed by I sat up. I mopped my sweat-ridden body down again with my shirt, and began to walk on. The suitcase was not getting any lighter so I decided to throw out some of its contents. Discovering it was still too heavy I discarded the whole thing in a ditch. It hurt me to leave the blazer with the Ovaltineys badge but the weather was much too hot to wear it, so it had to go, if I was to make any further progress in my escape plan. At several points in the journey I was tempted to return, and rescue the blazer but each time I managed to swallow such thoughts, and pressed on. Also I feared if I turned back, I might be tempted to walk back to Stamford, I soon quelled this notion.

I ambled through a small village, which was as quiet as a graveyard. There was a very sharp bend in the road, and when I reached it I collapsed down onto the wide grass verge for another rest. The thought of going to sleep was tempting. Suddenly, I was scared back into life by the screeching of an owl overhead I jumped up with a start, and carried on with my journey. I had other scary moments when rabbits bolting for cover scampered along the grass verge just in front of me. I plodded on, and each time they caused me much alarm, until I familiarised myself with their presence. Perspiration continued to flow down my young body, and again I mopped it with my shirt until the shirt itself was soaking wet. At times I found myself staggering into the middle-of-the-road, then staggering back onto the grass verge for more respite. When I heard a vehicle approaching I would dive under the hedge for cover and lay low until the danger of being spotted had past. On one occasion I almost fell asleep under the hedgerow, it was the sound of another vehicle that brought me back to reality I was now beginning to wish that I had never started out on this venture. Beginning to get very frightened of what might happen to me caused a cold shiver to pass through my sweltering body. I had come too far now to turn back I shuddered again and was ready to give into the harsh regime of the institution. Should I stop the next car going towards Stamford? As if by a miracle no vehicle passed that way. In a bemused state I chose to struggle on to on my village of Folkingham. By now I had walked about five miles. The Road seemed endless, and I couldn't discern the town of Bourne. I was completely exhausted, not only physically but also mentally with the relentless walking, and having to dive under the hedgerow whenever a vehicle approached. The sudden scampering rabbits, the screeching of the owls, the high pitched barking of foxes, and the oppressiveness of the night air were all beginning to take their toll. My alertness had forsaken me, and I wasn't aware of the big black car that had stopped on my side of the road just ahead of me. The driver reversed the car, peered through the passenger side window, and spied me inquisitively.

He called out. "*Now, where are you off to young man?*"

It was a reasonable question.

"*I'm on my way home to Folkingham.*" I called back.

"*Jump in,*" he replied. "*I'll soon get you there,*" he paused a second then continued in a very quizzical manner.

"*Where did you say your home was?*"

"Folkingham"

"No trouble at all, I'm going that way, you will soon be home." He joked.

Every limb in my body ached with weariness, and my resistance was very low indeed, I obediently climbed onto the back seat of the car. I realised the vehicle was, in fact, a taxi, and the driver told me he was returning to base after completing his last job in Stamford. As he spoke, I felt my eyelids drooping. Quickly I fell into a deep sleep. How long I slept for I do not know, but I woke up with a start as the car came to a sudden halt. The door on my side was swung open.

"Here we are sonny; it's just round the corner." He cheerfully said.

Just round the corner I mused, and still barely awake, I began to get very frightened.

"Follow me," he said, indicating the way with a half circle movement of his arm.

In the dim light the pavement and road were not at all familiar to me, and as we approach the corner of a stark looking building, a huge form suddenly loomed round the corner of the block, and swamped me with its huge bulk. Sheer terror caused my bladder to evacuate its contents on the pavement. I wanted to run but my feet were fixed firmly to the ground. The beam from the flashlight blinding my eyes caused me to blink rapidly as it completely blocked the view of the huge dark bulk standing before me, and locking me firmly where I stood. I was petrified. *"Now lad, where do you think you are you off to*?" Enquired the large dark shape looming over me with the flashlight scanning me as a searchlight in the wartime night, seeks out its victim.

This auditory interlude was something of a relief. My trembling hadn't subsided, crying weakly I answered the figure that stood before me, thus preventing me from any means of escape. With tears streaming down my cheeks I plaintively replied *"Home."*

By now I realised that the huge figure was a man of the law, and I was standing outside a police station

Strange as it may appear, this was a great relief to me being in the presence of the police, I felt very secure, and with hindsight I felt I was very lucky that I hadn't been molested. He continued to scan his torch all over by body.

"*Can I go home please*?" I asked weakly. "*I haven't done anything wrong!"*

"I think you had better come with me," he said grandly, Clearly not interested in my petty protestations. He took hold of my hand, and led me round the corner of the building. With the help of a very dim light positioned just inside the main entrance, I could just make out the words' Police Station'. This sent shafts of fear through my being, and I felt another trickled down the inside of my shorts, for up to now, I naively thought I would be taken home, not entering Bourne Police Station, as was the case now. The interior was stark, and foreboding. The policeman placed his torch on the counter, and led me into an adjourning office.

"Right lad, where would you like to sleep?" He asked, there was no real sense to the enquiry to his question. He knew exactly where he was taking me. Still holding my hand, he led me down a narrow stone passage, which was cold, and very poorly lit. "I think I'll put you in here." He said.

Peering into what I assumed would be a bedroom. Terrified, I saw it was a prison cell. He obviously had made his point, and no doubt he thought he had instilled into me the thought of running away again was out of the question.

Seeing my eyes jerk with fear, he took pity on me, and led me back to his office, and he sat me down on a long hard bench. *"You hungry then*?" he enquired.

"A bit," I replied.

"Well you will have something to eat later on. I should try, and get some sleep now while there is still something left of the night." Glancing at his watch he said. *"Put your shirt on properly."* He placed a blanket over me. I stretched out on the bench, and within seconds I was asleep. It wasn't long before my eyes opened to the scraping sound of the policemen sharpening his pencil. This activity I watched, fascinated by the dexterity, of how he managed to achieve the length, and sharpness of the graphite point. This continued for some time, and I continually opened my eyes to see if the point was getting any longer until at last sleep overwhelmed me. It was the delicious smell of sizzling bacon, and the clanking of cutlery that finally woke me.

"Here you are sonny, drink this," said the officer as he bore down on me with a very large mug of steaming hot tea. "When you have finished it you can have some breakfast. I bet you're ready for something to eat aren't you?"

"*I am*," I replied.

"Good, then when you've finished your breakfast we will have a little chat."

I don't believe that ever before had I enjoyed such a breakfast as I did on this particular Sunday morning, laid out in front of me, fried eggs, sausages, bacon, and sweet hot tea. I felt I was ready to face the rigours of what this day might bring. The taxi driver no doubt had supplied the constable with all the relevant information required. He knew where I hailed from, but now it was the policeman's turn to question me. To make sure everything was in order I had to confirm my name, where I had come from, how long I'd been walking, and many more searching questions. The institution no doubt had been notified of my present whereabouts. Thus, me being very prominent by my absence.

As the morning drew on, there was more activity in the station, and it wasn't very long before a policeman, with silver braid round the peak of his cap, appeared, and followed by a very handsome young constable. They both looked at me, and then they spoke to the duty sergeant. The gist of the conversation I could not grasp it obviously related to me, as I appeared to be the centre of much attention. All my hopes of reaching Folkingham were now completely dashed! I heard Stamford mentioned a few times. With each pronouncement of the place my heart missed a beat or two. Miserably, I thought, so that's where they'll be taking me?

My anxious thoughts were duly confirmed when immediately the very handsome young policeman looked at me, and smiled then said. "*Come on Sonny Jim; let's get you back to Stamford*."

It was no use protesting to this very handsome man of the law, as he gently squeezed my hand, leading me out of the station. I thought I like you, you seem so nice. I therefore I yielded to his kind, and encouraging voice. All this kindness from this delightful man was suddenly eroded, with the dreadful thought of the institution, and its proprietors, who no doubt, with fiery anger, and sadistic thoughts, would be waiting for their inmate, pray to be returned. The staff at the Bourne Police Station had been very kind to me during my brief visit. I remembered the advice given to me by the duty officer who told me that I might find myself sleeping in a prison cell if I ran away again. This dark thought resided in my being. It appeared to me there was a certain amount of relief on the face of each officer, seeing me safely tucked away in the rear of the police car. I wasn't aware of a vast amount of activity in the station whilst I was there; perhaps this brief visit by a wanderer added a little relief to the boredom of the night. They presumably had been informed of my first absconding from the institution so they were not going to take any unnecessary gambles, realising I was high risk escapee, and would probably try to escape from their custody. They were determined to get me back to the home intact, and obviously they were very much relieved when the car moved swiftly out of the police station yard. I sat very quietly in the rear seat of the police car as the journey progressed, much too fast for my liking. My eyes began to close; I was still tired from the previous night, and the intermittent sleep in the police station. Occasionally the handsome police officer in the front passenger seat would turn, and look at me; stupidly I thought he was making sure I hadn't run away already. He asked me if I was all right, no doubt noting my pallid colour. He had a concerned look on his face, probably thinking I might ask him to stop the car, and get out, because I was feeling sick, and then make good my escape. As the police car sped along, I could only think about how close I had been to Folkingham, and to reach Bourne in the middle of the night was quite an achievement. By the time we were nearing Stamford, I was oddly feeling a little pleased with myself, stupidly thinking I would be the envy of the other boys by managing to run away a second time my wits were beginning to shape up, and positive thoughts began crowding my head. These elated notions soon deserted me as we pulled up outside the institution. My stomach churned, I was very frightened. I pissed myself again. I began to feel sick at the thought of encountering the master, and matron, who would be waiting impatiently with cold hearts, and a scornful welcome at my return.

The proprietors of the miserable domicile stood outside the gate, the boys stood behind them in a semi-circle, to witness my chastisement as a warning to them that absconding was strictly unlawful. I considered the boys did not betray any trace of sympathy or emotion towards me. They stood like zombies, cold, and unforgiving. Ironically this picture of the boys as they stood motionless, trapped in fear, mixed almost with an air of menace, were going to be forever imprinted on my mind. I wanted to ignore and dash pass the master and matron and hug each boy and say how very sorry I was, for I knew in my heart they had and would be punished for my wrongdoing. As I stood outside the gate the master glared then began to pour his wrath on me, and then matron joined in with yet more verbal abuse. Their faces crimson with anger. No doubt they had been made to look fools in front of the police. My eyes darted from face to face, finally resting on the handsome policeman, pathetically searching his countenance for some solace. He smiled, but betrayed little in the way of comfort. I felt very small, and exposed as I searched for succor, and reassurance as the law towered over me. These policemen, hardy as they were, appeared very embarrassed by the affray they were witnessing. I felt I could not endure the anger of the master, and matron any longer so I dashed off from under their noses.

As I raced, with my heart thumping, along the footpath towards Stamford I knew, now that I had shot my bolt, there was no turning back. I had run away from the law I was a fugitive, and indeed this was a very serious offence. I am now on my own, and no one to help me. No friendly policeman to give me good advice, and no Richard to talk to about running away. Thoughts of the policeman giving chase or the master sending some of the bigger boys to capture me urged me on even faster. As I ran I dared not look back in case my speed was impeded. I raced on. Before I'd become completely breathless I found myself nearing the centre of Stamford. To allay any suspicion, and bringing attention to myself, I slowed down, and judiciously engaged a walking pace. There were a few people in the town on this Sunday morning, and I was hoping that I would not be recognised by any of them, this was most unlikely, as I had never experienced many visits into Stamford. An institution boy on the loose, and on his own, would be something of a rarity. There would always be some busybody ready to telephone the superintendent, informing him about the sighting of one of his inmates at large. I was out of breath, and confused. I needed to keep out of sight, and I must find somewhere to hide where I could collect my thoughts, sit down, and think what to do next. My meandering thoughts brought me automatically to the school I attended, and remembering there were outside toilets from my first encounter some weeks ago. I would have no problem finding them; the idea of hiding there seemed extremely feasible in the circumstances. I had no other choice but to hide. I would feel reasonably secure, and the likelihood of anyone appearing on the school premises on a Sunday morning was extremely remote. Finding the toilets I sat on one of the seats for about five minutes regaining my breath. After a while my thoughts began to resemble some form of sanity. I mustn't fall off to sleep, and I struggled for a while not to do so. Sitting quietly, I began to seriously consider my next plan of action. It wasn't possible I could sit in the toilet all day, I must make a move. I wondered if the hue and cry had died down. I feared that the superintendents had sent out a search party and at any moment the toilet door would crash open any second, and that I would be snared.

It was then that I remembered what Richard had told me about his grandma living at Great Gonnerby near Grantham, I thought, should I go there? It seemed a reasonable assumption in the circumstances. Probably Richard's grandma would let me stay with her? If I told her that Grantham was my birthplace this could possibly put me in good favour with her. Then a bombshell dropped. I suddenly thought, I haven't any money, how was I to get there? Having for a brief moment put this negative thought out of my mind, my next reasoning was, where would I catch a bus to take me to Great Gonerby? I also needed to know the time they departed, and if there were any buses on a Sunday going in that direction. I vaguely knew where I could board a bus so I cautiously ventured out from my hiding place, and made my way along the High Street trying to keep a low profile as possible, and hoping to see a Lincolnshire Green bus parked somewhere in the vicinity. Watching for any one that might be casting a suspicious eye on me, I strode down the street searching for the conveyance that would dispatch me from Stamford, and the horrid institution.

Eventually I saw a likely bus stop. There wasn't the luxury of a timetable, it being wartime, and the need for tight security. This omission meant I had to keep a look out for any bus that was heading in a northerly direction hoping it would be going to Grantham. For some time I wandered back and forth from the school toilets to this particular bus stop. On the odd occasion there was a bus standing there but I was reluctant to board, as an inner voice told me, it didn't appear to be going to my required destination. During the war there wasn't any information on buses to their designated destination for security reasons. I couldn't very well tell the conductor where I wanted to go, because I hadn't the money to offer for the fare. I needed to sneak on the vehicle unobserved. So I had to be certain when I got on the bus that it was going to Grantham. I had lost track of the time. I trekked back, and forth to the toilets. My route didn't take me past a clock. The only church clock I did see had stopped at eight o'clock. Being a Sunday, people were sparse on the ground. I dare not venture to ask the time from anyone, because I thought I must have been looking rather scruffy, and appallingly smelly by now, and I had no desire to bring any more attention to myself that was deemed necessary. I began to panic I thought it must be getting late? When would I ever get to Grantham? I plodded back, and forth to the school toilets once again, normally staying about a quarter of an hour. I worried if people had observed my movements; then again I remembered what the duty policeman had said to me. I could find myself back in a prison cell if I ran away again. I had been hanging around the area nearly all day and yet again I plodded down the high street, despondent, and tired and feeling very scruffy indeed. Not having had a wash for nearly thirty-six hours, I thought I would go back to the institution, and give myself up. Then a Green Lincolnshire bus came trundling along, and pulled up at the bus stop, as I ventured on my last excursion down the high street. Instinct told me that this could be the correct bus that I required sixth sense or whatever psychic phenomena told me, I was certain this was the one that I was to board. Excitedly I dashed from the rear, and scampered aboard making sure the driver and conductor didn't spot me. As luck fell in my lap, they were leaning on the radiator at the front of the vehicle smoking a cigarette before moving off. Not knowing where it was going for certain. It didn't matter, I ran to the back, squatted low in a rear seat, making myself as small as humanly possible. Within minutes we were moving away I panicked again, when I remembered I had no money. I thought when the lady conductor finds out; will she put me off the bus? From that day to this, I do not recall ever being asked my destination or being requested a fare, this was very strange indeed and it appeared to shape my destiny for the rest of my life. Having to make many stops, it was well into the late evening before we arrived at Grantham. I was utterly drained, feeling thoroughly spent, and completely lost. I had had little opportunity of sleep during the journey owing to the fact that this vehicle was a wartime utility version with wooden uncomfortable slatted seats. This Lincolnshire Green vehicle was extremely basic indeed.

Seven

Great Gonerby

Enter Grandma

To my utter relief I alighted without any problems from the driver or lady conductor. I still could understand why I had not been challenged in any way or form. As strange as it seemed, my feeling was, that is how it should have been. It was almost as if it was destined for me that day to reach Grantham unimpeded. For a while I wandered about the town as if I belong there. I tried to appear as normal as possible. However, I noticed I was beginning to get strange looks from people, and this concerned me so I used the side streets wherever possible in the hope I would not encounter so many people. I remembered very little about the town from the days when I used to visit with Uncle Alf and his excursions to the alehouses. Now, the last place I wished to be was in the vicinity of any public houses at this time of night, and there seemed to be an abundance of them in this town. It was said there were at one time thirteen on one street alone, No doubt a legacy from the eighteenth century coaching era. I tramped through the side streets for well over an hour. Then I seriously began to think about getting to great Gonerby, and Richard grandma's house. Strangely, I had not given great Gonerby much thought during the journey; no doubt my mind could only cope with the situation in hand. After all, being a very young and not highly intellectual lad I could only be expected to cope with one issue at a time as, and when it arose. To tackle many problems at once for me was impossible. I considered I had done very well to get this far. It appeared that Great Gonerby didn't exist, as no one was willing to direct me there. I could understand people during wartime reluctant to direct strangers to a particular place. I knew the place existed, and I thought people were taking the business of 'Mums the Word' rather too seriously again I thought, surely I wasn't considered an employee of the Third Reich, I was much too young? I was to discover late, that I was not too young to be conscripted into Hitler's Youth in the Third Reich.

The light was fading rapidly, and I knew I would have difficulty finding Great Gonerby in the dark. I panicked once again, worried what was to happen to me. There were neither street lights nor any kind of illumination emanating from the houses as I stumbled on. I was completely lost not knowing where to go next. I tripped over a wooden box lying across the path, and bruised my knee I then gave way to self-pity, and began to cry. I had nearly reached the end of one of the many side streets, when a shout added only more terror to my ominous night. "*Where is yer going to at this time 'o... night? Are yer lost boy?*" The voice echoed from the depths of the gloom. Still caressing my bruised knee I looked and saw a tall shadowy figure looming ominously out of the darkness. It leered down at me, and then said in slurred ambling tone punctuated by the odd hiccup. "*It looks ter me as if yer 've ert your sen laddie, I 'eard some of the noise of a few sssheconds ago it must have been yer.... falling over this 'ere box.*" The voice said swinging his large boot in the direction of the box, and completely missing the target, thus landing flat on his back on the pavement.

"*I want to go to great Gonerby,*" I said staring bewildered at the recumbent being before me. Being somewhat startled at the man's strange behaviour that seemed in the episode a rather comical sight. I temporally overcame my fear. He began waving an uncontrollable arm, he continued stammering intoxicating inaudible directions of where he considered it best that I should head. Not understanding a word he said, I thanked him, and made a hasty departure from his presents. I turn left at the end of the street in the general direction I thought the man intended me to go. I hadn't the faintest idea where Richard grandma's house was. All I knew for certain was that I needed to get out of this seedy area, and head for Great Gonerby, and grandma's house. I had a faint recollection of him mention a hill. I didn't know the lady's name. I thought, of whom should I ask? The prospect of finding the house seemed very remote indeed being enveloped in the darkness of the night. Although completely worn out, tired, and very hungry, I was determined not to give up, I was too scared to be outside in the night, and wished to be under the security of any roof. This state of mind pushed me on. I plodded on up the hill. The road, which now was devoid of any houses, was obviously leading out of the town. The hill was getting steeper, and caused much more effort to traverse its ever-increasing incline. I sat for a while on the grass verge, then in the distance, and almost at the brow of the hill I could just about discern what I thought were cottages.

I vaguely recalled Richard stating his grandma's house was second on the left in the main road. Depending on the way you approach the cottages made a difference to which was the left-hand side of the road. I considered that if Richard meant by leaving Grantham, and heading towards Great Gonerby, the house would be on the left-hand side of the road. I plumped for the second cottage, and elated I jumped up, and found a new energy, and reached the first block of semi-detached cottages. I tiptoed through the front gate of the second cottage. Very slowly and in the dark I crept up to the front door, and after hesitating for a minute, I gently tapped the door. Understandably there was no response to this very timid attempt to raise the occupants. I tapped gain a little harder this time. I repeated this exercise a few times to no avail. I guessed the inhabitants must be in bed, and fast asleep, after all it was quite late. To attend my bidding, I resorted to more desperate measures in my determination to rouse those dormant in the household. I scooped up a handful of earth from the front garden, and hurled it at the front bedroom window, I then waited. The shock of the bedroom window being violently flung open sent me reeling backwards over a garden gnome. A hair-curler adorned grey head thrust itself out of the window, and barked.

"Yeah, what do you think you are doing at this time of night?" At this well-deserved outburst I was more terrified than I sometimes was of matron, and for a brief moment I trembled, and could not utter a word. Scarcely making out her form in the poor light, but by the sound of her voice I imagined she concealed the best part of her anatomy that matched her very loud voice.

"Who are you?" I stupidly called up to the window where the huge bulk began to overflow the window ledge in an exceedingly precarious fashion, threatening to pitch forward any second.

"*Mind your own bloody business, and clear off!"* She screamed back.

I began to retreat backwards towards the front gate, and careful not to trip over the garden gnome again. When I reached the gate I called out. *"Richard said I could come, and see you,"* I lied, and then I plucked up more courage to say, *"I've come from Stamford."*

"*Bloody well wait there! Don't go away. Wait there!"* She fumed, loud enough to wake the whole neighbourhood.

The chance of me leaving now seemed very remote indeed, now that I'd found the right house. I mused, so this was Richard's grandma? While I waited for the hefty lady to emerge down the stairs I suddenly thought, what if she doesn't let me stay the night, what if she turns me away, or worse still, informs the home where I was? The front door was thrust open by this very capacious woman; she was in her dressing gown, and was still in the process of tying the cords which eventually vanished into the folds of her huge bulk. Her head was draped in a scarf that had obviously seen better days. Her hair curlers could be seen poking out through the scarf, adding a touch of comedy to this enormous female. She surveyed me for a few seconds, and to my relief she beckoned me inside. Meekly I followed her into the small dimly lit interior, and in my eagerness to get inside; I forgot to close the front door.

"For bloody well crying out loud, close the flaming door, there's a blackout on," she barked, reminiscent of matron. Once again I was reminded about the blackout, and the war that was still raging on. I thought that if anyone else in the house were asleep they would certainly be well awake by now. I felt very awkward; it was apparent that I was a nuisance. I thought I must not in any way displease this lady, and obey her every command in military fashion. Not wasting a second, I flew to the front door and closed it.

"You had better stay the night, and I'll sort you out in the morning, it's too bloody late now to do anything about you." She pronounced.

I made haste to follow her into the living room. With the aid of a night-light that she lit, and placed on the table, I could spy there was well-worn furniture, and dowdy looking pictures hanging on the equally dowdy looking walls. One's first impression of the room was that it was lived in. There were annuals, and hardback books strewn around on the chairs, and a large pile of newspapers stacked in a corner.

."Do *you know what time it is* "?" She barked. "*No Lady*" I replied.

"Well, I'll bloody well tell you, it's just gone midnight, so off to bed with you, come this way." She escorted me up a creaking staircase. In the gloomy interior, and not being familiar with the layout as she was, I stumbled against the wall. We finally made it to the top of the stairs. She opened the bedroom door; inside was a dim gaslight illuminating a large bed. When my eyes adjusted to the gloom, I could just discern three little heads resting on the

bolster. Pointing to the bed she commanded. "*There's where you'll sleep tonight,"* then within seconds she had left the room.

I stood motionless in the bedroom, perplexed, not knowing what to do. I certainly was not expecting this. I stared at the heads resting peacefully in the very large bed that occupied nearly all the available space in the bedroom I dare not disturb them. What was I to do? I looked around the cramped room I could see one little hard-backed chair, a very small wardrobe, and a picture hanging askew above the little fireplace. There was a large chest. I cautiously opened the lid to find it was empty. I toyed for a second with the idea of getting inside. At least I would be out of sight. It was then the thought of being enclosed in such a confined space shot shivers through my body. I remembered the time when I had had a jacket thrown over my head by the boys at Folkingham School. Claustrophobia wasn't my strong point, and I was terrified of ever being enclosed in a very small space. To add to the quandary, the room was very stuffy. I tried to open the tiny window but I discovered it was locked. I shuffled about as quietly as possible in the poor light, in the process of negotiating the bedroom; I stumbled on a chamber pot. Still wondering what to do, I looked at the sleeping heads again, thinking there isn't much space for anyone else in the bed even if I had the desire to jump in. I sat cramped in the little chair, which touched the bed. I thought there is little space to lay down on the floor either. I'd already tripped over a chamber pot and a motley collection of clothes. I began to doze off, and then I would wake up with a start, and then drop off again. I could not sleep in this tiny little chair but at least I tried.

Then a little while later I was woken by the touch of a hand on my shoulder. *"Come and get in here with us."* A boy's voice cordially invited me. *"Come on, we won't eat you."* he promptly jumped out of the bed to let me get in.

I was surprised how tall he was, he had long gangly legs, and I could see the best part of his legs well below the bottom of his pajamas. To the contrary that I had previously thought, I eagerly jumped into the already overcrowded bed. My body brought the total of four steaming, and sweaty bodies crammed tightly together in this very welcome bed, unless there were any more lurking further down between the sheets. To make sure this was the complete tally, I slid my hand down the bed. The boy that had invited me on to the snug little huddle of bodies, started to giggle, my last action had tickled his side. Still giggling he said. "*I like it, do it again"*

"I was just searching to see if there was anybody else lurking down the bottom of the bed besides us four." I informed him.

"We heard the shouting downstairs, so you've come from Stamford have you?" called out another boy.

"I'm sorry if I woke you all," I replied, in a weary voice.

"*That's all right,*" the boy answered. He asked. "*Do you know Richard*?"

I didn't wish to continue the conversation any longer. This lad wasn't to be put off, and kept me awake, and insisted I gave him more news about Richard. Very wearily I told him, *"I think he is alright, I'll tell you when we get up."* I was too tired to utter another word, and I very much hoped he would drop the subject, but it was not to be. He sat up in the overcrowded bed then said.

"Richard lived here before going to that home in Stamford."

His sudden activity in the bed partly aroused me and I became a little curious when he said that Richard had lived here. I then asked him. "*Did you know Richard very well?"*

"Nope, not very well, he wasn't here all that long. By the way, my name is James, what's yours?" He enquired.

"*My name's Roy."*

"The boy next to you is Steve, and the one next to him, on the outside is Michael." James informed me.

By now some of my dreariness had deserted me, and our talking had woken Stephen, and Michael, who began to show a certain amount of curiosity in the extra body that had, like a cuckoo, landed in their nest. When they came to terms with the stranger in their midst, James continued. "*Now let's all play a game.*"

"*What game?*" I asked.

"Tickling," laughed Stephen.

There was much giggling, and frolicking about. This woke me up completely, and I joined in with all the rollicking fun that was going on in this bed. I felt really at home, and wanted to stay with these very friendly boys. The amazing thing was that the large lady apparently hadn't heard what was going on; if she did she probably couldn't be bothered to get out of bed to silence the commotion we were making, and enjoying immensely.

Once the enjoyable sport had subsided, James said. "I *guessed you had come from the Boy's Home when I heard you tell grandma you had come from Stamford so I had an idea you had run away."* He said in a very knowledgeable fashion. So James was awake all the time and possibly the other two boys were also, and had just pretended to be asleep when I entered the bedroom.

Suddenly Steve shouted *" Anybody for a pillow fight?"* Within seconds the melee engulfed the bedroom in a fog of feathers. What a great bunch of lads I thought and for a brief while I had forgotten all my troubles, and tiredness, and with gusto pitched into the battle of pillows with all the strength I could muster. Unfortunately the fun didn't last very long, it being abruptly interrupted by grandma entering the bedroom fighting her way through a sea of feathers. She shouted very sternly to tidy the bed, and settle down immediately, or we would be for the high jump, within seconds of her leaving the room I snuggled down beside the other steaming hot bodies, and with what little was left of this eventful night, I slept heavily. I wanted to stay in bed the following morning when the other occupants aroused me. I sat up, and rubbed my sleep-ridden eyes. There was a swish as the little curtains were pulled back, revealing a bright sunny morning outdoors. Through a blur, I surveyed around me the shambles of the bedroom. There was a mad scramble by the inhabitants to find their own clothes trousers, shirts, socks, and shoes were strewn about in a nonchalant fashion. All I had to do was find my sandals. I didn't undress to retire. The boys threw items of clothing about willy-nilly like customers at a rummage sale. One second I saw one of my sandals being hurled across the bedroom, the next second I completely lost sight of it. I sat on the bed, and thought; I'll wait until this fiasco is over and see what's left. Steve had to take off a pair of trousers when he discovered weren't his; they were much too tight He eventually found them; they were hanging on the curtain rail. I thought, I wonder if this happy rumpus goes on every morning, there was much joy here in a strange way, a lot different to the Boy's Home at Stamford.

"This must be yours, it can't be mine, and I can't get it on," said James holding up a sandal. He bleary eyed looked around the bedroom. "*I've no idea where the other one is."*

"Thanks, I'll have a look myself," I replied with very little hope of finding it.

Moaning, James muttered. *"Come on you lot, or we'll be late for breakfast, it's Monday, and it's back to school."*

Within minutes the boys were dressed in their own attire, and made the bed, tidied the bedroom, and we all dashed downstairs. As we shuffled into the small living room a chair was put out for me I felt I had lived here for ages, I appeared to be very welcome. We sat down round the table, and waited patiently for our breakfast. Although I was hungry I wasn't very excited with the prospect of consuming the very fatty bacon which reclined on the plate in a puddle of grease accompanied by a chunk of black pudding. I was never enamoured with meat, and it took my foster parents quite a while to introduce me to the carnivorous eating habit. As I swallowed down the last dregs of my tea, I thought if I could stomach the food, I wouldn't mind living here. With all the excitement of the previous night, and the chaos of the morning I had not yet come to terms with what I should do, or say, to grandma?

James spotted the serious expression on my face, and when grandma had left the living room to replenish the teapot, he move closer towards me, and put a friendly hand on my knee in a reassuring manner, and whispered. *"Everything all right Roy? If you finished your breakfast lets go outside."*

I was touched by his concern when he asked me again. *"Is everything all right?"*
"Yes, I think so, although I don't know what is going to happen to me." I replied. I knew he had guessed I had run away from the home. I looked at him for some assurance, and what was to be my fate. This I knew he could not readily supply. I said, "*I suppose I ought to go back to Stamford."*

"Why should you go back to a place where you weren't happy?"

"How do you know I wasn't happy?"

"I just do," or you wouldn't have run away." Came his matter of fact reply

I sobbed." *What shall I do James, please help me?"*

"You know Richard lived here once," he said.

"Yes, I told you last night, it was Richard who told me about his Grandma, and that he used to live here. He didn't say anything about anymore boys living here, only his Grandma."

Before James said anything more he looked slightly bewildered, then said. *"Richard had to leave here because he was naughty so grandma had to send him to the Boy's Home in Stamford."*

"What did he do to make her send him to Stamford?" Thinking, I hadn't done anything wrong, but I had been sent to Stamford!

He continued. "*Richard swore at grandma rather a lot because she had told him to wash his hands before he sat down at the meal table. It wasn't just once, he was always swearing at her, she evidently got fed up with it, and that's what happened, he ended up at Stamford."*

Gosh! I thought, poor Richard. If he were sent to Stamford for using bad language because he wouldn't wash his hands, I considered myself lucky, my past wasn't exactly unblemished in that respect "*He must have done something worse than that!"* I said.

James's face presented a thoughtful expression before he spoke. "*He was always refusing to wash his hands, and swearing at grandma he was very upset when his mother died a couple of months ago, and he got really naughty one time, refusing to do jobs about the house, when asked to. He had a bit of a temper as well, and would throw things about. So for everyone's safety he had to leave. I hope one day he might come back."*

At least I knew how Richard felt having met him, although I'd only been away a short while, I wondered how he was getting on. We had built up a good relationship. I considered he had given me more hope while I was in the institution than I could ever imagine. After all, it was through him I was here now, and had for a few hours had been very happy in the company of the boys. My stomach churned once again with the thought of that place at Stamford. Now I was worrying about what my next move would be. Then suddenly it came to me. I would, give myself up.

James told me that he would have to go, and get himself ready for school and he hoped I would be able to sort things out. I felt sad as I waved goodbye to the three boys as they wandered their way to school. A large lump appeared on my throat, and with the thought of knowing that I wouldn't see any of them again, tears began to massage my eyes.

"*What are you going to do*?" asked grandma.

I thought this remark rather strange. I suspected she would have done something about me herself seeing the predicament I was in. As grandma had no interest regarding any responsibility for my welfare, it meant that now, I would go along with my plan, which was going to be a compromise.

Eight

Slea View Workhouse

Enter the Old Folk

"I'm going to Sleaford." I told her.

"Oh - why?"

"I'm going to see Miss Shee."

"Good, then you will need the bus fare." With this pronouncement she proffered the correct amount, and directed me to the nearest bus stop.

This reaction to my statement by grandma was all very matter-of-fact so I considered it prudent not to delay any longer getting to the bus stop. I never did know grandma's real name. It transpired that she fostered children, strangely enough all the children called her grandma. And this was the reason Richard had said that she was his grandma. She obviously liked children, the rough and ready manner appeared to manifest a rather aggressive woman, but deep down she had a real love for her charges. It wasn't long before a bus came along which would take me to Sleaford. I asked the conductor to put me off when we arrived, and offered him the correct fare. At this busy time of the day the bus was full, and I had to stand for the first part of the twenty-mile journey. A lady was staring embarrassingly at my hand as I held it on the back of the seat in front of her. Just before I had run away from Stamford, I had been pushed, and stumbled on to the kitchen stove. By instinct I rapidly pushed out my arm, and caught the back of my right hand on the hot metal chimney. The burn had healed up reasonably well but the pillow flight the previous night had knocked off the healing scab, and this was now causing a certain amount of sickly curiosity from the lady passenger. I could only think it was a very unpleasant sight for her. That is probably why the lady offered me her seat, knowing that if she stood, she was less likely to be in constant view of my unsightly injury. I had been aware of her aversion to my wound, and I politely accepted her offer.

Finally arriving at Sleaford bus depot, I alighted without the slightest idea where I was or where Miss Shee lived or if she would be at home at this time of day. What was I to do? At least I had got this far, and I knew that if I persevered I would find her. After all, it should be easy in the daylight having found grandma's place in the dark. Miss Shee was a very important person here in Sleaford and a lot of people would know of her, and her whereabouts, so I must ask the first person I saw of where she lived. I strode from the bus depot with a certain measure of confidence in my quest to find this lady. I had a niggling feeling at the back of my mind that I was not going to be very welcome, turning up on her doorstep out of the blue. There was nothing else I could do now, I come this far and I must locate Miss Shee, the Lincolnshire South Kesteven Children's Welfare Officer. Although only nine miles from Folkingham, a voice was telling me not to go there.. From time to time I had a feeling that the more I did in decision-making, the more it seemed to me to be the right decision, so I stuck with my instinct to lead me on the right path. I kept saying to myself, don't change your mind, do it! But how was I to find Miss Shee? and if I did, was I prepared for the outcome. A slightly happier feeling spurred me on and there was the fortuitous possibility that I would not see that horrible place at Stamford again. Was I correct in my thinking? The next few minutes are to me, and much later in my life, unbelievable. I had not walked more than a few yards from the bus depot when a lady, looking at me sauntering along the road stopped me, and said.

"Are you lost little boy?

My first reaction was of complete surprise. *"No, I want to find where Miss Shee lives, here in Sleaford."*

"You are in luck sonny, you are quite near to her home now. It's number fourteen Ickworth Road, and it is just there at the end of this road. It's only about a hundred yards or so, you can't miss it."

"Thanks Lady."

"You're welcome, goodbye," she cheerily said and continued on her way.

I couldn't believe my luck. Just minutes ago I hadn't any idea where Miss Shee lived, now here I was, almost on her doorstep. Suddenly, I was afraid to step any nearer her home. I trembled at the thought of her reaction at seeing me. Had I gone too far this time? I imagined what she would say when she saw me standing on her doorstep. Would she say, and what on earth are you doing here? I shall have to take you back to Stamford at once! This running away must stop! You are a very naughty boy indeed! For many anxious moments I stood at the end of Ickworth Road, not daring to venture another step closer to number fourteen. It was then that my mind was made up for me by a voice I thought very familiar.

"Go on, there it is, that's the house you want, the one with the green front door." It was the lady who earlier had given me directions.

"That's all right lady, I can see it now." I told her as I hesitantly walked nearer to the house. I grasped the doorknocker in my hand for a few seconds before acting upon its purpose in life. Then I remembered the little voice that had told me, don't change your mind, do it! A small neat little lady immediately answered my knock. She had silver wavy hair. She was very smartly attired in a mauve dress, and matching shoes. A silver necklace hung round her neck capturing the hue from her dress. There was a small trace of make-up on her mature face. I suspected her age to be about sixty. Knowing that this wasn't the lady whom I sought, I told her who I was and that I had come to see Miss Shee. She understandably eyed this scruffy spectre of a human being standing on the doorstep with a combination of suspicion, and disgust. The manner that she clung to the door struck me that she might slam it in my face any moment, as understandably there was a notable trace of horror on her face. After second thoughts, she half turned towards the interior of the hall, and in a very cultured voice called out. *"Elizabeth there's a boy here to see you."* She asked me my name.

"Roy," I timidly told her.

"*He says his name is Roy, do you know him?"*

I knew I'd blown it this time, I'd been announced, without an appointment, to a person I considered unjustly, an ogre. There was no turning back now. I couldn't run from this doorstep, like I had at the institution two days earlier. I trembled as I stood there, hardly daring to breathe lest I should offend the lady, who scanned me up, and down with an inkling of pity on her kind face. The waiting for Miss Shee to appear seemed endless, in reality it was only seconds. Then there she was, looking very formidable as she approached the half open door. Her hair was styled like the elderly lady, who now had moved unobtrusively into the interior of the hallway.

"Well, goodness Roy, what has happened this time?"

I was relieved it was a question directed at me, not a scalding. This is more than I'd hoped for. Emotions took over, my eyes filled with tears I could not answer her straight away.

"Come on in." Then addressing the elderly lady she said. *"Mother, could you ring my office, and tell them I have an emergency on my hands, and I won't be in this morning."*

As I entered the hall, and moved into the interior of the house, Miss She glanced in my direction then whispered to her mother. *"Phew, mother, I think a bath is in order"*. Her nostrils twitched aggressively as she spoke. In this very humid, and sticky weather I must have smelled dreadful, not having had a bath or wash for three days. In no time at all the bath water was run, and waiting for me to launch my smelly body into it. I struggled to strip off my sweaty shirt and shorts as they clung to my body in defiance. While I soaked my body in the very hot soapy water, my eyes wandered around the luxurious bathroom, with its pink décor, and thick matching pile carpet covering the floor. Huge bath towels hung on ornate rails along the walls. Everything about the bathroom shouted comfort, and well being. I was told to put on the bathrobe that hung on the door when I had finished my bath. After drying myself I put on the robe, it reached to the floor, and I needed to hold it up in case I tripped over. I had been instructed to stay in the bathroom until Miss Shee managed to acquire clothes from me which she duly presented sometime later. After discarding the sweaty clothes that I had been wearing for so long, the freshness of the new clothes she brought, were heaven. I had a new pair of everything, grey trousers, a smart shirt, a pullover, and three pairs of socks, shoes, a blazer, and a green cap. I was now a new boy, and almost had a new identity. I was ready for anything the world could pitch at me. I felt great.

I had partly got away with a scolding from Miss Shee, although I imagined she had soft-peddled a little in the presence of her mother, who had taken a liking to me. While I stayed at Miss Shee's home for a few hours, the friendship between her mother, and I had waxed, and she would slyly wink at me no sooner had her daughter warned me to behave myself? The time at number fourteen was uneventful, probably because I had to conduct myself in a manner becoming a well-brought up boy. This being the case, I recall very little of the brief period of my stay there. I didn't realise at the time; my next abode was to be not very far from number 14 Ickworth Road.

Slea View Workhouse, Sleaford, where I stayed from August to end October 1944 (Now a Car Park)

Packing my sparse belongings in a borrowed suitcase, Miss Shee deposited me in a very large building, with enormous grounds surrounding the house. The exact introductions to anyone in particular are now just a blur; in fact it was quite likely there were no introductions. As my stay in this establishment lengthened, all things appertaining to the building, its occupants, and myself became more unimpeded. My first memory was the first night at bedtime I was put to bed in a clean, spotless dormitory. The walls were coloured green; a white ceiling with large hanging lights. My bed was enormous, and comfortable. The space available in this monster piece of dormitory furniture was in stark contrast to the memorable one night stay in Great Gonerby.

The next morning a kindly lady in a blue and white uniform, with fair hair, a plump body, and a jovial round face, woke me. She had no doubt been aware of my previous activities. At this very moment of espying me snuggled in-between the bedclothes, she would, no doubt be relieved to see me still lying there in the morning. As I entered the very large dining room for breakfast, I noticed it was filled only with adults, and the men were segregated from the women. It was as quiet as a graveyard not a word was spoken. The clanking of cutlery on plates was all I heard. I thought where are the children? Then I realised it was much later than I had imagined, so all the children would have gone off to school, yes that was it, but I had not seen any children when I arrived yesterday, strange! Having finished my breakfast of stodgy porridge, I then encountered a tall dark man wearing a white coat. His jet black hair was strewn back, and layered with greasy looking hair lotion, which caused gleaming streaks to dance haphazardly over his head as he moved about. He was very tall, and thin, and his voice had a very commanding ring about it. He placed a hand on my shoulder, and said.

"I know all about you young man, if you behave yourself here then we'll get along fine, but if you don't, watch out! While you're here you call me Porter, okay!" He barked.

Not another one going to shout at me again I thought before I answered. "Yes."

"Yes what?"

"Yes Mr. Porter," I nervously answered.

"*No, not Mr. Porter, Just Porter*," he corrected me, putting the emphasis on Porter.

The harsh tone of his voice prompted me not to antagonise this man any more than necessary, so I timidly replied. "*Yes Porter, I'm sorry,"* and cringing I added, "*I won't do it again*."

"I'm sure you won't. Now if you've finished eating, you had better come with me, I've got a job for you."

Now where I heard this before?

The feeling of security that I had enjoyed when staying with Miss Shee was completely dashed by this man's manner. And again I was being instructed as if I was a criminal; nevertheless, I was getting very accustomed to this type of treatment by now, and began to accept it as normal behaviour with the adult population.

The porter took me into a very small storeroom, which was cluttered with heavy looking galvanised buckets, floor mops, and brooms, and on a shelf, a pile of floor cloths. Large blocks of yellow soap were piled precariously on another shelf partly blocking out what little light was coming in through the tiny window that was draped in huge cobwebs, giving the place is an air of foreboding. A cold shudder shot through my body, I wanted to flee this spooky little hole there, and then, but my instinct told me to keep my ground, and not to upset the porter.

"Here you are, take this broom, and come with me," his voice briefly broke the chilly atmosphere.

Obediently, and without delay, I followed him, anything to get away from that grotesque little room, and whatever he had for me in mind to do, I considered it would be better than staying here. Then, a terrible thought struck me. I would probably have to go there later to take the broom back, and collect other items needed for the domestic chores that I was about to undertake in this gloomy place. The outlook didn't appeal to me one iota; I had had enough scares in my young life, this scare somehow was one of the worst I had encountered so far. The porter set me to work sweeping the passageway leading from the main door to the dining room. Having finished this task he told me to follow him. Again we entered the scary store containing the cleaning materials. After collecting a galvanised bucket, soap, scrubbing brush, and a floor cloth, he escorted me to a chapel situated in the large grounds.

"Right son, you can get on with this job here, sweep the floor first, then scrub, and mop the floor dry, got that?"

"Yes Porter," I answered with much trepidation in my voice.

"This little job should keep you happy until lunchtime." He said, and with a big slap on my back that almost winded me, he dashed off into the direction of the main building.

I muttered to myself, don't they ever bloody well give up? I began to get on with the task in hand. I swept, and then scrubbed the wooden block floor. I then took a breather. Looking around the interior of the chapel, I could see that the walls and ceiling were painted brilliant white. There were vases of flowers standing on wooden plinths. On the altar holding two very large candles stood two large brass candlesticks. In the wall above the altar there was a large stained glass window depicting many ecclesiastical scenes. Passing through a gate in the altar rail I walked up the altar steps. A green cloth shrouded this holy table with intricate motives interwoven in fine needlework. A very small lectern stood to one side of the altar steps. There was no pulpit. Religious pictures interspersed with brass memorial plaques adorned the sparse walls. There were no pews, just plain wooden chairs, giving the chapel a very clinical atmosphere. My perusal of the chapel was interrupted when I heard footsteps outside. It was the porter. He came to see how I was progressing with the job in hand. It was when I had to collect water from the kitchen's huge boiler that I encountered some of the very elderly women slaving at their culinary tasks. Many of them worked in the kitchen, and laundry, sweating away at the endless task day in, and day out. Rising very early in the morning to commence whatever jobs they were allotted for that day. They were lucky if they saw any of the men-folk during working hours, the only time they had the opportunity, would be at mealtimes. As I sat at one of the many long tables in the dining area, I realised I had not yet seen any children about the place. The people were mostly elderly, and appeared to have given up the rivalry of human life. There was a distinct odour about the place, an odour that lingers in the very foundations, and walls of the building that has stood for generations, and witnessed many events, and some, fearfully, not so good. The very atmosphere of the dining area was very foreboding, which somehow complemented its inhabitants. The serenity of the chapel probably compensated these old people for any ills life may have bestowed upon them, and no doubt they sought succor, and comfort when assembled there. I could not help feeling sorry for these very pitiful creatures as they ate their lunch. Some struggled with the dearth of teeth but still trying to uphold some dignity, doing this very commonplace human function. As I ate my lunch of stringy meat, cabbage, and boiled potatoes I pondered on the fact of how lucky I was. Already I had moved through many vistas of life in my juvenility, and now, here I was beginning a new life, living here at The Union Workhouse, in Sleaford.

A tooth in my lower jaw had been paining me for a few days after I arrived at Slea View. I was a coward but I was prepared to endure the pain with a forlorn hope that it would eventually go away. The pain was getting much worse, but I was much too frightened to mention it to the lady, as she performed her night duty in the dormitory. When she asked me why I was crying I would lie, and say I had a headache, knowing it would necessitate a visit to the dentist if I told the truth. Then lying there in the men's large dormitory I would sob with the constant throbbing in my face. An aspirin or some such medication would be dispensed, and to the sounds of' 'A Fantasia on Greensleaves' by Ralph Vaughan Williams floated surreally over the airwaves. With this soothing music I would eventually be caressed into peaceful sleep. After I had been at Slea View, being the name of this institution, for a short while, I was given regular tasks about the establishment. The chapel had to be scrubbed clean once a week, and there was also dusting to be taken care of in most areas. Friday mornings were never very welcome in my young memory, because this particular morning required the cleaning of the workhouse mortuary, and the task fell to me, a small boy to perform this frightful mission. Collecting the utensils from the ghostly little store room was fearful enough. A voice would say. "Be gone boy, be gone!" I believe some dreadful incident had occurred in this room in the past. With hindsight, I recall the porter never entered the room; he would stand in the doorway, and indicate with a finger the items required for a specific task that was to be undertaken. The added distress of cleaning the mortuary was as much as I could bear on Friday mornings. I endeavoured to accomplish the task as rapidly as possible. Just a cursory sweep of the floor would simply take a few minutes. Scrubbing the floor took much longer. As I scrubbed, my head would be forever turning round to ascertain if anyone, or spectre were stealthily creeping up behind me. As I scrubbed, I would glimpse wearily at the cold white slab standing in the middle of this very cold stark place. Singing in the church choirs eventually came to my rescue. Having to learn the hymns when in my previous church choirs, and memorise the words I found that if I sang some of the words I had learned they would give me a moderate amount of courage, in this place of death. The house of God I would seek for comfort at these extremely traumatic times, I would wander in and say a quiet prayer to Jesus as I looked at him in a stained glass window.

All were oblivious to my wretchedness at this time, and I desperately wanted to pour out my heartaches to anyone who would listen. There was no one. I would need to try, and put this anguish behind me. It was imperative that it was succor that I required, but this seemed far away in the remoteness of time. The labour continued in monotonous regularity, and I gradually began to imagine that this place was to remain my home forever. The diversity of jobs I was given to tackle assumed preposterous possibilities. Probably the most bizarre of all was the Saturday morning routine when all the male inmates were given their weekly shave. They had no choice, whether they wanted to be shaved or not, they had no say in the incident whatsoever. All would be placed in a circle in the communal wash room. They were decked in an institution towel tucked tightly into their shirt collars. The pathetic men sat patiently waiting for the soapy foam to be lathered on to their sorrowful faces. I was destined to be honoured with this cosmetic duty. Given a shaving brush, and a very large mug in which I had to mix the shaving soap into the desired consistency. With gusto I whisked up this sloppy mixture into a mountainous heap, resulting in the foam garnishing the floor, and anyone in close proximity. This performance of lathering faces was carried out on over forty inmates. Chins would be protruded out in anticipation of being doused by the foaming mixture. Letting my excitement run away with me, my initial attempts resulted in a mass of foam completely covering the unsuspecting faces. The porter was not amused because he, following with an open razor, almost scalped one terrified inmate.

One Saturday morning, with complete command, and dexterity, and which included three breaks to strop the open razor, between us we managed to lather, and shave over forty inmates in less than ten minutes. This feat was an exception, and countless times I would day-dream, and linger in my duty, then the porter would jostle me.

One inmate would intentionally try, and scare me whenever he had the opportunity, and I was always very wary of him. The spontaneous opportunity to get my revenge on his fellow presented itself during one of the Saturday morning barbershop sessions. The inmate in question unfortunately had not had a charisma transplant. He had only one eye this one making up for two, glared with brilliant intensity. He processed a very large grotesque nose with equally large nostrils. Just one twisted tooth in his lower jaw and this tooth protruded towards his upper lip. This feature of the inmate I would christen as central heating. This farcical picture was enough to frighten me without his resorting to sneaking up quietly behind me, and then suddenly pouncing, and bellowing unrecognisable pronouncements in my ear, I was at a loss to understand at the time. On this particular Saturday morning, I must stress the subsequent action was completely spontaneous. When it was his turn to be lathered I approached him in the normal manner, wielding the shaving brush high above my head, as I always did as a lark. He stared intently at the brush smothered in foam, and for a split second, gaped, and opened his mouth wide. This I took as an invitation, and promptly thrust the shaving brush, and its contents into the gaping orifice. I felt a twinge of contrition after this action as I watched the poor man spluttering and gasping for breath. However, I had no more alarming incidents from this inmate again.

The porter's reaction to this episode was unexpected. I was waiting for a severe reprimand, but it never came. I believe he probably had been aware of what had been taking place between the inmate, and me in the past. The only chastisement I received that morning was reproachful look. As the porter turned his head away from my direction, I do believe I detected a wry smile creeping across his face. I considered the porter was an enigma. It may have been a quirk of my imagination. All the same I found it somewhat odd. We worked extremely effectively together on the Saturday morning shaving sessions, and due to this I do think I was favoured a little more by him. I enjoyed the barbershop activities, if one can enjoy oneself assisting the shaving of forty inmates living in a workhouse. Later on and unsupervised, I began to lather the inmates as normal. The porter arrived holding an envelope in his hand. He strode up to me and said, in a very light-hearted manner. "*You know what this is?*" He proffered me the envelope.

"*Yes I do, it's a letter,*" I replied.

"Yes I know it is, but do you know what these lines mean?" He enquired, and then he pointed to the blue lines forming across on the envelope.

"Yes, that means it's a registered letter, and there might be money in it." I answered.

"That's right, I expected it has." He chuckled.

It dawned on me some little time later that he had not let me see the entire envelope, or to whom it was addressed, because he rapidly flicked it over back, and forth concealing the addressee. Only getting a fleeting glance, I believe I saw part of my name peeping through is partly open fingers. Did someone know where I was, and had sent me money?

The evenings I found very frustrating, there being no one of my age in the institution, and I would get really bored. All the old men, sat in farmhouse chairs, some would be reading newspapers; others sat staring vacantly towards the dingy walls, thinking, no doubt, how cruelly life had treated them. As I sat gazing at these lost souls, I would try to imagine what they, in turn, would be thinking as the foul-smelling smoke from their pipes ascended in blue coils upwards, carrying their thoughts as it rose, then it would dispersing high above them into the lofty regions of the dismal ceiling. Some of the older men, no sooner had they sat in their chairs, and settled themselves down, would be sound asleep. Intermittent snoring would resound throughout the hollow common room, and the wakeful inmates appeared to be completely oblivious of the thunderous rumblings around them. Once I was invited to play draughts by one of the old men but my lack of concentration in what I thought was a very boring game, the pastime was soon terminated, thus I was told in forthright terms to "bugger off and find something to read!"

Other inmates would replenish their pipes by cutting off chunks of Digger tobacco that was supplied in long square lengths. One old man never smoked the tobacco; he would chew it, and then would spit it out in a sickening yellow squirt on the ground. His action would turn my stomach over every time I was unfortunate to witness this spectacle from the obnoxious habit of this equally disgusting inmate. Luckily his actions were only ever carried on outside. There were no children's books or comics, and I would find myself reading the same old newspapers day after day. Occasionally the porter would bring me very old books, the literature I found in these volumes way above my understanding. The odd comic very rarely found its way into the common room. I would amuse myself by talking to the inmates, although it was not long before they grew weary of my jabbering. To emphasise their point of my unwanted presents, they would blow their foul-smelling pipe smoke into my face. Every day the routine was the same. I looked forward to Saturday lunchtime, having struggled through the first course of stringy beef, cabbage, and sometimes on extremely rare occasion's sausages, and chips.

The first course was always followed with jam roly-poly pudding, and if I had been exceptionally good during the week, the porter would see that I received an additional helping of this delicious pudding. The inmates after they had finished eating would receive their meagre pocket money. I would be given two old pence after lunch. This two old pence pocket money, to me, of course, was the highlight of the week. The summer days began to greet the autumn, and on one such day, on a Saturday afternoon, and not having to work, and being very bored with no one to play with, I found myself ambling through the big garden. I wandered among the vegetable plots, and along the high wall skirting the grounds; I aimlessly picked wild blackberries, from a large bramble, which had meandered over from waste land on the other side of the wall. I ate a few of the berries, and took the remainder into the house, and put them into a tall glass jar that I had found lying around in the spooky little utensils store, sometime earlier. Every day I would check the contents of the jar, and after a few weeks to my astonishment I noticed the fruit was beginning to turn into liquid. This metamorphosis fascinated me, and it began to monopolise most of my leisure moments during the long boring evenings. My continued obsession with the jar, and its contents also created much enthusiasm among the other residents in the common room. Before very long, there was an assembled throng of strange inquisitive faces peering closely, with much anticipation, at the jar that stood reverently on a large wooden cabinet at the end of the common room.

Some weeks following, the jar contained only a bubbling liquid. Occasionally I would pull out the cork stopper, and sniff the contents, and there was a distinct odour of alcohol. I had made wine! I was not, in my junior years aware of it but obviously the blackberries, and the coating of yeast on their surface, the warmth of the common room, and the periodic opening of the container letting in oxygen all contributed to the fermenting process. My fame as a brewer reached the ears of the porter. After sampling some of the wine, he immediately said. "Don't give them any; I have enough problems with them as it is." He indicated with a nod of his head at the dosing inmates. Little did he know some of them had already sampled the nectar? Eventually, the wine was consumed so now I was looking around for some other activity, which would relieve the tedium of my evening respite. I usually had to retire at about a quarter to nine. I was still having a lot of pain from the decaying tooth, and my face was swollen but nothing was done about it. After being tucked up in bed at night I would hope the pain would not return. It was always worse at night. The strains of 'The Fantasia on Green sleeves', filtered through the dormitory. I noticed I heard it once a week and it was always on Wednesday evenings. I would strain my ears to hear what was being said as the music died away. I can only surmise it must have been a weekly serial broadcast on the wireless set situated somewhere in the institution.

Autumn was drawing on, I was still in the workhouse, and I seriously believed I was destined to stay for the duration. After being here such a long time, and beginning to accept my fate, naively I thought, probably this was part of normal life, it was meant for all children, and it was my turn now. Some nights as I lay in bed, I would stare at the ceiling, and its corners. They would retreat into infinity as they had at Folkingham years before. Then, after a few moments everything again would return to normality. This time the experience of this phenomenon was probably caused by having to work in the mortuary, and mix with those strange people, and the weird store room that I would swiftly vacate having acquired utensils for the job I was given. That place terrified me, and it gave me the impression that in the past something evil had happened in that little store. The morbid thoughts that enslaved me during my times in the mortuary, and the singular people around me no doubt took their toll on my juvenile mind at this disturbing time in my boyhood. Wearily the weeks passed. The war would be the topic of conversation among the inmates most evenings in the common room. Whenever possible I would peer at the maps, on the war battle battles portrayed in the newspapers. Every time a new map appeared I would try, and judge the situation of the war, and more interestingly, which side was winning. The older men would have their own ideas on the war, and there were the usual arguments regarding the outcome of any particular battle that was raging on at the time. Very often the arguments were very heated, yet unresolved before it was time for them to retire.

There was demarcation between male, and female, as was then normal practice in the workhouses of the day. Also if they had children they were segregated from them. The children would be in a separate building, but still part of the Union Workhouse set up. Obviously there were no children here at Sleaford, or I would have probably been incarcerated with them. The only time the adults met was in the dining hall. I often wondered what the women would be talking about doing their rest periods. The times I had to collect hot water from the kitchen boiler, they would struggle to give me a cheery smile. They had sad countenances, and most of the time looked thoroughly worn out. Strangely, the urge to run away from the workhouse never crossed my mind, and during my stay there I never once left the grounds, or obtained any schooling. Sleaford at that time was a geographical mystery to me. The times I had visited the town with Uncle Alf were now, well in the past, and my brief walk after alighting from the bus before finding Ickworth Road had not left a vivid impression on my mind regarding the town's topography. This lack of knowledge appertaining to Sleaford may have been, subconsciously a deciding factor why any absconding never occurred. I sorely missed the company of boys, and girls, and to occupy my mind during these workhouse days. The older men tolerated me to a certain extent but it was not their place to entertain me. Not understanding the immense age gap, I would get extremely frustrated with them, and begin to throw tantrums when they tired of my attention seeking. Being full of boyish vivacity, and energy was in extreme contrast to the tranquility of the aged inmates that surrounded me. Again, I failed to understand what my predicament was, and fretted why there were no other boys here. My emotions filtered through to the staff in the institution, at the time I was not aware of it. I was resigned to the fact that my childhood days were over, and I was to become a permanent soul here. My longing for the company of children manifested itself in a strange way that could only be regarded as sinister, and unhealthy in a child of the tender age of eleven years. I was developing a very cynical attitude to life in general; in fact my young mind was now becoming an adult, and very premature for my age. With a normal pace of life experiences, one would expect the growing process of a child's mind to mature with each child-like experience, graduating through the teens to become an adult. I appeared to have skipped the child, and teenager phases being thrust directly into an adult. A sorry state of affairs for any child of tender years, but luckily for me, this disorder was halted, and thankfully never returned. The rescue came, only briefly but nevertheless was a tonic in my world of non-equilibrium, and initially secured my rightful place in childhood.

I was paid a visit by the porter. "*In ten minutes I'll come, and collect you and you can come to my lodge, and have tea with my family, so spruce yourself up, and be ready when I come.*" For many seconds I was completely dumbfounded, and believed it was all a dream what the porter had just said. It wasn't until he prompted me, in a much louder voice, that I realised it wasn't a dream, it was reality.

"Go on, move yourself, I won't tell you again!"

I didn't need telling a third time I shot off like a fulguration to the washroom, and changed from my workhouse clothes into clean attire. I spruced myself up as best I could, and as quickly as possible, and finally rubbed my shoes with a newspaper, dashed outside, and with great excitement, waited by the main door for the porter to collect me. Mary, his daughter was about a year younger than me. John, his son, was eighteen months her senior. They both greeted me on the doorstep of the lodge. Inside his wife was busy preparing the tea. There was a delicious smell of home-made cakes drifting from the kitchen. The fire in the large hearth blazed ferociously. This was in stark contrast to the large building I had just left, and my thoughts flew to those poor people there, the gloomy outlook of the place, and that infernal smell which still lingered in my nostrils. I thought to myself, now, I must for the moment, forget that place, and think of myself, and savour these few precious moments with Mary, and John. John excitedly began to display all his birthday presents that he had received that day. While he did this I felt he sensed my awkwardness, and disappointment, not being in a position to offer him or his sister a gift in return for their hospitality that I was receiving. Mary quietly watched us both as we talked about the presents. She then produced a pretty hand-made card, and offered it to me. Tears began to roll down my cheeks as I took it nervously from their beautiful, and delicate outstretched hands. There was a reverent silence, only to be broken by John also handing the card that he had specially designed for me. I was overcome with emotion, and shamefully had to weep aloud. This, probably, was what I truly needed at this particular juncture in my life. The porter, and his wife tactfully left the room, and vanished into the kitchen, leaving us to play a game of snap, with a pack of cards that had been given to me recently by one of the inmates of the institution. This pack had a variety of cartoon characters depicted on the face of each card, the cartoons being duplicated four times in the pack. One particular set I vividly recall displayed an old man in a nightgown, holding a candlestick, and the caption read 'Is there a doctor in the house?' We played Ludo, Snakes, and Ladders. Then Mary said she would go, and help her mother with the tea. John immediately saw this as the cue to unpack the new clockwork train set from its bright colourful box, and began to assemble it on the living-room carpet.

"We can play with this now," he laughed, as he took out more tracks from the box, and invited me to assemble the rolling stock. He assumed that Mary had indicated to father what could be happening in the living room. No sooner had we began to move the bright green engine around the track, the porter flung open the living room door. He gleefully suggested many new ways to create authentic layouts of the track with enthusiasm like any father; he commenced to demonstrate the way it should be done. After a delicious tea, and another game of snap with all the family this time, I was taken back to the gloom of the workhouse. This memorable visit to the porter's lodge, and mixing with the children of my own age group, proved psychologically very beneficial to me, and the day turned out to be a very enjoyable one indeed, and one I will never forget. My toothache seemed to be beyond all recollection that night, and I was soon fast asleep and ready for the rigours of the world the next day.

The next few days passed relatively quickly, and it was on a late autumn day, the 30th of October 1944 that the porter came to me, and said in his commanding voice.

"*Tomorrow you are leaving here, and you are going somewhere where you will not be able to escape. The place is runaway proof."* Then he laughed, and let me get on with the cleaning of the toilets. In the common room that evening I pondered where I might be going the next day. Naively I ventured to ask some of the older men were I might be going. Of course they wouldn't know but I was desperate to find out for myself. All the time after leaving Folkingham, I was never part of the picture that was likely to happen to me as each day dawned. Not like the children of today, who are given consultation on all aspects regarding their everyday life, typical of the Nanny State we endure in today's world. The notion that I might have say in respect concerning my life appeared to be out of the question. All was planned for me, or was it?

This last **q**uestion of planning now did not ring true in my boy's mind, for I knew perfectly well that I was to quit this place. I was not destined to devote the remainder of my life here, and why now, was I suddenly being told, I was to leave? Was it a panic decision on the part of the powers to move me on, or had it been planned long ago, and I had only been informed now, as an afterthought? I came to the conclusion that I was a problem individual, and that there was nowhere I could be placed because of my perpetual absconding. No specific plans could be formulated for me, and I was to remain excluded from any such plans or discussions that took place.

Many workhouses were houses of slavery. Andover for example was notorious for ill-treatment of its inmates. One horrible task the inmates had to perform was the crushing of animal bones, the end result being fertiliser. The male inmates would stand round a large metal drum, which contained the bones. Gripping long poles, they would pound the bones until they resembled a powder mixture. Being extremely hungry, the wretched people were known to chew at any bones that may have still contained remnants of meat, and they would throw scraps over the wall to their wives in the adjoining courtyard.

When Miss. Shee arrived to take me away, I had already said my good-byes to the elderly men with a lump in my throat with the notion of leaving them there on their own. At least there was one consolation for them, as I apparently appeared to bother everybody; I would not be bothering them anymore. Who now would have to clean the mortuary? I would miss the chapel, and the Sunday services I attended. I'd been asked by the chaplain to lead the singing. It could not be called a real choir, but again I was part of this community life, through my meagre talents as a chorister.

On the day of Halloween, I was about to depart this place, and for a brief moment, I felt I was leaving someone else in charge. My daydreams continued. I had done my quota it was now down to someone else to take on where I had left off. I was going to somewhere new, to where, I did not know? I did not even know the county I might be entering in my new world. I imagined it was some very far away place from the tenor of the porter's manner. When he had told me the place was runaway proof. This final statement, would keep percolating through my head as I squatted down in the car, and began in a weird way to feel homesick, to leave all those elderly folk behind, I thought would they miss me? A slight smile crept over my face, as I mused, they may! Having passed through Leicester, and Coventry, and at that time I was not aware these cities ever existed. This journey was to take me to the County of Warwick.

Nine

Guy's Cliffe House

Enter Paul Field

Miss Shee maneuvered the car by the Lodge, which stood at the commencement of a very long drive, which in turn led off from the main A429 Coventry Road to Warwick. Swinging on the gate as we approached the Lodge, was a boy dressed in a bright red pullover, who jumped off, swung open the gate to let us pass through to a long, and winding gravel driveway. Eventually we approached an Italian style arch with the frontage of the house on the left. Looking straight ahead through the arch, and standing majestically at the far end of the courtyard there is a chapel, with a beautiful tower. Parking her car in front of the house she led me to an ornate veranda with stylish stone architecture each side of the front door. The veranda was on the first floor of the house, and commanded a breathtaking vista of a very long, and wide grass drive, lined with tall trees which in turn led to an ornate rose garden with a statue of a black boy holding a large plate. A low wall positioned at the end of the grass drive prohibited access to the main road. The wall at the end of the avenue of the grounds was possibly erected many years after the earlier part of the house was built. This view of the house, from the main road, with its elegant design, and architecture, was stunning indeed. So this is where I was to live? This was Guy's Cliffe House; Warwick the house has a very long and fascinating history.

My first glimpse of Guys Cliffe - Lodge Cottage - Guys Cliffe House and Chapel of St Mary Magdalene

The charming chapel of St Mary Magdalene at the end of the courtyard dates back to the 15th century. In its very long history, the house had been occupied by various organisations. During the First World War it housed a Red Cross Hospital. The house has a mixture of building techniques, and originally it is thought that the original house stood a little distance away, and was built of wood. Samuel Greatheed built the current building. As one moves further down into the courtyard, on your left is the entrance that would have been used in the eighteenth century, and walking up winding steps one could reach the house's entrance. This area would allow coaches adequate room to draw up by the steps. At the top of the courtyard, and to the left of the chapel was the coach house On the right lining the court yard, caves of varying dimensions, would have stored commodities for use in the daily running of the house in the eighteenth century, and later. A little about Samuel Greatheed, he was Member of Parliament for Coventry City, and with his father, had connections in the slave trade in the mid eighteenth century. It is thought he may have probably brought slaves over from St Kitts in the triangle trade routes of the time. At one time he had a quarrel with Lord Brooke the Earl of Warwick, over fiscal matters, which was eventually resolved by an intermediary, a gentleman called Pelham, with the last resident of the house, Captain J R Heber Percy. He was the Son in Law of Lord Algernon Percy. Guy's Cliffe was inherited by his wife after the death of Lord Algernon in 1933, but the house not was permanently occupied by the family. It became a Boys Home for wartime evacuees at the outbreak of the Second World War in 1939 by courtesy of the Percy family. More information on Guy's Cliffe House and its history, can be found on guyscliffehouse.co.uk website.

The day I arrived was sunny and reasonably warm for the end of October. A medium, well built gentleman, who immediately offered his hand to Miss Shee, met us at the front door of the ante-room. I particularly noticed her relaxed manner after the salutations of this gentleman, a vast difference to her actions at Stamford. The tall gentleman asked how the journey had been. Miss Shee told him, that apart from infrequent errors in Leicester, everything was all right. This gentleman introduced himself to Miss Shee as Paul Field, who was the master of the Boy's Home here at Guy's Cliffe House.

Looking down towards me, he said "Good, now this must be Roy, our latest and last addition." He continued. "Come lets go into the house, and you can meet my wife, and mother."

We entered what was known as the ante-room of the mansion house, and the Field family occupied this area on the first floor. Paul Field had three daughters, Anne, Susan, and Rosemary, Anne the eldest. There was another child expected in about six months. His mother was known as Granny Field.

He chatted to me for some time, and I began to appear more relaxed, having only been here for about a quarter of an hour. He opened the glass-partitioning door of the ante-room, and called out. "Jack, come in here please." Jack was the boy who I had seen swinging, and opening the gate for us on our arrival. He was a little smaller than me, but stocky built. He strode into the ante-room with a large grin all over his cheeky face.

No sooner had he opened his mouth, there was a distinct Yorkshire accent. "Yes sir," he answered jovially, and at the same time eyed Miss Shee and me, inquisitively

Paul Field continued. "Jack, I want you to take Roy long to Lacy in the kitchen, and see that he gets something to eat. Lacy is expecting him, and you might as well get your lunch as well." He then turned to Miss Shee, and told her that he would had obtained permission for Jack to stay away from school so that he could look after me on my first day here.

Miss Shee was very pleased to hear this, and gratefully accepted his invitation to stay for lunch. After finishing my meal prepared by Lacy, a little tubby lady, her eyes I failed to see through the binocular type spectacles she wore. The sight of these lenses prodded my thoughts-I hope she can see what she puts in the dishes she prepares? It appeared occasionally that Lacy would have no real concept of hygiene, producing a long sniff, and then wipe her nose with the back of her hand as she prepared her culinary duties. Jack, and I, from the very beginning began to get on very well together; he appeared to have plenty of robust spirit, the type of company I was craving for just now. I knew he could lift me out of my misery that I was still enduring. Yes, Jack was going to be my tonic. Ironically, little did I know it at the time, that in a week's time he was going to bestow on me, a very large black eye! We reported back to the ante-room as ordered by Lacy, and from her manner there was the distinct impression she would always be glad to see the back of Jack.

"Have you enjoyed your lunch, and has Lacy looked after you?" Paul Field called out as we entered the anteroom.

"Yes thank you." Jack gleefully answered.

"Good, now then Jack, you can take Roy out and show him around."

"Can we go into Warwick?" pleaded Jack.

"Yes of course you can."

At this juncture, Miss Shee looked very anxious towards me, with the prospect of me running way at the first opportunity of freedom.

Before Paul Field could say any more, Jack put in. "Can we go to the pictures in Warwick?"

"Which Cinema?" he asked.

"The County cinema in Warwick, there's a Tarzan film, with Johnny Weissmuller, called, 'The Desert Mystery', can we go please?" Jack asked with an air of impatience.

"Well have you any money?"

"Yes, I have sir."

"Well what about Roy?" The master enquired, looking at me.

Miss Shee spoke up. "Yes, Roy has some pocket money; he told me that he had saved up."

I looked at her as she spoke to Paul Field; I perceived a worrying expression on her face, probably at the thought of me going away from the security of Guy's Cliffe House, practically unescorted. I considered she would be thinking he would give me more trouble if he runs away from here. I didn't know it then that I was in the County of Warwick, and perhaps Miss Shee of South Kesteven, Lincolnshire, had shed all responsibility for me now that I was safely tucked away in Warwickshire. I then remembered the words the porter at the workhouse had said to me. You are going somewhere where you will not be able to run away from, and the phrase rang again, 'the place is runaway proof'.

Paul Field's voice interrupted my thoughts by saying in a very commanding manner. "You boys can go to the pictures, and if you go now I expect you'll be in time for the matinee. Don't be late back or you will be in trouble with Lacy."

Guy's Cliffe house is situated along the main road to Coventry. The River Avon passes by the adjacent Saxon Mill, its waters tumbling over the weir, and then gently meandering close by the house, with a back-water creating an island of wild life tranquility. Wildflowers were still in abundance in the surrounding fields and it was through one of these meadows that Jack and I sped towards Warwick, and the County Cinema. Charging along the fields Jack, being slightly out of breath, said. "We had better jump over the gate, there by the road."

We had just scrambled over the gate, and charging along the grass verge. It was then a car I recognised very well, pulled up just ahead of us. When we caught up with the car Miss Shee leant over to the passenger side, and the wound down the window.

"You are not running away already are you Roy?" She called out with a very anxious look on her face.

"No," I sheepishly replied.

"No he ain't Miss, he's with me, and so he's got no chance." Shouted Jack reassuringly.

She called me closer to the open window, then opening her handbag she took out a purse, and from it she produced a half crown piece. This was about the equivalent of ten week's pocket money. My eyes gleamed with astonishment at the site of the shiny half crown piece.

"Thanks ever so much," I said, and tears began to well up in my eyes as I realised this lady really trusted me at last.

She gave us both a beaming smile, and bid us goodbye. Before she drove away she addressed the next remark to me, and said in a quiet voice. "Be a good boy."

"I won't run away again, honest I won't Miss Shee." I called to her as the car sped away on the return journey to Lincolnshire. I knew from this point onwards that I would never be running away from Guy's Cliffe House. Not just because she had given me the half crown. Although that was something I enjoyed as a bonus. I was not going to let her down that was a sure fact. I guessed there would be plenty of freedom here, and freedom is what I sorely needed at this point in my young life.

During the matinee interval to the strains of Bing Crosby, crooning," Would you like to swing on a star, and carrying moonbeams home in a jar and be better off than you are, or would you rather be a fish?" Jack told me a little about himself. He enquired about my previous life. He obviously was too young to understand, and at this happy moment in time, I didn't want to relate anything to do with my past experiences. It was all too sorrowful. All I wanted to do was to enjoy his company, and my new-found liberty, so selflessly I glossed over the subject, not realising how in considerate I had been. Not aware at the time, I had upset Jack for he had his own sorrows to bear. When I did talk to him, later that evening, of my past life history he understood, and we became good friends.

We did not realise how long the show had lasted, and had to make a mad dash home, not wanting to upset Paul Field or Lacy. We were some fifteen minutes late when, gasping for breath - raced headlong into the basement kitchen only to be greeted by Lacy. She was fuming at the mouth, and wielding a large wooden spoon above her head, she croaked. “I am not at all pleased with you two. You are very late; I don't know what to do about it?” Then turning her powerful lenses on me; spluttered. “And you a new boy at that.”

Jack grinned at me, and winked before he chuckled. “Never mind Miss Lacy we love your tea.” Then promptly in a forthright manner rammed an apportioned size slice of bread, and dripping into his wide-open mouth. Having gulped it down post-haste he produced a very broad grin.

With much relish we ate the bread, and dripping sandwiches, and drank large mugs of cocoa. I tentatively took the first few sips of cocoa - it being some time before I forgot the hygienic laxity of Lace's culinary efforts at Guy's Cliffe. When she was well out of earshot Jack whispered to me. “If you tell her that her cooking is the best in the world, you'll get on all right with her, and she'll not bother you at all.” This evidently was sound advice from my new-found-friend, and I locked it away my memory bank for future reference. When we arrived back in the ante-room a new governess had appeared, and was standing talking to Paul Field I wasn't aware until now that she had arrived while we were at the cinema. Paul Field proffered the introductions.

“This is, Mrs. Jessie Prior so you will know her as Aunt Jess, our new governess, and she will be working here with us. She only arrived today.” Then turning his gaze to me, he continued. “So Aunt Jess is also new to Guy's Cliffe House.”

Aunt Jess was tall, with dark wavy hair. She wore a dark green warm looking dress attached to it was a sparkling brooch, which glistened in the pale rays of the late autumn sun streaming through the window. The spectacles she wore wear very stylish, and looked very expensive, obviously not the tortoiseshell variety, the norm in those days. She took off her posh black leather gloves, and then offered her hand to Jack, and me, she smiled, and spoke in a very quiet, and cultured voice, saying. “Hello Roy, I hope you will like living here, and I am sure we will get on fine.”

Paul Field gave a long laugh, and then turned to Aunt Jess, and said. “You have yet to meet our Lacy, she is a treasure.”

Before I knew it, it was time for bed. I was ready for shut-eye, as it had been a very long day journeying from Sleaford. The rushing back from the cinema, the excitement of a new-found freedom was beginning to overwhelm me with a satisfied feeling of tiredness. I was taken down into the large basement of the house which originally was the servant's quarters, in the eighteenth and nineteenth centuries. Here it was all stone; the dormitory housed five beds. There was another dormitory in this quarter that played host to the same number of places to sleep. I very soon found out that there were fifteen boys living here, including myself. I thought, that means some of us will have to double up in bed, unless some poor soul had to sleep on the floor. All my clothes had been brought with me in my little suitcase, which was now beginning to bulge, threatening to burst apart any second, due to the large amount of items that I had accumulated. I was doubling up in bed with Jack for the time being until other beds were available. Evidently, some boys were to be fostered out in homes in the neighbourhood, and there were no more boys to be admitted to the home, I was the very last to be admitted.

Miss Jessie Prior had taken over the role of her sister Miss Oxtaby, whose marriage was imminent. Paul Field, for a time served as a lance corporal in the Home Guard. He owned a Le Enfield rifle. There was a time, during the Coventry blitz, it was said he scrambled onto the large roof of the house, and in typical ‘Dad's Army’ fashion, began taking pot shots at any German aircraft he considered should be felled to the ground.

It wasn't very long before I made friends with the other boys. The names I recall I got to know quite well. Were Jack Parkinson the lad I first saw swinging on the driveway gate. Leonard Rose, John Nash, Brian, and Dennis Appleby, Alan Cooper, Ron Forrest, Tony Belcher, Roy Billington, Edward Smith, Maurice Clarke, David Cooper, no relation to Alan Cooper, and Tommy Deakin. Another lad called Wiltshire; his first name eludes me. It wasn't until years after I had left Guy's Cliffe that I found out there were two other brothers that had lived for a short while in the home. They were George, and Dennis Gilbert. George was in the Royal Navy, and was posted onto the Royal Yacht, at the same time I was in the Royal Air Force.

Ron Forrest, Brian Appleby, David Cooper,
Dennis Appleby, Tony Belcher

Ruby and Paul Field

When our leave coincided, we would meet up and have enjoyable social times together. I was not aware that George and his brother Dennis had stayed at Guy's Cliffe. It was only a few years ago, by sheer chance I told him I was carrying out my family research that this fact came to light. Some of the old boys meet up every year at the Friends of Guy's Cliffe Garden Party, and Open Day, always the last Sunday in June.

The house sadly fell into disrepair in the late sixties. The lead had disappeared from its massive roof. Then in 1992 Granada Television made use of the building to shoot the film, 'The Last Vampire'. The opening scene required a fire, sadly the pyrotechnic device managed somehow to get out of control, setting what timbers were still on the roof, ablaze. The building had to have parts of its walls pulled down, for safety reasons. The chapel was not damaged. The house was, I gather, an emergency war home to begin with, some of the boys living here were evacuees, and with the end of the war more eminent, these boys would be returning to their own homes. This is possibly the reason why there weren't too many boys here as in the past; at one time there were forty. I discovered later that not all the evacuees returned home. This sad tale regarded two of the boys, they never had parents or home is to return to, Reichmarshal Goring's Luftwaffe had taken care of that.

The next day was All Saints Day, and the boys from Guy's Cliffe attended the All Saints School in Warwick. Warwick was in close proximity to Guy's Cliffe House, and had close connections with all Saints Church. Being a Church of England school, in those days All Saints Day was a religious festival holiday. We lads from Guy's Cliffe attended the church celebrations of All Saints Day, and then the rest of the day was a holiday. I had never experienced an aroma quite like this before, at first I wasn't sure whether I liked it or not, then as the service progressed I was beginning to get intoxicated by this strange fragrance. As a possession of choristers, and clergy moved around the church, I witnessed a pale blue haze ascending ever upwards into the roof of the nave, collecting, and taking the prayers of the faithful to heaven. A tall elegant acolyte led the procession swinging a thurible containing incense that created the ascending blue smoke accompanied by this exquisite aroma. By his side a small boy proudly carried the boat that contained the incense. From time to time the vicar would, with a small spoon stoke-up the thurible when it required replenishing. There were on occasions when some acolytes would swing the thurible in such a swift and vigorous manner, which caused large amounts of the burnt resin to engulf the nave and choir stalls, this action was frowned upon by the Rev Delanoy Saberton MA, vicar of All Saints Church, Emscote, Warwick. There was one devilish trick played on the clergy, when certain choristers, in cohesion with the acolytes would place small pieces of cut-up rubber bands into the boat, it was almost impossible to distinguish the difference of the rubber to the incense. Of course there was a distinct small of burnt rubber associated with the true incense.

The name Emscote is a derivative of Edmund's Coat. St. Edmund was the martyr slain with arrows, there being a small colourful, gold leaf inlaid statue of the Saint replete with arrows, secured to the wall near the vestry door. Saberton revived the mediaeval ceremony of the Boy Bishop on St. Nicholas Day, December 6th. A choirboy was elected, and clothed in the appropriate apparel, Episcopal robes, with crozier, and mitre, and enthroned at the chancel door, with his attendant chaplain to receive homage. The Boy Bishop was whipped from office at the end of his period of rule. I was never selected to officiate in this ancient ceremony.

I was very pleased I recognised the hymn the choristers were singing as they processed with much pomp, and ceremony around the nave, the words, which were set to the tune *Sine Nomine,* by Ralph Vaughan Williams. For all the Saints who from their labours rest, Who Thee by faith before the world confessed, Thy name, O Jesu, be forever blest. Alleluia! Williams's introduction arrangement of '*All People that on Earth do dwell'*. This arrangement has an outstanding, and resounding last melody line, where the organ's foot pedal notes below the tune, descend down in rich tone's, climaxing in a fortissimo G major chord.

The carving of the pew ends, at first sight all appeared to be of the matching pattern. On closer inspection, all were certainly different, and of extreme craftsman skill in the workmanship. The rood screen was also constructed of wood complementing the pews perfectly. Standing on the triforium above the rood screen stood a large crucifix with the figures of St John, and the Virgin Mary standing at the foot of the cross. This wonderful and vibrant life size masterpiece was the design, and creation of Ninian Comptor's outstanding piece of craftsmanship that stood proudly, dominating the nave, when viewed from the West End of the church. Looking through the rood screen, one could view the altar that was covered in a lavishly decorated white cloth, with six tall brass candlesticks, completing the altar furnishings. Large frescoes depicting the New Testament Biblical scenes, the Twelve Stations of the Cross, decorated the lower section of the nave walls. In the north, and south transepts there was the Lady Chapel, and a War Memorial Chapel, and each with its own individual colourful decorative reredos. Eucharist was celebrated at the church, and this was always a high celebration. The Sanctus Bell could be heard toning the separate three and the six continuous rings as the host was being offered at the altar. All the pomp, and ceremony mesmerised me, and it was some time before I knew most of the ecclesiastical terms appertaining to all the artifacts associated in the ceremonial rights. After a while, I began to love all this ritual, the ritual and ceremony and, thoroughly immersed myself into all that was destined for me to be involved with at the time. At Guy's Cliffe there was one specific job I had, this task was to supply a supportive hand to Aunt Jess on a Saturday mornings laundering fifteen pairs of smelly socks. A small holding of livestock at the home was now being wound down. No doubt in those days when it was in full swing there would be plenty of work for the boys to do, keeping them very busy, as the home was almost self contained at that time.

From snippets of intelligence gathered from some of the boys, the regime was less rigid than in the past. There was still one form of punishment in existence, if caught misbehaving in the dormitories we were made to stand in bare feet on the stone cold floor in the passage outside of the dormitory. I only fell prey to this form of chastisement once, and fortunately, it was only for about ten minutes. Providing one had the intellect to move one's feet alternatively up, and down, it was bearable. Some of the older boys were already working in local industry, and having to rise early, they were needful of a decent night's sleep. Paul Field frowned upon anyone in the habit of keeping these lads awake, and the punishment was always inevitable. Freedom was in abundance as long as we performed the tasks that we were expected to complete. There was much more flexibility of movement here at Guy's Cliffe, and all the boys fulfilled their task eagerly not wanting to jeopardise their privileges. What a refreshing change was this, from the Boy's Home in Stamford! An exceptionally powerful team spirit was in abundance at Guy's Cliffe, and we would help each other in times of difficulty. Many times we would be cruelly dubbed 'home kids' by some of the children at school. More of this later. This ragging did not bother me, and I had already faced much worse verbal abuse, and bullying at Stamford. I now discovered I could stand up for myself having the comradeship, and the confidence of my Guy's Cliffe chums. Once again I was recruited into a church choir, this being at All Saints Church in Warwick the church previously mentioned. I had my audition at the vicarage accompanied on the piano by the Rev Delanoy Saberton, and I sang the first verse of. There is a green hill far away without a city wall, Where the dear Lord was crucified, Who died to save us all. Very much to my surprise I passed the audition. As Stamford when enlisted to the choral ranks, I thought, there must have been a particularly severe shortage of choristers at the time? At one time the church boasted three choirs one from Guy's Cliffe House, one from the St Edith's Choir School, adjacent to the church, which was run by nuns, and of course the parish choir. There was not a Guy's Cliffe House choir serving in the church while I was there, only the two other choirs still performing. When both choirs sang together it was much akin to a cathedral choir. Father Saberton, as he was known, was previously organist at St Peter Bancroft in Norwich. He had a very musical ear. He trained both choirs to a very high standard indeed. Performing in the Leamington Spa Music Festival regularly the choirs would pick up many first prizes for choral singing. Occasionally Father Saberton would invite the composer Sir Sydney Nicholson former organist, and choirmaster at Westminster Abbey to our church, and he would conduct from the pulpit, his flock of snowy hair flowing in unison to the beat of his baton. Sir Sydney was the founder of the Royal School of Church Music.

His contribution to the Church Hymnal was well known. He is buried in Westminster Abbey, and his epitaph can be seen amongst many famous composers, and musicians of this country. Henry Purcell, Thomas Tallis, being notable references. The Saints Days were celebrated with much pomp. We sang overtime during Holy Week, a service every night, after choir rehearsal. On Maundy Thursday in Holy Week there was a twenty-four hour vigil. Posted in the church porch was a roster inviting parishioners to place their names in an appropriate slot with the hour they could watch. Alan Cooper, Leonard Rose, and myself volunteered an hour. This, being three o'clock in the morning! We plumped for this time, not because it was the only hour left, we just wanted to experience the excitement of steeling out of the house in the early hours of the morning. Shamefully to say that was our only motive. We did not understand the true meaning of the vigil; probably we will be forgiven for our misconduct committed at this time if we ever get to heaven? However, we did it, and we were not discovered slipping out of the house in the early hours of the morning.

There are events I will always recall were the trips to out-lying village churches. Here we would sing evensong. We would scramble to get into Mrs. Glover's Armstrong Siddley car, because she drove to our liking, very fast indeed. Mrs. Glover was the mother of the Rev Saberton's wife. One event took us to a village between Claverdon and Henley in Arden. This village was christened with the rather charming name of Preston Baggot. We cycled to this church, with Sabo (as we called him) leading us on, and urging us to ride ever faster and faster. When arriving at the church on this very sticky early evening in August, we were sweating profusely. Sabo leaned his bike by the church wall, then promptly whipped his dog collar from out of his saddlebag, and then said in a forthright manner. "Let's go and show 'em how to sing."

At Guy's Cliffe the grounds were massive with woodland, meadows, and pathways running along the bank of the River Avon. We would journey along the river footpath to school, or take the route that ran along the Upper Cliffe. There was another route we sometimes would follow, this was across the fields, and onto the main road, then following the towpath along the Grand Union Canal, and we finally would arrived at All Saints school We found our grounds were a delight for frolicking about. Occasionally on Saturday afternoons adults would join us, and organise a variety of adventure games. One such person, Peter Sealey-Bell who was a cousin of Paul Field, was always very welcome when he arrived. He would organise very exciting and stimulating games for us to join in. These times I will always cherish in my memory. When absolutely filthy after these romps in the woods we would all be cleansed in the steaming hot water from the kitchen boiler. Water collected from the river, was deposited into a very large sink with at least two lads being scrubbed down together. The common bathhouse would be engulfed in clouds of steam. We would emerge from the water very much akin to freshly boiled lobsters. Peter would also take a group to the New Cinema in Warwick (now a block of flats) we saw the current productions; Charlie Chan springs to mind. After the film show it was beans on toast at the Porridge Pot (now a Pizza Parlour) in Jury Street in Warwick. Peter died recently in Australia.

The verbal bullying we sustained eventually came to a head. We closed ranks on these bullying tactics of our adversaries in a novel way. At our specific invitation some of our schoolmates would be welcomed into the massive grounds of the home. On one of these occasions we planned our revenge. After segregating the bullies from the goodies, we decided to deal out a certain method of retribution. Then lulling them into a certain area of the woodland in the grounds we would then with great confidence pounce on them, and secure them to secluded trees. We watched their writhing bodies as they tried to free themselves from the bonds that held them securely, and then we nonchalantly wondered off for some time, knowing they would be fairly secure, and couldn't escape straight away, although they eventually did. Never again were we called 'home kids' from this group of bullies, and ultimately after saying sorry to us, we became good friends, and later on we invited them to join in our rollicking in the woods. They, with trepidation accepted our invite. Not having a full knowledge, and understanding of our lifestyle at Guy's Cliffe from some of these children was understandable. After some time, a significant bonding developed as we all battled out our games in the woods. Delivery of coal to the boiler in the master's quarters, and, the study was via the smooth cart track. The fuel was collected from a cave in the large courtyard adjacent to the side of the house. This incidentally was the main entrance at that time. This area was where the horse drawn coaches would assemble picking up, and dropping off passengers, and the like in times past. As autumn was well set in, I committed a misdemeanour of what, I cannot recall, suffice to express, my punishment was to help Paul Field with the clearing up of leaves from the very long gravel driveway in the grounds. The day was extremely cold, and the wind began to blow strongly, and I found myself continually chasing, and retrieving leaves. I was given two planks of wood to scoop up the uninvited fallen vegetation, and throw them into a truck. Paul Field with a witch's broom had swept the leaves into piles along the drive. All the time I was miserably toiling with this task, the other boys were playing soccer on the large lawn running the entire length of the drive, which at past times there was situated on part of this grassland, a tennis court. For one dreadful moment, I thought this misdemeanour meant I would be on my way back to Stamford. The clearing of the leaves was a bearable punishment in comparison in my hypothesis.

I occasionally missed the old people at the workhouse, and thought probably one day I would pay them a visit. One other punishment that I had to endure was when, having not been at the home very long, I was creating a considerable racket in the dormitory. Paul Field took me outside, and stood me in the cold passage outside of the dormitory. He said in a very commanding voice. "Wait there until I return." A few moments later he returned with two pairs of boxing gloves. Handing a pair to me, he said. "Put them on." I found them very large, he tied up the cords for me, and then putting the other pair on himself, he said. "Hit me," at the same time holding me well back by my head. There was no possibility of me having the slightest chance of reaching him, or for that matter, hitting him. But I thrashed out mercilessly, in the hope of making some method of contact, after a short while I was thoroughly exhausted, and gave in to this exhaustion. This action had spent all my energy. As far as Paul Field was concerned it worked, I staggered back into the dormitory, flopped into my bed, and never made another sound that night, or ever any other night. That, to me, I now realise, was a clever piece of psychology at the time by Paul Field. It worked out any aggression in me, and strangely, I enjoyed the experience. Paul Field at one time was very proficient with the gloves, and had won a number of competitions.

On the Christmas of 1944 after leaving Sleaford, American airmen visited the home at Christmas tea time, and brought with them a variety of presents. I was very much looking forward to this Christmas as I had settled in, and was very happy now with all the other boys, but it was not to be. I had enjoyed the dinner, then sitting at the tea table, just as the American airmen arrived; I suddenly felt very sick, and spent the next two hours in the toilet. I was very sick indeed, and I put the blame squarely at Lacey's door, and her cooking. This was the only time I ever cried while at Guy's Cliffe. The Lockheed factory in Royal Leamington Spa would produce some very good pantomimes. I saw one such a production, this being Cinderella. Aunt Jess, and volunteers would escort the boys to these events. This was the last enjoyable event that I remember while at the home. During the interval of this production, Aunt Jess, and some other volunteers, tripped away to bring us some refreshments. When Aunt Jess returned to see me being hauled off by another lady, she was horrified, and a great row erupted between the two ladies. I thought there was going to be a punch-up. Aunt Jess eventually won, and successfully rescued me from the clutches of this very disagreeable lady. This is an incident that I shall forever remember. What would have happened to me had this lady succeeded in her intention, where would I be, now, once again I often wonder? The war was almost over, and it was well into spring. The peacocks that ran on the mansion's roof, that we would cruelly chase to collect their tail feathers, and sell them to the children at school, to supplement our meagre pocket money, the peacocks are now gone. I was not aware of it at the time that the home was closing down. I thought the dwindling away of my friends was the normal procedure, and consequently there would be more lads filling up the vacant spaces sooner or later. Paul Field was ahead of his time regarding the fostering, and welfare of children. To this end, he wanted more money to develop new plans he had for Guy's Cliffe. One idea he had was to adopt all the children with his own surname. He had requested funds from various people; he approached the Children's Society with his plans hoping for some support. To my belief he was turned down, and during the time I was there, I believe he was preparing to leave Guy's Cliffe. He wanted to purchase the house, and when Ruby is wife discovered this she was horrified, knowing they could not afford to buy the mansion. According to Anne the eldest daughter, and in her own words to me (2007) she said, "...when mummy heard that daddy wanted to buy the house, she was horrified at the idea...'

The filling of the oil lamps (no electricity, running water or central heating in those days) for Granny Field we would help, and fill the lamps with oil. Granny would play the piano at prayer time every morning, and evening. All this was shortly to become a feature of the past. When the weather was fine we had much more free time on our hands, and began to become more independent. We took all the chores about the house very seriously, with pride, and with a great deal of responsibility. Even helping Lacy in the kitchen, and of course, our cherished Aunt Jess. This attitude towards responsibility was no doubt due to the training that we had been given by Paul Field, and we were becoming, be it premature, young men! This following episode in my life I never completely understood at the time. One morning during the month of May, Paul Field with his family, and five of the boys were all standing with their luggage, on the veranda, by the rose garden apparently waiting for some kind of transport. At the moment there were only two boys left, Alan Cooper, and myself. We were destined to be fostered locally, but not aware of this at the time. Father Saberton believed we had fine singing voices, and he cajoled the Children's Society into letting us stay on locally. Some of the lads went to Hatton Hall in Wellingborough. Alan went there eventually. To the best of my knowledge Alan, and I were the only two left in the house that night before we were fostered out the following day.

No history of Guy's Cliffe can be considered complete without reference to its most distinguished residents the fabulous Mrs. Sarah Siddons. Her father was Roger Kemble, actor, and imprecision area of a troupe of actors who toured the Provinces in a circuit, with frequent appearances in Coventry, and Warwick. They were, in fact, known as 'The Warwick Company of Comedians' at a time when theatrical performances were regarded as either 'tragedies' or 'comedies'. Sarah played bit parts in her father's productions, and so did a certain William Siddons, with whom Sarah was a little too friendly for her father's liking. While the company was playing in Warwick in 1772 father Kemble resolved to 'break it up', and paid a visit to Guy's Cliffe, where he prevailed upon Lady Mary Greatheed, whom was the daughter of Peregrine, Duke of Ancaster (and, then a widow); to take Sarah into her household. Sarah was seventeen, and her role as being variously described as 'lady's maid', and companion. At all events, the latest arrangements did not deter William, who contrived to maintain the liaison. It was a cold, and foggy morning in November the 25th 1773, when Sarah splashed her way down the avenue, and emerged from the lynch gate onto the Coventry Road, where William waited patiently in a chaise, which whisked them off to Coventry, where they were married in Holy Trinity Church by the Rev George Richards (by license) The actors were also appearing in the Drapers Hall in that fascinating comedy 'The provoked husband or a journey to London'. The entire cast attended the wedding, and father Roger was there to append his name as a witness. This seems to suggest that the father had, either relented or had decided to make the best of a poor job. Sarah went on to become an actress of great distinction, and celebrated name in the annals of Drury Lane. She was also a frequent visitor to Guy's Cliffe.

John Rous records that the present chapel was built by Richard Beauchamp, Earl of Warwick in circa 1430 AD. There is evidence that the term rebuilt would be more appropriate, because there is ample indication that Beauchamp reconstructed the Chapel from partial ruin. The most casual observer will notice that parts of the chapel are considerably more ancient than others. This is observable in the distinct difference between the type of stonework forming the North, and South portions of the building the 'north end' including Guy's statue comprising approximately one-third of the whole. it is constructed of casual stonework, contrasting markedly with the carefully prepared, and 'masoned' stone used in the remainder of the building. This ancient stonework clearly remained intact, possibly supported by the area of solid rock from which the effigy of Guy had been carved, and which was incorporated in the North East corner of the building of the buildings as it remains to day. Guy Earl of Warwick, The tale of Guy Earl of Warwick is alleging, so it is closely connected with the chapel that some reference to it seemed to an essential part of the team. There is little proof of supporting evidence though the names of some of the dramatic as person are enshrined in accepting Saxon history. The story of St George, and the Dragon seems to have some kinship, both as to period, and credibility. Guy was a Saxon, and is thought to have been born in Warwick. He was not of noble birth but soon established a formidable reputation for proficiency. and in the martial arts. He was by any standard a 'big lad'. His statue in the chapel reputed to be life-size suggests he was rather more than eight feet tall, and of corresponding build. He attracted the attention of Rohund Earl of Warwick, who is recorded to have held Warwick under Alfred the Great. There Guy fell for Rohund's daughter, the beautiful Felice (Felicia), but his lowly birth presented a barrier, and he realised he must prove himself before there could be further progress. So he went to Normandy, and then he found fame by defeating all comers in a series of tourneys, and combats. Returning to England he obligingly slaughtered an enormous dun cow which was ravaging Dunmore Heath, and also put paid to a dragon which was terrifying Yorkshire, but then went abroad to find more adventure. He fought Turks, and brigands and he came home to find Felice responsive. They were married at Warwick amid great rejoicing. Guy felt he had more to do, and with a company of other gentle knights set off for the Crusades, where he won countless classic battles against the Saracens, and all other infidels.

Meanwhile, there was trouble at home. King Athelston, now on the throne, was cooped up in Winchester by an army of Danes, who demanded the surrender of England. The position was one of stalemate, and the Danish generals, Olaf, and Golanus, demanded either surrender or settlement of the issue by personal combat between their prospective champions. Athelston selected the latter alternative but lamented that all his famous champions were overseas, and he had no one of the requisite caliber to meet the challenge. Unknown to Athelston help was at hand. Guy had returned, and was at Portsmouth, in the robes of a potential pilgrim, having forsaken his is bloodthirsty ways, and seeking only a life of remorse. Hearing of Athelston's problem he made his way to Winchester, weak, and emancipated, and for the sake of England condescended to do battle. After a period of recuperation he fought, and killed the Danish champion Colbrand. The Danes accepted the verdict, and Winchester was saved. Whereupon Guy resumed the brown robes of the palmer, and returned to Warwick, 'for three days taking all alms at the hands of its own lady as one of the poor people unto whom she daily gave relief, and repaired to a hermit that resided among the shady woods hard by, desiring by conference with him to receive some spiritual comfort' (Rous). Here he abode for a short time until the hermit's death, after which he occupied the cave until 'discerning death to approach', he sent to his lady their wedding ring, advising her that she would find him dead in the chapel before the altar. So Guy died aged seventy. Whereupon the gravely neglected but still devoted Countess Felicia committed suicide by hurling herself from the high cliff adjoining the chapel, and they were buried together at the hermitage. (Rouse's date is 959AD).

In 1421 King Henry V came to Warwick, and paid a visit to Guy's Cliffe, where he was so impressed with the beauty and serenity of the place he resolved to found a chantry, with accommodation for two priests. The king died the following year at the age of thirty-four, his dream unfulfilled. His friend Richard Beauchamp, Earl of Warwick accepted responsibility, and in the first year of Henry V1 applied for a license for two priests to sing Mass daily in the Chapel. It is interesting to note the chapel faces north-south, not the normal east-west orientation.

Nine

Moving On

Enter George Robbins

After leaving Guy's Cliffe House, for a short while I lived at the all Saints Parish vicarage until other arrangements could be made for me. Eventually I was fostered with the Jones family, in Humphries Street, Emscote in Warwick. I was escorted to this house by Father Saberton. In a hurry to get away Lacy had nicked my suitcase. My belongings were lodged in a kit bag. No sooner had I arrived, Father Saberton tipped all my possessions out of the kit bag, strewing them all over the carpet, and at the same time saying. "Let's see what you have got here, oh, I see you have a football jersey. What else have you got interesting to see?" I took a very dim view of his nosy attitude and his poking around in my sparse possessions. Ever since that time, I was always wary of the man.

In the Jones family there were two daughters, and two sons. The elder son was in the army. I stayed with his family for quite some time. The house was big, and there were times when I was very frightened of being left alone on Saturday nights. My nightmares began to return, and I never looked forward to these solitary Saturday evenings in this house. There was a large cellar in the house, and I was always frightened that someone was lurking in the dark shadows down there, and would creep up on me when I wasn't aware.

One day returning home from school I met Aunt Jess, she had found employment in a local children's home in Warwick. When she saw me she looked aghast, her first remark was. "Roy, you do look thin, and pale, have you been eating enough? I am very concerned for you."

I began to cry I was not happy, and seeing Aunt Jess again brought back memories of Guy's Cliffe, and all my friends whom I was sadly missing. I was always hungry, and at this juncture in my life thirteen years of age I needed my sustenance; I obviously was not getting it. She could see how sorrowful I looked, and she held my hand for a short while. I cried all that evening in bed. The camaraderie of the boys at the home meant so much to me; I sadly missed them all. How I wished I were back there with them all again, laughing, joking, and playing pranks as we often did. The war now over, Alan, and I often saw each other after we left Guy's Cliffe. We were good friends. We would have dialogue about the times when we were at Guy's Cliffe House. I remember we had really serious discussions regarding the Civil War, he was a staunch Royalist, and Cromwell was my hero at that time.

He didn't appear to miss Guy's Cliffe House as much as I did. When in his first foster home, the foster parents allowed him to keep some puppies, and he was a very proud owner of these canine miniatures, although when I saw them, I had misgivings, I thought they were being over fed. I eventually had to leave my current foster home. The war now over, meant that many young men were being demobilised from the fighting forces. The eldest son of the family was coming home from the war, so space had to be made for him. Although it being a large house meant yet again I was on the move. This time to another foster home, with the Robbins family, in nearby Royal Leamington Spa, and this being my last move. Mrs. Saberton acting as a social worker introduced me to the Robbins family. As I sat in their living room I could see through the window at terrier dog that was barking, and yapping, it was very obvious that it was anxious to get at the intruder that had invaded its domain. It was standing on a table bouncing up, and down in a ferocious manner I was very concerned. My assumption was, this dog is not as friendly as Rex.

Mr. Robbins said. "I will let Spot in." He handed me a tennis ball, then said. "Throw it for her to catch, and then you will be her friend for life."

As soon as Spot was allowed in the room I cringed back in the chair, hoping the ground would open up, and swallow the dog, or me. I was terrified what this animal may do to me. Apprehensively I threw the ball at Spot; this very intelligent dog caught it skillfully in her mouth. Wagging her stubby tail she pushed the soggy ball back onto my lap, nominating me to go through the whole ritual once again. Much later, I taught this dog many more tricks, the skill of how to balance a dog biscuit on her nose, and wait until told to flick it up, and catch it skillfully in her mouth. The dog would love to get outside, and at every opportunity that arose she would rush past me to be first through the garden gate whenever I went out. It was this routine by Spot that gave me the idea of how I might contrive to teach her the trick of jumping through a bicycle tyre. It was simple, all I had to do, was to hold the tyre by the partly opened gate, and in gradual stages open the gate until there was ample space for her to get through, via the tyre. This ploy eventually worked. I was happy with the result, and Spot would perform this trick every time I let her out, and when I held the tyre out, and called jump! Eventually, by forming my arm in a circle by my side, and at the command jump, through the formed circle she would jump through. I would take her out for her constitutional trek across the Guy's Cliffe fields. She always insisted taking her tennis ball or a stick with her on these jaunts. No sooner had we got within smelling distance of the river, she would lunge herself into the water. One Sunday morning she slipped out unnoticed, and it was a short while before we became aware that she had vanished. I knew where she would be; sure enough there she was, struggling to retrieve a tree root that was protruding from the riverbank, which was just above the water level. Luckily she had her collar on. I lay flat on the riverbank, and hauled her up onto the grass. She was choking with all the water she had swallowed due to her strenuous fight with the tree root. I grabbed her by her stubby tail, held her upside down, and I was amazed she let me perform the task of emptying most of the river water from out of her stomach. I secured her with the leash I had brought; then, as if nothing untoward had happened we trotted home.

At All Saints School on Friday mornings, Mr. Twigger our headmaster, who for our sins, was chairman of the magistrates. His brief was to attend the Warwick Assizes. In his absence another teacher, Mrs. May supervised our class, from the adjoining classroom. She would slide back the partition separating her classroom from Mr. Twigger's, and survey us all very keenly. We were always in trepidation of her, if we misbehaved or talked too much, and were not getting on with our work. She was considerably more challenging than our headmaster. On occasions, when Mr. Twigger would bring his Saint Bernard dog to school, and this animal was a massive brute. Its name was Ben, he could just about fit his enormous bulk onto a large stool placed in front of the class; he then would keep a beady eye on us all. If our headmaster had to entertain a visitor, meant that he would need to go into his study, Ben would then, so to speak, be left in charge of the classroom, surveying us all from his stool. Strangely we were very suspicious of this dog that would offer a muffled growl at the slightest movement or noise in the classroom. Big Ben as we eventually nick-named him would also accompany the class when we played cricket in the nearby park. When it was his master's turn to bat, he then would be left with his leash secured tightly round my wrist, as I lay watching on the grass. No sooner had Mr. Twigger struck the ball firmly over into the Warwick laundry premises, and began to run, this was Big Ben's cue to drag me across the park, pursuing his master as he ran between the wickets.

I also was in charge Ben's mid-day feast on school days. The leftovers from the school dinners were his daily diet. These scraps of unwanted morsels would be thrown into a bucket. I would then, with much trepidation pass the bucket of remnants over the garden gate. I was constantly in fear that one day Ben would favour my arm to the scraps in the bucket. This habit of feeding him over the garden gate led to Ben being leveled out by burglars throwing a drugged bone over the gate. Had someone been aware of the mid-day ritual, and took advantage of the situation they may have witnessed? I eventually began to grow more confident with him. One day I had to sit in the rear of Mr. Twigger's car, and hold Ben tightly in case he leapt on his master's shoulders while he was driving. This trip was to a dog show in the Warwick Pageant House. My responsibility was to walk Ben around the arena, keeping him close to me as feasible, and make sure he behaved himself, as instructed by Mr. Twigger. Holding a portion of raw meat, in a handkerchief close to my side this method achieved the desired obedience that was required from this canine monster. For all I know, this method could well have been cheating? However, it did the trick, and to Mr. Twigger's, and my great relief, Ben obediently walked to heel. I thought it mandatory, that all dogs should behave themselves in this manner, the bonus was, he won first prize. Mr. Twigger lived only a very little distance from the school, and on more than one occasion he would ride to class, seated regally upright on his green Raleigh cycle. After parking his trusty steed by the school porch, he would instruct me to pump up the tyres, saying. "Pump them up nice and hard Robinson, I want to fly."

After exhausting myself countless times at this assignment, I often would mumble, in very slight undertones, "I wish you would fly."

One morning at school a gentleman appeared wearing a tweed jacket, and grey flannel trousers. I thought for one horrid moment, that he looked very much like the superintendent from the Boy's Home in Stamford, thinking my day had come! He had caught up with me at last, and he was here to take me back. Then, when I discovered what his business was all about at the school, I breathed a great sigh of relief. Until then, I had never been so pleased to see a dentist. The headmaster's study served as a surgery, and the children visited the dentist in turn. There was not a nurse in attendance, he did not remove his jacket, or put on a white medical coat. I still had my decaying tooth, but I think it had given up the ghost on paining me. The dentist peered into my mouth, there being a gleam of sadistic pleasure in his eyes as he began to extract the offending molar. The pain was most excruciating. The tooth that had given me so much pain in the past was now to be drawn without any pain killer. I was informed later, the manner in which the tooth had been extracted, that I was very fortunate to have a jaw intact, and no complications afterwards.

One Sunday morning after the church service, we choristers would congregate outside the church before going home for lunch. On this particular morning, a gentleman appeared, and was in earnest conversation with the vicar. Eventually, they came to me, and the gentleman began to talk about my future. I did not get the entire gist of the conversation at first, and I began to show some anxiety. The vicar noticed my concern. It appeared again at this time, that I had little voice in the situation regarding my future. I began to grow really embarrassed when the conversation between the vicar, and the gentleman reached a very intense level. The topic of the discussion was that I was probably going to have to leave and travel to Hatton Hall in Wellingborough. This gentleman, a Mr. Silverwood appeared to be scouting for clients in the foster care business. Had it not been for the Reverend Saberton, I would have been on my way to yet another foster home. Now, over the age of fourteen, and I was beginning to ponder what I would be fitted out for when my school days were over. This was not of serious concern to me, and at school, I would often drift in to daydreams, and enter into a world of my own making. Mr. Twigger would read to the class extracts from some of his favourite plays. The works of Shakespeare in particular was his special choice. It was at these intervals when I would drift off into my other world. One of the Great literacy master's works was a Midsummer's Nights Dream. In the midst of these enjoyable reading sessions, I would take my leave of this world. This was a great escape route to wonder into the plot line, with no effort on my part of having to read it myself. Mr. Twigger's voice was hypnotic, here I was involved with all the characters, and they were all coming to life in my daydreaming world. Unfortunately for me Mr. Twigger had no sympathy in my preoccupations, and the interpretations I invoked, he was not aware of the immense pleasure I was capturing in my own idyllic world of make believe. "Pay attention Robinson," he called out and at the same time brandishing a ruler in a very menacing manner. He continued. "Carry on reading from where I stopped." This command sent shivers down my spine; this was a problem for me, as I dreaded reading out loud to the entire class. I found it extremely difficult reciting some of the lengthy words, and very often I did not understand the significance of some of Shakespeare's strange verse. I became very embarrassed, and awkward. There would be the odd titter from some of my classmates when I committed the numerous faux pas. This tittering would cause the head to scowl at the culprits; enough to cut short any more incidents of that nature. He would pounce on one of the offenders, and make them read to the class. I was then mercifully relieved for a while, not having to participate with more agonising reading.

One boy, Alan Cooper who was my companion at Guy's Cliffe House, towards the closing of the home, was an expert at reading, and very rarely made any mistakes. One of our master's favourite plays was A Mid-Summer's Nights Dream. Again his voice was hypnotic, and as he read. Once again, I would drift into a world of my own making. My day dreaming was natural for me, and time, and time again I would escape into the scenes and, characters as he read. I wanted to embrace the entire world of Shakespeare by listening to Mr. Twigger's narrative; this is where I wanted to be, in the theatre with the actors on stage as Puck, Titania, Cobweb, Mustard-Seed, and Oberon. To me, these were real people conjuring up the delights of another world; I could flee, to where? I cared not. To me in my make-up world everything was all right, and, it was wonderful. I did not seek to return to my ink stained desk.

I was whisked away in time to my village school in Folkingham, and to listening to Mrs Lees reading extracts from Black Beauty, and the tales of Robin Hood. The sheer depth of the Shakespeare works needed so much more concentration than Robin Hood or Black Beauty ever did. Once being immersed in the intensity of these works was thrilling being born aloft, and swept away hopefully, forever.

The town Stratford - upon – Avon, being only about eight miles from Warwick, meant it was not difficult to get to, or a time consuming journey. This enabled Mr. Twigger to take our class to the Shakespeare Memorial Theatre. On one particular visit were treated to a performance of Lorna Doone the story by R D Blackmore. This was an exciting outing for us all. During the scene changes there was incidental music, Greensleaves, I recalled this was the tune I heard the time I spent in the Sleaford Workhouse when I would hear it played as the signature tune to a serial on the radio. This particular version was an arrangement of the melody by Ralph Vaughan Williams. The Lorna Doone interlude version was a piano duet rendering. Richard Doddridge Blackmore was born on the 7th June 1825 in the village of Longworth, Berkshire. He was the third son of the Revered John Blackmore, his mother; Ann died of typhus fever in October 1825 a few months after Richard's birth. Of course we were expected to write the mandatory essay on the subject the next day at school, which I confess ruined the whole experience for me. Having seen the play, the televised version and the film, to my mind none of the media versions compare at all favourably with the book, which I have read at least twice.

Another of Shakespeare's plays he would recite extracts from, was The Tempest. When I saw this play some years later I found it rather hard-going. There is one stanza I do recall from this work.

Where the bee sucks there suck I.... In a cowslip's bell I lie

Visualising the fields around and the yellow blanket of cowslips dancing in the breeze, I found it difficult to imagine myself lying in a cowslip's bell; I had visions of squashing the poor thing.

The most famous Sonnet by Shakespeare that Mr. Twigger would require us to recite was;

Shall I compare thee to a summer's day.... Thou art more lovely, and temperate:

We never acted plays on a stage at All Saints that I recall. What made the reading of these plays more exciting was, when asked to take a particular character as we read aloud the play. For instance I would take on the role of Bottom in the 'Dream' play. I loved the scene where Quince allotted the parts of their play to his comrades, in which they were to perform in Act One Scene Two.

Quince would say. "Is all our company here?"

Then I would say. "You were best to call them generally, man by man, according to the script."

Further on in the play I would have to say.

"The raging rocks and shivering shocks shall break the locks of prison gates:"

This passage I could remember well, as it tripped off the tongue so easily.

Quince would tell Flute he was to play a woman. I shall always remember Flute's reply.

"Nay, faith, let me not play a woman; I have a beard coming."

These were very happy moments in my school days at All Saint's, Warwick. I do believe Mr. Twigger treasured these moments also. The customary school assembly was held in Mrs. Glover's classroom, because it was here that the school piano was situated, and Mrs. Glover was the only teacher that was a pianist. After the assembly, this always included a prayer, and a hymn. The hymns were always taken from the English Hymnal 1933 edition when Mr. Twigger announced. "Hymn number 260 Mrs. Glover please." I soon caught on that we would be singing one of my favourites.

New every morning is the love....Our wakening and uprising prove;

I soon got accustomed of recognising the hymns from hearing their numbers announced, as one would after singing in church choirs for some considerable length of time, assuming it was always the English Hymnal 1933 edition. Another old chestnut we would very often vocalise was.

He who would valiant be, .Gainst all disaster....Let him in constancy....Follow the master.'

After the religious part of the assembly was over there would be more singing to come. These numbers were usually of a traditional nature and were accompanied by Mrs. Glover. Mr. Twigger would conduct with a ruler. Occasionally clouds of chalk dust would float off the ruler, because the head had forgotten to wipe it clean after using it as a straight edge. Some of the motley of songs we were required to lend a voice to, were Widecombe Fair, Good Morning Gossip Joan, The Lass of Richmond Hill, Dashing Away With The Smoothing Iron and the Yeomen of England, to mention but a few. Mr. Twigger relished these singing moments, he was a chorister in The

Collegiate Church of Saint Mary in Warwick, and no doubt this activity brought out his singing talents, which we all had noticed. In the song Widecombe Fair some of the lads were asked to sing a character, when the moment came for a name to be rendered. I always seemed to plump for Jan Stewer, and of course, we all joined in at the end of every chorus *"And Uncle Tom Cobley and all"*. Mr. Twigger failed miserably when he endevoured to get us, for this song, to cultivate a Devonshire accent. So he eventually succumbed to our futile efforts. The fair at Widecombe began as a place for farmers to purchase stock, and after a particularly successful market in 1850, it has been held every year since then, with the exception of World War Two, and the outbreak of the foot and mouth decease in 2001.

Another song that was always high up on the agenda was *Good Morning Gossip Joan.* And the number went something like this *'Good Morning Gossip Joan, Where have you been a walking? I have for you at home; I have for you at home, a pocket full of talking'.* Etc. This song aroused strange visions for me, as in my naive way I failed to see how a person could possibly contain a pocket full of talking. Woodworking classes were held at the Coton End School in Warwick. I never really enjoyed these sessions, and I again would enter a fantasy world. Then, Mr. Parnaby the woodwork instructor would crack down a metal ruler on my bench, in a bid to arouse me from the other world in to which I had surrendered my being. All the time I spent there I just managed to create a pair of candlestick holders. The resounding tones of Mr. Parnaby's voice I still hear. "There's a place for everything and everything its place." Indicating with his steel rule where this particular woodworking device should be located on the wall.

After the assembly was over, we all would proceed to our respective classrooms. If it happened to be a Monday morning, we could expect one of Mr. Twigger's lectures on our weekend out of school activities On Saturday afternoons, we would take a trip to one of the local cinemas to watch the matinee show. The most frequented cinema was the County Cinema in Warwick. We would assemble by our favourite bust stop, and ride on the Midland Red bus service to our destination. It was not a considerable distance, and we could easily have walked. And this was one of the topics our teacher would elaborate consistently. "I saw you boys standing in the bus queue on Saturday afternoon, when there were people waiting behind you, whom had more need of the service than you idle beggars. Just to go the cinema, would have burnt a hole in my pocket."

We had overlooked the fact, that we had boarded the bus at a stop close to Mr. Twigger's house No. 70 Emscote Road. After this telling off from our head, we vowed to either walk, or use a different alighting point. If we, with nothing better to engage our minds we'd loaf about in Warwick on a Saturday morning, He would duly inform us on these regular Monday morning lectures, our weekend behaviour. Unbeknown to us he would use another strategy to observe our behaviour. He would seclude himself in some convenient shop doorway, where there was an abundance of glass. He would pretend to window shop, but at the same time, keeping a beady eye on us boys. To our utter astonishment on a Monday morning he would relate all our misdemeanors that we had committed that weekend. Being the chairman of the magistrate's court, and of course a Justice of the Peace, I believe at the time, he felt it is bounded duty to uphold the law. *"Woe betides any of you if you come in front of me, if I happen to be sitting on the bench."* Was his severe warning to all of us.

Being a staunch Tory, he would wax lyrical about his hero Sir Winston Churchill, and would relate Churchill's exploits during the Boar War. My school report from Mr. Twigger, goes: *Progress: Quite satisfactory progress though in actual attainment, he is still backward. Conduct: Excellent when in Saint Michael's Home (Guy's Cliffe House, Warwick). When the home closed Roy was put with a family close to his school and church. He sings in the choir, and sings well, and has a very happy friendly disposition. He has grown tall and a smart looking boy. He wants to be a motor mechanic when he leaves school early in 1946 and he should do well. He is popular, and a boy always willing to help. (The Children's Society Records 1945)* Having overrun my academic tuition time, Mr. Twigger deemed it prudent to locate me, and a friend, George Wooton, who also was over school leaving age, to the school allotment, which boarded the vicarage field, now a small housing estate. This allotment was Mr. Twigger's pride a joy, and to walk anywhere near the grass path edges would be at your peril. Many prizes he had collected for the grand appearance of the school garden. The cultivated area had to be kept tidy at all times, and Mr. Twigger had contrived a method to get rid of all the rubbish. He did not believe in burning anything, and what he could not use as compost, he would have it buried. This is where George, and I came in as useful horticultural labourers. At the far end of the garden, there was ground that was not suited for cultivation. This area was shaded by some very tall fir trees in Charles Street adjacent to the school. This location is where he instructed us to dig a large trench to bury the accumulated waste. One morning our brief was to dig. We strived all morning, then repeated the exercise all again the following morning. This project continued all that week, and the trench was about ten feet long, four feet wide and getting very deep indeed. Our head eventually paid us a visit to examine our progress. I was clearing some of *the earth away from the ground around the top of the trench when he arrived. "Where's Wooton?" He asked.*

"In the trench Sir" I replied. George was completely out of view. Because he had not visited the site until now, he assumed we were getting on with the job as instructed, and did not need supervising. For devilment, we decided to see how deep we could dig before we were stopped, or reached Australia.

Mr. Twigger was horrified when he arrived, and discovered that the trench was well over six feet deep, and he had not been able to see George, who was a very tall boy indeed for his age. His other more pressing concern was when he arrived, was that we had fir tree roots protruding from one side of the trench's wall. He also was unimpressed, when he visualised it was very imminent that the Charles Street fir trees would bow-out in an untidy heap. We were promptly told to fill in the trench.

Mr. Twigger would spend a considerable amount of time cutting the edges of the paths while the big lads would do much of the heavy digging; one boy was very adept at delving in the earth. He always finished with a neat, and level patch that he had dug. I was hopeless at this spadework, unless it involved a deep hole. All this agricultural malarkey put me off ever wanting to possess a garden, or manage one for myself in the future. The produce from the school allotment was sold, and the proceeds were used to finance the school's social calendar, which enabled us to participate in the occasional school outings. Near Christmas time there sometimes would be a visiting entertainer to the school. I particularly remember a magician Samuel Wittington –Wickes, known as The Amazing Chang. I had to stick my head in a guillotine, and trembled as the screeching of the blade traveled downwards. I breathed a sigh of relief, when I saw the carrot below me having been sliced in half, and that my head was still on my shoulders. I received great applause; since I was the only volunteer daft enough to put my head in the magician's contraption, with which Wittington-Wickes had performed his trick with adept skillfulness. Whittington-Wickes performed in New York and Paris, and also performed all over the U.K. Superstar magician David Copperfield has paid tribute to the pioneering illusionist from Leamington Spa.

We never experienced the full sports curriculum as many education establishments did. Twice in the soccer season we would challenge the local Emscote Junior Private School to football. I would play in goal. It was a futile task trying to beat this school at football. We were outclassed, and never strong enough to defeat this establishment, we were lucky if we managed to score more than one goal against them, and even luckier if we conceded less than ten goals. There were times when swimming was on the agenda, and accompanied by Big Ben. I could not join in, as I was not able to swim at this time in my life. The swimming venue was at the Warwick Saint Nicholas Park open-air baths. The baths were sited close by the River Avon, and the river entered the swimming area at one end through a rather crude filtration system, and the water made an exit at the opposite end. Very often there would be the odd fish, and frogs that somehow had slipped through the filter. There were times when I was very miserable; if the weather conditions were definitely chilly, and not been able to join in the swimming did not help. Mr. Twigger did not arrange any formal swimming tuition, had this been the case, no doubt I would have been much keener on these swimming bath excursions. My school days suddenly came to an abrupt end; we had broken up for the yearly summer break. I had been invited on holiday by some friends of the Robbins' family, who lived in Strood, near Rochester in Kent. I came back during the third week of the holidays. Whilst I was away, one of the Appleby brothers paid a visit to my foster home. Which one of the brothers I cannot recall. Strangely, neither can they remember visiting my home.

Mr. Twigger was strict tea-total. His friend, and colleague in the choir of The Collegiate Church of Saint Mary in Warwick, was the County Coroner, Stephen Tibbets. Stephen very much enjoyed a pint of beer; this caused a little friction when Mr. Twigger, Stephen Tibbets, and I were with the choir on tour in Germany in the late 1960s. Stephen had no drinking partner, but as is happened I was duly co-opted to this very enjoyable appointment. After choir rehearsals at Saint Mary, we would adjourn into the Punch Bowl Public House nearby to soothe our worn out throats.

On one occasion the Coroner looked at my glass, being half full, he then said: "You want to take that back to the barman; to me it looks a bit cloudy." I could see, or taste no fault in the drink. It transpired that he would often employ this tactic, and usually after he had supped half a pint. Being the County Coroner not a lot could be said against his view of the sad state of the ale. It was his way of getting extra for his money. Fortunately the barman and the assembled colleagues were well aware of his ploy. Stephen was a very friendly natured man, but he did have the odd memory lapse from time to time. Being a medical practitioner, he would have to pay visits to patients in the outlying villages. He, being a keen train spotter very often in the summer days, he would lounge on the railway embankments, and indulge in his favourite pastime. One day he didn't arrive at his patient's home until 7.30.pm, the appointment was booked for 2.pm. On this particular warm summer afternoon, whilst sitting on the embankment, he had nodded off to sleep.

One Sunday afternoon in late November, Mr. Robbins my foster father said *"I want you to take this letter to Mr. Twigger, wait until he has read it, then come back home."*

I stood on Mr. Twigger's doorstep, and not knowing the contents of the letter, I felt very apprehensive indeed. This letter meant that I was to start earning a living, at the ripe old age of fourteen, with Mr. Robbins, and his associates, in the decorating business.

My aspirations of becoming a motor mechanic had vanished. I started work the next day as an "apprentice" painter and decorator with my stepfather who was a business partner in the firm. I was whisked away on the back of his BSA M/Cycle to the business premises, which turned out to be a large dilapidated shed situated near to a bomb site in Coventry. I thought "*what a pity it hadn't succumbed to a bomb*".

My first job was the menial and task of cleaning out old paint kettles not in use by inserting a paraffin soaked rag, setting it alight and burning all the residue paint to a cinder, scraping, sandpapering and sealing it clean with a knotting agent. It was boring, mind blowing work and I was not at all impressed.

The very first time I was let loose on any resemblance of painting and decorating was outside painting of properties suffering from war damage following War Ministry contracts at £4.00 per house for this type of work. My job was to clean down and paint the outer side of guttering, drainpipes and upper windows with any old paint rubbish, working in wintry conditions from the upper rungs of a step ladder. Internal work involved in colour washing the walls and applying a stipple effect using a sponge. I was never taught any aspect of hanging wall paper during the 3 years I was in the trade, although in latter years found that I enjoyed doing it. *So much for apprenticeships.*

I attended the Coventry School of Art one day a week, but the majority of what was taught did not apply in reality to the decorating trade. The realm of geometry was beyond my comprehension.

I was now earning £2 16s 6p per week, which after paying for board, clothes, fares and NI left me with £1.00 spending money. I was invited to join the Senior choir at All Saints Church and enjoyed the social life which went with it. A trip to London was especially exciting when the choir sang in Westminster Abbey in the presence of the Queen Mother.

My work pattern changed when the firm split up for monetary reasons and Mr. Robbins had to fall back on his plumbing experience to supplement his income. I continued to work with him, mainly as an unqualified assistant, taking the brunt of his anger if anything went amiss. I recall on one occasion being on the receiving end of his aggressive behaviour receiving a vicious blow on the head for daring to answer him back. From that day on we very rarely spoke to each other again in friendly terms and I never really considered him a father figure any longer.

There was to come the time when the father of Mr. Robbins came to live with us, being unable to take care of himself. For the short time he was with us I had to share the bedroom with Grandfather Robbins and was shocked one day on returning home from work, to be told that he had died peacefully in his sleep during the night.

I became interested in music and bought a second hand 24 bass accordion player for £10.00, but received no encouragement from Mr. Robbins in learning to play the instrument, Mrs. Robbins advised me to take piano lessons to further my interest and do something which would help me to learn how to read and play music. I was becoming more proficient in my singing, occasionally asked to sing solo in the choir.

I had a very good mentor who was the organist at All Saints Church, also called Mr. Robbins (no relation) and became involved in musical social events throughout the parish, which are for ever some of my most treasured memories.

Chapter Ten

A New Beginning

Enter the R A F

My life was to change with my conscription into the RAF for National Service. The Cold War with Russia and the conflict in Korea were considered by the Government as threats to civilization.

I had to report for duty to **RAF Cardington,** arriving after four train journeys from Leamington to Bedford, to start a 3 month basic training course. We were subjected to a series of lectures and films during the first week advising us of all the danger associated with unprotected sex and expounding the virtues of service in the RAF, after which we were dangled a carrot, with an invitation to extend our service from 2 to 3 years following Government initiative to lower the minimum for regular service from 5 years to 3, with further opportunities opening up.

I jumped for it, a decision which did not go down well with my foster father, but it was my decision and the beginning of a future which I never thought possible.

The initial basic training was tough and rigid, discipline, equipment spit and polish, billet bullshit and regimental training brought out a camaraderie spirit previously experienced during my stay at Guys Cliffe and achieving a feeling of self satisfaction and self respect. After three months at Cardington, the passing out parade completed our basic training and I was now AC1 Robinson, and proud of it.

My next posting was to **RAF Cosford** embarking on a 6 month Physical Training course of endurance, body building and toughening up in general. The finer points of physical training became more and more interesting and we had to partake in 2 sporting activities other than field sports, fencing and boxing being my choices. I came to love fencing, but the training was very arduous especially when standing *En Guard* waiting to have the stance checked by the instructor. Over 100 continuous movements were required without instructions, exercises which certainly sharpened your wits. *"A healthy body means a healthy mind"* would be the cry from our superiors.

I chose boxing because of my interest in Randolph Turpin who was from Leamington and destined to become the World Cruiserweight champion, defeating the legendary Sugar Ray Robinson. Tommy Farr who fought Joe Louis for the World Heavyweight title in1937 before a crowd of 32,000 was a boxing instructor at Cosford. My boxing experience lasted only 2 minutes of absolute purgatory with the living daylights being knocked out of me by my more experienced opponent. I was relieved to hear the referee shout *"STOP."*

The PT course involved a considerable amount of theory work necessitating a written exam. Although I was OK with the physical aspect of it, the written part was something I dreaded and I decided to quit the course, which meant running the gauntlet with our officer in charge It took me three days to pluck up the courage to lay myself open to his ranting and raving against my decision and the wasting of RAF time, finally being advised I would put in the pool flight to await the outcome.

After two weeks I attended an interview to determine the next step in my career, photography was the trade I was interested in pursuing, which the career's officer immediately scoffed at, informing me that the only option open to me was a 3 month culinary technician course. In other words I was to become a bloody cook.

I was told to report to **RAF Innsworth** in Gloucestershire the next day. After the usual introductory lectures I started work on the course, soon getting to grips with the culinary aspect and enjoying the vast variety of menus that one worked with. I became proficient as a cook and passed the course with '*flying colours*'.

My next posting was to **RAF St Athan** in South Wales where I became one of the Hospital staff on the base. The hospital was nearly always full and we occasionally accommodated patients from Cardiff General Hospital. I was given training into the finer points of dietary preparation of food for individual patent care including calories, vitamin quantities and the like. Pastry making was one aspect of cooking I had difficulty with and it was not until my next postage I eventually got it right. I learned a lot from my posting to St Athan and was promoted to LAC prior to my overseas posting in September.

Following 3 weeks embarkation leave, I reported to the transit camp for the necessary course of injections, for my posting to **RAF Gibraltar,** yellow fever jab being the most painful. I found myself being transported in a Viking twin engine aircraft from RAF Lytham in Wiltshire, to land in Gibraltar later that day.

Gibraltar was beyond my wildest dreams, me, a boy from a small village, actually being given an opportunity of a lifetime, thanks to National Service and the RAF. The history of Gibraltar fascinated me, Phoenicians, Carthaginians, Romans had all occupied 'The Rock' prior to the conquest of Spain by the Arab armies of Islam in the 7th century. Gibraltar remained under Moorish occupation for over 600 years

I was soon to be moved to the Officers mess at New Camp as assistant to two Spanish civilian chefs from whom I gained valuable experience for which I am always extremely grateful, (including how to make and roll pastry).

Gibraltar was for me a wonderful experience, the history of the rock and Barbary apes, leisure time for sight seeing, swimming, table tennis, British Fleet visits and being selected in 1952 to be part of the Guard of Honour for the new Governor General of Gibraltar, Sir George McMillan. I gave considerable thought to extending my service in the RAF, finally deciding against it and was demobbed on 27th May 1953.

Guard of Honour Parade for the new Governer of Gibraltar.
Sir George MacMillan. April 1952.

Chapter Eleven

Back to the Future

Enter Civvy Street

With £22.00 in my pocket, I bought a 'Rudge' Cycle and having no desire to return to work with George Robbins, started looking for employment.

My first job was with Timothy White and Taylor (Gents Outfitters) in Leamington becoming relief manager at branches in Stratford, Stourbridge, Rugby and Worcester before taking over as manager at Ilkeston in Derbyshire, resigning in 1955 to take a position with Warwick Transport Department, happily employed there for 9 years, mainly on clerical work. This was followed by 9 years working for Benford's (Concrete Machinery engineers) in Warwick

My foster father passed away in June 1967, I regret to say I was honestly not sorry for myself on hearing of his death, but only felt compassion for Mrs. Robbins, my foster mother.

I answered an advertisement in the local newspaper for a supervisor working as a teacher in a local Adult Training College in Warwick for the Mentally Handicapped, successfully attending the interview and accepting an appointment on a temporary basis in October 1973, which would become a permanent position on successfully completing a year long Academic and Practical Training course.

I enrolled at Bournemouth College of Humanities starting the course in Sept 1974. After initial training, followed by training practice at Canning Town Hospital in London and Chelmsley Wood Psychiatric Hospital in Birmingham, I returned to Bournemouth, successfully completing the course and obtaining my diploma, qualifying as a teacher for the Mentally Handicapped Adult at the Adult Training Centre in Stratford on Avon eventually being placed in charge of the Speech Therapy Programme.

I formed a very close relationship to Lorraine, an extremely attractive nurse whilst at Chelmsley Wood Hospital, spending most of my leisure time in her company. Unfortunately it was not to be, I received some devastating and grievous news, Lorraine had returned home to Monmouth a short time later and sadly died of cancer. Later I met another girl called Deidre, also studying at Bournemouth, continuing to meet up after we had both qualified, spending time together whenever the opportunity arose. Again the relationship came to nothing, when Deidre took up a permanent position, emigrating to Australia.

Lorraine, Nurse at Chelmsley Wood

Deidre, Student at Bournemouth

After 9 years at the Centre in Stratford, I became Deputy Officer at a residential home for the Mentally Handicapped in Warwick, with 20 residents, some of whom came from the Chelmsley Wood Psychiatric Hospital under a Government initiated pilot scheme regarding the intake of residents. I believed that in some cases this was a disaster, especially where the disturbed clients were concerned. After 5 years in this arduous environment I decide to take early retirement, initially finding part time work with the Warwickshire Archaeological Department, being involved in Archaeological digs at Burton Basset and Stratford on Avon until lack of funding resulted in closure.

Having previous involvement with All Saints Youth Club in the 1950's, I again became involved with the forming of a successful drama group, with one of my own scripts reaching the finals held in London and the group presented with the runners up prize by the late Bill Owen. *('Compo', in Last of the Summer Wine)*. We also made many super eight films, again winning the novice event in the finals of the Film Festival at the Coventry Arts Centre.

My foster Mrs. Robbins died in the December of 1990 at the age of 91, in Warwick Hospital.

I was in charge of organising and coaching Table Tennis for the youngsters in Lillington, running 4 teams for 17 years, later coaching a team in Leamington Spa to 5 league championships, with individual champions emerging from the club. I had the pleasure of coaching the young daughter of the England Table Tennis team manager for a brief period at the purpose built Table Tennis Centre in Grantham, Lincolnshire, which by coincidence was the place of my birth. Canoeing and rock climbing were other activities I enjoyed.

In summarising this narration, I point out some of the important events in my life:

The time I spent in the R.A.F, the travel entailed and friendships I was privileged to form, being one of the most memorable and the start of a new beginning.

Obtaining my Diploma in Teaching for The Mentally Handicapped, and the personal satisfaction that it gave me from teaching.

My first solo flight from Baginton Airport Coventry, in a Cessna Airplane.

The gaining of a National Table Tennis Coaching Certificate and the pleasure I got from all the years of coaching in Birmingham and Leamington Spa.

The singing that I loved and for the short time being a Coventry Cathedral Lay Clerk.

Part Three

Footnote to the Narrative

Enter The Children's Society

For the last twenty years I have been searching through many various mediums in hope of finding the history of my Mother and events appertaining to my life from the first time I was fostered into care about the age of four.

Since beginning this narrative I have, with the very kind assistance of The Children's Society in London, now learned much about my mother, her mother and my two half brothers and one half sister.

As stated, I began my search sometime in the 1980's, for the first 15 years without any success. I knew my birthplace and where my mother was living at the time, which was Stamford in Lincolnshire. My first glimmer of hope in my research came when I paid a visit to the Public Library in Stamford. In a street directory that went back many years, I discovered that my mother was living at the time of my birth with a Mrs. Elizabeth Dennis at 6 School Terrace, Stamford during the years 1930 to 1932.

I spent much time trying to discover details of this Mrs. Dennis. One day a lady from Stamford wrote to me and suggested she put a message in the Rutland and Stamford Mercury newspaper. Two weeks later, I had a letter from a Mrs. Mee, saying that Mrs. Dennis was her paternal grandmother, but had died in 1947 and she could recall little about her. So this lady, whom I had been making exhausted enquiries about, turned out to have been my grandmother.

My research took a break for some time, until I met up with one of my old friends Tony Belcher who was with me at Guy's Cliffe Boys Home many years earlier. He suggested I contact The Children's Society in London to see if they held any records regarding my fostering. I found out that they did and after a few months I arrived in Peckham where their office is situated and collected my records in hard copy form.

One page intrigued me, because it stated that my mother May Robinson was 50 years old in 1944, so I worked out that she would be deceased by now, being born in 1892, approximately 110 years ago. It also stated that her husband deserted her in 1928. There was the name Dennis typed in one column that didn't mean anything to me at that immediate moment. I had kept the letter from Mrs. Mee and decided to telephone her. I asked her if she remembered the name Dennis that appeared on one of thre reports. The almost unbelievable revelation then transpired, it turned out that the lady I was speaking to, was my cousin, and I apparently had another cousin living in America.

The Children's Society did some research for me and discovered that my mothers maiden name was May Dennis. That she married an Arthur Newbold in 1915 and that he was killed in Belgium in 1917 during the First World War I also discovered that she had a child, born in 1916 called Rose who died at the age of 12 of TB. She married again in 1925 to a Richard Henry Robinson., at the time residing at the Golden Fleece public house in Stamford.

My mother died in the County Institution at Sleaford Lincolnshire, this home was just around the corner from the Boy's Home where I was living at the time. According to the research, she would not have been able to look after me, and unbeknown to me she was living only a stones throw away from me. On her death certificate registered in 1955, the informants name is L A Newbold, son. So it appears that I had two uncles, William and Robert, an aunt Amy, a half sister Rose and a half brother Leslie Arthur Newbold. The name Leslie Newbold had cropped up in various documents from around the time of the early 19oo's. This LA Newbold was residing at the George Hotel in Stamford. He could well still be alive if he was born between the years 1915 to 1918 and at the time of writing be in his late 80's. I myself have more research to contemplate.

Roy never made contact with any of his relatives. C'est la Vie THAT'S LIFE

The End

List of Appendices

1. Photographs of Roy Robinson 1945 & 2011
2. Public Assistance Records
3. School Report
4. Mother's Historical Record
5. All Saints Church, Warwick – Boy Bishops
6. All Saints Church, Warwick – 1960
7. All Saints Church, Warwick – Demolition

Me just after leaving Guy's Cliffe House. 1945.

Roy, Dennis Appleby and Tony Belcher at Guy's Cliffe. September 2011.

Children's Society Records.

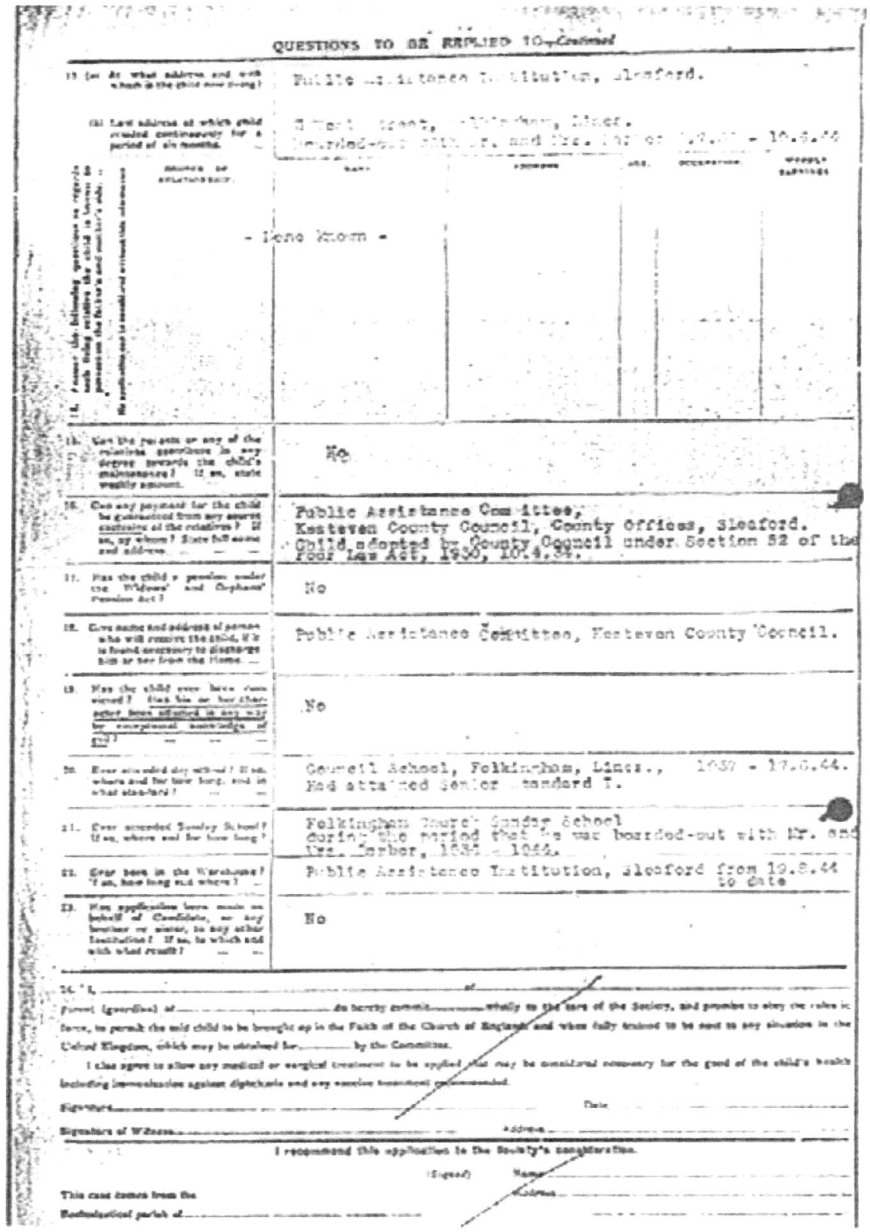

QUESTIONS TO BE REPLIED TO—Continued

Public Assistance Institution, Sleaford.

- None known -

No

Public Assistance Committee,
Kesteven County Council, County Offices, Sleaford.
Child adopted by County Council under Section 52 of the Poor Law Act, 1930, 10.4.34.

No

Public Assistance Committee, Kesteven County Council.

No

Council School, Folkingham, Lincs., 1937 - 17.8.44.
Had attained Senior Standard 7.

Folkingham Church Sunday School during the period that he was boarded-out with Mr. and Mrs. Barber, 1936 - 1944.

Public Assistance Institution, Sleaford from 19.8.44 to date

No

I recommend this application to the Society's consideration.

Public Assistance Institution Committee report, Sleaford. *Payments, School attended, Sunday school attended, boarded out with the Barber Family, from1936 to 1944. Resident in the Public Assistance Institution Sleaford from Aug 19th 1944 until left and went to Guy's Cliffe House, Warwick, October 31st 1944.*

1946 School Report

PLEASE NOTE: CHANGE OF NAME: CHURCH OF ENGLAND CHILDREN'S SOCIETY FORMERLY WAIFS AND STRAYS SOCIETY

THE CHURCH OF ENGLAND
WAIFS AND STRAYS SOCIETY
OLD TOWN HALL, KENNINGTON ROAD, LONDON, S.E.11.

REPORT. 56550.

NAME OF CHILD: ROBINSON, BERNARD R. AGE 14

HOME: 28, Albert St., Leamington Spa.

HEALTH: Excellent.

SCHOOL PROGRESS: Quite satisfactory. Bernard is not a clever boy. He was very backward when he came to this school. He has made satisfactory progress but I consider he is still a little below the average.

CONDUCT: Very good.

HEIGHT: 5'4" WEIGHT: not known.

GENERAL REMARKS (Please give a "chatty" account of the child's progress.): Bernard has taken quite a prominent part in School life. He has been a good 'sport', and he has gained a place in the School games teams.

Very popular in the Choir and a good staunch and regular boy - in music he has no great gift but plods along happily - very nice disposition and attractive appearance and manners and speech Excellent. He leaves at Xmas and his voice will be broken - but he is already a Server [illegible] Vicar

Date: Sep. 16. 46.

Signed: L.J. Twigger

(Address): All Saints School Warwick.

Printed by the Society's Apprentices at St. Aldhelm's Home Press, Frome.

School report by L.J. Twigger, Headmaster of All Saints School, Warwick. With additional remarks by The Rev. Delanoy Saberton. Who is stating, that my voice will be broken, by Christmas, but I am a Server in the Church's rituals. A good staunch and regular boy - in music he has no great gift, but plods along happily. A very nice chorister and attractive appearance and manners and speech excellent. September 1946.

Progress report on my mother's history and her health

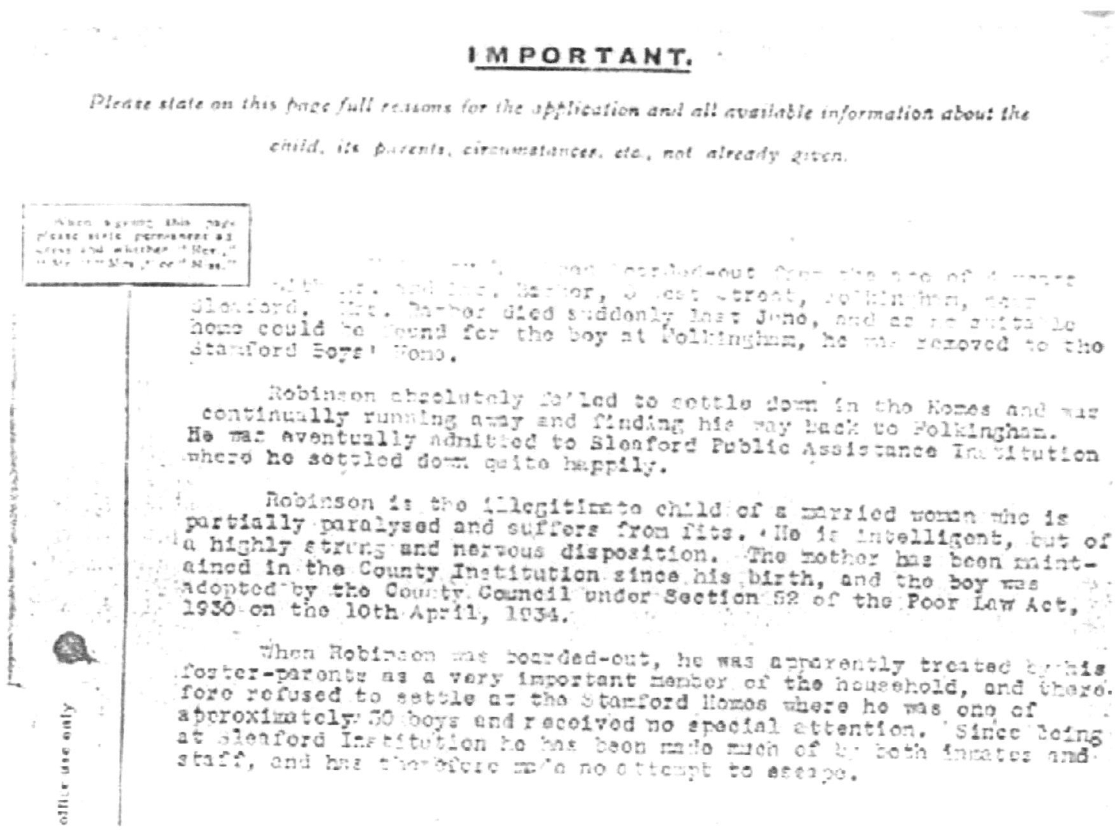

IMPORTANT.

Please state on this page full reasons for the application and all available information about the child, its parents, circumstances, etc., not already given.

Robinson absolutely failed to settle down in the Homes and was continually running away and finding his way back to Folkingham. He was eventually admitted to Sleaford Public Assistance Institution where he settled down quite happily.

Robinson is the illegitimate child of a married woman who is partially paralysed and suffers from fits. He is intelligent, but of a highly strung and nervous disposition. The mother has been maintained in the County Institution since his birth, and the boy was adopted by the County Council under Section 52 of the Poor Law Act, 1930 on the 10th April, 1934.

When Robinson was boarded-out, he was apparently treated by his foster-parents as a very important member of the household, and therefore refused to settle at the Stamford Homes where he was one of approximately 30 boys and received no special attention. Since being at Sleaford Institution he has been made much of by both inmates and staff, and has therefore made no attempt to escape.

Progress report on my mother's history and her health. How I was fostered with the Barbers, my Aunt Nin's death, my move to the Boy's Home in Stamford. How I settled in at the Sleaford Institution and according to this report, I didn't attempt to ESCAPE. Notice the brusque wiriting of this particular report, in comparison to the others.

Bernard Robinson has been boarded out from the age of 4 with a Mr. and Mrs. Barber of 3 West Terrace Sleaford, Mrs. Barber died suddenly last June and as no suitable home could be found for the boy at Folkingham, he was removed to the Stamford Boys Home.

Robinson absolutely failed to settle down in the home and was continually running away and finding his way back to Folkingham He was eventually admitted to Sleaford Public Assistance Institution where he settled down quite happily.

Robinson is the illegitimate child of a married woman who is partially paralysed and suffers from fits. He is intelligent, but of a highly strung and nervous disposition. The mother has been maintained in the County Institution since his birth and the boy was adopted by the County Council under Section 52 of the Poor Law Act 1930 on 1oth April 1944.

When Robinson was boarded out, he was apparently treated by his foster parents as a very important member of the household. And therefore refused to settle at the Stamford Home where he was one of approximately 30 boys and received no special attention. Since being at Sleaford Institution he has been made much of by both inmates and staff, and has therefore made no attempt to escape.

All Saints Church, Warwick

Left:
Gerald Potts, Boy Bishop.
George Gilbert, Chaplain

Right:
George Gilbert, Boy Bishop

Centre:
George and Dennis Gilbert

Bottom from left to right:
Robert Lines (Head Chorister)
George Gilbert
Don Wilkins

All Saints Church, Emscote, Warwick. The nave as seen from the choir.

All Saints Church, Emscote, Warwick. Before it was demolished in the 1960s.

Awesome - bulldozers move in to demolish All Saints Church, Warwick, and, right, the spire comes crashing down in a cloud of dust

Church comes crashing down

I abandon'd my originals, I left my guides, and delivered myself up to my ideas. I prescribed myself subjects, and laid down problems for my own solution.

Salomon Gessner 1730–88

Peter Coker

Peter Coker RA

David Wootton

with contributions by
John Russell Taylor and Richard Humphreys

CHRIS BEETLES LTD

Dedicated by Peter Coker 'to Vera and to the memory of our son Nicholas'

Chris Beetles Ltd
8 & 10 Ryder Street
St James's
London
SW1Y 6QB

Telephone: 020 7839 7551
Facsimile: 020 7839 1603
email: gallery@chrisbeetles.com
website: www.chrisbeetles.com

ISBN 1 871136 76 8

Edited by Fiona Pearce
Sketchbooks catalogued by Edwina Freeman

Design by Jeremy Brook, Graphic Ideas
Colour separation and printing by Hyway Printing Group

Cataloguing in Publication Data available from the British Library

Frontispiece
Self Portrait 1965 (**125**)

Contents

Introduction

David Wootton

Bold nos in brackets (**00**) refer to Catalogue Raisonné Numbers

It is a little over fifty years since Peter Coker first placed a work before the London public: *Still Life* (**6**) was exhibited in 1950 at the Royal Academy *Summer Exhibition*. The close of that half century seems to offer a perfect time at which to reassess the art of both an individual and an era.

We are not alone in making this assumption. At least in general terms, the visual culture of post-war Britain is now an object of wide interest. Last year, James Hyman published *The Battle for Realism*, a ground-breaking study of 'figurative art in Britain during the Cold War'. This year, the Barbican Art Gallery mounted *Transition*, a stimulating if uneven survey of 'the London Art Scene in the Fifties'. Both acknowledged the contributions of the critics John Berger and David Sylvester, who were so instrumental in shaping an understanding of contemporary art that their opinions continue to resonate. If Berger's current voice lacks its original insistence there is compensation, for a weighty selection of his earlier writings has recently appeared. And though Sylvester has just died, his very demise has ensured his survival, through a memorial exhibition at Tate Modern, the auction of his collection at Sotheby's and, most vitally, posthumous publications. Mention of Tate Modern also brings to mind the fact that its latest triumph, *Matisse/Picasso*, echoes a highly influential pairing of those artists, in a show which was held at the Victoria and Albert Museum in 1945–46. Even curatorial planning appears retrospective.

The post-war period is the context within which the young Peter Coker developed; and if he were only a part of its history his role would still need to be revalued. That Richard Humphreys should choose to illustrate Coker's *Table and Chair* (**49**) instead of a John Bratby in the *The Tate Britain Companion to British Art* demonstrates that such a revaluation is under way. References to the artist in Hyman's book indicate the same.

When Coker's career was properly launched, in 1956, with a solo show at the Zwemmer Gallery, he was well received, but immediately tarred with the same brush as the Kitchen Sink School. Such an association was perhaps understandable in the light of his butcher's shop paintings, but was also misleading. The term 'Kitchen Sink' had been coined by Sylvester two years earlier as a criticism of Bratby and other painters of domestic clutter who had been championed by Berger. It was just a single volley in that battle between two competing conceptions of Realism: Berger's Socialism and Sylvester's Modernism. Coker recognised no such distinction, and was willing to call on the muse of either camp – Courbet or Cézanne – in developing his highly independent approach to realist painting.

All three of the contributors to this volume make a case for Coker's independence. John Russell Taylor concludes that he built 'on a uniquely solid foundation', while the core of Kitchen Sink painters 'moved spectacularly on in the interim'. Richard Humphreys writes of the 'integrity of vision' and 'technical supremacy' that Nicholas Coker saw in his father's work, and remembers Nicholas in such a way as to give an insight into Peter's own free spirit. I compare him less to his contemporaries than to those he has emulated, placing him in the company of artists who transcend their age.

While he was still painting butchered meat, Coker defined himself as a landscape artist, and it is through that genre that he should be understood and judged. He has always responded directly to the impact of the many places that he visited, from Epping Forest to the Highlands of Scotland, and from Etretat to the Mediterranean coast. In so doing, he has produced an oeuvre that is replete with immediacy and alive to the range of terrains.

His experiences have also given him insights into the environments that affected masters as different as Courbet, Turner and Matisse. Though never derivative, he has been highly aware of those who have gone before, and of the tradition they embody. Over the decades, he has assimilated tendencies that might be labelled realist, romantic and modern, while remaining true to himself. And while his work has profoundly Gallic elements it is essentially British.

Landscape painting is surely the visual art for which the British are best known, a fact that was ably demonstrated by the Arts Council when, in 1983, it organised the memorable exhibition, *Landscape in Britain 1850-1950.* This spanned a century of talents from Turner's successors to such neo-Romantics as Piper and Sutherland, ending at the point at which Coker's career began. Whether or not an equivalent survey of the succeeding decades could prove so generally stimulating, Coker's achievement would shine out; for if not the finest landscapist to have emerged since the war, he is the finest native landscapist still painting.

July 2002

Chronology

1926 — 27 July. Born in the Royal Free Hospital, London; the only child of Elsie and Edwin Coker. Lived at Tredegar Road, Old Ford.

Moved to 1 Moyers Road, Leytonstone. Attended Canterbury Road School.

1937 — Moved to Maxwelton, Havering-atte-Bower, Romford. Attended Pettits Lane School.

1940 — Worked under his father as an assistant at Kerland & Haskin.

1941–43 — Studio assistant at Odham's Press, Covent Garden. Attended St Martin's School of Art and the Central School of Art.

1943–46 — During WWII, served in the Fleet Air Arm. Later moved to the Education Corps, teaching art and allied crafts.

1947–50 — Full-time student at St Martin's in the painting department.

1947 — Met Vera Crook, his future wife.

1949 — Italy, first trip abroad (3 months). Met with Vera in Paris.

1950 — Royal Academy *Summer Exhibition*: first exhibit *Still Life* (**6**).

Italy with Vera.

1950–54 — Studied in the Painting School of the Royal College of Art.

1951 — 31 March. Married Vera at St Andrew's, Gidea Park, London. Moved to 1 Moyers Road.

Won Royal Scholarship at the RCA.

Mevagissey, Cornwall with Vera. RCA sketch club prize for *Landscape China Clay Pits St Austell* (**13**).

1952 — 16 February. Birth of Nicholas Coker.

Llanelli, south Wales, made drawings of colleries.

1953 — Awarded diploma (ARCA) and a fourth year at the RCA; also a British Institution Scholarship.

1953–54 — Assisted Rodrigo Moynihan, RCA Professor of Painting.

1954 — Made first designs for printed textiles.

1955 — Began regular part-time teaching at St Martin's. Briefly taught History of Art and Architecture at Haberdasher Aske's School and painting at Ealing College of Art.

Fontainebleau, Barbizon, Fécamp and Etretat.

1956 — First regular use of sketchbooks.

Zwemmer Gallery, London: first solo show. Associated by critics with Kitchen Sink painters.

Etretat, Quimper and Audierne.

Devon with Nicholas, Vera and her parents.

1957 — Passed driving test. All painting trips from this time by car.

New Forest, first motor trip with Vera and Nicholas.

Etretat and Audierne with Vera and Nicholas.

Zwemmer Gallery, London: solo show.

1958 — Italy and France, including the first visit to the south of France, with Vera and Nicholas.

1959 — Zwemmer Gallery, London: solo show.

First of a series of medical problems. Diagnosed with Cushing's Disease.

Adrenalechtomy operation at Middlesex Hospital.

1961 — Mount Snowdon, Llanberis, Capel Curig and Pembrokeshire with Vera and Nicholas.

1962 — Became a visiting teacher in life painting at Colchester School of Art where he befriended John Nash.

Moved to the Red House, Mistley.

1964 — Zwemmer Gallery, London: solo show.

1965 — Elected Associate of the Royal Academy (ARA).

Brittany and the foothills of the Pyrenees with Vera and Nicholas.

1967 Malham, Yorkshire with John Nash.

Zwemmer Gallery, London: solo show.

David Murray Stewardship at the Royal Academy, for two seasons, supervising students in various locations in England and Scotland.

1968 Magdalene Street Gallery, Cambridge: solo show (drawings).

Stable Gallery, Ufford, Suffolk: solo show (drawings).

1969 Stone Gallery, Newcastle Upon Tyne: solo show (pastels).

Ostend, first of many visits.

Began experimenting with etching techniques.

1970 Thackeray Gallery, London: solo show.

Skye with John Nash.

1972 Elected Royal Academician (RA).

Mouthier-Haute-Pierre, in the Jura.

Thackeray Gallery, London: solo show.

Mollans-sur-Ouvèze, in the Côte de Ventoux, and Aurel with Vera.

The Minories, Colchester, and touring: retrospective.

1973 Leicester Fine Arts Gallery: solo show.

Mouthier-Haute-Pierre, Sault, Illiers-Combray and Paris.

1974 Thackeray Gallery, London: solo show.

Stopped regular teaching at St Martin's.

Lastours with Vera.

Became a teacher at the City and Guilds of London School of Art.

1975 Thackeray Gallery, London: solo show.

1976 Arts Council Award.

Published *Etching Techniques*.

Thackeray Gallery, London: solo show.

Gravelines.

1977 Bargemon, near Grasse, first of many visits.

1978 Thackeray Gallery, London: solo show.

Chelmsford and Essex Museum: retrospective.

Sault and Bargemon with Vera.

1979 University of Liverpool and touring: retrospective (butcher's shop paintings).

Poole Fine Art, Ampthill: retrospective (etchings).

Bargemon with Vera (two visits).

1980 Paris and Belgium with Vera.

Bargemon, and first visit to the Hanbury Gardens, La Mortola, Italy, with Vera.

Gallery 10, London: solo show.

1981 Etretat, Valmont, Tancarville and Fécamp with Vera.

Bargemon and Mouthier-Haute-Pierre with Vera.

1982 Greece with Vera.

Wrote obituary for *The Times* on his former teacher Vivian Pitchforth.

Gallery 10, London: solo show.

1982–85 Villa Clos du Peyronnet, near Menton with Vera.

1984 Gallery 10, London: solo show (May).

Gallery 10, London: solo show (October).

1985 22 March. Death of Nicholas Coker.

Resigned from the City and Guilds.

Gorse Bush (**60**) presented to the Tate Gallery in Nicholas's memory.

Badenscallie, Ross-shire, first of many visits, with Vera.

Wrote obituary for *The Times* on his former teacher James Stroudley.

1986 Gallery 10, London: solo show.

Bargemon with Vera (last visit).

1987 Badenscallie with Vera.

1988 Produced six self-portrait studies, entitled *Le Peintre au Travail* based on a Seurat drawing of the same name in Philadelphia Museum of Art.

Gallery 10, London: solo show.

Christchurch Mansion, Ipswich: retrospective.

1989 Fitzwilliam Museum, Cambridge; then Gallery 10, London: retrospective.

1990 Suffered serious heart attack.

Sketchbook drawings used to illustrate the fine wine list for Barwell & Jones. First of several.

Flying Colours Gallery, Edinburgh: solo show.

Suffered another serious heart attack and a debilitating stroke.

1991 Civil List Pension.

Varengeville and Etretat with Vera.

Flying Colours Gallery, Edinburgh: solo show.

Mayor Gallery, London: retrospective (textile designs).

James Hyman lecture at Tate: *British Realists: Bratby, Coker and Others.*

1992 Le Havre with Vera.

Menton with Vera.

Abbot Hall Art Gallery, Kendal, and touring: retrospective.

1993 Further Civil List Pension.

1995 Villa Costermano, Bardolino with Vera.

1998 Menton with Vera.

Awarded Honorary Fellowship of the Royal Society of Painter-Printmakers (HRE).

Menton with Vera (last visit).

1999 Lake Bolsena, Orvieto with Vera.

2000 Château Cordeillan-Bages, Pauillac with Vera.

Watermill Antiques, Nayland: retrospective.

Paris with Vera.

2001 Paris with Vera.

Bologna with Vera.

2002 Began to paint again after a gap of ten years.

Straight to the Heart of Things: the Achievement of Peter Coker

John Russell Taylor author and senior art critic of *The Times*

Labels invariably say at once too much and too little. They are convenient, of course. They are useful for headlines. With any luck they do not totally misrepresent, but neither can they be expected totally and accurately to represent. At a certain stage those involved may benefit from the label that has been applied to them, as it grabs the sort of attention they might otherwise miss. The question is, how is the quick fix to be balanced against later resentment at the constraints it imposes? No doubt people would eventually have heard of John Osborne even without the attention-grabbing label of 'Angry Young Man', but did it not eventually do him more harm than good, when he could not throw it off years after he had ceased to be either angry or young?

Peter Coker may well be in rather a similar bind with the label 'Kitchen Sink Painter'. Oddly – or perhaps not so oddly – the two labels were created at almost exactly the same time, in 1956. In that year, incredibly, an allegedly victorious Britain was still deep in a continuation of wartime austerity: the watchwords in home life were 'utility' and 'make do and mend'. The life most people, writers and artists like the rest, were forced to live was uniformly austere, drab and rather grim – and that, even five years after the Festival of Britain's proffered 'Tonic to the Nation'. Resentment against everyday restrictions was inevitable, and the Press eagerly read the auguries to find something which seemed to put this resentment into a newsworthy form.

The opening of John Osborne's play *Look Back in Anger* as part of a new theatre company's opening season at the Royal Court Theatre, long associated with the radical in drama almost instantly spawned dozens of headlines about those dangerous (but magnetic) Angry Young Men: this at the same time as the publication of novels like Kingsley Amis's *Lucky Jim* and John Wain's *Hurry On Down*, which seemed to reflect a similarly disaffected view of contemporary British life. All the excitement engendered speculation about whether it all signalled a new spirit in English life and culture. In the backwash a couple of other, parallel movements were hypothesised. One of them, Free Cinema, was based on some influential programmes of short films at the National Film Theatre. The other, Kitchen Sink painting, was based on a group of one-person shows, mostly at the Beaux Arts Gallery run by Helen Lessore, which in effect introduced to the public at large such artists as John Bratby, Edward Middleditch, Jack Smith and Derrick Greaves.

Peter Coker never showed at the Beaux Arts Gallery, but he was a contemporary at the Royal College of Art of the other four painters, and was linked with them, if not by anything so tangible as a manifesto or joint statement of intent, at least by bonds of acquaintanceship and a shared interest in painting the real world in a very direct and specific fashion. Since they were all young, impecunious, mostly married with babies or young children, and living in a London still in the cheerless grip of postwar austerity, inevitably the reality most of them found lying about them was that of the bedsit or basic basement flat, with cooking pans in the kitchen sink, washing on the line, and everything in uncomfortably close proximity to everything else. When the concept of Kitchen Sink painting materialised in some journalist's mind, it seemed for the moment graphically applicable.

Almost inevitably, Coker was swept in with the rest. And to begin with the label was not totally unfair. Admittedly his domestic circumstances were very different from those of the painters with whom he was, all arbitrarily, grouped by the press. He lived with his parents until 1951, and in 1952 moved to a spacious Victorian house where he and his wife Vera had most domestic chores looked after by a daily help. Vera doubts whether he had ever in his life at that time been anywhere near a kitchen sink, theirs or anyone else's. Undoubtedly in his early days Coker did his share of painting grim reality, haunting butcher's shops, observing the strange, opalescent hues of the sides of mutton or sheep's heads displayed in them, or laying out on his studio bench fish in pans and dead chickens or hares fresh from the shop, very much as though on a kitchen table. But even at the time of his first one-man show in London, at the Zwemmer Gallery in January 1956, he was painting many things far remote from a London kitchen, such as a variety of French landscapes, featuring especially the cliffs at Etretat so famously painted by Monet and, apparently more relevant where Coker is concerned, by Courbet.

All the same, once a catchy label like Kitchen Sink is affixed, it is very difficult to shift. Coker never belonged to any school or movement, and for that matter a Kitchen Sink School as such never really existed. But the school that never was has entered the mythology of British art history. In 1991 there was an exhibition in a Cork Street gallery entitled simply *The Kitchen Sink Painters*, and of course everyone knew who was meant, though all the painters represented had moved spectacularly on in the interim. Jack Smith had become a rigorous geometrical abstractionist, and totally rejected his realist phase. Derrick Greaves also had moved, though not so far, towards abstraction, developing a boldly simplified, linear style with extensive use of collage. John Bratby continued to paint in much the same fashion throughout his career, but considerably enlivened his range of colours and his geographical scope for landscape painting. Edward Middleditch concentrated on landscape, mostly British, often quite boldly formalised and using mostly very restrained colours.

And Peter Coker, always the odd man out? He, as ever, went his own way. It remains a mystery why, in anybody's estimation, he came to spend even the briefest of times in that particular galere. And what he has done since he, early and definitively, escaped from even the shadow of the misleading Kitchen Sink label has nothing to do with anyone or anything but himself.

Coker had a very successful art education studying at St Martin's School of Art under Vivian Pitchforth and James Stroudley (1947-1950), and then at the Royal College of Art (1950-54). During his time at the RCA, he won the Royal Scholarship (1951), and the British Institution Scholarship (1953). He was also commissioned – a great honour for a student – to paint a portrait of the recently retired Principal of the College, the painter Percy Jowett. He painted it in College, in the studio of the Principal, Robin Darwin, which he found intimidating. In fact he did two portraits, not liking the first one he did: eventually he left it on the doorstep of Jowett's London home. But the definitive version had a great success, both in the college and outside: it was shown at the Royal Academy *Summer Exhibition* in 1954, and was picked out for special commendation in most newspaper and magazine reviews of the show.

Among Coker's student contemporaries at the Royal College were such painters as Jack Smith (whom he had already encountered at the St Martin's), Edward Middleditch, Derrick Greaves, and John Bratby, and they were all influenced by the painters at that time showing in the West End galleries, which, student-like, they regularly haunted. Among the most important for them were Bernard Lorjou and André Minaux at the Adams Gallery, and Paul Rebeyrolle at Marlborough Fine Art, who all pioneered painting largely or entirely with the palette knife, applying paint to canvas in great thick slabs which sometimes achieved an almost sculptural quality. It was around this time that Coker first encountered the art of Nicolas de Staël, who shared some of these same qualities, but applied with more delicacy and finesse, and a much more refined sense of colour which Coker found more personally sympathetic.

The teachers Coker found particularly helpful during his art school days were mostly pretty conservative in their attitudes. At St Martin's, Pitchforth especially seemed almost to play up to the persona of a Victorian eccentric: when Coker first encountered him as a teacher he, being somewhat deaf, was still using an ear trumpet of positively Dickensian aspect. However, Coker found him in every way an excellent teacher, not only friendly and approachable, but well able to demonstrate as well as talk about the finer points of technique and aesthetics. Coker retained his affection and admiration for Pitchforth, and years later, when Pitchforth died at the age of 87 in 1982, Coker contributed an obituary tribute to *The Times*, doing the same for James Stroudley in 1985.

Someone else who proved friendly and helpful during Coker's student years at the RCA was Rodrigo Moynihan, Head of Painting. He never actually taught Coker, but used him as an assistant and had him around his Chelsea studio in the King's Road, working with him on various projects. The first was a portrait of Rowland Hill required to mark the centenary of the Penny Post, but then Coker stayed on to help Moynihan with a portrait commission from the Penguin Group: Moynihan would sketch the outlines in charcoal, then Coker would fix them with turpentine. At the end of this stint as a studio assistant Moyhihan thanked Coker and told him airily to help himself to some of the paints and brushes, but Coker, then in his last year at college, still felt too diffident to do so.

According to his own account, Coker was very retiring and quite solitary at college, pursuing his own interests and mixing little with the other students. Many of his contemporaries at college he never encountered until after they had all left. During his time there he knew John Bratby and was quite friendly with Jack Smith, in whose company he had moved from the St Martin's to the Royal College. He had also a nodding acquaintance with Derrick Greaves. But despite their being contemporaries, with sometimes a certain similarity in their approach to painting, Coker did not go along with Smith and Greaves and various others of the same generation to join the stable of Helen Lessore's Beaux Arts Gallery, then then flagship for the new wave of British realist art, shortly to be dubbed the Kitchen Sink painters. Smith had his first solo show at the Beaux Arts in 1952, Greaves in 1953, and Bratby and Middleditch in 1954, but Coker was not ready to show until 1956, when he had his first solo show at another gallery altogether.

This delay may well have had something to do with Coker's diffidence and independence of mind, but he was also determined that he would not go for a one-man show anywhere until he was certain in his own mind that he was ready. Meanwhile, his work was very favourably noticed in his graduation showing at the RCA, and a portrait of a six or seven-year-old girl, *Geraldine* (**26**), also had a big success when shown at the Royal Academy that summer. During other people's final shows Coker had remarked on the propensity of the staff to appropriate the best pictures for the college's permanent collection, so unbidden he sneaked his own canvases out of the place before anyone else could remove them. All went well for the moment, but later Carel Weight, then Professor of Painting at the College, expressed his surprise that there were no Cokers in the collection. Coker had to admit to having the two pictures in question at home, and bring them unwillingly back.

His first picture in the Royal Academy *Summer Exhibition* (1950) and his first sale, was a still life, painted at St Martin's in 1949. At the Royal College he took still-lifes almost as given, an extension of the drawing classes he had come to consider the necessary foundation of all good painting. After he left, he began to see them in a more informal light, as something to be consciously arranged and constructed. He began to buy hares and pigs' and sheep's heads from the butcher, and lay them out as compositions on a much used grained wood bench, deliberately manipulating things before he drew them, let alone started to paint them. From 1952 he began to tilt the pictorial plane by propping up the back legs of the table. This in its turn introduced a whole different range of colour values, the light falling very differently on the tilted table from the untilted. From there, moving his viewpoint to the source of the meat was just one natural step further, and Coker got in the habit of drawing in the butcher's shop every Wednesday afternoon, that being early closing day in the borough, so that he did not interrupt the shop's normal business.

There is a series of photographs of Coker drawing in the butcher's shop, watched by his four-year-old son Nicholas, born in 1952. One suspects that the pictures were taken, in a sense, after the event, for when Coker started painting sides of meat hanging in the shop he was certainly not famous enough for a photographic reporter to take any great interest in him. That all came about from his first one-man exhibition in London, in which the earliest of the meat paintings were prominently featured. Haunting the commercial galleries as he did, Coker had become conscious of a gallery attached to Zwemmer's art bookshop, just round the corner from St Martin's in the Charing Cross Road. One day he got into conversation with the gallery's manager, Michael Chase, who invited him to bring in some of his own work. Thus encouraged, he did so, and was offered a one-man show for the period of 10 – 31 January 1956. And part of the normal gallery routine was that the owner or manager would alert journalists to any 'story' connected with a forthcoming exhibition, in order to secure maximum publicity. Hence the visit of a press agency photographer to record Coker at work in the butcher's shop. And at once in his relations with Zwemmer's he established a convention which was to obtain throughout his career, with all his dealers: it was he, not they, who decided exactly what should go into the show, and how it would be shown.

Immediately Coker was associated by the critics (who gave this particular newcomer a gratifying amount of attention) with the so-called Kitchen Sink painters then fresh out of the Royal College and exhibiting at the Beaux Arts Gallery. In itself this was not unreasonable, though G S Whittet in *The Studio* did point out that 'to say that one sees in his work facets that call to mind the paintings of Edward Middleditch, Ginette Rapp and Rebeyrolle implies nothing more than that a community of climate exists as it did, say, among the Impressionists about the year 1880'.

Obviously there was something held in common between Coker's kitchen table still-lifes and the studies of similar subjects by the Beaux Arts painters, or between Coker's actual way of putting paint on canvas and the style of the then prominent but now virtually forgotten Rebeyrolle. But it is interesting to check in the catalogue of the Zwemmer's show to see of what exactly it consisted. Of thirty-one works – eighteen paintings, thirteen drawings, one lithograph , sixteen indeed rejoice in such titles as *Sheep Carcasses on Bench* (**45**) or *Fish with Grill* (**30**). But as against these reliably 'kitchen sink' subjects there were fifteen French landscapes, with titles like *Cliffs near Etretat* (**36**) and *La Plaine de Chailly* (**41**).

Kitchen Sink was in the news at the time, offering a newsworthy label like 'Angry Young Man' for young dramatists and novelists of the John Osborne generation. (*Look Back in Anger* was first produced five months after Coker's show opened.) Journalists – and even, it must be confessed, art critics – were more interested in a striking story than in a realistically qualified statement. The idea of a group, even a generation, of painters who never lifted their eyes from the gas ring and the basement clothes-line was striking and easily graspable. A painter like Coker, who regarded anything as grist to his mill, might paint a colour-drained interior if it happened to spark his imagination, but also would seize any opportunity that offered – in this era of strictly limited foreign travel – to head off to France and gleefully paint in locations made famous by the Barbizon painters and the Impressionists. He was just too difficult to force into any of their conventional pigeonholes.

Not surprisingly, Coker was pleased at the attention his first one-man show was accorded, but slightly irritated that he was so brusquely lumped in with so many diverse artists under some half-true, catch-all label. Though he knew most of the Beaux Arts artists, and shared many of the artistic experiences that had shaped them, in the way of current London exhibitions they had all seen, he was very aware that his own artistic interests and sympathies tended in some very different directions. How many of his contemporaries, for example, had any particular interest in such unfashionable nineteenth-century painters as Courbet, or knew anything about such dissident twentieth-century painters as Soutine? Yet these were vital to the evolution of his already highly personal style.

Not only that, but, more immediately apparent, his choice of subject. The butcher's shop he might quite easily have come to all on his own, without ever having seen a Soutine of raw meat. He would not be the only British painter to observe, provided one could put aside any crypto-vegetarian tendencies, the beautiful opalescent tints of uncooked meat – Francis Bacon, for one, had responded, though stylistically in a very different fashion. Coker now recalls that at the time he consciously regarded the butcher's shop paintings as virtually monochromatic, but looking at them again today he is intensely aware of the amount of delicately graded colour they contain, which must have affected him subliminally back in the 1950s. In any case, Coker's technique, with its heavy impasto, sufficiently resembles that of Soutine to suggest that Coker was already aware of that painter when he started turning his artist's eye on the local butcher – and indeed Coker recollects having been struck by a Soutine show in Paris on the Quai Voltaire in the early 1950s.

On the other hand, Courbet and the Barbizon School were directly and admittedly responsible for Coker's choice of Etretat and Barbizon Forest as the principal painting grounds of his French trip. For us today Etretat is inextricably linked with Monet: he first painted the famous arch formations in the cliffs by Etretat, the Porte d'Aval, the Porte d'Amont and the Manneporte, in 1882, and made several more visits during the next four years. But Monet was not the first to paint the coast at Etretat, nor the sole source of information about it. Courbet painted the Porte d'Aval in 1869 from roughly the same viewpoint used by Monet thirteen years later, and Monet himself commented on the problems of following in the older master's footsteps. Among later painters there are at least two pochades by Gerald Kelly, later PRA, showing the same subject from the other side and labelled 'Etretat – view from the first tee, 26th July 1908', suggesting that it was the quality of the golf rather than the quality of the landscape that brought him there. Also, on a more mundane level, Coker saw in the *Saturday Evening Post* an article on Courbet and a double-page spread on his painting of the Porte d'Aval at Etretat, which made Coker think he ought to see the place in real life.

Nonetheless, it was essentially Courbet who brought Coker there. During his first serious visit to Paris in 1950, Coker was able to study such classic works of Courbet as *The Funeral at Ornans* and *The Wave* in various public collections, and in the early 1950s there were some notable shows in London of Pre-Impressionist French art, notably of Courbet, and of the Barbizon School of landscapists, especially Millet. This, of course, was well before the tremendous vogue of the Impressionists which conquered the world in the 1980s. Consequently a preference for these immediate precursors of the Impressionists was not as strange then as it now seems, but the intense sympathy Coker felt for Courbet (and still does: when in Paris he always goes to the Musee d'Orsay to look at *The Funeral at Ornans*) was definitely exceptional.

What particularly drew Coker to Courbet was the solidity of his painting – the absolute opposite of Monet's practice – the way that forms were defined by solid slabs of (mostly very restrained) colour. Solidity and definition of form were something Coker was eager to achieve in his own work, and Courbet seemed to offer the perfect model: the rocks in his major landscapes, notably the cliffs at Etretat, appear practically sculptured, and the pebbles in the foreground are so solid one could almost stub a toe on them. It was just this quality that Coker sought in his own paintings: the fish on the newspaper or the side of pork hanging from a hook are apprehended in three dimensions, and rendered with a concern for volume that the moderns have learnt from the Cubists and the Cubists learned from Cézanne (when the moderns did not take their wisdom from Cézanne directly).

The same is true of the landscapes: they come from Coker's minute observation, noted down first in sketchbook drawings made on the spot, then sometimes worked over as drawings before being used as the basis for painting in the studio. At times in the surviving sketchbooks one can see evidences of Coker's rethinking: here and there he appears to have been worried by the perspective, and readjusted it before starting to paint. But more typically the relationship between drawing and painting is elliptical: the drawing has been used entirely as an aide-memoire, the painting related to it being clearly an autonymous creation, elaborated in its own terms on canvas in the studio, with only casual reference to any record made on the spot.

It was, no doubt, a sign of the times that Coker's first exhibition was discussed in some detail for the radio programme *The Critics* on the Home Service, the then equivalent of today's Radio 4. The art critic was J M Richards, the chairman Paul Dehn, and obviously the main subject raised by the show was deemed to be this possibly unpleasant, or at least unappealing, new realism which was in the air at the time. Doubts were expressed as to whether 'raw hanging meat in butchers' shops and so on' should be rejected as 'an ugly subject for an artist to tackle'. To his credit, Richards replied:

> Surely a painter has the right to use the raw material from which he gets stimulus, and I think that a good deal of the quality in Peter Coker's painting is certain discoveries he's made, such as the rather remarkable, exciting shapes that a skinned hare produces when it's laid out on a table. They're discoveries of his own and he's excited by them, and his paintings do convey some of that sense of excitement. I don't think you must look at subject matter in a sort of illustrative sense, and suggest that because it's a picture of an attractive object it's therefore attractive as a picture.

But it was Paul Dehn who made what was perhaps the most significant comment in terms of Coker's future:

> I think we are also stressing perhaps what I might call the 'meatscapes' as opposed to the landscapes and the cliffscapes and the seascapes that Mr Coker also paints, one of which I must confess to having found so enchanting that I went so far as to buy it. It's the first time I've ever done that when visiting an art exhibition for the BBC Critics. It was a lovely picture called *La Plaine de Chailly*, painted under a stormy grey windy sky, with one wet green field flanked on the left by a rutted lane leading to a white farmhouse with a red roof and a church spire behind some woods. And really, looking at it, one felt one had to put on a sou'wester and gum boots. It was an extraordinarily beautiful picture.

So, even at this early date, despite his works' more obviously newsworthy qualities, Coker's qualities as an artist built to last beyond any immediate vogue were recognised. Writing in *The Studio* a propos of his next one-man show at Zwemmer's in 1957, G S Whittet observed 'Peter Coker is, in my opinion, one of the younger artists now working who is more likely to stay the course in painting pictures that, while motivated by visible features, are far from being as tame as the abstractionists would imagine the term "representational" to imply.'

Of course, the subject matter of the paintings that inspired this comment had changed since the 'meatscapes'. Though the show did include two pictures of turbot, otherwise it consisted entirely of landscapes. Back in Leytonstone since 1952, Coker had taken to going sketching in nearby Epping Forest, and several large drawings in charcoal and conté in the show were derived from these visits. Most of the paintings, on the other hand, were drawn from trips to France, this time specifically Brittany, and the village of Audierne, which offered both the countryside depicted in *Bracken and Gorse, Audierne* (**57**), and the seaside subjects reflected in *White Buoys, Audierne* (**56**). Coker went first to Audierne in 1955, a trip remembered and recounted in 1986 in the *Tate Gallery Illustrated Catalogue of Acquisitions 1984–1986* (see page 61).

Several paintings of waves breaking on a pebbly shore at Audierne reiterated Coker's fascination with the patterns of moving water and the foreground beaches it was moving towards. The latter interest he says was partly from Courbet, but also, more immediately, derived from his devotion to the abstracted landscapes of Nicolas de Staël, the Russo-French painter who had a considerable vogue in the early 1950s, culminating for London in a retrospective at the Whitechapel Art Gallery in the Summer of 1956. De Staël had committed suicide in 1955 – actually by throwing himself from the lighthouse at Antibes, which may possibly have had some special significance, given that he was fascinated with lighthouses for much of his short working life.

Lighthouses also intrigued Coker, for their colouring, shape and placing against a backdrop of sea. The first time he went to Antibes Coker made an (unmorbid) pilgrimage to the de Staël lighthouse, and one of the three lighthouses at Audierne provided the subject for one of the more striking, and, in its virtuoso managing of plain blocks of colour, most de Staël-like pictures in the 1957 show. In general Audierne proved a very productive painting ground for Coker, and he returned there frequently with his family in subsequent years.

All the same, trees, and the right painting of trees, had become Coker's new obsession. Coker was always worried by the way that trees, when painted by strokes running up and down the trunk, tended to slip away and lack solidity. To counter this, he, as so often, looked back beyond the Impressionists to Courbet, the Barbizon School (centred on the Forest of Barbizon and painters of woodland par excellence) and to deeply unfashionable painters like Bastien-Lepage. What these did, he observed, was to paint *across* the trunk, modelling it by the weight and density of the crosswise stroke. Consequently, shadow and recession could be implied by the way that a left-to-right stroke starts thick and rich and gradually thins out as the brush or palette-knife passes across the canvas. Coker used this technique in many of the tree paintings he was making at that time.

While it is true that Coker, never by temperament a joiner, was not too happy to be lumped in regardless with several painters then exhibiting at the Beaux Arts Gallery, all under the catch-all heading of Kitchen Sink painting, there is no evidence that his artistic course was in any way deflected by these doubts. At the Royal College Coker had been very successful as a portrait painter, and he could no doubt have made this at the very least an important part of his subsequent career. But he just did not care for the idea of being a portraitist, so he naturally looked in other directions.

As a young married man, with a small child and a modest income, largely augmented by Vera's above-average salary, he was living in the house his father still owned in Leytonstone, and from which Coker's family had moved to Maxwelton, in Havering-atte-Bower, when he was eleven. As Coker wrote in an article for *House and Garden* in 1960:

> The advantages of this particular spot soon became apparent. We had only to pop around the corner to shop, and in the High Road we discovered a wood yard where moulding for frames could be cut, a builder's merchant who supplied paint at a discount, and the local butcher who allowed me to make drawings of his carcasses during closing hours. From time to time we think of returning to the more rural districts of Essex, and it is only then that we realize how fond we have become of this house – it is like an old coat, nobody would give it a second glance, but we feel at home in it (Coker 1959).

All the same, when the Cokers moved into his early childhood home in 1951, the neighbours' reaction was noticeably dubious, even after the place of the lace curtains normally omnipresent in Leytonstone had been substituted with draped opaque cotton producing the same effect at a more affordable price. The austerity of many of the Leytonstone paintings formed a natural part of Coker's art, which was, then as ever, firmly based on the notion of painting whatever was before his eyes. Of course, the process was not purely passive: the artist could choose what would be before him when his sketchbook was being deployed. In this still heavily controlled postwar world, travelling abroad was not as usual, and certainly not as easy, as it has subsequently become. Even a painting trip to Normandy and Brittany took some organizing, especially financial: the amount of money allowed to be exported for any particular trip was strictly limited.

Still, the evidence of Zwemmer's records suggests that Coker's early exhibitions sold pretty well: the first exhibition, while not an instant sell-out, raised, in immediate sales from the gallery, just under £400, and the second, which was half paintings, half drawings, brought in £686. Even allowing for the gallery commission, that was, in the terms of the time, a very reasonable return: in the case of the second, for just over a year's work. In addition, Coker had been teaching painting part-time at the St Martin's School since 1954. While still himself studying at the Royal College, he had gone back to the St Martin's to ask the then principal if he could be found some teaching to make ends meet, and had been told that they never took back old students. Little daunted, he had gone back a month later and talked instead to Frederick Gore, the Head of Painting, who immediately found him some work teaching life painting two days a week, which he continued to do for eighteen years. Not only that, but his wife Vera was working in the Scientific Civil Service until 1957, when she resigned to look after her mother, who was dying of cancer.

As a result of his first show at Zwemmer's Coker had seen his work politicized by no less an authority than John Berger. Reviewing the show in *The New Statesman* Berger hailed it as 'an important contribution to the school of English Realism, which is complementary to and equal with the French School'. The article opened by demanding:

> What is this movement? The kitchen-sink school? Social Realism? The name, deprecating or proud, doesn't matter. It is a movement of protest. A protest of young zeal against old expediency? Partly. A protest against art becoming a snob commodity? Partly also. But above all it is a protest against the squalor of indulgent dishonesty and deception.

Later the same year Berger curated a proselitising exhibition at the South London Art Gallery, *Looking Forward*, which included Coker's *Man Carrying Pig* (**42**) and *Still Life with Chicken* (**31**), both from the Zwemmer's show. In the foreword to the catalogue Berger extended his propaganda for this allegedly new kind of British painting, insisting that 'the artists here believe that imagination is the ability *to disclose that which exists*', and ending with one of Blake's more peremptory appeals to Englishmen to 'Know that every man ought to be a judge of pictures, and every man is who has not been connoisseured out of his senses'.

Though no doubt at the time Coker held the kind of liberal, vaguely left-wing views appropriate to a young and thoughtful man, Berger's reading seems much too specific. Coker himself says later, in a 1985 interview, 'For me, there was no political or social significance in what we were doing. One just worked on material one found interesting. I kept on my own, going my own way.' Certainly Coker's work of the 1950s, looked at overall, seems to throw some doubt on Berger's interpretation. Not only does Coker emerge as, politically, a much more ambiguous figure than Berger will allow. The influences at work on his art seem to be predominately aesthetic, and even the defiant reference by Berger to a specifically British movement, 'complementary to and equal with' the French (by which he means painters such as Rebeyrolle, then in the news as a result of a successful London showing), is slightly wide of the mark.

As Frederick Gore remarked in his introduction to the catalogue of Coker's 1972-73 retrospective, Coker was 'one of the first generation of English art students who were able to transcend the Englishness of their art education while still students' (Gore 1973). Coker was, in his artistic allegiences, more French than English, but it is fair to say that if he was in the first generation of anything definable, it was of an era when nationality made very little difference, art and art movements becoming more and more indefinably cosmopolitan and international. (Also the last time when artists worldwide would look to Paris for a lead, any leadership that might exist being about to transfer itself to New York.)

For the moment, though, Coker's aesthetic preoccupations continued to be expressed mostly at home. He had become increasingly interested in the challenge of painting trees, and a large part of his 1969 exhibition at Zwemmer's consisted primarily of paintings and drawings made in Epping Forest or from sketches made in Epping (though there were also a couple of still-lifes and flower-pieces). His technique, which was based on something he had learnt from de Staël, continued to develop in these pictures.

At art school he had learnt to prime his own canvases and lay a gesso base on them. But, once out of college, he took, largely for reasons of economy, to painting most frequently on hardboard. With this he rapidly found a much simpler and faster method of preparing for paint. What he did was initially to lay on the hardboard, literally by trowel, a mass of solid white lead, a kind of putty made of white lead and oil, generally used by plumbers to secure pipe joints. This, bought in industrial quantities, enabled one to cover large surfaces very quickly. Also, the white lead created an interestingly crusty surface, which appealed particularly to Coker at this time because he was becoming very conscious of paint surfaces and felt the need to build them up to create an almost sculptural effect.

The technique, apparently, was not applicable to canvas, as white lead would not stick to it, just rolling off. Even on hardboard it sometimes proved unstable – Coker recalls that in his famous 1955 picture *Table and Chair* (**49**) he originally painted the boy's head so thickly that the whole thing slid right off during the night. Once the white lead was in place, sometimes with the assistance of a bit of muslin to secure it to the hardboard, the more conventional oils would be applied on top of it, not with brushes but with implements which Coker made for himself, a sort of squeegee combined with a palette knife of very thin steel, sometimes as much as eighteen inches across, so that colour could be dragged across the surface with speed and amazing precision, and graded without the necessity of stopping to remix the paint.

The trees of Epping Forest offered perfect material for this form of painting: using one of his own special palette knives (no doubt much narrower than 18 inches), Coker could define the curvature of the trunks very precisely by dragging the appropriate colour across the primed canvas so that it thinned out or built up under the impulsion of the tool, while even on the heavily leaded hardboard it produced a richly textured effect. At this point in his career Coker was painting sometimes on canvas sometimes on hardboard, the choice depending on the subject. He normally stretched his canvases himself, immediately on return from a field trip, stretching a dozen at a time on the basis of the drawings he had brought back: twenty drawings would make him lay in twenty canvases, representing the expected workload of the two years that tended to elapse between exhibitions.

From the beginning he had been able to visualise the exact scale of the painting towards which the drawing was a first step, so he normally ordered his stretchers in bulk, readymade to standard formats. This might suggest that he was in the habit of following Old Master practice, squaring up drawings before transferring them literally to a canvas of the size envisaged. But in fact he never used this method of elaborating drawings into paintings. Rather, the drawings were used for general guidelines and as reminders of the initial visual experience. At most Coker would take a diagonal of the drawing, and work out from that the proportions of the painting: he worked first from instinct, and only then from mathematics. In relation to a particular canvas he would lay out all the related drawings on a table in his studio so that he could metaphorically pan over them and work directly from them, taking what he wanted from each without being confined to any one of them. For this reason he was always hesitant to sell his sketchbook drawings, regarding them as a sort of reference library which he would always be able to call on.

By the time he made his next appearance at Zwemmer's, in a mixed *Summer Selection* which also included John Bratby and Derrick Greaves and took place in May – June 1961, Coker was on the brink of making a radical move in his life. In 1960 he was stricken by the first of a series of medical problems which might well have stopped in his tracks anyone less determined and obsessed: he was diagnosed with Cushing's Disease, which required a massive operation and the removal of his adrenal glands, to be replaced by cortisone tablets. For a while he had extended his teaching practice, now he was forced to give up his two days of teaching. But before that he had been working at Ealing School of Art on Saturday mornings, and on returning to teaching at St Martin's in 1961 he was persuaded by a fellow exhibitor at the Zwemmer Gallery to be a visitor at Colchester School of Art. In Colchester he became very friendly with John Nash, who was also teaching there, and lived quite locally, in the village of Wormingford. Coker's Colchester experience and friendship with Nash gave him a good idea of the landscape of North Essex, and in 1962 he and Vera found a house in Mistley, just outside Manningtree, which seemed to fulfil most of their needs.

During these years trees had continued to be Coker's chief subject, so it was probably natural that, removed at last from Epping, he should look for a local alternative in East Anglia. Encouraged by John Nash, he went north into Suffolk to explore the ancient trees of Staverton Thicks, just outside Orford, but found little there to inspire him: like Monet on his first trip to the Riviera, he realized that just any old tree would not do, it had to be the right tree, and he would know it only when he saw it. However, the trip was not wasted, because he went on to Aldeburgh and found that the stormy weather, rough seas and Martello towers were very exciting to the painter in him. A friend of his had a flat in Tower House, Aldeburgh, and Coker found himself watching from there the bleak windswept beaches, observing the patterns made by people putting out windbreakers and then nestling in their shelter.

Aldeburgh renewed his interest in the sea, and inspired some of his first real seascapes after Etretat. It was a form to which he would revert very regularly throughout his career: at Etretat there were cliffs and rocks of extraordinary shapes to paint, while at Aldeburgh there were just the sea, the low pebbled beach, and the sky. Also, on his way back he passed through Rendlesham and Tunstall Forests, and found there plenty of trees that spoke to him, particularly at Rendlesham. He consequently made a lot of drawings on the spot, and, once the house was in shape and he could get back to work properly, produced a series of paintings which were included in his 1964 Zwemmer's exhibition. Retrospectively, Coker is less than happy with his paintings of the early 1960s, feeling that the pictures concerned come over as too comfortable, inclining towards (dread word) the picturesque.

Coker has always been very self-critical, with an almost puritanical mistrust of comfort and ease: while his greatest delight has always been found in the actual work process, it worries him if it seems to come too readily, with too little trouble. His 1964 show included the last of his Epping paintings, and the first of his tree paintings from Tunstall and Rendlesham Forests, but also three paintings of Aldeburgh, marking a new direction in his work, and a painting and a drawing from a trip to Wales, more wild than industrial, and in any case far from picturesque. Those inclined to be gloomy about the Royal Academy and all its works might worry that Coker's election as an Associate in 1965 would induce complacency, but there at least they would have underestimated their man: in the *Summer Exhibition* the following year the new ARA was singled out as signalling an invasion of the Academy by the dangerously modern and experimental.

One of Coker's six pictures in the show which was particularly remarked on was a 'sombre' painting of a cave in the Pyrenees, which Michael Webber, art critic of the *East Anglian Daily Times*, noted as having a romantic quality comparable with that of James Ward's masterpiece *Gordale Scar*. He also found paintings of local cataracts, such as the *Judas Gap* (**120**) at Flatford, in which the water pouring down over a shallow rock ledge is reduced almost to abstraction, comparable in their intensity to drawings by Leonardo da Vinci. As will be gathered, in the interim Coker, perhaps feeling the need to look further afield for inspiration than the Suffolk woods, had been in 1965 on a painting expedition to a pretty rugged terrain in the South of France, going by way of Josselin in

Brittany, where he made sketches for a painting of the local weir. The 'South' bit, with all its conventional connotations, was strictly coincidental: when Coker first visited Antibes some years earlier, partly on a de Staël pilgrimage, he was puzzled by his failure to find anything under the brilliant Mediterranean light that he wanted to paint, but his fellow Academician Frederick Gore was not surprised, remarking confidently 'But of course – you're a Northern painter'.

Coker recognised the justice of this: he just naturally responded to the cool, grey light of the North, the Channel coast always in preference to the Riviera. And naturally the rugged mountain scenery of the Pyrenees, though technically even further south than Antibes, was the opposite of lush. In any case, Coker's interests as a painter were becoming in a sense more and more abstract. Marina Vaizey said, reviewing Coker's next, and as it turned out last, Zwemmer's show in 1969, that 'Peter Coker paints and draws landscapes with a furious precision. The oils, with broad and vivid strokes of colour, capture the atmosphere of an untamed world, with movements of sky and water, sweeps of hill and earth, that reveal the passion of inorganic nature'. But this kind of furious precision betokens an increasing concern with form rather than content: the subjects obviously start with somewhere specific, but as reflected in the prism of the artist's sensibility, it becomes something much more universalised. These patterns of water in motion could have been observed anywhere or nowhere, but what matters finally is what the artist is moved to do with them in the studio, on the canvas.

Of course the nature of the scene that lies behind the painting remains vital, but increasingly the location seems tailored to the concept rather than the other way round. Perhaps that means just that we have a clearer and clearer vision of what kind of an artist Coker is, or maybe that Coker himself has a clearer vision of what kind of artist he is. He takes himself in the main to places he knows contain the kind of subject which will inspire him, though this admittedly changes and develops with time, becoming during the 1960s much more rugged and severe. Not that the inspiration had to be: the *Eastern Daily Press* noted of a picture in the 1967 show 'Even when he captures water in a peaceful frame of mind, as in the Stour Valley near his home at evening, there is a frown of cloud and a great sweep of red-tinged mud to suggest the violence of nature'. Which is only to say that, like any artist of true quality, Coker ultimately paints what is in his mind rather than what is in front of his eyes: the physical facts are merely the key which opens that particular door to the archetypal.

Nor need it be opened immediately. Both the 1967 and the 1969 exhibitions include a wide geographic range of subjects, some of them going back to sketches made several years before. This shows exactly what Coker means when he talks of his unreadiness to sell pages from his sketchbooks, even though they constitute perfectly self-sufficient works of art in themselves, regarding them as a storehouse of raw material, the full significance and potential of which might only gradually become apparent. Both shows include, for instance, paintings and drawings (finished drawings, that is, rather than sketches) based on sketches made in Epping Forest several years before, and in the 1969 show we find subjects drawn from visits made to Etretat, Audierne and Llanberis as well as from more recent trips to Scotland, Pembrokeshire and the Yorkshire Dales.

The Scottish and Yorkshire paintings arose from Coker's spell in 1967/68 as holder of the David Murray Stewardship at the Royal Academy. This was a job which required him to supervise, in a very hands-off fashion, the activities of students awarded a travel scholarship by the David Murray funds, enabling them to go to some part of Britain, work there, and bring their work into the Academy to be viewed and criticised by the Steward when the period of the grant ended. Sometimes, apparently, the grant-holders had such a good time that they had to be forced to come back and deliver, but Coker was determined to go out to see them in their chosen locations, or sometimes at their homes in exotic places like Blackpool. This took him to various parts of Scotland, including, among other places, Cape Wrath, Sutherland, and allowed him to take in visits to the wilder parts of Yorkshire.

On another occasion John Nash and Coker stayed at Malham, in the middle of the moor, where the rough upland scenery and the distinctive cataracts proved to match very closely Coker's current mood and interests as a painter. Together the two explored all the curious local formations of rock and water. Nash insisted on descending to the bottom of the precipitous Jenny's Fosse and having to be helped up, Coker carrying his bags, while Coker was drawn to the area of Gordale Scar, a dramatic cleft in the rocks already immortalised in paint by James Ward in the eighteenth century and John Piper in the twentieth. He also went with Nash to Skye, and was amused to see that the local paper, reporting their presence, noted an essential difference in their approaches, Nash coming out when the sun shone, Coker coming out only when it clouded over.

In 1969 Coker had been established in North Essex for barely six years, and was still exploring and responding to his own immediate vicinity. The scenery around Mistley, on the Essex/Suffolk border and just where the River Stour starts to open out into an estuary with the port of Harwich at its mouth, is notoriously flat and uneventful. The immediate area is famed as Constable Country, with Flatford Mill and Dedham Vale just a country walk away from the Cokers' house. And Constable is hardly famed as a painter of ruggedly dramatic scenes; rather, and understandably in the circumstances of his young manhood, he celebrates a green and pleasant land of neat fields and trees and calm waters. But, of course, he was also intensely interested in clouds and skyscapes – perhaps the one thing that he clearly has in common with Coker.

Indeed, the first thing that seems to have excited Coker about his new area was the enormous skies above the flats of East Anglia. His earlier works are more often than not interior, including the portraits and still-lifes, and when they are exteriors, like the minute examinations of trees in Epping Forest, there is still a certain claustrophobic closeness about them. One has the impression that Coker seldom if ever raises his eyes to the heavens. The visits to Etretat from 1954 and, even more, to Aldeburgh seem to have changed all that. At Etretat there was a lot more to look at than the lonely sea and the sky: what would be the point of a painter's going to Etretat if he did not paint the rocks and the cliffs? But the cold, grey spaces beyond, occupied by little but wind and water, were still there, humanly inescapable. In Aldeburgh these irresistibly occupy the centre of attention. And the fascination of troubled skies above uneventful land could readily be transferred to the otherwise unchallenging backwaters of the Stour.

But in general, since 1957, Coker established a clear painting routine. He would regularly go off on expeditions to what might prove interesting new places to paint. or, increasingly, places that he had already found inspiring. Once there, he would work very strenuously in his sketchbooks for a relatively short period, filling page after page with watercolours or charcoal sketches, or sometimes pencil or ink drawings. The point of these was to find a form of pictorial shorthand which would embody enough information but not too much. One might wonder how it was possible to have too much information in a sketch, but Coker found that if the notations in his sketchbook were too elaborate it was stultifying to any painting or finished drawing which might eventuate: too much information, too difficult to read, 'squashes out one's reaction to paint'.

Since the sketchbooks were intended for no one's eyes except the artist's, and conceived exclusively as preparatory work for art executed entirely in the studio, it did not matter whether they made sense to anyone else, provided they made sufficient sense to him. In practice, most of the sketchbook drawings and paintings constitute very satisfying works of art in their own right, though naturally in a much freer and more impressionistic style than one would ever expect to encounter in Coker's formally finished work. What he needed from them, to make the transition from sketch to finished painting, was basically a reminder of the first visual impact on him, and what it was in what he saw that made him think it might make an effective painting. This would include a general notion of the composition, and some notation of contrast and colour values. (This latter might be achieved through verbal notes on black-and-white drawings, very much as Victorian painters like Edward Lear did it.)

The structure of Coker's life at this time was clearly based on alternating periods of recharging in contact with the outside world and using the energy thus stockpiled when he got back to the studio. This had been a normal way of working for him ever since Royal College days: while he was still in college he generally worked the opposite way, painting his portraits and still-lifes on the spot, directly from the subject. Possibly one of the reasons that he changed method was the fascination he developed for the butcher's shop round the corner in Leytonstone: obviously it was impossible for him to settle down with the full equipment for making an easel painting in oils bang in the middle of a functioning business, though it was perfectly possible for him to draw there on early-closing afternoons.

But in any case the new way of working corresponded with something deep in his artistic nature. He was never by temperament anything of an impressionist – or certainly no more than Cézanne ever was. From the first he was little interested in evanescent effects of light and movement. Instead, he was concerned with rendering volume, producing an effect of strength and solidity. No doubt this desire for a certain monumentality in his work came from his admiration for Courbet – though here there is the chicken-and-egg question of whether he sought monumentality because of Courbet, or responded to Courbet because he already had an inbuilt taste for monumentality. In any case, Coker's kind of monumentality has never necessarily involved working on a large scale: it is worth remembering that another artist he greatly admires is Morandi, who had a remarkable ability to see the world in a grain of sand, or, more precisely, in an arrangement of small pots and bottles on a table.

Coker's range of media was not confined to painting and drawing. While a teenager studying part-time at the St Martin's School, he had taken classes in etching at the Central School of Art, Longacre, under W P Robins, and become very proficient in the medium – so much so that eventually, in 1976, he published a classic instruction book, *Etching Techniques*. He also learned to prepare lithographic stones, and experimented in various graphic media. At the time he chose subjects close to hand for his prints: the scene outside in Long Acre, the works of Old Masters, such as Rembrandt's etching *The Ratcatcher*, which it was part of his academic training to copy.

At the Royal College he was primarily occupied with painting, but shortly after he left, during 1954-56, his graphic training stood him in good stead when he was encouraged by a fashion designer on the staff of St Martin's to make designs for printed textiles, which were elaborated in a variety of methods and materials, including monotype, dyed papers, bleach, calligraphy, wax crayon, surface rubbings, oil paint, batik, collage, comb and marbling. Sometimes they were done on a large scale, and then what he considered the most interesting part cut out for display. He hawked the results around, with some success, to fabric manufacturers like Ascher's and printing warehouses like Bernard Ashley's at Victoria Station. Designing for printed textiles resulted in some of the very few abstracts Coker has ever made: looking back at the time of a show devoted to the designs at the Mayor Gallery in 1991, he noted 'These designs I now realize were my own way at that time of attempting to resolve the Abstract/Figurative conflict. I enjoyed the new found freedom, producing a quantity of designs in a very short time and for me in a quite uninhibited way' (Mayor 1991).

In the late 1960s Coker took up etching again and as his fascination with the seashore, the sea, and the chilly northern light grew, his printmaking took a new turn. Visiting Ostend he encountered a dealer-collector called Aerts, who was very enthusiastic about his work. Trips to Ostend thereafter became fairly regular for Coker, and each time he went over he would take with him a bundle of drawings and etchings for Monsieur Aerts's stock. Also, unsurprisingly for someone who found inspiration in the subdued beachscape of Aldeburgh, he found the low sandy beaches of Ostend, its watery flats at low tide and its shadowy breakwaters a fruitful source of imagery, which formed the basis of many drawings and a handful of Coker's finest etchings.

By the early 1970s Coker was amassing a small but loyal constituency of regular collectors. In the 1950s one Liverpool business man and amateur artist was so taken with a painting by Coker shortlisted and exhibited in the John Moores competition that he bought, not that but another Coker painting (minuscule, which Coker thought rather mean), and commissioned Coker to go up to Liverpool and tutor him in painting. The way this was done was that he and Coker would set up easels side-by-side, and paint exactly the same subject, the amateur trying as nearly as possible to reproduce the effects of the professional. Coker rarely managed to finish a painting at this time, but on this one occasion all went well, though he had to leave the finished work behind! Coker always refers to this incident as 'being wrung out like a damp dishcloth' – an experience never to be repeated. It was noticeable from the works on the Liverpool amateur's walls that William Scott, among other artists, had been similarly employed.

During the 1960s Coker found some more faithful admirers: Mr A N Provost would even fly over from America for each opening at the Zwemmer Gallery and always bought. Some of his collectors Coker suspected might be quite mad. There was one, for instance, who turned up in plimsolls to a Royal Academy Summer Exhibition and bought all the five or six pictures by Coker in the show in one fell swoop. He received a rather weird commission, when a lady called Ruth Borchard wrote to him out of the blue explaining that she was collecting self-portraits by contemporary artists and wondered if he had one he could let her have for 10-15 gns. ('I realize that you are well beyond this price range. On the other hand, I may well be asking for a painting which you may have outgrown.') Coker was rather charmed by her frank approach, and obliged with a classic small painting. This disappeared from view until the lady's death in 2000, when it reappeared with the rest of her hundred-strong collection, which retrospectively seemed like a visual who's-who of British painting in the second half of the twentieth century. But he was, of course, delighted to have such purchasers, as well as major public bodies like the Arts Council of Great Britain, the Contemporary Art Society and the Chantrey Bequest, not to mention the Tate Gallery, the National Portrait Gallery, the British Museum and innumerable regional galleries and museums.

Coker himself was also by this time getting into a regular routine – not so much with the work itself, but rather with his apportionment of time. As long as he was teaching, his painting trips abroad were governed to a large extent by the placing of his non-teaching periods. And then, always inclined to be a creature of habit, he fell into a pattern of returning regularly to places he knew and felt at home in. He always resented the feeling of wasting time: when he went to some unfamiliar place, as with Antibes in 1973, it took him some little time to acclimatise and find out whether it had anything to offer him, and the answer might well prove to be negative, while if he went to an old favourite like Bargemon or Varengeville he could start work right away, without the risk of disappointment.

Sometimes, of course, a disappointment would be followed by an exciting discovery: after finding nothing to his purpose in Antibes, Coker travelled north to Courbet country, up by the source of the Loue River in Franche-Comté, not far from Ornans. Here, as Coker well knew from a series of great landscapes painted by Courbet around 1864, the Loue dashes dramatically out of a huge cavern in the rockface and sets out on its at times precipitous course through lofty, interestingly sculpted chalk cliffs. This was a landscape after Coker's own heart, and a return from the unknown and, as it had proved, unsatisfactory to something relatively familiar, at least through the prism of Courbet's art.

Coker's frankly admitted attachment to familiar territories may make him sound a bit like the art-lover who insists that he knows what he likes but in reality likes only what he knows. In fact this focusing on the familiar does not in any way disqualify him from being taken seriously as an artist, but rather offers a helpful indication of what sort of artist he is. There are, clearly, artists who are turned on largely by novelty, but they are the world's extroverts, and even with them it probably remains true, unless they are confined to illustration, that ultimately they paint what is in their heads first and foremost, with what is before their eyes acting most importantly as a trigger to their getting in touch with the deeper levels of their psyche.

The quality of the work depends on the intensity with which these personal archetypes are accessed. In his last years Ben Nicholson's visual world was confined in effect to four or five short shelves in his studio, lined with perfectly agreeable but totally unremarkable pots. Many of his latest paintings and drawings were of just one of these, rendered as a flat pattern. This might have been very limiting, and no doubt many other artists would have found it so. But Nicholson's creative excitement never failed: for him there was unmistakably the same sort of vital inspiration in a simple blue and white banded jug that might have come from Woolworth's that another artist might have to navigate the Amazon or walk the Great Wall of China to find.

It seems to me that Coker's inspiration works in the same way. Remember Monet's realization that out of a hundred virtually identical trees on the Mediterranean, only one, for reasons inscrutable, actually spoke to him, responded to his interior needs as a subject for painting. Always, it was recognition rather than discovery. Coker seeks the same kind of subliminal recognition. He is really not interested in recording things: he is looking always for that something significant that lies beyond the scene. And once having found the right trigger, why should he waste time looking for more and different? Of course his artistic requirements gradually develop and change: for years he constantly painted trees in close-up, but then that interest ebbed, and he moved on to tumbling waters, eroded cliffs, fishing nets hanging to dry. In each case, it is the shapes above all that signify for him, both answering to some deep-buried need and lending themselves to the making of satisfactory patterns in paint.

One has only to look at the titles of paintings and drawings in show after show to see that for his inspiration Coker has turned most frequently to France. This, presumably, has more to do with with his intellectual allegiances and his physical and emotional comfort than with the uniqueness of the French landscape. After all, a cataract in the Pyrenees is unlikely to look, particularly in close-up, much different from a cataract in Yorkshire, a beach at Varengeville from a beach at Aldeburgh. But obviously Coker feels more at home in France – especially as a painter. So the routine became fairly fixed. During term time he would teach part-time, at the St Martin's until 1973 and then, on the urging of his friend Roger de Grey, at the City and Guilds of London School of Art: de Grey had just moved from being second-in-command at the Royal College to become Principal at the City and Guilds, and offered Coker the same conditions of work and pay he enjoyed at the St Martin's, plus travelling expenses. And then during vacations he would set off, sometimes by himself, sometimes with Vera, drive to his chosen sketching ground in France, have a concentrated bout of sketching on the spot, and return to work in his studio at Mistley on the paintings he had been planning from the moment he made the sketches.

Coker seems in general to have enjoyed teaching, provided it did not cut too radically into his painting time: since he was never at the best of times a socialiser and party-goer, and his natural tendency was to become more and more hermit-like, working by himself or in the midst of his own tight family circle, it was probably useful to have this enforced regular contact with other artists, both students and colleagues. And of course for most artists, even quite well established ones like Coker, the regular income was useful, both in itself and as a facilitator. It was not until 1985 that he decided to take the plunge and see if he could make a living entirely from painting – and even then, the decision was in part dictated by further severe medical problems and the tragically early death of his son Nicholas, the greatest single sorrow of his life.

In the practical sphere of Coker's life there had also been changes. The Zwemmer Gallery, where he had been happily exhibiting since 1956, closed in 1969, and Coker had to find another London showcase for his work. Fortunately he came into contact with a sympathetic gallery, the Thackeray Gallery in Kensington, where he was to have six shows between 1970 and 1978. After that, in October 1979, he was visited in Mistley by a Mr Marcou, who proved to be wildly enthusiastic about Coker's art and offered him a one-man show at Gallery 10 in Grosvenor Street, recently set up by Marcou and run by his daughter Ann. Part of the deal was that Marcou guaranteed to buy five or six of the paintings included in the show. Not only was he as good as his word, but continued to buy no fewer than four from each of the four other shows Coker had in the gallery between 1980 and 1988.

In 1972–73 Michael Chase, former manager of the Zwemmer Gallery and now director of the Minories in Colchester, organized the first Coker retrospective, of works from 1949 up to date, which toured to Bath, Sheffield and the Morley Gallery in London. Of its London showing Marina Vaizey wrote perceptively in *The Connoisseur*:

> In his paintings, whatever the subject, he seems to me more concerned with getting at, visually, the very structure, movement and life of what he is looking at so intensely. Texture is varied and vivid, although the unusually thick impasto of his earlier work has been somewhat refined down; colour is more tonal, blacks, whites, greys, but there is often a surprisingly vivid and subtle spectrum of beautifully modulated and variegated tones, unexpected shafts of blues and reds which punctuate with a controlled exuberance the deeply expressive qualities of his views of landscape. The exhilarating quality of the variegated surface of the paintings ensures that they are very tactile, almost as though the spectator in a curious manner were nearly brushing up against the gorse and bracken, feeling the splendidly harsh wood of the trees; but this is in no way affected. It is simply that the surface of the painting is a kind of analogue for the surfaces of natural things, of sea, beach and stone, of wood and vegetation, of window and balcony overlooking the Suffolk coast. He is particulally good too at catching the nuance of the moving, changing light of the sky, skimming clouds and gathering storm, dusk and the inevitable movement of the tide... Peter Coker... works from the particular to the universal, so that we who have never seen what he has seen accept the validity of his visual creations.

Another retrospective followed at the Chelmsford and Essex Museum in 1978. The following year there was an impressive show at the Royal Academy of early paintings and drawings of, and related to, the butcher's shop in Leytonstone, which also included some still-lifes of the turbot that Coker used to buy in Soho also in the mid 1950s. (This show also toured to Liverpool, Carlisle, Doncaster and Southport.) Writing jointly in *Art Monthly*, Juliet Steyn and Deborah Cherry drew attention to the technical revelations offered by the show in putting the paintings in the context of the preparatory drawings:

> The differences between the pencil drawing for the composition of *Butcher's Shop I* (**33**) and the finished painting (72 x 48 inches) reveal the means by which Coker arrives at a stable, monumental conception. In the painting the setting is radically revised, the depth of field contracted. The sharp angularity of line and the energetic activity of the butcher in the drawing is replaced in the painting by a rotundity of contour, a stillness of forms, a geometrically-plotted composition (in contrast to the oblique dynamics of the study) and the weighty solidity of the colouristic impasto contained within the insistent black outlines. The simultaneity of the viewpoint, seen in the depiction of the work-bench in the foreground of this painting, is a recurrent feature of Coker's work at this date, and is employed in *Butcher's Shop II* (**34**), *Fish and Newspaper* (**29**) and *Sheep Carcasses on Bench*, amongst others.

Many of the notices at the time did not seem able to get far beyond the old 'Kitchen Sink' label and the repetition (usually with a slightly dubious inflection) of John Berger's announcement that Coker's work made 'an important contribution to the school of English realism' – the doubt being apparently because there was some ambiguity attaching at the end of the 1970s to the whole school of English realism and how it should be rated. No one wanted to be seen espousing an outdated attitude or endorsing an aspect of recent art history which had been authoritatively dismissed as of no importance or contemporary relevance. However, the *Art Monthly* review was a straw in the wind, indicating that received wisdom on the subject of English realism was ripe for questioning, and that artists like Coker, instead of being tarred with some over-tidy capsule label brusquely applied two decades earlier, should be studied in their own right, with due consideration not only of the way they were (if they ever were), but of what they have subsequently become.

In 1979 Coker also had what amounted to a retrospective devoted exclusively to his etching mounted at a brand new gallery in Ampthill, Bedfordshire. The surprise here is not only the sheer number of prints on show, but the variety of techical variations included. No doubt in the light of Coker's book on etching technique this should not surprise, but there are thirty-five prints on show, for scarcely two of which the technical description is identical. Under the two headings, 'Etchings' and 'Colour Etchings' there are straight etchings, etchings with aquatint, etchings with aquatint and drypoint, soft ground etchings with open bite or aquatint, drypoints, and drypoints with mezzotint. And the subjects include landscapes from Scotland, Yorkshire, Aldeburgh, Ostend, Mouthier-Haute Pierre (a favourite French haunt of the Cokers at this time), Epping Forest and Malham, as well as portraits of *Nicholas* (**238**) and *Maisie* (**246, 247**) and such unclassifiable subjects as *Persian Kelim* (**224**) and *Orchestral Pit, Coliseum* (**223**). The prices, incidentally, ranged from £15 to £45.

Coker's first show at Gallery 10 in 1980 marked a notable change in his work. For all his earlier failure to respond to Antibes, and Frederick Gore's informed opinion that he was (irredeemably?) a Northern artist, the paintings in his new show, all executed in 1979-80, suddenly prove to be full of the warm south. Coker had in 1975 found at last in Bargemon, a small hill town in the Var, north of Dragignan and west of Grasse, a location with which he could identify. Coincidentally, or perhaps not so coincidentally, he appeared also to have discovered Matisse. Of course he had known the art of Matisse well ever since student days, but for a long time, however much he might admire it in the abstract, it did not seem relevant to his own case. But as his normal application of paint got lighter and thinner, and he was spending the summer of each year in Bargemon, relaxing into its warmth and sub-tropical luxuriance, the brighter colours and flat patterning of Matisse gradually came to look like a tempting option.

If there is one type of Matisse which must have exercised a radical influence on Coker, it has to be the many paintings which invite the spectator to look out from a darker interior towards the often brilliantly illuminated outside. Sometimes these can be very severe, like the almost abstract *Porte-fenêtre, Collioure* (1914), in which the 'view' outside the french window is a plain expanse of blue-green which one guesses, but only guesses, to be the sea. Here the colour is very thoroughly moderated, but elsewhere comparable window pictures such as *La fenêtre* of 1906, *Vue de la fenêtre* of 1912, or *La fenêtre ouverte* of 1921, glow with dazzling Mediterranean light blazing into the shade within. The idea of painting through a window is in many respects an obvious one, the window providing its own framing device. So it is hardly necessary to suppose that Coker's splendid, almost abstract *Window, Bargemon* (**399**) or *Blue, Black Interior: Two Windows* (**386**), both in the 1980 Gallery 10 show, are directly suggested by the Matisse. But the same idea of heat and colour simmering away outside, and it all observed from a cool and shady interior, certainly informs both paintings.

Perhaps this was the way that Coker emerged gradually from Northern gloom to the sensuous delights of the South, edging little by little out of a shadowy interior into the full blaze of noon. The Cokers first came to Bargemon at the invitation of a friend. It was a friend of hers who owned the nearby chateau in the grounds, gardens, and olive groves of which Coker did so much work. Even if Coker began by gazing doubtfully out of the shade, he very soon started drawing out in the gardens of the chateau, fascinated by the strange and exotic shapes of the vegetation. And from drawing the shapes he moved on to painting the colours. He even, wonder of wonders, exhibited in the 1980 show a painting of that same Antibes which a few years before he had found so dispiriting.

Bargemon remained central to Coker's inspiration throughout the early 1980s, and the main theme of the shows he had at Gallery 10 during most of the decade, up to the fifth in 1986. The spring 1984 show of oil paintings was dominated by Bargemon and vicinity, along with the first paintings of the Clos du Peyronnet, a villa at Menton on the Riviera, though the grimmer North was not forgotten: in a couple of paintings Coker reverted to Etretat. In the matching autumn show of drawings and watercolours the mix was much the same: two watercolours of Etretat out of 25 (and a screen print) dedicated to the nominal theme of the show, *Mediterranean Gardens*. The 1986 show suggested that Coker might be moving closer to abstraction, though the patterns on canvas were all unmistakeably based on details of Riviera landscape and vegetation.

The Cokers first stayed at the Clos du Peyronnet in late 1983/early 1984, having seen a flat in it advertised in *The Times* as a tempting holiday home. Needless to say, Coker was not the kind to take holidays, but he felt drawn to explore the lushness of the Riviera. The place had been owned by, and the garden made by, the painter Humphrey Waterfield, but was, by this time, in the charge of his nephew the botanist, William Waterfield. These gardens overlooked the Mediterranean, and were full of very exciting plants, which Coker delighted to draw and paint.

The second half of the 1980s was overshadowed for Coker by medical problems and personal tragedy, but at least he had finally decided in 1985 to give up teaching completely, and so could consecrate all his quality time to painting. The darkening of Coker's world was perhaps instrumental in the unexpected change marked in his sixth show at Gallery 10 in 1988. Instead of the Riviera, the show was devoted, all but one painting, to 'Scottish Landscapes'.

These, almost inevitably, were much more restrained in colouring – or at any rate much darker, for ever since his stint in the butcher's shop Coker has been able to find extraordinary richness and variety of colour at the heart of seemingly grim, colourless subjects. And there are certainly many other approaches to colour than the Matisse notion of *luxe, calme et volupté*. The Expressionist way, for example. Writing in *The Times* in 1988, I was merely one of many critics who found the concept of Expressionism springing to the tip of their pens: 'Some pictures here have an almost expressionist tinge: *Chrossavaig, Skye* (**520**), for instance, with its great hummock of blue heaving convulsively out of the massed greens, or *The Quirang, Skye* (**526**), where the paint is pasted on and scratched off again with quite demonic abandon.'

One might perhaps look to autobiographical reasons for this very evident increase in *sturm und drang*, seeing it as Coker's own version of 'Rail, rail against the dying of the light'. But then, Wordsworth said of Shakespeare's Sonnets 'With this key Shakespeare unlocked his heart', prompting Browning's irreverent riposte 'If so, the less Shakespeare he'. Alfred Hitchcock denied any interest in psychoanalytic explanations of his work, pointing out that even the existence of subconscious motivation was just an hypothesis, and 'I think I have enough silly hypotheses of my own, without listening to other people's silly hypotheses'.

Certainly the most sensible response to any such explanations in Coker's case is that (i) they are unproven and incapable of proof; and (ii) they do not matter anyway, since all that finally counts in the evaluation of Coker's changed manner is whether it is effective in its own terms. That it evidently is: the consensus of critical opinion was that the paintings in the 1988 show were among Coker's finest. His final show at Gallery 10, in 1989, shortly before the gallery closed, was something in the nature of a summation: devised originally for the Fitzwilliam Museum in Cambridge, it featured drawings and watercolours dating from as far back as 1956 and coming right up to date.

Among the most recent works included was a representation of the latest subject to fascinate Coker, *Salmon Nets* (**550**), arranged in slashing crisscross lines against a stormy sea and sky to almost Abstract Expressionist effect. Coker had first noted the effect of the nets in constant movement at Achiltibue on the windy northwest coast of Scotland in 1985, and he had returned there to observe it during the following three years, all of which activity resulted in a series of at least nine major paintings, exhibited in 1990. As Andrew Lambirth remarks in the catalogue of *The 1990 Contemporary British Painters Exhibition* at the Business Design Centre in Islington, in these paintings 'Coker walks the tightrope between figuration and abstraction, to great effect'.

Unhappily further misfortune was on the horizon for the Cokers: beginning in 1990, Peter suffered in rapid succession a serious heart attack and an equally serious stroke. Coker was no stranger to severe illness, which had dogged him, on and off, ever since his mid-thirties. With many people this double blow might have been the end of everything. But though the heart attack left him much enfeebled, and the stroke affected his coordination to some extent, he discovered he was still able to work. There was certainly some change in his style, but it seemed, and to a considerable extent was, a natural evolution

When Patrick Trevor-Roper published his book *The World Through Blunted Sight (1970)*, about the effect that various sight defects had on the work of artists suffering them, he was accused of trying to 'explain away' the genius of, say, El Greco. To this he reasonably replied that thousands of people might be suffering from the same eye condition as El Greco, but there was only one El Greco, with genius enough to turn his apparent disadvantage into a positive factor. In the same way, when the German painter Lovis Corinth suffered a serious stroke in 1911, his partial disablement forced him into a broader, more expressionistic style, the painting made up of little fluttery dashes and occasional broad, stabbing sweeps of the brush. Ironically, this moved him from conservative to avant-garde, and his later style exercised a more radical influence on later painters, such as his one-time pupil Oskar Kokoschka, than anything he had done before could conceivably have achieved.

So it proved with Coker. He had been moving in the direction of a much more jagged, expressionistic style already by 1988, in the paintings of fishing nets and some of the Scottish landscapes. So essentially he just had to keep working along the same lines. After the heart attack he was forced to stop painting for a while, and then, just when he felt ready to start again, he had the stroke. But, little daunted by the double blow, he determined to go to the old, familiar landscapes of Northern France and test the practicalities of the situation. He could no longer drive himself, but a friend of Vera's who lived near Paris volunteered to drive them round, and in the winter of 1990-91 they made a pilgrimage to Varengeville and then Etretat.

Coker found that he could make drawings and watercolours on the spot, as he always had, and sketched cliff faces all along the coast from Dieppe to St-Valery-en-Caux; all he needed was someone to drive, and Vera to hold his sketchbooks and tools while he worked. From the trip also resulted two major paintings done back in his studio in Mistley, one of them, of circular corn stooks, exhibited in the next RA *Summer Exhibition*. He had also become particularly interested in harbour scenes, working a lot on the distinctive shapes of piers and of nets hung up to dry and repair, and a number of paintings and drawings based on these subjects, observed not only in Scotland, but also on the French coast at Quiberville and other places, were included in the shows he had in Edinburgh at the Flying Colours Gallery in 1990 and 1991, and in several mixed shows in London.

Despite his relative success in working through and beyond his afflictions, by the beginning of 1992 Coker had become dispirited by the strict limitations to his freedom of movement (he could not even reach his upstairs studio in the Red House unaided), and virtually gave up the making of art, even though the principal result of one last painting trip to the Riviera, *Menton* (**590**), a view from a hotel balcony towards the sea with ghostly shapes which prove to be palm trees dissolving in the dusk, remains one of the finest and most haunting of all his works. As a lifelong workaholic, this diminution of activity cannot have been easy for him, though he admits that he was for a while happier than he would have imagined about doing nothing: the enforced lethargy had its own excuses. But he remained active – more active than ever in some ways – in the business of the Royal Academy, of which he had been a full member since 1972. In the controversy surrounding the *Sensation!* show there in 1997, for instance, he weighed in with a letter to *The Times*, in which he announced that 'The Academy has disgraced itself on both artistic and moral grounds.'

He began, eventually, to travel again. In the winter of 2000-01 he and Vera went twice to revisit old haunts in Paris, and they were both encouraged to find how much, including all the major galleries, could be negotiated by a wheelchair. Naturally Coker went to the Musée d'Orsay to renew direct acquaintance with his most-loved Courbets, such as *The Funeral at Ornans*, and among the exhibitions he took in was *Mediterranée* at the Grand Palais, which charted artistic reactions to the French Riviera, including Coker's old stamping-ground at Bargemon. Most significantly, he returned after a long interval to his favourite art suppliers in Paris, such as Sennelier, where he had always bought his stretchers: 'Probably the stretchers I could get in London were just as good, but there was a magic about going to Paris for them – you felt you were a real artist'. And, he bought a new supply of handmade papers, inks and other materials. He also had a chair-lift installed in his home, so that he could get into his studio again. He was going back to work.

Throughout his career, Coker has followed his own track with remarkable consistency. Now and then he has seemed to coincide with some group or movement, most obviously with the alleged Kitchen Sink School of the 1950s, but it has always been a genuine coincidence: what Coker has always done is to find his own means to his own ends. At times he has been fashionable, at times definitely not. His constituency has gradually shifted, so that when in the mid-1980s there was a rash of shows like *The Forgotten Fifties*, in Sheffield and London (1984), those who were reminded of Coker as he had been thirty years earlier did not necessarily connect this long-submerged artist with the happily surviving, regularly exhibited landscapist and Royal Academician.

But if so, that was their fault, not his. His preoccupations – one could not unfairly say obsessions – have always been rigorously consistent. Even as a Kitchen Sink painter he was always a formalist, constructing his paintings from a variety of sketches to make a satisfactory and considered composition: he was never a documentarist seizing the impression as it flies, And this has always remained his way of working. More expected, no doubt, of a mid-nineteenth-century, pre-Impressionist painter, so it is not surprising that his model painter should be Courbet. To begin with, while he was still effectively confined to London, where he had been born and returned to study, his subject-matter was totally different from Courbet's, and he was quite aware of what some French contemporaries, such as de Staël, Rebeyrolle and Lorjou, were doing, because they were exhibited in London, and seemed to share his post-Cézanne concerns with solidity of form. But when he was able with reasonable ease to get away, at least to the nearby parts of France, he immediately found his true, central form, the landscape. Of course he could still do other things: at the Royal College he had his notable success with portraits, and every now and then he might be moved to paint a flower piece or a still life, or even venture into abstraction if the needs of textile design invited it. But landscape was what he really responded to, and really wanted to construct paintings out of.

However, when he had settled on his chosen form, his artistic conscience drove him inexorably on, from solidity expressed in a quite sculptural build-up of pigment, highly appropriate for the beaches and cliffs of the Channel Coast, to a more fluid approach when water too became a major preoccupation. In the paintings of the sea itself, and the falling waters of the Yorkshire moors and the Pyrenees, the paint swirls and froths to reflect a world in movement. Yet still held firmly under the painter's control: the composition is always strict, and the movement within it is all the more intense because of that.

In the later 1970s Coker's work underwent another dramatic evolution, when he discovered Bargemon and the joys of the warm south, its brilliant colours and exotic shapes. It was easy to suppose that he had sacrificed his Northern puritanism to the heady influence of Matisse. But under the superficial, surface change he was the same painter exactly. His paintings were still firmly based on draughtsmanship, and his drawings of this period, of the palms and cacti and other spiky vegetation of the Riviera, have just the same attractive/repulsive quality as the 'northern' drawings of gorse and bracken and rough-barked English trees.

In any case, it was a transitory phase: in the later 1980s he was back in the rugged north of Scotland, piling on and scratching off the paint with expressionistic fierceness and abandon. Yet again he was visibly touching on the borders of abstraction, with his paintings of nets wildly billowing in the gale. But that is hardly surprising if one has followed closely his previous career: looking out of a window in Bargemon as much as peering closely at the irregularities of a northern beach, he has always been deeply concerned with the architecture of things, the archetypal patterns which lie beneath everyday appearances. Any representational painting worth its salt is abstract as well, and Coker's work, as well as fondling the surface, goes straight to the heart of things. His continuing achievement is the most substantial of anyone in his generation; where others have stagnated, sold out or faded away, he has been driven to build and build on a uniquely solid foundation, making a multitude of specifics into a statement of universal truth.

1 1926–1940: Wanting to be a Painter

Peter Godfrey Coker was born on 27 July 1926 at the Royal Free Hospital in Gray's Inn Road, London. He was the only child of Edwin Coker and Elsie Coker (née Goode) of Tredegar Road, in Old Ford, on the edge of London's East End. Both of his parents had grown up in the East End, as the children of skilled craftsmen. Edwin's father had been a book-edge marbler, while Elsie's father had founded a business in engraving and stencil cutting. Peter remembers the engraving workshop during the time that it was run by his uncle. Its range of tools, coloured bottles, rolls of zinc and copper contributed to a fascinating atmosphere which suggested to him the purpose and pleasure of craftsmanship. In time, he would echo those values in his painting, printmaking, even carpentry, and in the orderly studios in which he worked.

Edwin Coker did not follow his father into book-edge marbling. Instead he worked in trade, becoming the manager of Kerland & Haskin, a wholesale confectioner's based at Gardiner's Corner, Aldgate. Soon after the birth of Peter, he was able to move his family out of Old Ford, and buy a home in Leytonstone, Essex. At that time, Leytonstone was close to open countryside, so offering a pleasant environment in which to bring up a child.

No 1 Moyers Road lay at one end of a short Victorian terrace, between Vaughan's Dairy, which supplied the family's milk and butter, and the home of Mr Hanson, a local government officer. Years later, Peter described the house as:

> a typical example of the architecture found in the neighbourhood, yet…not without character. It grows on one as does the district, and is distinguished from the rest by the rakish angle at which the chimney leans and the ever-increasing dampness of the outside wall, attributed to the once mighty Lea. (Coker 1959)

Elsie Coker was 'terribly houseproud' (PC), and took charge of all the domestic tasks, including the cooking. In addition, she was an expert dressmaker, with an intense interest in style and design, who 'made all her own clothes with the greatest of flair' (JRT).

Music was the most important pastime of the Coker family, for Elsie was also a talented singer and pianist. She held musical evenings around the drawing room's Cramer piano, and sometimes took Peter to concerts and operas. As a pupil of a Miss Coe at the nearby school in Canterbury Road, he heard a memorable performance of Samuel Coleridge-Taylor's *Hiawatha* at the Royal Albert Hall. And as a member of the choir of St Catherine's Church, he sang 'the odd solo' (PC). Music would become, what Frederick Gore calls, 'his second string' (Gore 1973). Though musical events ensured that he mixed with others, much of his early childhood was spent alone, in drawing and reading. His favourite books included such tales of adventure and detection as Dumas' *The Count of Monte Christo* and those concerning Sherlock Holmes and Sexton Blake.

In 1937, Peter Coker moved with his parents further into Essex, though No 1 Moyers Road was retained for letting. They settled into Maxwelton, one of four new houses at Havering-atte-Bower, three and a half miles north of Romford. This large semi-detached property, with its generous amount of land, stood opposite a farm and set in countryside. It enabled Elsie Coker to develop her passion for gardening, and afforded Peter his 'first significant experience of landscape' (Gore 1973). Indeed he took full advantage of his new sense of freedom, playing in the fields and swimming with friends in the River Roding near Passingford Bridge. Everything seemed larger and more open. Thus his new school, at Pettits Lane, was two miles off, a distance that he first walked and later cycled (on a Raleigh that he still owns).

As a schoolboy, Peter showed most talent for art and games. He was encouraged in these pursuits by two masters, Walter Benson, who taught English and Games, and a Mr Rogerson, who taught Art.

Abbreviations
Abbreviations in the text refer to the following:

PC Peter Coker: interviews and statements
VC Vera Coker: interviews and statements
JRT John Russell Taylor: essays and drafts

Bold nos in brackets (**00**) refer to Catalogue Raisonné Numbers

SB in **bold** followed by **bold** numbers in brackets (**SB00:00**) refers to Sketchbook numbers:page numbers

Yorkshire-born Benson became a family friend and, as a result, involved Peter in a variety of activities, and in discussions of literature. Peter played chess with both Benson and Benson's father, and was taken to watch him play cricket.

Rogerson involved himself more gradually in Peter's education, for he tended to 'give his pupils a subject and let them get on with it' (PC). Yet, quite soon, from about the age of twelve, Peter decided that he 'really wanted to be a painter' (Lambirth 1989:14), not from any clear conception of the artistic life, but purely because he loved painting. Working at home in his bedroom as well as at school, he began to develop the thorough and orderly practice that would characterise his mature career. At this early stage, however, he took greatest pleasure in producing paintings and scraperboard drawings of birds and animals, especially polar bears. Inspiration for some of these pieces came from illustrations to *Zoo*, a magazine regularly passed on to him by his cousins.

Rogerson endorsed Peter's aspirations, and attempted to persuade his father to send him to art school, though with no immediate success. Attendance at an art school seemed particularly unrealistic with the onset of war, but the very conception of art as an occupation may have struck Edwin Coker as alien, for his artistic interests centred on a china collection, kept in a hallowed cabinet in the drawing room. While this was the only serious subject on which he and Peter ever disagreed, it was of such significance to both that each seemed determined in his resolve.

2 The 1940s: Becoming an Artist

When Peter Coker left school in the summer of 1940, the Second World War was well advanced. At fourteen, he was too young to be called up to fight, and was instead encouraged to take up work. His father was particularly keen that he enter the confectionery trade, and so employed him as his assistant at Kerland & Haskin. However, Peter remembers the ensuing period as 'the worst year of his life', during which he was at his father's beck and call from the break of day: 'his father had to shout in his ear to wake him at six in the morning and again in the car to prevent him falling asleep' (Gore 1973). The experience inevitably strengthened his artistic ambitions, and kept him worrying his father.

A resolution to this situation was eventually suggested by a customer, who bought confectionery for Odhams Press, a leading publisher of instruction manuals and children's books: as Peter was interested in art, he should apply to Odhams as a studio assistant, a position from which he was sure to benefit. With that customer's help he made his application and, in September 1941, began work at Odhams studio, based in Long Acre, Covent Garden.

On moving to the studio, Peter continued to live happily with his parents, and travel into town with his father. Yet he began a semi-independent way of life which probably affected him more deeply than the wider events of war. He was able to explore the bookshops in the Charing Cross Road, and to visit his first exhibitions, such as those at the National Gallery presenting the work of Official War Artists.

The Rat Catcher [after Rembrandt] c 1941-43 (**2**)

The Odhams studio was overseen by George Leech, a watercolourist and printmaker. He took a liking to Peter, and ensured that he learned the rudiments of his trade, as well as carrying out the more menial tasks of cleaning up and making tea. As a result, Peter worked alongside emerging young designers, and visited the studios of established artists, such as Thomas Dugdale and Feliks Topolski, who produced illustrations for Odhams on a freelance basis. He received particular attention from Frances Gorniot and Geraldine McKerrow, two designers in their twenties, who 'encouraged him to go to art school, to read seriously and to copy Rembrandt in the British Museum' (Gore 1973).

Following their advice, Peter went to St Martin's School of Art on Saturdays, Sundays and weekday evenings. Then, soon after, he discovered that a day release scheme was in operation with some firms in the area. As he had received a rise, on the arrival of a new assistant, he negotiated with Odhams to trade in the extra money for a full and regular day of courses. At this period, the St Martin's staff included Herbert Budd and John Farleigh (teaching life drawing), John Hadley Rowe (commercial art), and a Mr Lytton (general drawing), the latter praising a watercolour landscape that Peter had painted from his bedroom at Maxwelton. However, Peter learned more from Kalman Kemeny, an artist in his late forties, who sat beside him in weekend painting classes, and worked in an *intimiste* manner.

At the same time, Peter studied printmaking under William Palmer Robins, Head of Etching at the Central School of Art, along the road from Odhams. He was asked to copy Rembrandt's *The Rat Catcher* (**2**), which he executed in reverse, and then to produce a landscape. As an alternative, he chose the view from the studio window overlooking Long Acre (**1**) he remembers 'the perspective giving me a great deal of trouble, although it is surprising how errors can be concealed by clever printing!' (PC). As a culmination of this intensive education, George Leech allowed Peter to design a dust jacket, for a manual on knitting, the result being successful enough to be published.

~

In 1943, at the age of seventeen, Peter decided to enlist in the services. This distressed his father, who had been badly wounded in the arm during the First World War. But Peter wanted to volunteer for the Navy, so that he could serve alongside his closest friend, Andrew Stowe. In the event, his medical examination revealed that he had an auditory problem, a result which led to his eventual placement in the Fleet Air Arm, where he trained as an electrician.

During his first months of service, Peter was stationed at various air bases across England. Yet, whether at Havant or Warrington, he always managed to attend classes at the local art school, and maintain his devotion to drawing. Later, he entered the Education Corps, at Evesham, teaching art and allied crafts, and organising sessions of musical appreciation. There he made friends with 'some amazing people, masters and students of art and literature' (PC), whose conversations helped him develop his ideas and tastes. He also made more than one girlfriend among the WRNS.

Peter spent all his leave – official and unofficial – at home with his parents. On one visit, he submitted a *Self-Portrait in Striped Pyjamas* to a local art exhibition, which was bought by his first patron, a Mr Gillette. Gillette would then invite him to his home for coffee, and exchange books, from his impressive collection, for landscapes that Peter had painted in the forces. So Peter developed as an artist while building his own library of art books, which he supplemented each birthday, Christmas… indeed whenever possible.

On demobilisation, in December 1946, Peter returned to live at Maxwelton. As one qualified to receive a war service grant, he was able to take up a place at St Martin's School of Art as a full-time student of painting, and did so in the following January. Though always a workaholic, he proved particularly industrious at this time:

> All of us ex-service blokes worked like mad. We'd get into St Martin's at nine in the morning and come home at half-past eight every day of the week, with the odd Saturday morning class. (Lambirth 1989:14)

As a result, his work developed at a great rate, while he built up a close rapport with some of his most encouraging teachers, notably Vivian Pitchforth (who taught him life drawing) and James Stroudley (both life drawing and still life). They represented a generally realist tradition and were closely connected to the London Group. However, their personalities were in stark contrast.

Though somewhat deaf, Pitchforth was generally friendly and amusing, his use of an ear trumpet adding to his charming – positively Dickensian – appearance. An excellent teacher, he was well able to both talk about and demonstrate the finer points of technique and aesthetics. In his obituary of Pitchforth, written for *The Times* in 1982, Peter remembered that:

> The strength of Pitchforth's teaching was due in large measure to the clarity of his illustration. In spite of his deafness or perhaps because of it, his life classes became more concentrated and animated. One could also hear much of what was being said to the other students with the word 'form' echoing round the room…At the end of the day he would produce his book and draw for himself which was particularly stimulating and many of his demonstration drawings were kept by the students. (Coker 1982)

James Stroudley *Bather* 1958

Stroudley was a harder task master, though, as Peter wrote in his *Times* obituary in 1985, 'his matter-of-fact unpretentious criticism often belied a more sympathetic nature'. Peter always considered him both 'a deeply serious teacher' and a much underestimated artist. A pupil of the Rome Scholars, Alfred Kingsley Lawrence and Thomas Monnington, he taught Peter to mark out his figures in a careful, almost mathematical way. Peter would later demonstrate his affection for these teachers, not only by writing their obituaries, but by organising an exhibition, held at Long Melford, Suffolk, in 1971, entitled 'Pupil and Masters'.

While at St Martin's, Peter drew constantly and produced a number of paintings in a controlled tonal manner, but he did not then fully appreciate the relationship between the two activities. However, his studies as a draughtsman did contribute to his understanding of the art of the past, and compensated for the poor teaching in History of Art. With the approval of Edward Morss, the college principal, he applied successfully for a pass to the Print Room at the British Museum; there he copied drawings by artists that he wished to emulate, such as Michelangelo, Andrea del Sarto and Watteau. He also read more widely, supplementing loans from the 'college library' (a shelf space measuring six feet square) by making visits to the nearby Zwemmer's bookshop in the Charing Cross Road, where he browsed and bought.

In his precious spare time, Peter often attended ballets and classic plays at the New Theatre, in St Martin's Lane. On one occasion, in a queue for the ballet, in the spring of 1947, he met Vera Crook, the mathematics undergraduate who would become his wife. They met again by accident after the performance when both went backstage to see the same member of the corps de ballet, and on the following day at Liverpool Street Station. It transpired that Vera lived quite close to Peter, at Gidea Park, and like him travelled into London on the LNER. From that time, they often went together to the theatre, concerts and exhibitions.

above left
Carnival in Venice 1949 (**4**)

above right
Via Della Torre Rossa, Arezzo, 27 July 1949

In the summer of 1949, Peter was given the opportunity to travel to Italy. Vivian Bewick, a friend at St Martin's Painting School, had been asked to accompany a young disabled woman on a trip to Todi, and had suggested that Peter go with them; for Bewick thought that the two men could carry on with a tour of the country, seeing as much as possible. At that time of currency restrictions, British travellers were permitted to take only £50 abroad, exactly the amount that Peter had in his bank account. But he decided that a trip abroad would be a worthwhile, perhaps unrepeatable, experience. Indeed, the presence of Bewick, both older and more experienced than Peter, ensured that the most was made of their limited resources. He was very methodical and thorough, planning each day well in advance and taking with him the relevant guide books and timetables.

Peter found the trip a revelation. He made a few drawings, some of which were worked up later, but spent most of his time in looking. One highlight was a fresco of *The Last Supper* by Andrea del Sarto (in the refectory of the Convento di San Salvi, Florence) treasured for its extraordinary effect of space. Others can be gleaned by examining the collection of Alinari's famous facsimiles and photographs that Peter purchased at the time: works by Fra Bartolommeo, Correggio, Lorenzo di Credi, Raphael, Guido Reni, Tintoretto and Veronese. Managing to stretch the trip over nearly three months, Peter and Vivian stayed in Milan, Venice, Florence, Siena, Arezzo and Rome, and went on day trips from these bases to places round about. During this progress, they met Stroudley and his wife, who thought that Peter looked so thin and tired that they took him with them so that he could rest at Lake Como.

James Stroudley *Marine Still Life*

Still Life 1949 (**6**)

Peter and Vera, Pisa 1950

Peter and Vera, Pisa 1950

On the way back, Peter met up with Vera in Paris, for his first taste of the French capital. They stayed at a hotel in the Rue de Rome, and visited the Louvre, the Petit Palais, and the studios of Delacroix and Moreau. Focussing on French painting of the nineteenth century, Peter made a particular study of Courbet's major canvases, and was overwhelmed by the audacity of his achievement in scale, realism and variety. His enthusiastic response to the artist at this time marked the origin of his gradual realisation that landscape would be the ideal vehicle for his dedicated form of realism. This was soon confirmed when he encountered an article on Courbet in the *Saturday Evening Post*, and was transfixed by one of his views of Etretat reproduced as a centre-fold.

In his last year at St Martin's, Peter was able to work in a special room set aside for the more gifted students and often supervised by guest teachers. Prompted by memories of Italy, he produced two ambitious paintings of people eating melons, which attempted to combine figure with still life (**7**, **8**). He also worked on a more assured still life (**6**) that proved to be his first significant painting, if something of 'a one off' in its bright palette and smooth application of paint. The approach was partly inspired by Velasquez's *Old Woman Frying Eggs* (1618; then in the Cook Collection, and now in the National Gallery of Scotland); for Peter was especially stimulated by 'the painting of the insides of the dishes, the eggs and the knife resting over the dish casting a deep shadow, and also the shadow describing the form of the dish on which it is resting' (PC). Pitchforth, Stroudley and James Bateman (who taught composition) encouraged students to follow their example and send work to the Royal Academy. So Stroudley pushed Peter to complete the still life and submit it to the *Summer Exhibition*, which he did with success in 1950.

3 1950–54: The Royal College of Art

During his final year at St Martin's, Peter Coker was persuaded by both Vivian Pitchforth and James Stroudley to take the entrance examination for the Royal College of Art. He considers it to have been 'an awesome experience', for it lasted several days of spring 1950, and comprised various forms of assessment. Ahead of the exam itself, he submitted a portfolio of work, which included the still life he would exhibit at the Royal Academy and a life drawing of the rear view of a standing man. He then undertook a number of practical and theoretical exercises at the college: he produced a life drawing and spent a day on figure composition; he completed a written paper which tested his knowledge of art history and asked him to discuss a quotation from Degas's writings. Surviving the procedures of evaluation and selection, he was finally called to an interview with all the staff of the Painting School. It was no wonder that he valued his acceptance as 'something of a status symbol' (PC).

Nude 1950 (**9**)

When Peter took up his place at the RCA in the autumn of 1950, the college was undergoing a period of radical change. For its new principal, Robin Darwin, was busily establishing its independent status and reviving its relevance as the nation's premier institution for the teaching of design. Yet, as a painter, Darwin did not neglect the importance of the Painting School. He brought in Rodrigo Moynihan as the Professor of Painting, who, in turn, maintained a strong staff. Among its number were Robert Buhler (Peter's tutor), Rodney Burn and Charles Mahoney (both teachers of drawing), John Minton and Ruskin Spear. Indeed, Darwin's own red-damasked office was located in the Painting School at 'Exhibition Road', a wing of the Victoria and Albert Museum that constituted one of the college's numerous sites.

Old Man with Beard 1951 (**15**)

Nevertheless, Peter considers his development at the college to have been affected more by the general atmosphere than by the direct influence of any individual personality, whether teacher or student. For he knew few of his contemporaries at the time and tended to work apart:

> I made a lot of headway in my first year at the College, being left alone, able to make my own decisions. I can't remember anyone actually teaching anything though there was general encouragement. I think in real terms one got more teaching at an earlier level. The whole college ambiance was important, being surrounded by other students more developed than oneself. They worked more imaginatively, not so much from direct life and figurative situations which I opted to do and which really interested me. (Lambirth 1989:14)

One such imaginative painter, Peter Blake, has described the Painting School of a year or two later as 'all more or less life rooms – except for a still-life room and the composition room' (Huxley 1988: 86). Peter Coker would make sure that he reserved a spot for himself in each of these three spaces, so that he could take maximum advantage of what they offered, and make maximum progress. He enjoyed his work and felt in control:

> I was still very interested in working from the model, so I painted in the life rooms, and did portraits and still-lifes. My technical abilities were more mature and the actual pace of the painting developed. (Lambirth 1989:loc cit)

As at St Martin's, models would come to the office each day in the hope of employment:

> You'd still get Italian families who'd arrive with the child and equipment to dress up for 'costume life'. They'd put on the 'Spanish outfit' and the 'Roman outfit', and they loved to do the more difficult poses as a challenge. (Peter Blake in Huxley 1988:86)

John Minton, a popular teacher, would often set up a pose and then work at it alongside the students. Peter's *Nude* (**9**), and his earliest portraits, of an *Old Man with a Cap* (**10**) and an *Old Man with Beard* (**15**), arose out of such conditions. Yet the achievement of these works, and of parallel compositions in still life, is of a distinct kind, one that has been recognised by Frederick Gore:

> In very low-toned still-life and portraits he had served a faithful apprenticeship to Cézanne. His response to Courbet and his ability to make direct use of the French painters whom he admired marked him as one of a first generation of English art students who were able to transcend the Englishness of their art education while still students (Gore 1973)

It is perhaps no wonder then that Peter should have been singled out at the end of his first year and awarded the Royal Scholarship. As he was informed in a letter from the Registrar, J R P Moon:

> the Academic Board have accepted a recommendation that, as a result of the excellent work which you did in your first year here, and particularly in the First Year Examination, you should be awarded the title of Royal Scholar. You will be entitled to use this designation throughout your period at the College.

The scholarship provided, at once, an acknowledgement of Peter's calibre as a painter and a useful financial supplement to the grants he received as an ex-serviceman. Both aspects helped, in turn, to persuade his father that he could make his living as a painter; and this at a time when he was just settling into married life.

On 31 March 1951, Peter had married Vera Crook at St Andrew's, Gidea Park, with Andrew Stowe acting as his best man. In order to do this, he had had to receive permission from Robin Darwin, as Principal of the RCA, a procedure which may now seem old-fashioned. But, it was, in its way, understandable, for marriage certainly affected Peter's development as a painter. Most immediately, it provided a change of home, and gave him his own studio, the space in which he would produce most of the major works of the following decade.

Until his marriage, Peter had remained with his parents in the comfortable environment of Maxwelton. He then accepted his father's offer of the use of his old childhood home, in Moyers Road, Leyton, which had been retained and let. The property was not only economical; placed between central London and rural Essex, it proved convenient both for the couple's places of occupation and for sites that would increasingly inspire Peter's painting. At this time, Vera worked for the Scientific Civil Service, based in Whitehall, and contributed significantly to the household income.

The accommodation at Moyers Road was sufficiently spacious to allow for two spare bedrooms and generous storage space as well as a studio. The studio was allocated the large first floor room which stretched across the front of the house, and could take the double-sized studio easel that Vera had given Peter as a wedding present. The couple furnished the house to the best of their resources, and maintained it with care. As Vera remembers:

> We had no real hardship and certainly no squalor. The house was redecorated and well furnished. All was purchased from Heal's in Tottenham Court Road, the 'mecca' of Modern Scandinavian furniture and ceramics. (Most we still have, including a Gordon Russell sideboard.) We also employed a cleaning lady from the beginning. (VC)

Few of the neighbours had changed since Peter was a boy, and the Cokers behaved, and were generally treated as, model residents. However, one incident, described by Peter, suggests that they could be considered as slightly bohemian:

> All went smoothly until the white cotton covering the lower half of the studio windows, already rather paint splattered, began to disintegrate. These 'curtains' were there to minimise any distraction and to diffuse the light, but obviously had a limited exposure to the sun. I can't say that we had noticed this! However, we had a knock at the door and a complaint from the woman directly opposite (obviously a newcomer between 1937 and 1951!). Not only were we letting down the tone of the road but would we please do something about it – newspaper would be better – as she was expecting relatives from America to stay. (PC)

In summer 1951, Peter and Vera went to Cornwall, to stay in Mevagissey. However, the trip was less a belated honeymoon than a working holiday. Employing a sketchbook for the first time, Peter drew the fishing boats in harbour during the day, and at night went out with the herring fleet. He also painted the china clay pits, close to nearby St Austell. The resulting picture of the pits (**13**) would win him the RCA Sketch Club prize of a book, on his return to the college in the autumn, and he would choose a monograph of Modigliani.

This seemingly quiet coastal interlude actually had a marked influence on Peter's art. His decision to use a sketchbook instigated a regular practice in which drawing became integral to the preparation of painting. While his study of working environments helped him, however temporarily, establish an imaginative theme of his own. However, as Peter has suggested, the progression was gradual:

> During my second year I began to concentrate a lot on still-life, but I also began to feel that the imaginative side of my work was not really developing. I went to Wales, working out of doors in the mining districts. That was partly in preparation for the big painting required from each of us at the end of the second year. After that I started to rely on working from drawings. This was a crucial development. (Lambirth 1989:14)

above left
Mountain Ash, Rhondda 1952 (**19**)

above right
Tonypandy 1952 (**23**)

Peter's trip to Wales, in Easter 1952, occurred as a result of a friendship with Colin Allen, a student in the Department of Graphic Design, who captained the college football team. Peter would work alongside him when he painted in oils and play alongside him each Wednesday afternoon. Invited to stay with Allen's family in Llanelli, he agreed to go in order to avoid the chicken pox which Vera and Nicholas, his six-week-old son, had contracted. Once settled, he took up Allen's suggestion to look at nearby coal mines, and visited a different colliery each day by bus, producing in all about a dozen drawings.

On his return to London, Peter considered using the Welsh drawings as the basis of the required large-scale painting on the set theme of 'And then I saw eleven men'. However, he soon gave up the idea, perhaps affected by Minton's opinion that the drawings were too literal. Nevertheless, he was able to dispose of them with ease, selling to such leading dealers as the Leicester Galleries, the Redfern Gallery and Godfrey Pilkington at the Piccadilly Gallery. He then evolved a new response to the theme, producing a painting of a football crowd at Leyton (**16**). Another painting of the locality, of the nearby railway arches, was completed at about the same time (**17**).

~

From as early as his second year, Peter worked with equal resolve at college and home. For if at college he mastered still life and confronted imaginative themes, then at home he made progress in portraiture. Exploring the portrait form through images of relatives and acquaintances, he drew on the styles of James McNeill Whistler, Walter Sickert and Ruskin Spear – the last a teacher at the RCA – and so strengthened his own technique.

'Tubby' Webb 1951 (**14**)

John Jacobs 1951 (**22**)

And then I saw eleven men 1952 (**16**)
(now the reverse of *Cliff at Etretat* (**35**))

Vera's cousin, Alban Webb, was the first of those who agreed to sit for Peter (**14**). Taking a cue from his nickname, 'Tubby', Peter filled the picture plane with his bulky head, torso and arms, and emphasised each limb and feature through confident outline. In its combination of solidity and lucidity, it contrasts greatly with the slightly later portrait of John Jacobs, a friend of Peter's father (**22**). In this smaller canvas, Peter concentrated on the head of the sitter, painting it with looser, thicker brushstrokes, and setting it against a dark, indeterminate background.

Despite their differences, aspects of these two approaches were synthesised to great effect in Peter's portrait of Geraldine, perhaps the finest work of his student years (**26**). A girl of six or seven years' old, Geraldine was the daughter of the woman who looked after Nicholas while Vera was at work. Though young and inexperienced, she proved to be a surprisingly good model, both patient and sympathetic. As with Tubby Webb, Peter portrayed her in a half-length format, facing the picture plane and looking straight out. He found her face and details of her dress of great interest, and helpful in directing his intention. As in the image of John Jacobs, he used a relaxed handling, though to greater purpose, so that the finished painting demonstrated a development of both modelling and construction.

The discipline with which he worked greatly helped Peter in preparing for his diploma exhibition at the end of the third year. Indeed, he believes it was the presence of *Geraldine*, in particular, at that exhibition which ensured that he received the number of honours that he did; in addition to the diploma, he was awarded a fourth year at the college, was asked to assist Rodrigo Moynihan, the Professor of Painting, and received the commission to paint Percy Hague Jowett, former Principal.

Geraldine c 1952 (**26**)

Yet, while Peter was glad to receive the prestige, he was not so willing to give up possession of his work. He had noticed how, during the final shows of other students, members of staff would appropriate the finest paintings for the college's permanent collection. So he smuggled his own canvases out of the building before anyone else could remove them. Only some years later, in 1963, was it noticed by Carel Weight, then Professor of Painting, that the college held no Cokers!

To help support himself during his fourth year, Peter also applied for a British Institution Scholarship. To be considered, he had to submit a number of pieces, including a portrait and a large drawing from the antique (for which he returned to the Antique Room at St Martin's School of Art). The work of the applicants was then hung at the Royal Academy. Peter was notified in October 1953 that his application had been successful.

During his fourth year, Peter worked mostly at home. He did not rely on the life of the college to give him emotional support, and has since asked rhetorically, 'Why did I need to socialise? I had a very compact family unit' (PC). Nevertheless, the college encouraged his development as an artist, in giving him the opportunities to assist Moynihan and paint Jowett.

In his early forties, Rodrigo Moynihan had emerged as 'among the best-known and most accessible young painters in Britain' (Shone 1988:21). His much admired work on small landscapes, still lifes and figure compositions culminated in the production of two ambitious group portraits, following his arrival at the RCA. The first of those portraits commemorated his arrival, for, entitled *The Teaching Staff of the Painting School at the Royal College of Art, 1949-50* (1951; Tate), it comprised a confident and psychologically penetrating depiction of himself and his colleagues. The second recorded a parallel cultural elite, in being a commission from Penguin publishers to portray its editorial team. This was the most important project that Peter helped Moynihan to execute, while working with him at his private studio in the King's Road.

Peter first assisted Moynihan with a portrait of Sir Rowland Hill, commissioned by the Royal Mail to mark the centenary of Hill's introduction of the Penny Post. As this was a historical portrait, Moynihan worked from documentary material, and asked Peter to lay in the painting from a photograph. Moynihan then redrew and repainted the required adjustments, the finished image emerging through a process of collaboration. In remembering this working relationship, Peter has stated that 'the presence of the master always had a salutary effect'.

He learned even more from Moynihan's methods when together they embarked on preparation for *After the Conference: the Editors of the Penguin Group, 1951*. In order to study the many and varied people who comprised the Penguin editors, Moynihan first filmed them at a drinks party held to celebrate the close of a publishing conference. The particular configurations of people talking together inspired his composition, which would replicate loyalties and sympathies within the group in a way similar to that of the painting of his colleagues at the Royal College. In order to achieve this effect, various negatives from the film were projected onto the large canvas, Peter then drawing around the outlines of the figures. As before, Moynihan would readjust the relationship between the figures until he was satisfied with the outcome, while Peter fixed the outlines with varnish and laid in the foundation of the painting. At the end of this stint as studio assistant, Peter was thanked and told to help himself to some paints and brushes, but he felt too diffident to do so. Perhaps, the lessons that he had received from Moynihan were payment enough.

P H Jowett Esq, CBE c 1952–53 (**28**)

Of an earlier generation than Moynihan, the painter, Percy Hague Jowett, had been Principal of the RCA from 1935 until his retirement in 1947. During that time he had established a workshop in which industrial processes could be followed practically, thus preparing the way, in some respects, for the reforms of Robin Darwin. Peter painted the shy and retiring Jowett in Darwin's studio, where the quiet atmosphere of the sittings was often disturbed by Darwin himself wishing to pass the time of day. It may be this that led Peter, who found Darwin terrifying, to feel dissatisfied with the first of the portraits of Jowett that he completed (**27**). (This he eventually left on the doorstep of Jowett's London home.) So he set about painting a second – definitive – version, which was considered a great success both inside and outside the college (**28**). Shown at the Royal Academy's *Summer Exhibition* in 1954, alongside *Geraldine*, it was singled out for special commendation in many of the reviews. In the following year, the *Summer Exhibition* included Moynihan's *After the Conference*. Ostensibly, his experiences at the Royal College had made Peter a portrait painter ready to follow in the footsteps of Moynihan. But the experiments that he was undertaking in his studio at home were leading his career in quite another direction.

4 1954–57: From Still Life into Landscape

Peter Coker has stated that 'at the Royal College of Art, I couldn't find a theme, but I found one with the butcher's shop' (PC). From his final year at the college (1953-54), he worked apart, determined to use motifs distinct from those conventionally associated with still life, the still life as defined by the oeuvre of Cézanne. So he 'started introducing different, less formal subject matter', such as 'hares and big turbots, and deer's heads and pig's heads' (Lambirth 1989:14), which he laid out on 'an old much used, grained wooden bench' (PC). Some significant drawings were made in the local butcher's shop itself and they, in turn, helped to generate a series of striking large-scale paintings.

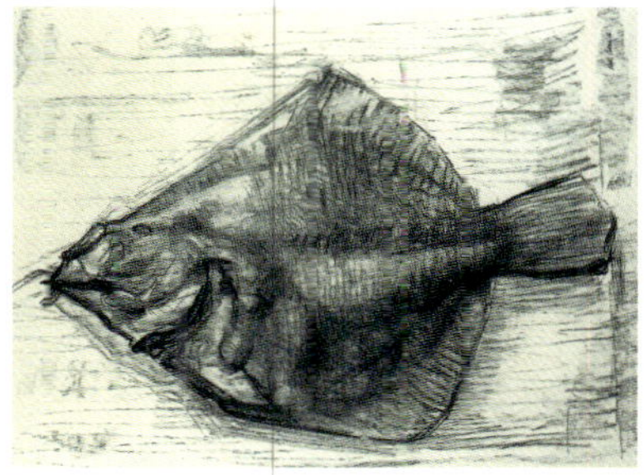

Turbot I 1956

The results were far reaching. During this period, Peter confirmed his mature practice of developing paintings extensively from drawings; those paintings grew into a body of work large and impressive enough to make possible the solo show that launched his career; that body of work demonstrated a gradual evolution from still life to landscape, the subject that would become central to his art.

Thus Peter established himself as a realist artist in the French tradition, at once fiercely independent and of his time. He compensated for his apparent dissociation from Cézanne by revealing a devotion to Courbet, which he cultivated through many visits to France. At the same time, he showed an awareness of – and affinity with – a number of contemporary French painters, most crucially André Dunoyer de Segonzac and Nicolas de Staël. While convinced of his individuality, he slowly discovered that he was considered a protagonist in a realist movement that had both national and international breadth.

Years of artistic training had encouraged Peter to believe in a close relationship between drawing skills and still life subjects. At the Royal College, he had taken 'still-lifes almost as a given, an extension of the drawing classes he had come to consider the necessary foundation of all good painting' (JRT). And when he subsequently saw still life 'in a more informal light, as something to be consciously arranged and constructed' (JRT), drawing remained an essential element in its representation. For in using drawing to explore a novel range of motifs, he both satisfied his formal fascination with line and freed his imagination. As still life had once seemed an extension of drawing, so the purpose of drawing became properly understood through the depiction of still life:

> After College it was a question of trying to learn to use my drawings in relation to my paintings and to find a way of collecting the material, finding a system of notation that I could read when back at the studio. It took me some time to achieve that. (Lambirth 1989:14)

The novel motifs that Peter introduced habitually comprised fish and meat, 'strong subjects chosen initially for their shock value to escape from the neutered subject matter of the conventional Cézannesque still life' (Gore 1973). At first, he concentrated on 'fishes and patterns of newspapers on scrubbed top tables' (Gore 1973), producing drawings in conté, and completing an oil – *Fish and Newspaper* (**29**) – towards the end of 1954. In describing this work, Peter's son, Nicholas Coker, highlighted texture as well as structure, so suggesting that the evolution from drawing to painting was already somewhat successful:

> The table top is parallel to the picture plane and the freedom of design that this facilitates is expressed in a very formal composition. Newspaper being flat in section breaks up the grain of the table. A second viewpoint is introduced to clarify the form of the fish and cup. The emphasis on texture relates as much to developing interest in paint itself as to a desire to keep the eye on the surface. (N Coker 1979)

Fish and Newspaper 1954 (**29**)

The play between space and surface, linearity and tactility, that is essayed here, would be explored more intensively by Peter as he altered his attention, away from fish to the more visceral matter of 'flayed hares, chicken carcasses and sheep's heads' (Gore 1973). He did this unequivocally by making the butcher's shop itself his subject.

Watson's shop was in the Hainault Road, just around the corner from Peter's home in Moyers Road, and 'the butcher was almost a friend, for he had known Peter's family since he started as a boy' (Gore 1973). Peter would spend each Wednesday afternoon on the premises, following 'early closing', in what he would

Drawing for Butcher's Shop I 1955

Butcher's Shop I 1955 (**33**)

depict as 'an enclosed space in which the contours of the carcases and hooks and cleavers are thrown against the back wall' (N Coker 1979). Under such circumstances, he would 'not interrupt normal business' (JRT), could 'draw unselfconsciously' (Gore 1973), and was even allowed to 'ask for specific carcases to draw' (N Coker 1979). The butcher was 'vaguely sympathetic and not too curious' of Peter's activities, becoming really interested only 'when a reproduction appeared in the journal *Meat Marketing*' (Gore 1973).

The drawings resulting from these sessions included those of pigs and sheep made in chalk and conté. However, the only significant compositional studies for *Butcher's Shop I* (pencil, 1955; Tate) and *Butcher's Shop II* (charcoal and chalk, 1955; Victoria and Albert Museum) 'were drawn from memory' in the studio, though Peter did have 'the idea in the shop itself' (N Coker 1979), and '"a few rough sketches developing the idea" would have been done *in situ*' (Vera Coker, in Tate 1988:313).

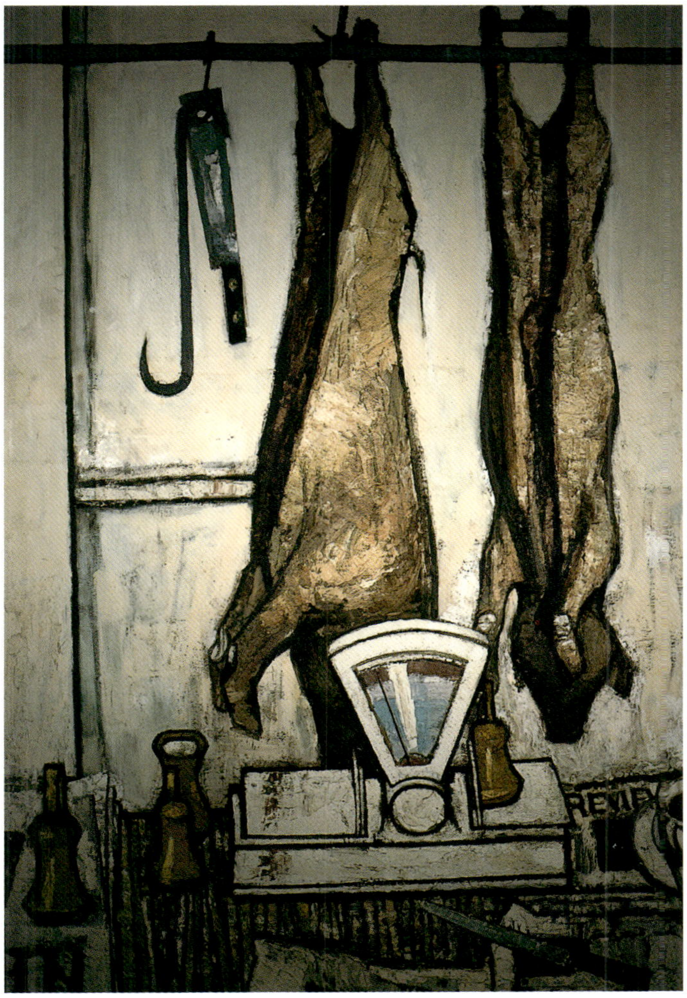

Butcher's Shop II 1955 (**34**)

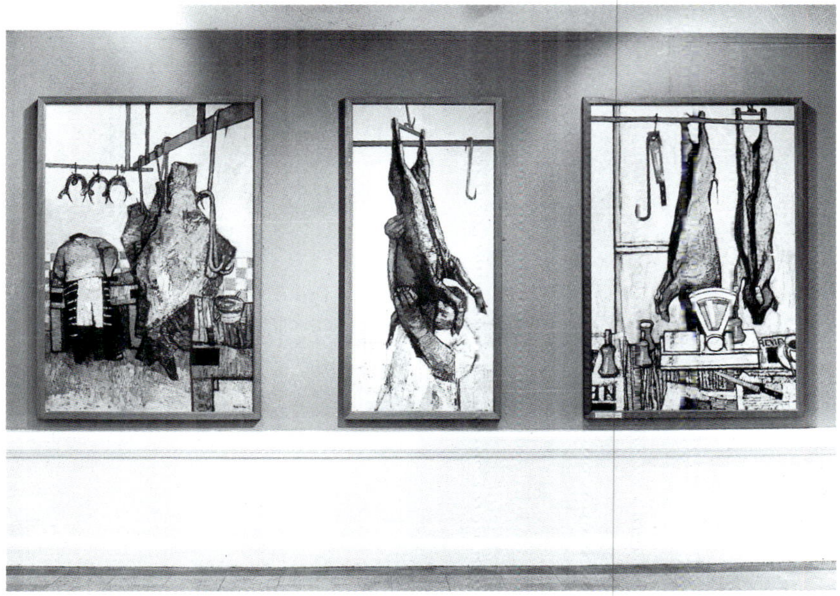

Touring exhibition 1972–73 at Mappin Art Gallery, Sheffield

Peter did not radically alter the composition of *Butcher's Shop I* in developing the image from drawing to painting (**33**). The 'vast slab of meat' (Tate 1988:313) dominates both, in the former as dynamic outline, in the latter as dense pigment. The most significant change between the two resides in the addition 'of a table in the foreground at bottom right, on which lie a knife and a skewered joint of meat…The artist also slightly modified the leaning pose of the butcher' (Tate 1988:313) These changes resulted in creating a shallower, more enclosed space than that of the drawing, Peter's intention, in this and subsequent paintings, being 'to develop an idiom subject to his own perception and innate pictorial logic' (N Coker 1979).

Butcher's Shop I is one of only two works in the sequence actually to 'include the figure of the butcher himself' (Tate 1988:313), the other being *Man Carrying Pig* (**42**). *Butcher's Shop II* (**34**) instead invokes his presence by displaying the stuff of butchery. In the painting, the knives and hooks, the scales and weights sit close to the surface below and beside the heavy hanging bodies of the pigs. Yet such details are inspired less by the desire to depict a trade than the need to construct an image. As Nicholas Coker has explained, objects were 'sought for the composition' of *Butcher's Shop II* 'as it evolved', so that 'the weight on the scale [is] placed so as to make the scale recede' while the 'knife keeps the paper lying flat on the table'. The paintings that derived from such attention are as solid as the subjects they portray:

> The reality of the carcase in *Butcher's Shop I* is in the weight of the form in the thickness of the paint. The visual puns in *Butcher's Shop II* of weights and carcase seem to make that point. (N Coker 1979)

Peter is not the first painter to have signalled a raw approach to figuration through the parallel of animal flesh. But, while the tradition stretches back at least as far as Rembrandt, the work of Chaim Soutine was his most likely inspiration, probably seen, in 1953, at an exhibition at the Galérie Weil, in Paris. Even then, Peter

> might quite easily have come to [the subject] all on his own, without ever having seen a Soutine of raw meat. He would not be the only British painter to observe…the beautiful opalescent tints of uncooked meat – Francis Bacon, for one, had responded, though stylistically in a very different fashion. (JRT)

And in identifying another – religious – aspect of his association of painting to butchery, Frances Spalding implies that Coker may relate to Rembrandt and Soutine more analogically than sequentially:

> In *Man Carrying Pig* the character of the man is submerged in his task as he forms a single unit with the carcass that he carries. The falling movement carries overtones of a Deposition scene and enhances the mood of religious dedication, of the man to his task, of the painter to his subject. (Spalding 1992:10)

Furthermore, whatever his indebtedness, Spalding, for one, is sure that Coker made an original contribution to the tradition, by being, 'the first to show how clean white walls of a butcher's shop could enhance the drama of hung carcasses and metal hooks' (loc cit). In some works, even the wall tiles have been painted out, so exaggerating the contrast between the clinical and visceral.

Sheep Carcasses on Bench 1955 (**45**)

It should be kept in mind, however, that Peter, working in the studio from drawings, only occasionally employed the motif of the butcher's shop in an overt fashion. Most of the compositions from this time close in on a carcass and the surface which supports it to the exclusion of a wider environment. And if they suggest an atmosphere other than that of the studio, it is likely to be one that is domestic, even culinary: garlic and gruyere go with a chicken, grapes accompany a hare. This is also the atmosphere of the ambitious *Table and Chair* (**49**), which, while similar in structure to *Butcher's Shop I*, elicits its power from its homely context; a severed sheep's head lies on a kitchen table, close to the figure of young Nicholas.

It is perhaps unsurprising that Nicholas Coker should have become the most sensitive interpreter of these of his father's paintings. For he sometimes accompanied Peter on his visits to the butcher, as well as sitting for him at home. And his lucid yet intimate examinations might be traced back to the searching gaze that he exhibits in *Table and Chair*. His description of *Sheep Carcasses on Beach* (**45**), a work which he considered 'better than the others', reveals a close familiarity with both the image and its subject. Epitomising the type, it deserves to be quoted in full:

> the form works in a limited space, the carcasses curve from neck over the edge of the bench, up over the belly through to the legs. Yet they sit firmly on a surface flattened to the picture plane. Their rounded irregular shapes lie enclosed in a strange formal composition of horizontals and verticals fronted by a symmetrical bench end. There is no escape into perspective and the eye is kept firmly on the surface by the complexity of the textures. The carcases have a disturbingly human likeness and posture not normally associated with four legged animals. The statement is unequivocally direct. (N Coker 1979)

Peter Coker in his studio 1956

Equally alive to its formal and psychological qualities, Nicholas touched on all the essential tensions that make his father's work so engrossing.

In its early stages, *Table and Chair* included neither Nicholas nor the sheep's head. As its title suggests, it developed from an interest in exploring and enlivening a seemingly inanimate space, furniture becoming characters in a drama. The door at the right was originally balanced with a stretcher to the left, two verticals stressing the vertiginous tilt of table and floor. The chair acted as an intermediary, communicating between stretcher and table, and so setting up a rhythm across the picture surface. At the centre of this composition lay a dead hare. Such was the state of the painting sometime after his seminal trip to France, in Easter 1955, when he first visited Etretat; for, as is recorded in a photograph of Peter in his studio, it was painted concurrently with *Cliff at Etretat* (**35**), preoccupations with meatscape and landscape overlapping.

Nicholas 1956

Table and Chair 1955 (**49**)

Deciding to add a figure, Peter made some sensitive drawings of Nicholas in various positions, including one of him seated at the table, side on to the viewer (sanguine; Fitzwilliam). However, it was through producing two more economical sketches that he fixed both the boy's general pose and the shape of his head (pencil; Tate). The head of the sheep that replaced the hare was similarly, if more simply, essayed in studies before being added to the painting (mixed media; Tate). The outcome created 'a contrast between the live and enquiring face of the child and the impassive face of the dead animal' (Tate 1982:70).

Peter most remembers the changes made to *Table and Chair* for the technical challenges that they imposed, and has instanced them in describing the problems he had in thickening his pigment with white lead:

> I began then to get very conscious of paint surfaces and actually wanted to fill out the paint. For years I had been using solid white lead as a cheap expedient. It's kind of putty made of white lead and oil, used for plumbing joints. I'd put that on the board and paint over it, or sometimes break it down slightly and then add the colour. I tried once or twice on canvas but it just rolled off, I couldn't get it to adhere. In *Table and Chair*, I painted the boy's head so thickly one evening that the whole thing slid off. Later on I used to put in a few grips or tacks or sometimes a bit of butter muslin to secure the white lead to the board. I occasionally used sand to granulate the texture and sometimes it would impact the colour. It dries up the pigment and makes it more controllable. The solidity of those paintings is all to do with recreating nature and making an equivalently solid object. (Lambirth 1989:16)

Such increasing confidence in the handling of pigment was just one of the rudiments that Peter learned from his paintings of meat. Others included 'manipulating the composition', and subsequent familiarity with 'a whole different range of colour values':

> I worked from drawings, finding much greater imaginative freedom, lifting the tables up (inclining the plane by propping up the back legs) creating the impetus for particular distortions … I had to think about how you organize disparate objects, how you place them. Sometimes the placing developed through the process of the painting. (Lambirth, 1989:16)

Though Peter came to appreciate many of the basic concerns of his art through that process of painting, he confronted one important issue through a parallel activity. In fallow periods between painting, during the period 1954-56, he developed a facility for designing printed textiles. These he offered with some success to fabric manufacturers, such as Ascher; printing warehouses, such as Bernard Ashley and Berne Silks; and the French textile printer, Garique. He was encouraged in this endeavour by Annie Frankel, a fashion designer whose daughter, Gerda Flöckinger, was a student at St Martin's School of Art (and has since become a successful jewellery designer). Frankel was a friend of Garique, and shared with him and Peter a taste for the French realists.

As a textile designer, Peter experimented with a prodigious range of materials and techniques; these included bleaching, calligraphic writing, collage, combing, dyeing, marbling, monotype printing, oil painting and wax rubbing. Trials were often made on a large scale, the most interesting area being isolated and cut out for use as the final pattern. Peter produced 'a quantity of designs in a very short time and for me in a quite uninhibited way' so that he 'enjoyed the new found freedom' (see Mayor 1991) and was given 'a release from my over-serious nature' (see Lambirth 1991).

However, the variety of texture and subtlety of colour that characterise his textiles often revealed kinship with his painting, and the medium informed his approach to his art. As he has stated, 'these designs I now realise were my own way at that time of attempting to resolve the Abstract/Figurative conflict' (see Mayor 1991). More than provide a satisfying outlet for pure decoration, they allowed him to rehearse the integration of figure and ground that he so successfully achieved in the major oils.

illustrated opposite page
Textile designs 1954–56

While Peter tended to engage practically with theoretical issues, working them through alone in his studio, he also experienced the ideas and achievements of others, by reading, visiting exhibitions and travelling.

He may have dissociated himself from aspects of the contemporary art world, but he was aware of, and stimulated by, a range of significant painters and writers, and by their own sources of inspiration. The progress of his work was mirrored by the progress of his taste, his identity as a realist emerging essentially from within a context of Francophilia.

From his first visit to Paris, in 1949, Peter established a profound love of both French art and the land that had engendered it. Through the 1950s, he returned to the city on several occasions, and also began to explore coastal and rural areas. However, a more general renewal of interest in French art in Britain, following the Second World War, made it possible for him to be equally stimulated by works shown in London.

This was certainly true of Gustave Courbet, the first and most important of the artists to have influenced Peter. The knowledge that he gained from initial encounters with his images - in Paris museums, and through an article in the *Saturday Evening Post* - may have been amply supplemented by visits to London exhibitions. For Courbet was not only represented in such mixed shows as *Oeuvres Choisies*, mounted at the Hanover Gallery in 1950, but was the subject of 'a major survey of thirty-seven works' held in 1953 at the Marlborough Gallery (Hyman 2001:73). And the wider reaction to this retrospective reveals that Peter was not alone in his admiration for this nineteenth-century painter. Indeed, James Hyman has written that:

> In Britain Courbet's status for champions of social and Socialist Realism was comparable to that of Cézanne for those of Modernist abstraction and Modernist realism (loc cit).

Yet Peter's response to Courbet was intensely personal, and unusually advanced and thorough. He had discovered the artist for himself while still a student, soon identified closely with his approach, and – as described below – would travel in order to work from some of his favourite motifs.

Peter Coker 1955

Even before he made the first of such pilgrimages, in 1955, Peter drew on fundamental elements of Courbet's mastery in producing his 'butcher's shop' still lifes. In the words of Nicholas Coker, 'the authority and weight of the images is resonant of Courbet as is the scale of the pictures' (1979). That Courbet imbued a range of subjects with such solidity also gave Peter a precedent in his transition from meatscape to landscape, one paralleling the other, each equally emphasising the paint surface.

Another precedent for such a parallel – of still life and landscape – was suggested by Frederick Gore, when he wrote that Peter saw, and expressed,'the edge of the vertical table top as a reminder of the horizon line used by Van Gogh in his Arles subjects' (Gore 1973). Peter would have had the opportunity to examine those 'Arles subjects' of Vincent Van Gogh – an honorary Frenchman – both in Parisian collections and in London, in 1951, at a retrospective mounted at the Tate Gallery. Like Courbet, Van Gogh was a figure of the moment, influencing British artists both directly and indirectly, through contemporary French realists. However, Gore's statement implies that Peter once again responded to the artist in a personal way, drawing as much on Van Gogh's approach to composition as on his 'strong drawing, saturated colour and bold handling of paint' (Hyman 2001:76).

Paul Cézanne seemed to make a more equivocal contribution to the formation of Coker's art than did Courbet and Van Gogh. Coker may have considered his work 'very bold', when he first saw it in Paris (PC); but the fact that he 'served a faithful apprenticeship to Cézanne…in very low-toned still-life and portraits' (Gore 1973), suggests that his example was almost too easily absorbed, and indeed Cézanne became a talisman to many contemporary British painters. Peter needed to dissociate himself from the conventional still life subjects and approaches so often denoted by the name of Cézanne, as much to understand the artist for himself as to establish his own creative personality. And his immediate allegiance to Courbet did not discount an increasing appreciation of Cézanne. So he would comment later in his career that 'one is still learning; sometimes it seems to me I haven't even started, especially when I look at Cézanne or late Degas' (Lambirth 1989:16). The respective association of Courbet with 'social realism' and Cézanne with 'Modernist realism' by which Hyman characterises British art of the post-war period was alien to Coker. His independent interpretation of realism made possible an absorption and synthesis of the two figures.

Peter may have gained only gradual awareness of the realist debate that would lead, at the time of his debut show, in 1956, to his being tarred with the brush of 'the Kitchen Sink School'. Nevertheless, he was quick to acquaint himself with various French exponents of contemporary realist painting. For him, this was a loose designation that included Maurice de Vlaminck and André Dunoyer de Segonzac, two senior painters who provided a link for the younger generation to the great tradition – or traditions – represented by Courbet and Cézanne.

In 1951, the Royal Academy mounted an important exhibition which rehearsed the significance of the Ecôle de Paris through the twentieth century. If the inclusion of work by Vlaminck and Segonzac demonstrated their general importance, it also allowed Peter an opportunity to remind himself of their particular value to him. So Vlaminck was perhaps the most 'modern' of the painters he then admired, well known for the fierce palette of his Fauve period, with an increasing reputation as a realist, as promoted by leading dealers, the Hanover Gallery and Arthur Tooth & Sons. However, Segonzac would have the more profound effect on Peter, who coupled him as an inspiration with Nicolas de Staël, by identifying him as 'a realistic de Staël', as Staël, in turn, would be identified as 'the realist among abstract painters' (Gore 1973).

Other French realists, contemporary to Staël, had an influence on Peter that may have been more immediate but was also more ephemeral. Bernard Lorjou, André Minaux and Paul Rebeyrolle were among those who pioneered painting with a palette knife in thick slabs. As such they were taken up in Britain – by the Arts Council, the Institute of Contemporary Arts and a number of dealers – for inclusion in realist showcases. But if their work bore superficial similarities to that of Peter in his early phase, they did not provoke the same sustained enthusiasm as Segonzac and Staël.

Peter had first encountered Segonzac's work at the Tate Gallery, which possessed a varied group of four paintings. He was particularly struck by the *La Ferme dans la Terre* (1923), a landscape representative of a new phase in the Frenchman's art, more lyrically naturalistic than his earlier geometricism. According to Nicholas Coker:

> he admired…the immediacy of the response inherent in it and the simplicity of treatment, paint vigorously applied with a knife, allowing a direct statement to be made. (N Coker 1979)

The primary qualities that he sought to embody in his own art were here seen freshly mastered not by a young contemporary but by an established figure, and demonstrated through landscape, the subject to which he was gravitating. The trajectory of Segonzac's career was such that his mature work seemed to Peter to achieve a satisfying synthesis of the conceptual and the visual, and to be truly painterly in both structure and surface.

Peter has stated that 'de Staël had an enormous influence on the lot of us' (Lambirth 1989:16), his intense works being regularly displayed at such leading dealers as Arthur Tooth and the Matthiesen Gallery. He embodied a set of painterly values that were similar to, yet distinct from, those of Segonzac, in which saturated colour played a more essential role in the articulation of structure and surface. For Peter, his example offered a way of breaking free from 'three dimensional space' by lifting 'things up vertically and [placing] them like a series of playing cards, thus creating the space on a vertical plane' (loc cit). When the thick slabs of pigment were spread with a palette knife to effect this formal device, 'fragments of underlying colour' showed through (Spalding 1992). The rich layering of such marks contributed to a construction of pictorial space that was physical rather than illusionistic, an insight Peter would make use of in many of his paintings.

So an ideal lineage could be traced for Peter from Courbet, who inspired the earliest of Segonzac's exhibited works, through Segonzac and Staël. Peter certainly scrutinised the works of these artists, when the opportunity arose, and was attentive to their strengths, as can be seen in the gestures that he attempted and achieved in his own painting. But he also went further, by rehearsing the context in which they had developed, in his reading and travel. Realism, as practised by Peter, was in every way an experiential art.

In the early 1950s, Peter began to read a number of texts intrinsic to the French aesthetic tradition. The first of these included translations of Eugène Delacroix's journals and André Malraux's *Les Voix de Silence* (both published in 1953). However, one work by the English writer, George Moore, proved equally inspiring in its articulation of an episode of the tradition. An exponent of Naturalism in fiction and a champion of Impressionism in painting, Moore set his short story, 'Henrietta Marr' (first published in the collection, *In Single Strictness*, in 1922), in the artistic community established in Barbizon. For Peter, the most memorable element was the phrase 'the forest is the studio' used by the character, Elsie Lawrence, and summing up the Naturalist, or Realist, credo. Though he would always distinguish between the forest and the studio in his own practice, Moore's elision of the two seemed sufficiently seductive for him to experience the atmosphere of Barbizon at first hand.

So in Easter 1955, Peter began to explore areas of France outside of Paris. Travelling alone, by train and bus, he visited Barbizon to the south-east of the capital, and then headed north to Etretat, on the Normandy coast. While Barbizon and Etretat had been popular with painters since the Romantic era, Courbet was alone among Realists of the mid nineteenth century in working extensively at each site. Peter, in turn, drew inspiration from the two for his first major statements as a landscape painter.

Barbizon had developed as an artistic centre because of its proximity to the forest of Fontainebleau, the forest being a manifestation of nature in essence, and so key to the development of naturalism in painting. Consider Corot, Rousseau, Monet. The arboreal motif would gradually work its power on Peter, so that he would produce entire series of forests through the late 1950s and early 60s; but the drawings that he made in Fontainebleau were exhibited as ends in themselves rather than as studies for paintings. Other – less obvious, more cultivated – aspects of the area had more immediate potential: farmland near Chailly to the north of Barbizon, and allotments and orchards in the village itself.

Cliff at Etretat 1955 (**35**)

Cliffs near Etretat 1955 (**35**)

Etretat attracted artists by its magnificent setting, a sweeping bay terminating at each end in high cliffs eroding into arches. The meeting of vertical rock face and the horizontals of beach and sea not only offered many interesting views but suggested a wealth of strong compositions. Yet the village was relatively unknown when Peter first arrived there, and still essentially a fishing community; only later would it develop into a resort.

Peter stayed at Le Corsaire, taking advantage of the hotel's central position facing the sea. On the first full day, he set out to draw under the cliffs with paper clipped to a piece of hardboard. But, eager to confront the elements directly, he failed to notice the sign that warned against falling rock. A little later, he was surprised when the elements confronted *him*, a piece of rock only just missing him and splitting both drawing and board. For many years, these items would be produced as chief exhibits of his ordeal, but also as evidence of how close to nature his work had brought him. J M W Turner lashed to a mast comes to mind.

The Rock, Etretat 1955 (**44**)

During this visit, Peter was observed by the owner of Le Corsaire sitting on the beach making a large drawing of a rock. He asked him to design a flag for the hotel, and Peter agreed to do something on returning to England. What resulted was a skull and crossbones in linocut printed in white on black cotton. On his second visit to the hotel, in the summer of the same year, Peter was thanked and given 'special rates'. This second trip was similar to the first, for it was again made alone and on public transport, and though Fécamp was added to the itinerary, Peter did not tarry there being eager to get on to Etretat.

The purpose and proof of Peter's travels in France reside in the drawings that he made. These tend to comprise individual sheets rather than sketchbook studies, and – as with preparation for the 'butcher's shop' paintings – are few in number, only one or two relating to each composition. Mostly in conté, they are at once spare and highly informative, recording the salient details in both image and written note. For, back in the studio, they would be instrumental in aiding the recreation of the experience of landscape. And while the paintings added weight, texture and colour to outline, they retained the economy of drawing by emphasising particular elements and establishing a certain mood.

So, in taking up the conté drawing of an allotment to paint *Landscape at Barbizon* (**40**), Peter focussed on the wooden stakes that populate its foreground. He increased their dominant verticality, through tone and density, and created a foil in the wide horizontal of a wall bisecting the picture space. The result is a dynamic grid made out of the elements of space yet revelling in surface.

A much greater transformation occurred between *Apple Tree* (**32**) and the two pencil drawings on which it is based. In each drawing, Peter singled out a complete tree and set it high on the paper against a context of building or orchard, so achieving a sense of balance and distance. But in the painting, a more skeletal, if fruiting, tree appears over the top of a wall which counters space and, in flatness and texture, accentuates the picture plane. Monumental in scale and effect, it seems to parallel the images of the butcher's shop.

Allotment 1955

Landscape at Barbizon 1955 (**40**)

Apple Tree, *Barbizon* 1955

Apple Tree 1955 (**32**)

La Plaine de Chailly (**41**) differs in actually increasing the sense of space delineated in its preparatory drawing in conté. The strip of farm buildings is placed high on the canvas, against a screen of trees, so that most of the area is give over to the fields. Yet the effect is not airy but sombre, a lowering sky appearing to reflect the furrowed soil itself. In its extreme earthiness it is a fitting homage to Segonzac's *La Ferme dans la Terre*, and a worthy successor to the visceral character of Peter's own meatscapes. It has remained a favourite among his works.

These 'Barbizon' paintings comprise a transitional phase from still life to pure landscape, in their suggestion of human activity. Those of Etretat replace culture with nature more comprehensively, while discovering in the cliff face an ideal metaphor for the painter's surface.

Barbizon
study for *La Plaine de Chailly* 1955

La Plaine de Chailly 1955 (**41**)

Through the autumn of 1955, Peter worked with great energy and efficiency, as he balanced painting with teaching, in various part-time positions. While still studying at the Royal College of Art, in 1954, Peter had returned to St Martin's School to ask the principal, Morss, if he could be found some teaching to help ends meet. The initial response was negative, his being told that the school never employed its former students. Nevertheless, he went back and asked again. His persistence paid off, for he was sent to Frederick Gore, the Head of Painting, who immediately found him an evening a week, teaching General Drawing in the Antique Room, as successor to John Napper. By early in 1955 he had began to teach Life Painting on two days each week. He also taught Painting on Saturday mornings at Ealing School of Art, and the History of Art and Architecture for one day a week at Haberdasher Aske's School, Hampstead, though he found so many commitments too time consuming, and kept up only that at St Martin's for any length.

Gore has rehearsed Peter's approach to teaching, which in obvious ways reflected his practice:

> For him painting starts with the study of exterior reality and to be eloquent must preserve a balance of various means – drawing, colour, texture, mass, volume and so on … He prefers to teach in terms of the craft and not ideas. (Gore 1973)

Though Peter taught more from necessity than vocation, his renewed association with St Martin's would surely have reminded him that tuition had a value for both teacher and student. It was at St Martin's that he had received the best of his formal training, under Pitchforth and Stroudley; so, in taking on their role, he could honour them and give something back. And as a young artist, experienced but not quite established, he could act as an exemplar to the ensuing generation.

While teaching at St Martin's, Peter often visited Zwemmer's Bookshop, on the Charing Cross Road and its associated gallery, at 26 Litchfield Street. One day he got into conversation with Michael Chase, the gallery's manager, and, mentioning his work, was invited to bring in some photographs. As a result, he was offered a solo show for the following January. Though the gallery had opened in the 1920s, and had shown examples of many a famous artist, Peter was its first significant 'discovery'. Furthermore, the owner, Anton Zwemmer, 'although more than twice Coker's age … seems to have warmed more to him than to

left
Michael Chase and Peter Coker outside the Zwemmer Gallery 1956

right
Peter Coker hanging *Butcher's Shop II*, Zwemmer Gallery 1956

most other young artists coming through the gallery' (Halliday 1991:238). Peter was given the freedom both to decide on the choice of pictures and to arrange their hanging; eighteen paintings, thirteen drawings and a lithograph made it to the walls. A period of almost two years of intense exploration and development was about to come to fruition, as his oeuvre was revealed to the public, and he emerged properly on the artistic scene.

The most significant and influential review of Peter Coker's first solo show was not necessarily the most perceptive. For John Berger, writing 'The Battle' in the *New Statesman* (21.1.56), treated Coker as just one exponent of the supposed international movement of Social Realism. Admittedly Berger approved of this movement, considering it to be a positive form of protest in opposition to 'the pathological self-deception' of such American Abstract Expressionists as Jackson Pollock and Willem de Kooning. Yet his approach was as detrimental to the reputation of the artists concerned as that of David Sylvester. Two years earlier, Sylvester had coined the term 'Kitchen Sink' (*Encounter*, 12.54) in order to dismiss those painters of domestic clutter who Berger championed; for he preferred a Modernist Realism practised by Francis Bacon and others of 'the School of London'. Ironically, the opposing groups were both represented by Helen Lessore of the Beaux-Arts Gallery. (For further details of the intellectual positions of Berger and Sylvester, see Hyman 2001:passim.)

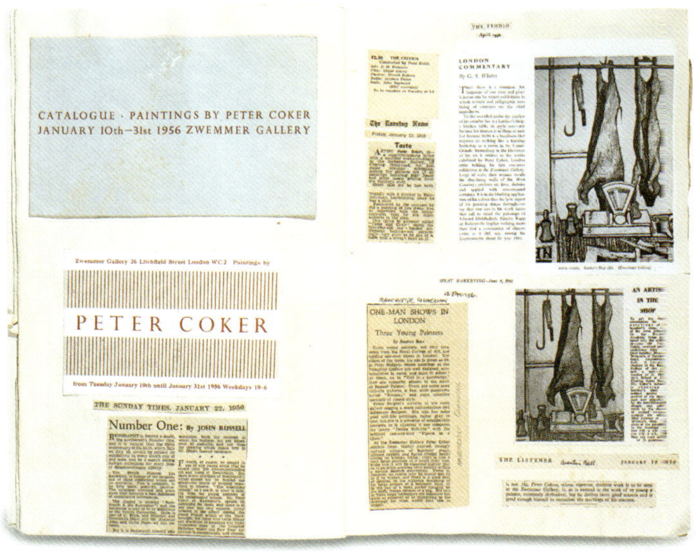

From the first of Peter Coker's scarapbooks: items relating to the Zwemmer Gallery exhibition 1956

Other critics tended to take their cue from Berger, interpreting the work of Coker through the application of a somewhat simplistic Social Realist context. This resulted in frequent comparisons with Derrick Greaves (ex RCA) and other Kitchen Sink painters and, perhaps more pertinently, with such French contemporaries as Paul Rebeyrolle.

Possibly the most searching and prescient examination of the show appeared not in print, but on the radio, in the highly popular arts review, *The Critics*, broadcast on the BBC Home Service each Sunday lunchtime. Its designated art critic, J M Richards, did begin by making a comparison between Coker and Jack Smith, Coker's contemporary at St Martin's and the RCA, and also a confrère of Greaves; but he soon considered the artist as an individual with his own preoccupations and passions:

> Surely a painter has the right … to use the raw material from which he gets stimulus and I think a good deal of the quality in Peter Coker's paintings is certain discoveries he's made, such as the rather remarkable exciting shapes that a skinned hare produced when it's laid out on a table and so on. They're discoveries of his own and he's been excited by them and his paintings do convey some of that sense of excitement.

Michael Chase and Peter Coker, Zwemmer Gallery 1956

Prompted by the admission of Paul Dehn, the Chairman of the programme, that he had purchased Coker's *La Plaine de Chailly*, the panel then opened up their discussion to consider the artist's work as a whole, 'the landscapes and the cliffscapes and the seascapes' as well as what Dehn called the 'meatscapes'. This approach was an accurate reflection of both Coker's then current practice of working simultaneously in various genres, and his increasing concentration on landscape. Similarly astute was the comment by Richards that 'he chose exactly the same cliffs that Courbet painted': for this took seriously his ambitions as a landscape painter and showed understanding of a possible wish to learn from and measure himself against exemplars of a greater realist tradition.

Some of the more visceral works from the Zwemmer show reappeared in further exhibitions during 1956, and were used to endorse the construction of Coker as Social Realist. Unsurprisingly Berger included *Man Carrying Pig* (painting) and *Dead Chicken on Table* (drawing) in *Looking Forward*.

For this exhibition, held at the South London Art Gallery, was a form of practical polemic in favour of the work of young British realist painters. However, the hanging committee of the *Summer Exhibition* at the Royal Academy also chose to treat Coker's submissions as symptomatic of a native realist movement. For it hung the two versions of the *Butcher's Shop* and *Sheep Carcasses on Bench* alongside the work of John Bratby and Edward Middleditch (with Greaves and Smith the core of the Kitchen Sink School). This encouraged some critics to treat these painters en masse, and respond to them as revolutionaries unparalleled in the history of the Royal Academy since the Pre-Raphaelite Brotherhood. T W Earp, writing in the *Daily Telegraph and Morning Post* (5.5.56), went so far as to say that 'Galleries 7 and 8 have become a stamping ground for art's Teddy-boys', and that Coker's *Butcher's Shop* was an 'average and repulsive example' of 'this pictorial anarchy'! But others took Social Realism for granted as an acceptable, even commercial, style, and were more interested in distinguishing the qualities of particular practitioners. Benedict Nicolson, reviewing 'Looking Forward' in the *New Statesman and Nation* (21.4.56), singled out Coker as an 'excellent painter' because:

> He senses the weight of the meat, and which way the bones go, and whether a hook can carry the carcass in the fleshy part – all this inside knowledge is relevant to the kind of monumental picture that he paints. For it is not enough nowadays just to see, you have to know. He is at ease with massive shapes, and … would make a fine fresco painter if he were ever given the chance.

Nicolson seemed to see in Coker an artist who could actually reconcile the past and present of painting: an exponent of the large format who, through a knowledge of his subject, transforms image into object.

The critical excitement – and profits – generated by his debut, led the Zwemmer Gallery to offer Peter a follow-up. A second exhibition tends to be less traumatic an experience than a second novel, for though it is as much a measure of staying power, it does not need to impress by its novelty. Peter's second exhibition, held in autumn 1957, might have seemed to emphasise his dissociation from the Kitchen Sink School, but its concentration on landscape was not new, and had already been noticed as intrinsic to his art by the more perceptive observer. His latest paintings showed him sustaining and expanding a strand in his work that was at once traditional and original: Etretat led to Audierne, Barbizon to the New Forest. If they revealed a new approach, it was because Peter 'didn't really wake up to space until the time of the first Zwemmer show' (PC). However, while an exploration of space led him to treat landscape as more separate from still life, it actually enriched his initial passion for paint as a physical substance that animates a surface.

In the Easter of 1956, Peter made a third trip along the French coast, alone and by public transport. From Etretat, in Normandy, where he again stayed at Le Corsaire, he travelled to Quimper, in western Brittany. He was led there by 'a photograph I saw in a book on Medieval France of the 11th Century Romanesque Church of Notre Dame de Locmaria that caught my attention and stimulated my interest' (Tate 1986:128). However, on arriving, he found that its bastion-like form and its slate spires were at the same time more challenging and less interesting than they had appeared in print. 'So I moved to the coast, making notes and drawings of the lighthouse, coastal fields, stonewalls, cabbage plots and close-ups of gorse and bracken bushes' (loc cit). This list, which almost itemises the contents of the second Zwemmer exhibition, indicates why Peter considered it a 'very happy and productive time for me', and why 'as a family we visited Audierne on a number of occasions afterwards with great enthusiasm' (loc cit). Moreover, Peter's discovery of Audierne coincided with his initial use of regular sketchbooks, so that he could make those 'notes and drawings' more quickly and effortlessly than on large sheets of paper. The first two sketchbooks (including one held by the British Museum (**SB1**)) date from this time, and contain the earliest studies for such major paintings as *Gorse Bush* (**60**) and *Lighthouse, Audierne* (**62**).

Though Peter did not make any other significant journeys during 1956, he soon learned to drive, passing his test on the first attempt early in 1957, and immediately buying a secondhand green Ford Escort. From that time all painting trips were made by car. His first motor trip took place that Easter, when he went, with Vera and Nicholas, to stay with an aunt of Vera who lived in the New Forest, in Hampshire. Attracted by the trees, he began to make drawings, resorting to the kind of large loose sheets he had used at Barbizon. Then, in the summer, he made his first motor journey abroad, taking Vera and Nicholas to stay at Le Corsaire in Etretat and L'Hotel de la Plage in Audierne; the latter has been likened by Vera to the establishment in Jacques Tati's film, *Monsieur Hulot's Holiday*. As the date of his second show neared, Peter did some painting on site.

Forest II 1957 (**59**)

The paintings included in Peter's second solo exhibition impress by their diversity, a diversity deriving in part from the variety of terrain, but as much from the variety of treatment. For, while Peter had earlier drawn parallels between the distinct genres of landscape and still life, he increasingly emphasised differences within landscape itself, each new change of subject signalling a modification in style. So the coasts of Normandy and Brittany called for the use of distinct palettes and techniques, as did the foliage of Brittany and the woodland of Hampshire.

The Wave 1956 (**52**)

Lighthouse, Audierne 1957 (**62**)

It is therefore not surprising that *The Wave* (**52**) and *Waves and Rock* (**55**) should remain close in character to the earlier paintings of Etretat. Land and sea are again represented, respectively, in terms of solidity and power. Cliff and beach have a literal density, slabs of pigment recreating the geology from rock face to pebble; broader, more dynamic strokes enact the movement of the breakers. Yet the two not only meet – in depicting water on the shore – but are united in both their stress on pictorial surface and their deceptively restricted range of colour.

In the contemporary depictions of Audierne, colour is heightened and form simplified. Pigment is as thickly applied, but with fewer broken strokes and less detail. And where outlines exist – as around the stones in *White Buoys, Audierne* (**56**) – they are formed through the placing of a light patch over a dark. The results sustain a sense of visual drama, most notably in *Lighthouse, Audierne*, in which strong diagonals lead the eye to the beacon set against a brooding slate grey sky. Such emotional intensity is grounded in secure technique, and it still greatly pleases Peter that – by scraping with tin and blending – he so successfully unified the tone and treatment of the sky on either side of the lighthouse.

Tree and Hedge I 1956 (**50**)

Tree and Hedge II 1956 (**51**)

Gorse Bush 1957 (**60**)

Study for *Tree and Hedge I* 1956

Peter's approach to inland topographies demonstrates a greater interest in adopting the appropriate manner for the particular subject than in strict stylistic development; for, while the two versions of *Tree and Hedge* (both 1956) (**50**, **51**) introduce a new fluidity, *Bracken and Gorse, Audierne* (**57**) as well as *Gorse Bush* (**60**) (both 1957) 'retains much of the characteristics of the Butcher Shop paintings of 1955' (PC in Tate 1986:128). Of course, the first two *Forest* paintings (both 1957) (**58**, **59**) look both forward and back, for they originate in drawings made in Barbizon and presage a major preoccupation of the next few years.

If the spirit of Courbet presided at Etretat, and even in the New Forest, then at Audierne it was that of Staël. Peter invoked his presence through both his general handling of paint and his choice of the lighthouse motif. Not only had Staël himself painted lighthouses, but he had worked in the one at Antibes, and had committed suicide by thrown himself from it on 16 March 1955. His death had been announced just before Peter set off on his first French sojourn, and sparked a series of British memorials through the following year which culminated, in summer 1956, in a retrospective at the Whitechapel Gallery.

Nicholas Sleeping c 1956

Vera c 1956

Though Peter initially felt incredulous at the artist's violent end, he then took up the unprecedented opportunity to examine his work in depth, the paintings at Audierne being the result. Yet when Peter attempted to extend this act of homage, by visiting the South of France, in summer 1958, his reaction was almost entirely negative. The extensive motor tour, made with Vera and Nicholas, first took in Northern Italy, and especially Venice, before heading for the French border. Arles as well as Antibes was included on the itinerary that followed, for at its Musée Réattu a further Staël retrospective was in progress. Such delights could prove no compensation for Peter, for he found the harsh light and bright colour alien to his sensibility. He turned away from France and, for the next seven years, explored landscapes nearer home.

Bracken and Gorse, Audierne 1957 (**57**)

The artist wrote to the Tate Gallery about *Gorse Bush* (**60**) on 19 May 1986:

'*The Gorse Bush, Audierne* was one of a number of paintings I made from drawings after visiting Audierne in 1957 which were all exhibited in my second one man exhibition at the Zwemmer Gallery, 26 Lichfield Street, London in 1957 (the gallery was in the side street next to Zwemmer's Bookshop in Charing Cross Road).

During the mid 50s I visited France regularly (the gaps between part-time teaching at St Martin's School of Art allowing). Audierne resulted from a visit to Quimper during Easter 1957. Why Quimper? It was a photograph I saw in a book on Medieval France of the 11th Century Romanesque Church of Notre Dame De Locmaria that caught my attention and stimulated my interest. Quimper was not to my liking, so I moved to the coast, making notes and drawings of the lighthouse, the sea, coastal fields, stonewalls, cabbage plots and close-ups of gorse and bracken bushes. Everything happened at eye level, the fields were separated from the shore by stone walls some four feet above the water line. It was a very happy and productive time for me and as a family we visited Audierne on a number of occasions afterwards with great enthusiasm.

The Gorse Bush was a companion work to the *Bracken and Gorse* purchased by the Friends of Birmingham City Art Gallery in 1957, which Mr Zwemmer had purchased from me earlier in the year. I will remember Dr Mary Woodall and the Friends visiting my studio in Leytonstone and not being able to decide between the *Bracken and Gorse* and *Sheep Carcasses on a Bench* 1955 (now my Diploma Work at the RA) finally choosing *Bracken and Gorse* for its companionability. One of the working drawings for *The Gorse Bush* was purchased from the Magdalene Street Gallery, Cambridge at the exhibition of drawings of mine in 1968 by Malcolm Cormack the then Keeper of Paintings and Drawings at the Fitzwilliam Museum.

The Gorse Bush retains much of the characteristics of the Butcher Shop paintings of 1955. Board being used as a support allowing the paint to stand on the surface, thick paint modelling the form and solid white lead paste the main material applied to the colour. I had thought to remove three or four inches from the right side of the wall, to enclose the bush more, decided against it but failed to remove the pencil line from the painting where I intended to cut the board. The encrusted textured surfaces of the table tops and benches of previous years found their expression in the tangled mass of twigs and branches, trees and hedges, rocks and sea. Thirteen paintings and twelve drawings were exhibited in my second one man show at Zwemmer's in October – November 1957, two thirds were Breton subjects, the exhibition was well received by the critics who in the main were relieved that the angry young painter of the butcher's shops had now passed on to less provocative subjects.'

Tate Gallery Illustrated Catalogue of Acquisitions 1984-1986: 128

East Anglia

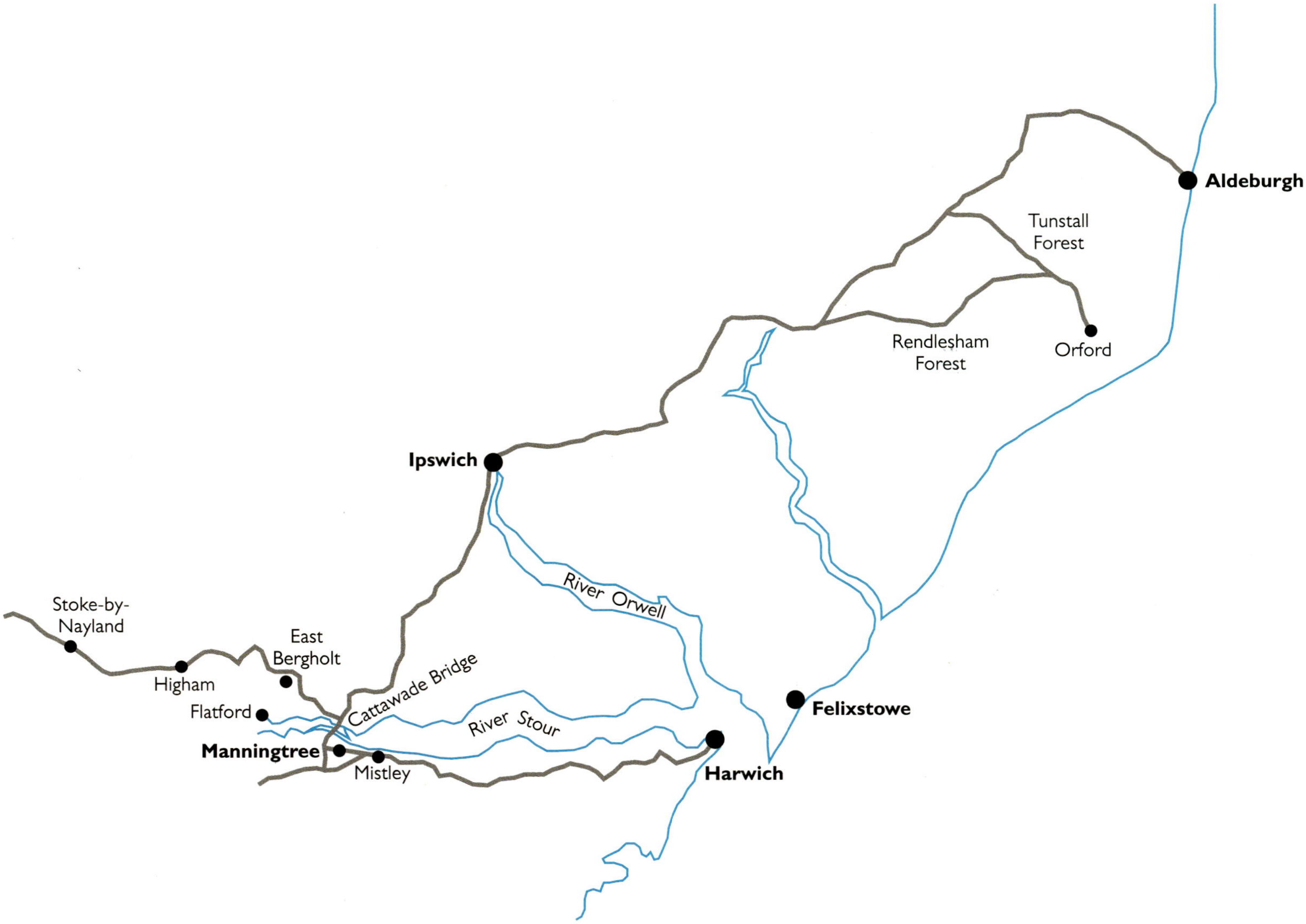
Aldeburgh
Tunstall
Forest
Rendlesham
Forest
Orford
Ipswich
River Orwell
Stoke-by-
Nayland
East
Bergholt
Cattawade Bridge
Higham
Flatford
River Stour
Manningtree
Mistley
Felixstowe
Harwich

5 1957–1970: An East Anglian Artist

From the late 1950s, as Peter focussed on native landscape, he began to be re-presented as an East Anglian artist. To a great extent this was only proper, for though born in London, he had moved to Leyton as a baby, and thence to Havering, in the Essex countryside. One of his first student landscapes was painted at Havering, from his bedroom window. During early married life he again lived in his Leyton home, and explored the immediate landscape, especially Epping Forest. Then, rehearsing his earlier trajectory, he began to teach at Colchester School of Art, and soon moved out to Mistley, on the borders of Essex and Suffolk, where he continues to live. A sense of north Essex as home was enhanced by friendships with neighbouring artists: Edward Bawden, John Nash and John O'Connor. Local exhibitions followed, most notably at the Minories, in Colchester, and local critics began to champion his work.

While he never relinquished his devotion to France, or its artistic tradition, Peter broadened his understanding of realism by finding vernacular parallels in both landscapes and landscape painters. His proximity to what is now known as 'Constable Country' was particularly pertinent. This development would be echoed a decade later, when painting trips to other parts of Britain encouraged his study of Turner. These two phases coincided with his election to the Royal Academy, in 1965 as an Associate, and seven years later as a full Academician. His recognition by this institution, so central to the then artistic establishment, helped place him in a line from those earlier Academicians, Constable and Turner, and thus confirmed his status not only as an East Anglian artist but as a truly English landscape painter.

Epping – situated north of Leyton – is one of Europe's most ancient forests, and one of Britain's largest. Yet, despite its proximity to London, it has never attracted major painters to the same degree as Fontainebleau. That Peter should explore it, as part of his continuing preoccupation with the motif of woodland, was thus a typically individual action. Indeed, he might be characterised as reviving the spirit of Barbizon on his own doorstep, and so sustaining the realist project as he returned to work closer to home.

Epping 1958

As at Barbizon, and in the New Forest, Peter utilised large loose sheets of paper for the drawings that he made on site. Back in the studio, he remained equally concerned with representing the trees through scale, and so chose canvas rather than board as a support. This was made more viable by his employing a fluid paint no longer mixed with a heavy substance such as sand or white lead.

Only one of his many Forest paintings is on board, though Peter used that solid support for other subjects during the same period: the last of the 'butcher's shop' still lifes, the flower pieces, and other landscapes. The advantage of board was that it could be more easily reused, fresh images being painted over discarded ones. This had a positive aesthetic outcome, as well as a practical one, for the older pigment would show through at the edges of the fresh forms, so emphasising outline and adding to visual excitement through rich multicolour. Similar effects were achieved on the Forest canvases, and contribute greatly to their success.

In producing the Forest pictures, Peter was particularly concerned to counter 'the ways that trees, when painted by strokes running up and down the trunk, tended to slip away and lack solidity'. So:

> as so often, [he] looked back beyond the Impressionists to Courbet, the Barbizon School … and to deeply unfashionable painters like Bastien-Lepage. What these did, he observed, was to paint *across* the trunk, modelling it by the weight and density of the crosswise stroke. Consequently, shadow and recession could be implied by the way that a left-to-right stroke starts thick and rich and gradually thins out as the brush or palette-knife passes across the canvas. (JRT)

Epping Forest 1959 (**71**)

However, for Peter, the results embodied his idea of 'modern painting', as exemplified by Segonzac and Staël, as much as an older tradition. Indeed, he even moved towards abstraction in the predominantly red *Epping Forest* (1959) (**71**), an oil on paper not exhibited until 1991. He has said, in the context of these

Forest IV 1959 (**75**)

Forest III 1959 (**74**)

Forest IX 1959 (**80**)

works, that 'though it took him an awfully long time to begin to experiment, he was not prepared to stay still, and was willing to take a chance when the moment was right' (PC).

Nine oils of Epping – supported by a further seven drawings – comprised the centrepiece of Peter's third solo exhibition, held at the Zwemmer Gallery in autumn 1959. Though suggestive of a range of terrain, they clearly express a single purpose, that of unifying a varied paint surface. The tree provides an ideal motif through which to do this, in its colonisation of space, thrusting up as a trunk and out in the form of branches, active against the light. Its vertical emphasis is balanced by the earth and, occasionally, the skyline, but also, in Peter's approach, by those horizontal strokes of brush and knife. A grid results, but one that is dynamic and flexible rather than schematic. A sense of design, so well exemplified by the landscapes of Barbizon, is explored with greater richness; a concentration on saplings and new shoots allows for a special degree of intricacy.

In the most significant review of the exhibition, Eric Newton, writing in the *Guardian* (26.10.59), particularly favoured these 'studies of a tangle of vigorous young trees in the fringes of a forest'. Appreciating the possibilities inherent in the motif, he stated that:

> No subject could be more tempting to a landscape artist and few subjects could be more difficult, for unless he can sort out the essentials, select and emphasise the dominant forms, jettisoning all the rest, note the fitful play of light that filters down from above, and realise the recession from foreground to distance with extreme precision the result will be an intolerable muddle.

For Newton, Peter so successfully solved 'all these problems … with authority and ease', that he made him the compliment of comparing him to Cézanne, while admitting that, as yet, 'something is missing'.

Forest VI 1959 (**77**)

Newton's review stated that Peter had made 'a remarkable advance' in his art and had the potential for greatness. Yet before he was more able to fulfil such promise, he became seriously ill. Exhausted and bloated, he was diagnosed as having contracted Cushing's Syndrome, a disorder caused by an over-active adrenal gland. For a while he produced very little work, and was forced to give up his two days of teaching at St Martin's School of Art. At most, he could exhibit existing works, and undertake some personal tuition. There would be a gap of five years before his next solo show.

In the spring of 1960, Peter underwent extensive tests, first at London Hospital and then at Middlesex Hospital, which he preferred. One of the consultants involved told Vera that Peter had become so ill that he doubted he would work again. Nevertheless, he underwent one of the first ever adrenalectomy operations, at Middlesex Hospital in August, in which hydrocortisone was introduced to substitute for the function of his adrenal glands. During the month's convalescence in the hospital that followed visitors included Zwemmer's son, Desmond, who brought him copies of *Burlington Magazine* and *L'oeil*, some of which contained references to Staël. Even while he was unable to paint, ideas fermented.

Foot of Snowdon, Wales c 1960–61

Through the long period of slow recovery, Peter took some tentative drawing trips to Wales, in the company of Vera and Nicholas. While renting a very basic holiday cottage at the foot of Mount Snowdon, in the winter of 1961, he made drawings and paintings of Llanberis and Capel Curig, and – though soon decamping to a comfortable hotel – rented another cottage in the area in the following year. During the same period, he also stayed at Broadhaven on St Bride's Bay, Pembrokeshire, inspired by the work of Augustus John.

However, Peter was drawn more definitely and permanently towards East Anglia. Soon after he returned to teaching at St Martin's, in 1962, he was persuaded by his fellow Zwemmer exhibitor, John O'Connor, as Principal of Colchester School of Art, to become a visiting teacher in life painting. Through the irregular weekly visits that ensued, he befriended other painter-teachers, and particularly John Nash and Edward Bawden; he remembers that 'we were all pretty sociable from early 62, and frequently dined together with other mutual friends' (PC). This, in turn, encouraged him to move closer to Colchester, buying his present house at Mistley, Manningtree, on the estuary of the River Stour, which divides Essex from Suffolk.

The Red House, Mistley

Peter and Vera purchased the Red House on the New Road for £4000, with the financial assistance of £1000 from each of their fathers. This red-brick Georgian property overlooked a quarter of an acre of garden which, at that time, was laid to grass and 'surrounded by old fruit trees, apples, pears and plums, plus a very mature cherry in which the birds took up residence every year and cropped despite all our efforts' (PC). The studio window looked out onto a similarly semi-rural landscape of 'seed testing beds, old maltings and through to the river'. This studio, constructed on the first floor a little while after the move, was made possible by a £500 advance from Zwemmer: two rooms were knocked into one by adding a reinforced steel joist, the ceiling was raised to allow for the easel, and the floor was levelled. It would act as the centre for Peter's activities for the remainder of his career.

Always self-critical, Peter retains particular reservations about the work that he produced during the early 1960s, the period that may be dubbed his 'return to painting':

> Some of my paintings in the early 1960s seem to me too naturalistic. I think they became too picturesque and closed in on themselves, too concerned with the actual *view*. I think I stayed too close to the subject rather than going to nature, confronting it and then beginning to use it. Painting is about this sort of confrontation. Those early 1960s paintings are too half-hearted: they don't delve enough into the subject in a closely described way nor move far enough away imaginatively. (Lambirth 1989:16)

This retrospective statement sets out the ideal towards which he was striving, and against which he occasionally fell short: Nature should be less a subject to depict, with superficial mimesis, than a model to which to respond, whether as a challenge, an experience or a metaphor. Viewed in the context of this clear – and rigorous – notion of intention, remarkably few of the paintings are, in fact, 'half-hearted'. Of those that are, some fail mainly through the choice of motif for, after the butcher's shop, flowers are likely to seem at best pleasant. Others cannot match motif with material, so that paint is reduced to the role of merely picturing a scene rather than producing an equivalent sensation.

The solo exhibition mounted at the Zwemmer Gallery in 1964 demonstrated the degree to which Peter was back on course. It married the continuing inspiration of woodland with a revival of interest in moving water, and so offered native parallels to the earlier pairing of Barbizon and Etretat. Epping was complemented by the Suffolk forests of Rendlesham and Tunstall; the sea at Aldeburgh and the River Brett introduced varieties of aqueous interest.

Peter was prompted to begin a proper exploration of Suffolk by John Nash, who had a patron near Staverton Thicks, close to Orford, and thought that its ancient trees would appeal. But, as John Russell Taylor has stated:

> [he] found little there to inspire him: like Monet on his first trip to the Riviera, he realized that just any tree would not do, it had to be the right tree, and he would know it only when he saw it.

However, on driving northwards, he discovered in Aldeburgh a place that did excite, though for quite different reasons. There he rented the flat on the first floor of Tower House which belonged to Bruce Killeen, Senior Lecturer in History of Art at Colchester. Again and again, he was drawn to its windows to study the low, flat land, exposed to inclement sea and sky, and the Martello towers that rise up from it. Then, on his way back, he passed through Tunstall and Rendlesham forests, discovering many trees to which he did respond, particularly in the latter. He would return to Aldeburgh, Rendlesham and Tunstall on many occasions during the following few years, drawing and painting them with an intensity as strong as that provoked by equivalent French sites. He and Vera would also become regular visitors to the Aldeburgh Festival.

The paintings of East Anglian wood and water, exhibited in 1964, continued the established interplay between surface texture and the illusion of space, while introducing some new approaches to composition and some fresh uses of pigment. This can be exemplified by one of each of the paintings inspired by Epping, Rendlesham and Tunstall forests, and by a small group of coastal and river scenes.

Though utilising a regular rectangular canvas (measuring 34 x 44 inches), the oil of *Epping Forest II* (**93**) unequivocally emphasises the horizontal. Set above broad rich foreground stripes, a mature tree spreads out its branches and canopy to left and right, while a broad band of sky sits aloft. Such a spreading motif acts as a perfect signal for the more fluid application of pigment characteristic of this period. This fluid horizontality is all the more striking when the painting is compared to the very different drawing on which it is based. It is constructed out of a more varied set of marks, made with charcoal and conté. As excited clusters of lines indicate shadow, and rhythmic curls suggest foliage, so a three-dimensional form, as strong in each and every direction, emerges from the paper.

By contrast, *Rendlesham Forest* (**112**) is resolutely vertical in both its drawn and painted versions. Indeed the charcoal drawing – made on [two] sheets of paper – is twice as high as it is wide, at 40 x 22 inches. And charcoal is, in its shape and material, such an apposite medium for the depiction of tall young saplings, growing close and straight. However, the wider oil stresses verticality in other ways, its greater tonal contrast directing attention to the few bright trunks, and particularly the twisted one that stands at the centre, energising the image like a fork of lightening.

Rendlesham Forest 1964 (**112**)

Tunstall Forest I 1964 (**113**)

Tunstall Forest I (**113**) lies between these compositional extremes; for it comprises a series of strong diagonals which create a deep central perspective and, at the same time, negate any potential vertical or horizontal stress. While the result is all enveloping, it is not purely illusionistic, for the areas of foliage which contribute so much are palpably constructed from sweeps of pigment. Its atmosphere of early evening, and the uncanny inner glow perceivable in low natural light, are also intrinsically painterly effects.

What distinguishes these works, in general, is the tendency of paint, and painterly effect, to support and strengthen monumental design; while, in the earlier Epping group, the paintwork is itself monumental, being built up into slabs with the aid of a palette knife.

To create a parallel set of monumental compositions from aqueous motifs proved more challenging. For, while the growth of a tree from the ground provides an obvious basic framework of height and breadth, the relation of river or sea to land that is characteristically low does not. Aldeburgh is nothing like Etretat; neither are the banks of the River Brett comparable to Malham (a place that appears in his paintings from 1967).

One solution was to use a square support, a format which imposes its own logic on a subject, and can give rise to unconventional elegance. When combined with a high viewpoint, taking in little or no sky, the result is often simultaneously economical, powerful and intriguing. Consider *River Brett* (**100**) and *Aldeburgh I* (**101**), paired by their scale (48 x 48 inches) and their content (firm wedges of bank or beach abutting turbulent whirls of water).

Aldeburgh I 1964 (**101**)

Aldeburgh II 1964 (**102**)

River Brett 1963 (**100**)

Study for *Judas Gap* (**120**) (**SB5**:4)

Judas Gap 1966 (**120**)

In the first, the reflections of land and sky in the flowing river are at once playful and unifying, while the tension set up between dynamic brushwork and tight regular framing expresses a barely restrained turbulence. (This tension provided the prototype for succeeding paintings of various terrains, produced in 1965-66, from local *Judas Gap* (**120**) to the French locations, *Weir, Josselin* (**118**) and *Mountain Stream, Pyrenees* (**122**, **123**).)

In the second, a restricted chalky palette draws together the different elements that fan out across the surface, while tonal range indicates their depth and distance. Apparently at odds, palette and tone actually combine to give the sense that the picture space is slowly filling with the incoming tide.

Aldeburgh I, like the different and vertical *Aldeburgh II* (**102**), seems to adapt the composition of *The Wave* (**52**) to the conditions of the Suffolk coast. In remembering the occasions on which he painted these two places, Peter once said that 'I don't know how you can distinguish between the English coastal waters and those of France'; however, his tone suggested that he could but try, and his paintings attest that he succeeded. In dispensing with the almost crystalline strata of *Wave, Etretat*, the Aldeburgh paintings gain a sense of space, but a space that is constantly threatened by excited water, that is by energetic applications of paint. As a result, the monumentality of their design appears provisional, which is wholly appropriate to their subject.

Study for *Evening: Train Ferry Pier, Harwich*

Evening: Train Ferry Pier, Harwich by 1975 (**304**)

Evening, River Stour 1967 (**134**)

Responses to the 1964 exhibition concentrated less on these paintings of river and sea than on those of woodland. Not only did the most substantial review – by Frederick Laws – make this emphasis; one of the forest sites – Tunstall – also provided the background for an item on Peter filmed for BBC's *Look East* (on 28 October); however the interview, recording his aims and ideas, had to be rerecorded at his home in Manningtree (on 2 November), when the original voice level was found to be too low.

Laws, writing in the *Guardian* (20.11.64), considered Peter to be 'a realistic painter of landscape in an old and good tradition', the earthy tradition of 'Constable, Courbet and Derain'. He particularly commended his 'way with trees', that 'he does not call them mere oaks or beeches or birches', and that 'he allows them to be, dramatic, elegiac, pure pattern or simple botany'. And, while he distinguished Peter from 'the academicians', his presentation of the artist seems far removed from that of T W Earp, eight years earlier, when he characterised him as'one of art's Teddy-boys'.

The identification of Peter with 'an old and good tradition' seems to have prepared the way for his election as an Associate of the Royal Academy. However, Frederick Gore (elected an Associate in 1964) has suggested that, conversely, 'his election…may have contributed to…an alteration in the mood of his painting, for he joined without reluctance a body where so many members in the past and not a few in the present have shown skilful devotion to landscape' (Gore 1973) It is probably best to consider that a growing awareness of the native tradition and recognition by the academy had a mutual effect on Peter's development and helped to define a new phase in his career.

Peter knew the election was in the offing, as he had been asked if he was willing to stand, but still considered the event 'a very pleasurable surprise' when it occurred on 23 April 1965. From that date, he actively participated in the functions of the Royal Academy, serving on several committees, especially the selection and hanging committee. His new position helped seal his relationship with such other East Anglian Academicians as Edward Bawden and John Nash, both of whom he would drive to the annual banquet, general assemblies and voting days. Additionally, it spurred him to explore the history of the institution, by reading such works as Sir Joshua Reynolds' *Discourses* and Joseph Farington's *Diaries*.

An Associateship of the Royal Academy obviously increased Peter's opportunities for exhibiting, in allowing him to show six works at each *Summer Exhibition*; and this at a time when he was working hard on three distinct areas of landscape: East Anglia, other parts of Britain and – once again – France. But it also introduced an element of stability into Peter's life as an exhibiting artist. For he remained loyal to the institution throughout his career, while changing dealers with each decade. Indeed, that very stability may have helped make such changes all the easier, and particularly the first, forced by the closure of the Zwemmer Gallery soon after he held his fifth show there in autumn 1967.

Sampling his current painting and drawing, the last Zwemmer show signalled the new breadth of his subject matter, including works inspired by the Yorkshire Moors, Western Sutherland and the Pyrenees (works surveyed in Chapters 6 and 7). However, its contents failed to demonstrate the degree to which Peter remained drawn to East Anglian sites, and especially those close to his Manningtree home. From Judas Gap, beyond Flatford in the west, to Harwich, on the estuary in the east, he thoroughly explored the River Stour. The results of these forays appeared in exhibitions at various venues through the late 1960s and 70s.

In addition, the proximity of Manningtree to 'Constable Country' meant that Peter was able to arrange and supervise trips for those of his students from St Martin's School of Art who were interested in painting *en plein air*. They stayed in the students' quarters at Flatford Field Centre and were invited to some jolly evenings at Peter's home. He particularly enjoyed these times as he did not have to travel to London for six weeks of the summer term, but could immerse himself in a landscape that he had made his own.

Balnakeil
Durness
Kinlochbervie
Scourie
Achiltibuie
Skye
Mull
Dunoon
Helensburgh
West Kilbride
Leadgate
Whitehaven
Whitby
Seascale
Starbotton
Malham
Blackpool
Rochdale
Llanberis
Hadleigh
Stour Valley
Harwich
St David's
Pembroke
Rhondda Valley
London
Welcombe
Places chosen by students who were awarded David Murray scholarships and where they were visted by Peter Coker as visitor to the students 1967 & 1968
Places visted and painted by Peter Coker

6 1967–1976: The Life of the British Landscape

The more extensive periods of travel that Peter undertook from the late 1960s, beyond East Anglia to other parts of Britain, have been considered, by Frederick Gore, to mark 'the beginning of a new phase in his work'. Gore elaborated this remark, tracing the deeper impetus and broader implications of such a change, when he wrote:

> It was not only the opportunity to see a wider and nobler range of northern landscapes which enlarged his subject matter but also his vision changed as he became fully conscious of the landscape itself. He felt that until now he had to some degree always used landscape as a reason for producing a picture, subjecting it to the requirements of what he thought necessary to a good painting. At first he had used particular motifs or landscape details which he could treat in much the same way as he had originally treated the ingredients of still life. His observant sympathy had therefore gone to the turbulent thicket of the forest, the rough cliff face, the cavern, the beach with the wave, things which the mind could isolate and grasp in their entirety, interpret in paint and reorganise. Now he saw as paintable something different; landscapes which surrounded him and which were in perpetual movement, landscapes structured not only by geological strata but also by light, landscapes which live and change with the seasons and by the hour. The life of the landscape had become at least as important as the ritual of painting. Thus the very breadth of Yorkshire's high countryside and its atmospheric changes led him to altogether thinner paint. (Spalding 1992)

This emergent, almost holistic, relationship between 'the life of the landscape' and the interpretation of it was underpinned by the example of J M W Turner. Peter confessed in an interview with a journalist from the *Post-Mercury Series*, 'I hope I've grown out of influences completely but I still find Turner a tremendous inspiration' (13.3.70). Though Peter would continue to value Courbet's Realism for providing one way of directly experiencing the landscape, he perceived another in Turner's Romanticism. In his impasto application of pigment, Courbet had always paralleled the depicted surface and the painting's support, so that the finished work seems almost a detached fragment of nature. But, even at their thickest, Turner's images suggest the enveloping space that he inhabited, unlimited nature appearing to fill the room. The pictures that Peter produced in the light of such an understanding may not always be obviously tactile but still involve the viewer immediately and intensely.

Bernard Dunstan, Peter Coker, Raymond Teague Cowern, 1970

Soon after his election as an Associate of the Royal Academy in 1965, Peter revived his interest in Turner, being fired by his tenure of the David Murray Stewardship. He read extensively in the literature, and was particularly impressed by the contributions of John Gage, author of such works as *Colour in Turner* (1972). Then elected a Royal Academician seven years later, he acted as a member of the committee for the major Turner exhibition in 1974, which was co-organised by the Royal Academy and the Tate Gallery. His major concern was to bring Gage on to the committee, for he believed him to be the only person who could do justice to Turner's travels and the sketchbooks used during them. Having succeeded in this, he decided to stand down and leave affairs in the hands of the scholars. One can imagine Turner reacting with similar concern over an exhibition of, say, his beloved Claude Lorrain.

Royal Academy Summer Exhibition hanging committee 1973: Peter Coker, Norman Blamey, Gertrude Hermes, Sir Thomas Monnington (PRA), James Fitton, William Dring, Geoffrey Clarke, Frederick Gore and Sir Basil Spence

Travel and the related sketchbooks were two components of Turner's practice which chimed particularly well with Peter's own. Sketchbooks became essential to Peter during the many travels that he undertook in the decade 1967-77, eight different books being used during the period. The range of the sizes of these books, and the variety of media employed within them, enabled Peter to respond quickly and appropriately to the visual challenge of any of the many different landscapes that appealed to him, from the flats of Seascale to Yorkshire fells. As a result, they soon developed into a record of a career, not only as a straightforward topographical diary but as a direct revelation of the artist's essential aesthetic. Perhaps, even more than the drawings made on individual sheets, those made in sketchbooks played an instrumental role in the genealogy of an image from first thoughts to finished painting.

During the Easter of 1967, Peter made his first trip to Yorkshire, joining John Nash for a week in and around Malham. Though Nash had been on similar trips with Edward Bawden and their respective wives, this was the first time that he and Peter had spent any length of time together. Peter would always find it a pleasure to travel with Nash, who was ever ready with a good story quietly told. They offered no threat to each other, being at different stages of their careers, and producing almost complementary kinds of image.

The two artists stayed at The Buck Inn, in Malham itself, 'a nice, comfortable hotel' which, according to Peter, may have been suggested by John Lewis, the specialist in printing and illustration who also lived in Manningtree. They would go out together after breakfast to explore the surrounding landscape, and especially the curious formations of rock and the water that tumbled down Gordale Scar. However, they usually worked independently, and only rarely drew from the same motif.

Waterfall, Malham [also known as Jenny's Fosse] 1967 (**137**)

When they later visited Skye together, in the summer of 1970, a local journalist would note the basic difference between their approaches. This was elaborated in a later report by the *Eastern Daily Press*:

> Peter Coker specialises in cold black skies and rain lashing down on desolate hillsides, so when a storm broke he sailed off excitedly, leaving Nash, who prefers brighter scenes, moping indoors. Later the sun broke through, Coker returned to their friend's house with his tail between his legs and Nash ventured into the open air feeling full of the joys of spring. (1.3.72)

Peter made most of his drawings on the Yorkshire trip in pencil in a spiral-bound sketchbook (**SB5**). He built these up out of a wide variety of marks, from fine etched-like lines to areas of flat shading, and again added written notes on colour. As in contemporaneous images of East Anglia and France, he pushed the sky to the edge or excluded it entirely, so concentrating attention towards the essential theme, that of powerfully flowing water. He also tended to choose a predominantly vertical format, emphasising the height from which the water falls, and the rock and vegetation that it passes on the way. This dynamic spirit was successfully sustained by the paintings that immediately resulted from the drawings, and especially by *Jenny's Fosse* (**137**), a depiction of the waterfall between Gordale Scar and Malham.

On 26 April 1967, soon after his return from Malham, Peter attended the Royal Academy Annual Banquet. At this event, he had the good fortune to be seated next to W T Oliver, sub-editor of the *Yorkshire Post*. For Oliver was a great enthusiast for his work, and invited him to make use of his stone cottage in the tiny village of Starbotton, Wharfedale. This opportunity enabled him to build on his recent introduction to Yorkshire, developing a relationship with the county that was almost as strong as that with his home area of East Anglia. He stayed at Oliver's cottage on several occasions, both on independent visits and during his tenure of the David Murray Stewardship.

Cranham, Welcombe, Devon.

Peter took on the David Murray Stewardship after he was approached by Peter Greenham, Keeper of the Royal Academy Schools. In this role he was required to supervise the activities of art students – drawn in alternate years from art schools in and out of London – who were travelling in Britain on scholarships financed by the David Murray funds. He could have carried out these duties satisfactorily simply by assessing their work at the RA itself; however, he decided it would be more rewarding to visit them in situ. Certainly, it gave him the opportunity to see a number of places he might otherwise have missed, and so expand his repertoire. In addition to north-east England, he visited the Lake District and many parts of Scotland, including Balnakeil, in Sutherland.

In the following year, Peter actively chose to take on a second David Murray Stewardship, so that he might work his way by stages across the north of England as he visited the students. This took most of the summer, and included stays at Starbotton (in Yorkshire); at Leadgate below Cross Fell, and between Buttermere

Rain, Rainbow and Stormy Seas, North Cliff Whitby 1974 (**287**)

Mallow Cottage 1972 (**248**)

and Crummock Water (in Cumbria). These experiences also encouraged him to make other, independent trips across England, from Welcombe in North Devon to Whitby on the North Yorkshire coast.

This increased exposure to the British landscape greatly expanded Peter's pool of rich and resonant motifs. He was frequently drawn back to a number of the locations in subsequent years, and would stay in a place for up to three months, usually in the company of Vera. Indeed, so frequent were the travels at this time, and so closely did place dictate approach, that the favourite destinations are here outlined topographically rather than chronologically.

Through the late 1960s and early 70s, Bill Oliver's cottage at Starbotton provided so regular a base for Peter that, while in residence, he was able to produce numerous small paintings, as well as making drawings in sketchbooks and on loose sheets. Its locale also inspired some of the earliest etchings during a concentrated period of printmaking (described in Chapter 8). This was because the terrain and its weather were very different from those of East Anglia, and together provided an entirely new set of stimuli.

Small steep valleys, such as Wharfedale, rise to high moors punctuated by stone walls that keep in the sheep. Contrasts in height and space actually emphasise the sky. Misty rain blurs clean edges, and can obliterate an entire fell, but may give way to strong contrasts of light and shade.

View from Ivy Cottage by 1971 (**208**)

Peter first captured these characteristic effects and features in conté, often mixed with charcoal or sanguine, or in pastel. He retained the immediacy of such drawing in the paintings that resulted, through the loose handling and thin paint described by Gore. He also sustained their power through a modesty of scale and concentration of motif.

The intensity of this response was well articulated by Bill Oliver himself when he reviewed an exhibition of pastels and other drawings by Peter, held in 1969 at the Stone Gallery, Newcastle upon Tyne. Writing in the *Yorkshire Post*, he stated that:

he loves the sweep and power of [the Northern countryside's] fells, the tumultuous rush of its rivers and mountain streams, the brilliance of its skies.

Starting with Malham and Upper Wharfedale, he has gone higher and higher … seeking always to get on paper or canvas the rough vitality of the Northern dales and moors. (28.10.69)

Some several miles north-west of Wharfedale lies the South Tyne Valley. This provided an eastern base from which to explore Cumbria, as Buttermere would provide a western base. Peter tended to stay at Ivy Cottage, in Leadgate, a hamlet which sits close to the confluence of the South Tyne and Black Burn, between Cross Fell and the village of Alston. In addition to its many interesting local features, it was in easy driving distance of Teesdale, and the two impressive waterfalls, High Force and Low Force. Similarly, Buttermere – at the heart of the Lake District – offered access to Seascale and Whitehaven.

The South Tyne Valley inspired a further set of small paintings invoking the spirit of the English countryside through form and atmosphere. Most of the images provide free interpretations of distant views across hilly fields to a high or low horizon, where fresh green meets steel grey. However, some draw the viewer into a closer proximity with nature – down a lane, along a wall, towards a tree – and do so with a sense of design that is parallel to the artist's contemporaneous achievements in etching.

Low Tide: Seascale by 1969 (**160**)

Though the paintings of Seascale are equally associated with the etchings, in themselves they probably comprise a more distinctive group. For the place itself – a flat expanse stretching out to the Irish Sea – is native landscape at its most visually uncompromising, more extreme than the low land of East Anglia, and the complete antithesis of the variousness of Yorkshire dales and fells. Only an artist at ease with the bare essentials, of craft and motif, could rise to such a challenge. The sky was no longer an optional element, and at times provided the chief interest, while the patterns in the sand eroded by the tide proved highly compelling. Peter produced a particularly successful balance of sky and sand in the square composition, *Low Tide: Seascale* (**160**), the empty air deflecting attention to the textures of the shore, while a single figure in red stands out on the horizon surrounded by a predominance of blue. (Fittingly, the work was much praised by Edward Bawden, himself a master of design.)

Chrossavaig, Skye 1971 (**213**)

Each topography that Peter encountered brought new challenges and encouraged fresh responses. So it was when he visited Sutherland, in northern Scotland, to supervise students at Balnakeil. Indeed his introduction to the country would have far-reaching consequences, through familiarisation with a number of its mainland and island regions, including Argyllshire, Ayrshire, Mull and Skye, and later Easter Ross. Its remote character would eventually stand as one extreme of his aesthetic, the antithesis of the bounty, the lushness of the South of France.

left
Storm Clouds – Kyle of Durness 1967-68 (**140**)

right
Dark Sea, Carsaig 1977 (**343**)

Kyle of Durness by 1969 (**158**)

Ostensibly, his time in Sutherland offered almost holiday pleasures; for he stayed in comfort at the very grand Durness Hotel, and socialised with Sally and Mike Arnup former contemporaries of the Royal College of Art, who had set up a craft centre in old nissen huts at Cape Wrath. Yet he explored the exposed coastline thoroughly, as far as Kinlochbervie in the west and – in what had become a thorough and habitual practice – recorded his discoveries in drawing.

The paintings that resulted from this study reveal an unparalleled freedom of handling, oil being treated almost with the liquidity of watercolour. Thus the boundaries of the spare, simple terrain are depicted as provisional, as if earth, sea and sky might merge or engulf each other. This counters any austerity or rigidity in the landscape, as does the accentuation of intense highland hues. A rich, even profligate, use of colour stands out, for instance, in *Kyle of Durness* (**158**), a representation of clouds speeding over the tidal estuary, where land and water are thrown variously into light and shade. It provides a fascinating comparison with the contemporaneous *Low Tide: Seascale*, in being constructed from the same essential elements. (The works were exhibited together at the Royal Academy in 1969). Where the one suggests calm and stillness by emphasising the order of an inherent natural pattern, the other embodies movement, from the slightest flickering brushstroke to the over-arching structure.

This new phase of Peter's painting developed in parallel with his public profile as an artist. Following his election as an Associate of the Royal Academy in 1965, Peter regularly contributed six works to each *Summer Exhibition*. As has already been suggested, this gave him a degree of stability, particularly while transferring his allegiance from one dealer to another. However, following the closure of the Zwemmer Gallery in 1967, he was able to mount three substantial exhibitions of drawings at provincial galleries, so emphasising the importance of the activity within his art; these were held at the Magdalene Street Gallery, Cambridge (1968), the Stable Gallery , Ufford (1968), and the Stone Gallery, Newcastle upon Tyne (1969). Then, in 1969, he accepted an offer to exhibit at the Thackeray Gallery, in London, and in the following year held a solo show, so establishing a relationship that would last for a decade.

Forest VIII 1959 (**79**)

Poster of the Touring Exhibition 1972-73, showing *The Wave* (**52**)

The presentation of new work was balanced by opportunities to review achievements to date, opportunities for both the public and Peter alike. These included the appearance of *Forest VIII* (**79**) in the Royal Academy's *Bicentenary Exhibition 1768-1968*; the unusual *Pupil & Masters* (Long Melford 1971), in which Peter placed himself in the context of Vivian Pitchforth and James Stroudley; and a full-scale retrospective which was mounted by the Minories, in Colchester, and toured to Bath, London and Sheffield (1972-73). (An early version of the statement by Frederick Gore which heads this chapter was included in the catalogue to this retrospective.) Such retrospection had less immediate effect on his way of working, it would seem, than on his role as a teacher; for, in 1974, he moved from St Martin's to City and Guilds of London School of Art, on the urging of Roger de Grey, the school's Principal and an established friend.

The numerous exhibitions of his work received wide coverage, both locally and nationally, and some sensitive critical response. One of his most consistent champions, Michael Webber stated boldly in a review of the first Thackeray Gallery exhibition that, 'aloof from fashion, Peter Coker continues along his own path, as one of the finest painters of landscape now working in this country' (*Arts Review*, 14.3.70). However, in common with other critics, he was keen to characterise him more precisely, and so situate him within the history of art. In a further review of the same exhibition, he wrote of 'the link between Constable and Cézanne' that he detected in the drawings (*East Anglian Daily Times*, 11.3.70), while another – anonymous – writer substituted Turner for Constable (*Post-Mercury Series*, 13.3.70).

William Packer defined this balance of tradition and modernity as 'Romantic Expressionism' (*Art and Artists*, 3.70), and others would follow suit in articles on subsequent exhibitions. It is a convenient shorthand for Peter's use of often free handling of paint to describe the spaces and atmospheres of the natural world. The most sympathetic critics were touched by his ability to create a sense of place that was emotional as well as physical; so A P Maguire, Bill Oliver's successor on the *Yorkshire Post*, wrote of the first Thackeray show, that:

> Some of us with regional attachments will be moved to nostalgia by several of the views and not in the current sense of mere wistfulness, but an aching to return to places. There is one large square canvas, *Towards Old Cote Moor Top* (**170**), which has the effect of a challenge to return. (4.4.70)

Beyond such degrees of local association, there was a wider appreciation of the grandeur of the artist's project, his ability to convey size, weight and elemental force through each mark and every image. As Ray Rushton would state, 'There is no sign of preciousness, not even in his drawings' (*Essex County Standard*, 15.9.72).

Those critics who had followed Peter's career most closely tried to distinguish the qualities of his latest work from those of his existing oeuvre, even before the opening of the retrospective. At the Royal Academy *Summer Exhibition*, in 1971, Webber noticed that Peter 'submits landscapes which show a slight, but significant change of style'; so that while *Black Burn and the South Tyne* (**194**) remained consistent with 'his earlier concern with the tactile quality of pigment lavishly and skilfully applied', *Trees at Leadgate* (**231**) revealed 'a more Cézanne-like interest in forms and design' (*East Anglian Daily Times*, 30.4.71). In the following year, at the second solo show at the Thackeray Gallery, Packer observed that 'the large studio paintings have given way to small-scale works, often modest in scope, but freely and surely established with quiet bravura…the shift in emphasis has recaptured a spontaneity'.

Peter Coker 1972

However contradictory these opinions might seem in themselves, they together acknowledged the degree to which Peter's aesthetic had matured; that his recent experience of the range of British landscape had instilled him with the ability to utilise spontaneity or strength of design – or a combination of the two – as was appropriate to his subject. And the general assessments generated by the retrospective were in accordance with this view; for Virginia Chapman wrote of the artist's 'greater understanding of the constant change in nature' (*Arts Review* 4.11.72), while Marina Vaizey remarked that 'the mood of landscape is anchored to specific scenes' (*Financial Times*, 20.1.73).

At the time of the retrospective, Peter gave a revealing interview to Vivienne Loomes for the *Essex County Standard*. However, when he spoke of the stylistic shifts that had occurred in his work, he did so in conventional, linear terms, stating that 'any painter worth his salt will find his painting changing at intervals. That's because he's not interested in stating the same thing over and over again. One is avoiding stylistic clichés' (20.10.72). Though this may have held true for the larger pattern of his career, it did not accurately describe his most recent achievement. The sketchbooks demonstrate a fundamental unity of vision and purpose, while the paintings manifest an original response to 'the constant change of nature' through the simultaneous mastery of many styles.

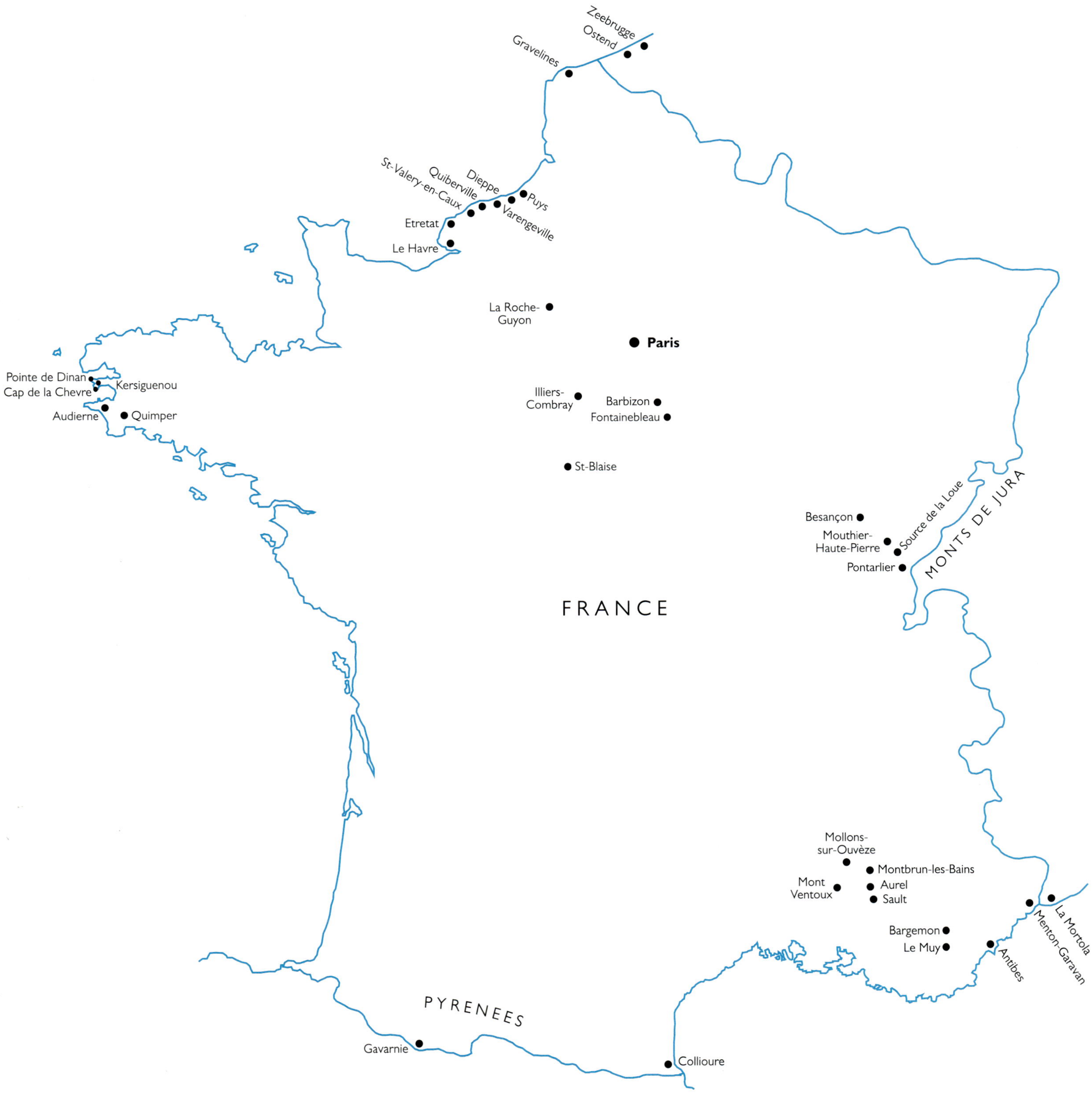
Zeebrugge
Ostend
Gravelines
Dieppe
Puys
Quiberville
St-Valery-en-Caux
Varengeville
Etretat
Le Havre
La Roche-Guyon
Paris
Pointe de Dinan
Kersiguenou
Cap de la Chevre
Audierne
Quimper
Illiers-Combray
Barbizon
Fontainebleau
St-Blaise
Besançon
Mouthier-Haute-Pierre
Source de la Loue
Pontarlier
MONTS DE JURA
FRANCE
Mollons-sur-Ouvèze
Montbrun-les-Bains
Mont Ventoux
Aurel
Sault
Bargemon
Le Muy
Antibes
Menton-Garavan
La Mortola
PYRENEES
Gavarnie
Collioure

7 1965-1977: The Return to France

The mastery of many styles that manifested itself in Peter's work during the late 1960s and early 70s appears all the more radical when it is realised that he was responding to French topography as well as English. In 1965, after a gap of seven years, he returned to France, and so began to broaden his knowledge of the country through a series of increasingly extensive – and extended – tours. At the close of the 1960s, he may have made mostly short trips to Belgium and northern France, but by the mid 1970s he could cover some hundreds of miles during stays of a month, and would return to favourite places again and again. So, as before, this chapter can only attempt to sample the range and depth of Peter's travels. Most enterprising was his exploration of some of the southern regions of the country, regions which had previously yielded little in the way of inspiration. The Pyrenees, Languedoc and especially parts of Provence would prove enormously fruitful as subjects in themselves, while also laying the way for the more complete surrender to the south that would occur from the late 1970s on encountering Bargemon, in the Var, and then Menton, on the Riviera.

The close proximity of Manningtree to Harwich gave Peter easy access to the Continent; for though the ferry to Zeebrugge was intended to transport railway freight trucks, it also carried a few cars when space permitted. Because this passenger service was never advertised, Peter's car was often the only one on board and, as a result, he and Vera would receive excellent service from the crew.

Sunset over Calm Sea, Ostend 1975 (**313**)

As this developed into a regular route, through the late 1960s, Peter became familiar with Ostend, which lies along the Belgian coast to the west of Zeebrugge. Indeed, it proved to be both an inspiration and a market for his art. On an early visit, he showed examples of his work to Frans Aerts, a dealer and collector based in the town. These were received with such enthusiasm that, on each subsequent journey through Belgium, he would take a folio of drawings and etchings for Aerts to view and buy. Aerts also persuaded the curators of the Museum voor Schone Kunsten to add the etchings *Jetty at Night, Ostend* (**284**) and *Night Sea, Ostend* (**285**) to its collections, and to buy other works for themselves. These purchases gave Peter a little more currency at the beginning of a trip.

Peter had been aware of certain Belgian artists since the 1950s, and therefore visited the Ostend museums with some interest. He may have disliked the 'Catholic atmosphere' of the James Ensor House, but was fascinated by some of that painter's imagery, and especially his interpretation of the locale. However, he preferred the work of Constant Permeke, which was on show at his former home in nearby Jabbeke; the vigorous handling of paint and use of large-scale figures was to him particularly impressive.

Les sables d'or, Ostend 1975 (**312**)

Of more direct relevance to Peter's work, however, was the place itself. In the words of John Russell Taylor, the artist 'found the low sandy beaches of Ostend, its watery flats at low tide and its shadowy breakwaters a fruitful source of imagery, which formed the basis of many drawings and a handful of [his] finest etchings'. Additionally, Peter painted several major oils of the town, which were completed over the two years between 1974-75 after a long period of gestation. However strong the design of these images, what most astonishes the viewer is the quality of colour. The often bleak North Sea coast is interpreted in a range of hues and tones from the serene glow of *Les sables d'or, Ostend* (**312**) to the almost violent primaries of *Sunset over Calm Sea* (**313**).

Ostend, the Café (**293**) stands apart from these essays in pure seascape in its presentation of a busy resort. Through a careful organisation of the picture plane, articulated by colour, the eye is taken from a café window across its terrace out to the beach and beyond to the sea. The late afternoon light is signalled by the setting sun in a still blue sky; it stains the window frame, the blinds and the closest chairs a deep and

Ostend, the Café 1974-75 (**293**)

solid red. Some human figures and a dog stand out in silhouette. The lighter central strip, denoting sand, is marked out in diminutive detail indicative of holiday life in all its relaxed clutter. The first such work in Peter's oeuvre, it offers a response to the example of Pierre Bonnard, and particularly to *La Place Clichy* (1912) and the *Café 'Au Petit Poucet'* (1928), both in the Musée des Beaux-Arts in Besançon. A decade later, *Promenade, Etretat* (**525**) would offer a parallel response to the example of Raoul Dufy. In the spirit of these French masters, Peter appears to have revitalised the north with the warmth of the south.

A burgeoning interest in the south was suggested by the first trip that Peter made on his return to France, that to the Pyrenees in August 1965. But the destination was prompted less by Peter's aesthetic considerations than by Nicholas's love of butterflies, and proved to embody the least luxuriant or comfortable aspects of the southern terrain.

Travelling via Brittany, the family went back to Audierne and visited Josselin, where Peter made drawings of a weir on the River Oust. On 9 August, they arrived at Gavarnie, in the foothills of the Pyrenees. To their dismay they discovered that it was a 'shanty town' with just one street and one hotel, the L'Astazou, in which they had booked to stay. Each morning the village became busy with donkeys and their drivers waiting to take visitors into the mountains, so that by the evening the street smelled so badly that it had to be hosed down.

Disassociating themselves from this rabble, the Cokers braved the wild qualities of land and weather, and went up to the snowline of the mountains without a guide. There they were able to see the moths and butterflies, including swarms of clouded yellows, which famously migrate through the Port de Gavarnie, on the Spanish border. Yet, intrepid though they were, their studies were often aborted, for the alternation of the electric current through the night made the light bulb in their moth-trap fluctuate.

Though Peter could share in Nicholas's passion for lepidoptery, he initially found limited aesthetic stimulation in the countryside. Gore recounts that 'only the streams in the lower foothills were interesting and faute-de-mieux he took to water, making notes on small sheets of paper' (Gore 1973).

On the 14 August, the Cokers moved north to Garzaupony, a hamlet near Condom, in Gers, where they stayed in an eighteenth-century watermill. However, this proved even less inspiring to Peter and, soon after returning to Gavarnie a week later, he and his family left the south to stay with Vera's friend, Jacqueline Thiraux, at Menilles, near Vernon, west of Paris.

Mountain Stream, Pyrenees 1966 (**123**)

Eventually, the groups of drawings that Peter made in Brittany and the Pyrenees together proved extremely useful in sparking the important series of paintings concerned with the energy of moving water. It is interesting to note that *Weir, Josselin* (**118**) and the versions of *Mountain Stream, Pyrenees* (**122**, **123**) represent the theme at its most elemental, even abstract, while subsequent variations are relatively naturalistic. (See Chapters 5 and 6 for more detailed information on the English paintings in the series.) In the French examples, the characteristic square format, use of diagonals and omission of an area of sky are combined with thick undulating brushstrokes and a strongly contrasting palette to project an extraordinary emotional intensity. Here, north and south seem very close, the south even being remade in the image of the north. This is similarly true of *Pyrenees Cave* (**124**). As with the images of moving water, its 'paint is still very thick', though it has a distinct presence as 'a statement by mass without line, reflective in mood, and showing a subtle interest in the fall and loss of light on different surfaces' (Gore 1973). Reviewing its appearance at the Royal Academy *Summer Exhibition*, in 1966, Michael Webber compared the character of this 'sombre painting' to 'the romantic quality of the huge painting of Gordale Scar in the Tate, by James Ward' (*East Anglian Daily Times*, 6.5.66).

Weir, Josselin 1965 (**118**)

Francophile friends of the Cokers took an interest in Peter's painting trips. They appreciated his subjects and were keen to suggest areas of France that he had not explored but that might appeal. In 1972, the Benhams and the Doncasters, living on either side of Colchester, both recommended the Côte de Ventoux, in Vaucluse. The former even went so far as to book and pay for a small dwelling for Peter in Mollans-sur-Ouvèze, a village set among lavender fields. He and Vera gratefully took up this offer but, on arriving in the August, discovered that the accommodation, attached to a farmstead called Le Toulourenc, was a small structure with a corrugated roof best described as a 'glorified chicken hut'. In the summer heat this became unbearably claustrophobic. Worse still was the lack of privacy that it offered, the Cokers' every movement being watched by Madame Marin and her friends as they sat stripping haricot beans. Peter and Vera coped with these conditions for about a fortnight before decamping to the more civilised surroundings of a hotel in Aurel, on a higher, cooler part of Mont Ventoux. From there they visited the other mediaeval villages of Montbrun-les-Bains and Sault, and in the latter attended a recital by Aurèle Nicolet, the internationally known French flautist.

The main achievement to derive from the stay at Le Toulourenc was the painting, *Stripping Haricots at Mollans* (**250**). Built up from a series of drawings in various media made on the spot, it might almost be considered an act of revenge on Peter's part, in that it makes Madame Marin the ultimate object of the gaze. However, the result is a benign, even idyllic representation of rural life, which at once extends a long tradition in French painting and lays the foundations for Peter's later compositions of arbours, pergolas and terraces.

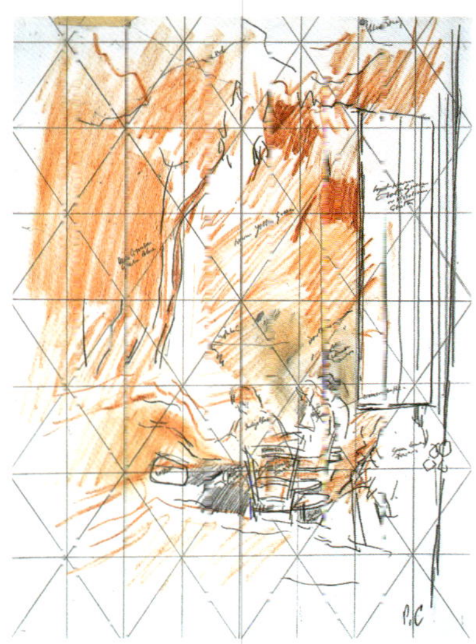

Study for *Stripping Haricots at Mollans* (**250**)

Peter returned to this area in October 1973, during an ambitious trip that he made alone. By negotiating a term's sabbatical from St Martin's School of Art, he was able to undertake a month-long trip which had at its centre an exploration of the places associated with Courbet and Proust; Mont Ventoux was also included on the itinerary.

La Loue, Jura 1972 (**245**)

Source of the Loue, Mouthier-Haute-Pierre

On Tuesday 2 October, Peter arrived in Mouthier-Haute-Pierre, which sits above the source of the Loue and lies ten miles upstream from Courbet's birthplace of Ornans. He stayed at La Cascade, a hotel already known to the Cokers from the year before. The high position of the village offered extensive views of a terrain long familiar to Peter from the landscapes that Courbet had painted from the 1850s. As described by John Russell Taylor, 'the Loue dashes dramatically out of a huge cavern in the rock face and sets out on its at times precipitous course through lofty, interestingly sculpted chalk cliffs'. Peter surveyed this area and the surrounding region in some detail, both on foot and by car. He took long walks along the river, crossing by the point of a great sluice so that he could take in the views from the other side. He also drove up on to the plateau, taking his art equipment with him; for, as on his travels across Britain, he was painting increasingly on the spot. Further afield, he visited Besançon, Salins-les-Bains and Ornans itself. At Besançon he discovered the 'two marvellous Bonnards' that would inform the making of *Ostend, The Café*, while at Ornans he took much pleasure in Courbet's landscapes and seascapes hanging in the birthplace museum.

During his previous stay at Mouthier, in 1972, Peter had focussed attention on the source of the Loue, producing drawings and a painting in oil on paper (**245**). In so doing, he had not only rehearsed Courbet's interest in the subject, but extended the challenge he had set himself when working on *Pyrenees Cave*: to represent a space with limited yet complex signs of light. On his return to the area, in 1973, he chose a very different perspective, looking down on the village from on high, as he had already learned to do at Starbotton in Yorkshire. He gained an understanding of the view through making a large drawing in conté and sanguine, and then began two paintings (*Mouthier-Haute-Pierre*, Nos 1 and 2 (**268**, **269**). These offer very different configurations of the same space, a tall narrow canvas emphasising altitude, and a broader one opening to a gentle and generous vista. Extracts from a postcard and a letter, both written to Vera, indicate the speed at which he developed these, while also suggesting his mixed feelings at working for so long alone:

> Rained today after three splendid days; still painting the same two canvases – the days are OK but the boredom in the evenings – I go to bed about 8.30 or 9pm and then get indigestion – I hope I shall manage to stay the time or rather, serve time, that's how it seems.
> Just came back from dinner, and feel a bit more jolly – ½ bottle of wine, and watching the French is amusing … – just eaten Rabbit. (Saturday 6 October, Mouthier-Haute-Pierre)
>
> The work seems to have slowed down - the two paintings of Mouthier were rained off so with the aid of photos I shall try to finish them when I get home. I have done one good drawing (I think) which should enlarge to a sizeable painting. Out of eight days only 4 were workable, its so depressing – how I remain and don't come home – well! (Thursday 11 October, Sault)

That 'good drawing', in pencil and sanguine, showed another distant view of the village, but on a level and through trees. Back in his Manningtree studio, after the trip, he would use it as the basis of a painting, *Picking Pears at Mouthier* (**274**) (bought by the Chantrey Bequest), and of colour and monochrome etchings. Again as redolent of the south as of the north, the painting in particular rhymes in its pastoral mood with *Stripping Haricots at Mollans*.

Leaving Mouthier on Wednesday 10 October, Peter travelled south via Annecy to Grenoble, where he visited the Musée des Beaux-Arts, and was particularly drawn to paintings by Bonnard and Matisse that he had not seen before. Then, on the Friday, he reached the Côte de Ventoux. On this occasion he went straight to Sault, and booked in at the 'reasonably priced' Hotel Signoret, recommended by the Doncasters. Surveying the number of works inspired by Sault, and its neighbouring hilltop villages, and appreciating their strength and serenity, it is surprising to read of the conditions under which many of them were conceived. On 13 October, Peter wrote Vera a somewhat lugubrious letter, which he followed four days later with a postcard:

I got your letters yesterday and was very pleased to receive them – they both put my efforts to shame – really because I am too busy feeling sorry for myself. Am sitting in the car – it's pouring with rain – did some work yesterday, I think most will have to be done when I get home – I'll do some drawings and hope to use them – The Hotel is typically French of the ordinary class – However I arrived as you already know on Friday midday – then went out to look for work, I came back when it got dark about 6pm or 6.30pm and saw an ambulance outside unloading a stretcher, on it a body completely covered over which was carried into the hotel, accompanied by crying relatives – this gave me a shock as you might imagine knowing my reactions to such things. I thought it might be somebody staying in the hotel – but it is now clear that it is somebody in the family – though who I cannot ascertain – whether its male, female or a child I don't know – judging by the weeping it must be very sudden & youngish – any way the proceedings are very gloomy – this morning as I was leaving 8am, the coffin was being manoeuvred outside my door – I can't wait to get out of the hotel each day – there are lots & lots of flowers in the Bar (which has been closed) where I assume the body will rest today – maybe its the funeral today? – I half expected them to ask me to leave but they have not done so. On Friday night there were lots of men eating and I should think some were staying in the Hotel – they have since disappeared – They were not holiday types – maybe workers in the area of some sort. The first floor where my bedroom is – has a large square landing which echoes every sound, I shan't be sorry to leave I can assure you but the landscape around here is really very good except for this morning – where I am sitting over, looking at what I can see of the gorge through the driving rain – I must hold out till Sunday and get some work. You should have got my letter by now, can't wait to see you. Love in abundance.

PS … here it will [cost] about £30 for ten days, wine included (vin ordinaire) – you have what is given – food is not bad, ordinary really – still under the circumstances I am lucky to be able to stay on. (Saturday 13 October, Sault)

The Hotel has settled down after the upset and one gets used to it eventually. Done another drawing or two – but can't get the paintings very far so I concentrate on the drawings, then paint, and when I get back – try to finish them off or use them for larger ones … I purchased a bottle of whisky on the boat and am very glad I did, I sit and have a cup with some evian, at the dull hours between 5pm – 6.30 when I am worn out. I get up at 7am the racket in the hotel wakes me and I am out by 8 or 8.30 and usually working by that time – the latest 9am. (Wednesday 17 October, Sault)

As recounted in this correspondence, the rain fell so often that Peter put away his wet canvases – beneath the car seats and in the tyre well – and turned to work on paper. But the drawings that he then produced not only served as the basis for the paintings but were achievements in themselves. (As such they were exhibited at the Thackeray Gallery in 1974.) Though some obviously impress by their imperial dimensions ($22\frac{1}{2}$ x $30\frac{3}{4}$ inches), all communicate well-defined and exciting graphic statements through a considered mix of media, such as chalk and crayon or conté and sanguine.

Though Bonnard and Matisse would act increasingly as major points of reference for Peter's vivid portrayal of the South of France, it is the spirit of Cézanne that seems to have presided at Mont Ventoux. Peter's drawings and paintings of Sault, Aurel and Montbrun-les-Bains bring to mind particularly the exploratory constructivism of Cézanne in his many responses to Mont Sainte-Victoire.

Yet if this echo resounds, it is as a result not of simplistic influence but of Peter's established practice; the resonant lessons of such a master as Cézanne had to be tested at length both on the ground and in the studio.

Be they hilltops and rocks or the walls and pinnacles of buildings, all forms were pared down by Peter to their essential shapes, as revealed by light and shadow, and as understood within their setting. Much was made at Sault and Montbrun of the heights on which they were built, whether as distant horizon or immediate and dominating planes. Aurel was valued more for the patterns of its surrounding fields.

Picking Pears at Mouthier 1973 (**274**)

Gnarled Olive Trunk, Aurel

Aurel 1973 (**262**)

Sault-de-Vaucluse, 1973 (**276**)

Bridge at Sault 1973 (**263**)

However, one view of the bridge near Sault in the late afternoon was interpreted (when painted rather than drawn) (**263**) more in terms of strong, pure colour, so offering a sign of preoccupations to come.

On Saturday 20 October, Peter left Sault and began the long drive to Illiers, close to Chartres in Normandy. The little town had played host to Marcel Proust during childhood holidays and, as 'Combray', became central to the world of his great novel sequence, *A la recherche du temps perdu*. Literature could affect Peter's aesthetic almost as strongly as any visual stimulation, as had been demonstrated by his response to the descriptions of Barbizon in George Moore's 'Henrietta Marr'. In 1972, he read Proust's work in the translation by C K Scott-Moncrieff, and was taken by the sensitivity of the author/narrator to his surroundings, be it the light on the sea at Cabourg or the countryside watered by the River Loir.

Arriving three days later, Peter discovered that sometimes the power of the written word could indeed surpass that of the image, for he was inspired by nothing in Illiers-Combray itself. Only when he began to explore its hinterland did he find a promising motif: the church of St-Blaise at Mézières-au-Perche rising up above a flat terrain. Even then his work did not immediately go smoothly, for having set himself up unobtrusively on a grass verge, he was interrupted by an angry farmer who thumped his drawing board. On recovering his cool, he produced a composition in pencil and sanguine that has remarkable weight and clarity. In some ways it revives the structure of the preparation for *La Plaine de Chailly* (**41**), in that a horizon line replete with topographical detail divides the barer spaces of sky and land. But this latest drawing is in itself more finished, and the resulting paintings are quite different from each other. While *La Plaine de Chailly* fixes on a sombre parallel between the turned earth and impasted pigment, *St-Blaise, Mézières-au-Perche* (**275**) demonstrates the potential luminosity of paint. In producing the canvas, Peter lowered the horizon line and painted what remained below in blocky shadow, so privileging an exciting sky of patterned clouds obscuring the illuminating sun.

On Thursday 25 October, Peter brought his work to an end, and drove into Paris, where he had arranged to meet Vera. Though time would prove that he had achieved much during their weeks apart, separation had not been easy. From the stay in Lastours in 1974, Vera would again accompany Peter on his painting trips abroad.

While those trips continued to have a peripatetic character, a more permanent base presented itself, in 1977, when Peter and Vera were invited to Bargemon by Elsbeth Juda. Peter would gradually appreciate the full potential of this village in the Var: as a community in itself and for its proximity to inspiring galleries and museums, as well as a rich and ever-present source of subjects. Thus the works sparked by these surroundings communicate a real sense of pleasure and plenitude, and of being at home in the south at last.

8 1971–1974: Etchings

The concentrated period of printmaking that Peter undertook in the early 1970s may have arisen circumstantially. Yet, of all of his activities, printmaking epitomises the balance of tradition and experimentation that lies at the heart of his mature artistic practice. To follow tradition, as he has increasingly understood it, it is not only necessary to appreciate a canon, but to master established skills. Only when those skills have been mastered can one deviate from them, and so experiment with purpose. While most great painting is founded on sure technique, an equivalent standard of printmaking is nigh impossible without it. Each of the more sophisticated processes of printmaking demands proficiency with a succession of tools, materials and procedures. However, that proficiency will in turn release the potential of those elements, and so facilitate individual artistic expression. Soon after Peter stopped making prints, he confirmed the degree to which he had succeeded in both the craft and the art of the activity. He published a handbook on *Etching Techniques* (1976) and held a retrospective of etchings (1979) which demonstrated 'not only the sheer number of prints … but the variety of technical variations' that he had undertaken (JRT).

Balcony, Aldeburgh 1971 (**209**)

Peter had derived a general pleasure from craftsmanship ever since he first visited the engraving workshop managed by his uncle (see Chapter 1). However, his first opportunity to engage properly in a craft arose at the age of fifteen when, on day release from Odhams, he studied printmaking under William Palmer Robins, Head of Etching at the Central School of Art. There he not only learned the rudiments of intaglio printing, lithography and other processes, but produced his first etchings (see Chapter 2). While he did not capitalise on these particular lessons in his early days as an artist, he put his manual dexterity to use in such tasks as making his own frames. Then, in the mid 1950s, as a spin-off from his painting, he developed a facility for designing printed textiles. In this endeavour, fundamental skills acted as a springboard for a liberating and radical exploration of pattern, and thus of the relationship between abstraction and figuration (see Chapter 4). Issues of form would prove similarly important in Peter's etchings.

Malham Night 1971 (**220**)

Peter began to visit the Etching Rooms at St Martin's School of Art late in the 1960s, during what he has called 'dull moments' of his teaching. Fascinated by the craft of etching, he would make trial images on spare pieces of zinc, and try out the various intaglio processes. Andrew Freeth, the Head of the Printmaking Department at St Martin's was always willing to answer any technical questions that arose from these sessions, as was Richard Bawden at Colchester School of Art. Additionally, he read key works on printmaking, including volumes by S W Hayter and E S Lumsden, and Anthony Gross's *Etching, Engraving and Intaglio Printing* on its publication in 1970. His study of the subject enhanced his admiration for, in particular, Rembrandt, Charles Meryon, Frank Brangwyn and André Dunoyer de Segonzac.

Of the forty prints that Peter completed between 1971 and 1974, the largest proportion – of over a quarter – combine etching and aquatint. In its widest sense, the term 'etching' covers both of these methods for, as explained by Peter, it 'is a process by which a design is eaten into metal by acid, for the purpose of printing from it' (Coker 1976:8). However, in its narrower sense, etching is a linear medium, in which 'the design is drawn with a needle through a layer of acid-resistant wax on a thin metal plate' (loc cit). Its tonal counterpart is aquatint, in which 'small particles of resin are laid on the plate [and heated] so that they adhere to it and act as an acid resist, allowing the acid to bite between them' (Coker 1976:72). Etching and aquatint are traditionally used together because their joint potential facilitates a range of effects equivalent to those in drawing and painting.

Malham Night, early state

Peter's work in etching and aquatint was extremely varied, and reflects his versatility in other activities undertaken at the same time. This can be exemplified by *Balcony, Aldeburgh* (**209**) and *Malham Night* (**220**), two contrasting prints both produced in 1971. *Balcony, Aldeburgh* is close in spirit to contemporaneous paintings of the same subject. It translates their strong design and restrained brushwork into clearly etched outlines infilled by flat aquatint planes. The tone of each plane is subtly differentiated from each other as the result of the patient and confident repetition of the addition of resin, yet together they build up to a strong effect of contre-jour. The greatest contrast of tone occurs between the top of the balustrade and the frame of the door, while the most complex combination occurs in the waves of the sea.

'Covering the dry print with tissue paper' (Coker 1976:55)
The Persian Kelim 1971 (**224**)

Low Force 1971 (**218**)

Seascale 1971 (**226**)

The Quirang towards Staffin 1971-72 (**234**)

Yorkshire Landscape 1973 (**279**)

If *Balcony, Aldeburgh* embodies the cool clarity of an architectural setting, *Malham Night* offers a natural parallel, in representing the nocturnal illumination of the Yorkshire fells. However, the means by which the two convey a similar mood are quite different. The etched lines of *Malham Night* are as expressive as they are descriptive, and so merge with areas of aquatint to produce a variety of textures as well as tones. The effect seems to replicate the immediacy of sketchbook drawing, while suggesting both the probing and provisional qualities of moonlight.

Peter also produced pure etchings, without the addition of aquatint, though mostly of the type known as 'soft ground etching'. In the more standard form of etching, the 'layer of acid-resistant wax' or 'ground must be sufficiently hard to allow handling and to ensure that it does not stick to the needle in drawing' (Coker 1976:13). A soft ground – containing a large proportion of grease – 'will adhere to anything with which it comes into contact' so is 'not used when direct drawing is required' (loc cit), but may take the imprint of drawings traced through paper or of such textured substances as fabrics.

The potential variety of soft ground etching may again be exemplified by two works from 1971, with *The Persian Kelim* (**224**) representative of the human environment and *Low Force* (**218**) of the natural world. *The Persian Kelim* depicts a music room with a pianist performing on his instrument though, as the title indicates, much emphasis is given to the highly decorated covering on the floor. It is a work in which action is subdued and emotion at its most implied. On the other hand, *Low Force* rehearses the powerfully energetic motif of water flowing through the countryside, as essayed in a significant series of paintings. Yet despite the difference between their compositions as well as their subjects, they exhibit a fundamental similarity in the bold intricacy of their patterning; for each figure in the carpet, each rivulet and rock, makes its distinct contribution to the image. It is easier to achieve such detailed definition when the design is transferred through paper rather than drawn directly into the ground. But more than ease the process, the soft ground invests the line with graininess and can incorporate rough shade, qualities which seem particularly suitable to both woven material and rugged terrain.

Though these examples demonstrate that pure soft ground etching can express tone as well as line, Peter also used the medium on occasion in conjunction with aquatint. That such a combination should be necessary, even imperative, can be seen in *Seascale* (1971) (**226**) which offers a similar, but wider, perspective to *Low Tide, Seascale* (**160**), the oil of two or so years earlier. The manual shading that can be produced through the soft ground process could never have achieved the nuanced tones of the furrowed sand flats or the pools of reflecting water that they contain. But neither could the outline have been satisfactorily set down straight on to a hard ground.

The need to sustain the essential concept of each design stimulated experimentation and encouraged the search for the appropriate technique. In the instance of *Seascale*, soft ground and aquatint together could alone produce the desired effect. On other, singular occasions, three or four techniques were employed on a plate. *The Quirang towards Staffin* (1971-72) (**234**) combines drypoint with etching and aquatint, while *Yorkshire Landscape* (1973) (**279**) includes those three *and* mezzotint.

Drypoint 'is the simplest and most direct manner of setting down a line on a metal plate that can be printed' (Coker 1976:68). The line is scored directly into the metal with a steel or diamond-tipped needle, held at an appropriate angle, so that a ridge or burr develops which then holds the ink; for 'a line with a good burr will print with a distinctive velvety richness' (loc cit). Though drypoint is often used in conjunction with etching, it is a satisfactory medium in itself, and the richness described by Peter can create a strong sense of atmosphere, as in the lowering cloudscapes, *Rain, North Sea* (1971-72) (**235**) and *Sun through Cloud, North Sea* (1974) (**290**). Another in this group, *North Sea Clouds* (1974) (**286**), is actually a mezzotint, which supports Peter's view that 'mezzotint is a process similar to drypoint', despite the fundamental difference that 'it is a method of working from black to white' (loc cit).

A powerful version of a favourite composition, *The Quirang towards Staffin* demonstrates how the addition of drypoint to etching and aquatint emphasises outline in what is otherwise an essentially tonal image. *Yorkshire Landscape*, however, is of quite a different order, in that its patchwork of fields appear as a technical

On the Moors 1970 (**183**)

showcase, each square of land being represented by a different medium and approach, mezzotint included. Yet, despite the extraordinary range of effects that Peter here achieved, he did not restrict himself to monochrome printmaking, but also tested the possibilities of colour.

Mouthier-Haute-Pierre 1973 (**272**)

Colour can be added to a print in two ways, either as part of the printmaking process, or by colouring each impression by hand. Peter tried both methods, using the former for Continental landscapes, and the latter for a still life. But even the landscapes are each produced in a different way. *Mouthier-Haute-Pierre* (1973) (**272**) is an etching and aquatint, *La Manneporte* (1973-74) (**253**) is a drypoint, while *Jetty at Night, Ostend* (1974) (**284**) is an etching. Peter added the colour to their plates by hand, carefully cleaning it off after each printing if he needed to change hue. The lightest colour would be added first. A painstaking and time-consuming activity, it did not encourage the production of large editions. By contrast, hand-coloured prints do not necessitate uniformity and can each be treated as a unique work of art; so it was with *Fruit Bowl* (1974) (**281**). Early in his exploration of printmaking, Peter had also experimented with monotype, another process for making single prints, including ones in colour, by taking an impression onto newspaper directly from the oil, *Yorkshire Dales* (1970). The result was *On the Moors* (**187**).

La Manneporte c 1972–73 (**253**)

Peter invariably printed his own work. On the one occasion that he secured professional help, in printing the colour version of *Mouthier-Haute-Pierre*, he was extremely disappointed. (These impressions were destroyed.) As a result of his extensive first-hand experience of every stage of the printmaking process, he attained a definite expertise which added gravitas to his images and helped his reputation. The etchings were first exhibited in a substantial group at the Thackeray Gallery in 1972, and made a significant contribution to the retrospective mounted by The Minories late in the same year. They sold well and were received with enthusiasm by his contemporaries.

Fruit Bowl 1974 (**281**)

John O'Connor even suggested that Peter write a book on etching for the same Batsford series for which he was writing on landscape drawing. Though *Etching Techniques* was not published until 1976, Peter wrote it two or three years earlier, as he produced his prints, a circumstance which injected the text and its accompanying photographs with a sense of immediacy. However, he received much help at transforming his knowledge into language from his son, Nicholas, who was then reading English at Cambridge. Judged to be highly readable and instructive, so simplifying a complex subject, it quickly sold out. Particularly heartening was the use made of it by fellow artists, including Sandra Blow and Jean Cooke.

Perhaps more important was the effect that the etchings had on Peter's own work and the position that they now hold within his oeuvre. When he first experimented with the medium, he would turn to drawings near at hand for conversion into print, and so treat the activity almost as an extension of his sketchbook practice, that is as considered yet spontaneous. Then, as he mastered printmaking techniques, a more formal relationship seemed to develop between drawings, paintings and prints, with established motifs and compositions being reconsidered and reinvented. The prints contributed to the extreme stylistic variety characteristic of the period by introducing an uncompromising aspect less apparent elsewhere. Designs are often pared down to their barest elements, tones are frequently sombre. The sense of place that is so carefully caught in drawings and paintings has been relinquished in favour of a greater abstraction. The results are not lacking in richness, yet expose every working of medium and technique. Closer than the textiles to the central concerns of Peter's art, they are at the same time a complete achievement in themselves.

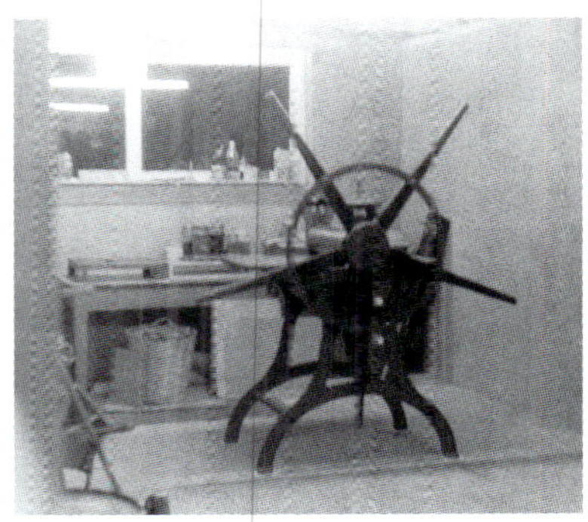

Peter Coker's star wheel etching press in his garage at Mistley

9 1977–1986: Bargemon

Throughout the 1970s, Peter had again travelled widely in France, and had re-established the balance between French and British subjects in his painting. However, he was fully able to accept the light and landscape of the Mediterranean only once he had gained a secure and regular base in the south. This was made possible by Elsbeth Juda, whom he met in 1975 through Roger de Grey, Principal of the City and Guilds. She invited him to stay at Bargemon, in the Var, and did much to enrich his first and subsequent visits. Her enthusiasm and energy reawakened his response to such exemplary moderns as Matisse. And it was her friend, Elisabeth Collins, who allowed him the freedom to work in the extensive gardens of her home, Le Vieux Château. The various experiences gradually instilled him with a new confidence. This showed in his painting through an ambitious approach to composition and, increasingly, a relaxed application of strong form and colour. Such qualities are epitomised by his magnificent series of arbours, the theme of which would spark parallel achievements when he went on to work at the Clos du Peyronnet, in Menton.

Elsbeth Juda and her husband, Hans, had moved from Germany to England in 1933. Together they founded *The Ambassador*, the 'British Export Magazine' for trade in textiles and other products. Enthusiastic patrons and collectors, they commissioned full-page illustrations for this publication from such prominent artists as Henry Moore, John Piper and Graham Sutherland. Hans was a trustee of the Royal College of Art, and sold his art collection before his death in 1975 in order to set up a scholarship fund for its students.

Window, chez Arcadio (**SB11**:1)

Elsbeth had additionally pursued an independent career as a freelance fashion and advertising photographer and, in 1963, founded a design studio to teach industrial practice to arts graduates. Since the death of her husband, she has also worked as a painter and collagist. Roger de Grey had known her since from days as senior Tutor in Painting at the RCA, and it was he who invited her to work under the guidance of Peter in the life room at the City and Guilds of London School of Art.

As a rapport developed between them, Elsbeth invited Peter to stay in the hill village of Bargemon, near Grasse, in the Var; though he needed to be persuaded before he accepted. She had bought part of a house built into the ramparts, which overlooked the gardens and orchards of Le Vieux Château, owned by her friend, Elisabeth Collins, the widow of a perfumer. Later, she would buy the remainder of the property, and convert part into a studio and part into a self-contained guest apartment. However, on their first visit in 1977, the Cokers stayed in a flat that Elsbeth rented for her friends; this was in the home of Mme Arcadio, on the second floor above a bakery. (Peter remembers how, on one occasion, a pastry cook with a violent temper threw confectioner's custard against the back wall of the rear yard - a kind of action painter manque!)

Window (**SB11**:4)

Bargemon offered Peter a wealth of experience, most crucially as an inspiration for his painting, but also as a base from which to make cultural and other visits across the region. Somewhat tentatively, even uneasily at first, he participated in the events that Elsbeth enthusiastically planned, and mixed with other residents and visitors, including Roland Penrose, the English surrealist who influenced Elsbeth's collages. Elsbeth herself would paint at speed, dashing off sketch after sketch, and so often find time to swim in the pool at Le Vieux Château. In the evenings she entertained with inventive food and excellent wines.

Elsbeth was perhaps even more keen to share her great love of the artistic tradition that had developed in the area through the twentieth century, and which seemed still very much alive. It was epitomised for her most triumphantly by the achievements of Henri Matisse (died 1954) and Pablo Picasso (died 1973), to which Peter would add that of Pierre Bonnard (died 1947). All three spent much of their later careers in south-east France, and are well represented in such major local collections as the Musée Matisse in Nice, the Musée Picasso in Antibes, and the Fondation Maeght in St-Paul-de-Vence. St-Paul is also home to the

Chapelle du Rosaire, decorated by Matisse in the period 1947-51. While Peter knew these venues, and made plans to see the many current exhibitions, it was Elsbeth who coaxed him away from his painting and so make time to look and respond to other artists.

Peter had, of course, long been familiar with these artists, and certain of their works had for him a powerful resonance. His painting had already begun to develop a particular dialogue with that of Bonnard, as instanced by *Ostend, the Café* (**293**), which, as explained earlier, expands on the tropes of such major figure compositions as *La Place Clichy* (1912; Musée des Beaux-Arts, Besançon). This evaluative relationship would not only continue but be matched by one with Matisse during Peter's time at Bargemon, and later at the Clos du Peyronnet in Menton.

Picasso, who rivalled Matisse and disliked Bonnard, stands apart as being of lesser and more limited importance to Peter. The fundamental lessons that his work could teach him, such as those regarding constructive design, had already been assimilated from elsewhere, and especially from Cézanne, one of Picasso's own essential sources of inspiration. That Peter did look to Picasso during this period is revealed most obviously in his rare ceramic decorations, many of Picasso's pots being on display at the museum in Antibes. Yet so pervasive a presence as Picasso inevitably intrudes into the work of as attentive a painter as Peter.

Terracotta vase decorated by Peter Coker with Palm leaves c 1984

Peter reacted with growing confidence to both the place and the people on each visit that he made to Bargemon between 1977 and 1986, a confidence that manifested itself strongly in his work. Though sustaining his existing range of subjects, including landscapes of the surrounding area, he also evolved a new dynamic between interior and exterior. This was signalled by series of paintings of the rooms that he stayed in, some of which are depicted as enclosed and private, while others open onto extensive vistas. The dynamic came to full florescence in his representations of the garden of Le Vieux Château – and of the Hanbury Gardens and the Clos du Peyronnet – which comprise complex, fluid spaces that break down distinctions between inside and out.

That Peter was allowed unrestricted access to the garden was greatly advantageous, enabling him to explore it at his own pace. He gained awareness of such luxuriant plants as agapanthus, agaves and chamaerops, and the fruit and olive trees; for until then, he had amassed little botanical knowledge, despite his friendships with such artist-plantsmen as Cedric Morris and John Nash. He also assessed the potential of these plants as motifs, singularly and en masse, and began to understand the relationships between their strong colours. More practically, he could leave his equipment wherever he was working, and did not have to carry it back and forth from his accommodation in the heat. On any one day at Bargemon, he might use a range of sketchbooks and draw in a wide variety of mixed media. These formed the basis of the paintings and large-scale chinese ink drawings that he produced on his return to Manningtree.

~

The earliest of Peter's Bargemon sketchbooks (**SB11**) reveals that he developed various themes in parallel, alternating images of windows with landscapes, views of the garden and studies of individual plants. However, the dates of the paintings and of their exhibition indicate that the most intense interpretations of the garden and its plants took longer to evolve.

Collioure 1979 (**388**)

Turning the pages of that sketchbook, the drawings of windows appear to fall into two broad types, those in which the window acts as a frame for a view beyond, and those in which the window is itself the main subject. But just as it would be crude to associate the former more with Bonnard and the latter with Matisse, so it would be wrong to divide the thematic group simplistically at all. Peter's drawings and paintings of this period prove the window to be an extraordinarily potent and flexible motif. At one extreme the window acts minimally as a secondary frame, as in his painting of Collioure (1979) (**388**),

Blue Interior by 1980 (**394**)

Blue, Black interior–Two Windows 1979 (**386**)

Interior 1979-80 (**393**)

the fishing village near the Spanish border immortalised by Matisse and his fellow Fauves. At the other it illuminates a seamstress, modelled by Vera chez Arcadio (*Interior,* 1979-80 (**393**)). Between these, it undergoes numerous stylistic and compositional variations, even being multiplied in the four ambitious versions of *Two Windows*. Psychologically, it seems to suggest degrees of openness to the external world, while formally it rehearses issues of pictorial space and proportion in the relation of figure to ground.

Windows, and associated balconies, were introduced by Peter into his paintings early in the 1970s, in such works as *View from Ivy Cottage* (**208**) and *The Balcony, Aldeburgh* (**210**). The mimetic detail with which they were depicted, each catch and baluster being carefully included, was in keeping with the accessible naturalism of that phase. But the explicit viewpoint, distinguishing the outside world from the inside, was a surprising departure, given the degree to which Peter had been concerned to capture 'the life of the landscape' (Gore 1992) (see Chapter 6).

From the later 1970s, while at Bargemon, Peter would explore more deeply the relationship between inside and out, the effect of the one on the other. Even that image of Collioure, in its framing of vertical stripes, problematises an observer's appreciation of the seascape beyond, by making it a view of a view. In the compositions conceived at Bargemon, a varying configuration of elements – glass, shutters, curtains, fragments of building and hill – contributes to the presentation of vistas which are complex, indirect or obscured. Not that the exploration was exclusively intellectual. Such works as *Blue, Black Interior – Two Windows* (1979) (**386**) and *Blue Interior* (by 1980) (**394**) are essentially atmospheric, their tonalities offering a cool retreat from the heat of the day. More generally, the palette is of greater warmth and intensity than that employed before. Indeed, the combination of the cerebral and the sensuous is highly characteristic of the specific French tradition with which Bargemon enabled Peter to engage.

Peter's initial sketches of single shuttered windows are undoubtedly reminiscent, in both colour and composition, of certain works by Bonnard. The view from the kitchen window at Chez Arcadio – out to the hills, over a tiled roof and the chateau gardens – is especially close to that in Bonnard's *La Fenêtre* (1925; Tate). In this type of image, the window not only opens onto a bountiful landscape, but ingests its light, warmth and fertility, conveying them directly to the viewer. In so doing it evokes an earthly paradise, a notion to which Matisse also acceded. Though Matisse had originally associated the Mediterranean with Charles Baudelaire's primitivist phrase, 'luxe, calme et volupté' (in the 1905 painting of that name in the Musée d'Orsay), he later portrayed it, and Nice in particular, as a civilised even domesticated Eden.

Interestingly, the most successful of the oils that Peter based on the composition do not communicate this sense of plenitude. Rather, they work to very different effect, unifying the picture plane by recreating space as solidity. At the outset of his career, Peter had been preoccupied with motifs that emphasised the material nature of pigment and support, whether a slab of meat or a cliff face. Later, his aesthetic evolved

Two Windows by 1980 (**398**)

Two Windows, Bargemon by 1982 (**418**)

in response to extensive travels, as he tried to capture the qualities of each particular terrain. The latest challenge returned him to first principles, and had him setting out to sustain materiality even in depicting distance, by reconciling the extreme difference between the far horizon and the immediate window frame. To realise this aim, he rehearsed the achievement of Cubism and, in *Window at Bargemon* (by 1980) (**399**) and *Window, Bargemon* (1979) (**391**), alluded respectively to the examples of Cézanne and Picasso. So the spirits of both place and painting were kept alive.

Window at Bargemon by 1980 (**399**)

The series of pictures featuring two windows comprise a more unusual subject, and bear a more subtle relation to the modern tradition. Like the paintings of the single window, they are based on the setting of Chez Arcadio, though its living room rather than the kitchen. However, they are not concerned with the view or its implications. The view from the living room at Chez Arcadio is, in fact, extremely limited, looking as it does onto a narrow street lined with plane trees. Of greater relevance is the window as light source, especially in the dramatic *Blue, Black Interior – Two Windows* (1979), which sits well within the strong tradition of contre-jour painting developed through the nineteenth century. This emphasis on light, together with the potential for juxtaposing planes of colour, suggests Matisse as the chief point of reference. The series seems to strike up a particular dialogue with the work of Matisse produced into the period of the First World War, both the flat decoration of such Moroccan scenes as *Sur la terasse* (1912-13; Pushkin Museum of Fine Arts), and subsequent experiments in near abstraction.

Blue, Black Interior provides a response to *Porte-fenêtre à Collioure* (1914; Centre Georges Pompidou), one of Matisse's most uncompromising compositions, in which the window opening is represented by an area of flat black. Though Peter retained the more naturalistic balance of pale windows set in dark surrounds, he treated each individual form and the relationship between them with almost equal restraint, so creating a similarly spare majesty. He showed that he appreciated Matisse's ability to indicate space without destroying the integrity of the surface. The motif itself directed the design through its arresting asymmetry, one rectangular window distanced from another with a curved top. Divided and decorated by signs of framing, louvres and safety rails, these shapes take on strong identities. To the attentive eye, they variously puncture the darkness, sit snug against it and float free. The effect is simultaneously solid and alive.

Window, Bargemon 1979 (**391**)

The other canvases in the series are variations on this theme. However, they comprise a distinct group, marked by a lighter palette and, perhaps, a sequential departure from pure observation. The first (**397**) seems to offer the clearest sense of space, through the presence of a corner of the room and the angling of open casements. Yet in subdued colouring and scumbled handling even it enacts a claustrophobic *intimisme*. Its very windows open playfully onto further obstructions. The second (**398**) has greater clarity and stillness but its inviting pleasures lie on the surface, as is also often true with the painting of Matisse: a strip of floor allows no foothold, cushions stand proud. The third rehearses modernist disruption, but in a strangely seductive fashion, dazzling fragments of Cubist light appearing in Fauve colours (**418**).

Agave, Bargemon 1980

Agave 1980 (**400**)

The views that there are from the windows and balconies depicted by Peter give a clear indication of the potential for painting in the area around Bargemon. However, the resulting landscapes, including those of Callas and Claviers, and those of nearby olive groves, tend to echo the qualities of his existing French subjects rather than breaking new ground. Far more innovative were the images of the garden of Le Vieux Château, in both their sensuous blend of colour and form, and their approach towards issues of inside and out.

The first plants in the chateau garden that Peter studied closely were agaves, the spiky succulents native to the Americas. The clear outlines of their variegated leaves variously curling would have been of obvious interest. But the sketchbook drawings also reveal a preoccupation with their relation to their setting, for they are shown in conjunction with the back gate, mesh fencing and stone walls. Thus the pairing of inside and out is here considered in terms not only of space but also of the contrast between the man-made and the organic. This can best be seen in the evolution of *Agave* (1980) (**400**). A sequence of more than half a dozen drawings and watercolours (mostly in **SB11**) explores what might almost be described as a power struggle between nature and culture. Sometimes the curves of the plant dominate, sometimes the angles of the walls. Power is finally balanced in the finished oil.

The possibility of such equilibrium is due in part to the structural quality of the agave. Even more architectonic – and sculptural – is the palm, and especially *chamaerops humilis*, known as the European fan palm. Images of palms appear throughout the sketchbooks that Peter used in and around Bargemon, and form the basis of some important paintings, including two delightful views of Antibes (**379**, **380**), which originated in a stay there in 1978. Though these views betray no ambiguity between interior and exterior, there are degrees of culture and nature, with palms acting as intermediary between a foreground terrace or balcony and a distant prospect.

Antibes–Palm by 1979 (**379**)

Antibes: Palm by 1979 (**380**)

The Palm, Chateau Garden by 1980 (**396**)

Palm, Antibes 1978

The form of the chamaerops, in both the individual leaf and the plant as a whole, offered Peter even greater body and variety than more conventional palms. For instance, one pencil drawing (**SB15**:8) represents a chamaerops as if it were a carving, the shadows appearing as deep cuts, the leaves standing out as surface. Then on the next page the many jagged fronds are vigorously emphasised in ink. It is therefore perhaps unsurprising that Peter should recruit the chamaerops to signal the fluidity between inside and out that so exemplified conditions at Le Vieux Château.

In four watercolours and drawings (**SB11**:65-70), Peter sketched out a dramatic composition in which the viewer looks down on a robust example of a chamaerops, caught in the angle of the house, and partly seen through railings. An urn defines the foreground at left; a pool indicates the background at right. The organic lines of the plant overlaps with the straight edges of the domestic environment. However, the sensation is of tension rather than of harmony. The two elements remained unresolved even in the canvases that resulted: *The Palm, Chateau Garden* (by 1980) (**396**) and *Chamaerops, Le Vieux Château* (by 1982) (**410**), the second of which was probably destroyed.

Resolution was achieved simultaneously in a composition of an arbour – which also focussed on a chamaerops – and in its subsequent variants. The arbour seems to occupy a long narrow space terminating in a wall. To the left is a building, to the right a low parapet. Wooden supports rise vertically from this parapet to meet those stretching from the building at an angled horizontal. Strung across this framework are cords creating a mesh. The arbour is essentially a room, but one open to the elements and populated by plants, and as such solves the problems posed by the motif of the window. Oppositions of inside/outside, culture/nature and private/public dissolve in this luxuriant and civilised space, which can be inhabited at ease.

Palm Arbour 1979 (**389**)

Palm Arbour, Chateau Garden 1979 (**390**)

Palm Arbour, Le Vieux Château, Bargemon

Study for *Palm Arbour* (**389**) and *Palm Arbour, Château Garden* (**390**) (**SB14**:14)

The motif of the arbour at Bargemon spawned at least seven major canvases. The first two (**389**, **390**) each comprise an impressive vertical format dominated by a chamaerops rising against the wall. A footpath of stepping stones leads the eye across strips of sun and shadow to be welcomed by its branches and dwell in its green heart. These paintings could be described as monumental, if they were not so inviting, comfortable, even healing. Most of those that follow exchange this airiness and clarity for cool shade and intense sensation. Strong form is replaced by vivid texture. However, the overall sense of pleasure is sustained. The spirit of Bargemon had been absorbed.

10 1980–1985: The Hanbury Gardens and the Clos du Peyronnet

By 1980, Bargemon had become Peter's established base in the south of France. Not only an inspiration in itself, it was the starting point for further exploration of the wider Mediterranean region, and for sealing his devotion to it. One important discovery, made in that same year, was the Hanbury Gardens, at La Mortola, just over the border into Italy. Then, two years later, Peter became aware of the private Villa Clos du Peyronnet, near Menton, through an advertisement offering apartments to let. That, too, was surrounded by a magnificent garden. The move that Peter made from Bargemon to La Mortola and on to the Clos had a profound effect on his artistic development, and can be clearly seen in the resulting paintings, which offer an increasingly sophisticated examination of the relation of colour to space, and especially those ambiguous spaces that are at once inside and out.

The celebrated botanical garden of La Mortola, near Ventimiglia, was founded by Sir Thomas Hanbury in 1867 with the help of his brother, Daniel, an eminent botanist, and Ludwig Winter, a young German gardener. Bounded by mountains on three sides, with the fourth running down to the sea, the extensive site enjoys a microclimate in which plants from many countries live as freely as in their natural habitats.

Peter was inspired to visit the garden on reading a publication by Sir Thomas, sent to him by Doncaster, his book-dealer friend. So during a stay in Bargemon in the summer of 1980, he and Vera made the first of four or five highly pleasurable visits. In that period, access to the garden was restricted, and visitors were not allowed off the pathways; and, though Peter could use small sketchbooks and take photographs, he was not allowed to set up an easel.

La Mortola (**SB15**:26)

The drawings that resulted appear in at least two sketchbooks, though some were produced on smaller sheets of paper and laid down in books at a later stage. They indicate three areas of interest: the pattern of overlapping banana leaves (**SB14**:25-28), pathways enclosed and shaded by mature plants (**SB15**:32, 34), and views from the balcony of a nearby hotel (**SB15**:26). While these were not developed into paintings, they presage subsequent compositions inspired by the garden of the Clos du Peyronnet. Indeed balconies and pathways also provide a link to Bargemon, and so suggest the continuing fascination with that indeterminate space between inside and out.

The Clos du Peyronnet is situated in Garavan, a mile from Menton towards the Italian border. Peter first became aware of this turn-of-the-century villa in 1982, when he read an advertisement in *The Times* regarding its apartments available to let. The booking that he made in response led to the first of several trips. On that occasion he never went beyond the garden. Once captivated, he and Vera returned repeatedly over the following three years and during various seasons, on each occasion occupying a different apartment. Later visits were made while staying in Menton proper.

Setcreasea Pallida 1985 (**480**)

Since 1912, the Clos du Peyronnet has been owned by the Waterfield family. Its garden was created in the late 1930s by Humphrey Waterfield, a painter, and is now maintained by his nephew, William Waterfield, an Oxford botanist. An unpublished memoir of Humphrey describes 'the magic beauty of the garden, its olive trees, wistaria, banksia roses, its view over the sea, and its background of mountains; it also explains how, following his division of the property into apartments at the end of the Second World War, 'gradually both house and garden, especially the latter, became with its bassins, its vistas and scala nobile even more beautiful than ever'.

Of the three Mediterranean gardens that so stimulated Peter, the Clos is much the smallest and most contained. The grounds around Le Vieux Château, while always called 'the garden', are sizable and varied, and include an olive grove, an orchard and a vineyard; altogether the property typifies the smaller estates of the south of France. La Mortola is closer in location to the Clos, in being near the coast, but is on a larger scale, with paths zig-zagging right down to the sea across both a railway and a road; its planting is also comprehensive and systematic, as befits a botanical garden Some of the contents of the Clos are similar to those of La Mortola, reflecting the owner's expertise, but it is still essentially a private garden, walled and separated from the sea by a road; indeed this is signified by the name 'clos', which means enclosed. While Bargemon had heightened Peter's awareness of plant life in general as a subject, La Mortola secured his interest in particular plant forms. And, when arrangements at La Mortola restricted him from developing that interest, the Clos provided the ideal conditions for further investigation.

Garden Clos du Peyronnet 1985 (**475**)

The work that originated at the Clos falls essentially into two categories: studies of particular plants and wider views of their setting. However, typically, it reveals great stylistic variety, as Peter engaged thoroughly, and imaginatively, with his subjects. At one extreme lies the self-contained, solidly described still life of a pot of *Setcreasea Pallida* (1985) (**480**); at the other the ambitious and intense evocation of *Bamboo Path* (by 1984) (**434**). Uniting the range is a dedicated exploration of colour and space or, more accurately, space through colour.

Peter worked almost exclusively in sketchbooks during his stays at the Clos, and the many finished pages that he produced there have functioned both as studies for paintings and as independent works of art. Some were extracted as early as 1984 for inclusion in the exhibition, *Mediterranean Gardens*, held at Gallery 10. In a review of that show, Graham Hughes concluded that, 'it makes an enticing argument that a quick sketch can carry more conviction than a bigger oil' (*Arts Review*, 26.10.84). However, while the larger canvases may convey a sense of magnitude achieved only at length, those devoted to individual plants retain the immediacy of the initial watercolours. Freedom of handling and freshness of colour characterise both.

Garden of the Villa Clos du Peyronnet

Take, for instance, the images of the *Beschorneria Yuccoides* or yucca, a plant related to the agave, to which Peter had paid close attention while at Bargemon (see Chapter 9). From the very first trip to the Clos, he made studies of yuccas which record both botanical detail and organic vitality (**SB14**:35–36). In these works, watercolour has been applied swiftly and confidently without any pencil underdrawing, so that strong broken outlines act as fields of energy, while washes simultaneously support this sense of movement and add body.

When, on the last of the regular trips to the Clos, in April 1985, Peter again focussed on individual plants, he produced a particularly vibrant watercolour of yuccas (**SB19**:21–22). Stalks thrust diagonally from lower right up to the centre of this composition, and burst into heavy flower heads; the palest of the leaves continue the line of direction across to the left. On translating the study into an oil (**474**), Peter strengthened this emphasis by heightening the contrast between the featured plant and its background. However, in all other respects he remained true to his first thoughts, and sustained the original atmosphere. That this approach was typical, rather than exceptional, can be indicated by another comparison, that between an oil of white irises (**479**) and the study on which it was based (**SB19**:33–34).

Study for *Irises* (**479**) (**SB19**:33–34)

The general format of the flower paintings inspired by the Clos is a regular rectangle (such as 24 x 30 inches) presenting a very shallow perspective with no horizon and no sky. The plants themselves crowd the surface, suggesting an atmosphere of luxuriant fertility. The wider views convey a similar sense of enclosure, though usually combined with a greater illusion of depth. Lighting is of fundamental importance, though its source is never seen. Indeed, certain of these views have a theatrical air, due perhaps as much to the work of William Waterfield as to Peter's representation of it. Akin to a stage designer or director, Waterfield was always making changes to the layout and the planting, and Peter often needed to revise his expectations and intentions when he arrived at the garden and set to work.

Irises 1985 (**479**)

Bamboo Path by 1984 (**434**)

One undoubtedly theatrical feature of the Clos is the *scala nobile*, a grand double stairway that connects the house to much of the upper garden. Urns and other pots bustle against each other at its base, and stand to attention at the sides of the stairs. Each is a character contributing to the show, and the challenge for the painter is to distinguish these individual elements while integrating them into the whole.

At least three large oils take as their subject an ascending flight of garden steps. As with the earlier images of the arbour at Bargemon (see Chapter 9), these create inviting spaces which are at once exterior and interior. The pots add to this ambiguity, even artificiality, though they hardly restrain nature. It spills out in a riot of form, its many different blooms and leaves growing close, and intertwining. If the first of the oils places some distance between the viewer and the steps (**426**), those that follow describe a more confined sense of space, the steps rising immediately from the lower edge of the canvas. One results in a reminiscence of the tilted table top of a Cézannesque still life (**486**), while another treats the steps as a scintillating waterfall of Fauve colour, areas of light and shadow standing out in solid primaries (**438**).

Garden of the Villa Clos du Peyronnet 1983 (**426**)

Clos du Peyronnet 1985-86 (**486**)

Garden of the Villa Clos du Peyronnet 1983 (**438**)

Peter's understanding and communication of the relation of colour to space culminated in two related paintings of one area of the garden: *Bamboo Path* (by 1984) (**434**) and *The Bamboo Pathway* (by 1986) (**490**). The most important study for each of these may be found among a fascinating series of drawings, some made on site and others in the studio, inserted into a sketchbook (**SB15**:32–44). This series rehearses Peter's fascination with enclosed pathways, and traces its evolution from those at La Mortola (1980) to those at the Clos (1983-84). With every consecutive image there is an increasingly intense sense of confinement, as if the viewer is adjusting to a change from light to dark, and still sees the light in the darkness. Each form becomes less comprehensible, but each colour more vivid. At this stage there may be echoes of the work of Graham Sutherland, who had lived latterly in Menton, at the Villa Blanche, until his death in 1980; the early neo-romantic *Entrance to a Lane* (1939; Tate) comes particularly to mind. But in developing these ideas into paintings, Peter banished such comparisons. He also transformed the mood, turning it away from anxiety, first to vivacity (in *Bamboo Path*), and then to tranquility (in *The Bamboo Pathway*).

Study for *The Bamboo Pathway* (**490**) (**SB15**:38)

For both the drawing and the painting of *Bamboo Path*, Peter made use of an exact square, a format in which he often worked at his best. The former, in wax crayon, indicates the topography in firm black outlines, and so retains a trace of naturalistic space: a path snakes clearly past a clump of bamboo out to the light beyond. However, in its forceful palette – predominantly of prussian blue – it is expressive rather than descriptive, conjuring up the feeling of cool in the dark corner of the garden near the back gate. In the painting, the outlines are free of anchorage and take on an active life; thus they lead the eye intuitively rather than logically across the picture space. Blue still predominates, but much of it has a lighter, brighter tonality which makes the whole less cool than refreshing.

The Bamboo Pathway offers a distinctly different interpretation of the same spot. An elongated portrait format narrows the space and stretches the key features. The drawing differs greatly from that for *Bamboo Path*, in being built from blended layers of wax crayon in a palette devoid of blue; and it guides the eye up the surface of the paper less by the residual outlines than by a smear of greyish-white, the lightest of the colours applied. The forms remain exploratory, the atmosphere uncertain. In a development opposite to that of *Bamboo Path*, the painting clarifies lines and shapes, so that even leaf patterns emerge. However, its chief strength lies in its inner glow, created by an increased contrast between light and shade, and having the quality of stained glass. Path, bamboo and the air beyond all shine out and, in so doing, still the spectator.

The Bamboo Pathway c 1986 (**490**)

11 1985–1989: Badenscallie

By the mid 1980s, Coker had established himself definitively as a painter of the Mediterranean south. However, he then threw this achievement into relief by turning to work in what was to him the extreme north. Though he had visited Sutherland and Skye from the late 1960s, his regular painting trips to Easter Ross still constituted a new phase of his art. The obvious contrast of Scotland to the South of France may have been accentuated for him by the circumstances under which the area was first viewed. For he initially went to Badenscallie at the invitation of his friends, the Ellises, following the sudden death of his son, Nicholas, in 1985. Yet he did not treat the landscape as a comfortable retreat or a conventional wilderness, but as a further site for exploration. Such exploration reached a new peak from his third visit to the area, in June 1987, when he unexpectedly encountered fishermen drying and mending their nets. These nets became central to his work, not only in defining a sense of place but extending the emotional power of landscape. The critical consensus has been that his later Scottish subjects are among the greatest successes of his career.

On the western edge of the mouth of Loch Broom lies a string of isolated crofting settlements, from Reiff in the north to Culnacraig in the south. It is reached by a circuitous route from Ullapool, the nearest town of substantial size, through mountainous countryside and around a series of small lochs. The steeply undulating coastal strip, dotted with stunted trees, is bleakly beautiful in itself, and offers superb views of the Summer Isles, out beyond Badentarbat Bay. Here the local population survives on farming, fishing and, more recently, a small amount of tourism.

Colin and Maggie Ellis own a holiday home at Badenscallie, one of the more southerly of the villages, which looks across to Horse Island. Collectors of Peter's work since the early 1970s, they gradually developed a friendship with the artist and his wife. As a consequence, they offered them the use of their Scottish house on numerous occasions, thinking that it would be a good base from which Peter could work. However, the Cokers accepted this offer only in the wake of personal sadness: the death of their only child, Nicholas, on 22 March 1985. (Later in the year, Peter presented *Gorse Bush, Audierne* (**60**) to the Tate Gallery in Nicholas's memory.)

On his son's death, Peter resigned from his teaching position at the City and Guilds of London School of Art. This freed up his time for reflection, and made travel possible at times other than outside the academic year. So he and Vera first went up to Badenscallie in the autumn of 1985, and returned in the following spring.

Sheep Croft, Badenscallie 1987 (**533**)

During these first visits, Peter concentrated on two aspects of the landscape: the crofts close to the Ellises' house and the views towards the Summer Isles. Working on loose sheets and in sketchbooks (**SB17, 20**), he produced numerous drawings and watercolours, the spontaneity of which was transferred, with apparent ease, onto canvas. As direct responses to a very particular terrain, the resulting paintings hark back to earlier Scottish subjects, and stand in direct contrast to the major achievements of Bargemon and Menton. However, careful scrutiny reveals that they too are considered and controlled.

Harold Brown's Croft 1986 (**509**)

An important feature of the paintings of the crofts is the proliferation of fence posts. They seem to pin down the wild open spaces and impose a structure upon them. In the panoramic composition, *Sheep Croft, Badenscallie* (**533**), a long post not only introduces a vertical element, but even bisects the picture space and so isolates a square to the right. Though reminiscent of the wooden stakes in the early *Landscape at Barbizon* (**40**), these posts conversely stand out for the most part as light against dark and also contribute to the animated handling. More pertinently, they presage the poles that are so essential to the subsequent images of salmon nets. This is particularly true of *Harold Brown's Croft* (**509**), in which the distant cottage is viewed through open-meshed fencing and dwarfed by two posts, a relationship highlighted by the use of white paint to pick out both building and shafts. Despite the absence of human figures, an unnerving drama is enacted. Elsewhere it is the land that is unsettling, the hills less rolling than rocking and tossing with the energy of moving water. It is no wonder that a drawing made on a subsequent visit should be labelled *Sea of Peat* (**SB23**:73-74). The sea itself, in views towards Tanera Mór and Horse Island, is comparatively serene.

Mending Salmon Nets, Achiltibuie 1987 (**522**)

The Cokers made their third visit to Badenscallie in June 1987. Not having been there before in the summer, they were greeted by an astonishing sight, and one which would become for Peter the central motif of his work in the area. In such coastal villages as Achiltibuie and Badentarbat, fishermen had put out their salmon nets for drying and mending, both stretched high on poles and spread out on the grass. These nets made the terrain seem unfamiliar by providing an indeterminate frame through which it could be viewed. In surprising reminiscence of the plants at the Clos du Peyronnet, they both created vistas and instilled those vistas with life. It is the nets, rather than the fishermen that use them, which truly provide the dynamism of the finished canvases and bear their significance; they that best represent the local character and way of life, and even bare the signs of a wider humanity's trials and triumphs.

Salmon Nets No 4 1987 (**531**)

Though executed in a characteristically confident mixture of media, the earliest drawings that Peter made of the salmon nets (**SB26**) seem to assess the role of each individual element. One drawing, in sanguine and pencil, provides a kind of key as to how these might fit together. The landscape, already known to Peter, is reduced to a high diagonal horizon, and bisected by the long strong verticals of the poles. Between and across those verticals lies a complex of curves representing the main lines of nets. Human figures provide scale, while floats and weights add detail and decoration. A few pages later, a watercolour explores the relation of poles and landscape to the exclusion of all else. Further on, the shapes of the nets are accentuated in black ink and white bodycolour against a sombre background.

Salmon Nets, Badentarbat 1987 (**528**)

It was necessary for Peter to understand the visual language with which he was working, in both its form and content. He was then able to express himself in painting with fluency and freedom. While the spirit of the place is rarely lost in the resulting canvases, they are extraordinarily varied, ranging from the solidly realistic to the allusively abstract, and indicative of many moods. Some comprise a numbered series, but nothing essential sets those apart and, indeed, deeper themes and variations cut across such a designation. Given that the paintings are based on distinct groups of drawings made on different visits, a chronological examination of them is perhaps as satisfactory as any other.

Salmon Nets No 2 1987 (**529**)

Of the first six paintings, produced in 1987, *Mending Salmon Nets, Achiltibuie* (**522**) stands out as a record of that initial encounter with the nets. Such telling details as the textured mesh and a number painted on a post convey an almost palpable sense of being there. Yet, at the same time, it presents those details as elements of a highly sophisticated composition. The two most dominant poles cut the picture plane into a triptych, and the more distant nets – set securely in their environment – take on a strong symmetry. While other objects rise to the surface as distinct identities, a solitary human figure remains ambiguously within the netting, neither certainly caught nor controlling. So detail and design develop into something alive with meaning and emotion. Indeed, if the structure suggests a Christian altarpiece, the netting might denote the fisher of men, and his power for both giving and taking life. Perhaps not consciously intended by Peter, this import remains in tune with his thorough and continuous absorption in the history of western painting.

Salmon Nets, Achiltibuie 1987 (**530**)

Salmon Nets No 4 (**531**) is as legible as *Mending Salmon Nets* but more condensed, for it excludes particulars in favour of essential balance and rhythm. As such, it reveals a potential for abstraction that is more fully exploited in the other works from early in the series. Each is built on a shared set of marks including, most notably, the straight lines of the poles, the curves of the ropes and the cross-hatching of the nets; but each expresses a unique statement, from unrestrained expressionism (**528**) through surprisingly intense exoticism (**529**) to freely-handled rhythmic geometricism (**530**).

Salmon Nets, Badentarbat 1988 (**551**)

Salmon Nets, No 8 1988 (**553**)

Mending Salmon Nets, NW Scotland 1988 (**548**)

Study for Salmon Nets, drying and ready for inspection, Badentarbat (**556**) (**SB26**:67)

The fourth and fifth visits to Badenscallie (on July 1988 and August 1989) yielded paintings of nets that are generally more naturalistic. The poles stand firm upon the vivid grass and under an intense sky, an environment visible both around and through the semi-transparent netting. Nevertheless, the variation between images is not wholly physical or climatic. Some have an almost oriental elegance (**548**, **551**), while others are brighter and more emphatic (**552**, **553**).

Salmon Nets, drying and ready for inspection, Badentarbat 1988 (**556**)

To an artist constantly concerned with the relation of figure to ground, the grid-like nature of the salmon nets, extended against a landscape high on poles, proved an ideal motif, and Peter mined it thoroughly. He then turned to the nets spread on the ground, from which he developed a further two compositions.

Salmon Nets, drying and ready for inspection, Badentarbat (**556**) presents a net stretched out across the canvas, each of its folds and ridges scrutinised and delineated. Interest is concentrated on the surface, perspective being merely hinted at by poles sketched in along the upper edge of vision. This stretched net cannot but call to mind a human body, and so invoke the splayed beings so present in the oeuvres of such modern painters as Jean Dubuffet and Willem de Kooning. Equally pertinent, perhaps, in the light of Peter's loss, is a much earlier work, Titian's *Flaying of Marsyas* (1575-76; State Museum of Kromeriz). This highly affecting, even shocking, masterpiece spurred many

Salmon Net Poles, Badentarbat 1989 (**574**)

Study for Salmon Net Poles, Badentarbat (**574**) (**SB31**:1-2)

Salmon Net Poles, Badentarbat 1989 (**574**) (**SB27**:87-88)

an artist into action when it was included in *The Genius of Venice*, an exhibition mounted in 1983 by the Royal Academy. A symbol of mortal fallibility and suffering, the satyr Marsyas is shown strung upside down, his skin being carefully stripped by Apollo as punishment for presuming to challenge the god's divine gift for music.

Salmon Net Poles, Badentarbat (**574**) revives the topographical space familiar to the fishermen – a field backed by a hill - but transforms it into a calvary. Relieved of their burdens, the poles lean and sway; long narrow nets lie exhausted below. If the former composition seems to associate the net with skin, this latter treats it as a shroud, and what a shroud contains. Remember the description by Frances Spalding of Peter's early painting, *Man Carrying Pig* (**42**), that 'the falling movement carries overtones of a Deposition scene and enhances the mood of religious dedication' (Spalding 1992:10).The point is not to accept Peter's art as an affirmation of belief; rather it is to understand its ability to express emotion at its most intense even through still life and landscape. An ambitious and passionate series, the salmon net paintings are at once extremely original and essentially faithful to Peter's initial preoccupations.

12 Since 1986: France and Beyond

Surveying a list of the landscape subjects that Peter has painted since he first visited Badenscallie seems initially like rehearsing his career: Etretat, Ostend and Menton stand out from numerous places on the Brittany and Normandy coasts. To look at the paintings, however, is to realise the degree to which he has continued to experiment, and has succeeded in reinventing even the most familiar locations. This may be demonstrated in exemplary fashion by a comparison between *Cliff at Etretat* (1955) (**35**) and *Promenade, Etretat* (1987) (**525**). While both keep faith with the fundamental desire to keep alive the picture surface, the geological quality of the former is entirely contrary to the airy atmosphere of the latter. The contrast between these particular works is indicative of the change that has occurred both to Peter's painting and to the areas that he has painted; indeed it marks the development of three or four decades. Yet his oeuvre as a whole does not obviously reflect artistic fashion or social modification. Rather it is a singular achievement which is, perhaps, best measured on its own terms and against established tradition.

Promenade, Etretat 1987 (**525**)

Early in Peter's career, Etretat had seemed like a touchstone, the place and the painters it had attracted embodying all that he most valued. Yet, while he continued to draw on its inspiration over the years, it seems significant that he should have made it the subject of another major statement in 1987. For at that time, he was beginning to evolve another maritime theme, that of fishing nets hanging to dry. Though it has certain techniques and effects in common with the series that resulted, *Promenade, Etretat* is as far removed in spirit from the paintings of Achiltibuie as it is from *Cliff at Etretat*. Its mood is signalled by its central motif, of windsurfers launching themselves out to sea. It is adventurous and ambitious, but in a relaxed and playful way. As such, it is antithetical to the passionate imagery of fishermen at work in an

North Sea 1987 (**523**)

North Sea 1987 (**524**)

often harsh environment, and to the undertone of personal loss. If the handling suggests the jauntiness of a work by Raoul Dufy, the palette corresponds to that of Peter's own *Bamboo Path* (by 1984) (**434**), and is similarly refreshing. In imbuing La Manche with the civilised pleasures of the Mediterranean, he here declared his fundamental sanity.

Not that this was the only interpretation of the northern shore of France and Belgium that Peter produced in this period. In fact, by again becoming a preoccupation, it provided proof of his versatility. From Etretat in the west to Ostend in the east, he made frequent visits to numerous sites. Especially favoured was a cluster of communities along the coastline of Haute-Normandie: St-Valery-en-Caux, Veules-les-Roses, Quiberville, Ste-Marguerite-sur-Mer, Varengeville-sur-Mer… Their hinterland, and the wider surroundings, also provided a wealth of subjects.

North Sea by 1988 (**539**)

The return to Ostend gave rise most notably to *North Sea* (by 1988) (**539**), a large-scale canvas that is the equivalent, and pendant, of *Promenade, Etretat*. It has even received the subtitle of *Promenade, Ostend*. Yet, despite this shared nomenclature, and the essential subject it describes, the paintings are marked more by their distinctions than their similarities. The image of Etretat has a highly-unified composition, the sailing boats and surfboards linking the limitless sea to the generous curve of the shore. Conversely, the image of Ostend is so clearly zoned into parallel bands that subtle puncturing of this structure – by boats, by people – actually accentuates the divisions between sky, sea and land.

Such variance and variation characterise this phase in Peter's painting when, more than ever, he could capitalise on his rich body of work as if he were his own tradition. So, if *Promenade, Etretat* offers a review of *Cliff at Etretat*, then *Promenade, Ostend* revises *Ostend, The Café* (1974-75) (**293**). It reverses the differences in tone between its bands, and eschews its uses of distance and detail. These changes fit the representation of a day that is overcast, and seems out of season; as a result, the viewer is exposed to the elements and feels the chill.

Study of *Cliffs, St-Valery-en-Caux* (**561**) (**SB29**:48)

Sparer still are two other paintings of the North Sea produced in 1988. One revives the emptiness of recent views 'towards Tanera Mór' (**523**); the other embodies an intense crepuscular obscurity (**524**). They are also akin to *Cliffs, St-Valery-en-Caux*, completed a year later (**561**). In their combination of minimal form and saturated palette, all three seem intrinsic to an artistic tradition that links Whistler's nocturnes and Monet's late waterlilies to more recent colour-field painting. However, measured against Peter's output, they are only the most extreme examples of his then current tendency to use a simple compositional trope to spark sophisticated facture, a tendency that manifests itself especially in the group of coastal scenes. These three examples demonstrate how that trope might be as basic as a shoreline.

Cliffs, St-Valery-en-Caux 1989 (**561**)

Cliffs at Quiberville 1989 (**559**)

Veules-les-Roses 1991 (**584**)

Such others as *Cliffs at Quiberville* (1989) (**559**) and the versions of *Veules-les-Roses* (1991) (**584**, **585**) make use of the solid silhouette of cliff formation.

More complex and more potent a subject was the small fishing port of St-Valery-en-Caux, with its harbour and lighthouse. The lighthouse, in general, had long been a particularly resonant motif for Peter, associated in his mind with the work of Nicolas de Staël and with his own hard-won early masterpiece, *Lighthouse, Audierne* (1957) (**60**). Over the three years between 1989 and 1991, St-Valery inspired a number of drawings and six paintings. While the first four oils are small in scale (as small as 4½ x 10 inches (**578**)), the last two are substantial and act as fitting culmination to the series (**582**, **583**).

St-Valery-en-Caux 1991 (**583**)

In themselves, they make an interesting comparison, offering very different developments of the same sketchbook drawing (**SB33**:3). One retains such topographical details as the posts that rise from the water and demarcate the deeper channels; indeed it accentuates them as elements in a rich play of verticals and horizontals. The other excludes them entirely and focusses on the lighthouse, the sail and a small square building, perhaps the harbourmaster's office. In this minimal treatment, these objects stand out in white on the horizon against a grey-blue sky, as figures in a possible drama. The first of these canvases is rhythmically active, the second taut with potential.

Cleaning Nets, Quiberville 1989 (**558**)

Study of *Cleaning Nets, Quiberville* (**558**)

The emotive quality of Peter's recent painting often suggests a human presence, whether he is himself the implicit figure in the landscape, or others are the subject. The Achiltibuie series demonstrates this quality triumphantly, for the motif of the nets denotes the fishermen and binds them to their environment without recourse to explicit narrative. The works produced on and near the Normandy coast are, in general, similarly subtle and coherent in their allusions, the land and the sea bearing traces of man's activities: field and orchard, lighthouse and sailing boat.

Peter had been drawn to manual labour and working environments from the beginning of his career, and conceivably as a metaphor for his own discipline; painting has always been to him a craft as well as an art, a task demanding physical endurance and technical accomplishment. Even before he had decided on the theme of the butcher's shop, he had depicted a china clay pit, an oil refinery and several collieries. More lasting was his fascination with the fishing industry. His response to an early experience of sailing with the herring fleet at Mevagissey, in 1951, was greatly magnified – and deepened – on encountering the Achiltibuie fishing nets in 1987. However, his most overt expression of this interest was sparked by visits to Quiberville in the period 1988-89. He made a number of small sketches on site, some showing a fishing boat and a tractor close to the shore (**SB28**, **29**). Then, back in the studio, he produced a large wash and chalk drawing of fishermen cleaning nets in a very different manner from those of Scotland. This became the basis for *Cleaning Nets, Quiberville* (1989) (**558**).

Peter Coker, Quiberville 1989

Cleaning Nets, Quiberville is manifestly a figure composition, for the men are the focus, as they sit closely together concentrating on the job in hand, surrounded by their boats. This is accentuated by the pictorial space, which is shallow and confined, excluding horizon or sky. Such an arrangement is common within Peter's oeuvre, but the handling is not, and signals a new approach developed through the five paintings finished in 1992 (discussed below). This handling is characterised by patches of bright jewel-like colour laid in at apparent speed, and contained within strong yet relaxed outlines. Applied to the subject of fishermen, it seems to suggest affirmation if not heroism.

Sea and Tractor, Quiberville (**SB29**:33)

Seascape, Quiberville 1989 (**575**)

The studies of fishermen also gave rise to *Seascape, Quiberville* (1989) (**575**), one of a grouping of oils of Normandy distinguished by their small size and panoramic format (mostly about 5 x 22 inches). Though Peter had made use of the format on previous occasions – as for *Aldeburgh, Yellow Kite* (by 1975) (**296**) – he here matched it with particular fitness to various, yet complementary, views. The ideas were generated in a number of sketchbooks (**SB28**, **29**, **32**) which, as often before, Peter had made to his own specifications. These contain many other, equally fine compositions, still awaiting development into paintings.

Orchard, Varengeville 1989 (**573**)

The subjects which Peter immediately transferred to canvas or board comprise an orchard at Varengeville (1989) (**564**, **573**) and the River Seine at La Roche-Guyon, in addition to the coast at Quiberville; for a row of trees, a length of river and a stretch of breakers eminently suit the low wide shape. The heights of La Roche-Guyon proved particularly inspiring, for in five paintings (all 1989) the artist explored the prospect down across an area of water. Some of the results are reminiscent of the view from the Quirang, and particularly comparable are the layout of *The Quirang, Skye* (1987) (**526**) and *La Roche-Guyon* (**565**). However, those that are most tight and economical have no such precedent. They treat the Seine as a streak of pigment echoing the breadth of sky, and so unifying the upper and lower portions of the picture space. If the more elongated of them (**566**) provides an exact and satisfying balance between sky and land, the other (**567**) contains all within a single sweep of dark foliage. As in so many of these recent images of northern France, landscape seems poised between the provisional and the eternal, an atmospheric effect never quite frozen in pigment.

In 1989, Peter was undoubtedly at the height of his powers, and was recognised as being so. The Fitzwilliam Museum, Cambridge, mounted a retrospective of his working drawings and sketchbooks, and in so doing treated his ideas, techniques and methods as seriously as his canvases. This was to appreciate him on his own terms, as an artist who always perceives the world through his own vision, and who comprehends it actively through his materials, especially the materials of drawing. Indeed, as he gained in confidence and freedom, his painting almost became an extension of drawing.

At the time of this exhibition, Peter was interviewed by Andrew Lambirth, and spoke with unparalleled eloquence about his own art. Certain comments in the resulting article, published in *The Artist's and Illustrator's Magazine*, are particularly revealing about his then current thinking, even when appearing retrospective:

La Roche-Guyon 1989 (**566**)

> As one goes on working, naturally one's mind moves in different directions. One had seen other things, other paintings, exhibitions, what's happening around one. I found in myself a much greater response imaginatively to landscape. The whole question of subject matter is finding something to identify with, and I've felt that I can really identify with landscape, particularly the dramatic and elemental. Painting out of doors re-energises one, makes one reassess the colour and everything else…
>
> For many years I've drawn in conté and charcoal…Now I occasionally use pastel and pencil, any materials that come readily to hand that are going to suit the purpose and create the sort of density I want. I probably over-densify things anyway, no doubt because of the physical nature of the work, the pressure, possibly because of the speed and directness of statement that I want. (Lambirth 1989:16)

Energy, physicality, speed and directness: these are the terms with which he characterised himself, and the work that he was then producing proved them to be accurate and fitting.

A more dangerous proof of this very driven nature manifested itself violently a few months later. Peter suffered the first of two heart attacks in February 1990, and the second in the early May. A serious, debilitating stroke followed during the same month while he was in Colchester General Hospital. It is quite remarkable that these events did not stop him working. By August 1991 he was again producing drawings and watercolours on site in northern France. Some of the paintings discussed above originated on this trip, notably those of St-Valery-en-Caux and Veules-les-Roses. He was assisted in these endeavours by Norman Starling, his then regular driver, and by Nelson Blowers, his framer, who adapted his wheelchair to take a drawing board. Vera was, of course, a continual support.

In January 1992, Peter thought himself well enough to undertake a two-week trip to the south of France. He and Vera flew to Nice, and were then taken on to Menton by car. Basing themselves at the Hôtel Pin Doré, they visited the Clos du Peyronnet by taxi and wheelchair. Despite his restricted mobility, Peter worked hard, producing numerous drawings in three sketchbooks (**SB34-36**). Then, in the ensuing months, he developed these into four paintings. A fifth painting took as its subject the pond at the Red House. To write of these five works of 1992 in terms of 'triumph over adversity' would be to diminish them. Knowledge of the infirmities of Paul Klee and Henri Matisse does not damage perceptions of their later achievements. And as they may be judged by the highest standards, so may those of Peter.

As already noted, this new phase in Peter's painting was signalled by *Cleaning Nets, Quiberville*. The subsequent works expand on its rich texture of loose bright patches of pigment. They also revive such important and consistent concerns as the relation of surface to space, of colour to form, and of figure to ground. However, there are differences between them, and they are best considered by topographical division: first Menton, then the Clos, and finally the Red House, Mistley.

Fenêtre Ouverte à Menton 1992 (**586**)

Menton 1992 (**590**)

From the Pin Doré, Menton 1992

The paintings of Menton are based on views from the Hôtel Pin Doré (a building which has since been demolished). While *Fenêtre Ouverte à Menton* (**586**) features the shutters and balcony of the room in which Peter stayed, *Menton* (**590**) focusses on the promenade below. The former is the culmination of the artist's lasting preoccupation with the motif of the window, and offers perhaps his most complete statement on the relationship between inside and out. Of its preparatory drawings, the most substantial dissolves such distinctions in a delicious fusion of wet white bodycolour and ink (**SB34**:1). The painting achieves the same effect through more emphatic form and, especially, strong outline. Outlines link the horizon to the wrought iron railing of the balcony by way of the reflection of a sunset across the sea. Thus light is brought into the room like a balloon being drawn in by its string, and is welcomed by the open embrace of shutters and windows. The long narrow format assists the eye to scan down from the sky to the very threshold.

In producing *Menton*, Peter returned to the canvas size of 48 square inches, a format he had often adopted and had used particularly for river and seascapes. It is salutary to compare the oil with the drawings, for they reveal that the artist compressed his composition when he turned to painting. To encompass all of the view available from the hotel room, some of the drawings span a sketchbook spread of two squares wide (probably made in **SB34**, but subsequently extracted). These studies depict palm trees and street furniture

The Grand Staircase, garden of the Clos du Peyronnet, late afternoon 1992 (**589**)

The Garden, Clos du Peyronnet, evening 1992 (**587**)

laid out along the strong yet gentle diagonal of the road; that in watercolour provides the blocking, the other in ink records the detail. And there are many details. In the painting these overlap each other, a plethora of verticals uniting the picture space from high horizon to low diagonal. Interlinked with these is the long reflection of the setting sun. Beneath this busy surface lies an equally unifying structure, a series of radiating lines, starting with the horizon, and ending with the window sill.

Study for *The Grand Staircase, garden of the Clos du Peyronnet, late afternoon* (**589**) (**SB34**:5-6)

If these images of Menton are essentially spatial, those of the Clos are organised by colour (**587**, **589**). Though they too rehearse an established motif – that of the garden steps – it is in a more uncompromising fashion. In earlier representations of the *scala nobile* and even in the latest studies (**SB34**:5-6), forms appeared ambiguous and restricted, but still relatively secure. Here, in these oils, they are reduced to frames for fields of pigment. However, the application of that pigment is layered and modulated, imbuing the surface with rich texture and sustaining a solidity of design. Like the best of Peter's paintings, they are objects which parallel the world, rather than openings into it; and the objects that they most suggest are cloisonné enamels, blocks of sparkling opaque glass fused together into patterns.

Water Reflections I, Pond, Red House

Garden Pond, The Red House 1992 (**588**)

Water Reflections II, Pond, Red House

Winter Pond Frost 1990

Pond, Red House

Perhaps inevitably, *Garden Pond, The Red House* (**588**) stands apart from these French paintings. Their production had followed Peter's established practice, in which the distance between the studies made on site and work on the canvas in the studio imposed a discipline; whatever the result, it would be an act of construction rather than depiction. By contrast, the artist's own garden pond is ever-present, can be returned to at will, but is less easily recollected in tranquillity. The positive outcome of this situation is that though ideas regarding the pond evolved over a long period, a great degree of spontaneity was maintained even into the final canvas.

Peter tended to make drawings of the pond on loose sheets and in an extreme mix of media. They call to mind the experimentalism of his earlier textile designs, which were exhibited at this time in a retrospective at the Mayor Gallery. In the brochure to that retrospective, Peter was quoted as saying that 'these designs I now realise were my own way at the time of attempting to resolve the Abstract/Figurative conflict' (see Mayor 1991). And in drawing the pond, he seems to have returned to this preoccupation. For instance, the studies known as *Water Reflections* attempt to integrate the glittering shape that is the pond to its more sombre surround. This intention had also lain behind the equivalent figure and ground in *Salmon Nets, drying and ready for inspection, Badentarbat* (**556**), of just a few years before. However, the painting of *Garden Pond, The Red House* suggests even more complex intent, for it combines a much greater sense of depth with marks that accentuate the surface. The viewer is encouraged to enjoy the physical process as much as the pictorial illusion.

Water has made a fundamental contribution to Peter's visual language, and to his finished landscapes, since he first visited Etretat. He understands – as Monet did before him – that the substance offers three aspects: the transparent, the solid and the reflective. Peter's paintings combine these same aspects, as *Garden Pond, The Red House* demonstrates. It is thus perhaps appropriate to sum up his recent phase with Ariel's words from Shakespeare's *The Tempest*: his work has suffered a sea-change into something rich and strange.

On finishing on these paintings, Peter began to feel dispirited by the strict limitations to his freedom of movement, and virtually gave up the making of art. Existing work was kept in the public consciousness by a major travelling retrospective, in 1992, by the annual Royal Academy *Summer Exhibition*, and by some other events. Perhaps, more importantly, he thought continually about his work and about the possibility of future projects. This thinking was fuelled by extensive reading and by intermittent travel to France and Italy. In the spring of 1998, he even made a return visit with Vera to Menton and the Clos du Peyronnet, where he managed to fill several pages of a new sketchbook (**SB36**). As much as any medical help, his very belief in himself as an artist sustained him through his disabilities and bouts of severe illness.

Then, soon after Easter 2002, following a gap of ten years, he began to paint again.

Peter Coker c 1989

Catalogue Raisonné of major oils, watercolours and etchings

> **Key**
> **date**
> *title* [and *alternative title*]
> description, including size in inches,
> to the nearest quarter inch
> (Exhibited place date/exhibition number)
> (last known owner)

circa 1941-43

1 *Long Acre*
etching, dimensions unknown

2 *The Rat Catcher [after Rembrandt]*
etching, 4 x 2½ inches
illustrated page 31

1946

3 *Thames Wharf*
oil on canvas, approximately 16 x 20 inches
(whereabouts unknown)

1949

4 *Carnival in Venice*
ink with watercolour and bodycolour,
19½ x 28 inches
(Exh Flying Colours at Watercolour and Drawings Fair 1999)
(Peter Coker)
illustrated page 33

5 *Pollarding at Trafalgar Square outside the National Portrait Gallery*
oil on canvas, 30 x 30 inches
(destroyed)

6 *Still Life*
signed; signed and inscribed with title on reverse, oil on board, 25 x 30 inches
(Exh RA 1950/141; Touring 1972-73/1)
(Peter Coker)
illustrated page 34

1949-50

7 *Melon Eater*
oil, approximately 30 x 24 inches
(Exh RBA 1951)
(destroyed)

8 *Melon Stall*
oil, approximately 24 x 30 inches
(Exh RBA 1951)
(destroyed)

1950

9 *Nude*
oil, 30 x 20¼ inches
(Royal College of Art)
illustrated page 35

10 *Old Man with a Cap*
oil on canvas, approximately 13 x 12 inches
(Richard Cory Smith)

circa 1950-52

11 *Still Life [with French Blue Enamel Jug]*
oil, 24 x 30 inches
(Exh RA 1952/261)
(whereabouts unknown)

12 *Still Life with Rhubarb and Black Earthenware Jug*
oil, 24 x 30 inches
(possibly destroyed)

1951

13 *Landscape China Clay Pits St Austell*
oil, 26 x 38 inches
(whereabouts unknown)

14 *[Portrait of Alban] 'Tubby' Webb*
signed on reverse, oil on canvas,
30 x 24 inches
(Exh Chelmsford 1978/1; Mayor 1991/15)
(Private Collection)
illustrated page 38

15 *[Portrait of] Old Man [with Beard]*
oil on canvas, 30 x 24 inches
(Exh Touring 1972-73/2; Ipswich Art Club 1991/50)
(Ipswich Borough Council Museums & Galleries)
illustrated page 35

1952

16 *And then I saw eleven men* [also known as *The Football Ground, Leytonstone*]
oil on canvas, 36 x 48 inches
(now the reverse of *Cliff at Etretat* (**35**))
illustrated page 38

17 *The Brick Arches of Leyton Midland Road Station*
oil on paper, dimensions unknown
(whereabouts unknown)

18 *Dowlas Steel Works, Cardiff*
watercolour, dimensions unknown
(Exh Piccadilly Gallery 1954/9)
(whereabouts unknown)

19 *Mountain Ash, Rhondda*
watercolour, dimensions unknown
(Exh Piccadilly Gallery 1954/12)
(Anglesey Heritage)
illustrated page 37

20 *Patty Page*
oil, 36 x 28 inches
(whereabouts unknown)

21 *Penycraig Colliery* [also known as *Penny Craig, Naval Colliery*]
watercolour, dimensions unknown
(Exh Piccadilly Gallery 1954/13)
(whereabouts unknown)

22 *[Portrait of] John Jacobs*
signed and dated 1952 on reverse, oil on board, 19¾ x 13¾ inches
(Exh Mayor 1991/16)
(Private Collection)
illustrated page 38

23 *Tonypandy [Naval Colliery Rhondda Valley S Wales]*
inscribed with title and dated 'April 9th 52',
watercolour, 15 x 22 inches
(Exh Piccadilly Gallery 1954/10)
(National Museums and Galleries of Wales, Cardiff)
illustrated page 37

24 *Tonypandy-Rhondda Valley*
watercolour, dimensions unknown
(Exh Management House 1954/37)
(whereabouts unknown)

25 *Ystrad, Rhondda* [also known as *Pit Head Rhondda*]
watercolour, dimensions unknown
(Exh Piccadilly Gallery 1954/11)
(whereabouts unknown)

circa 1952

26 *[Portrait of] Geraldine*
oil on canvas, 22 x 16 inches
(Exh RA 1954/493; Castle Colchester 1962; Touring 1972-73/3)
(Royal College of Art)
illustrated page 39

circa 1952–53

27 *[Portrait of] F H Jowett Esq, CBE* (first version)
oil, 30 x 25 inches
(Percy Hague Jowett)

28 *[Portrait of] P H Jowett Esq, CBE* (second version)
oil on canvas, 30 x 25 inches
(Exh RA 1954/398; RCA 1962/143; Touring 1972-73/4; RCA 1988/89)
(Royal College of Art)
illustrated page 40

1954

29 *Fish and Newspaper*
signed, oil on canvas, 50 x 40 inches
(Exh St Martin's School of Art 1955; Zwemmer 1956/14; Touring 1966/21; Touring 1979/1)
(Mr and Mrs Alan Ellis)
illustrated page 41

1954-55

30 *Fish with Grill*
oil on canvas, 33 x 23¼ inches
(Exh Zwemmer 1956/8; Jeffress 1956/8)
(H Dickson)

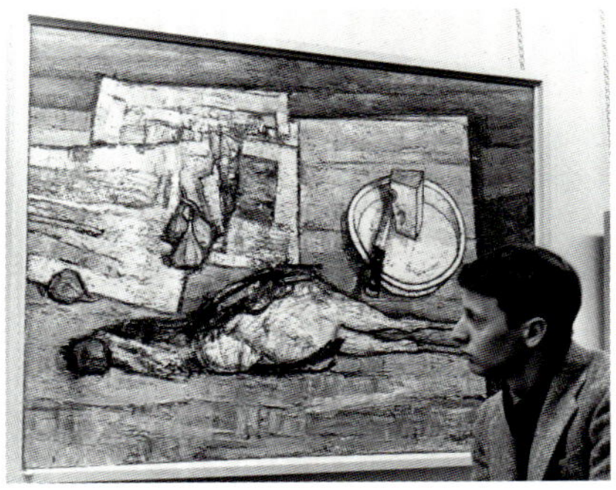

31

31 *Still Life with Chicken [on Table with Gruyere Cheese]*
signed, oil on canvas, 35½ x 47½ inches
(Exh Zwemmer 1956/15)
(whereabouts unknown)

1955

32 *Apple Tree*
signed, oil on board, 72 x 48 inches
(Exh Zwemmer 1956/3; Zwemmer Summer 1956; RA 1957/502; Chelmsford 1978/5)
(Accenture Art Collection)
illustrated page 53

33 *Butcher's Shop I*
signed, oil on board, 72 x 48 inches
(Exh Zwemmer 1956/1; RA 1956/348; Touring 1972-73/5; Touring 1975-76/28; RA British Painting 1977/76; Touring 1979/4; Touring 1984/18d; Critic's Choice 1984-85; RCA 1988/90; Norway 1997-98/20)
(Sheffield City Art Galleries)
illustrated page 42

34 *Butcher's Shop II*
signed, oil on board, 72 x 48 inches
(Exh Zwemmer 1956/5; RA 1956/440; Touring 1972-73/ex-cat; Touring 1979/6; Touring 1984/18b; Mall 1989)
(Doncaster Museum and Art Gallery)
illustrated page 43

35 *Cliff at Etretat*
signed, oil on canvas, 52 x 78 inches
(Exh Zwemmer 1956/11; RA 1957/446; Touring 1972-73/8; Fieldborne 1973/4; Chelmsford 1978/6; Minories 1979/20; Touring 1992/7)
(Sheffield City Art Galleries)
illustrated page 50

36 *Cliffs near Etretat*
signed, oil on canvas, 36 x 48 inches
(Exh Zwemmer 1956/13)
(Estate of Derek Hill)
illustrated page 51

37

37 *Dead Hare on Table*
signed, oil on canvas, 50 x 40 inches
(Exh Zwemmer 1956/10; Bournemouth 1956/6; Arts Council 1962; Arts Council 1966/7; Touring 1966/22; Touring 1972-73/10; Touring 1979/14)
(Arts Council Collection, Hayward Gallery, London)

38 *Hare on Table* [also known as *Still Life with Dead Hare*]
lithograph, 15 x 20½ inches
(Exh Zwemmer 1956/32; Touring 1972-73/92; Touring 1979/26)

39 *Hare Skinned*
oil on paper, 16 x 29 inches
(Exh Touring 1979/17)
(Patrick Dearsley)

40 *Landscape at Barbizon* [also known as *Allotments, Barbizon* and *Barbizon Landscape*]
signed, oil on canvas, 32 x 48 inches
(Exh Zwemmer 1956/7; Bournemouth 1956/41; CAS 1959/ex-cat; Touring 1972-73/9; Touring 1992/8)
(Huddersfield Art Gallery)
illustrated page 52

41 *La Plaine de Chailly*
oil on board, 36 x 48 inches
(Exh Zwemmer 1956/6; Zwemmer Spring 1959/2; Zwemmer Summer 1959)
(Mrs Thelma Seear)
illustrated page 54

42 *Man carrying Pig*
signed; signed and dated 1955 on reverse, oil on board, 72 x 33 inches
(Exh Zwemmer 1956/4; South London 1956/10; Austria 1960/5; Touring 1972-73/6; RA 1973/511; Touring 1979/9)
(Tate)

43 *Pig's Head*
signed, oil on canvas, 25 x 30 inches
(Exh Zwemmer 1956/9; Chelmsford 1978/3; Touring 1979/30)
(Castle Museum, Norwich)

44 *The Rock, Etretat*
oil, dimensions unknown
(Zwemmer 1956/16)
(Private Collection, China)
illustrated page 51

42

45 *Sheep Carcasses on Bench*
signed, oil on board, 60 x 45 inches
(Exh Zwemmer 1956/2; RA 1956/592; Touring 1972-73/7; RA 1973/578; Touring 1979/11; Leicester 1982/18; Ellingham Mill 1983; Glynn Vivian 1985; Mayor 1991/ex-cat)
(Royal Academy: diploma work)
illustrated page 44

46 *Sheep's Head*
pencil, charcoal, pastel and watercolour, 15¼ x 22 inches
(Exh Touring 1979/23)
(Tate)

47 *Sheep's Head on Newspaper*
signed, oil on canvas, 36 x 19 inches
(Exh Zwemmer 1956/17; Chelmsford 1978/4; Touring 1979/20; Michael Haas 1995)
(Private Collection)

48 *Still Life with Hare [and Grapes]*
signed, oil on board, 32 x 48 inches
(Exh Zwemmer 1956/12; Chelmsford 1978/2; Touring 1979/19)
(Chelmsford & Essex Museum)

49 *Table and Chair*
signed; signed, inscribed with title and dated 1955 on reverse, oil and sand on fibreboard, 60 x 48 inches
(Exh Zwemmer 1956/18; Touring 1972-73/11; Tate 1982)
(Tate)
illustrated pages 45 and 174

1956

50 *Tree and Hedge I*
signed, oil on hardboard, 48 x 72 inches
(Exh Zwemmer 1957/1; Zwemmer Summer 1958; Zwemmer Spring 1959/5; Liverpool 1959/23; Northampton 1960; Touring 1972-73/12)
(Provost family)
illustrated page 60

51 *Tree and Hedge II*
signed, oil on hardboard, 37 x 57 inches
(Exh Zwemmer 1957/8; Contemporary Art Society 1959/11; Touring 1972-73/13; Chelmsford 1978/8; Touring 1992/9)
(Alfred East Art Gallery, Kettering)
illustrated page 60

52 *The Wave [Etretat]*
signed, oil on canvas, 49 x 40 inches
(Exh Zwemmer 1957/9; Touring 1972-73/14; Touring 1992/10)
(Mrs Mandley)
illustrated page 58

by 1957

53 *Brittany Landscape*
oil on canvas, 40 x 50 inches
(Exh Zwemmer 1957/3; RA 1962/356)
(Private Collection)

54 *Wave*
oil on canvas, 33 x 23½ inches
(Exh Zwemmer 1957/13)
(Peter Winckworth)

55 *Waves and Rock*
oil on hardboard, 48 x 32 inches
(Exh Zwemmer 1957/11; RA 1964/82)
(Sheffield City Art Galleries)

56 *White Buoys, Audierne*
oil on hardboard, 48 x 36 inches
(Exh Zwemmer 1957/10; Zwemmer Spring 1959/11; RA 1961/468)
(H W Robinson)

1957

57 *Bracken and Gorse, Audierne* [also known as *Gorse and Bracken, Audierne*]
signed, oil on hardboard, 48 x 60 inches
(Exh Zwemmer 1957/2; Touring 1972-73/17; Touring 1992-93/11)
(City of Birmingham Museum and Art Gallery)
illustrated page 61

58 *Forest I*
signed, oil on canvas, 48 x 36 inches
(Exh Zwemmer 1957/4; Touring 1972-73/15; Touring 1992-93/1)
(Herbert Art Gallery and Museum, Coventry)

59 *Forest II*
oil on hardboard, 48 x 32 inches
(Exh Zwemmer 1957/7)
(Private Collection, USA)
illustrated page 57

60 *Gorse Bush [Audierne]*
signed; dated 1957 on reverse, oil on hardboard, 57¼ x 47¼ inches
(Exh Zwemmer 1957/5; Zwemmer Spring 1959/13; RA 1961/460; Zwemmer 1967/10; Thackeray 1970/12; Beecroft 1972; RA 1973/524; Leicester 1973/2; Radlett 1975/5; Chelmsford 1978/7; Minories 1979/21)
(Tate)
illustrated page 60

61 *Jetty*
oil on hardboard, 14 x 10¼ inches
(Zwemmer 1957/12; Touring 1972-73/37)
(G R Kennerley)

62 *Lighthouse, Audierne*
signed, oil on hardboard, 48 x 32 inches
(Exh Zwemmer 1957/6; Touring 1972-73/16; Chelmsford 1978/9; Touring 1992-93/12)
(Geoffrey White)
illustrated page 59

63 *Nicholas Asleep*
signed, oil on canvas, 15½ x 26 inches
(Exh Mayor 1991/17)
(Private Collection)

64

64 *Still life with Fish*
signed, oil on hardboard, 48 x 32 inches
(Exh Zwemmer 1959/1)
(Julian Hartnoll)

1958

65 *Smoked Mackerel on Table*
signed on reverse, oil on board, 16 x 31¼ inches
(Exh Mayor 1991/18)
(Private Collection)

66 *Fish and Bread*
signed, oil on board, 48 x 36 inches
(Exh Tate 1958/10; Zwemmer 1964/ex-cat; Touring 1972-73/13)
(Provost family)

1958-59

67 *Clouds I*
oil on hardboard, 48 x 32 inches
(Exh Zwemmer 1959/5)
(Atlantic Steam Navigation Co Ltd)

68 *Clouds II*
oil on canvas, 48 x 36 inches
(Exh Zwemmer 1959/14a)
(destroyed)

69 *Sunflowers*
oil on hardboard, 47¼ x 38¼ inches
(Exh Zwemmer 1959/3)
(Kemper)

1959

70 *Epping*
medium and dimensions unknown
(Exh Phoenix 196?/21)
(whereabouts unknown)

71 *Epping Forest*
signed on reverse, oil on paper laid on canvas, 13¾ x 15¼ inches
(Exh Mayor Gallery 1991/19)
(Private Collection)
illustrated page 63

72

72 *Forest I*
signed, oil on canvas
48 x 36 inches
(Exh Zwemmer 1959/6; Tib Lane 1959/20; RA 1997/621)
(Berardo Collection, Portugal)

73 *Forest II*
oil on canvas, 48 x 36 inches
(Exh Zwemmer 1959/7)
(Private Collection)

74 *Forest III* [also known as *Epping Forest III*]
signed, oil on hardboard, 48 x 36 inches
(Exh Zwemmer 1959/8; RCA 1962/139; Arts Council 1963/45; Chelmsford 1978/10; Ipswich Art Club 1991/52; Touring 1992-93/3)
(Ipswich Borough Council Museums & Galleries)
illustrated page 64

75 *Forest IV*
oil on canvas, 48 x 32 inches
(Exh Zwemmer 1959/9; Tib Lane 1959/21)
(Dr Gil Park)
illustrated page 64

76 *Forest V*
oil on canvas, 48 x 36 inches
(Exh Zwemmer 1959/10; RCA 1962/138)
(Private Collection)

77 *Forest VI*
signed, oil on hardboard, 58½ x 40¼ inches
(Exh Zwemmer 1959/11; Touring 1972-73/21; RA British Painting 1977/77; Touring 1992-93/4)
(Chris Beetles)
illustrated page 65

78 *Forest VII*
oil on paper, 13¼ x 9½ inches
(Exh Zwemmer 1959/12)
(Cole)

79 *Forest VIII*
signed, oil on canvas, 76¾ x 51 inches
(Exh Zwemmer 1959/13; RA 1961/482; RA Bicentenary 1968/D9; Touring 1972-73/22; Touring 1992-93/5)
(Scottish National Gallery of Modern Art)
illustrated page 78

80 *Forest IX*
signed, oil on canvas, 62¾ x 51½ inches
(Exh Zwemmer 1959/14; Austria 1960/4; Liverpool 1961/33; Touring 1972-73/23; Chelmsford 1978/11; Cheltenham 1990/89; Touring 1992-93/6)
(Rugby Borough Council Collection)
illustrated page 64

81 *Sea[-]scape*
signed, oil on hardboard, 60 x 48 inches
(Exh Zwemmer 1959/4; RA 1960/169; Zwemmer Summer 1965; Zwemmer 1967/9; Touring 1972-73/20)
(Provost family)

82 *Still[-]Life with Hare*
signed, oil on hardboard, 36 x 48 inches
(Exh Zwemmer 1959/2; RA 1967/570; Touring 1972-73/19; Carlisle 1975/110; Touring 1979/40; RCA 1988/91)
(Carlisle Museum and Art Gallery)

83 *Village in Brittany*
oil, 48 x 48 inches
(Exh Zwemmer Spring 1959/16)
(Private Collection, USA)

by 1960

84 *Sunflowers*
oil on board, approximately 48 x 36 inches
(Private Collection)

by 1961

85 *Copse*
oil on canvas, 47¾ x 37¾ inches
(Exh Zwemmer Summer 1961)
(Provost family)

1961

86 *Sunflowers*
signed, oil on board, 48 x 36 inches
(Exh Zwemmer 1961; Chelmsford 1978/12)
(Mrs Mary O'Donovan)

1962

87 *Hydrangea*
oil, dimensions unknown
(Private Collection)

88 *Llanberis Pass*
pen and watercolour, 30 x 32 inches
(Exh Zwemmer 1964/27)
(James Galway)

89 *Study, Tree Trunks*
oil on paper, 13¼ x 8¾ inches
(Exh Zwemmer 1964/31)
(Mrs M Barr)

1963

90 *Avenue of Trees*
oil on board, 48 x 36 inches
(Exh Zwemmer 1964/12)
(Taylor)

91 *The Brett, Study*
oil on board, 14 x 12 inches
(Exh Zwemmer 1964/14)
(Provost family)

92 *Epping Forest I*
oil on canvas, 24 x 20 inches
(Exh Zwemmer 1964/1)
(destroyed)

82

93 *Epping Forest II*
oil on canvas, 34 x 44 inches
(Exh Zwemmer 1964/2)
(Essex Education Committee)

94 *Epping Forest III*
oil on canvas, 40 x 20 inches
(Exh Zwemmer 1964/3)
(Mr Barr)

95 *Epping Forest IV*
oil on canvas, 30 x 20 inches
(Exh Zwemmer 1964/4)
(Colchester Art Society)

96 *Garden Copse*
oil on board, 48 x 36 inches
(Exh RA 1966/79; Thackeray 1970/3)
(Whitelands College, Putney)

97 *Landscape near Audierne*
oil on canvas, 30 x 25 inches
(Exh Zwemmer 1964/6)
(Thorn Industries)

98 *Late Summer, Epping*
oil on canvas, 48 x 36 inches
(Exh Zwemmer 1964/5)
(Mr George)

99 *Pen-y-Gwyrd Pass*
oil on canvas, 30 x 20 inches
(Exh Zwemmer 1964/11; RA for Schools 1967/27)
(Derbyshire Education Committee)

100 *River Brett* [also known as *Essex Stream*]
signed, inscribed with title and dated 'November 1963' on reverse, oil on board, 48 x 48 inches
(Exh Zwemmer 1964/16; Touring 1972-73/25)
(The Pyms Gallery, London)
illustrated page 69

1964

101 *Aldeburgh I*
signed with initials, inscribed 'High Sea, Aldeburgh, Suffolk', dated 'April 1964', oil on board, 48 x 48 inches
(Exh Zwemmer 1964/17; RA 1965/156; Touring 1972-73/26; Chelmsford 1978/15)
(Peter Coker)
illustrated page 69

102 *Aldeburgh II* [probably the same as *High Seas at Aldeburgh, Suffolk No 2*]
signed; signed, inscribed 'Clouds over Sea, Aldeburgh, Suffolk, No 2' on reverse, oil on canvas, 48 x 32 inches
(Exh Zwemmer 1964/18; Peckova House 1965/3)
(Julian Hartnoll)
illustrated page 69

103 *Aldeburgh III*
oil on canvas, 36 x 26½ inches
(Exh Zwemmer 1964/19)
(M Parkinson)

104 *Ardleigh*
pen and watercolour, 22 x 15 inches
(Exh Zwemmer 1964/29)
(Lord de la Warr)

105 *Autumn Forest, East Bergholt*
oil on canvas, 30 x 25 inches
(Exh Zwemmer 1964/10)
(Mrs Mary O'Donovan)

106 *Brett Bank*
signed, oil on canvas, 38½ x 47½ inches
(Exh Zwemmer 1964/15; Touring 1972-73/24)
(Provost family)

107 *The Brett, Suffolk* [also known as *Suffolk Landscape*]
oil on canvas, 60 x 50 inches
(Exh Zwemmer 1964/13; RA 1965/152)
(E C Sosnow)

108 *Landscape near Mistley*
oil on canvas, 48 x 36 inches
(Exh Zwemmer 1964/7)
(destroyed)

109 *Landscape near Mistley*
signed; signed, inscribed with title and dated 1964 on reverse, oil on board, 12 x 14½ inches
(Exh Zwemmer 1964/8; Touring 1972-73/38)
(John & Caroline Stevens)

110 *Landscape near Ardleigh*
signed, oil on canvas, 38 x 24 inches
(Exh Zwemmer 1964/9; Chelmsford 1978/14)
(Private Collection)

111 *Mistley*
watercolour, 30 x 22 inches
(Exh Zwemmer 1964/28)
(Mr Christopher)

112 *Rendlesham Forest*
oil on canvas, 60 x 48 inches
(Exh Zwemmer 1964/20; RA 1965/437; Chelmsford 1978/13)
(whereabouts unknown)
illustrated page 67

113 *Tunstall Forest I*
signed; signed, inscribed with title and dated June 1964 on reverse, oil on canvas, 34 x 44 inches
(Exh Zwemmer 1964/21; Fieldbourne 1979/55)
(Chris Beetles)
illustrated page 68

114 *Tunstall Forest II*
oil on canvas, 48 x 36 inches
(Exh Zwemmer 1964/22)
(possibly destroyed)

115 *Tunstall Forest III*
oil on canvas, 38 x 42 inches
(Exh Zwemmer 1964/23)
(Solomon)

116 *Tunstall Forest*
signed; inscribed with title on reverse; inscribed with title and dated 'July 1964' on stretcher, oil on canvas, 47¾ x 32 inches
(Exh RA 1967/573)
(Piano Nobile)
(This is possibly the same work as *Tunstall Forest II*)

117 *Tunstall Forest*
bodycolour, 30 x 22 inches
(Exh Zwemmer 1964/30; Stable Gallery 1968/1)
(Private Collection)

1965

118 *[The] Weir, Josselin [Brittany]*
signed; inscribed with title on reverse, oil on board, 43 x 48 inches
(Exh Zwemmer 1967/3; RA 1968/434; Thackeray 1970/1; Westgate House 1971/1; Beecroft 1972; Fieldborne 1973/1; Leicester 1973/1; Chelmsford 1978/16; Whittington 1997)
(Peter Coker)
illustrated page 83

by 1966

119 *Apple Tree*
oil on canvas, 49 x 59 inches
(Exh RA 1966/864)
(given to the Bishop of Coventry by his parishioners)

1966

120 *Judas Gap*
signed, oil on canvas, 38 x 47 inches
(Exh RA 1966/78; Touring 1972-73/27)
(David B Kenning)
illustrated page 69

121 *Judas Gap[, Flatford]*
oil, 8 x 13½ inches
(Exh Westgate House 1971/4; Thackeray 1972/18; Phoenix 1976/16)
(R McCausland-White)

125 *Self Portrait*
oil on board, 14¾ x 6 inches
(Exh Touring 1972-73/39)
(Ruth Borchard Collection, in the custody of Piano Nobile)
illustrated page 2 (frontispiece)

by 1967

126 *Audierne*
oil on board, 48 x 48 inches
(Exh Zwemmer 1967/6; RA 1968/80)
(Private Collection, USA)

1967

131 *Durness Landscape*
oil on paper, 22 x 30 inches
(Exh Zwemmer 1967/41)
(Financial Times)

132 *Dusk, Western Sutherland*
oil on board, 12¼ x 12 inches
(Exh Zwemmer 1967/46; Touring 1972-73/41)
(Private Collection)

133 *Evening, Malham*
oil on board, 15¾ x 21¼ inches
(Exh Zwemmer 1967/13; RA 1968/914)
(Alvin R Martin)

134 *Evening, River Stour*
signed, oil on canvas, 36 x 48 inches
(Exh Zwemmer 1967/12)
(Private Collection)
illustrated page 70

135 *Overlooking the Stour*
oil on canvas, 12 x 11¾ inches
(Exh Zwemmer 1967/45; Touring 1972-73/40)
(Mrs Averil Williams)

136 *Running Stream, Malham*
oil on canvas, 36 x 48 inches
(Exh Zwemmer 1967/5; RA 1968/762)
(The Hon Mr Justice C D Steward)

127

122 *Mountain Stream, Pyrenees [No 2]*
signed, oil on board, 48 x 48 inches
(Exh RA 1966/77; Zwemmer 1967/1; Touring 1972-73/28)
(Provost family)

123 *Mountain Stream, Pyrenees [No 3]*
oil on board, 48 x 48 inches
(Exh RA 1966/540; Zwemmer 1967/2; Thackeray 1970/2)
(Beecroft Art Gallery, Southend)
illustrated page 82

124 *Pyrenees Cave* [also known as *Cave, Pyrenees*]
signed, oil on canvas, 38 x 47 inches
(Exh RA 1966/80; Touring 1972-73/29)
(Mrs Moxon)

127 *Clouds over Sea*
signed, oil on board, 32 x 40 inches
(Exh RA 1967/571; Zwemmer 1967/11)
(Chris Beetles)

128 *Copse*
oil on board, 48 x 36 inches
(Exh Zwemmer 1967/7)
(Mrs M M Saunders)

129 *Evening Sea*
oil on canvas, 38½ x 47¾ inches
(Exh Zwemmer 1967/8; RA 1968/766)
(N C Howson)

1966-67

130 *[Tiger] Lilies*
signed, oil on canvas, 48 x 32 inches
(Exh Chelmsford 1978/20; Piano Nobile 1998)
(Private Collection)

130

137 *Waterfall, Malham* [also known as *Jenny's Fosse*]
oil on canvas, 60 x 50 inches
(Exh Zwemmer 1967/4; RA 1968/425; RI 1969/7)
(Leeds City Art Gallery)
illustrated page 74

138 *Western Sutherland*
signed, oil on canvas, 60 x 40 inches
(Exh Zwemmer 1967/14; Touring 1972-73/30)
(Provost family)

1967-68

139 *Durness*
watercolour, dimensions unknown
(Exh Fraser 1984/17)
(whereabouts unknown)

140 *Storm Clouds - Kyle of Durness*
signed, oil, 24 x 32 inches
(Mr & Mrs Richard Strover)
illustrated page 77

by 1968

141 *Audierne, Brittany*
bodycolour, dimensions unknown
(Exh Magdalene 1968/20)
(Mr & Mrs Malcolm Cormack, USA)

142 *Cloudscape at Seascale*
watercolour, 11½ x 8 inches
(Exh Deeside 1978/22)
(whereabouts unknown)

143 *Clouds, Seascale, 1*
watercolour, 11¼ x 8 inches
(Exh Thackeray 1976/37; Phoenix 1976/17)
(whereabouts unknown)

144 *Clouds, Seascale, 2*
watercolour, 11 x 8 inches
(Exh Thackeray 1976/38; Phoenix 1976/18)
(whereabouts unknown)

145 *Kyle of Durness*
oil, dimensions unknown
(Exh Phoenix 1976/15)
(whereabouts unknown)

146 *Kyle of Durness in Mist*
oil on board, 13 x 27 inches
(Exh Thackeray 1976/32)
(destroyed)

147 *Rendlesham, Suffolk*
bodycolour, dimensions unknown
(Exh Magdalene 1968/19)
(Private Collection)

1968

148 *Durness, Scotland*
mixed media including watercolour; 10 x 14¼ inches
(Exh Flying Colours at Watercolours and Drawings Fair 1999)
(whereabouts unknown)

149 *Moor End Fell, Starbotton*
ink and watercolour, 12 x 8¼ inches
(Exh Fraser 1984/5; Flying Colours 1990/28)
(whereabouts unknown)

150 *Moor End Fell, Starbotton*
sanguine and watercolour, 11¾ x 8 inches
(Exh Fraser 1984/2)
(Peter Coker)

151 *Starbotton Rain* [also known as *Rain, Moor End Fell, Starbotton*]
watercolour, 11¾ x 8¼ inches
(Exh Thackeray 1976/40; Phoenix 1976/19; Fraser 1984/3)
(Peter Coker)

152

152 *Storm*
signed, oil on canvas, 36 x 48 inches
(Exh Touring 1972-73/31; Chelmsford 1978/18; Flying Colours at Art London 1999)
(Flying Colours Gallery)

153 *Stour from Brantham*
watercolour, 10½ x 15 inches
(Exh Fraser 1984/13)
(whereabouts unknown)

154 *Stour from Brantham*
pencil, chalk and watercolour, 10½ x 15 inches
(Exh Fraser 1984/14)
(Brafield)

155 *Stour from Brantham*
pencil, chalk and watercolour, 10½ x 15 inches
(Exh Fraser 1984/15)
(Private Collection)

by 1969

156 *Dark Pond, Mistley*
signed, oil, 7½ x 13½ inches
(whereabouts unknown)

157 *Evening: Durness*
medium and dimensions unknown
(Exh RA 1969/27)
(whereabouts unknown)

158 *Kyle of Durness*
oil on canvas, 36 x 51 inches
(Exh Phoenix 1969/18; RA 1969/1037; Thackeray 1970/4)
(Fleming-Wyfold Art Foundation)
illustrated page 77

159 *Late Evening, The Storm*
medium and dimensions unknown
(Exh Phoenix 1969/20)
(whereabouts unknown)

160 *Low Tide: Seascale*
signed, oil on board, 48 x 48 inches
(Exh RA 1969/811; Touring 1972-73/33)
(Rochdale City Art Gallery)
illustrated page 76

161 *Night, Malham*
oil on hardboard, 17 x 34 inches
(Exh RA for Schools 1969/19)
(Leicestershire Education Committee)

162 *Rain, Old Cote Moor, Starbotton*
oil, dimensions unknown
(Richard Cory Smith)

163 *River Stour from Cattawade*
oil on cardboard, 20 x 30 inches
(Exh Stone Gallery 1969/6; Thackeray 1970/10)
(Richard Cory Smith)

1969

164 *Clouds over Cross Fell*
oil on canvas, 32¼ x 40½ inches
(Exh Thackeray 1970/6; RA 1970/592)
(Richard Cory Smith)

165 *Moor End Fell from Starbotton*
oil on canvas, 48 x 36 inches
(Exh Thackeray 1970/7; RA 1970/586)
(Richard Cory Smith)

166 *[Sea] Near Durness*
oil on canvas, 48 x 60 inches
(Exh RA 1969/569; Thackeray 1970/5; Westgate House 1971/2; Beecroft 1972)
(Provost family)

167 *Seascale*
signed, oil on canvas, 48 x 48 inches
(Exh RA 1969/427; Touring 1972-73/32)
(Mrs Ronald Ottey)

168

168 *Stour, Evening*
signed, oil on canvas, 24 x 20 inches
(Exh Thackeray 1970/11; Chelmsford 1978/19)
(North East Essex Technical College)

169 *The Stour from Cattawade, Evening*
signed, oil on canvas, 48 x 48 inches
(Exh Thackeray 1970/9; RA 1970/89; Touring 1972-73/34)
(Richard Cory Smith)

170 *Towards Old Cote Moor Top*
signed, oil on canvas, 48 x 48 inches
(Thackeray 1970/8; Exh RA 1970/585; Touring 1972-73/35)
(Richard Cory Smith)

By 1970

171 *Towards Dewley Fell, Alston* [also known as *Dewley Fell, Cumbria*]
ink and watercolour, 29½ x 21½ inches
(Exh Flying Colours at Watercolours and Drawings Fair 1999; RA 2000/564)
(Ann Murphy)

1970

172 *Clouds over Cross Fell*
signed on reverse, oil on board, 11 x 12 inches
(Exh Touring 1972-73/46)
(Richard Cory Smith)

173 *Clouds, South Tyne*
signed on reverse, oil on board, 5 x 6 inches
(Exh Touring 1972-73/44)
(Richard Cory Smith)

174 *Cross Fell*
oil on hardboard, 11 x 12 inches
(Richard Cory Smith)

175 *Cross Fell*
oil on plywood, 4¾ x 5¾ inches
(Richard Cory Smith)

176 *Dewley Fell [near Alston]*
signed, oil on canvas, 48 x 36 inches
(Exh RA 1971/478; Touring 1972-73/36)
(Richard Cory Smith)

177 *Harwich*
mixed media including watercolour, 10 x 21¼ inches
(Exh Flying Colours at Watercolours and Drawings Fair 1999)
(whereabouts unknown)

178 *Leadgate*
signed on reverse, oil on board, 16½ x 11 inches
(Exh Touring 1972-73/43)
(Richard Cory Smith)

179 *Leadgate*
oil on plywood, 7½ x 10 inches
(Richard Cory Smith)

180 *Leadgate*
signed on reverse, oil on board, 7½ x 9¾ inches
(Exh Touring 1972-73/47)
(Richard Cory Smith)

181 *Leadgate, Cumbria*
signed and inscribed with title, pencil and watercolour, 22 x 30½ inches
(Exh RA 2000/568)
(destroyed)

182 *Leadgate in the Rain*
signed on reverse, oil on board, 7½ x 9¾ inches
(Exh Touring 1972-73/48)
(Richard Cory Smith)

183 *On the Moors*
signed with initials and dated '70, oil on newspaper, 11 x 12 inches
(monotype taken from *Yorkshire Dales*)
(Peter Coker)
illustrated page 89

184 *Self Portrait*
signed on reverse, oil on board, 10 x 5 inches
(Cheltenham & Gloucester Building Society)

185 *Starbotton*
signed on reverse, oil on board, 9¾ x 7½ inches
(Exh Touring 1972-73/42)
(Richard Cory Smith)

186 *Trees, Leadgate*
signed on reverse, oil on board, 7½ x 9¾ inches
(K C Parry)

187 *Yorkshire Dales*
oil, dimensions unknown
(Provost family)

by 1971

188 *Along the Beach, Aldeburgh*
oil, 9 x 15 inches
(Exh Westgate House 1971/5)
(Private Collection)

189 *The Balcony, Aldeburgh*
oil on canvas, 44 x 34 inches
(Exh Thackeray 1972/8)
(Mr & Mrs J B Hanshaw)

190 *Balcony, Aldeburgh*
oil on board, 15¼ x 10½ inches
(Exh Thackeray 1972/17)
(Mrs A Wyard)

191 *The Beach at Aldeburgh*
oil on board, 8¾ x 15½ inches
(Exh Thackeray 1972/19)
(Mrs M Barr)

192 *Behind Leadgate*
oil on cardboard, 23 x 30 inches
(Exh RA 1971/876)
(RH Calvert)

193 *Behind Leadgate*
oil on cardboard, 23 x 30 inches
(Exh Thackeray 1972/4; RA 1972/867)
(Richard Cory Smith)

194 *Black Burn and the South Tyne*
medium and dimensions unknown
(Exh RA 1971/477)
(whereabouts unknown)

195 *Clouds over South Tyne*
watercolour, 8 x 10¾ inches
(Exh Thackeray 1972/20)
(Colin Clark)

196 *Cranham, Welcombe*
oil on board, 12½ x 9¾ inches
(Exh Thackeray 1972/16)
(Colin Clark)

197 *Cuillin Hills, Bruack na Frithe*
oil on paper, 20 x 29 inches
(Exh Thackeray 1972/7)
(Fleming-Wyfold Art Foundation)

198 *Evening, Loch Eishort, Skye*
watercolour, 8 x 11½ inches
(Exh Thackeray 1972/21)
(Private Collection)

199 *Leadgate*
oil on board, 23 x 30 inches
(Exh Fieldborne 1973/2)
(whereabouts unknown)

200 *Leadgate*
watercolour, dimensions unknown
(Exh Westgate House 1971/17)
(Miss Jackson)

201 *Loch Eishort, Skye*
watercolour, 8 x 11½ inches
(Exh Thackeray 1972/22)
(Norman Harris)

202 *Marsland Cliff*
oil on board, 11 x 16½ inches
(Exh Thackeray 1972/12)
(Mrs A Wyard)

203 *Mead Farm, Welcombe*
oil on board, 9½ x 7½ inches
(Exh Thackeray 1972/13)
(H P Lee)

204 *Moss Bank, Penifiler, Skye*
oil on paper, 20 x 29 inches
(Exh Thackeray 1972/5)
(Mrs S Harmel)

205 *Quirang, Loch Mealt, Skye*
oil on paper, 22 x 30 inches
(Exh Thackeray 1972/6)
(E B Harris)

206 *Sea off Welcombe*
oil on canvas, 7½ x 9¾ inches
(Exh Thackeray 1972/10; Minories 1974)
(Private Collection)

207 *Sea, Welcombe*
oil on board, 6¾ x 9¼ inches
(Exh Thackeray 1972/11; Fieldborne 1973/3; Leicester 1973/3)
(whereabouts unknown)

208 *View from Ivy Cottage*
oil, 36 x 30 inches
(Exh RA 1971/521)
(Chris Beetles)
illustrated page 76

1971

209 *Balcony, Aldeburgh*
etching and aquatint, 12 x 9½ inches
(edition of 10)
(Exh Thackeray 1972/56; Touring 1972-73/79; Fieldborne 1973/23; Leicester 1973/25; Thackeray 1976/14; Phoenix 1976/24; Chelmsford 1978/51; Poole 1979/14)
illustrated page 87

210 *[The] Balcony[, at] Aldeburgh*
oil on canvas, 36 x 48 inches
(Exh Thackeray 1972/9; RA 1972/505)
(Ivanovic Co)

211 *Black Burn*
soft ground etching, 7 x 9½ inches
(edition of 10)
(Exh Thackeray 1972/38; Touring 1972-73/85; Fieldborne 1973/10; Leicester 1973/12; Thackeray 1976/19; Phoenix 1976/32; Poole 1979/19)

212 *Buckden*
drypoint, 10½ x 14 inches (edition of 10)
(Exh Thackeray 1972/39; Touring 1972-73/84; Fieldborne 1973/11; Leicester 1973/13; Thackeray 1976/11; Chelmsford 1978/49; Poole 1979/11)

213 *Chrossavaig, Skye*
watercolour, 22 x 30 inches
(Exh RA 1996/21)
(Peter Coker)
illustrated page 76

214 *Concert at Aldeburgh[, 1971]*
etching and aquatint, 10 x 7½ inches
(edition of 25)
(Exh Westgate House 1971/16; Thackeray 1972/50; Touring 1972-73/83; Fieldborne 1973/17; Leicester 1973/20; Thackeray 1976/16; Phoenix 1976/25; Chelmsford 1978/53; Poole 1979/16)

215 *Cranham, Welcombe*
etching and aquatint, 11 x 14½ inches
(edition of 10)
(Exh Fieldborne 1973/20; Leicester 1973/23; Thackeray 1976/17; Chelmsford 1978/54; Poole 1979/17)

216

216 *Epping Forest*
soft ground etching and aquatint, 18¾ x 15 inches (edition of 10)
(Exh Thackeray 1972/42; RA 1972/962; Touring 1972-73/78; Fieldborne 1973/27; Thackeray 1976/6; Chelmsford 1978/45; Poole 1979/6; RA 1998/255)

217

217 *Leadgate*
signed, oil on canvas, 25 x 30 inches
(Exh Thackeray 1972/3;
Chelmsford 1978/21)
(Chelmsford and Essex Museum)

218 *Low Force[, Teesdale]*
soft ground etching, 15 x 19¾ inches
(edition of 15)
(Exh Thackeray 1972/52; RA 1972/992;
Fieldborne 1973/19; Leicester 1973/22;
Thackeray 1976/5; Chelmsford 1978/44;
Poole 1979/5; Atkinson 1984/12;
RA 1995/753
illustrated page 88

219 *Low Force, Teesdale*
soft ground etching, 14¾ x 19½ inches
(edition of 15)
(Exh Thackeray 1972/51; Touring
1972-73/91; Fieldborne 1973/18;
Leicester 1973/21; Thackeray 1976/7;
Chelmsford 1978/46; Poole 1979/7;
RA 1995/1159)

220 *Malham[,] Night*
etching and aquatint, 14½ x 10¾ inches
(edition of 10)
(Exh Thackeray 1972/43; Touring
1972-73/77; Fieldborne 1973/12;
Leicester 1973/16; Thackeray 1976/ex-
cat; Chelmsford 1978/56; Poole 1979/28;
RA 1979/755)
illustrated page 87

221 *The Maltings, Wednesday, 16th June, 1971*
oil on canvas, 48 x 48 inches
(Exh Thackeray 1975/4; RA 1975/503)
(destroyed)

222 *Moor End Fell, Starbotton*
oil on canvas, 48 x 48 inches
(Exh RA 1971/475; Thackeray 1972/1)
(Mr & Mrs J A Hanshaw)

223 *Orchestral pit, Coliseum*
etching and aquatint, 12 x 9½ inches
(Exh Thackeray 1972/55; Fieldborne
1973/22; Thackeray 1976/24; Poole
1979/24)

224 *[The] Persian Kelim*
soft ground etching, 15 x 11 inches
(edition of 10)
(Exh Thackeray 1972/57; Touring
1972-73/81; Fieldborne 1973/24;
Leicester 1973/26; Thackeray 1976/9;
Poole 1979/9)
illustrated page 88

225 *Portrait [of] Nicholas*
etching, 12¾x 7½ inches (edition of 15)
(Exh Thackeray 1972/48; Touring
1972-73/86; Fieldborne 1973/15;
Leicester 1973/18; Thackeray 1976/12;
Poole 1979/12)

226 *Seascale*
soft ground etching and aquatint,
15½ x 19½ inches
(first edition of 25: Exh Thackeray
1972/58; RA 1972/988; Touring
1972-73/89; Thackeray 1976/3;
Chelmsford 1978/42; Poole 1979/3;
Atkinson 1984/6; Exh RA 1995/754)
(second edition of 33)
illustrated page 88

227 *Self Portrait*
etching and aquatint, 5 x 2½ inches
(Exh Poole 1979/23)

228 *Sgiath[-]Bheinn Chrossavaig, Skye*
drypoint, 9 x 13½ inches (edition of 15)
(Exh Thackeray 1972/54; Touring
1972-73/82; Leicester 1973/24;
Thackeray 1976/10; Chelmsford 1978/48)

229 *Starbotton, Rain* [or *Rain, Starbotton*]
etching and aquatint, 12 x 8¾ inches
(edition of 10)
(Exh Thackeray 1972/44; Touring
1972-73/90; Fieldborne 1973/13;
Leicester 1973/15; Thackeray 1976/15;
Chelmsford 1978/52; Poole 1979/15)

230 *[The] Stour [from the Cattawade, Late Evening]*
signed on reverse, oil on board,
10 x 15 inches
(Exh Westgate House 1971/3; Touring
1972-73/49)
(Miss E M Jackson)

231 *Trees at Leadgate*
oil on canvas, 48 x 36 inches
(Exh RA 1971/476; Thackeray 1972/2)
(Richard Cory Smith)

232 *Waterfall, Tynehead*
soft ground etching, 10½ x 7¾ inches
(edition of 10)
(Exh Thackeray 1972/46; Poole 1979/31)

233 *Waterfall, Tynehead*
soft ground etching and aquatint, 10½ x 7¾
inches (edition of 10)
(Exh Thackeray 1972/47; Touring
1972-73/80; Fieldborne 1973/14;
Leicester 1973/17; Poole 1979/32)

1971-72

234 *The Quirang towards Staffin*
etching, aquatint and drypoint, 13 x 17½
inches (edition of 15)
(Exh Thackeray 1976/2; Chelmsford
1978/41; Exh Poole 1979/2)
illustrated page 88

235 *Rain, North Sea*
drypoint, 3¾ x 3¼ inches (edition of 10)
(Exh Thackeray 1976/25; Phoenix
1976/29; Poole 1979/25)

236

236 *Vaternish[,] from Cuidrach*
etching and aquatint, 14½ x 10½ inches
(edition of 19)
(Exh Phoenix 1976/22; Chelmsford
1978/47; Poole 1979/8)

by 1972

237 *Epping Forest*
soft ground etching, 18¾ x 15 inches
(edition of 20)
(Exh Leicester 1973/14; Poole 1979/4;
RA 1995/756)

238 *Nicholas*
etching and aquatint, 8¾ x 7½ inches
(Exh Thackeray 1972/49; Fieldborne
1973/16; Leicester 1973/19; Thackeray
1976/20; Poole 1979/20)

239 *River Tees*
oil, dimensions unknown
(Richard Cory Smith)

240 *Self Portrait*
drypoint, 7¾ x 6 inches
(Exh Thackeray 1972/45)

241

241 *Self Portrait*
drypoint, 8¼ x 5 inches

242 *Windswept Trees*
drypoint, 17½ x 23½ inches
(Exh Thackeray 1972/40; Chelmsford 1978/59)

243

1972

243 *Balcony Aldeburgh*
oil on board, 8 x 10½ inches
(Exh Minories 1975/46)
(Natalie Bevan)

244 *Hartland Point*
watercolour, dimensions unknown
(Exh Fraser 1984/4)
(Private Collection)

245 *La Loue, Jura*
oil on paper, 30¼ x 22 inches
(Exh Fitzwilliam 1989/13; Gallery 10 1989/12)
(Mr and Mrs John Paré)
illustrated page 84

246 *Maisie*
etching, 11¼ x 6¼ inches (edition of 4)
(Exh Poole 1979/29)

247 *Maisie*
hand-coloured etching, 11¼ x 6¼ inches
(Exh Poole 1979/35)

248 *Mallow Cottage*
oil on board, 14 x 12 inches
(Exh Thackeray 1972/14)
(Private Collection)
illustrated page 75

249 *Mollans sur Cuvèze*
oil, 28 x 30 inches
(Exh RA 1973/571)
(Richard Cory Smith)

250 *Stripping Haricots at Mollans*
oil, 30 x 25 inches
(Exh RA 1973/91)
(Richard Cory Smith)
study illustrated page 83

circa 1972

251 *Self Portrait*
drypoint, 5 x 5½ inches (edition of 10)

252

circa 1972-73

252 [*Etretat*]
oil, dimensions unknown
(whereabouts unknown)

253 *La Manneporte*
colour drypoint, 9¼ x 7¼ inches
(Exh Chelmsford 1978/58; Poole 1979/34)
illustrated page 89

by 1973

254 *Balcony, Aldeburgh*
oil on canvas, 48 x 32 inches
(Exh Thackeray 1974/5; RA 1974/555; Chappel 1996)
(Richard Cory Smith)

255 *Balcony - Aldeburgh*
oil on board, 6½ x 5¼ inches
(Exh Fieldborne 1973/27a
(Private Collection)

256 *Epping Forest*
etching, 19¼ x 12½ inches
(Exh Fieldborne 1973/26; Thackeray 1976/4; Chelmsford 1978/43)

257 *Sault*
oil, dimensions unknown
(Exh RA 1973/947)
(Chapman)

258 *Sault*
oil, dimensions unknown
(whereabouts unknown)

259 *Welcombe Bay*
watercolour, dimensions unknown
(Exh Fraser 1984/8)
(whereabouts unknown)

260 *Welcombe Bay*
pencil and watercolour, 7¾ x 15 inches
(Exh Fraser 1984/9)
(Private Collection)

1973

261 *Aurel*
oil on board, 23 x 29 inches
(Exh Thackeray 1974/13)
(Piano Nobile)

262 *Aurel* [from a sketchbook]
ink and watercolour, 15½ x 22 inches
(Exh Gallery 10 Autumn 1984/15; RA 1985/874)
(BP International Ltd)
illustrated page 85

263 *Bridge at Sault*
oil on canvas, 25 x 30 inches
(Exh Thackeray 1974/15)
(Mrs Mandley)
illustrated page 86

264 *Evening Storm, from Aird of Kinloch*
signed, oil on board, 36 x 48 inches
(Exh Thackeray 1974/3; Chelmsford 1978/22)
(Mr and Mrs A G P Stuart)

265 *Garden at Mistley*
oil on canvas, 48 x 32 inches
(Exh Thackeray 1974/6; RA 1974/531)
(Richard Cory Smith)

266 *Montbrun-les-Bains*
oil on canvas, 28 x 36 inches
(Exh Thackeray 1974/12)
(Corporate Collection)

267 *Mont Ventoux in Mist from Reilhanette*
oil on board, 48 x 57¼ inches
(Exh Thackeray 1974/1; RA 1974/517)
(destroyed)

268 *Mouthier-Haute-Pierre, 1*
oil on canvas, 40 x 24 inches
(Exh Thackeray 1974/9)
(Richard Cory Smith)

269 *Mouthier-Haute-Pierre, 2*
oil on canvas, 36 x 28 inches
(Exh Thackeray 1974/10; RA 1974/36)
(whereabouts unknown)

270 *Mouthier-Haute-Pierre*
oil on board, 6 x 8 inches
(Exh Thackeray 1978/15)
(Eric & Roberta Smith)

271 *Mouthier-Haute-Pierre*
etching and aquatint, dimensions unknown
(Exh Poole 1979/30)

272 *Mouthier-Haute-Pierre*
colour etching and aquatint,
21¼ x 14¼ inches
(Exh Poole 1979/33)
illustrated page 89

273 *Night, Killiemore from Aird of Kinloch*
signed, oil on canvas, 36 x 26 inches
(Exh Thackeray 1974/8; Chelmsford 1978/23)
(Private Collection)

274 *Picking Pears at Mouthier*
oil on canvas, 48 x 36 inches
(Exh Thackeray 1974/4; RA 1974/71; Winchester 1989)
(Doncaster Museum and Art Gallery)
illustrated page 85

275 *St-Blaise, Mézières-au-Perche*
oil on canvas, 34 x 44 inches
(Exh Thackeray 1974/7; RA 1974/554)
(Richard Cory Smith)

276 *Sault-de-Vaucluse, 1*
signed, oil on canvas, 26 x 36 inches
(Exh Thackeray 1974/11; Chelmsford 1978/24)
(Private Collection)
illustrated page 85

277 *Sault-de-Vaucluse, 2*
oil on canvas, 25 x 30 inches
(Exh Thackeray 1974/14)
(Private Collection)

278 *Towards Hawes from Greenside, Wensleydale*
oil on board, 48 x 48 inches
(Exh Thackeray 1974/2)
(Private Collection)

279 *Yorkshire Landscape*
etching, aquatint and drypoint and mezzotint, 17½ x 24 inches (edition of 15)
(Exh Thackeray 1976/1; Phoenix 1976/20; Chelmsford 1978/40; Poole 1979/1; RA 1995/1157; RA 1998/256)
illustrated page 88

by 1974

280 *Vaternish from Cuidrach*
chalk and watercolour, 11 x 7 inches
(Exh Thackeray 1978/24)
(whereabouts unknown)

1974

281 *Fruit Bowl* [also known as *Turkish Plate*]
hand-coloured deep etching,
13 x 17½ inches (unique)
(Exh Chappel 1990)
(Dr Ayache)
illustrated page 89

282 *Gathering Storm, Ord*
drypoint and mezzotint, 2½ x 8 inches (edition of 12)
(Exh Thackeray 1976/22; Phoenix 1976/31; Poole 1979/22)

283 *Jetty at Night, Ostend[e]*
etching and aquatint, 5¾ x 6¾ inches (edition of 15)
(Exh Thackeray 1976/21; Phoenix 1976/27; Poole 1979/21)

284 *Jetty at Night, Ostend* [also known as *Lighthouse at Night, Ostend*]
three-coloured etching, 7½ x 11 inches (unique)
(Exh Chappel 1990)
(National Maritime Museum)

285 *Night Sea, Ostend*
drypoint and mezzotint, 7½ x 11 inches (edition of 12)
(Exh Thackeray 1976/13; Chelmsford 1978/50; Poole 1979/13)

286 *North Sea Clouds*
mezzotint, 2 x 3 inches (edition of 8)
(Exh Thackeray 1976/27; Poole 1979/27)

287 *[Rain, Rainbow and Stormy Seas, North Cliff] Whitby*
signed, oil on canvas, 40 x 80 inches
(Exh Thackeray 1975/2; RA 1975/104; Ivor Weiss 1976/20; Chelmsford 1978/26; National Maritime Museum 2000)
(National Maritime Museum)
illustrated page 75

288 *Setting Sun, Ostend*
signed, oil on canvas, 34 x 44 inches
(Exh Thackeray 1975/8; Chelmsford 1978/25)
(Private Collection)

289 *Storm, Ostend*
drypoint, 7½ x 11 inches
(Exh Thackeray 1976/18; Chelmsford 1978/55; Poole 1979/18)

290 *Sun through Cloud, North Sea*
drypoint, 3½ x 5 inches (edition of 10)
(Exh Thackeray 1976/26; Poole 1979/26)

1974-75

291 *Lastours, 1*
oil on canvas, 30 x 36 inches
(Exh Thackeray 1975/9; RA 1976/349)
(C Lewis)

292 *Lastours, 2*
oil on canvas, 36 x 28 inches
(Exh Thackeray 1975/11)
(Mr and Mrs Brian Gilmore)

293 *Ostend, The Café* [also known as *View from a Café, Ostend*]
signed, oil on canvas, 56 x 68 inches
(Exh Thackeray 1975/1; RA 1975/494; Chelmsford 1978/27)
(Private Collection, USA)
illustrated page 81

294 *Staffin from the Quirang*
oil on board, 6 x 8 inches
(Exh Thackeray 1976/34; Phoenix 1976/14)
(R McCausland-White)

295

295 *Towards Vaternish from Cuidrach*
oil on canvas, 48 x 32 inches
(Exh Thackeray 1976/29)
(Miss Marjorie Walpole)

by 1975

296 *Aldeburgh, Yellow Kite*
oil on plywood, 8 x 30 inches
(Exh Thackeray 1975/13)
(Private Collection)

297 *Balnakeil Bay, Sutherland*
oil, 9 x 15½ inches
(Exh Deeside Gallery 1978/4)
(whereabouts unknown)

298 *Balnakeil [Beach] Sutherland*
oil on board, 6 x 8 inches
(Exh Thackeray 1976/36; RA 1977/221)
(Mrs Needham)

299 *Balnakeil, Faraid Head*
oil on board, 9 x 15 inches
(Exh Thackeray 1976/33)
(whereabouts unknown)

300 *Balnakeil, Sutherland*
oil, 9 x 15½ inches
(Exh Deeside Gallery 1977/35)
(whereabouts unknown)

301 *East Cliff, Whitby*
oil on canvas, 48 x 36 inches
(Exh Thackeray 1975/6;
Press Association 1976)
(Private Collection)

302

302 *East Lighthouse, Whitby*
oil on board, 8 x 5¾ inches
(Exh Thackeray 1975/14;
Thackeray 1976/30)
(Miss Marjorie Walpole)

303 *East Yorkshire Moors*
oil on canvas, 32 x 48 inches
(Exh Thackeray 1975/7; RA 1975/928)
(destroyed)

304 *Evening: Train Ferry Pier, Harwich*
oil, 30 x 36 inches
(Exh RA 1975/63)
(James Butler)
illustrated page 70

305 *Fishing Boat and Rainbow*
oil on canvas, 24 x 30 inches
(Exh Thackeray 1975/12)
(Private Collection)

306 *Grey September Sea*
oil on canvas, 26 x 36 inches
(Exh Thackeray 1975/10)
(Harry Anderson)

307 *Mist, Parkeston Quay from the Train Ferry Pier, Harwich*
oil on canvas, 26 x 39 inches
(Exh Thackeray 1975/20)
(Private Collection)

308 *The Rainbow, Barmouth*
oil on canvas, 60 x 40 inches
(Exh Thackeray 1975/3; RA 1975/874)
(destroyed)

309 *Sea Mist, Balnakeil Bay*
oil on board, 6 x 8 inches
(Exh Thackeray 1976/35)
(Private Collection)

310 *Sea off Aldeburgh*
watercolour, dimensions unknown
(Exh Fraser 1984/6)
(whereabouts unknown)

311 *Whitby Bay*
oil on plywood, 5¼ x 7¾ inches
(Exh Thackeray 1975/15)
(Private Collection)

1975

312 *Les sables d'or[, Ostend]*
signed, oil on canvas, 48 x 48 inches
(Exh Thackeray 1976/28; Chelmsford 1978/28)
(Private Collection)
illustrated page 81

313 *Sunset over Calm Sea, Ostend*
oil on canvas, 50 x 40 inches
(Exh Thackeray 1975/5; RA British Painting 1977/78)
(W D Day)
illustrated page 81

by 1976

314 *Autumn Sky*
oil, dimensions unknown
(whereabouts unknown)

315 *The Breaking Wave*
oil, 7 x 9 inches
(Exh Deeside Gallery 1977/36)
(whereabouts unknown)

316 *Calm Sea, Aldeburgh*
watercolour, 11 x 7½ inches
(Exh Thackeray 1976/39)
(Private Collection)

317 *Carsaig from Mull*
watercolour, dimensions unknown
(Exh Harrower 1986/21)
(whereabouts unknown)

318 *Carsaig Rain, Mull*
oil on board, 5¾ x 6¾ inches
(Exh Deeside 1978/28)
(whereabouts unknown)

319 *Carsaig, Mull*
oil, 4½ x 7¾ inches
(Exh Deeside 1978/30)
(whereabouts unknown)

320 *Clouds over the Sea*
oil on board, 5 x 9 inches
(Exh Deeside 1977/25)
(whereabouts unknown)

321 *Clouds over the Sea, Carsaig*
oil on board, 3 x 15 inches
(Exh Thackeray 1978/13)
(Mr and Mrs P Hartzis)

322 *Cloud over Sun, Carsaig, Mull*
oil, dimensions unknown
(Exh RA 1977/179)
(Cheetham)

323 *Clouds over the Sea, Carsaig, Mull*
oil, dimensions unknown
(RA 1977/130)
(whereabouts unknown)

324 *Cloudscape, Isle of Mull, Carsaig*
oil, 4½ x 7½ inches
(Exh Deeside Gallery 1977/23)
(whereabouts unknown)

325 *Cloudscape, Isle of Mull, Carsaig*
oil, 4½ x 7¾ inches
(Exh Deeside Gallery 1977/24)
(whereabouts unknown)

326 *From Carsaig*
watercolour, dimensions unknown
(Exh Fraser 1984/41)
(Private Collection)

327 *Grey Sea, Carsaig*
watercolour, 11 x 7 inches
(Exh Thackeray 1978/25)
(Jonathan Poole)

328 *Lighthouse, Gravelines*
watercolour, dimensions unknown
(Exh Fraser 1984/23)
(Mr & Mrs John Paré)

329 *Overcast Sea, Carsaig*
oil on board, 8 x 15 inches
(Exh Thackeray 1978/12)
(whereabouts unknown)

330 *Overcast Sea, Carsaig*
watercolour, 11 x 7 inches
(Exh Thackeray 1978/26)
(whereabouts unknown)

331 *Sea off Carsaig*
watercolour, dimensions unknown
(Exh Fraser 1984/18)
(Private Collection)

332 *Sea off Carsaig*
oil on canvas, 57 x 33 inches
(Exh Thackeray 1978/1)
(destroyed)

333 *The Wave*
oil on plywood, 6¾ x 9¼ inches
(Exh Thackeray 1976/31; Phoenix 1976/13)
(whereabouts unknown)

334 *Windbreakers Aldeburgh*
oil on board, 7¼ x 5 inches
(Thackeray 1976/ex-cat)
(Private Collection)

1976

335 *Porte d'Amont, Etretat*
watercolour, 10½ x 15 inches
(Exh Fraser 1984/11; Flying Colours 1990/25)
(whereabouts unknown)

336 *Porte d'Amont, Etretat*
watercolour, 10½ x 15 inches
(Exh Fraser 1984/12; Flying Colours 1990/26)
(whereabouts unknown)

337 *Self Portrait*
signed on reverse, oil on canvas, 25 x 15½ inches
(Exh RA 1976/352; Deben 1983/17)
(Private Collection)

338 *Still Life with Oranges and Pears* [also known as *Persian Bowl on Red Tablecloth* and *Still Life with Fruit*]
signed; signed on reverse, oil on canvas, 25 x 30 inches
(Private Collection)

by 1977

339 *La Manneporte, Etretat [1]*
oil, 25 x 30 inches
(Exh RA 1977/either 297 or 427; Thackeray 1978/8)
(Mr Costa Georgopoulos)

340

340 *La Manneporte, Etretat [2]*
oil on board, 8 x 10¼ inches
(Exh RA 1977/either 297 or 427; Thackeray 1978/14)
(James Swartz)

341 *La Manneporte, Etretat, 3*
watercolour, 10 x 7 inches
(Exh Thackeray 1978/27)
(Mr Costa Georgopoulos)

342 *Mouthier-Haute-Pierre, Jura*
oil, dimensions unknown
(Exh RA 1977/243)
(Safier)

337

1977

343 *Dark Sea, Carsaig [Isle of Mull]*
oil on canvas, 42 x 30 inches
(Exh Thackeray 1978/3; Exh RA 1978/100; Flying Colours at Art London 1999)
(Private Collection)
illustrated page 77

344

344 *Le Rameur*
oil and chalk on paper, 8 x 5½ inches
(Exh Fraser 1984/38; Flying Colours 1990/27)
(Flying Colours Gallery)

by 1978

345 *Bargemon, 1*
oil on canvas, 24 x 40 inches
(Exh Thackeray 1978/6)
(whereabouts unknown)

346

346 *Bargemon, 2*
oil on canvas, 24 x 30 inches
(Exh Thackeray 1978/9)
(Miss Marjorie Walpole)

347 *Bargemon towards Claviers*
oil on canvas, 32 x 48 inches
(Exh Thackeray 1978/2)
(Private Collection)

348 *Callas*
oil on canvas, 30 x 36 inches
(Exh Thackeray 1978/5; RA 1978/1364)
(Cooke Collection, Salford)

349 *Etretat, La Porte d'Aval*
watercolour, 7 x 9 inches
(Exh Thackeray 1978/30)
(Mr M Marcou)

350 *Olive Trees, Bargemon*
oil on canvas, 20 x 30 inches
(Exh Thackeray 1978/11; RA 1978/487)
(Private Collection)

351 *Olive Trees at Claviers*
oil on canvas, 24 x 30 inches
(Exh Thackeray 1978/10)
(whereabouts unknown)

352 *Road from Claviers*
oil on canvas, 36 x 28 inches
(Exh Thackeray 1978/7)
(Mr and Mrs Brian Gilmore)

353

353 *[Study for] 'La Plage' Etretat*
oil on canvas, 48 x 32 inches
(Exh Thackeray 1978/4; RA 1978/107;
Gallery 10 Summer 1979;
Touring 1992/14)
(Mrs Chandris)

1978

354 *Antibes*
oil on canvas, 36 x 48 inches
(Exh Gallery 10 1980/12)
(Mr and Mrs C Caroussis)

355

355 *Olives, Bargemon* [also known as *Bargemon: Olives*]
oil on canvas, 48 x 48 inches
(Exh RA 1979/1058; Touring 1992/15)
(Abbot Hall Art Gallery, Kendal)

356 *Studio Window*
oil on canvas, 48 x 48 inches
(Exh RA 1978/494)
(destroyed)

357 *Two Windows* [also known as *Study for Blue Black Interior, Bargemon*]
ink and oil on paper, 22 x 30 inches
(Flying Colours Gallery)

358 *Yellow Diving Board[, Etretat]*
pencil and watercolour, 4½ x 6¾ inches
(Exh Fraser 1984/22; Flying Colours 1990/22)
(whereabouts unknown)

circa 1978-79

359 *Bateaux*
signed, watercolour, 3½ x 4½ inches
(Exh Fraser 1984/28)
(Private Collection)

360 *Bateaux*
watercolour, dimensions unknown
(Exh Fraser 1984/25)
(whereabouts unknown)

361 *Beach Studies, Etretat*
four sheets, each signed, watercolour and pencil, 5 x 3½ inches
(Exh Chris Beetles 2000/116)
(Jane Moyes)

362 *Boy, Dog, Bather*
watercolour and pencil, dimensions unknown
(Exh Fraser 1984/30)
(whereabouts unknown)

363 *Boy with Towel*
watercolour and pencil, dimensions unknown
(Exh Fraser 1984/31)
(whereabouts unknown)

364 *Etretat Bathers* [from a sketchbook]
signed with initials, watercolour with pencil, 10½ x 7¼ inches
(Exh Chris Beetles 2000/113)
(Chris Beetles)

365 *Figures on Beach, Etretat*
watercolour, dimensions unknown
(Exh Fraser 1984/34)
(whereabouts unknown)

366 *Figures on Beach*
watercolour, dimensions unknown
(Exh Fraser 1984/35)
(whereabouts unknown)

367 *Figures on Beach*
watercolour, dimensions unknown
(Exh Fraser 1984/36)
(whereabouts unknown)

368 *Girl in Check Towel with Dog*
watercolour, dimensions unknown
(Exh Fraser 1984/37)
(whereabouts unknown)

369 *Girl, Red Shirt*
watercolour and pencil, dimensions unknown
(Exh Fraser 1984/32)
(whereabouts unknown)

370 *The Inquisitive Dog, Etretat* [from a sketchbook]
signed with initials, watercolour, 10½ x 7 inches
(Exh Chris Beetles 2000/114)
(Dr and Mrs R P H Thompson)

371

371 *La Plage, Etretat*
oil on board, 14 x 20 inches
(Athena Strutt)

372 *La Plage, Etretat*
watercolour, dimensions unknown
(Exh Fraser 1984/10)
(Private Collection)

373 *Man and Dog, Etretat* [from a sketchbook]
signed with initials, watercolour and pencil,
10½ x 7 inches
(Exh Chris Beetles 2000/115)
(Paul Collins)

374 *On the Beach, Etretat* [from a sketchbook]
signed with initials, watercolour,
4½ x 7¾ inches
(Exh Chris Beetles 2000/112)
(Chris Beetles)

375 *Out to Sea, Etretat*
watercolour and pencil, dimensions unknown
(Exh Fraser 1984/39)
(Private Collection)

376 *Red Sail*
signed, watercolour, 3½ x 4½ inches
(Exh Fraser 1984/29)
(Private Collection)

377 *Two Figures on Beach*
watercolour and pencil, dimensions unknown
(Exh Fraser 1984/33)
(whereabouts unknown)

378 *Yellow Sail [Etretat]*
signed with initials, watercolour,
7 x 10 inches
(Exh Fraser 1984/27)
(Peter Coker)

by 1979

379 *Antibes – Palm*
oil on canvas, 40 x 24 inches
(Exh Gallery 10 Summer 1979)
(Mrs Chandris)
illustrated page 95

380 *Antibes: Palm*
oil on canvas, 36 x 48 inches
(Exh RA 1979/94)
(David Gilmour, USA)
illustrated page 95

381 *Bargemon from the Window*
oil on canvas, 36 x 20 inches
(whereabouts unknown)

382 *Bargemon: The Window*
oil on canvas, 48 x 36 inches
(Exh RA 1979/690)
(David Gilmour, USA)

383 *Etretat: The Balcony*
medium and dimensions unknown
(Exh RA 1979/691)
(whereabouts unknown)

384

384 *Etretat: The Beach*
oil, 60 x 40 inches
(Exh RA 1979/81)
(Marcou)

1979

385 *Agaves*
signed; signed and dated 'Nov-Dec 1979' on reverse, oil on canvas, 60 x 52 inches
(Exh Gallery 10 1980/4)
(Piano Nobile)

386 *Blue, Black Interior - Two Windows* [also known as *Blue Black Interior, Bargemon*]
oil on canvas, 52 x 70 inches
(Exh Gallery 10 1980/2; Touring 1992/17)
(Private Collection)
illustrated page 92

385

387

387 *Chateau Garden [(Yellow Olives)]*
oil on canvas, 48 x 36 inches
(Exh Gallery 10 1980/9; Touring 1992/16)
(Mrs Chandris)

388 *Collioure*
oil on canvas, 22 x 16 inches
(Exh Gallery 10 1980/17)
(Mr and Mrs D Caroussis)
illustrated page 91

389 *Palm Arbour*
signed and dated November 1979, oil on canvas, 48 x 32 inches
(Exh Gallery 10 1980/10)
(Chris Beetles)
illustrated page 96

390 *Palm Arbour, Chateau Garden*
signed; signed and dated 'Nov-Dec 1979' on reverse, oil on canvas, 64 x 51¼ inches
(Exh Gallery 10 1980/3; RA 1981/73; Ellingham Mill 1983)
(Peter Coker)
illustrated page 96 and detail page 28

391 *Window, Bargemon*
oil on canvas, 60 x 50 inches
(Exh Gallery 10 1980/5; Touring 1992/18)
(Mr & Mrs Pittas)
illustrated page 93

395 *Palm Arbour*
oil on canvas, 40 x 48 inches
(Exh Gallery 10 1980/11)
(Private Collection)

396 *The Palm, Chateau Garden*
oil on canvas, 70 x 63 inches
(Exh Gallery 10 1980/1)
(G Rodopoulos)
illustrated page 95

397 *Two Windows, Bargemon*
oil on canvas, 24 x 30 inches
(Exh Gallery 10 1980/15)
(Mr and Mrs Anthony Rosner)

398 *Two Windows*
oil on canvas, 48 x 60 inches
(Exh Gallery 10 1980/6)
(Hawksfield Incorporated)
illustrated page 93

392

392 *The Yellow Diving Board, Etretat*
oil on canvas, 40 x 60 inches
(Exh RA 1979/89; Touring 1992/13)
(James Swartz)

1979-80

393 *Interior [Chez Arcadio]*
oil on canvas, 50 x 40 inches
(Exh Gallery 10 1980/8)
(Mr and Mrs Becerra)
illustrated page 92

by 1980

394 *Blue Interior*
oil on canvas, 36 x 30 inches
(Exh Gallery 10 1980/14)
(Mr & Mrs M Zolotas)
illustrated page 92

399 *Window at Bargemon*
oil on canvas, 40 x 30 inches
(Exh Gallery 10 1980/13)
(Mr and Mrs Doxiades, Greece)
illustrated page 93

1980

400 *Agave*
signed; dated 'Oct 79–Feb 80' on reverse, oil on board, 48 x 48 inches
(Exh Gallery 10 1980/7; RA 1981/47)
(Peter Coker)
illustrated page 94

401 *Bargemon*
watercolour, pen and bodycolour, 21¾ x 30 inches
(Exh Gallery 10 1989/25)
(Mr Costa Georgopoulos)

402 *Landscape Le Muy*
oil on canvas, 18 x 24 inches
(Exh Gallery 10 1980/16)
(Mr and Mrs Cu[illegible]ucundis)

403 *Landscape Le Muy*
oil on canvas, 13 x 27 inches
(Exh Gallery 10 1980/18)
(Miss Marjorie Walpole)

404

1980-81

404 *Chateau Arbour* [also known as *Yellow Enclosure*]
oil on canvas, 51½ x 64 inches
(Exh Gallery 10, date unknown)
(Mr Costa Georgopoulos)

1981

405 *Chamaerops*
signed; signed and dated '1980–81' on reverse, oil on canvas, 60 x 80 inches
(Exh Gallery 10 1982/3; Gallery 10 1985)
(Private Collection, China)

1981-83

406 *Artichokes*
oil on board, 5 x 4½ inches
(Exh Gallery 10 Spring 1984/7)
(Hassell)

407 *Artichokes*
pen and watercolour, 13½ x 9½ inches
(Exh Gallery 10 Autumn 1984/16; RA 1985/878) (Monique Sandoz)

408

by 1982

408 *Arbour*
oil on canvas, 45 x 57½ inches
(Exh Gallery 10 1982/5) (Joanna Hogg)

409 *Blue Enclosure*
oil on canvas, 48 x 60 inches
(Exh Gallery 10 1982/16; RA 1983/700)
(destroyed)

410

410 *Chamaerops, Le Vieux Château*
oil on canvas, 51½ x 77 inches
(Exh Gallery 10 1982/13)
(probably destroyed)

411 *Chateau Arbour*
oil on canvas, 32 x 40 inches
(Exh Gallery 10 1982/19)
(Mrs Chandris)

412 *Chez Arcadio [pages from sketchbook]*
pencil and watercolour, 11 x 20½ inches
(Exh Gallery 10 1982/6; RA 1983/247)
(Mr Boyd)

413 *Claviers [pages from sketchbook]*
pen and watercolour, 23½ x 15½ inches
(Exh Gallery 10 1982/12; RA 1983/165)
(whereabouts unknown)

414 *Room at Bargemon*
oil on paper, 22½ x 29½ inches
(Exh Gallery 10 1982/20)
(Private Collection)

415 *St-Saturnin*
pen and watercolour, 15½ x 23½ inches
(Exh Gallery 10 1982/8)
(Marcou)

416 *St-Saturnin*
signed and dated 1976 on reverse, pen and watercolour, 15½ x 22½ inches
(Exh Gallery 10 1982/11)
(Private Collection)

417 *St-Saturnin*
pen and watercolour, 15½ x 23½ inches
(*Artichoke*, pen and watercolour, on reverse)
(Exh Gallery 10 1982/21)
(Marcou)

418 *Two Windows, Bargemon*
oil on canvas, 52 x 77 inches
(Exh Gallery 10 1982/18; Touring 1992/19)
(Mr Costa Georgopoulos)
illustrated page 93

1982

419 *Arbour [(The Garden) Chateau Bargemon]*
signed and dated 1982 on reverse,
oil on canvas, 57½ x 33¾ inches
(Exh Gallery 10 1982/9)
(sold Sotheby's, 28 September 1994, no 209)

420 *Aurel [pages from sketchbook]*
pen and watercolour, 15½ x 23½ inches
(Exh Gallery 10 1982/7; RA 1983/166)
(whereabouts unknown)

421 *Aurel [pages from sketchbook]*
pen and watercolour, 15½ x 17 inches
(Exh Gallery 10 1982/10; RA 1983/170)
(whereabouts unknown)

422

422 *Balcony, Bargemon [, towards Clavier]*
oil on canvas, 48 x 60 inches
(Exh RA 1989/59)
(Piano Nobile)

423

423 *Cycas*
oil on canvas, 51½ x 64 inches
(Exh Gallery 10 1986/3)
(Tarik A Alireza)

424

424 *Montbrun-les-Bains*
oil on canvas, 36 x 48 inches
(Exh Gallery 10 1982/17)
(Mr Parathiras)

425 *Towards Claviers*
oil on board, 19½ x 37¼ inches
(Exh RA 1985/679)
(BP International)

1983

426 *Garden of the Villa Clos du Peyronnet*
signed, oil on canvas, 52 x 70 inches
(Exh Gallery 10 Spring 1984/18;
Chris Beetles 1999/72)
(Norman J Arnold)
illustrated page 101 and detail page 116

by 1984

427 *Agapanthus*
signed, oil on canvas, 32¼ x 40¼ inches
(Exh Gallery 10 Spring 1984/21;
RA 1985/619)
(sold Sotheby's, 23 March 1987, no 8;
given by the artist in aid of the
Courtauld appeal)

428 *Agapanthus*
oil on canvas, 25 x 30 inches
(Exh Gallery 10 Spring 1984/19)
(Miss Marjorie Walpole)

429 *Agapanthus*
watercolour, 15 x 19½ inches
(Exh Gallery 10 Autumn 1984/22)
(Private Collection)

430 *Aldeburgh Beach*
watercolour, 7 x 10½ inches
(Exh D'Arcy 1998/6)
(whereabouts unknown)

431 *Balcony*
oil on canvas, 24 x 24 inches
(Exh Gallery 10 Spring 1984/16)
(Private Collection)

432

432 *Balcony at Bargemon*
oil on canvas, 32 x 32 inches
(Exh Gallery 10 Spring 1984/2)
(Private Collection)

433 *Bamboo*
watercolour, 13½ x 9½ inches
(Exh Gallery 10 Autumn 1984/19)
(Mrs C Kalamotusis)

434 *Bamboo Path*
signed, oil on canvas, 48 x 48 inches
(Exh Gallery 10 Spring 1984/6;
Chris Beetles 1999/73)
(David Ciclitira)
illustrated page 100

435 *Beschorneria Yuccoides*
watercolour, 15½ x 22 inches
(Exh Gallery 10 Autumn 1984/21)
(Mr & Mrs O S Soderblom)

436 *Cherry*
watercolour, 15½ x 22 inches
(Exh Gallery 10 Autumn 1984/2)
(Mr Costa Georgopoulos)

437 *Falaise d'Aval, Etretat*
watercolour, 15½ x 22½ inches
(Exh Gallery 10 Autumn 1984/14)
(Patrick Dearsley)

438 *Garden of the Villa Clos du Peyronnet*
oil on canvas, 63 x 70 inches
(Exh Gallery 10 Spring 1984/3)
(Mr & Mrs R Hamilton)
illustrated page 101

439 *Garden of the Villa Clos du Peyronnet*
oil on canvas, 36 x 48 inches
(Exh Gallery 10 Spring 1984/9)
(Dr D Holt)

440 *Landscape Below Chateau*
oil on board, 10 x 14¾ inches
(Exh Gallery 10 Spring 1984/1)
(Mr M Marcou)

441 *Landscape from Chateau Garden*
oil on canvas, 26 x 36 inches
(Exh Gallery 10 Spring 1984/17)
(Mr & Mrs A Stamatiou)

442 *Les Environs d'Etretat*
oil on canvas, 33½ x 47½ inches
(Exh Gallery 10 Spring 1984/12)
(Mr M Marcou)

443 *[La] Manneporte [Etretat]*
oil on canvas, 47½ x 31½ inches
(Exh Gallery 10 Spring 1984/11)
(Phillips Petroleum Co)

444 *La Manneporte, Etretat*
watercolour, 15½ x 22½ inches
(Exh Gallery 10 Autumn 1984/12)
(Mr & Mrs E Guitar)

445

445 *Olives*
oil on canvas, 24 x 36 inches
(Exh Gallery 10 Spring 1984/13)
(Mr G Lewis)

446 *Olives*
oil on canvas, 26 x 36 inches
(Exh Gallery 10 Spring 1984/14)
(Private Collection)

447 *Olives*
oil on canvas, 25 x 30 inches
(Exh Gallery 10 Spring 1984/15)
(Mr & Mrs M Logothetis)

448 *Olives*
oil on canvas, 21¼ x 28¾ inches
(Exh Gallery 10 Spring 1984/20)
(Private Collection)

449 *Olives*
pen and watercolour, 15 x 23 inches
(Exh Gallery 10 Autumn 1984/8)
(Mr & Mrs C Coccolatos)

450 *Olives*
watercolour, 14 x 22 inches
(Exh Gallery 10 Autumn 1984/10)
(Mr & Mrs Peter Horbye)

451 *La Porte d'Aval*
watercolour and pencil, dimensions unknown
(Exh Fraser 1984/40)
(Jane Strutt)

452

452 *Putti, Clos du Peyronnet*
oil on canvas, 36 x 48 inches
(Gallery 10 Spring 1984/8)
(Mr G Rodopoulos)

453 *Road to Bargemon*
watercolour, 10¾ x 7½ inches
(Exh Gallery 10 Autumn 1984/18)
(Charles T Cavanagh)

454 *Sea off Etretat*
watercolour, 7 x 8 inches
(Exh Fraser 1984/26)
(Private Collection)

455 *Sea off Etretat*
watercolour, dimensions unknown
(Exh Fraser 1984/24)
(the Deben Gallery)

456 *Skye near the Cullin Hills*
watercolour, dimensions unknown
(Exh Fraser 1984/7)
(Private Collection)

457 *Strelitzia*
watercolour, 15 x 22½ inches
(Exh Gallery 10 Autumn 1984/4)
(Private Collection)

458 *Studio*
oil on canvas, 20 x 48 inches
(Exh Gallery 10 Spring 1984/4)
(Mr & Mrs W Armstrong)

459 *Studio at Bargemon*
oil on a pair of canvases, 36 x 96 inches
(Exh RA 1984/110)
(destroyed)

460 *Studio Bargemon*
watercolour, 15 x 21½ inches
(Exh Gallery 10 Autumn 1984/13)
(Elsbeth Juda)

461 *Studio Bargemon*
watercolour, 14 x 19½ inches
(Exh Gallery 10 Autumn 1984/25)
(Elisabeth Collins)

462

1984

462 *Callas, Summer in Provence*
oil on canvas, 36 x 48 inches
(Exh Touring 1992/21)
(James Capel & Co)

463 *Salix*
watercolour, 21¾ x 16½ inches
(Exh Gallery 10 Autumn 1984/9; RA 1985/844)
(Marcou)

464 *Sea off Aldeburgh*
oil, 34 x 48 inches
(Exh RA 1985/59)
(James Bolton)

465

465 *Willow*
oil on canvas, 36 x 28 inches
(Exh Gallery 10 Spring 1984/10)
(Dr C Dale Parker)

466

466 *Yellow Abutilon*
oil on canvas, 28½ x 38½ inches
(John Wilson, Australia)

467 *Yuccas*
watercolour, 15½ x 22 inches
(Exh Gallery 10 Autumn 1984/20)
(Private Collection)

1985

468 *Agapanthus*
signed with initials, oil on canvas, 28½ x 19 inches
(Exh Gallery 10 1986/10; Flying Colours 1990/2)
(John & Caroline Stevens)

469 *Badenscallie*
oil on canvas, 34 x 48½ inches
(Exh Touring 1992/28)
(Private Collection)

470 *Badenscallie I*
watercolour, approximately 20 x 25 inches
(Exh Harrower 1986/26)
(whereabouts unknown)

471 *Badenscallie II*
watercolour, approximately 20 x 25 inches
(Exh Harrower 1986/25)
(whereabouts unknown)

472 *Badenscallie III*
watercolour, approximately 20 x 25 inches
(Exh Harrower 1986/27)
(whereabouts unknown)

473 *Badenscallie IV*
watercolour, approximately 20 x 25 inches
(Exh Harrower 1986/28)
(whereabouts unknown)

474

474 *Beschorneria Yuccoides*
oil on canvas, 24 x 30 inches
(Exh Gallery 10 1986/1; Flying Colours 1990/10)
(AstraZeneca Ltd)

475 *Garden [of the Villa] Clos du Peyronnet, Garavan, Menton* [also known as *Phormium*]
signed, oil on canvas, 26 x 36 inches
(Exh Gallery 10 1986/7; Flying Colours 1990/12; Whittington 1997; City Gallery 1999; Chris Beetles 2000/69)
(Chris Beetles)
illustrated page 99

476 *[Garden Villa* or *Pergola] Clos du Peyronnet*
oil on canvas, 28½ x 36¾ inches
(Exh Gallery 10 1986/17; Flying Colours 1990/9)
(Private Collection)

477 *Horse Island from Acheninver, Scotland*
oil on canvas, 32 x 40 inches
(Exh Ipswich Art Club 1991/49; Touring 1992/27)
(Ipswich Borough Council Museums and Galleries)

477

478 *Horse Island from Achiltibuie*
watercolour, 15 x 21 inches
(Exh Harrower 1986/23)
(whereabouts unknown)

479 *Irises*
oil on canvas, 24 x 30 inches
(Exh Gallery 10 1986/19; Flying Colours 1990/8; Flying Colours at Art London 1999)
(Private Collection)
illustrated page 99

480 *Setcreasea Pallida*
oil on canvas, 30 x 25 inches
(Exh Gallery 10 1986/14; Flying Colours 1990/11)
(AstraZeneca Ltd)
illustrated page 98

481 *Towards Tanera Mór*
oil on canvas, 24 x 30 inches
(Exh Gallery 10 1986/25; RA 1986/511; Touring 1992/29)
(CH Mangen)

482 *Towards Tanera Mór*
oil on paper laid on board, 20½ x 28½ inches
(Exh Flying Colours 1991/8)
(whereabouts unknown)

476

483

483 *Towards Tanera Mór*
oil on paper laid on board, 20 x 30 inches
(Exh RA 1992/1010)
(David & Helma Collins)

484 *Towards Tanera Mór*
watercolour, dimensions unknown
(Exh Harrower 1986/22)
(whereabouts unknown)

485 *Towards Tanera Mór II*
watercolour, dimensions unknown
(Exh Harrower 1986/24)
(whereabouts unknown)

1985-86

486 *[Garden Villa] Clos du Peyronnet*
oil on canvas, 52 x 75 inches
(Exh Gallery 10 1986/11; Flying Colours 1990/20)
(AstraZeneca Ltd)
illustrated page 101

487

by 1986

487 *Achvraie from Tigh A'Sgiobair*
oil on canvas, 48 x 48 inches
(Exh RA 1986/608)
(Fleming-Wyfold Art Foundation)

488 *Agave Attenata*
oil on canvas, 28 x 36 inches
(Exh Gallery 10 1986/9)
(Nathalie Bardelle-Thiraux)

489

489 *Balcony Clos du Peyronnet*
oil on canvas, 36 x 48 inches
(Exh Gallery 10 1986/4)
(Mr & Mrs Azouz)

490 *The Bamboo Pathway*
oil on canvas, 48 x 32 inches
(Exh RA 1986/649)
(Mr de Rougemont)
illustrated page 101

491 *Cap de la Chèvre*
oil on canvas, 28 x 36 inches
(Exh Gallery 10 1986/22; ROI 1989/56; RA 1991/1220)
(Private Collection)

492 *Cercis*
oil on canvas, 45½ x 58 inches
(Exh Gallery 10 1986/5)
(Private Collection)

493 *Dark Pond, Strelitzia*
oil on canvas, 26 x 36 inches
(Exh Gallery 10 1986/15)
(Private Collection)

494

494 *Dark Pond, Strelitzia*
oil on canvas, 52 x 65 inches
(Exh Gallery 10 1986/16)
(Private Collection)

495 *Daturas*
oil on canvas, 16 x 20 inches
(Exh Gallery 10 1986/6)
(Private Collection)

496 *Fig*
oil on canvas, 40 x 50 inches
(Exh Gallery 10 1986/8)
(Banque Belge)

497

497 *Forêt de Landévennec*
oil, 36 x 48 inches
(RA 1986/529; Ohio 1989)
(Mr & Mrs Christopher Dunn)

498

498 *Garden Clos du Peyronnet [,Garavan, Towards Ventimiglia]*
oil on canvas, 36 x 48 inches
(Exh Gallery 10 1986/18)
(Private Collection)

499 *Green Curtain, Aldeburgh*
oil on canvas, 28 x 36 inches
(Exh Gallery 10 1986/24)
(destroyed)

500 *Hedera*
oil on canvas, 32 x 40 inches
(Exh Gallery 10 1986/2)
(Tarik A Alireza)

501 *Kersiguenou*
oil on canvas, 30 x 36 inches
(Gallery 10 1986/13)
(Jacqueline Thiraux)

502 *Kersiguenou*
oil on canvas, 16 x 24 inches
(Exh Gallery 10 1986/21)
(Mr & Mrs Azouz)

503

511

514

503 *Pointe de Dinan*
oil on canvas, 26 x 36 inches
(Exh Gallery 10 1986/12)
(Mr & Mrs C Steane)

504 *Sea Off Vaucottes*
oil on canvas, 36 x 48 inches
(Exh Gallery 10 1986/20)
(Mrs Mary Fox Linton)

505 *Window, Aldeburgh*
oil on canvas, 28 x 36 inches
(Exh RA 1986/194)
(destroyed)

506

1986

506 [*Badenscallie*]
oil, 36 x 46 inches
(whereabouts unknown)

507 *Bargemon, [in] April*
oil on canvas, 34 x 48 inches
(Exh RA 1986/531; Touring 1992/22)
(Private Collection)

508 *Cliff at Vaucottes*
oil on canvas, 30 x 30 inches
(whereabouts unknown)

509 *Harold Brown's Croft*
oil on canvas, 22 x 30 inches
(Exh Gallery 10 1988/13; RA 1989/36)
(C Leonard Kirby)
illustrated page 102

510 *Monsieur Benoit's House, Bargemon*
oil, dimensions unknown
(Marcou)

511 *Rowans, Badenscallie*
oil on canvas, 36 x 48 inches
(Exh RA 1987/159; Touring 1992/30)
(Dr A J Horan)

512 *Vaucottes [(near Etretat) Normandy]*
[also known as *Cliffs at Vaucottes*]
oil on canvas, 30 x 30 inches
(Exh Gallery 10 1986/23; Flying Colours 1991/10; Piano Nobile 1998)
(whereabouts unknown)

circa 1986

513 *Homage to John Singer Sargent (The Daughters of Edward D Boit)*
oil on canvas, 36 x 36 inches
(Exh RA 2002/405)
(Peter Coker)

513

by 1987

514 *Abandoned Sheepcroft, Badenscallie*
oil, approximately 24 x 36 inches
(Exh RA 1987/435)
(L A Fulford)

515 *Achiltibuie*
medium and dimensions unknown
(Exh RA 1987/1320)
(Dr M A Coates)

516 *Drumrunie*
oil on canvas, 36 x 48 inches
(Exh RA 1987/1067)
(L Johannesson)

517

517 *La Forêt, Claviers*
signed with initials, ink and watercolour, 30½ x 21½ inches
(Exh RA 1996/3)
(Peter Coker)

1987

518 *Badenscallie*
oil on canvas, 28 x 36 inches
(Exh RA 1987/1309; Gallery 10 1988/12; Flying Colours 1991/6; Flying Colours at Art London 1999)
(Flying Colours Gallery)

519 *Balcony, Etretat*
oil, dimensions unknown
(destroyed)

520 *Chrossavaig, Skye*
dated 1987 on reverse, oil on canvas, 36 x 48 inches
(Exh Gallery 10 1988/2; RI 1990/63; Gallery 10 at Art London 1990; Touring 1992/36; RA 2002/403)
(Mr M Marcou)

521 *Lobster*
watercolour, 19½ x 15 inches
(Exh Gallery 10 1989/6)
(Mr & Mrs John Paré)

522 *Mending Salmon Nets, Achiltibuie*
oil on canvas, 60 x 72 inches
(Exh RA 1988/417; Touring 1992/31)
(Cheltenham and Gloucester Building Society)
illustrated page 103

523 *North Sea*
signed with initials, oil on board, 27½ x 31 inches
(Exh RA 2001/154)
(Private Collection)
illustrated page 107

524 *North Sea*
oil on paper (laid on board), approximately 4½ x 10 inches
(Exh Flying Colours 1991/11)
(Peter Coker)
illustrated page 107

525 *Promenade, Etretat*
signed; signed, inscribed with title and dated 1987 on stretcher, oil on canvas, 51½ x 77 inches
(Exh Minories 1988; Chris Beetles 2000/66)
(Mr & Mrs Nick Ross)
illustrated page 106 and detail page 12

526 *The Quirang, Skye*
oil on canvas, 45 x 57¾ inches
(Exh Gallery 10 1988/11; RA 1990/82)
(Mr & Mrs Christopher Dunn)

527 *Salmon*
watercolour, 19¼ x 8¾ inches
(Exh Gallery 10 1989/17)
(Private Collection)

528 *Salmon Nets, Badentarbat*
[also known as *Salmon Nets No 1*]
oil on canvas, 36 x 60 inches
(Exh RA 1991/465; Flying Colours 1991/2)
(Mulberry Gallery, Wantage, Oxfordshire)
illustrated page 103

529 *Salmon Nets No 2*
oil on canvas, 52 x 60 inches
(Exh Business Design Centre 1990)
(Mr & Mrs John Paré)
illustrated page 103

530 *Salmon Nets, Achiltibuie [No 3]*
oil on canvas, 36 x 48 inches
(Exh RA 1991/466; Flying Colours 1991/5)
(Cargill Europe)
illustrated page 103

531 *Salmon Nets No 4*
signed with initials; signed and dated 1987 on reverse, oil, 34 x 58 inches
(Exh RA 1990/1136)
(Mrs Wood)
illustrated page 103

532

532 *Salmon Nets No 5*
oil on canvas, 52 x 75 inches
(Mr & Mrs Christopher Dunn)

533 *Sheep Croft, Badenscallie*
oil on canvas, 20 x 60 inches
(Exh Gallery 10 1988/5; Gallery 10 at Art London 1989; RI 1988/67; Flying Colours 1991/4)
(whereabouts unknown)
illustrated page 102

534

534 *Terrace, Le Vieux Château – Towards Claviers*
oil on canvas, 48 x 48 inches
(Exh RA 1987/434; Touring 1992/20)
(D B Lundell)

535

by 1988

535 *Badenscallie*
oil on canvas, 26 x 36 inches
(Exh Gallery 10 1988/1)
(Richard Attenborough)

536 *Badenscallie*
oil on canvas, 24 x 30 inches
(Exh Gallery 10 1988/3)
(Mr & Mrs Parkin, Canada)

537 *Badenscallie*
oil on canvas, 26 x 36 inches
(Exh Gallery 10 1988/10;
City Gallery 2000)
(whereabouts unknown)

538 *Badentarbat Bay*
watercolour, 15 x 20 inches
(Exh Gallery 10 1988/6)
(Mr & Mrs Rougemont)

539 *North Sea* [also known as *Promenade, Ostend*]
oil on canvas, 53½ x 85½ inches
(Exh Gallery 10 1988/7)
(Mr Costa Georgopoulos)
illustrated page 107

540 *Sea Badentarbat*
oil on canvas, 28 x 41½ inches
(Exh Gallery 10 1988/4)
(whereabouts unknown)

541 *Sea, Summer Isle*
oil on canvas, 24 x 85½ inches
(Exh Gallery 10 1988/8)
(whereabouts unknown)

542

542 *Towards Polbain*
oil on canvas, 22 x 30 inches
(Exh Gallery 10 1988/9; Ohio 1989;
Flying Colours 1991/1)
(Strutt)

543 *Towards Polbain*
oil, 22 x 30 inches
(whereabouts unknown)

544 *Vines, Le Vieux Château*
oil on canvas, 28 x 36 inches
(Exh Gallery 10 1988/14)
(Mr Gabriel Kaplan, USA)

1988

545 *Achiltibuie*
oil on canvas, 32 x 48 inches
(Exh RA 1989/547)
Lord Tollemache of Helmingham)

546 *Badenscallie*
oil on canvas, 48 x 48 inches
(Exh RA 1989/8; Touring 1992/37)
(G Minden)

547

547 *Evening Towards Westminster from Cranley Gardens* [also known as *London from Cranley Gardens*]
oil, 32 x 47 inches
(Exh ROI 1989/55; Gallery 10 1989;
RA 1993/852)
(Myles Pepper, West Wales Art Centre)

548 *Mending Salmon Nets, N W Scotland* [also known as *Mending Nets, Achiltibuie* and *Willie Muir with his Dog*]
signed with initials; signed and dated 1988
on reverse, oil on canvas, 24 x 30 inches
(Exh Flying Colours 1990/5; Whittington
1997; Chris Beetles 1999/71)
(Chris Beetles)
illustrated page 104

549 *Peat Landscape, Achiltibuie*
signed with initials; signed and dated 1988
on reverse; oil on canvas, 30 x 39¾ inches
(Exh RA 1989/885; Flying Colours
1991/3; Chris Beetles 2000/68)
(Chris Beetles)

550 *Salmon Nets*
watercolour and pen, 23 x 31 inches
(Exh Fitzwilliam 1989/21; Gallery 10
1989/26; Touring 1992/35)
(Private Collection)

551 *Salmon Nets, Badentarbat*
[also known as *Salmon Nets No 6*]
oil on canvas, 45 x 57½ inches
(Exh RA 1991/513; Flying Colours
1991/9)
(whereabouts unknown)
illustrated page 104

552

552 *Salmon Nets No 7*
oil, 45 x 57 inches
(Exh RA 1990/531)
(Private Collection)

549

553 *Salmon Nets [Badentarbat] No 8*
oil on canvas, 38 1/2 x 57½ inches
(Exh Business Design Centre 1990)
(Private Collection)
illustrated page 104

554 *Salmon Nets [Badentarbat] No 9*
oil on canvas, 35 x 51½ inches
(Exh Business Design Centre 1990;
Flying Colours at Art London 1999)
(Private Collection)

555

555 *Salmon Poles, Badentarbat*
watercolour and bodycolour, 22 x 30 inches
(Exh Fitzwilliam 1989/19; Gallery 10
1989/15; Flying Colours 1991/13;
RA 1996/20)
(Dr Williams)

556 *Salmon Nets, drying and ready for inspection, Badentarbat [Salmon Nets No 11]*
signed with initials, oil on canvas,
34 x 48 inches
(Peter Coker)
illustrated page 104

557 *Self Portrait [in Studio Mirror]*
signed; signed and dated 1988 on reverse,
oil on canvas, 57½ x 35 inches
(Peter Coker)

1989

558 *Cleaning Nets, Quiberville*
signed, inscribed with title and dated 1989
on reverse, oil on board, 44 x 57 inches
(Exh RA 1999/356)
(Peter Coker)
illustrated page 109

559 *Cliffs at Quiberville*
oil on board, 12¼ x 16 inches
(Exh Flying Colours 1990/3)
(Christopher Dowling)
illustrated page 108

560 *Cliffs at Quiberville*
oil on board, 7 x 22 inches
(Exh Flying Colours 1990/6)
(Private Collection)

561 *Cliffs, St-Valery-en-Caux*
oil on canvas, 20 x 30 inches
(Exh Flying Colours 1990/21)
(Richard Strover)
illustrated page 107

562

562 *Cornfield, Higham*
oil, 32 x 48 inches
(Private Collection)

563

563 *Jim Muir Mending Nets, Coigach in Distance*
[also known as *Mending Salmon Nets No 12*]
oil on canvas, 40 x 60 inches
(Exh RA 1990/527; Flying Colours at Art
London 1999)
(Private Collection)

557

564 *Landscape, Varengeville-sur-Mer*
[also known as *Orchard at Varengeville*]
oil on canvas, 19 x 48 inches
(Exh Touring 1992/24; Flying Colours at
Art London 1999)
(Private Collection)

565 *La Roche-Guyon*
oil on canvas, 27½ x 48 inches
(Exh Flying Colours 1990/1;
Touring 1992/23)
(Private Collection)

566 *La Roche-Guyon*
signed with initials; signed and inscribed
with title on reverse, oil on board,
7 x 22½ inches
(Peter Coker)
illustrated page 111

567

567 *La Roche-Guyon*
oil on canvas, 19 x 48 inches
(Jane Strutt)

568 *La Roche-Guyon*
oil on board, 12 x 31¼ inches
(Exh Flying Colours 1990/7)
(Mr & Mrs Richard Cobbold)

569 *La Roche-Guyon*
oil, 50 x 60 inches
(destroyed)

570 *Lighthouse, St-Valery-en-Caux*
oil on board, 12¼ x 16 inches
(Exh Flying Colours 1990/4)
(Private Collection)

571 *Lighthouse, St-Valery-en-Caux*
oil on board 9 x 9½ inches
(Exh Flying Colours 1990/17)
(Private Collection)

572 *Lighthouse St-Valery-en-Caux*
oil on board, 7 x 14 inches
(Exh Flying Colours 1990/19)
(Private Collection)

573 *Orchard, Varengeville*
oil on board, 6½ x 21½ inches
(Mr & Mrs Richard Cobbold)
illustrated page 110

574 *Salmon Net Poles, Badentarbat*
signed with initials; signed and dated 1989 on reverse, oil on canvas, 27½ x 48 inches
(Pen and Ron Zimmern)
illustrated page 105 and detail page 160

575 *Seascape, Quiberville*
oil, 6½ x 21½ inches
(Mr & Mrs Richard Cobbold)
illustrated page 110

576

582

1991

576 *Cornfield, Ste-Marguerite-sur-Mer*
oil, 13 x 14 inches
(Exh RA 1993/881)
(Lisa Mesdag)

577 *Harvest, Normandy*
oil, 20 x 30 inches
(Exh RA 1992/1060)
(Private Collection)

578 *Lighthouse, St-Valery-en-Caux*
oil on board, 4½ x 10 inches
(Exh Flying Colours 1991/12)
(Private Collection)

579 *[Marine,] Varengeville*
oil, 13 x 14 inches
(Exh RA 1993/880)
(Private Collection)

580 *[Mending Salmon] Nets*
signed with initials, watercolour, ink and oil pastel with chalk and bodycolour, 26 x 39 inches
(Exh Touring 1992/38; RA 1996/34)
(Peter Coker)

581 *Paysage, Normandy* [also known as *Near St-Marguerite-sur-Mer*]
signed and inscribed with title on reverse, oil on board, 4 x 9¼ inches
(Peter Coker)

582 *St-Valery-en-Caux*
signed with initials; signed, inscribed with title and dated 1991 on reverse, oil on board, 21 x 30 inches
(Exh Chris Beetles 2000/67)
(Chris Beetles)

583 *St-Valery-en-Caux*
signed with initials; signed, inscribed with title and dated c 1991 on reverse; oil on board, 15¾ x 26 inches
(Chris Beetles)
illustrated page 108

584 *Veules-les-Roses*
signed with initials, oil on board, 15½ x 30½ inches
(Exh RA 1993/882; Chris Beetles 1998/294)
(Dr A J Horan)
illustrated page 108

585 *Veules-les-Roses*
signed with initials; inscribed with title on reverse, oil on board, 13¾ x 19¼ inches
(Exh RA 1993/835; Chris Beetles 1998/295)
(Barbara Tucker)

580

1992

586 *Fenêtre Ouverte à Menton*
oil, 48 x 32 inches
(Exh RA 1992/530)
(J R S Boas)
illustrated page 112

587 *The Garden, Clos du Peyronnet, evening*
signed; signed and dated 1992 on reverse,
oil on canvas, 57¾ x 35 inches
(Peter Coker)
illustrated page 113

588 *Garden Pond, The Red House*
signed; signed and dated 1992 on reverse,
oil on canvas, 51¾ x 64 inches
(Peter Coker)
illustrated page 114

589 *The Grand Staircase, garden of the Clos du Peyronnet, late afternoon*
signed; signed and dated 1992 on reverse,
oil on canvas, 45 x 57½ inches
(Peter Coker)
illustrated page 113

590 *Menton*
signed, oil, 48 x 48 inches
(Exh RA 1999/329)
(Peter Coker)
illustrated page 112 and detail page 144

585

45

List of Exhibitions

1950
Royal Academy of Arts, London:
Summer Exhibition (29 Apr – 7 Aug)
141 *Still Life*

1951
Royal Society of British Artists, Suffolk Street Galleries, London: *Young Contemporaries* (15 Jan – 5 Feb)
Melon Eater
Melon Stall

Paul Alexander Gallery, London: *New Painting, '51* (Nov)
Still Life
[and one other work]

1952
Leicester Galleries, London: *Artists of Fame and of Promise, Part 1* (Jul)
182 *Ystrad, Rhondda*

Redfern Gallery, London: *Summer Exhibition* (3 Jul – 30 Aug)
499 *Tonypandy Colliery*
500 *Penycraig Colliery*

Royal Academy of Arts, London:
Summer Exhibition (2 May – 16 Aug)
261 *Still Life*

1953
The Shell Petroleum Company Limited, London: *The Artist's View of an Industry*
13 *Rail Tank Cars (Stanlow Refinery, Cheshire)*
14 *Pipes (Stanlow Refinery, Cheshire)*

1954
Management House, London: *Life in Industry. An exhibition of paintings by Contemporary Artists* (15 Jan – 14 Feb)
37 *Tonypandy-Rhondda Valley*

Royal Academy of Arts, London:
Summer Exhibition (1 May – 15 Aug)
398 *P H Jowett Esq, CBE*
493 *Geraldine*

The Piccadilly Gallery, London: *Exhibition of Contemporary Watercolours* (Jun – Jul)
9 *Dowlas Steel Works, Cardiff*
10 *Tonypandy*
11 *Ystrad Rhondda, South Wales*
12 *Mountain Ash, Rhondda*
13 *Penny Craig, Naval Colliery*

1955
St Martin's School of Art, London (Mar)
Fish and Newspaper

Royal Academy of Arts, London:
Summer Exhibition (30 Apr – 14 Aug)
714 *Ystrad Rhondda, South Wales*

1956
Zwemmer Gallery, London: solo exhibition: *Paintings by Peter Coker* (10 – 31 Jan)
Paintings
1 *Butcher's Shop I*
2 *Sheep Carcasses on Bench*
3 *Apple Tree*
4 *Man carrying Pig*
5 *Butcher's Shop II*
6 *La Plaine de Chailly*
7 *Landscape at Barbizon*
8 *Fish with Grill*
9 *Pig's Head*
10 *Dead Hare on Table*
11 *Cliff at Etretat*
12 *Still Life with Hare*
13 *Cliffs near Etretat*
14 *Fish and Newspaper*
15 *Still Life with Chicken*
16 *The Rock, Etretat*
17 *Sheep's Head on Newspaper*
18 *Table and Chair*
Drawings
19 *The Cliff at Etretat*
20 *The Wave*
21 *Sheep's Head*
22 *The Rock, Etretat*
23 *Cliffs near Etretat*
24 *Fish*
25 *The Forest, Fontainebleau*
26 *Apple Tree, Barbizon*
27 *Wave on Shingle Beach*
28 *Cliffs at Etretat*
29 *Dead Chicken*
30 *Chicken on Table*
31 *The Forest, Barbizon*
Lithograph
32 *Hare on Table*

1956
South London Art Gallery: *Looking Forward. An exhibition of realist pictures selected by John Berger* (18 Apr – 5 May)
10 *Man Carrying Pig*
50 *Dead Chicken on Table (drawing)*

Royal Academy of Arts, London:
Summer Exhibition (5 May – 19 Aug)
348 *Butcher's Shop*
440 *Butcher's Shop II*
592 *Sheep Carcasses on Bench*

Arthur Jeffress (Pictures), London
Contemporary British Painting & Sculpture. Some unusual juxtapositions (29 May – 29 Jun)
8 *Fish with Grill*

Zwemmer Gallery, London: *Summer Exhibition* (22 Aug – 19 Sep)
Apple Tree
[and possibly other works]

Bournemouth Arts Club: *Painting Today*
6 *Dead Hare on Table*
41 *Barbizon Landscape*

1957
Royal Academy of Arts, London
Summer Exhibition (4 May – 18 Aug)
446 *Etretat*
502 *Apple tree*

Zwemmer Gallery, London: solo exhibition: *Peter Coker* (21 Oct – 16 Nov)
Paintings
1 *Tree and Hedge I*
2 *Bracken and Gorse, Audierne*
3 *Brittany Landscape*
4 *Forest I*
5 *Gorse Bush*
6 *Lighthouse, Audierne*
7 *Forest II*
8 *Tree and Hedge II*
9 *The Wave*
10 *White Buoys, Audierne*
11 *Waves and Rock*
12 *Jetty*
13 *Wave*
Drawings (all charcoal and conté)
14 *Turbot*
15 *Tree and Hedge*
16 *Turbot II*
17 *Tree and Hedge*
18 *Waves and Rock*
19 *Bracken, Audierne*
20 *Forest I*
21 *Forest II*
22 *Forest III*
23 *Forest IV*
24 *Forest V*
25 *Forest VI*

1958
The Cafe Royal, London: *The Arts and the Cafe Royal: Twenty Contemporaries – a collection of invited paintings together with a retrospective exhibition of works by some of the artists who have visited the Cafe Royal since 1865* (24 Jun – 19 Jul)
[exhibits unidentified]

Tate Gallery, London: Contemporary Art Society: *The Religious Theme* (10 Jul – 21 Aug)
10 *Fish and Bread*

Zwemmer Gallery, London: *Summer Exhibition* (Sep)
Tree and Hedge

Jordan Gallery, Toronto, Canada: *Contemporary British Artists* (24 Oct – 15 Nov)
[exhibits unidentified]

1959
The Arts Council of Great Britain, London: The Contemporary Art Society: *Recent Acquisitions. An Exhibition of works shortly to be distributed to public galleries* (25 Feb – 26 Mar)
11 *Tree and Hedge II*
Ex-catalogue *Landscape at Barbizon*

Zwemmer Gallery, London: *Spring Selection*
2 *La Plaine de Chailly*
4 *Study for Tree and Hedge* (conté)
5 *Tree and Hedge I*
11 *White Buoys, Audierne*
13 *Gorse Bush*
16 *Village in Brittany*

Zwemmer Gallery, London: *Summer Exhibition* (Sep)
La Plaine de Chailly

Zwemmer Gallery, London: solo exhibition: *Peter Coker* (22 Oct – 19 Nov)
Paintings
1 *Still life with Fish*
2 *Still life with Hare*
3 *Sunflowers*
4 *Seascape*
5 *Clouds I*
6 *Forest I*
7 *Forest II*
8 *Forest III*
9 *Forest IV*
10 *Forest V*
11 *Forest VI*
12 *Forest VII*
13 *Forest VIII*
14 *Forest IX*
14a *Clouds II*
Drawings
15 *Tree I* (charcoal and conté)
16 *Tree II* (conté and ink)
17 *Pollards, Epping* (charcoal)
18 *Forest I* (conté)
19 *Forest III* (charcoal and conté)
20 *Forest IV* (charcoal and conté)
21 *Forest VI* (charcoal)
22 *Landscape near Audierne* (conté and ink)
23 *Head* (charcoal)
24 *Figure* (charcoal)
25 *Still life with fish* (charcoal and pencil)

1959/1960
Walker Art Gallery, Liverpool: *The John Moores Liverpool Exhibition 2* (18 Nov 1959 – 17 Jan 1960)
23 *Tree and Hedge*

Tib Lane Gallery, Manchester: *A Selection of Young Contemporaries* (30 Nov 1959 – 2 Jan 1960)
20 *Forest I*
21 *Forest IV*
22 *Forest I* (drawing)

1960
Northampton Museum and Art Gallery: *Art Alive* (5 Mar – 9 Apr)
Tree and Hedge I

Royal Academy of Arts, London: *Summer Exhibition* (29 Apr – 14 Aug)
100 *Forest No 1*
169 *Seascape*
201 *Forest No 4*

Europaisches Forum, Alpbach, Tirol, Austria (19 Aug – 7 Sep) and Neue Galerie Der Stadt, Linz, Austria (25 Nov – 31 Dec): *Das Junge England*
4 *Forest IX* [Wald]
5 *Hanging Pig* [Schweinträger]

1961
Zwemmer Gallery, London: *Summer Selection* (16 May – 20 Jun)
Copse
Sunflowers

Royal Academy of Arts, London: *Summer Exhibition* (29 Apr – 13 Aug)
460 *Gorse Bush*
468 *White buoys, Audierne*
482 *Forest No 8*

Wildenstein Gallery, London: *Contemporary Portrait Society. Inaugural Exhibition* (25 Oct – 18 Nov)
1 *Vera and Nicholas Coker* (drawing)

1961/1962
Walker Art Gallery, Liverpool: *The John Moores Liverpool Exhibition 1961* (16 Nov 1961– 14 Jan 1962)
33 *Forest IX*

1962
The Arts Council of Great Britain: *The Arts Council as Patron. A Selection of Paintings Purchased 1957-1962* (5 Apr – 5 May)
Dead Hare on Table

Royal Academy of Arts, London: *Summer Exhibition* (4 May – 26 Aug)
133 *Tree & Hedge, No 1*
356 *Brittany Landscape*

Castle Museum, Colchester: (15 – 27 Oct)
Geraldine

Royal College of Art, London: *Towards Art? The Contribution of the RCA to the Fine Arts 1952-62* (7 Nov – 1 Dec)
138 *Forest V*
139 *Forest III*
143 *Portrait of the late P H Jowett, CBE, Principal 1935-48*
162 *Charcoal Drawing*

1963
The Minories, Colchester: *John Hutton, Peter Coker, Peter Searle* (14 Jan – 2 Feb)
41 *Llanberis* (conté and charcoal)
42 *Llanberis Pass I* (conté and charcoal)
43 *Llanberis Pass II* (conté and charcoal)
44 *Llangranog* (conté and charcoal)
45 *Forest I* (conté and charcoal)
46 *Forest II* (conté and charcoal)
47 *Tree* (conté)
48 *Copse I* (conté and charcoal)
49 *Copse II* (conté and charcoal)
50 *Rocks, Pembrokeshire I* (conté and charcoal)
51 *Rocks, Pembrokeshire II* (conté and charcoal)
52 *Waves, Etretat* (conté and charcoal)
53 *Chicken* (conté)
54 *Turbot* (charcoal)
55 *Still Life with Fish* (pencil and charcoal)
Ex-catalogue *New Forest* (drawing)

Royal Academy of Arts, London: *Summer Exhibition* (4 May – 18 Aug)
364 *Forest No 5*
1011 *Pembrokeshire Coast* (pencil and chalk)

The Arts Council of Great Britain: *Towards Art?* (a selection of the exhibition held in 1962 at the Royal College of Art). Touring to: The Arts Council Gallery, Cambridge (18 May – 8 Jun), Graves Art Gallery, Sheffield (15 Jun – 6 Jul), Laing Art Gallery, Newcastle (13 Jul – 3 Aug), Municipal College of Art, Bournemouth (10 – 31 Aug), Victoria Street Art Gallery, Nottingham (7 – 28 Sep), National Museum of Wales, Cardiff (5 –26 Aug):
45 *Forest III*

The Minories, Colchester: *An Exhibition of English Drawings* (1 – 20 Jul)
18 *Waves and Rock*
19 *Mountain Landscape*

1964
Royal Academy of Arts, London: *Summer Exhibition* (2 May – 16 Aug)
82 *Waves and Rock*
900 *Forest* (conté and charcoal)
997 *Waves and Rock* (conté and charcoal)

Zwemmer Gallery, London: solo exhibition: *Peter Coker. An exhibition of recent forest paintings and other works* (10 Nov – 7 Dec)
Paintings
1 *Epping Forest I*
2 *Epping Forest II*
3 *Epping Forest III*
4 *Epping Forest IV*
5 *Late Summer, Epping*
6 *Landscape near Audierne*
7 *Landscape near Mistley*
8 *Landscape near Mistley*
9 *Landscape near Ardleigh*
10 *Autumn Forest, East Bergholt*
11 *Pen-y-Gwyrd Pass*
12 *Avenue of Trees*
13 *The Brett, Suffolk*
14 *The Brett, Study*
15 *Brett Bank*
16 *River Brett*
17 *Aldeburgh I*
18 *Aldeburgh II*
19 *Aldeburgh III*
20 *Rendlesham Forest*
21 *Tunstall Forest I*
22 *Tunstall Forest II*
23 *Tunstall Forest III*
Drawings
24 *Epping* (conté and charcoal)
25 *Rendlesham Forest* (charcoal)
26 *Tunstall Forest* (pencil and charcoal)
27 *Llanberis Pass*
28 *Mistley*
29 *Ardleigh*
30 *Tunstall Forest*
31 *Study, Tree Trunks*
Ex-catalogue *Fish and Bread*

1965
The Minories, Colchester: (22 Mar – 10 Apr) *Rendlesham Forest* (drawing)

Royal Academy of Arts, London: *Summer Exhibition* (1 May – 15 Aug)
152 *Suffolk Landscape*
156 *Aldeburgh*
487 *Rendlesham Forest*

Zwemmer Gallery, London: *Summer Exhibition* (Aug)
Sea-scape

Peckova House, Wisbech: *English Shores* (Enterprise Neptune) (20 Jul – 2 Aug)
3 *High Seas at Aldeburgh, Suffolk No 2*
71 *Pembrokeshire Coast* (conté and charcoal)

1965/1968
The Arts Council of Great Britain: *British Painting 50-57*
Touring to: Bristol (1965), London (1966), Reading University (1966), Wales (1967), Scotland (1968)
7 *Dead Hare on Table*

1966
The Arts Council of Great Britain: *Painters in East Anglia:*
Touring to: Cambridge Arts Council Gallery (22 Jan – 12 Feb), Southampton Art Gallery (19 Feb – 12 Mar), Plymouth City Art Gallery (19 Mar – 9 Apr) Keighley Art Gallery and Museum (16 Apr – 7 May), Glynn Vivian Art Gallery, Swansea (14 May – 4 Jun), Stafford Art Gallery (11 Jun – 2 Jul)
21 *Fish and Newspaper*
22 *Hare on Table*
23 *Dead Hare* (conté and charcoal)
24 *Vera and Nicholas Coker* (conté and charcoal)

Royal Academy of Arts, London: *A Selection of Pictures for Schools* (16 Feb – 4 Mar)
51 *Llanberis Pass I* (conté and charcoal)
52a *Still Life with Fish* (charcoal and pencil)
52b *Llanberis Pass II* (conté and charcoal)

Royal Academy of Arts, London: *Summer Exhibition* (7 May – 14 Aug)
77 *Mountain Stream, Pyrenees, No 2*
78 *Judas Gap*
79 *Garden Copse*
80 *Pyrenees Cave*
540 *Mountain Stream, Pyrenees, No 3*
864 *Apple Tree*

1967
Royal Academy of Arts, London: *A Selection of Pictures for Schools* (15 Feb – 3 Mar)
26 *Epping Forest*
27 *Pen-y-Gwyrd Pass*

Royal Academy of Arts, London: *Summer Exhibition* (29 Apr – 30 Jul)
569 *Forest* 1959
570 *Still Life with Hare* 1958
571 *Clouds over Sea*
573 *Tunstall Forest*
1050 *Epping Forest* (conté and charcoal)
1061 *Rendlesham Forest* (conté and charcoal)

Zwemmer Gallery, London: solo exhibition: *Peter Coker. An exhibition of paintings and drawings* (4 Oct – 3 Nov)
Paintings
1 *Mountain Stream, Pyrenees II*
2 *Mountain Stream, Pyrenees III*
3 *Weir, Josselin*
4 *Waterfall, Malham*
5 *Running Stream, Malham*
6 *Audierne*
7 *Copse*
8 *Evening Sea*
9 *Seascape*
10 *Gorse Bush*
11 *Clouds over Sea*
12 *Evening, River Stour*
13 *Evening, Malham*
14 *Western Sutherland*

Drawings
15 *Sluice* (conté and chalk)
16 *Judas Gap* (conté and chalk)
17 *Running Stream, Malham* (pencil)
18 *Epping Forest* (pencil)
19 *Waterfall, Malham* (conté and chalk)
20 *Forest* (conté)
21 *Bracken* (conté)
22 *Bracken Field* (conté)
23 *Bracken Field* (conté)
24 *Derelict Lighthouse, Audierne* (conté)
25 *The Copse* (conté and chalk)
26 *Cliffs near Etretat* (conté and crayon)
27 *Epping Forest* (conté)
28 *Seashore, Normandy* (conté)
29 *Epping* (conté)
30 *Epping* (conté)
31 *Rush Bank* (conté)
32 *Landscape near Audierne* (pencil)
33 *Waves, Etretat* (conté and charcoal)
34 *Forest* (conté and charcoal)
35 *Rocks, Pembrokeshire* (conté)
36 *Llanberis* (conté and charcoal)
37 *Rendelsham Forest* (ink)
38 *Slate quarry near Llanberis* (conté and charcoal)
39 *Towards Arncliffe* (chalk)
40 *Durness Landscape* (chalk)
41 *Durness Landscape*
42 *The Strath Beag* (charcoal)
43 *Evening, Malham moor* (chalk)
44 *Llangranog* (charcoal and pencil)
Paintings
45 *Overlooking the Stour*
46 *Dusk. Western Sutherland*

1968
Royal Academy of Arts, London: *A Selection of Pictures for Schools* (28 Feb – 15 Mar)
127 *Llangranog* (charcoal and pencil)
128 *The Copse* (conté and chalk)

Magdalene Street Gallery, Cambridge: solo exhibition: *Drawings by Peter Coker* (20 Apr – 11 May)
1 *Forest*
2 *Bracken Field I*
3 *Bracken Field II*
4 *Seashore, Normandy*
5 *Derelict Lighthouse, Audierne*
6 *Landscape near Audierne*
7 *Sluice Gates, Ulting, Essex*
8 *Life Study*
9 *Near Fordingbridge*
10 *Mill House, near Fordingbridge*
11 *Near Etretat, Normandy*
12 *Coast Scene, Etretat*
13 *Epping Forest*
14 *Sluice Gate, near Fordingbridge*
15 *Barbizon Orchard*
16 *Nicholas*
17 *Nude*
18 *Reclining Nude*

19 *Rendlesham, Suffolk*
20 *Audierne, Brittany*
21 *Hare*
22 *Llanberis*
23 *Apple Tree, Mistley*
24 *Epping Forest*

Royal Academy of Arts, London:
Summer Exhibition (4 May – 4 Aug)
80 *Audierne*
425 *Waterfall, Malham*
434 *Weir, Josselin*
762 *Running Stream, Malham*
766 *Evening Sea*
914 *Evening, Malham*

Stable Gallery, Ufford: solo exhibition:
An exhibition of drawings by Peter Coker
(30 Jun – 21 Jul)
1 *Tunstall Forest*
2 *Epping Forest* (conté and charcoal)
3 *Hare* (conté and charcoal)
4 *Fish* (pencil)
5 *Sluice Gates, Ulting Essex* (pastel)
6 *Coast, Etretat* (conté)
7 *Sluice Gate, Fordingbridge* (conté)
8 *Barbizon, Orchard* (conté)
9 *Epping Forest* (conté)
10 *The Copse* (conté and chalk)
11 *Normandy coast* (conté)
12 *Epping* (pencil)
13 *Epping* (conté)
14 *Nicholas* (pencil and charcoal)
15 *Running Stream* (pencil)
16 *Bracken Field* (conté)
17 *Bracken* (conté)
18 *Epping Forest* (conté)
19 *Tunstall Forest* (ink)
20 *The Copse*

1968/1969
Royal Academy of Arts, London:
Bicentenary Exhibition 1768-1968
(14 Dec 1968 – 2 Mar 1969)
D9 *Forest VIII*

1969
Royal Institute Galleries, London:
East Anglian Art Today (27 Jan – 15 Feb)
7 *Waterfall, Malham*

The Scottish Arts Council Gallery, Glasgow:
Painting 1950-57, (a selection of paintings from the Permanent Collection of the Arts Council of Great Britain) (8 Mar – 5 Apr)
[Probably included *Dead Hare on Table*]

Royal Academy of Arts, London:
Summer Exhibition (3 May – 27 Jul)
27 *Evening: Durness*
94 *Night: Malham*
427 *Seascale*
569 *Near Durness*
811 *Low Tide: Seascale*
1037 *Kyle of Durness*

Royal Academy of Arts, London:
A Selection of Pictures for Schools (15 – 31 Oct)
19 *Night, Malham*

Stone Gallery, Newcastle Upon Tyne: solo exhibition: *Peter Coker ARA. Pastels*
(25 Oct – 29 Nov)
1 *Kinlochbervie, Sutherland* (conté and charcoal)
2 *Near Garrigill* (pastel)
3 *Leadgate* (pastel)
4 *Evening, Malham* (pastel)
5 *Kyle of Durness* (pastel)
6 *River Stour from Cattawade*
7 *Towards Arncliffe* (pastel)
8 *Low Force, Teesdale* (charcoal and chalk)
9 *Black Burn* (chalk)
10 *Garrigill* (chalk)
11 *Waterfall, Tynehead* (chalk)
12 *Low Force* (chalk)
13 *Forest* (conté and charcoal)
14 *Strath Beg* (charcoal)
15 *Starbotton* (chalk and charcoal)
16 *Kinlochbervie, Sutherland* (chalk and wash)
17 *Llanberis Pass* (conté and charcoal)
18 *Towards Old Cote Moor* (chalk)
19 *Overlooking Starbotton* (chalk)
20 *Moor End Fell* (pastel and chalk)
21 *The Copse* (conté and chalk)
22 *Epping* (conté and charcoal)
23 *Below Low Force* (chalk and wash)
24 *Ash Gill* (ink)
25 *Rendlesham* (ink)
26 *Kyle of Durness* (pastel)
27 *Night, Malham* (pencil)
28 *Coast, Durness* (chalk)
29 *Sea, Durness* (chalk)
30 *River Wharfe, Starbotton (chalk)*
31 *Leadgate* (pencil)
32 *Running Stream, Malham* (pencil)
33 *Epping Forest* (pencil)
34 *Bracken Field* (conté)
35 *Derelict Lighthouse, Audierne* (conté)

The Phoenix Gallery, Lavenham:
Sixty Good Pictures
18 *Kyle of Durness*

196?
The Phoenix Gallery, Lavenham:
60 Good Pictures (25 Aug – 9 Sep)
20 *Late Evening, The Storm*
21 *Epping*

1970
Thackeray Gallery, London: solo exhibition:
Peter Coker ARA. Paintings and Drawings
(3 – 26 Mar)
Paintings
1 *Weir, Josselin*
2 *Mountain Stream, Pyrenees*
3 *Garden Copse*
4 *Kyle of Durness*
5 *Near Durness*
6 *Clouds over Cross Fell*
7 *Moor End Fell from Starbotton*
8 *Towards Old Cote Moor Top*
9 *The Stour from Cattawade, Evening*
10 *River Stour from Cattawade*
11 *Stour, Evening*
12 *Gorse Bush*
Drawings
13 *Kinlochbervie, Sutherland (conté and chalk)*
14 *Near Garrigill (pastel)*
15 *Leadgate (pastel)*
16 *Evening, Malham (pastel)*
17 *Kyle of Durness (pastel and chalk)*
18 *Towards Arncliffe (pastel)*
19 *Low Force, Teesdale (charcoal and chalk)*
20 *Black Burn (chalk)*
21 *Garrigill (chalk)*
22 *Waterfall, Tynehead (chalk)*
23 *Low Force (chalk)*
24 *Forest (conté and charcoal)*
25 *Strath Beg (charcoal)*
26 *Starbotton (chalk and charcoal)*
27 *Kinlochbervie, Sutherland (chalk and wash)*
28 *Llanberis Pass (conté and chalk)*
29 *Towards Old Cote Moor (chalk)*
30 *Overlooking Starbotton (chalk)*
31 *Moor End Fell (pastel and chalk)*
32 *The Copse (conté and chalk)*
33 *Epping (conté and chalk)*
34 *Below Low Force (chalk and wash)*
35 *Rendlesham (ink)*
36 *Kyle of Durness (pastel)*
37 *Night, Malham (pencil)*
38 *Coast, Durness (chalk)*
39 *Sea, Durness (chalk)*
40 *River Wharfe, Starbotton (chalk)*
41 *Leadgate (pencil)*
42 *Running Stream, Malham (pencil)*
43 *Epping Forest (pencil)*
44 *Bracken Field (conté)*
45 *Derelict Lighthouse, Audierne (conté)*
46-5 *figures*

Royal Academy of Arts, London:
Summer Exhibition (2 May – 26 Jul)
89 *The Stour from Cattawade: evening*
585 *Towards Old Cote Moor Top*
586 *Moor End Fell from Starbotton*
592 *Clouds over Cross Fell*
654 *Black Burn (chalk)*
671 *Waterfall, Tynehead*

1971
Royal Academy of Arts, London:
Summer Exhibition (1 May – 25 Jul)
475 *Moor End Fell, Starbotton*
476 *Trees at Leadgate*
477 *Black Burn and the South Tyne*
478 *Dewley Fell, near Alston*

521 *View from Ivy Cottage*
876 *Behind Leadgate*

Westgate House, Long Melford: *Pupil & Masters* (joint exhibition with Vivian Pitchforth and James Stroudley) (15 –31 Oct)
Paintings
1 *Weir, Josselin*
2 *Near Durness*
3 *The Stour from the Cattawade, Late Evening*
4 *Judas Gap, Flatford*
5 *Along the Beach, Aldeburgh*
Drawings
6 *Near Garrigill* (pastel)
7 *Low Force, Teesdale* (charcoal & chalk)
8 *Forest* (conté & charcoal)
9 *Strath Beg* (charcoal)
10 *Towards Arncliffe* (pastel)
11 *The Copse* (conté and charcoal)
12 *Llanberis Pass* (conté and charcoal)
13 *Low Force* (chalk)
14 *Moor End Fell* (pastel & chalk)
15 *Stoke by Nayland* (sanguine & pencil)
Etching
16 *Concert at Aldeburgh*
Watercolour
17 *Leadgate*

1972
Thackeray Gallery, London: solo exhibition (29 Feb – 29 Mar)
Paintings
1 *Moor End Fell, Starbotton*
2 *Trees at Leadgate*
3 *Leadgate*
4 *Behind Leadgate*
5 *Moss Bank, Penifiler, Skye*
6 *Quirang, Loch Mealt, Skye*
7 *Cuillin Hills, Bruack na Frithe*
8 *The Balcony, Aldeburgh*
9 *Balcony at Aldeburgh*
10 *Sea off Welcombe*
11 *Sea, Welcombe*
12 *Marsland Cliff*
13 *Mead Farm, Welcombe*
14 *Mallow Cottage*
15 *Trees, Leadgate*
16 *Cranham, Welcombe*
17 *Balcony, Aldeburgh*
18 *Judas Gap, Flatford*
19 *The Beach at Aldeburgh*
Drawings
20 *Clouds over South Tyne*
21 *Evening, Loch Eishort, Skye*
22 *Loch Eishort, Skye*
23 *Sea off Welcombe mouth* (chalk and crayon)
24 *Trees at Leadgate* (pencil)
25 *Dewley Fell* (conté crayon)
26 *Windswept Trees, Welcombe* (sanguine and charcoal)
27 *Mead Farm* (pencil)
28 *Sgiath-bheinn Chrossavaig, Skye* (chalk)
29 *Sgiath-bheinn Chrossavaig, Skye* (pencil and sanguine)
30 *From Mallow Cottage* (sanguine and pencil)
31 *Mead Farm* (sanguine and pencil)
32 *Near Cranham Mill* (pencil)
33 *Cranham* (pencil)
34 *Cranham* (sanguine and pencil)
35 *Trees, Mead Farm* (sanguine and pencil)
36 *The Balcony, Aldeburgh* (sanguine and pencil)
37 *Breakwater at Aldeburgh* (sanguine and pencil)
Etchings
38 *Black Burn*
39 *Buckden*
40 *Windswept Trees*
41 *Epping Forest*
42 *Epping Forest*
43 *Malham, Night*
44 *Starbotton, Rain*
45 *Self Portrait*
46 *Waterfall, Tynehead*
47 *Waterfall, Tynehead*
48 *Portrait, Nicholas*
49 *Nicholas*
50 *Concert at Aldeburgh, 1971*
51 *Low Force, Teesdale*
52 *Low Force*
53 *Cranham, Welcombe*
54 *Sgiath-bheinn Chrossavaig, Skye*
55 *Orchestral Pit, Coliseum*
56 *The Balcony, Aldeburgh*
57 *The Persian Kelim*
58 *Seascale*

Royal Academy of Arts, London: *Summer Exhibition* (29 Apr – 23 Jul)
238 *Trees, Leadgate*
505 *The Balcony, Aldeburgh*
867 *Behind Leadgate*
962 *Epping Forest*
988 *Seascale*
992 *Low Force*

Beecroft Art Gallery, Southend-on-Sea: *The Essex RAs. John Aldridge. Edward Bawden. Peter Coker. John Nash* (26 Aug – 24 Sep)
Gorse Bush
Weir Josselin
Sea near Durness
Epping Forest (charcoal)
The Copse (conté and chalk)
Strathbeag (charcoal)
Near Garrigill (pastel)
Moor End Fell (pastel and chalk)
Llanberis (conté)
Mead Farm (pencil)

The Minories, Colchester: *Colchester Art Society: 26th Annual Winter Exhibition* (Nov) [exhibits unidentified]

1972/1973
The Minories, Colchester: retrospective exhibition: *Peter Coker RA. paintings, pastels, drawings, etchings* (14 Oct – 4 Nov). Touring to: Victoria Gallery, Bath (1 – 30 Dec), The Morley Gallery, London (10 Jan – 3 Feb 1973), Mappin Art Gallery, Sheffield (10 Feb – 11 Mar)
Oil Paintings
1 *Still Life*
2 *Portrait of Old Man*
3 *Portrait of Geraldine*
4 *Portrait of P H Jowett, CBE*
5 *Butcher's Shop I*
6 *Man Carrying Pig*
7 *Sheep Carcasses on Bench*
8 *Cliff at Etretat*
9 *Landscape at Barbizon*
10 *Dead Hare on Table*
11 *Table and Chair*
12 *Tree and Hedge I*
13 *Tree and Hedge II*
14 *The Wave, Etretat*
15 *Forest I*
16 *Lighthouse, Audierne*
17 *Bracken and Gorse, Audierne*
18 *Fish and Bread*
19 *Still Life with Hare*
20 *Seascape*
21 *Forest VI*
22 *Forest VIII*
23 *Forest IX*
24 *Brett Bank*
25 *River Brett*
26 *Aldeburgh*
27 *Judas Gap*
28 *Mountain Stream, Pyrenees*
29 *Cave, Pyrenees*
30 *Western Sutherland*
31 *Storm*
32 *Seascale*
33 *Low Tide Seascale*
34 *The Stour from Cattawade Evening*
35 *Towards Old Cote Moor Top*
36 *Dewley Fell*
Small Paintings
37 *Jetty*
38 *Landscape near Mistley*
39 *Self Portrait*
40 *Overlooking the Stour*
41 *Dusk, Western Sutherland*
42 *Starbotton*
43 *Leadgate*
44 *Clouds, South Tyne*
45 *Self Portrait*
46 *Clouds over Cross Fell*
47 *Leadgate*
48 *Leadgate in the Rain*
49 *Stour*
Drawings
50 *Study of Hanging Hare* (charcoal)
51 *Dead Chicken on Table* (charcoal and conté)
52 *The Cliff at Etretat* (conté and chalk)
53 *Studies for Butcher's Shop II* (conté and chalk)
54 *Nicholas at Table* (sanguine)
55 *Nicholas, Back of Head* (pencil)
56 *Turbot* (charcoal and conté)

57 *Bracken, Audierne* (conté)
58 *Waves and Rock* (conté and charcoal)
59 *Tree II* (conté and ink)
60 *Nicholas in Bed* (pencil)
61 *Forest III* (charcoal and conté)
62 *Epping Forest* (conté)
63 *Epping Forest* (conté)
64 *Study for Fish and Frying Pan* (pencil)
65 *Llanberis* (conté and charcoal)
66 *Rendelsham Forest* (charcoal)
67 *Towards Arncliffe* (chalk and pastel)
68 *Durness Landscape* (chalk and pastel)
69 *Towards Withermarsh* (pastel and charcoal)
70 *Black Burn* (chalk)
71 *Towards Old Cote Moor* (chalk)
72 *Garrigill* (chalk)
73 *Waterfall, Tynehead* (chalk)
74 *Low Force* (chalk)
75 *Starbotton* (chalk and charcoal)
76 *Trees at Leadgate* (pencil)
Etchings
77 *Malham Night*
78 *Epping Forest*
79 *The Balcony, Aldeburgh*
80 *Waterfall, Tynehead*
81 *The Persian Kelim*
82 *Sgiath Bheinn Chrossavaig, Skye*
83 *Concert at Aldeburgh*
84 *Buckden*
85 *Black Burn*
86 *Portrait, Nicholas*
87 *Cranham Welcombe*
88 *Low Force*
89 *Seascale*
90 *Starbotton Rain*
91 *Low Force, Teesdale*
Lithograph
92 *Hare on Table*
Ex-cat. *Butcher's Shop II*

1973
Royal Academy of Arts, London:
Summer Exhibition (5 May – 29 Jul)
91 *Stripping Haricots at Mollans*
511 *Man Carrying Pig 1955*
524 *Gorse Bush*
571 *Mollans-sur-Ouvèze*
578 *Sheep Carcasses on Bench* (Diploma Work deposited on election as an Academician)
947 *Sault*

Fieldborne Galleries, London: *Peter Coker RA. Alfred Cohen. Keith Grant. Barbara Tribe FRBS* (14 June – 4 Jul)
Paintings
1 *Weir Josselin*
2 *Leadgate*
3 *Sea, Welcombe*
4 *Cliff at Etretat*
Drawings
5 *Dewley Fell* (pencil)
6 *Low Force* (chalk)
7 *Sgiath-Bheinn Chrossavaig, Skye* (chalk)
8 *Staffin* (pencil and sanguine)
9 *Mead Farm* (pencil and sanguine)
Etchings
10 *Black Burn*
11 *Buckden*
12 *Malham, Night*
13 *Starbotton, Rain*
14 *Waterfall, Tynehead*
15 *Portrait, Nicholas*
16 *Nicholas*
17 *Concert at Aldeburgh*
18 *Low Force, Teesdale*
19 *Low Force*
20 *Cranham, Welcombe*
21 *Sgiath-Bheinn, Chrossavaig, Skye*
22 *Orchestral Pit, Coliseum*
23 *The Balcony, Aldeburgh*
24 *The Persian Kelim*
25 *Seascale*
26 *Epping Forest*
27 *Epping Forest*
27a *Balcony - Aldeburgh*

Leicester Fine Arts Gallery, Leicester: solo exhibition: *Paintings, Drawings and Etchings by Peter Coker RA* (28 Sep – 20 Oct)
Paintings
1 *Weir Josselin*
2 *Gorse Bush*
3 *Sea, Welcombe*
Drawings
4 *Strath Beg* (charcoal)
5 *Dewley Fell* (conté crayon)
6 *Near Garrigill* (pastel)
7 *Moor End Fell* (pastel and chalk)
8 *Low Force* (chalk)
9 *Staffin, Skye* (pencil and sanguine)
10 *Staffin, Skye* (pencil and sanguine)
11 *Reclining Nude* (charcoal)
Etchings
12 *Black Burn*
13 *Buckden*
14 *Epping Forest*
15 *Starbotton, Rain*
16 *Malham Night*
17 *Waterfall, Tynehead*
18 *Portrait, Nicholas*
19 *Nicholas*
20 *Concert at Aldeburgh 1971*
21 *Low Force, Teesdale*
22 *Low Force*
23 *Cranham, Welcombe*
24 *Sgiath-Bheinn Chrossavaig, Skye*
25 *The Balcony, Aldeburgh*
26 *The Persian Kelim*
27 *Seascale*
28 *Epping*

1974
Thackeray Gallery, London: solo exhibition (19 Feb – 15 Mar)
Paintings
1 *Mont Ventoux in Mist from Reilhanette*
2 *Towards Hawes from Greenside, Wensleydale*
3 *Evening Storm, from Aird of Kinloch*
4 *Picking Pears at Mouthier*
5 *Balcony, Aldeburgh*
6 *Garden at Mistley*
7 *St-Blaise, Mézières-au-Perche*
8 *Night, Killiemore from Aird of Kinloch*
9 *Mouthier-Haute-Pierre, 1*
10 *Mouthier-Haute-Pierre, 2*
11 *Sault-de-Vaucluse, 1*
12 *Montbrun-les-Bains*
13 *Aurel*
14 *Sault-de-Vaucluse, 2*
15 *Bridge at Sault*
Drawings
1 *Mollans-sur-Ouvèze* (pencil and sanguine)
2 *Montbrun-les-Bains* (chalk and charcoal)
3 *Aurel* (conté)
4 *St-Blaise, Mézières-au-Perche* (pencil and sanguine)
5 *Sault* (chalk and crayon)
6 *Sault-de-Vaucluse* (conté and sanguine)
7 *Mouthier-Haute-Pierre* (pencil and sanguine)
8 *Cray Gill, Buckden* (conté and sanguine)
9 *Kilmuir, Skye* (pencil)
10 *Loch Scridain from Aird of Kinloch* (pencil)
11 *Aros, Tobermory* (sanguine)
12 *Stripping Haricots at Mollans* (pencil and pen)
13 *Evening, Sault* (pencil and sanguine)
14 *Mouthier-Haute-Pierre* (conté and sanguine)
15 *Bridge at Sault* (pencil)

Royal Academy of Arts, London:
Summer Exhibition (4 May – 28 Jul)
36 *Mouthier-Haute-Pierre*
71 *Picking Pears at Mouthier*
517 *Mont Ventoux in Mist from Reilhanette*
551 *Garden at Mistley*
554 *St-Blaise, Mézières-au-Perche*
555 *Balcony, Aldeburgh*

The Minories, Colchester: *Colchester Art Society* (17 Nov – 8 Dec)
Kilmuir on Skye (pencil)
Sea Off Welcombe

1975
Thackeray Gallery, London: solo exhibition (4 – 26 Mar)
Paintings
1 *Ostend, The Café*
2 *Rain, Rainbow and Stormy Seas, North Cliff, Whitby*
3 *The Rainbow, Barmouth*
4 *The Maltings, Wednesday, 16th June, 1971*
5 *Sunset over Calm Sea, Ostend*
6 *East Cliff, Whitby*
7 *East Yorkshire Moors*
8 *Setting Sun, Ostend*
9 *Lastours, 1*
10 *Grey September Sea*
11 *Lastours, 2*
12 *Fishing Boat and Rainbow*

13 *Aldeburgh, Yellow Kite*
14 *East Lighthouse, Whitby*
15 *Whitby Bay*
20 *Mist, Parkeston Quay from the Train Ferry Pier, Harwich*
Drawings
16 *Lastours, 1* (pencil and sanguine)
17 *Lastours, 2* (pencil and sanguine)
18 *Waterfall from Llyn Cau, Cader Idris* (pencil and sanguine)
19 *Mollans-sur-Ouvèze* (pencil and sanguine)

The Radlett Gallery, Radlett: *Artists of East Anglia, Part 1* (4 – 29 Mar)
5 *Gorse Bush*
31 *Dewley Fell* (pencil)

Royal Academy of Arts, London:
Summer Exhibition (3 May – 27 Jul)
63 *Evening: Train Ferry Pier, Harwich*
104 *Rain, Rainbow and Stormy Seas, North Cliff, Whitby*
494 *Ostend, The Café*
503 *The Maltings: Wednesday, 16th June, 1971*
874 *The Rainbow, Barmouth*
928 *East Yorkshire Moors*

Carlisle City Art Gallery: *The Purchase Scheme* (21 Jun – 27 Aug)
60 *Aurel* (conté)
110 *Still Life with Hare*

The Minories, Colchester: *The R A Bevan Collection* (26 Jul – 31 Aug)
46 *Balcony Aldeburgh*

1975/1976
Mappin Art Gallery, Sheffield: *British Painting 1900-1960* (Nov 1975 – Jan 1976)
Touring to: Aberdeen Art Gallery (Jan – Feb)
28 *Butcher's Shop I*

1976
Thackeray Gallery, London: solo exhibition: *Paintings, Drawings and Etchings by Peter Coker* (27 Apr – 14 May)
Etchings
1 *Yorkshire Landscape*
2 *The Quirang towards Staffin*
3 *Seascale*
4 *Epping Forest*
5 *Low Force*
6 *Epping Forest*
7 *Low Force, Teesdale*
8 *Vaternish from Cuidrach*
9 *Persian Kelim*
10 *Sgiath-bheinn Chrossavaig, Skye*
11 *Buckden*
12 *Portrait of Nicholas*
13 *Night Sea, Ostend*
14 *Balcony, Aldeburgh*
15 *Rain, Starbotton*
16 *Concert at Aldeburgh, 1971*
17 *Cranham, Welcombe*
18 *Storm, Ostend*
19 *Black Burn*
20 *Nicholas*
21 *Jetty at Night Ostend*
22 *Gathering Storm, Ord*
23 *Self-Portrait*
24 *Orchestral Pit, Coliseum*
25 *Rain, North Sea*
26 *Sun through Cloud, North Sea*
27 *North Sea clouds*
Ex-catalogue *Self-Portrait*
Ex-catalogue *Malham, Night*
Paintings
28 *Les sables d'or, Ostend*
29 *Towards Vaternish from Cuidrach*
30 *East Lighthouse, Whitby*
31 *The Wave*
32 *Kyle of Durness in Mist*
33 *Balnakeil, Faraid Head*
34 *Staffin from the Quirang*
35 *Sea Mist, Balnakeil Bay*
36 *Balnakeil Beach, Sutherland*
Ex-catalogue *Windbreakers Aldeburgh*
Watercolours
37 *Clouds, Seascale, 1*
38 *Clouds, Seascale, 2*
39 *Calm Sea, Aldeburgh*
40 *Rain, Moor End Fell, Starbotton*
Drawings
41 *Dewley Fell (conté crayon)*
42 *Low Force (chalk)*
43 *The Quirang towards Staffin* (pencil and sanguine)
44 *Boreaig from Ord* (pencil and sanguine)
45 *Loch Langaig* (pencil and sanguine)
46 *Persian Kelim* (pencil and sanguine)

Royal Academy of Arts, London:
Summer Exhibition (8 May – 1 Aug)
349 *Lastours*
352 *Self Portrait*
1011 *Waterfall from Cader Idris* (pencil and sanguine)
1013 *Lastours II* (pencil and sanguine)
1014 *Mollans-sur-Ouvèze* (pencil and sanguine)
1015 *Lastours I* (pencil and sanguine)

Ivor & Joan Weiss, Colchester:
East Anglia – contemporary work (Jun)
19 *Ostend, The Café*
20 *Rain, Rainbow and Stormy Seas, Whitby*
21 *Sluice Gate at Fordingbridge* (conté)
22 *Chicken on Table* (conté)
23 *Hanging Pig* (conté and chalk)

The Phoenix Gallery, Lavenham:
Summer Exhibition (19 Jun – 17 Jul)
Drawing
12 *Low Force*
Paintings
13 *The Wave*
14 *Staffin from the Quirang*
15 *Kyle of Durness*
16 *Judas Gap*
Watercolours
17 *Clouds, Seascale*
18 *Clouds, Seascale II*
19 *Rain, Moor End Fell, Starbotton*
Etchings
20 *Yorkshire Landscape*
21 *The Quirang towards Staffin*
22 *Vaternish, from Cuidrach*
23 *Sgiath-Bhein, Chrossavaig*
24 *Balcony, Aldeburgh*
25 *Concert at Aldeburgh 1971*
26 *Cranham Welcombe*
27 *Jetty at Night, Ostende*
28 *Orchestral Pit, Coliseum*
29 *Rain, North Sea*
30 *North Sea, Clouds*
31 *Gathering Storm, Ord*
32 *Black Burn*

Press Association, London
East Cliff, Whitby
[and possibly other unidentified exhibits]

1977
New Ashgate Gallery, Farnham:
mixed exhibition (1 – 26 Feb)
[unidentified oil and print landscapes]

Fieldborne Galleries, London:
Contemporary British Landscapes (Feb)
[exhibits unidentified]

Leonie Jonleigh Studio, Wonersh, Guildford:
Painting & Sculpture by 20th Century Artists (4 – 19 Jun)
[exhibits unidentified]

Royal Academy of Arts, London:
Summer Exhibition (21 May – 14 Aug)
179 *Cloud over Sun, Carsaig, Mull*
180 *Clouds over the Sea, Carsaig, Mull*
221 *Balnakeil, Sutherland*
243 *Mouthier-Haute-Pierre, Jura*
297 *La Manneporte, Etretat*
427 *La Manneporte, Etretat*

Fieldborne Galleries, London: *Summer Exhibition*
[exhibits unidentified]

Thackeray Gallery, London: *Summer Exhibition*
[exhibits unidentified]

Royal Academy of Arts, London: *Modern Drawings for Sale, small groups of works on paper by Royal Academicians and other Artists* (8 Jul – 14 Aug)
[work unidentified]

St James's Deeside Gallery, Dinnet, Aberdeenshire: *Silver Jubilee Exhibition* (13 Aug – 15 Oct)

23 *Cloudscape, Isle of Mull, Carsaig*
24 *Cloudscape, Isle of Mull, Carsaig*
25 *Clouds over the Sea*
35 *Balnakeil, Sutherland*
36 *The Breaking Wave*

Royal Academy of Arts, London: *British Painting 1952-1977* (24 Sep – 20 Nov)
76 *Butcher's Shop I*
77 *Forest VI*
78 *Sunset over Calm Sea, Ostend*

1978
Thackeray Gallery, London: solo exhibition (28 Feb – 22 Mar)
Paintings
1 *Sea off Carsaig*
2 *Bargemon towards Claviers*
3 *Dark sea, Carsaig*
4 *Study for 'La Plage', Etretat*
5 *Callas*
6 *Bargemon, 1*
7 *Road from Claviers*
8 *La Manneporte, 1*
9 *Bargemon, 2*
10 *Olive Trees at Claviers*
11 *Olive Trees, Bargemon*
12 *Overcast Sea, Carsaig*
13 *Clouds over the sea, Carsaig*
14 *La Manneporte, Etretat, 2*
15 *Mouthier-Haute-Pierre*
Drawings
16 *Bargemon, 3* (chalk and sanguine)
17 *Sea at Welcombe* (chalk and charcoal)
18 *Apple Tree, Mistley* (conté and charcoal)
19 *Apple Trees, Barbizon, 1* (conté)
20 *Apple Trees, Barbizon, 2* (conté)
21 *Mistley Pond* (conté)
22 *Leadgate* (conté)
23 *The Wave, Aldeburgh* (chalk)
24 *Vaternish from Cuidrach*
25 *Grey Sea, Carsaig*
26 *Overcast Sea, Carsaig*
27 *La Manneporte, Etretat, 3*
28 *Jetty, Ostend, at Night* (chalk)
29 *Jetty Lights, Ostend* (chalk and pencil)
30 *Etretat, La Porte d'Aval*
31 *Train Ferry Pier, Harwich* (pencil)

Royal Academy of Arts, London: *Summer Exhibition* (20 May – 13 Aug)
100 *Dark Sea, Carsaig*
107 *Study for 'La Plage', Etretat*
487 *Olive Trees, Bargemon*
494 *Studio Window*
1364 *Callas*

Chelmsford and Essex Museum: retrospective exhibition (2 Jun – 11 Jul)
Paintings
1 *Tubby Webb*
2 *Still Life with Hare*
3 *Pig's Head*
4 *Sheep's Head on Newspaper*
5 *Apple Tree*
6 *Cliff at Etretat*
7 *Gorse Bush*
8 *Tree and Hedge II*
9 *Lighthouse, Audierne*
10 *Forest III*
11 *Forest IX*
12 *Sunflowers*
13 *Rendlesham Forest*
14 *Landscape near Ardleigh*
15 *Aldeburgh*
16 *Weir Josselin*
17 *Evening, River Stour*
18 *Storm*
19 *Stour, Evening*
20 *Lilies*
21 *Leadgate*
22 *Evening Storm from Aird of Kinloch*
23 *Night, Killiemore from Aird of Kinloch*
24 *Sault de Vaucluse*
25 *Setting Sun, Ostend*
26 *Rain, Rainbow and Stormy Seas, North Cliff, Whitby*
27 *Ostend, The Café*
28 *Les sables d'or*
29 *Self Portrait*
Drawings
30(1) *Via della Torre Rosa, Arezzo* (pen and wash)
30(2) *Vera and Nicholas Coker* (pencil and charcoal)
31 *Tree Study I* (conté and charcoal)
32 *Pembrokeshire Coast* (pencil and chalk)
33 *Waterfall, Malham* (conté and chalk)
34 *Towards Withermarsh* (pastel and charcoal)
35 *Low Force, Teesdale* (charcoal and chalk)
36 *Windswept Trees* (sanguine and charcoal)
37 *Sgiath-bheinn Chrossavaig, Skye* (pencil and sanguine)
38 *Sault de Vaucluse* (conté and sanguine)
39 *Lastours I* (pencil and sanguine)
Etchings
40 *Yorkshire Landscape*
41 *The Quirang towards Staffin*
42 *Seascale*
43 *Epping Forest*
44 *Low Force, Teesdale*
45 *Epping Forest*
46 *Low Force, Teesdale*
47 *Vaternish from Cuidrach*
48 *Sgiath-bheinn Chrossavaig, Skye*
49 *Buckden*
50 *Night Sea, Ostend*
51 *Balcony, Aldeburgh*
52 *Rain, Starbotton*
53 *Concert at Aldeburgh*
54 *Cranham, Welcombe*
55 *Storm, Ostend*
56 *Malham Night*
57 *Mouthier Haute Pierre*
58 *La Manneporte*
59 *Windswept Trees*

Gainsborough's House, Sudbury: *The Bevan Collection. A selection of paintings by British artists including The Camden Town Group and memorial tribute to John Nash* (5 – 27 Aug)
49 *Evening, Malham Moor* (pastel)

St James's Deeside Gallery, Dinnet, Aberdeenshire: *Nineteenth Summer Exhibition* (12 Aug – 14 Oct)
4 *Balnakeil Bay, Sutherland*
5 *Sgiath-Bheinn, Chrossavaig, Skye*
22 *Cloudscape at Seascale*
28 *Carsaig Rain, Mull*
30 *Carsaig, Mull*

Fieldborne Galleries, London: *Landscapes by Royal Academicians*
[exhibits unidentified]

1979?
Gordon Fine Arts, Poole: *Exhibition of Sculpture, Drawings and Paintings by Five Royal Academicians and Kiril Sokolov*
[exhibits unidentified]

1979
Peter Coker. Paintings & Drawings of the Butcher's Shop
Touring to: The University of Liverpool (15 Jan – 3 Feb), Carlisle Museum and Art Gallery (17 Feb – 17 Mar), Doncaster Museum and Art Gallery (13 Apr – 13 May), Atkinson Art Gallery, Southport (26 May – 16 Jun), Royal Academy of Arts, London (14 Jul – 19 Aug)
1 *Fish and Newspaper*
2 *Fish on Plate* (conté)
3 *Fish in Scoop* (conté)
4 *Butcher's Shop I*
5 *Butcher's Shop I* (pencil)
6 *Butcher's Shop II*
7 *Butcher's Shop II* (charcoal and chalk)
8 *Hanging Pig* (conté and chalk)
9 *Man Carrying Pig*
10 *Hanging Pig* (conté and chalk)
11 *Sheep Carcasses on Bench*
12 *Sheep Carcass* (conté)
13 *Sheep Carcass on Bench* (conté)
14 *Dead Hare on Table*
15 *Hanging Hare* (charcoal)
16 *Hare on Table* (charcoal)
17 *Hare Skinned*
18 *Two Studies of Skinned Hare* (conté)
19 *Still Life with Hare and Grapes*
20 *Sheep's Head on Newspaper*
21 *Sheep's Head* (conté)
22 *Photograph (detail): Table and Chair*
23 *Sheep's Head (charcoal, chalk and wash)*
24 *Nicholas, Two Studies for Table and Chair* (pencil)
25 *Sheep's Head on Newspaper* (black crayon and ink)
26 *Hare on Table*
27 *Dead Chicken on Table* (charcoal and conté)

28 *Chicken on Table* (conté)
29 *Hanging Chicken* (charcoal)
30 *Pig's Head*
31 *Pig's Head* (conté)
32 *Pig's Head* (conté)
33 *Nicholas, back of Head* (pencil)
34 *Nicholas at Table* (sanguine)
35 *Turbot I* (charcoal and conté)
36 *Turbot II* (charcoal and conté)
37 *Still Life with Fish and Frying Pan* (charcoal and pencil)
38 *Fish and Frying Pan* (pencil)
39 *Fish and Frying Pan* (pencil)
40 *Still Life with Hare*
41 *Still Life with Hare* (pencil)
42 *Two Photographs of Zwemmer Gallery, 26 Litchfield Street, Charing Cross Road, London WC2*

The Minories, Colchester: *Twenty-Four Essex & Suffolk Artists 1900-1978* (31 Mar – 29 Apr)
20 *Cliff at Etretat*
21 *Gorse Bush, Audierne*

Poole Fine Art, Ampthill: a retrospective exhibition: *Peter Coker RA. Etchings* (19 May – 16 Jun)
1 *Yorkshire Landscape*
2 *The Quirang towards Staffin*
3 *Seascale*
4 *Epping Forest*
5 *Low Force*
6 *Epping Forest*
7 *Low Force, Teesdale*
8 *Vaternish from Cuidrach*
9 *Persian Kelim*
10 *Sgiath-bheinn, Chrossavaig, Skye*
11 *Buckden*
12 *Portrait of Nicholas*
13 *Night Sea, Ostend*
14 *Balcony, Aldeburgh*
15 *Rain, Starbotton*
16 *Concert, Aldeburgh, 1971*
17 *Cranham, Welcombe*
18 *Storm, Ostend*
19 *Black Burn*
20 *Nicholas*
21 *Jetty at Night, Ostend*
22 *Gathering Storm, Ord*
23 *Self Portrait*
24 *Orchestral Pit, Coliseum*
25 *Rain, North Sea*
26 *Sun through Cloud*
27 *North Sea Clouds*
28 *Malham Night*
29 *Maisie*
30 *Mouthier-Haute-Pierre*
31 *Waterfall, Tynehead*
32 *Waterfall, Tynehead*
33 *Mouthier-Haute-Pierre*
34 *La Manneporte*
35 *Maisie*

Royal Academy of Arts, London: *Summer Exhibition* (19 May – 12 Aug)
81 *Etretat: The Beach*
89 *Etretat: The Yellow Diving Board*
94 *Antibes: Palm*
690 *Bargemon: The Window*
691 *Etretat: The Balcony*
1058 *Bargemon: Olives*

Gallery 10, London: *Summer Exhibition* (Jun)
Antibes – Palm
Study for 'La Plage' Etretat

Fieldborne Galleries, London: *City and Guilds of London Art School. One Hundred Years* (7 – 27 Jul)
55 *Tunstall Forest*

1980
Gallery 10, London: solo exhibition (4 Nov – 6 Dec)
1 *The Palm, Chateau Garden*
2 *Blue, Black Interior - Two Windows*
3 *Palm Arbour, Chateau Garden*
4 *Agaves*
5 *Window, Bargemon*
6 *Two Windows*
7 *Agave*
8 *Interior*
9 *Chateau Garden*
10 *Palm Arbour*
11 *Palm Arbour*
12 *Antibes*
13 *Window at Bargemon*
14 *Blue Interior*
15 *Two Windows, Bargemon*
16 *Landscape Le Muy*
17 *Collioure*
18 *Landscape Le Muy*

1981
Tate Gallery, London: *Recent Chantrey Purchases* (29 Mar – 26 Apr)
Man Carrying Pig

Royal Academy of Arts, London: *Summer Exhibition* (16 May – 16 Aug)
47 *Agave*
73 *Palm Arbour, Chateau Garden*

1982
Tate Gallery London: *Acquisitions 1980-81* (19 Jan – 28 Mar)
Man Carrying Pig [The Butcher's Shop]
Table and Chair
[and two drawings relating to the latter]

Leicestershire Museum and Art Gallery: *Royal Academy Works 1921-1981* (24 Apr – 27 Jun)
18 *Sheep Carcasses on Bench*

Gallery 10, London: solo exhibition: *An exhibition of paintings watercolours and drawings by Peter Coker RA* (19 Oct – 15 Nov)
1 *Chez Sandoz* (ink)
2 *Palm* (ink)
3 *Chamaerops*
4 *Chamaerops* (ink and chalk)
5 *Arbour*
6 *Chez Arcadio*
7 *Aurel*
8 *St-Saturnin*
9 *Arbour*
10 *Aurel*
11 *St Saturnin*
12 *Claviers*
13 *Chamaerops, Le Vieux Château*
14 *Arbour* (ink)
15 *Arbour* (ink)
16 *Blue Enclosure*
17 *Montbrun-les-Bains*
18 *Two Windows Bargemon*
19 *Chateau Arbour*
20 *Room at Bargemon*
21 *St Saturnin*

1983
Royal Academy of Arts, London: *Summer Exhibition* (28 May – 28 Aug)
165 *Claviers: Pages from Sketch-book* (pen and watercolour)
166 *Aurel: Pages from Sketch-book* (pen and watercolour)
170 *Aurel: Pages from Sketch-book* (pen and watercolour)
247 *Chez Arcadio: Pages from Sketch-book* (pencil and watercolour)
700 *Blue Enclosure*
952 *Arbour* (ink and wash)

Ellingham Mill Art Society's Gallery, Bungay: *20th Century East Anglian Members of the Royal Academy* (9 Jul – 7 Aug)
Sheep Carcasses on Bench
Palm Arbour, Chateau Garden

Deben Gallery, Woodbridge: *Critic's Choice: (Works chosen by Michael Webber, London critic of the East Anglian Daily Times)* (21 Nov – 3 Dec)
16 *Vera and Nicholas* (pencil)
17 *Self Portrait*

1984
The Forgotten Fifties:
Touring to: Graves Art Gallery, Sheffield (31 Mar – 13 May), Norwich Castle Museum (26 May – 24 Jun), Herbert Art Gallery and Museum, Coventry (7 Jul – 5 Aug), Camden Arts Centre, London (15 Aug – 23 Sep)
18a *Butcher's Shop I* (pencil and chalk)
18b *Butcher's Shop I*
18c *Hanging Pig* (charcoal and chalk)
18d *Butcher's Shop I*

Gallery 10, London: solo exhibition (1 – 26 May)
1 *Landscape below Chateau*
2 *Balcony at Bargemon*
3 *Garden of the Villa Clos du Peyronnet*
4 *Studio*
5 *Towards Claviers*
6 *Bamboo Path*
7 *Artichokes*
8 *Putti, Clos du Peyronnet*
9 *Garden of the Villa Clos du Peyronnet*
10 *Willow*
11 *Manneporte*
12 *Les Environs d'Etretat*
13 *Olives*
14 *Olives*
15 *Olives*
16 *Balcony*
17 *Landscape from Chateau Garden*
18 *Garden of the Villa Clos du Peyronnet*
19 *Agapanthus*
20 *Olives*
21 *Agapanthus*

Atkinson Art Gallery, Southport:
Print-Making - Making Prints (12 May – 9 Jun)
6 *Seascale*
12 *Low Force*

Christopher Hull Gallery: *Flower Pot Art 1984:* Touring to: Contemporary Arts Fair, Bath (25 – 27 May), Christopher Hull Gallery, London (29 May – 9 Jun), Sutton Manor Arts Centre (11 – 30 Jun), Liverpool International Gardens Festival (2 Jul – 6 Oct)
[a decorated flower pot]

Royal Academy of Arts, London:
Summer Exhibition (19 May – 19 Aug)
110 *Studio at Bargemon*

Gallery 10, London: solo exhibition:
Mediterranean Gardens. Villa Clos du Peyronnet, Garavan and Le Vieux Château, Bargemon. watercolours and drawings (17 Oct – 8 Nov)
1 *Néflier* (ink & sanguine)
2 *Cherry*
3 *Collection of Plants* (ink)
4 *Strelitzia*
5 *Aloes and Agaves* (ink)
6 *Garden* (ink)
7 *Putti* (ink)
8 *Olives*
9 *Salix*
10 *Olives*
11 *Putti* (ink)
12 *La Manneporte, Etretat*
13 *Studio Bargemon*
14 *Falaise d'Aval*
15 *Aurel*
16 *Artichokes*
17 *Beschorneria Yuccoides* (ink)
18 *Road to Bargemon*
19 *Bamboo*
20 *Yuccas*
21 *Beschorneria Yuccoides*
22 *Agapanthus*
23 *Aloes & Agaves*
24 *Strelitzia* (ink)
25 *Studio Bargemon*
26 *Palm*

The Fraser Gallery, Woodbridge: *Christmas Exhibition. Watercolours & Drawings. Peter Coker RA. Denis Burroughs* (1 – 15 Dec)
1 *Epping Forest* (ink)
2 *Moor End Fell, Starbotton*
3 *Starbotton Rain*
4 *Hartland Point*
5 *Moor End Fell, Starbotton*
6 *Sea off Aldeburgh*
7 *Skye near the Cuillin Hills*
8 *Welcombe Bay*
9 *Welcombe Bay*
10 *La Plage, Etretat*
11 *Porte d'Amont, Etretat*
12 *Porte d'Amont, Etretat*
13 *Stour from Brantham*
14 *Stour from Brantham*
15 *Stour from Brantham*
16 *From Carsaig, Mull* (chalk on sepia wash)
17 *Durness*
18 *Sea off Carsaig*
19 *Sea off Carsaig* (sepia and white)
20 *North Sea, Ostend* (sepia and wash)
21 *La Plage, Etretat* (chinese ink)
22 *Yellow Diving Board, Etretat*
23 *Lighthouse, Gravelines*
24 *Sea off Etretat*
25 *Bateaux*
26 *Sea off Etretat*
27 *Yellow Sail*
28 *Bateaux*
29 *Red Sail*
30 *Boy, Dog, Bather*
31 *Boy with Towel*
32 *Girl, Red Shirt*
33 *Two Figures on Beach*
34 *Figures on Beach, Etretat*
35 *Figures on Beach*
36 *Figures on Beach*
37 *Girl in Check Towel with Dog*
38 *Le Rameur*
39 *Out to Sea, Etretat*
40 *La Porte d'Aval*
41 *From Carsaig*

1984/1985
Critic's Choice (works chosen by Bill Oliver): Touring to: Mappin Art Gallery, Sheffield (17 Nov 1984 – 6 Jan 1985), Cartwright Hall, Bradford (19 Jan – 17 Feb), Elizabethan Gallery, Wakefield (28 Mar – 24 Apr), Leeds City Art Gallery (16 May – 16 Jun)
Butcher's Shop

1985
Gallery 10 at *2nd International Contemporary Art Fair*, Olympia, London (17 – 20 Jan)
Chamaerops
Olives

Royal Academy of Arts, London:
Summer Exhibition (1 Jun – 25 Aug)
59 *Sea off Aldeburgh*
619 *Agapanthus*
679 *Towards Claviers*
844 *Salix* (watercolour)
874 *Aurel* (pen and watercolour)
878 *Artichokes* (pen and watercolour)

Fieldborne Galleries, London:
Heads – Selected Artists (4 – 29 Jun)
[exhibits unidentified]

Glynn Vivian Art Gallery and Museum, Swansea:
Fine Art. A Selection of Paintings, Sculptures and Drawings by Royal Academicians 1770-1980 (Diploma Works)
Sheep Carcasses on Bench

1986
Gallery 10, London: solo exhibition (7 – 31 May)
1 *Beschorneria Yuccoides*
2 *Hedera*
3 *Cycas*
4 *Balcony Clos du Peyronnet*
5 *Cercis*
6 *Daturas*
7 *Phormium*
8 *Fig*
9 *Agave Attenta*
10 *Agapanthus*
11 *Garden Villa Clos du Peyronnet*
12 *Pointe de Dinan*
13 *Kersiguenou*
14 *Setcreasea Pallida*
15 *Dark Pond, Strelitzia*
16 *Dark Pond, Strelitzia*
17 *Clos du Peyronnet*
18 *Garden Clos du Peyronnet*
19 *Irises*
20 *Sea Off Vaucottes*
21 *Kersigenou*
22 *Cap de la Chèvre*
23 *Vaucottes*
24 *Green Curtain, Aldeburgh*
25 *Towards Tanera Mór*

Gallery 10 at *3rd International Contemporary Art Fair*, Olympia, London (25 May – 1 Jun)
Villa Clos du Peyronnet

Royal Academy of Arts, London:
Summer Exhibition (31 May – 24 Aug)
194 *Window, Aldeburgh*
511 *Towards Tanera Mór*
529 *Forêt de Landevennec*
531 *Bargemon, April*

608 *Achvraie from Tigh A'Sgiobair*
649 *Bamboo Pathway*

National Portrait Gallery, London: *Faces for the Future. New 20th Century Acquisitions at the National Portrait Gallery* (11 Jul – 5 Oct)
Self Portrait

John Harrower at Aigas Field Centre, Beauly, Inverness-shire: *The Face of the Highlands. Exhibition of Oils and Watercolours*
(2 Aug – 13 Sep)
21 *Carsaig from Mull*
22 *Towards Tanera Mór*
23 *Horse Island from Achiltibuie*
24 *Towards Tanera Mór II*
25 *Badenscallie II*
26 *Badenscallie I*
27 *Badenscallie III*
28 *Badenscallie IV*

1987
Royal Academy of Arts, London:
Summer Exhibition (6 Jun – 21 Aug)
159 *Rowans, Badenscallie*
434 *Terrace, Le Vieux Château – Towards Claviers*
435 *Abandoned Sheepcroft, Badenscallie*
1067 *Drumrunie*
1309 *Badenscallie*
1320 *Achiltibuie*

John Harrower at Aigas Field Centre, Beauly, Inverness-shire: *4th Highland Exhibition of Oils and Watercolours* (8 Aug – 12 Sep)
[exhibits unidentified]

1987/1988
Fine Art Society, London: *Landscapes and Interiors. Drawings chosen by William Packer for the International Association of Art Critics*
(7 Dec 1987 – 17 Jan 1988)
Barbizon 1955 (conté)
Nicholas 1956 (pencil)
Sunflower 1958 (charcoal)
Llanberis Pass 1962 (conté and charcoal)
Vera, Chez Arcadio (charcoal)
Cycas, Clos du Peyronnet 1984 (chinese ink)

1988
The Minories, Colchester: *For Sale. Contemporary Art for personal and corporate collectors. Over 150 works by British artists. £25-£6000*
(21 Feb – 3 Mar)
Promenade, Etretat

Royal College of Art, London: *Exhibition Road. 20th Century Painters from the Royal College of Art*
(10 Mar – 24 Apr)
89 *Portrait of Percy Jowett*
90 *Butcher's Shop I*
91 *Still Life with Hare*

The Arts Club, London: *Images of Italy*
(23 Mar – 13 May)
Via della Torre Rosa, Arezzo (pen and wash)

Royal Academy of Arts, London:
Summer Exhibition (14 May – 7 Aug)
417 *Mending Salmon Nets, Achiltibuie*

Gallery 10, London: solo exhibition:
An Exhibition of Scottish Landscapes (2 – 30 Jun)
1 *Badenscallie*
2 *Chrossavaig, Skye*
3 *Badenscallie*
4 *Sea Badentarbat*
5 *Sheep Croft Badenscallie*
6 *Badentarbat Bay*
7 *North Sea*
8 *Sea, Summer Isle*
9 *Towards Polbain*
10 *Badenscallie*
11 *The Quirang, Skye*
12 *Badenscallie*
13 *Harold Browns Croft*
14 *Vines, Le Vieux Château*

Christchurch Mansion, Ipswich:
An Artist in Focus (Jul)
[exhibits unidentified]

Mall Galleries, London: *Royal Institute of Oil Painters: 101st Exhibition* (8 – 21 Dec)
67 *Sheep Croft, Badenscallie*

1989
Mall Galleries London: *This Land is Our Land. Aspects of Agriculture in English Art* (4 – 29 Jan)
Butcher's Shop No II
Hanging Pig (drawing)

Mall Galleries, London: *Royal Institute of Oil Painters: 102nd Exhibition* (20 Feb – 3 Mar)
55 *Evening Towards Westminster from Cranley Gardens*
56 *Cap de la Chèvre*

The Great Hall, Winchester: *Paintings from the Chantrey Bequest* (23 Mar – 1 May)
Picking Pears at Mouthier

Gallery 10 at *Art London 89. 4th International Contemporary Art Fair*, Olympia, London
(30 Mar – 2 Apr)
Sheep Croft Badenscallie

Gallery 10, *10th Anniversary Exhibition: Views of Westminster* (17 May – 10 Jun)
Evening Towards Westminster from Cranley Gardens

Royal Academy of Arts, London:
Summer Exhibition (9 Jun – 20 Aug)
8 *Badenscallie*
36 *Harold Brown's Croft*

59 *Balcony, Bargemon*
547 *Achiltibuie*
885 *Peat Landscape, Achiltibuie*

Ruthven Gallery, Lancaster, Ohio, United States: *Classically British. The Enduring Appeal of English Painting* (21 Jul – 5 Aug)
Clos du Peyronnet
Forêt de Landevennec
Towards Polbain

Fitzwilliam Museum, Cambridge: retrospective exhibition: *Peter Coker: Working Drawings and Sketchbooks 1955-1988* (14 Aug – 15 Oct)
1 *Barbizon* (conté)
2 *Nicholas* (pencil)
3 *Gorse* (conté and charcoal)
4 *Reed Bank* (conté and charcoal)
5 *Cornfield, Audierne* (conté)
6 *Vera* (charcoal)
7 *Nicholas* (charcoal)
8 *Sunflower* (charcoal)
9 *Llanberis* (conté and charcoal)
10 *Strath Beg, Sutherland (charcoal)*
11 *Chrossavaig, Skye* (conté and charcoal)
12 *The Quirang, Skye* (charcoal)
13 *La Loue, Jura*
14 *Olives, Bargemon* (charcoal)
15 *The Quirang* (sanguine)
16 *La Roche Guyon* (ink)
17 *'Le Peintre au Travail'* (pastel and chalk)
18 *'Le Peintre au Travail'* (pastel and chalk)
19 *Salmon Poles, Badentarbat*
20 *Salmon Nets* (conté crayon and charcoal)
21 *Salmon Nets*
22 *Coigach* (charcoal)
23 *Badenscallie* (charcoal)
24 *Drying Nets* (conté and sanguine)
Sketchbooks
25 *Etretat*
26 *Bargemon, Antibes, Etretat and Clos du Peyronnet*
27 *Mistley, Harwich, Bargemon, Antibes, Etretat and Fécamp*
28 *Le Vieux Château and Bargemon*
29 *Villa Clos du Peyronnet and Menton*
30 *Le Vieux Château, Bargemon and the Villa Clos du Peyronnet*
31 *Bargemon, Aldeburgh and Achiltibuie*
32 *Bargemon*
33 *Bargemon, Kersiguénou, Aldeburgh, Achiltibuie and Badenscallie*
34 *Stoke-by-Nayland, Skye and Badenscallie*
35 *Skye and Badenscallie*

Gallery 10, London: solo exhibition: *An exhibition by Peter Coker RA of drawings and watercolours 1955-1989* (24 Oct – 16 Nov)
1 *Sunflower* (charcoal)
2 *Badenscallie* (charcoal)
3 *Coigach* (charcoal)
4 *Salmon Nets* (conté crayon and charcoal)
5 *Drying Nets* (conté and sanguine)

6 *Lobster*
7 *Olives* (charcoal)
8 *Olives, Bargemon* (charcoal)
9 *Barbizon* (conté)
10 *Reed Bank* (conté and charcoal)
11 *Llanberis* (conté and charcoal)
12 *La Loue, Jura*
13 *The Quirang* (sanguine)
14 *Le Peintre au Travail* (pastel and chalk)
15 *Salmon Poles, Badentarbat*
16 *Le Peintre au Travail* (pastel and chalk)
17 *Salmon*
18 *Gorse* (conté and charcoal)
19 *Cornfield, Audierne* (conté)
20 *Chrossavaig, Skye* (conté and charcoal)
21 *La Roche Guyon* (ink)
22 *The Quirang, Skye* (charcoal)
23 *Nicholas* (pencil)
24 *Vera* (charcoal)
25 *Bargemon*
26 *Salmon Nets*

1990

Chappel Galleries, Chappel, near Colchester: *Original Prints and Drawings by Selected Artists* (3 Feb – 24 Mar)
Lighthouse at Night (coloured etching)
Seascale (etching and aquatint)
Strath Beg. Sutherland (conté and charcoal)
Turkish Plate (coloured etching and monotype)

Cheltenham Museum and Art Gallery: *Modern Masterpieces. 20th Century British Art from the Rugby Collection* (10 Feb – 10 Mar)
89 *Forest IX*

Flying Colours Gallery, Edinburgh: solo exhibition: *Peter Coker RA. Oils and Drawings* (7 Mar – 4 Apr)
1 *La Roche-Guyon*
2 *Agapanthus*
3 *Cliffs at Quiberville*
4 *Lighthouse, St-Valery-en-Caux*
5 *Mending Nets, Achiltibuie*
6 *Cliffs at Quiberville*
7 *La Roche-Guyon*
8 *Irises*
9 *Garden Villa Clos du Peyronnet*
10 *Beschorneria Yuccoides*
11 *Setcreasea Pallida*
12 *Phormium*
13 *Beschorneria Yuccoides* (ink)
14 *Aloes and Agaves*
15 *Collections of Plants*
16 *Epping Forest*
17 *Lighthouse, St-Valery-en-Caux*
18 *Putti* (ink)
19 *Lighthouse, St-Valery-en-Caux*
20 *Clos du Peyronnet*
21 *Cliffs St-Valery-en-Caux*
22 *Yellow Diving Board*
23 *La Plage*
24 *Yellow Diving Board*
25 *Porte d'Amont, Etretat*
26 *Porte d'Amont, Etretat*
27 *Le Rameur*
28 *Moor End Fell*

Gallery 10 at *Art London 90, 5th International Contemporary Art Fair'*, London, Olympia (29 Mar – 1 Apr)
Chrossavaig, Skye

Aldeburgh Festival (Royal British Legion Hall, Aldeburgh): *Spaces* (9 – 28 Jun)
River Brett

Royal Academy of Arts, London: *Summer Exhibition* (9 Jun – 19 Aug)
82 *The Quirang*
527 *Mending Salmon Nets, No 12*
531 *Salmon Nets, No 7*
1136 *Salmon Nets, No 4*

Contemporary British Painters Exhibition, Business Design Centre, London (21 –24 Jun)
Salmon Nets No 2
Salmon Nets No 8
Salmon Nets No 9

John Harrower at Aigas Field Centre, Beauly, Inverness-shire (4 Aug – 15 Sep)
[exhibits unidentified]

Mall Galleries, London: Royal Institute of Oil Painters (12 – 21 Dec)
63 *Chrossavaig, Skye*

1991

Ipswich Borough Museums & Galleries: *Art is Our Speciality* (16 Mar – 12 May)
[exhibits unidentified]

Mayor Gallery, London (in association with Julian Hartnoll): *The Kitchen Sink Painters* (19 Mar – 26 Apr)
15 *Portrait of Alban 'Tubby' Webb*
16 *Portrait of John Jacobs*
17 *Nicholas Asleep*
18 *Smoked Mackerel on Table*
19 *Epping Forest*
Ex-cat. *Sheep Carcasses on Bench*

Royal Academy of Arts, London: *Summer Exhibition* (9 Jun – 18 Aug)
465 *Salmon Nets, Badentarbat*
466 *Salmon Nets, Achiltibuie*
513 *Salmon Nets Badentarbat*
514 *Salmon Net Poles Badentarbat*
1215 *Badenscallie*
1220 *Cap de la Chèvre*

Corn Exchange, Ipswich: *Ipswich Art Club* (12 – 26 Jul)
49 *Horse Island from Acheninver, Scotland*
50 *Old Man*
51 *Nicholas Coker*
52 *Epping Forest III*

Chappel Galleries, Chappel, near Colchester: *A Survey of East Anglian Artists* (19 Jul – 11 Aug)
Towards Westminster from Cranley Gardens

Flying Colours Gallery, Edinburgh: solo exhibition: *Oil Paintings and Drawings by Peter Coker RA* (19 Nov – 7 Dec)
1 *Towards Polbain*
2 *Salmon Nets, Badentarbat*
3 *Peat Landscape, Achiltibuie*
4 *Sheep Croft, Badenscallie*
5 *Salmon Nets, Achiltibuie*
6 *Badenscallie*
7 *Salmon Net Poles, Badentarbat*
8 *Towards Tanera Mór*
9 *Salmon Nets, Badentarbat*
10 *Cliffs at Vaucottes*
11 *North Sea*
12 *Lighthouse, St-Valery-en-Caux*
13 *Salmon Net Poles, Badentarbat*
14 *Strath Beg* (charcoal)
15 *Badenscallie* (charcoal)
16 *Chrossavaig, Skye* (conté and charcoal)
17 *The Quirang, Skye* (sanguine)
18 *Coigach* (charcoal)
19 *The Quirang* (charcoal)
20 *Badenscallie* (pencil)

Mayor Gallery, London: solo exhibition: *Peter Coker RA. Textile Designs 1954-56* (2 – 20 Dec)

1992

Royal Academy of Arts, London: *Summer Exhibition* (7 June – 16 Aug)
530 *Fenêtre Ouverte à Menton*
1010 *Towards Tanera Mór*
1060 *Harvest, Normandy*

1992/1993

Peter Coker. Landscapes 1955-1991
Touring to: Abbot Hall Art Gallery, Kendal (18 Jul – 25 Oct), Royal Academy of Arts, London (a selection of works transferring from Abbot Hall: 20 Aug – 11 Oct), Tullie House, Carlisle (30 Oct – 29 Nov), Christchurch Mansion, Ipswich (9 Jan – 21 Feb 1993)
1 *Forest I*
2 *Tree II* (conté and ink)
3 *Epping Forest III*
4 *Forest VI*
5 *Forest VIII*
6 *Forest IX*
7 *Cliff at Etretat*
8 *Landscape at Barbizon*
9 *Tree and Hedge II*
10 *The Wave, Etretat*
11 *Bracken and Gorse, Audierne*
12 *Lighthouse, Audierne*
13 *The Yellow Diving Board, Etretat*
14 *Study for 'La Plage' Etretat*

15 *Olives, Bargemon*
16 *Chateau Garden*
17 *Blue Black Interior, Bargemon*
18 *Window, Bargemon*
19 *Two Windows, Bargemon*
20 *Terrace, Le Vieux Château – Towards Claviers*
21 *Callas, Summer in Provence*
22 *Bargemon in April*
23 *La Roche-Guyon*
24 *Landscape, Varengeville-sur-Mer*
25 *Chrossavaig, Skye* (conté and charcoal)
26 *The Quirang, Skye* (charcoal)
27 *Horse Island from Acheninver*
28 *Badenscallie*
29 *Towards Tanera Mór*
30 *Rowans Badenscallie*
31 *Mending Salmon Nets, Achiltibuie*
32 *Badenscallie* (charcoal)
33 *Coigach* (charcoal)
34 *Salmon Nets* (conté and charcoal)
35 *Salmon Nets*
36 *Chrossavaig*
37 *Badenscallie*
38 *Salmon Nets*
39 *Le Peintre au Travail* (pastel and chalk)

1993
Royal Academy of Arts, London:
Summer Exhibition (6 Jun – 15 Aug)
835 *Veules-les-Roses*
852 *London from Cranley Gardens*
880 *Marine, Varengeville*
881 *Cornfield, Ste-Marguerite-sur-Mer*
882 *Veules-les-Roses*

1993/1994
Arthur Andersen Art Collection, London:
The Spirit of Place: Highlights from the Permanent Collection (27 Sep 1993 – 4 Jan 1994)
Badenscallie (charcoal)

Harris Museum and Art Gallery, Preston:
Drawing on these Shores. A View of British Drawing & its Affinities
(27 Nov 1993 – 8 Jan 1994):
Touring to: Wolsey Art Gallery, Christchurch Mansion, Ipswich (22 Jan – 20 Mar), Holburne Museum, Bath (15 Apr – 8 Jun), Brighton Art Gallery and Museum (18 Jun – 31 Jul)
23 *Nicholas at Table* (red chalk)

1994
Cleveland Gallery, Middlesborough:
The Kitchen Sink Painters. British Painting from the 1950s (7 May – 25 Jun)
[exhibits unidentified]

Royal Academy of Arts, London:
Summer Exhibition (5 Jun – 14 Aug)
7 *Le Peintre au Travail 1988* (pastel, chalk and conté)
9 *Le Peintre au Travail 1988* (pastel, chalk and conté)
71 *Chrossavaig Skye 1970* (conté and charcoal)
72 *Coigach 1938* (charcoal)
73 *The Quirang, Skye 1970* (charcoal)
1277 *The Quirang, Skye 1987* (sanguine)

Mayor Gallery, London: *The Kitchen Sink and the Beaux Arts Gallery* (15 Nov – 23 Dec)
(included within this show was Julian Hartnoll's show 'Kitchen Sink and other drawings of the Fifties in black chalk')
3 *Study of a butcher carrying a carcass* (black chalk heightened with white)
4 *Study of a butcher carrying a carcass* (black chalk heightened with white)
5 *Study for the painting Man Carrying a Pig* (grey black chalk)
6 *Study of dead chicken on a chair* (ink and pencil)
7 *Study of a hanging dead chicken* (chalk)
8 *Study of a skinned hare* (chalk)
9 *Study of a dead hare* (pencil)
10 *Study of a dead pouting* (black chalk heightened with white)
11 *Study of a hanging dead pollock* (chalk)
12 *Study of two hanging dead pollock* (chalk)
13 *Study of a tree* (grey and black chalk heightened with white)
14 *Study of a tree and buildings* (grey and black chalk)
15 *The Tees at Teesdale* (black chalk heightened with white)
16 *The Cliffs at Etretat* (black chalk heightened with white)
17 *The Weir at Little Baddow* (black chalk heightened with white)
18 *The Cliffs at Durness* (black chalk heightened with white)
19 *Study of a sunflower* (chalk)
20 *Study of a sunflower* (chalk)
21 *Study of the artist's wife, Vera* (chalk)
22 *The artist's son, Nicholas, asleep* (pencil)

1995
Galerie Michael Haas, Berlin-Charlottenburg:
The Kitchen Sink Painters (24 Mar – 29 Apr)
Sheep's Head on Newspaper (painting and drawing)

Gainsborough's House, Sudbury:
Contemporary Portraits from Suffolk and Essex
(25 Mar – 21 May)
John Nash, painter and plantsman circa 1970 (pencil and chalk)

Royal Academy of Arts, London:
Summer Exhibition (4 Jun – 13 Aug)
753 *Low Force, Teesdale* (soft ground etching and open bite)
754 *Seascale, 1972* (soft ground etching and aquatint)
755 *Malham Night* (etching and aquatint)
756 *Epping Forest* (soft ground etching)
1157 *Yorkshire Landscape* (etching, aquatint, drypoint and mezzotint)
1159 *Low Force, Teesdale* (soft ground etching and open bite)

1996
Mead Gallery, University of Warwick:
Earthbound: Landscape to Abstraction
(6 Jan – 3 Feb)
[probably included *Forest IX*]

Royal Academy of Arts, London:
Summer Exhibition (9 Jun – 18 Aug)
3 *La Forêt, Claviers* (pen and watercolour)
20 *Salmon Nets Poles, N W Scotland* (watercolour and chinese white)
21 *Chrossavaig, Skye* (watercolour)
34 *Mending Salmon Nets* (mixed media)

Mayor Gallery, London: *Works on Paper*
(15 Jun – 31 Aug)
[exhibits unidentified]

The Minories, Colchester: *Colchester Art Society: Colchester Art Society: 1946–1996 – A Celebration* (15 Jul – 31 Aug)
Epping Forest IV

Chappel Galleries, Chappel near Colchester:
(3 – 24 Aug)
Balcony Aldeburgh, 1973

Christchurch Mansion, Ipswich: *100 Years of Collecting at Christchurch Mansion*
(20 Jul – 15 Sep)
[exhibits unidentified]

1997
Royal Academy of Arts, London:
Summer Exhibition (1 Jun – 10 Aug)
621 *Forest I, 1959*

Christchurch Mansion, Ipswich: *Points of Contact. A Selection from the 20th Century Fine Art Collections* (5 Jul – 31 Aug)
[exhibits unidentified]

Julian Hartnoll, at 20th Century Art Fair, Royal College of Art, London (24 – 28 Sep)
[exhibits unidentified]

Whittington Fine Art, Old Amersham:
An Exhibition of Leading 20th Century Artists
(30 Nov – 20 Dec)
Mending Salmon Nets, N W Scotland
Garden of the Villa Clos du Peyronnet, Garavan, Menton
The Weir, Josselin, Brittany

1997/1998
A Century of Change. Twentieth Century British Art from the Collection of Sheffield City Art Galleries
Tour of Norway: Haugar Museum, Tønsberg

(22 Feb – 20 Apr), Rogaland Kunstmuseum, Stavanger (1 Jun – 10 Aug), Bergen Billedgalleri, Bergen (23 Aug – 5 Oct), Nordnorsk Kunstmuseum, Tromsø (18 Oct 1997 – 4 Jan 1998)
20 *Butcher's Shop I*

1998
Piano Nobile Fine Paintings, at *Art 98, London Contemporary Art Fair*, Business Design Centre, London (20 – 25 Jan)
Vaucottes (near Etretat) Normandy

D'Arcy Gallery, Ipswich (17 Jan – 28 Feb)
3 *View from the Balcony, Aldeburgh*
4 *Jetty at Ostend*
5 *Changing Sky*
6 *Aldeburgh Beach*

Chris Beetles Ltd, London: *Summer Show* (2 Jun – through the summer)
294 *Veules-les-Roses*
295 *Veules-les-Roses*

Royal Academy of Arts, London: *Summer Exhibition* (2 Jun – 16 Aug)
255 *Epping Forest* (etching and aquatint)
256 *Yorkshire Landscape, 1st state* (etching)
770 *The Seine, La Roche Guyon* (chinese ink)

Piano Nobile Fine Paintings at *20th Century British Art Fair*, Royal College of Art, London (23 – 27 Sep)
Tiger Lilies

1999
Flying Colours Gallery at *The Watercolour and Drawings Fair*, Park Lane Hotel, London *(28 – 31 Jan)*
Paris at Night, Pont Neuf
Carnival in Venice (ink with watercolour and bodycolour)
Window, Bargemon (chinese ink)
Coigach (charcoal)
Chrossavaig, Skye (conté and charcoal)
Dewley Fell, Cumbria (watercolour and ink)
Durness, Scotland (mixed media)
Harwich (mixed media)

Chris Beetles Ltd, London: *Summer Show* (25 May – 30 Jul)
70 *Salmon Net Poles, Badentarbat*
71 *Willie Muir with his Dog*
72 *Garden of the Villa Clos du Peyronnet*
73 *The Bamboo Path*

Royal Academy of Arts, London: *Summer Exhibition* (7 Jun – 15 Aug)
329 *Menton 1992*
356 *Cleaning Nets, Quiberville 1989*
461 *Leadgate, Cumbria* (pastel)
510 *The Seine – La Roche Guyon* (sanguine)
514 *Study for Cleaning Nets, Quiberville 1989*

The City Gallery, London: *The Royal Academicians* (2 – 18 Jun)
Garden, Clos du Peyronnet, Menton

Flying Colours Gallery: *Peter Coker RA and Charlie Mackesy*, at Art London, Duke of York Barracks, London (16 – 20 Jun)
Storm
Dark Sea, Carsaig, Isle of Mull
Irises
Badenscallie
Salmon Nets, Badentarbat No 9
Landscape, Varengeville-sur-Mer
Mending Salmon Nets No 12

2000
National Maritime Museum, London: *Beside the Sea. the British coast in art* (17 Feb – 6 Jun)
Whitby

Chris Beetles Ltd, London: *Summer Show* (16 May – 30 Jun)
66 *Promenade, Etretat*
67 *St-Valery-en-Caux*
68 *Peat Landscape, Achiltibuie*
69 *Garden, Clos du Peyronnet, Garavan, Menton*
112 *On the Beach, Etretat*
113 *Etretat Bathers*
114 *The Inquisitive Dog*
115 *Man and Dog, Etretat*
116 *Beach Studies, Etretat* (four sheets)

Royal Academy of Arts, London: *Summer Exhibition* (29 May – 7 Aug)
561 *Palm* (chalk)
564 *Towards Dewly Fell, Alston* (pen and watercolour)
565 *Towards Menton from the Balcony Clos du Peyronnet* (chalk and charcoal)
565 *Orchard, Vieux Château, Bargemon* (chinese ink)
568 *Leadgate, Cumbria* (mixed media)
569 *Balcony, Clos du Peyronnet, Garavan* (chinese ink)

The City Gallery, London: *The Royal Academicians* (13 – 30 Jun)
Badenscallie

Watermill Antiques, Nayland: solo exhibition: *A small exhibition of paintings, watercolours, drawings, etchings and a group of original fabric designs for Bernard and Laura Ashley* (8 Jul – 5 Aug)
[exhibits unidentified]

2001
Royal Academy of Arts, London: *Summer Exhibition* (5 Jun – 13 Aug)
154 *North Sea*

The Picture Gallery, Hintlesham Hall, Suffolk (5 Aug – 18 Sep)
[exhibits unidentified]

2002
Royal Academy of Arts, London: *Summer Exhibition* (11 Jun – 19 Aug)
403 *Chrossavaig, Skye*
405 *Homage to John Singer Sargent (The Daughters of Edward D Boit)*

The Picture Gallery, Hintlesham Hall, Suffolk (4 – 30 Aug)
[details not finalised at time of going to press]

Chris Beetles Ltd, London: major retrospective exhibition: *Peter Coker RA* (16 Oct – 9 Nov) (Over 200 exhibits, in the process of organisation at the time of going to press)

List of Sketchbooks

'Throughout Coker's career, sketchbooks have been central to the development of his ideas. In [almost] every case they are made from high quality hand-made paper, bound to the artist's specifications. It is not uncommon for two, three or even more sketchbooks to be used simultaneously; this makes it possible to consider a number of different approaches to the subject, and to use a range of media - chalks, watercolour, charcoal and ink – depending on the size and absorbancy of the paper surface.'

Peter Coker. Working Drawings and Sketchbooks 1955 to 1988. Cambridge: Fitzwilliam Museum, 1989

Key to list of sketchbooks

bc = bodycolour
d = dated
dr = dated on the reverse
i = inscribed
ink = chinese ink
ins = inches
ir = inscribed on the reverse
iwss = inscribed with studio stamp
iwt = inscribed with title
iwtr = inscribed with title on the reverse
s = signed
swi = signed with initials
wc = watercolour

Dimensions are given only when they deviate from those of a single or double page.
Bold numbers in brackets (**00**) denote Catalogue Raisonee numbers

---

No 1

1956
George Rowney, black cloth, 8½ x 5½ ins, 80 leaves
Brittany: villages, churches and other buildings, figure studies inc female nudes
(owned by the British Museum)

No 2

1956–57, 1959
George Rowney, black cloth, 8½ x 5½ ins
Studies after Ensor and for the Tate exhibition *The Religious Theme*; Audierne, Etretat
(owned by Peter Coker)

1 [no image:] iwss
2 Nude study after Segonzac
pencil
4 Nude study after Segonzac
pencil
The following six drawings are all studies for *Lighthouse, Audierne* (**62**)
5 Study of lighthouse, Audierne
pencil
6 Study of lighthouse, Audierne
pencil
7 Study of lighthouse, Audierne
pencil
9 Study of lighthouse, Audierne
pencil
11 Study of lighthouse, Audierne
pencil
12 Study of lighthouse, Audierne
pencil
13 Study of figures on beach, Audierne
pencil
14 Study of figures on beach, Audierne
pencil
16 Head of Negro model
pencil
18 Sea, Audierne
pencil
The following two drawings are studies for *Bracken and Gorse. Audierne* (**57**)
21 Studies of bracken bush
pencil
22 Studies of bracken bush
pencil
25 Sea study
pencil
26 Sea study
pencil
28 Sea study
pencil
29 Etretat, cliffs
conté
30 Etretat, cliffs
conté
31 Studies of the golden section
33 Study for *The Religious Theme*
pencil ink
34 Study for *The Religious Theme*
pencil ink
35 Study for *The Religious Theme*
pencil ink
36 Study for *The Religious Theme*
pencil ink
37 Study for *The Religious Theme*
pencil ink
38 Study for *The Religious Theme*
pencil ink
39 Nude study after Matisse
pencil
40 Nude study after Matisse
pencil
41 Nude study for *The Religious Theme*
pencil
43 Study after Ensor
pencil
44 Study after Ensor
pencil
45 Study after Ensor
pencil
46 Study after Ensor
pencil
49 Sea study
pencil
50 Sea study
pencil
55 Sea study
pencil
58 Lighthouse, Audierne at night
pencil
75-76 Audierne
pencil
77-78 Sea study
pencil
91-92 Male nude studies for *The Religious Theme*
pencil
93 Male nude studies for *The Religious Theme*
pencil
94 Male nude studies for *The Religious Theme*
pencil
95 Male nude studies for *The Religious Theme*
pencil
96 Male nude studies for *The Religious Theme*
pencil
99 Rocks
pencil
114 Study of tree, Devon
pencil
115 Study of tree, Devon
pencil
116 Study of tree, Devon
pencil
117 Study of tree, Devon
pencil
118 Fishing boat and sea, Hastings
i 'Hastings , d 1959

No 3
1958-59, 1961, 1967-68, 1970
George Rowney, black canvas spine,
8½ x 5½ ins
Epping, Leadgate, Seascale, Norfolk, Wales
(owned by Peter Coker)

1 [no image:] iwss
2 Study of trees, Epping Forest
conté
3 Study of trees, Epping Forest
conté
4 Study of trees, Epping Forest
conté
5 Study of trees, Epping Forest
conté
6 Study of trees, Epping Forest
conté
7 Study of trees, Epping Forest
conté
8 Study of trees, Epping Forest
conté
9 Study of trees, Epping Forest
conté
10 Study of trees, Epping Forest
conté
11 Study of trees, Epping Forest
conté
12 Study of sunflower heads
pencil
14 Whirlpool, seagulls, jetty
pencil
15 Whirlpool, seagulls, jetty
pencil
16 Whirlpool, seagulls, jetty
pencil
17 Whirlpool, seagulls, jetty
pencil
18 Whirlpool, seagulls, jetty
pencil
19 Sea and clouds
d 1959; pencil
20 Sea and clouds
pencil
21 Sea and clouds
pencil
22 Sea and clouds
pencil
23 Sunflowers
pencil
24 Sunflowers
pencil
25 Sunflowers
pencil
26 Sunflowers
pencil
27 Epping
pencil
28 Epping
pencil
29 Wales – Pembrokeshire
pencil
30 Wales – Pembrokeshire
pencil
31 Wales – Pembrokeshire
pencil
32 Wales – Pembrokeshire
pencil
33 Wales – Pembrokeshire
pencil
34 Wales – Pembrokeshire
pencil
35 Wales – Pembrokeshire
pencil
36 Wales – Pembrokeshire
pencil
37 Wales – Pembrokeshire
pencil
38 Wales – Pembrokeshire
pencil
39 Lighthouse, Pembrokeshire
pencil
40 Lighthouse, Pembrokeshire
pencil
41 Lighthouse, Pembrokeshire
pencil
43 Lighthouse, Pembrokeshire
pencil
44 Lighthouse, Pembrokeshire
pencil
45 Rock faces, Pembrokeshire
pencil
46 Rock faces, Pembrokeshire
pencil
47 Rock faces, Pembrokeshire
pencil
48 Rock faces, Pembrokeshire
pencil
50 Llanberis, quarry, North Wales
pencil
52 Lighthouse, Happisburgh, Norfolk
pencil
54 Lighthouse, Happisburgh, Norfolk
pencil
56 Leadgate
d 1970; pencil
59-60 Leadgate
d 1970; pencil
62 Window, Ivy Cottage
pencil
64 Trees, Ivy Cottage
pencil
66 Leadgate, Ivy Cottage
pencil
68 Leadgate, Ivy Cottage
pencil
70 Dewley Fell, Alston
d 1970; pencil
72 Black Burn, late evening
pencil
73-74 Study of farmer and dog from the sitting room, Ivy Cottage
pencil
75 Study of tractor
pencil
76 Study of landscape with farmer
pencil
78 Annotated sketch
pencil
80 Black Burn, Leadgate, clear sunny morning
pencil
82 Leadgate
pencil
84 Rough sketch
pencil and sanguine
86 Rough sketch
pencil and sanguine
88 Cliff face
pencil
90 Wave breaking over rock
pencil

No 4
1962, 1965, 1967-68
George Rowney, black canvas spine,
8½ x 5½ ins
Mistley, Norfolk, Seascale, Yorkshire,
Menilles, Pyrenees
(owned by Peter Coker)

1 [no image:] iwss
2 Mistley, trees
pencil
4 Mistley, trees
pencil
5-6 Mistley, pond and pathway
pencil
8 Mistley, pond and pathway
pencil
10 Nude, figure
pencil
12 Mistley trees
pencil
15-16 Cave, Pyrenees
pencil conté ball point pen
17 Cave, Pyrenees
d 1965; pencil conté ball point pen
18 Cave, Pyrenees
d 1965; pencil conté ball point pen
19-20 Cave, Pyrenees
d 1965; pencil conté ball point pen
21-22 Cromer, low lying cliff face
conté
24 Cave, Pyrenees
d 1965; pencil conté ball point pen
25-26 Cave, Pyrenees
d 1965; ball point pen
27-28 Sheringham, Norfolk
pencil
29-30 Sheringham, Norfolk, sea and jetty
pencil
32 Audierne, corn stooks
pencil
33-34 Audierne
pencil
35-36 Audierne
pencil
38 Audierne
pencil conté
39-40 Menilles, river, bank and trees
pencil charcoal
50 Malham
d 'August 68'; pencil
Study for *Night, Malham* (**161**)
54 Durness
s iwt; sanguine chalk
56 Bushes, towards Old Cote Moor
pencil
57 Study of tree, Starbotton
pencil
58 Study of tree, Starbotton
pencil
59 Study of horses, Starbotton
pencil
60 Study of horses, Starbotton
pencil
62 Study of tree, Starbotton
Charcoal
65-66 Bridge, Leadgate
pencil conté charcoal
67-68 Waterfall
pencil conté
Study for *Waterfall, Tynehead* (**232**, **233**)
70-71 Tractors and farm machinery – drawn by Nicholas Coker 5 Aug 1969
pencil

71 End of bridge – Leadgate
pencil
72 Cross Fell from Leadgate
pencil
73 Old Cote Moor, Starbotton
pencil
74 Old Cote Moor, Starbotton
pencil
76 Starbotton
pencil
77 Starbotton
pencil
78 Starbotton
pencil
80 Starbotton
pencil
83-84 Buckden, Yorkshire
pencil
Study for *Buckden* (**212**)
86 Seascale, sand and sky
pencil
87 Figures on beach, Seascale
pencil
88 Figures on beach, Seascale
pencil
89 Figures on beach, Seascale
pencil
90 Figures on beach, Seascale
pencil
92 Figures on beach, Seascale
pencil

SB5:12

No 5

1964, 1967-68, 1970
sprial bound, cardboard, 10¾ x 14¾ ins
Aldeburgh, Judas Gap, Malham, Kinlochbervie, Audierne, Pyrenees
(owned by Peter Coker)

2 Pyrenees, cave
pencil
Study for *Pyrenees Cave* (**124**)
4 Working drawing for Judas Gap No 1, Flatford
swi; conté
Study for *Judas Gap* (**120**)
6 Working drawing for Judas Gap No 2
swi; conté chalk
Study for *Judas Gap* (**120**)
8 Working drawing for Cattawade Bridge
conté, white chalk
(See paintings of Cattawade, **163** and **169**)
10 Near Orford, coastal defences
sepia chalk
11 Study of Stour from Cattawade Bridge
sepia
12 Stour from Cattawade Bridge
swi; pastel chalk pencil
13 The Cattawade
chalk
14 Audierne
swi iwt; pencil
15-16 Stooks Audierne
swi i 'Audierne'; conté pencil
17 Green colour study
wc
The following 8 drawings are all studies for *Waterfall, Malham* (**137**)
18 Study of Jenny's Fosse Malham, Yorkshire
pencil
20 Study of Jenny's Fosse Malham, Yorkshire
pencil
21 Study of Jenny's Fosse Malham, Yorkshire
pencil
22 Study of Jenny's Fosse Malham, Yorkshire
pencil
23 Study of Jenny's Fosse Malham, Yorkshire
pencil
24 Study of Jenny's Fosse Malham, Yorkshire
pencil
25 Study of Jenny's Fosse Malham, Yorkshire
pencil
26 Study of Jenny's Fosse Malham, Yorkshire
pencil
28 Gnarled trees, Malham, Yorkshire
conté
The following 2 drawings are studies for *Waterfall, Malham* (**137**)
29 Study for Jenny's Fosse Maham, Yorkshire
pencil
30 Study for Jenny's Fosse Maham, Yorkshire
pencil
31-32 Malham, Yorkshire Night
swi iwt d 68; conté chalk
33 Sketch of Kinlochbervie
pencil
34 Kinlochbervie
swi iwt; conté chalk
35 Sketch of Kinlochbervie
pencil
36 Balcony, Aldeburgh
pencil
Study for Balcony, Aldeburgh (**209**)
37 Aldeburgh
swi iwt d 1971; pencil
38 Aldeburgh
s; pencil sanguine
39-40 Aldeburgh
swi; pencil chalk

No 6

1965-66, 1970
George Rowney, black cloth, 11 x 8½ ins
Flatford; Kelim
(owned by Peter Coker)

1 [no image:] s iwss i artist's address
2 Flatford, or the River Stour
pencil
4 Fall of the water, Judas Gap, Flatford
d 66; penci
6 Looking towards Manningtree from Judas Gap
pencil
The following 2 drawings are studies for *Judas Gap* (**120**)
9-10 The sluice gates, Flatford
ink sepia
13-14 The sluice gates, Flatford
ink sepia
16 Reed beds by the sluice
conté pencil
18 Reed beds by the sluice
conté pencil
20 From the sluice towards Manningtree
conté pencil
21 Sequential drawings of the river bank
conté pencil
22 Sequential drawings of the river bank
conté pencil
23 Sequential drawings of the river bank
conté pencil
24 Towards Manningtree
conté pencil
25-26 River flow
conté pencil
27 Skyline towards Manningtree
pencil
28 Sluice gates with figures
pencil
29 Figures walking along the bank
pencil
30 From Flatford towards Manningtree
ball point pen
31 Figure walking
pencil
32 Grasses
conté pencil
34 Bridge across the sluice
conté pencil
36 Looking across the bridge
conté pencil
38 Sluice flaps and banks
conté pencil
40 Looking down on flaps and hinges
conté pencil
42 River
pencil
The following 13 drawings are studies for *The Persian Kelim* (**224**)
44–56 all pencil
58 Self portrait
pencil
60 Self portrait
s; pencil
62 Study for Kelim etching
pencil
Study for *The Persian Kelim* (**224**)
65 Female nudes
ball point pen
66 Female nudes
ball point pen

No 7

1970
George Rowney, black cloth, 8½ x 5½ ins
Coliseum, Aldeburgh, Welcombe, Wales, Mull, Skye, Mollans
(owned by Peter Coker)

1 [no image:] iwss
2 Figures on the beach, Aldeburgh, windbreakers
pencil
4 Figures on the beach, Aldeburgh, windbreakers
pencil
6 Figures on the beach, Aldeburgh, windbreakers
pencil
8 Figures on the beach, Aldeburgh, windbreakers
pencil
10 Window and balcony, Tower House, Aldeburgh
pencil

12 Aldeburgh, towards Martello tower
pencil
14 Head
pencil sanguine
16 Aldeburgh, towards Martello tower
pencil
18 Old coastguard's building
pencil
20 Aldeburgh breakwaters and dog
pencil
22 Coastguard lookout, Aldeburgh
pencil
23 Figures on the beach, Aldeburgh
pencil
24 Figures on the beach, Aldeburgh
pencil
26 Aldeburgh looking south towards Martello tower
pencil
Figure on balcony, Tower House
pencil
28 Orchestra pit, Coliseum
pencil
30 Orchestra pit, Coliseum, musicians
conté sanguine
32 Orchestra pit, Coliseum, conductor
conté
34 Orchestra pit, Coliseum, four studies of conductor
conté ball point pen
36 Orchestra pit, Coliseum
pencil
37 Orchestra pit, Coliseum
pencil
38 Orchestra pit, Coliseum
pencil
39 Orchestra pit, Coliseum
pencil
40 Orchestra pit, Coliseum
pencil
41 Orchestra pit, Coliseum
pencil
42 Orchestra pit, Coliseum
pencil
44 Skye, Staffin
pencil
45 Uig, Skye, study of fishing boats
pencil
46 Uig, Skye, study of fishing boats and sea
pencil
48 Rainbow, Staffin, Skye
pencil
50 View from the cottage, Staffin, Skye
pencil
52 View from the cottage, Staffin, Skye
pencil
54 View from the cottage, Staffin,Skye
ball point pen
56 Staffin, cows
pencil
58 Staffin, the Quirang towards Staffin
conté
60 North Wales towards Berin Edra
d 1974; conté
62 North Wales towards Berin Edra
d 1974; pencil
64 Skeabost Bridge – Skye, Swizon Chapel
pencil
66 Skeabost Bridge – Skye, Swizon Chapel
pencil
68 Toward the Cuillins, Skye
pencil
70 Tower House, Aldeburgh
pencil conté sanguine
72 Tower House, Aldeburgh
pencil conté sanguine
74 Tower House, Aldeburgh
pencil conté sanguine
76 Tower House, Aldeburgh
pencil conté sanguine
80 Tower House, Aldeburgh
pencil conté sanguine
84 Mollans, stripping beans
d 1973; ink
88 Cliff and rocks, Welcombe
conté
89 Cliff and rocks, Welcombe
conté sanguine
90 Cliff and rocks, Welcombe
conté sanguine
92 Pathway through forest, Welcombe
pencil sanguine
94 Cliff and rock, Welcombe
pencil conté
96 Cliff and rock, Welcombe
pencil conté
98 Cliff and rock, Welcombe
pencil
100 Trees, Welcombe
pencil conté
105-6 Lighthouse, Kinloch, Mull
pencil
108 Mull, 9 pm
iwt; pencil
110 Kinloch at night
pencil
Study for *Night, Killiemore from Aird of Kinloch* (**273**)

No 8

1974
George Rowney, black cloth, 8½ x 5½ ins
Whitby, Scotland, France, Ostend
(owned by Peter Coker)

1 [no image:] s iwss
2 Sault, 5pm the bridge
d 1974; pencil
Study for *Bridge at Sault* (**263**)
4 Sault
pencil
6 Impressions of Ravel's *L'enfant et les sortileges*
ink
9 Ostend
pencil
10 Café Melrose
pencil
11-12 Sunset over calm sea
pencil
14 Sunset over calm sea
pencil
16 Dark sea
pencil
17-18 Sea piece
pencil sanguine
20 Figure on beach
pencil
22 Figure in cafe
pencil
Study for *Ostend, The Café* (**293**)
24 Clouds over Sea, Harwich-Zeebrugge
conté sanguine pencil
26 Study of sea and sky for etchings
pencil
28 Study of sea and sky for etchings
pencil
30 Study of sea and sky for etchings
pencil
31 Overcast sea, Ostend
d 1974; conté sanguine
Study for *Night Sea, Ostend* (**285**)
36 Study of sea and sky for etchings
pencil
38 Study of sea and sky for etchings
pencil
40 Decorated plate with fruit
pencil
Study for *Fruit Bowl* (**281**)
42 Lastours
pencil
44 Dog
pencil
46 Dog
pencil
48 Narbonne beach
pencil
50 Narbonne beach
pencil
52 Cahors from window
pencil
54 Jetty, Cahors
pencil
56 Whitby, East Cliff
d 'Sept 1974'; pencil
58 Whitby, East Cliff
d 'Sept 1974'; pencil
60 Whitby, East Cliff
d 'Sept 1974'; pencil
62 Whitby, East Cliff
d 'Sept 1974'; pencil
64 Whitby, rain – a grey day
d 'Sept 1974'; pencil
66 Tiny fishing boats
pencil
69 Ostend
pencil
70 Ostend at night
pencil
73 Tractor, Tongue, Scotland
pencil
74 Landscape, Tongue
pencil
76 Clouds and sun
pencil
78 Evening clouds, Skye
pencil sanguine
80 Skye landscape
pencil

No 9

1976-78
canvas, 11 x 7½ ins
Harwich, Mistley, Antibes, Bargemon, Etretat, Fécamp
(owned by Chris Beetles)

1- 2 Winter landscape
s; oil pastel pencil
3 Sketch of cliffs
pencil
4 Sketch of cliffs
pencil
5 Sketch of cliffs
pencil
6 Sketch of cliffs
pencil sanguine
7 Sketch of cliffs
pencil

8 Sketch of cliffs
pencil conté
9 Bather
pencil
10 Bathers
pencil
11 Sketch of garden
pencil
Colour study
wc
12 Open window
wc
13 Open window
ink
14 Open window
ink
16 Sailing boats
wc bc ink
17 Palm
ball point pen
18 Palm
pencil
Study for *Antibes – Palm* (**379**)
19 Palm
wc
20 Palm garden
wc
Study for *Antibes – Palm* (**379**)
22 Study of Bargemon landscape
pencil blue pencil
24 Study of Bargemon landscape
wc conté ink
25-26 Olive trees
wc pencil; 11 x 13 ins
27-28 Study of olive trees
conté; 11 x 13 ins
29-30 Study of olive trees
pencil
31-32 Colour study of trees
wc pencil; 11 x 11½ ins
33 Study of trees
conté
34 Study of trees
pencil
35-36 Bargemon landscape
wc pencil
37-38 Canna, Bargemon
iwtr; pencil; 11 x 9½ ins
40 Canna, Bargemon
wc pencil
42 Valley landscape
irw colour notes; wc pencil
43-44 Canna, Bargemon
pencil
45-46 Bathers
wc
48 Seascape
wc
49-50 Cliffs at Etretat
wc
51 Beach study
wc ink
52 On the beach
wc pencil
53 Window
ink & wash
54 Window
wc bc
73-74 Hillside landscape
pencil
75 Maisie (inversed)
pencil
Study for *Maisie* (**246**, **247**)

No 10

1977 onwards
George Rowney, black cloth, 8½ x 5½ ins
Bargemon, Clos du Peyronnet, Halkidiki
(owned by Peter Coker)

1-2 Above Bargemon
s iwss i artist s address d 77; pencil
4 Towards Claviers from Bargemon
pencil
6 Bargemon
wc pencil
8 Olive trees, flowers on a grassy bank
sanguine pencil
9-10 Olive terrace, Bargemon
pencil
12 Olive tree trunk
pencil
13-14 Blue terraces below the chateau, Bargemon
wc pencil
15-16 Claviers, road to Bargemon
pencil sanguine
18 Claviers
pencil
22 Rear window, chez Arcadio
ink
24 Rear window, chez Arcadio
ink
25-26 Rear window, chez Arcadio
wc ink
28 Rear window, chez Arcadio
pencil ink wash
30 Rear window, chez Arcadio
pencil
32 Church spire from upper road, Bargemon
pencil
34 Bargemon
pencil
37 Lion's head and agave, Jardin Méditerranéan, Villa Clos du Peyronnet
pencil
38 Exit from the Clos
pen ink wash
41-42 Putti, the Clos
pencil
45-46 From the balcony flat towards Menton
ink
46 Roof tiles
pencil
50 Sketch of Ouranoupolis, Halkidiki
pencil
51 Sketch of Ouranoupolis, Halkidiki
pencil
52 Sketch of Ouranoupolis, Halkidiki
pencil
54 Sketch of Ouranoupolis, Halkidiki
pencil

SB11:19-20

No 11

1977 onwards
biscuit buckram, 11 x 7 1/2 ins
Antibes, Bargemon
(owend by Peter Coker)

1 Window, chez Arcadio
wc bc
2 Window
wc bc
3 Vera sewing
wc ink
Study for *Interior [Chez Arcadio]* (**393**)
4 Window
bc wc
5-6 Yellow windows
wc
7-8 Black windows
bc wc
Study for *Blue, Black Interior – Two windows* (**386**)
The following 6 drawings are all studies for *Agave* (**400**)
9 Agave
pencil
10 Agave
pencil
11 Agave
wc bc ink
12 Agave
wc bc ink
13 Garden
wc
14 Agave
wc
15-16 Agaves
wc ink; 11 x 10½ ins
Study for *Agaves* (**385**)
18 Agaves
wc bc ink pencil
Study for *Agaves* (**385**)
19 Agave
wc ink sanguine
20 Agave Americana
wc ink sanguine
21 Back gate
wc
22 Back gate
wc ink
23-24 Agave Americana and window sketch
wc ink pencil
25 Sketch of window, chez Arcadio
ink
26 Window, chez Arcadio
wc ink
Study for *Window at Bargemon* (**399**)
27 Agave Americana
iwt; pencil
28 Agave
wc ink
Study for *Agave* (**400**)
29 Agave Americana, Marginata
iwt; pen ink
30 Agave, Back Gate
wc ink
31-32 Les Agaves Americana Marginata
iwt; pencil
33-34 Olive trees
pen ink
35-36 Olive trees
wc
37 Palms
wc
38 Olive trees
pencil sanguine

39 Palms through the window
wc
40 Palms, Antibes
wc ink
41-42 Sketches of palms, Antibes
ink
43-44 Sketches of palms, Antibes
pencil
45-46 From Bargemon towards Claviers
wc ink; 11 x 12¼ ins
47-48 From Bargemon towards Claviers
wc; 11 x 9 ins
49 Olive trees
wc ink
Study for *Olives, Bargemon* (**355**)
50 Olive trees
pencil
Study for *Olives, Bargemon* (**355**)
51-52 Olive trees
bc wc
53-54 Olive trees, chateau garden
wc ink
55-56 Bargemon landscape
wc ink
Study for *Bargemon towards Claviers* (**347**)
57-58 Olive plantation
wc bc
59-60 Sketch of olive trees
pencil
61-62 Road to Claviers
swi; pen ink
63-64 Road to Claviers
wc
65-66 Palm
wc ink; 11 x 14 ins
67 Sketch of Chamaerops palm
pencil
68 Chamaerops palm
wc
Study for *Chamaerops* (**405**)
69-70 Chamaerops palm
pencil sanguine; 11 x 11 ins
71-72 Montbrun
bc wc 10 x 11 ins
Study for *Montbrun-Les-Bains* (**424**)

No 12

1977- 78 onwards
black buckram, 7 x 5 ins
Bargemon
(owned by Peter Coker)

1 [no image:] iwss
2 Bargemon
pencil coloured pencil
4 Towards Claviers from Elsbeth's balcony
pencil
6 Bargemon from the Claviers road
pencil coloured pencil
7- 8 Olives, Bargemon
sepia ink wc
9-10 Road down towards Bargemon
sepia pencil bc
12 Olives, Claviers
sepia pencil bc
14 Red tablecloth with fruit
pencil wc
Study for *Still Life with Oranges and Pears* (**338**)
16 Towards Bargemon from the Claviers road
sepia ink
19 Twisted trees
pencil
20 Twisted trees
pencil

No 13

1978-82
Daler, smooth black, 8½ x 6 ins
Antibes, Bargemon, Clos du Peyronnet, Etretat
(owned by Peter Coker)

1 [no image:] iwss
2 Café Melrose, Ostend
ink
4 Window, Bargemon
pen wc bc
6 Window, Bargemon
ink
9 Open window, Villa Claire, Antibes
wc
10 Open window, Villa Claire, Antibes
wc
12 Open window, Villa Claire, Antibes
d 78; wc
14 From the rear window, Chez Arcadio, Bargemon
pencil
16 Rough sketches
pencil
18 Rough sketches
pencil
21-22 Olives, Le Vieux Château, Bargemon
wc
23 Sketch of olives, Bargemon
pencil
24 Sketch of olives, Bargemon
pencil
25 Sketch of olives, Bargemon
pencil
26 Sketch of olives, Bargemon
pencil
28 Sketch of olives, Bargemon
pencil
30 Sketch of olives, Bargemon
pencil
32 Figures on beach, Etretat
pencil
33 Figures on beach, Etretat
wc
34 Figures on beach, Etretat
wc
36 Etretat, La Manneporte
pencil
39-40 Figures on beach, Etretat
wc
42 Surfboarding, Etretat
ink
44 Canoeist
wc
46 Figures entering the water, Etretat
wc
48 Swimming figure and blue sails, surfboards
wc
50 Water and sky
wc
54 Putti, the Clos du Peyronnet
ink wc
57-58 Grand staircase with plants, garden of the Clos du Peyronnet
ink
62 Bamboo pathway
ink
64 Left side of the grand staircase, the Clos
pencil wc

SB14:30

No 14

1980-82
black cloth, 15¾ x 12 ins
Bargemon, Clos du Peyronnet, La Mortola, Montbrun-les-Bains
(owned by Peter Coker)

1-2 Palm
swi; wc bc ink; 15½ x 12¾ ins
3 Sketch of palm
wc
4 Palm
swi; wc bc pencil
5-6 Chamaerops
swi; wc bc ink
7-8 Chamaerops
swi; ink
9-10 Chamaerops
swi; bc ink wc
12 Chamaerops and swimming pool
swi; wc bc ink
13 Palm arbour
swi; wc bc
14 Palm arbour
swi; wc bc ink pencil
Study for *Palm Arbour* (**389**) *and Palm Arbour, Chateau Garden* (**390**)
15-16 Arbour, palm and vines
swi; wc bc ink; 15¼ x 18½ ins
17-18 Figs and vines
swi; ink
19-20 Palm arbour
swi; ink
21-22 Chamaerops
swi; ink
23-24 Artichoke heads
swi; wc ink; 15 x 12 ins
25-26 Banana leaves, Hanbury Gardens
swi i 'Hanbury'; ink wc
27 Banana plants
ink
28 Sketch of banana leaves
ink
29 Sketch of artichokes
swi; ink
30 Artichokes
swi iwt; ink bc wc
31 Study of artichokes
swi; wc ink
33-34 Montbrun
swi; chalk
Study for *Montbrun-Les-Bains* (**424**)
35 Yuccoides, the Clos
swi; wc bc

36 Yuccoides, the Clos
swi; wc bc ink

39 Montbrun-les-Bains, 2 sketches
wc bc pencil

40 Montbrun-les-Bains
swi; wc bc pencil
Study for *Montbrun-les-Bains* (**424**)

SB15:5-6

No 15

1980-84
canvas, 11 x 10½ ins
Bargemon, La Mortola, Clos du Peyronnet
(owned by Peter Coker)

3 Palm study
ink charcoal

4 Palm study, Bargemon squared for transfer to canvas
swi i 'Bargemon' d 81; ink bc pencil

5-6 Palm study, Bargemon squared for transfer to canvas
swi i 'Bargemon' d 81; ink sanguine pencil; 11 x 12 ins

8 Palm study
swi; pencil

9-10 Palm study
swi; ink sanguine; 11 x 16 ins

13-14 Palm sketches
swi; pencil ink

16 Sketch of palm arbour
swi; ink

18 Sketch of palm arbour
ink wc

19-20 Sketch of palm arbour
swi; ink wc; 11 x 15½ ins

21-22 Artichokes, Bargemon
swi, iwt d 81; ink; 11 x 11½ ins

24 Study of an artichoke
swi; pencil; 10 x 10 ins

25 La Mortola
swi, iwt, d 80; wc

26 La Mortola
swi, iwt, d 80; wc bc pencil

28 Rough sketch
pencil

29-30 Palm sketches
pencil

32 Hanbury Gardens pathway, La Mortola
swi; ink wc; 9 x 6½ ins (paper laid down)

34 Hanbury Gardens pathway, La Mortola
swi, d 80; ink wc; 7 x 5 ins (paper laid down)

36 Pathway to back gate, Clos du Peyronnet
swi, i 'Clos du Peyronet', d '83-84'; wax crayon; 8 x 5½ ins (paper laid down)

38 Bamboo pathway, Clos du Peyronnet
swi; wax crayon; 7½ x 5¼ ins
(paper laid down)
Study for *The Bamboo Pathway* (**490**)

SB15:42

40 Bamboo pathway, Clos du Peyronnet
swi, i 'Clos du Peyronnet' d '83-84'; wax crayon; 6 x 7½ ins (paper laid down)

42 Bamboo pathway, Clos du Peyronnet
swi, d 'July'; wax crayon; 6½ x 5½ ins
(paper laid down)
Study for *Bamboo Path* (**434**)

44 Bamboo pathway, Clos du Peyronnet
(inverted)
swi iwt; wax crayon; 8 x 4½ ins
(paper laid down)

46 Chez Sandoz, Bargemon, two windows and table
swi; wax crayon; 5½ x 7¾ ins
(paper laid down)

48 Chez Sandoz, Bargemon
swi; wax crayon; 6 x 7½ ins
(paper laid down)

50 Chez Sandoz, Bargemon
swi; wax crayon; 5½ x 7½ ins
(paper laid down)

52 Palm, Bargemon
swi; wax crayon; 6 x 5 ins (paper laid down)

54 Colour study of palm, Bargemon
swi; wax crayon; 6½ x 3½ ins
(paper laid down)

No 16

1981
canvas, 11 x 7½ ins
Bargemon, Etretat
(owned by Chris Beetles)

4 Palm arbour
wc bc sanguine pencil

5 Balcony
Ball point pen pencil; 11 x 4¾ ins

5-6 Palm arbour
wc ink; 11 x 10¼ ins

8 Palm arbour
wc ink bc

9-10 Palm arbour
wc; 11 x 12½ ins

12 Palm sketch
pencil

13 Bargemon landscape
pencil

14 Bargemon landscape
wc pencil

16 Bargemon road
wc bc pencil ink

17 Bargemon road
pencil

18 View from a window
wc

19 Sketch for arbour
ink

20 Sketch for arbour
ink

21-22 Sketch for arbour
ink

23-24 Bargemon window
swi i 'Bargemon'; wc bc pencil

25-26 Sketch of arbour
ink

27-28 Sketch of arbour (portrait format)
ink bc

29-30 Olive trees and wall
swi; ink wc

31-32 Olive trees and wall
ink

33 Sketch of allée
ink

34 Sketches of olive trees and wall
ink and pastel

37-38 Vera, Bargemon
swi iwt d 81; wc bc

40 Chez Sandoz, Bargemon
iwt; wax crayon

41-42 Chez Sandoz, Bargemon
swi iwt d 81; pencil & ink

43-44 Chez Sandoz, Bargemon
swi wc bc

47-48 Medlar, chez Sandoz, Bargemon
swi iwtr dr 1931; wc bc ink

51-52 Cliff at Etretat (inverted)
bc ink wc

53-54 Cliff at Etretat
wc bc ink pencil

SB16:56

56 Windsurfers and beach
swi; wc ink

57-58 Cliff at Etretat
wc bc; 11 x 10½ ins

59-60 Beach at Etretat
swi; bc ball point pen

61-62 Cliffs at Etretat
ink

65-66 Cliff at Etretat
swi; wc bc

68 Vera, Bargemon, Mme Fanenel's balcony
(landscape format)
iwt; wax crayon; 6 x 8¼ ins
(Chatham paper, laid down)

70 Vera, Bargemon, chez Arcadio
iwt, d 79; pencil; 5¼ x 7½ ins
(paper laid down)

72 Putti, Clos du Peyronnet
iwt d 84; coloured pencil (Heritage woodfree blotting paper laid down)

74 Vera, Bargemon, chez Arcadio
iwt d '79; pencil ; 7½ x 5¼ ins
(paper laid down)

76 Putti, Clos du Peyronnet
iwt; pencil; 3½ x 7 ins
(Somerset paper laid down)
Vera, Bargemon balcony
iwt d 82; pencil; 6 x 3½ ins
(Somerset paper laid down)

No 17

1983-85
black cloth, 15¾ x 11½ ins
Badenscallie, Bargemon
(owned by Peter Coker)

2 Aurel
swi iwt; ink sanguine pencil

5 Open window
swi; wc bc

6 Interior, chez Sandoz
swi; pencil wc; 6½ x 11¼ ins

8 Bargemon
swi; wc bc

10 Willow, Bargemon
swi; wc bc
Study for *Willow* (**465**)

11-12 Towards Tanera Mór
iwt d 85; bc wc

13 Artichokes
swi; ink

15-16 Etretat
swi iwtr dr 'Oct 84'; wc bc

19-20 Badenscallie
swi iwtr dr 85; ink

21-22 Badenscallie
swi iwtr dr 85; ink

25-26 Etretat
swi dr 84; wc bc

29-30 Etretat
swi; ink

33-34 Etretat, detail
wc bc

35-36 Etretat, detail
wc bc

NB some images removed from this book prior to cataloguing, including some of Clos du Peyronnet

No 18

c1984
Clos du Peyronnet
(owned by Julian Hartnoll)

SB19:3

SB19:5-6

No 19

April 1985
black cloth, 15½ x 11¼ ins
Bargemon, Clos du Peyronnet
(owned by Peter Coker)

2 Sketch
pencil

3 Cycas palm
swi wc; 8½ x 10½ ins

5-6 Olives Bargemon
swi; wc ink bc

9-10 Dark Pond, Strelitzia
swi iwtr; wc ink

13-14 Farm buildings
swi; charcoal

17-18 Vines below the chateau, Bargemon
swi ir 'Bargemon'; wc

SB19:21-22

21-22 Beschorneria Yuccoides
swi iwtr; wc
Study for *Beschorneria Yuccoides* (**474**)

SB19:25-26

25-26 Garden pathway, Clos du Peyronnet
swi iwtr; wc

29-30 Cercis (inverted)
swi iwt; wc

33-34 Irises
swi iwtr; wc
Study for *Irises* (**479**)

37-38 Study of Judas tree, Clos du Peyronnet
sanguine pencil

41-42 Towards Ventimiglia from the Clos du Peyronnet, overcast
swi; ink

45-46 Towards Ventimiglia from the garden of the Clos du Peyronnet
swi; wc

No 20

1985-86
Aldeburgh, Achiltibuie, Badenscallie, Drumrunie, Bargemon, Cap de la Chèvre, Clos du Peyronnet, Forêt de Landévennec, Kersiguenou, Vaucottes
(owned by Robert Travers, Piano Nobile)

No 21

1985-86
inc Aldeburgh, Bargemon
(owned by Lowell Libson)

SB22:17-18

No 22

1986
canvas, 11 x 7½ ins
Bargemon, Fayence
(owned by Peter Coker)

4 Flower bank, Bargemon
iwt d 'June 86'; wc pencil

5-6 Flower bank, Bargemon
swi i colour notes d 86; pencil sanguine

7-8 Sketch of Bargemon fields
pencil

9-10 Towards ramparts of Bargemon from chateau garden
swi i colour notes; wc pencil

12 Looking up toward the chateau, from the valley: sketch
pencil

13-14 Mme Benois, Le Vieux Château - olives, vines and stone wall
swi i 'Mme Benois'; pencil sanguine

15-16 Geraniums on Elsbeth's balcony: sketch
pencil

17-18 Geraniums on Elsbeth's balcony
swi; wc

19-20 View from Elsbeth's balcony: sketch
pencil

21 Study for Terrace, No 1
swi iwt i 'preliminary for large painting 48"x48", RA ex'; wc pencil
Study for *Terrace, Le Vieux Château - Towards Claviers* (**534**)

22 Study for the terrace, Le Vieux Château
swi i colour notes; pencil
Study for *Terrace, Le Vieux Château – Towards Claviers* (**534**)

23 No 2, Study for Terrace
swi iwt 'RA ex'; wc
Study for *Terrace, Le Vieux Château - Towards Claviers* (**534**)

24 Alliums
pencil

25 Sketches of grasses
swi i notes; pencil

SB22:49-50

26 Alliums
swi; wc pencil
27-28 Study of olive trees
sanguine
29-30 Study of olive trees
pencil
31-32 Study of olive trees
i colour notes; pencil
33-34 Bargemon, towards Claviers
swi; wc
35-36 Bargemon apricots
swi; pencil sanguine
37-38 Bargemon apricots
wc pencil
39 Colour notes
wc
40 Colour notes
wc
41 Colour notes
wc
42 Colour notes
wc
43-44 Fayence
swi iwt; wc; 9 x 14½ ins
45-46 Fayence
iwt and colour notes; ink
47-48 Arbour
swi; wc bc
49-50 Arbour
swi; wc bc
53-54 Sketch for a Bargemon landscape
pencil wc bc
57-58 Sketch for arbour
pencil

SB23:93-94

No 23

1986-87
black cloth, 15¾ x 11¼ ins
The Red House, Bargemon, Clos du Peyronnet, Eure
(owned by Peter Coker)

1-2 Yellow iris, Bargemon
swi i 'Bargemon' d 'June 1986'; wc bc ink
5-6 Poppies, Bargemon
swi; wc bc ink
9-10 Olive trees, Bargemon
swi; wc bc ink

SB23:104

13-14 Bargemon landscape
swi; wc
17-18 Vanishing field to olive trees
swi; wc ink
21-22 Blue orchard
swi; wc ink
25-26 Bargemon landscape
swi; wc ink
29-30 Le Vieux Château, Bargemon, towards Claviers
swi; wc bc
Study for *Terrace, Le Vieux Château – Towards Claviers* (**534**)
33-34 Bargemon landscape
swi; ink
37-38 Bargemon landscape
swi; wc
41-42 From Elsbeth's balcony
swi; ink
45-46 Bargemon Garden
swi; wc ink
49-50 Olive tree, Bargemon
swi; wc
53-54 Bargemon landscape
swi; wc
57-58 Olive trees, Bargemon
swi; wc ink
61-62 Forest, Claviers
s i 'Claviers'; wc ink; 22 ¾ x 15 ins
Study for *La Forêt, Claviers* (**517**)
65-66 Fayence
swi iwt; wc bc
69-70 Apricot tree Bargemon
swi; wc bc
73-74 Olive trees, Bargemon
swi; wc ink bc
77-78 Jardin Méditerranéan, overhanging pergola, Clos du Peyronnet
swi; wc bc; 11 x 15 ins

SB23:17-18

81-82 Menilles, Eure
swi; wc bc ink
85-86 Chez nous, the Red House, front garden and red brick wall
swi; wc ink
89-90 Cherry blossom, the Red House
swi, iwtr, dr 'April 87'; ink
93-94 Beschorneria Yuccoides, Red House grown from Clos du Peyronnet
swi, iwtr; wc bc ink
104 From Elsbeth's balcony;
swi; wc bc
105-6 Bargemon
swi, iwt d 'June-July 1986'; wc; 15½ x 12 ins

SB23:5-6

SB23:1-2

SB23:21-22

No 24

1987
Red House, Stoke-by-Nayland, Badentarbat, Badenscallie, salmon nets, Skye, Etretat
(owned by the British Museum)

No 25

1987
black cloth, 11½ x 8 ins
Aldeburgh, Achiltibuie, Ostend
(owned by Peter Coker)

1 [no image:] iwss
2 Nets, Badentarbat
wax crayon wax resist
Study for *Salmon Nets No 2* (**529**)
2 Nets, Badentarbat
pencil
Study for *Salmon Nets No 2* (**529**)
4 Sketch of nets
ink wc bc wax resist
Study for *Mending Salmon Nets, Achiltibuie* (**522**)
4 Sketch of nets
swi; pencil wc
Study for *Mending Salmon Nets, Achiltibuie* (**522**)
7-8 Sea, Ostend
swi; wc
9 Sea off Aldeburgh towards the Martello tower
swi; wax crayon
10 Sea off Aldeburgh towards the Martello tower
swi; wax crayon wc pencil

SB26:31-32

No 26

June 1987 and July 1988
black cloth, 15 ½ x 11½ ins
Achiltibuie, Badenscallie, Badentarbat,
Salmon Nets, Skye
(owned by Peter Coker)

1-2 Skye 1987, overlooking Staffin from the Quirang
swi i 'Skye & Badenscallie', d 'June 1987 July 88'; wc bc pencil
Study for *The Quirang, Skye* (**526**)
5-6 Skye 1987, overlooking Staffin from the Quirang
swi; wc bc pencil
Study for *The Quirang, Skye* (**526**)
9-10 Skye overlooking Staffin from the Quirang
swi; wc pencil
Study for *The Quirang, Skye* (**526**)
13-14 Skye overlooking Staffin from the Quirang
swi; wc bc pencil
Study for *The Quirang, Skye* (**526**)
15-16 Badenscallie June 1987, reworked July 1988
swi iwtr; bc wc ink
19-20 Langoustines, Achiltibuie
swi; wc bc pencil
23-24 Mending salmon nets
swi iwtr; sanguine pencil
27-28 Salmon poles, Badenterbat Bay
swi iwtr dr 87; wc bc
31-32 Salmon nets, Achiltibuie
swi iwt d 87; wc bc ink
35-36 Badenscallie
swi iwtr dr 88; wc bc
39-40 Badentarbat Bay
swi iwtr dr 'July 88' sepia
41-42 Salmon nets
swi; ink
43-44 Rusting buoys on the shoreline
swi; wc bc ink
47-48 Jim Muir's nets
swi iwtr; sepia ink wc
51-52 Badentarbat
swi iwtr, dr 88; ink wc
55-56 Badenscallie
swi iwtr dr 88; ink wc bc
59-60 Towards Coigach
swi iwtr; wc bc ink
63-64 Drying salmon nets
swi iwtr; wc sepia
Study for *Salmon Nets, drying and ready for inspection, Badentarbat* (**556**)
67-68 Ground net
swi; wc ink bc
Study for *Salmon Nets, drying and ready for inspection, Badentarbat* (**556**)
71-72 Approaching Achiltibuie
swi; wc bc ink
75-76 Sea of peat, Achiltibuie
swi iwtr dr 88; sepia ink wc
79-80 Behind Tigh A' Sgiobair
swi iwtr; wc bc ink

SB27:15-16

SB27:55-56

No 27

1987-89
black cloth, 12 x 11½ inches
Badenscallie, La Roche-Guyon, Ostend, Pourville
(owned by Peter Coker)

3-4 La Roche-Guyon
swi iwtr dr 87; wc bc
7-8 The Epte and Seine, La Roche-Guyon
swi iwt; wc bc
11-12 Ostend, window out to sea
swi ir 'Ostend'; wc
15-16 Pourville
swi iwtr; wc
19-20 Pourville
swi iwtr; wc pencil
23-24 Salmon poles, Badentarbat Bay
swi iwtr dr 'July 88'; wc bc charcoal

SB27:57-58

25-26 Salmon net poles, Badentarbat, looking towards Achiltibuie
s; sepia wash; 12 x 16 ins
27-28 Salmon net poles, Badentarbat
pencil; 11 x 17 ins
29-30 From Badentarbat Bay towards Coigach (Ben Mor)
pencil
31-32 Gathering storm, Badentarbat, salmon net poles
swi; conté ink wc pencil
33-34 Salmon net poles, Badentarbat
swi; pencil wc
35-36 Badenscallie
swi iwt; conté chalk ink
39-40 Approaching storm, Badentarbat
s; wc conté ink
43-44 Badentarbat, gathering storm
s, ir 'Badentarbat'; wc wax resist conté
46 Sketch of Badentarbat
pencil; 7½ x 21½ ins
47-48 Salmon net poles, Badentarbat
wc pencil
51 Towards the Summer Isles from Achiltibuie
swi; bc wc
52 Salmon nets, Badentarbat
swi; conté bc wc
53 Sketch of figures with salmon net poles
swi; pencil
54 Sketch of figures with salmon net poles
swi; pencil
55-56 Salmon net poles, Badentarbat
wc bc pencil
57-58 Salmon net grounded
swi; sanguine wc bc conté; 12 x 14½ ins
Study for *Salmon Nets drying and ready for inspection, Badentarbat* (**556**)
59-60 Inspecting nets, with figures
s; pencil ink
61-62 Sketch of figures with salmon nets
pencil
63-64 Badenscallie, red roof, Ben Mor Coigach, Badenscallie
i 'Ben Mor Coigach, Badenscallie'; wc bc
65-66 Sketch of figures with salmon nets
pencil
67-68 Sketches of salmon net poles
pencil
Study for *Salmon Nets drying and ready for inspection, Badentarbat* (**556**)
69-70 Sketches of salmon net poles
pencil sanguine

SB27:79-80

73-74 Sea of peat
swi iwt; pencil
77 Sea of peat
swi; ink wc
79-80 End of the fishing season, Badentarbat
s iwtr d 'August 89'; wc sepia
83-84 Badentarbat
swi; wc bc
Study for *Salmon Net Poles, Badentarbat* (**574**)
87-88 Poles and net on the ground
swi; wc bc (painted Aug 1989)
Study for *Salmon Net Poles, Badentarbat* (**574**)
91-92 Badentarbat Bay, Achiltibuie
swi d 89; wc bc

No 28

1988-89
canvas, 10¾ x 13½ ins
London, Etretat, Quiberville, St-Valery-en-Caux, Varengeville
(owned by Peter Coker)

3-4 Westminster, evening
s; sepia wc
Study for *Evening towards Westminster from Cranley Gardens* (**547**)
5-6 St-Valery-en-Caux
swi d 'May 89'; wc
7-8 St-Valery-en-Caux
swi iwt d 'May 89'; wc
Study for *Lighthouse St-Valery-en-Caux* (**570**)
9-10 St-Valery-en-Caux
swi iwt d '1989'; wc
Study for *Lighthouse St-Valery-en-Caux* (**570**)
11-12 Etretat
s iwt d 'May 1989'; wc bc ink; 10½ x 23½ ins
15-16 Quiberville
swi iwt d 89; wc bc
Study for *Seascape, Quiberville* (**575**)
17-18 St-Valery-en-Caux,
swi iwt d 89; pencil
19-20 Quiberville,
swi iwt d 'May 89' wc bc
Study for *Cliffs at Quiberville* (**559**)
21-22 Quiberville
swi iwt d 'May 89'; wc bc
Study for *Seascape, Quiberville* (**575**)
23-24 Cliffs at Quiberville
swi i 'drawings for the watercolours Quiberville and painting' d 'May 89'; wc bc pencil sanguine
Study for *Cliffs at Quiberville* (**559**)
25-26 Quiberville
s iwt d 89; bc wc
Study for *Seascape, Quiberville* (**575**)
27-28 Varengeville
swi; pencil; 8½ x 17¼ ins
Study for *Orchard, Varengeville* (**573**)
30 Quiberville
swi iwt d 89; wc; 8½ x 12½ ins
31-32 Orchard, Varengeville
swi iwt d 89; pencil sanguine
Study for *Orchard, Varengeville* (**573**)
33-34 Varengeville
swi d 'May 89' iwtr; wc
Study for *Orchard, Varengeville* (**573**)
52 Groyne, St-Valery 10¼ x 4¾ ins
swi iwt d 91; oil on newspaper

NB numerous images removed from this book prior to cataloguing, including some of tractors

No 29

1989
black, 7 x 11½ ins
Etretat, Quiberville, St-Valery-en-Caux, Varengeville
(owned by Peter Coker)

1 Beach
swi; wc bc; 6 x 7 ins
2 St-Valery-en-Caux and lighthouse
swi; wc bc
3-4 Varengeville between the cliffs from the terrace
swi ir 'Varengeville'; wc bc
7-8 Varengeville between the cliffs from the terrasse
swi; wc bc 7 x 14 ins
9-10 St-Valery-en-Caux
iwt; sepia ink; 7 x 18½ ins
Study for *Lighthouse, St-Valery-en-Caux* (**578**)
13-14 Etretat on the cliff top out to sea
s ir 'Etretat'; wc bc
17-18 Etretat out to sea from the cliff top
swi ir 'Etretat'; wc bc
19-20 Harbour, St-Valery-en-Caux
s; wc bc
23-24 Sea, Quiberville
swi ir 'Quiberville'; wc
Study for *Seascape, Quiberville* (**575**)
25 Jetty, St-Valery-en-Caux
swi; wc
26 Lighthouse and jetty, St-Valery-en-Caux
swi; wc
29-30 Quiberville, cliffs & sky from shore
swi ir 'Quiberville'; wc bc
Study for *Cliffs at Quiberville* (**560**)
33 Sea and tractor
swi; wc bc; 6½ x 8½ ins
34 Sea and tractor
swi; pencil
35-36 Horizon and sky from the cliffs, Varengeville
swi; wc bc
39-40 Quiberville beach
swi; wc bc; 7 x 21 ins
Study for *Cliffs at Quiberville* (**560**)
41 Study of Quiberville beach out to sea
swi; wc
42 Cliffs, Quiberville
swi; wc
Study for *Cliffs at Quiberville*
45-46 Varengeville
swi iwtr; wc bc
Study for *Orchard, Varengeville* (**573**)
47 Layout of St-Valery-en-Caux
pencil
48 St-Valery-en-Caux, sea piece looking towards Dieppe
swi iw 'St-Valery-en-Caux' d 1989; wc bc; 7 x 10 ins
Study for *Cliffs St-Valery-en-Caux* (**561**)
51-52 Red House garden, Mistley
s swi i 'Mistley' d 1991; wc bc ink

No 30

1989
Sennelier, canvas, 10¾ x 13½ ins
Badentarbat Salmon Net Poles
(owned by Peter Coker)

2-3 Salmon poles, Badentarbat
s; wc bc
8-9 Salmon poles, Badentarbat
wc bc

SB31:5-6

No 31

1989-90
black cloth, 15¾ x 12 ins
Red House, Badenscallie, La Roche-Guyon, Quiberville, St-Valery-en-Caux
(owned by Peter Coker)

1-2 Salmon poles, Badentarbat
swi; wc bc
Study for *Salmon Net Poles, Badentarbat* (**574**)
5-6 Salmon Nets, Badentarbat
swi ir 'Badentarbat' dr 'Aug 1989'; wc bc ink
Study for *Salmon Net Poles, Badentarbat* (**574**)
9-10 Rowans, Tigh A' Sgiobair, Mr Brown's cottage
swi; wc bc ink

SB31:17-18

13-14 St-Valery-en-Caux
swi iwtr dr 'Sept 1989'; wc bc
17-18 Quiberville
swi iwtr; wc bc
21-22 La Roche-Guyon
swi iwtr; wc bc ink
25-26 La Roche-Guyon
swi; wc bc
29-30 La Roche-Guyon
swi; wc bc ink
33-34 La Roche-Guyon
swi; wc bc ink
Study for *La Roche-Guyon* (**567**)
49-50 Lily Pond Red House
swi iwt, d 'September 28th 1990'; wc bc

No 32

1989, 1991
black cloth, 7 x 11 ins
Aldeburgh, Higham, Badentarbat, Varengeville
(owned by Peter Coker)

1-2 Cornfield Higham
iwss; pencil sanguine
Study for *Cornfield, Higham* (**562**)
3-4 Layout for nets lying Badentarbat (drying) poles to left
iwt d 'Aug 1989'; pencil
5-6 Badentarbat, beach detritus
swi; pencil sanguine

7-8 Badentarbat beach towards Coigach
swi; wc
10 St-Valery-en-Caux
swi; wc
11 Sea, Quiberville
swi; wc
12 Sea, Quiberville
swi; wc
13-14 Sea, Quiberville
swi; wc bc
15-16 La Roche-Guyon
s; wc bc
Study for *La Roche-Guyon* (**567**)
17-18 La Roche-Guyon
swi iwt, d 89; pencil
21-22 La Roche-Guyon
s; wc bc
25-26 La Roche-Guyon
sepia
27-28 La Roche-Guyon
iwt d 'Sept 89'; pencil; 6½ x 16½ ins
29-30 La Roche-Guyon
s; sepia
33-34 La Roche-Guyon
swi; wc bc
Study for *La Roche-Guyon* (**567**)
35-36 Aldeburgh from the Wentworth, fishermen's huts and out to sea
swi; wc bc ink
39-40 Morning clouds over sea from the Wentworth
swi i 'Morning Aldeburgh 7am'; wc bc ink
41-42 Aldeburgh from the Wentworth, fishermen's huts and out to sea
swi; wc bc ink
44 Beach Aldeburgh
swi; pencil
46 Aldeburgh
iwt d 1990; pencil
47-48 Aldeburgh from the Wentworth, fishermen's huts and out to sea
s; pencil
51-52 Red House garden
swi i 'Mistley' d 1991; wc bc sepia
55-56 Aldeburgh, overcast sea
swi iw 'Aldeburgh' d 'Jan 1991'; wc ink bc
65 St-Valery-en-Caux
swi; pencil
66 Jetty, St-Valery-en-Caux
swi iwt; pencil; 4 x 11 ins

No 33

1991
Sennelier, red canvas, 12¼ x 9¾ ins
Etretat, Ste-Marguerite-Sur-Mer, St-Valery-en-Caux, Varengeville, Vaucottes, Veules-les-Roses
(owned by Peter Coker)

1-2 St-Valery-en-Caux
iwss; wc
3-4 St-Valery-en-Caux
swi; wc bc
Study for *St-Valery-en-Caux* (**583**)
25-26 Etretat from the Hotel Dormy
swi; pencil
27-28 Etretat from the Hotel Dormy
swi i 'Etretat Dormy'; wc bc
31-32 Harvest, Varengeville, Ste-Marguerite-sur-Mer
swi; wc bc
Study for *Harvest, Normandy* (**577**)
33-34 Near Ste-Marguerite-sur-Mer
swi iwt; sepia
Study for *Harvest, Normandy* (**577**)
41 St-Valery-en-Caux
swi iwt; wc bc
42 Vaucottes
swi iwt; wc bc
44 Vaucottes cliff and sea – 2 sketches
swi iwt d 'Aug 91'; pencil
49-50 Harvest stooks, Ste-Marguerite-sur-Mer
swi; pencil
Study for *Harvest, Normandy* (**577**)
51 Preliminary sketch for Veules-les-Roses
swi iwt; pencil
52 Preliminary sketch of Veules-les-Roses
swi; pencil
Study for *Veules-les-Roses* (**584**, **585**)
53 Preliminary sketch of Veules-les-Roses
swi i 'Veules-les-Roses'; pencil
54 Preliminary sketch of Veules-les-Roses
swi; pencil
55 Preliminary sketch of Veules-les-Roses
swi i 'Veules-les-Roses'; pencil
63-64 Late Afternoon Harvest, Ste-Marguerite-sur-Mer
swi; wc bc
Study for *Cornfield, Ste-Marguerite-sur-Mer* (**576**)
65-66 Cornfield, Ste-Marguerite-sur-Mer, with circular bales
swi; pencil sanguine
66 Cornfield, Ste-Marguerite-sur-Mer, with circular bales
swi; wax crayon
Study for *Cornfield, Ste-Marguerite-sur-Mer* (**576**)
73-74 Cornfield, Ste-Marguerite-sur-Mer, Normandy
iwtr d 1991; pencil sanguine
Study for *Harvest, Normandy* (**577**)

No 34

Jan 1992
black cloth, 12 x 11 ins
Hôtel Pin Doré Menton, Clos du Peyronnet
(owned by Peter Coker)

1-2 Window at the Hôtel Pin Doré,
s i 'Hôtel Pin Doré' d 'Jan 92'; wc bc & ink; 22¾ x 12 ins
Study for *Fenêtre Ouverte à Menton* (**586**)
5-6 Clos du Peyronnet
s iwt d 92; wc bc sepia & ink
Study for *The Garden, Clos du Peyronnet, late afternoon* (**589**)
8 Cycas
s iwt d 1992; wc & pencil
9 Clos du Peyronnet, verandah
swi; wc sanguine conté & pencil
10 Clos du Peyronnet
wc
12 Sketch of Clos du Peyronnet, verandah
conté
14 Putti, Clos
swi iwt; pencil & sanguine
15-16 Terrace and verandah, Clos du Peyronnet
s; sepia
18 Verandah, Clos du Peyronnet
sanguine
20 Palms
swi; ball point pen
Study for *Menton* (**590**)
21-22 Study from Hôtel Pin Doré, Menton
swi; ball point pen
Study for *Menton* (**590**)

No 35

Jan 1992–98
black cloth, 15¾ x 11½ ins
Clos du Peyronnet, Menton
(owned by Peter Coker)

1 Studies of the Clos du Peyronnet
s iwss i 'Terrace, 4 studies Clos du Peyronnet' d 'January 1992';
wc pencil
2 Putti
iwt d 1991; wc ink bc pencil
3 Kumquat
swi iwt; wc ink bc (painted Sep 1998)
4 Kumquat
swi iwt; wc ink bc (painted Sep 1998)
7 L'escalier d'honneur, Clos du Peyronnet
swi; pencil sanguine
8 L'escalier d'honneur, Clos du Peyronnet
swi iwt; pencil sanguine
10 Study of balcony Hôtel Pin Doré, Menton
swi; ink (drawn 1992)
Study for *Fenêtre Ouverte à Menton* (**586**)
14 L'escalier d'honneur, Clos du Peyronnet
pencil
16 From the balcony, Hôtel Pin Doré, Menton, towards Ventimeglia
swi iwt d 1992; pencil sanguine
Study for *Menton* (**590**)
18 Study of the grand staircase, Clos du Peyronnet
swi iwt; sanguine
29 Preliminary sketch of Clos du Peyronnet
pencil
30 Clos du Peyronnet
pencil
31 Preliminary sketch of Clos du Peyronnet
pencil
32 From the top of the path at Clos du Peyronnet down to the sea
swi; sanguine
34 Menton
swi iwt; ink

No 36

1998
black cloth, 15 x 11½ ins
Clos du Peyronnet, Menton
(owned by Peter Coker)

3-4 Clos du Peyronnet
s d 1998; wc ink
7-8 Pots and terracotta brick wall , Clos du Peyronnet
s iw 'Clos du Peyronnet' d 1998; wc ink
12 Study of the terrace, Clos du Peyronnet
swi d 1998; wc sepia
15-16 Red mullet, Menton
s iwt d 'Sept 98'; wc bc
17-18 Rough sketch
pencil
21-22 Sketch of the Clos du Peyronnet
swi; pencil wc
26 The pond, Clos du Peyronnet
swi iwt d 'Sept 1998'; wc
29-30 Entrance to the Clos du Peyronnet
s iwt d 98; 15 x 19 ins; wc
33-34 Terrace at the Clos du Peyronnet
s d 'September 1998'; wc; 15 x 15½ ins

Public Collections containing Works by Peter Coker

Arts Council of Great Britain; Victoria Art Gallery, Bath; Bagshaw Art Gallery, Batley; Birmingham City Museums and Art Gallery; Eastern Arts Association, Cambridge; Fitzwilliam Museum, Cambridge; Carlisle Museum and Art Gallery; Chelmsford and Essex Museum; The Minories, Colchester; Contemporary Art Society of Wales; Herbert Art Gallery, Coventry; Doncaster Museum and Art Gallery; Scottish National Gallery of Modern Art, Edinburgh; Ipswich Museums and Galleries; Abbot Hall Art Gallery, Kendal; Kettering Art Gallery; City Art Gallery, Leeds; Leicester Museums and Art Gallery; Walker Art Gallery, Liverpool; British Museum, London; Contemporary Art Society, London; Chantrey Bequest, London; National Maritime Museum, London; National Portrait Gallery, London; Royal Academy of Arts, London; Royal College of Art, London; Tate, London; Victoria and Albert Museum, London; City Art Gallery, Manchester; Norwich Castle Museum; Rugby Art Gallery and Museum; Rochdale Art Gallery and Museum; Salford Museum and Art Gallery; Sheffield City Art Galleries; Beecroft Art Gallery, Southend-on-Sea Atkinson Art Gallery, Southport; Stedelijk Museum, Ostend, Belgium; Berardo Collection, Lisbon, Portugal.

Picture Credits

Bold numbers refer to Catalogue Raisonné Number;
others refer to page number on which picture appears

Abbot Hall Art Gallery, Kendal (**355**)
Accenture Art Collection (**32**)
Alfred East Art Gallery, Kettering (**51**)
Anglesey Heritage (**19**)
Arts Council, London (**37**)
AstraZeneca Ltd (**480**, **486**)
Beecroft Art Gallery, Southend (**123**)
Berardo Collection, Portugal (**72**)
BP International Ltd (**262**)
Cargill Europe (**530**)
Carlisle Museum and Art Gallery (**82**)
Chelmsford and Essex Museum (**217**)
Cheltenham and Gloucester Building Society (**522**)
City of Birmingham Museum & Art Gallery (**57**)
Doncaster Museum and Art Gallery (**34**, **274**)
Fitzwilliam Museum, Cambridge (45: *Nicholas*)
Fleming-Wyfold Art Foundation, London (**158**)
Flying Colours Gallery, London (**152**, **344**, **487**)
Hawksfield Incorporated (**398**)
Huddersfield Art Gallery (**40**)
Ipswich Borough Council Museums & Galleries (**15**, **74**, **477**)
James Capel & Co (**462**)
Julian Hartnoll (**64**, **102**)
Leeds City Art Gallery (**137**)
Mulberry Gallery, Wantage (**528**)
National Maritime Museum, London (**287**)
National Museums and Galleries of Wales, Cardiff (**23**)
North East Essex Technical College (**168**)
Piano Nobile Fine Paintings, London (**125**, **385**, **422**)
The Pyms Gallery, London (**100**)
Rochdale City Art Gallery (**160**)
Royal Academy of Arts, London (**45**)
Royal College of Art, London (**9**, **26**, **28**)
Rugby Borough Council Collection (**80**)
Scottish National Gallery of Modern Art, Edinburgh (**79**)
Sheffield City Art Galleries (**16**, **33**, **35**; 41: *Turbot I*)
Tate, London (**42**, **49**, **60**; 42: *Drawing for Butcher's Shop I*)
Victoria and Albert Museum, London (47: textile designs)

Table and Chair 1955 (**49**)

Town and Country – Fatal Englishman: Memories of Nicholas Coker

Richard Humphreys Senior Curator: Programme Research, Tate Britain

I can never look at Peter Coker's *Table and Chair* without thinking of the Sex Pistols, Essex and a muddy weekend in Gloucestershire.

The painting shows the artist's son Nicholas standing by a table and chair in 1955 in a bare room in East London reminiscent of a farmhouse setting. The extreme right-hand edge of the canvas reveals part of an open door. On the table are various items which suggest a meal is being prepared. The most striking object is a sheep's head on sheets of newspaper. Although this a measured piece of very fine and sophisticated painting about the facts of life and looking, it also has a remarkable edgy, contradictory energy – the sheep's head seems to look at you as if emerging still-born out of contemporary events; a fully alive three-year old boy stares up inquiringly and tentatively as if posing a question; the open door compresses the space and gives the sense of a very particular moment. The image is apparently full of unspoken or unknown implications, suggesting a mute drama. And one culinary thought I still have is what on earth you do with a sheep's head for lunch.

Twenty years later I first met this little boy, Nick, as I knew him, at the Courtauld Institute of Art where we had both gone to do MAs in art history following English degrees at Cambridge. I didn't know his father or his painting then. We immediately hit it off and I realised he was exactly the sort of person who you could learn much strange knowledge from – what to do with a sheep's head for instance. Or how to make beef tea or how to poach eggs in your moules marinière sauce from the night before. And he was, besides, a brilliant flautist which clinched it for me.

Nick was very leftishly and anarchistically politicised and began some brilliant research on Sir Peter Lely and the iconoclasm of the Civil War period involving analyses of radical pamphlets, aristocratic dress and Stuart and Cromwellian coinage. Whether he was a Roundhead or Cavalier at heart, though, I wasn't sure. He argued energetically and intelligently about revolution and culture and I remember him saying often that he saw everything politically - all this during the years immediately prior to Anthony Blunt's disgrace, it may be telling to recall. He also had, as might suit someone with that kind of loaded theatrical outlook, a number of disguises or personae which interested me – one was that of a late nineteenth century dandy; another was that of a City gent; another was the countryman in plus fours. You might of course expect this of a pupil from Christ's Hospital where they dress more strangely than Etonians. There was something Edwardian and expansive about all of these images. The wardrobe which clothed them was impressive – he introduced me to the expensive, exclusive joys of Jermyn Street and was forever on the lookout for bargains at sales at places such as Hilditch and Key. Church's shoes were sacrosanct. His addresses were usually central and impressive-sounding and he would arrange to meet you in Johnsonian chop houses in the City. Girl friends were top-drawer, beautiful and interesting. It might sound precious and tiresome but it wasn't at all – it was all done with great conviction, power and pleasure, and a great love of well-made things. Life was rich and exciting and you should be at the heart of it and that involved looking the part wherever you might find yourself. Life was a stage but the drama, even in the illusory late twentieth century, was pretty much for real.

Nick was friendly with all sorts of people worth knowing in art, music, film, business and so on and was forever hatching schemes and intrigues. Risk and adventure were all and he told me my own laconic detachment was paper-thin and evasive. He was right. But I always protected myself from fate, or its appearance, more than he did.

He had a way, so to speak, of facing the dead sheep's head in the news which I took much longer to acquire. Taking me to the old London Film Makers' Co-op in Primrose Hill to see Franju's compelling and horrifying film about Parisian slaughterhouses was a memorably bracing experience I wouldn't have tried without Nick's impulse.

When the 'punk thing' happened in 1976 Nick dived in with his usual gay abandon and not least in his new DIY attire of safety pins, torn and paint-splattered trousers and shock of tousled hair – Rupert Brooke and Sid Vicious merged in some peculiar and charming way. His bosom friend from Cambridge Julien Temple, was filming the rise of the Sex Pistols and their manager Malcolm MacLaren, along with The Clash and other new bands. Nick was close to all these people, not as a star-struck hanger on and fashion addict but as an engaged partner – he designed fabrics and clothes, as Peter had in very different circumstances years before, he discussed the politics of popular culture and he contributed original ideas of all kinds for all-comers. He also brought unlikely people together. Although he was himself an unlikely person in some respects he was also direct and practical and above all generous-spirited and good-humoured – even when I ruined the silk lining of his best tailor-made suit with ink. He could always cook a meal or make some clothes and thought things were there to be shared. Meantime he was also to be found at posh weddings in the country in immaculate morning dress, just like the Americans imagine such Brits always are.

1977 saw the Queen's silver jubilee and the notorious Sex Pistols Thames boat trip. Nick was there in body and spirit. There was also a show of British painting from the years 1952-1977 at the Royal Academy. Nick was unconvinced by the version of history it presented but even more so he was affronted by the lazy and uninformed critical responses it elicited. We decided rather grandly to write an article and to revive the critical debates of John Berger and David Sylvester from the heroic post-war years of communists and liberals. In a spirit worthy of *Withnail and I* we found our way to a remote, cold and primitively equipped farm cottage in Gloucestershire. We drank red wine and ate, if not sheep's head, then a number of slightly obscure dishes cooked by Nick with my assistance and prepared on an old wooden table by an open range. In the evenings we would head out across muddy fields towards pubs where the locals looked upon us with some gratifyingly quiet suspicion. Staggering back through dark uncharted fields, drunk, we'd try to compose our piece before facing a freezing night of alcohol-fuelled dreams. We spent hours trying to find the telling phrase or watertight, nutcracking argument. In the end Nick wrote it later and had it published in some obscure new wave magazine. Nobody noticed but it was a pretty good piece all the same.

What struck me then was how much Nick was arguing the case for his father's art and how fiercely proud and protective he was about it. It wasn't a political case, as John Berger's had rather misguidedly been in the 1950s, but one about a power and integrity of vision and of technical supremacy. In fact it was against the words in newspapers and fashionable rebellion and for a patient inquiry and crafting endeavour. It stood for something traditional and uncompromising.

After that, asides from a rather existential and mind-broadening trip to Paris and a few other excursions, our paths slowly started to diverge. Nick went onto another level of adventure and I was too cautious and laconic to join him. I was devastated some years later, by which time I was a dad and fully employed, to learn of his death. And not entirely surprised to hear various intriguing rumours about his life towards the end.

It now seems entirely appropriate, even fateful, that *Table and Chair* was acquired by the Tate in 1981, the year I joined the staff there and relieved my wife and family by seeming to have grown up at last. And when I look at it again today I think of a little English boy, like so many, growing up in a world somewhere between the steady, rural, artisanal world both Nick's father and mine had known as boys, and the crazy, unreal urban world of image and fast words which most of us live in today. Nick, eternally curious and creative, was always trying to bridge gaps which many people hadn't even noticed. It is a great painting as well as moving for me personally as I think incoherently about the strange web of things and a life lived unsafely and to the full.

Nicholas Coker was born on 16 February 1952, and educated at Christ's Hospital, Horsham, Sussex. During his schooldays he played flute in the National Youth Orchestra (1968-70), and subsequently studied the instrument under James Galway in Berlin (1971). He then went on to read English at King's College, Cambridge (1971-74) and History of Art at the Courtauld Institute (1975-79). As an art historian, he specialised in English art of the seventeenth century, and particularly Peter Lely and Iconoclasm. He assisted his father on the writing of *Etching Techniques* (1976), and wrote catalogue essays for three of his exhibitions, including *Paintings and Drawings of the Butcher's Shop* (1979). He died on 22 March 1985.

Select Bibliography

A. Texts by Peter Coker

Coker 1953 'The Language of Painting' [publication details unidentified, c 1964] (based on the dissertation written at the Royal College of Art, 1953)

Coker 1959 'Peter Coker's Leyton', *House & Garden*, December 1959 – January 1960, Page 83

Coker 1971 'Introduction', *Pupil & Masters*, Long Melford: Westgate House, 1971

Coker 1976 *Etching Techniques*, London: B T Batsford, 1976

Coker 1982 'Vivian Pitchforth', *The Times*, 8 September 1982, Page 12

Coker 1983 *Critic's Choice*, Woodbridge: Deben Gallery, 1983, Page 3

Coker 1985 'James Stroudley', *The Times*, 18 May 1985, Page 10

B. Texts about, or including images of work by, Peter Coker

Chase 1960 Michael Chase, 'Peter Coker', *Studio*, volume 160, December 1960, Pages 214-217

Christian 1960 Roy Christian, 'Derby Home Brewers', *The House of Whitbread*, Spring-Summer 1960, Pages 21-[24] (illustrated by Peter Coker)

N Coker 1978 Nicholas Coker (introduction), *Works by Peter Coker RA*, Chelmsford & Essex Museum, 1978

N Coker 1979 Nicholas Coker (introduction), *Peter Coker. Painting & Drawings of the Butcher's Shop*, [publisher unidentified], 1979

Collins 1990 Ian Collins, *A Broad Canvas. Art in East Anglia since 1880*, Norwich: Parke Sutton Publishing, 1990

Eustace 1986 Katherine Eustace, *Artists of Promise and Renown*, University of Warwick, 1986

Gore 1973 Frederick Gore (introduction), *Peter Coker*, Sheffield: Mappin Art Gallery, 1973

Halliday 1991 Nigel Vaux Halliday, *More than a Bookshop. Zwemmer's and art in the 20th century*, London: Philip Wilson, 1991

Holst 1957 Dr Neils von Holst, *Moderne Kunst und Sichtbare Welt*, Berlin: Springer-Verlag, 1957

Humphreys 2001 Richard Humphreys, *The Tate Britain Companion to British Art*, London: Tate Publishing, 2001

Huxley 1988 Paul Huxley (editor), *Exhibition Road. Painters at the Royal College of Art*, Oxford: Phaidon-Christie's and the Royal College of Art, 1988

Hyman 2001 James Hyman, *The Battle for Realism. Figurative Art in Britain During the Cold War 1945-1960*, The Paul Mellon Centre for Studies in British Art, New Haven and London: Yale University Press, 2001

Lambirth 1989 Andrew Lambirth (interviewer), 'Peter Coker. A Search for Identification', *The Artist's and Illustrator's Magazine*, September 1989, Pages 14-17

Lambirth 1991 Andrew Lambirth, 'Peter Coker', *Galleries*, Volume IX, No 7, December 1991, Page 18

Loomes 1972 Vivienne Loomes (interviewer), 'A young RA rooted in tradition', *Essex County Standard*, (magazine section), 20 October 1972

Mayor 1991 *Peter Coker RA. Textile Designs 1954-56*, London: The Mayor Gallery, 1991

Morgan 1972 Edward Morgan, *Artists in Camera. Photographs of Artists in East Anglia*, Colchester: The Minories, 1972

National Maritime Museum 1988 *Concise Catalogue of Oil Paintings in the National Maritime Museum*, Woodbridge: Antique Collectors' Club, 1988

National Portrait Gallery 1983 *National Portrait Gallery, Illustrated Report & List of Acquisitions 1982-83*, London: National Portrait Gallery, 1983

National Portrait Gallery 1987 *National Portrait Gallery. Acquisitions 1985-86*, London: National Portrait Gallery, 1987

O'Connor 1977 John O'Connor, *Landscape Drawing*, London: B T Batsford, 1977 (numerous illustrations)

Packer 1989 William Packer (introduction), *Peter Coker. Working Drawings and Sketchbooks 1955 to 1988*, Cambridge: Fitzwilliam Museum, 1989

Parry-Crooke 1979 Charlotte Parry-Crooke (editor), *Contemporary British Artists with Photographs by Wallia*, London: Bergstrom & Boyle, 1979

Spalding 1990 Frances Spalding, *Dictionary of British Art – Volume VI. 20th Century Painters and Sculptors*, Woodbridge: Antique Collectors' Club, 1990

Spalding 1992 Frances Spalding (introduction), *Peter Coker*, Kendal: Abbot Hall Art Gallery/Bristol: Redcliffe Press, 1992

Spargo 1989 Demelza Spargo (editor), *This Land is Our Land*, London: Mall Galleries, 1989

Tate 1979 *The Tate Gallery. An Illustrated Companion*, London: Tate Gallery, 1979 (revised 1984)

Tate 1982 *The Tate Gallery Illustrated Catalogue of Acquisitions 1980-82* London: Tate Gallery, 1984

Tate 1984 *The Tate Gallery Illustrated Catalogue of Acquisitions 1982-84*, London: Tate Gallery, 1986

Tate 1986 *The Tate Gallery Illustrated Catalogue of Acquisitions 1984-86*, London: Tate Gallery, 1988

Tate 1988 Leslie Parris (editor), *The Tate Gallery Illustrated Catalogue of Acquisitions 1986-88*, London: Tate Gallery, 1996

Tate 1991 *Concise Catalogue of the Tate Gallery Collection*, London: Tate Gallery, 1991 (9th edition)

Webber 1972a Michael Webber, 'Profile of Peter Coker', *Arts Review* Volume XXIV, No 4, 26 February 1972

Webber 1972b Michael Webber, 'Peter Coker ARA', *East Anglian Magazine*, April 1972, Number 6, Volume 31, Pages 250-251

Windsor 1998 Alan Windsor (editor), *Handbook of Modern British Painting and Printmaking 1900-1990*, Aldershot: Ashgate Publishing, 1998 (2nd edition)

C. Other texts cited

Shone 1988 Richard Shone, *Rodrigo Moynihan. Paintings and Works on Paper*, London: Thames & Hudson, 1988

Acknowledgements by Peter Coker

I should like to begin by thanking Chris Beetles for proposing the idea of this project in the first instance and for having faith in its result. Little did I know of what was to be expected of me and my wife, endless questions and identification of images of works over fifty years.

I am indebted to the team at the Chris Beetles Gallery who have worked like Trojans on my behalf, especially Fiona, Edwina and David. Fiona on the production and layout of the book, Edwina who has catalogued the seemingly endless number of sketchbooks and David, a perfectionist at all times, for the mammoth task of compiling the chronology, and for the writing of the text.

I thank Richard Humphreys for his appreciation of our son Nicholas, and John Russell Taylor for his response to my work. To the owners, both public and private of the works illustrated, I express my gratitude for their permission to reproduce them and often for having provided the photographs as well.

I wish to thank Mr and Mrs Colin Ellis of Achiltibuie, Mrs Elsbeth Juda and Mrs Elisabeth Collins of Bargemon and Mr William Waterfield of Garavan, Menton who all made their gardens and houses readily available to me from which to work without interruption. Also my medical team Dr and Mrs David Read, Dr Fayez Ayache and Dr Brian Williams and, finally, my framer and friend Nelson Blowers, whose practical help over the years has been invaluable. It is one thing writing posthumously but quite another when the artist is still alive. I am not given to answering questions, believing that the work should speak for itself. I hope that it does and that all those concerned find this result worth waiting for.

Peter Coker
Mistley, 2002

Further Acknowledgements

Photography: Douglas Atfield; Hughie Kelly (Red Apple); Peter W Wedgewood
Production: Penny Dudley and Mark Fairman (Hyway Printing Group); Phil Tite (proof-reading)

For information, thanks to: Kim Baker (Tate Archives); Joanne Barber (New Ashgate Gallery); Guy Baxter (Archive of Art and Design, Victoria and Albert Museum); Frances Carey (British Museum); Hon Secretary, Colchester Art Society (Archive); Sally Dummer (Ipswich Borough Council Museums & Galleries); Essex Records Office(Colchester Branch); Jan Green (Tib Lane Gallery); Julian Hartnoll; Andrew Haslen (The Wildlife Art Gallery); Jane Houldsworth (Flying Colours Gallery); Andrew Hunter (Gainsborough's House, Sudbury); Elsbeth Juda; Lowell Libson; Beth McIntyre (National Museums & Galleries of Wales, Cardiff); Edna Mirecka (Chappel Galleries); Godfrey Pilkington (The Piccadilly Gallery); Juliet Thorp (Royal College of Art); Robert Travers (Piano Nobile Fine Paintings).

Index of names and places mentioned in the text

Bold numbers refer to illustrations; *italicised* numbers refer to other chief references; ***bold italicised*** numbers refer to maps

SCULPTURE IN THE AGE OF DONATELLO

Renaissance Masterpieces
from Florence Cathedral

SCULPTURE IN THE AGE OF DONATELLO

Renaissance Masterpieces from Florence Cathedral

Edited by Timothy Verdon and Daniel M. Zolli
With contributions by Timothy Verdon, Daniel M. Zolli, Amy R. Bloch, Marco Ciatti, Stefano Nicastri, and a new corpus of photographs by Antonio Quattrone

Museum of Biblical Art, New York, in association with D Giles Limited, London

This catalogue accompanies the exhibition *Sculpture in the Age of Donatello: Renaissance Masterpieces from Florence Cathedral* organized by Opera di Santa Maria del Fiore, Florence, and the Museum of Biblical Art, New York, and on display at the Museum of Biblical Art from February 20 to June 14, 2015.

OPERA DI SANTA MARIA DEL FIORE
DAL 1296

MOBIA

The exhibition is under the patronage of His Excellency Matteo Renzi, Prime Minister of the Italian Republic.

Sculpture in the Age of Donatello: Renaissance Masterpieces from Florence Cathedral is made possible by the generous support of Howard and Roberta Ahmanson, the Davis Foundation, Samuel H. Kress Foundation, Robert Lehman Foundation, Gladys Krieble Delmas Foundation, Jean and Eugene Stark, the National Endowment for the Arts, and the Friends of Donatello.

ART WORKS. National Endowment for the Arts arts.gov

Major support for MOBIA's exhibitions and programs is provided by the American Bible Society and by the New York City Department of Cultural Affairs in partnership with the City Council.

AMERICAN BIBLE SOCIETY

NYCULTURE Department of Cultural Affairs City of New York

The exhibition was curated by Mons. Timothy Verdon, Director, Museo dell'Opera del Duomo, and Daniel M. Zolli

Contributions by Timothy Verdon, Daniel M. Zolli, Amy R. Bloch, Marco Ciatti, Rita Filardi, and Stefano Nicastri

MOBIA is grateful to those who contributed to the exhibition by joining the Friends of Donatello: Mr. and Mrs. J. Tomilson Hill, Jon and Barbara Landau, Hester Diamond, Barbara and Hans Jepson, Bowden Family Fund, Furthermore Foundation, Roberta and Richard Huber, David Loch, Salvatore Ferragamo S.p.A., and Frances Beatty and Allen Adler.

First published jointly in 2015 by GILES
An imprint of D Giles Limited
4 Crescent Stables
139 Upper Richmond Road
London SW15 2TN, UK
www.gilesltd.com

and the Museum of Biblical Art
1865 Broadway (at 61st Street)
New York City
NY 10023, USA
Phone: 212-408-1500
Fax: 212-408-1292
info@mobia.org
www.mobia.org

ISBN: 978-1-907804-56-4

For D Giles Limited
Copy-edited and proofread by Sarah Kane
Designed by Alfonso Iacurci and Helen McFarland
Produced by GILES, an imprint of D Giles Limited, London
Printed and bound in China

All measurements are in centimeters and inches; height precedes width.

Library of Congress Cataloging-in-Publication Data
Sculpture in the age of Donatello: Renaissance masterpieces from Florence Cathedral / edited by Timothy Verdon and Daniel M. Zolli ; with contributions by Timothy Verdon, Daniel M. Zolli, Amy R. Bloch, Marco Ciatti, Stefano Nicastri.
pages cm
Includes bibliographical references and index.
"This catalog accompanies the exhibition Sculpture in the Age of Donatello: Renaissance Masterpieces from Florence Cathedral on display at the Museum of Biblical Art from February 20th-June 14th, 2015."
ISBN 978-1-907804-56-4 (hardback)
1. Sculpture, Renaissance–Italy–Florence–Exhibitions. 2. Sculpture, Italian–Italy–Florence–Exhibitions. 3. Santa Maria del Fiore (Cathedral : Florence, Italy)–Exhibitions. 4. Donatello, 1386?-1466–Exhibitions. 5. Donatello, 1386?-1466–Friends and associates–Exhibitions. I. Verdon, Timothy, editor. II. Zolli, Daniel M., editor. III. Museum of Biblical Art. IV. Opera di S. Maria del Fiore (Florence, Italy). Museo.
NB621.F6S38 2015
730.945'5110747471–dc23
2014024853

Front cover:
Donatello, *St. John the Evangelist*, cat. 10

Back cover:
Nanni di Banco, *St. Luke the Evangelist*, cat. 9

Front cover (jacket):
Donatello, *St. John the Evangelist* (detail), cat. 10

Back cover (jacket):
Nanni di Banco or Donatello, *Hercules* (detail), cat. 4

Frontispiece:
Attributed to Giovanni d'Ambrogio, *Archangel Gabriel of the Annunciation* (detail), cat. 1

Opposite:
Attributed to Giovanni d'Ambrogio, *Virgin Mary of the Annunciation* (detail), cat. 2

Page 6: Attributed to Nanni di Banco, *Profetino* (detail), cat. 6

CONTENTS

The Museum of Biblical Art is grateful to the individuals and organizations whose generosity has made *Sculpture in the Age of Donatello* possible.

Sponsors

Howard and Roberta Ahmanson
Davis Foundation
Samuel H. Kress Foundation
Jean and Eugene Stark
Robert Lehman Foundation
Gladys Krieble Delmas Foundation
National Endowment for the Arts

Friends of Donatello

Mr. and Mrs. J. Tomilson Hill
Jon and Barbara Landau
Hester Diamond
Barbara and Hans Jepson
Bowden Family Fund
Furthermore Foundation
Roberta and Richard Huber
David Loch
Salvatore Ferragamo S.p.A.
Frances Beatty and Allen Adler

Foreword

Opera di Santa Maria del Fiore

The exhibition hosted by the Museum of Biblical Art—*Sculpture in the Age of Donatello: Renaissance Masterpieces from Florence Cathedral*—is a truly exceptional endeavor, made possible only because Florence Cathedral's Museo dell'Opera del Duomo, where the works in the show are normally to be seen, is closed for an extended period to allow for the expansion and renovation of the museum's galleries. The new, larger museum, scheduled for completion in fall 2015, is designed to show the works to best advantage, recreating the atmosphere and context of their intended sites, and the specific places for which the works were conceived and produced by the great masters of the Florentine Renaissance.

The Opera's commitment to emphasizing the historical and religious meaning of the masterpieces in its museum explains our choice of MOBIA as partner for the exhibition in New York, which we hope will call attention to an epoch and a city—Florence—that, in a short span of time, deeply touched all of Western culture. We also hope that the New York exhibition will give a sense of the extraordinary experience the new Museo dell'Opera will offer. Thus the present exhibition is also an ambassador, as it were, sent not to rouse curiosity or create sensation but to prompt a discovery—an experience of religious feeling through art—and to deepen our understanding of a moment in Western history to which we are all indebted, a moment that will be fully illuminated in our new museum in Florence.

Allow me to add that the majority of works exhibited at MOBIA are traveling outside Italy for the very first time, and it is unlikely they will ever repeat the journey, underscoring the unique quality of this endeavor. Credit for realizing this singular opportunity is due to MOBIA and former Board Chair Roberta Green Ahmanson, who responded with enthusiasm to our willingness to lend the works. Our thanks also go to MOBIA's director, Richard P. Townsend, who has carried out her vision with competence and passion.

Finally, on behalf of the Opera, I wish to thank Monsignor Timothy Verdon, the director of our museum and the present exhibition's principal curator. It is a source of great satisfaction to me that through this project we can bring to the attention of that global capital of finance and culture, New York City—which is, in a sense, a new Florence—and share with its many millions of residents and visitors an unparalleled display of the treasures managed by our foundation since 1296, and which we hold in trust for the benefit of humanity.

Franco Lucchesi
President
Opera di Santa Maria del Fiore

Foreword
Museum of Biblical Art

Sculpture in the Age of Donatello: Renaissance Masterpieces from Florence Cathedral represents a renaissance—not only the historical period in Florence around 1400 which indelibly shaped Western civilization, but also for its two organizing institutions, the Museum of Biblical Art in New York on the occasion of its tenth anniversary and the Opera di Santa Maria del Fiore with its newly expanded and renovated museum in Florence. The Museo dell'Opera del Duomo reopens later this year and will certainly become an essential stop on any visitor's Italian sojourn.

The present exhibition of monumental Florentine Renaissance sculpture is, quite simply, without precedent in the United States or, indeed, in the Western Hemisphere. The works that comprise our highly focused exhibition were produced to decorate Florence's Duomo (or cathedral) in the first fifty years of the fifteenth century. Never before in this country has quite such a project been attempted, despite the important exhibitions that preceded it in Detroit and Ft. Worth in 1985–86, New York's Metropolitan Museum of Art in 1993, and in Atlanta, Chicago, and the Metropolitan Museum of Art in 2007–8. Nine sculptures alone by Donatello—the greatest Italian sculptor before Michelangelo—guarantee the significance and beauty of the present endeavor. In fact, most of the sculpture included herein has never before left Italy, representing a once-in-a-lifetime opportunity for New Yorkers and visitors to our city to experience and better understand the early Florentine Renaissance.

The spirit of autonomy and liberty that informed early Renaissance Florence was already characteristic of the civic foundation—the Opera di Santa Maria del Fiore or Opera del Duomo (the cathedral's board of works)—founded in 1296 and still functioning today. The Opera continues to be responsible for projects at the cathedral, and in it the spirit and virtues of the Florentine Renaissance live on. It has therefore been a great privilege to work with the Opera on this tremendous undertaking and we thank its President, Franco Lucchesi, its Secretary General Enrico Viviano, and its board of trustees for placing their confidence in us. It has been my distinct pleasure and privilege to work with Monsignor Timothy Verdon, the Museo dell'Opera's director and our exhibition's principal curator and catalogue editor; Registrar Rita Filardi and the Opera's close collaborator Stefano Nicastri. Likewise, I thank both Daniel Zolli, the exhibition's co-curator and catalogue co-editor, and Professor Amy Bloch for their assistance and new perspectives on Donatello's and Ghiberti's oeuvres as well as Dr. Marco Ciatti, Superintendent of the Opificio delle Pietre Dure. We are deeply honored that the exhibition enjoys the high patronage of His Excellency Prime Minister Matteo Renzi and that His Eminence Cardinal Giuseppe Betori, Archbishop of Florence, has lent his support to the project.

An undertaking such as this requires great vision and resources, and we would especially like to recognize former Board Chair Roberta Green Ahmanson and her husband Howard for generously contributing both to *Sculpture in the Age of Donatello*. We are also grateful to the Samuel H. Kress Foundation, the Davis Foundation, Eugene and Jean Stark, the Robert Lehman Foundation, the Gladys Krieble Delmas Foundation, the National Endowment for the Arts, and to the Friends of Donatello.

I am proud of MOBIA's staff in making this exhibition and catalogue a reality, especially the efforts of Adrianne Rubin, Taylor Catalana, Daniel Beaudoin, Nathaniel Prottas, Alisa Lycheva, Bruno Nouril, and Dean Ebben. I salute Wendy Evans Joseph and Chris Cooper of Cooper Joseph Studio for the evocative architectural installation and D Giles, London, for producing this beautiful publication.

Richard P. Townsend
Director
Museum of Biblical Art

Cat. 5, detail

FLORENCE CATHEDRAL, RENAISSANCE SCULPTURE, SACRED SCRIPTURE

Timothy Verdon

This exhibition is about a building, the Duomo, or cathedral, of Florence, begun in 1296 and nearing completion in the early fifteenth century. It is also, and more specifically, about the art chosen to communicate that building's meaning: sculpture as it developed in the period known as the "Early Renaissance." Finally, it is about the idea of human dignity that the cathedral and its sculpture took from Judeo-Christian scripture, which in fact shaped the conceptual background of the building and the iconography of its carved and painted decoration.

Fig. 1
Piazza del Duomo, Florence, looking east, with the baptistery of San Giovanni, the cathedral or duomo of Santa Maria del Fiore surmounted by Brunelleschi's dome, and Giotto's bell tower

The Cathedral Project

For more than half a millennium, the main creative project of Florence, a city famous for art, was the complex of large buildings dominated by the cathedral (fig. 1).[1] From the reconstruction of the baptistery, begun in 1059, to the completion of the cathedral, whose decoration was still underway in the 1580s, work went forward almost without interruption, impressing the project on the citizens' imagination, making it a part of their collective identity. This massive commitment of time, energy, and resources paid off, and, as early as 1436, when the cathedral's structure was finally complete, Florence could boast the biggest covered space in the pre-modern world, together with one of the boldest engineering undertakings known to history: the titanic dome designed by Filippo Brunelleschi (1377–1446). What is more, the "cathedral project" generated masterpieces in such astounding quantity—works in marble, bronze, precious metals, stained glass, ceramic, painting, and textiles—that Florentines knew they had fathered a Golden Age, a modern version of what Athens had achieved in the time of Pericles and Rome in that of Augustus: the phenomenon known as the *Rinascita*, the Rebirth, the Renaissance.

Why did this wealthy city and its culturally advanced inhabitants invest so heavily and for so long in a single project? Obviously there were *material* reasons such as civic pride, regional prestige, the political ambitions of successive city governments, rivalry among the guilds commissioning artworks, and competition among the artists called to make them. But the dominant motivation was *spiritual*: the cathedral and baptistery are, after all, places of worship, and the bells in Giotto's campanile even today call people to prayer. The buildings, indeed, express the inner life of those who commissioned and paid for them—of women and men who took seriously St. Paul's words to a faith-community of the first century: "You are God's building ... you are a temple of God with the Spirit of God living in you ... God's temple is holy, and you are that temple" (1 Corinthians 3:9b,16–17). The cathedral and its related structures gave visual form, that is, to a sense of "election" and "vocation" that Florentines felt strongly.[2]

Historical Coefficients

This religious self-awareness coexisted with an equally strong historical identity. Florence is an ancient city, founded in the Roman era some fifty years before the birth of Christ, and this past has always been legible in the rational layout of the oldest part of town and in surviving relics of antiquity such as sarcophagi and marble columns. Of particular importance was the fact that *Florentia* had been born when Rome was still a republic: Florentines saw themselves as heirs of an ancient freedom, and in the fourteenth and fifteenth centuries, when they called their city-state the "Florentine Republic," among its political emblems was a shield displaying the Latin word *Libertas*, "Liberty."[3]

A turning point in the history of the republic had come in 1289, when a Tuscan army led by Florence defeated its opponents in the hills to the east of the city, at Campaldino, some sixty kilometers distant. The "opponents" were also Tuscan, and the battle was the final act of an ideological struggle that had dragged on for more than a century, between the two principal factions in the region, Guelphs and Ghibellines. "Guelphs" were the new-rich merchants of the Tuscan city-states, desirous of political autonomy; Ghibellines were the landed aristocrats who wanted the cities to remain satellites of the Holy Roman Empire with its Germanic ruler, from whom they had received titles and power.

The Tuscan Guelphs, Dante Alighieri among them, were victorious at Campaldino, thus confirming the leadership of Florence in central Italy. And that is why the cathedral was begun: the city that had guided its neighbors to victory, guaranteeing regional *libertas*, freedom, wanted a visible sign of its new role, and seven years after the epochal victory rejected a plan to enlarge and improve its old main church for the much more ambitious idea of an entirely new one, which Florence hoped would be "the finest and most honorable place of worship anywhere in Tuscany," as a document of 1300 would state: "... venustius et honorabilius templum alioquo alio quod sit in partibus Tusciae".[4] The new cathedral, called "duomo" from the Latin word *domus*, "house," was born, that is, in public recognition of the divine favor that had allowed Florence to defeat its enemies and to surpass other cities in the size and magnificence of its monuments. For when the document of 1300 says that Florentines hoped to have the "finest and most honorable place of worship anywhere in Tuscany," it is in fact alluding to the cathedrals of rival city-states such as Pisa and Siena, then already built or nearing completion, which Florentines wanted to eclipse with their new Duomo, their "house" made for God and for the city they believed He loved. The century and a half from the beginning of the cathedral's construction to its effective completion

Fig. 2
The baptistery of San Giovanni, looking west

would see the gradual confirmation of the city's pre-eminence in Tuscany which Florentines considered their God-given calling.

Size, Growth, Wealth

The new Duomo was also meant to signal the maturity of several processes then rapidly transforming Florence and other European cities. One of these was the wave of church building that had begun after the year 1000, leading communities to substitute older places of worship with more modern ones, usually on a much larger scale. Florence was no exception, and from 1059 through the 1280s had replaced its small, early Christian baptistery with the grandiose, sumptuously decorated structure we see today (fig. 2).[5] As the baptistery neared completion in the mid- and later 1200s, the city built immense churches for then new religious orders like the Dominicans and Franciscans in developing areas on the perimeter of the Roman center. The vast size of these rising churches, like that of the new cathedrals in neighboring Tuscan cities, established a "modern" standard of scale which the Duomo would seek to surpass, and an early fourteenth-century writer, Giovanni Villani, commenting on the reasons for choosing to build the new Florence Cathedral, in fact notes that the old one "was small and very crude in form, in comparison with the city Florence was becoming."[6]

Florence then was rapidly becoming one of Europe's major cities.[7] The population, perhaps 30,000 to 40,000 people when the reconstruction of the baptistery began in 1059, had swollen to more than 100,000 by the time the new cathedral got underway in 1296. This demographic growth had obliged the city to expand its system of defensive walls, first in 1173–75, and then, far more ambitiously, in 1284–1333; these more comprehensive defenses enclosed the churches of the new religious orders, originally outside the walls, and the churches themselves were enlarged to suit the needs of the growing population: beginning in 1279 the Dominican church, Santa Maria Novella, acquired a nave that trebled its size, and from 1294 onwards the Franciscan church, Santa Croce, was rebuilt on a scale larger than that of any existing structure in Tuscany. The new Duomo, whose cornerstone was laid barely two years after that of Santa Croce, would be the definitive expression of this process, the physical and symbolic declaration of all that Florence had achieved. Almost all the modifications introduced during the 140-year long construction process had the objective of increasing the building's length and height, and make it clear that enthusiasm did not cool as the decades passed.

All this required an uninterrupted flow of money, and the cathedral, together with the baptistery and bell tower (campanile), in fact proclaimed that the city which had built them was very rich. The wealth derived from industry and commerce: Florence was one of

Fig. 3
Andrea Pisano
The Art of Weaving,
1337–42
Marble,
83 x 69 cm
(32⅝ x 27⅛ in.)
Museo dell'Opera del Duomo, Florence

the capitals of the medieval "industrial revolution," producing high-quality wool cloth which it then sold throughout Europe; the above-mentioned demographic explosion was in fact due to immigration, as thousands left the surrounding countryside to man the city's factories. Even women worked, not in the factories but at home, weaving on rented looms, and it is significant that a carved relief illustrating the art of weaving—one of a series made for the bell tower showing the arts, sciences, professions, and crafts of fourteenth-century Florence—in fact depicts a woman whose work is directed by another woman (fig. 3).

So important was this industry in the economic life of Florence that the city entrusted the cathedral project's financial management to the Arte della Lana or wool guild, whose emblem became that of the foundation created to superintend the work in progress, the Opera del Duomo or cathedral board of works. This typically Florentine practice, the assignment of financial oversight of churches to one or another of the guilds, reflected the city's mercantile spirit, for it was taken for granted that the guilds would compete in lavishly embellishing these buildings which bore their coats of arms. And it made an even more important statement than wealth itself, proclaiming that Florentines knew how to invest resources and were willing to use private money for public goals. The city's second major "industry" in fact was international banking.

The Choice of Sculpture

From the very beginning, Florence chose the most costly form of art available, sculpture, to adorn the cathedral and then the baptistery and bell tower.[8] This was by no means an obvious choice or a common one: most medieval Italian churches had no exterior sculpture, and in the thirteenth century even the new Florence Baptistery was entirely without statuary. The great exception was Siena, which in the 1280s commissioned Giovanni Pisano to create a richly carved façade for its cathedral, thus introducing Italy to what had been common practice in France and elsewhere in northern Europe for more than a hundred years.[9] It was the Sienese example that spurred Florence to want its new Duomo lavishly adorned with figural sculpture, and probably played a part as well in the choice of Arnolfo di Cambio as architect: Arnolfo was a famous sculptor, and in his youth had worked alongside Giovanni Pisano in the shop of Giovanni's father, Nicola Pisano. Significantly, among the first things Arnolfo did when he took charge of the Duomo project was to carve statues and reliefs that were mounted on the façade before this reached half its intended height (fig. 4)![10]

From the façade, described in a contemporary document as a "magnificent beginning" awakening great hopes,[11] the passion for sculpture spread to the facing baptistery,

where between 1310 and 1320 an artist who had worked in Siena, Tino di Camaino, was called to create groups of life-size marble figures over the building's three portals.[12] The motivation was probably more than aesthetic: the guild responsible for the baptistery, the Arte di Calimala or cloth-merchants' corporation, must have been alarmed to see the "magnificent beginning" across the piazza financed by the Arte della Lana, a rival guild. The decision to enrich the hitherto unadorned baptistery exterior with sculpture was thus a response, at barely forty meters distance, to the statues and reliefs carved by Arnolfo for the rising Duomo façade.

The Arte di Calimala made the contest more interesting by deciding, in 1322, to create the first of what would ultimately be three monumental bronze doors for the baptistery, actually commissioning the work in 1330. Since everyone knew that, after gold and silver, bronze was the most expensive material in which to create sculpture, it is clear that the Calimala merchants were making a point: namely that, despite the smaller size of the baptistery, the resources they were willing to invest in it equaled what the Arte della Lana was spending for the Duomo. There was also the "added value" of modernity, for the new door was conceived in a contemporary style far from that of Arnolfo's classical statues for the Duomo façade: each of its twenty-eight reliefs is in fact framed by a Gothic quatrefoil, and the scenes recounting the life of St. John the Baptist are inspired—in some cases perhaps

Fig. 4
Arnolfo di Cambio
Pope Boniface VIII,
ca. 1296–1310
Marble
280 × 81 × 95 cm
(110¼ × 31⅞ × 37⅜ in.)
Museo dell Opera
del Duomo Florence

Fig. 5
Andrea Pisano
South Doors of Florence
Baptistery, 1330–36:
panel with the *Beheading of St. John the Baptist*
Bronze, 52 × 45 cm
(20½ × 17¾ in.)
Baptistery of San Giovanni,
Florence

personally designed—by the period's avant-garde painter, Giotto (fig. 5). Author of the bronze doors was Andrea da Pontedera, usually called Andrea Pisano.[13]

The answer from across the piazza was not long in coming, and, even as the Calimala doors were being fashioned, beside its unfinished Duomo façade the wool guild in 1334 began a titanic bell tower meant to host sixteen life-size statues and fifty-six figured reliefs.[14] The artists called to build and carve were those just mentioned: Giotto as architect, Andrea Pisano as sculptor and, after Giotto's death in 1337, as overall director of the project. Before Andrea Pisano left Florence in 1343, eight of the statues and forty-nine of the reliefs had been carved;[15] the tower itself was finished in 1359 by a third architect, Francesco Talenti, to whom responsibility for the Duomo project, interrupted during the twenty-five years needed to build the tower, was entrusted. Work resumed on the façade, with the addition of numerous new statues, and the rising cathedral's side doors too were enriched with sculpture. The last of these to be done, the north-east door later known as the Porta della Mandorla, was begun in 1391.[16] And that in fact is where our exhibition opens, with six pieces of sculpture carved for the Porta della Mandorla.

Fig. 6
Andrea Pisano
The Art of Sculpture,
1336–43
Marble,
83 × 69 cm
(32⅝ × 27⅛ in.)
Museo dell'Opera
del Duomo, Florence

The Meaning of Sculpture

Before turning to specific works, however, a further clarification is in order regarding what sculpture signified—what it *meant*—in the context of the Duomo project (fig. 6). For, beyond its obvious economic implications and the cultural message it conveyed in a city then without public statuary, the sculpture made for the cathedral and baptistery exteriors also resounded with biblical significance, and indeed it was this scriptural significance that saved it from being mere decoration. Particularly the stone sculpture would have recalled the exhortation: "Listen to me, you who are in search of justice, you who seek the Lord; look to the rock from whom you are cut, and to the quarry from which you are extracted. Look to Abraham, your father, and to Sara, who bore you…" (Isaiah 51:1–2a). That is, the sculpture would have been read in relation to the community's own identity as "cut" from a rock-like prototype and "extracted" like quarried stone from a faith tradition going back to Abraham, who, at God's bidding, had left Chaldea in search of a promised land.

Christian Scripture had developed this Old Testament figure in architectural terms, speaking of Christ as a "living stone, rejected by men but chosen and precious to God" (1 Peter 2:4)—a characterization,

Fig. 7
After Bernardo Poccetti
The Medieval Façade of Santa Maria del Fiore, before 1536–37
Pen and ink on paper, 72.3 × 58.2 cm (28½ × 22⅞ in.)
Archivio dell'Opera del Duomo, Florence

this, based on other words of Isaiah: "Behold, I lay in Zion a cornerstone, chosen, precious, and all who believe in it will not be disappointed" (1 Peter 2:6–7: cf. Isaiah 28:16; 8:14ff). The same text asserts that those who draw near to this cornerstone will, in turn, "like living stones," themselves be built into "a spiritual edifice," the Church (1 Peter 2:5). The whole scriptural image thus regards an edifice, the Church, made from human beings who are "like living stones" because they have adhered to Christ, himself a "living stone." In this poetic framework, it is clear that marble statues of saints and prophets become, again, images of the community; distributed across the Duomo façade, these "living stones" seemed in effect structural elements, as if the new cathedral incorporated the heroic personages represented on its front (fig. 7). A well-known early medieval hymn used for the dedication of churches—*Urbs Jerusalem beata*—exploits this imagery, describing a heavenly city built of living stones shaped by resounding blows that fit them in place.[17] The "blows" are the sufferings endured by the saints.

Another context of meaning we should mention is the new interest in the human body that characterized Italian art of the thirteenth century, due in part to the spirituality of St. Francis of Assisi and his followers.[18] At La Verna in 1224 Francis's body was said to have received the wounds of Christ's Passion—the stigmata—and that fact, which deeply impressed his contemporaries, called attention to the body as a vehicle of Christian spiritual experience, promoting its rediscovery as a subject for church art. More eloquently than mosaic or painting, sculpture spoke of the first Christian mystery, that of God's Word made flesh in Christ, and artists responded to Francis's vision of a *Dio umanato*, a God-made-human, with new attention to the body. In their search for models, some turned to classical statuary, and in general monumental sculpture at this time became an important option in church ornament, as the cathedral façades in Siena and Florence make clear. "Sculpture" indeed meant *figural sculpture*, with the body as its main theme—what Ghiberti and others would, in the early fifteenth century, call *statua virile*, fully human statuary.[19]

Fig. 8
The Porta della Mandorla on the north side of the cathedral of Santa Maria del Fiore

The Porta della Mandorla

The body theme emerges with force in the earliest works in the exhibition, six pieces of marble sculpture for the last of the Duomo doors, the northeast entry known as the Porta della Mandorla (fig. 8). Begun in 1391, this complex assemblage was realized in three phases, the first of which, completed by 1397, features handsome late Gothic decorative carving by masters such as Giovanni Tedesco and Giovanni d'Ambrogio in the door's left and right jambs. An alternative orientation is apparent in the surprisingly classical figure in the left reveal—an ancient Hercules enlisted to act the part of the Christian virtue Fortitude (fig. 9)—in which figure the artist's interest in the male nude has led him to imitate a Roman prototype. Today it is thought that the sculptor may be the same Giovanni d'Ambrogio who in other works appears far more traditional.[20]

The second phase of decoration, involving the arch springing from the jambs of the Porta della Mandorla, continues the style of the first phase but after an interruption of seven years. The first work included here dates from 1404–9 (cat. 4): it is a component of the right archivolt, again depicting Hercules but clearly not by the same master who did the one lower down. Archival documents associate two artists with the archivolt, Niccolò Lamberti, who had been among the finalists for the bronze doors for the baptistery

LEFT
Fig. 9
Attributed to Giovanni d'Ambrogio
Hercules-Fortitude,
ca. 1391–97
Marble
Porta della Mandorla, cathedral of Santa Maria del Fiore, Florence

RIGHT
Cat. 4, detail

finally commissioned from Lorenzo Ghiberti in 1402, and the less distinguished Antonio di Banco, who was assisted however by his son Nanni, destined to emerge a few years later as one of the creators of the new sculpture style. An attractive hypothesis is thus that this small Hercules may be a youthful work by Nanni di Banco, carved in homage to the lower Hercules figure, which seems to be its source.[21] This hypothesis invites us to imagine a "collective style" developed among the different artists employed on the door, and is particularly interesting since in 1414 the third and final phase of decoration of the Porta della Mandorla—the monumental relief of Mary lifted to heaven by angels—would be entrusted to Nanni di Banco, who may have been expected, among other things, to guarantee continuity with what had been realized in earlier stages.

Our second work, also made in the 1404–9 phase of the Porta della Mandorla's evolution, is the keystone of the arch, with a half-figure of Christ as *Vir Dolorum*, "Man of Sorrows" (cat. 3). The iconographic sense is drawn from the New Testament text cited above, the first letter of St. Peter, which—after asserting that believers are living stones, and quoting: "Behold, I lay in Zion a cornerstone, chosen, precious, and all who believe in it will not be disappointed"—adds a verse from Psalm 118 which clarifies that "the stone that the builders rejected has become the corner stone..." (1 Peter 2:6–7; cf. Isaiah 28:16; 8:14f. and

LEFT
Cat. 3, detail

RIGHT
Fig. 10
Donatello
Crucifix, ca. 1408–12
Wood with polychromy
168 × 173 cm
(66⅛ × 68⅛ in.)
Santa Croce, Florence

LEFT
Cat. 5

RIGHT
Cat. 6

Psalm 118:22). In this context, "rejection" means the refusal of the religious authorities of Christ's time to acknowledge him, and thus alludes to his passion and death, which, the text argues, are now the cornerstone of a new temple. This suffering Christ on the keystone of the arch is thus a deeply meaningful image, as the sculptor who carved it seems to have understood, emphasizing the figure's pathos in the inclination of Christ's head, in the facial expression, in the long-fingered, half-open hands.

Once attributed to Nanni di Banco, today this Christ is generally accepted as an early work by Donatello, whose name appears in the Porta della Mandorla payment records in these years.[22] It has, indeed, striking analogies with that master's painted wood crucifix in the Florentine church of Santa Croce—particularly in the soft but sure modeling of the musculature (fig. 10). Here there is no sense of an inherited style, and the antiquarian nostalgia of the little Hercules gives way to a moving naturalism supported by accurate anatomical portrayal. The juxtaposition in the same decorative project of classical heroes like Hercules and this sensitive, suffering Christ is surprising, yet the improbable admixture was typical of early fifteenth-century Florence, reflecting a new body of artistic and cultural information that supplemented without supplanting more traditional styles and subjects; indeed the contemporaneous representation of Hercules and Christ opened new perspectives for each, "humanizing" the Greek hero, "classicizing" the Jewish teacher.

A clear instance of the stylistic variety of the Porta della Mandorla sculptors is furnished by two statues of youthful personages from the door's right and left pinnacles. In the right-side statue (cat. 6), known as the *Profetino* ("Small Prophet") because of the scroll the figure holds, a certain autonomy in the stance and the tight, full-packed volumes of the face have led many to invoke the name of Nanni di Banco and date the work to the second phase of elaboration of the door in 1404–9; the figure indeed has a conceptual affinity with a large statue of the prophet Isaiah done by Nanni in 1408, now inside the cathedral (fig. 19). The little prophet's head, with its air of bright purposefulness, is moreover similar to the heads of Nanni's angels in the *Assumption of Mary* relief of the door's third phase, datable from 1414–22, and in fact some have ascribed our statuette to that period, imagining the assistance of a younger member of Nanni's shop, perhaps Luca della Robbia. This thorny question remains open, and gives a glimpse of the complex attribution and dating problems surrounding the Porta della Mandorla, the inaugural monument of Renaissance sculpture.[23]

The second statue—the one from the left-hand pinnacle—is also fraught with problems. Unlike its neighbor, it seems not to have been born as a prophet, since it has no scroll, the normal attribute of prophet figures (cat. 5). Apparently moving forward, with a dreamy look on its face and crowned with a garland of laurel, it has been thought to be the angel from an Annunciation group, used here simply to fill a gap in the decoration—an unflattering but not unrealistic view of how big projects sometimes got completed on the Duomo work site.

The real interest of this statue arises from its attribution to Donatello, today generally accepted.[24] The work, perhaps datable around 1406–9, has indeed a remarkable resemblance to this master's first documented freestanding statue, a *David* carved in 1408–9 as a pendant to a statue by Nanni di Banco—the Isaiah now in the Duomo—both works intended for buttresses on the cathedral's north transept (see figs. 19 and 20). Indeed Donatello's *David*, today in the Museo del Bargello in Florence, has the same dreamy, youthful visage and sway-backed pose as our Porta della Mandorla figure, which thus may represent the artist's first effort ever to carve a statue. Realized in the collective framework of the ongoing Porta della Mandorla project, it is also the first instance of a creative face-off between Donatello and Nanni destined to be repeated in the years to come—a side-by-side pairing of their works in which each must distinguish himself from the other—ending only with Nanni's premature death in 1421.

Fig. 11
Lorenzo Ghiberti
North Doors of Florence Baptistery, 1403–24: panel with the *Adoration of the Magi* (detail),
Bronze with gilding, full panel 52 × 45 cm (20½ × 17¾ in.)
Museo dell'Opera del Duomo, Florence

Ghiberti, the International Gothic, the Antique

If we take the Porta della Mandorla figure as Donatello's first marble statue, we may be puzzled at the lack of definition of the body, all but lost beneath the abundant drapery, in striking contrast to Nanni's stand-up *Profetino*. This interest in the cadenced fall of pliant cloth reflects Donatello's beginnings in the shop of the great Florentine sculptor at the dawn of the fifteenth century, Lorenzo Ghiberti, who in 1402 had won the public competition for a second set of monumental bronze doors for the baptistery and was already an independent master when young Donatello and Nanni were still part of the Porta della Mandorla "collective."[25] It is Ghiberti's fluid drapery style that Donatello adapts, as a comparison of his statue with an early relief for Ghiberti's door, the *Adoration of the Magi*, makes clear; the youthful king in the *Adoration*, at the viewer's left (fig. 11), has the same tubular, light-catching folds in his cloak that Donatello gives to his small statue, whose oneiric beauty too seems close to this figure. The new baptistery doors executed by Ghiberti from 1403 to 1424, in fact made a deep impression on contemporaries, as three Abruzzese reliefs of the 1440s present in the exhibition suggest; even in their ruined condition, these carvings obviously reproduce compositions devised by Ghiberti for his doors.

Ghiberti's success was in part due to an ability to bend the decorative elegance of then popular International Gothic art to the serious narrative requirements of his door's theme, the life of Christ, occasionally introducing the classical allusions that had begun to appeal to educated viewers. In all those respects it is interesting to compare his *Annunciation* relief for the baptistery door with a marble *Annunciation* group made for the tympanum above

Fig. 12
Lorenzo Ghiberti
North Doors of Florence Baptistery, 1403–24: panel with the *Annunciation*
Gilded bronze, 52 × 45 cm (20½ × 17¾ in.)
Museo dell'Opera del Duomo, Florence

the Porta della Mandorla (fig. 12; cats. 1 and 2). The Ghiberti relief was modeled in the years corresponding to the Porta della Mandorla's second stage of decoration; the marble statuary group has sometimes been assigned to the same years, sometimes to the earlier phase, 1391–97; hypotheses of authorship include attributions to Nanni di Banco and—more widely accepted today—to Giovanni d'Ambrogio.[26]

The marble statues have a rhythmic grace not unlike that which Ghiberti gives his paired figures, and their luxuriant robes evince similar pleasure in the depiction of drapery, albeit in a style more clearly indebted to antiquity than Ghiberti's is. Antiquarian above all are the two heads: the wingless angel's is in fact Hellenistic, through a Byzantine lens, while the Virgin Mary's is Roman, based (astonishingly) on a portrait type used for adolescent males. This pair of statues too could have influenced young Donatello's Porta della Mandorla statue; in any case the Annunciation group was part of his visual culture, a stimulus—or perhaps foil—for his emerging personal style.

The Seated Evangelists

A distinctive personal style emerges with force in Donatello's first monumental work, a seated figure of St. John the Evangelist commissioned by the Opera del Duomo in mid-December 1408 for a position of great visibility, one of four niches to the right and left of the main door of the Duomo (cat. 10).[27] Similar statues were to fill the other three niches as well, and two other masters also received commissions, the more mature Niccolò Lamberti and Donatello's young contemporary Nanni di Banco, thus reconstituting part of the Porta della Mandorla team. There was a particular incentive to work well, for the contract stipulated that the fourth Evangelist figure would be assigned to the member of this group whose statue turned out best: thus what *may* have been competition between Donatello and Nanni at the Porta della Mandorla now definitely was. In the event, in May 1410 the Opera del Duomo, impatient with the progress of the three original contestants, gave the commission for the remaining Evangelist to an outsider, Bernardo Ciuffagni; but in the first seventeen months of work Donatello, Nanni and Lamberti must have seen themselves as vying for individual recognition. Lamberti was a known quantity, and in fact would produce a rather conventional figure, as would Ciuffagni, also an older man; the real contest was between the young artists, Donatello and Nanni di Banco.

The new statues were not simply "additions" to the ongoing decoration of the Duomo front. Their scale—taller than most of the earlier figures despite the fact that the Evangelists are *seated*—and their prominent position, in semi-circular niches cut a bare meter above eye-level, suggest their importance in what must have been an early fifteenth-century attempt to modernize the façade begun by Arnolfo di Cambio in far off 1296 (fig. 13).[28] They would in fact be among the last sculptures commissioned for the façade, which remained unfinished until finally dismantled in the 1580s, and their task was to imbue the seemingly endless Duomo project with a new sense of urgency.

Cats. 1 and 2

OVERLEAF
Cat. 9 (left)
Cat. 10 (right)

One of the Evangelists in the exhibition is Donatello's *St. John*, carved between 1408 and 1415; he is shown not as the young "beloved disciple" described in John's own Gospel, but with the long beard that artists attribute to him in old age, when, according to church tradition, he wrote the Book of Revelation; the volume on which his left hand rests alludes to one or other of these texts, or perhaps to his collected writings, which include three letters. But the solemnity of Donatello's figure, and his grave yet visionary gaze, make it clear that the artist meant to depict the courage of this old man who, exiled for his faith, heard and saw mysterious truths which he communicated in writing to his persecuted fellow-Christians. To those who entered the cathedral this statue seemed to say:

> I, John, your brother and companion in tribulation, in the Kingdom and in the perseverance in Jesus, was on the island called Patmos due to the word of God and my bearing witness to Jesus. On the Lord's day I was lifted up by the Spirit and heard, behind me, a voice from the West, like a trumpet, which said: "That which you see, write it in a book and send it to the seven Churches: at Ephesus, Smirne, Pergamon, Theatira, Sardis, Philadelphia and Laodicea" (Revelation 1:9–11).

"On the Lord's day": John's inspired visions occurred on Sunday, and this statue, placed at the right of those entering the cathedral through the main door, reminded Sunday worshippers that the liturgical functions in which they would take part were "mysteries" that allowed them to spiritually contemplate, "amidst the candlesticks" of the altar (Revelation 1:13), the Christ who had told John: "Fear not, I am the First and the Last, the Living One. I was dead, but now I live forever and possess the keys of death and of the underworld" (Revelation 1:17–18). The Duomo was already in full use by 1380, with Mass said at a temporary altar positioned at the east end of the nave, against a brick wall that separated the completed western section from the incomplete eastern transept and apse area. Thus Donatello's Evangelist, positioned on the façade in October 1415, would have interacted with worshippers; in fact, he seems to be turning slowly to his right, as if aware of those

entering the cathedral; a miniature showing Pope Eugenius IV's arrival at the portal, on the occasion of the cathedral's consecration in 1436, illustrates the effect (fig. 13).

This slow movement is a sign of the new age which soon would be called the "renascence" or rebirth. Unlike Arnolfo's early fourteenth-century *Pope Boniface VIII*, the only prior seated figure on the façade (see fig. 4), Donatello's statue gives the impression of integral movement, with the knees veering toward the viewer's right while the torso and head gradually move in the opposite direction—precisely as if, originally poised toward the right, St. John had become aware of our presence and was beginning to turn. The simultaneity of dawning psychological awareness and incipient physical response implies a grasp of the real-life coordination of mind and body that Greek and Roman sculptors had possessed but that the Middle Ages had lost. A century later, this Evangelist slowly beginning to turn would inspire one of the most powerful Renaissance essays in unfolding movement, Michelangelo's *Moses*. Michelangelo, a Florentine born in 1475, would have seen Donatello's *St. John* every time he passed before the Duomo.

Donatello's figure, at the viewer's right, was complemented by Nanni's at the left: the Evangelist Luke, in whom the "purposefulness" of the Porta della Mandorla *Profetino* has developed into an intelligent presence that captures and holds our attention (cat. 9).[29] This figure too seems to turn toward those who would have entered the Duomo at its left, and clearly gazes downwards. Nanni, who admired Roman sculpture, gives his St. Luke tousled hair and a close-curled beard derived from ancient prototypes, along with an unfolding movement that, in analogy with Donatello's statue, suggests spontaneity. But the figure's pose is awkward, as if St. Luke were perched on the edge of his seat: Nanni has not grasped that the only way to avoid this effect, in the shallow block furnished to him as to the others, is to swing the legs to one side as Donatello does. What is more, St. Luke's upper body is strangely pneumatic, muffled in drapery; by contrast, the close-fitting tunic of Donatello's *St. John* lets us intuit the figure's chest, reinforcing our perception of a real body beneath the drapery.

The chief beauty of Nanni's statue—what "saves" it, as it were—is the lively intelligence with which the sculptor imbues his figure (cat. 9, detail). Like Donatello's emphasis on mystic grandeur in his *St. John*, this underscoring of intellectual vitality reflects what Scripture tells us of the Evangelist's character. In fact St. Luke was a learned man, who in the opening paragraph of his Gospel set forth his objectives and method as a scholar might do:

Fig. 13
Francesco di Antonio del Chierico
Pope Eugenius IV Consecrates the Cathedral of Santa Maria del Fiore in 1436 (detail), ca. 1471
Page 79 × 53 cm (31 × 22⅞ in.)
Ink, tempera, and gold on parchment
Florence, Biblioteca Medicea Laurenziana, Ms. Edili 151, c. 7v
By permission of MiBACT; further reproduction by any means prohibited

Cat. 9, detail

ABOVE
Cat. 11

OPPOSITE
Cat. 11, detail

> Seeing that many others have undertaken to draw up accounts of the events that have reached their fulfillment among us, as these were handed down to us by those who from the outset were eyewitnesses and ministers of the word, I in my turn, after carefully going over the whole story from the beginning, have decided to write an ordered account... (Luke 1:1–3).

The Bell Tower Statues

The esteem of the Opera del Duomo for both Nanni di Banco and Donatello can be gauged by the importance of the commissions each received after the Evangelist figures. In 1414 Nanni was assigned the third and final phase of the Porta della Mandorla: the five meter-high relief of Mary raised to heaven in an almond-shaped glory (whence the name *mandorla*, which means "almond," see fig. 8).[30] And in 1415 Donatello was commissioned to carve the first two of what would ultimately be five statues of Old Testament personages for the bell tower.[31] Each master thus found himself called to complete a major fourteenth-century program: Nanni the northeast cathedral door, begun in 1391, and Donatello the series of statues initiated in the 1330s for Giotto's campanile. It was a decisive moment, for what hitherto had been "insider" competition between sculptors of the same generation now became a public contest in which the art of earlier generations would be seen and judged in relation to what Nanni di Banco and Donatello produced. In the latter's case, the judgment of his contemporaries would be clarified in 1464, two years before the master's death, when four of his statues were moved from the less-visible positions in which originally placed, on the tower's north side, to niches on the west—the main front facing the baptistery—changing places with fourteenth-century statues by Andrea Pisano held to be "very crude in comparison."[32]

The earlier of the two campanile statues in this exhibit is the *Sacrifice of Isaac* (cat. 11), a two-figure group in which Donatello captures the dramatic dénouement of the Bible story that Ghiberti, Brunelleschi, and others had illustrated in their 1401–2 trial reliefs for the bronze baptistery doors (see figs. 31 and 32). With the assistance of the sculptor Nanni di Bartolo, known as Rosso ("Redhead"), Donatello extracts from a single block of marble two closely intertwined figures, the patriarch Abraham and his son Isaac, in the process anticipating a compositional formula to which the artist would return thirty years later in his *Judith and Holofernes*, and which late fifteenth- and sixteenth-century masters including Michelangelo would perfect: the so-called *figura serpentinata e moltiplicata* or "coiled, multiple-figure grouping." Donatello's Isaac figure, unclassical but beautiful in an angular, adolescent way, is the first life-size nude of the Renaissance.

In this work of 1421, Donatello chooses a point in the scriptural account subtly different from the ones illustrated nineteen years earlier by his famous contemporaries: neither the moment before Abraham learned God did not want the sacrifice of Isaac (Ghiberti's theme in the competition relief) nor the instant in which the angel actually stayed Abraham's hand (Brunelleschi's subject), but rather the split second after the father learned his son would not

ABOVE AND OPPOSITE
Cat. 11, details

die but live. The patriarch's left hand, pulling back the boy's hair to bare his neck, is still tense; the right hand, gripping the knife, relaxes as the blade slides away (cat. 11, detail, left). Beyond the moment illustrated, however, Donatello's "subject" is the interior drama in Abraham, whose upturned face conveys infinite gratitude (cat. 11, detail, page 33). Donatello in fact expresses in Abraham a gratitude that the Bible attributes to God, who is described as moved by Abraham's willingness to obey him even to the point of sacrificing his son.[33] "'Do not raise your hand against the boy', the angel said. 'Do not harm him, for now I know you fear God. You have not refused your own beloved son'" (Genesis 22:12); and God promises Abraham: "I will shower blessings on you and make your descendants as numerous as the stars of heaven and the grains of sand on the seashore" (Genesis 22:17).

The New Testament makes the point that the same God who spared Abraham's son would not, later, spare his own (Romans 8:32), and sees in Isaac saved from death a prophetic figure of Christ's resurrection (Hebrews 11:17). Indeed in the Christian tradition Isaac, who had carried the wood for the burnt offering on his back to the mountain where the sacrifice was to take place (Genesis 22:6), was interpreted as adumbrating Christ who, according to the Evangelist John, carried his own wooden cross to the hill where he would die (John 19:17).[34] The vulnerable nudity of Donatello's Isaac, and his calm inwardness, probably reflect this Christian reading of the Old Testament text (cat. 11, detail, opposite), just as Abraham's upward gaze—which, in the statue's placement on the east side of the bell tower, was directed toward the Duomo, may allude to the sacrifice of God's son Jesus re-presented every time Mass is said in the cathedral.

The second bell tower statue shown in the exhibition is one of those moved in 1464: Donatello's *Zuccone* or "Squash Head," as the figure was popularly known: a prophet of ancient Israel whose specific identity is difficult to ascertain, perhaps Habakkuk, Jeremiah, or Elisha (cat. 12). The figure's baldness would suggest Elisha,[35] who according to the Bible was ridiculed for being bald (2 Kings 2:23), as would the cloak over his left shoulder, falling to the prophet's feet in heavy folds: Elisha, a disciple of the prophet Elijah, recovered his master's mantle, which had fallen to the ground when, at the end of his life, Elijah was borne to heaven in a fiery chariot (2 Kings 2:11–13).

The relevant archival sources do not really put much emphasis on specific identification of Donatello's prophet statues, and it may be that these were meant simply to evoke the drama of the prophetic vocation, illustrating the range of spiritual, moral, and psychological responses described in various of the writings of different personages in this biblical category. Poised in his niche twenty meters above the piazza, "Squash Head," with his half-open mouth, could be Isaiah, whose lips had been purified with a burning coal so that he might speak in God's name to the people (Isaiah 6:6–7), or Jeremiah, to whose objection that he did not know how to speak God responded by stretching out his hand and touching the prophet's mouth (Jeremiah 1:6–9). With his intense downward gaze, he could

Cat. 12

be Habakkuk, who asked the God whose eyes "are so pure that You cannot look upon evil" why, although he sees the wicked, he keeps silent (Habakkuk 1:13). The qualities Donatello seems to want us to see in this figure—righteous anger in the face of sin and injustice; an irrepressible need to correct error, giving voice to truth; and supernatural courage in doing God's will—in fact belonged to many Old Testament prophets.

Arguably what Donatello's contemporaries admired in this statue was the artist's capacity to fuse Judeo-Christian spiritual grandeur with the moral dignity of ancient Greece and Rome. The *Zuccone* in fact appears as a toga-clad orator, and his furrowed bald brow and grave visage recall Roman portrait heads of the Republican period, reminding Florentines of their own origins in the age before Rome became an autocratic state. "Prophecy" here in fact implies political as well as religious correction, and it is unsurprising that later Renaissance sources saw the *Zuccone* as a portrait of a defender of the Florentine Republic, the fifteenth-century enemy of the Medici family's power, Giovanni di Barduccio Cherichini. While probably erroneous, this view suggests the extraordinary lifelikeness of the statue and its passionate individuality, making it almost credible that, as some Renaissance writers say, while carving the *Zuccone* Donatello repeatedly ordered the statue to speak to him. More than any sculpture since classical antiquity, this prophet, probably carved in the mid-1430s, seems a living person.

The Vault of Heaven

In the years Donatello was carving the bell tower prophets, his friend and youthful companion, the architect Filippo Brunelleschi, began work on the final architectural component of the Duomo, the vast cupola rising above the church's nave and transepts (fig. 14). Lifted high over the building's roof line by a massive drum, the dome is the most imposing part of the entire complex, visible not only from the surrounding streets and squares but from the hills that ring the city and, across the Arno river valley plain, from the neighboring city of Pistoia. A younger contemporary of Brunelleschi's, the classical scholar and architect Leon Battista Alberti, who arrived in Florence in 1434 as the dome was nearing completion, summed up what must have been everyone's impression of this looming wonder, asking:

> Who could ever be hard or envious enough to fail to praise Pippo the architect [Filippo Brunelleschi] on seeing here such a large structure, rising above the skies, ample to cover with its shadow all the Tuscan people, and constructed without the aid of centering or great quantities of wood? Since this work seems impossible of construction in our time, if I judge rightly, it was probably unknown and unthought of among the Ancients...[36]

The form of Alberti's question—"Who could ever be hard or envious enough to fail to praise Pippo the architect"—was not a mere rhetorical device. In the early phases of the dome's construction, Filippo had in fact been subjected to harsh criticism from real or would-be experts, some of whom wrote to the Opera del Duomo explaining the reasons for their distrust of his project. Indeed, the sixteenth-century art historian Giorgio Vasari says that Brunelleschi was so embittered by these attacks that he often considered abandoning Florence; stronger still, however, was his desire to finish the dome, and so he stayed.[37] The soaring structure is thus more than a technical and stylistic achievement: it is a personal victory, a sign of the human capacity to defend deeply held ideas, a trophy of inspired perseverance.

Why were so many opposed to Brunelleschi's plan? There are various reasons, among which obviously the envy mentioned by Alberti. But perhaps the main cause of resistance was fear of failure. For generations Florentines had dreamed of seeing their cathedral finished, as a famous fourteenth-century fresco showing the church makes clear (fig. 15); painted before Brunelleschi was born, it imagines the dome already built, and, beneath it, on the north flank of the church, the religious and civil authorities arrayed in serried ranks, as if the new cathedral were to symbolize the entire social order, the prestige of "Christendom." The city's identity was at stake, that is, and with it the Florentine claim to artistic superiority: if Filippo failed, all Florence would seem to have failed, its costly, century-long project shown to be unrealizable, its pride ridiculous.

A second reason for opposition was that Brunelleschi kept his plan for building the dome secret, at least as long as he could. And when it became clear how he meant to set

Fig. 14
Filippo Brunelleschi
The dome of Santa Maria del Fiore

Fig. 15
Andrea di Bonaiuto
The Church on Earth and in Heaven, with an Ideal View of Florence Cathedral, 1365–68
Fresco, 7.5 × 11.6 m (436¾ × 295¼ in.)
Santa Maria Novella, Florence, Chapter House

about the task, there were grave doubts that his ideas would work. Alberti alludes to one of Filippo's most improbable solutions when he says that the dome was "constructed without the aid of centering or great quantities of wood." "Centering" is the term for wood templates employed in constructing arches; here it implies what everyone believed to be ineluctable, namely the use of a titanic wooden support structure spanning the width of the cathedral crossing, forty-three meters, and rising ninety meters to the height of the dome itself: a structure over whose upper contour the dome's masonry would then be laid. The Florentine Republic had long before made available thousands of acres of woodland in the Casentino, a mountainous area east of Florence, to meet this and other construction needs.[38]

But Filippo Brunelleschi solved the problem in an entirely different way, creating a "floating" work platform on beams cantilevered from the base of what would become the dome, at sixty meters from the ground. Through a wide opening at the center of this aerial platform a huge crane, the *magna rota* or "great wheel," hoisted materiel to the work site from which the thirty-meter-high dome would rise, and new series of scaffolding holes were built into the structure as work advanced, allowing secondary platforms to be created nearer the dome's apex.

Short of the dome itself, still firmly in place after almost six centuries, nothing can really suggest the grandeur of Brunelleschi's achievement. The two wood models in the exhibit, believed to have been made in the 1430s to his specifications to illustrate structural features of the cupola and lantern (cats. 22 and 23), nonetheless put us in touch with the excitement of those last years of the Duomo project, when Florentines saw the immense building their great-great-grandfathers had begun reach completion.

When he died in 1446 Brunelleschi was considered equal and even superior to the greatest ancient architects, as his admirer, Leon Battista Alberti, had implied in the text cited above, and this profound veneration for the architect's genius and courage, which would last into the sixteenth century and beyond, became a constituent part of the new Renaissance identity of Florence. Filippo Brunelleschi was what his contemporaries called an "illustrious man": one of the people who changed human history.

Cat. 22

Cat. 23

Philosophy, Grammar, Music

The completion of the dome and formal consecration of the cathedral in 1436 inaugurated an *aurea aetas* or "golden age" which saw the culmination of numerous other works. Among these were the handsome organ lofts commissioned from Luca della Robbia and Donatello in 1431–33 for the Duomo interior, and Lorenzo Ghiberti's second set of doors for the baptistery—the one Michelangelo would call the "Gates of Paradise"—begun in 1425 and installed in 1452. A still older project completed in these years was the series of hexagonal reliefs on the lower level of the bell tower, begun in the fourteenth century but lacking five components. These

FROM LEFT
Cat. 15
Cat. 16
Cat. 17

"marble stories," as Vasari would later call them,[39] were commissioned from Luca della Robbia on May 30, 1437 and set in place in 1439.[40] Three of the five constitute the next-to-last section of the exhibition: *Philosophy* (or *Dialectic*), *Grammar*, and *Music*.

Where the fourteenth-century reliefs in this series illustrate human work, starting with Adam and Eve and including modern Florentine arts and crafts such as wool weaving, farming, painting, and sculpture (see figs. 3 and 6 above), the fifteenth-century additions by Luca represent the *studia humanitatis* or "liberal arts" and evoke the new ideal of education which the early Renaissance pursued. The first shows two men engaged in a lively debate, one of whom supports his arguments by referring to a book he holds open (cat. 15). The "art" illustrated is thus logical argumentation, and the debaters are perhaps, as Vasari later says, Plato and Aristotle, whose works were known in fifteenth-century Florence. The relief was carved on the eve of one of the great "disputes" of that age, the Council of Florence, an ecumenical gathering of Eastern and Western bishops and theologians held in the cathedral and in other Florentine churches in 1439–40, and Luca della Robbia anticipates what would be the heat of theological discussion; an inscription in the Duomo recalling the council speaks of the "long debates" that characterized its sessions. To such learned hypotheses, however, we must add that Florentines genuinely love debate, and Luca della Robbia's gesticulating pair in ancient dress describes what even today is an admired skill: the outstripping of intellectual opponents through eloquence, vehemence, and clarity of reasoning.

According to Vasari, Luca's second relief, *Grammar*, also represents an ancient master of this art: one of the main authors studied in the Renaissance scholastic curriculum, Aelius Donatus, a fourth-century Roman grammarian who had numbered St. Jerome among his pupils (cat. 16). The great dignity Luca gives this schoolmaster, and the handsome classical portal of his schoolroom, recall that one of the achievements of the period was the rediscovery of the Latin of the age of Virgil and Horace, as opposed to the corrupt *Latinitas* of the Middle Ages. The well-dressed schoolboys also have a recognizable identity—not as individuals, but as representatives of the privileged class whose parents paid famous humanists to tutor their children. In the late fifteenth century, Lorenzo de' Medici would hire Angelo Poliziano to oversee the education of his sons, among them the future pope Leo X

The third relief probably shows Orpheus, son of the Thracian king Oeagrus and of the Muse of music, Calliope (cat. 17). Orpheus could subdue birds and wild beasts with music, and that is how Luca della Robbia represents him, enchanting an audience of animals with rhapsodic song. This mythological hero's inclusion in a series of accounts that opens with biblical personages—Adam, Eve, Jabal, Jubal, Tubalcain, Noah—suggests the ambitious goal that early Renaissance humanism had set itself: to ascribe to classical culture a dignity comparable to that of Judeo-Christian revelation. Luca's *Music* was set into the north side of the bell tower, below the line of niches which until 1464 hosted Donatello's bald-headed prophet *Zuccone*.

The Bronze Heads

The last works in the exhibition are also products of the "golden age" of Brunelleschi's cupola and instances of Renaissance interlace of classical with Christian subjects. They are two bronze heads, clearly Hellenistic in inspiration, made for the organ loft or "cantoria" commissioned from Donatello in 1433[41] as a companion piece to that ordered a year earlier from Luca della Robbia (see figs. 27 and 28). An archival document authorizing consignment to Donatello of a quantity of bronze for "a certain head" for the cantoria, and specifying that it should resemble "the other head," dates from 1439,[42] the year in which the cantoria was finished, and the heads may thus belong to the last phase of the cantoria's manufacture and could be an afterthought—a classical note that the artist added when the work was all but complete. Because of their subtly different interpretation of the antique theme, the heads are believed to be by different hands, one being assigned to Donatello himself (cat. 13), the other to his collaborator Michelozzo (see cat. 14).

In reality the entire cantoria by Donatello, like that by Luca della Robbia, is "classical" in feeling, with architectural elements derived from antiquity and figural sculpture similarly evoking Greco-Roman art. In the figurative sections, both artists depict children: Luca della Robbia with ten reliefs illustrating Psalm 150 (inscribed above and below the scenes) and Donatello in a continuous frieze showing *putti* running joyously to and fro. The classical dress of the adolescents in the former and the nudity of the children in the latter both allude to pagan Greece and Rome. Despite this, the overall message remains decidedly Christian and Florentine. The psalm text illustrated describes a concert in God's honor and was used to connect the liturgy of ancient Israel with that of Florence Cathedral. These organ lofts were in fact made for the altar area of the Duomo beneath Brunelleschi's newly finished dome. In each, the use of small children to express biblical joy probably also had

OPPOSITE
Fig. 16
Interior of Florence Cathedral looking toward the southeast pier, which once supported Donatello's cantoria above the sacristy portal, in the position now occupied by the 19th-century organ loft

ABOVE
Cat. 13

a pastoral message: to show babies at play above the altar, in an age of high infant mortality such as the fifteenth century, was a kind of sermon, reassuring those assembled for Mass that God does not forget innocents who die.

What then was the function of our two heads, whose disheveled hair and anguished gazes are at odds with the theme of joy in the cantoria's other figural elements? Were they intended precisely as foils, juxtaposing adult despair to the frolicking babes of the marble frieze? Did they perhaps serve to contrast a pagan world without hope with the child-like exuberance of Christian faith? We do not know, yet the emotional intensity of these works makes it hard to believe their purpose was merely ornamental.

Two facts that came to light in a recent restoration of the heads may help us grasp their meaning. The first is the angled contour of the necks, from which we deduce that, when attached to the cantoria, the heads necessarily looked downwards. Donatello's cantoria was installed on the massive southeast pier of the crossing of the Duomo, and below it was the chancel and high altar with its crucifix (fig. 16). Thus it may be that the air of dismay in these visages expresses pagan surprise at the Christian mystery of salvation—in the spirit in which St. Paul asked the believers of Corinth, many of whom had converted from paganism:

Fig. 17
Donatello
Penitent St. Mary Magdalene, detail, 1454–55
Poplar wood, polychromy, and gilding, height 188 cm (74 in.)
Museo dell'Opera del Duomo, Florence

> Do you not see how God has shown up the foolishness of human wisdom? If it was God's wisdom that human wisdom should not know God, it was because God wanted to save those who have faith, through the foolishness of the message that we preach. And so, while the Jews demand miracles and the Greeks look for wisdom, here are we preaching a crucified Christ; to the Jews an obstacle that they cannot get over, to the pagans madness, but to those who have been called, whether they are Jews or Greeks, a Christ who is the power and the wisdom of God. For God's foolishness is wiser than human wisdom, and God's weakness is stronger than human strength (1 Corinthians 1:21b–25).

The second fact to which the recent restoration calls attention is the gilding Donatello applied to the heads, of which traces have again become visible. A document in the Duomo archives reveals that the gold leaf was applied, however, many years after the installation of the cantoria in 1439: in 1456, in fact,[43] after Donatello's return from a decade of work in north Italy. In the mid-1450s the artist was probably again employed by the cathedral authorities—his *Penitent St. Mary Magdalene* almost certainly dates from this period (fig. 17)—and we can imagine him going into the Duomo to check the cantoria he had made seventeen years earlier and being unhappy with the effect of the two heads, placed below the jutting upper singing-gallery and not very evident, except on bright days. He was applying gold leaf to the *Mary Magdalene* and may have felt that this could help the bronze heads too, which—placed as we said above the chancel in the cathedral crossing—were just a few meters above the chancel lighting system, comprised of candles and torches grouped on a raised architrave around the octagonal choir enclosure designed by Brunelleschi in 1436. The living flames from the torches had probably always been part of Donatello's idea for the cantoria, which he in fact adorned with light-reflecting gold mosaic *tesserae*; now he planned to extend this effect to the bronze heads, which evidently he wanted to be visible in relation to the altar.

Toward the Future

The question of the meaning of the cantoria's bronze heads in the liturgical context of the Duomo high altar suggests a further reflection. In the last work he made, a pair of so-called "pulpits" for the Florentine church of San Lorenzo, Donatello would again use an ancient pagan image to dramatize a Christian theme: a wildly disheveled maenad (female mourner) at the foot of Christ's cross in the bronze *Deposition* relief of the pulpit on the left side of the nave, looking at the altar.[44] The extremity of this figure's grief, a very paroxysm of weeping, stands in strong contrast to the more reserved sorrow shown in the scene's other figures, and at odds as well with the viewer's awareness that two days later Christ would rise from the dead. In theological terms, the Resurrection renders desperation futile, but Donatello may have felt that the human reality of grief needed expression, and that one Greco-Roman maenad opened a horizon lacking in Judeo-Christian thought and iconography: a universe of inner chaos.

For, beneath its cultivated surface, Renaissance "humanism" really hungered to know human nature, as many works in this exhibition attest. The gradual rediscovery of the body, of motion and of emotion all served this end, whose value seemed indisputable to people who believed that God himself had shared our humanity and, as man, had known suffering and death. Paradoxically, however, the vehicle that would permit the Renaissance to express its Christian faith was pagan art, the rediscovery of which revealed to artists and their public a new and more inclusive world.

This exhibition charts the beginning of their journey toward that future shore.

DONATELLO'S VISIONS

The Sculptor at Florence Cathedral

Daniel M. Zolli

> For the main façade of the campanile of Santa Maria del Fiore [Donatello] wrought in marble…[a statue that is] now called il Zuccone. [It is] considered a very rare work and the most beautiful that [Donatello] ever made, such that whenever he wished to take an oath, to make others believe him he would say: "By the faith that I have in my Zuccone." And while he was carving [the statue], he would gaze at it and exclaim: "Speak, speak, or may the bloody dysentery take you."[1]
>
> —Giorgio Vasari, *Lives of the Artists*, 1568

Introduction

An artist who could make mute stone seem to speak. Since antiquity writers had invoked the trope in countless celebrations of figural sculptors, but perhaps nowhere more memorably than in the above anecdote, vividly articulated by Giorgio Vasari in the mid-sixteenth century. The sculpture in question, popularly known as the *Zuccone* ("Squash Head," for its balding pate), belonged to a series of Old Testament prophets that Donatello (ca. 1386–1466) had chiseled for the bell tower of Florence's cathedral roughly between the years 1415 and 1436. By the time Vasari was writing, nearly a century after the sculptor's death, the *Zuccone* had come to stand as a paradigm of sculptural mimesis (cat. 12, detail). Here, Vasari suggests, was a creature so perfectly crafted, so persuasive in its lifelikeness, that even its *maker* believed it might speak (speech, it bears mentioning, was a prophet's central duty). While Vasari's drama of Donatello jawing away at an inert block of marble is almost certainly apocryphal, it nevertheless retains a kernel of truth. Even viewers today are struck by the extraordinary realism and psychological urgency of Donatello's *Zuccone*: his face ravaged, neck craned forward and lips parted, almost apoplectic with purpose as he delivers God's word (see pages 65–67). Confronted with this startling vision of prophetic mission, it can be difficult *not* to imagine that the figure possesses the breath of life.

Probably completed in 1435–36, Donatello's scowling prophet was among the last assignments that he would tackle for the Opera del Duomo, the body in charge of supervising the construction and embellishment of Florence's cathedral (its members were called "operai"). The affiliation spanned nearly four decades of the sculptor's career, and it was the making of him. From his formative years as an apprentice to his full-fledged artistic maturity, Donatello built his reputation through a steady stream of projects for the church's

Cat. 12, detail

interior and exterior, its bell tower, and baptistery (see fig. 1). These commissions, while apparently wide-ranging in function and subject, shared one consistent goal: to give compelling material form—often a body—to the immaterial truths of Christianity.

During the period in question—the "age" to which this exhibition's title refers—no task could have seemed more important. Completed during protracted conflicts with rival cities, amidst increasing factionalism in Florentine politics, and against the constant threat of plague outbreak, these works offered hope to a world framed by uncertainty. Indeed, the very choice of sculpture signaled the seriousness and public nature of the church's message. For unlike the altarpieces within the cathedral, these sculpted similitudes of divine figures, their lives and deeds, were largely displayed *outside*. Visible in the world, this race of new sculptures "spoke"—was voluble—to anyone who entered the center of the city, regardless of social station or rank. That many of these works, like the *Zuccone*, mimicked the volumes, masses, and even scale of human forms made their appeal to viewers more powerful still. To call Donatello's works decorative, then, does not begin to countenance the vital role that they played in the life of every Florentine. They were emblems of civic pride, ethical statements, vehicles of communication between their viewers and God, and investments in collective salvation.

What follows is an overview of Donatello's activities at Florence's cathedral complex. Given the content of this exhibition, I focus mainly on the sculptor's work in marble, although, as we shall see, these undertakings drew on sensibilities that he developed in other media such as wax, clay, gold, and bronze. To discern the appeal of Donatello's sculptures—both to his contemporaries and to later viewers—we must attend throughout to how he *made* them. The decoration of Florence Cathedral was an ongoing project, subject to continuous redesign, and Donatello often had to work within constraints that he inherited from its earlier phases. Each assignment posed unique challenges that affected Donatello's design, his techniques, and his choice of materials. Focusing on key considerations that structured Donatello's approach to each commission—e.g. site, scale, style—this essay is meant to introduce his practice in carving marble, tracking its evolution, its negotiation of tradition and novelty, the sculptor's triumphs and failures. For this it is necessary to glimpse beneath the patina of myth at Donatello's beginnings.

Beginnings

Long before posterity would crown him as Florence's patron saint of sculpture, Donatello was known simply as Donato di Niccolò di Betto Bardi, son of a wool stretcher (*tiratore di lana*). His father's professional background distinguished Donatello from others in the cohort of artists highlighted in this exhibition, for unlike his slightly older peers Lorenzo Ghiberti (1378/80–1455) and Nanni di Banco (ca. 1380/85–1421), who trained in workshops run by their families, Donatello found his way to sculpture from the outside.

Regrettably, few details exist concerning the route by which Donatello arrived at the sculptor's trade. It is reasonable to suppose that he first entered the profession as an apprentice in his early teens, as was common, although available documents are completely silent on the matter.[2] The earliest reference to Donatello, from 1401, alerts us to one possible trajectory.

Fig. 18
Lorenzo Ghiberti
North Doors of Florence Baptistery, 1403–24: panel with the *Nativity*
Bronze with gilding, 52 × 45 cm (20½ × 17¾ in.)
Museo dell'Opera del Duomo, Florence

It locates the teenager in nearby Pistoia, where he was arrested for a skirmish with one Anichino di Piero, whom he bludgeoned with a stick.[3] Beyond its psychological interest, the episode hints at a potential link with Filippo Brunelleschi (1377–1446), who was then completing a silver altar for Pistoia's cathedral, and who may well have employed the young Donatello in his shop.[4] That the two developed an affinity early on is well attested. Indeed, should Brunelleschi's later biography prove reliable, the pair even traveled to Rome together in 1402–3, where they embarked on an exhaustive study of ancient architecture and sculpture, while supporting themselves with a steady stream of goldsmithing assignments.[5] At the same time, it is plausible that Donatello instead—or also—trained in stone carving, as a later payment record implies.[6]

Whatever the case, there can be little doubt that when Donatello returned to Florence, around 1404, he encountered a scene flush with professional opportunities. Foremost among these, both in importance and scope, was the commission for a new set of bronze doors for the east portal of the cathedral's baptistery, famously won in a public competition of 1401–2 by Ghiberti, and begun the following year (on the history of the project see pages 75–81). This was the city's most ambitious undertaking in bronze in nearly a century. To fulfill the task Ghiberti—then only in his twenties—had to enlist swarms of assistants, who would aid him in completing the doors' projected twenty-eight panels and massive framework.[7]

It is within this context, as one of the eleven assistants comprising Ghiberti's initial shop crew, that Donatello first enters the light of history.[8] Donatello probably joined the *bottega* sometime between 1404 and 1406, and initially he may have performed routine tasks for Ghiberti, such as maintaining the master's tools and equipment, or acquiring his materials. There is reason to believe, however, that the teenager quickly proved himself able beyond his years, for after Ghiberti signed a new contract for the project in 1407 Donatello received an annual salary of seventy-five florins; several others drew the same wage, but among Ghiberti's twenty-one (!) assistants nobody made more.[9] What this suggests, at least circumstantially, is that in a matter of months the young sculptor had graduated to some of the shop's most important tasks, and was being compensated on a par with much more experienced hands.

What sorts of responsibilities fell to the younger sculptor? A glance at the *Nativity*, among the roughly four panels completed during Donatello's assistantship, helps one to

Cat. 5, detail

appreciate how diverse his activities must have been (fig. 18).[10] After experimenting with drawings and preliminary models, Ghiberti and his assistants would have translated their composition into wax, filling the field within the quatrefoil design with figures, rocks, and trees (on the division of labor see page 77). The completed ensemble was then cast, cleaned, chased, and its surface textures differentiated. The torsos of the shepherd boys were polished with abrasives, for instance, while the jagged outcrop and foliage were left relatively coarse.[11] Certain details were then picked out with tools (called "cold working")—the delicate calligraphic lettering on Mary and Joseph's robes, for example, or the plumed wings of the angel that irrupts from the relief's ground. While Ghiberti surely modeled and finished many of the relief's most prominent features, as his contract stipulated, there is little reason to doubt Donatello's participation in every stage of its realization.[12]

It is tempting to peruse these early panels for traces of Donatello's hand, to attempt to identify in this or that detail the tremors of an emerging artistic persona. That such exercises invariably prove futile is telling. Indeed, one of Ghiberti's guiding concerns seems to have been that his assistants hewed closely to his style the better to bring overall cohesion to the doors. That Donatello's specific contributions could be so lost within the doors' overall design attests not only to the success of Ghiberti's approach, but to how thoroughly the younger sculptor had assimilated his master's lessons.

His tenure in Ghiberti's shop schooled Donatello in activities that he would fall back on throughout his career: among them drawing, casting bronze, and modeling and finishing sculpture.[13] But it also versed him in a style that well suited other projects underway in the cathedral complex. The decorative elegance of Ghiberti's reliefs, and their artful fusion of naturalism and lyrical grace, were hallmarks of the International Gothic idiom that had inundated Florence from the north in the late Trecento.[14] Where sculpture was concerned, the other great manifestation of this style in the city was on the northern entrance to the cathedral, known as the Porta dei Servi (it was only later dubbed the Porta della Mandorla).

The first burst of activity at the Porta spanned roughly the years 1391–97, when the Opera enlisted hoards of stone carvers to populate the great door's jambs with thickets of foliate ornament and half-length figures of angels (five in each reveal), and mythological figures. By 1404, the Opera had shifted its attention to the arch above the door, which continued the decorative program from the previous decade (on the chronology of the program, and its participants, see pages 20–21).[15] It is in connection with this second phase of activity that Donatello is first recorded as a marble sculptor. That his name appears in the Opera's account books as early as 1406 suggests that he may have begun working on cathedral projects while still a member of Ghiberti's shop, which Donatello seems to have left in early 1407.

There is every reason to believe that Donatello's activities at the Porta della Mandorla ranged widely, but the available documentary evidence, unfortunately, makes it difficult to say precisely what they were. Nor is it easy to attribute works to Donatello on stylistic grounds alone. Like Ghiberti's doors, the decoration of the Porta was an ongoing project, and individuals were often asked to imitate the style of more established hands to ensure consistency in the program's many parts. Aiming at uniformity, the Opera even levied fines on those whose work strayed from the Porta's master design.[16]

Individual sculptors nonetheless expressed, in places, their own stylistic tendencies. A significant portion of the sculptural decoration is deeply influenced by the International Gothic style, but the program also teems with classicizing elements, most notably a series of *all'antica* figures punctuating the door's inner reveals and archivolt (the figures were begun in the 1390s, and finished by 1409). The *Hercules* on exhibit here might serve as representative of the general stylistic traits of this group (see cat. 4). The figure's dependence on ancient Roman sculpture is palpable: not only in its classical subject, but in its deftly modeled musculature, its near-accurate proportions, and its *contrapposto* pose. It might strike today's reader as strange that the Opera would allow such seemingly varied stylistic forms to enter into its program. Such eclecticism was common in early fifteenth-century Florence, however, and the Opera would not have viewed it as detrimental to the Porta's appearance of unity. Donatello's presence at the Porta would thus have allowed him to engage with a plurality of styles.

Cat. 3, detail

Examination of the two works most commonly ascribed to Donatello during his years at the Porta della Mandorla helps to focus the issue. The so-called *Profetino*, probably carved around 1406–9, is unmistakably Ghibertesque in character (cat. 5, detail).[17] Its torpid expression, the rippling folds of its cloak, and the use of drapery to reinforce the figure's corporeality, all have strong precedents in the early reliefs for the North Doors.[18] The statue's debt to Ghiberti becomes more pronounced still when one compares the piece to its companion, also a "small prophet," here given to Nanni di Banco (the figures were installed, respectively, atop the door's left and right finials no later than 1422). The assured stance of Nanni's boy-prophet, and the thick—almost vertical—masses of cloth that invest its right leg differ markedly from the rhythmic grace of its counterpart. What we see here, in other words, are two alternative stylistic orientations: where Nanni's statue is conspicuously un-Ghibertesque, its sibling appears to adapt the goldsmith's lessons to a larger scale.

An entirely different style obtained in the keystone for the arch above the door, it, too, carved around 1408 (for the relief's placement see fig. 8). The relief's subject is a three-quarter-length figure of Christ, depicted as Man of Sorrows, here nested against a cartouche.[19] In contrast to the gentle Gothic air of the *Profetino*, this figure is racked with suffering: his neck slack, Christ's head succumbs to the force of gravity, his facial features tinged with pathos. The musculature of the figure, the veins in his forearms, and every bit of his luminescent flesh are rendered with startling naturalism (cat. 3). These details suggest a sculptor attuned to the classicizing rhetoric on view elsewhere on the door—Christ's torso, for example, resembles that of the diminutive *Hercules* almost to the letter. The relief is distinguished from its *all'antica* neighbor, however, in its emotional urgency—a quality that better suited its subject.

Although the attribution has spawned considerable debate among scholars, few have doubted that the relief was created during the years that Donatello was actively involved with the Porta's decoration. Whether or not Donatello authored the piece himself, its example appears to have lingered in his mind long enough to inspire his subsequent work. One notes, in particular, the relief's strong affinity with the sculptor's wooden crucifix for the nearby church of Santa Croce (ca. 1408–12), which exhibits a similarly anguished mien, and the same anatomical precision, and heightened sensitivity to modeled flesh.

That Donatello may have simultaneously crafted two works (the *Profetino* and *Man of Sorrows*) so apparently divergent in style—or, at least, witnessed their realization—attests to the variety of influences that engaged him early in his career, each mobilized by the sculptor, to varying degrees, in the years to come.

Fig. 19
Nanni di Banco
The Prophet Isaiah, 1408
Marble,
height 193 cm (76 in)
Cathedral of Santa Maria del Fiore, Florence

Scale

Whatever his activities were, Donatello clearly impressed the operai with his performance at the cathedral's northeast portal, for in February 1408 they awarded the sculptor his most impressive commission yet: a marble statue of David, freestanding and slightly over life-size, to be placed just above the Porta della Mandorla on the church's north tribune.[20] With the assignment, Donatello joined a program that was already underway. One month earlier, the Opera had tasked Nanni di Banco with carving a figure of the Old Testament prophet Isaiah, it, too, scaled to life and destined for the cathedral's roofline (fig. 19). The pair was the first in a planned series of twelve Hebrew prophets that would crown the buttresses surrounding the exteriors of the three tribunes of the building, where together they would act as a stone militia keeping watch over the city's most sacred precinct.[21]

Although the *David* is Donatello's first securely documented commission, in certain respects the ground here is no more stable than before. While Donatello's contract stipulates his salary, as well as the statue's subject and dimensions, it cannot be linked conclusively to any of his extant works. Indeed, the quest to identify the *David* remains an active one on art-historical turf, with several candidates emerging in recent decades.[22] The most commonly cited among these is currently housed in Florence's Bargello museum (fig. 20). Some have noted the artifact's kinship with the *Profetino* discussed earlier: a shared heritage is suggested by the figures' almond-like eyes, delicate nose and mouth, and in the grammar of their gently turning bodies.

And yet none of this quite prepares us for the sheer corporeality and psychic presence of Donatello's ephebe. In this his first full-sized figural undertaking, Donatello has delivered his referent with astonishing fidelity, conjuring an image of the biblical hero that is convincing in both spirit and letter. Witness the care with which the sculptor has rendered the shepherd boy's flesh, his taut leather armor, and suffused his young warrior with swagger—arms akimbo, cape tossed over his right shoulder, David gazes outward, seemingly conscious of being seen.[23]

Fig. 20
Donatello
David, 1403–9
Marble,
height 191 cm
(75¼ in.)
Museo Nazionale
del Bargello, Florence

If the *David* was Donatello's most accomplished work to date—a marvel of mimesis—it was also arguably his greatest disappointment. In early 1409, just as Donatello was bringing his statue to completion, the Opera took measures to put its counterpart—Nanni's *Isaiah*—in place on the church's buttress. The endeavor proved inauspicious. For in setting the statue's scale, artist and patron alike had not accounted fully for the vast distance between the work's intended site and its audience far below. To be sure, Nanni's prophet cut a formidable figure when viewed head on. Exhibited atop the cathedral's soaring architecture, however, it would have resembled nothing more than a fleck to passersby, a shortcoming duly noted by the operai, who ordered that the *Isaiah* be removed from its perch and returned to the ground ("elevetur et ponatur in terram").[24] Since the height of the *David* was identical to its ill-fated companion, the operai must have concluded that it, too, would be unsuitably small for its lofty setting. In fact, the sculpture never saw the light of day; it was left to languish in the cathedral workshop for nearly a decade, until 1416, when the Florentine government acquired the statue for its town hall (later called the Palazzo Vecchio). There, presented to the intimate address of city councilmen, its scale would have been less controversial.[25]

Although shadowed by frustration, the *David* did not shake the Opera's confidence in Donatello. Hardly had the marble dust settled than the Opera was making arrangements for Donatello to create its successor, identified in documents as the prophet Joshua, and, elsewhere, simply as the "large white man" ("homo magnus et albus"). Clearly both parties had taken to heart their past missteps, for at nearly eighteen feet tall (almost three times the size of its earlier predecessors) the giant statue, wrought from whitewashed brick and plaster, would have been impossible for spectators to ignore.[26] The *Joshua* disintegrated sometime in the eighteenth century, but several illustrations predating its disappearance bear testimony to how commanding its profile once was against the Florentine skyline. In one such image (fig. 21) the prophet appears to grow from the very fabric of the church like a miniature spire, arms cantilevered away from its body, and hands directed skyward in prayer.

Fig. 21
Ferdinando del Migliore
"View of Piazza del Duomo with *Joshua* at Left", in *Firenze città nobilissima*
Etching, 1684,
Ital 3365.1
Houghton Library, Harvard University

If the *Joshua* gripped Florence's collective imagination, as eyewitness accounts suggest, it was at least in part because of Donatello's technique. The increase in scale demanded resourcefulness. No stone colossus had been attempted in living Florentine memory, and the feat must have raised concerns about whether, in practical terms, a figure so large could be carved, and, if so, whether it would fall (how would the Opera hoist something so ponderous onto the cathedral in the first place?). Faced with such uncertainties, Donatello turned to terracotta (baked clay), which was more easily modeled, comparatively lighter, and cheaper (should the commission fail). In all probability, he built up the giant, one layer at a time, with individual terracotta pieces—Vasari calls them *mattoni* or "bricks"—eventually coating its entire exterior with stucco and white lead paint (*biaccha*). Payment records suggest that Donatello even applied a final oil-based varnish, which would have served not only to protect the fragile statue, but to give its surface the appearance of polished stone, an effect similar, one imagines, to what Luca della Robbia would later achieve with his glazed earthenware.[27] No wonder that Donatello's final payment specifies that, in addition to labor and expenses incurred, the artist was being rewarded for his *magisterium* (roughly "superior craftsmanship"), a recognition of the ingenuity with which he had tackled the problem of site, scale, and medium.

Optical Corrections

The *Joshua* foregrounds a key issue that would guide each subsequent commission that Donatello undertook at the cathedral. It registers his growing consciousness that, in order to be effective, sculpture had to take into account the *subjective* experience of the beholder. In the example above, Donatello recognized that, when seen at a distance, the factual reality of the *Joshua*'s materials crumbled away. What mattered to him, in this case, was not the cost or prestige of the stuffs he used, but their ability to simulate the optical properties of marble (its luster and texture), and to do so on a previously unimaginable scale.

Donatello's monumental likeness of *St. John the Evangelist* (cat. 10), an assignment that he tackled contemporaneously with the *Joshua*, introduced an altogether different set of concerns. The artist's solutions, while different, exhibit a similar sensitivity to the sculpture's conditions of viewing, and a similarly empirical approach toward facture. The *John* was planned as early as 1405, when the Opera began making provisions to frame the cathedral's central west portal with marble effigies of the authors of the New Testament (called the Four Evangelists).[28] These sculptures would inhabit preexisting niches that flanked the portal in pairs, each set roughly ten feet above the ground. By 1408, the Opera had entrusted the first three *Evangelists* to artists who had already proved themselves at the Porta della Mandorla—Niccolò Lamberti (ca. 1370–1451), Nanni di Banco, and Donatello—with the added incentive that whoever was to carve the better sculpture would receive the final commission (the cathedral board later changed its mind, entrusting the fourth to Bernardo Ciuffagni).

Once in place, Donatello's *John* and its companions would become central nodes of attention on the vast façade. Not only would they mark the threshold between the secular world and the cathedral's sacred interior, but they would serve as backdrop and stimulus for the many ritual events that took place in the piazza (see fig. 13). It follows that the sculptures demanded a monumentality to match these lofty imperatives. That the Opera had such considerations in mind may be inferred from their choice to represent the Evangelists *seated*, which implied that the figures' actual height far surpassed that of their architectural containers (a standing figure, cut from the same block, was much less monumental). The sculptures were installed within their respective niches by 1415, where they remained until the 1580s, when the Opera transferred the group indoors following the destruction of the church's façade.

In the years separating Donatello's era and our own, authorities would relocate nearly every one of his sculptures for the cathedral, often more than once, owing to changing political sympathies at times, or to shifts in artistic taste, or simply out of practical need. For this reason, the works under consideration rarely appear in the settings for which Donatello originally intended them. As we have seen already, and as many of his contemporaries recognized, a fundamental strength of Donatello's work was its site-specificity: its delicately engineered relationship to a *specific* setting and audience. It is this same site-specificity, however, that can make his sculptures look altogether unusual when displayed in different contexts.

St. John the Evangelist is no exception. When seen only slightly above ground level, as is typically the case in modern museum installations or photographs, *John* often strikes viewers as eccentric in its treatment of the human form. The figure's torso and right arm

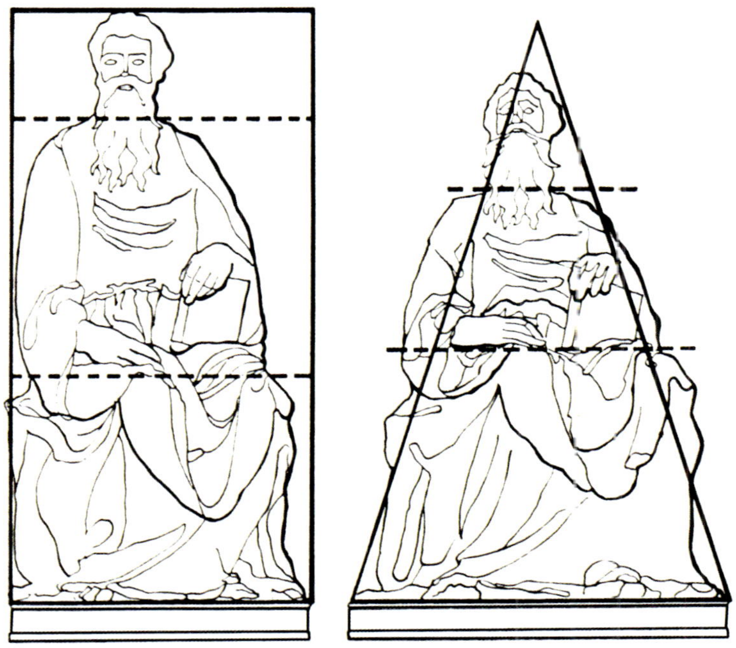

OPPOSITE
Cat. 10

ABOVE
Fig. 22
Donatello
St. John the Evangelist,
1408–15
Diagram of composition depending on viewer's point of view (from Charles Seymour, *Sculpture in Italy 1400–1500,* Harmondsworth and Baltimore, 1966, 57)

are attenuated, its head thrust forward awkwardly, drapery cumbersome, the whole pose languid: hardly what we would expect for someone of John's spiritual pedigree.

How different these same traits appear when seen from below. When Donatello undertook to carve the statue, he recognized that its base would be set roughly four feet above human height, and made formal adjustments to accommodate this low vantage point (cat. 10).[29] Not only are John's proportions far closer to nature when observed from this angle, but his presence is much more formidable: the fabric of his raiment hangs heavily from the frame of his body, and the whole composition organizes itself into a stable pyramid (fig. 22). Gone is every trace of passivity. John is in the act of physically turning to his right, his expression smoldering with intensity, gaze lost somewhere in the distant space of thought (the two nicks indicating pupils may have been later interventions).[30] If a writing instrument once lay between the fingers of John's right hand, as some have suggested, one might understand this to be a representation of the author in the process of writing down his visions, the book he holds—perhaps his Gospel or Revelation—unfinished. In the *St. Luke* for the niche flanking the portal's other side, Nanni likewise used optical corrections, but to entirely different effect. Taken together, his adjustments would have supported the impression that Luke glances downward imperiously, as though reflecting upon—or addressing—the crowd beneath (see cat. 9). Of the three sculptors to join the project originally, only Lamberti did not compensate for a lower viewpoint.

In important respects, Donatello was working with tools that others in his profession had honed before him. Already in the 1280s, the sculptor Giovanni Pisano (ca. 1250–ca. 1315) had applied a similar logic of distortion to his prophets for the upper stories of the cathedral façade in nearby Siena. Realizing that his figures would be seen from a great distance, Giovanni enlarged their eyes, for instance, and elongated their necks to ensure

Fig. 23
Giovanni Pisano
The Prophet Haggai, ca. 1285–97
Marble,
64 × 48 × 36 cm
(25⅛ × 19 × 14¼ in.)
Victoria and Albert Museum, London

OPPOSITE
Cat. 10, profile view of block

their heads would be legible to the distant spectator (fig. 23). The overall effect must have been remarkably theatrical, with the figures peeling themselves from the fabric of the façade to engage in a choreographed exchange of glances and gestures. More immediately, Donatello may have drawn inspiration from Ghiberti, whose panels for the north portal of the baptistery betray a profound sensitivity to the beholder's angle of vision. Take, for example, the relief depicting the *Resurrection* (see fig. 37).[31] Here, the decisions to elongate Christ's torso, to model his head in high relief, and inclined downward, were clearly made in view of the panel's eventual location, around thirteen feet above the ground (one finds, by contrast, no such compensations in those reliefs exhibited at human height, e.g. see fig. 18). The clay and wax that Ghiberti used to make preliminary sketches and then models (to be cast in bronze) well suited such corrective efforts. These soft, tactile media could be heated and reworked, allowing the goldsmith to adjust his composition continuously, the better to gauge how his finished sculpture would appear on site. Ghiberti's example was not lost on Donatello, who used clay and wax models (*modelli*) frequently in the design process, possibly even while preparing *St. John the Evangelist*.[32] The sculptor apparently even "scaled up" to full-size models on occasion, which could be tested in their intended setting—later sources recommend covering a wooden armature with cloth "skins" dipped in thick clay slip.[33]

In other respects, the *John* posed problems—and invited solutions—of a different sort. When Donatello and his fellow sculptors planned their figures, they had to reckon with niches whose shape and size were predetermined by the earlier design of the façade. As circumstance would have it, the depth of these alcoves—and thus of the statues they could accommodate—was remarkably shallow, a fact that threatened to undermine the Opera's monumental intentions. How, then, to maximize the figures' appeal—to worshippers entering the church or passersby—within these inherited constraints? A photograph of the *John* in profile helps us to appreciate just how remarkable was Donatello's solution to the dilemma (cat. 10, profile view of block). In fact, what reads as a statue in the round is nothing more than a thin marble block carved in exceptionally high relief, even if viewers below the niche would not perceive this. Working from a slab that was no more than twenty-two inches thick, Donatello excavated the stone at substantially varied depths, leaving the base virtually unaltered, but reducing the piece to less than nine inches at the saint's abdomen.

If Donatello took utmost advantage of the slender block, his colleagues, and particularly Lamberti, proved less intrepid. The older sculptor made his bid for viewers' attention by way of a dazzling use of the International Gothic style, describing in careful strokes the roiling curls of Mark's beard, lyrical folds in his robe, and straps on his codex (fig. 24). The figure is, in spite of its exquisite workmanship, remarkably flat, and almost mannequin-like in its immobility.

Fig. 24
Niccolò Lamberti
St. Mark the Evangelist,
1408–15
Marble,
210 × 88 cm
(82⅝ × 34⅝ in.)
Museo dell'Opera del Duomo, Florence

OPPOSITE
Cat. 10, detail

While Lamberti trained his chisel on minutiae to the detriment of figural depth, Donatello reversed these priorities. Eschewing nearly all decorative niceties, Donatello focused his carving on those areas that would most animate his figure, in both a physical and psychic sense. If one looks closely at the *John*, as we may do in this exhibition, there is clearly an emphasis given to those parts that determine the saint's character and action. Note the undercuts below the tendrils of the saint's beard, or beneath his stormy brows, which intensify the play of light and shadow around his face (cat. 10, detail). Or the deeply gouged—almost cavernous—hollows in his drapery, which invest the figure's lower half with apparent volume. Such tactics support the illusion of a three-dimensional body straining from its chair; they unleash the saint from his architectural straitjacket the more directly to interact with the city space before him.

When the adjudicating committee evaluated the finished sculptures they awarded Donatello, the youngest participant, the highest compensation for his work (160 florins). On the other end of the pay scale fell Lamberti, the oldest in the group, who received 130 florins (Nanni and Ciuffagni collected 137 and 150 florins, respectively). This disparity may not necessarily reflect an aesthetic verdict on the part of the Opera, which often determined payment on the basis of practical factors such as number of hours worked and cost of materials. It can be no coincidence, however, that Lamberti left Florence mere months after the Evangelists were put in place. Perhaps sensing a sea change underway, the elder sculptor set out to remake his career in Venice, where the decorative surface patterning characteristic of his *Mark* would be warmly welcomed, and not soon outpaced.

St. John the Evangelist was no isolated experiment. In these same years, Donatello accepted a commission for an over-life-size figure of *St. Mark* (1411–13) to adorn the southern exterior of Orsanmichele, Florence's guild church and other major arena for sculpture (fig. 25). As with the *John*, the sculpture was intended for a niche set just above human height, and not surprisingly, Donatello availed himself of similar techniques. As in the *John*, the very qualities that appear ungainly when seen straight on—exaggerated features, deep undercutting, and so forth—become elements that reinforce the statue's physical, as well as moral, weight. The *Mark* also appears severe and lost in contemplation, and it, too, reads as a statue fully in the round. The saint turns, his left foot raised, suggesting that were he to rotate more still, we would see what remains of his body—an illusion, to be sure, since, like the *John*, the figure is no more than a deep relief, its back flat and unfinished. To bolster this illusion further, Donatello stands Mark on a cushion, whose contours fictively bulge as

though compressed under the saint's weight—a conceit that can make one forget that the whole ensemble is, in reality, hewn from a single heavy stone. Indeed, upon seeing the statue in its enclosure, "so gracefully arranged and situated," no less an authority on sculpture than Michelangelo was reported to have said that, "if Saint Mark really resembled [Donatello's figure] then every word that he spoke would inspire belief."[34]

Optical feats like those on offer in the examples above became a mainstay in later appreciations of Donatello. In 1481, for instance, the writer and philosopher Cristoforo Landino lauded the sculptor for attaining "great vivacity through both the arrangement and positioning of his figures, all of which appear to move."[35] Some even attached Donatello's play with optics to a playful personality. This is true of an anecdote from the sixteenth century about Donatello's *Mark*, recounted by Vasari, but possibly known earlier.[36] According to the writer, Donatello's patrons—the consuls of the linen guild—deemed the figure unacceptable when they first examined it at ground level. Recognizing that he could change their minds with a different perspective, as it were, Donatello persuaded his clients to let him set the sculpture in its niche, where he promised to rework it to their satisfaction. In an irreverent sleight of hand, Donatello then hid the piece from view, waiting fifteen days before unveiling it, untouched, to the universal admiration of his critics. The story is almost certainly fictional, an amusing yarn that Vasari, or one of his contemporaries, spun as proof of Donatello's precocious genius, which emerges here in contrast to the ignorance of his patrons. Fiction though it may be, the anecdote does raise an important point: it registers an awareness, nearly a century after Donatello's death, that the belief his sculptures awakened, both aesthetic and religious, extended from his site-specific approach to design.

OPPOSITE
Fig. 25
Donatello
St. Mark, 1411–13
Marble,
height 236 cm (including cushion and plinth);
width 74 cm at the base)
(93 × 29⅛ in.)
Orsanmichele, Florence

Narrative

Donatello's successes at the cathedral and Orsanmichele did not go unnoticed by his contemporaries. That the sculptor had gained the esteem of his patrons is apparent from the next assignment the Opera gave him: he was called on to help complete the program of Old Testament figures on the cathedral's bell tower. The plan was one of long standing. The Opera had initiated the project in the 1330s, when sixteen niches were constructed on the campanile's third story (four on each side), eight of these filled with statues by Andrea Pisano (ca. 1270/90–ca. 1348/49). In 1415, Donatello was commissioned to carve two of the eight statues that remained to be completed (he finished these by 1420).

The sculptor's third contribution to the program was an *Abraham and Isaac,* begun in March 1421 and finished just eight months later (cat. 11).[37] The statue differed from its predecessors in important respects. In the first place, the commission was not Donatello's alone, but awarded jointly to his younger colleague at the cathedral workshop, Nanni di Bartolo (known as Rosso, or "Redhead", active 1419–51). Timing might help to explain the Opera's insistence on collaboration. Donatello had been dilatory in delivering his first two campanile statues, and by 1421 the Opera would have had good reason to make provisions for the timely completion of his assignments. The year before—in 1420—Brunelleschi's dome had begun to rise over the cathedral site, and, with its completion on the horizon,

the Opera may have felt an added urgency to finish outstanding decorative projects. Another possibility is that the sculpture's complexity demanded an additional hand. For unlike its siblings—figures who preach, instruct, or ruminate—this block would represent *two* figures, and it would relate a narrative: the Old Testament story of Abraham nearly sacrificing his son Isaac (Genesis 22:1–13).

The Opera's choice of subject would have aroused immediate associations with the competition for the baptistery's doors from roughly two decades earlier, in which contestants had been asked to produce trial reliefs representing the same episode. Donatello and Rosso's group departs from these reliefs—the two that survive, at least—in its choice of moment (see figs. 31 and 32). Where Ghiberti had shown Abraham readying himself for the deadly blow, and Brunelleschi the instant of angelic rescue, Donatello and Rosso fixed on a later point in the biblical psychodrama. This is the second after Abraham hears the angel's voice, and understands that his son will live. Certain details hint at the mayhem that has just transpired: the father's left hand still grips the boy's disorderly coils of hair, the right sleeve of his robe is still raised in preparation for death-dealing, and his right foot is still perched atop the kindle for the sacrificial altar. But Abraham's right arm grows slack, and the edge of the blade he holds slides away from the boy's throat, his gaze directed skyward in wonder (cat. 11, detail).

It may have been that the sculptor's decision to focus on the episode's dénouement was motivated by practical necessities. The niche that the sculptors inherited was both shallow and narrow, a fact that allowed neither frenzied movement in his composition (cf. Brunelleschi's relief), nor additional characters. By homing in on a moment of relative calm—the father pauses, his gaze apparently lingering on the elevated site of his epiphany—they could accommodate the formal constraints of the assignment while still honoring the story's psychological demands.

Cat. 11

OPPOSITE
Cat. 11, detail

Surface

The Opera's account books do not specify how labor was divided between Donatello and Rosso. In the absence of concrete evidence, scholars generally endorse the idea that Donatello was responsible for the group's design and most of its carving, while Rosso—the less established sculptor—confined himself to surface work. This type of arrangement was hardly unusual. The later stages in a marble sculpture's production could be enormously time-consuming: its surface was often filed to erase chisel marks, meticulously polished with pumice and straw, and occasionally colored with pigment. In Donatello's time, it was not uncommon for sculptors to delegate some of these activities to others, owing to lack of time or expertise. Indeed, what evidence exists of Donatello's early workshops suggests that he often, if not always, followed this approach, especially when working on a larger scale. It does not follow, however, that the handling of surface was low in Donatello's hierarchy

of priorities, mere technical drudgery that he passed on to assistants or younger collaborators like Rosso. On the contrary, it appears to have been an organizing concern for the sculptor, even if some of the more repetitive work fell to different hands. Not only was surface treatment instrumental in how his works *looked,* but it could, as we shall see later, factor into their narrative meaning.

What sorts of considerations guided Donatello's management of surface? Later commentators hinted that the distance at which a work was displayed bulked heavily in the sculptor's mind. Writing in 1677, Giovanni Cinelli noted that Donatello refrained from giving certain works too high a finish to enhance "their effectiveness [from afar], even though they became somewhat less striking when viewed at close range."[38] Cinelli's remark and others like it orient us toward an important—and by now familiar—idea: that Donatello adjusted his technique according to the circumstances of viewing.

The works themselves would seem to confirm Cinelli's intuition. On the one hand, there is *St. John the Evangelist*, which, in comparison to other sculptures we have encountered, was exhibited relatively close to the beholder. What is apparent, even if the surface has lost some of its original finish, is just how much care Donatello took to differentiate the marble's textures. He indicated the figure's eyebrows with short, irregular strokes, the strands of its beard with wending, almost draftsman-like incisions, the fringe on its garment with repetitive, vertical gashes: all this in contrast to the vast expanses of robe where traces of the chisel are nowhere to be found. Donatello added further tactile variety by giving more or less polish to areas of the stone: note how markedly the smooth sheen and deep tone of John's hands, finished with abrasives, differs from those sections that are treated more coarsely, such as the beard, which appear much brighter (cat. 10, detail). Not only were these variations perceptible to the viewer, but they contributed directly to the illusion that the sculpture was not marble, but flesh, hair, and cloth. We do not know whether, or to what extent, Donatello added polychromy to the figure, or if and how selectively it was gilded. Such practices were indeed quite common, and both have been shown to pertain to near-contemporary marble works by the sculptor.[39] Should Donatello have heightened the *John* with colors and gold, the figure's diversity of texture and hue would have been still more pronounced.

In the series of bell tower prophets, on the other hand, such surface subtleties were of little account. More than ten times distant from the beholder's eye than the *John*, these statues' placement necessitated a different approach entirely. To illustrate this point, we would do well to look at one of Donatello's final contributions to the program, the *Zuccone*, originally placed in a niche on the north side of the campanile (cat. 12). Scholars remain divided over the specific identity of the prophet, in part because the Opera's payment records and deliber-

OPPOSITE
Cat. 10, detail

ABOVE
Cat. 12, detail

OPPOSITE
Cat. 12, detail

LEFT
Fig. 26
Donatello
The Prophet Jeremiah, 1423–25 (?)
Marble,
194 × 45 × 45 cm
(76⅜ × 17¾ × 17¾ in.)
Museo dell'Opera del Duomo, Florence

RIGHT
Cat. 12

ations rarely name figures explicitly.[40] As Timothy Verdon suggests in his essay, it may be that the Opera's interest—and Donatello's—centered not on *who* the prophet was, but on *how* he, and his marble counterparts, evoked the Old Testament ethic that they preached.

Here, as elsewhere, legibility was of utmost importance. Recent conservation efforts have helped the marble regain some of its original appearance, enough to establish that Donatello did not give the figure a high polish, leaving unrefined, for instance, the file marks that limn its arms, nape, and lone exposed shoulder (cat. 12, detail).[41] The emphatically scratched lines of the beard, and the deeply cut eye sockets—which create pooling shadows beneath the figure's craggy brows—together relay a sense of inner turmoil (cat. 12, above, and cat. 12, detail, page 65). Donatello's emphatic surface marks thus contribute to the statue's expressiveness and render it clearly visible from a distance.

As with other prophets, like the *Jeremiah* (fig. 26), Donatello pared the *Zuccone* down to its emotional nucleus. No decorative adornments or iconographic prompts: even the scroll was done away with to enhance the figure's psychological immediacy. His neck thrust forward in speech, the *Zuccone* glowers downward to address the populace. But where the *Jeremiah* is athletic, this figure is physically frail. The crenellation of his teeth is irregular, for instance, and his flesh seemingly worn out from severe asceticism.[42] In his gritty appearance, the figure embodies the very message of selfless devotion to God that Old Testament prophets advocate. This renders the urgency of his message all the more poignant. For in spite of its wilted state, the *Zuccone*'s body pulsates with energy, the tendons of his neck tensed as though his voice strains.

As we have seen, praise for the *Zuccone* and its affecting realism echoed loudly in later estimations of the sculptor. Some even attributed its success directly to Donatello's technique. Writing in 1596, the scholar Bernardo Davanzati noted that the eyes of the figure as one sees them "on high look as though they were dug out with a spade; had [Donatello] worked them for a near view, the figure would now appear blind, for distance

Fig. 27
Donatello
Cantoria, 1433–39
Marble with gold and colored mosaic inlay, bronze heads,
348 × 570 cm
(137 × 224⅜ in.)
Museo dell'Opera del Duomo, Florence

devours all refinements."[43] Davanzati's observation—that "everything depends on context," as he put it—registers an awareness of the practicalities that underpinned Donatello's approach to surface.

Likewise sculpted for a location far over head, but utterly different in appearance, tone, and subject, is Donatello's organ loft, or "cantoria," which he made to adorn the cathedral's formidable southeast pier (fig. 27).[44] In the early 1430s, with Brunelleschi's massive dome above the altar area nearing completion, the Opera turned its attention to furnishing the newly renovated space beneath. Among their priorities was a larger organ to enrich the acoustic life of the church, planned as early as 1426.[45] This new instrument, and its smaller predecessor, would be mounted in architectural galleries set well above the cathedral's north and south sacristies (immediately to the left and right of the main altar, respectively). Given the organs' indispensable role in church ceremony and their high visibility, these structures were destined to become central nodes of attention in the cathedral. Responsibility for the first gallery, that which would house the main organ, fell to Luca della Robbia, his contract likely drawn up in 1431. Donatello was then in Rome (he had based himself there from 1430), but when he returned to Florence in 1433 the Opera awarded him the second commission forthwith, later adding that he would receive up to ten more florins than Luca for each panel that surpassed his in quality.[46]

How did each artist approach the assignment? Luca set ten figural reliefs within an architectural framework, each panel closely portraying one verse of Psalm 150, which enjoins the faithful to "praise the lord" through music, song, and dance. These reliefs throb with details of an almost ethnographic sort: adolescent boys jockey for space around a book of hymns; a child loses his place in the text; and instruments, sandals, even hairstyle all appear with studied authenticity (fig. 28). Although classicizing in style, this content would have struck churchgoers as familiar, for in age and action the youth resemble the confraternity of boys that daily sang the church's canonical hours.[47] Indeed, classicism pervades the whole

Fig. 28
Luca della Robbia
Cantoria, 1432–38
Marble,
323 × 560 cm
(129⅛ × 220½ in.)
Museo dell'Opera del Duomo, Florence

ensemble, evident in the Roman lettering of the inscriptions, or in the paired Corinthian pilasters that punctuate the gallery's face. Although similar in size and format, Donatello's cantoria departs from its counterpart in almost every other respect. Abandoned are the anecdotal particulars of everyday life, replaced by winged infants that know no real-world referent. And where Luca exhibited each relief discretely, Donatello arrayed his cavorting creatures along a continuous horizontal band, the sum total conjuring an ongoing sense of movement *around* the gallery (in reality, the frieze comprises four slabs—two spanning the front, and one on either side—evidence that a desire to out-earn Luca was not foremost among Donatello's motives). Donatello drew from ancient sources, as well, but his approach was emphatically *sui generis*: while he borrowed motifs from classical sarcophagi, for example, the variegated mosaic that sheaths the construction recalls, instead, early Christian or medieval inlay work (called *opus sectile*), familiar to the sculptor from his Roman sojourn.

In their finish and facture, too, the ensembles could not be less alike. Predictably, Donatello tailored his treatment of materials to the work's eventual location. In the first place, and along lines similar to his prophets, he refrained from polishing the marble (fig. 27, detail, page 71). Strong modeling and exaggerated—almost unthinkable—poses are likewise deployed with respect to the viewer below.[48] Luca, by contrast, fashioned his compositions delicately, meticulously finishing every square inch of his panels, especially those completed in the initial stages of the assignment (fig. 29). Documents indicate that the sculptor came to recognize early on the perils of his approach, for when Luca renegotiated his contract in 1434, roughly midway through work on his cantoria, he pledged to produce reliefs that were "better and more beautiful."[49] There is a notable difference, in fact, between these two phases: Luca modeled his later panels more robustly, in higher relief, and with less finish, no doubt in an effort to enhance their legibility to the viewer on the pavement below (fig. 30). Could it be that seeing Donatello's reliefs in progress had led Luca to revise his approach?

LEFT
Fig. 29
Luca della Robbia,
Group of Tambourine-Playing Children
(detail of cantoria),
1432–35 (?)
Marble,
98½ × 94 cm
(38¾ × 37 in.)
Museo dell'Opera del Duomo, Florence

RIGHT
Fig. 30
Luca della Robbia,
Children Singing (detail of cantoria), 1435–38 (?)
Marble,
103 × 64 cm
(40½ × 25⅓ in.)
Museo dell'Opera del Duomo, Florence

But there is more at play in Donatello's cantoria. As Timothy Verdon notes in his essay, the sculptor's design took carefully into account his cantoria's principal light source: mere feet below the work was a group of torches and candles elaborately ordered atop an architrave, their purpose to illuminate the space surrounding the church's main altar. In this respect, Donatello's use of materials cannot have been arbitrary. Consider the glass *tesserae* that so densely populate the cantoria, or the variegated pigments that Donatello applied selectively to accentuate decorative motifs. Both media are highly reflective, and would have endowed the monument with a shimmering quality, enhancing its visual impact in the otherwise subdued light of the church interior. Crucially, Donatello extended this effect to the stone itself. Left unfinished, marble exudes an inner luminosity, and appears extraordinarily bright, qualities that are greatly reduced once the substance is polished. In leaving his surfaces only roughly chiseled, then, the sculptor unleashed the brilliant qualities inherent in the stone (Luca's finished reliefs exhibit, by comparison, a uniformly deeper tone). This rendered the frieze of turbulent children not only more conspicuous, but more *animated*. Light from nearby candles would have flickered across the raw, grainy surface, picking out individual crystals in the rock, and enhancing the children's uncanny illusion of continuous motion. In the cantoria, finish—or lack thereof—became a vehicle for expressive meaning.

It bears mentioning that Donatello's treatment of surface was not only a bravura show of artistry, but directed to the function of the cantoria. To those who gazed upon his gallery during the Mass, and especially when music was sung or played, these children would have been understood as responding to a concert celebrating God. To viewers aware

Fig 27, detail

Cat. 14

of philosophical interpretations of how sound traveled, they also perhaps evoked ideas about the ways music stirred the human soul. As Charles Dempsey has shown, Donatello's exuberant infants belong to an iconographic type well known to the sculptor and his contemporaries: the *spiritello*.[50] A venerable tradition with its origins in the Greek philosopher Aristotle and current in fifteenth-century Tuscany held that these "little sprites" occupied the air: immaterial entities whose movements were excited by the melodies and rhythms of music, their activity arousing the emotions of listeners. These personified spirits well suited the purpose of Donatello's cantoria, and during the celebration of the liturgy their role would have been especially pronounced. The *spiritelli* (they are called this explicitly in the documents) would have appeared to react to the playing of the organ, as though its noise produced a sudden surge propelling them into frenzied dance.[51] Here, glinting marble and mosaic were the privileged media with which Donatello brought these ethereal beings to life.

By 1439 work on the cantoria had all but concluded, with one notable exception.[52] The bronze heads in this exhibition were probably the last elements that Donatello added to his ensemble (see cats. 13 and 14). The sculptor set them below the loft's projecting face, in the two central spaces between the consoles, each head nested against a disc of purple porphyry, and each inclined downward toward the pavement below. As a document from October 1439 implies, these iridescent likenesses are, in reality, the same person twice portrayed. Whereas Donatello quarried many sources in the zone above, this pair is *explicitly* classical in form, material, and style. Along these lines, it might be tempting to view these "pseudo-antiques" as an improvisational afterthought, a curiosity that the sculptor added to the cantoria as testimony of his own classical interests, which were at fever pitch after his trip to Rome—a veiled artistic signature, in other words. Given their commanding place in the cantoria's lower register, however, and the sheer cost of bronze and porphyry, it is unlikely that these objects were mere antiquarian whimsy. What role might they have served, then, in the original program for the cantoria?

At the most basic level, the heads acted as foils for the *spiritelli* above them. This occurred, first, materially. As Donatello knew well, bronze offered aesthetic possibilities that the other media in his ensemble did not. The metal's smooth, finished surfaces and dark, earthy tones could powerfully evoke human hair and flesh, here in opposition to the glimmering marble of the *spiritelli*, which implied something almost incorporeal. Emotionally, moreover, the heads' haunted air offers the strongest contrast imaginable to the manic glee of the *spiritelli*. A premium is placed on pathos: disheveled hair, furrowed brows, and parted lips—all boldly modeled for the spectator below—suggest the duo is gripped by internal drama. Were these denizens of antiquity unnerved by the Christian jubilation that surrounded them? Or were they not pagan at all? Do they, too, respond to the music of the organ, modeling its effects to churchgoers, as it were?

Within this sea of interpretative uncertainties, one fact remains undeniable: as the cantoria's largest anthropomorphic features, and angled toward viewers, the two heads delivered the most direct human appeal in the entire structure. Scanning the cantoria during Mass, the spectator may have felt that the heads addressed him or her directly, their enlivened—and very recognizable—gazes meeting the viewer's own, forcing participation with the work at large. Thus, above and beyond their antique visual references, these heads may also have been—perhaps most saliently—human points of entry into the cantoria's more rarefied realms.

What is clear is that the Opera deemed the aesthetic impact of the pair important. This may be inferred from the fact that in 1456, some seventeen years after the heads were installed, the Opera made arrangements to have them gilt with gold leaf (traces of which still remain).[53] In all probability, the Opera, or Donatello himself, found that the dark bronze objects were not sufficiently visible within the shaded recesses below the gallery and required gilding to make them more eye-catching. Able thus to respond more dynamically to the candles below, the heads would have become full-fledged actors in Donatello's multi-media tour de force. Bronze, porphyry, gold, marble, mosaic, and paint—the surface of each material essaying a different effect—joined together in theatrical accompaniment to the church's ceremony.

The End of Marble

The cantoria was, in all probability, the last major commission that Donatello completed in marble. By 1443, and perhaps earlier, the sculptor had left Florence for the city of Padua to the north, where he would complete some of the century's most ambitious projects in bronze. Even when Donatello returned to Florence in the mid-1450s, he focused his energies on other materials. It is difficult to say with certainty what motivated Donatello to relinquish marble for the last two decades of his life. Given the sculptor's absolute silence on the matter—indeed on any matter—the question must remain open-ended. It may be that Donatello's taste—or the taste of his patrons—had changed. Or perhaps the expressive possibilities offered by other media—wax/bronze, stucco, limestone—proved more appealing.

When Donatello's great age of marble came to an end, the sculptor had left behind a substantial—and varied—corpus of works in that medium, many of these for Florence's cathedral. As we have seen, each of these sculptures was an individually wrought solution to a specific set of demands—and many drew on the sculptor's experiences in other media. So, as well, would each endure beyond the circumstances and the era in which it was made. As Vasari's anecdote at the beginning of this essay hints, artists in the sixteenth century continued to learn from the lessons these works had to teach. They still marveled at the skill with which Donatello had made his stony figures—how it was that these "visions" seemed to speak, to move, to come to life. Even viewers today might wonder the same.

LORENZO GHIBERTI

From the Early Workshop to the Gates of Paradise

Amy R. Bloch

In 1401 the Arte di Calimala, the guild that supervised the decoration of the Florence Baptistery of San Giovanni, announced a competition for the commission to sculpt the church's second set of bronze doors. News of the contest crossed the Italian peninsula and reached Pesaro, where the Florentine Lorenzo Ghiberti, then in his early twenties, was helping a painter fresco a room in a palace of the Malatesta family. In the autobiography he wrote many years later, Ghiberti describes his decision to leave Pesaro—and painting—behind and outlines the parameters of the contest he entered upon his return home.[1] The Calimala, which asked each competitor to make a trial relief, selected the subject (the sacrifice of Isaac from the Old Testament), apportioned the materials (four sheets of bronze per sculptor), and determined the time allowed each entrant to finish the work (one year). Seven sculptors submitted panels that were judged by guild officials and artists who, Ghiberti claims, all declared his entry (fig. 31) the winner. Despite his assertion of unanimity, the decision clearly divided opinion in the city and remained controversial deep into the fifteenth century. In the 1480s Antonio Manetti, the biographer of Filippo Brunelleschi, whose relief (fig. 32) was one of the final two considered, recounted a different outcome in which the judges deemed the contest a tie and asked Brunelleschi and Ghiberti to share the commission, a proposal, states Manetti, that Brunelleschi refused to entertain.[2]

In his account Ghiberti omits to explain a fundamental aspect of the competition: where and how he learned to cast a figural relief in bronze. Manetti similarly leaves out any discussion of who taught Brunelleschi, trained, like Ghiberti, as a goldsmith, to cast.[3] Whereas young marble sculptors could develop and refine their skills at the workshop of Florence Cathedral, which had been a training ground for carvers since the end of the thirteenth century, bronze casting was not used to produce statues and reliefs in Florence before 1400.[4] To fashion images in bronze, the sculptor, often using the so-called lost-wax method, builds up figures and forms in wax, uses the wax models to produce molds, and then casts the relief or statue by pouring molten metal into them. To complete the baptistery's first set of bronze doors, which were made between 1330 and 1336, the Calimala and the Opera (board of works) it administered at San Giovanni had the sculptor Andrea Pisano prepare the wax models and then called from Venice a skilled caster to transform them into bronze panels.[5] Given the absence of bronze sculptors in Florence around 1402, the Calimala and Opera could not enlist experts in the medium to help judge the competition for the second doors, and Ghiberti writes that painters, goldsmiths, and marble carvers offered opinions on the entries.[6]

During their apprenticeships both Ghiberti and Brunelleschi would have learned lost-wax casting, which goldsmiths often employed to turn silver and gold alloys into small-scale objects for domestic and sacred contexts.[7] The steps of their technique parallel those used by bronze sculptors, although casting bronze figural relief on a large scale, which requires the

Fig. 31, detail

Fig. 31
Lorenzo Ghiberti
The *Sacrifice of Isaac*, 1401–2
Bronze with gilding, 45 × 38 cm (17¾ × 15 in.)
Museo Nazionale del Bargello, Florence

Fig. 32
Filippo Brunelleschi
The *Sacrifice of Isaac*, 1401–2
Bronze with gilding, 46.5 × 40 cm (18¼ × 15¾ in.)
Museo Nazionale del Bargello, Florence

careful mixing of copper alloys, the creation of large and intricate molds, the construction of a furnace, the building of a spacious casting pit, and the precise regulation of the pit's temperature, is far more laborious and complex. By 1401 Ghiberti, whose competition panel manifests a high level of technical sophistication, had evidently learned the process. Unlike Brunelleschi, who cast seven solid bronze elements and bolted or soldered them onto a flat bronze sheet, Ghiberti cast his relief hollow and fashioned separately just two pieces: Isaac's body and the front of the altar on which he kneels, the details, perhaps not coincidentally, that most vividly demonstrate Ghiberti's youthful embrace of classicism.[8] To create the relief's smoothed surfaces and intricate details, which are added through the process known as chasing, Ghiberti relied to some degree on skills developed during his training as a goldsmith, when he would have learned the art of finishing cast metal.[9] Bronze alloys, however, are on average much harder than gold and silver alloys, and to chisel and stamp bronze surfaces the sculptor must use a particular combination of force and control not required when working with precious metals.[10] Some have speculated that Ghiberti learned to fashion bronze reliefs during his time in Pesaro, where he might have come into contact with casters from Venice, a city renowned for its thriving bronze industry.[11] Such a hypothesis has not been confirmed, and we remain in the dark regarding the origins of Ghiberti's skill in creating figural relief in bronze, an art he had mastered, and without known precedent in Florence, by 1402.

The commission Ghiberti received as a result of his victory represented, in every sense, a monumental challenge. He had neither a local workshop model on which to rely nor immediate access to a community of trained bronze sculptors from which he could hire qualified assistants. His achievement in creating his first doors (fig. 33) was therefore not only to fashion in twenty-eight bronze quatrefoil panels a New Testament cycle along with the Evangelists and four Doctors of the Church, but also to assemble a shop capable of creating and managing everything needed to design, model, cast, and finish the massive doors.

Fig. 33
Lorenzo Ghiberti
North Doors of Florence Baptistery, 1403–24
Bronze with gilding, height ca. 4.6 m (181⅛ in.); each panel 52 × 45 cm (20½ × 17¾ in.)
Museo dell'Opera del Duomo, Florence

The Calimala's generous funding of the commission helped Ghiberti assemble a crew to assist in the completion of these tasks. In the contract he and his stepfather Bartolo signed on November 23, 1403, which specifies that Ghiberti was to carry out "the figures, trees, and similar objects" and finish three panels per year, the guild promised them the substantial annual salary of 200 florins and pledged to pay all assistants Ghiberti deemed necessary.[12] Between 1404 and 1407 at least eleven individuals were brought into the shop.[13] The teenage Donatello, who was working on marble sculptures for Florence Cathedral in these years, joined Ghiberti's workshop sometime after 1403. Bernardo Ciuffagni, also a member of Ghiberti's shop before 1407, went on to complete several sculptures for the cathedral. Their presence at the earliest stage of the doors project strongly implies that they participated in the design process. Others, like Giuliano di Ser Andrea, who remained with Ghiberti for nearly three decades, perhaps acted as shop managers. The painter Masolino appears among those hired to help with the doors in this early period, but the nature of his participation is unknown. A number of workers would have helped with routine but crucial tasks, like bringing equipment and supplies to the shop, repairing tools, and maintaining the casting pit.

By 1407 Ghiberti had probably cast at most four reliefs.[14] In that year, he signed a revised contract in his own name that, although it tightened oversight, maintained the annual salary of 200 florins, a sum he no longer had to share with Bartolo, who was paid separately.[15] The Calimala understood that workshop assistants participated in the sculpting, but this new contract asserts that Ghiberti was to work in both "wax and bronze," and especially on "hair, bodies, and [other] similar [things]." Very often the head of a workshop, no matter the profession, provided designs that were carried out by assistants. In this case, however, the Calimala, in specifying that Ghiberti was both to design and to finish prominent elements, attempted to ensure the quality of the costly commission it was funding. The contract's language also demonstrates a basic understanding of the casting process: Ghiberti was to model in wax the important portions of the reliefs and then clean and chase those same sections in the cast bronzes. Between 1407 and 1415 the workshop hummed as workers were hired, departed if no longer needed or when other opportunities called, and then sometimes returned.[16] Donatello continued at a top salary for a few weeks in 1407 and then left, probably to focus on cathedral commissions. Well paid for several years were Bandino di Stefano and Giuliano di Ser Andrea, senior members of the crew. Masolino stayed on for several years, and Ciuffagni, making less than the others, drew his salary for a brief time before leaving and then returning, again for a relatively short period, at a higher rate of pay.

After 1407 the workshop not only produced bronze sculptures but also trained apprentices. In the 1410s Paolo Uccello joined as an apprentice (a *garzone*), left after about three years, and then, having matriculated in the Arte dei Medici e Speziali, the guild to which painters belonged, returned at a salary four to five times higher and stayed for a little over a year.[17] The panels themselves give some indication of the tasks assigned to apprentices or less experienced sculptors. Many of the reliefs were modeled in two sections—the ground level below and the portion containing figures, buildings, and landscape elements above—that were joined and cast, and in many panels one can still see the seams between the parts (fig. 34 and fig. 34, detail). Ghiberti, along with the shop's more experienced sculptors, must have fashioned the upper zones but perhaps allowed apprentices to try their hands at modeling and finishing the lower segments. The movements in and out of the shop of Ghiberti's more skilled assistants probably followed the course of work. We might imagine, for example, that Ciuffagni helped with the models, left before the casting began, and then returned to assist with either the cleaning and chasing of reliefs that had been cast or the modeling of the next set of wax panels. When around 1417 Ghiberti needed another sculptor to help with chasing, gilding, and the casting of the doors' final reliefs, he brought in Michelozzo, a skilled goldsmith and metalworker whose earliest experience with large-scale figural relief came during this time with Ghiberti.[18] In the same period Antonio Averlino, commonly called Filarete, quite possibly entered the shop to learn the art of bronze sculpture, a skill he later put to use when he fashioned a new set of doors for St. Peter's at the Vatican.[19]

A number of artists worked in the shop, a wellspring of creativity and artistic energy, during their formative years. For the young Donatello the opportunity to learn the art of bronze casting must have been almost impossible to pass up.[20] His time in the shop, moreover, gave him the chance to work with various substances such as wax, bronze, and gold, as well as the clay used to make both molds and preliminary models in which Ghiberti and his assistants sketched their ideas, adjusting roughly formed bodies to explore the effects of various poses, gestures, and expressions. Ghiberti's panels indeed share a number of details with contemporary

FROM TOP
Fig. 34
Lorenzo Ghiberti
North Doors of Florence Baptistery, 1403–24: panel with the *Crucifixion*
Bronze with gilding, 52 × 45 cm (20½ × 17¾ in.)
Museo dell'Opera del Duomo, Florence

Fig. 34, detail

Fig. 35
Lorenzo Ghiberti
North Doors of Florence Baptistery, 1403–24: panel with the *Transfiguration*
Bronze with gilding, 52 × 45 cm (20½ × 17¾ in.)
Museo dell'Opera del Duomo, Florence

Fig. 36
Lorenzo Ghiberti
North Doors of Florence Baptistery, 1403–24: panel with *Christ Debating with the Doctors in the Temple*
Bronze with gilding, 52 × 45 cm (20½ × 17¾ in.)
Museo dell'Opera del Duomo, Florence

Fig. 36, detail

statues attributed to Donatello or those close to him: the *Profetino* (see cat. 5), for example, and the Christ of Ghiberti's *Transfiguration* (fig. 35) both step on the corners of their cloaks, producing a taut, arcing swath of drapery crossing between the figures' legs; the "Small Prophet" also holds up folds of his garment to remove them from the area around his feet, an action that Ghiberti frequently included in his reliefs—in the *Transfiguration* Moses and Elijah perform such an act—to imply movement; and a knotted belt of cloth pulls tight around the chest of both the prophet and several of Ghiberti's figures (fig. 36 and fig. 36, detail), a device allowing for the clearer visualization of the bodies' forms beneath the voluminous cloaks covering them.[21] Donatello also found in Ghiberti's practice a consideration of the effects of viewpoint not unlike the concerns that animated his own approach from at least 1409, when he began carving his *St. John the Evangelist* (see cat. 10), a figure whose proportions he calculated in accordance with its placement in an elevated niche on Florence Cathedral's façade.[22] In Ghiberti's *Resurrection* panel (fig. 37), sculpted for the doors' uppermost register perhaps before 1407, plants and flowers cover the underside of a shelf of ground curving beneath the scene.[23] Their placement below the ground rather than atop it provides those who gaze up towards the panel—and not the image's protagonists—with a view of natural forms that sprout from the earth and parallel Christ's emergence from his earthly tomb.

Fig. 37
Lorenzo Ghiberti
North Doors of
Florence Baptistery,
1403–24: panel with the
Resurrection
Bronze with gilding,
52 × 45 cm
(20½ × 17¾ in.)
Museo dell'Opera del
Duomo, Florence

Ghiberti's first doors influenced many Florentine sculptors not directly connected to the shop, such as Nanni di Banco, who worked at the cathedral and associated with many of Ghiberti's assistants.[24] Largely because of the constant movement of sculptors into and out of the workshop, Ghibertian motifs began appearing in other sculptures even before the doors were mounted on the baptistery's east side in 1424.[25] The bronze of the completed panels had hardly solidified when, in 1417, the Sienese sculptor Giovanni di Turino borrowed copiously from them to complete his *Birth of St. John the Baptist* for the Siena Baptistery font (fig. 38). He copied Ghiberti's *Luke* (fig. 39) in representing Zacharias, his Virgin from the *Nativity* (see fig. 18) in depicting Elizabeth, as well as at least four other figures from four different panels.[26] Echoes of Ghiberti's first doors reverberated into the fifteenth century. Luca della Robbia, like Giovanni di Turino, looked to Ghiberti's *Luke*, borrowing a version of his pose for the foreground student in the *Grammar* hexagon he made for the

Florence campanile around 1438 (see cat. 16). Motifs from the doors migrated throughout the Italian peninsula, perhaps because the many assistants who came from afar to work for Ghiberti—they hailed not only from Florence but also Bologna, Rome, Verona, and Sicily—helped spread his innovations after they left the shop to seek other jobs or return home.[27] Ghibertian motifs even appear outside Italy in the early fifteenth century. In 1418, a sculptor called in the documentary record Julià lo Florentì—Giuliano the Florentine—carved alabaster reliefs for Valencia Cathedral in Spain that quote figures and compositions from the doors.[28] Ghiberti's first doors provided artistic models into the seventeenth century. In the 1620s or 1630s, the two pulpits that Donatello, at the end of his life, made for the Florentine church of San Lorenzo were detached from the church's crossing piers, placed atop small columns, and transformed into freestanding pulpits; in conjunction with this change, wooden relief panels were added to the back sections of the pulpits.[29] One of the panels inserted into the so-called Passion pulpit on the basilica's south side includes a close copy of the *John the Evangelist* from Ghiberti's first doors (figs. 40 and 41).

This exhibition gives us the chance to study up close quintessential examples of Ghiberti's influence in the early fifteenth century. Sometime around 1430 an anonymous sculptor from the Abruzzo, whom art historians typically connect to the circle of the goldsmith Nicola da Guardiagrele, carved in Maiella stone, a local limestone quarried south of L'Aquila, three reliefs that copy several of Ghiberti's compositions in his first doors (see cats. 18, 19, and 20).[30] These sculptures, along with three others, the latter indebted to Ghiberti's style if not to specific panels of the doors, were at some point immured in the courtyard of a house in the Abruzzese town of Castel di Sangro. Their surfaces, damaged by exposure to the elements and by their dismantling and movement, were covered with dark varnish and white plaster after they were carved. Flakes of the plaster are still visible in places, and the use of such surface treatment, which masks the natural beige color of the stone, was perhaps intended to make the reliefs seem as if carved in white marble.[31]

Fig. 38
Giovanni di Turino
Birth of St. John the Baptist, ca. 1417–27
Gilt bronze, 60 × 60 cm
(23⅝ × 23⅝ in.)
Baptistery of San Giovanni, Siena

Fig. 39
Lorenzo Ghiberti
North Doors of Florence Baptistery, 1403–24: panel with *St. Luke the Evangelist*
Bronze with gilding,
52 × 45 cm
(20½ × 17¾ in.)
Museo dell'Opera del Duomo, Florence

Fig. 40
Anonymous sculptor
St. John the Evangelist, detail showing early 17th-century panel in wood added to one side of Donatello's Passion pulpit, 1463–66
Bronze, 137 × 280 cm (54 × 110¼ in.)
San Lorenzo, Florence

Fig. 41
Lorenzo Ghiberti
North Doors of Florence Baptistery, 1403–24: panel with *St. John the Evangelist*
Bronze with gilding, 52 × 45 cm (20½ × 17¾ in.)
Museo dell'Opera del Duomo, Florence

These panels were not initially intended for the domestic context in which they were discovered. Although their original use and location are unknown, their link to Ghiberti is undeniable. Art historians have suggested that their author copied either his completed panels or preliminary sketches of them—in clay or on paper—accessible in the workshop.[32] Certain elements in the stone reliefs, like the drapery hanging from and wrapping around the Virgin's left leg in the *Adoration of the Magi*, or the folds of cloth enveloping Christ's hips in the *Flagellation*, repeat almost exactly the corresponding sections of Ghiberti's images (fig. 42; for the *Adoration*, see fig. 73). In other places they depart from them. The carver, for example, omitted part of the architectural backdrop in Ghiberti's *Adoration*, and Joseph, who in the *Adoration* of the doors shyly peeks between and from behind two piers, seems in the Castel di Sangro version as if he is moving through and stepping in front of the vertical supports. The carved reliefs replace the fluid, curving bodies in Ghiberti's *Flagellation* with figures standing in more upright poses. It is impossible to determine with certainty whether such changes reflect free variations of Ghiberti's final, cast panels or if they are faithful representations of his early ideas as reflected in preparatory drawings or clay models, which, with perhaps one exception, long ago disappeared.

That exception, a drawing in the Albertina in Vienna (fig. 43), contains what may be preliminary studies, either by Ghiberti or a workshop assistant, for the figures in the *Flagellation* who reach back, coiling their arms in the moment before they whip them forward and unleash their aggression.[33] At the drawing's top left the artist sketched a figure who holds his arms low; the figure at the top right elevates both arms; and in the top center the artist has combined the poses, placing one arm up and one down as if demonstrating the merits of balance in pose. This body, which has been reinforced with repeating pen strokes that render it almost sculptural, resembles the figure at left in the bronze relief. Ghiberti did not adopt the pose twice explored in the drawing's lower part, nor did he include the sketch's architectural backdrop, which comprises a room topped by a ceiling (covered with a perspectival grid) and bordered in the back by an arcade in which vertical supports carry summarily sketched arches. A simpler building, in which two rows of five columns hold up a perfectly flat ceiling, appears in Ghiberti's panel. We do find arches, however, running along the background of the Castel di Sangro *Flagellation*. If we assume that the drawing was produced in the shop as part of Ghiberti's design process, the appearance of arches in the background of the stone panel perhaps suggests that these images together reflect an initial planning stage, when Ghiberti and his assistants were working their way through ideas about the appearance of the *Flagellation* relief's architectural elements.

Having demonstrated his skill as a sculptor, Ghiberti was in high demand after 1410. In the years before and after he finished his first baptistery doors he worked on a number of projects for other sites, most prominently the church of Orsanmichele, for which he made three colossal bronze statues. The guilds owned the rights to the niches located in the church's exterior walls, and in the early fifteenth century they turned to Donatello, Nanni di Banco, and Ghiberti to fill them with statues. Ghiberti fashioned three in bronze: *John the Baptist* for the Calimala (1412–17); *Matthew* (1419–22) for the Arte del Cambio, the bankers' guild; and *Stephen* (1425–29) for the Arte della Lana, the guild of the woolen cloth manufacturers and merchants. Between 1417 and 1427 he also sculpted two bronze reliefs for the Siena Baptistery font.

The commission for the *Stephen* came just months after he signed, on January 2, 1425, a contract for a second set of baptistery doors.[34] For these doors, known today as the Gates of Paradise (fig. 44), Ghiberti fashioned ten Old Testament narratives in square, rather than quatrefoil, reliefs that measure thirty-one inches on each side. He modeled and cast the panels, as well as twenty-four statuettes in high relief for the niches flanking them in the frame, with astonishing speed: by 1437 these relief elements were done, ready to be cleaned and chased.[35] Between 1437 and 1452, when the doors were mounted on the baptistery's east side (displacing his first set to the north portal), Ghiberti and his assistants cleaned, chased, and gilded the panels and frame elements. They also fashioned the doors' massive back sections and frames (each door was cast in a single pour), the twenty-four small gilded busts adorning the doors, including Ghiberti's self-portrait, and the threshold, lintel, and jambs. Once again he organized a large shop of laborers and skilled assistants, the latter group including Michelozzo (who helped design and chase the cycle's architectural structures), the painter Benozzo Gozzoli (who chased figural and landscape elements), the goldsmith Bernardo Cennini, Ghiberti's son Vittorio, and, possibly, Luca della Robbia.[36] As with Ghiberti's first doors, the Gates of Paradise influenced generations of painters and sculptors in Florence and outside the city.[37]

Ghiberti sculpted the doors in his large workshop in Florence, which was located across the street from the hospital of Santa Maria Nuova. His shop was, first and foremost, a

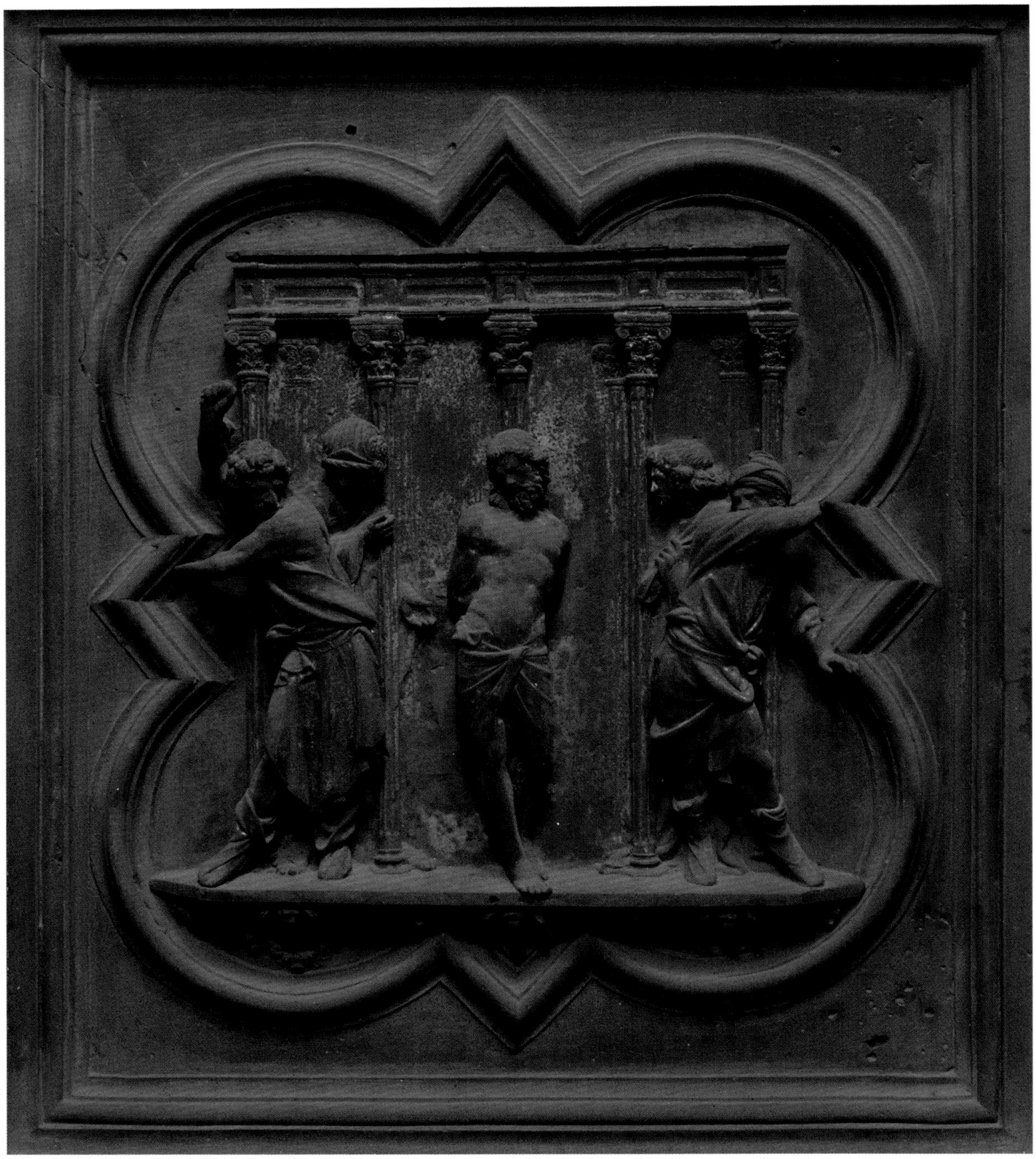

Fig. 42
Lorenzo Ghiberti
North Doors of Florence Baptistery, 1403–24: panel with the *Flagellation*
Bronze with gilding
52 × 45 cm
(20½ × 17¾ in.)
Museo dell'Opera del Duomo, Florence

OPPOSITE
Fig. 43
Lorenzo Ghiberti (or circle)
Sketch for the Flagellation of Christ (detail), n.d.
Pen and bister ink on paper,
page 21.6 × 16.6 cm
(8½ × 6½ in.)
Albertina, Vienna

place for the creation of bronze sculpture, and upon entering it in the busiest periods one must have been overwhelmed by noise, smoke, heat, and light. By the 1420s, however, the workshop had also evolved into a place of study and contemplation—of both images and books. Excerpts from Ghiberti's will and later documents reveal that it contained a *scrittoio*—a place for reading and writing—and that he kept in the shop books, writings, reliefs and statues in bronze and marble, drawings, ancient busts and carved vases, and cut and uncut gems.[38] Later descriptions hint at the richness of Ghiberti's art collection, which possibly included a bronze relief attributed to Polykleitos and a version of the *Medici Venus*.[39] Curious artists probably went to the shop to study Ghiberti's works in bronze and preparatory models and drawings, as well as, perhaps, the antiquities in his collection.[40] Visitors to Florence were also sometimes granted access to his working spaces. In 1433 Cyriac of Ancona went to the city and saw, in the workshops of Donatello and Ghiberti, modern and

ancient works in bronze and marble.[41] By this point these workshops straddled the line between private and public.

Ghiberti's collecting habits reflect his connection to intellectual currents in the opening decades of the fifteenth century. If after 1403 Ghiberti created and shaped a collective of artists and craftsmen who helped him revive bronze casting in Florence, by the late 1420s he had gravitated towards another community, namely the humanist intellectuals who directed their attention to the history and literature of ancient Greece and Rome, making it their aim to learn about these civilizations by recovering lost texts or amending those that had reached the fifteenth century in corrupted form. They also studied ancient images, coins, carved gems, and inscriptions, often exchanging ideas about them with artists and architects. Poggio Bracciolini, a member of the humanist group, discussed ancient sculptures with Donatello.[42] The late fifteenth-century biographer Vespasiano da Bisticci wrote that Niccolò Niccoli, known for his dogged search for ancient manuscripts and his immense library, befriended a number of contemporary artists, including Brunelleschi, Donatello, Luca della Robbia, and Ghiberti.[43] In his autobiography Ghiberti recounts a meeting with Niccoli in which the two men examined an ancient chalcedony intaglio whose delicate carving, he states, could only be appreciated in low light.[44] Ghiberti also accepted commissions from, and was a close associate of, Palla Strozzi, one of the wealthiest men of early fifteenth-century Florence and a member of the supervisory committee that administered the project for Ghiberti's first doors. Strozzi participated in the humanist movement and amassed a large and diverse library of Greek and Latin books.[45]

Ghiberti engaged with the heritage of antiquity from the earliest stages of his career. To fashion figures in his competition panel and first doors he drew heavily on ancient models, both those he saw in Florence and others he encountered during his travels to other cities, Rome included, on the Italian peninsula. By about 1425 his interest in antiquity had expanded to include not just images but also texts—and he sometimes sought quite obscure ones he learned about while engaged in conversation with contemporary intellectuals. Around 1430, for example, he wrote to the humanist Giovanni Aurispa, asking to borrow a rare manuscript copy of Athenaeus Mechanicus's *On Machines*, a treatise in Greek on siege engines from the first century BCE.[46] Ghiberti could have learned about its contents only with assistance from a member of the humanist circle who knew Greek.

The clearest evidence for his engagement with ancient textual sources comes in the *Commentaries*, the three-book treatise he probably began writing in the late 1420s and worked on until the end of his life. This remarkable, unprecedented text contains a history of ancient art, a history of late medieval Italian art that opens with Cimabue and Giotto and culminates in Ghiberti's autobiography (mentioned above), the first ever written by an artist, and, in its final section, a compilation of excerpts from medieval optical treatises that explain the functioning of human vision. Ghiberti's account of ancient art, the first written after antiquity, derives largely from Pliny's *Natural* History and Vitruvius's *Ten Books on Architecture*, sections of both of which Ghiberti probably translated into Tuscan himself. His account of the development of Italian art is entirely original. Although for the *Commentaries* and other projects Ghiberti directed much of his intellectual energy towards examining ancient textual sources, his interests expanded to include medieval literary

Fig. 44
Lorenzo Ghiberti
East Doors of Florence Baptistery, known as the "Gates of Paradise," 1425–52
Bronze with gilding, height 4.6 m (181⅛ in.); each panel 79.4 × 79.4 cm (31 ¼ × 31 ¼ in.)
Museo dell'Opera del Duomo, Florence

works, including Dante's *Divine Comedy*, a copy of which he acquired in the late 1420s.[47] In seeking and exploring ancient and medieval texts, Ghiberti reflected the widespread literacy of his society. During the late 1420s the literacy rate among men in Florence was around seventy to eighty percent, and Florentines of all social levels sought and read books.[48] The activities represented in Luca della Robbia's campanile images of *Dialectic* and *Grammar* (see cats. 15 and 16), where figures discuss and debate texts, would have seemed very familiar indeed to their fifteenth-century viewers.

Ghiberti's ideas about how artists could take advantage of book learning are encapsulated in his comments on a painted map of the earth (a *mappamundo*) that Ambrogio Lorenzetti, whom Ghiberti praises highly in the *Commentaries*, made for the Palazzo Pubblico in Siena in 1345.[49] After describing Ambrogio's work, he writes that its representation of the land was imperfect because, in the time of Lorenzetti, "there was not then knowledge of the *Cosmography* of Ptolemy."[50] Ptolemy's cartographic treatise was translated into Latin around 1405 after Palla Strozzi brought it to Florence, and Ghiberti may have seen Ptolemy's book, both in Greek and in Latin translation, in Palla's library.[51] From Ghiberti's perspective, Ptolemy's authoritative text offered its readers knowledge previously inaccessible. Reading such books, his words suggest, helps the artist understand the world so that he can correctly represent its people, forms, history, and structures. Ghiberti drew ideas about the physical world and its human communities from a range of ancient and medieval texts, and his approach might thus be likened to that of Augustine, who, in *On Christian Learning*, recommends that his readers use their knowledge of the Greek and Hebrew languages, of history, of natural forms like animals, trees, plants, stones, and stars, and of human activities like the mechanical arts, no matter the source for the information, to comprehend and interpret biblical events.[52] Certainly Ghiberti's ties to the humanist community gave him access to pagan and Christian sources, many of which he must have discussed with contemporary intellectuals, that explain the earth's natural environment and describe the human communities that grew and developed throughout history.

The world that Ghiberti imagined and sculpted in the Gates of Paradise changes according to ideas he found in these books. His landscapes, for example, evolve in accordance with geological theories propounded by ancient and medieval philosophers. The episodes in the *Adam and Eve* relief (fig. 45) are set in a landscape of gently rippling sheets of ground that slope upward at the panel's sides. This landscape reflects ideas found in Augustine, who states in one of his Genesis commentaries that the earth's surface, immediately after its creation, was relatively flat.[53] Medieval philosophers, Dante among them, wrote at length on precisely how topographical elements—hills, mountains, and, eventually, mountain ranges—emerge from the earth, eventually settling on

OPPOSITE
Fig. 45
Lorenzo Ghiberti
East Doors of Florence Baptistery, known as the "Gates of Paradise," 1425–52, panel with the stories of Adam and Eve
Bronze with gilding, 79.4 × 79.4 cm (31¼ × 31¼ in.)
Museo dell'Opera del Duomo, Florence

ABOVE
Fig. 46
Lorenzo Ghiberti
East Doors of Florence Baptistery, known as the "Gates of Paradise," 1425–52, panel with the stories of David
Bronze with gilding, 79.4 × 79.4 cm (31¼ × 31¼ in.)
Museo dell'Opera del Duomo, Florence

Fig. 47
Lorenzo Ghiberti
East Doors of Florence Baptistery, known as the "Gates of Paradise," 1425–52: panel with the stories of Noah
Bronze with gilding, 79.4 × 79.4 cm (31¼ × 31¼ in.)
Museo dell'Opera del Duomo, Florence

a theory first developed by Pliny, who hypothesized that stars exert an upward pull on the earth's land.[54] In the lower panels of the Gates of Paradise, which represent subsequent events in Old Testament history, one indeed finds distant mountains and, in the *David* relief (fig. 46), a peak that nearly reaches the panel's upper edge. The cycle also marks the emergence of the seasons. A tradition with its roots in the Bible (Genesis 8:22) and sustained by many medieval authors held that the seasons began changing only after the Flood.[55] Accordingly, Ghiberti dresses his protagonists in long-sleeved, multi-layered garments only in the episodes following the recession of the Flood's waters. In the representation of Noah, his wife, sons, and daughters-in-law exiting the ark (fig. 47 and fig. 47, detail)—here envisioned as a pyramid—Ghiberti gave to the son at the far left of the group activated drapery that billows outward, an indication of the presence of wind, which, according to ancient and medieval thought, causes and accompanies meteorological events.

In subsequent panels Ghiberti, a keen observer of nature, devised novel means of visualizing natural phenomena in the celestial and earthly realms. In the *Moses* panel (fig. 48), for example, members of a large crowd standing beneath the summit on which God hands the tablets of the law to Moses (Exodus 31:18) gaze upward, cover their faces, or

Fig. 47, detail

stare at the ground, stunned, it seems, by something they have witnessed, or now see, in the sky. In the biblical account, the sky and the land evince the supernatural status of the events happening atop Sinai: in the moment when God descends to earth to speak to Moses, lightning and thunder flash and rumble and, according to some readings of the passage, the ground shakes (Exodus 19:16–18).[56] Representing nature's dramatic spectacles presented Ghiberti with certain challenges. How, he must have wondered, could one suggest in bronze the presence or imminence of thunder and earthquakes, phenomena heard and felt but not seen? And how is it possible to indicate lightning, which even human sight strains to capture given the speed with which bolts flash across the sky? To solve these dilemmas he turned to widely read texts that investigate the natural forces and elements that cause thunder, lightning, and earthquakes. Most ancient and medieval writers repeated the ideas of Aristotle, who first proposed that hot, dry winds, when they tear through sheets of surrounding, cool clouds, make thunder; when these winds catch fire, as, he says, they often do, they appear as jagged lightning bolts.[57] The only step in the process that Aristotle does not explain pertains to the ways such winds are ignited, and later authors—the ancient Roman philosophical poet Lucretius, for example, or the seventh-century encyclopedist Isidore of Seville—theorized that, when clouds collide, they set the air on fire.[58]

Viewers of Ghiberti's *Moses* panel find precisely these processes and natural forces in the sky above Sinai (fig. 48), where angels flit through the air and, at points, pierce the curtain of clouds trailing behind God. Their drapery responds to the force of their flight, but in places it also billows out in the opposite direction, responding, it seems, to moving air that whips through the sky. Several of the little angels pull their garments back towards their bodies, attempting to counter the wind's blustery force. This same wind perhaps also causes the fragmentation of the bank of clouds at the panel's upper left edge, where clusters of cloud have been sheared away from the larger sheet. Ghiberti thus illustrates the forces that give rise to thunder, as winds pass through and break up the expanse of clouds surrounding the angels. The individual shards of cloud, moreover, slice into each other, crashing together to produce the heat needed to ignite air and produce lightning. Ghiberti suggests the imminence of an earthquake by alluding to phenomena preceding it. Pliny summarizes Aristotle's theory that two signs portend earthquakes: ocean waves swell, and a streak of cloud stretches across the sky.[59] Appropriately, then, in the panel the waves of the body of water in the lower left corner roil, and a figure standing at the water's edge looks fixedly into the sky as if gazing at some unusual occurrence.

In the Gates of Paradise, human communities change over time just as nature evolves. Individuals (Adam and Eve) create families that increase in size, extend into multiple generations, and eventually become, in the last four panels, teeming crowds that populate communities living within cities like Jerusalem, which appears twice, first in the *David* panel's background and then again in the *Solomon* relief (fig. 49), where Ghiberti takes his viewers directly into the city square beside Solomon's temple. Architecture similarly evolves

OPPOSITE
Fig. 48
Lorenzo Ghiberti
East Doors of Florence Baptistery, known as the "Gates of Paradise," 1425–52: panel with the stories of Moses
Bronze with gilding.
79.4 × 79.4 cm
(31¼ × 31¼ in.)
Museo dell'Opera del Duomo, Florence

ABOVE
Fig. 49
Lorenzo Ghiberti
East Doors of Florence Baptistery, known as the "Gates of Paradise," 1425–52: panel with the story of Solomon and the Queen of Sheba
Bronze with gilding.
79.4 × 79.4 cm
(31¼ × 31¼ in.)
Museo dell'Opera del Duomo, Florence

Fig. 50
_orenzo Ghiberti
East Doors of Florence
Baptistery, known as the
"Gates of Paradise,"
1425–52: panel with the
Stories of Cain and Abel
Bronze with gilding,
79.4 × 79.4 cm
(31 1/4 × 31 1/4 in.)
Museo dell'Opera
del Duomo, Florence

Fig. 50, detail

Fig. 51
Lorenzo Ghiberti
East Doors of Florence Baptistery, known as the "Gates of Paradise," 1425–52: panel with the stories of Jacob and Esau
Bronze with gilding, 79.4 × 79.4 cm (31¼ × 31¼ in.)
Museo dell'Opera del Duomo, Florence

Fig. 52
Lorenzo Ghiberti
East Doors of Florence Baptistery, known as the "Gates of Paradise," 1425–52: panel with the stories of Joseph and his brothers
Bronze with gilding, 79.4 × 79.4 cm (31¼ × 31¼ in.)
Museo dell'Opera del Duomo, Florence

Fig. 53
Lorenzo Ghiberti
East Doors of Florence Baptistery, known as the "Gates of Paradise," 1425–52: panel with the stories of Joshua
Bronze with gilding,
79.4 × 79.4 cm
(31¼ × 31¼ in.)
Museo dell'Opera
del Duomo, Florence

Fig. 45, detail

from simple to complex: rustic fences (*Adam and Eve*) are followed by thatched huts (*Cain and Abel*; fig. 50 and fig. 50, detail), pyramids and shelters made of forked posts, beams, and sloped roofs (*Noah*), elegant halls made with arcuated supports and adorned with Corinthian pilasters (*Jacob and Esau*; fig. 51), perfectly round buildings supported by slender piers and graced by Composite pilasters (*Joseph*; fig. 52), and, finally, entire cities filled with large and small structures and enclosed within crenellated walls (*Joshua* [fig. 53] and *David*). In the final relief, the temple of Jerusalem, its vaulted interior resembling that of Florence Cathedral, seemingly takes us into Ghiberti's own time. The cycle's classicizing buildings reflect Ghiberti's careful study of ancient architecture, but the earlier part of his architectural history, in which biblical protagonists create rudimentary structures, comes straight from the most sophisticated understanding of the history of architecture available in his time: Vitruvius's *Ten Books on Architecture*.[60] Humans, says Vitruvius, first built huts of mud and leaves, sometimes covered with straw, and then devised more advanced structures made of "forked props and sticks," often with walls made of mud and wood and roofed with inclined planes composed of "reeds and leafage." The earliest peoples, he adds, also fashioned pyramidal structures, a detail that perhaps led Ghiberti to suggest that Noah, one of the Bible's earliest builders, designed the ark as a pyramid. If Ghiberti learned, as some have suggested, that the third-century theologian Origen described the ark's shape as pyramidal, he must have found satisfying this confluence of Christian and pagan beliefs, which proved the potential compatibility of Judeo-Christian ideas and those put forward by revered ancient authors whose ideas on art and architecture Ghiberti and his humanist contemporaries deemed authoritative.[61]

The doors' ten reliefs, which individually depict narratives unfolding over discrete amounts of time, collectively show how the world evolved over the four millennia that Ghiberti and his contemporaries believed had elapsed between the Creation of Adam, which appears in the first panel, and the meeting of Solomon and the Queen of Sheba, the final relief's subject.[62] The cycle is as much history as art. The practice of sculpture, however, was never far from Ghiberti's mind, and a number of details manifest his experience as a sculptor and reveal his interest in investigating, through the reliefs, the origins of his art. His consideration of the sculptural act, for example, tinged his visualization of the Creation of Adam (fig. 45, detail), whom God fashions, in the Bible, in his own "image and likeness" and by manipulating wet earth (Genesis 1:26 and 2:7). Images of the episode typically show Adam sitting on a pedestal unrelated to the shape of his body or reclining atop a flat sheet of earth (e.g., fig. 54). But in Ghiberti's *Adam and Eve* panel, he reclines within a mound of land, its outline surrounding and also resembling the silhouette of his body. The surface of the land directly around him is smooth, unlike the ridged, bumpy ground elsewhere in this panel and in the cycle's other reliefs. The same manipulated earth can be found in the upper surfaces of several concavities appearing in the triangle of land beneath Adam's body, the results, a viewer might assume, of God having scooped up earth to use in creating him.

The similarity between Adam's body and the mound of earth around him implies that the contour and shape of this earthy mass have inspired God's creation. And the presence of manipulated ground suggests that he took mud from the mound in order to model the body of the first man. Ghiberti, one might say, gave to God the abilities possessed by sculptors of marble and bronze, who, in the former case, size up a roughened block of stone to determine what can be sculpted from it before the carving begins and, in the latter, gather and manipulate wax to build up and shape a model that is then cast. To emphasize that this God has used his hands to make Adam, Ghiberti arranged his outer cloak differently compared to the relief's other episodes. In the Expulsion and Creation of Eve this raiment sweeps across God's forearms and, in places, covers his wrists. By contrast, to create Adam God has thrown his cloak over his right shoulder, from which it hangs in heavy, columnar folds, and has also rolled up the sleeves of his inner garment to keep them away from his hands—the hands, one assumes, he has used to make man. Ghiberti gives us an image of a divine artist whose working methods are in the image and likeness of the human artists who labored in his workshop. The image, moreover, attributes divine origins to sculpture in representing God as a creator who crafted man out of mud, as indeed the biblical passage says. Because this sculptor-God creates humans in his own image, the panel suggests that God and man share both a likeness and creative instincts.

The impulse to create, and often without local or immediate models to imitate, might indeed be considered the major motivating force of Ghiberti's career. He resuscitated the art of bronze sculpture in Florence, organized a new workshop capable of managing all aspects of the design and casting processes, helped train an entire generation of artists, and, of course, produced two massive sets of bronze doors as well as three monumental statues and a number of other reliefs. Such accomplishments were without precedent in the Florence of his time. The trajectory of his career recalls Leon Battista Alberti's famous dedicatory letter to Brunelleschi preceding the Tuscan version of his treatise *On Painting*, written around 1435.[63] Alberti praises Brunelleschi, Donatello, Ghiberti, Luca della Robbia, and Masaccio for displaying "a genius for every laudable enterprise" and for discovering without "preceptors and without any model ... arts and sciences hitherto unheard of and unseen." Alberti's list includes an architect, an artist known for his skill in working with marble, a bronze sculptor, a marble sculptor who around 1435 invented glazed terracotta, and a painter. Each major material or medium used, and art practiced, in early fifteenth-century Florence is represented in his enumeration of illustrious contemporaries. The presence, in his list, of two sculptors who worked with techniques not used in Florence before 1400 reminds us that the fifteenth-century renaissance of sculpture saw not only the focused

study of ancient models, but also an intense investigation of materials and how to use them in novel ways. Donatello, Nanni di Banco, and Luca della Robbia took marble carving and terracotta modeling to new heights. Ghiberti reinvigorated the lost art of bronze casting, working alongside a generation of artists who assisted him and learned from him. In fashioning fifteenth-century Florence's most expansive and impressive cycles of biblical imagery in bronze, Ghiberti affirmed for his contemporaries the possibility of renewal and the idea that forgotten or mislaid knowledge—of artistic techniques and of the history of nature and human life—could be revived and regained.

Fig. 54
Attributed to Salerno di Coppo and Corso di Buono
Creation of Adam,
13th century
Mosaic, height ca. 350 cm (137¾ in.
Baptistery of San Giovanni, Florence

"...WITH IMMENSE DILIGENCE AND DISCIPLINE"

Lorenzo Ghiberti's North Doors and the Opificio delle Pietre Dure's Conservation and Restoration Project

Marco Ciatti

The North Doors of the baptistery in Florence are the product of a famous competition held in 1401 when the guild of merchants in foreign cloth known as the Arte di Calimala (or Arte dei Mercatanti) decided to fit the building they patronized with a second set of bronze doors akin to those made by Andrea Pisano in the previous century (1330–36).[1] Around 1400 other projects were about to get underway in the city, both for the cathedral of Santa Maria del Fiore—then largely unfinished—and for Orsanmichele, which still lacked many statues in the tabernacles on its four external walls. All of this was designed to underscore the city's renewed economic prosperity and its willingness to use the profits from its business interests to adorn its most representative spaces with magnificence and splendor, highlighting its religious faith while simultaneously enhancing the image of the city and its illustrious citizens.

Fig. 55
Lorenzo Ghiberti
North Doors of Florence Baptistery, 1403–24
Bronze with gilding,
height ca. 4.6 m (181⅛ in.)
each panel 52 × 45 cm (20½ × 17¾ in.)
Museo dell'Opera del Duomo, Florence

Unfortunately, history and art history rarely dovetail neatly with a simplistic subdivision of time into centuries. During the first two decades of the fifteenth century in Florence, for instance, the transition between the late Gothic stylistic mode (deriving from Giotto) and the early Renaissance approach to making images was not seamless, as though each style were a successive chapter in an art history manual. Real life is far more multifaceted and interwoven. Cennini's *Libro dell'Arte* (*Craftsman's Handbook*), for example, which still holds Giotto up as a paradigm of technique and style, appeared in the first years of the fifteenth century, the very years in which Brunelleschi, Ghiberti, Donatello, and Nanni di Banco were conducting their first innovative experiments.[2] Another alternative to Giotto's models was the International Gothic style, an idiom then popular in the courts in northern Italy and indeed in a large part of Europe. Gentile da Fabriano, at the time one of the leading painters in Italy, was in Florence in the early 1420s and influenced Florentine artists from Masolino to Fra Angelico, thus showing a different path to renew figurative painting. The greatest innovations, however, occurred in the field of marble and bronze sculpture.

The fact that the competition for the North Doors was held in 1401, however, may appear to suggest that it marked a turning point between the past and the future of Florentine art. The most famous contestants—Brunelleschi, Ghiberti, Francesco di Valdambrino, Niccolò Lamberti, and Jacopo della Quercia—are considered the leading players in the art of their day, and they certainly do represent a truly exceptional concentration of talent. So many artists of such outstanding skill have rarely been known to compete for a single commission. A celebration of this new artistic civilization, developed through the genius and hard work of these pioneering Florentine artists, may be found in the vernacular version of Alberti's *On Painting*, composed around 1435. In the prologue of his treatise Alberti credits the Florentines for elevating art to heights not achieved since the ancients.[3]

It is astonishing that Lorenzo Ghiberti won the 1401 competition at such a young age, before he received any prominent commissions and when he was certainly not a famous artist. But then, the other contestants mentioned above were also young. Francesco di Valdambrino, born in 1363, was the oldest, followed by Jacopo della Quercia (born ca. 1374), and Brunelleschi (born 1377). That makes Ghiberti, who was born in 1378 or 1380, the youngest of those whose dates of birth are known.[4]

One of the most interesting and much-debated aspects of scholarship on Ghiberti concerns his training and what work he may have produced before the North Doors. Before 1401 Ghiberti had worked, as an assistant to another painter, for the Malatesta family in Pesaro in the Marche.[5] Giuseppe Marchini has suggested that before Ghiberti began work on his first doors, and perhaps during this sojourn in the Marche, he may have sculpted a bronze *Assumption of the Virgin* for the church of Sant'Angelo in Vado, a *Virgin Annunciate* for the church of San Filippo in the same city, and a relief of the *Madonna and Child* (the latter now in the Galleria Nazionale della Marche in Urbino).[6] These works, however, may not have been made there or could simply be evidence of Ghiberti's influence on local artists. Certainly Bartolo di Michele, known as Bartoluccio the Goldsmith—the second husband of his mother Fiore, to whom Ghiberti refers as either his father or his stepfather according to the social or fiscal requirements of the occasion—must have trained him in the techniques pertaining to that branch of art, including casting, embossing, and chasing. Numerous objects of the goldsmith's art have now been more or less unanimously attributed to Ghiberti, the most outstanding example being the reliquary of St. James in Pistoia.[7]

To date, scholarship has tended to underestimate Ghiberti's status as a goldsmith—an obvious fact yet one whose full significance has often been overlooked. Working in this field in the Middle Ages was considered to be one of the loftiest achievements in the arts. Gold symbolized royalty, and light reflected by precious stones and enamels evoked divine light according to an ancient philosophical tradition still very much alive in medieval times. In the historic connections between the various branches of the arts, the fifteenth century represented a golden era of balance in which the unity of medieval art still effectively prevailed, ensuring that every kind of material and every work, from the tiniest reliquary to the grandest cathedral, enhanced the depiction of collective values, yet with the new addition of the ideals of humanism that were to lead to the rediscovery of the artistic values of the classical era. One should not forget that Ghiberti trained as a goldsmith and mastered metalworking—indeed, there is not a single work by his hand that is not made of metal of some kind. In his *Commentaries*, in which he celebrates his own skill as an artist, he assigns the same importance to objects of the goldsmith's art as he does to large works in bronze, for example the miter, cope, and clasp he made for Pope Martin V and the gold miter he made for Pope Eugene IV.[8]

It is not clear exactly what happened in the competition of 1401 that ultimately led to Ghiberti being given the commission. While in his autobiography in the *Commentaries* Ghiberti highlights his role as the undisputed victor of the competition, a biography of Brunelleschi written by Antonio Manetti sometime between 1475 and 1497 tells us that the commission should have gone to both artists, who were judged to be equally skilled, but that Brunelleschi rejected the prospect of a dual award and left Ghiberti the lone victor.[9] The fact that their two panels alone have survived may bolster this contention. In any event, the two men were to vie with one another again in the future for the commissions for Florence Cathedral's dome and lantern, only this time the winner would be Brunelleschi.

After the contract was drawn up on November 23, 1403, the Arte di Calimala made significant changes to the iconographical program.[10] They decided that these doors should show scenes from the New Testament rather than the Old, and they added the figures of the Evangelists and Doctors of the Church. Archival documents reveal that the competition panel representing the *Sacrifice of Isaac* (see fig. 31) was to be set aside with a view to commissioning another set of doors: "It was then decided to place the New Testament in the aforesaid door and the aforesaid Story was set aside to be placed in the other door if ever the Old Testament were made."[11] It seems clear that in the meantime the idea had taken hold to commission both of the still lacking sets of doors, but that the first would contain a New Testament cycle. The contract specified that the commission was given to Lorenzo di Bartolo and to Bartolo di Michele, his father, noting that the figures in the quatrefoils should be the work of the young artist while his father and his assistants should merely play a supporting role. A document dated to sometime between 1404 and 1407 lists a total of eleven assistants, among them the young Donatello, then only a teenager. The initial contract was revised in 1407 when Ghiberti proved that it was impossible to produce three panels a year. In this new contract Ghiberti earned a salary of 200 florins a year, while the Opera agreed to foot the bill for all of the materials and assistants. The artist was asked to make sure that he worked on the commission daily, while his father, Bartolo, moved decidedly into the background, now figuring as one of the assistants and paid separately. We should note that the number of assistants helping Lorenzo in his herculean task rose to as many as twenty-one after 1407. For short periods of time the list even included Donatello and Paolo Uccello, while Giuliano di Ser Andrea was to prove his most loyal aide, working alongside the master from 1405 to 1433. The experience was to prove of crucial importance also in the formative years of Michelozzo, who first worked with Ghiberti from 1417 to 1425. With the new arrangement after 1407, work proceeded apace. Richard Krautheimer correctly argued that 1420 should be considered the starting date for work on the frame, the decorative reliefs, and the small heads on the doors.

This massive frame proved extremely difficult for Ghiberti to cast. According to Vasari, the sculptor produced a model of the structure in wood, which he then attempted to cast in a workshop located opposite Santa Maria Nuova: "as chance would have it [the cast] did not come well" and so "without losing heart or giving way to depression, [Ghiberti] promptly made another mold and cast it again, without telling anyone about it, and it came out very well."[12] A new document recently published by Luca Boschetto offers a somewhat different version of Vasari's account.[13] There were indeed three major

problems when the frames were cast, and on February 3, 1422 three Burgundian masters, Domenico di Diveth, Iacop Ghaglieth, and Nicolas Andrat, swore before an official of the Mercanzia (merchants' court) to "recast and make good those frames which they promised the aforementioned Lorenzo and his companions they would do." Taking his cue from a note in the *Libro del Pilastro di Orsanmichele*, Boschetto argues that the three men were already in Florence and that Ghiberti had involved them both in casting his *St. Matthew*, in connection with which he would later admit to having had problems, as well as with the North Doors (cf. his deposition before the consuls of the bankers' and money-changers' guild or Arte del Cambio on July 16, 1421). A likely trace of Ghiberti's technical problems, which may still be seen today, is a crack found by restorers crossing the door from top to bottom. In any event, the North Doors were completed on April 19, 1424, having been made, as Lorenzo himself was to remark, "with immense diligence and discipline." Ghiberti put in two decades of hard work to complete the doors, which cost the Calimala roughly 16,000 florins, a portion of which paid for the 34,000 pounds of bronze used in casting them. These doors were, in 1424, set up on the baptistery's eastern portal, across from the façade of Santa Maria del Fiore.[14]

The twenty-eight individual panels maintain the Gothic quatrefoil shape that had been used also for Andrea Pisano's doors. They are set in the center of elegant borders filled with plants and small animals, these separated in the corners by small heads of prophets and sybils (figs. 56 and 57). The freshness and compositional freedom of the design framing the panels makes it a masterpiece in its own right. The iconographical structure of the doors considers the two doors to form a single, unbroken space that should be read from left to right. In stylistic terms, the overall composition reveals an impressive unity of hand, thus complying with the patrons' demand that the figurative parts be entirely the work of Ghiberti; in fact it is impossible to identify the work of his numerous assistants, however prestigious they may have been in their own right. It is also very difficult to assign dates to each of the panels within the twenty-year period over which the doors were made or to know in what order they were produced. In his fundamental analysis of the artist's career, however, Richard Krautheimer has endeavored to group them together on the basis of compositional and formal considerations. The first group includes reliefs developed along lines similar to Ghiberti's trial relief: parallels may be found in the figures' facial features, their flowing robes, and the strong S-curve—in short, those features which betray the influence of Gothic models. The panels in this group are the *Annunciation*, the *Nativity*, the *Adoration of the Magi*, the *Baptism of Christ* (figs. 58, 59, and 60) and the *Agony in the Garden*, some of which are divided diagonally by rock formations echoing the rocks in the competition panel.

Fig. 56
Lorenzo Ghiberti
North Doors of Florence Baptistery, frame of left door: small head set between the *Transfiguration* and the *Baptism of Christ*, before cleaning

OPPOSITE
Fig. 57
Lorenzo Ghiberti
North Doors of Florence Baptistery, frame of left door: small head set between the *Transfiguration* and the *Baptism of Christ*, during cleaning

Fig. 58
Lorenzo Ghiberti
North Doors of Florence Baptistery: panel with the *Baptism of Christ*, before cleaning

Fig. 59
Lorenzo Ghiberti
North Doors of Florence Baptistery: panel with the *Baptism of Christ*, during cleaning

Krautheimer identified a second group comprising *Christ among the Doctors*, the *Temptation* (figs. 61, 62, and 63, fig. 61, detail, and fig. 63, detail), the *Transfiguration*, the *Crucifixion*, and the *Last Supper*, in which we can perceive a looser and more personal style and in which the figures adapt to the quatrefoil with elegant movement: see, for instance, the figures of Christ and Satan in the *Temptation*. While the first group may have been completed in the first phase before 1407, the second may tentatively be assigned to the period after the contract was revised in that year. Krautheimer's third group is distinguished by its greater compositional richness. These reliefs are less constrained by the shape of the quatrefoil frame, and the figures adopt movements previously unseen. The panels with these features are the *Expulsion of the Money-Changers from the Temple* (figs. 64, 65, and 66), the *Entry into Jerusalem*, *Christ before Pilate*, the *Raising of Lazarus*, and *Christ Walking upon the Water*. In the fourth group of reliefs, the compositions highlight a central figure that is the narrative's focus, and many of these last reliefs demonstrate Ghiberti's greater confidence in the handling of perspective in the classicizing architecture. According to Krautheimer, this group includes the *Arrest of Christ*, the *Flagellation*, the *Way to Calvary*, and the *Pentecost* (figs. 67 and 68, and fig. 68, detail).

It is also worth pointing out that the setting for the scenes taking place inside and outside buildings determines the base supporting the composition: a rock in the latter case and a platform in the former. The rhythm dictating the alternation of solids and voids must also have been calculated to allow the quatrefoil panels to be inserted into the individual frames, which are part and parcel of the structure. Rivets and small wedges fix the panels in place. Technical investigations conducted to date suggest that Ghiberti employed the lost-wax method of casting, using a fairly soft alloy that allowed him to take all the time

Fig. 60
Lorenzo Ghiberti
North Doors of Florence Baptistery: panel with the *Baptism of Christ*, after cleaning

he needed to chase the composition, which he finished to a degree worthy of the finest goldsmith's work but on a monumental scale. After the lengthy and meticulous chasing process was complete, the panel was gilded using the heated mercury amalgam method which produces an extremely high-quality sheen on the finished product. Currently the restorers are seeking to determine whether it was intended to gild the entire surface of each panel, including both the figures and the setting, as was the case with the two surviving panels from the competition of 1401, or whether only the figures were meant to be gilded in order to cause them to stand out against the background. In many of the panels the background bears only traces of gilding, as though it had been intentionally removed or had overflowed by mistake from the figures on which, on the contrary, the gilding is still remarkably intact.

In pursuit of additional clues that might shed light on the chronological order in which Ghiberti completed his panels, several scholars have turned to the many contemporary artists who attentively studied and imitated the reliefs on the North Doors, many of them not directly involved in the doors' production. One such example is Giuliano di Nofri,

Fig 61
Lorenzo Ghiberti
North Doors of Florence Baptistery: panel with the *Temptation of Christ*, before cleaning

Fig 61, detail

Fig. 62
Lorenzo Ghiberti
North Doors of Florence Baptistery: panel with the *Temptation of Christ*, during cleaning

Fig. 63
Lorenzo Ghiberti
North Doors of Florence Baptistery: panel with the *Temptation of Christ*, after cleaning

Fig. 63, detail

who served as a witness when Ghiberti signed a contract to complete reliefs for the Siena baptismal font, and who thus had a connection—professional or personal—to Ghiberti. When Giuliano carved twelve alabaster reliefs for the choir of the Chapel of the Holy Chalice in Valencia Cathedral between 1418 and 1424, he exhibited a familiarity with Ghiberti's scenes of *Christ Walking upon the Water*, the *Expulsion of the Money-Changers from the Temple*, and *Christ before Pilate*, thus giving us a *terminus ante quem* for these particular reliefs. Along similar lines, Lorenzo Monaco painted his *Christ in the Garden of Gethsemane* (now in the Galleria dell'Accademia, Florence) in 1408, which may owe a debt to the same scene on the North Doors, perhaps providing us with a date indicating the end of the first phase of Ghiberti's work. There may be many other derivations and instances of Ghiberti's sculptures influencing the art of his day, which would indicate that the North Doors may rightly be considered, to quote a term so aptly coined by Benvenuto Cellini, a "school of the world" for the early Renaissance in Florence, a claim similar to that made by Ghiberti himself, who wrote that "few things of importance have been made in our region that were not designed and ordered by my own hand." Further instances of derivation may be found in Nicola da Guardiagrele's altar frontal (1433–48) for the cathedral of Teramo, and in a cycle of six panels by the so-called Master of Castel di Sangro that are now in the Museo dell'Opera del Duomo, Florence. Three of the panels, the *Adoration of the Magi*, the *Flagellation*, and the *Crucifixion* (see cats. 18, 19, and 20), are clearly based on Ghiberti's work, while the other

Fig. 64
Lorenzo Ghiberti
North Doors of Florence Baptistery: panel with the *Expulsion of the Money-Changers from the Temple*, before cleaning

Fig. 65
Lorenzo Ghiberti
North Doors of Florence Baptistery: panel with the *Expulsion of the Money-Changers from the Temple*, during cleaning

three, the *Flight into Egypt*, the *Presentation in the Temple*, and *Judas's Betrayal of Christ*, while stylistically akin to the first three, are of subjects not depicted on the North Doors. All of them, however, are included in the altar frontal in Teramo Cathedral, and it has thus been suggested that the latter three compositions may also have been based on panels designed by Ghiberti but never produced owing to a change in the iconographical program for the doors.

It is interesting to compare the relief of the *Baptism of Christ* on the North Doors with the panel of the same subject that Ghiberti produced for the baptismal font in Siena. In the Siena relief, modeled between 1424 and 1425 and delivered after gilding in 1427, Ghiberti shows that he has made further progress, producing figures of greater plasticity yet without sacrificing their grace. Most importantly, it is in the background that he has enriched his composition. A group of angels in low relief frames the figure of Christ, while the Almighty appears above the dove of the Holy Spirit, imparting His blessing. Ghiberti's Siena panels have a painterly quality with layered planar development, features that would culminate in the baptistery's Gates of Paradise and that may well have been facilitated by the new-shaped format Ghiberti used in the Siena reliefs. In fact, it is perfectly possible that his work on the baptismal font in Siena, falling as it did between his commissions for the two sets of baptistery doors, convinced him of the need to adopt a new format for the scenes in the later commission. The panel depicting the *Arrest of John the Baptist*, also for the Siena Baptistery font, appears to have been designed earlier, around 1420. Krautheimer argues that it refers directly to the composition of the episode from the North Doors showing *Christ before Pilate*, yet is imbued with the dynamic energy to be found in the scene of the *Expulsion of the Money-Changers from the Temple*. If we look closely, we can see that here, too, Ghiberti increases the depth of the scene. The building in the background is not simply a depiction of classical architecture providing a stage for the scene as it does in the North Doors; it is the depiction of interior space in a depth achieved by varying the levels of the modeling, which could well make it closer in date to the *Baptism*.

Another of Ghiberti's inventions may be found on the back of the doors, where squares contain round frames housing circular reliefs showing lions' heads in various poses. We should also note that the division of space on the back and front of the doors is not identical because there are no plant borders on the back. Our restorers are currently using X-ray and other non-invasive techniques to explore the methods that Ghiberti used to assemble his doors. An initial assessment suggests that the panels were inserted from the front, fixed, as mentioned earlier, to the frames which are part and parcel of the overall main frame structure (with or without the additional use of wedges) and possibly also using the round aperture on the back to help place them. These apertures were then sealed with the reliefs of lions' heads described above, which appear to have been held in place by iron dowels.

After completion of the major conservation and restoration project on Lorenzo Ghiberti's Gates of Paradise in the summer of 2012, the Opificio delle Pietre Dure, the institute in Florence responsible for research and conservation of works of art in stone and metal, was commissioned by the Opera di Santa Maria del Fiore to start work on the North Doors.[15] The experience gained with the Gates of Paradise and the numerous technological innovations devised to resolve its conservation issues have had an immediate and positive impact on work on the North Doors. The project, initially directed by Anna Maria Giusti (whose place was taken by Maria Donata Mazzoni when the former retired), was thus able to avail itself of the expertise that restorers Stefania Agnoletti, Annalena Brini, and other technical authorities at the Opificio had gained during the many years they spent working on the Gates

OPPOSITE
Fig. 66
Lorenzo Ghiberti
North Doors of Florence Baptistery: panel with the *Expulsion of the Money-Changers from the Temple*, after cleaning

ABOVE LEFT
Fig. 67
Lorenzo Ghiberti
North Doors of Florence Baptistery: panel with the *Pentecost*, before cleaning

ABOVE
Fig. 68
Lorenzo Ghiberti
North Doors of Florence Baptistery: panel with the *Pentecost*, during cleaning

of Paradise. This particularly with regard to the cleaning phase, which is now being conducted partly by mechanical means and partly using the laser devised by the Italian National Council for Research in Florence.

The initial results of the cleaning have been truly exceptional, albeit with a certain lack of uniformity to be expected with objects of this age, due to both the techniques originally adopted to produce them and to local conservation conditions. Two aspects of the doors instantly caught our attention: first, the extraordinary refinement and quality of their execution; and second, the splendid mercury gilding of the figures, which causes them to stand out against the now predominantly bronze background. The slow and deliberate action of the laser produced results of extraordinary quality, fully respecting the work's textural and aesthetic features, which were enhanced considerably by the cleaning. The conservation and restoration project began with a series of diagnostic inspections and investigations *in situ*, prior to dismantling. After this phase the North Doors were moved from the baptistery to the Opificio's laboratory on the night of March 18/19, 2013, an operation carried out by specialized companies with assistance and advice from the Opificio's experts (fig. 69). This second phase saw the start of a detailed photographic campaign to record the doors' condition before, during, and after restoration, which is being conducted throughout the different phases of the project. The restoration process proper then got underway with the microaspiration of fine dust on the surface, the dust being analyzed to allow us to address safely the next phase involving washing. A structure specially designed and produced for the purpose was then installed to allow us to wash the doors with deionized water vapor (fig. 70). This initial cleaning of the surface was conducted on one part of the doors at a time, each individual part being of an appropriate size to allow us constantly to monitor and assess the results. The washing of the front was also monitored in an onging manner by the Opificio's scientific laboratory to allow it to examine the quantity and nature of the soluble salts dissolved. The backs of the two doors, on the other hand (fig. 71), were washed with a microvaporizer, but only after protecting the lions' heads because the sporadic traces of gilding still on them, presumably applied using the gold-leaf gilding method, might have proved sensitive to moisture. The washed surfaces were immediately dried after each application.

The diagnostic inspections, which began while the doors were still *in situ* in the baptistery, continued in an attempt to gain a deeper understanding of the state of conservation of the surfaces and of any attendant deterioration issues and their causes, in order to allow us to identify the most appropriate cleaning method. After a comprehensive picture of all these facets had been built up, cautious cleaning trials were conducted on small marginal parts of the doors, choosing areas in different positions with differing conservation issues (fig. 72). For instance, we compared the potential results of chemical and mechanical cleaning on an inner strip of the left-hand door in ungilded bronze. The chemical process involved the use of various kinds of solvent, these applied with different types of gel, while the mechanical process centered on the use of a scalpel and other appropriate tools. In those areas where it was possible to detect the presence of gilding—the figures, for example—cleaning trials were conducted using the sophisticated technique of photoablation by laser based on the experience gained while restor-

Fig. 68, detail

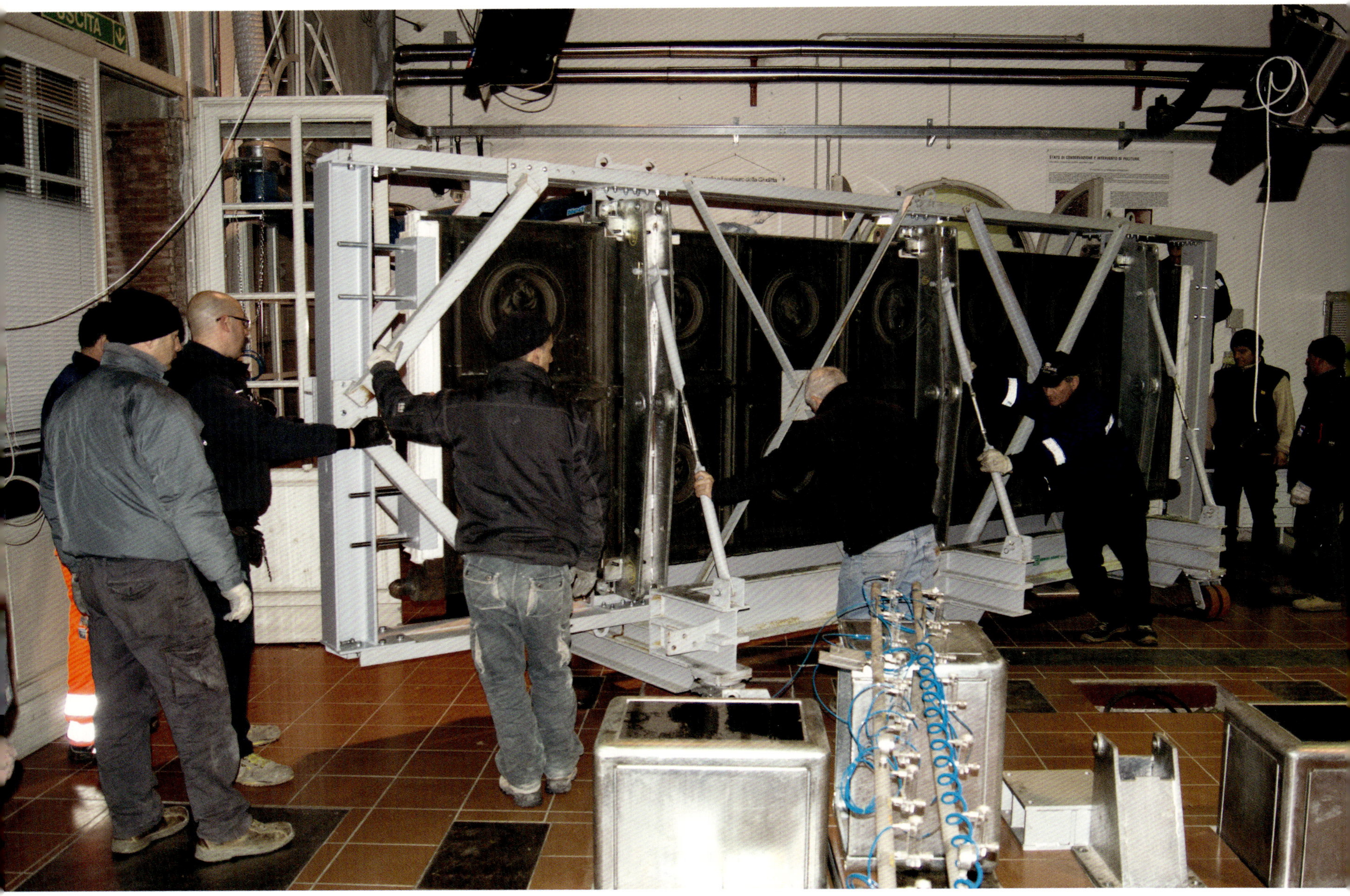

Fig. 69
Moving one of the two doors into the Opificio delle Pietre Dure

ing the Gates of Paradise. All of these various cleaning techniques are now being used by the restorers who are currently conducting the restoration and, as mentioned above, good results have been obtained for both the bronze and gilded components. Naturally, the individual panels are in very different states of conservation, especially with regard to cleaning. This is a result primarily of the greater or lesser degree of success achieved by Ghiberti when originally gilding each panel, but also of the panels' higher or lower position on the doors which resulted in a difference in their exposure to atmospheric agents, human risk, and random events. Finally, the cleaning of the North Doors demands meticulous care and gradual, measured intervention in order to achieve a uniform result despite the vastness of the surface involved and the large number of restorers at work—to the extent that such uniformity is possible given the doors' far-from-consistent state of conservation. In this way, one might say that the restoration is being conducted in exactly the way Ghiberti himself made the doors: "with immense diligence and discipline."[16]

Translated from the Italian by Stephen Tobin

Fig. 70
The surface of the two doors after careful washing with a deionized water vapor

Fig. 71
The back of the North Doors during washing

Fig. 72
Cleaning trials on the front of the left-hand door

CATALOGUE

All works, unless otherwise indicated, are in the collection of the Museo dell'Opera del Duomo, Florence.

Catalogue contributors:

AB	Amy Bloch
RF	Rita Filardi
SN	Stefano Nicastri (translations by Stephen Tobin)
DZ	Daniel Zolli

1—2

1
Attributed to Giovanni d'Ambrogio (active 1382–1418)
Archangel Gabriel of the Annunciation
Late 14th century
Marble
144 × 44 × 30 cm (56¾ × 17¼ × 11⅞ in.)
Inv. no. 2005/276

2
Attributed to Giovanni d'Ambrogio (active 1382–1418)
Virgin Mary of the Annunciation
Late 14th century
Marble
144 × 44 × 30 cm (56¾ × 17¼ × 11⅞ in.)
Inv. no. 2005/277

—

This sculptural ensemble was originally intended for the Porta della Mandorla, the side entrance leading into the north aisle of Florence Cathedral. The decoration of the door, which spanned roughly the years 1391–1423, required a vast number of sculptors (for a list of contributors, see pages 20–24). The door's sculptures have played a role of considerable importance in art history because they were made during the transition between the final flowering of Gothic art and the early Renaissance, ranking among the earliest examples of the classicizing taste that would soon overtake Florence. The first phase of construction, lasting from 1391 to 1397, consisted of the erection of the portal's geometrical structure and of part of its cladding up to the impost of the arch, still in the Gothic style, and including the two tabernacles and the statues in the lunette. The sculptors who worked on this phase included Giovanni d'Ambrogio, Jacopo di Piero Guidi, Pietro di Giovanni Tedesco, and Niccolò Lamberti. The latter, together with the father-and-son team of Antonio and Nanni di Banco, also took part in the second phase of decoration which was to produce the cornice for the crowning tympanum with its plant volutes, the carved borders of the lunette, and two small prophets, one attributed to Donatello and the other to Nanni de Banco (cats. 5 and 6). A third phase was completed between 1414 and 1421, when Nanni di Banco carved the relief for the pediment. It was during this last phase that the Opera placed this pair of statues depicting the Annunciation in the portal lunette. Documentary evidence suggests that the group was initially placed on the Altar of the Trinity inside the cathedral, and it is only described as being in the lunette on April 2, 1414, where it would remain until 1489–90, when a mosaic by Domenico del Ghirlandaio and his brother David—it, too, an Annunciation—replaced it. The group is next heard of in 1886, when it was described as being on display in the forecourt of the Museo dell'Opera del Duomo.[1]

Although the two statues are doubtless by the same hand, their attribution remains the subject of considerable dispute.[2] While scholars have put forth a range of possibilities, the most likely attribution is to Giovanni d'Ambrogio, arguably the most important sculptor in Florence during the final two decades of the fourteenth century. A follower of Andrea Pisano, d'Ambrogio was influenced by the work of Orcagna and also studied classical sculpture, this latter sensibility crucial in paving the way for the Renaissance. His work made a major impression on the first sculptors of the early Renaissance in their youth, especially on Nanni di Banco. Giovanni d'Ambrogio was appointed master of works (*capomaestro*) at Florence Cathedral in 1401, holding the post until 1418 with several interruptions, the longest of which lasted from December 1413 until July 1415. It was during this period that the chapels, the tribunes, and the drum over the choir were built. No sculptures by Giovanni d'Ambrogio are recorded in these years, but he is known to have produced a design, dated 1408, for the decorations on the archivolts of the Porta della Mandorla, for which he continued the decoration of the splays and cornice. He resigned as master of the works of Florence Cathedral in 1418 on the grounds that he had grown too old to continue in the post.

The first of the two statues exhibited here (cat. 1) depicts the Archangel Gabriel, his right leg bent to suggest movement. Although dressed in elegant classicizing garb, this figure simultaneously possesses an International Gothic sensibility, especially in its swaying posture. Gabriel's face, with its clear echoes of classical Roman and Hellenistic portraiture, turns slightly to the left, its soft features framed by flowing locks of hair pulled back from his forehead by a diadem. The pupils

Cat. 2, detail

1–2

of Gabriel's eyes—made of lead inserts—not only reflect classical taste, but they act to enliven his gaze, directed toward the Virgin Mary (her pupils also have lead inserts). His right arm is raised in a gesture of blessing, while his left bends slightly (his left hand—now empty—originally held a lily). Almost all of the statue's fingers and the point of the diadem are the result of later restoration. The back of the statue is fitted with a bronze ring that served to fasten the statue to the façade, and it exhibits two holes that once held wings (these, too, are lost). The angel's pose is designed to complement that of the Virgin.

The second statue (cat. 2) depicts the Virgin Mary, who reacts with surprise—almost alarm—as she receives the Archangel's message. Here, too, the reference to classical portraiture is unmistakable. Her right arm is raised, her hand lifted in a gesture at once astonished and defensive. Cradled in her left arm is an open book, alluding to the Word of God made flesh in her womb. Some of the fingers on either hand and the patina of her face are the result of later restoration. Like Gabriel, the back of this statue is fitted with a bronze ring. The figure of the Virgin, like Gabriel, has asexual features that seem deliberately designed to underscore her purity and divinity. The Virgin's pose is intended to complement that of the angel in a kind of mirror image highlighting the group's compositional and formal unity.

– SN

1. C. J. Cavallucci, *Vita ed opere del Donatello* (Milan, 1886), 11.
2. On the history of the attribution of this work, see Luisa Becherucci and Giulia Brunetti, eds., *Il museo dell'Opera del Duomo a Firenze*, 2 vols. (Venice, [1970]), vol. 2, 211–14, with additional bibliography.

OPPOSITE
Cat. 1 (left) and Cat. 2 (right)

3

Nanni di Banco (ca. 1380/85–1421) or Donato di Niccolò di Betto Bardi, known as Donatello (ca. 1386–1466) (?)
Vir Dolorum (Man of Sorrows)
ca. 1407–9
Marble
48 × 66 × 12 cm (18⅞ × 26 × 4¾ in.)
Inv. no. 2005/280

This relief originally served as the keystone for the arch that dominated the upper register of Florence Cathedral's northeast entrance, called the Porta dei Servi (it was only later labeled the Porta della Mandorla). Although the relief is relatively small in size, its scope is monumental. It depicts a three-quarter-length figure of Christ, his arms outstretched, neck slack with fatigue, and facial features tinged with suffering. This particular convergence of elements corresponds closely to late medieval representations of Christ as Man of Sorrows (*Vir Dolorum*), an iconography not attached to any episode in the Passion narrative, but meant to rivet beholders' attention on the Savior's suffering more generally (on this tradition and its meaning, see pages 21–24). This particular portrayal of Christ is rendered all the more affecting for its naturalism: the musculature of the figure, for example, the veins in his forearms, and every bit of his luminescent flesh are delivered with startling fidelity. The *Vir Dolorum* remained on site until around 1870, when restorers replaced the relief with a copy. In 1886, after two decades in the Opera's storerooms, the relief, along with those decorative elements that once flanked it on the arch, entered the Museo dell'Opera del Duomo.[1]

The campaign to decorate the Porta began in the last decade of the fourteenth century. During the first wave of activity, which took place between 1391 and 1397, the Opera enlisted swarms of sculptors to populate the jambs surrounding the great door with thickets of foliate ornament and half-length figures of angels. A second phase of activity, which spanned the years 1404 to 1409, extended this program to the band of decoration surrounding the arch—or archivolt—above the door (on this chronology, see pages 20–21). It is likely that the *Vir Dolorum* relief was made during the latter half of this second period of work (i.e., 1407–9). This may be inferred from the relief's slightly uneven shape, which suggests that the object was made to fit the space left vacant by the (presumably) already completed reveals to either side—it was, in other words, one of the last elements designed for the archivolt.

While scholars are in general agreement about these dates, they have shown little unanimity concerning the authorship of the relief. With good reason, attributions have tended to cluster around those sculptors who were active at the Porta from roughly 1404 to 1409. Along these lines, some have ascribed the relief to Niccolò Lamberti (ca. 1370–1451), who appears to have played a significant role in the archivolt's carvings.[2] A more likely candidate for most, however, is Nanni di Banco (ca. 1380/85–1421), who had worked in the cathedral workshop—alongside his father Antonio—since the 1390s, and whose name, like Lamberti's, appears in the Opera's payment records in connection with the archivolt zone.[3] There is much to recommend Nanni's authorship. Particularly noteworthy is the relief's classicizing sensibility, one hallmark of the young Nanni's emerging style. The deftly modeled musculature of Christ's torso, for example, resembles almost to the letter that of the diminutive *all'antica Hercules* on view nearby, it, too, often attributed to Nanni (see cat. 4).

Others have assigned the work to Donatello, who was then active in the cathedral workshop, and who completed—at minimum—one additional statue for the Porta during these same years.[4] Those who give the relief to Donatello have tended to adduce two pieces of evidence to support the attribution. There exists, on the one hand, a document, dated February 1408, that records payment from the Opera to Donatello for "a marble figure 1⅓ *braccia* long" destined for the Porta, which some have interpreted as a reference to the relief.[5] Scholars have detected, on the other hand, stylistic similarities with other juvenilia by the sculptor, and particularly his wooden crucifix for the nearby church of Santa Croce (ca. 1408–12), which exhibits a similar sensitivity to anatomical detail, to modeled flesh, and a similarly tilted head as the relief.[6] Laura Cavazzini perceived in the two works—the relief and its larger wooden sibling—*both* a debt to Lorenzo Ghiberti (she cites the lyrical treatment of Christ's loin cloth), *and* an expressive urgency that is utterly distinct from the goldsmith's figures.[7] What we might see here, in other words, are the earliest tremors of Donatello's emerging artistic identity, characterized, among other things, by a desire to imbue his subjects with psychological immediacy. Still others have assigned the relief to an "unidentifiable master," an individual, that is, whose name does not appear in the Opera's account books in relation to the archivolt.[8]

That scholars have nominated so many sculptors as the relief's author is revealing. The Porta was an ongoing project, and artists involved in its decoration were often asked to hew closely to *particular* styles the better to bring general cohesion to the program's many parts (on this point see page 48). It follows that many of the relief's stylistic particulars—its avowed naturalism, its Gothic elegance, its attunement to classicism—were practiced by more than one hand. Rather than adjudicate between these competing attributions, then, it is also possible to view the relief as part of a larger collaborative project, one that often subsumed individual identities in the interest of the Porta's overall coherence. In this way, the *Vir Dolorum* relief may be viewed as part of a "collective style" that developed at the Porta, one to which artists like Donatello, Nanni di Banco, and Niccolò Lamberti were heirs and beneficiaries.

– DZ

1. On the circumstances surrounding the relief's removal, see Mary Bergstein, *The Sculpture of Nanni di Banco* (Princeton, NJ, 2000), esp. 89.
2. E.g., Hans Semper, *Donatello: seine Zeit und Schule* (Vienna, 1875), 61; and Giuseppe Fiocco, "I Lamberti a Venezia," *Dedalo* 8 (1927–28): 292 and 299.
3. For a full treatment of Nanni's contributions to the archivolt, see Bergstein, *The Sculpture of Nanni di Banco*, esp. 89–93. Bergstein's entry on the *Vir Dolorum* also includes an exhaustive bibliography of the relief, as well as an impressive and even-handed treatment of questions of attribution.
4. A payment record dated November 1406 confirms that Donatello made—or was making—"marble prophets" for the Porta. See Giovanni Poggi, ed., *Il Duomo di Firenze* (Berlin, 1909), doc. 362. On this document and its implications see also cat. 5.
5. See Poggi, *Il Duomo di Firenze*, doc. 366. Margit Lisner was the first to relate this document to the *Vir Dolorum*. It should be noted that the length of the relief (roughly 66 cm) is shorter than the 1⅓ *braccia* mentioned in the document, a fact that Lisner and others have sought to explain away by noting that the Porta documents tended to be imprecise in their measurements. See Lisner, "Zum Frühwerk Donatellos," *Münchner Jahrbuch der bildenden Kunst* 13 (1962): 63–68.
6. On the relief's connection with the Santa Croce crucifix, see, for example, Laura Martini, "Crocifisso" and "Cristo in Pietà," in *Lorenzo Ghiberti: "materia e ragionamenti,"* exh. cat. (Florence, 1978), 212–16; and George R. Goldner, *Niccolò and Pietro Lamberti* (New York, 1978), 246 n. 53. H. W. Janson expressed reservations about the connection, arguing that the similarity is "one of type, rather than of personal style" (see Janson, *The Sculpture of Donatello* [Princeton, NJ, 1963], 10 n. 1).
7. Laura Cavazzini, "1400–10: the Dawn of the Renaissance," in *The Springtime of the Renaissance: Sculpture and the Arts in Florence 1400–60*, eds. Beatrice Paolozzi Strozzi and Marc Bormand (Florence, 2013), esp. 72.
8. E.g., Manfred Wundram, "Antonio di Banco," *Mitteilungen des Kunsthistorischen Institutes in Florenz* 10 (1961): 23–32; and Michael Phillips, "A New Interpretation of the Early Style of Nanni di Banco," *Marsyas* 11 (1962–64): 63–66.

Cat. 3, detail

4

Nanni di Banco (ca. 1380/85–1421) or Donato di Niccolò di Betto Bardi, known as Donatello (ca. 1386–1466) (?)
Hercules
ca. 1404–9
Marble
122 × 41 × 10 cm (48 × 16⅛ × 4 in.)
Inv. no 2005/282

This small relief image of *Hercules*, the legendary hero of ancient Greek and Roman mythology, was originally part of the elaborate sculptural decoration of Florence Cathedral's so-called Porta della Mandorla, the church's northeast entrance. The *Hercules*, removed from the door in the nineteenth century, occupied a place in the right side of one of the outer archivolts, in a wide relief strip in which angels, enclosed in hexagonal frames, alternate with elaborate wreaths of acanthus leaves surrounding standing figures (the *Hercules* among them). The Porta was the focus of an extensive decorative campaign that can be divided into three periods: 1391–97; 1404–9; and 1414–22.[1] Most scholars agree that the *Hercules* was fashioned in the second phase of work. Authorship has been assigned to a variety of sculptors, including Nanni di Banco (whose name, along with that of his father Antonio di Banco, appears in payment records for the archivolt carvings), Donatello (who completed at least one statue for the Porta during this period), and others among the many sculptors hired by the Opera to carry out the decoration of the portal (Niccolò Lamberti, whom documents also connect to the archivolt sculptures, has often been proposed).[2]

Certain stylistic elements of the *Hercules* can be connected with later, documented works. The pronounced hip thrust, for example, appears again in Nanni di Banco's *Isaiah* of 1408; the left hand of the *Hercules*, resting on his hip with fingers extended, resembles closely the right hand of the statue carved by a sculptor in the relief below Nanni di Banco's *Quattro Santi Coronati* for Orsanmichele (1409–16/17). Despite such similarities, the fragmentary state of the documentation and the undefined nature of the oeuvres of many who worked at the Porta contribute to the likelihood that authorship of the *Hercules* will remain an open question.

Much of the sculpture of the Porta della Mandorla manifests the lyricism of line and elegance of form associated with the so-called International Gothic style. The *Hercules* highlights the presence of another stylistic tendency, namely classicism, among artists working at the cathedral at the turn of the century. The figure, identified by his club, stands in subtle *contrapposto*, his left hip jutting outward, his right leg bent at the knee, and his left leg—its muscles bulge as they strain—supporting much of the body's weight. The sensitively carved torso and muscular legs reveal the sculptor's study of ancient models and idealized human anatomy in nature. On the other hand, certain features, like the figure's proportions, which produce relatively large hands and feet, depart from the ideals of antiquity and nature and recall instead earlier, local treatments of the male nude (e.g., Nicola Pisano's *Fortitude*, sometimes identified as Hercules, from the Pisa Baptistery pulpit). Aspects of the standing pose of this *Hercules* draw on a representation of the triumphant hero made for the left jamb of the Porta della Mandorla—there were, as will be discussed, many images of him in the cycle—in the previous decade. This earlier *Hercules*, similarly inspired by ancient models, also stands in subtle *contrapposto* and grasps a club (now mostly missing) with his right hand.[3]

Hercules is one of several figures from pagan mythology in the Porta della Mandorla cycle. For the jambs and lintel sculptors created cavorting *putti*, a personification of Abundance based on an ancient model, figures identified as Prometheus and Apollo, and a host of other *all'antica* figural and decorative elements.[4] Hercules, however, dominates in this crowd of mythical pagans, for five images of him were included in the program—the relief in this exhibit, the earlier example mentioned above, and three scaled-down narratives made, during the first stage of work, for the relief strip covering the left jamb abutting the doorway: Hercules slaying the Hydra, Hercules and the Nemean lion, and the triumph of Hercules over Antaeus. This profusion of Herculean imagery in part resulted from his exalted place in Renaissance Florence, where since the thirteenth century, when he appeared on the city's seal, he was considered an emblem of Florentine fortitude and virtue.[5] Richard Krautheimer suggested that Coluccio Salutati, the humanist chancellor of the city, influenced the decision to highlight Hercules at the Porta della Mandorla.[6] Salutati wrote, between ca. 1382 and the mid-1390s, the *De*

4

laboribus Herculis, which includes an analysis of Seneca's ancient tragedy about Hercules and an account of the mythological figure's life.[7] Medieval Christian theologians interpreted Hercules's life allegorically and his labors as examples of the triumph of good over evil.[8] Erwin Panofsky considered the images of Hercules at the Porta della Mandorla as one component of an allegory in which pagan figures symbolize the Cardinal Virtues, with Hercules personifying Fortitude.[9] Such interpretations, which transform the pagan hero into a symbol of Christian virtue, as well as his civic status in Florence, explain his prominent presence at the city's cathedral.

– AB

1. For a summary of these stages of work in diagrammatic form, see Charles Seymour, *Sculpture in Italy 1400–1500* (Harmondsworth and Baltimore, 1966), 33.
2. For documentary evidence connecting Nanni di Banco, Antonio di Banco, and Niccolò Lamberti to the archivolt decoration and other parts of the Porta della Mandorla in this period, see Giovanni Poggi, ed., *Il Duomo di Firenze* (Berlin, 1909), docs. 361, 363–65, and 367–70; and Manfred Wundram, "Antonio di Banco," *Mitteilungen des Kunsthistorischen Institutes in Florenz* 10 (1961): 23–32, esp. 27, n. 52. For documentary evidence of Donatello's work for the portal in 1406–8, see Poggi, *Il Duomo di Firenze*, docs. 362 and 366. For a summary of the opinions concerning the attribution of the archivolt reliefs, see Mary Bergstein, *The Sculpture of Nanni di Banco* (Princeton, NJ, 2000), 90–93, esp. 92 where Bergstein gives the *Hercules* to Piero di Niccolò Lamberti, the son of Niccolò Lamberti); and Aldo Galli's entry on the *Hercules* relief in *The Springtime of the Renaissance: Sculpture and the Arts in Florence 1400–60*, eds. Beatrice Paolozzi Strozzi and Marc Bormand, exh. cat. (Florence, 2013), 310.
3. On this older *Hercules*, see pages 20–21.
4. On the mythological figures on the Porta della Mandorla, see Richard Krautheimer, *Lorenzo Ghiberti* (Princeton, NJ, 1982), 279–81.
5. Leopold D. Ettlinger, "Hercules Florentinus," *Mitteilungen des Kunsthistorischen Institutes in Florenz* 16 (1972): 119–42.
6. Krautheimer, *Lorenzo Ghiberti*, 280.
7. On the *De laboribus Herculis*, see Berthold L. Ullman, *The Humanism of Coluccio Salutati* (Padua, 1963), 21–26; and Ronald G. Witt, *Hercules at the Crossroads: The Life, Works, and Thought of Coluccio Salutati* (Durham, NC, 1983), 213–26.
8. Henri de Lubac, *Medieval Exegesis: The Four Senses of Scripture*, trans. E. M. Macierowski, 4 vols. (Grand Rapids, MI, 2000), vol. 2, 100. On Hercules's integration into Christian thought, see Marcel Simon, *Hercule et le christianisme* (Paris, 1955).
9. Erwin Panofsky, *Renaissance and Renascences in Western Art* (New York, 1972), 149–50, esp. n. 4.

Cat. 4, detail

5—6

5
Attributed to Donato di Niccolò di Betto Bardi, known as Donatello (ca. 1386–1466)
Profetino
ca. 1406–9
Marble
128 × 32 × 29 cm (50⅜ × 12½ × 11⅜ in.)
Inv. no. 2005/287

6
Attributed to Nanni di Banco (ca. 1380/85–1421)
Profetino
ca. 1406
Marble
130 × 48 × 30 cm (51¼ × 18⅞ × 11⅞ in.)
Inv. no. 2005/288

These two sculptures were designed and carved to crown the pinnacles on the sides of the Porta della Mandorla. Called *Profetini*, or "small prophets," these statues likely belonged to the second phase of the door's decoration (1404–9), carved, that is, after the construction of the Porta's geometrical structure and part of its cladding. Among the sculptors to participate in this second phase of activity were Antonio and Nanni di Banco, the father-and-son team that produced the cornice for the crowning tympanum with its plant volutes and the carved borders of the lunette; Nanni was likely also responsible for one of the two boy-prophets exhibited here, the other is probably by Donatello.

The placement of the *Profetini* on the pinnacles of the door probably coincided with the installation of Nanni di Banco's large relief of the Assumption, which took place between 1422 and 1423 (thus after Nanni's death). Although Donatello's *Profetino* was almost certainly completed before 1422, some scholars have suggested that Nanni's ephebe may have been carved alongside the Assumption relief, its execution timed to correspond with that relief's installation.[1] The sculptures, while being set at some distance from each other on the side pinnacles, nevertheless mirror one another, the leg closest to the door being bent in both cases, the head of each *Profetino* turned slightly inward. The two prophets were removed from the door in 1990 and restored prior to display in the Museo dell'Opera del Duomo.

Donatello's prophet (cat. 5) is a smaller-than-life-size white marble sculpture in the round, finely modeled in the front but unfinished in the back, possibly because the statue was only intended to be seen from a fixed vantage point—a feature found elsewhere in Donatello's work, for instance in his *St. Mark* (1411–13) and *St. Louis of Toulouse* (ca. 1423) for Orsanmichele. The figure has none of the *contrapposto* of classical sculpture, but sways forward as if advancing. The stylized drapery, festooned tightly around the body, is Gothic in inspiration and echoes the style of Ghiberti. The broad swaths of the mantle fall on the shoulders and down to the arms, enhancing the figure's formally complex configuration. The head, crowned by a foliate wreath, is framed by delicately chiseled hair; the eyelids are heavy, the mouth fleshy, and the facial features—as with the drapery—reminiscent of Ghiberti's figures.

The statue's attribution has been the subject of some dispute. Scholars have continued to compare the left-hand *Profetino* to the work of Donatello. An alternative that scholars often propose is Bernardo Ciuffagni, who received a commission in these same years for an unidentified prophet and angel to be placed somewhere on the cathedral.[2] Ciuffagni produced three additional statues for the cathedral façade (*St. Matthew*, 1410–15; *Isaiah*, 1424–27; and *David*, 1425–35) in which he endeavored to bring his late Gothic training into line with the innovative style of Donatello. The most plausible attribution is to the young Donatello, who here displays his debt to Ghiberti, for whom he worked between roughly 1404 and 1407, when the goldsmith recruited him to assist in the early stages of the North Doors of the baptistery.[3]

The second prophet (cat. 6), also smaller than life size, features the full, oval face of a young man with large eyes, a small nose and tight lips. This *Profetino* wears a tunic held at the waist by a belt, while a cloak covers his legs with swirling drapery reaching to his bare feet. This figure does assume a *contrapposto* pose and grips an unfurled scroll (a traditional attribute of prophets). Unlike the drapery of its counterpart, the fabric of this *Profetino* does not cling to the body, but envelops the figure in thick and deeply tooled swaths. While the work's attribution is uncertain, many scholars have

pointed to Nanni di Banco based on stylistic affinities with other works that sculptor carved for Florence Cathedral.[4] Other critics are inclined to think that the statue is a youthful work by Luca della Robbia, who may well have studied under Nanni di Banco.[5] Among the features supporting this attribution, according to Luciano Bellosi, are "the roundness of the head, the tender fleshiness of the mouth and the hint of bags under the eyes," qualities reminiscent of Luca's figural work elsewhere (the children in his reliefs for the cantoria, for example). Although the similarities are suggestive, without further findings the authorship of this diminutive prophet—indeed its very identity as a prophet—must remain open-ended questions.

– SN

1. Giulia Brunetti, "L'Angelo del Metropolitan Museum di New York e qualche contributo nuovo a Piero Tedesco," *Metropolitan Museum Journal* 6 (1972): 163.
2. Hans Semper, *Donatello: seine Zeit und Schule* (Vienna, 1875), 53; Albert Jansen, review of *Donatello: seine Zeit und Schule*, by Hans Semper, *Zeitschrift für Bildende Kunst* 11 (1876): 316–19; J. Lányi, "Le statue quattrocentesche dei Profeti nel campanile e nell'antica facciata di S. Maria del Fiore," *Rivista d'arte* 17 (1935): 121–59, 245–80.
3. Luciano Bellosi, "I problemi dell'attività giovanile," in *Donatello e i suoi: scultura fiorentina del primo Rinascimento*, exh. cat. (Florence, 1986), 122–24; Beatrice Paolozzi Strozzi and Marc Bormand, eds., *La primavera del Rinascimento: la scultura e le arti a Firenze 1400–1450*, exh. cat. (Florence, 2013).
4. See, for example, Frida Schotmüller, *Die Gestalt des Menschen in Donatellos Werk* (Zurich, 1904), 21; Aldo Galli in *La primavera del Rinascimento* (2013), 308, with additional bibliography; and H. W. Janson, *The Sculpture of Donatello* (Princeton, NJ, 1963), 219–22.
5. Charles Seymour, "The Young Luca della Robbia," *Allen Memorial Art Museum Bulletin* 20 (1963): 92–119; G. Gentilini, entry on Luca della Robbia in the *Dizionario biografico degli Italiani* (Rome, 1989), vol. 37, 280.

7—8

7
Attributed to Donato di Niccolò di Betto Bardi, known as Donatello (ca. 1386–1466) or Nanni di Bartolo, known as Rosso (active 1419–51)
Prophet
ca. 1406–10
Marble
87.5 × 30 × 25 cm (34½ × 11¾ × 9⅞ in.)
Inv. no. 2005/425

8
Attributed to Donato di Niccolò di Betto Bardi, known as Donatello (ca. 1386–1466) or Nanni di Bartolo, known as Rosso (active 1419–51)
Prophet
ca. 1410
Marble
88 × 25 × 31 cm (34⅝ × 9⅞ × 12¼ in.)
Inv. no. 2005/427

In February 1431 the Opera placed these two statues, carved some time earlier, on the pinnacles framing either side of the door on the east side of the bell tower of Florence Cathedral.[1] It is likely that they were conceived as companion pieces, owing not only to their extraordinary formal and stylistic similarities, but because they were positioned to mirror one another. The two statues were moved to the Museo dell'Opera del Duomo in 1965, due to their poor state of conservation.

Vasari assigned the two statues to Andrea Pisano (after a design by Giotto), an attribution that has since won endorsement from several scholars, who have read the pair as the prophets Moses and Elijah on Mount Tabor.[2] Others assign the works to Niccolò Lamberti or Nanni di Bartolo.[3] Volker Herzner, for his part, considered them to be youthful works by Donatello while still apprenticed to Ghiberti because, he argued, "the powerful vigour of their bodies overshadows the rendering of the drapery"—a feature that can be found only in Donatello's sculpture at this time. Herzner thus dated them to sometime between 1406 and 1408.[4]

Cat. 7 depicts a prophet whose face is framed by a thick, curling beard. He wears a loose tunic remarkable for its soft, graceful folds of drapery. The prophet stands barefoot, his weight balanced on his left leg, his torso twisting slightly to his left, and with his gaze directed upward. His (now mutilated) left hand is slightly raised, while his right hand holds an unfurled scroll.

Cat. 8 is likewise bearded and barefoot, and it, too, is dressed in a tunic, this one slightly longer than that worn by its counterpart (it extends to the ground, spilling over the base on which the statue stands). The lack of headgear further distinguishes this statue from its companion. These small differences notwithstanding, cat. 8 is an almost exact mirror of cat. 7; the figure's torso twists, one arm raised, the other holding a scroll (only a small fragment of which has survived); its gaze is directed skyward possibly in a moment of divine revelation.

– RF

1. Giovanni Poggi, ed., *Il Duomo di Firenze* (Berlin, 1909), doc. 307.
2. Giorgio Vasari, *Le vite de' più eccellenti pittori, scultori ed architettori*, ed. Gaetano Milanesi, 9 vols. (Florence, 1906), vol. 1, 488; Giuseppe Richa, *Notizie istoriche delle chiese fiorentine*, 10 vols. (Florence, 1754–1762), vol. 6 (1757), 66; M. Rastrelli and V. Follini, *Firenze antica e moderna illustrata* (Florence, 1790), vol. 1, 372.
3. On these competing attributions see, among other sources, Luisa Becherucci and Giulia Brunetti, eds., *Il museo dell'Opera del Duomo a Firenze*, 2 vols. (Venice, [1970]), vol. 1, 264–65, with additional bibliography.
4. Donatella Reggioli in *Lorenzo Ghiberti: "materia e ragionamenti,"* exh. cat. (Florence, 1978), 107–8; V. Herzner, "Zwei Frühwerke Donatellos: die Prophetenstatuetten von der Porta del Campanile in Florenz," *Pantheon* 37 (1979): 27–36; V. Herzner in *Donatello e i suoi: scultura fiorentina del primo Rinascimento*, exh. cat. (Florence, 1986), 121.

OPPOSITE
Cat. 7

OVERLEAF
Cat. 7, detail (left)
Cat. 8 (right)

9

Nanni di Banco (ca. 1380/85–1421)
St. Luke the Evangelist
1408–13
Marble
207 × 91 × 63 cm (81½ × 35⅞ × 24⅞ in.)
Inv. no 2005/112

The fifteenth-century history of the project to place marble Evangelists on Florence Cathedral's façade goes back to 1405, when the blocks for the statues were quarried at Carrara.[1] In December 1408 Nanni di Banco, along with Donatello and Niccolò Lamberti, was commissioned to carve seated Evangelists for elevated niches—their bases were approximately ten feet above the ground—inserted into the façade of the cathedral and flanking its main portal.[2] The project, a continuation of the decorative campaign for the façade begun around 1300, was at once a commission and a competition, for the cathedral operai announced that the author of the work deemed best would be given the job of sculpting the fourth Evangelist. Nanni's commission, which resulted in the *Luke*, followed immediately his successful completion of another cathedral statue, the *Isaiah*, which he carved in 1408 for a buttress on the church's north side. By June 1410 Nanni had begun the *Luke*, and payment records indicate that he continued working on it through the summer of 1412.[3] The disbursement of the final payment in February 1413 indicates that the statue was finished. The operai's desire for the swift completion of the Evangelist project evidently trumped their interest in fostering a competitive spirit among the sculptors, because they assigned the commission for the fourth statue to Bernardo Ciuffagni in 1410.[4]

By October 1415 all of the statues were finished and had been placed in the façade niches (Artur Rosenauer gives their design to Ghiberti while Michaela Kalusok suggests Brunelleschi).[5] Attributions of the four Evangelists rely on stylistic comparison with other documented autograph works, and Wilhelm Bode was the first modern scholar to attribute the *Luke* to Nanni.[6] Certainly the voluminous, active drapery and the classicizing head of the *Luke*, which owe much to ancient Roman models, recall the clothing and heads of the four figures comprising Nanni's roughly contemporary *Quattro Santi Coronati* (1409–1416/17) for Orsanmichele. The drapery folds, in places wide and flattened, resemble those of the robes of Nanni's *Isaiah*.[7] Sixteenth-century sources, including Vasari, indicate that the *Luke* occupied one of the niches to the left of the cathedral's entrance, and a majority of scholars, most recently Mary Bergstein, believe that the *Luke* was positioned directly next to the portal on the left.[8] After the façade's destruction in 1587 all of the Evangelists were taken down and installed in the cathedral's east tribune.[9] They were transferred to the Museo dell'Opera del Duomo in the middle of the twentieth century.

In sculpting the *Luke* Nanni combined sensitive carving with the construction of an assertive pose. He fashioned the face and robes of the statue, for example, with immense care. The individually defined locks of the beard and mustache of the *Luke* curl above and below his lips.[10] A delicately carved belt, which seems to be made of twisted cloth, encircles the saint's waist, producing activated folds in his inner robe and giving definition to his torso. The heavy swaths of drapery covering his legs, at once softly curving and ponderous, wrap around, and fall from, his knees. Although the *Luke* represents a seated figure, no part of the statue's body is relaxed. He sits with his arms extended and bent at the elbow, a pose that gives the work a roughly hexagonal shape that differs from the pyramidal form Donatello used to structure the *St. John the Evangelist*. Such an arrangement helped the *Luke* fill the width of the niche.[11] The figure's elongated, straightened torso and neck lift his head far above ground level, enhancing the sense of height already imparted by the *Luke*'s originally elevated position. The figure shifts slightly backward and towards his right and lifts his left shoulder higher than his right.

When placed in the façade niche the figure would have seemed to gaze down and to his left, as if focusing his attention on those passing him and entering the cathedral's main portal. This downward gaze, which functions in accordance with the viewpoint of those who encounter the figure from below, gives the statue a sense of confidence and authority.[12] The right hand of the *Luke* tugs at a section

9

of his cloak, and his left hand grasps his Gospel book, which is open. The inclusion of an open book implies that, in the fiction of the work, Luke has been reading. Viewers who passed the statue as they walked towards the cathedral's main entrance were perhaps meant to understand their action as interrupting him. Seeming as if momentarily distracted from a text he had been reading, Luke glanced down in their direction.

– AB

1. Giovanni Poggi, ed., *Il Duomo di Firenze* (Berlin, 1909), docs. 162–64.
2. Ibid., doc. 172.
3. Ibid., docs. 184, 189, 198, and 205 (doc. 205 records Nanni's final payment).
4. Ibid., doc. 173.
5. Ibid., doc. 220. The niches were inserted into the façade in the fourteenth century, but their architectural adornment was likely added in the early fifteenth century. On the fifteenth-century artist responsible for this decoration, see Artur Rosenauer, "Die Nischen für die Evangelistenfiguren an der Florentiner Domfassade," in *Essays Presented to Myron P. Gilmore*, eds. Sergio Bertelli and Gloria Ramakus, 2 vols. (Florence, 1978), vol. 2, 345–52; and Michaela Kalusok, *Tabernakel und Statue: die Figurennische in der italienischen Kunst des Mittelalters und der Renaissance* (Münster, 1996), 182–85.
6. Jacob Burckhardt, *Der Cicerone: eine Anleitung zum Genuss der Kunstwerke Italiens*, ed. Wilhelm Bode (Leipzig, 1884), 346. On the history of the attribution of the work, see Luisa Becherucci and Giulia Brunetti, eds., *Il museo dell'Opera del Duomo a Firenze*, 2 vols. (Venice, [1970]), vol. 1, 262; and Mary Bergstein, *The Sculpture of Nanni di Banco* (Princeton, NJ, 2000), 107–10.
7. Leo Planiscig, *Nanni di Banco* (Florence, 1946), 24. For a brief comparison between the *Luke* and other works by Nanni, see Paolo Vaccarino, *Nanni* (Florence, 1950), 30.
8. Giorgio Vasari, *Le vite de' più eccellenti pittori, scultori, ed architettori*, ed. Gaetano Milanesi, 9 vols. (Florence, 1906), vol. 2, 164; and Bergstein, *Sculpture of Nanni di Banco*, 107–13. Robert Munman argues for a different configuration in "The Evangelists from the Cathedral of Florence: A Renaissance Arrangement Recovered," *Art Bulletin* 62 (1980): 207–17. For a discussion of sixteenth-century evidence concerning the placement of the statues, see Becherucci and Brunetti, *Il museo dell'Opera*, vol. 1, 262; and Bergstein, *Sculpture of Nanni di Banco*, 107–10.
9. Joachim Poeschke, *Donatello and His World: Sculpture of the Italian Renaissance*, trans. Russell Stockman (New York, 1993), 372.
10. On the face of the *Luke*, see Mary Bergstein, "Nanni di Banco, Donatello, and Realism in the *Testa Virile*," *Source: Notes in the History of Art* 5 (1986): 8–11, esp. 8–9.
11. As noted by John Pope-Hennessy in *Italian Renaissance Sculpture* (London and New York, 1971), 5.
12. This presence of the downward gaze has been noted often. See, for example, Charles Seymour, *Sculpture in Italy 1400–1500* (Harmondsworth and Baltimore, 1966), 56. On the figure's gaze, see also Manfred Wundram, *Donatello und Nanni di Banco* (Berlin, 1969), 158.

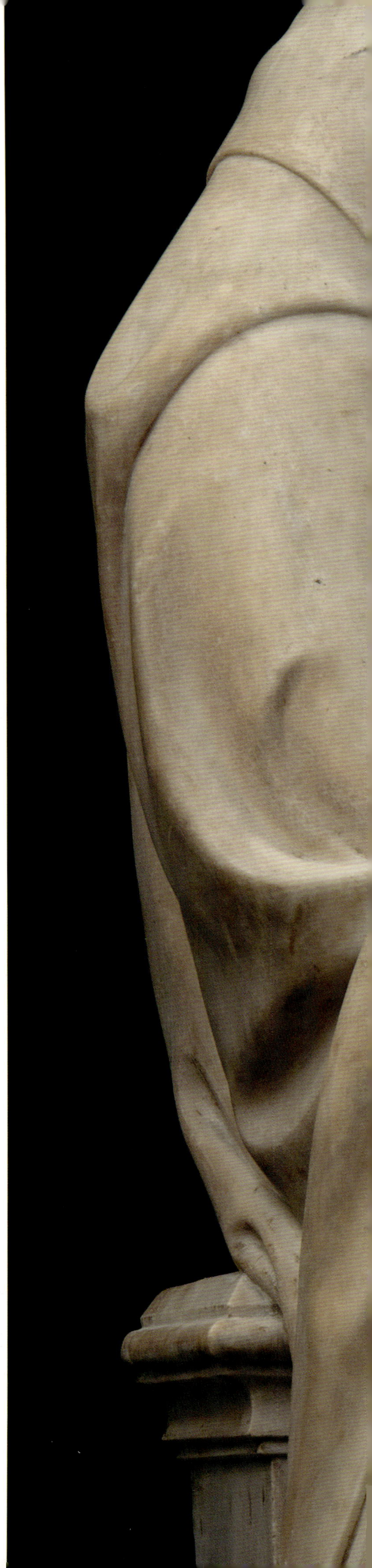

Cat. 9, detail

10

Donato di Niccolò di Betto Bardi, known as Donatello
(ca. 1386–1466)
St. John the Evangelist
1408–15
Marble
212 × 91 × 62 cm (83½ × 35¾ × 24½ in.)
Inv. no 2005/113

Donatello's *St. John the Evangelist* was one of three seated Evangelists commissioned in December 1408 for the façade of Florence Cathedral.[1] Payments were made to Donatello in 1412 and 1413 specifically for work on the statue, and then again in early 1415.[2] In April of that year the cathedral operai urged him to complete the work, ordering Donatello to finish by the end of May and specifying a hefty fine of 25 florins if he did not meet this deadline.[3] Work continued apace, and he received payments in mid-May and early June.[4] By October 1415 all of the Evangelists were completed and had been installed on the façade.[5] Donatello's *John* was valued at 160 florins, more than the amounts assigned to the façade statues by Niccolò Lamberti and Bernardo Ciuffagni.[6] Fifteenth-century images of the cathedral façade imply strongly that the *John* was located in the niche directly to the right of the main portal, and most scholars support this suggestion.[7] After their installation in the cathedral interior in 1589 (following the destruction of the façade in 1587), Wilhelm Bode was the first modern writer to attribute the statue to Donatello, a suggestion based on clear stylistic affinities with the sculptor's contemporary works.[8]

The period between 1408 and 1415 was a busy one for Donatello that saw him complete not only the *John*, but also a marble *David* (1408–9) and terracotta *Joshua* (1409–10) for the buttresses supporting the cathedral's north tribune, and the *St. Mark* (1411–13) for the Orsanmichele niche of the guild of the used cloth dealers and linen manufacturers. Through comparison with these and other contemporary works, scholars have attempted to assign the *John* a more specific date within the time—1408–15—during which, according to extant documents, Donatello received payments. Some, like Joachim Poeschke, believe it was carried out late in this period, and others, for example H. W. Janson (who carefully surveyed earlier art-historical opinion on the point), conclude that Donatello carved the majority of the sculpture between 1409 and 1411.[9] To be sure, the *John* shares features with the *David* (that is, the Bargello statue often considered the work Donatello carved for the north tribune) and the *Mark*. Like both, for example, the *John* engages emotionally, through purposeful gaze, the space before him. His brow heavily furrowed, he directs his head up and to his right, staring over and above his viewers as if observing something in the distance. The eyes' pupils, roughly and almost haphazardly carved into the marble (perhaps, Janson suggested, by a later hand), give the intense gaze directionality and focus.[10]

As he did when fashioning the *Mark*, Donatello kept in mind the assumed viewpoint of passersby, who would have seen the *John* in its elevated niche (the base of the statue was approximately ten feet above the ground), when determining the statue's pose and calculating its proportions. Indeed, scholars, most prominently Charles Seymour and Robert Munman, have explicated the adjustments Donatello made to the figure so that it would appear correctly proportioned and powerfully posed when examined from a point beneath it.[11] When viewed at eye level the statue's torso seems unnaturally elongated, the thighs bend towards the ground, the left hand hangs over the book—the Gospel of John, the Book of Revelation, or another text—listlessly and without evident strength, and the right hand rests limply on the right thigh, as if not capable of grasping anything. The work is utterly transformed when seen from below. The extra length of torso falls behind the draped knees, which point toward the figure's left. Simultaneously the lengthened torso elevates the head, which becomes the pinnacle of the figure's pyramidal form. The hands, rather than succumbing to the effects of gravity, work against it. The left hand holds the book upright, and the fingers of the right hand curl as if grasping something. This hand probably held a metal pen that Donatello added to the sculpture after its completion.[12] The writing implement perhaps rested in the indentation carved beside the thumb.

Donatello also accounted for the placement of the statue above eye level by cutting deeply into the marble block in order to create dark shadows that outline and thus emphasize John's face, the locks of his flowing beard, and his draped body.[13] The desire to insert deep pockets of space, and thus

10

dark shadows, into the statue's lower half required Donatello to carve the upper part of the body from a section of marble of limited depth, and indeed when one examines the statue from the side one sees that the torso and shoulders (from front to back) are extremely narrow.[14] When viewed from below, however, the forms take on greater bulk and the work appears to represent a massive, draped body existing fully in the round and animated by an inner force that causes the legs to shift and the head to turn.[15] Donatello's skill as a carver and unmatched ability to tailor the work to its site and with the viewers' perspective in mind resulted in the creation of a powerful portrait of John. If indeed he held a writing implement, the statue can be read not only as an image of a man ruminating on what he has just written, but also as a figure in the process of composing his text. In this scenario his distant gaze indicates not the contemplation of previously recorded ideas but a search for inspiration in the heavens to guide the formation of new ones.

– AB

1. On the circumstances of the project, see the essays in this volume by Timothy Verdon and Daniel Zolli, as well as the catalogue entry on Nanni di Banco's *St. Luke the Evangelist*. For the document recording the commission in 1408, see Giovanni Poggi, ed., *Il Duomo di Firenze* (Berlin, 1909), doc. 172.
2. Ibid., docs. 199, 206, and 211.
3. Ibid., doc. 215.
4. Ibid., docs. 216 and 218.
5. Ibid., doc. 220.
6. Ibid., docs. 213 and 220.
7. On the fifteenth- and sixteenth-century evidence regarding the original location of the *John*, see Luisa Becherucci and Giulia Brunetti, eds., *Il museo dell'Opera del Duomo a Firenze*, 2 vols. (Venice, [1970]), vol. 1, 262–63. For affirmations of this location, see, for example, H. W. Janson, *The Sculpture of Donatello* (Princeton, NJ, 1963), 14; and Charles Seymour, *Sculpture in Italy 1400–1500* (Harmondsworth and Baltimore, 1966), 56.
8. Jacob Burckhardt, *Der Cicerone: eine Anleitung zum Genuss der Kunstwerke Italiens*, ed. Wilhelm Bode (Leipzig, 1884), 350.
9. Joachim Poeschke, *Donatello and His World: Sculpture of the Italian Renaissance*, trans. Russell Stockman (New York, 1993), 380; and Janson, *Sculpture of Donatello*, 13–16.
10. Janson, *Sculpture of Donatello*, 16.
11. Seymour, *Sculpture in Italy*, 54–58; and Robert Munman, *Optical Corrections in the Sculpture of Donatello* (*Transactions of the American Philosophical Society*, vol. 75, n. 2) (Philadelphia, 1985), 1–96, esp. 10–14.
12. Poeschke, *Donatello and His World*, 379.
13. On the treatment and carving of the block, see also pages 56–58.
14. Bonnie A. Bennett and David G. Wilkins, *Donatello* (Oxford, 1984), 106.
15. On the figure's sense of movement and energy, see John Pope-Hennessy, *Donatello Sculptor* (New York, 1993), 25; and Artur Rosenauer, *Donatello* (Milan, 1993), 16.

Cat. 10, detail

11

Donato di Niccolò di Betto Bardi, known as Donatello (ca. 1386–1466) and Nanni di Bartolo, known as Rosso (active 1419–51)
Abraham and Isaac (the *Sacrifice of Isaac*)
1421
Marble
188 × 56 × 45 cm (74 × 22 × 17¾ in.)
Inv. no 2005/366

Extant documents outline clearly the chronology of the *Abraham and Isaac*, which Nanni di Bartolo and Donatello were commissioned to make for the east side—in the upper row of niches, the second from the right—of the campanile of Florence Cathedral. The marble group was carved relatively quickly: Donatello and Nanni received the commission in March 1421 and had completed it by November of that year, when documents record a final payment for their work.[1] They received 125 florins in total, a substantial sum probably reflecting the labor involved in sculpting the complex multi-figural group. The *Abraham and Isaac* is the only campanile statue to include more than one figure and was the first large-scale sculpture of the Italian Renaissance consisting of two figures and fashioned from a single block of marble.[2]

It is also the only statue for a campanile niche that relates a narrative: the sacrifice of Isaac (Genesis 22:1–13), the biblical story in which God tests Abraham by ordering him to kill his son Isaac and then, seeing his willingness to carry out the act as adequate proof of faith, sends an angel to stop the sacrifice.[3] Twenty years earlier, the entrants in the contest to sculpt Florence Baptistery's second set of doors represented this episode in their competition reliefs. The two that survive, by Ghiberti and Brunelleschi (see figs. 31 and 32), represent moments different from the one depicted in the campanile group. In Ghiberti's, Abraham readies the knife, unaware of the angel bursting into the scene; Brunelleschi shows the angel physically stopping Abraham by restraining his arm. The campanile image visualizes a later instant, after the angel has intervened to announce God's decision that Isaac should live. Although in the campanile statue Abraham still holds aside Isaac's cascading locks of hair to expose his neck, he dramatically turns his head to look over his left shoulder, his right hand begins to slacken, and the knife's cutting edge points away from Isaac's neck, signs that Abraham has heard and understood the angel's order. Isaac's placid expression perhaps communicates his resignation. The statue remains true to the biblical account and dominant theological interpretations of it. In the Bible Abraham hears the angel's voice but does not perceive it through sight, and the fact that Abraham looks up into an empty space emphasizes that he did not visualize the angel and only heard it calling out to him.

Although most scholars assign to Donatello primary authorship of the *Abraham and Isaac* and consider Nanni to have played at most a minor role in its creation, some do hypothesize that Nanni shared equally in the work or even did much of the carving.[4] The statue was fashioned from a relatively narrow (from front to back) piece of marble, a requirement imposed by the restricted depth of the niche for which it was made. Donatello, with Nanni perhaps working alongside him, fit the two figures into the composition by elevating Abraham's right leg, which bends at the knee, atop a stack of wood intended for use in the sacrifice and carving in high relief, rather than in the round, his left leg. Isaac's body, its chest and head twisting back and towards his left, occupies the open space between Abraham's legs and at points merges with them. The group contains several optical adjustments typical of Donatello's approach. The sculptor responsible for carving Abraham's body, probably Donatello, undercut the swaths of drapery surrounding Abraham's waist and carved away marble between his left arm and flank, deepening the shadows outlining these forms, and he fully freed Abraham's right arm from his torso, silhouetting both the inner and outer contours of this arm against the shadowy space of the niche. Such techniques rendered Abraham's upper body, and especially the active arms, more easily seen from below. Donatello also took care to insert details of human anatomy, like the delicately carved veins and bones of Abraham's right arm, wrist, and hand. The arm and hand are revealed because Abraham, in the fiction of the image, has rolled up the right sleeve of his shirt, presumably in an earlier moment when he anticipated using this hand and arm to make his deadly strike. Donatello also differentiated the

11

materials represented, from the heavy cloth of Abraham's sleeves to the long, thin folds of the lighter, seemingly silken material of the raiment covering his torso to the soft waves of the figures' hair and Abraham's beard. Although difficult to see from below, the superb representation of anatomy and clothing was surely appreciated by those who encountered the sculpture before it was elevated into the niche.

– AB

1. Giovanni Poggi, ed., *Il Duomo di Firenze* (Berlin, 1909), docs. 245, 248–49, and 251 (the last document records the final payment of 125 florins).
2. Marc Bormand, catalogue entry on *Abraham and Isaac*, in *The Springtime of the Renaissance: Sculpture and the Arts in Florence 1400–60*, eds. Beatrice Paolozzi Strozzi and Marc Bormand, exh. cat. (Florence, 2013), 326–27.
3. Bonnie A. Bennett and David G. Wilkins, *Donatello* (Oxford, 1984), 205.
4. H. W. Janson and Joachim Poeschke argue that Donatello carried out the majority of the work. See Janson, *The Sculpture of Donatello* (Princeton, NJ, 1963), 37; and Poeschke, *Donatello and His World: Sculpture of the Italian Renaissance*, trans. Russell Stockman (New York, 1993), 383. For the possibility that Nanni di Bartolo and Donatello shared the work, see Luisa Becherucci and Giulia Brunetti, eds., *Il museo dell'Opera del Duomo a Firenze*, 2 vols. (Venice, [1970]), vol. 1, 269–70; and John Pope-Hennessy, *Donatello Sculptor* (New York, 1993), 62–63. And for the hypothesis that Nanni di Bartolo was responsible for most of the design and carving, see Hans Kauffmann, *Donatello: eine Einführung in sein Bilden und Denken* (Berlin, 1935), 32.

Cat. 11, detail

12

Donato di Niccolò di Betto Bardi, known as Donatello
(ca. 1386–1466)
Prophet (possibly Habakkuk), known as the *Zuccone*
1435–36
Marble
195 × 54 × 38 cm (76¾ × 21¼ × 15 in.)
Inv. no. 2005/374

This statue belongs to a series of sixteen Old Testament prophets made for niches on the third story of Florence Cathedral's bell tower (on the history of this project, see pages 16–18 and 32–36). It was one of four statues carved for the bell tower's north side between roughly 1420 and 1436, and as such ranks among the last statues completed in the program, which had been underway already for nearly a century. These four sculptures were evidently of such high quality, the Opera so delighted with them, that in 1464 they were moved to the bell tower's highly visible—and therefore highly prestigious—western side, where they replaced a group of sibyls and kings produced by Andrea Pisano and his workshop (the bases of these older statues were retained, however). This statue and its companions on the campanile's west side were removed from their niches in 1937 and replaced with copies.[1]

Scholars have tended to link this prophet with another statue from the same program—the prophet Jeremiah—it, too, attributed with certainty to Donatello. There is less agreement, however, about the chronological order in which the statues were carved. Both statues are acknowledged to be products of Donatello's maturity, works of extraordinary realism that go well beyond the references to classical portrait busts recognizable in the figures' heads. Documents held in the Opera del Duomo's archives explicitly mention a statue by Donatello portraying the prophet Habakkuk, on which the sculptor was working in 1435 and which he completed in 1436. It is probable—if not certain—that these documentary references are to this statue, which therefore stands as Donatello's last contribution to the program.

The so-called Habakkuk is widely celebrated as one of Donatello's greatest sculptures. Compared to the sculptor's

Cat. 12, back and front views

12

earlier figural work—the three statues on the bell tower's eastern side, for example—this prophet exhibits a much higher degree of naturalism and expressivity. The prophet is portrayed bald (whence its nickname, "lo Zuccone," or "Squash Head") and ascetically thin, his tunic hanging heavily from his left shoulder and creating deep, vertical drapery folds that underscore the figure's inner torment, and which draw attention—by way of contrast—to the figure's emaciated body beneath. His half-open mouth, deep-set eyes, and aquiline nose suggest a person at once dignified and intense. So pronounced is the statue's individuality, in fact, that by the end of the fifteenth century some Florentines had come to believe that it was a portrait of a *specific* person—one Giovanni Cherichini, a politician and adversary of the Medici family who died in 1416. Giorgio Vasari later reported that Donatello proclaimed the statue his masterpiece, and would even on occasion demand that it speak.[2]

The prophet Habakkuk is known as the author of the Bible's Book of Habakkuk, which comprises three chapters divided into fifty-six verses. In them, the prophet addresses a variety of themes ranging from divine justice and loyalty to the covenant which leads to salvation and to theophany (the manifestation of God through his works). The etymology of the name Habakkuk is uncertain, some scholars arguing that it comes from a Hebrew word meaning he who embraces or struggles. Habakkuk's moral and religious doctrine is rich and profound, taking its cue from the basic problem besetting history and mankind's existence: why does injustice exist in the world? Like other prophets, he too is moved by the oppression of the weak and cries out for justice, but unlike any other prophet he points to a vital principle that instills courage and guides the spirit: "Write the vision [God tells him] and make it plain upon tables, that he may run that readeth it ... the just shall live by his faith."[3] The most accurate philological interpretation of Habakkuk's meaning in this phrase, which St. Paul was to adopt as one of the keystones of his own theology, is the constancy of good, upheld by faith in God's justice which governs the world and by faith in the fulfillment of God's promises.[4]

– SN

1. See Giovanni Poggi, ed., *Il Duomo di Firenze* (Berlin, 1909), e.g., docs. 323–34; and H. W. Janson, *The Sculpture of Donatello* (Princeton, NJ, 1963), 33–41.
2. Giorgio Vasari, *Le vite de' più eccellenti pittori, scultori, ed architettori*, ed. Gaetano Milanesi, 9 vols. (Florence, 1906), vol. 2, 404–5; Hans Semper, *Donatello: seine Zeit und Schule* (Vienna, 1875); C. Frey, *Il Codice Magliabechiano, cl. XVII.7, contenente notizie sopra l'arte degli antichi e quella de' Fiorentini da Cimabue a Michelangelo Buonarroti, scritte da Anonimo Fiorentino* (Berlin, 1892), 75–76; J. Lányi, "Le statue quattrocentesche dei Profeti nel campanile e nell'antica facciata di S. Maria del Fiore," *Rivista d'arte* 17 (1935): 121–59, 245–80.
3. Habakkuk 2:2–4.
4. Romans 1:17; Galatians 1:13; see Hebrews 10:3.

Cat. 12, detail

13—14

13
Donato di Niccolò di Betto Bardi, known as Donatello (ca. 1386–1466) and workshop
Head
ca. 1439
Bronze with traces of gilding
45 × 35 × 30 cm (17¾ × 13¾ × 11¾ in.)
Inv. no. 2005/379a

14
Donato di Niccolò di Betto Bardi, known as Donatello (ca. 1386–1466) and workshop (Michelozzo di Bartolomeo Michelozzi, known as Michelozzo [1396–1472] ?)
Head
ca. 1439
Bronze with traces of gilding
45 × 35 × 33 cm (17¾ × 13¾ × 13 in.)
Inv. no. 2005/379b

These two bronze heads once belonged to the organ loft, or "cantoria," that Donatello and his workshop made to adorn the southeast pier flanking Florence Cathedral's main altar. The sculptor set them below the loft's projecting face, in the two central spaces between the brackets, each piece nested against a disc of purple porphyry, and each inclined downward toward the pavement below. The Opera's account books suggest that the heads were among the last elements that Donatello added to the structure. A document from October 1439 shows the Opera allocating a substantial amount of bronze to the sculptor for a certain "texta" that would appear in the "hole or opening below [the pulpit]." The document specifies, further, that this bronze head should be "the same as the other head," it, too, destined for the zone beneath the pulpit.[1] The heads were separated from the cantoria at an unknown date, and only reunited with the ensemble in the 1930s, when the Museo dell'Opera del Duomo acquired them from the Museo Nazionale del Bargello.[2]

Donatello accepted the commission for the cantoria shortly after his return from Rome, where he had based himself between roughly the years 1430 and 1433, and where he had ample occasion to study the city's classical heritage. In the years that followed, Donatello's interest in the ancient past reached fever pitch. Not only had the sculptor begun to collect classical pieces himself, but, according to the humanists with whom he kept company, he had become a recognized authority—a connoisseur—of antiquities.[3]

Not surprisingly, perhaps, the cantoria reflects Donatello's energetic engagement with ancient Rome's material culture. This is particularly true of these heads, which appear to be copied directly from an ancient prototype. So closely do the heads resemble classical portraits, in fact, that they were, until their arrival at the Museo dell'Opera in the 1930s, classified as ancient bronzes.

In material and format, too, these iridescent likenesses are explicitly classical in inspiration. As Donatello knew well, bronze smacked of antiquity, especially when affixed to a porphyry *tondo*. What strikes one immediately is the heads' dependence on the imperial Roman tradition of the *imago clipeata*, which set the hieratic portrait of an emperor—often cast in bronze—into a circular shield or medallion (as though it had been "clipped" from one context and introduced into another). Without denying this association, H. W. Janson suggested that Donatello may also have looked to Roman fountain basins, in which paired heads such as these were used as spouts.[4]

As the document from October 1439 hints, these objects are, in reality, the same person twice portrayed: an adult male with tousled hair and beard, brows knit with concern, seemingly caught on the horns of some internal predicament. Subtle differences between the objects, however, suggest that they may be the work of different artists. The modeling of the left head (cat. 13), for example, is more expressive and assured than that of its sibling (cat. 14): in the figure's furrowed forehead, or its dramatically parted lips (which reveal a row of teeth), or its deeply set eye sockets. One possibility is that Donatello produced cat. 13 shortly before 1439, and delegated responsibility for cat. 14—its matching copy—to one of his assistants. In large assignments like the cantoria, such a division of labor was quite common. Allocating the second head to an assistant would not only have proved more efficient, but would have granted that assistant a chance to imitate his master as part of a learning process within the workshop. It is equally possible that Donatello made neither of the heads, and merely provided instructions for their realization.[5]

What is almost certain, however, is that Donatello did not cast the heads himself. Throughout his career, the sculptor preferred to entrust his wax models—or his assistants' models—to professional bronze founders, a tendency well documented in contracts, account books, and—later—in the writings of his commentators.[6] One candidate for casting the heads is the bell-maker, architect, and sculptor Michelozzo (1396–1472). That artist had collaborated with Donatello on assignments regularly since 1425—most recently the outdoor pulpit at Prato's cathedral (ca. 1433–38)—and wherever bronze was involved, he had assumed casting responsibilities.[7] In the absence of further documentation, however, the question of who modeled and/or cast the heads must remain open.

An equally refractory problem is defining what purpose the heads served in the overall program for the cantoria. Given the objects' highly visible placement in the ensemble's lower register, and the extraordinary cost of bronze and porphyry, it is unlikely that they were mere decorative whimsy. Robert Corwegh labeled the heads Old Testament prophets, an interpretation that few scholars have since endorsed.[8] A more plausible hypothesis, first advanced by Janson, designates the heads and the two reliefs flanking them (the latter depict, in his words, "pagan offerings") as the "zone of antiquity" here knowingly juxtaposed with the "Christian jubilation on the balustrade."[9] Questions of iconography aside, one fact remains undeniable: as the cantoria's largest anthropomorphic features, and angled toward viewers, the two heads delivered the most direct human appeal in the entire structure. Scanning the cantoria during Mass, the spectator may have felt that the heads addressed him or her directly, their gazes meeting the viewer's own, providing a human point of entry into the structure at large.

Whatever the case, the operai clearly thought the aesthetic impact of the heads was important, for in 1456 they made arrangements to have the heads gilt with sheets of gold leaf.[10] What this suggests, perhaps, is that the Opera felt the dark tone of the metal was not sufficiently legible within the shadowy niches below the cantoria's projecting face, and required gilding to enhance its appeal to viewers below.

– DZ

1. Giovanni Poggi, ed., *Il Duomo di Firenze* (Berlin, 1909), doc. 1312. The heads were in place no later than 1446, and probably well before. This may be inferred from a record for the cantoria dated February 26, 1446, in which Donatello is paid, among other things, for the "two bronze heads that [he] has made and installed" (Poggi, *Il Duomo di Firenze*, doc. 1315). See also Luisa Becherucci and Giulia Brunetti, eds., *Il museo dell'Opera del Duomo a Firenze*, 2 vols. (Venice, [1970]), vol. 1, 280–82.
2. One reason for the transfer of the heads may have been to test Robert Corwegh's hypothesis—then unsubstantiated—that they had originally belonged to the cantoria. See Robert Corwegh, *Donatellos Sängerkanzel im Dom zu Florenz* (Berlin, 1909), 12–13, 26f.
3. In his biography of Cyriac of Ancona, Francesco Scalamonti wrote that the former had visited the houses of Donatello and Ghiberti in the mid-1430s and saw "many statues, both antiquity pieces and their own modern works in bronze and marble." See the *Vita viri clarissimi et famosissimi Kyriaci anconitani* (*Transactions of the American Philosophical Society*, vol. 86, n. 4), eds. and trans. Charles Mitchell and Edward W. Bodnar, S.J. (Philadelphia, 1996), 132. Donatello's ability to judge the quality of antiquities is mentioned by his contemporaries Nanni di Miniato and Poggio Bracciolini (see Hans Semper, *Donatello: seine Zeit und Schule* [Vienna, 1875], 281, 311).
4. See H. W. Janson, *The Sculpture of Donatello* (Princeton, NJ, 1963), 125 n. 5; and Janson, "Donatello and the Antique," in *Donatello e il suo tempo* (Florence and Padua, 1968), 84.
5. Janson made this claim, although he maintained that one of the heads (cat. 13) was an antiquity, the other (cat. 14) its exact copy. See Janson, *Sculpture of Donatello*, 124. Conservators at the Opificio delle Pietre Dure have since disproved Janson's hypothesis, demonstrating that both works are indeed from the fifteenth century. See Stefania Agnoletti, Annalena Brini, Andrea Cagnini, Maria Donata Mazzoni, and Simone Porcinai, "Le teste in bronzo della Cantoria di Donatello: aspetti conoscitivi e conservativi," *OPD Restauro 25* (2013): 201–12.
6. On this point, see page 187, note 13.
7. On Donatello and Michelozzo's partnership see R. W. Lightbown, *Donatello & Michelozzo: An Artistic Partnership and Its Patrons in the Early Renaissance* (London, 1980); and Harriet McNeal Caplow, "Sculptors' Partnerships in Michelozzo's Florence," *Studies in the Renaissance* 21 (1974): 145–75.
8. Corwegh, *Donatellos Sängerkanzel*, 12.
9. Janson, *Sculpture of Donatello*, 125.
10. Poggi, *Il Duomo di Firenze*, doc. 1318.

15—17

15
Luca della Robbia (1399/1400–1482)
The Art of Dialectic (Plato and Aristotle?)
1437–39
Marble
83.5 × 69 × 13 cm (32⅞ × 27⅛ × 5 in.)
Inv. no. 2005/437

16
Luca della Robbia (1399/1400–1482)
The Art of Grammar (Aelius Donatus or Priscian instructing students?)
1437–39
Marble
81.5 × 68.5 × 13 cm (32 × 27 × 5 in.)
Inv. no. 2005/436

17
Luca della Robbia (1399/1400–1482)
The Art of Music (Orpheus or Arion?)
1437–39
Marble
81.5 × 69 × 13 cm (32 × 27⅛ × 5 in.)
Inv. no. 2005/438

In May 1437 the Opera charged Luca della Robbia with finishing a series of reliefs for the lower level of Florence's bell tower, a program begun in the mid-fourteenth century by Andrea Pisano and his school, but still lacking five components.[1] The hexagonal panels exhibited here—*Dialectic*, *Grammar*, and *Music*—are three of the original five that Luca produced. The cycle depicted the activities of man. Unlike other cycles of its type, however, this one does not correlate the depiction of work with the rhythm of the months or seasons, perhaps because Florence was a mercantile republic (and thus more divorced from the seasons than an agrarian community, for example). Here, the city of Florence extolled the basis of success, which is not a glorious tradition or wealth deriving from its land, but the activities of a city built on the industrious labor of its inhabitants. The bell tower is divided into two levels, with hexagonal panels on the first level and rhomboid lozenges on the second (these latter panels depict the Seven Sacraments). The hexagonal reliefs are made of marble alone, while the lozenges have a blue maiolica ground.

According to Timothy Verdon, the fourteenth-century cycle was inspired by a Florentine writer named Fra Remigio de' Girolami, a Dominican friar from the convent of Santa Maria Novella traditionally thought to have been Dante's mentor and who was, in turn, a pupil of St. Thomas Aquinas. The text enabling us to understand the iconographic program of the bell tower's sculptural decoration is his *Contra falsos ecclesie professores*, in which Fra Remigio expounds the theory that the Catholic Church "renews" all the different disciplines of human knowledge and highlights their function in revealing the perfection of Christ.[2] The fourteenth-century cycle was partly rearranged later on: the panels depicting painting and sculpture were moved to the north side of the bell tower, where they joined Luca's five hexagonal panels depicting the liberal arts and their founders.

Luca's panels are an interesting indication of a change of era. Luca's work on the bell tower, which is extraneous to the legibility of the previously completed cycle, became necessary when a walkway linking the cathedral to the bell tower was demolished in 1431 and a small door was opened in the tower to provide access to it from the east. The Middle Ages' grandiose, all-embracing vision of work had already fallen out of fashion by the fifteenth century; thus, aesthetic

considerations aside, Luca's contributions are total departures from the logic governing Andrea Pisano's preexisting cycle. The panels on the north side of the bell tower were arranged as follows (from left to right):

- *The Art of Sculpture* (Andrea Pisano)
- *The Art of Painting* (Andrea Pisano)
- *The Art of Grammar* (Luca della Robbia)
- *The Art of Dialectic* or *Philosophy* (Luca della Robbia)
- *The Art of Music* (Luca della Robbia)
- *The Art of Geometry and Arithmetic* (Luca della Robbia)
- *The Art of Astronomy* (Luca della Robbia)

The hexagonal panels illustrate human activity, which scholastic philosophy divided into *artes mechanicae*, *artes liberales*, and *artes virtutis*.[3] The Trivium, which referred in medieval times both to three of the liberal arts and to their teaching, was followed thematically by the Quadrivium. The Trivium included the three philosophical and literary disciplines: Grammar (which basically meant Latin), Rhetoric (the art of composing speeches and public speaking), and Dialectic (or philosophy). The Quadrivium, on the other hand, included four disciplines related to the sphere of mathematics: Arithmetic, Geometry, Astronomy, and Music. The liberal arts are generally taken to refer to those creative activities that demand intellectual application and the production of which is denoted by their unique content value. So they stand in opposition to the mechanical arts, which were techniques that later developed into specialized skills, or manual disciplines.

The first relief exhibited here represents Dialectic, one of the liberal arts in the Trivium. Giorgio Vasari was the first to decipher this relief's allegorical sense, identifying the two figures engaged in debate as Aristotle and Plato. The two philosophers fill the entire field of the relief, and are modeled with sobriety and simplicity. In this respect, Luca's relief hews closely to the style of Andrea Pisano, probably in an attempt to maintain overall consistency in the program.

The second relief exhibited here is an allegory of Grammar. The nature of the allegory remained uncertain until the mid-sixteenth century, when Vasari identified the main figure as either Priscian or Aelius Donatus. Priscian of Caesarea (Priscianus Caesariensis, born in Caesaria in Mauritania) was a Roman grammarian who lived between the late fifth and early sixth centuries AD, teaching Latin in Byzantium during the reign of Emperor Anastasius (491–518). Aelius Donatus, on the other hand, lived in Rome sometime around the middle of the fourth century, and was the author of the *Ars Grammatica*. Probably of African origin, he also taught rhetoric and his pupils included St. Jerome and Rufinus. These two Latin grammarians, Donatus and Priscian, spawned both the Modists who studied the different modes of meaning in words most likely to accentuate their logical function, and the Terminists who based their beliefs on the premise that every term is closely bound to an individual substance and that universal terms have no other reality but are simply the result of relations (thus there are no different modes of meaning; terms simply need to be studied from a strictly grammatical viewpoint). The allegory of Grammar is generally depicted employing a scroll, a book, or a desk at which a boy is writing. The teacher may also be holding a knife or a small scraper to correct mistakes.

Luca's panel shows one of these two learned scholars—Priscian or Donatus—in the schoolmaster's chair, lecturing to two students. In the background, modeled in *stiacciato* or low relief, we see a classicizing door surmounted by a Renaissance-style pediment. It is interesting to note that the door is shown half-open, a conceit that not only enhances the sense of depth in the relief, but which might allude to the opening of the "door of knowledge" through teaching.

The third panel represents the liberal art of Music, a component of the Quadrivium. Vasari identified the central figure as either Orpheus or Arion, who enchants a group of animals with his music making. Ancient sources claim that Orpheus was a native of Pieria, a distant and mysterious region thought to host shamans with the ability to influence the natural world and entrance their audiences through music. Born to the Muse Calliope and to the Thracian king Oeagrus (or, according to another version, to the god Apollo), Orpheus belonged to the generation preceding the era of classical Greek religion. With the spellbinding power of his lyre and his singing he would tame wild beasts and breathe life into rocks and the elements of nature. Arion of Methymna (also known as Arion of Lesbos) was a citharede (a player of the lyre, or cithara) in ancient Greece. Herodotus tells us that he invented the dithyramb, a hymn sung and danced in honor of Dionysus. Of these two figures, the one that appears to be iconographically closest to Luca's sculpture is Orpheus. The composition is rich in detail and figures which take up all the available space. The panel is dominated by the central figure of the musician, who is shown seated, wearing early fifteenth-century costume and playing a lute. The choice of a lute as his instrument is a way of underscoring the setting's references to the contemporary culture of della Robbia's day. Luca fills the background surrounding the musician with animals—a mythological unicorn among them—which together emerge from the thick undergrowth and vegetation that cover the relief's ground. In this case the artist has deliberately sought to break the panel's geometrical pattern by filling all the available space and more with a richly detailed background. Even the lower point of the hexagon, which generally contains decoration designed to fill an obvious gap, is taken up here by the rocky ground on which the musician is sitting, and has thus become part and parcel of the scene depicted. The original panels were moved to the Museo dell'Opera del Duomo between 1965 and 1967.

– SN

1. Luisa Becherucci, *Andrea Pisano nel Campanile di Giotto* (Florence, 1965), 1–3; Becherucci, "La bottega pisana di Andrea da Pontedera," *Mitteilungen des Kunsthistorischen Institutes in Florenz* 11 (1965): 227–63, esp. 227; Becherucci and Giulia Brunetti, eds., *Il museo dell'Opera del Duomo a Firenze*, 2 vols. (Venice: [1970]), vol. 1, 276–77.
2. T. Verdon, "Il Campanile di Giotto," in *Alla riscoperta di Piazza del Duomo in Firenze* (Florence, 1994), 84–115.
3. Julius von Schlosser, "Giusto's Fresken in Padua und die Vorläufer des Stanza della Segnatura," *Jahrbuch der Kunsthistorischen Sammlungen* 17 (1896): 37–76.

18—20

18
Master of Castel di Sangro
Adoration of the Magi
First half of the 15th century
Maiella stone
56 × 57 × 14.5 cm (22 × 22 × 5¾ in.)
Museo dell'Opera del Duomo,
Florence (deposit of Gallerie Fiorentine,
inv. Bargello sculture 483)
Inscription on lower edge in Gothic letters:
"QUANDO FO PRESENTATO AD LI MAGI"
Inv. no. 2005/893

19
Master of Castel di Sangro
Flagellation
First half of the 15th century
Maiella stone
56 × 52.5 × 14.5 cm (22 × 20 × 5¾ in.)
Museo dell'Opera del Duomo,
Florence (deposit of Gallerie Fiorentine,
inv. Bargello sculture 487)
Inscription on lower edge in Gothic letters:
"QUANDO XPO FO LEGATO A LA COLONNA"
Inv. no. 2005/896

20
Master of Castel di Sangro
Crucifixion
First half of the 15th century
Maiella stone
57 × 57 × 14.5 cm (22½ × 22½ × 5¾ in.)
Museo dell'Opera del Duomo,
Florence (deposit of Gallerie Fiorentine,
inv. Bargello sculture 488)
Inv. no. 2005/898

Castel di Sangro—a town in the province of L'Aquila in the region of Abruzzo—is situated on the edge of a stark, barren limestone outcrop rising at the northern tip of a long plateau. The now-ruined castle that gave the village its name is perched on top of this rocky outcrop, in a strategic position that allowed the village to enjoy a certain degree of prosperity and security for many centuries. During the course of the fifteenth century, ties with the Florentine cloth manufacturing industry developed. Given these trade relations, both artists and their compositions migrated from one region to the other. The stone reliefs exhibited here bear vivid testimony to these exchanges.[1]

Scholars have shown clear iconographic and stylistic affinities between these works and Ghiberti's nearly contemporary reliefs for the North Doors of Florence's baptistery. The stone used in these sculptures is known as *pietra bianca*, a creamy white limestone quarried on the Maiella, a mountainous area of Abruzzo. Maiella stone was never used either in Florence

Fig. 73
Lorenzo Ghiberti
North Doors of Florence Baptistery, 1403–24: panel with the *Adoration of the Magi*. Bronze with gilding, 52 × 45 cm (20½ × 17¾ in.)
Museo dell'Opera del Duomo, Florence

or in Tuscany, however, and it is therefore likely that these panels were carved in the region from which the stone itself came. Scholars have drawn similar conclusions based on their analysis of the wording engraved on the panels' lower frames, which contains clear instances of Abruzzo dialect.

A document in the archive of the Opera del Duomo relates that these panels and their three companions (the cycle comprises six reliefs in total) were sold by the painter Teofilo Patini to antique dealer Godefroy Brauer in 1904, who gave them to the Italian state around 1936.[2] They were then given to the Museo dell'Opera del Duomo in 1938 or 1939 and put in storage. Most scholars agree that the time the panels spent in the Patini family's courtyard was simply one stage in a long journey from what was probably their original location on the outside of the church of Santa Maria Assunta in Castel di Sangro. There is little consensus among critics over the panels' attribution, however. One possible candidate is Nicola da Guardiagrele (1385–1462), who was arguably the most important goldsmith, painter, and sculptor in Abruzzo during the fifteenth century. Accepting the panels' association with the North Doors of the baptistery in Florence, Lionello Venturi gave them to Nicola da Guardiagrele, an attribution based on analogies with Nicola's silver altar frontal for Teramo Cathedral (1433–48), some panels of which recall the style and subject matter of Ghiberti's work. Other scholars have assigned the panels to an anonymous master whom they call Amico di Bartolomeo, tracing the work back to that name through an inscription under the portico of Castel di Sangro's principal church, the lettering of which is similar to that on the panels. This has led some to posit that the artist in question traveled to Florence—either in Nicola's company or on his own—where he studied Ghiberti's work, eventually bringing Ghiberti's innovations with him back to Abruzzo.

The panels are in a poor state of conservation and are partly covered by a layer of plaster and a layer of gray paint imitating stone. Where this patina has worn off, the carving showing through is of the highest quality and shows a remarkable similarity with the style of Nicola da Guardiagrele, although only a thorough, careful, and extremely necessary restoration of the panels could confirm such an attribution.

The *Adoration of the Magi* is missing several key structural parts including its top right-hand corner and details such as the heads of the Madonna and the Christ Child. The panel, which is quadrangular in shape, closely echoes the iconography of the corresponding panel in Ghiberti's North Doors for the baptistery in Florence (the first panel in the third row from the bottom of the right-hand door; fig. 73). The composition also emulates Ghiberti's panel in that the Holy Family—the Virgin Mary, the Christ Child, and St. Joseph—are depicted in the shelter of a Gothic loggia. A figure in adoration—perhaps one of the Three Wise Men—is also heavily damaged, shown kneeling, with one hand resting on the ground. Above this figure, a group of four other figures stands in the foreground, with further figures in the background. Those in the foreground include the Wise Men, or Magi, whose faces are still (miraculously) almost intact and free of the layers of plaster overlaid on other parts. They bear a close resemblance to some of the figures in the Lanciano Cross (the first of the crosses that can be attributed to Nicola da Guardiagrele). It is precisely this kinship with the Lanciano Cross that has suggested to scholars that the panel was carved shortly after 1423, while the many analogies that can be detected with Ghiberti's panel include an exact reproduction of a figure—the last figure on the upper left-hand side of the panel—carrying a small monkey on his shoulder, copied with extraordinary fidelity and sophistication. In both instances the animal's snout projects slightly more than the rest of its body, which is carved in *stiacciato*, or flattened relief. This can be explained by the fact that the panel for the door was designed to sit higher than eye level; thus, in rendering the figure's perspective, the sculptor allowed for the fact that it would be viewed from below. The composition, which is particularly well balanced despite its serious lacunae, wholeheartedly espouses the style of Florentine Gothic sculpture.

The Adoration of the Magi symbolizes the acknowledgement of Jesus as the long-awaited Messiah, such recognition being offered even by the kingdoms and religions of the distant Orient, where his coming was mentioned in ancient tradition by the oracle of Balaam—identified with Zoroaster—when he announced that "there shall come a Star out of Jacob, and a Sceptre shall rise out of Israel" (Numbers 24:17). The Magi who "came from afar" are considered to stand for all those who "came from afar" and were eyed with suspicion at that time, because the Gospels make it quite clear that the Magi were Gentiles rather than Jews.

Cat. 19, above and Cat. 20, below

18–20

Several parts of the figures on the severely damaged *Flagellation* panel are unfortunately missing: the figure of Christ in the center is missing its head, part of an arm and part of the left leg, while the flagellants to Christ's left and right are missing their left arms. Iconographically, it closely echoes the corresponding panel in Ghiberti's North Doors in the baptistery in Florence (the first panel in the sixth row from the bottom of the right-hand door; see fig. 42). The composition also emulates Ghiberti's panel in that the scene takes place in an architectural setting with a classical trabeation, or horizontal lintel, supported by five columns, Christ being bound to the central column. Its overall appearance reveals a less careful and confident hand at work. The panel is also fairly difficult to decipher, although we can make out the presence of spectators above the two flagellants, again echoing Ghiberti's panel.

The story of the Flagellation of Christ is one of the most important accounts of betrayal and suffering in the Gospels, marking the start of Christ's painful journey that would lead to the expiation of human sin. The Gospel account tells us that Jesus was bound to the column by Pontius Pilate, the Roman governor who presided over the trial of Jesus after he was charged with plotting against the Roman Empire and proclaiming himself King of the Jews. The panel depicts Christ bound to the column by his wrists with a flagellant to either side, although their precise actions are difficult to make out, not least because of damage to key parts of the figures. The rendering of the scene nevertheless manages to be highly dramatic. The iconography of the Flagellation is designed to prompt the faithful to contemplate the Passion of Christ and thus to understand the suffering of the Church in this world.

The *Crucifixion* is also badly damaged (the heads of Christ and of the figure seated beneath the Cross on the right are both missing, for example). The panel's iconography echoes Ghiberti's relief of the same subject for the North Doors (see fig. 34), although the Abruzzese sculptor omits the angels on either side of the Cross. In the absence of detailed analysis resulting from restoration, the panel's present condition makes it impossible for scholars to determine whether the sculptor deliberately omitted the two angels seen in Ghiberti's panel or whether they have simply been removed or have disappeared through natural causes over time.

– SN

1. These reliefs are discussed, among other sources, in Luisa Becherucci and Giulia Brunetti, eds., *Il museo dell'Opera del Duomo a Firenze*, 2 vols. (Venice, [1970]), vol. 1, 275–76, with additional bibliography; Aldo Galli, "Echi di Lorenzo Ghiberti in Abruzzo," in *Nicola da Guardiagrele: orafo tra Medioevo e Rinascimento. Le opere, i restauri*, ed. Sante Guido (Todi, 2008), 369–98; *Lorenzo Ghiberti: "materia e ragionamenti"* (Florence, 1978), 121–24; C. Seymour, *Sculpture in Italy 1400–1500* (Harmondsworth and Baltimore, 1966), 44; G. Fiocco, "Arte quattrocentesca in Castel di Sangro," *Rassegna d'Arte* 7 (1913), 117; M. Reymond, "A proposito dei bassorilievi di Castel di Sangro," *L'Arte* 5 (1902): 112–14; A. De Nino, "Bassorilievi medievali in Castel di Sangro," *L'Arte* 4 (1901), 422, 424.
2. The original cycle originally comprised six panels. In addition to the three reliefs exhibited here, the series also included the *Presentation in the Temple*, the *Flight into Egypt*, and *Judas's Betrayal of Christ*. There was a further panel depicting the Madonna and Child, subsequently lost, although known from a photograph. On Nicola da Guardiagrele see, among others, A. Venturi, *La scultura del quattrocento*, Storia dell Arte Italiana (Milan, 1908), 176.

Cat. 20, detail

21

Luca della Robbia (1399/1400–1482)
and Antonio di Salvi Salvucci (1450–1527)
Processional Cross: Christ Crucified, the Evangelists, Allegory of the Sun
15th century (after 1460, before 1475)
Gilded copper (repoussé and chased), gilded bronze, and enamel
76 × 57 cm (total height with staff 160 cm) (30 × 22½ in.)
(total height with staff: 63 in.)
Inv. no. 2005/347

Luca della Robbia, the artist likely responsible for the figure of the crucified Christ on this processional cross, learned metalwork at a very young age. As an adolescent, Luca became an apprentice to the goldsmith Leonardo di Ser Giovanni, in whose workshop he would have developed the ability to draw, to model in wax, and to work metal with a high degree of polish and finish. Given the absence of firm documentary evidence, the attribution of Christ to Luca is the result of stylistic comparison with other works by him. Considering its evident kinship with the Gothic style, the cross itself was, in all probability, produced earlier, and only later adapted to take the figure of Christ.[1]

In use as far back as the thirteenth century, processional crosses usually had half-figures adorning the ends of their arms. In this case the cross has six quatrefoils with four half-figures on the front, three on the back, and smaller figures at the crossing of the arms and below Christ's feet, in the now-traditional "Gothic compass" shape. Four of these panels, at the end of the cross's four arms, contain the figures of the four Evangelists portrayed with their iconographic attributes (St. John with an eagle, Luke an ox, Matthew an angel, and Mark a lion). The body of Christ occupies the two central quatrefoil panels, his head rests against a bird—probably a swan or pelican—and a sun is at his feet. An elaborate ornamental border frames each of the cross's figural elements.

Much of the cross is smooth, with small golden stars adorning a matt blue enamel ground. It is worth noting that plant motifs are to be found on numerous crucifixes from the Romanesque era, which depict the dead Christ on a cross made from a tree in full bloom.

The depiction of a sunburst is intended to symbolize an element that clarifies, enlightens, and evokes divinity in the shape of a radiant sun. The swan, moreover, may be seen as further bolstering the symbol of the sun, a reference taken from Greek mythology where the god Apollo was venerated as the sun god governing the harmony of the universe. One of Apollo's attributes was the swan, which signified his connection to music (swans, it was believed, sang a final haunting melody before they died, which Renaissance interpreters used, by analogy, to describe the final spark of life). The pelican, on the other hand, was used in the Middle Ages as a symbol of Christ's compassion: the mother pelican was thought sometimes to strike its breast with its beak, sacrificing its life in order to nourish its young with its blood. Here the creature's appearance is that of a swan, but its meaning probably relates to this pelican symbolism.

– SN

1. M. W. Wackernagel, *Der Lebensraum des Künstlers in der florentinischen Renaissance* (Leipzig, 1938), 96; and Luisa Becherucci and Giulia Brunetti, eds., *Il museo dell'Opera del Duomo a Firenze*, 2 vols. (Venice, [1970]), vol. 2, 246–47.

Cat. 21

OVERLEAF
Cat. 21, details

22—23

22
Attributed to Filippo Brunelleschi (1377–1446)
Model for the Dome of Santa Maria del Fiore
ca. 1420–52
Wood
Dome: 100 × 70 cm (39⅜ × 27½ in.);
Apses: 55 × 63 × 35 cm each (21⅝ × 24¾ × 13¾ in. each)
Inv. no. 2005/493

23
Attributed to Filippo Brunelleschi (1377–1446)
Model of the Lantern for the Dome of Santa Maria del Fiore
15th or 16th century
Wood (elm and walnut), wax, and plaster
84 × 70 cm (base) (33 × 27½ in.)
Inv no. 2005/485

The dome of Florence Cathedral, which today dominates the city's skyline, was built following a design by Filippo Brunelleschi (1377–1446). Work began in 1420, and concluded in 1436, when Pope Eugenius IV solemnly consecrated the cathedral, with the dome more or less resembling the wooden model exhibited here (cat. 22).[1]

While not completely faithful to the dome as finally built, this model's shape and structure convey an accurate idea of the innovative approach devised by Brunelleschi in the first phase of planning. The date of the model remains controversial, often hovering between 1420 and the years immediately following Brunelleschi's death, as does the work's authorship. Giuseppe Marchini, who conducted the first reliable study of the model, argued that it is by Brunelleschi's hand, identifying close similarities with the architecture itself, especially with the irregularity of the dimensions of the octagonal drum, four of whose sides are longer than the others (Marchini dated the model to 1429).

The model—built to provide a complete view of the project, its volume, and its structure—today looks bare and devoid of ornament, but this was not always the case. The wax putty and polychromy that originally adorned the model were lost during restoration efforts following the flood in Florence in 1966.[2] Brunellechi's assistant and later biographer, Antonio di Tuccio Manetti (1423–1497), tells us that the model was made under his master's supervision: "...Filippo's tendency—or rather his custom—concerning the models he made for the buildings that were required and that he built was to indicate little about the symmetrical elements. He took care to have only the principal walls built and to show the relationship of certain members without the ornaments."[3]

This model consists of three separate, fragmentary parts: two apsidal tribunes devoid of their respective domes, and the octagonal drum on which the cathedral dome rests. The tribunes, which were only reunited with the model of the dome after the restoration following the flood of 1966, are on two levels with two superimposed semioctagonal *exedrae*. The five walls of the semipolygon on the first (lower) level are each divided into three blind, round-headed arcades, with a lancet window in each of the walls' middle sections. The upper level reproduces the semipolygonal *exedra* of the lower level but on a smaller scale, with the difference that its sides each have a single blind arcade with a tall lancet window, matching those on the first level in both number and size. The second level also has a buttress on each of the four corners where the walls join. These buttresses perform the function of structural elements supporting the tribune's semidomes. A molded cornice runs around the top of the tribunes. The two smaller parts are missing their semidomes, and thus resemble a cross-section that reveals the process by which they were constructed.

The drum of the cathedral dome model, which is octagonal in shape, is divided into two levels separated and crowned by strip cornices with molding, held in place by projecting corner pilasters; the cornice separating the two levels is interrupted where the tribunes' semidomes would connect with the drum, while the points at which the semidomes' "dead tribunes" meet the drum are highlighted by pointed-arch openings. The walls of the drum's second level have circular openings splayed inwards; and one can clearly make out the structural ribs strengthening the corners of the segments both on the drum and on the dome.

The second model exhibited here (cat. 23) was almost certainly produced later than the first. Its focus is the lantern that crowns and seals Brunelleschi's dome. Three segments

Cat. 22

of the dome proper are deliberately omitted to display its internal structure. When Brunelleschi completed the dome in the 1430s, a huge debate took place over how it should be crowned.[4] A competition was held in which six models were submitted by various architects, among them Lorenzo Ghiberti (1378/80–1455). On December 31, 1436 a commission chaired by Cosimo de' Medici chose Brunelleschi's design. Construction did not begun until 1446, and when Brunelleschi died—mere months later—responsibility for the execution of his design fell to Manetti, Michelozzo di Bartolomeo Michelozzi (1396–1472), and Bernardo Rossellino (1409–1464). They finished the lantern in 1467.

Although Giorgio Vasari mentioned this model in his biography of Brunelleschi, its attribution and date are uncertain. Some have argued that the base is original but that the lantern is a late seventeenth-century replacement, adducing both the date "1673" scratched on it and the baroque style of the volutes and trim. What is certain is that Brunelleschi was accustomed not only to producing designs but also to building models to allow his workmen to gain a better understanding of his construction methods. Possibly in an attempt to highlight the way in which Brunelleschi maintained control over his projects, Manetti tells us that Brunelleschi was concerned "that whoever would make the model should not discover his every secret, expecting to make all things precisely and well as they followed bit by bit in the actual building."[5] The model was made of various kinds of wood, with the addition of parts modeled in wax and plaster (capitals, pilasters, and decorative elements).

– SN

1. The models discussed here have received extensive scholarly treatment. See, for example, Luisa Becherucci and Giulia Brunetti, eds., *Il museo dell'Opera del Duomo a Firenze*, 2 vols. (Venice, [1970]), vol. 2, 211–14; and Beatrice Paolozzi Strozzi and Marc Bormand, eds., *La primavera del Rinascimento: la scultura e le arti a Firenze 1400–1460* (Florence, 2013), 289–91.
2. The very presence of these materials supports the attribution to Brunelleschi. Manetti tells us that the architect used several models to show his workmen how to build the dome, the details of which were made from a wide range of materials including clay, wax, wood, and even *calicioni* (large winter turnips). On this point see, for example, *Catalogo del Museo di Santa Maria del Fiore* (Florence, 1891), 35; Becherucci and Brunetti, *Il museo dell'Opera*, vol. 2, 15; Brunetti, "Il Museo dell'Opera del Duomo," in *Atti della Società Leonardo da Vinci* 6 (1975), 19–32, esp. 22; G. Marchini, "La cupola: medievale e no," in *Filippo Brunelleschi: la sua opera e il suo tempo*, 2 vols. (Florence, 1977), vol. 2, 916ff.; H. Millon, *Rinascimento da Brunelleschi a Michelangelo: la rappresentazione dell'architettura* (Milan, 1994), 19–22; A. Giusti and C. Acidini Luchinat, eds., *Masters of Florence: Glory and Genius at the Court of the Medici*, exh. cat. (Memphis, 2004); M. Bietti, A. Giusti, and M. Sframeli, eds., *The Splendour of the Medici: Art and Life in Renaissance Florence*, exh. cat. (Budapest, 2008), 88–89; Beatrice Paolozzi Strozzi and Marc Bormand, *La primavera del Rinascimento: la scultura e le arti a Firenze 1400–1460*, exh. cat. (Florence, 2013), 90.
3. A. Manetti, *Vita di Filippo di Ser Brunellesco*, eds. D. De Robertis and G. Tanturli (Milan, 1976), 116: "...i modelli c'è faceva [Brunelleschi] è gli faceva che intorno à fatti delle simmetrie poco v'appariva, ma attendeva solamente a fare le mura principali alla rispondenza di qualche membro senza ornamenti...."
4. Paolo Sanpaolesi, *La cupola di Santa Maria del Fiore* (Rome, 1941), 11; Sanpaolesi, "La lanterna di Santa Maria del Fiore e il suo modello ligneo," *Bollettino d'Arte* (1956): 11–29; Sanpaolesi, *Brunelleschi* (Milan, 1962), 157.
5. H. Saalman, *Filippo Brunelleschi: The Cupola of Santa Maria del Fiore* (London, 1980), 145–46.

THE NEW MUSEO DELL'OPERA DEL DUOMO

Timothy Verdon

Founded in 1891, Florence's Museo dell'Opera del Duomo or "Cathedral Works Museum" has the world's largest concentration of Florentine monumental sculpture of the Middle Ages and Renaissance: statues and reliefs in marble, bronze, and precious metals by Arnolfo di Cambio, Andrea Pisano, Lorenzo Ghiberti, Donatello, Luca della Robbia, Antonio Pollaiuolo, Andrea del Verrocchio, Michelangelo Buonarroti, and others. Almost all these works were made for exterior or interior areas of the ecclesiastical structures that stand in front of the museum: the baptistery of San Giovanni, the cathedral of Santa Maria del Fiore or "Duomo," and Giotto's bell tower. And that is what defines the Museo dell'Opera's character—its unique mission to display works made for the large buildings at its doorstep, themselves part of what today is called the "Grande Museo del Duomo" or "Greater Duomo Museum."

For the first 120 years of the museum's life, severe space limitations made this almost impossible. Two exhibit halls—opened to the public in 1891—did slowly grow to eighteen, but these remained insufficient for the collection's hundreds of works, the largest of which remained crated in a warehouse. Still worse, the available rooms were without exception too small for the works shown, most larger than life and meant to be seen from a distance. In the 1990s it became clear that various works removed from the cathedral complex buildings for restoration would, for conservation reasons, have to be displayed in the museum, which, however, lacked space for them

It was therefore with considerable relief that in 1997 the Opera acquired a vast building adjacent to the existing museum: 3,000 square meters of space that could be added to the 2,500 of the old museum. Erected as a theater in 1778, this structure had served various purposes in the nineteenth century, finally becoming a parking garage. Happily free of distinguishing architectural features, it could, by Italian law, be remodeled according to the purchaser's needs, with no obligation to preserve anything more than its roof line.

The Opera asked me to propose a new installation for the museum that would result from the fusion of the new building with the existing one. And the first site visit made clear what we could do, for the vast, bare interior offered a chance to solve our thorniest museological problem: that of exhibiting more than 100 fragments of the cathedral's lost medieval façade, dismantled in 1586–87—forty statues, many monumental in scale, and some sixty architectural elements with carved decoration and mosaic inlay. Looking at

Fig. 74, detail

the former theater's 36-meter length, 20-meter height, and 20-meter width, I saw that we could reconstruct virtually the whole façade, which had never reached more than a third of its planned height and whose final form is known from a drawing made at the time of its disassembly.

Thus, according to the plan developed by the Florentine architects chosen for the project—Adolfo Natalini, Piero Guicciardini, and Marco Magni—the new first hall of the museum will, on one of its long walls, recreate the fourteenth-century cathedral front, resituating our statues in the positions indicated in the sixteenth-century drawing. Particularly important works which in that arrangement would be visually inaccessible will be exhibited at eye level, with plaster casts in the niches on the reconstructed façade (fig. 74). And, in the same hall, Ghiberti's Gates of Paradise will be installed just as they were in 1452, right across from the main cathedral portal with its marble sculpture; the other two bronze baptistery doors will occupy positions at right and left of the Gates of Paradise (fig. 75). Above these doors then will stand the three groups of monumental sixteenth-century statues made for those positions, and the same hall will also host two large Roman sarcophagi known to have stood outside the baptistery throughout the Middle Ages and Renaissance. Reuniting works made to stand in close proximity but later separated, the installation in this 486-square-meter space seeks to reactivate the dialogue between antiquity, the Middle Ages, and the early and later Renaissance that once made Florence unique.

After this experience evoking public grandeur, three smaller rooms suggest the private piety that also characterized art made for the baptistery and cathedral: a "reliquary chapel" with masterpieces of medieval, Renaissance, and baroque goldsmith's work; a hall of votive paintings whose images of saints include portraits of the donors in prayer, and at whose center stands Donatello's wood statue of the penitent Mary Magdalene; and a gray sandstone sanctuary where Michelangelo's penultimate sculpture stands alone (fig. 76). The *Pietà*, meant for the artist's own tomb, portrays him lowering Christ's body into Mary's arms. For those with limited time, these two opening sections—the great hall with the reconstructed façade and the smaller "rooms of piety"—constitute an abbreviated itinerary, and visitors can in fact move directly from the *Pietà* to the exit.

Fig. 74
Architect's rendering of the main hall of the new museum, with its scale reconstruction of the medieval façade of the Duomo dismantled in 1586 but known from a contemporary drawing

For those able to devote more time, the visit continues on the upper level in a thirty-six-meter-long gallery hosting sculptures made for Giotto's bell tower: sixteen larger-than-life statues by Andrea Pisano, Donatello, and their collaborators, and almost sixty reliefs, including several by Luca della Robbia (fig. 77). One of the long walls of this gallery is pierced with openings looking back into the great hall with its reconstituted cathedral façade, which was in fact the visual point of reference for the bell tower, begun later; the statues are positioned between these "windows" open-

ing on the façade, and thus are necessarily seen in relation to it. An adjacent gallery then, twenty meters in length and six high, gathers objects and artifacts related to the building of Brunelleschi's dome: fifteenth-century models and construction materials, Brunelleschi's death mask, the sixteenth-century "shrine" with the architect's bust portrait created in the Opera del Duomo rooms he occupied in the years he directed the raising of the cupola (fig. 78).

On the museum's third level, another thirty-six-meter-long gallery opening onto the great hall brings together sixteenth- and early seventeenth-century works reflecting the efforts of the ruling Medici family to "modernize" the cathedral: large wooden presentation models by Bernardo Buontalenti, Giovan Antonio Dosio, Gherardo Silvani, and others for a new façade to replace the unfinished medieval one dismantled in 1586, and ephemeral statues and paintings made for the marriage of Grand Duke Ferdinando I de' Medici to Christina of Lorraine in 1589. Again, ceiling to wall apertures in the outer wall of this gallery make the reconstructed façade in the great hall continually present, and a small theater area helps visitors visualize the cathedral's documented role as dynastic church.

Fig. 75
The hundred-foot-long wall opposite the reconstructed façade, with the three bronze doors of the baptistery and their 16th-century statuary groups

At this point the itinerary leads back to the old museum's historic rooms on the intermediate level, where a completely revamped installation evokes the cathedral interior, with a further selection of gold-backed medieval and Renaissance altarpieces, the marble organ lofts or "cantorie" by Luca della Robbia and Donatello, twenty-five reliefs from Baccio Bandinelli's sixteenth-century choir enclosure, and the fourteenth–fifteenth-century silver altar made for the baptistery, with its monumental crucifix by Antonio Pollaiuolo. Precious liturgical textiles are exhibited alongside these furnishings, including the twenty-seven embroidered panels designed by Pollaiuolo in the 1460s for the set of vestments used on the Feast of St. John the Baptist, the city's patron saint.

A final enfilade of rooms is dedicated to the sixty-year-long design process that would finally, in the 1880s, produce the neo-Gothic façade that today adorns Florence Cathedral: drawings, paintings, statues, plaster casts, and models offer a rich panorama of the architectural and decorative impulses of the decades corresponding to the "Risorgimento" or period of national unification. Florence was indeed Italy's capital from 1865 until 1871, when the government transferred to Rome, and the Florence Cathedral façade was the first major monument of the new nation state.

OPPOSITE
Fig. 76
Architect's rendering of the hall containing Michelangelo's unfinished *Pietà*

Fig. 77
Architect's rendering of the gallery containing the sixteen statues and fifty-four reliefs originally on the exterior of Giotto's bell tower

ABOVE
Fig. 78
Architect's rendering of the gallery containing 16th- and 17th-century wood models made to illustrate proposals for a modern façade for the Duomo, whose medieval front had been dismantled in 1586–87

Notes

Florence Cathedral, Renaissance Sculpture, Sacred Scripture
Timothy Verdon

1. Most recently see Timothy Verdon, "Der Florentiner Dom im städischen Kontext," in *Florenz!*, eds. A. Giusti, B. Roeck, and G. Wolf, exh. cat. (Bonn, 2013), 57–65. But see also Verdon, *Firenze cristiana: cammini di fede e arte* (Florence, 2012), 60–92.
2. Timothy Verdon, "The Baptistery of San Giovanni: A Religious Monument Serving the City," in *The Baptistery of San Giovanni, Florence*, Mirabilia Italiae, ed. A. Paolucci (Modena, 1994), 9–32; and Verdon, "Spiritualità e arti figurative," in *La cattedrale di Santa Maria del Fiore a Firenze*, eds. F. Gurrieri and C. Acidini Luchinat, 2 vols. (Florence, 1995), vol. 2, 19–30.
3. G. Brucker, *Florence 1138–1737* (London, 1984), 109–39.
4. See Cesare Guasti, *Santa Maria del Fiore: la costruzione della chiesa e del campanile* (Florence, 1887), 20, doc. 24.
5. Gabriele Morolli, "The Architecture of the Baptistery and the 'Good Antique Style,'" in Paolucci, *Baptistery of San Giovanni*, 33–132, and, more recently, A. Giusti, *Il Battistero di San Giovanni a Firenze* (Modena, 2014).
6. "…Era molto di grossa forma e piccola a comparazione di si fatta cittade…": cf. Giovanni Villani, *Cronica*, ed. F. G. Dragomanni, 4 vols. (Florence, 1844–45), vol. 2, 16.
7. G. Fanelli, *Firenze*, Le Città nella Storia d'Italia (Rome and Bari, 1980), 13–52.
8. See Margaret Haines, ed., *Santa Maria del Fiore: The Cathedral and its Sculpture. Acts of the International Symposium for the VII Centenary of the Cathedral of Florence, Villa I Tatti, June 5–6 1997* (Florence, 2001), and particularly the two sections entitled "The Choice of Sculpture," with an introduction by K. Weil-Garris Brandt, 15–17, and "The Meaning of Sculpture," with an introduction by T. Verdon, 97–100.
9. T. Verdon, "Il Duomo come libro aperto: i messaggi della facciata," in *La facciata del Duomo di Siena: iconografia, stile, indagini storiche e scientifiche*, ed. M. Lorenzoni (Milan, 2007), 17–76.
10. See Enrica Neri Lusanna, "Venustius et honorabilius templum," in *Arnolfo: alle origini del Rinascimento fiorentino*, ed. E. Neri Lusanna, exh. cat. (Florence, 2005), 201–78.
11. See note 4.
12. John Pope-Hennessy, *Italian Gothic Sculpture* (London and New York, 1972), 15–18, 183–85.
13. Anita Fiderer Moskowitz, *The Sculpture of Andrea and Nino Pisano* (Cambridge, 1986), 7–30.
14. Marvin Trachtenberg, *The Campanile of Florence Cathedral: "Giotto's Tower"* (New York, 1971).
15. Moskowitz, *Sculpture of Andrea and Nino Pisano*, 31–50.
16. Charles Seymour, *Sculpture in Italy 1400–1500* (Harmondsworth and Baltimore, 1966), 31–35.
17. *Urbs Jerusalem beata,/ dicta pacis visio, / quae construitur in coelis /vivis ex lapidibus, / et angelis coronata, / ut sponsata comite … Tunsionibus, pressuris / expoliti lapides, / suis coaptantur locis / per manus artificis, / disponuntur permansuri / sacris aedificiis.* Cf. M. Britt, ed., *The Hymns of the Breviary and Missal* (New York, 1924), 348, n. 168.
18. T. Verdon, "Costruire una casa per il Signore," in *Alla riscoperta di piazza del Duomo in Firenze*, vol. 1, *Dal Battistero al Duomo*, ed. T. Verdon (Florence, 1992), 93–115. See also Verdon, *L'arte sacra in Italia: l'immaginazione religiosa dal paleocristiano al postmoderno* (Milan, 2001), 76–83, and Verdon, "1200–1400: da San Francesco alla fine del Trecento," in *L'arte cristiana in Italia*, ed. T. Verdon, 3 vols. (Milan, 2005–9), vol. 1, 279–394.
19. See Seymour, *Sculpture in Italy*, 4–8.
20. G. Kreytenberg, "Le sculture trecentesche all'esterno e all'interno," in Gurrieri and Luchinat, *La cattedrale di Santa Maria del Fiore*, vol. 2, 73–155. Seymour, *Sculpture in Italy*, 34–35, attributed this figure to Niccolò Lamberti. See also Mary Bergstein, *The Sculpture of Nanni di Banco* (Princeton, NJ, 2000), 83–87, who reconsiders the traditional dating of this part of the portal and attributes the Hercules to Nanni di Banco.
21. Beatrice Paolozzi Strozzi and Marc Bormand, eds., *La primavera del Rinascimento: la scultura e le arti a Firenze 1400–1460*, exh. cat. (Florence, 2013), 310.
22. Kreytenberg, "Le sculture," but see Bergstein, *Nanni di Banco*, 89–93.
23. See Aldo Galli's catalogue entry in Paolozzi Strozzi and Bormand, *La primavera del Rinascimento*, 308. Kreytenberg, "Le sculture," tentatively attributes this figure to Donatello, Bergstein, *Nanni di Banco*, 179–81, to a follower of Nanni, perhaps Luca della Robbia.
24. See Laura Cavazzini's catalogue entry in Paolozzi Strozzi and Bormand, *La primavera del Rinascimento*, 306, with full bibliography.
25. See Amy Bloch's essay in this catalogue.
26. A. Natali, E. Neri Lusanna, and A. Tartuferi, eds., *Bagliori dorati: il gotico internazionale a Firenze 1375–1440*, exh. cat. (Florence, 2012), entry by G. Kreytenberg, 134–35.
27. H. W. Janson, *The Sculpture of Donatello* (Princeton, NJ, 1963), 12–16.
28. The façade niches and the Evangelist figures were not planned simultaneously. The niches, which were not part of Arnolfo's original decoration, may have been cut at the time of the modernization of the main door with deep embrasures containing small niches, after 1357, but perhaps more likely date from the time of the making of a second series of statuettes—the fifteen today in the Museo dell'Opera—for those embrasures. These statuettes, made from 1387 to 1390 and discussed in Luisa Becherucci and Giulia Brunetti, *Il museo dell'Opera del Duomo a Firenze*, 2 vols. (Venice, [1970], vol. 1, 253 (nn. 90–104) belong to the period of maximum sculptural enrichment of the cathedral and, gilded and painted, suggest that particular attention was being paid to the main entry area.

    It is precisely in the following years—1396–1400—that Pietro di Giovanni and Niccolò Lamberti received commissions for the four statues of Doctors of the Church today in the museum, badly eroded by the elements and with their heads recut. These were meant to go "in quattuor tabernaculis mangnis [*sic*] existentibus duobus ex utraque parte, prope terram et juxta ianuam maiorem ecclesie s. Reparate in facie anteriore," as a document of August 29, 1396 states (cf. Giovanni Poggi, ed., *Il Duomo di Firenze*, [Berlin, 1909], doc. 122). Later this destination was changed, and the "four big existing tabernacles" were used for the Evangelists, but it remains uncertain for how long before the commission of the Doctors of the Church the tabernacles "existed."

    In any case the niches must have been very shallow, since the Doctors were commissioned to be 1 *braccio* wide, 4 high and barely ¾ of a *braccio* deep (cf. Poggi, *Il Duomo di Firenze*, doc. 109 and this author's analytic discussion at p. xxxiii). A Florentine *braccio* was 58 cm, so the thickness of the statues was barely 46 cm, requiring niches of remarkably little depth. In the event, the depth of the four Doctors is from 50 to 60 cm; their heights do not exceed 2.38 cm. The Doctors of course were standing figures, and so the shallow niches were not a problem. When however the choice was made to use the niches for seated Evangelists, it became a question of how to compose these figures in such little depth, whence Donatello's brilliant solution. In the event, the depth of the Evangelists is 67 cm (St. Mark), 51 cm (St. Luke), 54 cm (St. John) and 60 cm (St. Matthew), so they may have projected a bit from their niches. The heights of the Evangelists are never more than 2.24 cm.

    The niches must have been high enough to take the standing Doctors. The decision to replace them with seated Evangelists, quite apart from iconographical considerations, must also have been a choice for more monumental figures: a seated figure with practically the same height as another one, standing, obviously seems grander.
29. Bergstein, *Nanni di Banco*, 107–13. The position of Nanni's *Saint Luke* at the viewer's left of the main portal is clear in the drawing after Bernardo Poccetti, reproduced in fig 7. By contrast, in the fifteenth-century miniature by Francesco d'Antonio del Chierico shown in our fig. 13, the statue in the niche at the viewer's left of the door seems to be Bernardo Ciuffagni's *St. Matthew*. There is no documentary evidence that, once set in their niches, these statues were ever moved, so one of the two depictions must be mistaken. The miniature, which was not intended primarily as "documentation" of the appearance of the façade, takes other liberties in its description of the portal, whereas the drawing after Poccetti was specifically made to be an accurate image of the façade that was then about to be demolished. Thus I have preferred the sixteenth-century version of the facts to that provided by Francesco d'Antonio del Chierico.
30. Bergstein, *Nanni di Banco*, 153–63.
31. Janson, *Sculpture of Donatello*, 33–41.
32. Ibid.
33. See T. Verdon, "Il corpo, il volto, la persona di Gesù," in *Gesù: il corpo, il volto nell'arte*, ed. T. Verdon, exh. cat. (Turin, 2010), 19–69.
34. An early source for what becomes the standard Patristic identification of Isaac as a Christ-figure is Origen, who in his eighth homily on the Book of Genesis states: "Isaac who bears the wood for his own sacrifice is a figure of Christ who bore his cross." *Patrologia Graeca*, ed. Jacques-Paul Migne, 161 vols. (Paris, 1857–66), cols. 206–09.

35. P. Rose, "Bears, Baldness and the Double Spirit: The Identity of Donatello's *Zuccone*," *The Art Bulletin* 63 (1981): 31–41.
36. Alberti, *Della pittura/De pictura* (in *Opere volgari*, vol. 3 of 3 vols.), ed. Cecil Grayson, 3 vols. (Rome and Bari, 1960–73), vol. 3 (1973), 7–8. Reproduced here is the English rendering of the phrase in Alberti, *On Painting*, trans. and with an introduction by John R. Spencer (New Haven and London, 1956), 39–40.
37. See Vasari's biography of Filippo Brunelleschi: *Le vite de' più eccellenti pittori, scultori, ed architettori*, ed. Gaetano Milanesi, 9 vols. (Florence, 1906), vol. 2, 327–87.
38. A. Gabbrielli and E. Settesoldi, *La storia della foresta casentinese nelle carte dell'archivio dell'Opera del Duomo di Firenze dal secolo XIV al XIX*, Collana Verde 37 (Rome, 1977).
39. In his biography of Luca della Robbia. See Vasari, *Le vite*, vol. 2, 167–89.
40. Giancarlo Gentilini, *I Della Robbia: la scultura invetriata nel Rinascimento*, 2 vols. (Milan, 1992), vol. 1, 90–91.
41. Janson, *Sculpture of Donatello*, 119–29.
42. Ibid., 120, where Janson summarizes the document published in Poggi, *Il Duomo di Firenze*, doc. 1312. Janson discusses the two bronze heads at length in *Sculpture of Donatello*, 123–25.
43. Poggi, *Il Duomo di Firenze*, doc. 1318.
44. F. Antal and E. Wind, "The Maenad Under the Cross," *Journal of the Warburg and Courtauld Institutes* (1937–38): 70–73. Cf. also T. Verdon, "Donatello and the Theater: Stage Space and Projected Space in the San Lorenzo Pulpits," *Artibus et Historiae* 14 (1986): 29–55.

Donatello's Visions: The Sculptor at Florence Cathedral

Daniel M. Zolli

In preparing this essay, I have benefited from the advice and encouragement of many individuals, among them Michael Cole, Alina Payne, Luke Syson, Amy Bloch, Frank Fehrenbach, John Paoletti, and Stephan Wolohojian. I am especially grateful to the latter four individuals for reading a version of the manuscript in its entirety, and for their valuable criticisms and commentary. Jesse Feiman likewise sacrificed time from his work to scrutinize an earlier draft, as did Trevor Stark. Finally, my heartfelt thanks to Richard Townsend, Monsignor Timothy Verdon, and the staffs of their respective institutions: for their kindness, good sense, and for providing every sort of practical support imaginable. Unless otherwise acknowledged, translations are mine.

1. "Lavorò di marmo, nella facciata dinanzi del campanile di Santa Maria del Fiore, quattro figure di braccia cinque; delle quali due ritratte dal naturale sono nel mezzo: l'una è Francesco Soderini giovane, e l'altra Giovanni di Barduccio Cherichini, oggi nominato il Zuccone; la quale, per essere tenuta cosa rarissima e bella quanto nessuna che facesse mai, soleva Donato, quando voleva giurare, sì che gli credesse, dire: Alla fé ch'io porto al mio Zuccone; e mentre che lo lavorava, guardandolo, tuttavia gli diceva: favella, favella, che ti venga il cacasangue!" In Giorgio Vasari, *Le vite de' più eccellenti pittori, scultori, ed architettori*, ed. Gaetano Milanesi, 9 vols. (Florence, 1906), vol. 2, 404–5.
2. On the relative ages at which sculptors and painters began apprenticeships see, for example, Peter Burke, *The Italian Renaissance: Culture and Society in Italy* (Cambridge, 1995), esp. 51–56; for statistics see Richard Goldthwaite, *The Economy of Renaissance Florence* (Baltimore, 2009), 373.
3. See Lucia Gai, "Per la cronologia di Donatello: un documento inedito del 1401," *Mitteilungen des Kunsthistorischen Institutes in Florenz* 18/3 (1974): 355–57.
4. James Beck discusses this possibility in "Ghiberti giovane e Donatello giovanissimo," in *Lorenzo Ghiberti nel suo tempo*, 2 vols. (Florence, 1980), vol. 1, 111–34.
5. See Antonio di Tuccio Manetti, *The Life of Brunelleschi*, ed. Howard Saalman and trans. Catherine Enggass (University Park, PA and London, 1970), 52–55.
6. The first reference to Donatello at the Porta della Mandorla, from November 1406, refers to him as "carver" (*scarpellator*), which implies that he had already had some training in marble work. See Giovanni Poggi, ed., *Il Duomo di Firenze* (Berlin, 1909), doc. 362.
7. On the collaborative nature of Ghiberti's workshop, and its implications, see Adrian Randolph, "Republican Florence, 1400–34," in *Florence*, ed. Francis Ames-Lewis (Cambridge, 2012), 121–24.
8. The very fact that Donatello was hired into Ghiberti's shop suggests that he had prior training as a goldsmith. On this possibility see Richard Krautheimer, *Lorenzo Ghiberti* (Princeton, NJ, 1982), 369, doc. 28. On the original documentation concerning Ghiberti's North Doors see page 188, note 5.
9. See Krautheimer, *Lorenzo Ghiberti*, 369–70, doc. 31.
10. According to Richard Krautheimer, the *Nativity* belonged to a group of four reliefs on which Donatello probably worked. See Krautheimer, "Ghibertiana," *The Burlington Magazine* 71 (1937), esp. 69, 75. The scholar revised his overall chronology somewhat in his 1982 monograph, but kept the *Nativity* in the 1403–7 group (see Krautheimer, *Lorenzo Ghiberti*, esp. 121–22 n. 15 and 127).
11. A useful overview of these activities may be found in Francesca G. Bewer, "Bronze Casting: The Art of Translation," in *Bronze*, ed. David Ekserdjian, exh. cat. (London, 2012) 24–31.
12. For the contract of 1403, of which only a summary survives, see Krautheimer, *Lorenzo Ghiberti*, 368–69, doc. 26
13. Although bronze works are not the focus of this essay, they comprised a substantial portion of Donatello's oeuvre, especially in the latter half of his career. On Donatello's relationship to bronze casters see, for example, H. W. Janson, *The Sculpture of Donatello* (Princeton, NJ, 1963), esp. 45–64; Bruno Bearzi, "La tecnica fusoria di Donatello," in *Donatello e il suo tempo* (Florence, 1968), 97–105; and Andrea Calore, "Andrea Conti 'da le caldiere' e l'opera di Donatello a Padova," *Il Santo* 33 (1993): 247–72.
14. On the impact of French Gothic art on Ghiberti, see Richard Krautheimer "Ghiberti and Master Gusmin," *The Art Bulletin* 29/1 (1947): 25–35.
15. A brief but lucid account of the political and cultural context in which each phase unfolded may be found in Charles Seymour, *Sculpture in Italy 1400–1500* (Harmondsworth and Baltimore, 1966), 31–35.
16. In May 1408, for example, Niccolò Lamberti was admonished by Giovanni d'Ambrogio, then *capomaestro*, for deviating from the master design, and was fined twenty-five florins unless he corrected his mistakes. See Poggi, *Il Duomo di Firenze*, doc. 367.
17. For further elaboration on this point see page 79.
18. The absence of a scroll has led some to speculate that the statue was not born as a prophet, but rather as the Archangel Gabriel. See Wilhelm Reinhold Valentiner, "Donatello and Ghiberti," *The Art Quarterly* 3 (1940), esp. 182–86. It may be that the statue originally belonged to an Annunciation filling the lunette above the door. On this possibility see Janson, *Sculpture of Donatello* 221–22.
19. On the iconography of the relief, and its relationship to the Porta della Mandorla, see pages 21–24.
20. In Poggi, *Il Duomo di Firenze*, doc. 405.
21. On the talismanic function of these statues, and particularly their role in defending Florence against Milan, see Frederick Hartt, "Art and Freedom in Quattrocento Florence," in *Essays in Memory of Karl Lehmann*, ed. Lucy Freeman Sandler (New York, 1964), 114–31.
22. Many have drawn the connection between Donatello's Bargello statue and the 1408–9 commission. See, for example, Janson, *Sculpture of Donatello*, 3–7. Another plausible candidate is the so-called *Bearded Prophet* in the Museo dell'Opera del Duomo. This attribution is supported by John Pope-Hennessy, *Donatello Sculptor* (New York, 1993), 17–20, among others. A useful summary of the debate may be found in John T. Paoletti and Gary M. Radke, *Art in Renaissance Italy*, 4th edn. (London, 2011), 208–9.
23. For a brilliant discussion of Donatello's treatment of the subject, and specifically his later bronze statue, see Adrian W. B. Randolph, *Engaging Symbols: Gender, Politics, and Public Art in Fifteenth-Century Florence* (New Haven, 2002) 139–92 (the Bargello *David* figures on 153–55).
24. Poggi, *Il Duomo di Firenze*, doc. 413.
25. For a different interpretation of these events, see Manfred Wundram, *Donatello und Nanni di Banco* (Berlin, 1969), esp. 7–10, 26–29, 62–69; Volker Herzner, "David Florentinus I. Zum Marmordavid Donatellos im Bargello," *Jahrbuch der Berliner Museen* 20 (1978), 43–115; and Pope-Hennessy, *Donatello Sculptor*, 17–20.
26. Some scholars have suggested that the Joshua may have been a trial piece intended to test the size necessary for the buttress statues. See, for example, Paoletti and Radke, *Art in Renaissance Italy*, 210.
27. Poggi, *Il Duomo di Firenze*, docs. 415, 421.
28. In June 1405, the Opera had four pieces of marble, each roughly seven feet tall, harvested from the quarries in nearby Carrara. See ibid., doc. 162. For a translation and analysis of this document see Mary Bergstein, *The Sculpture of Nanni di Banco* (Princeton, NJ, 2000), 188, doc. 49.
29. Charles Seymour first noted Donatello's optical adjustments in *Sculpture in Italy*, 66–69. Robert Munman later examined

the topic exhaustively, and across the sculptor's oeuvre, in *Optical Corrections in the Sculpture of Donatello* (Philadelphia, 1985).

30. On the carving of John's pupils see Janson, *Sculpture of Donatello*, 16; and cat. 10 here.
31. See note 10 above.
32. See Bonnie A. Bennett and David G. Wilkins, *Donatello* (Oxford, 1984), 98; Irving Lavin, "Bozzetti and Modelli: Notes on Sculptural Procedure from the Early Renaissance through Bernini," in *Visible Spirit: The Art of Gianlorenzo Bernini*, 2 vols. (London, 2007), vol. 1, esp. 37; Pope-Hennessy, *Donatello Sculptor*, 38–39, 61.
33. See Giorgio Vasari, *Vasari on Technique*, trans. Louisa Maclehose and ed. Gerard Baldwin Brown (London, 1907), 150–51.
34. Giovanni Battista Gelli, reprinted as G. Mancini, ed., "Vite d'artisti di Giovanni Battista Gelli," in *Archivio storico italiano*, fifth series, XVII (1896), 59.
35. Cristoforo Landino, *Comento sopra la Comedia*, ed. P. Procaccioli, 4 vols. (Rome, 2001), vol. 1, 242.
36. Vasari, *Le vite*, vol. 2, 403.
37. For relevant documents see cat. 11, note 1. The statue was made for the campanile's eastern side, but the Opera had it moved in 1464 to the western face, the latter facing the piazza and therefore probably more prestigious. On the implications of this relocation, see page 32.
38. Janson, *Sculpture of Donatello*, 18.
39. On Donatello's use of gilding see Carlo Sisi, "San Marco," in *Restauro del marmo: opere e problemi*, OPD Restauro, eds. Antonio Paolucci and Anna Maria Giusti (Florence, 1986), 134–50; and Anna Maria Giusti, Carlo Biliotti, and Cristina Samarelli, "Alcuni casi di utilizzo del laser nella pulitura dei marmi," *OPD Restauro* 8 (1996): 120–26. Documents on polychromy in Donatello's marble sculptures, specifically for the Bargello *David* when it was transferred to the town hall, are published in Poggi, *Il Duomo di Firenze*, docs. 426–27.
40. E.g. Poggi, *Il Duomo di Firenze*, docs. 272, 279.
41. Restorers at the Museo dell'Opera del Duomo conserved the *Zuccone*, as well as Donatello's four additional bell tower prophets, in 1999. I thank Rita Filardi for sharing their findings with me.
42. That Donatello drew inspiration from ancient Roman busts for his *Zuccone* and other prophets is noted widely in the literature. See, for example, Pope-Hennessy, *Donatello Sculptor*, 56–70, p. 61. See also page 36.
43. Bernardo Davanzati, *Opere di Tacito*, vol. 2 (Padua, 1755), 656. Here I use the translation provided by Janson, with some modifications (Janson, *Sculpture of Donatello*, 36).
44. The term "cantoria," retained here for convenience, refers to the loft's later function as a gallery that housed singers. See Pope-Hennessy, *Donatello Sculptor*, 103–12; Pope-Hennessy, *Luca della Robbia* (Oxford, 1980), esp. 19–29; and Janson, *Sculpture of Donatello*, 119–29.
45. Poggi, *Il Duomo di Firenze*, doc. 1336.
46. Ibid., docs. 1286–7.
47. For an interesting contextual study of Luca's cantoria and the confraternity that sang at Florence Cathedral see Robert L. Mode, "Adolescent Confratelli and the Cantoria of Luca della Robbia," *The Art Bulletin* 68/1 (1986): 67–71.
48. On the compositional strategies that Donatello used to enhance the children's illusion of movement, see E. H. Gombrich, "Moment and Movement in Art," *Journal of the Warburg and Courtauld Institutes* 27 (1964), esp. 304–5. I thank Frank Fehrenbach for this reference.
49. Poggi, *Il Duomo di Firenze*, doc. 1262.
50. See Charles Dempsey, *Inventing the Renaissance Putto* (Chapel Hill, NC, 2001), esp. 1–61. Ulrich Pfisterer likewise reads the children as *spiritelli*, in *Donatello und die Entdeckung der Stile: 1430–1445* (Munich, 2002), 201–16.
51. Poggi, *Il Duomo di Firenze*, doc. 1315. Cited in Dempsey, *Inventing the Renaissance Putto*, 14. For an alternative interpretation of this document see Francesco Caglioti, "Tra dispersione e ricomparse: gli spiritelli bronzei di Donatello sul pergamo di Luca della Robbia," in *Santa Maria del Fiore: The Cathedral and its Sculpture*, ed. Margaret Haines (Florence, 2001), 263–78, esp. 267.
52. A document from February 1439 refers to the cantoria that Donatello "has made." See Poggi, *Il Duomo di Firenze*, doc. 1311.
53. Ibid., doc. 1318.

Lorenzo Ghiberti: From the Early Workshop to the Gates of Paradise
Amy R. Bloch

1. Ghiberti, *I commentarii*, ed. Lorenzo Bartoli (Florence, 1998), 92–93.
2. Antonio di Tuccio Manetti, *The Life of Brunelleschi*, ed. Howard Saalman and trans. Catherine Enggass (University Park, PA and London, 1970), 46–51.
3. On Ghiberti's early training in his stepfather's goldsmith shop, see Dora Liscia Bemporad, *La bottega orafa di Lorenzo Ghiberti* (Florence, 2013), 9–18.
4. Certain bronze objects, like bells and mortars, were cast in Florence.
5. Most of the original documentation for baptistery commissions was lost in an eighteenth-century fire that destroyed the Calimala archive. Fortunately, in the seventeenth century Carlo Strozzi copied, summarized, and excerpted a number of the original records. I cite the versions of Strozzi's records published in appendices of the following two volumes: Anita Fiderer Moskowitz, *The Sculpture of Andrea and Nino Pisano* (Cambridge, 1986); and Richard Krautheimer, *Lorenzo Ghiberti* (Princeton, NJ, 1982). A document of 1329 suggests that the Calimala at first planned to bring in a Venetian sculptor to carry out the entire project; see Moskowitz, *Sculpture of Andrea and Nino Pisano*, 198, doc. 2. For the record of a payment to the Venetian artisan who, along with two assistants, cast Andrea Pisano's reliefs in bronze, see Moskowitz, *Sculpture of Andrea and Nino Pisano*, 199, doc. 12.
6. *I commentarii*, 93: "...pictori e scultori, d'oro e d'argento e di marmo."
7. Massimo Bernabò, ed., with Mario Scalini, "Le tecniche e gli strumenti," in *L'oreficeria nella Firenze del Quattrocento* (Florence, 1977), 203–32, esp. 205–6.
8. *Lorenzo Ghiberti: "materia e ragionamenti,"* exh. cat. (Florence, 1978), 66; and Francesca G. Bewer, Richard E. Stone, and Shelley G. Sturman, "Reconstructing the Casting Technique of Lorenzo Ghiberti's Gates of Paradise," in *The Gates of Paradise: Lorenzo Ghiberti's Renaissance Masterpiece*, ed. Gary M. Radke (New Haven and London, 2007), 157–182, esp. 175.
9. The Calimala called in a local Florentine goldsmith, Piero di Donato, to help chase Andrea Pisano's doors; see Moskowitz, *Sculpture of Andrea and Nino Pisano*, 199–200, docs. 13, 15–17, 27, and 29.
10. For his first set of doors Ghiberti used alloys with a high white-metal content (around 17–26%), making them especially hard and thus difficult to chase; see Salvatore Siano, Piero Bertelli, Ferdinando Marinelli, and Marcello Miccio, "Casting the Panels of the Gates of Paradise," in *The Gates of Paradise: Lorenzo Ghiberti's Renaissance Masterpiece*, 141–55, esp. 147.
11. Giuseppe Marchini, "Ghiberti *ante litteram*," *Bollettino d'arte* 50 (1965): 181–93. On the bronze industry in medieval and Renaissance Venice, see Victoria Avery, *Vulcan's Forge in Venus' City: The Story of Bronze in Venice, 1350–1650* (New York, 2011).
12. For the contract of 1403, of which only a summary survives, see Krautheimer, *Lorenzo Ghiberti*, 368–69, doc. 26.
13. Ibid., 369, doc. 28.
14. On the chronology of Ghiberti's first doors, and on the progress of work, I follow Richard Krautheimer, "Ghibertiana," *The Burlington Magazine* 71 (1937): 68–70, 75–76, and 79–80, here 69 and 75.
15. Krautheimer, *Lorenzo Ghiberti*, 369, doc. 27.
16. On the membership of the shop in this period, see ibid., 369–70, doc. 31.
17. James Beck, "Uccello's Apprenticeship with Ghiberti," *The Burlington Magazine* 122 (1980): 837.
18. Krautheimer, *Lorenzo Ghiberti*, 109 and 370, doc. 34. On Michelozzo's contribution, see also Harriet McNeal Caplow, "Sculptors' Partnerships in Michelozzo's Florence," *Studies in the Renaissance* 21 (1974): 145–75, esp. 159–60.
19. On this possibility, see Robert Glass, "Filarete at the Papal Court: Sculpture, Ceremony, and the Antique in Early Renaissance Rome," PhD dissertation, Princeton University, 2011, 133–40.
20. Later in his career, Donatello often made the wax models for his bronzes but left their casting to others. On this, see Bruno Bearzi, "La tecnica fusoria di Donatello," in *Donatello e il suo tempo* (Florence, 1968), 97–105; and Andrea Calore, "Andrea Conti 'da le caldiere' e l'opera di Donatello a Padova," *Il Santo* 33 (1993): 247–72.
21. H. W. Janson mentions the generally Ghibertian mien of the *Profetino* in *The Sculpture of Donatello* (Princeton, NJ, 1963), 220.
22. On this point, see pages 53–61, as well as the catalogue entry on Donatello's *St. John the Evangelist* (cat. 10).
23. On the dating of the *Resurrection* panel, see Krautheimer, "Ghibertiana," 69 and 75. Krautheimer redated the panel to ca. 1414–16 in *Lorenzo Ghiberti*, 121–22, n. 15 and 127.
24. Mary Bergstein, *The Sculpture of Nanni di Banco* (Princeton, NJ, 2000), 103–4.
25. On the influence of Ghiberti's first doors, see Aldo Galli, "Nel segno di Ghiberti," in *La bottega dell'artista: tra Medioevo e Rinascimento*, ed. Roberto Cassanelli (Milan, 1998), 87–108, esp. 92–94.

26. Krautheimer, *Lorenzo Ghiberti*, 117.
27. Ibid., 369–70, docs. 28 and 31.
28. Ibid., 118, esp. n. 10.
29. Artur Rosenauer, *Donatello* (Milan, 1993), 290.
30. On these reliefs, see Luisa Becherucci and Giulia Brunetti, eds., *Il museo dell'Opera del Duomo a Firenze*, 2 vols. (Venice, [1970]), vol. 1, 275–76 and Donatella Reggioli's entry in *Lorenzo Ghiberti: "materia e ragionamenti,"* 121–24. On Nicola da Guardiagrele, see Antonio Cadei, ed., *Nicola da Guardiagrele: un protagonista dell'autunno del Medioevo in Abruzzo* (Milan, 2005).
31. On the varieties of limestone quarried in the Abruzzo (and especially near L'Aquila), see Francesco Rodolico, *Le pietre delle città d'Italia* (Florence, 1995), 316–24.
32. The debates concerning the models for the Castel di Sangro reliefs are reviewed in Aldo Galli, "Echi di Lorenzo Ghiberti in Abruzzo," in *Nicola da Guardiagrele: orafo tra Medioevo e Rinascimento. Le opere, i restauri*, ed. Sante Guido (Todi, 2008), 369–98. Galli suggests that Nicola da Guardiagrele, after a trip to Florence, brought back to the Abruzzo drawings after Ghiberti as well as casts of both his finished bronzes and preparatory models (392–93).
33. Krautheimer (*Lorenzo Ghiberti*, 129 and n. 17) attributes the drawing to Ghiberti and likewise emphasizes the darkening of the figure in the center of its upper section. Luciano Bellosi gives it to Masolino in "A proposito del disegno dell'Albertina (dal Ghiberti a Masolino)," in *Lorenzo Ghiberti nel suo tempo*, 2 vols. (Florence, 1980), vol. 1, 135–46.
34. Krautheimer, *Lorenzo Ghiberti*, 370, doc. 36.
35. On the chronology of the Gates of Paradise, see ibid., 159–68, and Francesco Caglioti, "Reconsidering the Creative Sequence of Ghiberti's Doors," in *The Gates of Paradise: Lorenzo Ghiberti's Renaissance Masterpiece*, 86–97. The following pages anticipate the analysis offered in my forthcoming book, *Lorenzo Ghiberti's Gates of Paradise: Humanism, History, and Artistic Philosophy in the Italian Renaissance* (Cambridge University Press).
36. On Michelozzo's work on the Gates of Paradise, see Caplow, "Sculptors' Partnerships in Michelozzo's Florence," 163–65. On Benozzo Gozzoli's participation, see Maria Grazia Ciardi Dupré Dal Poggetto, "Sulla collaborazione di Benozzo Gozzoli alla Porta del Paradiso," *Antichità viva* 6 (1967): 60–73. On Cennini, see Krautheimer, *Lorenzo Ghiberti*, 420, dig. 277. The evidence for Luca's connection to the Gates of Paradise comes from the 1427 *catasto* (tax) declaration of the goldsmith Antonio del Vagliente, in which Luca della Robbia, who "fa le porte" ("is making the doors"), is included in a list of debtors; on this document and Luca's connection to Ghiberti, see Giancarlo Gentilini, *I Della Robbia: la scultura invetriata nel Rinascimento*, 2 vols. (Florence, 1992), vol. 1, 19–23.
37. Diane Cole Ahl, "'Captured by the Sight of Such Wonders': Renaissance Painters and the Gates of Paradise," in *The Historian's Eye: Essays on Italian Art in Honor of Andrew Ladis*, eds. Hayden B. J. Maginnis and Shelley E. Zuraw (Athens, GA, 2009), 113–21; and Keith Christiansen, "Ghiberti and Painting," in *Renaissance Studies in Honor of Joseph Connors*, eds. Machtelt Israëls and Louis A. Waldman, 2 vols. (Cambridge, MA and Milan, 2013), vol. 1, 76–100.
38. Trude Krautheimer Hess, "More Ghibertiana," *Art Bulletin* 46 (1964): 307–21, esp. 309 and 311; and Phyllis Pray Bober, "Polykles and Polykleitos in the Renaissance: The 'Letto di Policreto'" in *Polykleitos, the Doryphoros, and Tradition*, ed. Warren G. Moon (Madison, WI, 1995), 317–26, esp. 317–18.
39. Julius von Schlosser, "Über einige Antiken Lorenzo Ghibertis," *Jahrbuch der kunsthistorischen Sammlungen des Allerhöchsten Kaiserhauses* 24 (1903): 125–59, esp. 125–29 and 141–50.
40. Christiansen, "Ghiberti and Painting," 87–90.
41. Francesco Scalamonti wrote, probably in the 1450s, a biography of Cyriac of Ancona, drawing on Cyriac's travel diary and writings; see the *Vita viri clarissimi et famosissimi Kyriaci anconitani* (*Transactions of the American Philosophical Society*, vol. 86, n. 4), eds. and trans. Charles Mitchell and Edward W. Bodnar, S.J. (Philadelphia, 1996), 70 and 132.
42. George Holmes, *The Florentine Enlightenment: 1400–1450* (New York, 1969), 226–27.
43. Vespasiano da Bisticci, *Le vite*, ed. Aulo Greco, 2 vols. (Florence, 1970–76), vol. 2 (1976), 237: "Non solo Nicolaio prestò favore a uomini litterati, ma intendendosi di pitura, scoltura, architettura, con tutti ebbe grandissima notitia, et prestò loro grandissimo favore nel loro exercicio, Pipo di ser Brunelesco, Donatello, Luca della Robia, Lorenzo di Bartoluccio, et di tutti fu amicissimo."
44. *I commentarii*, 109–10.
45. On Palla Strozzi's role in the commission for the first doors, see Krautheimer, *Lorenzo Ghiberti*, 106. On his library, see Aubrey Diller, "The Greek Codices of Palla Strozzi and Guarino Veronese," *Journal of the Warburg and Courtauld Institutes* 24 (1961): 313–21; Giuseppe Fiocco, "La biblioteca di Palla Strozzi," in *Studi di bibliografia e di storia in onore di Tammaro de Marinis*, 4 vols. (Verona, 1964), vol. 2, 289–310; and Vittorio Fanelli, "I libri di Messer Palla di Nofri Strozzi (1372–1462)," *Convivium* 15 (1949): 57–73.
46. Krautheimer summarizes the peregrinations of the Athenaeus manuscript and Ghiberti's engagement with, and use of, the text in *Lorenzo Ghiberti*, 311–12, esp. n. 21.
47. Archivio di Stato di Firenze, Catasto 388, 170r–170v, esp. 170v, where, in the list of his debts, Ghiberti includes the following: "[Debbe] avere la detc opera [di Santa Croce] per uno Darte ebi da lloro – f. 5 l. 2."
48. Robert Black, "Education and the Emergence of a Literate Society," in *Italy in the Age of the Renaissance*, ed. John M. Najemy (Oxford, 2004), 18–36, esp. 18; and Black, "Literacy in Florence, 1427," in *Florence and Beyond: Culture, Society and Politics in Renaissance Italy*, eds. David S. Peterson with Daniel E. Bornstein (Toronto, 2008), 195–210, esp. 205–6.
49. On Ambrogio's painting, which no longer survives, see Marcia Kupfer, "The Lost Wheel Map of Ambrogio Lorenzetti," *Art Bulletin* 78 (1996): 286–310.
50. Ghiberti, *I commentarii*, 89: "Non c'era allora notitia della Cosmografia di Tolomeo, non è da maraviglare se lla sua non è perfetta."
51. Sebastiano Gentile, "Emanuele Crisolora e la 'Geographia' di Tolomeo," in *Dotti bizantini e libri greci nell'Italia del secolo XV. Atti del convegno internazionale, Trento 22–23 ottobre 1990*, eds. Mariarosa Cortesi and Enrico V. Maltese (Naples, 1992), 291–308.
52. Augustine, "De doctrina Christiana," in *Patrologia Latina*, ed. Jacques-Paul Migne, 221 vols. (Paris, 1844–55 and 1862–65) (henceforth *PL*), vol. 34, cols. 42–43 and 55–57 (2.11 and 2.28–30).
53. Augustine, "De Genesi ad litteram," in *PL*, vol. 34, col. 330 (5.10).
54. Pliny, *Natural History*, trans. H. Rackham, 10 vols. (London and Cambridge, MA, 1938), vol. 1, 245–51 (2.38–39); and Dante, *De situ et forma aque et terre*, ed. Giorgio Padoan (Florence, 1968), 34.
55. See, for example, the thirteenth-century encyclopedic text known as the Book of Sidrach: Adolfo Bartoli, ed., *Il libro di Sidrach* (Bologna, 1868), 50: "E sapiate tutti di vero che dal tenpo d'Adamo infino al tenpo di Noè, non piove unque, e non aparvono nuvoli in cielo. E non mangiavano carne e non beveano vino; e tutto quello tenpo era così bello come la state; e si era abondanza di tutte le cose…"
56. The biblical text (Exodus 19:16–18) mentions lightning and thunder and describes the fearful appearance of Sinai. Interpreters frequently assumed that the mountain shook in these moments. Certainly Ghiberti, who mentions in his description of the Moses panel in the *Commentaries* that "earthquakes, lightning, and thunder" accompany the giving of the law, accepted this interpretation; see *I commentarii*, 96.
57. Aristotle, *Meteorologica*, trans. H. D. P. Lee (Cambridge, MA and London, 1952), 222–25 (2.9.369a).
58. Lucretius, *De rerum natura libri sex*, ed. Jacob Bernays (Leipzig, 1879), 168 (6.160–163); and Isidore, *Etymologiarum sive originum libri xx*, ed. W. M. Lindsay, 2 vols. (Oxford, 1911), vol. 2, 90 (13.9.1–2).
59. Pliny, *Natural History*, vol. 1, 326–27 (2.83 196)
60. For Vitruvius's account, which I summarize in this paragraph, see Vitruvius, *On Architecture*, ed. and trans. Frank Granger, 2 vols. (Cambridge, MA and London, 1998), vol. 1, 76–87 (2.1.1–9).
61. Origen, "In Genesim homilia," in *Patrologia Graeca*, ed. Jacques-Paul Migne, 161 vols. (Paris, 1857–66), vol. 12, cols. 161–62. On the possibility that Ghiberti learned of Origen's idea, see Edgar Wind, "The Revival of Origen," in *Studies in Art and Literature for Belle da Costa Greene*, ed. Dorothy Miner (Princeton, NJ, 1954), 412–24.
62. Isidore of Seville, in the influential chronology in the *Etymologies*, claims that 4,204 years elapsed between the creation of the world and the building of the Temple of Jerusalem by Solomon; see *Etymologiarum sive originum libri xx*, vol. 1, 211 (5.39.13).
63. Alberti, *Della pittura/De pictura* (in *Opere volgari*, vol. 3 of 3 vols.), ed. Cecil Grayson (Rome and Bari, 1960–73), vol. 3 (1973), 7–8. I cite in this paragraph the Grayson translation: *On Painting* (New York, 1991), 34–35.

"…with immense diligence and discipline": Lorenzo Ghiberti's North Doors and the Opificio delle Pietre Dure's Conservation and Restoration Project
Marco Ciatti

1. This essay owes a debt to a number of crucial works on Ghiberti and the North Doors: Richard Krautheimer, *Lorenzo Ghiberti* (Princeton, NJ, 1982); Krautheimer, *Ghiberti's Bronze Doors* (Princeton, NJ, 1971); *Lorenzo Ghiberti: "materia e ragionamenti,"* exh. cat. (Florence, 1978). Gary M. Radke provides an accurate, in-depth analysis of the North Doors, from the competition of 1401 to their completion, in Annamaria Giusti and Gary M. Radke, *La Porta del Paradiso: dalla bottega di Lorenzo Ghiberti al cantiere del restauro* (Florence, 2012), 27–57.
2. Cennini, *Il libro dell'arte*, ed. F. Frezzato (Vicenza, 2003).
3. Alberti, *Della pittura / De pictura* (in *Opere volgari*, vol. 3 of 3 vols.), ed. Cecil Grayson (Rome and Bari, 1960–73), vol. 3 (1973), 7–8.
4. We have no certain information regarding the dates of birth of the other contestants: Simone da Colle, Niccolò di Luca Spinelli from Arezzo, and Niccolò Lamberti.
5. Ghiberti, *I commentarii*, ed. Lorenzo Bartoli (Florence, 1998), 92–93.
6. Giuseppe Marchini, "Ghiberti *ante litteram*," *Bollettino d'Arte* 50 (1965):181–93.
7. Dora Liscia Bemporad has recently taken a fresh look at the topic of Ghiberti's early goldsmith work, making several interesting new suggestions. See Bemporad, *La bottega orafa di Lorenzo Ghiberti* (Florence, 2013).
8. Ghiberti, *I commentarii*, 94.
9. Ibid., 93; A. Manetti, *Vita di Ser Filippo di Ser Brunellesco*, eds. D. De Robertis and G. Tanturli (Milan, 1976), 61–64.
10. For all archive documents cited here, see summary by G. Nunziati in *Lorenzo Ghiberti: "materia e ragionamenti,"* 82–86, which contains all of the references to the archive papers published by Krautheimer, *Lorenzo Ghiberti*.
11. Quoted in Krautheimer, *Lorenzo Ghiberti*, 370, doc. 33.
12. Giorgio Vasari, *Le vite de' più eccellenti pittori, scultori, ed architettori*, ed. Gaetano Milanesi, 9 vols. (Florence, 1906), vol. 2, 227–28. Although Ghiberti's doors proved extremely difficult to cast, the challenge was not unprecedented. Seven decades earlier, Andrea Pisano had to summon experts from Venice to cast his doors for the baptistery.
13. L. Boschetto, "Ghiberti e i tre 'compari': un nuovo documento sulla fusione dei telai della seconda porta del nuovo Battistero," *Mitteilungen des Kunsthistorisches Institutes in Florenz* 53 (2009): 145–49. My thanks to Anna Maria Giusti for bringing this article to my attention.
14. The weight of the bronze is equivalent to 11,544.428 kg (roughly 11.5 tons). This number undoubtedly includes the waste material not used in some of the cast, because the estimated overall weight of the doors, like the Gates of Paradise, is around 8 tons.
15. For further information on the North Doors conservation project, see the initial reports filed by Bruno Santi, Marco Ciatti, Maria Donata Mazzoni, Stefania Agnoletti, and Annalena Brini in *La Porta Nord del Ghiberti: primi risultati del progetto di conservazione e restauro*, eds. B. Agostini and B. Santi (Florence, 2013).
16. The restoration of the North Doors has been planned, directed, and carried out by the Opificio delle Pietre Dure (OPD): Supervisor and Sole Project Manager: Marco Ciatti; Section Manager: Maria Donata Mazzoni; Design and Planning: Anna Maria Giusti; Supervision of Works: Maria Donata Mazzoni; Collaboration on Design, Planning, and Supervision of Works: Andrea Montanari, Stefania Agnoletti, and Annalena Brini; Technical Managers and Restorers: Stefania Agnoletti and Annalena Brini, with the cooperation of restorers (all of whom are graduates of the OPD's restoration school): Elena Della Schiava, Sveta Gennai, Saskia Giulietti, Antonio Mignemi, Merj Nesi, Ludovica Nicolai, Elisa Pucci, Nicola Salvioli, and Chiara Valcepina; Diagnostic Investigations by the OPD's scientific laboratory: Simone Porcinai, Andrea Cagnini, Monica Galeotti, Isetta Tosini, and Maria Rizzi; Scientific Consultant: Salvatore Siano, IFAC-CNR; Digital X-Ray: Thierry Radelet; OPD Photographic Workshop Manager: Alfredo Aldrovandi; Photographers: Marco Brancatelli and Pino Zicarelli.

    The set of doors was dismantled, moved, and set up for restoration by the Opera di Santa Maria del Fiore with the coordination of the Technical Office managed by Paolo Bianchini.

    A crucial premise for this major conservation project, of which the OPD is extremely proud, was the memorandum of understanding with the Opera di Santa Maria del Fiore, which bore a majority of the operation's costs while setting a definite deadline for its completion, namely the reopening of the museum after renovation in the fall of 2015. Only the fact that we have been able to count on the experience gained with the Gates of Paradise, together with the cooperation of a group of nine restorers who graduated from this very institute, have made it possible to accomplish such a major restoration in such a short time. I would like to underscore that all of this attests to the enormous potential of the restoration sector of the OPD, which, like the ten others that make up the OPD as a whole, has immense potential to improve the conservation of our artistic heritage—this provided that new staff members are brought in, a move that can no longer be postponed.

Selected Bibliography

Fifteenth-Century Florentine Sculpture (General)

Charles Avery, *Florentine Renaissance Sculpture* (London and New York: J. Murray, 1970).

Wilhelm von Bode, *Florentine Sculptors of the Renaissance* (London: Methuen, 1928).

Penelope Curtis, ed., *Depth of Field: The Place of Relief in the Time of Donatello*, exh. cat. (Leeds: Henry Moore Institute, 2005).

Frederick Hartt, "Art and Freedom in Quattrocento Florence," in *Essays in Memory of Karl Lehmann*, ed. Lucy Freeman Sandler (New York: Institute of Fine Arts, 1964), 114–31.

Jules Lubbock, *Storytelling in Christian Art from Giotto to Donatello* (New Haven and London: Yale University Press, 2006), esp. 149–74, 227–44.

Joachim Poeschke, *Donatello and His World: Sculpture of the Italian Renaissance*, trans. Russell Stockman (New York: Harry N. Abrams, 1993).

John Pope-Hennessy, *Italian Renaissance Sculpture* (3rd edn.) (Oxford: Phaidon, 1986).

Adrian W. B. Randolph, "Republican Florence, 1400–1434," in *Florence*, ed. Francis Ames-Lewis (Cambridge: Cambridge University Press, 2011), 119–66.

Charles Seymour, *Sculpture in Italy 1400–1500* (Harmondsworth and Baltimore: Penguin, 1966).

Carl Brandon Strehlke, ed., *Orsanmichele and the History and Preservation of the Civic Monument*, Studies in the History of Art Series, National Gallery of Art, Washington, D.C. (New Haven and London: Yale University Press, 2012).

Beatrice Paolozzi Strozzi and Marc Bormand, eds., *The Springtime of the Renaissance: Sculpture and the Arts in Florence 1400–60 / La primavera del Rinascimento: la scultura e le arti a Firenze 1400–1460*, exh. cat. (Florence: Mandragora, 2013).

Florence Cathedral

Luisa Becherucci and Giulia Brunetti, eds., *Il museo dell'Opera del Duomo a Firenze*, 2 vols. (Venice: Electa, [1970]).

Luciano Bellosi, "I problemi dell'attività giovanile," in *Donatello e i suoi: scultura fiorentina del primo Rinascimento*, exh. cat. (Florence: La Casa Usher, 1986), 47–54.

Domenico Cardini, ed., *Il bel San Giovanni e Santa Maria del Fiore: il centro religioso di Firenze dal tardo antico al Rinascimento* (Florence: Le Lettere, 1996).

Richard A. Goldthwaite, *The Building of Renaissance Florence. An Economic and Social History* (Baltimore: Johns Hopkins University Press, 1980).

Cesare Guasti, *Santa Maria del Fiore: la costruzione della chiesa e del campanile* (Florence: M. Ricci, 1887).

Francesco Gurrieri and Cristina Acidini Luchinat, eds., *La cattedrale di Santa Maria del Fiore a Firenze*. 2 vols. (Florence: Cassa di Risparmio, 1995).

Margaret Haines, "Firenze e il finanziamento della cattedrale e del campanile," in *Alla riscoperta di piazza del Duomo in Firenze*, vol. 3, ed. T. Verdon (Florence: Centro Di, 1994), 71–83.

Margaret Haines, "L'Arte della Lana e l'Opera del Duomo a Firenze con un accenno a Ghiberti tra due istituzioni," in *Opera: carattere e ruolo delle fabbriche cittadine fino all'inizio dell'età moderna*, eds. M. Haines and L. Riccetti (Florence: Olschki, 1996), 267–86.

Margaret Haines, ed., *Santa Maria del Fiore: The Cathedral and Its Sculpture* (Florence: Cadmo, 2001).

Margaret Haines, ed., *Gli anni della cupola: archivio digitale delle fonti dell'Opera di Santa Maria del Fiore* (Florence, 2009): http://duomo.mpiwg-berlin.mpg.de/home.html.

Ludwig Heydenreich and Wolfgang Lotz, *Architecture in Italy 1400–1600* (Harmondsworth: Penguin, 1974).

Antonio Paolucci, *The Origins of Renaissance Art: The Baptistery Doors, Florence*, trans. Françoise Pouncey Chiarini (New York: George Braziller, 1996).

Alessandro Parronchi, "Le statue per gli sproni," *Antichità viva* 28 (1989): 80–85.

Giovanni Poggi, ed., *Il Duomo di Firenze: documenti sulla decorazione della chiesa e del campanile tratti dall'Archivio dell'Opera*, 2 vols. (Berlin: Bruno Cassirer, 1909); reprint edited by Margaret Haines (Florence: Edizioni Medicea, 1988).

Marvin Trachtenberg, *The Campanile of Florence Cathedral: "Giotto's Tower"* (New York: New York University Press, 1971).

Marvin Trachtenberg, *Dominion of the Eye: Urbanism, Art, and Power in Early Modern Florence* (Cambridge: Cambridge University Press, 1997).

Timothy Verdon, "The Baptistery of San Giovanni: A Religious Monument Serving the City," in *The Baptistery of San Giovanni, Florence*, Mirabilia Italiae, ed. A. Paolucci (Modena: Pannini, 1994), 9–32.

Timothy Verdon, "Spiritualità e arti figurative," in *La cattedrale di Santa Maria del Fiore a Firenze*, eds. F. Gurrieri and C. Acidini Luchinat, 2 vols. (Florence: 1995), vol. 2, 19–30.

Timothy Verdon, "*Gratia plena*: modernità teologica e stilistica nel cantiere di Santa Maria del Fiore," in *Bagliori dorati: il gotico internazionale a Firenze 1375–1440*, eds. A. Natali, E. Neri Lusanna, and A. Tartuferi, exh. cat. (Florence: Giunti, 2012), 53–61.

Timothy Verdon, "Der Florentiner Dom im städischen Kontext," in *Florenz!*, eds. A. Giusti, B. Roeck, and G. Wolf, exh. cat. (Bonn: Bundeskunsthalle, 2013), 57–65.

Timothy Verdon and Annalisa Innocenti, eds., *La cattedrale e la città: saggi sul Duomo di Firenze. Atti del VII centenario del Duomo di Firenze*, 3 vols. (Florence: Edifir, 2001).

Donatello

Bonnie A. Bennett and David G. Wilkins, *Donatello* (Oxford: Phaidon, 1984).

Monika Cämmerer, ed., *Donatello-Studien* (Munich: Bruckmann, 1989).

Donatello e il suo tempo. Atti dell'VIII convegno internazionale di studi sul Rinascimento (Florence: Istituto Nazionale di Studi sul Rinascimento; Padua: Civelli, 1968).

Michael Greenhalgh, *Donatello and His Sources* (London: Duckworth, 1982).

Frederick Hartt, *Donatello: Prophet of Modern Vision* (New York: Harry N. Abrams, 1973).

H. W. Janson, *The Sculpture of Donatello* (Princeton, NJ: Princeton University Press, 1957; reprinted 1963 and 1979).

Hans Kauffmann, *Donatello: eine Einführung in sein Bilden und Denken* (Berlin: Grote, 1935).

R. W. Lightbown, *Donatello & Michelozzo: An Artistic Partnership and Its Patrons in the Early Renaissance* (London: Harvey Miller, 1980).

Gernot Lorenz, *Donatellos Prophetenstatuen am Campanile des Florentiner Doms. Studien zur Ikonographie und Bedeutung der Propheten in Florenz* (Weimar: VDG, 2002).

Francesca Petrucci, *La scultura di Donatello: tecniche e linguaggio* (Florence: Le Lettere, 2003).

Ulrich Pfisterer, *Donatello und die Entdeckung der Stile 1430–1445*, Bibliotheca Hertziana 17 (Munich: Hirmer Verlag, 2002).

John Pope-Hennessy, *Donatello Sculptor* (New York: Abbeville, 1993).

Artur Rosenauer, *Studien zum frühen Donatello: Skulptur im projektiven Raum der Neuzeit* (Vienna: Holzhausens, 1975).

Enzo Settesoldi, *Donatello e l'Opera del Duomo di Firenze* (Florence: Scala, 1986).

Manfred Wundram, "Donatello e Nanni di Banco negli anni 1408–1409," in *Donatello e il suo tempo* (Florence: Istituto Nazionale di Studi sul Rinascimento, 1968), 59–75.

Lorenzo Ghiberti

Diane Cole Ahl, "'Captured by the Sight of Such Wonders': Renaissance Painters and the Gates of Paradise," in *The Historian's Eye: Essays on Italian Art in Honor of Andrew Ladis*, eds. Hayden B. J. Maginnis and Shelley E. Zuraw (Athens, GA: Georgia Museum of Art, 2009), 113–21.

Amy R. Bloch, "The Evolution of Lorenzo Ghiberti's Approach to the Narrative Relief," in *Depth of Field: Relief Sculpture in Renaissance Italy*, eds. D. Cooper and M. Leino (Oxford: Peter Lang, 2007), 125–48.

Amy R. Bloch, "Lorenzo Ghiberti, the Arte di Calimala, and Fifteenth-Century Florentine Corporate Patronage," in *Florence and Beyond: Culture, Society, and Politics in Renaissance Italy*, eds. D. S. Peterson and D. E. Bornstein (Toronto: Centre for Reformation and Renaissance Studies, 2008), 135–51.

Amy R. Bloch, "Perspective and Narrative in the Jacob and Esau Panel of Lorenzo Ghiberti's *Gates of Paradise*," in *A Scarlet Renaissance: Essays in Honor of Sarah Blake McHam*, ed. V. Coonin (New York: Italica Press, 2013), 1–34.

Keith Christiansen, "Ghiberti and Painting," in *Renaissance Studies in Honor of Joseph Connors*, eds. Machtelt Israëls and Louis Waldman, 2 vols. (Cambridge: Harvard University Press; Milan: Officina Libraria; and in conjunction with Villa I Tatti, 2013), vol. 1, 76–100.

Lorenzo Ghiberti, *Lorenzo Ghibertis Denkwürdigkeiten (I Commentarii)*, ed. Julius von Schlosser, 2 vols. (Berlin: J. Bard, 1912).

Lorenzo Ghiberti, *I commentarii*, ed. Lorenzo Bartoli (Florence: Giunti, 1998).

Lorenzo Ghiberti: "materia e ragionamenti," exh. cat. (Florence: Centro Di, 1978).

Annamaria Giusti and Gary M. Radke, *The Gates of Paradise: From the Renaissance Workshop of Lorenzo Ghiberti to the Modern Restoration Studio / La Porta del Paradiso: dalla bottega di Lorenzo Ghiberti al cantiere del restauro* (Florence: Giunti, 2012).

Richard Krautheimer, with Trude Krautheimer-Hess, *Lorenzo Ghiberti* (Princeton, NJ: Princeton University Press, 1956; reprinted 1970 and 1982).

Lorenzo Ghiberti nel suo tempo. Atti del convegno internazionale di studi (Firenze, 18–21 ottobre 1978), 2 vols. (Florence: Olschki, 1980).

Gary M. Radke, ed., *The Gates of Paradise: Lorenzo Ghiberti's Renaissance Masterpiece* (New Haven and London: Yale University Press, 2007).

Julius von Schlosser, *Leben und Meinungen des florentinischen Bildners Lorenzo Ghiberti* (Basel: Holbein-Verlag, 1941).

Filippo Brunelleschi

Eugenio Battisti, *Filippo Brunelleschi: The Complete Work*, trans. Erich Wolf (New York: Rizzoli, 1981).

Luciano Bellosi, "Filippo Brunelleschi e la scultura," *Prospettiva* 91/92 (1998): 48–69.

Samuel Y. Edgerton Jr., *The Renaissance Rediscovery of Linear Perspective* (New York: Basic Books, 1975), esp. 124–52.

Margaret Haines, "Brunelleschi and Bureaucracy: The Tradition of Public Patronage at the Florentine Cathedral," *I Tatti Studies* 3 (1989): 89–125.

Antonio di Tuccio Manetti, *The Life of Brunelleschi*, ed. Howard Saalman and trans. Catherine Enggass (University Park, PA and London: The Pennsylvania State University Press, 1970).

Frank D. Prager, *Brunelleschi: Studies of His Technology and Inventions* (Cambridge, MA: MIT Press, 1970).

Howard Saalman, *Filippo Brunelleschi: The Buildings* (University Park, PA: Pennsylvania State University Press, 1993).

Diane Finiello Zervas, *The Parte Guelfa: Brunelleschi & Donatello* (Locust Valley, NY: Augustin, 1987).

Other Sculptors Active at Florence Cathedral

Mary Bergstein, *The Sculpture of Nanni di Banco* (Princeton, NJ: Princeton University Press, 2000).

Harriet McNeal Caplow, "Michelozzo: His Life, Sculpture and Workshops," PhD dissertation, Columbia University, 1970.

Harriet McNeal Caplow, "Sculptors' Partnerships in Michelozzo's Florence," *Studies in the Renaissance* 21 (1975): 145–75.

Giancarlo Gentilini, *I Della Robbia: la scultura invetriata nel Rinascimento*, 2 vols. (Milan: Cantini, 1992).

George R. Goldner, *Niccolò and Pietro Lamberti* (New York, 1978).

H. W. Janson, "Nanni di Banco's Assumption of the Virgin on the Porta della Mandorla," in *The Renaissance and Mannerism*, ed. Millard Meiss (Princeton, NJ: Princeton University Press, 1963), 98–107.

Enrica Neri Lusanna, "Venustius et honorabilius templum," in *Arnolfo: alle origini del Rinascimento fiorentino*, ed. E. Neri Lusanna, exh. cat. (Florence: Pagliai Polistampa, 2005), 201–78.

Anita Fiderer Moskowitz, *The Sculpture of Andrea and Nino Pisano* (Cambridge: Cambridge University Press, 1986).

John Pope-Hennessy, *Luca della Robbia* (Oxford: Oxford University Press, 1980).

Charles Seymour, "The Young Luca della Robbia," *Allen Memorial Art Museum Bulletin* 20 (1963): 92–119.

Charles Seymour, *Michelangelo's David: A Search for Identity* (Pittsburgh: University of Pittsburgh Press, 1967).

Photo Credits

Photographs in the book have been provided by the owners or custodians of the work. The following list applies to those photographs for which a separate credit is due. Individual photographer names are provided when available. Every effort has been made to obtain rights from image rights holders. Any information on unlocated rights holders forwarded to the Museum will be acted upon for future editions.

Holly Hayes / Art History Images, p. 56

Erich Lessing / Art Resource, NY, pp. 37 (right), 76

Kunsthistorisches Institut in Florenz/pr. ECHO, p. 37 (left)

© Opera di Santa Maria del Fiore / Nicolò Orsi Battaglini, pp. 17 (left), 50, 58

© Opera di Santa Maria del Fiore / Ottaviano Caruso-Antonio Mignemi, pp. 108 (right), 110

© Opera di Santa Maria del Fiore / Franco Cosimo Panini SpA, pp. 12, 15, 17 (right), 99

© Opera di Santa Maria del Fiore / Antonio Quattrone, pp. 2, 5, 6, 10, 16, 18, 20, 21, 22, 24, 25, 26, 27, 28, 29, 30, 32, 33, 34, 35, 36, 38, 39, 40, 41, 42, 44, 47, 48, 49, 54, 57, 59, 62, 63, 64, 65, 66, 67, 68, 69, 70, 71, 72, 74, 77, 78, 79, 80, 81 (right), 82 (right), 84, 86, 88, 89, 90, 91, 92, 93, 94, 95, 96, 97, 100, 104, 105, 106, 107, 108 (left), 109, 111, 112, 113, 115, 118, 121, 123, 124, 126, 128, 130, 133, 134, 137, 138, 139, 141, 143, 144, 146, 149, 150, 152, 153, 155, 156, 159, 160, 162, 165, 166, 167, 169, 170, 173, 174, 175, 176, 179

© Opera di Santa Maria del Fiore / Nicola Salvioli, p. 116

© Opificio delle Pietre Dure, p. 117

© Lorenzo Mennonna, Firenze, p. 23

Scala / Art Resource, NY, pp. 51, 60, 81 (left)

Photo © Tarker / The Bridgeman Art Library, p. 82 (left)

Board Members & Staff

Acknowledgments

The organizers wish to thank the following friends and colleagues for their tremendous support and assistance: Cristina Acidini, Silvio Amori, Olivia d'Aponte, Rose-Anne Bartholomew, Pat Barylski, Frances Beatty, Peter Bell, Gail Brewer, Sabrina Brogelli, Lucio Caputo, Ken Carbone, Katherine Cartwright, Elizabeth Chapman, Jocelyn Chuang, Samantha Cohen, Alessandra Di Curzio, Alain Elkann, Julie Ember, Meryl Feinstein, Monica Fiorini, Kimberly Fry, Dan Giles, Robert Gottheim, Margaret Grace, Sara Griffin, Gruppo Esponenti Italiani New York, Alfonso Iacurci, Jade Jiambutr, Elizabeth Kelley, Rick Landers, Ethan Lercher, Eric Lindveit, Gail and Barry Lord, A. Edward Major, Mark Mann, Eddie McAveney, Helen McFarland, Sarah McLaughlin, Enrico Marinelli, Paul Mehl, Renato Miracco, Celine Mizrahi, Congressman Jerrold Nadler, Marco Pellegrini, Maggi Peyton, Consul General Natalia Quintavalle, Anne-Imelda Radice, Joe Regina, David Resnicow, Gary Schutz, Margaret Schwartz, Maria Matilde Simari, Deputy Consul Dino Sorrentino, Ines Theodoli, Ralph Veerman, George Wachter, Ian Wardropper, and Rena Zurofsky.

Statement from the Guild of the Dome

GUILD OF THE DOME ASSOCIATION

It is with enthusiasm and gratitude that the Guild of the Dome is participating in the exhibition *Sculpture in the Age of Donatello: Renaissance Masterpieces from Florence Cathedral*. As it is not possible for Ghiberti's great masterpieces for the Duomo's baptistery —the North Doors and the Gates of Paradise, which are so eloquently described elsewhere in this volume—to be part of this exhibition, we are pleased to lend precise cast replicas of panels from the former and an entire replica of the latter. Prior to the display of the Gates of Paradise in New York in conjunction with *Sculpture in the Age of Donatello*, they have been exhibited in Mumbai and Seoul.

It is through efforts such as these that our mission to "share universal values through art" is being met. The Guild of the Dome is an association of entrepreneurs from around the world who have committed their time, expertise, and financial resources to promoting the values common to all mankind as conveyed by great works of art.

Our initial project is the restoration of the North Doors, the first set of doors created by Lorenzo Ghiberti for Florence Baptistery. The cast replica, made using the original lost-wax bronze technique, is to be fitted in place of the original doors when finished (the originals will be installed in the Museo dell'Opera del Duomo nearby). This novel approach, made possible thanks to cutting-edge 3D technology, will produce for the very first time absolutely precise replicas, avoiding the shrinkage of the bronze that traditional techniques cause. In order to support this work, members of the Guild will underwrite the production of each of the twenty-eight panels of the North Doors.

The Guild is actively seeking new members from all over the world, individuals who believe in the mission of the Guild, individuals who believe that they can make a difference and can leave a better world for others, individuals who take pride in building bridges between different cultures all over the world.

James and Nancy Greenleaf
Lawrence and Illana Raia
Enrico and Gloria Marinelli
Founders of the Guild of the Dome

Index

Page numbers in **bold** indicate illustrations

Meze griegas

Cielo rojizo al atardecer, del pastor el mayor placer... Puesta de sol en Hóra Sfakion.

Meze griegas

100 exquisiteces para picar

Sarah Maxwell

KÖNEMANN

NOTA:

En general se utiliza la medida taza –con una capacidad de 250 ml– aplicada tanto a ingredientes líquidos como sólidos.

Este libro ha sido diseñado y producido por
Quintet Publishing Limited
6 Blundell Street
London N7 9BH

Título original: Meze Cooking

Director creativo: Richard Dewing
Diseñador: Chris Dymond
Director de proyecto: Damian Thompson
Editor: Diana Vowles
Ilustrador: Marianna Ziffo
Fotógrafo: Trevor Wood

Könemann Verlagsgesellschaft mbH
Bonner Str. 126, D – 50968 Köln
Redacción y maquetación:
LocTeam, S.L., Barcelona
Traducción del inglés: Ester Galindo
para LocTeam, S.L., Barcelona
Impresión y encuadernación: Sing Cheong Printing
Impreso en Hong Kong
ISBN 3-8290-0399-4

Contenido

Introducción

Las meze constituyen, sin duda alguna, la característica más auténtica de la cocina griega y, si bien el nombre de meze suele presentar variaciones en la ortografía, su significado permanece inalterable. Las meze son porciones pequeñas de manjares exquisitos, que deben acompañarse con algún tipo de bebida refrescante. Están concebidas para disfrutar de todo su sabor de una manera relajada, mientras se yace bajo el sol del Mediterráneo y en distendida tertulia con amigos y paseantes.

En Grecia, las meze se sirven en todos los cafés, en todas las casas y en los numerosos puestos de comida que proliferan por las esquinas. La gran variedad existente va desde unas cuantas pipas de calabaza tostadas hasta un surtido de tentadoras ensaladas, platos de legumbres, salsas, pinchitos, hortalizas rellenas, o sin rellenar, y muchas recetas más que dan lugar a un conjunto armonioso de sabores, colores y texturas.

Si al igual que a una servidora, le resulta difícil escoger los platos de un menú o decidir qué va a cocinar en una ocasión especial, aquí tiene la solución. Con las meze disfrutará de todo un poco y sus invitados quedarán fascinados ante el interminable desfile de platos que irán apareciendo de la cocina. Llegado el momento, no podrán tomar ni uno más... o, bueno, sólo otro más.

Este libro le ofrece un sinnúmero de recetas para preparar una comida a base de meze. Algunas de ellas pertenecen al recetario tradicional, otras son clásicos griegos y muchas más han sido adaptadas con cierta licencia poética, sustituyendo algún que otro ingrediente o cambiando los métodos de cocción, a fin de hacerlas más accesibles a nuestros lectores.

Seleccione sus platos preferidos y cree su propia comida a base de meze; para ello, consulte los capítulos siguientes, o bien pruebe uno de los menús recomendados para las ocasiones especiales que figuran de manera esporádica a lo largo del libro. Presente los platos a la mesa por grupos; empiece por los entrantes, siga con una selección de meze consistentes y termine con los dulces.

Ésta no es la única manera posible de servir las meze, sino que también puede incluirlas en cualquier menú, como almuerzo ligero, aperitivo o postre, siempre que le apetezca conferir cierto aire helénico a la ocasión. Estas preparaciones permiten aumentar, asimismo, la cantidad de los ingredientes según convenga o en el supuesto de querer servir una meze como plato principal; no olvide, en tal caso, aumentar a su vez el tiempo de cocción. El mayor atractivo de las meze griegas radica precisamente en esta posibilidad de añadir siempre un poco más ante la llegada de un invitado inesperado o cuando apetezca repetir.

Este tipo de preparación culinaria ejemplifica a la perfección el modo de vida de los griegos, que se caracteriza por una actitud relajada y distendida. No existen pautas para la presentación de las meze; sencillamente se eligen unas cuantas al gusto y se dejan en la mesa para que cada comensal se sirva por sí mismo. La mayoría de las recetas puede prepararse con antelación, mientras que otras pueden cocerse o calentarse pocos minutos antes de servirlas. Así que olvídese del reloj y disfrute preparando su selección de meze con toda tranquilidad.

A LA IZQUIERDA
De camino al mercado de hortalizas de Heraklion... La fruta, el tabaco, el aceite y las telas constituyen la base de la exportación del país.

PÁGINA SIGUIENTE
El palacio de Knosos en Creta, centro de la cultura minoica hacia el año 2000 a. C. Según la leyenda, aquí fue donde Teseo se enfrentó al Minotauro.

AMPHORA
HOTEL
ΔΕΣΠΟΙΝΑ

Acerca del vino

Grecia posee más de 300 variedades de uva y produce un surtido impresionante de vinos tintos de mucho cuerpo, además de algunos vinos de postre de gran calidad y una amplia selección de vinos blancos y rosados.

El Retsina es seguramente el vino más conocido de Grecia. La mayoría de los extranjeros que lo prueba por primera vez coincide en afirmar que posee un sabor cargado de misterio que todo el mundo debería catar. Se elabora siguiendo el mismo método que para los vinos blancos, con la única variante de que se le añaden unas gotitas de resina de pino al comienzo de la fermentación, lo que le confiere ese aroma tan inconfundible. El Retsina, que debe consumirse bien frío y cuando todavía es joven, constituye el mejor acompañamiento para cualquier plato de la cocina griega.

El Naoussa y el Naoussa Grande Reserve son dos vinos muy distinguidos que provienen de la región vinícola de Macedonia. Se trata de vinos tintos, secos y con cuerpo que se han dejado envejecer durante un mínimo de cuatro años hasta alcanzar su punto óptimo de maduración. Se reservan para ocasiones más especiales y deben servirse a temperatura ambiente, como complemento de una comida rica y sabrosa.

La uva blanca de moscatel se extiende por toda la isla griega de Samos, que fue una de las primeras regiones vinícolas del país. La bebida que se elabora en Samos, de color dorado pálido, constituye uno de los vinos más populares de Grecia. Ligero, chispeante y de sabor más bien dulce, este vino blanco debe servirse bien frío, como acompañamiento de platos de pescado o carne blanca, así como para los postres.

Si bien no se trata de un vino, sí constituye la bebida nacional de Grecia, y por ello debemos mencionar el Ouzo. Clasificada como licor, y de los fuertes, esta bebida alcohólica de color claro, sabor a regaliz y consistencia más bien espesa, se destila a partir de los restos de la uva, después de que ésta haya sido prensada para la elaboración del vino. El Ouzo debe tomarse a temperatura ambiente, con o sin un chorrito de agua helada, pero siempre con algo de comer y en compañía de buenos amigos o familiares.

Llamativas barcas multicolores alegran el puerto de Haniá durante el verano.

C A P Í T U L O 1

Entrantes

Sopa de pollo con salsa de huevo y limón

KOTOSOUPA AVGOLEMONO

Esta sopa, de sabor más bien picante, resulta deliciosa, refrescante y ligera. Su consistencia la hace ideal para el invierno, mientras que su frescor la adecúa al verano.

Tiempo de preparación: unos 30 minutos
Tiempo de cocción: unas 3½ horas

PARA 6 PERSONAS

- *1 pollo de 1,5 kg, sin los despojos y preparado para asar al horno*
- *1 cebolla grande*
- *2½ l de agua*
- *sal y pimienta negra recién molida, al gusto*
- *2 clavos*
- *1⅓ tazas de arroz de grano largo*
- *2 huevos*
- *el zumo de 1 limón recién exprimido*

1 Introduzca el pollo en una cacerola grande, junto con la cebolla, los clavos y el agua. Deje hervir lentamente los ingredientes y espume la superficie; déjelos cocer entre 2½ y 3 horas a fuego lento, hasta que la carne se desprenda de los huesos con facilidad.

2 Retire la cacerola del fuego y pase el pollo a una tabla de trinchar. Con la ayuda de una espumadera, retire también la cebolla y los clavos, y deséchelos. Separe la carne del pollo de los huesos con un trinchante y un tenedor, y córtela en trozos o en tiras. Deseche los huesos.

3 Devuelva el pollo a la cacerola y deje que la sopa vuelva a hervir. Añada el arroz, tape la cacerola y déjelo cocer a fuego lento entre 15 y 20 minutos, hasta que el arroz esté tierno.

4 En un bol de tamaño mediano, bata los huevos junto con el zumo de limón, hasta que la mezcla quede espumosa; vierta 4 ó 5 cucharones de sopa, de uno en uno, y bátala bien después de cada adición. Vierta la mezcla de huevo y sopa en la cacerola, y remuévalo todo mediante una cuchara de madera hasta que la sopa adquiera una textura homogénea. Rectifíquela de sal y pimienta y sírvala enseguida.

ABAJO
La claridad incomparable de la luz mediterránea aporta un resplandor inusual a cualquier escena, como en esta fachada de una vivienda de Psichró.

Sopa de hortalizas clásica

HORTOSOUPA

Sirva esta sopa griega clásica acompañada de pan de aceitunas recién hecho (*eliopitta*).

Tiempo de preparación: unos 15 minutos
Tiempo de cocción: 1 hora y 35 minutos
PARA 6-8 PERSONAS

- *½ taza de aceite de oliva*
- *2 dientes de ajo, majados*
- *2 cebollas, picadas*
- *2½ tazas de col, en juliana*
- *3 zanahorias, picadas*
- *3 tallos de apio, picados*
- *2 patatas grandes, peladas y cortadas en dados*
- *2½ l de agua o caldo vegetal*
- *4 tomates pelados, sin semillas y troceados*
- *sal y pimienta negra recién molida, al gusto*
- *4 cucharadas de perejil fresco, picado*
- *50 g de queso feta o kefalotyri, rallado*

1 Ponga a calentar el aceite de oliva en una cacerola grande y sofría la cebolla y el ajo durante 5 minutos, hasta que la cebolla esté tierna pero no dorada. Vierta la col y prosiga la cocción durante 3 ó 4 minutos más.

2 Añada las zanahorias y el apio a la cacerola, remuévalo y déjelo cocer otros 5 minutos más. Agregue las patatas, remueva y cuézalo todo a fuego lento durante 5 minutos, hasta que las hortalizas estén tiernas.

3 Vierta el caldo vegetal o el agua y remuévalo bien. Suba el fuego para que la sopa rompa el hervor; tape la cacerola y déjela cocer a fuego lento entre 12 y 15 minutos. Incorpore el tomate y sazónelo al gusto con sal y pimienta negra recién molida. Vuelva a tapar la cacerola y deje cocer la sopa durante 1 hora a fuego lento. Añada el perejil poco antes de agotarse el tiempo de cocción y sirva la sopa con el queso rallado por encima.

Crema de berenjena

MELITZANOSALATA

Utilice berenjenas grandes y frescas y obtendrá una crema con todo su aroma. En cuanto a la textura de la crema, puede variarla de más a menos gruesa según sus preferencias.

Tiempo de preparación: unos 20 minutos
Tiempo de cocción: 1 hora aproximadamente
Temperatura del horno: 190°C

PARA 4-6 PERSONAS

- *2 berenjenas grandes*
- *4 dientes de ajo, pelados*
- *¼ taza de aceite de oliva y un poco más para untar*
- *1 cucharada de vinagre*
- *½ cucharadita de azúcar*
- *sal y pimienta negra recién molida, al gusto*
- *aceitunas maduras picadas y perejil fresco picado, para decorar*

1 Precaliente el horno a 190°C. Lave las berenjenas, séquelas con papel de cocina y pínchelas con un tenedor por toda la superficie; dispóngalas en una bandeja de horno bien engrasada. Hornéelas durante 1 hora aproximadamente, hasta que la piel se arrugue y la pulpa se ablande; retírelas del horno.

2 Deje que las berenjenas se enfríen a temperatura ambiente, pélelas y córtelas por la mitad a lo largo. Con una cuchara, extraiga las semillas y deséchelas. Vierta la pulpa en el robot de cocina junto con el ajo y tritúrelo todo hasta que la mezcla adquiera la consistencia de una crema.

3 Con el robot en marcha, vierta el aceite de oliva dejándolo caer en un chorrito continuo; agregue también el vinagre y el azúcar, y condiméntelo al gusto con sal y pimienta. Tritúrelo todo hasta obtener la textura deseada, páselo a un bol de servir y esparza por encima las aceitunas y el perejil

Salsa de yogur con ajo y pepino

TZATZIKI

Esta salsa, ligera y refrescante, debe servirse siempre bien fría. Además de ser muy fácil de preparar, resulta deliciosa tanto si se toma acompañada de pan pita recién hecho como si se sirve para completar un plato de fritos variados.

Tiempo de preparación: unos 10 minutos
Tiempo de cocción: ninguno
PARA 4–6 PERSONAS

- *500 g de yogur natural*
- *½ pepino*
- *3 dientes de ajo, majados*
- *2 cucharadas de menta fresca, picada*
- *2 cucharadas de aceite de oliva*
- *1 cucharada de vinagre de vino blanco*
- *sal, al gusto*
- *menta fresca picada, para decorar*

1 Vierta el yogur en un bol de tamaño mediano. Pele el pepino y rállelo; exprima la pulpa entre las manos para extraer el exceso de agua. Vierta el pepino escurrido en el yogur.

2 Añada el ajo, la menta fresca, el aceite de oliva y el vinagre a la mezcla anterior, y sazónela con sal al gusto. Tape la salsa y refrigérela hasta el momento de servir; decórela con la menta fresca picada justo antes de presentarla a la mesa.

Sopa de Pascua con carne de cordero

MAGEIRITSA

***Mageiritsa* significa, en griego, "los restos de la comida de Pascua". Lo tradicional consiste en no desperdiciar nada del cordero o de la cabra asados, por lo que algunos llegan a utilizar hasta los pies. En esta receta el cordero se corta en tiras y se acompaña del pan griego típico de Pascua (*Tsoureki*), con el que se interrumpe el ayuno una vez oficiada la misa de medianoche. (Véase página 37, menú de Pascua.)**

Tiempo de preparación: unos 30 minutos
Tiempo de cocción: unas 3 ½ horas
PARA 6–8 PERSONAS

- *2 kg de espalda de cordero*
- *2 tallos de apio, picados*
- *1 zanahoria grande, picada*
- *1 cebolla grande, picada*
- *sal y pimienta negra recién molida, al gusto*
- *2½ l de agua*
- *4 cucharadas de eneldo fresco, picado*
- *4 cucharadas de menta fresca, picada*
- *⅔ taza de arroz de grano largo*
- *3 huevos*
- *el zumo de 1 limón grande recién exprimido*
- *eneldo y menta frescos y picados, para decorar*

1 Introduzca el cordero en una cacerola grande con el apio, la zanahoria y la cebolla; condiméntelo y agregue el agua.

2 Deje que rompa a hervir, baje el fuego y cueza el caldo a fuego lento entre 2½ y 3 horas hasta que la carne esté tierna y se desprenda de los huesos con facilidad; espume el caldo durante la cocción.

3 Retire el cordero de la cacerola y páselo a una tabla de trinchar. Con la ayuda de un trinchante y un tenedor separe la carne de los huesos y córtela en tiras finas. Devuelva la carne a la cacerola y añada el eneldo y la menta picados; incorpore el arroz y remuévalo. Deje que el caldo rompa a hervir otra vez, remuévalo de vez en cuando y déjelo cocer a fuego lento hasta que el arroz esté tierno.

4 En un bol de tamaño mediano bata los huevos junto con el zumo de limón; añada 3 ó 4 cucharones de caldo, bátalo y devuelva la mezcla a la cacerola. No deje de remover el caldo mediante una cuchara de madera, hasta que presente una textura homogénea. Sirva la sopa en boles individuales y decorada con las hierbas aromáticas bien picadas.

Salsa de huevas de bacalao

TARAMOSALATA

La receta tradicional de la *Taramosalata* es a base de huevas de carpa pero hoy en día se prepara siempre con huevas de bacalao. Y es que, si bien el sabor final varía ligeramente, el bacalao resulta mucho más asequible, en todos los aspectos.

Tiempo de preparación: unos 10 minutos
Tiempo de cocción: ninguno
PARA 4 PERSONAS

- *75 g de huevas de carpa o de bacalao, sin membranas*
- *1 rebanada de pan blanco más bien gruesa, sin corteza*
- *1 patata mediana, hervida hasta dejarla tierna y pelada*
- *1 cebolla, picada*
- *½ taza de aceite de oliva*
- *el zumo de 1 limón recién exprimido*
- *gajos de limón y perejil fresco picado, para decorar*

1 Vierta las huevas de pescado en el robot de cocina. En un plato aparte, coloque la rebanada de pan y rocíela con agua fría hasta empaparla; exprima el pan con las manos, para extraer el exceso de agua y viértalo también en el robot.

2 Trocee la patata más bien gruesa y añádala al robot, junto con la cebolla; tritúrelo todo a velocidad mínima, si es posible. Con el robot en marcha, agregue el aceite de oliva y el zumo de limón, dejándolos caer en un chorrito continuo, hasta que la mezcla quede fina y cremosa. Sirva la salsa bien fría y decorada con los gajos de limón y el perejil fresco picado.

ABAJO
Las barcas de pesca llenan de colorido el puerto de Hóra Sfakion cada vez que descargan sus capturas de gambas, calamares, sardinas y pez espada.

Ensalada griega clásica

HORIATIKI SALATA

El secreto de esta ensalada, conocida en el mundo entero, no radica en el método de preparación sino en sus ingredientes. Es preciso contar con lo más fresco del mercado para recrear la sensación de ociosidad de los días bajo el sol del Mediterráneo.

Tiempo de preparación: unos 20 minutos
Tiempo de cocción: ninguno
PARA 4–6 PERSONAS

- *2 tomates grandes maduros*
- *½ pepino, en dados*
- *1 pimiento verde, sin semillas y en rodajas*
- *50 g de aceitunas kalamata*
- *1 cebolla roja grande, cortada en aros finos*
- *150 g de queso feta, cortado en dados de 2,5 cm*
- *la ralladura y el zumo de ½ limón*
- *¼ taza de aceite de oliva*
- *1 cucharadita de orégano seco*
- *sal gorda, al gusto*

1 Corte los tomates en gajos más bien finos y póngalos en un bol de tamaño mediano. Añada el pepino, el pimiento verde y las aceitunas.

2 Incorpore la mitad de la cebolla roja y la mitad del queso feta cortado en dados, y revuelva bien la ensalada; esparza el resto de la cebolla y del queso por encima.

3 Rocíe la ensalada con el zumo de limón y esparza la ralladura por encima; condiméntela con el aceite de oliva y termine de sazonarla con la sal y el orégano seco; revuélvala una sola vez justo antes de servirla.

Ensalada de patatas a la griega

PATATOSALATA

Prepare esta ensalada con dos días de antelación, guárdela bien tapada en el frigorífico y olvídese de ella. Al ir a servirla, comprobará que el sabor es mucho más intenso.

Tiempo de preparación: unos 20 minutos
Tiempo de cocción: 20–25 minutos
PARA 4–6 PERSONAS

- *1 kg de patatas nuevas pequeñas, lavadas*
- *1 cebolla roja mediana, cortada en aros finos*
- *50 g de aceitunas kalamata, lavadas y escurridas*
- *4 cucharadas de aceite de oliva*
- *2 cucharadas de vinagre de vino tinto*
- *sal y pimienta negra*
- *1 cucharadita de tomillo seco*

1 Introduzca las patatas en una cacerola grande y vierta agua hirviendo hasta cubrirlas. Llévelas a ebullición y cuézalas entre 20 y 25 minutos hasta que estén tiernas; escúrralas y déjelas enfriar un poco.

2 Corte las patatas en rodajas de ½ cm de grosor y dispóngalas en círculo en una fuente de servir, alternándolas con los aros de cebolla. Esparza las aceitunas por encima.

3 Vierta el aceite, el vinagre, la sal, la pimienta negra recién molida y el tomillo en un tarro con tapa de rosca, y agítelo bien. Rocíe la ensalada con el aliño obtenido, tápela y guárdela en el frigorífico hasta el momento de servirla a la mesa.

Crema de garbanzos

HUMMUS

Todo un clásico que debe servirse acompañado de pan pita. No es necesario utilizar garbanzos secos, puesto que los envasados resultan mucho más prácticos y el resultado que se obtiene es igual de delicioso.

Tiempo de preparación: unos 15 minutos
Tiempo de cocción: ninguno
PARA 4–6 PERSONAS

- *375 g de garbanzos envasados, lavados y escurridos*
- *½ taza de pasta tahini*
- *¼ taza de agua*
- *2 dientes de ajo, majados*
- *¼ taza de aceite de oliva*
- *4 cucharadas de zumo de limón recién exprimido*
- *sal y pimienta negra recién molida, al gusto*
- *1 cucharadita de pimentón*
- *perejil fresco, picado, para decorar*

1 Vierta los garbanzos en el robot de cocina y tritúrelos hasta obtener una masa más bien grumosa. En un bol aparte, mezcle la pasta tahini con el agua y remuévalo con un tenedor, hasta que adquiera una textura fina y homogénea.

2 Incorpore la mezcla de tahini y el ajo a los garbanzos, y tritúrelo todo hasta que adquiera la consistencia de una crema. Con el robot en marcha, vierta el aceite de oliva y el zumo de limón de manera alternativa y dejándolos caer en un chorrito continuo a fin de que la mezcla quede fina y cremosa. Salpimiente el *hummus* al gusto, espolvoréelo con el pimentón y decórelo con el perejil fresco picado.

ABAJO
Aquí, cerca de Frangokastello, en la costa sur, no hay lugar a dudas sobre la reputación de Creta por la belleza de sus flores silvestres en primavera.

Atún con garbanzos

TONOS ME REVITHIA

Esta fabulosa combinación del atún con los garbanzos constituye una meze fría excelente por ser fácil y rápida de preparar y poseer, además, un alto valor nutritivo.

Tiempo de preparación: unos 10 minutos
Tiempo de cocción: ninguno
PARA 4–6 PERSONAS

- *375 g de garbanzos, envasados*
- *375 g de atún en salmuera*
- *4 chalotes, picados*
- *1 tallo de apio, picado*
- *½ taza de aceite de oliva*
- *4 cucharadas de zumo de limón recién exprimido*
- *la ralladura de ½ limón*
- *3 cucharadas de perejil fresco, picado*
- *1 cucharada de eneldo fresco, picado*
- *sal y pimienta negra recién molida, al gusto*
- *2 dientes de ajo, majados*
- *¼ cucharadita de mostaza en polvo*
- *perejil y eneldo frescos, para decorar*

1 Vierta en un bol los garbanzos y el atún escurridos. Añada los chalotes y el apio, y remuévalo todo con cuidado.

2 En un tarro con tapa de rosca, vierta el aceite, el zumo y la ralladura de limón, el perejil, el eneldo, la sal y la pimienta, el ajo y la mostaza; agítelo bien para que se mezcle y viértalo sobre la ensalada de atún y garbanzos. Revuélvalo y páselo a una fuente de servir. Ganará en sabor, si lo tapa y lo deja refrigerar unas cuantas horas antes de servirlo. Presente la ensalada decorada con las hierbas aromáticas.

Ensalada de pimientos asados

PIPERIES OREKTIKO

Cuanto más variado sea el color de los pimientos, más atractiva resultará la ensalada.

Tiempo de preparación: unos 30 minutos
Tiempo de cocción: unos 20–25 minutos
Temperatura del horno: 230°C

PARA 4 PERSONAS

- *6 pimientos de colores distintos*
- *2 cebollas, picadas*
- *sal y pimienta negra recién molida, al gusto*
- *3 cucharadas de vinagre de vino blanco*
- *¼ taza de aceite de oliva*
- *3 cucharadas de perejil fresco picado, para decorar*

1 Precaliente el horno a 230°C. Coloque los pimientos enteros en la bandeja del horno y áselos entre 20 y 25 minutos, hasta que estén tiernos y la piel se arrugue.

2 Déjelos enfriar un poco, pélelos y córtelos por la mitad; extraiga las semillas y retire las membranas.

3 Corte la pulpa de los pimientos en tiras y dispóngalas en una fuente de servir; condiméntelos con la cebolla, la sal y la pimienta, el vinagre y el aceite de oliva. Aderécelos con el perejil picado y póngalos a enfriar en el frigorífico antes de servirlos.

Albóndigas marinadas

KEFTEDAKIA ME SALTSA

Estos pequeños y apetitosos bocados no pueden faltar en una comida a base de meze. Y no se preocupe por la cantidad, porque seguro que se las comen todas.

Tiempo de preparación: unos 15 minutos
más el tiempo en marinada
Tiempo de cocción: unos 55 minutos
Temperatura del horno: 230°C, y luego 200°C

PARA 4 PERSONAS

- *250 g carne magra de vacuno, picada*
- *1 taza de pan blanco fresco, rallado*
- *1 huevo, batido*
- *1 cucharadita de mostaza*
- *1 cucharada de perejil fresco, picado*
- *una pizca de orégano seco*
- *1 cebolla, rallada*
- *sal y pimienta negra recién molida, al gusto*
- *1 cucharadita de menta seca*
- *una pizca de canela en polvo y otra pizca de clavo molido*
- *2 dientes de ajo, majados*
- *aceite de oliva, para engrasar*
- *375 g de tomates en lata*
- *¼ taza de agua*
- *perejil y menta frescos, picados, para decorar*

1 Precaliente el horno a 230°C. Vierta todos los ingredientes, menos los tomates y el agua, en un bol y mézclelos bien. Humedézcase las manos ligeramente y moldee la masa obtenida en bolitas de 2,5 cm de diámetro; dispóngalas en una bandeja de horno untada con un poco de aceite.

2 Hornéelas durante 20 minutos, dándoles la vuelta durante la cocción para que se doren de manera uniforme. Deje escurrir las albóndigas sobre papel de cocina y páselas luego a una fuente grande y llana; resérvelas

3 Vierta los tomates en lata en el robot de cocina y tritúrelos hasta hacerlos puré; páselos por el chino a fin de separar las semillas de la pulpa. Vierta el tomate tamizado en un cazo, agregue el agua, y déjelo cocer durante 5 minutos a fuego lento; nape las albóndigas con la salsa resultante. Déjelas enfriar, tápelas y refrigérelas durante varias horas o toda la noche.

4 Para calentar las albóndigas, precaliente primero el horno a 200°C y déjelas entre 25 y 30 minutos. Déles la vuelta durante la cocción. Sírvalas aderezadas con las hierbas frescas picadas.

Queso frito

SAGANAKI

Saganaki **es el nombre que los griegos dan al tipo de sartén que se usa para cocinar este plato: una meze clásica y fácil que se sirve acompañada de un vaso de Ouzo.**

Tiempo de preparación: unos 15 minutos
Tiempo de cocción: unos 10 minutos

PARA 4–6 PERSONAS

- *200 g de queso haloumi*
- *½ taza de harina*
- *pimienta negra recién molida, al gusto*
- *¼ taza de aceite de oliva*
- *2 cucharadas de zumo de limón, recién exprimido*

1 Corte el queso en lonchas de 7 cm de largo y 1 cm de grosor; lávelas bien bajo el chorro de agua fría y séquelas con papel de cocina.

2 Vierta la harina en un plato y condiméntela con la pimienta; pase las lonchas de queso por la mezcla, de modo que queden bien rebozadas.

3 Caliente el aceite de oliva en una sartén de fondo pesado. Sacuda las lonchas de queso para que suelten el exceso de harina y fríalas por tandas. Déjelas cocer unos 2 ó 3 minutos por cada lado y páselas a una fuente precalentada; seque el exceso de aceite con papel absorbente, si fuera necesario.

4 Sirva las *saganaki* rociadas con el zumo de limón.

Rollitos de pollo

BOUREKAKIA ME KOTA

La pasta filo se utiliza con profusión en la cocina griega. Con sólo seguir un par de reglas obtendrá unos resultados excelentes de la forma más sencilla.

Tiempo de preparación: unos 35 minutos
Tiempo de cocción: unos 45 minutos
Temperatura del horno: 190°C
PARA 8–10 PERSONAS

- *450 g de pechugas de pollo en filetes, sin piel*
- *1 cebolla grande, cortada en cuartos*
- *2 tallos de apio, picados*
- *3 granos de pimienta*
- *una pizca de sal*
- *1 ramita de perejil fresco*
- *¼ taza de mantequilla*
- *2 cucharadas de eneldo fresco, picado*
- *50 g de queso feta, rallado*
- *1 huevo, batido*
- *200 g de pasta filo*
- *1 taza de mantequilla, fundida*

1 Disponga los filetes de pollo en una sartén honda, junto con la cebolla, el apio, los granos de pimienta, la sal y la ramita de perejil. Agregue suficiente agua como para cubrir el pollo y déjelo cocer entre 20 y 25 minutos hasta que esté hecho.

2 Retire el pollo de la sartén con la ayuda de una espumadera y páselo a un robot de cocina, junto con la cebolla y el apio; deseche el líquido de la cocción y limpie la sartén para poder utilizarla de nuevo.

3 Triture el pollo y las hortalizas hasta obtener una mezcla sin grumos. Por otra parte, derrita la ¼ taza de mantequilla en la sartén limpia; saltee la mezcla de pollo y hortalizas entre 5 y 10 minutos, hasta que presente un tono más bien dorado. Incorpore el eneldo picado y el queso rallado, y déjelo aparte para que se enfríe del todo. Añada el huevo y bátalo todo bien. Precaliente el horno a 190°C.

4 Para preparar los rollitos de pasta filo, extienda la masa sobre la superficie de trabajo y cúbrala con un paño ligeramente humedecido. Saque la primera lámina de pasta y extiéndala sobre la superficie; mantenga el resto cubierto con el paño para evitar que se seque. Córtela en tres tiras de igual tamaño y píntelas con la mantequilla fundida.

5 Coloque 2 cucharaditas colmadas de la mezcla de pollo sobre uno de los extremos de cada tira de pasta. Pliegue los laterales de la masa hacia adentro, aproximadamente unos 5 mm. Enrolle la tira de masa sobre sí misma, empezando por el extremo con el relleno, de modo que el rollo quede compacto y bien cerrado.

6 Repita la operación del paso anterior con cada una de las tiras de masa, y haga lo mismo con el resto de las láminas de pasta filo. Es probable que necesite más de una bandeja de horno para cocerla toda.

7 Hornee los rollos durante unos 20 minutos, hasta que estén crujientes y presenten un tono ligeramente dorado.

Empanadillas de carne

COUPES

La crujiente cobertura de bulgur encierra en su interior un relleno de carne que sorprende por su delicado sabor. Otra tentación griega a la que resulta difícil resistirse.

Tiempo de preparación: unos 20 minutos
Tiempo de cocción: unos 20 minutos
PARA 8–10 PERSONAS

- *2 tazas de bulgur*
- *1½ tazas de agua hirviendo*
- *sal y pimienta negra recién molida, al gusto*
- *2 cucharaditas de canela*
- *1 cucharada de aceite vegetal, más para freír*
- *150 g de carne magra de cerdo, picada*
- *4 chalotes, picados*
- *2 cucharadas de perejil*

1 Vierta el bulgur en un bol de tamaño mediano y el agua hirviendo por encima. Sazónelo con sal y pimienta negra recién molida, añada 1 cucharadita de canela molida y remuévalo. Déjelo enfriar y remuévalo de vez en cuando.

2 Mientras tanto, prepare el relleno: caliente 1 cucharada de aceite en una sartén y rehogue la carne de cerdo y los chalotes entre 10 y 15 minutos, hasta que la carne cambie de color y esté bien cocida. Agregue el perejil fresco picado y el resto de la canela molida; remuévalo y sazónelo con sal y pimienta negra recién molida. Déjelo aparte para que se enfríe.

3 Para moldear las *coupes*, humedézcase las manos, tome una pequeña cantidad de la mezcla de bulgur y forme con ella una bola. Con la ayuda del dedo índice y una cucharilla, practique un hueco en el centro de cada bola y rellénelas con la carne picada. Pellizque los extremos de las bolas a fin de darles una forma más oval; déjelas reposar.

4 Caliente el aceite en una freidora y fría las empanadillas por tandas entre 3 y 5 minutos; deberían quedar doradas, crujientes y bien hechas. Coloque las *coupes* ya hechas sobre papel de cocina para que escurran el aceite y déjelas en el horno a temperatura baja para que no se enfríen mientras cocina el resto. Sírvalas bien calientes.

Triángulos de queso

TIROPITTES

Una meze del recetario griego clásico. Le sugerimos que prepare el doble de cantidad y congele la mitad de los *tiropittes* antes de hornearlos. De este modo siempre tendrá algo a mano ante cualquier visita inesperada.

Tiempo de preparación: unos 25 minutos
Tiempo de cocción: unos 20 minutos
Temperatura del horno: 200°C

PARA 8–10 PERSONAS

- *250 g de queso feta*
- *¾ taza de requesón*
- *2 huevos, batidos*
- *2 cucharadas de perejil fresco, picado*
- *1 cucharada de menta fresca, picada*
- *sal y pimienta negra recién molida, al gusto*
- *250 g de pasta filo, descongelada, si no es fresca*
- *1 taza de mantequilla fundida*

1 Precaliente el horno a 200°C. Introduzca el queso feta y el requesón en un bol de tamaño mediano y mézclelos bien. Agregue los huevos, el perejil y la menta, y bátalo todo bien.

2 Para preparar los *tiropittes*, extienda la masa sobre la superficie de trabajo y cúbrala con un paño ligeramente humedecido. Saque la primera lámina de pasta filo y extiéndala sobre la superficie; mantenga el resto cubierto con el paño para evitar que se seque. Corte la lámina en tres tiras de igual tamaño y úntelas con la mantequilla fundida.

3 Coloque 2 cucharaditas de la mezcla de queso sobre el extremo inferior derecho de la tira de pasta. Pliegue ese extremo en diagonal, hacia el extremo superior izquierdo, de modo que resulte un triángulo. Pliegue luego el extremo inferior izquierdo en dirección al extremo superior derecho y así sucesivamente hasta terminar la tira de pasta y obtener un triángulo compacto y bien cerrado.

4 Repita la misma operación del paso anterior con el resto de las tiras y con las demás láminas de pasta filo.

5 Disponga los *tiropittes* en una bandeja de horno untada con mantequilla y hornéelos entre 15 y 20 minutos, hasta que empiecen a dorarse y estén crujientes. Páselos a una rejilla metálica y sírvalos calientes, o bien déjelos enfriar.

Pinchitos

SOUVLAKIA MEZE

Con la palabra *souvlakia* los griegos denominan los trozos pequeños de carne (y, en ocasiones, también de hortalizas), que se ensartan en una brocheta y se asan a la barbacoa. Esta receta, sin embargo, se prepara al horno, aunque si lo prefiere puede utilizar la barbacoa.

Tiempo de preparación: unos 15 minutos
Tiempo de cocción: unos 15–20 minutos
Temperatura del horno: 190°C
PARA 6–8 PERSONAS

- *1 pierna de cordero de 1 kg, deshuesada*
- *½ taza de aceite de oliva*
- *1 cucharadita de comino, molido*
- *1 cucharadita de orégano seco*
- *2 hojas de laurel, picadas*
- *2 dientes de ajo, majados*
- *1 cebolla, picada muy fina*
- *¼ taza de vino tinto*
- *¼ taza de vinagre de vino tinto*
- *2 cucharadas de zumo de limón recién exprimido*
- *sal y pimienta negra recién molida, al gusto*

1 Corte el cordero en dados de 2 cm y colóquelos en una fuente grande y llana. Mezcle el resto de los ingredientes aparte, en un tarro con tapa de rosca, y agítelo bien.

2 Rocíe la carne con la marinada obtenida y revuélvala para que quede napada de manera uniforme. Tápela y déjela marinar en un sitio fresco durante varias horas o toda la noche.

3 Precaliente el horno a 190°C. Ensarte los trozos de cordero en las brochetas y colóquelas en bandejas de horno llanas. Hornéelas entre 15 y 20 minutos, dándoles la vuelta con frecuencia, hasta que presenten un tono dorado y estén bien hechas. Sirva las *souvlakia* ensartadas en las brochetas y preséntelas a la mesa acompañadas de pan pita y un buen plato de ensalada verde.

CAPÍTULO 2

Hortalizas y legumbres

Calabacines fritos crujientes

TEGANITA KOLOKYTHAKIA

Si bien el rebozado utilizado en esta receta es una mezcla especial, por lo general las hortalizas se pasan por harina condimentada antes de freírlas.

Tiempo de preparación: unos 10 minutos, más refrigeración
Tiempo de cocción: unos 3–5 minutos
PARA 4–6 PERSONAS

- *2¾ tazas de harina*
- *sal y pimienta negra recién molida, al gusto*
- *una pizca de canela en polvo*
- *¾ taza de agua*
- *450 g de calabacines*
- *aceite vegetal para freír*

1 Vierta 1¾ tazas de harina en un bol de tamaño mediano y condiméntela con la sal, la pimienta y la canela. Practique un hueco en el centro de la mezcla de harina y vierta el agua mientras lo remueve con un tenedor. La masa debe quedar espesa y presentar una textura fina y sin grumos. Tápela y refrigérela de 2 a 3 horas antes de utilizarla.

2 Deseche los extremos de los calabacines y córtelos en rodajas de unos 3 mm de grosor. Pase las rodajas por la harina restante y luego por la masa del rebozado.

3 Fría los calabacines por tandas de 3 a 5 minutos en abundante aceite caliente, hasta que estén crujientes, dorados y cocidos. Retírelos con una espumadera y escúrralos sobre papel de cocina. Déjelos en el horno para que no se enfríen y sírvalos calientes.

Hortalizas rellenas sin carne

YEMISTA ORPHANA

Esta receta es originaria de la isla de Creta, donde los rellenos a base de arroz ocupan un puesto importante en la cocina. La mezcla de uvas pasas, piñones y almendras que se añade al arroz delata su auténtico origen.

Tiempo de preparación: 1 hora aproximadamente
Tiempo de cocción: 1 hora y 30 minutos
Temperatura del horno: 180°C
PARA 8–10 PERSONAS

- *8–10 hortalizas maduras pero firmes, por ejemplo, calabacines, berenjenas, tomates y pimientos*
- *6 cucharadas de aceite de oliva*
- *6 chalotes, picados*
- *1⅓ tazas de arroz de grano largo*
- *2 dientes de ajo, majados*
- *1 cucharadita de canela molida*
- *½ taza de uvas pasas sin pepitas*
- *½ taza de piñones tostados*
- *sal y pimienta negra recién molida, al gusto*
- *4 cucharadas de perejil fresco, picado*
- *3 cucharadas de menta*

1 Preparación de las hortalizas: corte el extremo superior de los tomates, los pimientos, los calabacines y las berenjenas. Con una cuchara extraiga las semillas y la pulpa de los tomates y páselos a un bol. Repita la operación con las berenjenas y los calabacines y no se olvide de desechar las semillas amargas de las primeras. Haga lo mismo con los pimientos. No tire la parte superior de las hortalizas, ya que se utilizan como tapadera, una vez rellenas.

2 En una sartén de tamaño grande, caliente 2 cucharadas de aceite de oliva y sofría la cebolla durante 3 minutos; añada el arroz, el ajo, la canela, las uvas pasas y los piñones junto con las semillas y la pulpa de las hortalizas. Vierta agua hasta que llegue a cubrir el arroz, tápelo y cuézalo a fuego lento entre 7 y 10 minutos, o hasta que el arroz esté tierno y se haya embebido casi todo el líquido.

3 Agregue la sal, la pimienta y las hierbas a la mezcla de arroz, remuévalo y retírelo del fuego. Precaliente el horno a 180°C. Rellene las hortalizas con la mezcla y coloque encima la parte superior de las mismas, a modo de tapadera. Dispóngalas en una fuente de horno con un poco de agua.

4 Rocíelas con el aceite de oliva restante y hornéelas entre 50 y 60 minutos o hasta que las hortalizas estén tiernas. Báñelas con frecuencia durante la cocción, pero no intente moverlas porque podrían desmontarse con facilidad. Estas *yemista* pueden servirse calientes, pero también resultan deliciosas frías.

Estofado de habas y corazones de alcachofa

ANGINARES ME KOUKIA

Esta meze clásica requiere cierta dosis de paciencia a la hora de preparar las hortalizas y la salsa, pero comprobará que el resultado final bien merece la pena.

Tiempo de preparación: 1 hora aproximadamente
Tiempo de cocción: 1 hora y 30 minutos
PARA 6-8 PERSONAS

- *el zumo recién exprimido de 3 limones*
- *2½ tazas de agua*
- *8 alcachofas frescas*
- *3 cucharadas de aceite de oliva*
- *1 cebolla grande, picada fina*
- *3 dientes de ajo, majados*
- *900 g de habas frescas desvainadas, lavadas y escurridas (o 450 g de habas congeladas)*
- *⅔ taza de hinojo, en rodajas*
- *sal y pimienta negra recién molida, al gusto*
- *½ cucharadita de azúcar*

PARA LA SALSA
- *¼ taza de aceite de oliva*
- *1 cucharada de harina*
- *el zumo recién exprimido de 1 limón*
- *sal y pimienta negra recién molida, al gusto*

1 Vierta el zumo de 2 limones en un bol de tamaño grande y agregue el agua. Para preparar las alcachofas utilice unas tijeras de cocina y corte los tallos de las mismas dejando tan sólo unos 2,5 cm. Retire también las hojas más duras y corte unos 6 cm de la punta de cada alcachofa. Separe las hojas, raspe un poco la pelusa del corazón y deséchela. Sumerja las alcachofas limpias en el bol con agua y limón.

2 Caliente el aceite de oliva en una sartén grande y honda; saltee la cebolla y el ajo durante 3 ó 4 minutos, hasta que la cebolla esté tierna. Incorpore las habas y rehóguelo todo durante 3 ó 4 minutos más. Añada entonces las alcachofas, junto con el hinojo, la sal y la pimienta negra recién molida, el azúcar y el zumo de limón restante. Vierta suficiente agua hasta casi cubrirlo todo, baje el fuego y déjelo cocer entre 50 y 60 minutos, hasta que las hortalizas estén tiernas. Añada más agua durante la cocción, si lo cree necesario.

3 Con la ayuda de una espumadera, pase las alcachofas y las habas a una fuente de servir precalentada y cúbralas con papel de aluminio para mantenerlas calientes. Prepare la salsa en una cacerola mediana; vierta 3 cucharadas de aceite de oliva, añada la harina y remuévalo todo bien hasta que la mezcla se espese. Cuézalo durante 1 ó 2 minutos a fin de que adquiera un tono ligeramente dorado.

4 Incorpore a la cacerola el zumo de limón y el jugo de cocer las hortalizas, y bátalo bien. Remueva constantemente mientras cuece a fuego lento, hasta obtener una salsa bien espesa y sin grumos. Condiméntela con sal y pimienta negra recién molida. Retire el papel de aluminio que cubre las hortalizas y nápelas con la salsa; sirva el plato caliente y acompañado de una buena ración de pan para mojar en la salsa.

Patatas asadas con ajo

PATATES ME SKORTHO

Saben tan bien como suena. Prepárelas con orégano y zumo de limón y descubrirá, con tan solo probarlas, que no hay mejor forma de asar las patatas.

Tiempo de preparación: unos 10 minutos
Tiempo de cocción: 1 hora aproximadamente
Temperatura del horno: 230°C
PARA 6–8 PERSONAS

- *900 g de patatas grandes, mondadas*
- *¼ taza de aceite de oliva*
- *½ taza de zumo de limón recién exprimido*
- *2 cucharaditas de orégano seco*
- *3 dientes de ajo, majados*
- *sal y pimienta negra recién molida, al gusto*
- *½ taza de agua*

1 Precaliente el horno a 230°C. Corte las patatas en cuartos o en octavos, en sentido longitudinal, y colóquelas en una fuente de horno grande y llana.

2 Añada los demás ingredientes y remueva las patatas, para cubrirlas con el condimento. Hornéelas 1 hora en la parte superior del horno, sin tapar, hasta que se doren ligeramente y estén crujientes por fuera y tiernas por dentro. Remuévalas de vez en cuando y agregue más agua durante la cocción, si lo cree necesario.

Croquetas de espinacas

KROKETES SPANAKI

En esta receta se ha utilizado pan de centeno crujiente para empanar las croquetas. Si no puede conseguirlo, utilice harina de trigo integral en su lugar.

Tiempo de preparación: unos 30 minutos
Tiempo de cocción: unos 20 minutos
PARA 6–8 PERSONAS

- *2 cucharadas de mantequilla*
- *1 cebolla, picada*
- *900 g de espinacas frescas, troceadas*
- *150 g de queso feta, rallado*
- *3 huevos*
- *sal y pimienta negra recién molida, al gusto*
- *1½ tazas de pan blanco fresco, finamente rallado*
- *1½ tazas de pan de centeno crujiente, rallado*
- *aceite de oliva, para freír*

1 Derrita la mantequilla en una sartén y saltee la cebolla durante 3 minutos, hasta que esté tierna. Añada las espinacas y rehóguelo todo otros 5 minutos, hasta que las espinacas también estén tiernas. Retire la sartén del fuego.

2 Pase la mezcla de las espinacas a un bol mediano y añada el queso feta, un huevo entero y las yemas de los otros dos huevos, sin dejar de remover; condiméntelo con sal y pimienta negra recién molida e incorpore el pan rallado.

3 Ponga el pan de centeno crujiente rallado en un plato y las claras de huevo en otro. Humedézcase un poco las manos y moldee la mezcla obtenida en forma de pequeñas croquetas; páselas primero por el pan crujiente, luego por las claras de huevo y, finalmente, otra vez por el pan. Repita la misma operación con todas las croquetas.

4 Caliente un poco de aceite de oliva en una sartén y fría las croquetas por tandas entre 5 y 8 minutos, hasta que estén bien hechas y doradas; déles la vuelta con frecuencia durante la cocción. Utilice una espumadera para pasar las croquetas a un plato forrado con papel de cocina, a fin de que escurran el aceite. Manténgalas calientes dentro del horno, a temperatura baja, mientras termina de freír el resto. Puede servirlas tanto frías como calientes.

Coliflor al horno con tomates y queso feta

KOUNOUPITHI KAPAMA

La canela molida, de uso muy extendido dentro de la cocina griega, combinada con el sabor fuerte de los tomates, confiere a este plato un sabor y una riqueza exquisitos.

Tiempo de preparación: unos 30 minutos
Tiempo de cocción: 1 hora y 30 minutos
Temperatura del horno: 190°C

PARA 4–6 PERSONAS

- *6 cucharadas de aceite de oliva*
- *1 cebolla, cortada en aros*
- *2 dientes de ajo, majados*
- *8 tomates, pelados y picados*
- *una pizca de canela molida*
- *2 cucharaditas de orégano seco*
- *sal y pimienta negra recién molida, al gusto*
- *1 coliflor grande, cortada en ramilletes*
- *1 cucharada de zumo de limón, recién exprimido*
- *75 g de queso feta, rallado*

1 Caliente 2 ó 3 cucharadas de aceite de oliva en una sartén de fondo pesado y saltee la cebolla y el ajo durante unos 3 ó 4 minutos, hasta que la cebolla esté tierna.

2 Añada los tomates troceados, la canela y el orégano, y condiméntelo con sal y pimienta. Remuévalo, tápelo y déjelo cocer durante 5 minutos.

3 Precaliente el horno a 190°C. Agregue la coliflor a la mezcla de tomate, tápelo y cuézalo entre 10 y 15 minutos más, hasta que la coliflor esté tierna. Retírelo del fuego.

4 Pase la coliflor junto con la mezcla de tomate a una fuente grande y llana, y rocíelo todo con el aceite de oliva restante. Vierta también por encima el zumo de limón y el queso feta rallado; hornee el plato entre 45 y 50 minutos, hasta que la coliflor se ablande y el queso se derrita. Sírvalo caliente.

Menú de Pascua

Empanadillas de carne
Coupes
◆
Sopa de Pascua con carne de cordero
Mageiritsa
◆
Estofado de cordero con menta y salvia
Arni me Diosmo kai Fascomilo
◆
Pinchos de cordero
Souvlakia
◆
Patatas asadas con ajo
Patates me Skortho
◆
Judías verdes estofadas
Fassolakia Yiahni
◆
Pan de Pascua
Tsoureki
◆
Pastitas de queso dulces
Kaltsounia Cretis
◆
Galletas de Pascua
Koulourakia Lambriatika
◆
Vino: Naoussa Grande Reserve
(Vino tinto de mucho cuerpo)
◆

Hojas de parra rellenas

DOLMADES

Utilice, a ser posible, hojas de parra frescas y elija las que sean jóvenes, fuertes y de tamaño más bien grande. Lávelas, séquelas bien y corte los tallos con unas tijeras de cocina. Hierva las hojas durante unos 15 minutos en agua salada, escúrralas y aclárelas bajo el chorro de agua fría.

Tiempo de preparación: unos 45 minutos
Tiempo de cocción: unas 2 horas y 30 minutos
PARA 10-12 PERSONAS

- *30 hojas de parra en salmuera, aclaradas*
- *¼ taza de aceite de oliva*
- *1 cebolla grande, picada*
- *⅔ taza de arroz de grano largo*
- *2 dientes de ajo, majados*
- *⅓ taza de piñones*
- *⅓ taza de uvas pasas*
- *1 cucharadita de comino*
- *2½ tazas de agua, más 3 cucharadas*
- *4 cucharadas de eneldo fresco, picado*
- *4 cucharadas de perejil fresco*
- *2 cucharadas de menta fresca, picada*
- *sal y pimienta negra*
- *1 huevo, batido*
- *el zumo de 1 limón*

1 Llene una cacerola grande con agua y llévela a ebullición. Vierta las hojas de parra en el agua y hiérvalas entre 3 y 5 minutos, hasta que estén tiernas. Escúrralas bien y resérvelas.

2 Saltee la cebolla entre 3 y 5 minutos en una sartén grande con 2 cucharadas de aceite de oliva, hasta que se ablande. Añada el arroz y cuézalo de 3 a 5 minutos hasta que se dore. Remuévalo continuamente con una cuchara de madera.

3 Añada el ajo, los piñones, las uvas pasas y el comino molido; vierta 1¼ tazas de agua y remuévalo todo bien. Tápelo y déjelo cocer unos 10 minutos, hasta que el arroz esté tierno y se haya embebido todo el líquido. Retírelo del fuego y déjelo enfriar.

4 Incorpore a la mezcla de arroz las hierbas aromáticas picadas y condiméntelo bien con sal y pimienta negra recién molida. Añada 1 cucharada del aceite de oliva restante junto con el huevo batido.

5 En una cacerola grande mezcle el resto del aceite de oliva con 3 cucharadas de agua. Forre el fondo de la cacerola con 3 ó 4 hojas de parra. (Para ello puede utilizar hojas de parra rotas o de forma irregular.) Rellene las demás hojas con 1 cucharadita de la mezcla de arroz; colóquela en el centro de cada hoja y enróllela con cuidado, de modo que resulte un paquetito perfectamente cerrado.

6 Coloque las hojas de parra rellenas en el fondo de la cacerola, con las costuras en la parte de abajo, y apile el resto con cuidado, formando capas. Rocíelas con el zumo de limón y 1¼ tazas de agua. Coloque un plato boca abajo encima de las *dolmades* para que no se muevan durante la cocción. Tape la cacerola y déjelas cocer a fuego lento durante unas 2 horas, hasta que las hojas estén tiernas y el arroz esté bien hecho. Puede servirlas tanto frías como calientes.

ABAJO *Desde las montañas de la isla de Mikonos se divisa la hermosa silueta de la vecina Delos, isla donde, según la mitología griega, nacieron Apolo y Artemisa.*

Judías verdes estofadas

FASSOLAKIA YIAHNI

Grecia cuenta con una gran variedad de judías verdes y todas son aptas para preparar esta receta. Aunque, por lo general, se trata de un plato frío, también es posible servirlo caliente.

Tiempo de preparación: unos 15 minutos
Tiempo de cocción: unas 2 horas
PARA 6–8 PERSONAS

- *¼ taza de aceite de oliva*
- *2 cebollas, picadas*
- *700 g de judías verdes frescas, sin las puntas*
- *3 patatas medianas, peladas y cortadas en cuartos*
- *2 dientes de ajo, majados*
- *4 tomates maduros, pelados, sin semillas y troceados*
- *¼ taza de agua*
- *sal y pimienta negra recién molida, al gusto*
- *75 g de queso feta, rallado*

1 En una cacerola grande con aceite, rehogue la cebolla durante unos 3 ó 4 minutos, hasta que se ablande pero sin que llegue a dorarse. Añada las judías verdes y las patatas, y remuévalo todo para que quede bien untado de aceite; incorpore el ajo y rehóguelo otros 5 minutos más.

2 Incorpore los tomates y el agua, y condiméntelo con sal y pimienta negra recién molida; baje el fuego y déjelo cocer lentamente durante 1½ horas, hasta que las patatas y las judías estén tiernas. Agregue más agua, si lo cree necesario. Espolvoree el queso feta rallado por encima, en caso de servir el plato caliente.

PÁGINA SIGUIENTE
¿Que le parecería saborear una copa de retsina en esta entrañable taberna del puerto de Réthimnon?

Pastel de espinacas

SPANAKOPITTA

Los *Pites*, que es como llaman en griego a los pasteles salados, son bien recibidos en todas partes. Ya sean rellenos de espinacas, queso, carne o calabacín, cortados en rodajas o en porciones, son lo más apropiado para una ocasión informal.

Tiempo de preparación: unos 45 minutos
Tiempo de cocción: 1 hora aproximadamente
Temperatura del horno: 190°C
PARA 8–10 PERSONAS

- *6 láminas de pasta filo, descongelada, si no es fresca*
- *½ taza de mantequilla*
- *6 cucharadas de aceite de oliva*
- *1 manojo de chalotes, picados*
- *1 puerro, lavado y picado*
- *700 g de espinacas frescas*
- *6 cucharadas de eneldo fresco*
- *4 cucharadas de perejil fresco*
- *1 huevo, batido*
- *350 g de queso feta, desmenuzado*
- *2 cucharadas de queso kefalotyri o queso parmesano fresco, rallado*
- *½ cucharadita de nuez moscada, rallada*
- *½ cucharadita de comino*
- *sal y pimienta negra*
- *1 yema de huevo mezclada con 2 cucharadas de leche*

1 Extienda una lámina de pasta filo sobre la superficie de trabajo y mantenga el resto bien cubierto con un paño ligeramente humedecido. Unte la lámina de manera uniforme con mantequilla fundida y coloque otra lámina encima. Unte esta segunda y cúbrala asimismo con una tercera lámina untada. Páselo todo a una fuente de horno honda y ovalada de unos 26 cm y previamente untada con mantequilla.

2 Precaliente el horno a 190°C. Prepare el relleno en una sartén grande. Caliente 2 cucharadas de aceite de oliva y sofría los chalotes y el puerro durante unos 5 minutos o hasta que se ablanden. Añada las espinacas y rehóguelo todo otros 5 ó 7 minutos, hasta que éstas se marchiten. Cuele la mezcla obtenida, a fin de extraer el exceso de líquido, y déjela enfriar.

3 En un bol de tamaño grande mezcle las espinacas con las hierbas aromáticas picadas, el huevo batido, los quesos y las especias; salpimiéntelo y remuévalo todo bien. Extienda la mezcla obtenida, de manera uniforme, sobre la pasta dispuesta en el fondo de la fuente. Repita la operación de las capas de pasta filo untadas con mantequilla, hasta terminarlas todas y cubrir con ellas el pastel. Pellizque los bordes de la pasta de modo que queden pegados y recorte la que sobre.

4 Practique una pequeña incisión en el centro del pastel y pinte la superficie con la mezcla de leche y huevo batido. Hornéelo entre 40 y 45 minutos, hasta que la masa esté crujiente y dorada. Déjelo enfriar un poco en la misma fuente antes de cortar las porciones. Frío, sabe igual de delicioso.

Rollitos de col

LAHANODOLMADES

Los griegos tienen preferencia por las hojas de col a la hora de preparar rollitos. El relleno puede ser a base de carne o arroz, pero todos se sirven calientes y se acompañan, muy a menudo, con yogur griego o crema agria.

Tiempo de preparación: unos 45 minutos
Tiempo de cocción: unas 3 horas
PARA 6-8 PERSONAS

- *1 col savoy*
- *el zumo de 1 limón recién exprimido*

PARA EL RELLENO
- *6 cucharadas de aceite de oliva*
- *1 cebolla grande, picada*
- *⅔ taza de arroz de grano largo*
- *100 g de carne magra de cordero o vacuno, picada*
- *2 dientes de ajo, majados*
- *3 cucharadas de eneldo fresco, picado*
- *2 cucharadas de perejil fresco*
- *1 cucharadita de comino molido*
- *1 cucharadita de menta seca*
- *sal y pimienta negra recién molida, al gusto*
- *⅔ taza de agua*

1 Con un cuchillo para hortalizas afilado extraiga el corazón de la col y separe las hojas de la misma con cuidado, de modo que no se rompan. Lávelas, escúrralas y viértalas en una olla grande con agua hirviendo; cuézalas durante unos 2 ó 3 minutos a fin de que se ablanden un poco. Escúrralas y aclárelas bajo el chorro de agua fría; resérvelas.

2 Para preparar el relleno, caliente 2 cucharadas de aceite en una sartén grande y rehogue la cebolla durante unos 3 minutos o hasta que se ablande. Añada el arroz y rehóguelo otros 2 minutos más; vierta entonces la carne picada y saltéela durante 5 minutos hasta que pierda su tono rosado. Agregue el ajo, las hierbas y las especias, y salpimiéntelo. Vierta el agua, tape la sartén y cuézalo a fuego lento entre 15 y 20 minutos, hasta que la carne esté prácticamente hecha y el arroz esté tierno. Añada más agua durante la cocción, si lo cree necesario.

3 Vierta 2 cucharadas más de aceite de oliva en una cacerola grande. Cubra el fondo de la misma con 3 ó 4 hojas de col. (Utilice las que se hayan roto o presenten una forma irregular.) Rellene el resto de las hojas con 2 cucharaditas de la mezcla de carne; colóquela sobre el extremo inferior de la hoja y pliegue ambos lados de la misma, de modo que el relleno quede encerrado en su interior. Enrolle la hoja, empezando por el extremo inferior, y colóquela con cuidado sobre su costura en el fondo de la cacerola. Repita la operación con todas las hojas y dispóngalas por capas, unas encima de las otras.

4 Agregue suficiente agua para cubrir las hojas rellenas y vierta el aceite de oliva restante, junto con el zumo de limón. Coloque un plato boca abajo sobre las hojas de col rellenas, a fin de que no se muevan durante la cocción. Tape la cacerola y déjelas cocer entre 2 y 2½ horas, hasta que las hojas estén casi transparentes y el relleno esté tierno. Añada más agua durante la cocción, si lo cree necesario.

EN LA PÁGINA SIGUIENTE
Un molino de viento en Mikonos a principios de otoño... Esta isla del Egeo cuenta con una iglesia para cada día del año.

Moussaka con berenjenas

MOUSSAKA ME MELITZANES

Esta es la variante vegetariana de este clásico de la cocina griega. El arroz, el queso feta, las pasas de Corinto y las semillas constituyen un delicioso relleno alternativo.

Tiempo de preparación: unos 30 minutos, más tiempo en remojo
Tiempo de cocción: 1 hora y 30 minutos
Temperatura del horno: 190°C
PARA 10–12 PERSONAS

- *3–4 berenjenas*
- *sal*
- *aceite de oliva, para freír*
- *¾ taza de arroz integral de grano corto*
- *375 g de tomates triturados, en lata*
- *1 cebolla, picada*
- *3 cucharadas de perejil fresco, picado*
- *½ taza de aceite de oliva*
- *3 dientes de ajo, picados*
- *pimienta negra recién molida, al gusto*
- *2 cucharadas de semillas de girasol*
- *2 cucharadas de piñones*
- *½ taza de pasas de Corinto*
- *100 g de queso feta, rallado*

PARA LA SALSA

- *1½ tazas de harina*
- *½ taza de mantequilla*
- *3½ tazas de leche caliente*
- *5 huevos, más 1 yema*
- *sal y pimienta negra recién molida, al gusto*
- *300 g de queso kefalotyri o feta, rallado*

1 Corte las berenjenas en rodajas finas en sentido longitudinal y colóquelas en un plato llano. Cúbralas con agua fría y espolvoréelas con abundante sal; déjelas en remojo durante unos 30 minutos. Aclare las rodajas de berenjena bajo el chorro de agua fría y séquelas con papel de cocina. Caliente un poco de aceite de oliva y fría las rodajas, por tandas si es necesario, entre 10 y 15 minutos, hasta que estén tiernas y doradas. Déles la vuelta de vez en cuando durante la cocción y, con una espumadera, páselas a un plato llano forrado con papel de cocina, a fin de que escurran el aceite; resérvelas.

2 Lave el arroz y escúrralo. Hiérvalo entre 20 y 25 minutos, hasta que esté tierno. Escúrralo y devuélvalo a la cacerola junto con los tomates, la cebolla, el perejil, el aceite de oliva y el ajo; condiméntelo con sal y pimienta negra recién molida. Déjelo cocer a fuego lento durante 10 minutos y remuévalo de vez en cuando, hasta que el arroz se haya embebido casi todo el líquido. Retírelo del fuego e incorpore las semillas, los piñones, las pasas de Corinto y el queso. Resérvelo.

3 Precaliente el horno a 190°C. Para elaborar la salsa mezcle la harina con la mantequilla en un cazo grande y caliéntelo a fuego lento, sin dejar de remover, hasta que la mantequilla se derrita y la mezcla adquiera una textura fina. Vierta la leche caliente de manera gradual y con cuidado para que no se formen grumos. Lleve la salsa a ebullición y no deje de remover hasta que se espese. Retire el cazo del fuego y agregue los huevos, la yema, la sal, la pimienta negra recién molida y el queso.

4 Coloque la mitad de la berenjena frita formando una capa en el fondo de una fuente de horno de unos 25 x 30 cm. Vierta la mezcla de arroz y espárzala de manera uniforme, añada el resto de las rodajas de berenjena. Nápelo todo con la salsa de queso espesa y hornee la *moussaka* entre 35 y 40 minutos, hasta que la superficie esté dorada y esté todo bien caliente. Déjela enfriar un poco antes de cortarla en porciones para servir.

Champiñones a la griega

MANITARIA

El secreto de este plato radica en su simplicidad. Para prepararlo tan sólo se precisan champiñones frescos y firmes y aceite de oliva de primera calidad.

Tiempo de preparación: unos 10 minutos
Tiempo de cocción: unos 15 minutos
PARA 6–8 PERSONAS

- *⅔ taza de aceite de oliva*
- *½ taza de vino blanco seco*
- *sal y pimienta negra recién molida, al gusto*
- *1 cucharadita de tomillo seco*
- *3 dientes de ajo, majados*
- *4 cucharadas de perejil fresco, picado*
- *500 g de champiñones pequeños, limpios*
- *el zumo de 1 limón recién exprimido*
- *perejil fresco picado, para decorar*

1 Vierta todos los ingredientes, menos los champiñones y la mitad del zumo de limón, en una cacerola; deje que rompa el hervor. Baje el fuego y añada los champiñones; remuévalos y cuézalos tapados a fuego lento de 8 a 10 minutos.

2 Pase los champiñones con el líquido de la cocción a una fuente de servir y déjelos enfriar del todo. Sírvalos a temperatura ambiente rociados con el zumo de limón restante; decórelos con el perejil fresco picado.

ABAJO
Bares y tabernas, puestos de cuero y otros tenderetes se amontonan en el paseo marítimo del puerto de Haniá en busca de clientes. En primavera, que es temporada baja, el paseo resulta más apacible.

Berenjenas estofadas

MELITZANES YIAHNI

Esta meze tan condimentada debe acompañarse a la mesa con abundante pan recién hecho, queso feta y un vino tinto de mucho cuerpo.

Tiempo de preparación: unos 20 minutos, más tiempo en reposo
Tiempo de cocción: unos 50–60 minutos
PARA 4–6 PERSONAS

- *3 berenjenas grandes*
- *sal*
- *½ taza de aceite de oliva*
- *2 cebollas, cortadas por la mitad y en rodajas*
- *4 dientes de ajo, majados*
- *700 g de tomates pelados, sin semillas y troceados*
- *3 cucharadas de perejil fresco, picado*
- *sal y pimienta negra recién molida, al gusto*

1 Corte las berenjenas en rodajas de unos 5 cm de grosor y colóquelas en un colador. Espolvoréelas con abundante sal y déjelas reposar entre 30 y 45 minutos. Enjuague las berenjenas bajo el chorro de agua fría y escúrralas bien.

2 En una cacerola grande con aceite de oliva, rehogue la cebolla entre 3 y 5 minutos hasta que esté tierna. Añada entonces los trozos de berenjena y remuévalos para que se unten bien con el aceite.

3 Vierta el ajo, los tomates y el perejil en la cacerola, y condiméntelo con sal y pimienta negra recién molida. Agregue un poco de agua para humedecer la mezcla, si lo cree necesario. Tape la cacerola y cuézalo a fuego lento durante unos 50 ó 55 minutos, hasta que la berenjena esté muy tierna y la salsa se espese. Sírvalo caliente o frío.

Ensalada de hortalizas asadas

BRIAM

Este plato ligero y fácil de preparar es uno de los favoritos en toda Grecia durante los meses de primavera y verano.

Tiempo de preparación: unos 10 minutos
Tiempo de cocción: unas 2 horas
Temperatura del horno: 180°C

PARA 6–8 PERSONAS

- *6 cucharadas de aceite de oliva*
- *3 cebollas, cortadas en aros*
- *700 g de patatas pequeñas, peladas, cortadas por la mitad y en rodajas gruesas*
- *700 g de calabacines, cortados en rodajas gruesas*
- *8 tomates maduros, pelados y troceados*
- *2 pimientos, sin semillas y cortados en rodajas*
- *4 dientes de ajo, picados*
- *1 cucharadita de orégano seco*
- *4 cucharadas de perejil fresco, picado*
- *2 cucharadas de eneldo fresco, picado*
- *sal y pimienta negra recién molida, al gusto*
- *½ taza de agua*

1 Precaliente el horno a 180°C. En una sartén con 2 cucharadas de aceite de oliva, rehogue la cebolla durante 3 ó 5 minutos hasta que se ablande, pero sin que llegue a dorarse. Retírelo del fuego.

2 En una fuente para asar mezcle la cebolla salteada con las patatas, el calabacín, los tomates, el pimiento, el ajo, las hierbas aromáticas, la sal y la pimienta. Agregue el agua y hornéelo todo entre 1½ y 2 horas, hasta que las hortalizas estén tiernas y bien cocidas; remueva dos veces durante la cocción. Sirva el plato frío o caliente.

Judías de careta con espinacas

LOUVIA ME LAHANA

Plato típico griego que se sirve en primavera, una vez pasadas las lluvias, cuando las verduras se encuentran en su máximo esplendor. La acelga es la más adecuada para esta receta pero las espinacas son un buen sustituto.

Tiempo de preparación: unos 30 minutos
Tiempo de cocción: unos 30 minutos
PARA 4-6 PERSONAS

- *1½ tazas de judías de careta, en remojo toda la noche*
- *450 g de acelgas o espinacas*
- *aceite de oliva*
- *2 cucharadas de zumo de limón recién exprimido*
- *sal y pimienta negra recién molida, al gusto*
- *perejil fresco, picado, para decorar*

1 Vierta las judías de careta en una cacerola mediana y cúbralas con agua. Llévelas a ebullición, escúrralas y enjuáguelas.

2 Devuelva las judías a la cacerola y cúbralas con agua fresca; deje que rompa el hervor y cuézalas a fuego lento entre 25 y 30 minutos, hasta que estén prácticamente tiernas. Agregue un poco más de agua durante la cocción, a fin de que las judías queden sumergidas en todo momento.

3 Corte las acelgas o las espinacas en tiras y añádalas a las judías; cuézalo otros 3 ó 4 minutos, hasta que la verdura se ablande. Escurra todo bien y páselo a una fuente de servir. Rocíelo con el aceite de oliva y el zumo de limón, salpimiéntelo y sírvalo caliente; aderécelo con perejil fresco picado.

A LA IZQUIERDA
La bendición de la palma el domingo de Pascua constituye toda una tradición en Grecia.

C A P Í T U L O 3

Carne

Albóndigas en salsa de tomate

Moussaka

Rollitos de cordero

Gratinado de pasta

Albóndigas de carne y arroz en salsa de limón

Carne de cerdo con trigo

Hamburguesas a la griega

Estofado de cordero con menta y salvia

Estofado de salchichas con pimientos

Bistec estofado

Estofado de carne con cebolla

Chuletas de cordero con queso

Pinchos de carne de cordero

Macarrones con jamón

Cordero en papillote

Pinchos de carne picada

Albóndigas en salsa de tomate

GIOUVARLAKIA

Este plato, rico y sabroso, puede prepararse con antelación y guardarse en el frigorífico; de hecho, sabe mucho mejor si se consume al día siguiente, recalentado.

Tiempo de preparación: unos 30 minutos
Tiempo de cocción: unos 30 minutos
PARA 6–8 PERSONAS

- *700 g de carne de cordero, picada*
- *2 rebanadas de pan integral de trigo*
- *¼ taza de leche*
- *1 cucharada de aceite de oliva*
- *1 cebolla, picada*
- *1 tomate pelado, sin semillas y troceado*
- *⅔ taza de arroz de grano largo*
- *1 cucharada de menta fresca, picada*
- *una pizca de canela molida*
- *2 cucharadas de perejil fresco, picado*
- *1 huevo, batido*
- *¼ taza de vino tinto*
- *sal y pimienta negra recién molida, al gusto*
- *5 tazas de agua*
- *4 cucharadas de concentrado de tomate*
- *1 diente de ajo, majado*
- *perejil fresco picado, para decorar*

1 Introduzca la carne de cordero picada en un bol. Aparte, separe la corteza del pan y ponga éste en un plato; rocíelo con la leche y déjelo 10 minutos a remojo, hasta que se haya embebido todo el líquido. Pase el pan al bol con la carne y amase la mezcla con las manos, a fin de dejarla homogénea.

2 En una cacerola pequeña, rehogue la cebolla y la pulpa de tomate troceado durante unos 5 minutos. Vierta la mezcla obtenida en el bol y añada el arroz, la menta, la canela, el perejil, el huevo batido, el vino, la sal y la pimienta negra recién molida; mézclelo todo bien.

3 Vierta el agua en una sartén grande y honda junto con el concentrado de tomate y remuévalo. Añada el ajo y déjelo a fuego lento hasta que rompa el hervor; cuézalo a fuego lento durante unos 5 minutos.

4 Humedézcase las manos ligeramente para moldear la mezcla de carne en forma de albóndigas, del tamaño de una pelota de golf, y colóquelas con cuidado en la sartén con la salsa de tomate. Tape la sartén y deje cocer todo unos 30 minutos, hasta que el arroz esté hecho y la salsa se espese. Sirva las albóndigas aderezadas con perejil picado.

Moussaka

Considerada como el plato nacional griego, la *Moussaka* se prepara alternando capas de berenjena, cebolla y carne picada de cordero, que se recubren con salsa bechamel.

Tiempo de preparación: 1 hora aproximadamente
Tiempo de cocción: unas 2 horas y 30 minutos
Temperatura del horno: 180°C
PARA 10–12 PERSONAS

- *5 berenjenas grandes, lavadas y cortadas en rodajas longitudinales*
- *sal*
- *aceite de oliva, para untar*
- *2 tazas de pan blanco fresco, rallado*
- *150 g de queso feta, rallado*

PARA LA SALSA BECHAMEL

- *½ taza de mantequilla*
- *¾ taza de harina*
- *5 tazas de leche caliente*
- *sal y pimienta negra recién molida, al gusto*
- *una pizca generosa de nuez moscada, rallada*
- *3 yemas de huevo*

PARA LA SALSA DE CARNE

- *2 cucharadas de aceite de oliva*
- *4 cebollas, troceadas*
- *1 kg de carne magra de cordero, picada*
- *750 g de tomates triturados, en lata*
- *3 dientes de ajo, majados*
- *½ cucharadita de canela*
- *una pizca de pimienta de Jamaica, molida*
- *sal y pimienta negra*
- *4 cucharadas de concentrado de tomate*
- *½ taza de vino tinto seco*

1 Disponga las rodajas de berenjena sobre la superficie de trabajo y sálelas bien por ambas caras. Déjelas reposar unos 30 minutos para que "suden" y suelten todo el líquido; aclárelas bajo el chorro de agua fría.

2 Coloque en una parrilla tantas rodajas de berenjena como le quepan y úntelas con abundante aceite de oliva. Áselas entre 5 y 10 minutos; déles la vuelta una vez y vuélvalas a untar con aceite de oliva durante la cocción. Ase todas las rodajas hasta que presenten un tono dorado por ambas caras.

3 Unte una fuente de horno de 28 x 38 x 7,5 cm con aceite de oliva y esparza el pan rallado por el fondo de manera uniforme. Para la salsa bechamel, derrita la mantequilla en un cazo grande, vierta la harina y remuévala bien hasta obtener un roux espeso; déjelo cocer unos 30 segundos y retírelo del fuego. Añada la leche de manera gradual y remueva la salsa después de cada adición para evitar que se formen grumos. Vuelva a poner el cazo al fuego y déjelo cocer a fuego lento hasta que rompa el hervor; no deje de remover hasta que la salsa se espese y empiece a hervir. Retírela del fuego y condiméntela con sal, pimienta negra recién molida y nuez moscada. Déjela enfriar un poco e incorpore las yemas de huevo; bátalo todo bien. Cubra la salsa con una lámina de papel encerado, así evitará que se forme una película en la superficie. Resérvela.

4 Para la salsa de carne, caliente el aceite de oliva en una cacerola grande y pesada. Saltee la cebolla hasta que esté tierna. Añada la carne picada y remueva. Cuézalo todo durante 10 minutos, sin dejar de remover, hasta que la carne pierda su tono rosado. Incorpore los tomates, el ajo y las especias, y condiméntelo con sal y pimienta negra recién molida. Vierta el concentrado de tomate y el vino tinto.

5 Baje el fuego, tape y deje cocer a fuego lento durante 45 minutos. Agregue más agua durante la cocción, si lo cree necesario. Destape la cacerola durante los últimos 15 minutos de la cocción, a fin de que se evapore la humedad. Deje la salsa aparte para que se enfríe.

6 Precaliente el horno a 180°C. Disponga una capa de rodajas de berenjena en el fondo de la fuente ya preparada y cúbrala con otra capa de salsa de carne. Alterne otra capa más de berenjena con otra de carne y así sucesivamente hasta terminar con una capa de berenjena; con cuidado vierta la salsa bechamel por encima y extiéndala de manera uniforme. Espolvoree todo con el queso feta rallado y hornéelo durante 1 hora o hasta que la superficie esté dorada y la *moussaka* esté bien caliente. Sírvala enseguida.

ABAJO
Vista de la meseta de Lesithi, un paisaje típicamente griego.

Rollitos de cordero

ARNI EXOHIKO

***Exohiko* es la palabra griega para campo y, tal como su propio nombre indica, esta meze resulta ideal para tomar en picnics. Como resulta muy fácil de preparar, hágala con antelación y congélela cruda. Luego sólo deberá descongelarla y hornearla según se indica a continuación.**

Tiempo de preparación: 1 hora aproximadamente
Tiempo de cocción: unas 3 horas
Temperatura del horno: 190°C
PARA 10–15 PERSONAS

- *3,5 kg de pierna de cordero*
- *4 dientes de ajo, cortados en astillas*
- *sal y pimienta negra recién molida, al gusto*
- *2 cucharaditas de orégano seco*
- *1½ tazas de mantequilla, derretida*
- *3 cucharadas de zumo de limón recién exprimido*
- *2 zanahorias, peladas*
- *2 tallos de apio, limpios*
- *1 cebolla, en cuartos*
- *450 g de pasta filo*
- *8 tazas de pan blanco fresco, rallado*
- *200 g de queso feta, rallado*

ABAJO
Las delicadas rejas de hierro forjado son características de la arquitectura helénica.

1 Precaliente el horno a 190°C. Con un cuchillo afilado practique pequeñas incisiones por toda la pierna de cordero e inserte en ellas las astillas de ajo. Pase el cordero a una fuente de asar, salpimiéntelo y esparza por encima el orégano. Rocíelo con un poco de mantequilla fundida y todo el zumo de limón. Añada la zanahoria, el apio y la cebolla a la fuente de asar y áselo todo entre 2 y 2½ horas hasta que la carne esté tierna y el jugo de la cocción presente un tono más bien claro. Pase la carne a una tabla de trinchar y córtela en trozos de unos 2,5 cm; deseche la grasa y los huesos. Deje enfriar la carne.

2 Separe una lámina de pasta filo y úntela con un poco de mantequilla fundida; mantenga el resto de la pasta cubierta con un paño ligeramente húmedo. Pliegue la lámina por la mitad y úntela de nuevo con mantequilla. Esparza un poco de pan rallado por encima.

3 Coloque unos cuantos trozos de carne sobre un extremo de la pasta filo y espolvoree un poco de queso por encima. Enrolle la pasta de modo que el relleno quede bien encerrado y coloque el rollito, con la costura hacia abajo, en una bandeja de horno ligeramente engrasada. Repita la operación con la pasta y el relleno restantes. Unte los rollitos con el resto de la mantequilla derretida y hornéelos durante 30 minutos hasta que estén crujientes y dorados.

A LA DERECHA
La vespa para ir de compras y la madera para la leña... esperan en Psichró a que se termine la hora de la siesta.

Gratinado de pasta

PASTITSIO

Sin duda alguna el nombre de este plato proviene del italiano, pero el método de cocer la pasta y la carne en una misma fuente sólo podía ser griego.

Tiempo de preparación: 1 hora aproximadamente
Tiempo de cocción: unas 2 horas
Temperatura del horno: 180°C
PARA 10–12 PERSONAS

- *6 cucharadas de aceite de oliva*
- *3 cebollas, picadas*
- *700 g de carne magra de vacuno, picada*
- *2 dientes de ajo, majados*
- *750 g de tomates triturados*
- *2 cucharaditas de canela*
- *1 ½ cucharaditas de pimienta de Jamaica*
- *1 cucharadita de nuez moscada, molida*
- *sal y pimienta negra, recién molida*
- *700 g de espaguetis*

PARA LA SALSA DE QUESO

- *½ taza de mantequilla*
- *¾ taza de harina*
- *5 tazas de leche caliente*
- *sal y pimienta negra*
- *200 g de queso feta o kefalotyri, rallado*
- *3 yemas de huevo*

1 Caliente 2 cucharadas de aceite de oliva en una cacerola grande y rehogue las cebollas hasta que estén tiernas, pero no doradas. Añada la carne de vacuno picada y cuézala, sin dejar de remover, hasta que pierda su tono rosado.

2 Agregue el ajo, los tomates triturados y las especias, y condimente todo con sal y pimienta negra recién molida. Tape la cacerola y deje cocer a fuego lento durante 40 minutos. Agregue más agua durante la cocción, si lo cree necesario. Destape la cacerola durante los últimos 10 minutos, a fin de que se evapore la humedad retenida; déjelo enfriar.

3 Mientras tanto, lleve a ebullición una olla grande con agua y vierta los espaguetis; déjelos hervir entre 10 y 15 minutos hasta que estén al dente, es decir, hasta que la pasta esté hecha, pero no blanda. Escúrrala y aclárela bajo el chorro de agua caliente. Devuelva la pasta a la olla y añada 2 cucharadas más de aceite de oliva.

4 Para la salsa de queso, derrita la mantequilla en un cazo grande y vierta la harina; remueva la mezcla hasta obtener un roux espeso y cuézalo durante 30 segundos; retírelo del fuego. Agregue la leche caliente de manera gradual y remueva bien después de cada adición para que no se formen grumos. Devuelva la salsa al fuego y condiméntela con sal y pimienta negra recién molida. Vierta el queso rallado y déjelo cocer a fuego lento hasta que arranque el hervor; no deje de remover, hasta que la salsa se haya espesado y borbotee. Incorpore las yemas de huevo y bátalo bien.

5 Precaliente el horno a 180°C. Unte una fuente de horno de 28 x 38 x 7,5 cm con aceite de oliva y reparta la mitad de los espaguetis por el fondo. Vierta la salsa de carne y espárzala de modo uniforme sobre la pasta. Coloque otra capa de espaguetis y nápela con la salsa de queso; hornee todo durante unos 45 minutos o hasta que la superficie esté bien dorada y el *pastitsio* esté caliente.

Albóndigas de carne y arroz en salsa de limón

YUVERLAKIA

Este plato, cuyo nombre, *Yuverlakia*, significa "bolitas", se encuentra a medio camino entre una sopa consistente y un estofado.

Tiempo de preparación: unos 30 minutos
Tiempo de cocción: unos 50 minutos
PARA 8–10 PERSONAS

- *450 g de carne picada de cerdo*
- *¾ taza de arroz de grano largo*
- *1 cebolla grande, picada*
- *2 dientes de ajo, majados*
- *4 cucharadas de perejil fresco, picado*
- *2 cucharadas de menta fresca, picada*
- *1 cucharadita de orégano seco*
- *1 yema de huevo*
- *sal y pimienta negra recién molida, al gusto*
- *harina, para rebozar*
- *3 cucharadas de aceite de oliva*
- *3 huevos, batidos*
- *el zumo de 2 limones recién exprimido, colado*
- *perejil fresco, para decorar*

1 Mezcle, en un bol grande, la carne picada de cerdo con el arroz, la cebolla, el ajo y las especias. Añada la yema de huevo y condiméntelo todo con sal y pimienta negra recién molida; remueva todo bien. Con las manos ligeramente humedecidas, moldee la mezcla resultante en forma de bolitas de unos 5 cm de diámetro; espolvoréelas con harina.

2 Introduzca las albóndigas en una sartén grande y honda con el aceite de oliva, y vierta suficiente agua hirviendo para cubrirlas. Tape y deje cocer todo a fuego lento entre 35 y 40 minutos, hasta que la carne y el arroz estén cocidos. Agregue más agua durante la cocción, si lo cree necesario, a fin de que las albóndigas queden sumergidas en el agua todo el tiempo.

3 Para la salsa de limón, bata los huevos junto con el zumo de limón hasta obtener una mezcla espumosa. Añada 2 cucharadas del jugo de la cocción de las albóndigas y bátalo enérgicamente para evitar que se cuaje. Retire la sartén del fuego y vierta la mezcla de huevo sobre las albóndigas. Devuelva la sartén al fuego y remuévalo constantemente hasta que la mezcla se espese, pero sin que llegue a romper el hervor. Pase las albóndigas y la salsa a una fuente de servir precalentada y aderécelo con el perejil fresco picado.

Carne de cerdo con trigo

KISKEKI

Este plato simple y de larga tradición rural se solía preparar con manteca de cerdo o "gleena". En esta receta se ha substituido por aceite de oliva con la intención de obtener un plato más saludable. El trigo entero puede adquirirse en establecimientos de productos naturales.

Tiempo de preparación: unos 30 minutos
Tiempo de cocción: unas 4 horas

PARA 8–10 PERSONAS

- *¼ taza de aceite de oliva*
- *1 kg de filete de cerdo, cortado en trozos grandes*
- *sal y pimienta negra recién molida, al gusto*
- *2–3 guindillas rojas, sin semillas y picadas*
- *1⅓ tazas de granos de trigo*
- *¼ taza de mantequilla*
- *2 cebollas, peladas y picadas*
- *1 cucharadita de comino molido*
- *yogur natural o al estilo griego, para servir*

1 En una cacerola grande con aceite caliente, rehogue la carne de cerdo hasta dorarla de manera uniforme. Añada agua hasta cubrir la carne y cuézala a fuego lento, hasta que rompa el hervor. Condimente todo con sal y pimienta negra. Añada las guindillas rojas, baje el fuego, tape la cacerola y deje cocer la carne lentamente durante 2 horas o hasta que esté muy tierna.

2 Mientras tanto, vierta los granos de trigo en una cacerola de tamaño mediano; agregue agua hasta una altura de 7 cm por encima del trigo. Deje que rompa el hervor, remueva y baje el fuego. Tape la cacerola y deje cocer el trigo a fuego lento durante 1½ horas o hasta que esté tierno. Retírelo del fuego y escúrralo.

3 Derrita la mantequilla en una sartén y rehogue la cebolla hasta que esté tierna, pero no dorada; resérvela. Pase la carne de cerdo cocida a una tabla de trinchar y, mediante dos tenedores, desmenuce la carne en trozos pequeños; pásela a una fuente de servir precalentada junto con el trigo. Revuelva todo y vierta por encima la cebolla salteada y la mantequilla. Esparza el comino molido también por encima y sirva el plato acompañado de yogur griego.

Hamburguesas a la griega

KEPHTEDES

Las hamburguesas al estilo griego pueden servirse frías o calientes; lo más importante es no cocerlas demasiado.

Tiempo de preparación: unos 30 minutos
Tiempo de cocción: unos 40 minutos
PARA 6-8 PERSONAS

- *500 g de carne picada de vacuno*
- *2 rebanadas de pan, sin corteza*
- *2 cucharadas de leche*
- *3 cucharadas de aceite de oliva*
- *¼ taza de mantequilla*
- *1 cebolla pequeña, picada*
- *1 diente de ajo, majado*
- *1 zanahoria pequeña, rallada*
- *1 tomate, pelado y picado*
- *4 cucharadas de perejil fresco, picado*
- *2 cucharadas de vino tinto*
- *sal y pimienta negra recién molida, al gusto*
- *1¾ tazas de harina*

1 Vierta la carne picada en un bol y, en un plato aparte, el pan junto con la leche. Deje el pan a remojo durante 5 minutos hasta que se embeba toda la leche y añádalo a la carne; mezcle todo bien y resérvelo por el momento.

2 En una sartén con 1 cucharada de aceite de oliva y 1 cucharada de mantequilla bien caliente, rehogue la cebolla, el ajo, la zanahoria y el tomate durante unos 7 minutos o hasta que la cebolla se dore.

3 Añada las hortalizas rehogadas al bol con la carne y agregue el perejil, el vino, la sal y la pimienta negra recién molida; remuévalo bien y déjelo reposar unos 30 minutos.

4 Espolvoree una bandeja de horno con harina. Con las manos ligeramente humedecidas, moldee la mezcla de carne en forma de hamburguesas y reboce ambas caras con harina. Disponga las hamburguesas enharinadas en una bandeja de horno limpia y forrada con papel encerado.

5 Caliente la mantequilla y el aceite de oliva restantes en una sartén grande, hasta que empiecen a chisporrotear. Fría las hamburguesas por tandas durante 5 minutos cada lado. Déles la vuelta con cuidado y añada un poco más de aceite de oliva y mantequilla, si lo cree necesario, con cada una de las tandas. Pase las hamburguesas hechas a una fuente de servir precalentada, mientras termina de freír el resto. Sírvalas frías o calientes.

Estofado de cordero con menta y salvia

ARNI ME DIOSMO KAI FASCOMILO

Se trata de un *pilau* tradicional griego, para el que se puede utilizar tanto carne de cordero como de ternera.

Tiempo de preparación: unos 30 minutos
Tiempo de cocción: 1 hora y 20 minutos
PARA 6–8 PERSONAS

- *¼ taza de aceite de oliva*
- *1 kg de filete de cordero magro, cortado en dados de 2 cm*
- *1 cebolla picada*
- *2 zanahorias, en dados*
- *½ taza de vino blanco seco*
- *sal y pimienta negra recién molida, al gusto*
- *⅔ taza de almendras fileteadas*
- *3¾ tazas de agua*
- *1⅓ tazas de arroz de grano largo*
- *⅓ taza de uvas pasas*
- *⅓ taza de sultanas*
- *½ cucharadita de salvia seca*
- *1 cucharadita de menta seca*

1 En una cacerola grande con aceite caliente, rehogue la carne cortada en dados y remuévala con frecuencia, hasta que adquiera un tono dorado uniforme. Añada la cebolla y la zanahoria y rehóguelo todo otros 5 minutos más. Vierta el vino, remuévalo y salpimiéntelo. Deje que rompa el hervor, tape la cacerola y cuézalo todo durante 10 minutos.

2 Mientras tanto, tueste las almendras en el horno o en una sartén de fondo pesado hasta que se doren; resérvelas.

3 Vierta el agua en la mezcla de carne y déjela cocer a fuego lento durante unos 30 minutos; remueva de vez en cuando. Agregue el arroz, las sultanas, las pasas, la salvia y la menta, y condimente todo de nuevo, si lo cree necesario. Tape la cacerola y deje cocer de 30 a 35 minutos más, hasta que el arroz esté hecho y la carne esté bien tierna. Agregue más agua durante la cocción, si fuera necesario. Esparza las almendras tostadas sobre el *pilau* y sírvalo bien caliente.

Estofado de salchichas con pimientos

SPETSOFAI

Esta receta es la versión en cazuela de un plato griego que, tradicionalmente, se cuece al horno en boles de arcilla individuales. Es una preparación simple que se sirve tanto en los hogares como en las tabernas rurales de Grecia.

Tiempo de preparación: unos 15 minutos
Tiempo de cocción: 1 hora y 20 minutos
PARA 6–8 PERSONAS

- *3 cucharadas de aceite de oliva*
- *700 g de salchichas de buena calidad, pinchadas con un tenedor*
- *2 cebollas, cortadas en aros*
- *5 pimientos de distinto color, sin semillas y cortados en rodajas de 1 cm*
- *700 g de tomates, pelados y cortados en rodajas*
- *3 dientes de ajo, majados*
- *2 cucharaditas de orégano seco*
- *½ taza de vino tinto seco*
- *sal y pimienta negra recién molida, al gusto*
- *salvia fresca, picada, para aderezar*

1 En una sartén grande con aceite caliente, fría las salchichas hasta que adquieran un tono dorado uniforme; remuévalas con frecuencia durante la cocción. Páselas a un plato con papel de cocina para que escurran el aceite.

2 Vierta la cebolla y los pimientos en la sartén, y rehóguelos durante unos 10 minutos, hasta que se ablanden. Añada los tomates, el ajo y el orégano.

3 Devuelva las salchichas a la sartén y rocíelas con el vino. Condimente todo con sal y pimienta negra recién molida y déjelo cocer, tapado y a fuego lento, durante 1 hora, hasta que las salchichas estén cocidas. Vierta un poco más de agua durante la cocción, si lo cree necesario. Sirva las salchichas con salvia fresca picada por encima.

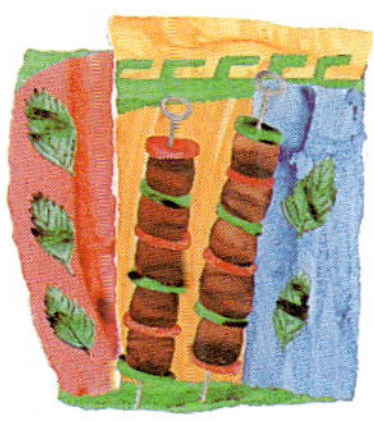

Bistec estofado

SOFRITO

Esta especialidad, típica de la isla de Corfú, es la manera más fácil y sabrosa de servir la carne en una comida a base de meze.

Tiempo de preparación: unos 10 minutos
Tiempo de cocción: unas 2 horas
PARA 6–8 PERSONAS

- *1 kg de carne de vacuno, en lonchas de unos 2 cm*
- *4 cucharadas de harina*
- *sal y pimienta negra recién molida, al gusto*
- *1 cucharadita de tomillo seco*
- *¼ taza de aceite de oliva*
- *6 cucharadas de vinagre de vino tinto*
- *6 cucharadas de agua*
- *2 dientes de ajo, majados*
- *1 cucharada de concentrado de tomate*
- *2 cucharadas de perejil fresco, picado, para aderezar*

1 Vierta la carne en un bol y espolvoréela con la harina, la sal, la pimienta negra recién molida y el tomillo. Revuélvala bien para que quede rebozada con la mezcla.

2 Caliente la mitad del aceite en una sartén y rehogue la mitad de la carne durante unos 5 minutos o hasta que adquiera un tono dorado uniforme. Remuévalo a menudo durante la cocción. Pásela a un plato de servir y vierta el resto del aceite en la sartén; una vez caliente, fría el resto de la carne y, cuando esté dorada, devuelva la primera tanda a la sartén.

3 Añada el vinagre, el agua, el ajo y el concentrado de tomate; remuévalo. Deje que rompa el hervor, tápelo y cuézalo a fuego lento entre 1 y 1½ horas, o hasta que la carne esté tierna y la salsa se espese. Agregue más agua durante la cocción, si lo cree necesario. Aderécelo con perejil picado.

Estofado de carne con cebolla

STEFADO

Este estofado, perteneciente al recetario clásico, también puede elaborarse con carne de ternera.

Tiempo de preparación: unos 15 minutos
Tiempo de cocción: unas 2 horas
PARA 8–10 PERSONAS

- *¼ taza de mantequilla*
- *1,5 kg de aguja de vacuno, en dados de 5 cm*
- *1¼ tazas de vino tinto seco*
- *375 g de tomates triturados, en lata*
- *4 cucharadas de concentrado de tomate*
- *1¼ tazas de agua hirviendo*
- *3 cucharadas de aceite de oliva*
- *3 cebollas, picadas*
- *3 dientes de ajo, majados*
- *1 cucharadita de canela molida*
- *½ cucharadita de orégano seco*
- *sal y pimienta negra*
- *4 cucharadas de perejil fresco, picado, para aderezar*

1 Derrita la mantequilla en una cacerola grande y pesada, y vierta la carne en dados; remuévala de modo que se dore de manera uniforme.

2 Agregue la mitad del vino y cuézalo a fuego lento durante 5 minutos. Vierta los tomates triturados, el concentrado de tomate y el agua hirviendo; tape la cacerola y deje cocer todo durante 10 minutos.

3 Mientras tanto, en una sartén con aceite caliente, rehogue la cebolla y el ajo durante unos 5 minutos hasta que estén dorados. Añádalos a la cacerola con la carne, junto con la canela, el orégano, la sal y la pimienta negra recién molida. Tape la cacerola y déjelo cocer a fuego lento entre 1 y 1½ horas, hasta que la carne esté muy tierna; agregue el resto del vino durante la cocción. Espolvoree el perejil fresco picado por encima antes de servirlo.

Chuletas de cordero con queso

ARNI PALIKARI

Esta combinación a base de queso y carne de cordero puede sonar atípica, pero no por ello menos deliciosa. Se asa envuelta en papel de aluminio, a fin de retener todo el aroma.

Tiempo de preparación: unos 20 minutos
Tiempo de cocción: unas 2 horas
Temperatura del horno: 180°C
PARA 4 PERSONAS

- *4 chuletas de cordero*
- *2 cucharadas de mantequilla*
- *1 cebolla, cortada en aros*
- *2 dientes de ajo, majados*
- *3 tomates, cortados en rodajas*
- *3 cucharaditas de orégano seco*
- *sal y pimienta negra recién molida, al gusto*
- *100 g de queso kaseri o gruyere, cortado en lonchas finas*

1 Fría las chuletas en una sartén, sin nada de grasa, unos 3 minutos por cada lado, hasta que se doren uniformemente. Corte 4 piezas cuadradas de papel de aluminio de 30 cm de lado y coloque una chuleta en el centro de cada una de ellas.

2 Precaliente el horno a 180° C. Derrita la mantequilla en una sartén y sofría la cebolla y el ajo durante unos 3 minutos. Con una cuchara de madera, reparta la mezcla de cebolla entre las chuletas; reparta también las rodajas de tomate entre los paquetes de aluminio y colóquelos encima de la cebolla. Espolvoree todo con el orégano y salpimiéntelo. Esparza el queso por encima de cada una de las chuletas.

3 Lleve los cuatro extremos de la hoja de papel de aluminio hacia el centro y retuérzalas con los dedos de modo que resulte un paquetito bien cerrado. Pase los paquetitos a una bandeja de horno y hornéelos entre 1½ y 2 horas, hasta que la carne esté tierna y bien caliente. Sirva las chuletas en sus respectivos envoltorios de aluminio.

Pinchos de carne de cordero

SOUVLAKIA

Estos pinchitos de carne se suelen asar a la barbacoa y pueden servirse como tentempié, aperitivo, plato principal, o bien como parte integrante de una comida a base de meze. El limón es el ingrediente secreto de esta receta y debe ser recién exprimido.

Tiempo de preparación: 20 minutos, más tiempo en marinada
Tiempo de cocción: unos 10 minutos
PARA 4-6 PERSONAS

- *3 cucharadas de aceite de oliva*
- *3 cucharadas de zumo de limón, recién exprimido*
- *2 cucharaditas de tomillo seco*
- *2 dientes de ajo, majados*
- *pimienta negra, recién molida*
- *1 kg de carne magra de cordero, cortada en dados de 2,5 cm*
- *unas 14 hojas de laurel*
- *gajos de limón, para decorar*

1 Para la marinada mezcle el aceite de oliva, el zumo de limón, el tomillo, el ajo y la pimienta negra recién molida en un tarro con tapa de rosca. Ciérrelo bien y agítelo bien para que todos los ingredientes se entremezclen.

2 Disponga la carne en un plato llano. Trocee 2 hojas de laurel y espárzalas por encima de la carne; rocíe ésta con la marinada y remuévala para que quede bien napada. Cúbrala y refrigérela durante unas 2 horas.

3 Ensarte el resto de las hojas de laurel en cuatro brochetas y altérnelas con los dados de carne. Precaliente la parrilla y ase los pinchos de 5 a 10 minutos, hasta que la carne esté hecha. Úntelos con la marinada reservada y déles la vuelta durante la cocción. Sirva los pinchos acompañados con gajos de limón.

Macarrones con jamón

HIRINO YAHNI MAKARONADA

Una receta griega sencilla y de influencia claramente italiana.

Tiempo de preparación: unos 30 minutos
Tiempo de cocción: unas 3 horas
PARA 10-12 PERSONAS

- *½ taza de mantequilla*
- *1 pieza de jamón de 700 g, cortada en dados de 5 cm*
- *sal y pimienta negra recién molida, al gusto*
- *½ cucharadita de canela molida*
- *1 cebolla grande, picada*
- *8 cucharadas de concentrado de tomate*
- *5 tazas de agua hirviendo*
- *1 ramita de canela*
- *450 g de macarrones*
- *200 g de queso kefalotyri o parmesano, rallado, para servir*

1 Derrita la mitad de la mantequilla en una sartén grande y vierta la mitad del jamón cortado en dados. Condiméntelo con sal y pimienta negra recién molida y añada la canela molida. Sofría el jamón durante unos 5 minutos, dándole la vuelta con frecuencia, hasta que se dore de manera unifome.

2 Derrita la mitad de la mantequilla restante en una cacerola grande y sofría la cebolla de 5 a 7 minutos hasta que esté dorada. Añada la mezcla de carne, junto con el concentrado de tomate, el agua hirviendo y la ramita de canela; déjelo cocer a fuego lento y sin tapar entre 2 y 2½ horas, hasta que la carne esté bien tierna y la salsa empiece a espesarse.

3 Cueza los macarrones en una olla grande con agua hirviendo, hasta que estén al dente. Escúrralos y páselos a una fuente de servir previamente calentada; cúbralos con papel de aluminio para que no se enfríen. Derrita el resto de la mantequilla en una sartén pequeña y sofríala durante unos 3 minutos hasta que esté dorada; viértala sobre los macarrones y esparza el queso rallado por encima. Sirva la pasta napada con la salsa de jamón.

Cordero en papillote

ARNI KLEFTIKO

El auténtico *kleftiko* griego se cuece hasta el punto en que la carne se desprende del hueso por sí sola. El secreto está en la cocción, que es prolongada y se realiza en envoltorios de papel de aluminio, los cuales retienen todo el sabor de la carne hasta que ésta está tan tierna que se deshace en la boca. Se sirve con gajos de limón para refrescar el paladar.

Tiempo de preparación: unos 10 minutos
Tiempo de cocción: unas 2 horas
Temperatura del horno: 180°C
PARA 8 PERSONAS

- *8 chuletas de cordero*
- *4 dientes de ajo, cortados en tiras finas*
- *¼ taza de mantequilla, derretida*
- *3 cucharadas de zumo de limón recién exprimido*
- *sal y pimienta negra, al gusto*
- *1 cucharada de orégano seco*
- *1 cucharada de menta seca*

1 Precaliente el horno a 180°C. Con un cuchillo pequeño y afilado, practique incisiones en las chuletas e introduzca las tiras finas de ajo en las mismas. Coloque una chuleta en el centro de cuadrados de papel de aluminio de unos 30 cm de lado.

2 Distribuya el resto de los ingredientes entre las ocho chuletas y cierre el papel de aluminio juntando los extremos del cuadrado en el centro y retorciéndolos con los dedos.

3 Coloque los paquetitos de aluminio en una bandeja y áselos al horno entre 1½ y 2 horas, hasta que la carne esté muy tierna y bien caliente. Sirva los paquetitos cerrados para que cada comensal abra el suyo.

Pinchos de carne picada

KOFTA

Los ingredientes de las *kofta* varían de una casa a otra y de una región a otra. Esta receta es una invitación a que pruebe su propia variante de uno de los platos griegos más populares.

Tiempo de preparación: unos 15 minutos
Tiempo de cocción: unos 10 minutos
PARA 8–10 PERSONAS

- *1 kg de carne magra de cordero o de vacuno picada, o bien una mezcla de ambas*
- *2 cebollas, picadas o ralladas*
- *1 cucharadita de canela molida*
- *1 cucharadita de pimentón*
- *1 cucharadita de comino molido*
- *1 cucharadita de cilantro molido*
- *2 cucharadas de perejil fresco*
- *2 dientes de ajo, majados*
- *aceite de oliva, para engrasar*

1 Vierta todos los ingredientes en un bol de tamaño grande y remuévalos bien para entremezclarlos.

2 Distribuya la mezcla obtenida entre las brochetas de metal y moldéela con las manos para darle forma de salchicha a lo largo de la brocheta. Unte con aceite la rejilla del grill para evitar que la carne se adhiera a ella. Áselas a fuego alto de 5 a 10 minutos o hasta que la carne esté dorada y bien hecha; déles la vuelta durante la cocción. Sirva los pinchos acompañados de pan pita recién hecho, un buen surtido de ensaladas y gajos de limón, si lo desea.

CAPÍTULO 4

Pollo

Pollo a la parrilla con yogur griego

Pinchos de pollo con ajo

Pollo al orégano

Pollo al limón

Pollo con macarrones

Albóndigas de pollo fritas

Pinchos de pollo

Pollo con queso feta y aceitunas verdes

Pollo guisado con tomate

Alitas de pollo con ajo y zumo de lima

Pollo guisado con patatas

Pollo asado con pistachos

Pastel de pollo

Pollo asado con hortalizas

Pilaf de pollo

Pollo a la parrilla con yogur griego

KOTOPOULO YIAOURTI

En esta receta se han utilizado muslos de pollo, pero puede prepararse con cualquier otra parte de esta ave. El yogur no sólo aporta sabor al plato, sino que además deja la carne más tierna, jugosa y suculenta.

Tiempo de preparación: 10 minutos, más marinada
Tiempo de cocción: unos 20–40 minutos

PARA 6 PERSONAS

- *6 muslos de pollo*
- *3 dientes de ajo, majados*
- *sal y pimienta negra, al gusto*
- *1 cucharadita de pimentón*
- *1 cucharadita de canela*
- *una pizca de pimienta de Cayena*
- *el zumo de 1 limón*
- *¼ taza de aceite de oliva*
- *8 cucharadas de yogur griego*
- *gajos de limón, para decorar*

1 Disponga los muslitos de pollo en un plato grande y llano. En un bol de tamaño mediano, mezcle el ajo con la sal, la pimienta negra recién molida, el pimentón, la canela, la pimienta de Cayena, el zumo de limón, el aceite y el yogur.

2 Vierta la marinada sobre los muslos de pollo y remuévalos de modo que queden bien recubiertos. Tápelos y déjelos marinar en el frigorífico de 2 a 3 horas, o bien durante toda la noche.

3 Sazone otra vez los muslos con abundante sal y pimienta negra recién molida, y páselos a una rejilla de grill untada con aceite. Áselos a la parrilla, previamente calentada, de 20 a 40 minutos, hasta que estén dorados y crujientes por fuera y bien hechos por dentro; déles la vuelta con frecuencia durante la cocción. Sírvalos con gajos de limón.

Pinchos de pollo con ajo

KOTA ME SKORTHO

Un consejo muy práctico: empape las brochetas de metal en zumo de limón durante unos 30 minutos antes de utilizarlas. De este modo el pollo adquiere un ligero sabor ácido y las brochetas no se queman durante la cocción.

Tiempo de preparación: 20 minutos, más marinada
Tiempo de cocción: unos 5–10 minutos

PARA 6 PERSONAS

- *6 filetes de pechuga de pollo, sin piel ni huesos*
- *6 dientes de ajo, majados*
- *sal y pimienta negra recién molida, al gusto*
- *el zumo de 2 limones recién exprimidos*
- *¼ taza de aceite de oliva*
- *6 cucharadas de perejil fresco, picado*

1 Corte los filetes de pollo en trozos de 2,5 cm y páselos a un plato llano.

2 En un bol de tamaño pequeño, mezcle el ajo, la sal y la pimienta negra recién molida, el zumo de limón y el aceite de oliva. Vierta la marinada sobre el pollo, remueva todo, tápelo y déjelo marinar de 2 a 4 horas en el frigorífico. Remueva de vez en cuando.

3 Esparza el perejil picado sobre un plato. Corte los trozos de pollo en seis porciones iguales y ensártelas en seis brochetas de metal; páselas por el perejil para que queden bien cubiertas.

4 Disponga las brochetas de pollo sobre una rejilla untada con aceite y áselas a la parrilla, previamente calentada, de 5 a 10 minutos, hasta que la carne esté dorada por fuera y bien hecha por dentro. Dé la vuelta a las brochetas y báñelas con la marinada restante durante la cocción; así ganarán en sabor.

Pollo al orégano

KOTOPOULO RIGANATO TIS SKARAS

Este plato, sencillo y sabroso, es ideal para una barbacoa veraniega; si desea una meze rápida, ásela a la parrilla.

Tiempo de preparación: 10 minutos, más marinada
Tiempo de cocción: unos 30 minutos
PARA 6–8 PERSONAS

- *6–8 trozos de pollo*
- *½ taza de aceite de oliva*
- *½ taza de vino blanco seco*
- *2 cucharadas de orégano seco*
- *sal y pimienta negra recién molida, al gusto*
- *2 dientes de ajo, majados*

1 Disponga las porciones de pollo en un plato grande y llano.

2 En un bol de tamaño pequeño mezcle el aceite, el vino, el orégano, la sal, la pimienta negra recién molida y el ajo; remueva todo bien. Esparza la marinada sobre el pollo, cúbralo y déjelo marinar de 2 a 3 horas; déle la vuelta de vez en cuando.

3 Coloque los trozos de pollo sobre una rejilla untada con aceite y áselos a la parrilla, previamente calentada, durante unos 30 minutos, hasta que el pollo esté crujiente y dorado por fuera y bien hecho por dentro; déle la vuelta varias veces durante la cocción. Sírvalo frío o caliente.

Menú rápido y fácil

Ensalada griega clásica
Horiatiki Salata

◆

Crema de garbanzos
Hummus

◆

Pollo asado con hortalizas
Kota me Ladera

◆

Pinchos de carne picada
Kofta

◆

Pan pita

◆

Galletas de almendra
Amygthalota

◆

Vino: Santorin
(vino blanco seco)

◆

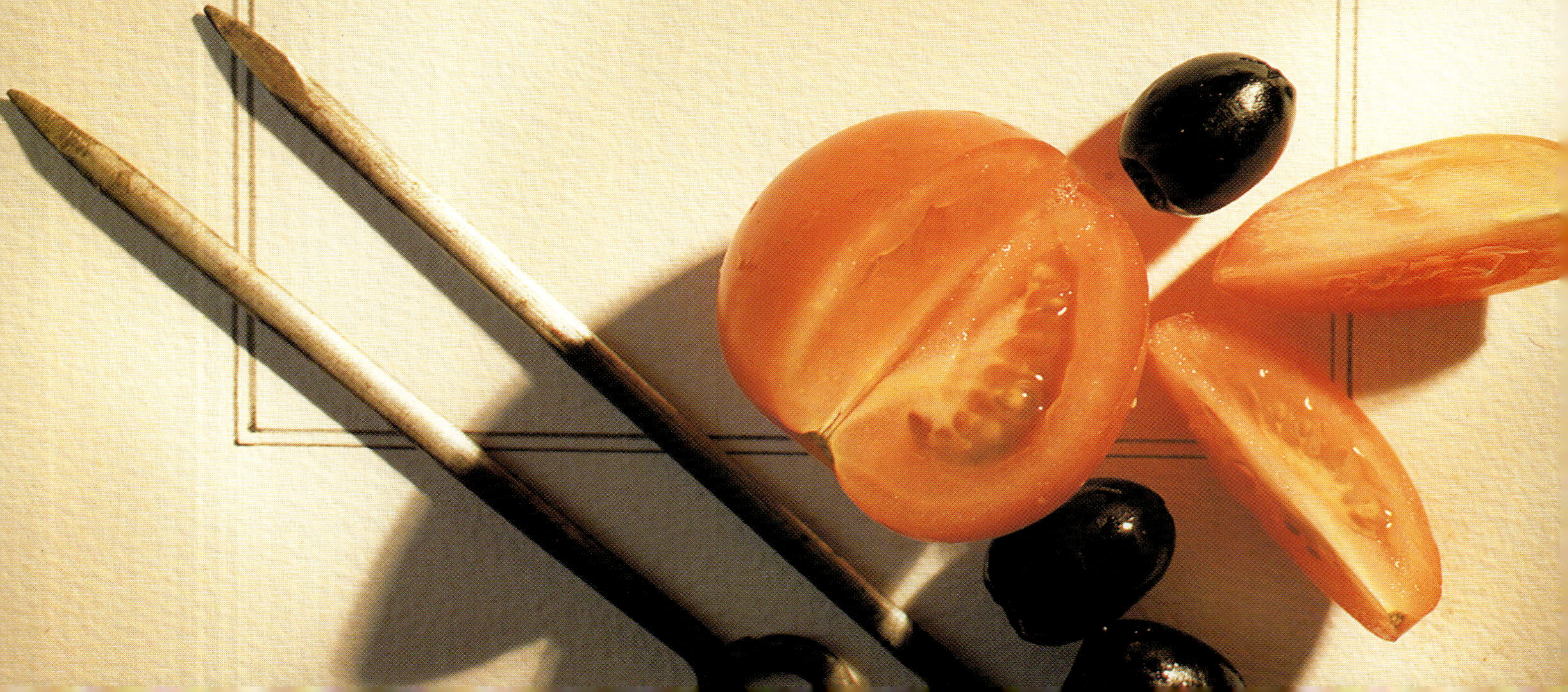

Pollo al limón

KOTOPOULO ME AVGOLEMONO

El pollo aromatizado con limón resulta en una combinación de sabores de lo más exquisita, que se da con mucha frecuencia en la cocina griega. El arroz constituye el acompañamiento perfecto para disfrutar de la salsa.

Tiempo de preparación: unos 20 minutos
Tiempo de cocción: unos 45 minutos

PARA 6-8 PERSONAS

- *1,5 kg de pollo, sin los despojos y cortado en porciones pequeñas*
- *¼ taza de mantequilla*
- *sal y pimienta negra recién molida, al gusto*
- *1 ¼ tazas de agua hirviendo*
- *1 manojo de cebolletas, limpias y cortadas en trozos de 2,5 cm*
- *3 huevos*
- *3 cucharadas de zumo de limón recién exprimido*
- *2 cucharadas de eneldo fresco, picado, para decorar*

1 Derrita la mantequilla en una cacerola grande de fondo pesado y cueza el pollo durante unos 5 minutos, hasta que esté dorado; revuélvalo con frecuencia durante la cocción.

2 Sazone el pollo con sal y pimienta negra recién molida; añada el agua hirviendo y las cebolletas. Tape la cacerola y deje cocer todo a fuego lento de 35 a 40 minutos, hasta que el pollo esté tierno y caliente.

3 Casque los huevos en un bol pequeño y bátalos bien. Para evitar que la mezcla se corte, agregue el zumo de limón de manera gradual e intermitente, y bátalo. Vierta asimismo 300 ml del jugo de la cocción del pollo y bátalo. Nape el pollo con la mezcla resultante y no deje de removerlo hasta que la salsa se espese un poco. Evite que rompa el hervor.

4 Pase el pollo y la salsa a una fuente de servir precalentada y esparza el eneldo fresco picado por encima.

Pollo con macarrones

KOTA KAPAMA

Prepare la salsa con antelación y refrigérela hasta el momento de servir. Puede recalentarla mientras cuece los macarrones y, de este modo, obtendrá, en cuestión de minutos, un plato sustancioso para su selección de meze.

Tiempo de preparación: unos 20 minutos
Tiempo de cocción: 1 hora y 15 minutos
PARA 6–8 PERSONAS

- *1 kg de muslos de pollo, sin piel*
- *sal y pimienta negra recién molida, al gusto*
- *una pizca de canela molida*
- *6 cucharadas de mantequilla*
- *750 g de tomate triturado, en lata*
- *8 cucharadas de concentrado de tomate*
- *1 cucharadita de azúcar*
- *¾ taza de agua hirviendo*
- *2 ramitas de canela*
- *1 cebolla, rallada*
- *2 dientes de ajo, majados*
- *500 g de macarrones*
- *200 g de queso kefalotyri o parmesano, rallado*

1 Coloque los muslos de pollo sobre una tabla de trinchar y espolvoréelos de manera uniforme con sal, pimienta negra recién molida y canela.

2 Derrita la mitad de la mantequilla en una cacerola grande de fondo pesado y rehogue el pollo durante unos 5 minutos, revolviéndolo bien, para que se dore de manera uniforme.

3 Añada el tomate triturado, el concentrado de tomate, el azúcar y el agua hirviendo; remueva y agregue la canela en rama. Tape la cacerola y cueza todo a fuego lento durante 5 minutos.

4 Derrita la mantequilla restante en una sartén y sofría la cebolla y el ajo de 3 a 5 minutos o hasta que se ablanden. Incorpórelos a la mezcla de pollo y suba el fuego para que rompa el hervor. Tape la sartén y deje cocer todo a fuego lento durante 1 hora, o bien hasta que el pollo esté tierno y la salsa se espese; remueva de vez en cuando durante la cocción.

5 Durante los últimos 20 minutos de cocción, cueza los macarrones en una olla grande con agua hirviendo, hasta que estén al dente. Aclárelos bajo el chorro de agua caliente y páselos a una fuente de servir precalentada. Nape la pasta con la salsa de pollo y espolvoree el queso rallado por encima. Sirva el plato inmediatamente.

Albóndigas de pollo fritas

KOTO TIGHANITO

La mezcla de pollo de esta receta puede moldearse en forma de salchicha alrededor de una brocheta y así obtener *koftas* de pollo para asarlas a la parrilla o a la barbacoa.

Tiempo de preparación: unos 15 minutos
Tiempo de cocción: unos 8 minutos
PARA 6–8 PERSONAS

- *3 filetes de pechuga de pollo, deshuesados y picados finos*
- *1 taza de pan blanco fresco, rallado*
- *⅓ taza de piñones, molidos*
- *3 cucharadas de perejil fresco, picado*
- *½ cucharadita de cúrcuma molida*
- *1 huevo, batido*
- *sal y pimienta negra recién molida, al gusto*
- *harina, para espolvorear*
- *aceite de oliva, para freír*
- *el zumo de 1 limón recién exprimido*

1 Ponga el pollo en un bol y añada el pan rallado, los piñones, el perejil y la cúrcuma; remuévalo todo bien.

2 Vierta el huevo batido en la mezcla de pollo y condiméntelo con sal y pimienta negra recién molida. Con las manos ligeramente humedecidas, moldee la mezcla resultante en forma de bolitas del tamaño de una nuez; colóquelas en una bandeja de horno forrada con papel encerado.

3 Espolvoree las albóndigas ligeramente con harina. Caliente aceite en una sartén honda antiadherente y rehogue las albóndigas por tandas de 5 a 8 minutos, o bien hasta que estén crujientes y bien hechas; remuévalas para que se cuezan de manera uniforme. Páselas a una fuente e introdúzcalas en el horno, a temperatura baja, para que se mantengan calientes mientras fríe el resto. Sírvalas frías o calientes, y rociadas con zumo de limón.

Pinchos de pollo

SOUVLAKIA ME KOTA

Este plato típico griego debería servirse a la mesa de las meze junto con abundante *tzatziki* y pan pita caliente.

Tiempo de preparación: 20 minutos, más marinada
Tiempo de cocción: unos 20–25 minutos

PARA 6 PERSONAS

- *½ taza de aceite de oliva*
- *1 cucharada de zumo de limón recién exprimido*
- *1 cucharada de vinagre de vino*
- *¼ taza de vino tinto seco*
- *2 dientes de ajo, majados*
- *1 cucharadita de menta seca*
- *4 filetes de pechuga de pollo, deshuesados y cortados en dados de 2,5 cm*
- *200 g de higaditos de pollo, troceados*
- *2 pimientos verdes, sin semillas y troceados*
- *12 champiñones medianos, lavados*
- *12 tomates "cherry"*

1 En un bol pequeño mezcle el aceite, el zumo de limón, el vinagre de vino, el vino tinto, el ajo y la menta; remuévalo bien.

2 Disponga los filetes y los higaditos de pollo en un plato llano, vierta la marinada por encima y remueva todo para que quede bien recubierto. Tape el plato y déjelo marinar en el frigorífico durante 2 ó 3 horas; remueva los ingredientes de vez en cuando.

3 Ensarte el pollo, los higaditos, los pimientos, los champiñones y los tomates en seis brochetas de metal. Unte todo con el resto de la marinada y colóquelo sobre una rejilla de grill untada con aceite. Ase los pinchos de 20 a 25 minutos o hasta que estén crujientes y bien hechos; déles la vuelta con frecuencia durante la cocción.

Pollo con queso feta y aceitunas verdes

KOTO BARTHOUNIKIOTOU

Este plato proviene originariamente del pequeño pueblo de Barthouna, cerca de Esparta. Se prepara con uvas pasas o aceitunas, ya que ambos productos abundan en la región.

Tiempo de preparación: unos 30 minutos
Tiempo de cocción: unos 40 minutos

PARA 4 PERSONAS

- *4 filetes de pechuga de pollo*
- *harina, para espolvorear*
- *sal y pimienta negra molida, al gusto*
- *6 cucharadas de aceite de oliva*
- *300 g de cebollitas (o cebollas grandes, cuarteadas)*
- *375 g de tomates troceados, en lata*
- *½ taza de agua hirviendo*
- *250 g de aceitunas verdes sin hueso, lavadas y escurridas*
- *1 cucharada de vinagre de vino tinto*
- *100 g de queso feta*

1 Coloque los filetes de pollo sobre una tabla de trinchar, espolvoréelos con la harina y condiméntelos por ambas caras con sal y pimienta negra recién molida .

2 Caliente el aceite en una sartén grande y honda, y coloque los filetes de pollo de modo que la parte con piel quede debajo. Fríalo por ambas caras entre 3 y 5 minutos, hasta que esté dorado. Retire el pollo de la sartén y resérvelo.

3 Añada la cebolla a la sartén y sofríala, sin dejar de remover, durante unos 5 minutos o hasta que esté tierna. Devuelva el pollo a la sartén y añada los tomates troceados y el agua hirviendo. Condiméntelo todo con sal y pimienta negra recién molida, tape la sartén y deje cocer a fuego lento entre 25 y 30 minutos, hasta que el pollo esté tierno y bien caliente. Agregue más agua durante la cocción, si lo cree necesario.

4 En los últimos 10 minutos de la cocción, agregue el vinagre de vino tinto y remueva. Coloque una loncha de queso feta encima de cada filete de pollo y siga cociéndolo, sin tapar, otros 10 minutos más o hasta que el queso se haya fundido por completo. Sirva el plato inmediatamente.

Pollo guisado con tomate

KOTOPOULO KOKKINISTO

***Kokkinisto* es el nombre que se suele dar a los guisos hechos a base de carne y salsa de tomate.**

Tiempo de preparación: unos 15 minutos
Tiempo de cocción: 1 hora y 15 minutos
Temperatura del horno: 190°C
PARA 4–6 PERSONAS

- *¼ taza de aceite de oliva*
- *1,5 kg de pollo, cortado en porciones*
- *harina, para espolvorear*
- *2 cebollas rojas grandes, cortadas en aros*
- *750 g de tomate triturado, en lata*
- *3 dientes de ajo, majados*
- *sal y pimienta negra recién molida, al gusto*
- *6 cucharadas de agua hirviendo*
- *2 cucharadas de vinagre de vino tinto*
- *perejil fresco, picado*

1 Precaliente el horno a 190°C. Caliente el aceite en una cazuela grande y resistente al fuego. Coloque las porciones de pollo sobre una tabla de trinchar y espolvoréelas con harina. Páselas a la cazuela y cuézalas durante unos 5 minutos, o bien hasta que presenten un tono dorado uniforme; remuévalas durante la cocción. Con una espumadera, pase el pollo a un plato y resérvelo.

2 Agregue la cebolla a la cazuela y sofríala durante 3 minutos hasta que esté tierna. Devuelva el pollo a la cazuela, incorpore el tomate triturado y el ajo, y condiméntelo todo con sal y pimienta negra recién molida. Agregue el agua hirviendo, tape la cazuela y hornee de 45 a 55 minutos, hasta que el pollo esté tierno y la salsa se espese.

3 En los últimos 5 minutos de cocción, vierta el vinagre de vino tinto y un poco más de agua, si lo cree necesario; remueva. Sirva el guisado con perejil fresco picado por encima.

Alitas de pollo con ajo y zumo de lima

KOTOPOULO MARINATO

Siempre que compre un pollo entero, congele las alitas, en el caso de no necesitarlas. Cuando ya disponga de unas cuantas, utilícelas para preparar este delicioso plato de sabor ácido.

Tiempo de preparación: 10 minutos, más marinada
Tiempo de cocción: unos 25 minutos

PARA 8–12 PERSONAS

- *12 alitas de pollo*
- *4 dientes de ajo, majados*
- *sal y pimienta negra recién molida, al gusto*
- *el zumo de 4 limas recién exprimidas*
- *una pizca de pimienta de Cayena*

1 Coloque las alitas de pollo en un plato llano y frótelas bien con el ajo majado; condiméntelas luego con sal y pimienta negra recién molida.

2 Rocíe las alitas con el zumo de lima y espolvoréelas con la Cayena. Cúbralas y déjelas marinar en el frigorífico durante 3 ó 4 horas; remuévalas de vez en cuando.

3 Disponga las alitas en una sartén grande y rocíelas con la marinada. Vierta agua fría hasta cubrirlas y deje que rompa el hervor rápidamente. Deje cocer, sin tapar, entre 20 y 25 minutos, hasta que el pollo esté hecho y la salsa se haya reducido ligeramente. Sirva este plato en seguida o, mejor todavía, sírvalo frío al día siguiente.

Pollo guisado con patatas

KOTOPOULO ME PATATES

Si lo prefiere, puede utilizar porciones de pollo deshuesadas; aunque sea menos auténtico, el plato será igual de sabroso.

Tiempo de preparación: unos 20 minutos
Tiempo de cocción: unas 2 horas

PARA 4–6 PERSONAS

- *1,5 kg de pollo, sin los despojos y cortado en porciones pequeñas*
- *el zumo de 1 limón recién exprimido*
- *2 cucharadas de aceite de oliva*
- *2 cebollas, picadas*
- *1 pimiento rojo, sin semillas y picado*
- *4 tomates grandes, pelados, sin semillas y troceados*
- *3¾ tazas de agua hirviendo*
- *1 cucharada de concentrado de tomate*
- *2 dientes de ajo, majados*
- *3 hojas de laurel, troceadas*
- *4 cucharadas de perejil fresco, picado*
- *2 patatas medianas, peladas y cortadas en trozos*
- *una pizca de azúcar*
- *sal y pimienta negra recién molida, al gusto*
- *perejil fresco, picado, para aderezar*

1 Coloque las porciones de pollo sobre una tabla de trinchar y rocíelas con el zumo de limón. Caliente el aceite de oliva en una cazuela grande de fondo pesado y rehogue el pollo de 5 a 10 minutos, hasta que esté dorado de manera uniforme; remuévalo durante la cocción. Incorpore las cebollas a la cazuela y deje cocer otros 5 minutos, hasta que estén tiernas.

2 Añada los pimientos y el tomate, y cuézalos entre 3 y 4 minutos. Vierta el agua hirviendo y deje que vuelva a arrancar el hervor. Agregue el concentrado de tomate, el ajo, las hojas de laurel, el perejil, las patatas y el azúcar, y condiméntelos con sal y pimienta negra recién molida. Remueva todo, tápelo y déjelo cocer a fuego lento durante 1½ horas, hasta que el pollo esté hecho y las patatas estén tiernas. Esparza un poco más de perejil picado por encima, para aderezar el plato.

ABAJO
En pleno verano, y a diferencia de los turistas hambrientos de sol, los griegos de avanzada edad buscan con toda sensatez una sombra donde cobijarse.

Pollo asado con pistachos

KOTOPOULO ME PISTACHIO

Esta receta es una variación de uno de los platos más populares de Grecia. El pollo debería trocearse y servirse con el relleno por separado.

Tiempo de preparación: unos 25 minutos
Tiempo de cocción: unas 2 horas
Temperatura del horno: 230°C y, posteriormente, 180°C

PARA 6–8 PERSONAS

- *¼ taza de aceite de oliva*
- *2 cebollas, picadas*
- *1⅓ tazas de arroz de grano largo*
- *4 tomates grandes, pelados, sin semillas y picados*
- *1⅓ tazas de pistachos sin cáscara, troceados*
- *⅔ taza de uvas pasas, sin pepitas*
- *una pizca de canela molida*
- *sal y pimienta negra molida, al gusto*
- *2¼ tazas de agua hirviendo*
- *3 cucharadas de perejil fresco, picado muy fino*
- *1 pollo de 1,5 kg, sin los despojos*
- *¼ taza de vino blanco seco*

1 Precaliente el horno a 230°C. Caliente la mitad del aceite en una sartén grande y pesada, y rehogue la cebolla durante unos 5 minutos o hasta que esté tierna.

2 Vierta el arroz en la sartén y deje cocer otros 3 minutos más, o hasta que el arroz empiece a dorarse; remuévalo de vez en cuando. Agregue la mitad de los tomates, los pistachos, las pasas, la canela, la sal, la pimienta negra recién molida y ¾ taza de agua hirviendo. Déjelo cocer a fuego lento, sin dejar de remover, durante unos 10 minutos o hasta que el arroz esté casi cocido y se haya embebido casi todo el líquido. Retírelo del fuego, agregue el perejil y remuévalo.

3 Introduzca la mezcla de arroz dentro del pollo con la ayuda de una cuchara, pero sin apretarlo demasiado. Coloque el pollo en una fuente para asar y reparta la mezcla de arroz que haya podido sobrar por su alrededor; salpimiente el pollo.

4 Distribuya los tomates restantes alrededor del pollo y vierta 1½ tazas de agua hirviendo y el vino en la fuente para asar. Reduzca la temperatura del horno a 180°C; de este modo, la piel del pollo se soasa y se vuelve más crujiente mientras el horno se ajusta a la nueva temperatura. Rocíe el pollo con el aceite de oliva restante y áselo durante 1½ horas, hasta que esté bien hecho y el arroz esté tierno, tanto dentro como fuera del pollo. Báñelo varias veces durante la cocción y añada un poco más de agua, si lo cree necesario. Deje reposar el asado durante unos 10 minutos antes de cortarlo en porciones y servirlo junto con el relleno.

Pastel de pollo

KOTOPITTA

Este pastel resulta ideal para una comida veraniega al aire libre. Sabe delicioso tanto frío como caliente, es fácil de preparar y, además, tiene un aspecto exquisito.

Tiempo de preparación: unos 45 minutos
Tiempo de cocción: unos 50 minutos
Temperatura del horno: 180°C
PARA 8–10 PERSONAS

- *½ taza de aceite de oliva*
- *6 láminas de pasta filo, descongelada, si no es fresca*
- *2 filetes de pechuga de pollo, sin piel ni huesos y cortados en trozos pequeños*
- *1 manojo de chalotes*
- *3 cucharadas de eneldo fresco, picado*
- *2 tallos de apio, picados*
- *sal y pimienta negra recién molida, al gusto*
- *2 cucharaditas de tomillo*
- *1 cucharadita de menta seca*
- *½ cucharadita de mejorana*
- *½ cucharadita de estragón*
- *150 g de queso feta, desmenuzado*
- *2 cucharadas de queso kefalotyri o parmesano fresco, rallado*
- *2 huevos batidos*
- *½ cucharadita de Ouzo (opcional)*
- *1 yema de huevo, batida, para glasear*

1 Precaliente el horno a 180°C. Unte una fuente honda y ovalada de unos 25 cm con un poco de aceite de oliva. Extienda la pasta filo sobre la superficie de trabajo y cúbrala con un paño ligeramente húmedo para que no se seque.

2 Ponga las porciones de pollo en un bol grande con los chalotes, el eneldo, el apio, la sal, la pimienta negra recién molida y las hierbas aromáticas secas. Añada el queso feta desmenuzado y el queso rallado, y remuévalo todo bien. Incorpore los huevos batidos y el ouzo (si lo desea), así como 2 cucharadas de aceite de oliva; remuévalo bien.

3 Separe una lámina de pasta filo del resto y extiéndala sobre la superficie de trabajo. Mantenga el resto de la pasta cubierta con el paño. Unte la lámina con un poco de aceite de oliva y extienda otra lámina encima; unte ésta también con aceite y repita la operación con una tercera lámina. Úntela con aceite y páselas todas al fondo de la fuente, de modo que la pasta que sobre sobresalga por encima del borde.

4 Con la ayuda de una cuchara, pase la mezcla de pollo a la fuente con la pasta y espárzala de manera uniforme. Extienda y unte las láminas restantes como en el paso anterior y colóquelas encima del relleno de pollo.

5 Enrolle los extremos de la pasta filo de modo que se entrecruzen y encierren en su interior el relleno. Practique unas cuantas incisiones en la superficie del pastel para que pueda salir el vapor mientras se cuece. Píntelo con la yema de huevo batida para glasearlo y hornéelo entre 45 y 50 minutos hasta que la pasta esté crujiente y el pollo esté cocido. Corte el pastel en porciones y sírvalo frío o caliente.

Pollo asado con hortalizas

KOTA ME LADERA

Escoja a su gusto las hortalizas para esta receta, pero no olvide que cuanto más blandas son, menos tiempo de cocción necesitan; ajuste, por consiguiente, el tiempo de cocción de la receta al tipo de hortaliza.

Tiempo de preparación: unos 15 minutos
Tiempo de cocción: unas 2 horas
Temperatura del horno: 230°C y, posteriormente, 180°C

PARA 6–8 PERSONAS

- *6–8 porciones de pollo*
- *6 cucharadas de aceite de oliva*
- *sal y pimienta negra recién molida, al gusto*
- *el zumo de 2 limones recién exprimidos*
- *2 cucharaditas de tomillo seco*
- *½ cucharadita de mejorana seca*
- *3 dientes de ajo, majados*
- *2 patatas grandes, peladas y cortadas en gajos a lo largo*
- *3 zanahorias, cortadas en trozos grandes*
- *1 pimiento rojo, sin semillas y en cuartos*
- *1 pimiento verde, sin semillas y en cuartos*
- *6-8 champiñones, limpios*
- *3 calabacines medianos, cortados en trozos grandes*

1 Precaliente el horno a 230°C. Coloque el pollo en porciones en una fuente para asar grande y frótelo con 2 cucharadas de aceite de oliva. Sazónelo con sal y pimienta negra recién molida.

2 En un bol pequeño mezcle el aceite de oliva restante, el zumo de limón, el tomillo, la mejorana, el ajo y un poco más de pimienta negra recién molida. Mézclelo bien y unte con ello el pollo de manera uniforme.

3 Esparza las hortalizas alrededor del pollo y salpimiéntelas. Reduzca la temperatura del horno a 180°C. La piel del pollo se volverá crujiente antes de que la temperatura llegue al mínimo. Agregue el agua hirviendo y ase todo durante unas 2 horas o hasta que el pollo esté bien cocido y las hortalizas estén tiernas, pero no blandas. Báñelo todo bastante a menudo con el jugo de la cocción. Sirva el plato caliente.

ABAJO
Al comienzo del verano, las amapolas inundan con su intenso color la árida meseta de Lesithi.

Pilaf de pollo

KOTOPOULO PILAFI

La manera típica griega de ultimar este plato, y otros tantos a base de pasta o arroz, consiste en dorar un poco de mantequilla en una sartén pequeña y verterla por encima justo antes de servir. En esta versión se trata de un paso opcional por lo que, en caso de estar controlando la ingestión de grasas, mejor será que no lo incluya.

Tiempo de preparación: unos 10 minutos
Tiempo de cocción: unos 45 minutos

PARA 6–8 PERSONAS

- *½ taza de mantequilla*
- *1 kg de filetes de pechuga de pollo, sin piel ni huesos y troceados*
- *sal y pimienta negra recién molida, al gusto*
- *una pizca de canela molida*
- *una pizca de pimienta de Jamaica, molida*
- *2 cebollas, picadas*
- *3 cucharadas de concentrado de tomate*
- *2½ tazas de agua hirviendo*
- *1⅓ tazas de arroz de grano largo*
- *¼ taza de mantequilla*
- *menta fresca, para decorar*

1 Derrita la mantequilla en una cacerola grande de fondo pesado y rehogue el pollo de 5 a 10 minutos o hasta que empiece a dorarse; déle la vuelta durante la cocción. Añada la sal, la pimienta negra recién molida, la canela y la pimienta de Jamaica, y remueva todo bien.

2 Agregue la cebolla a la cacerola y deje cocer hasta que esté tierna. Incorpore el concentrado de tomate y el agua hirviendo, tape la cacerola y deje cocer otros 20 minutos. Añada el arroz, tape de nuevo y cueza otros 20 ó 25 minutos más, hasta que el pollo esté cocido y el arroz esté tierno.

3 Destape la cacerola durante los 10 últimos minutos, a fin de que se embeba todo el líquido. Derrita la mantequilla en una sartén pequeña y cuézala hasta dorarla. Pase el *pilaf* a una fuente de servir calentada previamente y vierta la mantequilla dorada por encima. Sirva el plato decorado con la menta fresca picada.

CAPÍTULO 5

Pescado y marisco

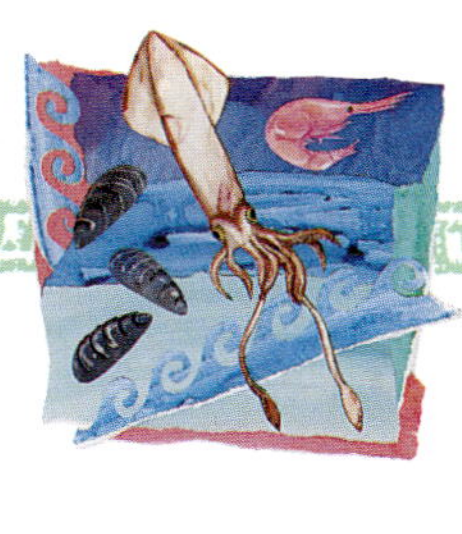

Filetes de pescado con tomate y queso feta

FETES PSARI ME FETA KAI DOMATES

Los griegos demuestran tener una gran estima por el mar y por todas las criaturas que en él viven; es por esto que no acostumbran a sumerger el pescado en salsas fuertes, ni a cocerlo durante mucho tiempo. Consumen el pescado lo más fresco posible y lo cocinan muy brevemente, de modo que la delicadeza de su sabor y de su textura sigan siendo las principales características del plato.

Tiempo de preparación: unos 10 minutos
Tiempo de cocción: unos 5–10 minutos

PARA 6–8 PERSONAS

- *1 kg de filetes de platija, sin piel*
- *aceite de oliva, para untar*
- *1 cebolla grande, rallada*
- *sal y pimienta negra recién molida, al gusto*
- *4 tomates pelados, sin semillas y troceados*
- *½ taza de mantequilla, fundida*
- *150 g de queso feta, desmenuzado*
- *perejil fresco picado, para aderezar*

1 Disponga los filetes de platija en una sola capa en una fuente resistente al fuego, grande y llana, y untada con aceite.

2 Esparza la cebolla sobre los filetes y sazone todo con la sal y la pimienta negra recién molida. Distribuya también el tomate troceado por encima de la cebolla.

3 Rocíe los filetes con la mitad de la mantequilla fundida y colóquelos bajo el grill del horno, previamente calentado, entre 5 y 7 minutos. Vierta el resto de la mantequilla y el queso feta por encima; deje cocer de 3 a 5 minutos más, hasta que el pescado esté cocido. Espolvoréelo con perejil fresco picado.

ARRIBA
Un puesto de salmonetes, pinchos de pez espada, pulpo, doradas y gambas capta la atención de los transeúntes en el puerto de Réthimnon.

Fritada de marisco

OSTRAKA

Esta meze, sencilla pero deliciosa, debería servirse con abundantes gajos de limón fresco.

Tiempo de preparación: unos 10 minutos
Tiempo de cocción: unos 5–10 minutos
PARA 8–10 PERSONAS

- *1 kg de marisco variado (p.ej. gambas peladas, calamares en rodajas, filetes de pescado blanco troceados, chanquetes)*
- *harina, para rebozar*
- *sal y pimienta negra recién molida, al gusto*
- *aceite de oliva, para freír*
- *el zumo de 1 limón recién exprimido*
- *gajos de limón, para acompañar*

1 Disponga el pescado en un bol de tamaño grande y espolvoree con harina hasta cubrirlo todo con una leve capa y de manera uniforme; remueva con cuidado.

2 Sazone el pescado enharinado con sal y pimienta negra recién molida. Caliente el aceite en una sartén honda y fría el pescado por tandas de 5 a 7 minutos, hasta que se dore y esté hecho. Con una espumadera, páselo a un plato preparado con papel de cocina, a fin de que escurra el aceite.

3 Rocíe el pescado frito con el zumo de limón y sírvalo caliente, acompañado con los gajos de limón adicionales.

Pescado al vino

PSARI PLAKI

***Plaki* es el nombre que recibe en Grecia el método de cocción de este plato. También se aplica, no obstante, a recetas a base de legumbres u hortalizas cocidas de este modo.**

Tiempo de preparación: unos 15 minutos
Tiempo de cocción: unos 55 minutos
Temperatura del horno: 180°C
PARA 8–10 PERSONAS

- *½ taza de aceite de oliva*
- *2 cebollas grandes, cortadas en aros*
- *4 tallos de apio, troceados*
- *4 chalotes, picados*
- *4 cucharadas de perejil fresco, picado*
- *4 tomates, cortados en rodajas*
- *3 dientes de ajo, majados*
- *1 kg de filetes de lubina, sin piel*
- *2 cucharaditas de orégano seco*
- *sal y pimienta negra recién molida, al gusto*
- *2 limones, cortados en rodajas finas*
- *1¼ tazas de vino blanco seco*
- *3 cucharadas de zumo de limón recién exprimido*
- *1½ tazas de pan blanco, rallado*
- *perejil fresco picado, para aderezar*

1 Precaliente el horno a 180°C. En una sartén con todo el aceite menos dos cucharadas, rehogue la cebolla durante unos 3 minutos hasta que esté tierna. Añada el apio, los chalotes, el perejil, los tomates y el ajo; remuévalo todo ligeramente y deje cocer otros 5 minutos más.

2 Unte una fuente de horno grande y llana con el aceite restante y disponga los filetes de pescado. Esparza el orégano por encima y condiméntelos con sal y pimienta negra recién molida. Pase la mezcla de cebolla cocida a la fuente con el pescado y esparza por encima las rodajas de limón.

3 Vierta el vino y el zumo de limón, y espolvoree el pan rallado por encima; hornéelo todo, sin tapar, durante unos 45 minutos, hasta que el pescado esté bien hecho y la cobertura esté dorada. Sirva el plato aderezado con perejil fresco picado.

Calamares fritos

KALAMARIA TIGANITA

Esta meze es todo un clásico y especialmente popular en los meses de verano.

Tiempo de preparación: unos 20 minutos
Tiempo de cocción: unos 5–10 minutos
PARA 8–10 PERSONAS

- *1 kg de calamares pequeños, lavados y cortados en aros de 1 cm*
- *harina, para rebozar*
- *sal y pimienta negra recién molida, al gusto*
- *aceite vegetal, para freír*
- *gajos de limón, para acompañar*

1 Ponga los calamares en un bol. Espolvoree la harina por encima de modo que queden recubiertos con una capa fina y uniforme. Sazónelos con sal y pimienta negra recién molida, y remuévalos bien.

2 Caliente el aceite y fría los calamares por tandas de 3 a 5 minutos, hasta que estén crujientes y dorados por fuera, y tiernos por dentro. Con una espumadera, páselos a un plato forrado con papel de cocina, a fin de que escurran el aceite. Sírvalos con los gajos de limón.

Gratinado de gambas

GARIDES ME SALTSA

Este plato sabe mucho mejor si no se le añade sal durante la cocción, ya que ésta suele endurecer las gambas. Si considera que la sal del queso feta no es suficiente para su gusto, añada más una vez servido a la mesa.

Tiempo de preparación: unos 10 minutos
Tiempo de cocción: unos 45 minutos
Temperatura del horno: 220°C

PARA 6–8 PERSONAS

- *3 cucharadas de aceite*
- *2 cebollas grandes, ralladas*
- *2 dientes de ajo, majados*
- *3 cucharadas de perejil fresco, picado*
- *1 cucharada de eneldo fresco, picado*
- *una pizca de mostaza en polvo*
- *una pizca de azúcar*
- *375 g de tomate triturado, en lata*
- *1 cucharada de concentrado de tomate*
- *450 g de gambas frescas, peladas y sin el intestino*
- *200 g de queso feta*
- *eneldo fresco, picado*

1 Caliente el aceite de oliva en una cacerola grande y saltee la cebolla durante 5 minutos o hasta que esté tierna y empiece a dorarse. Añada el ajo, las hierbas aromáticas picadas, la mostaza en polvo, el azúcar, los tomates troceados y el concentrado de tomate. Deje cocer la mezcla, sin tapar, durante unos 30 minutos o hasta que la salsa se espese y se reduzca ligeramente. Mientras tanto, precaliente el horno a 220°C.

2 Añada las gambas a la salsa y remuévalas. Siga cociendo de 3 a 5 minutos más, hasta que las gambas adquieran un tono rosado y estén hechas.

3 Vierta la mezcla resultante en un plato de servir resistente al calor y esparza por encima el queso feta desmenuzado; hornéelo todo entre 5 y 10 minutos, hasta que el queso se derrita. Sirva el gratinado inmediatamente y con eneldo fresco picado por encima.

Croquetas de huevas de bacalao

TARAMA KEFTEDES

Fuera de la frontera griega, las huevas de bacalao se asocian normalmente con la *taramosalata*, pero en realidad se utilizan para distintas mezes, como, por ejemplo, ésta misma.

Tiempo de preparación: unos 20 minutos más refrigeración
Tiempo de cocción: unos 5–10 minutos
PARA 8–10 PERSONAS

- *450 g de huevas de bacalao ahumadas*
- *1 cebolla, picada*
- *1½ tazas de pan blanco fresco, rallado*
- *2 cucharadas de zumo de limón recién exprimido*
- *3 dientes de ajo, majados*
- *pimienta negra recién molida, al gusto*
- *5 cucharadas de perejil fresco, picado*
- *2 claras de huevo, batidas*
- *harina, para rebozar*
- *aceite de oliva, para freír*
- *gajos de limón, para acompañar*

1 Pele las huevas de bacalao y deseche la membrana que las envuelve. Vierta las huevas en el robot de cocina o la batidora, junto con el pan rallado, el zumo de limón, el ajo, la pimienta negra recién molida y el perejil. Tritúrelo hasta que adquiera una textura fina y añádale un poco de clara de huevo para reblandecer la masa. Pase la mezcla a un bol de tamaño mediano, tápela y refrigérela por un mínimo de 2 horas.

2 Humedézcase las manos y moldee la masa obtenida en forma de bolitas del tamaño de una nuez. Esparza la harina en un plato y pase por ella las bolitas, de modo que queden bien rebozadas.

3 Caliente el aceite y fría las croquetas por tandas de 5 a 8 minutos, hasta que estén crujientes por fuera y tiernas por dentro. Con una espumadera, páselas a un plato forrado con papel de cocina, a fin de que escurran el aceite. Sírvalas calientes o frías y con gajos de limón.

Salmonete con ajo

BARBOUNI ME SKORTHO

Por su tamaño, los salmonetes resultan ideales para servirlos a una mesa de meze; si no encuentra salmonetes pequeños, cocine uno grande y trocéelo en la mesa.

Tiempo de preparación: unos 10 minutos
Tiempo de cocción: unos 5–10 minutos
PARA 6 PERSONAS

- *6 cucharadas de perejil fresco, picado*
- *6 dientes de ajo, majados*
- *sal y pimienta negra recién molida, al gusto*
- *6 salmonetes pequeños, lavados*
- *harina, para rebozar*
- *aceite de oliva, para freír*
- *perejil fresco picado, para aderezar*
- *gajos de limón, para acompañar*

1 En un bol pequeño, mezcle el perejil con el ajo y sazónelo con sal y pimienta negra recién molida. Introduzca 1 cucharadita de la mezcla obtenida en cada uno de los salmonetes y frote la piel con la mezcla restante. Enharine el pescado ligeramente y de manera uniforme.

2 Caliente el aceite en una sartén honda y fría los salmonetes, como máximo de dos en dos, entre 5 y 7 minutos hasta que estén crujientes por fuera y tiernos por dentro. Con una espumadera, páselos a un plato forrado con papel de cocina, a fin de que escurran el aceite. Espolvoree el perejil por encima y sírvalos acompañados de los gajos de limón.

Cazuela de pescado con hortalizas

PSARI YIAHNI ME LAHANO

El bacalao, el eglefino o el rape son los pescados más indicados para esta receta originaria de la isla de Corfú. El ingrediente más importante de este plato es el ajo, que se emplea con abundancia.

Tiempo de preparación: unos 15 minutos
Tiempo de cocción: unos 40 minutos
PARA 8-10 PERSONAS

- *6 cucharadas de aceite de oliva*
- *1 cebolla grande, cortada en aros*
- *1 kg de patatas nuevas pequeñas, cortadas en rodajas de 1 cm*
- *2 zanahorias, cortadas en dados de 2,5 cm*
- *1 tallo de apio, picado*
- *sal y pimienta negra recién molida, al gusto*
- *6 dientes de ajo, majados*
- *1 kg de pescado blanco en filetes, cortados en dados de 5 cm*
- *¼ taza de zumo de limón recién exprimido*

1 Caliente ¼ taza de aceite de oliva en una cazuela grande de fondo pesado y rehogue la cebolla durante unos 3 minutos, hasta que esté tierna.

2 Añada las patatas, las zanahorias y el apio, y sazónelo todo con sal y pimienta negra recién molida. Deje cocer durante 4 ó 5 minutos más, hasta que las hortalizas empiecen a ablandarse.

3 Agregue el ajo y vierta suficiente agua para cubrirlo todo. Deje que rompa el hervor, tape la cazuela y cueza a fuego lento entre 10 y 15 minutos, hasta que las hortalizas estén prácticamente tiernas.

4 Incorpore el pescado a la cazuela con cuidado, tápela y deje cocer de 10 a 15 minutos, hasta que el pescado esté tierno; añada algo más de agua, si lo cree necesario. Poco antes de agotar el tiempo de cocción, retire la tapa y agregue el zumo de limón y el aceite de oliva restante; remueva. Rectifique el plato de sal y sírvalo.

Pescado relleno con salsa de huevo y limón

FETES PSARI GEMISTES AVGOLEMONO

Este plato resulta perfecto para las ocasiones especiales. Y aunque requiere algo más de tiempo que la mayoría de las meze, merece la pena prepararlo para poder disfrutar de su delicioso sabor y su buena presentación.

Tiempo de preparación: unos 45 minutos
Tiempo de cocción: unos 40 minutos
Temperatura del horno: 180°C

PARA 6–8 PERSONAS

- *6 cucharadas de mantequilla*
- *2 dientes de ajo, majados*
- *1 cebolla, picada*
- *½ pimiento verde, sin semillas y picado*
- *150 g de gambas peladas, cocidas y troceadas*
- *1 taza de pan blanco fresco, rallado*
- *1 cucharada de perejil fresco, picado*
- *sal y pimienta negra recién molida, al gusto*
- *4 filetes de platija o lenguado, sin piel*
- *3 huevos*
- *6 cucharadas de zumo de limón recién exprimido*
- *1¼ tazas de caldo de pescado caliente*
- *perejil fresco picado, para aderezar*

1 Precaliente el horno a 180°C. Derrita dos cucharadas de mantequilla en una sartén grande y rehogue el ajo, la cebolla y el pimiento verde durante unos 5 minutos, hasta que la cebolla esté dorada.

2 Añada las gambas a la mezcla de cebolla, junto con el pan rallado, el perejil, la sal y la pimienta negra; remueva. Cueza el relleno 1 minuto más, retírelo del fuego y déjelo enfriar.

3 Distribuya la mezcla de las gambas entre los filetes de pescado y espárzala bien. Enrolle los filetes y colóquelos, con la costura hacia abajo, en una fuente de horno grande y untada con mantequilla. Derrita la mantequilla restante en un cazo y unte con ella los filetes de pescado enrollados. Hornéelo todo entre 25 y 30 minutos o hasta que la carne del pescado se desprenda con facilidad y esté tierna. Corte los rollos en rodajas de 1 cm y dispóngalas en una fuente de servir precalentada. Coloque papel de aluminio encima para que no se enfríen.

4 Para la salsa de huevo y limón, bata los huevos en un bol mediano y agregue el zumo de limón de manera gradual; bátalo. Añada, asimismo, el caldo de pescado caliente muy poquito a poco. Pase la salsa a un cazo y caliéntela a fuego lento, sin dejar de batir, hasta que empiece a espesarse. Nape con ella los rollos de pescado y espolvoréelos con el perejil.

ABAJO
Peces de todos los colores del arco iris en el puerto de Heraklion.

Fritos de bacalao con ajo

BAKALIAROS SKORTHALIA

Adquiera el bacalao en un puesto especializado y recuerde que debe empezar esta receta con un día de antelación, ya que el bacalao debe estar en remojo durante 24 horas.

Tiempo de preparación: 1 hora y 30 minutos, más remojo
Tiempo de cocción: unos 5–10 minutos
PARA 6–8 PERSONAS

- *750 g de bacalao, puesto a remojo durante 24 horas, renovando el agua*
- *¾ taza de harina*
- *sal y pimienta negra recién molida, al gusto*
- *1 cucharada de aceite de oliva*
- *⅔ taza de agua caliente*
- *1 clara de huevo*
- *aceite de oliva, para freír*
- *gajos de limón, para servir*

PARA LA *SKORTHALIA*

- *4 rebanadas de pan blanco, sin la corteza*
- *6 dientes de ajo, majados*
- *sal, al gusto*
- *⅓ taza de almendras blanqueadas, molidas*
- *⅔ taza de aceite de oliva*
- *el zumo de 1 limón recién exprimido*

1 Para la *skorthalia,* vierta el pan en el robot de cocina y tritúrelo bien fino. Agregue al pan 4 cucharadas de agua fría y déjelo en remojo durante 5 minutos. Añada el ajo, la sal y la almendra molida y tritúrelo todo bien fino.

2 Con el robot en marcha, deje caer el aceite de oliva en un chorrito continuo, hasta que la mezcla se espese y esté bien fina. Vierta el zumo de limón de la misma manera que el aceite. Páselo todo a un bol de servir, tape y reserve.

3 Retire la piel y las espinas del bacalao y deséchelas. Corte la carne en dados de 5 cm. Prepare el rebozado para el pescado en un bol con la harina tamizada, la sal y la pimienta negra recién molida. Rocíelo todo con el aceite de oliva y agregue el agua caliente; bata la mezcla hasta que adquiera una textura bien fina. Déjela reposar durante 1 hora a temperatura ambiente.

4 Bata la clara de huevo a punto de nieve en un bol limpio y seco, y añádala a la mezcla del rebozado. Caliente el aceite, sumerja los trozos de pescado en el rebozado y viértalos con cuidado en el aceite. Fría el pescado por tandas de 5 a 7 minutos, o bien hasta que esté crujiente y dorado. Con una espumadera, pase los fritos a un plato forrado con papel de cocina, a fin de que escurran el aceite. Sírvalos acompañados con gajos de limón y la *skorthalia.*

ABAJO
La antigua ciudad de Epidauros es conocida por la belleza del Templo de Asklepios (siglo IV a.C.) y por su teatro, que aparece en la ilustración.

Menú veraniego de pescado

Atún con garbanzos
Tonos me Revithia

◆

Crema de huevas de bacalao
Taramosalata

◆

Roscas de sésamo
Semit

◆

Pinchos de pez espada
Xifias Souvlakia

◆

Salmonetes con ajo
Barbouni me Skortho

◆

Champiñones a la griega
Manitaria

◆

Judías de careta con espinacas
Louvia me Lahana

◆

Hortalizas rellenas sin carne
Yemista Orphana

◆

Pastel de crema
Galaktoboureko

◆

Crêpes con mermelada
Krep me Marmelada

◆

Vino: Retsina
(vino blanco seco)

Mejillones rebozados

MITHIA TIGANITA

En Grecia abundan los mejillones frescos y, por lo tanto, resultan bastante económicos. En el caso de utilizar mejillones congelados, ya cocidos, lo único que debe hacer es descongelarlos bien antes de usarlos.

Tiempo de preparación: unos 30 minutos
Tiempo de cocción: unos 15–20 minutos
PARA 6–8 PERSONAS

- *1 kg de mejillones frescos*
- *aceite vegetal, para freír*
- *gajos de limón, para servir*

PARA EL REBOZADO
- *2 huevos*
- *½ taza de harina*
- *sal y pimienta negra recién molida, al gusto*
- *2 cucharadas de perejil fresco, picado*
- *½ cucharadita de canela molida*

1 Lave y frote los mejillones bajo el chorro de agua fría, retire las "barbas" y deseche aquellos que estén entreabiertos. Coloque los mejillones limpios en una cacerola grande.

2 Cubra los mejillones con agua y deje que rompa el hervor; cuézalos durante unos 10 minutos, hasta que se abran las conchas y los mejillones estén tiernos. Escúrralos y deseche aquellos que no se hayan abierto. Deje que se enfríen ligeramente y sepárelos de su concha.

3 Para preparar el rebozado, casque los huevos en un bol de tamaño mediano y bátalos hasta que estén espumosos. Agregue la harina y bátalo todo bien fino. Vierta 4 cucharadas de agua fría y sazone con sal y pimienta negra recién molida. Incorpore el perejil picado y la canela molida; remueva todo bien.

4 Caliente abundante aceite. Moje los mejillones, uno por uno, en la mezcla del rebozado y déjelos caer con cuidado en el aceite caliente. Fríalos por tandas durante unos segundos, o bien hasta que estén crujientes por fuera. Con una espumadera, páselos a un plato con papel de cocina, a fin de que escurran el aceite. Sírvalos calientes y con los gajos de limón.

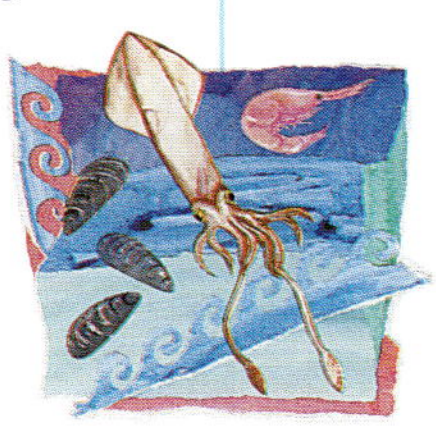

Pinchos de pez espada

XIFIAS SOUVLAKIA

El pez espada es el más indicado para esta receta, puesto que posee una carne firme y un sabor intenso; no se deshace durante la cocción y los pinchos quedan deliciosos.

Tiempo de preparación: 15 minutos, más marinada
Tiempo de cocción: unos 15–20 minutos
PARA 6–8 PERSONAS

- *½ taza de aceite de oliva*
- *el zumo de 2 limones recién exprimidos*
- *2 cucharaditas de orégano seco*
- *sal y pimienta negra recién molida, al gusto*
- *1 kg de pez espada, sin piel, en filetes y cortado en dados de 5 cm*
- *4 tomates, en cuartos*
- *2 pimientos verdes, sin semillas y troceados*
- *3 cebollas, cortadas en cuartos*

1 En un bol pequeño mezcle el aceite de oliva, el zumo de limón, el orégano, la sal y la pimienta negra recién molida al gusto. Coloque el pez espada en una fuente grande y llana, y vierta la mezcla de aceite por encima; tápelo y déjelo marinar durante 2 horas.

2 Reserve la marinada y reparta los dados de pescado, los cuartos de tomate, los trozos de pimiento verde y los cuartos de cebolla entre seis u ocho brochetas de metal. Disponga los pinchos sobre una rejilla para asar al grill.

3 Precaliente el grill y ase los pinchos de 10 a 15 minutos o hasta que el pescado esté hecho y las hortalizas estén tiernas; báñelos con frecuencia con la marinada reservada y déles la vuelta varias veces durante la cocción. Sírvalos inmediatamente.

28.773
ΛΙΑΝΙΚΗΣ ΠΩΛΗΣΕΩΣ
№ 10569
ΕΙΔΟΣ

Pescaditos en hojas de parra

PSARI STA KLIMATOFILLA

Las hojas de parra constituyen un envoltorio perfecto para el pescado pequeño y aceitoso, pues retienen el sabor y evitan que el pescado se deshaga durante la cocción. Se trata de una especialidad griega poco habitual que puede asarse también a la barbacoa.

Tiempo de preparación: unos 30 minutos
Tiempo de cocción: unos 10–15 minutos

PARA 6 PERSONAS

- *6 arenques o caballas pequeños, sin escamas y limpios*
- *el zumo de 1 limón recién exprimido*
- *sal y pimienta negra recién molida, al gusto*
- *aceite de oliva, para sazonar*
- *3 cucharaditas de tomillo seco ó 4 cucharaditas de tomillo fresco*
- *12 hojas de parra, cocidas durante 5 minutos, escurridas y enfriadas*
- *ramitas de tomillo frescas, para decorar*
- *gajos de limón, para servir*

1 Lave el pescado bajo el chorro de agua fría y séquelo con papel de cocina. Páselo a una tabla de trinchar y rocíelo con el zumo de limón. Sazónelo con sal y pimienta negra recién molida.

2 Rocíe el pescado con un poco de aceite de oliva y esparza el tomillo por encima. Extienda las hojas de parra sobre la superficie de trabajo y úntelas con un poco de aceite de oliva. Utilice dos hojas de parra para cada pescado y envuélvalo de modo que quede bien encerrado.

3 Disponga el pescado envuelto sobre una rejilla ligeramente untada con aceite y áselo al grill durante unos 6 minutos por cada lado, hasta que la carne esté tierna. Páselo a una fuente de servir y decórelo con ramitas de tomillo frescas. Sírvalo con los gajos de limón.

Pilaf de gambas

PILAFI ME GARIDES

Pruebe esta misma receta con mejillones cocidos sin concha en lugar de las gambas; es una variante exquisita.

Tiempo de preparación: unos 20 minutos
Tiempo de cocción: unos 25 minutos
PARA 6–8 PERSONAS

- *4 cucharadas de aceite de oliva*
- *2 dientes de ajo, majados*
- *1 cebolla grande, cortada en aros*
- *2 tallos de apio, picados*
- *⅔ taza de arroz de grano largo*
- *375 g de tomate triturado*
- *2 cucharaditas de mejorana seca*
- *sal y pimienta negra recién molida, al gusto*
- *⅔ taza de caldo de pescado caliente*
- *1 cucharadita de azúcar*
- *2 cucharaditas de zumo de limón*
- *300 g de gambas grandes, peladas y cocidas*
- *100 g de queso feta*
- *perejil fresco, picado*

1 Caliente el aceite en una sartén grande y sofría el ajo, la cebolla y el apio durante unos 5 minutos o hasta que estén tiernos. Añada el arroz y deje cocer todo 1 minuto más.

2 Agregue los tomates picados y la mejorana, y sazónelos con la sal y la pimienta negra recién molida. Vierta el caldo de pescado, el azúcar y el zumo de limón, y deje que rompa el hervor. Tape la sartén y deje cocer a fuego lento de 10 a 15 minutos o hasta que el arroz esté hecho; remueva de vez en cuando.

3 Incorpore las gambas y cuézalas de 3 a 5 minutos más. Esparza el queso por encima y remuévalo, a fin de mezclarlo todo bien. Retire la sartén del fuego y manténgala tapada durante 1 ó 2 minutos, o bien hasta que el queso se derrita. Espolvoree el *pilaf* con el perejil fresco picado y sírvalo directamente de la sartén.

Sardinas con tomate y romero

SARTHELA MARINATA

Dicen que todo aquel que prueba este plato clásico griego, sueña con Grecia el resto de su vida.

Tiempo de preparación: unos 30 minutos
Tiempo de cocción: unos 35 minutos
PARA 8 PERSONAS

- *8 sardinas frescas, limpias y sin la cabeza*
- *harina, para rebozar*
- *aceite de oliva, para freír*

PARA LA SALSA

- *¼ taza de aceite de oliva*
- *1 cucharada de harina*
- *¼ taza de vinagre de vino tinto*
- *400 g de tomate triturado, en lata*
- *2 cucharaditas de romero seco ó 3 cucharaditas de romero fresco*
- *1 cucharadita de orégano seco*
- *2 dientes de ajo, majados*
- *sal y pimienta negra recién molida, al gusto*
- *1 cucharadita de azúcar*
- *ramitas de romero frescas, para decorar*
- *gajos de limón, para acompañar*

1 Lave las sardinas y séquelas con papel absorbente; extiéndalas sobre la tabla de trinchar y enharínelas.

2 Caliente el aceite y fría el pescado por tandas durante unos 5 minutos, hasta que esté dorado y tierno. Con una espumadera, pase el pescado a un plato forrado con papel de cocina, a fin de que escurra el aceite. Cúbralo con papel de aluminio para mantenerlo caliente.

3 Para preparar la salsa, caliente el aceite de oliva en un cazo de tamaño mediano y vierta la harina; remuévalo bien hasta obtener un roux. Cuézalo durante 30 segundos y agregue de manera gradual el vino tinto, el vinagre y el tomate triturado, el romero, el orégano y el ajo. Sazone con la sal y la pimienta negra recién molida; añada el azúcar y remueva. Tape el cazo y cueza la salsa a fuego lento de 15 a 20 minutos hasta que se espese; remueva de vez en cuando.

4 Disponga las sardinas en una fuente de servir precalentada y nápelas con la salsa. Decórelas con ramitas de romero frescas y acompáñelas con los gajos de limón.

Un buffet para fiestas

Ensalada de patatas a la griega
Patatosalata

◆

Ensalada de pimientos asados
Piperies Orektiko

◆

Albóndigas marinadas
Keftedakia me Saltsa

◆

Patatas asadas con ajo
Patates me Skortho

◆

Hojas de parra rellenas
Dolmades

◆

Moussaka

◆

Pinchos de carne de cordero
Souvlakia

◆

Albóndigas de pollo fritas
Koto Tighanito

◆

Fritos de bacalao con ajo
Bakaliaros Skorthalia

◆

Pastas rellenas de frutos secos
Thaktyla Kypriaka

◆

Pastitas de queso dulces
Kaltsounia Cretis

◆

C A P Í T U L O 6

Meze dulces

Crêpes con mermelada

Pastas rellenas de frutos secos

Tarta de chocolate helada

Pastel de coco

Pastitas de almendra

Pastelitos de frutos secos

Pastel de crema

Tortitas de miel

Pastas de Navidad

Buñuelos de miel

Pastitas de Pascua

Pastitas de queso dulces

Compota de fruta variada

Pastel de Año Nuevo

Fruta en almíbar

Crêpes con mermelada

KREP ME MARMELADA

Prepare estos crêpes con antelación y apílelos en un plato; cúbralos con papel de aluminio y caliéntelos en el horno a temperatura baja durante 15 minutos. Sírvalos con mermelada y azúcar aromatizado con canela.

Tiempo de preparación: unos 30 minutos
Tiempo de cocción: unos 15 minutos
PARA UNAS 24 UNIDADES

- *2 huevos, batidos*
- *1 cucharada de azúcar*
- *un par de gotas de extracto de vainilla*
- *2½ tazas de leche*
- *2 tazas de harina*
- *mantequilla, para untar*
- *mermelada, para servir*
- *canela mezclada con azúcar extrafino, para servir*

1 Casque los huevos en un bol de tamaño mediano, añada el azúcar y bata la mezcla, preferiblemente con una batidora eléctrica, hasta que se espese, adquiera un tono pálido y espumee. Agregue el extracto de vainilla y la leche de manera gradual, y bátalo todo bien.

2 Agregue la harina tamizada poco a poco a la mezcla de huevo y bátala bien después de cada adición a fin de que no se formen grumos.

3 Derrita un poco de mantequilla en una sartén para crêpes y vierta 2 cucharadas de la mezcla anterior; haga girar la sartén para que la masa cubra todo el fondo. Fríala a fuego alto durante unos segundos o hasta que la crêpe esté dorada por la cara de abajo. Déle la vuelta con una espátula y cuézala unos segundos más hasta que se dore.

4 Pase la crêpe a un plato y siga friendo el resto de la masa; añada más mantequilla a la sartén, si lo cree necesario. Apile las crêpes ya cocidas y sepárelas con una hoja de papel encerado, de modo que no se peguen las unas a las otras.

5 Para servir las crêpes, extienda un poco de mermelada sobre cada una y enróllelas holgadamente. Dispóngalas en una fuente de servir precalentada, ya sea superponiéndolas o apilándolas. Espolvoréelas con la mezcla de azúcar y canela mientras estén calientes.

Pastas rellenas de frutos secos

THAKTYLA KYPRIAKA

Una masa crujiente, bañada de jarabe y con un exquisito relleno de frutos secos; no dude en preparar muchas, porque sus invitados van a repetir una y otra vez. El agua de rosas se vende en tiendas de productos naturales.

Tiempo de preparación: 1 hora, más reposo
Tiempo de cocción: unos 5–10 minutos
PARA 30-40 UNIDADES

- *aceite vegetal, para freír*
- *150 g de pistachos, sin cáscara y troceados*
- *1 cucharadita de canela*

PARA EL JARABE
- *2¼ tazas de azúcar*
- *2½ cucharadas de miel clara*
- *1½ tazas de agua*
- *una tira de piel de limón*
- *2 cucharadas de agua de rosas (opcional)*
- *2 cucharadas de zumo de limón recién exprimido*

PARA LA MASA
- *4⅓ tazas de harina, más un poco para espolvorear*
- *¼ cucharadita de sal*
- *¼ taza de mantequilla*
- *2 cucharadas de manteca*
- *2 cucharadas de agua*
- *1 yema de huevo*

PARA EL RELLENO
- *1 clara de huevo*
- *2 cucharadas de azúcar*
- *1⅓ tazas de almendras blanqueadas, molidas*
- *2 cucharaditas de canela*

1 Para preparar el jarabe, vierta el azúcar y la miel en un cazo de tamaño mediano, y agregue el agua; remueva. Deje que arranque el hervor a fuego lento y añada la piel de limón y el agua de rosas, si lo desea. Deje cocer a fuego lento durante unos 5 minutos y retire el cazo del fuego. Agregue el zumo de limón, destape el cazo y deje enfriar el jarabe.

2 Para la masa, tamice la harina junto con la sal en un bol grande y practique un hueco en el centro. Añada la mantequilla y la manteca, y trabaje la mezcla con un cuchillo hasta que adquiera el aspecto de migas de pan. Agregue el agua y la yema de huevo, remueva y mézclelo hasta obtener una masa consistente. Pásela a una superficie de trabajo ligeramente enharinada y amásela hasta dejarla bien fina. Introdúzcala en una bolsa de plástico y déjela reposar durante 1 hora.

3 Para el relleno, vierta la clara de huevo en un bol de tamaño mediano, limpio y seco, y agregue el azúcar. Bata la mezcla a punto de nieve e incorpore las almendras y la canela molidas.

4 Extienda la masa con el rodillo sobre una superficie de trabajo amplia, limpia y ligeramente enharinada, hasta dejarla bien fina, casi transparente. Córtela en rectángulos de 5 x 10 cm. Coloque ½ cucharadita de la mezcla de relleno en uno de los extremos cortos de cada rectángulo y enróllelos de forma que queden como un dedo. Con un tenedor moje las pastitas en agua fría, presione los extremos para encerrar bien el relleno, y tire a la vez de ellos para alargar la forma.

5 Caliente el aceite en una freidora y fría las pastitas por tandas de 3 a 5 minutos, hasta que estén doradas y crujientes. Con una espumadera, páselas a un plato con papel de cocina, a fin de que escurran el aceite.

6 Mezcle los pistachos troceados y la canela molida en un bol; espárzalo todo sobre un plato. Moje las pastitas calientes en el jarabe enfriado y páselas inmediatamente después por los frutos secos picados. Disponga las pastitas en una fuente de servir y sírvalas frías o calientes.

Tarta de chocolate helada

TOURTA TSOKOLATAS PSIGIOU

La *tourta tsokolatas psigiou* constituye un postre realmente exquisito, con la ventaja de poder hacerla con antelación.

Tiempo de preparación: unos 20 minutos, más congelación
Tiempo de cocción: ninguno

PARA 10–12 PERSONAS

- *2⅔ tazas de galletas integrales, desmigajadas*
- *½ taza de leche*
- *2 cucharadas de brandy*
- *1 taza de mantequilla, ablandada*
- *1 taza colmada de azúcar extrafino*
- *3 huevos*
- *2 cucharaditas de extracto de vainilla*
- *4 cucharadas de cacao en polvo*
- *¾ taza de almendras blanqueadas, tostadas y troceadas*
- *aceite vegetal, para untar*

1 Vierta las galletas desmigajadas en un bol grande, vierta la leche y el brandy por encima, y déjelas a remojo hasta que se embeban todo el líquido.

2 Vierta la mantequilla ablandada y el azúcar en un bol mediano, y bata la mezcla hasta dejarla homogénea y cremosa. Agregue las yemas de huevo, el extracto de vainilla, el cacao en polvo y las almendras troceadas; bata todo bien.

3 Monte las claras de huevo en un bol limpio e incorpórelas a la mezcla de chocolate. Agregue las galletas remojadas en leche. Unte un molde para pan de 1¼ litros de capacidad, fórrelo con papel encerado y vierta la mezcla de chocolate; espárzala bien en el molde y congélela durante unas 4 horas, o hasta que se solidifique. Retire la tarta del congelador unos 30 minutos antes de servir y manténgala refrigerada; pásela a un plato de servir y córtela en porciones.

Pastel de coco

PASTA A LA POLITA

◆ ◆ ◆ ◆

Un bizcocho esponjoso que se embebe en jarabe para conferirle una textura irresistible. En un recipiente hermético se conserva bien hasta dos semanas.

Tiempo de preparación: 1 hora aproximadamente
Tiempo de cocción: unos 40 minutos
Temperatura del horno: 190°C
PARA 10-12 PERSONAS

PARA EL JARABE

- *1¾ tazas de azúcar*
- *1 ramita de canela*
- *1 cucharada de brandy*
- *1 taza de agua*

PARA EL BIZCOCHO

- *2 tazas de mantequilla fundida, más un poco para untar*
- *1¾ tazas de azúcar*
- *6 huevos*
- *1 cucharada de brandy*
- *1 cucharada de zumo de naranja recién exprimido*
- *3¾ tazas de harina*
- *1 cucharada de levadura*
- *1¾ tazas de coco, en tiras*

1 Para preparar el jarabe, vierta el agua en un cazo mediano y añada el azúcar; remueva de vez en cuando mientras cuece a fuego lento, hasta que el azúcar se haya disuelto por completo. Incorpore la ramita de canela y el brandy, y deje que rompa el hervor. Hierva el jarabe unos 5 minutos, retírelo del fuego y déjelo aparte para que se enfríe.

2 Precaliente el horno a 190°C. Unte una fuente para asar de 23 x 70 x 7,5 cm con mantequilla y fórrela con papel encerado. Para el bizcocho, mezcle la harina con el azúcar en un bol y bata bien la mezcla hasta dejarla esponjosa. Incorpore las yemas de huevo, una por una, y bátalas después de cada adición. Agregue el brandy y el zumo de naranja.

3 Tamice la harina junto con la levadura y añada la mezcla anterior de manera gradual. Agregue el coco en tiras y bátalo todo. Aparte, en un bol limpio y seco, monte las claras de huevo a punto de nieve e incorpórelas a la mezcla cremosa. Páselo todo a la fuente y hornéelo de 30 a 35 minutos hasta que el bizcocho esté dorado. Inserte una brocheta en el centro de la masa y, si ésta sale limpia, significa que el bizcocho está hecho.

4 Coloque el bizcocho, sin desmoldarlo, encima de una rejilla y utilice un cuchillo afilado para marcar las porciones en forma de rombo. Vierta el jarabe enfriado por encima del bizcocho y déjelo reposar durante al menos 15 minutos antes de proceder a cortarlo en porciones y servirlo.

Pastitas de almendra

AMYGTHALOTA

El agua de rosas o de azahar se vende en establecimientos de productos naturales y selectos. Utilice almendra molida y elabore la mezcla de forma manual en lugar de con el robot de cocina.

Tiempo de preparación: unos 20 minutos
Tiempo de cocción: unos 15 minutos
Temperatura del horno: 180°C

PARA UNAS 24 UNIDADES

- *2½ tazas de almendras blanqueadas*
- *1 taza colmada de azúcar extrafino*
- *1 cucharadita de extracto de vainilla*
- *3 claras de huevo*
- *2½ tazas de pan blanco fresco, rallado*
- *mantequilla, para untar*
- *1¼ tazas de agua de rosas o de azahar*
- *azúcar, para decorar*

1 Precaliente el horno a 180°C. Vierta las almendras junto con 2 cucharadas de azúcar en el robot de cocina y tritúrelo todo bien fino. Añada el azúcar restante y el extracto de vainilla. En un bol aparte, limpio y seco, bata ligeramente las claras de huevo y agréguelas a la mezcla, junto con el pan rallado. Mézclelo todo hasta obtener una masa de textura fina y pásela a la superficie de trabajo.

2 Unte dos bandejas para galletas con un poco de mantequilla. Humedézcase las manos ligeramente y moldee la mezcla de almendras en forma de bolitas del tamaño de una nuez. Colóquelas en las bandejas y hornéelas durante 15 minutos hasta que estén doradas y firmes por fuera.

3 Déjelas enfriar un poco y páselas a una rejilla. Vierta el agua de rosas o de azahar en un bol pequeño y moje las bolitas: vuelva a depositarlas sobre la rejilla, espolvoréelas con el azúcar extrafino y déjelas secar antes de servir.

Pastelitos de frutos secos

BAKLAVA

Para esta versión del postre clásico griego se ha utilizado una mezcla de nueces y almendras, pero siempre se puede optar por rellenarlo sólo de nueces, de almendras o, por qué no, de pistachos.

Tiempo de preparación: unos 45 minutos
Tiempo de cocción: 1 hora y 15 minutos
Temperatura del horno: 160°C

PARA UNAS 24 UNIDADES

- *¾ taza de mantequilla, fundida*
- *450 g de pasta filo, descongelada, si no es fresca*

PARA EL RELLENO

- *4 cucharadas de miel clara*
- *2 cucharadas de zumo de limón recién exprimido*
- *¼ taza de azúcar*
- *2 cucharaditas de canela molida*
- *1 cucharadita de ralladura de limón*
- *1⅓ tazas de almendras blanqueadas, troceadas*
- *1⅓ tazas de nueces peladas, troceadas*

PARA EL JARABE

- *1¾ tazas de azúcar*
- *5 cucharadas de miel clara*
- *2½ tazas de agua*
- *1 ramita de canela*
- *1 tira de piel de limón*

1 Precaliente el horno a 160°C. Unte una fuente para asar de 30 x 23 x 7,5 cm con mantequilla y recorte las láminas de pasta filo para que encajen en el recipiente.

2 Extienda la primera lámina de pasta filo sobre el fondo de la fuente y úntela con mantequilla de manera uniforme. Repita la operación hasta que tenga 12 láminas de pasta filo una encima de la otra, y untadas. Cubra el resto de la pasta con un paño ligeramente humedecido, a fin de que no se seque mientras trabaja.

3 Para preparar el relleno, vierta la miel en un bol de tamaño mediano, añada el zumo de limón y revuélvalo bien. Incorpore el azúcar, la canela molida, la piel de limón y los frutos secos; esparza la mezcla obtenida sobre la pasta filo.

4 Disponga tres láminas más de pasta filo untadas con mantequilla fundida encima de la mezcla del relleno. Esparza el resto del relleno encima de la pasta y cúbralo con las láminas de pasta restantes, también untadas con mantequilla. Unte la superficie con la mantequilla que haya sobrado y marque rombos de 5 cm en la masa con un cuchillo. Hornee el *baklava* durante una hora o hasta que esté dorado y crujiente; retírelo del horno y déjelo reposar encima de una rejilla.

5 Para preparar el jarabe, vierta todos los ingredientes en un cazo de tamaño mediano y caliéntelo bien hasta que el azúcar se disuelva por completo. Suba el fuego y déjelo hervir durante 10 minutos, sin remover. Retírelo del fuego y déjelo enfriar; deseche la ramita de canela y la piel de limón y nape la superficie del postre con el jarabe. Para un resultado óptimo, deje reposar el *baklava* a temperatura ambiente durante toda la noche; sírvalo cortado en porciones en forma de rombo.

Pastel de crema

GALAKTOBOUREKO

Otro postre del recetario griego tradicional, muy similar al *baklava*, e igual de dulce e irresistible.

Tiempo de preparación: 1 hora aproximadamente
Tiempo de cocción: 1 hora y 30 minutos
Temperatura del horno: 180°C
PARA UNAS 24 UNIDADES

- *450 g de pasta filo*
- *½ taza de mantequilla sin sal, fundida*
- *naranja recién exprimido*
- *2 cucharaditas de zumo de limón recién exprimido*

PARA EL JARABE
- *2¼ tazas de azúcar*
- *1¼ tazas de agua*
- *1 ramita de canela*
- *clavos enteros*
- *1 cucharada de brandy*
- *1 cucharada de zumo de*

PARA EL RELLENO
- *1 taza colmada de azúcar*
- *⅓ taza de sémola fina*
- *6¼ tazas de leche*
- *1 cucharada de brandy*
- *3 huevos*
- *la ralladura de ½ naranja*

1 Para preparar el jarabe, vierta el azúcar y el agua en un cazo grande y remueva a fuego lento hasta que el azúcar se disuelva. Añada la ramita de canela y los clavos de especia, y deje que rompa el hervor; hierva el jarabe de 10 a 12 minutos. Retírelo del fuego y agregue los demás ingredientes; déjelo enfriar y deseche la ramita de canela y los clavos.

2 Precaliente el horno a 180°C. Unte una fuente para asar de 30 x 23 x 7,5 cm con un poco de mantequilla

3 Para el relleno, vierta el azúcar y la sémola en un cazo grande. Agregue la leche de manera gradual, remueva la mezcla constantemente y caliéntela a fuego lento, hasta que se espese. Asegúrese de que no se forman grumos. Incorpore el brandy y retire el cazo del fuego.

4 Casque los huevos en un bol y bátalos hasta que estén pálidos y espumosos. Añada la mezcla de sémola y bata todo de nuevo, hasta mezclarlo bien. Agregue la ralladura de naranja y deje enfriar la mezcla un poco.

5 Extienda la mitad de la pasta filo sobre el fondo de la fuente preparada, y unte las láminas con mantequilla fundida. Con una cuchara, esparza la mezcla de relleno por encima. Cubra todo con las láminas de pasta restantes untadas con mantequilla.

6 Mediante un cuchillo afilado, marque en las capas superiores de pasta rombos o cuadrados de 5 cm de lado. Hornee el pastel durante 45 minutos o hasta que esté crujiente y dorado por encima, y el relleno haya cuajado. Retírelo del fuego y colóquelo sobre una rejilla, sin sacarlo de la bandeja. Nape el *galaktoboureko* con el jarabe y déjelo reposar al menos durante 4 horas o, preferiblemente, durante toda la noche. Sirva el pastel cortado en trozos pequeños.

Tortitas de miel

DIPLES

◆ ◆ ◆ ◆

Uno de los dulces preferidos de los griegos. Se trata de trozos finos de masa fritos en aceite, que se mojan en jarabe de miel y se recubren con nueces troceadas y canela.

Tiempo de preparación: unos 30 minutos
Tiempo de cocción: unos 20 minutos
PARA UNAS 60 UNIDADES

- *3 huevos, más 3 yemas*
- *2 cucharadas de zumo de naranja, recién exprimido*
- *2 cucharaditas de levadura*
- *6½ tazas de harina*
- *aceite vegetal, para freír*

PARA EL JARABE

- *1⅓ tazas de miel clara*
- *½ taza de agua*
- *2 cucharaditas de canela molida*
- *1⅔ tazas de nueces peladas*

1 Vierta los huevos y las yemas en un bol, y bátalo todo bien; agregue el zumo de naranja. Aparte tamice la levadura en polvo junto con 3¾ tazas de harina y añádalas a la mezcla de huevo; bata bien la mezcla resultante. Agregue más harina hasta obtener una masa consistente.

2 Pase la masa a una superficie de trabajo ligeramente enharinada y trabájela durante unos 10 minutos, hasta que aparezcan burbujas.

3 Corte la masa en cuatro partes iguales y extiéndalas con el rodillo sobre la superficie enharinada, hasta que estén tan finas como el papel. Corte la masa en rectángulos de 10 x 15 cm y déjelos reposar. Caliente el aceite y fría las tiras de masa por tandas, durante unos pocos segundos, hasta que estén doradas y crujientes. Con la ayuda de dos tenedores, déles varias vueltas durante la cocción. Con una espumadera, páselas a un plato con papel de cocina para que se escurran.

4 Para preparar el jarabe, vierta la miel y el agua en un cazo grande y caliéntelos a fuego lento, hasta que se funda la miel. Deje que rompa el hervor y cuézalo durante unos 15 minutos; espume la superficie cuando el jarabe hierva. Retírelo del fuego. Moje cada una de las tortitas en el jarabe caliente y colóquelas encima de la rejilla para que se enfríen. Espolvoréelas con la canela molida, páselas por las nueces troceadas y déjelas enfriar por completo antes de servir.

Pastas de Navidad

KOURABIETHES

Poco antes de que empiece la Navidad, las pastelerías griegas llenan sus escaparates con este tipo de pastas. Prepare muchas con antelación y guárdelas bien herméticas; así estarán a punto para las celebraciones navideñas.

Tiempo de preparación: unos 20 minutos
Tiempo de cocción: unos 20 minutos
Temperatura del horno: 190°C

PARA UNAS 26 UNIDADES

- *2 tazas de mantequilla, ablandada*
- *1 taza colmada de azúcar*
- *3 yemas de huevo*
- *4 cucharadas de brandy*
- *un par de gotas de extracto de vainilla*
- *7 1/3 tazas de harina de fuerza, tamizada*
- *1 1/3 tazas de almendras blanqueadas y tostadas*
- *4 cucharadas de agua de rosas*
- *azúcar glas, tamizado*

1 Precaliente el horno a 190°C. Vierta la mantequilla y el azúcar en un bol, y mézclelos hasta obtener una crema ligera y esponjosa. Añada las yemas de huevo, el brandy y el extracto de vainilla.

2 Tamice la harina y agregue las almendras; remueva bien hasta obtener una masa consistente. Pásela a una superficie de trabajo enharinada y trabájela durante unos segundos.

3 Extienda la masa con el rodillo hasta dejarla de 5 mm de grosor y córtela, con la ayuda de moldes, en forma de estrella, de media luna y de círculos. Coloque las pastas en placas previamente untadas con un poco de mantequilla y hornéelas durante unos 20 minutos, hasta que estén firmes pero no doradas.

4 Páselas a una rejilla para que se enfríen y rocíelas con el agua de rosas. Déjelas secar y espolvoréelas con abundante azúcar glas. Apílelas en un plato y sírvalas.

Buñuelos de miel

LOUKOUMADES

Una especialidad griega que se sirve con un buen café amargo, a fin de contrarrestar el dulce sabor y la textura melosa de estas delicias de almendra.

Tiempo de preparación: unos 30 minutos
Tiempo de cocción: unos 5–10 minutos
PARA 30 UNIDADES

- *1 ¼ tazas de agua templada*
- *20 g de levadura fresca*
- *2 ¾ tazas de harina*
- *½ cucharadita de canela*
- *una pizca de sal*
- *6 cucharadas de leche*
- *2 huevos, batidos*
- *aceite vegetal, para freír*
- *¼ taza de azúcar*
- *1 cucharadita de canela molida*
- *⅔ tazas de almendras blanqueadas, tostadas*

PARA EL JARABE

- *⅔ taza de miel clara*
- *½ taza de azúcar*
- *1 cucharada de zumo de limón recién exprimido*
- *1 ramita de canela*

1 Vierta ⅔ taza de agua templada en un bol y esparza la levadura por encima. Remueva bien hasta que ésta se haya disuelto por completo. Deje reposar la mezcla de 15 a 20 minutos en un lugar templado, hasta que espumee.

2 Tamice la harina con la canela y la sal en un bol, y practique un hueco en el centro de los ingredientes; vierta la mezcla espumosa de la levadura, la leche y el resto del agua templada. Agregue la mezcla de harina de manera gradual, dejándola caer desde los laterales del bol. Incorpore los huevos y bátalo todo, de manera que resulte una masa de textura fina. Siga batiéndolo hasta que aparezcan burbujas en la superficie y déjelo reposar.

3 Para el jarabe, vierta todos los ingredientes en una cacerola mediana y caliéntelo a fuego lento hasta que el azúcar se disuelva. Suba el fuego y hierva el jarabe unos 10 minutos; déjelo enfriar, retire la ramita de canela y resérvelo.

4 Caliente abundante aceite para freír. Vierta la masa en el aceite caliente cucharada a cucharada y fría los buñuelos por tandas, de 3 a 5 minutos, hasta que se hinchen y estén dorados. Remuévalos con frecuencia durante la cocción. Repita la operación con el resto de la masa. Con una espumadera, pase los buñuelos ya hechos a un plato forrado con papel de cocina, y déjelos que escurran el aceite.

5 Mezcle el azúcar extrafino y la canela molida en un plato. Pase los buñuelos por la mezcla a fin de que queden bien rebozados. Disponga los buñuelos en una fuente de servir llana, nápelos con el jarabe y déjelos reposar durante 1 hora; esparza la almendra troceada por encima. También puede apilar los buñuelos en un plato, esparcir la almendra por encima y servir el jarabe aparte.

Pastitas de Pascua

KOULOURAKIA LAMBRIATIKA

Estas pastas son un requisito indispensable de la comida de Pascua en Grecia. Semanas después de las celebraciones, se siguen mojando en el café del desayuno.

Tiempo de preparación: unos 30 minutos, más tiempo en reposo
Tiempo de cocción: unos 20 minutos
Temperatura del horno: 180°C

PARA UNAS 48 UNIDADES

- *6½ tazas de harina*
- *1 cucharada de levadura*
- *una pizca de sal*
- *¾ taza de mantequilla, reblandecida*
- *1¾ tazas colmadas de azúcar extrafino*
- *2 huevos*
- *½ taza de leche*
- *la ralladura de ½ naranja*
- *la ralladura de ½ limón*
- *un par de gotas de extracto de vainilla*
- *1 yema de huevo desleída con 1 cucharada de zumo de naranja, para glasear*
- *semillas de sésamo, para decorar*

1 Precaliente el horno a 180°C. Tamice la harina junto con la levadura y una pizca de sal en un bol de tamaño mediano.

2 Vierta la mantequilla y el azúcar en un bol, y bátalos bien hasta obtener una mezcla ligera y esponjosa. Incorpore los huevos, uno por uno, y agregue la leche; bátalo todo bien después de cada adición. Añada las ralladuras de naranja y de limón y el extracto de vainilla; bátalo de nuevo.

3 Añada la mezcla de harina de manera gradual y poco a poco, a fin de obtener una masa espesa y de textura fina. Pásela a una superficie de trabajo ligeramente enharinada y amásela hasta ablandarla. Déjela reposar unos 10 minutos.

4 Divida la masa en pequeñas porciones y moldéelas como bastoncitos; forme con ellos figuras en forma de S, espirales, aros o círculos. Compruebe que las figuritas tienen el mismo tamaño para que se cuezan de manera uniforme.

5 Disponga las pastitas en bandejas para galletas ligeramente engrasadas y píntelas con la mezcla de naranja y yema de huevo. Esparza las semillas de sésamo por encima y hornéelas entre 15 y 20 minutos, o bien hasta que estén doradas. Páselas a una rejilla para que se enfríen.

Pastitas de queso dulces

KALTSOUNIA CRETIS

Esta receta es originaria de Creta, donde las *kaltsounia cretis* se pueden adquirir recién salidas del horno las veinticuatro horas del día. El queso del relleno se vende en tiendas especializadas en productos selectos. Estas pastas se conservan hasta dos semanas, si se guardan en un recipiente hermético y en un lugar fresco y seco.

Tiempo de preparación: unos 40, más reposo
Tiempo de cocción: unos 25 minutos
Temperatura del horno: 180 °C
PARA UNAS 30 UNIDADES

- *azúcar extrafino, tamizado, para decorar*

PARA LA MASA
- *3¾ tazas de harina tamizada*
- *1 cucharadita de levadura*
- *1 cucharada de azúcar*
- *una pizca de sal*
- *¼ taza de mantequilla, en dados, y más para untar*
- *¼ taza de manteca en dados*
- *2 huevos*
- *2 cucharaditas de agua de azahar*
- *1–2 cucharadas de leche*

PARA EL RELLENO
- *450 g de queso fresco sin sal, como el mizithra, el anthotiro o el ricotta*
- *1 huevo*
- *⅓ taza de azúcar*
- *2 cucharadas de miel clara*
- *1 cucharadita de canela*
- *½ cucharadita de menta*

ABAJO
Las galletas son auténticas obras de arte en esta típica pastelería de Heraklion.

1 Para preparar la masa, tamice la harina, la levadura en polvo, el azúcar y la sal en un bol. Añada la mantequilla y la manteca y utilice un cuchillo para desmenuzarlas hasta que la mezcla tome la apariencia de migas de pan.

2 Incorpore los huevos, el agua de azahar y la leche, hasta obtener una masa blanda y elástica. Pásela a una superficie ligeramente enharinada y amásela durante 10 minutos, hasta que adquiera una consistencia fina y blanda. Devuelva la masa al bol limpio, tápela y déjela reposar.

3 Para el relleno, mezcle los ingredientes en un bol y remuévalos bien. Unte dos bandejas para galletas con un poco de mantequilla y precaliente el horno a 180 °C.

4 Divida la masa en porciones del tamaño de una nuez y extiéndalas con el rodillo en una superficie enharinada hasta obtener círculos de 10 cm de diámetro. Coloque 1 cucharadita del relleno en el centro de cada círculo y doble los cuatro lados hacia dentro hasta que se toquen, pero dejando que se vea un poco el relleno.

5 Coloque las pastitas de queso en las bandejas engrasadas y hornéelas de 20 a 25 minutos, hasta que empiecen a dorarse y estén crujientes. Páselas a una rejilla para que se enfríen y espolvoree el azúcar glas por encima.

Compota de frutas

KOMPOSTA ANAMIKTI

El mejor acompañamiento de este delicioso postre es una buena porción de yogur griego muy espeso.

Tiempo de preparación: unos 30 minutos
Tiempo de cocción: unos 15 minutos

PARA 8–10 PERSONAS

- *350 g de peras*
- *350 g de manzanas*
- *350 g de melocotones*
- *350 g de albaricoques*
- *2 cucharadas de zumo de limón recién exprimido*
- *3½ tazas de azúcar*
- *2 ramitas de canela*
- *3¾ tazas de agua*
- *3–4 clavos*
- *1 tira de piel de limón*

1 Para preparar la fruta para la compota, pele las peras y las manzanas, extráigales el corazón y córtelas en cuartos. Lave los melocotones y los albaricoques, y deseche el hueso. Corte los melocotones en cuartos y los albaricoques por la mitad.

2 Vierta los cuartos de pera y de manzana en una cacerola grande de fondo pesado, junto con el zumo de limón, el azúcar, la canela, el agua, los clavos y la piel de limón. Deje cocer a fuego lento hasta que rompa el hervor y hiérvalo durante unos 5 minutos.

3 Añada los melocotones y deje cocer durante otros 5 minutos; incorpore los albaricoques y cueza todo de 3 a 5 minutos más, hasta que estén tiernos. Con una espumadera, pase la fruta a un bol de servir, tápela y déjela reposar.

4 Deje que el jarabe vuelva a romper el hervor y cuézalo a fuego fuerte durante 10 minutos, o hasta que se reduzca un poco y se espese. Retire las ramitas de canela, los clavos y la piel de limón. Deje enfriar el jarabe y viértalo sobre la fruta; sirva la compota a temperatura ambiente, o bien recién salida del frigorífico.

Pastel de Año Nuevo

VASSILOPITTA

El *vassilopitta* se sirve por tradición el día de Año Nuevo. El afortunado que encuentre la moneda en su porción, deberá tener cuidado de no tragársela.

Tiempo de preparación: unos 40 minutos, más tiempo para subir
Tiempo de cocción: unos 50 minutos
Temperatura del horno: 190°C
PARA 10–12 PERSONAS

- *8 tazas de harina*
- *una pizca de sal*
- *1 taza de leche tibia*
- *50 g de levadura fresca*
- *4 huevos*
- *½ taza de azúcar extrafino*
- *1 taza de mantequilla fundida y más para engrasar*
- *leche, para glasear*
- *3 cucharadas de semillas de sésamo tostadas, para decorar*

1 Tamice la harina y la sal en un bol grande. Vierta la leche templada en un bol aparte y esparza la levadura por encima; remueva bien hasta que ésta se disuelva. Tape el bol y deje reposar la mezcla en un lugar cálido hasta que espumee.

2 Practique un hueco en el centro de la mezcla de harina y añada los huevos, uno por uno; bátalos bien. Agregue el azúcar, la mantequilla y la mezcla de levadura. Siga removiendo hasta obtener una masa, pásela a una superficie de trabajo enharinada y amásela hasta dejarla suave y elástica.

3 Devuelva la masa al bol limpio y cúbrala con film transparente. Déjela reposar durante 2 horas en un lugar cálido para que doble su volumen.

4 Precaliente el horno a 190°C. Pase la masa a una superficie de trabajo ligeramente enharinada y amásela de nuevo durante 5 minutos. Introduzca una moneda limpia en la masa y siga trabajándola de 1 a 2 minutos más. Moldee la masa en forma de bola e introdúzcala en un molde redondo de 20 cm, engrasado. Cúbrala con film transparente y déjela en un lugar cálido otros 10 minutos más, hasta que suba.

5 Moje la superficie del pastel con leche y esparza las semillas de sésamo tostadas por encima. Hornéelo durante 50 minutos, hasta que esté dorado por arriba y suene a hueco al darle golpecitos con la mano. Páselo a una rejilla para que se enfríe y sírvalo cortado en porciones.

Fruta en almíbar

GLIKA KOUTALIOU

Prepare varios tarros con estas dulces tentaciones cuando la fruta sea del tiempo, ya que se conservan durante meses si se guardan en un lugar fresco y seco. Los griegos solían ofrecer estos dulces a los invitados con una taza de café y un vaso de agua helada. Ofrezca varios platos con fruta y almíbar para que los invitados se sirvan por sí mismos.

Tiempo de preparación: unos 30 minutos, más reposo
Tiempo de cocción: unos 20 minutos
PARA UNOS 3 TARROS DE 450 G

- *1 kg de fruta fresca variada: cerezas, higos, uvas y uvas espina*
- *2½ tazas de agua*
- *3½ tazas de azúcar*
- *2 cucharadas de zumo de limón recién exprimido*
- *1 tira de piel de limón*
- *un par de gotas de extracto de vainilla*

1 Prepare la fruta: deshuese las cerezas y las uvas, limpie las uvas espina, etc.

2 Vierta el agua en una cacerola grande y añada el azúcar. Caliéntelos, sin dejar de remover, hasta que el azúcar se disuelva. Suba el fuego y deje hervir el almíbar durante 5 minutos, sin removerlo.

3 Vierta la fruta en el almíbar, junto con la piel de limón y el extracto de vainilla, y deje cocer la mezcla a fuego lento durante 10 minutos. Pásela a un bol resistente al calor, tápela y déjela reposar toda la noche en un lugar fresco.

4 Devuelva la fruta a la cacerola limpia con el almíbar y deje que rompa el hervor una vez más. Deje cocer todo a fuego lento durante 5 minutos y páselo luego al bol. Tápelo y déjelo reposar toda la noche.

5 Deseche la piel de limón. Con una cuchara, vierta la fruta y el almíbar en tarros con tapa de rosca esterilizados y todavía calientes. Enfríelos, etiquételos y guárdelos hasta el momento de consumirlos.

CAPÍTULO 7

Un pan para cada meze

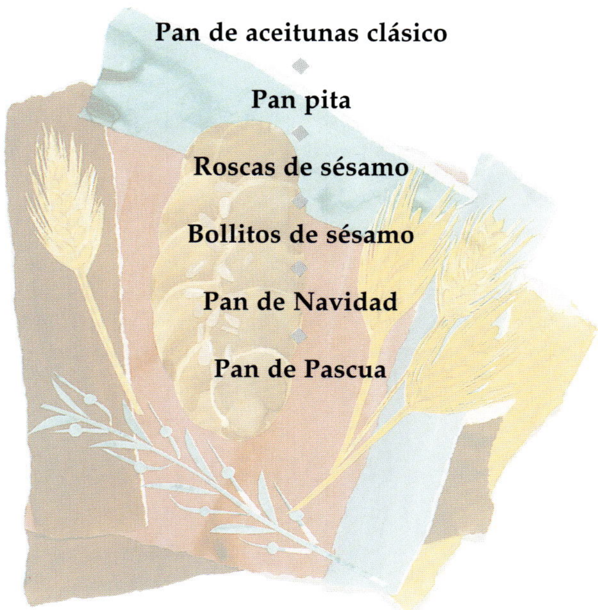

Pan de aceitunas clásico

Pan pita

Roscas de sésamo

Bollitos de sésamo

Pan de Navidad

Pan de Pascua

Pan de aceitunas clásico

ELIOPITTA

Las aceitunas que se añaden a este pan no siempre están deshuesadas. Para un toque excepcional, pinte el pan con yema batida 15 minutos antes de agotar el tiempo de cocción.

Tiempo de preparación: unos 30 minutos, más reposo
Tiempo de cocción: unos 50 minutos
Temperatura del horno: 190°C

PARA 1 PAN

- *6½ tazas de harina de trigo*
- *1 cucharada de levadura, en polvo*
- *una pizca de sal*
- *¾ taza de agua*
- *¼ taza de aceite de oliva, más un poco para untar*
- *1 cucharada de menta seca*
- *1 cebolla, picada*
- *350 g de aceitunas, deshuesadas, lavadas y secas*
- *1 yema de huevo, batida, para glasear*

1 Precaliente el horno a 190°C. Tamice la harina, la levadura y la sal en un bol, y practique un hueco en el centro.

2 Vierta el agua en el hueco, junto con el aceite de oliva, la menta seca, la cebolla picada y las aceitunas. Remuévalo todo con una cuchara de madera hasta obtener una masa consistente. Pase la masa a una superficie de trabajo ligeramente enharinada y trabájela durante al menos 10 minutos, hasta que adquiera una textura blanda y fina. Devuelva la masa al bol limpio, cúbrala con film transparente y déjela en reposo durante unos 10 minutos.

3 Vuelva a colocar la masa sobre una superficie de trabajo ligeramente enharinada; trabájela y moldéela en forma de bola de 24 cm de diámetro. Unte con un poco de aceite una fuente de horno honda y ovalada de 25 cm de diámetro; coloque la masa dentro y hornéela durante unos 50 minutos. Pinte la superficie con la yema batida 15 minutos antes de retirar el pan del horno. Déjelo enfriar sobre una rejilla.

Pan pita

PITTA

No hay nada comparable al sabor único del pan pita recién hecho, servido junto con toda una selección de deliciosas meze. El pan pita es ideal para congelar, ya que sólo es necesario calentarlo en el horno durante unos minutos a temperatura moderada antes de servirlo.

Tiempo de preparación: unos 30 minutos, más tiempo para subir
Tiempo de cocción: unos 10 minutos
Temperatura del horno: 240°C

PARA 12 UNIDADES

- *3 cucharadas de levadura*
- *1 cucharadita de azúcar*
- *2½ tazas de agua caliente*
- *11 tazas de harina de trigo, más un poco para decorar*
- *2 cucharaditas de sal*
- *6 cucharadas de mantequilla, fundida*

1 Vierta la levadura y el azúcar en un bol pequeño y añada 1¼ tazas de agua caliente. Remueva bien hasta que todo se haya disuelto. Cubra la mezcla con film transparente y déjela reposar 15 minutos en un lugar cálido, hasta que espumee.

2 Ponga la harina junto con la sal en un bol, y practique un hueco en el centro. Vierta 1¼ tazas de agua caliente en el centro de los ingredientes y añada la mantequilla fundida y la mezcla de levadura; remueva bien hasta obtener una masa pegajosa.

3 Pase la masa a una superficie de trabajo ligeramente enharinada y añádale un poco más de harina, si lo cree necesario. Trabájela hasta dejarla blanda y fina, y moldéela en forma de bola; pásela a un bol limpio. Cubra la masa con film transparente y déjela reposar en un lugar cálido durante 1½ horas, o hasta que haya doblado su volumen.

4 Vuelva a poner la masa sobre la superficie de trabajo ligeramente enharinada y golpéela hasta que adquiera de nuevo su tamaño original. Déjela reposar unos 20 minutos y mientras tanto espolvoree tres bandejas de horno con harina.

5 Corte la masa en 12 porciones iguales y moldéelas en forma de bola de unos 20 cm de diámetro. Dispóngalas en las bandejas, de modo que disten unos 2,5 cm las unas de las otras. Cúbralas con film transparente, pero sin presionarlas, y deposítelas durante 30 minutos en un lugar cálido para que sigan subiendo.

6 Precaliente el horno a 240°C. Coloque la primera bandeja en la parte inferior del horno y espere de 3 a 5 minutos, hasta que suba el pan. Retire el pan de la bandeja y deposítelo en la rejilla y a media altura del horno. Hornéelo otros 5 minutos más hasta que esté consistente y empiece a dorarse. Páselo a una fuente de servir precalentada y repita la operación con la masa restante. Sirva el pan caliente.

A LA DERECHA
Las paredes se blanquean para reflectar el calor, con lo que los pueblos como éste, cerca de Plakias, constituyen todo un reducto de frescor durante el verano.

Roscas de sésamo

SEMIT

Son el equivalente griego de los *brezels* alemanes y se conservan durante días en un recipiente hermético.

Tiempo de preparación: unos 20 minutos, más tiempo para subir
Tiempo de cocción: unos 15 minutos
Temperatura del horno: 190°C

PARA UNAS 12 UNIDADES

- *3¾ tazas de harina, más un poco para decorar*
- *1 cucharadita de azúcar*
- *una pizca de sal*
- *3 cucharaditas de levadura seca*
- *½ cucharadita de menta*
- *⅔ taza de agua caliente*
- *1 clara de huevo desleída con 2 cucharadas de agua fría, para glasear*
- *semillas de sésamo*

1 Vierta la mitad de la harina en un bol de tamaño mediano, junto con el azúcar, la sal, la levadura seca y la menta. Agregue el agua caliente y trabájelo todo hasta obtener una masa pegajosa.

2 Añada la mitad del resto de la harina y amase todo con las manos. Pase la masa a una superficie de trabajo ligeramente enharinada y siga trabajándola hasta que deje de ser pegajosa y adquiera una textura suave y blanda (añada la harina restante, si lo cree necesario). Vuelva a colocarla en el bol, cúbrala con film transparente y déjela reposar 5 minutos.

3 Corte la masa en cuatro porciones iguales y moldee cada porción en forma de salchicha de 60 cm de largo. Divida ésta en tres partes y forme roscas cerradas con cada una de ellas.

4 Precaliente el horno a 190°C. Espolvoree varias bandejas de horno con harina y disponga las roscas encima. Cúbralas con film transparente, de modo que quede suelto, y déjelas reposar 25 minutos en un lugar cálido hasta que suban.

5 Pinte las roscas con la mezcla de clara de huevo y esparza las semillas de sésamo por encima. Hornéelas durante unos 15 minutos, hasta que estén doradas y crujientes. Páselas a una rejilla y déjelas enfriar antes de servir.

Bollitos de sésamo

PSOMAKIA ME PROZIMI

Estos bollitos resuelven cualquier situación, pues siempre quedan bien. Congele los que sobren y descongele sólo los que vaya a necesitar.

Tiempo de preparación: unos 30 minutos, más reposo
Tiempo de cocción: unos 20 minutos
Temperatura del horno: 180°C

PARA UNAS 48 UNIDADES

- *2 cucharadas de levadura seca*
- *12¾ tazas de harina*
- *1 taza colmada de azúcar*
- *5 cucharadas de agua caliente*
- *2½ tazas de leche*
- *3 huevos, batidos*
- *extracto de vainilla*
- *½ taza de mantequilla*
- *aceite vegetal, para untar*
- *1 huevo batido, para glasear*
- *semillas de sésamo*

1 Vierta la levadura, 3 cucharadas de harina, ½ cucharadita de azúcar, ½ cucharadita de sal y el agua caliente en un bol de tamaño pequeño. Revuelva hasta que la levadura y el azúcar se disuelvan, cubra la mezcla con film transparente y déjela 15 minutos en un lugar cálido, hasta que espumee.

2 Vierta la leche en un bol grande y agregue el azúcar restante junto con la sal, los huevos batidos y el extracto de vainilla. Incorpore la mezcla espumosa de levadura y bátalo todo bien.

3 Tamice la mitad de la harina restante sobre el bol con la mezcla y bata de nuevo. Incorpore la mantequilla fundida y vuelva a batir. Añada la harina restante, pasándola por el tamiz, de modo que la masa resultante quede consistente. Pásela a una superficie de trabajo ligeramente enharinada y trabájela durante unos 10 minutos, hasta que la masa esté suave y elástica. Vuelva a ponerla en el bol limpio, cúbrala con el film transparente y déjela en un lugar cálido durante 1½ horas o hasta que haya doblado su volumen.

4 Retire la masa del bol y golpéela para que vuelva a su forma original. Póngala de nuevo en el bol, cúbrala y déjela en un lugar cálido durante 1 hora más para que suba.

5 Pase la masa a una superficie enharinada y golpéela para que vuelva a su forma original; divídala en 48 porciones del tamaño de una nuez. Moldéelas en forma de salchicha de unos 18 cm de largo y forme con ellas espirales, figuras en S o roscas. Coloque los bollitos en bandejas engrasadas y cúbralos con film transparente, pero sin ceñirlo demasiado. Déjelos 30 minutos en un lugar cálido para que suban.

6 Precaliente el horno a 180°C. Pinte los bollitos con el huevo batido y esparza por encima las semillas de sésamo. Hornéelos de 15 a 20 minutos (por tandas, si no cupiesen todos a la vez), hasta que suban, se doren y suenen a hueco al golpearlos por debajo. Déjelos enfriar antes de servir.

Pan de Navidad

CHRISTOPSOMO

Se trata de una receta tradicional que se cuece a lo largo y ancho de toda Grecia durante los días de Navidad. El ama de casa que elabora el pan lo marca con la huella de su mano y cuenta a los niños que Jesús bendice el pan mientras se cuece. Si no precisa las dos barras de pan, envuelva una, etiquétela y congélela. Cuando la necesite, descongélela a temperatura ambiente durante varias horas.

Tiempo de preparación: unos 30 minutos, más tiempo para subir
Tiempo de cocción: unos 30 minutos
Temperatura del horno: 180°C

PARA 2 PANES

- *3 cucharadas de levadura seca*
- *1¾ tazas de azúcar*
- *12¾ tazas de harina*
- *una pizca de sal*
- *½ taza de agua caliente*
- *5 huevos*
- *1½ tazas de leche*
- *unas gotas de extracto de vainilla*
- *1 taza de mantequilla*
- *100 g de higos secos, picados*
- *50 g de orejones, picados*
- *1⅓ tazas de almendras blanqueadas, picadas*
- *⅔ taza de sultanas*
- *la ralladura de 1 naranja*
- *la ralladura de 1 limón*
- *aceite vegetal, para engrasar*

1 Vierta la levadura, 1 cucharadita de azúcar, 2 cucharadas de harina, sal y agua caliente en un bol de tamaño pequeño. Remueva hasta disolver la levadura y el azúcar, cubra la mezcla con film transparente y déjela en un lugar cálido durante unos 15 minutos, hasta que espumee.

2 Casque los 4 huevos en un cuenco grande y agregue la leche y el azúcar restante; bátalo todo bien. Añada la mezcla de levadura espumosa, 6½ tazas de la harina restante y el extracto de vainilla; remueva bien. Incorpore la mantequilla fundida y el resto de los ingredientes.

3 Mezcle todo hasta obtener una masa consistente y pásela a una superficie de trabajo ligeramente enharinada; amásela,

añadiéndole el resto de la harina, si lo cree necesario. Trabájela durante 10 minutos, hasta que la masa esté blanda y suave.

4 Devuelva la masa al bol limpio y cúbrala con film transparente. Déjela en un lugar cálido durante 1½ horas para que doble su volumen. Vuelva a pasarla a la superficie ligeramente enharinada y golpéela hasta que adquiera de nuevo su forma original. Póngala otra vez en el bol, cúbrala y déjela en un lugar cálido otros 30 minutos, para que suba.

5 Divida la masa en seis porciones iguales y enróllelas en forma de salchicha de unos 30 cm de largo. Elabore una trenza con tres partes y junte los extremos para dejarla bien acabada. Haga lo mismo con las otras tres tiras de masa y coloque cada trenza en una bandeja de horno untada con un poco de aceite. Cúbralas con film transparente pero sin ceñirlas demasiado y déjelas en un lugar cálido de 30 a 40 minutos para que suban.

6 Mientras tanto, precaliente el horno a 180°C. Bata el huevo restante en un bol y pinte el pan. Hornéelo durante unos 30 minutos hasta que se dore y suene a hueco al darle golpecitos por debajo con la mano. Páselo a una rejilla para que se enfríe antes de servir.

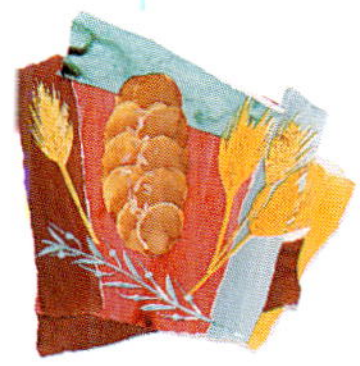

Pan de Pascua

TSOUREKI

Este pan de masa consistente se come tradicionalmente los días de Pascua. El huevo rojo simboliza la sangre de Cristo y se prepara hirviéndolo en agua mezclada con colorante rojo y vinagre. Se deja enfriar y se añade a la receta como se indica a continuación.

Tiempo de preparación: 1 hora, más reposo
Tiempo de cocción: unos 45 minutos
Temperatura del horno: 190°C

PARA 1 PAN

- *1¼ tazas de leche templada*
- *1 cucharada de levadura seca*
- *7⅓ tazas de harina*
- *¾ taza colmada de azúcar*
- *una pizca de sal*
- *la ralladura de ½ naranja*
- *la ralladura de ½ limón*
- *¼ taza de mantequilla en dados, más un poco para engrasar*
- *3 huevos, batidos*
- *2 cucharaditas de extracto de vainilla*
- *3 huevos, teñidos de rojo (opcional)*
- *1 yema desleída con 3 cucharadas de leche*

1 Vierta la leche en un bol grande y esparza la levadura por encima. Remueva hasta disolver la mezcla, agregue 1¾ tazas de harina y 2 cucharadas de azúcar. Cubra el bol con film transparente y déjelo en un lugar cálido durante 1 hora o hasta que la mezcle espumee.

2 Tamice la harina restante en otro bol grande y añada la sal y el azúcar. Incorpore la ralladura de naranja y de limón, así como la mantequilla; utilice un cuchillo para desmenuzarlo todo de tal manera que parezca migas de pan. Practique un hueco en el centro de la mezcla y vierta la levadura espumosa, los huevos batidos y el extracto de vainilla. Remuévalo todo hasta obtener una masa.

3 Pase la masa a una superficie de trabajo ligeramente enharinada y trabájela de 10 a 15 minutos, hasta que esté blanda y elástica. Devuélvala al bol limpio, cúbrala con film transparente y déjela subir en un lugar cálido entre 1 y 2 horas, hasta que doble su volumen.

4 Vuelva a pasar la masa a la superficie de trabajo enharinada y golpéela hasta que adquiera de nuevo su forma original. Divídala en tres partes iguales y moldéelas en forma de salchicha de 30 cm de largo. Disponga las tiras de masa una al lado de la otra y júntelas por uno de los extremos. Elabore una trenza partiendo del otro extremo y junte las tiras al llegar al final; acerque ambos extremos de la trenza hasta que se toquen y péguelos, de modo que resulte una rosca grande y trenzada.

5 Presione los huevos rojos en la masa y coloque el pan sobre una bandeja de horno engrasada. Cúbrala con film transparente y déjela en un lugar cálido durante 2 horas, hasta que doble su volumen. Mientras tanto, ponga a calentar el horno a 190°C.

6 Retire el film y pinte el pan con el glaseado de yema y leche; hornéelo de 40 a 45 minutos, hasta que se dore y suene a hueco al golpearlo con la mano por debajo. Páselo a una rejilla para que se enfríe antes de servir.

Índice

Q

R

S

T

V

X

Y

Z

Sir Hen. Hoc Keale Bar.
Lord Killmorey
Kingston Esq.
Doc. Kennew
Mr. Thomas King
Seventeen Mile
Eighteen Mile
the Road From
A Farm House
Tog Hill House
Trace Park
C O L D A S T
6 Mile
5 Mile
Beach Brook
Frisen Hill
Hamsel House
Mr. Whittington
Tyly's Farm
Davis's Farm
Taylors
The Kings Camp
Beach
P A R I S H
L O C E S T E R
4 Mile
Frisen Hill Bottom
Nimlet Down
To Catherine
Mr. Pierce's Farm
Beach Farm
Knowles Leazes
Beach Wood
To Tog Hill
Mr. Pierce's
Turney's Court
Mr. Gunning Jun.
Monument of Sr. Bevil Granville
To Beach
the Boundary of ye Countys
Gowdy's Farm
Tat Wick
To Cold Aston
T H
To Upton
Mr. Gunning's Farm
S T O K E
Stoke Wood
Lansdown
L A N G R I D G E
To Stoke
Langridge
Stoke Common
P A R I S H
Olivers Intrenchment
3 Mile
To Langridge
Langridge Brook
To Langridge Mile
P A R I S H
the old Chapel
Collins's Farm
Lansdown Houses
Gun Powder
Soupers Farm
Wolley
Wolley Farm
2 Mile
Hen Street Hill
Lansdown Barrows
Soupers Wood
a Barn
Farm
a Farm House
2 Mile
Lansdown

Gainsborough in Bath

Gainsborough in Bath

Susan Sloman

Published for
THE PAUL MELLON CENTRE FOR STUDIES IN BRITISH ART
by
YALE UNIVERSITY PRESS
New Haven and London

Designed by Elizabeth McWilliams

Printed in China

Library of Congress Cataloging-in-Publication Data

Legouix, Susan.
Gainsborough in Bath / Susan Sloman.
p. cm.
Includes bibliographical references and index.
ISBN 0-300-09711-5
1. Gainsborough, Thomas, 1727–1788. 2. Painters – England – Biography.
3. Bath (England) – Civilization – 18th century. I. Title.
ND497.G2 L44 2002
759.2 – dc21
2002001891

A catalogue record for this book is available from
The British Library

Frontispiece: detail of fig. 113.

Note on illustrations: dimensions given for prints throughout are to plate mark.

Contents

Acknowledgements

This book began life as a dissertation for the History of Art Department at the University of Bristol,under the guidance of Michael Liversidge. It has benefited from the generous support of many people over a long period, notably Hugh Belsey, Curator of Gainsborough's House, Trevor Fawcett, John Hayes, Michael Rosenthal and David Tyler. At Yale University Press Gillian Malpass has provided expert guidance and encouragement and Elizabeth McWilliams has been a tactful editor and thoughtful designer. Paul Sloman patiently helped prepare the text during the final stages. Without Brian Allen and the Paul Mellon Centre for Studies in British Art there probably would never have been a book.

My former colleagues at the Victoria Art Gallery, Bath and present colleagues at Agnew's have tolerated many Gainsborough-centred discussions and helped in a host of ways. I am greatly indebted to the staff of museums, libraries and record offices, both public and private, who have given time and advice. Chief among these are the curators, librarians and archivists at Bath Central Library, the Bath Record Office, the Bodleian Library, Bristol Central Library, the Department of Prints and Drawings at the British Museum, the British Library, the Witt Library at the Courtauld Institute of Art, C. Hoare & Co, the London Library, the National Gallery, the Heinz Archive and Library at the National Portrait Gallery, the Royal Commission on the Ancient and Historical Monuments of Wales, the Somerset Record Office, the Wiltshire and Swindon Record Office, the University of Bristol Library and the Yale Center for British Art. At Badminton, archivist Margaret Richards has regularly answered enquiries and shared her extensive knowledge of the history of the Somerset family. In an age when public institutions struggle with inadequate resources it is a joy to find dedicated and knowledgeable individuals who are still prepared to go to great lengths to provide an excellent service – the National Library of Wales and the National Monuments Record Centre at Swindon seem to be blessed with an unusually high proportion of such people. I am extremely grateful to them and to all the following who have contributed in one way or another, often giving up a great deal of valuable time: David Alexander, His Grace the Duke of Beaufort, Anthony Beeson, the late John Bensusan-Butt, Amanda Berry, Philippa Bishop, Michael Brennan, David Brenneman, Jack Calow, Mike Chapman, the Earl of Clarendon, Warwick Cole, Major D. J. C. Davenport, Emma Deakin, Elizabeth Einberg, the late Graham Finch, Emma Floyd, the Hon. Mrs C. Gascoigne, Mike Gray, Ken Hall, Janet Harris, Kate Harris, Elizabeth Holland, Victoria Hutchings, Colin Johnston, Jeremy Key-Pugh, Nicholas Kingsley, Godfrey Laurence, Emma Lauze, Philip McEvansoneya, Audrey Mead, James Methuen-Campbell, Tim Mowl, Evelyn Newby, Vivienne Rae-Ellis, Penelope Ruddock, Barbra Sands, Nancy Steele, Lady Cleone Versen, Peter Ward Jones, Henry Wemyss, Philip White, Christopher Woodward and Edward Yescombe. I am no less grateful to those who have allowed access to private collections but prefer to remain anonymous.

Ron, Paul and Beverley Sloman wholeheartedly backed the project from the very beginning, Hugh Belsey has been overwhelmingly generous in sharing his knowledge and Andrew Wyld gave me a job despite my preoccupation with Gainsborough – this book is dedicated to them.

Introduction

Thomas Gainsborough arrived at Bath at the age of thirty-one and left when he was forty-seven. He could not have been described as an unknown painter at the beginning of this period – he was already highly regarded by other artists – but his limited self-esteem at this date can be inferred from the modest five guineas he charged for a 'head' portrait, and the punishing workload he undertook in the first few years. By the end of his residence in Bath he was known to consider himself one of the foremost artists in Europe. How such a remarkable transformation occurred is explored in this book through a detailed examination of the artist's life in the city.

The major contribution of Michael Rosenthal's recent *The Art of Thomas Gainsborough* has been to show what a diverse and restless artist Gainsborough was, tirelessly absorbing influences, reacting to circumstances and manoeuvring within the cultural and commercial world in which he found himself.[1] This study of Gainsborough at Bath also uncovers a complex picture. Far from being aloof or removed from the commercial and social life of this city, the artist is shown to have thoroughly assimilated himself within Bath society and to have used the cyclical pattern of its social season to his own advantage. Bath was unlike any other provincial town of the mid-eighteenth century, a playground for the rich and a showcase for shopkeepers, but also, and most importantly, a serious medical and cultural centre. It was not a microcosm of London, but a particular (and in some senses peculiar) society, where, within a very small geographical area, a balance was maintained between overt commercialism and a spirit of philanthropy. As Josiah Wedgwood noticed, shop windows were *more* extravagant than in London, and yet, as records show, retailers were also quick to persuade their customers to make generous donations to the Bath Hospital. Visitors expected to be entertained as well as cured or fitted out with new clothes, and tightly regulated daily routines, presided over by a Master of Ceremonies or 'King' of Bath, allowed for a great flowering of artistic, theatrical and musical life. Using a wide range of unpublished and little-known documents, letters and contemporary literature, this study sets the scene and identifies the players who surrounded Gainsborough as he assumed the role of leading artist on this distinctive stage.

Remarkably little was known about Gainsborough's modus operandi in Bath. At the outset of this research it was not even entirely clear where he lived and worked between 1760 and 1766, the vital formative period that produced such masterpieces as the portraits of Ann Ford, Mary, Countess Howe and General Philip Honywood. It is now possible to say not just in which building, but in which room, these pictures were painted, and to postulate much else about the artist's working practice, thanks to the discovery of new documents concerning the properties he occupied. Having established some fundamental facts about the day-to-day business of Gainsborough's portrait-painting practice, the study shows how Bath provided the intellectual stimulus and financial independence that allowed him to develop an imaginative and distinctive style of painting. This was not achieved in a vacuum, and the presence of an existing artistic tradition in the city is described, as is the role of a number of important thinkers and theorists within the artist's circle of friends and patrons.

Two articles by Marcia Pointon have provided a particular impetus: 'Gainsborough and the Landscape of Retirement' of 1979 and 'Portrait-Painting as a Business Enterprise in London in the 1780s' of 1984.[2] Recognising that Gainsborough could not simply be perceived as an 'intuitive' or 'natural' painter, Pointon proposed that connections might be made between Gainsborough's landscape painting and the works of writers active in Bath: here some verifiable connections are looked at in more depth. Pointon's observations on the subject of Gainsborough's independence of mind and his approach to the business of portraiture are also developed here in relation to specific works of the Bath period.

The late John Bensusan-Butt and Hugh Belsey have shown how a close examination of the status, occupation and character of the artist's patrons can add immeasurably to our understanding of the pictures painted for them. Much of Bensusan-Butt's research related principally to

Gainsborough's East Anglian work, but by applying an equally rigorous approach to the artist's relationship with some of the Bath patrons, it is possible to see certain works, both landscapes and portraits, in a new light. More broadly, an examination of the landscape and portrait patronage of the Bath period uncovers a network of men and women who were connected not only with Gainsborough in Bath in the 1760s, but also with the development of the literature of the Picturesque later in the century. Taking a cue from Hugh Belsey's 1988 exhibition and accompanying catalogue, *Gainsborough's Family*, it has been possible to show how far-reaching an effect Gainsborough's marriage had on his career, and how some members of his wife's extended family were pivotal figures within this web of patrons and supporters.

A study of this kind, focusing on the particular circumstances of one stage of the artist's career, can only be carried out against a wider framework. The last half-century has been an especially fruitful period for Gainsborough studies. In 1958 Ellis Waterhouse compiled a catalogue of Gainsborough's paintings, a second edition of which appeared in 1966. Two editions were published, in 1961 and 1963, of Mary Woodall's collection of Gainsborough's letters, a vital new source that revealed much about the painter's life and character. By the mid-1960s John Hayes was already publishing new Gainsborough research and his major catalogues of the artist's drawings (1970) and landscape paintings (1982) were interspersed with catalogues to Gainsborough exhibitions at the Tate Gallery in 1980 and Grand Palais, Paris in 1981. Hayes curated the first exhibition of Gainsborough's work in Italy, in the Palazzo dei Diamanti, Ferrara, in 1998 and in 2001 he edited a new and attractively compact edition of the *Letters*, adding freshly discovered correspondence and providing a context by grouping the letters chronologically between linking explanatory passages.

The meticulous cataloguing undertaken by John Hayes throughout the 1960s and 1970s established the groundwork for all subsequent Gainsborough studies. Exhibitions and catalogues inevitably (and usefully) stimulate debate and the criticism of Hayes's approach has been that on occasion it presents a picture of Gainsborough as a painter imbued with a natural talent, whose work progresses inexorably forward and upward, prefiguring the romantic artists of the nineteenth century. A number of publications from the late 1970s and the 1980s illustrate a reaction to Hayes's work, while necessarily relying on it for essential information. Marcia Pointon's two articles of 1979 and 1984 have been mentioned; John Barrell's chapter on Gainsborough in *The Dark Side of the Landscape: The Rural Poor in English Painting, 1730–1840*, published in 1980, took a fresh look at the characters who inhabit Gainsborough's landscapes and linked them with a literary tradition, and the comic pastorals of John Gay in particular. Ann Bermingham's *Landscape and Ideology: The English Rustic Tradition, 1740–1860*, of 1987, drew attention to the socio-economic overtones of Gainsborough's landscapes, demonstrating the artist's apparent sensitivity to the issues of land enclosure and changing agricultural practice, points examined further by Michael Rosenthal in an article of 1994, 'The Rough and the Smooth: Rural Subjects in Later Eighteenth-Century British Art'.[3] While not attempting any broad interpretation of the iconography of the Bath landscapes, the present study takes account of notions formulated by Bermingham and Rosenthal and applies them to particular examples of the artist's work that suggest that certain figure types can only be properly understood in the context of rural life in the vicinity of Bath.

In his review of Hayes's Gainsborough exhibition at the Tate in 1980, Michael Kitson noted that the balance of the selection was tilted in favour of landscapes, rather than portraits, and that there appeared to be a reluctance to represent the more 'flashy' side of the artist's work. Undue emphasis was perhaps given to the early Dutch-inspired landscapes of the pre-Bath period.[4] To some degree this overriding interest in the early period has persisted, with the *Young Gainsborough* exhibition at the National Gallery in 1997 focusing on a number of exquisite 'portraits in little' painted in East Anglia and, strangely, omitting the life-sized portraits he also painted before moving to Bath.

Gainsborough's 'flashy' work (as Kitson characterised it) first emerged in Bath. William Whitley, author of a painstakingly researched biography of Gainsborough published in 1915, made a serious attempt to set the crucial middle period of the artist's life in context and was the first, and to an extent the only, author to do so. There have been a small number of Gainsborough exhibitions in Bath in the last hundred years, although none has significantly advanced Whitley's account of the painter's relationship with the city, its inhabitants and its landscape. The most sensational of the exhibitions to be held in Bath must have been the display of Gainsborough paintings from the Royal Collection at the Victoria Art Gallery in 1918: this included the late landscape *Diana and Actaeon*, the first time this picture was publicly exhibited. In 1949 Mary Woodall selected works from all periods of Gainsborough's life for an Arts Council exhibition that opened in Bath and toured to Ipswich and three other provincial centres. Woodall again curated a Gainsborough exhibition at the Victoria Art Gallery to coincide with the Festival of Britain in 1951. This focused more on Bath, and included drawings as well as paintings, but also encompassed the whole of the artist's career.[5] The 1988 bicentenary exhibition *Gainsborough in Bath* (at the Holburne Museum in Bath) was the first to rekindle an interest that had largely lain dormant since Whitley's time, and in her foreword to the catalogue of this exhibition Barley Roscoe expressed the show's aspiration to trace Gainsborough's transition from 'a Suffolk painter of great charm to an artist of European stature'.[6] The show concentrated exclusively on Bath works and illustrated the diversity of Gainsborough's achievement in the 1760s and early 1770s, but the limited scope of the exhibition did not allow for a reappraisal of the Bath period.

The present study has benefited from a number of facilities not available to earlier authors. Thanks particularly to the efforts of Trevor Fawcett, local history studies in Bath have been placed on a serious footing over the past decade and scholars from a wide range of disciplines have contributed to the periodical *Bath History*. The History of Bath Research Group and other organisations, such as the Bath Archaeological Trust and the Survey of Bath and District, have provided new opportunities for an exchange of ideas and information. Much material unavailable to William Whitley is now catalogued or published, and the movement of numerous family archives to public record offices in Wiltshire, Somerset, Hereford and Worcester has provided a rich new deposit of primary sources. In addition to these local developments, the unparalleled facilities now on offer at Gainsborough's House at Sudbury have aided this and much other new Gainsborough research. As well as housing an ever-expanding collection and library, the museum has mounted a series of stimulating exhibitions and publishes the *Gainsborough's House Review*, a unique annual periodical for original research on Gainsborough and East Anglian art. The Gainsborough's House catalogues *The Moysey Family* (1984), *Gainsborough the Printmaker* (1988) and *From Gainsborough to Constable* (1991) have all shown that Gainsborough was less of a lone artist than has often been suggested. These exhibitions, and *Gainsborough to Constable* in particular, also offered opportunities to see some extraordinary and little-known works from private and public collections. The *Gainsborough's House Review* has included important articles on the supporting figures in Gainsborough's life, such as Felicity Owen's 'Joshua Kirby (1716–1774): A Biographical Sketch' (1996), as well as new discoveries, such as Alex Kidson's 'Thomas Gainsborough and the Revd William Lowther: An Unpublished Letter' (1996), and Amal Asfour and Paul Williamson's publication of William Jackson's papers, to which the whole of the 1997 edition was devoted.

Drawing on this rich variety of sources, this book applies to Bath the sort of scrutiny that has been given to the East Anglian period of Gainsborough's life and looks at aspects of his career as a portrait and landscape painter from some fresh perspectives. Following William Whitley's lead, it presupposes the value of establishing a local context in order to understand the art of the Bath period and introduces a number of new figures not previously associated with the artist, as well as fleshing out some well-known names. Visual sources, from the local landscape to the work of local painters, are also given serious consideration, and a number of previously unrecognised parallels illustrated.

1 John Nixon (c. 1750–1818), *The Pump Room, Bath* 1790, pen and ink and ink wash, $7\frac{3}{4} \times 11\frac{3}{8}$ inches (19.6 × 28.9 cm), signed and dated 1790, Victoria Art Gallery, Bath and North East Somerset Council. This Pump Room, the one that was known to mid-eighteenth-century visitors, was replaced within a few years of the date of this drawing. The Tompion clock and sculpture of Beau Nash, seen on the left, were transferred and remain in the new Room.

I

Bath: 'the busiest idle place in the world'

Bath was commended as a 'proper preparation for the London world' by Lord Herbert, writing from his country seat at Wilton, just outside Salisbury, in 1784.[1] For Lord Herbert and his circle, Bath was a place where the young or socially inept might acquire a degree of 'polish' before launching themselves into London society. Gainsborough too must have regarded Bath as a suitable preparation for London, though for professional rather than social reasons. He doubtless recognised Bath's potential as a stepping stone in his career between the limitations of Ipswich and the demands of London. Having moved to Bath, Gainsborough then seemed reluctant to leave, finding the city a vibrant cultural and commercial centre, and one that particularly suited his needs as an aspiring portrait painter with an abiding love of landscape.

One of the principal reasons Gainsborough selected Bath rather than any other provincial town is that he had friends and associates from East Anglia who were already regular Bath visitors. Philip Thicknesse, who befriended the artist around 1753, had a house in Bath and frequently spent winters there. William Kirby, brother of Gainsborough's close friend Joshua Kirby, had made an excursion to Bath in September 1756, and there were others, some of whom were sitters, as will be shown in Chapter 3, and some business and family connections.[2] The artist's domestic life and business life were always closely intertwined and the fact that Bath was near Badminton, the seat of the Dukes of Beaufort and source of Mrs Gainsborough's valuable annuity, must have been a major consideration in his choice, as we shall see in the next chapter.

Another attraction of Bath was its location, close to the junction of the rich counties of Gloucestershire, Somerset and Wiltshire it was becoming increasingly well connected with London. The Great Bath Road underwent an important series of changes throughout the first half of the century, gradually providing a safer, swifter and more comfortable route between London and Bath.[3] The fastest journey time from London before 1680 was over sixty hours. By 1750 it was thirty-six hours (twenty-eight on the road) and by 1763 only twenty-four hours (all on the road).[4] The River Avon, which was made navigable between Bristol and Bath in 1727, was another vital element of the communication network that linked Bath with the whole of the British Isles and beyond.[5]

Above all, Bath was the most rapidly expanding social centre in England. It was Mrs Delany, writing in 1760, who called it 'the busiest idle place in the world'.[6] Large numbers of potential sitters from all over the country could be guaranteed to be in residence every year between the beginning of October and the end of May. As Peter Borsay has written, 'Whereas most towns identified closely with a particular region or locality, Bath was first and foremost a cosmopolitan centre, catering for the medical, recreational and aesthetic needs of the nation's elite'.[7] Spa towns such as Bath, rather than other predominantly commercial centres which were also expanding in the mid-century, attracted the noble as well as the simply rich, and having enticed them in encouraged them to stay for periods of leisure and entertainment of several weeks duration. Nearby Bristol was a much larger city than Bath, the second centre for business in the country It too possessed a spa and might appear to have been an equally ideal base for a portrait painter, but the combination of busy port, manufacturing and the leisure industry was not an entirely happy one. An unpublished letter of 1759, written by Margaret Fownes Luttrell of Dunster Castle, Somerset, neatly summarises Bristol's disadvantages:

> Bath is certainly a warm place but I believe ye Hot Well at Bristol exceeds it, for I thought it ye Hottest Place I ever was in, & often thank'd my Stars that since some waters were necessary for me it was those here & not ye Bristol ones, for it would half kill me I think to spend a Season there, ye City is ye most shocking Place I ever saw . . . we found it vastly dusty.[8]

Nevertheless Bristol was important to Bath. Gainsborough had some of his picture frames made there and may have used the city for other services.[9] Bristol certainly reinforced the commercial attraction of Bath for a professional painter.

By the mid-eighteenth century the only provincial town apart from Bath which could claim to accommodate visitors from all over England on a regular basis was Tunbridge Wells in Kent. Contemporary diaries, letters and journals show that many of Bath's regular seasonal visitors also frequented the Kentish resort. For most of the century Tunbridge Wells and Bath even shared the same Masters of Ceremonies. Richard Nash, MC at Bath from 1708–61; Samuel Derrick, MC from 1761–9 and Richard Tyson, MC from 1780–1805 all officiated at Tunbridge Wells in the summer months. However, it was Bath that was in the ascendancy at the time Gainsborough was seeking to advance his career. R. S. Neale judges the height of Bath's prosperity to have been in the late 1760s.[10] Building activity reached a peak between 1766 and 1773 when, on average, fifty-six houses were added each year.[11] The buoyancy of the building trade is reflected in local apprentice records: 15 per cent of the masters of apprentices belonged to building trades between 1706 and 1727, between 1750 and 1769 this figure had risen to 28 per cent.[12] But the growth of the 1760s slowed dramatically with the onset of war with America and, on average, only thirteen houses were built each year between 1773 and 1776.[13] Gainsborough, who invested heavily in property while in Bath, rode the wave of expansion and then moved out as values fell in the mid-1770s.[14]

The development of large numbers of new properties every year was a response to the demand for more visitor accommodation. Because so many people were continuously coming and going, it is difficult to calculate the resident population of Bath in the eighteenth century. Sylvia Mcintyre estimates that the resident population increased more than tenfold between 1660 and 1801, and R. S. Neale suggests that a total of around ten thousand in 1743 increased to fifteen thousand by 1771.[15] More important than the permanent residents were the seasonal visitors, but the numbers of these cannot be accurately assessed. It was estimated by the architect John Wood in 1749 that twelve thousand visitors could be accommodated.[16] Wood's source for this information was 'common Fame' rather than any scientific measure, but his figure has been accepted as reasonable by some scholars.[17] On one sunny January morning in 1780 it was estimated that three to four thousand people were promenading in front of the Royal Crescent, so many that 'It was quite full from point to point'.[18] The *Bath Journal* published lists of visitors which rose from 510 for the year of 1746 to 2,525 in 1760 and 3,091 in 1780, but it is not known how the names published were collected or selected.[19] The nature of the seasonal company can be more easily judged than the numbers of people who came. In the autumn of 1765 the visitors included three princes, four dukes, four duchesses, one marquess, two marchionesses, twenty-four earls, twenty-two countesses, fourteen viscounts, forty-three viscountesses, twelve barons, twelve baronesses, one ambassador, one archbishop and five bishops, a remarkable list by any standards.[20] There were claims that the quality of the company diminished as the numbers increased from the mid-century onwards, but Edmund Rack's entry in his 'Disultory Journal' for 3 January 1780 shows that a great many noteworthy visitors could still be found gathered together at this date: 'In the Morning went to Pump-Room – Saw there the Dukes of Leeds, Marlborough & Beaufort; Lords Grantham, Dillon, Mulgrave, Drogheda, Rivers, Donnegal, Cashill, Chichester, Tracy, Northington, Colvill and Ilchester, Baron Warnsdale, Judges Willes & Buller, Bishops of Worcester, Man, and Salisbury . . .'.[21]

The rapid economic and physical growth which took place in Bath in the 1750s and 1760s was not mirrored in Tunbridge Wells at the same date, but apart from this the principal difference between the two spas was that Bath's season was in the winter, while Tunbridge (like Bristol Hotwells), entertained visitors in the summer. At the beginning of the century Bath's season had likewise been in the summer, but competition from Tunbridge Wells led Bath to concentrate on autumn and spring seasons. By the 1750s these two seasons had almost merged into one. *Boddely's Bath Journal* for 12 March 1759 announced 'This Day the Music begins playing at the Pump-Room for the Spring Season' and the same newspaper for 8 October 1759, 'On Monday last [ie 1 October] the Music began playing at the Pump-Room for the ensuing season'. But in the same year the paper had also reported on 15 January, 'Tuesday last the Ball (being the first of the second Subscription) was opened . . .', indicating that by this date January and February were almost as busy as the 'official' spring and autumn seasons. A foreign visitor to Bath, Johanna Schopenhauer thought the idea of a winter season a typical example of British eccentricity: 'Somehow, in England, everything in life has to go against the ordinary course of nature', she wrote, '. . . it has pleased the powers that be to change the Season in Bath to the winter. From November to May the place swarms with visitors who rotate in a circle of endless jollifications to the point of becoming dizzy. In summer Bath is empty . . .'.[22]

For an artist such as Gainsborough, who by the late 1750s regarded himself a portrait painter by profession but dreamed of walking 'to some sweet Village' where he could paint landscapes and of lying in a waggon 'gazing at Green Trees & Blue skies', there was an obvious advantage in the arrangement of the Bath season.[23] The extended period of October to May allowed for a great many more portrait sittings than would have been possible in the shorter Tunbridge Wells or Bristol Hotwells seasons, while in the summer he was free to visit friends and indulge his fondness for landscape. On 25 May 1768 Gainsborough wrote from Bath to his friend and banker James Unwin, 'Thank God I shall now shut myself up for the summer and not appear til September comes in'.[24] James Vertue (*fl.* 1744–60), who kept a toy shop and taught drawing and painting at Bath, also made good use of the summer break. His brother, the antiquary George Vertue, recorded, 'In the intervalls of the seasons he rides about makes his tour comes to London etc – thus in augt. 1751 –

as he had done several years past. – about Michaelmas returns to Bath again to reside'.[25] In the summer of 1760 Gainsborough was visiting his friend Robert Price at Foxley in Herefordshire and in early July 1763 he was in London, but his letters show that he was often still resident in Bath during the summer, making local excursions to satisfy his hunger for landscape.[26] He wrote dejectedly to David Garrick from Bath in August 1768, during a period of exceptional rainfall, and he was also in Bath in July 1763, early September 1767, July 1770, June 1772 and July 1773.[27] Little is known of his summer activities, but in July 1770 he wrote to Unwin, 'I'll pack up all my Drawing things, and see Derbyshire next summer, if I'm alive'.[28] The promise of a summer break, allowing for a period of regeneration and relaxation, was a luxury not enjoyed by artists in other provincial towns. Of course not all painters could afford to use the time in this way. Thomas Beach (1738–1806) for example, who was based in Bath between 1772 and 1803, regularly set out from Bath in June on a portrait-painting tour of the West Country and southern England, returning before Christmas to take advantage of the winter season.[29]

If the annual cycle of Bath's social life was likely to appeal to Gainsborough, the daily routine also happened to be conveniently arranged for portrait painters, with social gatherings concentrated during the hours of least daylight at the beginning and end of each day. Bathing or drinking the waters normally took place between six and nine in the morning, followed by a general assembly in the Pump Room where music played from eight to ten (fig. 1).[30] After this the company was left to wile away what Oliver Goldsmith called Bath's 'tedious morning' before dining at two or three o'clock.[31] Gainsborough's daughter recalled that her father generally worked between eleven and three, although on his earliest visit to Bath in 1758 he apparently took sittings from before ten o'clock.[32] How many sitters were booked each day, and how long they sat, is not on record but the artist mentioned to Garrick in an undated letter that he had on one particular day 'three sitters one after another'.[33] At the height of his success in London, Sir Joshua Reynolds normally took sittings between eleven and four o'clock, lasting an hour each, but sitting times could vary and earlier in his career he often began working at nine or earlier.[34]

One further advantage of the Bath season for the painter of oil portraits was that visitors tended to stay for several weeks. At Tunbridge Wells, which could be reached quickly and easily from London, people often paid fleeting visits of two or three days. In Bath a six-week stay seems to have been quite normal. William Hickey recalled, 'In the month of December [1772] my father, by way of recreation, took me with him to Bath . . . Here I passed six weeks very agreeably'.[35] Lord Chesterfield wrote from Bath on 20 November 1757 to his son, 'I will stay here at least six weeks longer, where I am much quieter than I should be allowed to be in town'.[36] The visitor who spent weeks or months, rather than days, in Bath would have found no difficulty in fitting in several sittings and might even have stayed long enough to be able to take delivery of his portrait.[37]

The Earl of Chesterfield's comment that he would be allowed to be 'much quieter' in Bath is significant. David Garrick wrote that (in Bath) 'I do this, & do that, & do Nothing, & I go here and go there & go nowhere – Such is ye life of Bath & such the Effects of this place upon me – I forget my Cares, & my large family in London, & Every thing . . .'.[38] Mrs Delany told Jonathan Swift, 'I think Bath a more comfortable place to live than London. All the entertainments of the place, and you are at liberty to take them or let them alone just as it suits your humour . . .'.[39] Many other visitors expressed similar sentiments, indicating that they saw Bath as a place of retreat, removed from the pressures of business and the more formal social life of London. R. S. Neale concludes that for 'men and women of property and wealth [Bath] offered brief moments of social communion wrapped in a cocoon of pleasure in pleasant surroundings remote from the competitive reality of the economic life of property and wealth'.[40] In such an unhurried atmosphere the visitor's thoughts might well turn to sitting for a portrait, and in this respect Bath might even have had an advantage over London, where so many other activities and responsibilities competed for people's time and attention.

Apart from the benefits of the Bath social season, with its national clientele and its summer respite, the cost of living in Bath may have played a part in Gainsborough's decision to stay the best part of sixteen years. Many contemporary writers remarked how easy it was to sustain a high standard of living on a modest income. Johanna Schopenhauer noted that 'Those who wish to live elegantly but are not rich enough to do so in London, flock to Bath'.[41] Horace Walpole, who took 'an insuperable aversion' to Bath, nevertheless conceded, 'The place is healthy, everything is cheap, and the provisions better than I ever tasted'.[42] Tobias Smollett in *The Expedition of Humphry Clinker*, first published in 1771, had his character Matthew Bramble tell a friend, 'About a dozen years ago, many decent families, restricted to small fortunes, . . . were tempted to settle at Bath, where they could live comfortably, and even make a genteel appearance, at a small expense'.[43] As early as 1749 the portrait painter William Hoare (1707–1792) 'lived in a handsome, genteel manner' in Bath, as Gainsborough was no doubt aware.[44]

Finally, Gainsborough would have been attracted to Bath for the same reason as many of his patrons. He seems always to have been anxious about his own and his family's health. In January 1765 he asked the Duke and Duchess of Bedford's agent to inform the Duchess 'that 'tho my Ill Health forbids my following Business in London (to which I have frequent invitations) Her Grace may nevertheless command me at any time to paint any of The Family there'.[45] Many more of Gainsborough's letters, both earlier and later in date, make reference to his own health, which may always have been

2 Unidentified British artist, *Queen Square, Bath* c. 1810, pen and ink and ink wash, 6¾ × 10¾ inches (17.3 × 27.3 cm), Victoria Art Gallery, Bath and North East Somerset Council. The painter William Hoare and the jeweller and toyman Paul Bertrand occupied houses in the west-facing terrace seen to the right.

delicate.[46] Three other eighteenth-century artists came to Bath at least partly because of their own ill-health: Thomas Worlidge (1700–1766), who suffered badly from gout but managed to carry on working as a portrait painter and etcher; James Vertue who had 'a nervous paralecttick distemper'; and the German landscape painter Johann Hackert (1744–1773), whose cure was unsuccessful and who died in Bath in 1773.[47] Gainsborough's daughters' health also gave him cause for concern, so much so in 1771 that he himself became ill as a result of his devoted attention to Mary during a period of sickness that was diagnosed as 'delirious fever'.[48] Having lost one child in infancy, Gainsborough and his wife may well have considered that Bath, with its supply of eminent doctors, was a sensible place to bring up a family as well as a good place to become established as a society portrait painter.[49]

William Hoare lived handsomely as a portrait painter in Bath in the 1740s, and his presence may have encouraged others to involve themselves in artistic activity. There are some grounds for believing that there was a painting academy in the city as early as 1743. The evidence is frustratingly slight and as yet uncorroborated, but if, as it appears, an academy did exist, it would have been the earliest in a provincial town and one of the first in the British Isles. Beyond London only the Academy of St Luke in Edinburgh, founded in 1729, and that in Dublin of 1742 were established earlier.[50]

The background to the single unambiguous published reference to an academy is complex. Not long after the Bath General Hospital opened its doors to patients in 1742 (fig. 11), one of its assistant surgeons Archibald Cleland became embroiled in a scandal that led to his dismissal.[51] Cleland was judged guilty of professional misconduct by a committee of seventeen of the Hospital's governors who met to investigate complaints that he had carried out repeated and unnecessary vaginal examinations on two women patients. Cleland believed, possibly with some justification, that he was the victim of a conspiracy. In pamphlets published in his own defence he was at pains to point out that of the thirteen governors who voted to sack him, three were physicians to the Hospital (and might therefore have been motivated by professional jealousy) and ten were closely associated with each other, either through business or friendship.[52] Cleland was especially scornful of the behaviour of one of these governors, Paul Bertrand (d. 1755), whom he describes as 'a *French* Toyman'.[53] One of the two female complainants against Cleland subsequently died at the Hospital and was the subject of a post-mortem examination. Bertrand showed particular curiosity about this patient and asked to attend the post-mortem, enquiring at the same time if Cleland considered the woman to have been a virgin. In his pamphlet *A Full Vindication of Mr Cleland's Appeal to the Publick*, Cleland noted with some indignation,

> It may here not improperly be asked, From what Sort of Principle this extraordinary Curiosity of Mr *Bertrand's* did proceed? since he had, or might have fully satisfied a more modest Degree of it, in his frequent Examinations, or at least viewing of naked Women, in the *Academy of Painting*, as it is call'd, in this Place; which, I am inform'd, He, and some other *Governors* are Members; and where one can scarcely think any modest Maid, or Woman, wou'd expose herself.[54]

It is possible to make an informed guess as to which of the 'some other *Governors*' might have been members of this academy. The most likely candidates from Cleland's list of ten associates are the painter William Hoare; James Leake (1686–1764), publisher, book and print seller; John Morris (apothecary to the Hospital 1741–1757); and Ralph Allen (1694–1764), businessman and philanthropist. Paul Bertrand, goldsmith and toyman, was stated by Cleland to have been a member.

William Hoare would have been a pivotal character in the formation of an academy. Hoare seems to have been in Bath as early as 1738.[55] His name first appears in Bath rates books in 1742 when he took over a house in Barton Street, probably one of the terrace of five which made the east side of Queen Square (figs 2 and 40). Next door, or next but one, to Hoare was Paul Bertrand, who had been there since 1739.[56] In 1754 both Hoare and Bertrand were still in Barton Street and by this date other residents included Surgeon Peirce of the General Hospital, the subject of a portrait by Hoare (fig. 11), and Sir John Cope who had been commander-in-chief of forces in Scotland in the 1745 rebellion.[57]

While Hoare's place in Bath society is well known, Paul Bertrand, the one person named by Cleland as a member of the academy, is not mentioned in any account of the history of the arts in Bath.[58] Bertrand is known to have been a goldsmith in St Martin-in-the-Fields, London, between 1709 and 1711, was in Bath by 1733, and is recorded at a meeting of the Bath Freemasons at the Bear Inn on 2 November 1737.[59] He was presumably a member of one of the many Huguenot families of goldsmiths and silversmiths who came to Britain after the revocation of the Edict of Nantes in 1685. Bertrand seems to have maintained links with other Huguenots even after his move to Bath. An advertisement in the *Bath Journal* for 10 October 1748 announces, 'Moses Roubel, French Jeweller (Who was Chief, in the Working Part, to Mr Bertrand for several Years) . . . sets all Manner of Jewellery Work . . .'. In the same issue of the same newspaper one James Tilly, also calling himself 'Chief Workman to Mr Bertrand at Bath, for Many Years', is described as a 'French Jeweller'. Bertrand was an active governor of the Hospital, regularly handing over funds collected from eminent visitors to the town.[60] After his death an auction sale of his 'Valuable Collection of Pictures, Busts' and other works of art took place on 11 and 12 November 1755.[61] On 3 January 1748 the *Bath Journal* had advertised 'Messrs Bertrand, and Compy. Having left off Trade, the greatest Variety of Jewels and Toys, with Useful and Ornamental Dresden and China Ware, Are to be Sold at Davis's India-House, Adjoining Mr Wiltshire's Long Room, on the Lower-Walks . . .'. In fact Bertrand's wife may have continued to run the business after this date since Horace Walpole refers to her as 'the toy-woman of Bath' in a letter of 18 May 1749.[62] Mrs Bertrand's sister was the famous London toy-woman Mrs Daniel Chenevix, from whom Walpole leased Strawberry Hill in 1749.[63] Walpole recorded that when he signed a document relating to the lease of Strawberry Hill, Mrs Chenevix brought Mrs Bertrand as a witness. Rather than treating the women to wine, Walpole showed them his cabinet of enamels, at which Mrs Bertrand joked, 'Sir, I hope you don't trust all sorts of *ladies* with this cabinet', which remark Walpole regarded as 'an entertaining assumption of dignity'.[64]

The scraps of information that survive about Paul Bertrand paint a picture of a well-to-do businessman aspiring to be a gentleman, living at a good address, surrounded by a collection of works of art, eager to involve himself in charitable works. Employees who subsequently set up their own businesses were keen to use his name. In addition to Roubel and Tilly, a John Pyke, toyman in Orange Grove in the 1750s, used a flamboyant rococo trade card on which he described himself as 'From Mr. Bertrand'.[65]

Bertrand's toy shop near the two Assembly Rooms, or Long Rooms, on Terrace Walk was close to the internationally famous Terrace Walk bookshop run by James Leake. There is no way of assessing the extent of Leake's involvement with the visual arts, but his son Henry Leake was apprenticed to William Hoare in June 1760, when he was awarded a Premium for 'a Drawing after the Antique' by the Society for the Encouragement of Arts in London.[66] In order to have become proficient at drawing from antique sculpture, Henry Leake must have had access to a collection of casts, either belonging to William Hoare or William's brother the sculptor Prince Hoare, or perhaps belonging to an academy. Leake's was known as 'One of the finest bookshops in Europe'.[67] It is not known precisely when he came to Bath, but at the time of his marriage to a Bath girl in Bath Abbey on 23 April 1721, his address was given as St Martin's, Ludgate, London.[68] He probably moved to Bath soon afterwards.[69] When the contents of Leake's shop were advertised

3 Anthony Walker (1726–1765) after a drawing by the same artist, *Prior Park, the Seat of Ralph Allen Esqr near Bath* 1752, engraving, $11\frac{1}{8} \times 17\frac{5}{16}$ inches (24.8 × 44 cm), published 1752, Victoria Art Gallery, Bath and North East Somerset Council. Railway trucks transported the stone from Allen's quarries down an inclined plane past Prior Park to his wharf on the River Avon. The gardens at Prior Park were open to the public on Thursdays during Allen's lifetime.

for sale in 1762, two years before his death, there were six thousand volumes including important publications such as Giacomo Leoni's English translation of Palladio's *Quattro Libri dell'Architettura*.[70] Not all his stock was of this quality. The Earl of Orrery was amused by Leake's social pretensions and described him as 'the Prince of all the coxcomical Fraternity of Booksellers: and, not having any Learning himself, He seems resolved to sell it as dear as possible to Others'.[71] Leake had in fact attended the Merchant Taylors' School in London and so was not wholly uneducated, but he was a shrewd businessman and had no qualms about publishing and selling popular, as well as serious, literature.[72] In 1740 he printed *A New Description of Merryland* by Thomas Stretzer, a detailed account of the discovery of a woman's body set out in the form of a topographical tour. By 1742 this had run to ten editions and an illustrated version, *Merryland Displayed*.[73]

Of the two remaining characters listed by Cleland who might have been members of what he called 'the *Academy of Painting*', John Morris, apothecary, was the highest paid member of resident staff at the hospital, while Ralph Allen was possibly the single most influential personality in Bath's early eighteenth-century history.[74] The only hint that Morris might have had some involvement with the arts derives from the fact that he was probably the father of the painter Benjamin Morris (1722–1807), several of whose portraits remain in the Hospital collection.[75]

Ralph Allen (fig. 12) first made a fortune from developing an efficient national postal service, and then successfully promoted the use of Bath stone as a high quality building material. He was involved in almost every major business venture in Bath in the first half of the century, including the highly important Avon Navigation Company, and acted as unofficial banker to the Bath Corporation.[76] Although he is never known to have shown any personal inclination towards drawing and painting, he was a keen supporter of the arts in general, played host to writers, musicians and painters at his home at Prior Park (figs 3 and 6) and was a regular customer of the painter and print dealer Arthur Pond.[77]

As Archibald Cleland himself pointed out, a common thread linking the group of Hospital governors who voted for his dismissal was an association with Ralph Allen.[78]

Membership of an academy may also have centred on the same social circle. The clergyman-poet the Revd Richard Graves recalled, 'I met Mr. William Hoare, the painter, at Prior Park; who so long presided at the head of his profession in Bath; and who was not only one of the most virtuous, friendly, and inoffensive men, but one of the best classical scholars, both in Greek and Latin, with whom I was ever acquainted'.[79] If Hoare was something of a Renaissance man, so were some of the doctors employed at the General Hospital, and several of these may also have been connected with an academy. Roger Rolls has concluded, 'What distinguishes the early medical staff more than their medical qualifications, is the breadth of their interests, and the diversity of their achievements'.[80]

4 George Vertue (1684–1756) after James Vertue (*fl.* 1731–60), *A Perspective View of the Abbey Church of St Peter and St Paul at Bath* 1750, engraving, 23 × 14⅞ inches (58.5 × 37.8 cm), published 1750, Victoria Art Gallery, Bath and North East Somerset Council. This plate is dedicated by James Vertue to Charles Noel, Fourth Duke of Beaufort. At the east end of the Abbey the arched marble altarpiece containing the *Adoration of the Shepherds* painted by Johann Van Diest can just be seen.

One further artist who was not a governor of the Hospital but may well have been involved with an academy is James Vertue (fig. 4). He was certainly in Bath by the beginning of 1744 since he is recorded at a meeting of the Bath Lodge of Freemasons at the Bear Inn on 16 January of that year. Also present were John Morris, James Leake and Thomas Ross (*fl.* 1730–57), a landscape artist who was working for Allen around this time.[81] According to George Vertue, James had 'many years livd with Mr Richardson painter & sometime with J. Vandrbank painter' before moving to Bath where he dealt in 'small toys. etc. but by practiceing & teaching to draw from the rudiments he had learnt. many persons of distinction. were his scholars. and some made Great progress in drawing & painting'.[82] Through John Vanderbank (1694–1739), Vertue may have become acquainted with the Bath-born painter John Robinson (1715–1745), before coming to settle in Bath on account of his health.[83] Vertue was still active in Bath in 1760 when he placed an advertisement in *Boddely's Bath Journal* of 7 January. The full text reads,

> Mr James Vertue, now residing at Mrs Willmore's, at West-Gate-House in Bath, (where he is obliged for the Benefit of his Health to live constantly) and Brother to the late Mr George Vertue, Engraver and Member of the Society of Antiquaries, having been educated from his early Youth, in the Art of Painting, under the most eminent Masters, and having for several Years drawn in the Academy after the Life; by the general Advice of his Friends, begs Leave to acquaint the Public, that he teaches to draw and paint upon the true Rules and Principles of the Art, and that he is ready to attend such Gentlemen and Ladies as are desirous to be instructed therein, either in Town or Country.

Although no documentary evidence has been found to prove that Vertue played a part in any academy in Bath, it is clear that there were in Bath in the 1740s and 1750s two artists with direct links with the earlier London academies. Vertue had, according to his brother, lived with Jonathan Richardson who was involved in the foundation of Kneller's Academy in 1711, and John Vanderbank who founded the St Martin's Lane Academy in 1720. When in his advertisement Vertue said that he had 'for several Years drawn in the Academy after the Life', he may have been referring to Kneller's, the St Martin's Lane Academy or a Bath academy. William Hoare was linked with St Martin's Lane through his master Giuseppi Grisoni who was one of its first subscribers.[84]

The artist who most obviously influenced Gainsborough's early portrait-painting style was Francis Hayman (1708–1776) who was a leading instructor at the St Martin's Lane Academy.[85] Hayman's association with this London Academy was probably slightly later than Vertue's, although the two men could have drawn together there in the late 1730s. It is also conceivable that Hayman visited Bath in the 1740s. Around 1743–4 he painted a group portrait of John Jacob and his family of Bath (fig. 155), a patron whose family later purchased several paintings from Gainsborough.[86] On 19 December 1748 the *Bath Journal* included the name 'Mr Heymans', a possible distortion of Hayman, in its list of visitors who had arrived in the town during the previous week.

Michael Kitson and Brian Allen have shown that although the St Martin's Lane Academy was in a formal sense probably no more than a life class, it had an incalculable value as an arena for aesthetic debate.[87] Archibald Cleland's single reference to a Bath academy of painting suggests that it too was a life class and here, to an even greater extent, the drawings produced by its members (an assortment of doctors, retailers, amateurs and artists) must have been of little significance compared to the accompanying debate. Hoare, we know, was learned and eloquent. Vertue had spent his formative years in the company of eminent London artists and kept in touch with the London art world through his brother. Here, apparently, was a group of men linked by some form of academy, by friendship and by Freemasonry, whose discourse on matters of aesthetics and taste must have been of a much higher order than anything found in any other provincial town of the period.

The few facts that are known about artistic activity in Bath in the 1740s suggest that close links existed between the profession of painting and the luxury trade. While William Hoare was probably a friend as well as a neighbour of Paul Bertrand, the toyman and goldsmith, James Vertue was himself both toyman and artist.[88] Later on Gainsborough himself shared the commercial, or retail, space in his first town house in Bath with his sister Mary Gibbon, a milliner, and probably benefited from having her shop under his roof.[89] Painters were, to all intents and purposes, participants in the luxury business.

The luxury trade in Bath was more highly developed than that of any other provincial town. Josiah Wedgwood found 'the Toy and China shops are richer and more extravagant in their shew here [in Bath] than in London'.[90] Many of those involved in the trade were also extremely influential in the life of the city. Bertrand, for example, was a governor of the Hospital, and throughout the century the Corporation was dominated by tradesmen, including a high proportion who represented the luxury end of the market.[91]

Statistics show that a large number of artists practising in Bath were miniaturists, that branch of portraiture most closely allied to the luxury goods market.[92] Of a total of 166 painters recorded in the town between 1700 and 1800, fifty-three (32 per cent) painted miniatures. Of the sixty-two (37 per cent) who painted portraits in oil or pastel, sixteen produced miniatures as well as full-size paintings and some may have worked more often on a small scale. Only twenty-four (14 per cent) worked exclusively as landscape or topographical artists, although a further twenty-five combined landscape with another discipline such as portraiture or printmaking. Artistic activity was concentrated in the second half of the century, with only fifteen (9 per cent) of the 166 painters being in Bath before 1750. These statistics are probably somewhat distorted by a lack of records from before 1750, but they do give a broad indication of the spread of artistic activity in Bath, both before and after Gainsborough's arrival. Landscape painting was clearly the least-practised art, a point of interest when Gainsborough's own landscape career in Bath is considered.

The luxury market was well established in Bath before the mid-century. A writer noted in 1725, 'the streets though narrow have many handsome shops which are well accustomed by the great resort of nobility and Gentry to this place'.[93] By 1749 the architect John Wood noted 'Artificers in the most Curious Works begin to find such Encouragement in the City, as to induce them to settle in it; so that *Bath* now boasts her Painters, Carvers, Engravers, Jewellers, Guilders etc.'[94] He refers in particular to the art of stone seal engraving which he says, 'is already become no inconsiderable Fibre of the Business of the City . . .'.[95] The principal seal engraver was John Wicksteed (d. 1754) who was in Bath by 1733, and whose son was still trading in the town in the 1770s.[96] By the 1770s the Wicksteeds had capitalised on a fresh water spring, found in the grounds of their seal-cutting 'Machine' at the foot of Ralph Allen's Drive, and turned the property into a pleasure garden offering spa water and cures by subscription.[97] Just how highly prized seals were to their eighteenth-century owners can be judged from advertisements in the local press offering rewards for the recovery of lost treasures. In 1744 one owner offered half a guinea reward for the return of a carnelian seal engraved with a head and in 1758 another offered a guinea for 'a very small Seal, set in Gold, with a little Swivel'.[98] The poet Alexander Pope, in a letter, asked Dr Oliver to collect a seal from Wicksteed on behalf of a friend.[99]

Allied to the art of seal and gem engraving as practised by the Wicksteeds was armorial and metal engraving which was carried out in Bath in the 1740s by Jacob Skinner (d. 1754), at the sign of the Grasshopper (a clever pun on his name, since grasshoppers shed their skins), where he also exhibited shells, fossils and other curiosities.[100] Skinner executed some finely crafted rococo trade cards, including the one already mentioned for Bertrand's former employee John Pyke, who had a toy shop in Orange Grove in the 1750s.[101] Close to Pyke's shop was Wicksteed's Orange Grove retail premises, a toy shop run by Mrs Sarah Wicksteed who sold fine porcelain as well as engraved gems and seals made by her husband and son.[102] By the autumn of 1754 and probably at least a decade earlier, she was also marketing the work of Thomas Worlidge (1700–1766), the most original printmaker to work in Bath in the eighteenth century (fig. 5).[103] The place of Thomas Worlidge in the Bath art world is of particular interest since he, more noticeably than any other artist, criss-crossed the boundaries between the luxury trade and the business of fine art. It is not known precisely when Worlidge first worked in Bath, but a portrait drawing by him of Beau Nash, dated 1736, suggests an early association with the town and the link was cemented by his marriage on 12 June 1743 to Mary Wicksteed.[104] A daughter was baptised in Bath Abbey on 12 May 1744 and five more children (including a boy named Francis Correggio) were baptised in the Abbey between 1745 and 1759.[105]

Worlidge is usually only mentioned today in the context of the Rembrandt revival in England and his longstanding association with Bath has been generally overlooked. The most recently published brief account of his life suggests that he left Bath in the 1730s.[106] However, advertisements in the Bath press and the baptisms of children indicate that he was in Bath for several months of most years between 1743 and his death in 1766, although he always maintained his principal address in the Covent Garden area of London. He was keen to advertise his regular presence in Bath and inscribed his etchings of *Rembrandt's Head* (of c. 1755) and *Abraham Offering up his Son Isaac* (dated 1758) 'Thos. Worlidge Painter in Bath'.[107] An inscription in Horace Walpole's hand on the reverse of an impression of Worlidge's etched *Self Portrait* of 1754 in the collection of the Yale Center for British Art reads 'Thos Worlidge of Bath his own Portrait by himself'.[108] In 1756 Worlidge was admitted to the Bath Lodge of Freemasons which met at the Bear Inn.[109]

In Bath, Worlidge practised as painter, miniaturist, delineator of metalpoint portraits on vellum and printmaker. In the autumn season of 1754 he announced himself as 'Portrait-Painter from London . . . to be heard of at Mr Wicksteed's Toy-Shop in the Grove'.[110] Two months later a newspaper advertisement offered a huge ten-guinea reward for the return to Mr Worlidge of a miniature portrait of a gentleman set with diamonds which had been lost near the Pump Room.[111] While commissions for portraits were arranged through Wicksteed's shop, his prints were sold there and at Leake's and Frederick's bookshops.[112] His most ambitious print, depicting the installation of the Earl of Westmorland as Chancellor of the University of Oxford, was announced in Bath three months in advance of the actual event, inviting subscriptions which could be taken at both Coffee Houses, Leake's and Frederick's and at Worlidge's own house.[113] Subscriptions were at the relatively high price of one guinea for the print and people wishing to have themselves depicted in the scene could be included on payment of two guineas. One of the Wicksteeds, almost certainly James, was associated with Worlidge's project to etch a collection of *Drawings from Curious Antique Gems . . . Etched after the Manner of Rembrandt*, although the full extent of his involvement is not clear. Dr Richard Pococke, on a visit to Bath in September 1764, recorded, 'I went . . . to see Mr Wicksteds water engine for engraving seals . . . He is carrying on a work executed by Worledge in London of an Etching of the best antique Gems'.[114] The site of Wicksteed's 'machine', between Prior Park and the city, is marked on Thomas Thorpe's *Survey . . . of Bath* (fig. 6).

5 Thomas Worlidge (1700–1766), *Self Portrait* 1754, etching with drypoint, 7⅞ × 6⅛ inches (19.8 × 15.6 cm), signed and dated 1754, Victoria Art Gallery, Bath and North East Somerset Council.

Worlidge left one imitator in Bath, William Hibbart (1725–1808), a pupil of Jacob Skinner who, like Worlidge, worked in a drypoint technique inspired by the example of Rembrandt. Amongst other subjects, Hibbart etched in confident Worlidge style a portrait of Laurent Delvaux, the sculptor with whom the young William Hoare had shared lodgings in Rome between 1729 and 1732 (fig. 7).[115] Hoare commended Hibbart as a good etcher to the poet Christopher Anstey for the purposes of producing illustrations for his *Election Ball*, the designs for which were drawn by Gainsborough's friend Coplestone Warre Bampfylde.[116]

Thomas Worlidge must have found enough patronage in Bath to bring him back year after year over a period of well over twenty years. Like Hogarth in London, who marked his house with a sign of Van Dyck's head, he proudly advertised his status

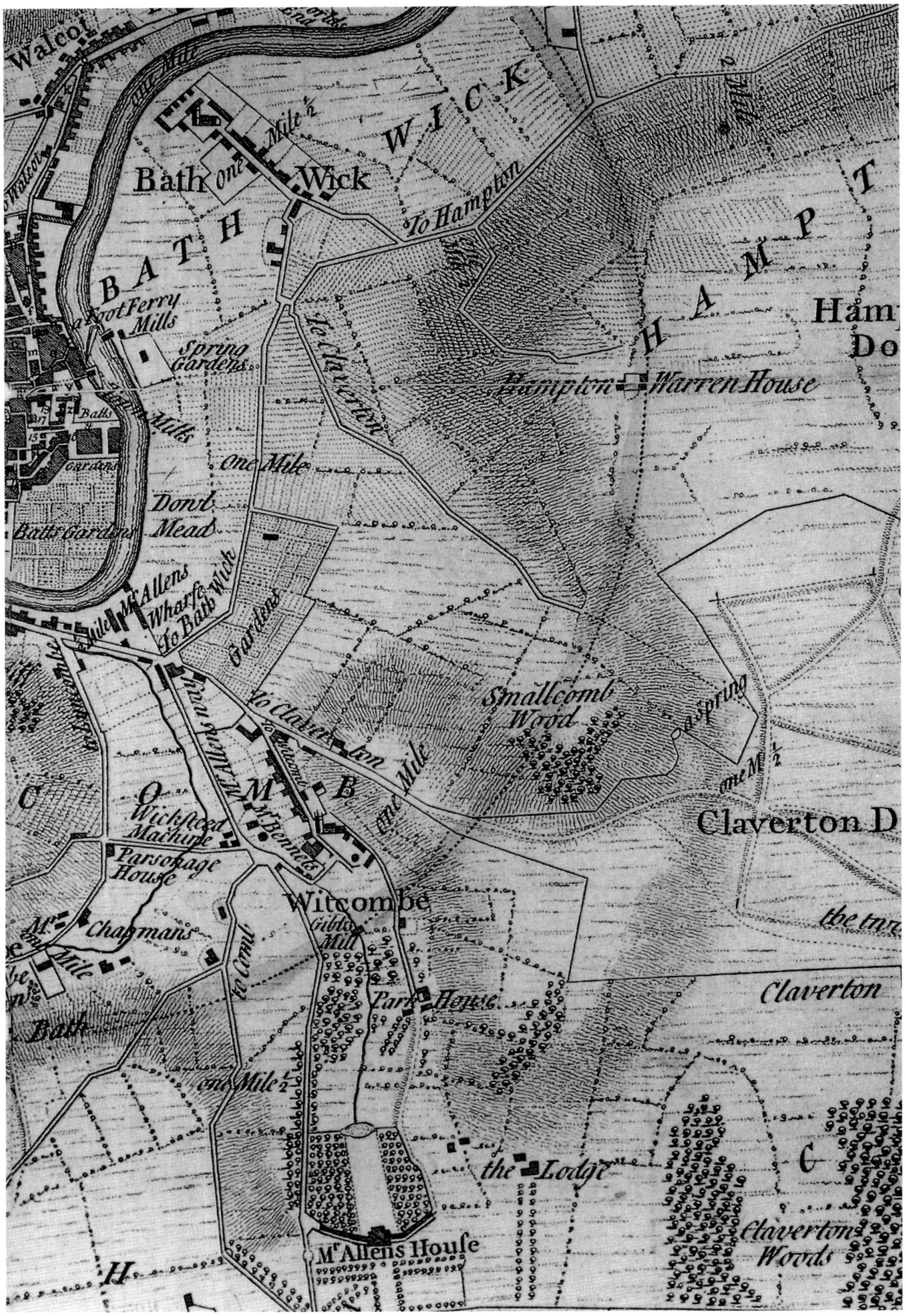

7 *(above)* William Hibbart (1725–1808), *Laurent Delvaux (1696–1778), sculptor* 1762, etching with drypoint, $6^{11}/_{16} \times 5^{1}/_{4}$ inches (17 × 13.3 cm), published 1762, British Museum, London.

6 *(left)* Thomas Thorpe, *An Actual Survey of the City of Bath . . . and of Five Miles Round* (detail) 1742, engraving (the whole) $75^{5}/_{8} \times 77$ inches (192.1 × 195.6 cm), published 1742, Bath Record Office, Bath. This detail (reproduced actual size) shows the area immediately to the east and south-east of Bath including part of the Revd Richard Graves's parish of Claverton. Between Prior Park and Bath the site of Wicksteed's seal-cutting 'machine' is marked.

with the sign of a Golden Head, an image which seems in itself to symbolise the link between portraiture and the luxury goods business.[117] Although he has never been seriously considered as a significant figure in the history of art in Bath, there is no doubt that his vigorous graphic style and his lively personality must have made an impression.[118] Some, such as Horace Walpole, identified him with Bath rather than London. He can be seen to be at the heart of the same social circle as William Hoare, selling his work at Leake's bookshop and possibly painting a portrait of Ralph Allen (fig. 12).[119] Like Ralph Allen, Paul Bertrand, James Leake, John Morris, Beau Nash, John Pyke, Thomas Ross, Jacob Skinner, James Vertue and John Wood, he was a Freemason.[120] Since only the Abbey separated Gainsborough's first house from Orange Grove and the Wicksteeds, Worlidge must have been known to Gainsborough. It is possible that Gainsborough's drawing *Peasants going to Market* (Gainsborough's House, Sudbury), reflects a knowledge of Rembrandt's graphic work acquired through Worlidge.[121]

Although Worlidge and Gainsborough were in no sense comparable artists, it may be that both flourished in Bath for similar reasons. Worlidge was able to exploit the Bath luxury market by the diversity of his activity, from the production of miniatures set with jewels, to full-scale oil portraits. His close association with, and marriage into, one of the leading business families, gave him an entrée into the heart of Bath's commercial life. Michael Rosenthal has recently pointed out that Gainsborough was 'acutely market-aware'.[122] Unlike Worlidge, he did not diversify his activity in order to maximise his clientele, but (as Rosenthal again has observed) he 'capitalized on an exclusive style, and an unparalleled capacity to catch a likeness'.[123] It is clear that both Worlidge and Gainsborough had a keen business sense that enabled them to use the opportunities of the Bath marketplace to advantage. Temperamentally too, they had things in common. Both enjoyed the good life (Worlidge was especially fond of good food), and were at ease in the company of wealthy patrons who might expect to be entertained by lively conversation while they sat for a portrait.[124] Those characteristics shared by Worlidge and Gainsborough may have been precisely the ones that were lacking in Joseph Wright of Derby's personality, and he, as is well known, completely failed to charm Bath society.[125]

Despite the interesting parallels between Worlidge and Gainsborough, it was William Hoare who was acknowledged to be the leading portrait painter in Bath before Gainsborough's arrival. Hoare's patrons of the 1740s and 1750s certainly outshone those of every other provincial artist in terms of social standing. Although artists such as John Theodore Heins in Norwich and George Beare in Salisbury managed to make a living without aristocratic sitters, Gainsborough's experience in Ipswich must have brought home to him the limitations of a career lived out at market-town level.[126] Even while he was still in Ipswich, Gainsborough was probably aware of the quality as well as the quantity of Hoare's sitters. By 1754 Hoare had painted a three-quarter length portrait of Pitt the Elder which became a standard and often-repeated likeness of the statesman.[127] The Third Duke of Beaufort also sat to Hoare, as did the Fourth Duke.[128] Hoare, like Gainsborough, came originally from Suffolk, but there is no evidence to suggest that he maintained links with East Anglia after his move to Bath. It must be assumed that whatever knowledge Gainsborough had of Hoare in advance of his first visit to Bath, must have been based on word-of-mouth accounts. He also might well have seen examples of Hoare's work in collections in London and East Anglia. Gainsborough must have believed that there were opportunities enough in Bath for more than one resident painter of full-scale portraits and he probably judged that Hoare, who was his senior by twenty years, might have passed the peak of his career. In the event, the increase in visitor numbers which coincided with Gainsborough's arrival helped to ensure that neither artist suffered from the competition of the other, and Hoare remained successful and respected throughout the entire duration of Gainsborough's residence. Quite a number of Bath visitors sat to both artists.[129] In 1764, five years after Gainsborough settled in Bath, Hoare was chosen by the Bath Corporation to paint a full-length portrait of the City's Recorder, Charles Pratt, First Earl Camden, and was able to charge sixty guineas, the same or more than Gainsborough then charged for a picture of the same size.[130] In 1767 the Corporation paid Hoare eighty guineas for a full-length of William Pitt, First Earl of Chatham, the City's Member of Parliament, a price twenty guineas higher than Gainsborough then charged.[131]

When Gainsborough arrived in Bath there were paintings to be seen in public buildings, churches and many private houses. The miniature painter Ozias Humphry (1742–1810), who was in Bath between 1760 and 1764, later recalled, 'This City [Bath] was certainly preferable to every other out of London; but still the latter City was to be preferred to Bath, on Account of its superior advantage for study to a young artist . . . There were few or no Pictures of old masters at Bath; nor did he [Humphry] see any Collections in the neighbourhood except Mr Methuen's at Corsham, and those of Mr Hoare at Stourhead'.[132]

It is true that many of the paintings to be seen in public buildings in Bath around the mid-eighteenth century were rather pedestrian in character. The painter who had been most active in the City before Hoare's arrival was Johann Van Diest (*fl.* 1695–1757), son of the Dutch landscape painter Adriaen Van Diest, who had come to England in 1672. Ellis Waterhouse aptly described Johann Van Diest's portraits as 'moderately wooden', but in the absence of any competition, Van Diest was busy in Bath for a decade from the mid-1720s.[133] He painted an altarpiece for Ralph Allen's private chapel at Prior Park and was involved in discussions between Allen and Alexander Pope about other decorative projects in the mansion and garden.[134] He also painted copies of allegorical pictures for Prior Park, again on themes chosen with Allen and Pope.[135] Van Diest was commissioned by Bath's Member of Parliament, General George Wade to paint all the members of the Corporation who had elected him to office: in return the Corporation asked Wade to sit to Van Diest for his own full-length. All these portraits hung and were cared for in the Guildhall.[136] The arrival of William Hoare in 1738 evidently dealt a severe blow to Van Diest. A letter from Van Diest's friend Dr William Borlase, dated 8 October 1739, urges him to try his hand at something other than portraiture:

8 Unidentified British artist, *Wiltshire's Assembly Rooms, Bath* c. 1737, etching, for a fan, image $6\frac{13}{16} \times 16\frac{7}{8}$ inches (17.3 × 43 cm), published by Jonathan Pinchbeck, c. 1737, private collection. These Rooms were managed by members of the Wiltshire family, including Gainsborough's friend Walter Wiltshire, for much of the eighteenth century. In this print the Master of Ceremonies Beau Nash is seen accompanying three ladies, others take tea, while two play at shuttlecock.

9 *(left)* Thomas Ross (*fl.* 1730–57), *William Shenstone (1714–1763), Poet and Landscape Gardener* 1738, oil on canvas, $29\frac{7}{8} \times 22\frac{1}{4}$ inches (75.9 × 56.5 cm), signed and dated 1738, National Portrait Gallery, London. Two versions of this portrait exist; the other, which originally belonged to the Revd Richard Graves, is at Pembroke College, Oxford where Shenstone and Graves were students in the 1730s.

10 *(facing page)* Thomas Ross (*fl.* 1730–57), *View Towards Prior Park, from the River Avon, Bath* c. 1740, oil on canvas, $36 \times 47\frac{1}{2}$ inches (91.5 × 121.5 cm), Victoria Art Gallery, Bath and North East Somerset Council.

> If you will take my advice . . . you must gett into quite another way. Change the serious primm traits of a face form'd by commanding constables and beadles, and flattered by the feasts of a Corporation, for the grimm terrors and majesty of a General in action. Instead of Cupids and soft and tender ladies, draw the fierce horse, the square batalion, the pale wounded heroe, the glittering swords, the level'd muskets, the streaming banners: in short, Van, I would have you quite lay aside the dull insipid face-painting; and, as I know you can easily master the difficulty of passing from one part of your profession to another (if you would be ru'd by me), go into battle; conform to the times; teach your mind to draw skirmishes, seiges, tents, and batteries; and, as Van Meulen did, mix the delicate groves and country with all the parade of war.[137]

Despite Dr Borlase's encouragement, Van Diest does not seem to have risen to this challenge and his portraits in the Guildhall were (and are) the best-known of his works in Bath. Also in the Guildhall was a pair of full-length portraits of Frederick, Prince of Wales and his wife Princess Augusta, presented by the Prince following a visit to Bath in 1738.[138] Hoare's portraits of Pratt and Pitt were added to this civic collection in the mid-1760s and Hoare also gave a portrait of Beau Nash following the famous Master of Ceremonies's death in 1761.[139] There was likewise a portrait of Nash in Simpson's Assembly Rooms, together with 'several very fine Landscapes' and another of Nash in Wiltshire's Rooms with 'many curious Landscapes' (fig. 8).[140] The full-length of Nash in Wiltshire's Assembly Rooms was in place before Hoare's arrival in Bath and is likely to have been the work of Van Diest, although it could conceivably have been by Thomas Ross, who was a portraitist as well as a landscape painter (fig. 9).[141] At this time there were no pictures in the Pump Room: the *Bath and Bristol Guide* of 1755 described the only objects of interest there as the full-length marble sculpture of Nash from the studio of William Hoare's brother Prince Hoare, and a fine clock by Thomas Tompion, both of which can be seen in John Nixon's drawing of the Room (fig. 1).[142]

The most accomplished landscape artist to live and work in Bath before 1750 was Thomas Ross. Ross painted views of Mount Edgcumbe (Devon), two of Chepstow and one of Twerton (just outside Bath) for Ralph Allen's drawing room.[143] One of a pair of landscapes by Ross, now in the collection of the Victoria Art Gallery, depicts the hills to the south-east of Bath with Prior Park as a focal point on the horizon (fig. 10).[144] Ross's four oils at Prior Park would have been seen by many visitors to Bath before Allen's death in 1764. Many others also saw Beau Nash's collection of 'beauties' that hung in his home in Bath. Lady Luxborough was surprised to find Nash, at an advanced age, busy rearranging these pictures in order to make room for additions.[145] Some of the 'beauties' were by William Hoare, but it is not clear whether all were.[146]

Apart from the Guildhall, the most prestigious location for paintings was the Hospital. While London artists, including the young Gainsborough, were giving paintings to the Foundling Hospital, Bath artists followed suit by giving paintings to the Bath Hospital. In Bath's case these were nearly all portraits. Benjamin Morris, who was probably the son of the Hospital's resident apothecary, gave several portraits, as did William Hoare.[147] It may be significant that

11 William Hoare (1707–1792), *Dr William Oliver and Mr Jeremiah Peirce, Physician and Surgeon to the Bath Hospital, Examining Patients* c. 1742, oil on canvas, 42 × 69 inches (125 × 169 cm), dated 1742 on the frame, Royal National Hospital for Rheumatic Diseases, NHS Trust, Bath. New patients are assessed on admission to the Hospital: Mr Peirce, the surgeon, tests a man's palsied hand while Dr Oliver, the learned physician, makes notes.

12 Attributed to Thomas Worlidge (1700–1766), *Ralph Allen (1694–1764)* c. 1742, oil on canvas, 30 × 25 inches (76.2 × 63.5 cm), Royal National Hospital for Rheumatic Diseases, NHS Trust, Bath. The Bath Hospital and other local causes benefited from Allen's philanthropy. This likeness bears comparison with the caricature of him in *The Knights of the Baythe, or the One Headed Corporation* (fig. 87).

13 William Hoare (1707–1792), *The Pool of Bethesda* 1767, oil on canvas, 68 × 82 inches (173 × 207.5 cm), Bath Masonic Trust, Old Orchard Street, Bath.

several of Hoare's best paintings at the Hospital were given *after* Gainsborough's arrival in Bath. In 1762 he donated his most successful group portrait, *Dr Oliver and Mr Peirce, Physician and Surgeon to the Bath Hospital, examining Patients* (fig. 11), a picture that he also exhibited at the London Society of Artists exhibition that year, although it must have been painted at least ten, if not twenty, years earlier.[148] A portrait of Ralph Allen in the Hospital collection is attributed to Jonathan Richardson, but may be the work of Thomas Worlidge (fig. 12).[149] All these paintings would have been seen by the many Bath visitors who toured the Hospital and their presence on the Hospital walls not only advertised the artists' technical abilities but also their worthy intentions. By supporting the Hospital in this manner the painters themselves acquired social standing, their gifts of paintings putting them on an equal footing with other benefactors.

Visitors to Bath also saw paintings in several places of worship. The Abbey had an altarpiece painted by Van Diest and St Michael's Church an altarpiece featuring the Tablets of the Law flanked by two figures, *Moses* by John Robinson, and *Christ Bearing his Cross* by William Hoare.[150] The *New Bath Guide* of 1762 described these as 'two very fine paintings', but the Revd John Penrose, visiting Bath in 1766, was less impressed.[151] The two pictures are still in the present St Michael's Church. In 1765–7 Hoare painted *The Pool of Bethesda* (fig. 13), a New Testament subject uniquely suited to a spa setting, for the altar of the fashionable new Octagon proprietary chapel in the centre of town.[152] Interestingly Hoare, who was also a governor of the London Foundling Hospital, seems to have borrowed from William Hogarth's *Moses before Pharaoh's Daughter* in the Foundling Hospital for the composition of this large painting; he, or the proprietors of the Octagon Chapel, also chose for it a frame which is similar in design to those used for the pictures in the General Court Room of the Foundling Hospital.[153]

As well as the paintings in public buildings, churches and well-known private homes such as those of Nash and Allen, there were often temporary exhibitions. Some of these were closer to entertainment than fine art, but they are worth mentioning, since they illustrate the range of visual attractions with which portrait painters had to compete. In 1744 visitors were invited to attend 'Gough's illuminated artificial Wilderness' where they could see fruit trees, busts and figures of the ancients, all 'in Roman and Italian Taste'.[154] In 1754 a Mr Corton, painter of perspective views, displayed an example of his work at Wiltshire's Assembly Rooms. He was in attendance at the Rooms for several hours every day and could otherwise be contacted through Moses Roubel, the jeweller and toyman.[155] In 1757 one Samuel Dixon exhibited 'Flower pieces in Basso Rilievo' and in 1758 the miniature painter John Brockmer showed a collection of 'Fancy Pieces' by 'an eminent Hand'.[156] Waxworks were popular, with Mrs Salmon's 1748 exhibition of members of the English Royal family being accompanied by a musical entertainment, both vocal and instrumental.[157] Twelve life-sized wax figures of the King of Prussia and his family could be seen in Bath towards the end of 1759 and another Royal waxwork exhibition was held in 1762.[158] An exhibition of sculptures after the antique and 'new and old prints after the best masters' was assembled in 1765 by a 'Mr Champione', an Italian who apparently travelled the country with his collection.[159]

Although Ozias Humphry's complaint about the dearth of old master pictures in Bath appears to be justified, there may in fact have been one or two genuine old master paintings in the town at various times in the late 1750s and early 1760s when both he and Gainsborough were first established there. In 1758 Thomas Worlidge advertised 'a curious Collection of Pictures, from the best Masters, which may be seen at his House'.[160] In the *Bath Advertiser* of 21 May 1764 an unnamed 'Person of Distinction' advertised a 'Magnificent Sedan

Chair' and 'several very good Pictures . . . amongst which are four painted by the celebrated Lemoine, who painted the Labours of Hercules at Versailles, and one of Titian, and various others'. In December 1760 the poet William Whitehead wrote to his former pupil Lord Nuneham, from Bath, 'I was much entertained the other morning with a very good copy of the famous Corregio [sic] Picture at Parma. Mr Webb, whom we saw in Italy, is in possession of it. He has likewise a holy family by Julio Romano touched up by Raphael, which is very fine. You must never pass thro' Bath without seeing them'.[161] 'Mr Webb' was Daniel Webb (1719?–1798) who in the same year had published *An Inquiry into the Beauties of Painting*, a book that made him something of a local celebrity.[162] Mrs Delany clearly knew of Webb and had just read his *Inquiry* when she went to Gainsborough's house in October 1760 and saw his portrait of Ann Ford amongst other paintings. In an often-quoted passage of a letter to her sister she expressed the view that Gainsborough's pictures 'may well be called what Mr. Webb *unjustly* says of Rubens, "they are *splendid impositions*"'.[163]

Later in the 1760s a painter of still life and art dealer named William Jones settled in Bath and regularly exhibited old master paintings which he described as 'Just arrived from Abroad'.[164] Jones charged a shilling for admission and claimed to show pictures by Poussin, Rubens, Murillo and Claude in his rooms.[165] Since it is more likely that the pictures to which lesser names were attached were correctly identified, it is of interest to note that between 1769 and 1772 he advertised landscapes by Waterloo, Teniers and Snyders, artists whose names are often cited with reference to Gainsborough.[166]

Mrs Delany was just one of a number of Bath visitors who recorded their impressions of painters' showrooms.[167] These rooms were separate from the painting rooms in which portrait sittings were carried out and were specifically set aside for exhibition (fig. 14). Miniaturists, who required less space (and could not expect to earn enough to afford the luxury of a display room), showed their work in a variety of commercial premises, from toy shops to wig shops. The viewing of paintings in artists' rooms became a regular morning pastime in Bath and most visitors must have gone away with stronger impressions of the pictures they saw in these rooms than the rather old-fashioned works that decorated some of the public buildings. Artists went to some lengths to attract visitors to their rooms, exhibiting showpiece portraits of well-loved actors and actresses, musicians, writers and other public figures, many of which must have been painted uncommissioned, specifically to advertise their ability. Members of the public could make up their own minds about an artist's success in catching a likeness only if they were familiar with the appearance of the sitter, as each artist must have been acutely aware. As well as a careful choice of showroom portraits, most artists also hung subject pictures, landscapes or even a few old master pictures in order to add interest to their exhibitions.

The portrait painter Thomas Beach is known to have staged a high quality musical entertainment in his picture room in Bath in 1781, featuring musicians of international reputation. Horace Walpole, who attended this concert, described the scene in poetic terms:

> A fine light and shade being thrown upon the paintings, every one found himself surrounded, as if by magic, by a number of his acquaintances, breathing in canvass . . . About fifty ladies and gentlemen formed the audience; and, in such natural shapes did the pictures look upon, and seem to listen to us, that it was difficult to persuade ourselves they were not auditors also.[168]

Beach's concert was presumably organised as a bait to attract visitors to his rooms and it appears to have been carefully stage-managed, with the pictures lit to advantage, and the subjects chosen to include faces that would be known to the audience. Although one of the earlier waxwork exhibitions was also accompanied by music, it is not known whether Beach's concert was a unique event in a serious portrait-painter's rooms, or whether it followed precedents arranged by Gainsborough or Hoare, both of whom were keenly musical. What is clear is that the principal oil painters who worked in Bath, Hoare and Gainsborough, and later Beach, Wright of Derby and Robert Edge Pine, all had exhibition rooms in their houses which were open to the public throughout the Bath season (fig. 40). These rooms were well furnished and well situated in order to be easily accessible to visitors. Visitors sometimes had to pay for admission, in other cases gratuities were expected at the door. The Bath picture rooms were no doubt modelled on London artists' rooms, but in Bath they were the most important means of advertising available to painters. In London public exhibitions became the principal showcases for artists from the 1760s, but no such equivalent existed in Bath, although Thomas Beach attempted to inaugurate an annual public exhibition in 1778, four years after Gainsborough left the city.

Outwardly eighteenth-century Bath appeared a place where commerce was all-absorbing and material success came to those who most ably exploited and indulged the whims of the idle rich. But Bath's *raison d'être* was its spa and it is evident that many who profited by the luxury business felt a moral obligation to support charitable causes, and above all, the General Hospital. Not only were men such as Leake, Bertrand and Hoare active participants in the administration of the Hospital, but they also played an important role in reminding the noble and moneyed visitors to Bath with whom they traded of *their* moral duty to contribute. By their own ostentatious charitable efforts, the tradesmen, craftsmen and artists came near to being the social equals of their customers. Bath had a peculiarly levelling effect on its visitors and inhabitants. As Trevor Fawcett has pointed out, the day-to-day social life of the town was governed by Masters of Ceremonies who lacked pedigree, landed property or exten-

14 Thomas Rowlandson (1756–1827), *A Portrait Painter's Show Room* 1809, pen and ink and watercolour, $4\frac{7}{8} \times 7\frac{7}{8}$ inches (12.4 × 20.1 cm), signed and dated 1809, Ashmolean Museum, Oxford. Visitors to a painter's house examine and discuss pictures in the showroom or exhibition room, while a sitter is ushered into the adjoining painting room by a footman.

sive private wealth and yet were able to lay down rules of behaviour, protocol and dress to which visitors of all ranks acceded.[169] Many contemporary commentators refer to the extraordinary social mix to be found in the city, where the upwardly mobile middle classes rubbed shoulders with the nobility in a manner that would have been unthinkable in London. Early in the century Sir Richard Steele wrote, 'It was no little Satisfaction to me, to view the mixt Mass of all Ages and Dignities upon a Level [in Bath], partaking of the same Benefits of Nature, and mingling in the same Diversions'.[170] More specifically, in the 1760s, Oliver Goldsmith noticed that at concert breakfasts at the assembly rooms, 'Persons of rank and fortune who can perform are admitted into the orchestra, and find a pleasure in joining with the performers'.[171]

Marcia Pointon has argued that in the last quarter of the eighteenth century 'Portrait painting offered probably one of the greatest opportunities for social mobility of the period'.[172] In Bath, where social distinctions were already blurred, the opportunities must have been even greater than in London. William Hoare appears to have crossed all social barriers. In later life he was often referred to as a gentleman rather than a painter, even, on occasion, on legal documents.[173] By 1770 Gainsborough too, according to Thicknesse, knew how to act, and think like a gentleman, as he does to contemn and despise those who dare to treat him in any other light'.[174] The capacity to think like a gentleman was considered a prerequisite for true taste and judgement, but was not easily attained. Daniel Webb restated the commonly held view that the technical constraints of painting denied most professional artists genuine intellectual freedom, '[Artists] seldom, like Gentlemen and Scholars, rise to an unprejudiced and liberal Contemplation of true Beauty. The Difficulties they find in the Practice of their Art, tie them down to the Mechanic . . .'.[175]

It does appear that the particular circumstances prevailing in Bath allowed Gainsborough a degree of freedom and self-confidence unusual in any artist of the period and especially unusual in any working outside London.[176] The Bath ambience provided not only a captive clientele, but an intellectual life that embraced a tradition of cultural debate and a social system that was flexible enough to allow talented individuals to flourish, whatever their background. Gainsborough's personal triumph over the 'mechanic' is an integral part of any account of his Bath career.

15 Thomas Gainsborough (1727–1788), *Mrs Margaret Gainsborough (1728–1798)* c. 1758, oil on canvas, 30 × 25 inches (76.2 × 63.5 cm), Staatliche Museen zu Berlin – Preussischer Kulturbesitz, Gemäldegalerie. The most sensuous of Gainsborough's portraits of his wife, and the one which most clearly demonstrates the influence of Sir Peter Lely's portrait style, this must have been painted around the time of the Gainsboroughs' move to Bath.

2

Mrs Margaret Gainsborough: 'a prince's daughter'

In 1799, shortly after the death of the artist's wife Margaret, the diarist Joseph Farington visited the Gainsboroughs' two daughters. The younger, Margaret, told Farington that their mother 'was a natural daughter of Henry, Duke of Beaufort, who settled £200 a yr. upon Her which was paid till the last half year which remains unsettled as she died on the 17th. of December last, and it was not due till the 25th'.[1] Documents have now been found that show that Mrs Margaret Gainsborough was indeed the daughter of Henry Somerset, Third Duke of Beaufort (1707–1745), the Duke who did most to turn Badminton in Gloucestershire into one of the great treasure-houses of England, but died young, leaving the title to his brother Charles Noel Somerset (1709–1756). The same documents also explain Miss Gainsborough's remark to Farington that the last half-year of her mother's annuity remained unsettled.[2]

Following the publication of his *Diary* in 1922, it was generally accepted that Farington provided a satisfactory explanation of Mrs Gainsborough's parentage. The further discovery, in the same year, of accounts between Gainsborough and his attorney James Unwin (1717–1774) (fig. 16) confirmed that the source of the annuity was indeed the Beaufort estate.[3] The annuity documents themselves show that the £200 came initially from the Third Duke's hunting estate of Netheravon in Wiltshire and then the Beaufort farms and properties at Skenfrith in Monmouthshire. The agreement was drawn up in June 1744, three months after he was granted a divorce from his errant wife, Frances Scudamore, from whom he had been separated since 1740.[4] It states that Margaret Burr is to receive £200 a year, 'from and after the decease of the said Duke for and during the natural Life of the said Margaret Burr Paiable and to be paid in and upon the Twenty fifth day of December and Twenty fifth day of June yearly . . .'. In fact the Duke died less than a year later on 24 February 1744/5 at Bath.[5] Gainsborough must have known about this valuable annuity when he married Margaret in July 1746, eighteen months after the Duke's death. Strangely, the annuity agreement is not signed by Margaret Burr. At the foot of the document is the Duke's signature and seal on the left hand side, but on the right is no signature, but the seal of the family of Darcy de Knayth, 'Per pale azure and gules, three lions rampant argent'.[6] This may have been a purely arbitrary utilisation of a seal that happened to be in the office of the lawyer, or, possibly, the seal may have belonged to Patrick Darcy or d'Arcy, a prominent Jacobite living in Italy at the time of the Duke's grand tour.[7] The witnesses to the Duke's signature on the annuity document were lawyer Kingsmill Evans, William Addams and William Conniers.[8]

Netheravon is the setting for John Wootton's painting of one of the Third Duke's hunters, *Poppet* (fig. 17) and another Wootton oil dating from 1744 of the Duke out hawking with friends on Salisbury Plain.[9] The house and stables still stand, inappropriately converted for use by the Ministry of Defence.[10] In 1773 Netheravon was sold to raise funds to cover massive debts on the Beaufort estates and Mrs Gainsborough's annuity was rewritten in order to transfer the source of income to the family estate of Skenfrith in Monmouthshire. This new document, dated 26 March 1773, was signed by both Margaret and Thomas Gainsborough in the presence of the artist's nephew Gainsborough Dupont and another witness Nicholas Shipton.[11]

In December 1798 Edmund Estcourt, lawyer and steward to the Fifth Duke of Beaufort, submitted a bill of £1.6.8 to the Duke for 'Attending Miss Gainsborough several times upon the Death of her Mother. Preparing Case for the Opinion of Mr Neyle as to the last half Years Annuity & fair copy and attending him . . .'.[12] As is mentioned by Farington, Miss Margaret Gainsborough had tried to claim a proportion of the final £100 half-year payment for the period from 25 June 1798 until her mother's death on 17 December, just short of the normal payment date of 25 December. In fact Mr. Neyle had decided on 7 January 1799 that the Beaufort estate was not obliged to pay anything more to the Gainsborough family.[13] Miss Gainsborough had clearly not yet heard the result of this ruling when she saw Farington on 5 February.

16 Thomas Gainsborough (1727–1788), *James Unwin (1717–1774)* 1758–60, oil on canvas, 29 × 24 inches (73.7 × 61 cm), whereabouts unknown.

17 John Wootton (?1678–1764), *'Poppet', a Hunter belonging to the Third Duke of Beaufort* c. 1744, oil on canvas, 38 × 50 inches (96.5 × 127 cm), private collection. The horse is depicted on Salisbury Plain, with Netheravon, the source of Mrs Gainsborough's annuity, visible in the background.

The newly discovered annuity documents not only make sense of Farington's record of his conversation with Miss Gainsborough, but they contribute in a number of ways to our understanding of other aspects of the artist's family life. By marrying Margaret Burr soon after she had been granted a handsome settlement, the artist assured himself a degree of financial stability he could not necessarily expect from his career as a painter in the mid-1740s. By moving to Bath in the late 1750s the family became established close to the Beaufort seat at Badminton and not far from the source of the annuity, Netheravon in Wiltshire.

Mrs Gainsborough was not universally liked by her husband's friends: some found her aloof and judged her mode of dress too ostentatious for the wife of a painter. Philip Thicknesse harboured 'an implacable hatred' of her.[14] On one occasion she justified her elaborate dress, whispering to her young niece Sophia Gardiner, 'I have some right to this, for you know, my love, I am a prince's daughter'.[15] In parts of Europe dukes were sovereign princes ruling over small states and in England dukes stood next to princes in terms of status, so Mrs Gainsborough's remark to her niece was, perhaps, not as extravagant as it sounds. The Dukes of Beaufort were especially conscious of their noble lineage, boasting Royal descent from the Plantagenet kings of England through Edward III's son John of Gaunt. Their pride in their family history was expressed through building projects, the maintenance of large estates in England and Wales, and through collecting. It has recently been shown that the Third Duke was 'one of the most active and discerning English collectors to travel in France and Italy during the early decades of the eighteenth century'.[16] Perhaps Margaret Gainsborough was entitled to bask in the glory of her noble background, although she never seems to have openly discussed her illustrious parent with anyone outside the immediate family circle.

What the Badminton documents do not disclose is the identity of Margaret's mother. The original annuity agreement refers to Margaret Burr as being 'of Dukes Street near Grosvenor Square' in 1744, but the lists of names of ratepayers in the street are not illuminating.[17] Thicknesse called her 'a very pretty Scots girl, of low birth', Gainsborough himself mentioned a poor relative of his wife's 'from Scotland' and

Fulcher says she was the sister of a young man employed by Gainsborough's father as an agent in his textile trade.[18] Recent research by David Tyler suggests that Margaret Burr was a member of the Aikman family of Edinburgh, and related to the painter William Aikman (1682–1731) whose uncle John Aikman (1679–1752) and nephew William (1695–1784) were partners in the influential Aikman trading house of Leghorn in Italy.[19] It is a fact that the Third Duke of Beaufort was advised on his grand tour by the Scottish painter Patrick Cockburn and that the works of art he purchased in Italy were packed and shipped home by Messrs Winder and Aikman of Leghorn.[20]

The Duke set off on his travels in 1725, finally leaving Italy for home in August 1727.[21] Margaret Gainsborough is said to have been born in 1728.[22] To commemorate his grand tour the Duke was painted by Andrea Soldi (c. 1703–1771) in a Roman setting, gesturing towards the Coliseum (fig. 18).[23] His long nose, heavy-lidded eyes and deep chin are also apparent in William Hoare's profile drawing (fig. 19).[24] Gainsborough's portrait of his wife, painted at about the time they moved to Bath, shows that she seems to have inherited from her father a tendency towards a double chin, although her pretty eyes and nose must have owed more to her Scottish mother (fig. 15). Interestingly, the Gainsboroughs' older daughter Mary, seen to the right of *The Painter's Daughters with a Cat* (fig. 51) has her mother's roundish face, while the younger, Margaret, has heavy-lidded soulful eyes and a long nose, features common to her grandfather the Duke, and her father.

While in Italy the Third Duke commissioned the remarkable 'Badminton Cabinet' and purchased large quantities of antique sculpture and paintings including works by Claude and Poussin.[25] In his collecting he was helped by Cardinal Alberoni, a man at the centre of Jacobite circles, entrusted by

18 Attributed to Andrea Soldi (c. 1703–1771), *Henry Somerset, Third Duke of Beaufort (1707–1745)* c. 1740, oil on canvas, 39 × 59 inches (99 × 150 cm), private collection.

19 William Hoare (1707–1792), *Henry Somerset, Third Duke of Beaufort (1707–1745)* c. 1740, pencil, $6^{11}/_{16} \times 5^{5}/_{16}$ inches (17 × 13.5 cm), private collection.

20 John Wootton (?1678–1764), *Henry Somerset, Third Duke of Beaufort and Sir Watkin Williams Wynn with the Racehorse 'Little David' at Newmarket* c. 1744, oil on canvas, 40 × 50 inches (101.5 × 127 cm), private collection.

the Pope with the duty of supervising the finances of James III and his family in Rome.[26] Late in 1728 ninety-six cases sent by Winder and Aikman from Italy were safely unloaded for the Duke at Bristol and among these was one of the most treasured artefacts, subsequently known at Badminton as the Alberoni Urn.[27] On his return to England the Duke set about remodelling Badminton and commissioned John Wootton to paint the large equestrian and hunting scenes which decorate William Kent's Great Hall. Among Wootton's paintings for Badminton is one that shows the Third Duke leaning on the shoulder of his great friend and fellow patron of the arts Sir Watkin Williams Wynn (fig. 20).[28] Like the Duke of Beaufort, Sir Watkin had extensive estates in Wales and was a committed Jacobite. The two shared a close association with the Monmouthshire barrister and poet David Morgan who was executed for meeting Bonnie Prince Charlie in England.[29]

Gainsborough's marriage to the illegitimate daughter (and only child) of the Third Duke may have been arranged by James Unwin, the artist's attorney and banker. Unwin was a complex individual, a London lawyer and property agent who, through various quirks of fate, ended his life as the owner and occupier of one of the grandest houses in Staffordshire, Wootton Lodge near Ashbourne (fig. 96). There, for a period of fifteen months, he was neighbour to the philosopher Jean-Jacques Rousseau.[30] Gainsborough's one long excursion from Bath (apart from trips to London) appears to have been a visit to Wootton in 1771. Although it has been known since 1922 that Unwin acted in a business capacity for Gainsborough, little else has been said about him. The artist's letters to him that survive (there must have been many more) show that he was an intimate friend as well as a trusted business advisor.[31] Unwin also seems to have been genuinely fond of Mrs Margaret Gainsborough. The earliest personal correspondence that still exists between Gainsborough and Unwin is addressed to Unwin at Great Baddow, near Chelmsford in Essex and, most intriguingly, the artist wrote in March 1764 to Unwin at Great Baddow, 'I hope you are happily & pleasantly situated in the House you mention, which my Wife knows extreemly well'.[32] Margaret Gainsborough, it seems, had a longstanding knowledge of either the Unwin family or Great Baddow. A rare glimpse of Margaret's humour is found in Gainsborough's affectionate account of his wife's chiding over the unfinished portrait of Mrs Unwin in January 1765: 'What you scrubb said She, have not you been as long about a Shaddow as he have [sic] been in making three Substantial whole length figures', meaning that in the time it had taken the artist to fail to complete one painting, Unwin had succeeded in making his wife pregnant no less than three times.[33]

If Unwin had been instrumental in introducing Gainsborough to Margaret Burr it must have been because he knew Gainsborough well by the mid-1740s, and that he was also by this date associated with the Dukes of Beaufort. It

21 J. Ross (*fl.* 1730–57), *The Beaufort Hunt: The Hounds at Fault* 1733, oil on canvas, 36 × 57 inches (91.4 × 144.8 cm), signed and dated 1733, private collection. In the background is Troy House, the Monmouthshire seat of successive Dukes of Beaufort and members of the Somerset family. It was also the country residence of the Third Duke's receiver-general John Burgh and his son Bertie Burgh.

can be demonstrated that Unwin was linked with Beaufort business affairs from as early as 1737 and Gainsborough's connection with Unwin's business is documented from February 1749 and probably dates from earlier than this. It is quite possible that Gainsborough knew Unwin or some of his relatives from childhood, since an Unwin family of Flemish origin was established in Castle Hedingham, Essex, a few miles from Sudbury in Suffolk where Gainsborough grew up. A member of this Castle Hedingham Unwin family, the Revd William Cawthorne Unwin (1744–1786), was painted by Gainsborough in Bath in the 1760s.[34] These Unwins were engaged in cloth manufacturing: the artist's father was in the same trade in Sudbury.[35]

James Unwin and at least one other member of his family were in business with a John Burgh (d. 1740), steward to the Third Duke of Beaufort, whose London office was in Castle Yard, Holborn. When he was not in London, John Burgh occupied part of Troy House, an old Beaufort property at Mitchel Troy in Monmouthshire (fig. 21). Edward Somerset, Fourth Earl of Worcester, had purchased Troy around 1600 and it was then occupied by various members of the family at different times, with the western portion of the house set aside as the country home of the chief steward to the Dukes of Beaufort.[36] John Burgh became receiver-general in 1715, a year after Henry, the Third Duke had inherited the title at the tender age of seven. Since the Duke was a minor, John Burgh exerted considerable authority in the management of the estates and lived in some style at Troy. He and a local ironmaster by name of Rae were the first two men in Monmouthshire to keep a coach and the appearance of John Burgh driving to church in Monmouth with his ten children drew crowds to the church gates on a Sunday. He also built a road from Troy to Monmouth for the convenience of his coach.[37] John Burgh's post as receiver-general and the occupancy of Troy House was inherited by his son Bertie, who was probably named after his father's friend and political ally the Hon. James Bertie (1673–1735), the second son of the First Earl of Abingdon.[38] Bertie Burgh, his brother James Burgh (who predeceased his father in 1739) and James Unwin all had accounts with Hoare's Bank in Fleet Street, a short distance from their office in Castle Yard. Movements of money between these accounts show that James Unwin was certainly connected with the Burghs by 1737, perhaps as an employee in the Castle Yard office.[39] The earliest appearance of Gainsborough's name in the context of Burgh and Unwin's business is on 17 February 1749 when Bertie Burgh paid him a sum of £145.16.0.[40] At this date Gainsborough had been married just over two and a half years and was living in Hatton Garden, just north of Holborn, an address close to Burgh and Unwin's office, as David Tyler has pointed out.[41]

The post of receiver-general involved the collection of rents from the Beaufort estate's extensive properties in England and Wales, a highly responsible job, involving considerable sums of money. Bertie Burgh and James Unwin's accounts with Hoare's Bank show both men handling tens of thousands of pounds each year. Credits totalling £85,473.4.11 are noted in Unwin's account on 6 November 1758, for example.[42] It is not clear what proportion of these large sums was Beaufort estate money, but much of it probably involved rental payments. In the case of Bertie Burgh the trust placed in him by the Beauforts was abused and after the Fourth Duke's death in 1756 it was found that Burgh had submitted no proper accounts since 1748 and he personally owed the estate £8,000. His mismanagement was considered partly to blame for the estate's debts of £146,500 discovered by the Fifth Duke's Trustees, Norborne Berkeley (later Lord Botetourt) and George Henry, Earl of Lichfield.[43] The Trustees subsequently pursued Burgh (who was found to be bankrupt) and Unwin in an attempt to recoup, at the very least, the £8,000 owed personally by Bertie Burgh. Unwin steadfastly denied any responsibility for mismanagement and pointed out that he too was owed money by Burgh and that he had lent £4,000 of his own money to the Fourth Duke at a time when the Duke 'was almost beseiged [sic] by his tradesmen & other people that wanted their Money' and had never received any repayment of this loan.[44]

In an attempt to prove that Unwin was in a position to pay off his former partner's debts, Norborne Berkeley obtained a copy of the will of a Captain Edward Wheeler who died in 1761, leaving all of his considerable estates to James Unwin.[45] Wheeler was Bertie Burgh's brother-in-law, but evidently fell out with almost every member of his family, including Burgh, and decided to give everything to Unwin, unless it should happen that his 'much esteemed friend' Miss Fanny Stephenson of Newcastle-on-Tyne should bear him a child. In this case, the child should be named after him and, if a son, should inherit, since it was Wheeler's belief 'that the *Children of Love* are more naturally and properly the heirs of your inheritance'.[46] In the event Unwin inherited not only the Wheeler estates, but Miss Stephenson too. A year after Wheeler's death she had become Mrs Unwin. She is mentioned fondly in a number of Gainsborough's letters and was painted by the artist in a portrait which must have been started around the time of her marriage but was only completed a decade later (fig. 22).[47]

22 Thomas Gainsborough (1727–1788), *Mrs James Unwin (d. 1813/14)* c. 1763 and c. 1771, oil on canvas, 49½ × 42 inches (125.7 × 106.7 cm), private collection.

How much Margaret Gainsborough knew about her husband's use of her £200 annuity cannot be judged, but what is evident from the surviving accounts between Unwin and Gainsborough is that from as early as 1751 the annuity was being used as security for loans. Significantly, in February 1755, Gainsborough borrowed the large sum of £300 from Unwin's benefactor Edward Wheeler, a sum he paid back with interest in June 1757 using annuity funds.[48] In May 1756 Gainsborough wrote to a Mr Harris, to whom he owed money, asking him to be good enough to wait till midsummer, that is 25 June, the date the next annuity payment was due, for settlement of his debt.[49] Payments from Bertie Burgh to Gainsborough between February 1749 and January 1752, of amounts between £20 and £260, are all unidentified, but may be loans or part-payments of Mrs Gainsborough's annuity.[50] Similar payments to Gainsborough from Unwin's account, dated between May 1755 and August 1759 are also probably connected with the annuity or loans negotiated by Unwin.[51]

23 Luke Sullivan (c. 1725–1771), *The Fourth Duke of Beaufort's Family in the Park at Badminton* c. 1755, pencil and grey wash, 12¾ × 19½ inches (32.5 × 49.5 cm), private collection.

Gainsborough clearly owed a great deal to his wife's annuity and thus, indirectly, to the Dukes of Beaufort. There is no documentary evidence to suggest that he ever had any personal contact with Badminton and his close friendship with Unwin, if it was known about at Badminton, would certainly have rendered him *persona non grata* from around 1762 onwards. After 1756 Unwin tried to suggest a rescue plan for the Beaufort estates, but angry notes drafted by Norborne Berkeley in 1763 make it quite clear that the family was in no mood to forgive and still considered Unwin to have been a 'powerful Actor' in the partnership that it held responsible for so many of its troubles.[52] From 1762 Gainsborough only occasionally used Unwin as his banker, not because he had any personal quarrel with Unwin, but because the Unwin–Burgh business had ceased to exist and Unwin, since inheriting Wheeler's estates in 1761, no longer worked regularly as a banker and lawyer. One personal link with the Somerset family did, however, have a bearing on Gainsborough's artistic career and ultimately on the development of landscape theory and taste in the latter part of the eighteenth century. This was through the Price family of Foxley, related to the Beauforts through the marriage of Uvedale Tomkyns Price (1685–1764), Gainsborough's early Bath friend and patron, to Anne, daughter of Lord Arthur Somerset and granddaughter of the First Duke of Beaufort (see family tree, fig. 126).[53] A broader circle of people who might be termed 'cultural Jacobites', whose support for Gainsborough during his early years in Bath may have been influenced by a knowledge of his wife's identity, will be discussed in Chapter 6 below.

Living only a matter of yards away from Unwin's office in Castle Yard, Holborn, was the engraver Joseph Wood (d. 1763), the person who had assisted Gainsborough in producing his first etching in 1754, a landscape illustration for Joshua Kirby's *Dr Brook Taylor's Method of Perspective made easy* . . .[54] In the 1740s Wood had engraved a series of landscapes after Gaspard Dughet for the publisher Arthur Pond (fig. 133), one of the original paintings being a Dughet in the collection of Robert Price, the son of Uvedale Tomkyns Price.[55] Wood was in Cursitor's Alley, a narrow passage at the southern end of Castle Yard, and it was here that he 'had Mr Kirby's drawings under his care'.[56] These drawings must have been Kirby's studies of historic buildings in Suffolk that were engraved by Wood and published in 1748.[57] Joshua Kirby (1716–1774), painter and writer on perspective, was a lifelong friend of Gainsborough and the person next to whom he elected to be buried at Kew.[58] Gainsborough's association with Joseph Wood lasted into the Bath period of his career when Wood engraved and finished Gainsborough's print *The Gipsies* (fig. 121).[59] It is likely that Gainsborough visited Unwin, his banker and friend, and Wood, his mentor in the art of etching, on the same excursions to London.

Another important indirect connection between Gainsborough and Badminton should be mentioned here. The famous musical family the Linleys, who were to become some of the closest friends of the artist, came from Badminton. Thomas Linley (1733–1795), father of the 'Nest of Nightingales' (fig. 81), was born and baptised at Badminton, as was his brother William who became a builder in Bath.[60] Their father, also William, is said to have been a carpenter and Badminton documents include records of payments made to William Linley 'joiner' between 1756 and 1774.[61] In the 1730s the elder William Linley might well have been employed on the extensive building programme at Badminton undertaken by Mrs Gainsborough's father, the Third Duke.

A young painter also emerged from Badminton around the same time. Luke Sullivan (c. 1725–1771) was the son of a groom to the Duke of Beaufort and dedicated one of his earliest independent works, an engraving after Teniers, to Charles Noel, the Fourth Duke.[62] Sullivan went to London as a pupil of the French engraver Bernard Baron (perhaps on the recommendation of John Wootton who had employed Baron in the 1720s), worked as an assistant and engraver to Hogarth in London in the 1750s, and was also a fine miniature painter and topographical draughtsman (fig. 23).[63] Whether Gainsborough knew Sullivan is not established, but Sullivan engraved Hogarth's frontispiece for Kirby's *Dr Brook Taylor's Method of Perspective made easy* . . . in 1754 and subscribed to four copies of the book.[64] Sullivan's periodic visits to Badminton and Bath in the 1750s and 1760s serve as a reminder of the regular comings and goings of artists between London, Bath and Badminton in the mid-century.

Another important artist to work at Badminton and to bring the skills and traditions of the London academies to the area was Michael Rysbrack (1694–1770). In 1735 Rysbrack was painted by Gawen Hamilton as one of the participants in the *Conversation of Virtuosis . . . at the King's Armes*.[65] In the same group portrait are George Vertue, brother of the Bath painter James Vertue; John Wootton; Charles Bridgeman, the eminent landscape gardener who worked at Badminton; and James Gibbs, the architect who designed pavilions for Badminton in the 1730s. At Badminton Rysbrack designed monuments to the Second and Third Dukes of Beaufort and the Fourth Duke.[66] He was also responsible for the monument to the Third Duke's friend Sir Watkin Williams Wynn, the design for which was approved by the Fourth Duke.[67]

When James Unwin fell out of favour with the Fifth Duke of Beaufort's Trustees and became a gentleman of leisure after inheriting Captain Wheeler's estates in 1761, a new method of paying Mrs Gainsborough's annuity had to be found. Since Burgh and Unwin were longstanding account-holders at Hoare's Bank in Fleet Street, and the Trustees themselves also had an account there, this was the obvious bank for Gainsborough to use. This banking house also had a long association with the city of Bath. Its founder, Richard Hoare (1648–1718) had been a frequent visitor to Bath and regularly had crates of bottled Bath water sent to him in London. His sons Henry and Benjamin Hoare were Beau Nash's bankers and were involved with the Bath Hospital at its inception.[68] This Henry's son, known as Henry 'the Magnificent' (1705–1785), was Gainsborough's London banker from 1762 and the person who purchased the painter's *Peasants and Colliers going to Market* (fig. 158) in 1773. No designated bank existed in Bath until the Bath Bank, whose partners Cam, Clutterbuck, Whitehead, Danvers and Phillott opened in their first premises in 1768, although Isaac de Vic, a wine merchant, offered banking services from 1753.[69] As a result of Hoare's involvement with Bath a number of local businessmen, from Paul Bertrand to John and Walter Wiltshire, had accounts in Fleet Street, as did several of the artist's friends and patrons, including Jonathan Buttall senior, Dr Rice Charleton and Sir Charles-Kemeys Tynte.[70] Full details of Gainsborough's bank account, which was opened in May 1762, are given as Appendix II at the end of this book. The account seems to have been kept mainly for the twice-yearly payment of the annuity, but it is also occasionally used by sitters to settle accounts for pictures. The payments Gainsborough himself made out of his account are of considerable interest, and include the transfer of money to members of his family and a variety of tradesmen from artists' colourmen and picture framers to linen and woollen drapers and a Bath wine merchant. The large number of payments to drapers and mercers beg the question as to whether Gainsborough was still in some way involved in the family cloth trade or playing a part in his sister Mary Gibbon's millinery business, but they may simply be confirmation of Mrs Gainsborough's and her daughters' extravagant taste in clothes. Many of the sums paid out are in round figures, often £20 or £50, perhaps an indication that not all are for goods or services, but are evidence of the banking of money with local retailers or the loaning of money to these people. The regular payments between 1767 and 1774 to an Edward Parker, presumably the Bath wine and brandy merchant of that name, total £520, and while they may tell us something about the artist's thirst for fine wines, some of the payments may be evidence of local banking rather than the settlement of bills. The payment made to him in the summer of 1767 rather suggests this: on 8 August Mrs Gainsborough's £100 annuity is received, the next entry in the account is a payment of £100 to Edward Parker.[71] Parker may well have followed in Isaac de Vic's footsteps and offered banking in conjunction with wine selling in his Westgate Street premises. His will, which mentions stocks and securities, shows that at his death in 1785 or 1786 he was a wealthy man, able to leave £5,000 to his nephews in addition to other bequests including £100 to the Bath Hospital.[72]

The complexities of the business and family relationships linking Gainsborough, his wife and the Dukes of Beaufort, Bertie Burgh and James Unwin are still unfolding and it is likely that information will continue to surface. It is already clear that Badminton and people connected with the Dukes of Beaufort had an effect at every stage of Gainsborough's career. The names of those who were important figures in the artist's youth resonate throughout his life, even long after the people themselves ceased to belong to his immediate circle. Bertie Burgh, for example, was a major figure in his life in the 1740s and 1750s, only to disappear in disgrace around 1760. Gainsborough must, however, have been reminded forcefully of him when he painted Willoughby Bertie, Fourth Earl of Abingdon (1740–1799) in the mid-1770s.[73] What follows is a closer examination of Gainsborough's life in Bath and the pictures he painted from the time of his introduction to the west of England in 1758. The consequences of his marriage take the place of an underlying theme throughout.

3

'Mr. Gainsborough' Arrives: Bath 1758–1759

Gainsborough's career divides quite naturally into three phases, each associated with a different place of residence. During the first period the artist learnt his trade in London and East Anglia, he then acquired a national reputation while living in Bath and finally enjoyed a time of sustained prosperity in London. The general view that Gainsborough's decisive move to Bath took place late in 1759 must now be tempered by the knowledge that he made a preliminary visit, for a period of up to six months, in the winter of 1758–9.[1] It is now clear that a number of the portraits formerly thought to have been painted in Ipswich in fact belong to Bath, and it is also the case that some of the many portraits previously assigned to the period of 1760 to 1763 may have been painted earlier. A clear-cut stylistic break marking the transition between Ipswich and Bath can no longer be identified, since the technique Gainsborough used for life-sized portraits in Ipswich, characterised by a very obvious 'pencilling' of the flesh tones, is unchanged. While Gainsborough appears not to have painted any particularly memorable portraits during this first visit to Bath, the quality of the patronage he enjoyed within the space of a few weeks was indeed remarkable and was to have far-reaching consequences for the rest of his career.

Many of the facts of the artist's earlier working life in London and East Anglia have only recently been established.[2] The young Gainsborough went from Sudbury to London around 1740. There he came within the orbit of the St Martin's Lane Academy and two of its most influential teachers Hubert François Gravelot and Francis Hayman. He lived in Hatton Garden, an area to which he remained attached, and to which he seems to have returned periodically, even after moving to Bath. The artist's bank account demonstrates the extent to which he remained loyal to old friends in London and East Anglia after moving to Bath. As late as 1769, for example, he paid £20 to a Mileson Hingeston, a bookseller who was associated with Hatton Garden and must also have been a relative of the Hingestons of Ipswich whom the artist came to know in the 1750s.[3] While living in London, before and after his marriage in 1746, Gainsborough painted some accomplished landscapes and already, as Rica Jones has shown, possessed a 'remarkable ability to make paint sparkle'.[4] By the time he left Hatton Garden, early in 1749, to return to East Anglia, his name had been included in a list of leading British painters.[5]

Despite the fact that his abilities were recognised by the cognoscenti at this early date, Gainsborough quickly found that he could not make a living through landscape painting and turned to portraiture to make ends meet. The 'portraits in little' he painted in London, Sudbury and then Ipswich are exquisite, as the exhibition *Young Gainsborough* at the National Gallery in London in 1997 showed. In these pictures the small landscapes he had learnt to paint by imitating Dutch masters such as Wijnants and Ruisdael were effortlessly adapted to form settings for his portrait sitters (fig. 26). These jewel-like pictures, in which full-length figures are contained within a space seldom bigger than 30 × 25 inches, must have positively glowed on the walls of the traditional Suffolk homes of their owners. They were perhaps less suited to the much taller, lighter rooms of the new houses (that we now call Georgian) which were springing up in Ipswich and every other major city in England. This new architecture demanded larger-scale canvases of the kind Hudson, Ramsay and Reynolds were painting, and Gainsborough must have realised that he needed to adopt a larger format if he was to succeed in the competitive portrait market. It was in Ipswich that he gradually changed to the three standard life-sized canvases he almost invariably used at Bath: 30 × 25 inches for a 'head', 50 × 40 inches for a half-length and 90 or 94 × 60 inches for a full-length. The transition from painting full-length figures within a thirty by twenty-five inch canvas to painting a head and shoulder portrait within this same space was a difficult one. It demanded a different method of applying paint (hence the artist's preoccupation with 'pencilling' at this stage) and a broader approach to composition. Throughout his years at Ipswich, between 1752 or 1753 and 1758, Gainsborough experimented with this new way of working. The straightforward

24 Detail of fig. 121.

25 Thomas Gainsborough (1727–1788), *John Sparrowe (1689/90–1762)* 1755–7, oil on canvas, 50 × 40 inches (127 × 101.6 cm), Auckland Art Gallery Toi o Tamaki, Mackelvie Trust Collection. Sparrowe, who was Bailiff of Ipswich, holds a volume of *The Justice of the Peace and Parish Officer* by Richard Burn, a legal manual for local government officials published in 1755; the other volume lies on the table.

26 Thomas Gainsborough (1727–1788), *Charles Crockatt, William Keable and Peter Darnell Muilman, 'The Muilman Conversation Piece'* c. 1749–50, oil on canvas, 30 × 25 inches (76.3 × 63.5 cm), Gainsborough's House, Sudbury, and Tate Britain, London.

half-length of *John Sparrowe* (fig. 25), painted in the mid-1750s, is technically mature and shows an engaging feeling for character, but some of the full-scale figures painted during this period are tentatively drawn, and the artist had occasional difficulties with full-length figures well into the 1760s. The most successful large-scale figures of the 1750s were portraits of those nearest and dearest to the painter, the double portrait of *The Painter's Daughters Chasing a Butterfly* (fig. 27) of around 1756 exhibiting, as Michael Levey observed, a new-found 'boldness of conception'.[6] This picture became the property of the Revd Robert Hingeston, Master of Ipswich School, at an early date, perhaps when Gainsborough left Ipswich for Bath.

That move, as we now know, did not take place in one easy stage, but was preceded by an exploratory visit in 1758. When he was recovering from a serious illness in the late autumn of 1763, Gainsborough wrote to James Unwin, 'The truth is, I have apply'd a little too close for these last 5 years, That both my Doctors & Friends really think'.[7] The suggestion here is that he looked back on the preceding five years as a unit and thus, by implication, the autumn of 1758 had marked a turning point or new departure in his career. The generally accepted chronology has the painter settling in Bath in the autumn of 1759, around the date that his possessions in Ipswich were auctioned.[8] During the previous year he is usually said to have spent some time as an itinerant portrait painter in the Midlands.[9] However it is now possible to prove beyond doubt that Gainsborough was in Bath in the autumn of 1758, and to argue that he stayed until spring 1759 before returning through London to Ipswich for the summer when the Bath season closed.

Edward Edwards, writing in 1808, believed that 'Gainsborough removed to Bath, where he settled about the year 1758, and began his career as a portrait-painter, at the low price of five guineas, for a three-quarter canvas; however, his great facility in producing a likeness, increased his employment and fame, and he soon raised his price from five to eight guineas'.[10] Allan Cunningham in his *Lives of the Most Eminent British Painters*, published in 1829, says much the same: 'The increasing fame of Gainsborough demanded a wider field; he had exhausted the faces and scenery of Ipswich, and the counsel of Thicknesse agreeing with his own wishes, removed to Bath in the year 1758 . . .'.[11] The Bath historian Dr James Tunstall, writing in 1847, seems to be relying on Cunningham when he says, 'Here [ie. at Ipswich] he became acquainted with Thicknesse, governor of Landguard fort, by whose advice he removed to Bath in 1758 . . .'.[12] In 1856 George Williams Fulcher acknowledged Cunningham's date of 1758 but discounted it because of his knowledge of a letter written by Joshua Kirby proving the artist to be in Ipswich in August 1759.[13]

With hindsight it seems surprising that none of these historians referred to contemporary Bath newspapers. Reginald Wright, a long-serving librarian and curator of the Victoria Art Gallery in Bath, was the first person to search the local press for information about Gainsborough and his friends and fellow artists.[14] There in the *Bath Advertiser* for Saturday 7 October 1758 among the list of visitors who had arrived in Bath during the previous week is 'Mr. Gainsborough', and the same appears in *Boddely's Bath Journal* for Monday 9 October 1758.[15] 'Mr. Gainsborough' must therefore have arrived or registered his arrival in Bath between Monday 2 October and Saturday 7 October. The same week saw the opening of the official Bath season with a ball at Simpson's Assembly Rooms on Tuesday 3 October, the day that Richard 'Beau' Nash arrived in Bath from Tunbridge Wells, where he officiated during the summer months.[16] The *Bath Advertiser* for 23 September 1758 noted optimistically that the forthcoming autumn season promised to be the best in many years, as lodgings had been booked by 'such a Number of Families of Distinction'.

Between the autumn of 1758 and the autumn of 1774 when the artist finally left Bath, his name never again appears in any 'arrivals' list. It is likely that the names published were those of people who positively wished to register their presence in the town for social or professional reasons. The names may have been drawn from the subscription books at either the Pump Room or the Assembly Rooms. The Revd John Penrose, a Cornish clergyman who visited Bath in April 1766, wrote home to one of his daughters, 'If you do not see our Names among those of the Gentry arrived at Bath, in the Sherborne Paper, we have seen them in the *Bath Journal* . . .'.[17] Gainsborough, like Penrose, probably derived satisfaction from seeing his first visit to Bath announced in print, but his rapid professional success in the town soon rendered such social niceties superfluous.

Of course the identity of the Mr Gainsborough of the 'arrivals' lists could be questioned, but a letter written from Bath by the poet laureate William Whitehead to the young Viscount Nuneham proves that the artist was certainly in Bath in December 1758. Paradoxically, a published version of the same letter has been used as the principal argument against Gainsborough's presence in 1758, ever since William Whitley's biography of 1915. Whitley noted that 'There is a theory that [Gainsborough] had already passed a winter in Bath before leaving Ipswich for good, but the evidence in support of this appears to be untrustworthy. It is contained in a letter, given by several of Gainsborough's biographers as written from Bath, under date December 5, 1758'.[18] Two of these biographers were Arthur B. Chamberlain and A. E. Fletcher who did indeed refer to the letter and say it was written by Whitehead to Lord Harcourt from Bath.[19] Whitley goes on to argue correctly that in the published *Harcourt Papers* the letter in question is said to have been written from Middleton in Oxfordshire and dated 6 December 1758. The critical passage begins, 'We have a painter here,

27 Thomas Gainsborough (1727–1788), *The Artist's Daughters Chasing a Butterfly* c. 1756, oil on canvas, $44\frac{3}{4} \times 41\frac{1}{4}$ inches (113.5 × 105 cm), National Gallery, London. Mary (on the right) was baptised on 3 February 1750, and Margaret on 22 August 1751; both were born at Sudbury in Suffolk.

who takes the most exact likenesses I ever yet saw . . .', and concludes, 'The painter's name is Gainsborough'.[20] This leaves little room for doubt that Gainsborough was at that date at Middleton Park, the country seat of the Earls of Jersey, at Middleton Stoney near Oxford.[21] From this, the notion of Gainsborough as an itinerant portrait painter naturally evolved.

In fact the editor of the *Harcourt Papers* Edward William Harcourt was mistaken when he published the extract from Whitehead's letter. The letter is written by Whitehead to Viscount Nuneham, Lord Harcourt's eldest son, on 6 December 1758, from Bath.[22] This letter not only places Gainsborough in Bath in December 1758, but offers a glimpse of Bath life at that date and even offers a foretaste of some aspects of the artist's future in the town. The full text reads,

> My Lord
>
> Your Lordship seemed so well amused & in such very good company when I had the honour of hearing from you, that I thought I might very well postpone my answer 'till my return from Long-leat. I arrived at Bath again yesterday, & found the Ball of last night rather thinner than those I had been used to. Miss Ford is still here, but leaves us next week. Your friends the Players are very busy in getting up a new Comedy, called 'a Trip to the Bath', in which a good deal of the dialogue is very tolerable, & the whole, I think, like the common run of Plays. A new Actress is to make her appearance in it; the Green room calls her a young woman of *some fashion*, who, contrary to the inclinations of her friends, has so violent a passion for the stage, & so good an opinion of the Bath Company of Comedians, that in short, etc etc etc.
>
> We have a painter here who takes the most exact likenesses I ever yet saw, his painting is coarse and slight, but has ease and spirit. Lord Villiers set to him before he left Bath, & I hope we shall be able to bring his Picture to town with us, it is he himself & preferable in my opinion to the finest unlike picture in the Universe, tho' it might serve for a sign. He sate only twice. The Painter's name is Gainsborough.
>
> And now, my good Lord, give me leave to ask a little after poor London. How is Dodsley's Cleone recieved? & what is become of the Pritchards? I take it for granted Garrick makes you laugh in the Busy Body. Do the young actors improve, & is the Town favorable to them? I shall probably myself not reach Grosvenorshire 'till Christmas, & I really like Bath as well at present. The waters agree exceedingly with Lord Jersey & Lady Jersey finds Benefit from some new medecines. They both desire their compliments to your Lordship, and Capt. Stephens begs I would insert his respects, to which let me add my own, & that I have the honor to be
>
> My Lord
> Your Lordship's
> most obliged & most obedient
> Humble Servant
> W: Whitehead
>
> Bath. Dec: 6th, 1758

William Whitehead (1715–1785) was a regular visitor to Bath, often in the company of Lord Villiers and Villiers's parents Lord and Lady Jersey. His association with Bath and his role as poet laureate is acknowledged in an anonymous poem published on the front page of *Boddely's Bath Journal* shortly before the marriage of George III in 1761. One verse refers to Lord Villiers as well as Whitehead:

> Apollo cried . . . far, far from Home
> By Lordly Villiers taken,
> In *Bath* my Laureat loves to roam,
> *My sweeter streams* foresaken.[23]

In the autumn of 1758 Whitehead's arrival is announced in the *Bath Advertiser* on Saturday 18 November and in *Boddely's Bath Journal* on Monday 20 November. The Earl of Jersey's name appeared in both newspapers a week earlier.[24] As Whitehead's letter indicates, he must have spent a few days at Longleat before returning to Bath on 5 December. He remained in the town with the Jerseys until 27 December, when they returned together to Middleton.[25] Whitehead had been tutor to both George Bussy Villiers, later Fourth Earl of Jersey (1735–1805) and George Simon Harcourt (1736–1809) (styled Viscount Nuneham between 1749 and 1777) later the Second Earl Harcourt. Lord Nuneham, the recipient of the letter, has been described as 'one of the most pretentiously aesthetic men of his day' and Villiers is said 'greatly to have affected French manners and fashions'.[26] The two men were the closest of friends 'from their infancy' according to the poet William Mason.[27] Viscount Nuneham was himself a keen amateur artist, as was his sister Lady Elizabeth Harcourt (fig. 112). Both brother and sister took lessons in drawing and etching from Paul Sandby around 1758 when this artist was commissioned by their father, Lord Harcourt, to paint two oils of his new seat, Nuneham Park at Nuneham Courtenay.[28] Sandby was very closely connected with the family at this date, even designing a marble fireplace for the first floor drawing room at Nuneham.[29] He also completed a set of watercolours of the gardens at Nuneham and at Stanton Harcourt, and drew some charming informal studies of various members of the Harcourt family.[30] Under Sandby's influence Viscount Nuneham etched about twelve landscapes, half of these after Sandby designs.[31] He was regarded as something of an authority on prints by his friends.[32] So, when Whitehead communicated to Nuneham the news of Gainsborough's work in Bath, he was speaking to someone with a genuine interest in the visual arts. Whitehead himself also knew something about the business of portraiture, having very recently sat to Benjamin Wilson in London.[33]

In the first paragraph Whitehead briefly mentions 'Miss Ford'. This was Ann Ford (1737–1824), the subject of Gainsborough's portrait of 1760 (fig. 58). Whitehead spent much time in her company. He wrote on 16 November 1758, 'I have seen Miss Ford, nay almost lived with her ever since I have been here . . .'.[34] It was widely believed that Lord Jersey wished to make Ann Ford his mistress, but Whitehead was interested in commending her to his friend William Mason, or even Viscount Nuneham himself.[35] Given Ann Ford's prominence in Bath society and her association with the Jersey circle, it is most likely that Gainsborough would have seen her and possibly even made her acquaintance at this early date. Her potential as a colourful and sympathetic sitter cannot have passed unnoticed.[36]

The often mis-quoted paragraph of Whitehead's letter concerning Gainsborough is of considerable interest when set in context. Unfortunately the Villiers portrait by Gainsborough is only known today through a photograph dating from 1936, by which time it had clearly suffered at the hands of a restorer and had lost much of its surface quality (fig. 30).[37]

One other document, though a rather puzzling one, has something to say about Gainsborough's first visit to Bath. This is a published excerpt from an anonymous diary headed 'A very extraordinary Journal' printed in the *Town and Country Magazine* for September 1772.[38] The passage dates from 6–16 November 1758 and describes an encounter with Gainsborough in Bath. The story is said to be of a traveller who made a quest for undiscovered men of genius a lifetime's occupation. On coming across an early landscape painting by Gainsborough, he travels first to Ipswich and then on to Bath in pursuit of its author. The 'Journal' has been summarily dismissed as a work of fiction on the grounds that the artist was not in Bath in the autumn of 1758.[39] As it can now be proved that Gainsborough was there, the narrative may be viewed in a different light. The *Town and Country Magazine* was a periodical of somewhat dubious reputation whose primary intention was to entertain rather than to inform.[40] Nevertheless it is hard to think of a good reason for inventing the Gainsborough story, which is completely devoid of malice and appears to be designed to promote rather than satirize the artist.

The picture presented by the 'Journal' is of Gainsborough working methodically on sittings from ten o'clock in the morning, or even earlier, in an upstairs room, having brought with him from Ipswich a stock of landscape drawings and possibly some paintings for visitors to view. An acquaintance fulfils the role of a footman at the lodgings, protecting the painter from interruption while recommending his work and showing examples to the curious. This person's argument that 'He that takes up G[ainsborough]'s time, robs him in reality', finds an echo in a letter written in 1773 by Philip Thicknesse. At this date Thicknesse says that every five days, away from the artist's studio constitutes 'a loss to him of at least an hundred pound', and hints that it was Mrs Gainsborough who had her eye on the clock to ensure that the painter's earning hours were not wasted.[41]

Several factual errors in the 'Journal' are immediately obvious. Gainsborough had not been in Bath 'many months' by 7 November as the writer says, but arrived in the first week of October. Since he arrived precisely as the Bath social season commenced, he cannot have come 'from accident' or started to paint portraits 'by way of amusement'. The aspects of the document that point more convincingly to the truth are the writer's appreciation of the small oil landscape painting, which he describes as 'delicious', 'Ruysdael improved', the travel and accommodation arrangements (which in general ring true) and the account of Gainsborough's drawings in which 'so few parts are so much varied'. Some of the general observations about the artist's character are also convincing. One of the most revealing passages is that in which the writer expresses his disappointment at the 'common portrait stiffness' of the paintings he found the artist working on in Bath. These, he felt, compared poorly with his landscapes.

The 'extraordinary Journal' has been discussed recently by Michael Rosenthal in an article 'Testing the Water Gainsborough in Bath in 1758'.[42] Its author could have been Philip Thicknesse; another possible candidate is Daines Barrington (1727–1800), an eccentric man of wide-ranging interests who, notably, sought out prodigies, and in 1781 described an encounter with the very young Thomas Lawrence, then living at Devizes near Bath.[43] Barrington was the brother-in-law of Robert Price of Foxley (1717–1761), son of Uvedale Tomkyns Price (see family tree, fig. 126). Daines Barrington did write about Gainsborough at a later date, in the context of landscape gardening, as will be discussed below, in Chapter 8. In 1758 he could have seen in Gainsborough the undiscovered genius he so desired to promote. Gainsborough was by this date hardly a youthful prodigy like Lawrence, but he was certainly an artist whose exceptional talents were not yet widely recognised. By turning the pursuit of Gainsborough into a short and amusing drama, the author (whoever he was) successfully conveyed the sense of promise generated by Gainsborough's early work, and especially the landscape paintings. By 1772, when the 'extraordinary Journal' was published, Gainsborough was vying for position as one of England's leading artists, and, as Rosenthal has argued, difficulties with the Royal Academy may have prompted his supporters to draw attention to him in the press.

The terms used by the writer of the 'extraordinary Journal' and the poet Whitehead to describe Gainsborough's portraits in 1758 call to mind Philip Thicknesse's reaction to the Ipswich-period portraits he saw in Gainsborough's studio in 1753. Thicknesse described them as 'truly drawn, perfectly like, but stiffly painted, and worse coloured'.[44] Thicknesse's biography contains the final important pointer to Gainsborough's presence in Bath in 1758. Despite his own participation in the events, Thicknesse's memory of

28 *(above left)* Thomas Gainsborough (1727–1788), *William, Third Earl of Jersey (1706–1769)* 1758, oil on canvas, 30 × 25 inches (76.2 × 63.5 cm), private collection.

29 *(above)* Thomas Gainsborough (1727–1788), *Henry, Viscount Cornbury (1710–1753)* 1758–9, oil on canvas, 30 × 25 inches (76.2 × 63.5 cm), private collection.

31 *(facing page left)* Thomas Gainsborough (1727–1788), *Mrs Philadelphia Lee (d. 1799)* 1758–9, oil on canvas, 29½ × 24½ inches (75 × 62 cm), private collection.

32 *(facing page right)* Thomas Gainsborough (1727–1788), *William Lee (d. 1778)* 1758–9, oil on canvas, 29 × 24 inches (73.7 × 61 cm), private collection.

30 *(left)* Thomas Gainsborough (1727–1788), *George, Lord Villiers, later Fourth Earl of Jersey (1735–1805)* 1758, oil on canvas, 30 × 25 inches (76.2 × 63.5 cm), whereabouts unknown.

Gainsborough's introduction to Bath is confused: it is accurate in detail but not arranged chronologically.

In 1753 Thicknesse commissioned Gainsborough to paint a view of Landguard Fort, a coastal defence near Harwich to which he had been appointed Governor. Gainsborough's painting was engraved in 1754 by Thomas Major, a former pupil of Gravelot who was suspected of Jacobite leanings and had been interned for three months after the Battle of Culloden.[45] Thicknesse recalls 'That engraving made Mr. Gainsborough's name known beyond the circle of his country residence, and he was soon after by me, and several of his friends, urged to remove to Bath, and try his talents at portrait painting, in that fluctuating city, at which time I had a house there and resided during the winters'.[46] Thicknesse then describes the search for lodgings in Bath that culminated in the artist renting a town house for the considerable sum of £150 a year. This, we now know, took place in the winter of 1759–60.[47] The author then promptly reverts to what must be an account of the winter season of 1758–9: 'As at that time I was better known, and better loved at Bath, than I am at this . . . My head was held up as a decoy duck, but the first sitting (not above fifteen minutes) is all that has ever been done to it, and in that state it hangs up in my house at this day; business came in so fast, at five guineas *a head*, that though he did not much mend in his colouring, or style, yet he was obliged to raise his price from five to eight guineas . . .'.[48] It is known from the surviving receipt for the portraits of William Lee (fig. 32) and Mrs Philadelphia Lee (fig. 31) that Gainsborough charged eight guineas in April 1759. The five-guinea fee must therefore have applied some time before April 1759, presumably earlier in the Bath 1758–9 season. Thicknesse's text makes it quite clear that he considered the increase in price from five to eight guineas to have taken place in Bath. D. E. Williams, the biographer of Sir Thomas Lawrence, writing in 1831 stated, 'Gainsborough's price, for a head, in oils, when he was about thirty-five years of age, at Bath, was five guineas . . . [he] raised his price to 8*l*. 8*s* . . .'.[49] Local historian J. F. Meehan, writing in 1901, says that in Bath Gainsborough 'commenced, about 1758, to paint three-quarter portraits at five guineas each, which price he was soon able to raise to eight'.[50]

The portrait of Lord Villiers mentioned in William Whitehead's letter must be one of the earliest painted in Bath.[51] In the same period, between October and Christmas 1758, Gainsborough painted Lord Villiers's father William, Third Earl of Jersey (fig. 28).[52] At around the same time he also painted a posthumous portrait of the Earl of Jersey's relative Henry, Viscount Cornbury (fig. 29).[53] While the Villiers portrait can now only be considered a wreck, *Viscount Cornbury* is a striking picture, though something of an oddity, based as it is, on an earlier likeness. *William, Third Earl of Jersey* is a simply composed likeness, the sitter is dressed

33 Thomas Gainsborough (1727–1788), *Robert Price (1717–1761)* 1758 or earlier, oil on canvas, 29½ × 24½ inches (75 × 62 cm), whereabouts unknown.

plainly, but in a vivid red coat that lifts the picture out of the ordinary. Viscount Cornbury is dressed in brilliant blue. Both the *Viscount Cornbury* and *Earl of Jersey* portraits remain in the family collection and, since they have escaped the restoration that has damaged many of the first pictures Gainsborough painted in Bath, they are two of the most significant works of this closely defined period. How Gainsborough managed to secure commissions to paint such people immediately on his arrival in the city is an important question, since this highly prestigious patronage must have given the artist instant credibility in the city, and would have ensured a flow of further commissions. The clues seem to lie in Mrs Margaret Gainsborough's relationship with the Beauforts and, obliquely, in the posthumous portrait of Viscount Cornbury.

It is likely that the Jerseys were introduced to Gainsborough by Uvedale Tomkyns Price or Robert Price. The Prices were certainly acquainted with Gainsborough at or before the time of his first visit to Bath, since a portrait of Robert Price (fig. 33) must, on the grounds of style and the age of the sitter date from 1758–9 or earlier. The Prices took pride in their longstanding political alliance with leading Tories and former Jacobites, including the Beauforts and members of Lord Cornbury's family. Uvedale's father Judge Robert Price (1655–1732) had written to the First Duke of Beaufort, 'It has been one of the greatest blessings of my life to be known to your grace, and to have upon all occasions access to you, and your countenance'.[54] Mrs Anne Price, Uvedale's wife, had been close to her cousin, the Third Duke, Mrs Gainsborough's father.[55] Although the family estates were at Foxley in Herefordshire and in North Wales, Uvedale Tomkyns Price lived mainly in Bath from the early 1740s until his death in 1764.[56] Members of the family had owned properties in Bath as early as the sixteenth century, and Uvedale was one of the first to donate funds towards the foundation of a Bath Hospital.[57] Letters from the poet Alexander Pope, a mutual friend of the Beauforts and the Prices, show that Mrs Anne Price had also been close to Henry, Viscount Cornbury, the subject of Gainsborough's portrait, and travelled to Spa in Germany with him in 1740.[58] It appears that the Jersey-Cornbury family and the Prices had known one another for several decades and probably even for several generations.[59]

Since Uvedale Tomkyns Price was well known in Bath, it is likely that the 'Mr. Price, jun.' listed in the 'arrivals' column in *Boddely's Bath Journal* of 25 September 1758 is his son Robert Price.[60] This would suggest that both Uvedale and Robert Price were in Bath at the time Gainsborough and the Earl of Jersey arrived, on hand to bring about an introduction between artist and client. It appears that the presence of the Prices and the Jerseys in Bath in 1758–9 provided an important boost to Gainsborough's portrait-painting career at this critical moment, when a decision as to whether to move permanently from East Anglia hung in the balance.

Some time before April 1759 Gainsborough painted the pair of portraits of William Lee and his wife Philadelphia Lee.[61] The Lee family seat at Hartwell near Aylesbury was not more than twenty-five miles from the Harcourts' country home at Nuneham and the two families knew each other at this date.[62] William Lee's father Lord Chief Justice Sir William Lee and his wife are recorded as visitors to Bath in the 1740s.[63] Lord Chief Justice Lee had been painted by both Vanderbank and Ramsay, and like Lord Villiers, was also the subject of a pastel portrait by William Hoare that was probably painted in Bath.[64] Sir William Lee, Lady Elizabeth Harcourt's husband, was also portrayed in pastel by Hoare, as was Miss Sarah Lee.[65]

It is usually said that Gainsborough painted the Lees at Hartwell, but now that the artist's presence in Bath in the winter of 1758–9 is established, it seems certain that the sittings took place there. The Lees would have been perpetuating a family tradition by visiting Bath during the season. The local newspapers record the arrival of a 'Mr. and Mrs. Lee' in the first and last weeks of December 1758 and in mid-March 1759.[66] It is safe to say that the Lees must have been painted between the beginning of December 1758 and 19 April 1759. This latter date is that of the receipt which survives in the archive of the National Gallery, London.[67] The full text reads,

April 19 1759
Rec.d of Willm. Lee Esqr. The sum of sixteen guineas in full for a portrait of Mrs. Lee and another of himself
£16.16 Tho Gainsborough

Eight guineas was still a modest price to pay for a standard thirty by twenty-five inch portrait at this date. In London Allan Ramsay was charging fifteen, and Reynolds twenty guineas.[68] In Bath a framed and glazed pastel 'head' by William Hoare cost eight guineas in 1738.[69] It is not known what Hoare charged in 1758, but it cannot have been less than eight guineas for a pastel, and certainly more for an oil. The miniaturist Samuel Finney charged three guineas for a watercolour portrait in Bath in 1748 and Henry Millington three and a half guineas for a miniature portrait in 1757.[70]

If Gainsborough's first visit to Bath in the season of 1758–9 was an attempt to broaden the scope of his career as a portrait painter, it was certainly a success. At this early date he managed to secure introductions to several families whose social status far exceeded that of most of his Ipswich sitters It has already been shown that in the Jersey-Harcourt set Gainsborough encountered young men who were not only well bred but considered themselves arbiters of fashion and taste. The attractions of such new patronage for an ambitious painter like Gainsborough were obvious, and it appears he lost no time in capitalising on several other important introductions.

A portrait that is almost identical in composition to that of Lord Villiers is of Christopher Griffith Senior (fig. 34).[71]

34 Thomas Gainsborough (1727–1788), *Christopher Griffith Senior (d. 1767)* 1759, oil on canvas, 30 × 25 inches (76.2 × 63.5 cm), Restoration House, Rochester.

35 Thomas Gainsborough (1727–1788), *Portrait of a lady of the St Quintin family, here identified as Miss Mary St Quintin or Miss Charlotte Fane* 1758–9, oil on canvas, 30 × 25 inches (76.2 × 63.5 cm), private collection.

Portraits of Griffith's son and daughter-in-law *Christopher Griffith* and *Mrs Catherine Griffith*, which are much more 'rounded' in style, may well belong to the later date and perhaps commemorate their marriage in November 1759.[72] A 'Mr. Griffith', who might be the elder Christopher Griffith, is recorded amongst Bath visitor 'arrivals' in early January 1759.[73] Mrs Catherine Griffith was the daughter of Sir William St Quintin, Fourth Baronet (1700–1771) of Scampston in Yorkshire. From Gainsborough's early meeting with the Griffith and St Quintin families in 1758–9 a significant stream of subsequent patronage flowed. In late 1763 Gainsborough told James Unwin 'I have got a Horse which I had of my good Friend Sir William St. Quintin . . .' and in 1766 this same Sir William St Quintin purchased a major landscape from the artist.[74] Sir William the Fifth Baronet also purchased a number of landscapes from Gainsborough that he was later forced, through financial embarrassment, to sell back to Gainsborough's nephew, Gainsborough Dupont.[75] The first portrait of a member of the St Quintin family is that of one of Catherine's sisters, Rebecca, Mary, or their sister-in-law Charlotte, normally called *Rebecca St Quintin* (fig. 35). Circumstances suggest that the painting is much more likely to represent Mary St Quintin, later Mrs George Darby, or Charlotte Fane, later wife of Sir William St Quintin, the Fifth Baronet.[76] The elder Sir William and either Catherine or Mary arrived in Bath in the second week of December 1758 and a Miss Fane arrived in late September 1758.[77] Both Miss St Quintin and Miss Fane are reported in the local newspapers as leading the dancing at the public balls on various occasions during the 1758–9 winter season.[78]

The Miss St Quintin or Charlotte Fane of Gainsborough's portrait is formally dressed, presumably in her ballgown, as is the subject of another portrait that must have been painted in early 1759, Barbara, Lady Mostyn (fig. 36).[79] Lady Mostyn visited Bath in March 1759 (her arrival is noted in the *Bath Advertiser* of 10 March and *Boddely's Bath Journal* of 12 March). She was the granddaughter of Florence, third daughter and coheiress of Sir Charles Somerset of Troy House, Monmouthshire.[80] On her father's side she was the daughter and sole heiress of Sir George Browne of Kiddington Park near Oxford, a family that claimed descent from Charles II's mistress Barbara Villiers, a relative of the Earls of Jersey.[81] Lady Mostyn's husband was related to the Duke of Beaufort's friends the Williams Wynns.[82] Following the death of Sir Edward Mostyn, she married Edward Gore of Barrow Court, Somerset. One of her sons by this marriage took the name of Gore-Langton on his marriage to Bridget Langton, sole heiress of Joseph Langton of Newton Park near Bath. Two full-length portraits by Gainsborough of Joseph Langton and his wife descended in the Gore-Langton family

36 Thomas Gainsborough (1727–1788), *Barbara, Lady Mostyn (1729–1801)* 1759, oil on canvas, 30 × 25 inches (76.2 × 63.5 cm), Albany Institute of History and Art, Gift of Mrs David C. Hanrahan, Albany, New York.

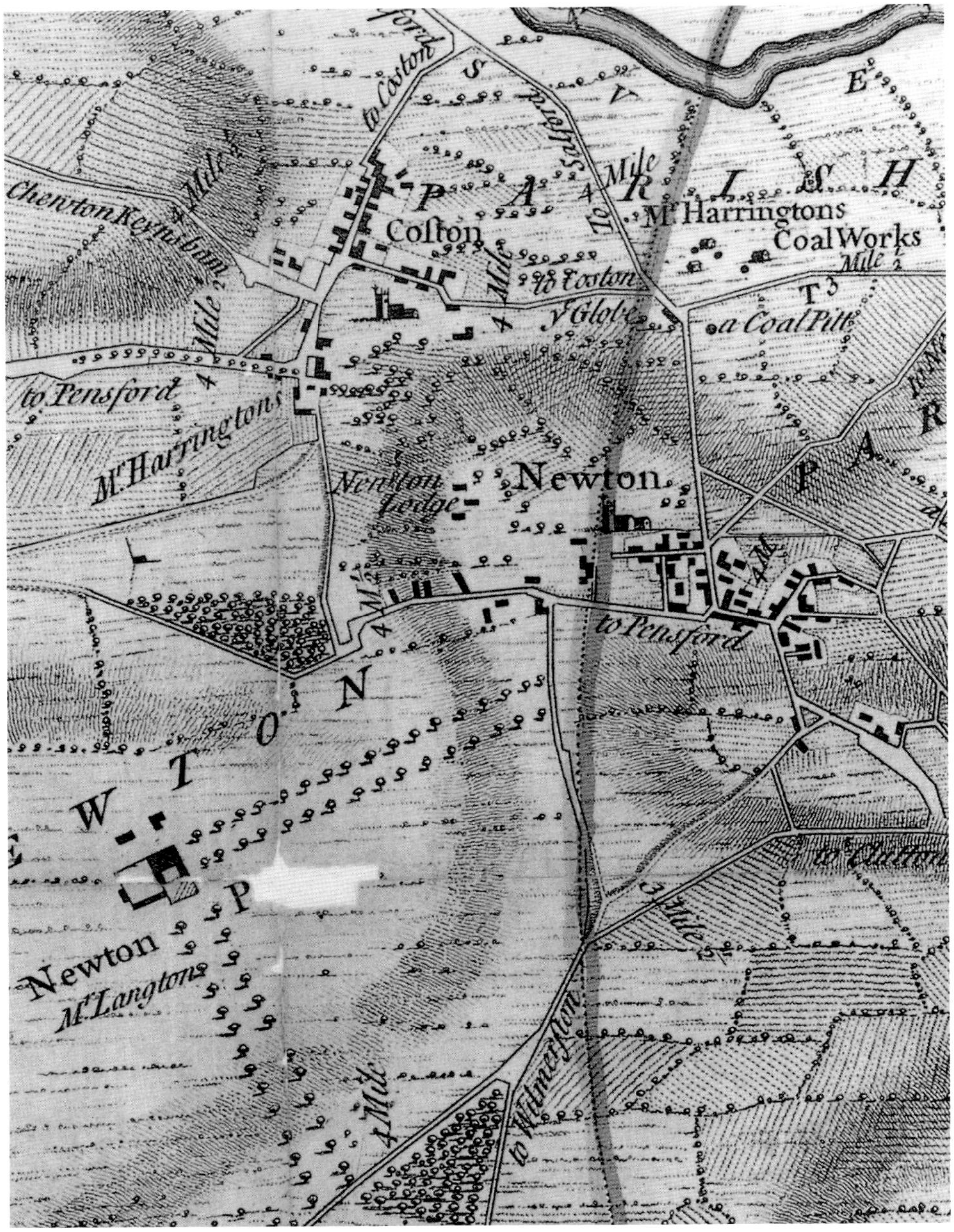

38 *(above)* Thomas Gainsborough (1727–1788), *Sir Francis Skipwith (d. 1778)* 1759, oil on canvas, 29½ × 24 inches (74.9 × 60.9 cm), private collection.

37 *(left)* Thomas Thorpe, *An Actual Survey of the City of Bath . . . and of Five Miles Round* (detail) 1742, engraving (the whole) 75⅝ × 77 inches (192.1 × 195.6 cm), published 1742, Bath Record Office, Bath. An actual size section of Thorpe's *Survey* showing an area immediately to the west of Bath, with Newton Park, the seat of Gainsborough's sitter Joseph Langton, and a coal pit and coal works within 3 miles of the centre of the city.

and are said to have been lost in the bombing of Bath in 1941.[83] The Langton portraits were probably painted to hang in the new mansion at Newton Park that was built near Bath for Joseph Langton between 1762 and 1765 by Stiff Leadbetter (see fig. 37). Lady Mostyn may have been one of Gainsborough's last sitters during his first Bath season. Sir Francis Skipwith of Newbold Hall, Warwickshire, arrived in the town the same week as Lady Mostyn and his portrait by Gainsborough must have been painted at the same time (fig. 38).[84]

All the earliest Bath portraits are painted on standard thirty by twenty-five inch canvases, usually called 'three-quarters'.[85] A certain flatness and plainness characterises the paintings. Where a landscape background is employed, as in *Mrs Philadelphia Lee*, there is a richness to the canvas that looks back to some of the most successful Ipswich portraits such as *Lady Innes* and forward to Bath masterpieces such as *Mary, Countess Howe*, but most of the portraits have plain backgrounds.[86] While he economised by excluding background detail and the hands of his sitters, Gainsborough paid careful attention to the sumptuous colours and surface texture of the dresses worn by his female sitters. The men, by contrast, are very simply clothed, without any trappings of wealth or status. John Hayes attributes this in part to the influence of Hogarth, but the sitters themselves must have acquiesced in the choice of their dress and attitude.[87] At this date Gainsborough's professional standing was not so well established that he could dictate terms to peers and baronets, though he certainly did a few years later.[88] The particular social circumstances prevailing in Bath clearly had a part to play. Although women used the Bath balls and concerts to dress as elaborately as they pleased, social divisions were less marked in Bath than in London. In his epistolary novel *The Expedition of Humphry Clinker*, based on first-hand knowledge of Bath, Tobias Smollet describes the absence of social barriers as being a singular advantage of the place. His character the young student Jery Melford marvelled at seeing some of the most eminent men of the day 'divested of their formal draperies, undisguised by art and affectation' and enjoyed 'the general mixture of all degrees assembled in our public rooms, without distinction of rank or fortune'.[89] Whatever the style of dress, most of Gainsborough's portraits of this period suffer from steeply falling shoulders, a natural consequence of painting the costumes on lay figures rather than on the sitter or a live model. Some years later, Gainsborough was aware of this potential problem and complained that the engraver Francesco Bartolozzi in copying his portrait of the Marquess of Lansdowne 'sloped the shoulders like my Layman stuff'd with straw . . .'.[90] The restricted format of these early portraits must have been dictated by the limited time Gainsborough anticipated being in Bath and the nature of his studio space. It was only with his move to large-scale premises in June 1760 that he began seriously to turn his attention to half- and full-length canvases.[91]

Thicknesse himself said that it was he and 'several of his [Gainsborough's] friends' who urged the artist to try his hand in Bath, and there is no reason to disbelieve this.[92] As we have seen, Gainsborough knew James Unwin and may well have known Uvedale Tomkyns Price and Robert Price before he came to Bath. Several of the artist's Suffolk sitters may also be tentatively identified in Bath and may have been regular visitors. The name 'Wollaston' and a variant or simply a misspelling 'Woollaston' occurs in published Bath visitor lists with some frequency, but it is impossible to tell which family or family members are referred to.[93] Better leads are offered by more unusual names. The 'Mr. and Mrs. Rustat' whose arrival is announced in the *Bath Advertiser* of 23 December 1758 must surely either be the painter's sitters of that name or relatives of the Suffolk family.[94]

The Peter Darnell Muilman of the *Muilman Conversation Piece* (fig. 26) could be the 'Mr. Muilman' noted in the *Bath Journal* of 17 October 1748 and the person of the same name who arrived in Bath when Gainsborough was there in December 1758.[95] Although he was a Suffolk man and had previously been painted by Gainsborough in Ipswich around 1755–6, Lambe Barry may have been a Bath visitor and could have had the second of his two portraits painted in Bath rather than Ipswich.[96] A 'Mr. Barry' is recorded in *Boddely's Bath Journal* on 4 September 1758, 23 April 1759 and 8 October 1759.

Now that Gainsborough's presence in Bath in 1758–9 is established beyond doubt, the theory that 'After a short tour of the Midlands as an itinerant painter in 1758–9 he suddenly moved to Bath . . .' can be safely discounted.[97] Gainsborough himself said that he disliked visiting the homes of the nobility and felt he had been taken prisoner when he was tricked into painting Lord and Lady Ligonier at their country residence in the summer of 1770.[98] The pattern of his studio practice, whereby sitters almost invariably came to him, had been established in Ipswich and was continued in Bath with little change. The artistic development over the years 1753 to 1759 is gradual, the impact of new patrons in Bath having no immediate effect on Gainsborough's technique. Commentators have rightly associated the major change in style that took place around 1760 with the opportunities offered in the West Country for the study of notable picture collections and the work of Van Dyck in particular. During the visit of 1758–9 the artist seems to have been fully occupied in painting portraits and it was only in 1760, when he was secure in the knowledge of regular work and settled accommodation that he was able to make the excursions which proved so influential. The Bath visit of 1758–9 is scarcely discernible in his work, but its impact was life-changing – it was this busy few months that convinced him to make a permanent break with East Anglia.

Some planning was required before this move could be made, and after painting the portraits of Lady Mostyn and Sir Francis Skipwith in March or April Gainsborough returned to Ipswich for the summer of 1759. He evidently broke his journey in London and visited old friends in Hatton Garden. A bill addressed to Gainsborough at 17 Hatton Garden and dated 9 May 1759, has recently been found. It records the sale to Gainsborough by Thompson Scott of a painting, 'Love at the Well', for £35 and a 'Frame etc etc' for £5.[99] Thompson Scott has not been identified, but he could have been connected with the colourman Scott of the Strand, from whom Gainsborough is said to have obtained pigments later in life.[100] Since £40 would have been a large slice of Gainsborough's earnings in Bath, this transaction was presumably a business one, with the artist buying on behalf of a client, as he is recorded doing in 1769, when he paid five guineas for a 'Fruit-piece' for the Revd Nicholas Bacon.[101] While at Hatton Garden in May 1759 Gainsborough may well have called on Joseph Wood to look at progress on the plate of *The Gipsies*, the first impressions of which are dated March 1759. In the autumn of 1759 Gainsborough's wholehearted integration into Bath society began.

4

'Your Likeness Man, Tho Gainsborough'

Gainsborough arrived in Bath a professional portrait painter and soon became a fully fledged Bath businessman, earning a secondary income by letting rooms to seasonal visitors. Property was to play an important role in the artist's life and in the lives of several members of his family from 1760 until the end of the century. One of the grandest buildings in the centre of the town was known as 'Gainsborough's' for twenty-five years. The artist and his relatives were associated with no less than four houses in the Circus, the architectural heart of Bath around which social life revolved from the late 1760s onward.[1] Gainsborough's properties supported his portrait-painting business by providing suitable premises in which he could work and display his work; they also contained enough rooms to generate an independent income.

It was common in the eighteenth century for tradesmen to diversify. In Bath shopkeepers of all kinds spread their business risks in this way. The bookseller James Leake sold medicines such as 'Dr Lobb's Tincture' and 'Pectoral Balsam of Honey' as well as books.[2] The wine merchant Isaac de Vic was also a banker, and Thomas Underwood, musical instrument maker and repairer, also sold 'Catchup, Mushrooms, and all other Sorts of Pickles'.[3] So Gainsborough's additional business activities were unexceptional. As the recently discovered Thompson Scott receipt indicates, he also engaged in picture dealing on one or two occasions and, when business was especially brisk, he may (like his close friend James Unwin) have earned a little extra through moneylending.[4] The letting of property was, however, the most important of his subsidiary business ventures. Indeed, so full of paying guests were his houses that the artist often could not accommodate his own friends. In 1770 he wrote with regret to James Unwin, 'We never had above a Bed & a half to spare in our lives . . .'.[5] The success of his ancillary business can be measured by the subsequent activities of his family. At least ten of the artist's relatives became involved in lodging house keeping in Bath before the end of the century, their migration from East Anglia prompted by news of profit in the property business rather than in the business of portrait painting.[6] Gainsborough's success in Bath may also have encouraged him to continue letting rooms in London as a form of insurance against any downturn in his portraiture. In September 1777, by which time he had been established in Schomberg House for three years, he wrote to his sister Mary Gibbon in Bath, 'I like to bragg when I let an Appartment as well as some Circus friends do, but I'm afraid I shall never be out of Business'.[7] By this date Mrs Gibbon was established as one of Bath's principal lodging house keepers, managing her business affairs from the centre south-facing house in the Circus.[8] The artist appears to have been unwilling to abandon what had become something of a family industry.

It is not known where Gainsborough lived on his first visit to Bath in 1758. He might have lodged in Thicknesse's house, or a Price property. All we are told by the 'extraordinary Journal' is that the writer called at a house in Bath and was told that Gainsborough was not at home, although he swore he heard the sound of a fiddle being played, which strongly suggested that the artist was inside.[9] The three-quarters format of all the known portraits produced during this initial visit suggest that Gainsborough was working in a limited space. He is unlikely to have risked paying out a large rent at this date, having been accustomed to spending only £11 a year on his Ipswich house.[10]

It is also not known where the artist lived or worked for the first six months after he moved more permanently to Bath in the autumn of 1759, but his payment of £70 to one Hanbury Pettingal on 31 December 1759 might provide a clue as to where he lodged in 1758 and 1759.[11] Two generations of Pettingal, father and son, both named Hanbury, were silk retailers in Bath, but like most other town-centre traders, they probably also took in lodgers. It is perhaps more likely that Gainsborough spent the considerable sum of £70 on accommodation than on silks at this particular time, although it is also possible that Pettingal was providing a banking service.[12] Pettingal was in Pierrepont Street, close to the house occupied by the Linley family from the early 1760s.[13] This may account for the friendship that existed between the Pettingals and the painter Ozias Humphry, who lodged with

39 Detail of fig. 45.

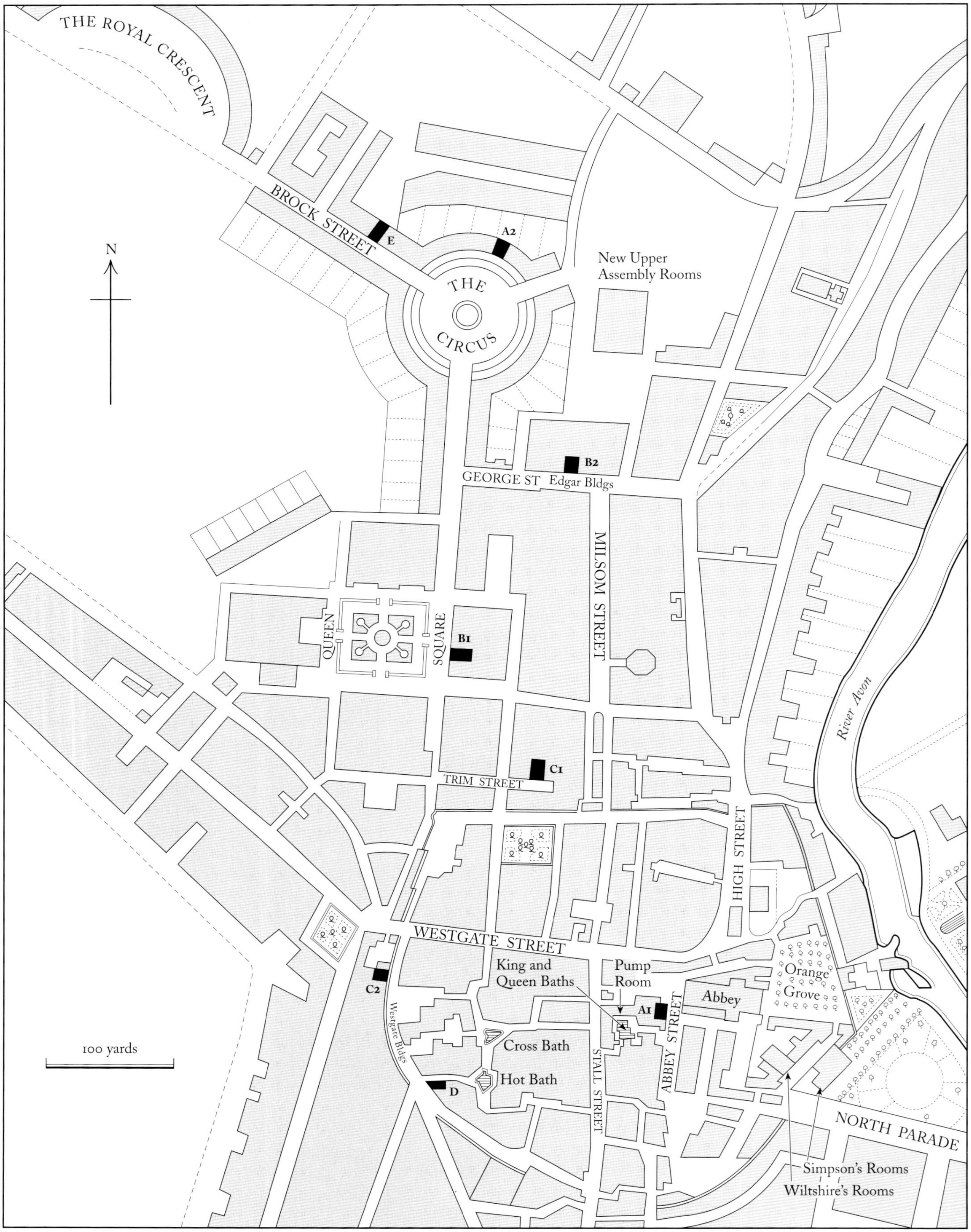

40 Plan of Bath illustrating the location of artists' houses. A1, A2 = Thomas Gainsborough; B1, B2 = William Hoare; C1, C2 = Thomas Beach; D = Robert Edge Pine; E = Joseph Wright of Derby.

the Linleys between 1762 and 1764. Towards the end of his life Humphry told a friend that he was anxious to visit Bath in order to support his 'dear and much valued friend' Winifred Pettingal in her application to become the next Pumper at the Pump Room.[14]

The first substantial house that Gainsborough could call his own was the one he took in Bath in 1760. That he was able at this date to shoulder the responsibility of a large property costing £150 a year in rent may be largely thanks to the sound business advice of Philip Thicknesse. Thicknesse's own account of his role in helping Gainsborough to find a suitable house does seem to be accurate. His recollection that the rent was £150 has been proved to be correct by the discovery of Gainsborough's lease and other documents.[15] Having long been associated with Bath, Thicknesse was well acquainted with the commercial life of the city. In May 1742 he had been admitted as a visitor to a Bath masonic meeting which was also attended by bookseller James Leake, painter Thomas Ross, engraver Jacob Skinner, carrier John Wiltshire, landlord of the Bear Inn Johnson Robinson and several other local gentlemen and tradesmen.[16] Thicknesse's experience of Bath's commercial life, over a period of twenty years, must have been invaluable to Gainsborough. If, as it seems, he encouraged the artist to rent a large house, parts of which could be sub-let as lodgings, his influence at this crucial stage of Gainsborough's career was indeed of overriding importance.

The house that Gainsborough occupied from June 1760 was ideally situated as a portrait-painter's premises and as lodgings for seasonal visitors. The only one of the Duke of Kingston's many properties in Bath to bear his arms, it was apparently built as a residence for the Duke himself, but for some reason was never occupied by him (fig. 41). The house itself was in many respects a symbol of the new direction of the artist's career: a confident new building whose very design announced a happy combination of gentlemanly status and commercial realism. Just yards away from the Pump Room and the Abbey (fig. 40), it was so close to the King's and Queen's Baths that its structure incorporated a public passageway for bathers (fig. 42). The passageway also gave access to the yard of the Three Tuns, which Mrs Delany described in 1760 as 'a *very* good inn'.[17] The position of the house was both prestigious and practical, being clearly visible as an imposing residence and easily accessible to potential patrons. The painter Robert Edge Pine was to choose a similarly situated house when he settled in Bath twelve years later, in 1772. Pine's had a door 'next the Hot Bath Pump Room in Hetling Court' at one end of its façade and a street entrance giving access to a direct carriage route to the Circus at the other end (fig. 40).[18] To some visitors, Pine's position by the Hot and Cross Baths seemed preferable, being in a quieter locality. Horace Walpole wrote in 1766, 'All my comfort is, that I lodge close to the Cross Bath by which means I avoid the Pump Room and all its works'.[19]

While it was undoubtedly in a prime trading position Gainsborough's Abbey Street house, which he called his 'House in the Smoake', afforded him no escape from work and must have been noisy as well as smoky.[20] After his serious illness in the autumn of 1763 he decided to let off all the rooms in this house as lodgings, apart from his painting room and the best parlour which he used as an exhibition room. By this means, he told James Unwin, he planned to ease himself 'of as much Painting work as the Lodgings will bring in'.[21] He and his family now lived in a 'sweetly situated' house on Lansdown Road, about three-quarters of a mile from the town centre.[22] Here Gainsborough paid £30 a year rent, and enjoyed the benefits of a good garden containing a cold bath.[23] The house may be identified as the one called Bellevue in the nineteenth century, now Lansdown Lodge (fig. 43).[24] It was one of the very few detached houses on the slopes of Lansdown and, as Gainsborough's own description and its later name imply, commanded splendid views. The atmosphere of Lansdown was considered particularly healthy. In fact so beneficial was its air, according to the architect John Wood, that almost every house on the hill boasted an inhabitant 'who had lived almost to the Age of one hundred Years'.[25] Such a reputation must have attracted Gainsborough at a time when he had been so ill that his death had accidentally been reported in the local newspaper.[26]

For three years the artist must have enjoyed the contrast between his Abbey Street workplace and his Lansdown retreat. The Abbey Street house had on the ground floor, in addition to the parlour, a large room called the 'shop' (fig. 42). Gainsborough's sister Mrs Mary Gibbon moved from Colchester to Bath in the spring of 1762 and brought her established millinery business to this shop at this date.[27] Mrs Gibbon quickly became well known as a fashionable milliner in Bath, even meriting a mention in Christopher Anstey's satirical verses *The New Bath Guide* of 1766, where she is called 'Mrs Gibbons', purveyor of 'Lace and Ribbons'.[28] Milliners at this time sold not just hats, but perfumes, powder, flowers, haberdashery and a host of other luxury goods for women. Mrs Gibbon's business would have handsomely complemented her brother's portrait practice and she remained in business in Gainsborough's Abbey Street house until 1776, when two other milliners Ann and Sophia Heaven took over the shop.[29] The Revd Richard Graves recalled the shop when occupied by the Heaven sisters: 'And all Arabia breathes from yonder shop: There bounteous Heavens their sweetest blooms display'.[30] This heavily scented hothouse atmosphere must also have pervaded the house during Mrs Gibbon and Gainsborough's occupancy, and it serves as a reminder that the artist was, like his predecessors Thomas Worlidge and James Vertue, working at the heart of the luxury business. Abbey Churchyard and Wade's Passage were favourite addresses for milliners, there being in addition to Mrs Gibbon a Miss Roach, Elizabeth Broderip, Janetta Cooke and Mrs Parkes.[31] Also very close to Gainsborough

41 Model of Gainsborough's house, Abbey Street, Bath. The house was built 1755–60, to designs attributed to John Wood the Elder (1704–1754). It was demolished in 1892, following the excavation of the Roman Baths immediately to the south (left) of the building.

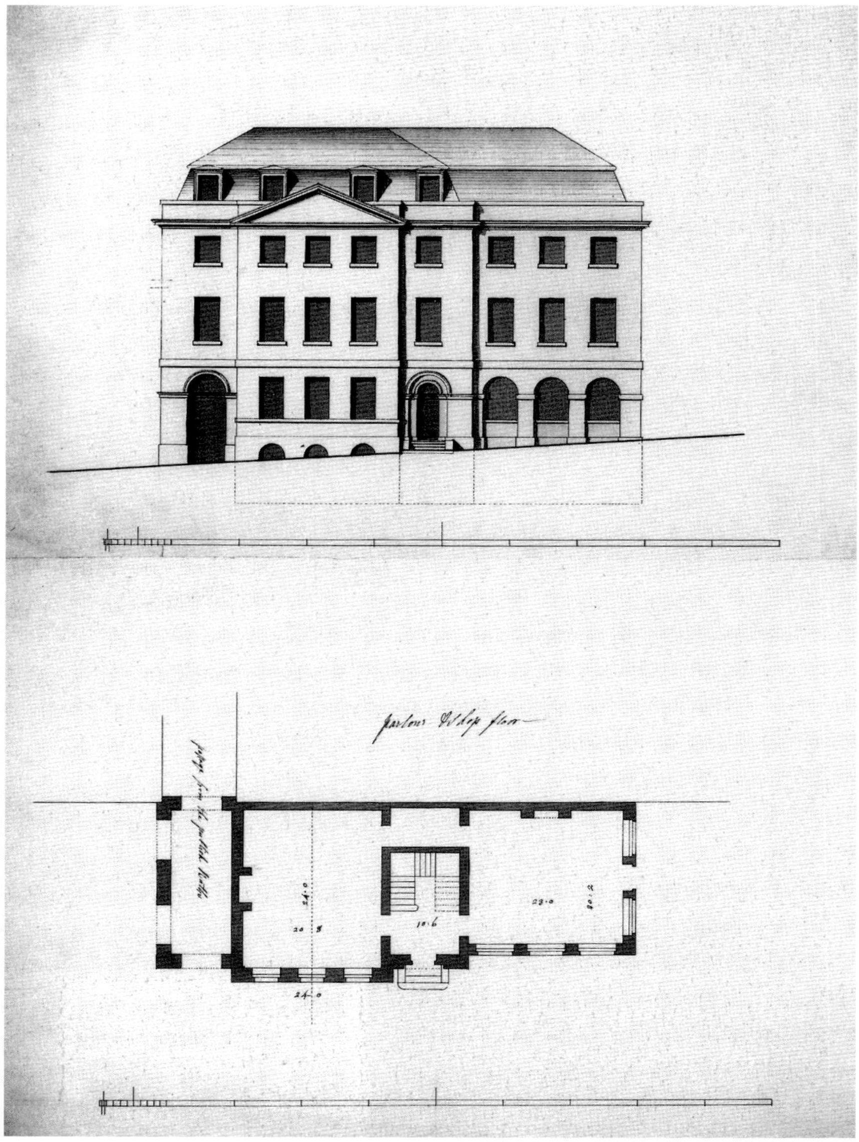

42 Attributed to John Wood the Elder (1704–1754), Elevation and ground plan of Gainsborough's house on the Duke of Kingston's estate in Bath, pencil, ink and ink wash, on two sheets, $9 \times 13\frac{5}{8}$ inches (22.8 × 34.6 cm); $9 \times 13\frac{5}{8}$ inches (22.9 × 34.5 cm), RIBA Library Drawings Collection, London. Gainsborough rented this house in Abbey Street from 1760 to 1774. The ground plan shows the 'passage from the publick Baths' and the 'parlour & Shop floor'. The parlour was Gainsborough's exhibition room from 1760 to 1766 and the shop Mrs Mary Gibbon's millinery from 1762.

43 *(facing page)* House on Lansdown Road now called Lansdown Lodge, rented by Gainsborough as a family home between autumn 1763 and Christmas 1766.

in Abbey Churchyard or Wade's Passage were Mrs Tucker's China Shop; Thornton's Linen Drapery Warehouse; Francis Bennett's linen and wool drapery (patronised by Gainsborough); Marmaduke Webb, a watchmaker; James Wall's linen drapery; Thomas Creaser's woollen drapery; W. Rogers' jewellery shop; W. Taylor's bookshop (he was a former employee of James Leake) and Mr Grandi, perfumer.[32] At the famous Gill's pastry shop in Wade's Passage was Johannes Zumpe, inventor of the square piano, who advertised in Bath as a maker of 'guittars' (popularised by Ann Ford), and a new instrument called the 'Amantor'.[33] Thomas Underwood, in Stall Street, just south-west of Abbey Street, advertised a whole range of musical instruments, including the 'Glassychord in the Manner of Mr Schuman'.[34] Mr de la Main, dancing master, operated from lodgings in Mr Wall's linen drapery.[35]

The majority of businesses that surrounded Gainsborough in Abbey Churchyard advertised their wares in the local newspapers. More directly, they advertised their shops with the use of painted signs. In 1762 Thomas Creaser's drapery sign was a 'Golden Fleece and Hat' and Elizabeth Broderip had the sign of the Sun over her millinery in 1763.[36] As has already been mentioned, artists too had painted signs, the engraver Jacob Skinner a Grasshopper and Thomas Worlidge a Golden Head.[37] The landscape and decorative painter Joseph Woolley used the sign of St Luke's Head and himself painted 'Signs and Shew-Boards'.[38] It is not known whether Gainsborough used a sign, but it is likely that he did. Thicknesse, writing on the subject of artists in Bath, deplored the fact that even painters 'of Eminence in their Profession, think it necessary to put their Names upon Boards in Public Places'.[39] Name boards attached directly to the façades of buildings, rather than projecting pictorial hanging signs, gradually became the norm, and were used by professional people, such as doctors, as well as tradesmen.[40]

Although the presence of a signboard could be important in identifying an artist's house in an era before street numbering, the position and appearance of the property, and the amenities it offered, were of greater significance. All the evidence is that Gainsborough always kept one step ahead of his rivals in Bath in this respect. His move at the end of 1766 from Abbey Street to the Circus also proves that he was keenly attuned to the shifting pattern of commercial and residential life in the city. Although many improvements had been made to the buildings, streets and drainage in the centre of town, the area around Bath Abbey still retained vestiges of its crowded seventeenth-century character and the advantages of John Wood's new developments on the upper northern slopes, were soon appreciated by visitors and residents. Wood's emerging Circus and its tributary streets offered cleaner air, wider roads and open spaces. By 1780 Lady Pembroke, a regular Bath visitor wrote, 'I cannot bear to go into the lower town', and when seeking lodgings she specified they 'must be in the Upper Town, that is, not lower than Bond Street, as much higher as you please'.[41] In 1766 Gainsborough selected a house on the north side of the Circus that belonged to a Mr Penny and became the first tenant there, just as he had been the first occupier of the Duke of Kingston's Abbey Street house.[42] No record has been found of what rent Gainsborough paid to Penny, but the Revd John Penrose noted in 1766 that no house in the Circus was let for less than £100 a year.[43] For some months in 1767 the artist was paying rent for three houses, Abbey Street at £150 a year, the Circus at £100 or more, and his house on Lansdown at £30 a year. It took some time for him to relet the Lansdown property, but from the beginning of 1767 he does seem to have reunited family life and business under one roof at the Circus.[44] At the same time, he maintained the lease on Abbey Street. The expiry of this lease in 1774 coincides with his departure to London, and may have been the deciding factor in the timing of his move.[45]

While Gainsborough based his portrait business in two large new houses both designed by John Wood, one by Bath Abbey and one in the Circus, William Hoare also worked from prestigious though slightly less prominent addresses (fig. 40). Beginning in Queen Square, Hoare, like Gainsborough, moved up hill to Edgar Buildings, just south of the new Assembly Rooms.[46] The New or Upper Rooms were built in response to the shift of visitors from the lower to the upper town, the foundation stone being laid in May 1768.[47] Proximity to the New Rooms must have been important to both Hoare and Gainsborough, and later the very young Thomas Lawrence was brought by his father to a house close to the Rooms where he made a reputation for himself painting small pastel portraits of visitors.[48] Of those artists who came to Bath in the 1770s, few could afford to be as well situated in the upper town as Gainsborough and Hoare. Pine, as has been shown, was near the Hot and Cross Baths. Close to him was Thomas Beach who had a 'House Elegantly Furnish'd . . . Very Roomy and Convenient', next

44 Pediment stones from Gainsborough's house, Abbey Street, photograph, 1992, Roman Baths Museum, Bath and North East Somerset Council. Carved with the Duke of Kingston's crest, flanked by swags of foliage and flowers, these are the only material fragments of Gainsborough's Abbey Street house to have survived.

door to the Bishop of Salisbury's house (fig. 40).[49] Thomas Hickey was in Abbey Churchyard, near the Pump Room, and the topographical artist Thomas Malton was opposite the Theatre.[50] The only other painter who took a relatively expensive property in the upper town in the 1770s was Joseph Wright of Derby who came to Bath a year after Gainsborough's departure, in November 1775. Wright rented a well-placed house in Brock Street, between the Royal Crescent and the Circus.[51]

Less is known about the interiors and furnishings of artists' houses in Bath, but again, Gainsborough must have set the standard. In 1761 George Lucy wrote that he was to be 'Enthroned in Mr Gainsborough's Painted Chamber', suggesting that a degree of luxury could be expected at Abbey Street (although he may also have been making an ironic reference to the London Court of Claims which was situated in the 'Painted Chamber' at Westminster).[52] The house certainly had a palatial air, and the exterior promised riches within. The carved pediment on east-facing Abbey Street façade, with the Duke of Kingston's crest, was a surprisingly rare embellishment for a Bath town house of this date (fig. 44).[53] This detail (the only fragment of the house to survive) probably set the scene for what was to be found inside. The house was fitted up with every modern convenience, 'Locks and Keys to all Doors fixed Grates in all Chimneys a Boyler and Copper and the Rooms of the first and second Floors and the Front Parlour hung with paper and a Smoak Jack in the Kitchen Chimney'.[54] The wallpaper must have been of good quality. When Gainsborough and his sister left the house, the cost of repapering for the next tenant came to £32.9.6, more than a year's rent on the artist's Lansdown house.[55] Though less favourably situated than Gainsborough's, Thomas Beach's house was spacious and 'Elegantly Furnish'd' and Robert Edge Pine's rooms were large enough to be used for the Bath showing of de Loutherbourg's *Eidophusikon* after Pine had moved away.[56] It is clear from Gainsborough's letter to Unwin that his business at Abbey Street was concentrated in two rooms, his 'Painting Room and best parlour to show Pictures in'.[57] In Abbey Street the best parlour or exhibition room was on the ground floor, while the painting room was upstairs, above Mrs Gibbon's shop. At the Circus it is more likely that Gainsborough's painting room and showroom adjoined on the first floor. Giles Walkley has described a very similar

45 Joseph Mallord William Turner (1775–1851), *The West Front of Bath Abbey* 1796, pencil, pen and ink and watercolour, $9^{5}/_{8} \times 11^{1}/_{4}$ inches (24.4 × 28.6 cm), Victoria Art Gallery, Bath and North East Somerset Council. This watercolour was exhibited by Turner at the Royal Academy in 1796, but is based on drawings of 1792 or 1793. The north elevation of Gainsborough's house, with an added Venetian window to the first floor painting room, can be seen to the right

arrangement in Francis Cotes's house in London.[58] Cotes had on his first floor an almost square north-facing painting room and an adjoining 'Shew Room', both of which were furnished with rich carpets and mahogany furniture.

It can be argued that in Bath Gainsborough was only following the London pattern, choosing a well-situated house to which customers could be easily attracted, but the details which are now known about Gainsborough's Bath properties serve to illustrate how supremely important the artist considered his trading situation and public image to be. During his tenancy the Abbey Street house was one of the most expensive in Bath (probably the most expensive in single family occupancy), and no other newly built house could have been considered more central.[59] The difference between the very high-profile image the artist presented in Bath, compared with his modest public face in Ipswich, is remarkable.

If Gainsborough's Bath properties were the outward expression of his status as a jewel in the crown of Bath's luxury trade, they also had to function in a practical way as a painter's rooms. In London a number of houses were occupied by several artists in succession, indicating that the adaptations made to a property by one artist could be of benefit to another.[60] Artists did follow to similar locations to those chosen by Gainsborough – Thomas Hickey and George Roth to Abbey Churchyard and Charles Gill to the Circus – but no artist lived or worked in either his Abbey Street house or 17 Circus, despite the fact that alterations had been made to both houses, both involving the lighting of the painting rooms.[61]

It has been said in the past that a north light was 'of little consequence' to Gainsborough, since 'he was accustomed to use either artificial or carefully controlled lighting for his painting'.[62] It is undoubtedly the case that he used controlled lighting, but in order to have maximum control, the daylight he did use had to be from the north or north-east. In c. 1600 Nicolas Hilliard had recommended, 'Let yr light be nothward somwhat toward the east which comonly is without sune Shining in. on [i.e. one] light great and faire let it be, and without impeachment . . . the dieper the window and farer, the better . . .'.[63] Most subsequent artists' manuals repeat similar advice. When James Northcote asked his brother to search for rooms for him in Plymouth, he asked that they should be 'very good ones and the room I am to paint in should have a north light or very nearly so'.[64]

46 North-facing first floor windows to Gainsborough's painting room at 17 Circus, photograph, 1991. A third window to the left has become a door to a nineteenth-century bathroom extension. The outline of the central 'cut up' window to Gainsborough's painting room, now filled in to the same height as that flanking it, can be seen in the stone. (17 Circus is a private property; the rear elevation cannot be seen from any public street.)

47 James Sant (1820–1916), *Self-portrait* c. 1842, oil on canvas, $23\frac{1}{4} \times 17\frac{3}{8}$ inches (59.1 × 44.1 cm), National Portrait Gallery, London. The interior appearance of a 'cut up' painting room window, and the use of blinds to block or diffuse low-level light, can be seen in this painting of c. 1842.

It is not known what the north-facing windows of the painting room at Abbey Street were like when Gainsborough leased the house, but it appears that during his time there he installed a tripartite Venetian window in this room. This window was not part of Wood's original plan for the house (and it had gone by 1816), but it can be clearly seen in Turner's watercolour of Bath Abbey (fig. 45).[65] Turner made studies for this watercolour in Bath around 1793, at a time when the house must have been remembered locally as Gainsborough's. The property was still called 'late Gainsborough's' in Kingston estate papers in 1785.[66] Turner's depiction of the Venetian window seems very unlikely to be a fiction, since he has drawn every other part of the house accurately, and applied the same amount of meticulous care to this area of his watercolour as to the Abbey and other buildings. If the Turner can be regarded as a record of the eighteenth-century appearance of the north side of Gainsborough's house, it shows that the artist enjoyed the benefits of a north-facing tripartite window at Abbey Street and the Circus. Just such lighting was valued by a London-based landscape painter who wrote, 'My large room has three windows in front. I shall make that my shop, having the light from the upper part of the middle window, and by that means I shall get my easil in a good situation'.[67] It is significant that the 'upper part of the middle window' is described here as the principal light source, since this also seems to have been Gainsborough's favoured lighting. By inserting a Venetian window at Abbey Street he created a central, elevated light source and at the Circus he had the middle window extended upwards (fig. 46). Using such an arrangement he probably had blinds to diffuse the lower light, leaving the upper part of the central window to provide the strongest directional illumination. A blind being used to restrict low-level light and the interior appearance of a 'cut up' window can be seen in a nineteenth-century self-portrait by James Sant (fig. 47). Every Bath house of the period was also equipped with internal wooden shutters such as can be seen in the portraits *Robert Craggs Nugent* (fig. 63) and *Mr and Mrs Dehany and their Daughter* (fig. 64), and these acted as a very simple means of controlling illumination. Gainsborough's careful attention to the control of light and the changes he had made to his Bath houses may have had a far-reaching influence. In Percy Street in London a terrace of north-facing houses built in the late 1760s has several first floor painting room windows cut up through the level of the floor above, their design perhaps reflecting a knowledge of Gainsborough's Circus painting room.[68]

While the architectural evidence of the artist's Bath properties shows that he did attach a great deal of importance to the control of natural light, there is no doubt that he also manipulated artificial light. Among others, Ozias Humphry in his unpublished 'Memoir' and Sir Joshua Reynolds in his fourteenth Discourse refer to the painter's practice of painting by candlelight. Fragments of Humphry's memoir are often quoted, but the passage about Gainsborough needs to be read in its entirety for what it has to say about the painter's ways of working, including his use of light and method of straining his canvases while painting. It also mentions several important portraits:

> When the Summer advanced, and the Luxuriance of Nature invited and admitted of it, he accompanied Mr. Gainsborough in his Afternoon Rides on Horseback to the circumjacent Scenery, which was in many Parts, picturesque, and beautiful to a high Degree. To those and succeeding Excursions the Public are indebted, for the greater Part of the Sketches, and more finished Drawings from time to time made public by that whimsical, ingenious, but very deserving Artist – Mr. Gainsborough painted during this year several Landscapes of extraordinary merit, that were mostly executed by Candle Light, to which he was much accustomed – In this City (as is well known) his general Practice was in Portraiture, in which also, he had peculiar Excellence, and frequently produced Pictures of surprizing Resemblance and Perfection. Likeness alone was all he avowed to aim at; from this circumstance it must often have happened, that, altho' his pictures were exactly like, and to the parties for whom they were painted and their Families highly satisfactory at the time, whilst the prevailing modes were daily seen, and the Friends approved and beloved in them; yet the satisfaction arising from this fixed Resemblance was lessening daily, as the fleeting Fashions varied and were changing from time to time – The portrait of Mr. Quin was painted about this period, and was of uncommon force and vigor – with a truth and animation beyond Mr. Gainsborough's usual Performances. – As the original had bold, and expressive Features, and was singularly calculated for representation; few Pictures have ever been more popular, or maintained their Credit with less Decadency, upon the minds of the beholders – This Portrait was painted within a few Months of that great Actors Death, which was very sudden (occasioned by a scratch with a Pin on his Thumb) so that his Dress and general appearance never varied from the time it was completed, and is therefore an exception to the above observation – Doctor Charlton's picture the physician was also of this Description, and painted about the same time – It was a walking figure in a familiar Dress, and absolutely seemed upon first entering the Room, like a living Person – It were useless to enumerate his other excellent Portraits – Those of Mr. Nugent when Member for Bristol (since created an Earl,) General Johnston, Mr. Medlicott, (a sprightly elegant Figure getting over a Style) Mr. Pointz in a shooting Dress with many fashionable Females well known having been publickly exhibited in London and universally admired. – Exact resemblance in his Portraits as has already been said was Mr. Gainsborough's constant Aim, to which he invariably adhered. – These Pictures (as well as his Landskips) were often wrought by Candle Light, and generally with great force, and likeness. But his Painting Room even by Day (a kind of darkened twilight) had scarcely any Light; and our young Friend has seen him, whilst his Subjects have been sitting to him, when neither they or their pictures were scarcely discernible – If the Canvasses were of three quarter size [added, '3/4 of a yard in length the common size for heads in oil'], he did not desire they should be loosened upon the straining Frames; – but if they were half lengths, or whole lengths, he never failed to paint with the Canvases loose, secured by small Cords, and brought to the extremity of the frames [added 'and having previously determind and marked with chalk upon what part of the Canvasses the faces were to be painted'] they were so placed upon the Eisel as to be close to the Subject he was painting, which gave him an opportunity (as he commonly painted standing) of comparing the Dimensions and Effect of the Copy, with the original both near and at a distance; and by this method (with incessant study and exertion) he acquired the power of giving the Masses and general forms of his models with the utmost exactness. Having thus settled the ground Work of his Portraits, he let in (of necessity) more light, for the finishing of them; but for him correct preparation was of the last Importance, and enabled him to secure the proportions of his Features [(with uncommon Truth) crossed out] as well as the general Contours of Objects with uncommon Truth.[69]

On occasion pressure of work forced Gainsborough to paint by artificial light, the best-known instance being in London when he and Gainsborough Dupont stayed up all night to paint the drapery in Queen Charlotte's full-length portrait.[70] More usually, as Humphry illustrates, he would have utilised candlelight by choice, in order to achieve a particular effect.

Certain portraits painted at Abbey Street such as the sumptuous and mysteriously dark *Gertrude, Lady Alston* (Louvre, Paris) appear to have been painted at least partly by artificial light.[71] What this and other paintings from the first half of the Bath period demonstrate is the use of a combination of controlled natural light and artificial light. Humphry was in Bath from 1760, leaving on 5 August 1764, so this account of the Abbey Street period is of great interest, though it should be borne in mind that his reminiscences were apparently written down in 1803, forty years after the event.[72] Humphry makes it clear that Gainsborough used this 'darkened twilight' in order to establish the groundwork, which Gainsborough considered 'of the last [ie the greatest] Importance'. He then let in more light in order to continue the painting. Candlelight, according to Humphry, was often used by Gainsborough for portraits and landscapes at this date.

The principal differences between portraits painted at the Circus, as opposed to Abbey Street, are that the lighting is from a higher angle and is more focused, the painting style is ever more fluid, and the sitters tend to be viewed from a lower angle. All three developments contribute to the increasingly grand manner of Gainsborough's work. The intimate, almost homely, character of some of the earlier portraits such as *Sir William St Quintin* (fig. 98), *Uvedale Tomkyns Price* (fig. 131) and *Mr and Mrs Philip Dehany and their Daughter Mary*, where viewer and sitter meet as if on the same level, is less frequently found in portraits painted at the Circus.[73]

The generally higher and more sharply defined lighting can be readily explained by the exceptionally tall window Gainsborough installed at the Circus, while other changes are less related to a change of premises and more to do with a general movement towards a more cosmopolitan style of portraiture. If the Abbey Street period saw Gainsborough adapting to the needs of the Bath clientele, the Circus was where he seriously prepared for London, utilising subtle changes of technique to add a greater formality and sophistication to his portraits. The question of viewpoint and the eventual hanging height of portraits must have concerned all thinking painters, but the evidence is that it vexed Gainsborough more than most, and it appears to be one of the issues that preoccupied him during his residence at 17 Circus. He fell out with the Royal Academy authorities, and did not submit any pictures to the exhibitions of 1773 to 1776, because the hanging committee would not display his paintings at what he considered a proper height.[74] He wrote to his friend David Garrick in 1772, 'a Word to the Wise; if you let your Portrait hang up so high, only to consult your Room, and to insinnuate somthing over the other Door, it never can look without a hardness of Countenance and the Painting flat: it was calculated for breast high & will never have its Effect or likenesss otherwise'.[75]

The important point seems to be the height at which the painting was *calculated* to hang. When he knew that a portrait must of necessity be hung high, as was the case with the portrait of Captain William Wade (fig. 75) of 1770–71, which was destined for a prepared site over a door in the new Upper Assembly Rooms, he made compensatory adjustments.[76] Wade was painted in a strikingly simple red suit, silhouetted against a bright sky, the landscape being seen from a very low viewpoint. An intriguing passage on the subject of viewpoint in portraits was written by Gainsborough's close friend William Jackson.[77] Since Jackson derived at least part of his artistic education from Gainsborough in Bath, it is likely that his views reflect some of the concerns of the artist. Jackson describes the way in which artists generally set their sitters near to their own eye level, but knowing that the painting (especially if it was a full-length) would be hung above eye level, they painted the background as if seen from below. The consequence of this practice was, as Jackson observed, that a conflict arose between the two different viewpoints, with the result that, in extreme cases, the figure appears to be falling forwards.[78] In a number of Gainsborough's full-length portraits painted at the Circus the horizon is set very low indeed. Some of the most notable examples are the full lengths of George Pitt, Lord Rivers (fig. 49), Isabella, Viscountess Molyneux (fig. 48), Abel Moysey (private collection, on loan to Gainsborough's House, Sudbury) and Captain William Wade.[79] It may be significant that the first two and the last of these were all exhibited at the Royal Academy, where an elevated hanging position was anticipated, but it is more likely that the artist had the eventual hanging site in mind. The problem of conflicting viewpoints is overcome by Gainsborough through the use of harmonising colour, consistent light, the style of his brushwork and the idealised nature of the landscape backgrounds. The paintings are woven in to an integrated whole through the deliberate unreality of the landscape backgrounds, and the way in which the brushwork expressive of drapery connects seamlessly with the brushwork depicting grass, foliage and sky. Helen Glanville has described how this integration even involved the carrying of pigments across the boundaries of costume and background, 'emphasising the "wholeness" of the work'.[80] The 'real' elements, such as fences and animals, found in the backgrounds of earlier portraits such as *Mary, Countess Howe* (fig. 69) have, by the later 1760s, given way to landscapes in which specifics have disappeared in favour of texture and colour. The figures do not appear to fall forward simply because the landscape is not perceived as an illusionistic perspective view. Difficulties do arise when an architectural background is used in a painting destined for a high hanging site. The brilliantly painted *John Campbell, Fourth Duke of Argyll*, full-length, dating from around the time of the artist's move to the Circus, has an architectural setting seen in sharp perspective which is somewhat at odds with the figure, even though the sitter is here placed at a high level in relation to the artist (fig. 50).[81]

It is known from Ozias Humphry's recollections that in the early 1760s Gainsborough set the sitter so that his or her

48 Thomas Gainsborough (1727–1788), *Isabella, Viscountess Molyneux, later Countess of Sefton (1748–1819)* 1768–9, oil on canvas, 92 × 60 inches (233.7 × 152.5 cm), Walker Art Gallery, Liverpool.

49 Thomas Gainsborough (1727–1788), *George Pitt, First Earl Rivers (1721–1803)* 1768–9, oil on canvas, 92¼ × 60¾ inches (234.3 × 154.3 cm), The Cleveland Museum of Art, Gift of the John Huntington Art and Polytechnic Trust, 1971.2.

50 Thomas Gainsborough (1727–1788), *John Campbell, Fourth Duke of Argyll (d. 1770)* 1766–7, oil on canvas, 91 × 60½ inches (231 × 153.7 cm), Scottish National Portrait Gallery, Edinburgh.

head was more or less at his own standing eye level, and that he manipulated the canvas so that the head he was painting was also at the same height. Gainsborough's practice in this respect may have been exceptional, as Humphry explains it at some length. Helen Glanville has postulated that Gainsborough prepared his own canvases (especially large-sized ones) rather than obtaining them ready-primed from a colourman: this would have allowed him complete freedom to stretch them in any way that suited him.[82] Working with the canvas suspended at a convenient height, rather than from steps (which was probably the more normal method), gave him the freedom to continually view the progress of the picture from a distance as well as at close quarters. The remarkable effect of Gainsborough's portraits from a distance was particularly admired by his contemporaries and was singled out by Reynolds and by the writer of his obituary in the *Gentleman's Magazine* who noted, 'his portraits are calculated to give effect at a distance'.[83] As well as walking back and forth in front of his canvas, it is said Gainsborough sometimes used brushes attached to sticks up to six feet in length.[84] This was presumably part of the groundwork preparation as described by Humphry, when he worked in a restricted light, 'setting' the main forms of the figure. One of the reasons he considered the groundwork to be of the greatest importance must have been because he often painted immediately at full-scale, directly on to canvas, without the aid of preparatory drawings. The unfinished double portrait *The Painter's Daughters with a Cat* (fig. 51) gives some idea of the direct 'drawing' on to the canvas that underlies the portraits. Compositional drawings on paper for a number of full- and half-length portraits of the later Ipswich and earlier Bath periods do survive, but, given the quantity of portraits painted, these are very few in number.[85]

In addition to an increased concern for the hanging height of portraits, and the evidence in the Circus period paintings of a conscious working out of the problems of viewpoint, one of the subtle shifts that give these later pictures a greater formality and authority is simply the raising of the sitter's chair. Although no hard and fast distinction can be made between pictures painted before and after 1767, many more of the later full-lengths show that the sitter's head was slightly above the painter's eye level. A simple comparison can be drawn between the portrait of Richard, First Earl Howe painted at Abbey Street and that of Augustus Hervey, Third Earl of Bristol, painted at the Circus, both in naval uniform (figs 52 and 53).[86] The depiction of the tricorn hat immediately defines the height of the sitter in relation to the painter, showing that the Earl of Bristol sat several inches higher than Earl Howe.

The year 1767 marked not only Gainsborough's move to the Circus, but a number of developments in London of which he must have been fully aware. Francis Cotes painted his first portrait of a member of the Royal family in 1767 and Allan Ramsay was appointed Principal Painter in Ordinary to King George III.[87] Reynolds, though less favoured by the Royal family, had won over London society by the breadth of his talent; his work ranging effortlessly from heroic male portraits to tender depictions of women and children. From the secure distance of Bath, Gainsborough was in a position to observe his competitors and concentrate on developing a unique style of his own. The sheer volume of work Gainsborough undertook at Abbey Street caused him frustration and even illness, but it was here that the portraits of Ann Ford, Mary, Countess Howe and large-scale pictures such as *Mr and Mrs George Byam and their Daughter Selina* and *General Philip Honywood* (fig. 74) revealed for the first time an artist who could be described as 'almost the only painter of this country who attempts the thin brilliant style of penciling of Vandyke'.[88] By the time he painted *John Campbell, Fourth Duke of Argyll* this 'brilliant style' of brushwork was fully formulated and the more settled years he spent at the Circus allowed him the breathing space to make refinements and explore its full potential.

Despite the relatively easygoing period he spent living at the Circus, Gainsborough never ceased worrying about money, as Thicknesse noted.[89] Between 1758 and 1774 Gainsborough's prices for portraits rose steadily from five guineas for a 'head' (or thirty by twenty-five inch canvas), to thirty guineas, and from fifteen guineas for a half-length (or fifty by forty inch canvas), to sixty guineas. His price for a full-length before 1766 is not known, but between 1766 and 1774 it rose from sixty to one hundred guineas.[90]

Although the majority of surviving receipts and other records of payments confirm this general and gradual increase in prices, there were exceptions. Some portraits, such as, for example, *Captain William Wade*, were painted without any expectation of payment.[91] Others were given to family or friends. It also appears that Gainsborough occasionally charged an 'old' or lower price in special circumstances. The most interesting instance is a portrait painted after the artist left Bath, but intimately connected with the Bath period, the portrait of *Paul Cobb Methuen*, still at Corsham Court, the Methuen family seat.[92] Ozias Humphry described Corsham as one of the very few places in easy reach of Bath where good old master paintings could be seen and Gainsborough is known to have been a visitor to the house.[93] Perhaps in appreciation of hospitality at Corsham, Gainsborough only charged Paul Methuen forty guineas for the half-length portrait of his son Paul Cobb Methuen in 1777 when his normal price for this size was sixty guineas. The portrait of Paul Cobb Methuen is one of a group of four half-lengths painted for Paul Methuen between 1776 and 1778 of his son Paul Cobb, daughter-in-law Matilda, daughter Christian and her husband Frederick, Second Baron Boston.[94] William Hoare painted Mrs Matilda Methuen and George Romney Lord and Lady Boston. The relevant payments recorded in Paul Methuen's 'Daybook' are of particular interest. They read,

51 Thomas Gainsborough (1727–1788), *The Painter's Daughters with a Cat* c. 1760–61, oil on canvas, $29\frac{3}{4} \times 24\frac{3}{4}$ inches (75.6×62.9 cm), National Gallery, London

52 Thomas Gainsborough (1727–1788), *Commodore Richard Howe, First Earl Howe (1726–1799)* 1763–5, oil on canvas, 96 × 59 inches (244 × 150 cm), private collection.

53 Thomas Gainsborough (1727–1788), *Commodore Augustus Hervey, later Third Earl of Bristol (1724–1779)* 1767–8, oil on canvas, $91\frac{1}{2} \times 60$ inches (232.5 × 152.5 cm), Ickworth, The Bristol Collection (The National Trust).

14 October 1776 'Pd. Mr Hoare for a half length Picture of Mrs P. Methuen 42.0.0'
18 June 1777 'Pd Mr. Gainsborough in full for my sons Picture 42.10.0'
2 May 1778 'Pd Mr Romney for two half length pictures of Lord & Lady Boston 73.0.0'
4 May 1778 'pd Mr Allwood for four Picture frames 34.11.0'.[95]

Since the payment to Thomas Allwood for frames was made just after Romney was paid, it seems likely the four frames were for these four pictures.[96] It appears from these records that Gainsborough and Hoare charged the same forty guineas for their portraits, the additional ten shillings to Gainsborough probably being for a case for transport from London.

The majority of payments for the Bath period show simple settlements, in full, for standard amounts. Although it was common practice to split payments for portraits into two halves, Gainsborough does not often seem to have been paid in this way at this stage of his career.[97] A considerable number of records of payments survive for 'heads' and a fair number for half-length portraits, but less is known of what was charged for full-lengths.[98] In July 1771 Lord Ligonier paid Gainsborough one hundred guineas, presumably for his or his wife's full-length portrait.[99] In the absence of any receipts for full-lengths between 1770 and 1774, one of the most valuable documents is a subscription list for the portrait of John Eld painted for the Stafford General Infirmary (fig. 54).[100] John Eld (1704–1794) who was a member of the Hospital's Quarterly General Board from its foundation in 1765 until at least 1780, lived at Seighford Hall, Stafford. His portrait is always said to have been painted in 1772, but the subscription list is dated 1774.[101] The document shows that the total money raised by the subscription was £101.17.0, but Gainsborough was paid one hundred guineas, Eld himself apparently meeting the deficit.[102]

Gainsborough's portrait prices as compared to other artists when he first visited Bath in 1758 have been discussed above. Taking the Bath period as a whole, a comparison with William Hoare is the most relevant, since Hoare was the only other artist to have remained in the city throughout. Gainsborough's prices in general seem to have been the same or lower than Hoare's until the last few years of his residence in Bath. Hoare charged thirty guineas for a half-length portrait in 1763, at a time when Gainsborough probably charged around the same price.[103] In October 1765 Hoare was paid sixty guineas for a full-length of the First Earl Camden for the Bath City Corporation, the picture having been commissioned (and the price presumably agreed) on 26 October 1764.[104] The Corporation commissioned a second full-length from Hoare of the First Earl of Chatham on 20 May 1766, when a price of eighty guineas was agreed.[105] From 1766 to 1769 Gainsborough's full-length price was sixty guineas, meaning that for at least three years his price was twenty guineas less than Hoare's for a picture of this size. Hoare was, indeed, capable of commanding extremely high prices, charging £200 for a pastel copy of a Rubens (or a picture then thought to be by Rubens) in 1762, almost double the figure Gainsborough received for any picture in Bath.[106]

In general, both Gainsborough's and Hoare's portrait prices were modest when compared to the leading London painters. In 1759 when Gainsborough raised his price for a 'head' from five to eight guineas, Ramsay, Reynolds and Hudson were asking fifteen guineas for the same size portrait.[107] In 1766 Reynolds was charging 150 guineas and Ramsay eighty guineas for a full-length, while Gainsborough asked sixty guineas.[108]

Some of the surviving receipts for Gainsborough's work also give the prices of frames, cases and delivery. In 1762 George Lucy paid 'Three Guineas and a half for a three quarter Frame Burnishd Gold, and seven shillings for a Case' for his thirty by twenty-five inch portrait which had cost eight guineas (fig. 78).[109] The frame was delivered to Lucy's home, Charlecote Park near Warwick, by 'Harper the Warwick Carrier'.[110] Also in 1762, Gainsborough's sitter Richard Stevens paid ten guineas for his portrait of the same size, two guineas for the frame and seven shillings for a case.[111] The cost of large frames could be considerable, that made for the full-length of Garrick for Stratford-on-Avon amounted to £68.14.0 and the case £3.12.0.[112] On 27 July 1768 Gainsborough wrote to Garrick from Bath, 'I beg Sir you'l leave the affair of Gossett to me, I shall give him a Bill payable at first sight I assure you'.[113] This must refer to one of the framemakers Gideon or Isaac Gosset who acted as London framers for both Gainsborough and Hoare.[114] In April 1762 Gainsborough wrote from Bath to a Captain Townsend in London, 'I would not have you trouble yourself to pay Gossett . . .' and in September of the same year Gainsborough's bank account shows him paying £15 to Isaac Gosset.[115] Sometimes clients did apparently pay the Gossets directly. In June 1761, two months after he had paid Gainsborough for one or more pictures, Sir Charles-Kemeys Tynte of Halswell House, Somerset, paid Isaac Gosset £12.[116]

One of the Gossets, probably Isaac, who sat for his portrait around 1779–80 (fig. 55), must have grown close to Gainsborough over a long period of association, for he was one of the mourners at the artist's funeral in 1788.[117] A foreman from one of the Gosset workshops set up in business in Bath in 1772, advertising himself in the *Bath Chronicle* of 23 January 1772 as 'James Guillet, Carver and Gilder, from Richmond in Surry (formerly Apprentice and Foreman to Messrs. Gossett's, in Berwick Street, London) in Axford Buildings . . . all Sorts of Picture and Glass Frames, Carlo Marat's, Italian and other Mouldings'. Also in Bath were Frime and Joy, from London, carvers and guilders of frames in 'Burnish, and Oil Gold', Thomas Smith, 'Carver and Guilder' of frames and Charles Davis, coach, sign and house painter as well as supplier and gilder of picture frames.[118] In a letter of 1768 to

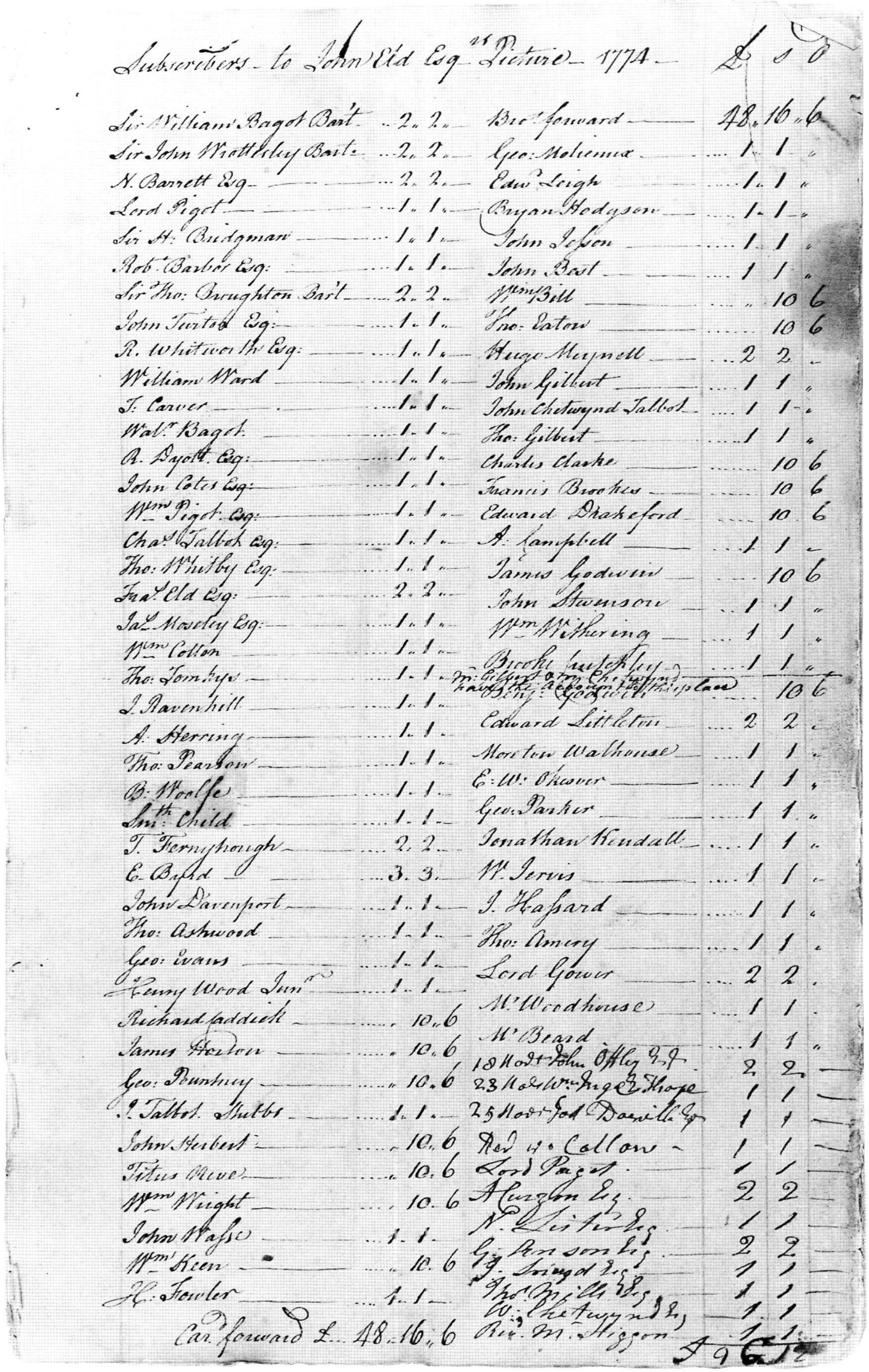

Subscribers to John Eld Esqrs. Picture 1774 — £ s d

Sir William Bagot Bart.	2. 2. –	Brot. forward	48. 16. 6
Sir John Wrottesley Bart.	2. 2. –	Geo: Molineux	1. 1. –
N. Barrett Esq.	2. 2. –	Edw. Leigh	1. 1. –
Lord Pigot	1. 1. –	Bryan Hodgson	1. 1. –
Sir H. Bridgman	1. 1. –	John Jesson	1. 1. –
Rob. Barbor Esq.	1. 1. –	John Best	1. 1. –
Sir Tho: Broughton Bart.	2. 2. –	Wm. Bill	10. 6
John Turton Esq.	1. 1. –	Jno. Eaton	10. 6
R. Whitworth Esq.	1. 1. –	Hugo Meynell	2. 2. –
William Ward	1. 1. –	John Gilbert	1. 1. –
T. Carver	1. 1. –	John Chetwynd Talbot	1. 1. –
Walr. Bagot	1. 1. –	Tho: Gilbert	1. 1. –
R. Dyott Esq.	1. 1. –	Charles Clarke	10. 6
John Cotes Esq.	1. 1. –	Francis Brookes	10. 6
Wm. Pigot Esq.	1. 1. –	Edward Drakeford	10. 6
Chas. Talbot Esq.	1. 1. –	A. Campbell	1. 1. –
Tho: Whitby Esq.	1. 1. –	James Godwin	10. 6
Fras. Eld Esq.	2. 2. –	John Stevenson	1. 1. –
Jas. Moseley Esq.	1. 1. –	Wm. Withering	1. 1. –
Wm. Cotton	1. 1. –	Brooke [illegible]	1. 1. –
Tho: Tomkys	1. 1. –	Mr. Gilbert [illegible] Benj. Godwin	10. 6
J. Ravenhill	1. 1. –	Edward Littleton	2. 2. –
A. Herring	1. 1. –	Moreton Walhouse	1. 1. –
Tho: Pearson	1. 1. –	E. W. Okeover	1. 1. –
B. Woolfe	1. 1. –	Geo. Parker	1. 1. –
Smth. Child	1. 1. –	Jonathan Kendall	1. 1. –
T. Fernyhough	2. 2. –	W. Jervis	1. 1. –
E. Byrd	3. 3. –	J. Hassard	1. 1. –
John Davenport	1. 1. –	Tho: Amery	1. 1. –
Tho: Ashwood	1. 1. –	Lord Gower	2. 2. –
Geo: Evans	1. 1. –	Mr. Woodhouse	1. 1. –
Henry Wood Junr.	1. 1. –	Mr. Beard	1. 1. –
Richard Caddick	10. 6	18 Novr. John Offley Esq.	2. 2. –
James Horton	10. 6	23 Novr. Wm. Inge Esq. Thorpe	1. 1. –
Geo: Pountney	10. 6	25 Novr. Jos. [illegible] Esq.	1. 1. –
J. Talbot Stubbs	1. 1. –	Revd. [illegible] Collow	1. 1. –
John Herbert	10. 6	Lord Paget	1. 1. –
Titus Neve	10. 6	A. Curzon Esq.	2. 2. –
Wm. Wright	10. 6	N. Lister Esq.	1. 1. –
John Wasse	1. 1. –	G. Anson Esq.	2. 2. –
Wm. Keen	10. 6	J. Sneyd Esq.	1. 1. –
H. Fowler	1. 1. –	Thos. Mills Esq.	1. 1. –
		W. Chetwynd Esq.	1. 1. –
Carr. forward £	48. 16. 6	Rev. M. Higgon	1. 1. –
			[illegible]

54 Subscription list for the portrait of John Eld for Staffordshire General Infirmary, Staffordshire Record Office. The list continues, the total subscriptions amounting to £102.17.0.

55 Thomas Gainsborough (1727–1788), *Isaac Gosset (1713–1799)* 1779–80, oil on canvas, 30 × 25 inches (76.2 × 63.5 cm), whereabouts unknown.

Richard Stevens, Gainsborough refers to a frame that 'was done after the Drawing you sent, by the best frame maker at Bristol'.[119] This is most likely to have been James Paty, carver and gilder of Broadmead, Bristol, a member of a highly regarded local family of architects, sculptors and craftsmen.[120] Among their many and varied projects, the Patys built castellated additions to Stoke Gifford, near Bristol, the seat of Norborne Berkeley.[121]

In May 1771 Gainsborough paid a Thomas King eighteen guineas through his Hoare's Bank account.[122] This payment may also be for a frame or frames, since a Thomas King (1741–1804) was a well-known Bath sculptor and mason who is known to have supplied carved picture frames. He was married to a daughter of Thomas Paty of Bristol.[123] King carved the memorial to the actor James Quin in Bath Abbey and a memorial to one Peter Muilman in the Church of Debden, Essex. This latter memorial may have been to the Peter Muilman who was the uncle of Gainsborough's sitter Peter Darnell Muilman (b. 1730) of *The Muilman Conversation Piece* (fig. 26).[124] The Muilmans must have come across Thomas King in Bath and preferred his work to that of any sculptor resident in Essex.

The John Deare to whom Gainsborough paid £48.6.0 on 22 May 1771, using his Hoare's Bank account, must be the carver, gilder and framemaker of that name who was in Kingsmead Street, Bath, from 1766.[125] This payment immediately follows the one to Thomas King. The date of May 1771 for these two payments may indicate a connection with the 'two handsome frames' that Gainsborough planned for his two large landscapes exhibited at the Royal Academy that year. On 21 March 1771 the artist wrote to Edward Stratford, 'I am daubing away for the Exhibition with all my might, and have done two large Landskips which will be in two handsome frames . . . and think whether you have recover'd your Riches or not, you ought to purchase them . . . the Landskips are the best I ever did'.[126] The two handsomely framed landscapes have never been conclusively identified, but one is thought to be the picture that was subsequently owned by Walter Wiltshire (fig. 118). It seems that in Bath Gainsborough used a variety of framers including Gosset of London, Paty of Bristol, John Deare of Bath and Thomas King of Bath, but the artist was not always responsible for supplying the frames for his pictures. At Corsham Court, for example, his portraits are in frames that match others in the rooms in which they hang, and were obviously chosen by the client rather than the artist. On occasion, frames were ready on the wall before portraits had been painted.[127]

There is every indication that Gainsborough took great pains to present his paintings carefully and ensure that they were safely delivered to clients. In a letter of 1763 to Philip, Lord Royston, concerning the delivery of a painting, he advises, 'I shall paper it up to secure the dust from lodging on the surface of the Picture'.[128] Thicknesse recalled how Gainsborough sent him the full-length of Ann Ford rolled up inside another canvas for protection; another later letter makes it clear that a canvas was rolled and put in a case for delivery.[129] Some full-length portraits appear to have been packed flat rather than rolled. The case used for the delivery of the portrait of John Eld to the Staffordshire Infirmary was so substantial that the wood was used to make partitions between beds in the upper ward of the infirmary and 'a Cratch in the Kitchen for the purpose of drying Cloths on'.[130]

George Lucy's portrait (or at least the frame for his portrait) was sent by Gainsborough by the Warwick carrier, Harper, and the artist may have used other cross-country carriers for delivery to specific localities. His relationship with the carrier Walter Wiltshire is well known and it was probably Wiltshire who most regularly transported his paintings between Bath and London, whether for exhibition or for delivery to London sitters. Walter Wiltshire was not merely a carrier but a wealthy and influential figure in Bath society. His father, John Wiltshire, and brother John had also been carriers and were Bath Freemasons, mixing with artists Thomas Ross, James Vertue and Jacob Skinner.[131] Walter Wiltshire was first elected a Bath councillor in 1746, went on to be Mayor in 1772, 1780 and 1791, and at one stage the Council was indebted to him to the very considerable sum of £7,700.[132] When he was elected Mayor in 1772 he treated the gentry to a lavish entertainment in the Guildhall, thereby offending many of his fellow tradesmen who were not invited.[133] From 1743 Walter Wiltshire paid £40 for the lease on a premises in Broad Street, from which his carriages and waggons set out for London and in 1762 he paid £60 for the lease of a 'newly built messuage with stables etc belonging in Broad Street'.[134] He was also connected with other properties and was probably the 'Mr Wiltshire' who owned the lease on a house in Milsom Street that Gainsborough's friend and sitter Sir William St Quintin occupied in 1766.[135] Three payments amounting to £400 made by Walter Wiltshire to Sir William St Quintin in 1770 suggest that Wiltshire not only acted as banker to the Bath Corporation, but also to individuals and local businesses.[136] Walter Wiltshire's payments of £100 and £600 to Dr Rice Charleton in 1771 also appear to be banking transactions, as also must be his payments to surgeon Philip Ditcher and wine merchant Edward Parker.[137] Like Bertie Burgh and James Unwin, Wiltshire handled very large sums of money through Hoare's Fleet Street bank. In eight months between 14 July 1764 and 28 March 1765, for example, a total of £27,037.18.0½ was credited to his account.[138]

Alongside their carrying and banking enterprises, members of the Wiltshire family were proprietors of one of the two lower Assembly Rooms which hosted many of the principal social events of the day and was ornamented with a 'Portrait Picture and Bust of the late Richard Nash, Esq. besides many curious Landscapes'.[139] Ann Wiltshire ran the Rooms from 1744 to 1747; John (Walter's brother) from 1747 to 1762 and Walter from 1762 to 1767.[140] Walter Wiltshire also claimed sole London agency for the sale of bottled Bath water at his depots at the White Bear, Piccadilly and the White Swan, Holborn.[141] It is clear that through friendship with Wiltshire, Gainsborough not only gained safe passage for his paintings, but a whole network of social and business contacts.[142]

As well as painting portraits and arranging their framing and delivery, Gainsborough sometimes supplied copies or other versions of his portraits, all apparently painted solely by himself until he took on his nephew Gainsborough Dupont as an apprentice in 1772.[143] Three versions are known of the pair of 'head' sized portraits of Mr and Mrs Thomas Prowse of Compton Bishop near Axminster in Somerset, all painted in the early 1760s.[144] Interestingly, the likeness of Thomas Prowse, an attorney, Member of Parliament and amateur architect, appears to be based on an earlier portrait by William Hoare.[145] The production of such repetitions must have been irksome; in this particular case the artist may have been spurred on by the fact that Prowse was a close friend of the wealthy Somerset landowners Sir Charles-Kemeys Tynte and Sir George Trevelyan, both of whom commissioned portraits around the same time.[146] Sometimes paintings which have traditionally been catalogued as versions are actually second portraits, painted from fresh sittings. This is the case with the two 'head' portraits of George Lucy painted between the beginning of 1760 and spring 1762. Having completed sittings and paid for his first portrait in February 1760, Lucy wrote home from Bath in March 1760, 'I like it so well myself, that if the money holds out, I don't know whether I may not sit for another, but I shall take some time to consider of it'.[147] A month later Lucy was sitting for the second painting (fig. 78). The two pictures are the same size and format but show the sitter facing in opposite directions and in different dress.

After he had painted David Garrick's portrait in 1772, Gainsborough apologised to Mrs Garrick for not sending the portrait, but explained, 'my chief reason for detaining it so long, was the hopes of getting one copy like, to hang in my own Parlour . . . but not one copy can I make which does not as much resemble Mr Garrick's Brother as Himself . . .'.[148] To Garrick himself he wrote, 'I will never consent that any body makes a present of your Face to Clutterbuck but myself, because I always intended a Copy (by my own hand) for Him . . .'.[149] Also by his 'own hand' must have been the two copies he painted of the Duke of Bedford's portrait in 1765.[150] The Duke and Duchess's agent asked the artist to send on to London the Duchess's and another portrait, instructing that 'they need not wait for His Grace's Picture if you have not finished the Copies you were to make of it, but if they are done that the original can be spared . . . .'.[151] Gainsborough charged exactly the same price, twenty guineas, for all three of the Duke's portraits, making no distinction between the 'original' and the copies.[152] The Duchess tried to tempt the painter to London for further work, offering to pay his travelling expenses but on condition that he kept to his usual prices for the portraits.[153]

How much people valued their portraits, or to what extent they considered they had received value for money, is hard to assess. At one stage of the protracted relationship between George Lucy and Gainsborough, the sitter petulantly declared that his second portrait 'will scarcely deserve the carriage', unless the painter can alter it 'much for the better'.[154] Thicknesse reported in 1770, 'We have been told a noble Duke advised Mr. Gainsborough never to raise his present price'.[155] In the light of the Duchess of Bedford's request in 1765, and further portraits painted for that family in 1768 and 1769, it seems more than likely that the 'Noble Duke' in question was the Duke of Bedford. The Duke must have been well aware that even by 1770 he was still paying less in Bath for portraits by Gainsborough than he would have to pay a comparable artist in London, and he was probably keen to prolong this advantage.

Portraits in general, and even portraits by an artist as accomplished as Gainsborough, must have been easily affordable for the majority of Bath's seasonal visitors. In 1763, for example, Gainsborough's charge of ten guineas for a 'head' portrait would have paid for two men's suits of average size. Richard Painter, tailor of James Street, Bath charged £4.14.6 for a suit, or, if the elements were sold separately, £2.16.0 for a coat, £1.5.0 for the waistcoat and £0.19.0 for the breeches, totalling £5.0.0.[156] At Corsham, Paul Methuen regularly paid out very large sums of money on his coaches, horses and associated expenses, far more than he ever paid for portraits of his family. In 1774 he paid £131 for a new coach and in 1779, £119.17.0 for another one.[157] A single coach horse cost over £50, £8 more than he paid Gainsborough for his son's portrait, and painting the coach £12.14.0, over a quarter as much as he paid for the portrait.

Paul Methuen's 'Daybook' records that in 1775 he paid Edward Francis Cunningham (known as 'Calze') £26.5.0 for updating the costume on a portrait of himself, a payment that supports Gainsborough's own observation that drapery painting could be almost as profitable as portraiture.[158] When comparing Gainsborough's prices during his residence in Bath with those of other artists, or prices for other commodities, it should be remembered that until he took on his nephew as an apprentice, he painted every part of his pictures himself. This, in an age when the use of drapery painters was accepted as normal practice in any successful studio, set Gainsborough's work apart. As Thicknesse particularly noted in 1770, 'Mr. Gainsborough not only paints the face; but finishes with his own hands every part of the drapery, this, however trifling a matter it may appear to some, is of great importance to the picture as it is fatigue and labour to the Artist'.[159]

As well as painting unaided until 1772, Gainsborough was exacting in his technique. In general his pictures did not fade (as Reynolds's did), nor did the paint surface deteriorate as a result of the use of drying accelerators. He appears to have been fastidious in his choice of materials. These were available in Bath from suppliers such as the house painter Francis Woolley who sold 'Oils and Colours for Painting; Whiting Balls' and a 'Variety of Prints and Paintings' in 1760, but as Gainsborough's Hoare's Bank account reveals, he used London colourmen during his stay in Bath.[160] These were men he must have known and trusted since his Hatton Garden days, specialists with a reputation for supplying high quality and reliable products.[161] His principal suppliers seem to have been Charles Sandys of Long Acre and John Middleton of St Martin's Lane, colourmen who went into partnership as Sandys & Middleton at 79 Long Acre in the 1780s (fig. 172).[162] The bank account shows payments of £50 to Charles Sandys in 1763 and £37 in 1768, while John Middleton was paid £52 in December 1774, just after the artist moved to London.[163] These scattered payments probably only represent a tiny fraction of Gainsborough's transactions with colourmen: as has already been mentioned, the artist's London bank account was mainly used to receive Mrs Gainsborough's annuity and it was only called upon intermittently for making payments for goods and services. It is possible that Sandys' and Middleton's goods could also have been obtained through the agency of a Bath retailer. A Mr Middleton, 'pencil maker' of London, possibly a relative of the colourman, regularly sold through Bath bookshops and when a fire devastated his Piccadilly premises in 1786 the booksellers of Bath appealed to their customers for donations to support the elderly tradesman and his family in their distress.[164] John Middleton the colourman supplied Paul Sandby, Reynolds and other leading painters of the day, and was respected for his knowledge. He was said to be one of the few who could prepare ultramarine properly. While ultramarine could be obtained at three guineas an ounce, Middleton's highest quality ultramarine cost ten guineas.[165] Gainsborough is also said to have used the colourman John Scott of 417 Strand, London, perhaps a member of the same family as the Thompson Scott from whom he purchased a painting in 1759.[166] The only slight hint that Gainsborough might have occasionally used a Bath colourman is contained in his payment of £30 to a William Townsend in 1766.[167] A William Townsend, jeweller of Walcot Street, Bath, may be the same Mr Townsend who, at his death at the age of eighty-six in 1813, was said to have been 'an ingenious jeweller' who also had 'considerable skill in chemistry, and prepared some fine colours for miniature-painting superior to any man of his time'.[168] There is nothing to suggest Townsend was a supplier of colours to painters in general, however, and it is equally possible that Gainsborough was simply buying silver or jewellery from him.

If Gainsborough used only the best materials for his oil paintings, it is also evident from his letter to William Jackson of 1773 that he was keen to experiment with pigments when making landscape drawings, which on the whole he did not intend for sale. He suggested Jackson try using Bristol white lead, which could be bought in lumps at any house painters' supplier, as a chalk highlighter in ink drawings.[169] These lumps of white lead may have been the 'Whiting Balls' advertised by Francis Woolley in Bath. The eighteenth-century lead industry in Bristol provided a number of by-products that were used in the manufacture of colours, but not, it appears, colours for artists.[170]

Gainsborough, like any other painter, would have been helped in the preparation of his materials. Gainsborough Dupont lived 'under his wing from a child', according to Thicknesse, before becoming his apprentice in 1772.[171] Although Dupont can only have made a limited contribution to the works of the Bath period, entries in the Hoare's Bank account ledgers suggest that his input thereafter was more significant than has usually been supposed. From 1774 onwards Gainsborough made regular payments to his nephew. The first, recorded on 31 December 1774, is for £30; another £31.10.0 was paid six weeks later, on 11 February 1775; and £45.17.0 on 24 July 1775.[172] Subsequently Dupont was paid a total of £79 in 1776; £120 in 1777; £100 in 1778; £50 in 1781 and £93 in 1783.[173] These payments (again, probably only a proportion of the full amount paid) certainly compare favourably with the £100 a year Reynolds is said to have paid his principal assistant Giuseppe Marchi.[174] As John Hayes has noted, Gainsborough also occasionally used other assistants after moving to London, his payment of twenty guineas to Peter Toms in 1776 being evidence of this.[175]

While there is every indication that Gainsborough's approach to portraiture in Bath was much more businesslike than has usually been recognised, it is also on record that the artist was impulsively generous and not infrequently inspired to paint portraits for his own pleasure and the delight of his friends. His touching portrait of his daughters Mary and Margaret playing with a cat (fig. 51) must have been painted purely for his own and his wife's enjoyment, probably within a year or two of settling at Abbey Street. A letter by James Clutterbuck, written to Garrick in 1771, describes the immense pleasure he took in the portrait of Garrick which the artist gave him. He was, he said, overwhelmed by the 'unbounded liberality' of the painter who had even given him a frame as well as the 'exquisite portrait' itself.[176]

5

'Daubing away for the Exhibition': Show Pictures and Exhibitions

When Gainsborough sent his portrait of Ann Ford (fig. 58) to Philip Thicknesse in London he included a note thanking Thicknesse for having 'procured me the favor of her sitting for it', adding, 'it has done me great service . . .'.[1] In 1772 he wrote to Garrick, 'I ask pardon for having Kept your Picture so long from Mrs. Garrick – It has indeed been of great service in keeping me going . . .'.[2] When he says the pictures were of 'great service', Gainsborough must have meant that they functioned extremely effectively as show pictures in his rooms in Bath, attracting visitors and bringing in new business. Gainsborough had a keen eye for characters whose portraits would make good show pictures. He is supposed to have said to the actor James Quin, 'If you will let me take your likeness, I shall live for ever', and by this he may have meant 'survive financially' as much as earning a place in the annals of British art.[3] While many commissioned portraits must have hung in the artist's showroom while drying out or awaiting delivery, some were further detained if they were particularly useful show pictures and others were painted solely for that purpose.

It is known that Gainsborough referred to these portraits as 'show pictures' because in the same letter to Garrick he explains that one reason he has kept the picture so long is that he was trying to make a satisfactory copy of it, 'not as a show Picture, but for my own enjoyment'.[4] As has already been mentioned, portraits of actors, musicians and other stage performers were favourite subjects for show pictures, but well-known society personalities, and even those who had earned a certain notoriety through some real or imagined scandal in their private lives, could make ideal sitters for show pictures. Ann Ford, who was the subject of much gossip as a result of a supposed relationship with the Earl of Jersey, could be seen to fall in to this last category, as could Captain William Wade who famously fell in love with Mrs Elizabeth Campbell, wife of the Lord Lyon of Scotland, John Hooke Campbell.[5] The private life of the Revd Thomas Wilson, son of the Bishop of Sodor and Man, held great fascination for the public in Bath in the mid-1770s and this may be one of the reasons that Joseph Wright of Derby chose to paint a portrait of him for display in his Bath picture room in 1776. A developing intimate relationship between Wilson and the writer and historian Mrs Catherine Macaulay caused Wilson to indulge in several reckless and ill-advised gestures of generosity, from giving her his Bath house to adopting her young daughter. Wright confided to his brother that he painted the picture of Wilson and his adopted daughter Miss Macaulay 'for reputation only, but you must not say so'.[6] Wright presumably painted this portrait without payment, purely for use in his rooms, and Gainsborough's note to Thicknesse suggests that the portrait of Ann Ford was also primarily intended as a show picture and had not been commissioned.

It appears that Gainsborough attached more than usual importance to the production of show pictures, considering them more useful than reproductive prints in establishing his reputation. As André Rouquet had observed in 1755, most British painters were keen to see their work reproduced in the form of mezzotint engravings, where 'the painter's name is at the bottom of the plate, he reads it with a secret satisfaction, as he runs thro' the collections in printsellers' shops; this is a public testimony of his existence . . .'.[7] For Gainsborough a remarkable series of show pictures, beginning with *Ann Ford*, was his testimony. The accessibility of these pictures, at Abbey Street and then the Circus, obviated the need for the production of prints. It has been claimed that the reason for the scarcity of prints after his work was his 'complete lack of interest in publicity' as well as the difficulty of transcribing his highly individual painting style into the mezzotint medium.[8] However, the discovery of Gainsborough's prominently situated house in Abbey Street, as well as references in his letters to particular pictures being of 'great service', show that he had as much interest in publicising his work as any other artist, but in his case this was done directly, by facing the man in the street with his original paintings, undiluted by the process of reproductive engraving. The practice Gainsborough established in Bath of showing his work in his own rooms became the modus

56 Detail of fig. 14.

operandi for the rest of his career. Although he also submitted pictures to the London public exhibitions from 1761 onwards, he always continued to exhibit in his own house, reverting to this method alone in London from 1784 when he finally lost patience with the Royal Academy.

Mrs Delany's account of the portrait of Ann Ford, as she assessed it armed with a copy of Daniel Webb's *Inquiry*, is just one chance record of an individual's response to the painting.[9] She found it too bold for her liking, and it was indeed an even bolder picture than Mrs Delany seems to have realised, since its composition is, in essence, a reversed image of Sir Peter Lely's famous portrait of King Charles II's mistress Barbara Villiers, Countess of Castlemaine.[10] Given that the Earls of Jersey were relatives of Barbara Villiers, Gainsborough seems to have been quietly poking fun at Lord Jersey and, perhaps, at Ann Ford herself. He was also paying homage to Lely, an artist he seems to have admired almost as much as Van Dyck at this time. Apart from Mrs Delany, there is no way of telling how many other people saw *Ann Ford*, what effect the picture had on them, or how long it remained with Gainsborough, but there is an important clue in the form of Johan Zoffany's portrait of Mrs Warren Hastings, painted in India in the mid-1780s (fig. 57). The upper part of the body and head of Mrs Hastings is modelled very closely on *Ann Ford*. Since the Ann Ford portrait was not exhibited in London, or engraved, it must have been seen by Zoffany either in one of Gainsborough's premises or in one of Thicknesse's homes. Zoffany visited Gainsborough in Bath in late 1771 or early 1772, and so he may have seen the picture then.[11] What is significant is the fact that Zoffany, by the 1780s an extremely well-established artist, should still hold in his mind (and presumably his notebook or sketchbook), such a vivid memory of one of Gainsborough's earliest full-length portraits, a picture that was used by the artist to mark the beginning of his Abbey Street career in Bath.

57 Johan Zoffany (1733–1810), *Mrs Warren Hastings (d. 1837)* 1783–4, oil on canvas, 81 × 60 inches (205.7 × 152 cm), Victoria Memorial Hall, Calcutta.

A striking male show picture which must have been painted within a year or two of that of Ann Ford is *Colonel James Johnston* (fig. 59). As boldly conceived as *Ann Ford*, the dashing Colonel Johnston's portrait is drawn from a low viewpoint which accentuates his elegant physique. Known as 'Irish' Johnston, although he was in fact Scottish, he was apparently 'a great favourite with the fair sex and considered so handsome and fashionable, that Gainsborough requested him, as a great favour, to sit to him for his portrait, in order to bring himself into vogue – which he did; and after the picture had been exhibited the usual time, the artist made him a present of it . . .'.[12] Unfortunately the 'usual time' the portrait was exhibited at Abbey Street is not recorded, but the picture might have been slightly less appealing to the fair sex once Colonel Johnston was married in 1762. Using a tree as a 'prop' for the figure, rather as he had done in earlier portraits such as *Mr and Mrs Andrews* (National Gallery, London) Gainsborough set Colonel Johnston in magnificently painted leafy countryside, advertising his skills as a landscape artist almost as much as his portraiture. The brilliant red of Johnston's jacket must have made as bold a splash in the parlour at Abbey Street as the red of Captain William Wade's suit did in the new Assembly Rooms a decade later (fig. 75). There is also a strong similarity between Colonel Johnston's good looks and the classic features and graceful bearing of Captain Wade: in an age when different standards apply, it is instructive to note that these were the men who proved irresistible to women in the 1760s. The lady who married Colonel Johnston was, like Ann Ford, a well-known amateur musician, Henrietta Cecilia West, appropriately nicknamed 'the divine Cecilia' or 'Saint Cecilia'.[13]

The most remarkable show picture of the Bath period is the portrait of a boy in Van Dyck dress, *The Blue Boy* (fig. 60), generally considered to be a portrait of Jonathan Buttall (1752–1805), the son of a London ironmonger also named Jonathan Buttall (1717–1768). This smaller than usual full-length portrait cannot have been a commissioned picture as it is painted on a previously used canvas, something that would not have been acceptable in a picture painted for a paying client. The only other portrait painted on a spoiled canvas is the full-length of Johann Christian Fischer (fig. 82),

58 Thomas Gainsborough (1727–1788), *Ann Ford, later Mrs Philip Thicknesse (1732–1824)* 1760, oil on canvas, $77\frac{5}{8} \times 53\frac{1}{8}$ inches (197.1 × 135 cm), Cincinnati Art Museum, Cincinnati, Bequest of Mary M. Emery.

59 Thomas Gainsborough (1727–1788), *Colonel James Johnston later General Johnston (1721–1797)* c. 1761–2, oil on canvas, 81¼ × 55½ inches (206 × 141 cm), National Gallery of Ireland, Dublin.

60 Thomas Gainsborough (1727–1788), *The Blue Boy* c. 1768–70, oil on canvas, 70 × 48 inches (178 × 122 cm), Henry E. Huntington Library and Art Gallery, San Marino, California.

61 Jonathan Spilsbury (1737–1812) after Joshua Reynolds (1723–1792), *Giuseppe Marchi, 'The Turkish Boy'* 1761 (after a painting of c. 1753), mezzotint, $13\frac{1}{8} \times 9\frac{1}{16}$ inches (33.2×23 cm), published by John Boydell, 1761, British Museum, London.

a picture that was 'not to be paid for'.[14] It is not known when *The Blue Boy* was painted, but it has been identified with the 'Portrait of a young gentleman' exhibited in the second Royal Academy exhibition in 1770. If the portrait does indeed represent Jonathan Buttall it must have been painted well before that date. Jonathan Buttall was born in 1752 and so would have been aged around eighteen in 1770. The size of canvas used for *The Blue Boy* (20 inches less tall than a normal full-length) in itself indicates that this is a youth, little more than a child. A boy of eighteen was certainly considered adult at this date (Gainsborough himself was only just nineteen when he married). The 'Blue Boy' cannot be more than fourteen or fifteen years old and so, if he is Jonathan Buttall, the picture must have been painted around 1766–7. It is possible that it was painted at this time, in which case it may have been designed as a spectacular attraction to draw visitors to Gainsborough's new rooms at the Circus, to which he moved towards the end of 1766.

The Blue Boy may not, however, be a portrait of Buttall at all. The earliest explicit reference to the picture was made by the diarist Joseph Farington, as Robert Wark has pointed out. Farington attended the Buttall sale on 15 December 1796, when Jonathan Buttall was still very much alive, and reported, 'Gainsborough's picture of a Boy in a Blue Vandyke dress sold for 35 guineas'.[15] The picture is first described as a portrait of a 'Master Brutall' in Edward Edwards' *Anecdotes of Painters . . .* published in 1808, and written a few years earlier.[16] It may be that *The Blue Boy* was a show picture painted in response to Reynolds's *The Turkish Boy*. The latter picture, a fancy dress portrait of Reynolds's principal studio assistant Giuseppe Marchi, hung as a show picture in Reynolds's house in Leicester Fields.[17] Painted around 1753 in a consciously Rembrandtesque manner, it shows Marchi wearing a turban devised (as Aileen Ribeiro has shown) from a fringed sash that would commonly have been worn by a lady at the waist.[18] For Reynolds, Marchi was an ideal subject for a show picture as most visitors to his rooms would have come across him. They must have been impressed and entertained to see the studio assistant ennobled by his exotic costume of turban and fur-lined scarlet coat. The most dis-

62 Thomas Gainsborough (1727–1788), *Gainsborough Dupont (1754–1797)* c. 1768, oil on canvas, 17½ × 14¼ inches (44.5 × 36 cm), Tate Britain, London.

cerning would have appreciated the reference to Rembrandt and perhaps drawn parallels between this picture and Rembrandt's depictions of his son Titus. For Reynolds, who did not have a son, his most trusted assistant was the nearest equivalent model. If Gainsborough was aware of *The Turkish Boy* and its reference to Rembrandt he might well have planned *The Blue Boy* as his own show picture par excellence, paying homage in his case to Van Dyck. There is no indication that Gainsborough visited Reynolds's rooms in the 1750s or 1760s, but it is quite possible that he did. Even if he had not seen the painting, he would almost certainly have known the mezzotint of the portrait that was made by Jonathan Spilsbury (1737–1812) and published in 1761 (fig. 61).[19] Spilsbury was associated with Gainsborough on two occasions in the 1760s. His mezzotint of Gainsborough's portrait of Mrs Richards, wife of the Bath violinist David Richards, was published in 1768 and he also made a mezzotint of the picture *Two Monks Reading*, thought to be by Rubens, which hung on Gainsborough's wall in Bath.[20]

If, by whatever means, Gainsborough knew Reynolds's *Turkish Boy* and wished to go a step further in the creation of a fancy dress show picture of his own, at full-length, the choice of Van Dyck costume for his model was an obvious one. Van Dyck was the portrait painter he most admired in the 1760s, and seventeenth-century costume symbolised the Stuart age to which so many of Gainsborough's patrons remained emotionally attached. If the model for *The Blue Boy* was not Jonathan Buttall, then Gainsborough's nephew Gainsborough Dupont is the most likely candidate. He was two years younger than Jonathan Buttall and was depicted by Gainsborough wearing a Van Dyck collar when still in his teens (fig. 62). Although he was only apprenticed to Gainsborough in 1772, he had lived with the artist's family since childhood, and would have been an available model, but no full-face likeness of him is known, so it is not possible to make a convincing case for identifying him as the 'Blue Boy'. Another possible sitter is the boy known as *The Pitminster Boy* (fig. 111), but there must also have been any number of boys known to the artist who would, for a fee or a favour, have sat for the picture.

It is not known how early *The Blue Boy* was known by that title. William Jackson wrote in 1798 that it was 'known among the painters by the name of the Blue-boy'.[21] The blue in itself is significant. In Italian Renaissance painting the Madonna was always depicted in blue, simply because blue was the most precious pigment, and even in the eighteenth century, as we have seen, the best blues were very expensive, with Middleton's pure ultramarine costing ten guineas an ounce. Gainsborough's emphatic use of blue would, therefore, have been recognised (by artists at least) for the 'showy' and extravagant gesture that it was.

One of the few certainties about *The Blue Boy* is the fact that it entered the collection of an ironmonger named Buttall in Soho. The Bath newspapers record the presence of a 'Mr. and Mrs. Butall' in Bath in April 1764; 'Mr. and Mrs. Buttalls' in February 1774 and 'Mr. and Mrs. Buttall' at the end of June 1774.[22] The Buttall family came from Wrexham in Denbighshire, the home county of the Price family. Wrexham is also just a few miles from Hawarden in Flintshire, the birthplace of the artist-printseller John Boydell who published four landscapes after Gainsborough in the 1740s and *The Gipsies* in 1764.[23] The elder Jonathan Buttall (1717–1768) was the son of Joshua and Deborah Buttall of Penybryn, Wrexham. Ironmongers by name of Buttall are recorded in Wrexham in the seventeenth century.[24] The Mr and Mrs Buttall who visited Bath in 1774, a few months before Gainsborough moved to London, may have been the ironmonger James Buttall (1718/19–1793) of London and his wife.[25] The young Jonathan Buttall was not married in 1774 and his father had died by this date. The Buttall sale in 1796, at which *The Blue Boy* was sold, and which included other works by Gainsborough and Gainsborough Dupont, may have been occasioned by the death of James Buttall in 1793. It is known that Gainsborough was close to one or other member of this family, since a Mr Buttall attended the artist's funeral in 1788, but it is by no means clear which Buttall acquired *The Blue Boy*, or when they acquired it.[26] If it was James Buttall who visited Bath in 1774 and who was the particular friend of the artist, Gainsborough (knowing that he would shortly be moving to London) may have given him the picture then. By this time it must have done sterling service as a show picture at the Circus.

Had Gainsborough settled in London rather than Bath in the late 1750s he might, like Reynolds and other painters, have relied less on show pictures and more on prints for his reputation. The concept of the show picture fits particularly comfortably within the Bath context. Bath was overwhelmingly concerned with show, whether it was in the form of the gaudy splendour of shop windows or the elegance of society ladies at the assembly balls and out walking on the specially designed parades. Andrew Wilton has very reasonably argued that 'The English are embarrassed by show for its own sake', an attitude he attributes to the Protestant ethic, going on to quote Hazlitt's observation that religious painting is at odds with the British sensibility, 'pictures for Protestant churches are a contradiction in terms'.[27] But Bath was less inhibited by the Protestant ethic than any other city in Britain. Show for its own sake was entirely acceptable and even expected, and all the principal places of worship had painted altarpieces, from Van Diest's *Adoration of the Magi* in Bath Abbey to William Hoare's *Pool of Bethesda* (fig. 13) in the Octagon Chapel. Men assiduously studied the relative beauty of different ladies as they showed themselves off in the Assembly Rooms, Philip Thicknesse even going to some lengths to discover whether the lighting in the Upper or the Lower Rooms was more flattering. Interestingly, Thicknesse compares the actuality of the effects of candlelight in the Rooms with the lighting used by artists (and perhaps Gainsborough in particular), 'we much doubt, whether it be true that the Upper Rooms shew Female Beauty so advantageously as the Lower. There is a certain Degree of Light to see nature, as well as Art, to Advantage; and we know that the Painters give us only a small Proportion, not ALL the Light they could throw upon their Works'.[28]

Thicknesse makes it clear that for him, one of the pleasures of the social life of Bath was unashamed people-watching, and in this he was certainly not alone. It was only a small step from admiring the different attractions of real people in the Rooms, or comparing the goods in one toy shop with those in another, to contemplating the relative merits of paintings exhibited in artists' rooms. The new London exhibitions of contemporary art, inaugurated in 1760, provided similar entertainment and instruction, but here visitors could make immediate comparisons between the work of one artist and another.

Since Gainsborough only established himself at Abbey Street in June 1760, it is no surprise that he was not ready to send any paintings to the first public exhibition at the Society of Arts' Great Room in the Strand on 21 April of that year.[29] William Hoare also failed to exhibit in 1760 at the Strand, but his daughter Mary won a gold medal for the 'best drawing by young Ladies under 16 years'.[30] By October 1760 Gainsborough was exhibiting the *Ann Ford* portrait at Abbey Street and by the following spring he was ready to send to London his portrait of Robert Craggs Nugent (fig. 63).[31] This year there were two exhibitions, one presented by the Society of Arts at the Strand (with Peter Templeman as Secretary) from around the 27 April and a second by the Society of Artists of Great Britain (with Francis Milner Newton as Secretary) at the Great Room at Spring Gardens, Charing Cross from 9 May.[32] Gainsborough submitted his picture to the latter exhibition. Among the other exhibits were 'A Family; a Gentleman, his Lady and Child. By Mr. Hoare', and 'An old Woman, half length. Mr. Worlidge', and no less than five paintings by Reynolds, including an imposing equestrian portrait.

From 1761 onwards Gainsborough sent paintings to the Spring Gardens Society of Artists exhibitions every year until

1769 when he and William Hoare were the only two artists based outside London to be invited to be founder members of the Royal Academy.[33] During this period a number of other artists also sent from Bath to the London exhibitions. John Thomas Seaton, a pupil of Hayman (and son of Christopher Seaton, a gem-engraver like the Wicksteeds of Bath), sent portraits to the Society of Artists exhibitions from Bath in 1766 and 1767.[34] The wax-modeller Joachim Smith of Bath exhibited a portrait of the Duke of Newcastle at Spring Gardens in 1766 and a Miss Sophia Smith some miniatures and flower studies in 1766 and 1767.[35] Between 1768 and 1770 the miniature painters Simon Pine (brother of Robert Edge Pine) and Thomas Redmond exhibited from Bath at the Society of Artists and in 1769 William Jones of Bath showed flower and fruit pictures.[36] Thomas Worlidge favoured the original Society of Arts exhibitions, which became known as the Free Society in 1763. His portrait of William Kenrick, shown in 1766, was described as 'capital' in the *Public Advertiser*.[37] At the Free Society in 1764 the sculptor John Ford the Younger of Bath exhibited a marble bust of Worlidge's young son Thomas.[38] The landscape painter and friend of Gainsborough, Edmund Garvey, also supported the Free Society.[39]

Of all the artists who sent work from Bath to London, only Gainsborough and Hoare attracted serious attention from the critics. David Brenneman has recently shown how Gainsborough was assessed throughout the 1770s and 1780s, when a serious body of critical writing emerged in the London press.[40] The art of newspaper criticism was in its infancy during Gainsborough's Bath period, but there are nevertheless a number of indications of contemporary responses to both Gainsborough and Hoare. Hoare's work was always well received but on occasion the response to Gainsborough was unfavourable. The author of the *Critical Review of the Pictures, Sculptures etc.* of 1765 wrote of the equestrian portrait of General Philip Honywood (fig. 74), 'the intire piece wants great correction, the whole being too heavy, and the performance too large'.[41] Horace Walpole, however, found the same picture 'very good', and the King is said to have admired it so much he wanted to buy it.[42] Gainsborough's portrait of John Campbell, Fourth Duke of Argyll (fig. 50) also met with a mixed response, 'The likeness is very great, as is usual with this artist, and the face well painted; but the attitude is bad, the background unfinished, and the sky intolerable'.[43] By 1772, however, the correspondent of the *Middlesex Journal* wrote with confidence, 'No one need to be informed of Mr. Gainsborough's excellence in portrait painting . . .'.[44]

Gainsborough clearly selected with care the pictures he sent to London, no doubt bearing in mind the qualities of the sitters as well as the quality of his performance. Sitters, of course, had to be willing to wait for their pictures if they were to be shown in London, and, perhaps to tolerate extra sittings so that the artist could achieve precisely his desired effect. Gainsborough wrote to William Johnstone Pulteney, husband of the Bath heiress Henrietta Laura Pulteney, asking him the favour of just one more sitting, 'either to morrow morning, or any other, most agreeable to yourself. I am fired with the thoughts of Mrs. Pulteney's giving me leave to send you to the Royal Exhibition, and of making a good Portrait of you, therefore hope Sir you will be so good to pardon my giving you all this trouble'.[45]

63 Thomas Gainsborough (1727–1788), *Robert Craggs Nugent, later Earl Nugent (1702–1788)* 1760–61, oil on canvas, 81 × 59 inches (231 × 150 cm), private collection, on loan to the Holburne Museum of Art, Bath. Nugent's arrival in Bath is noted in *Boddely's Bath Journal* on 22 September 1760. The picture must have been painted between that date and the beginning of May 1761 when it was exhibited in London. The sitter was Member of Parliament for Bristol between 1754 and 1774; he became Earl Nugent in 1776.

65 *(above)* Thomas Gainsborough (1727–1788), *Mr and Mrs George Byam and their Daughter Selina* c. 1761 and c. 1763–6, oil on canvas, 98 × 94 inches (249 × 238.8 cm), The Andrew Brownsword Arts Foundation, on loan to the Holburne Museum of Art, Bath. Recent technical analysis has shown that Mrs Byam wore a pink dress and her husband a blue waistcoat when the picture was first painted. The costumes must have been changed when Gainsborough added little Selina Byam (who was born in 1760) to the group.

64 *(facing page)* Thomas Gainsborough (1727–1788), *Mr and Mrs Philip Dehany and their Daughter Mary* c. 1760–61, oil on canvas, 94 × 58 inches (238.3 × 147.43 cm), private collection. Mary Dehany was born in June 1759.

66 Thomas Gainsborough (1727–1788), *Mrs Henry William Berkeley Portman (1707–1781)* 1764–5, oil on canvas, 84½ × 60½ inches (214.5 × 153.5 cm), Trustees of the Portman Settled Estates.

On occasion, it seems, pressure to exhibit came from the sitter. There are several hints to the effect that some friends or acquaintances of the artist attempted to take advantage of his good nature and persuade him to exhibit portraits of themselves for their own personal gain or glory. In 1770 Thicknesse published his *Sketches and Characters of the most Eminent and most Singular Persons now Living* which included a list 'of those who have made a mean and contemptible figure in some action or circumstance of their lives'. One of this list was 'Dr. C—rl—on, When he employed Mr. Gainsborough, to enable him to exhibit his full length Portrait, in the exhibition room at Spring Gardens'.[46] Thicknesse seems to be suggesting that Dr Rice Charleton engineered the production and exhibition of his portrait (fig. 88) for his own ends. It could be argued that this is simply a case of Thicknesse's malicious imagination getting the better of him, but Bath's doctors were notoriously powerful and ambitious men, and Charleton could certainly have seen the portrait as a means of publicising his practice.[47] Another Bath character also seems to have attempted to promote himself via Gainsborough. This was the young poet Underwood who claimed that Gainsborough had promised to paint his portrait for the Spring Gardens exhibition:

> Gainsbro', an Artist in this Place,
> I told you was to draw my Face;
> And, *gratis*, promis'd to supply,
> A Picture for the public Eye:[48]

It appears that Gainsborough either never intended such a gesture, or made a rash promise and changed his mind on reflection. Whitley describes the quarrel that developed between the two men and the well-meaning intervention of Simon Pine, which only resulted in the poet's bitterness being directed towards the miniature painter as well as Gainsborough.[49] Charleton and Underwood were certainly not the only individuals to attempt to exploit the public exhibitions. The actor Samuel Reddish commissioned Robert Edge Pine to paint his full-length portrait in the character of Posthumus, with the express purpose of seeing it exhibited at Spring Gardens in 1768. Reddish then strutted about the exhibition himself 'above 4 hours every day, for the space of 6 weeks, like a second Narcissus'.[50]

At the time Gainsborough was exhibiting from Bath at the Society of Artists exhibitions at Spring Gardens and at the Royal Academy it was normal for the printed catalogues to these exhibitions to identify sitters only as 'a lady, whole length', or 'an officer, whole length', unless the person depicted was a public figure such as an actor, in which case he or she was normally named. Despite this practice, the majority of Gainsborough's exhibited portraits from the Bath period can be identified from contemporary catalogue annotations or other clues. Having satisfactorily matched known and named portraits with pictures listed in the printed catalogues, it has become common to date the portraits to the years in which they were exhibited. In a number of cases this is untenable, however. By 1 March 1762 Gainsborough had already painted his full-length of Charleton, but he only exhibited the picture in London in 1766.[51] Of *The Hon. Mrs Thomas Graham* (National Gallery of Scotland, Edinburgh), painted shortly after he left Bath, he is reported to have said that he had 'no thoughts of finishing it within the twelve month' and the portrait of Johann Christian Fischer (fig. 82) exhibited at the Academy in 1780 was painted in 1774.[52] It has been shown that the earliest Bath portraits, including those painted in 1758–59, were executed quickly and in some cases delivery took place within a few weeks. The time Gainsborough spent on his pictures gradually became longer and longer, however, and since the London exhibitions took place in April or May, it is often incorrect to date them to the year of exhibition. Sometimes the arrival of sitters in Bath can be established from the local newspapers and this can assist in dating, but all too often sitters came regularly for the season. The Byams, for example, who commissioned a full-length family portrait (fig. 65), made frequent visits to Bath.[53] It appears that Waterhouse and others who have associated the double portrait exhibited at Spring Gardens in 1766 with the Byam picture are unlikely to be correct.[54] Hugh Belsey has now convincingly demonstrated that the Byam picture was painted in two stages, the first around 1761–2 and the second, when the Byam's infant daughter was added and the costumes of Mr and Mrs Byam completely changed, between 1763 and 1766.[55] The Byam portrait appears to have been in Gainsborough's showroom at Abbey Street on 21 April 1766 when the Spring Gardens exhibition opened. On 18 April the Revd John Penrose wrote from Bath to his daughter in Cornwall,

> Your Mama and Fanny have both been to see the Pictures, and are much pleased with them. Among the rest is a fine portrait of a father, mother and child: the finest Portrait she ever saw, and she liked it the better for the child's being very like little Molly.[56]

This description sounds very like the Byam picture, and the Penroses were staying just a matter of yards from Gainsborough's house, in Abbey Green.[57] The only other painting Mrs. Penrose could have been describing is the family group of *Mr and Mrs Dehany and their Daughter* (fig. 64) an appealing picture which could well have elicited a similar maternal response.[58] The child, Mary Dehany, was born in June 1759, however, which would place the portrait around 1761–2 at the latest, and the composition is altogether less assured than the Byam picture. The best clue as to the identity of the double portrait exhibited in 1766 is contained in the *Critical Review* of that year. The writer says, 'There is so much confusion in this picture, owing to the ill distribution of light and shadow, that I think it does the artist no credit'.[59] This rather harsh comment might possibly refer to the portrait of Mr and Mrs Richard Neave (later Sir Richard and Lady Neave) (fig. 72), a curious picture full of dashes of

67 Thomas Gainsborough (1727–1788), *Mrs Mary Carr, later Lady Carr* 1763–5, oil on canvas, 50 × 40 inches (127 × 101.6 cm), Yale Center for Studies in British Art, New Haven, Bequest of Mrs Harry Payne Bingham. Mary Carr's husband Robert Carr was a London mercer, a point of some significance given the large number of payments in Gainsborough's bank account to drapers and mercers and the artist's proximity to his sister Mary Gibbon's millinery business between 1762 and 1766.

light, brilliant colour and spiralling movement.[60] Though little known today, the Neave portrait appears to have had some influence on other artists in the 1760s and '70s, a fact that would lend weight to the theory that it was the picture exhibited in London.[61]

In 1764 Gainsborough only sent one 'Portrait of a gentleman, three quarters' to the Society of Artists exhibition at Spring Gardens, perhaps the *Joshua Kirby* now in the Fitzwilliam Museum, Cambridge. The *Public Advertiser* of 2 May 1764 reported that Mr Gainsborough 'Has only favoured the Exhibition with one Portrait this year, which is not so good as either of his last'.[62] Gainsborough's failure to show anything of particular note that year must be related to his severe illness of the previous autumn and his consequent change of working pattern. Having just moved to Lansdown and arranged to let off all of Abbey Street except for his painting room and showroom, he was probably too unsettled to have a major picture fully ready for London, although he told Unwin he had painted 'a whole length, three half lengths and seven Heads, exclusive of a full length of Doctor Charleton, and a half length of Doctor Moysey's son' by the beginning of March.[63]

The portraits Gainsborough sent to the Society of Artists exhibitions between 1761 and 1768 did not, by any means, demonstrate the full range of his abilities (Appendix IV provides the full list). Over this eight-year period he sent only one female portrait (and one 'Lady and gentleman, whole length', perhaps the Neaves), a quite extraordinary statistic, when it is considered that he painted such masterpieces as *Mary, Countess Howe* (fig. 69) and *Mrs Henry William Berkeley Portman* (fig. 66) at this time, as well as a remarkable series of female half-lengths such as *Lady Mary Carr* (fig. 67) and *Lady Harriet Tracy* (fig. 68). His failure to send a truly representative selection of works to Spring Gardens underlines the importance he attached to his own exhibition rooms in Bath. When the Royal Academy exhibitions began in 1769 he sent more pictures (an impressive total of five full-lengths in 1771) and seems to have selected them with greater care. The two full-lengths exhibited at the first Academy exhibition, *Isabella, Viscountess Molyneux* (fig. 48) and *George Pitt, First Lord Rivers* (fig. 49) are among his greatest portraits. Lady Molyneux is painted, like *The Blue Boy*, in cool hues against a warm-coloured sky. The painting of the drapery, at a time when Gainsborough still executed every area of the picture unaided, is, as John Hayes has noted, particularly fine, and the bearing of the figure nothing short of 'regal'.[64] Waterhouse called the portrait 'an eighteenth-century version of Van Dyck of hardly surpassable refinement'.[65] George Pitt, one of the few 'Great Men'

68 Thomas Gainsborough (1727–1788), *Harriet, Lady Tracy (d. 1795)* 1763–5, oil on canvas, $49\frac{3}{4} \times 39\frac{3}{4}$ inches (126.4 × 101 cm), Gainsborough's House, Sudbury, Suffolk.

Gainsborough truly respected, is a commanding figure, set against a very low horizon.[66] His manner of holding his sword in his left hand is exactly the same as the way Peter Muilman holds his cane in the canvas painted twenty years' earlier and it is interesting to compare these two figures (fig. 26). The change is from one kind of refinement to another, and once again, the comparison brings home the realisation that new architecture had much to do with a new style of portraiture. A portrait the size of the Muilman picture, however exquisitely painted, would have been lost on the walls of Gainsborough's house in the Circus, the Academy or Stratfield Saye, Pitt's country seat.

The portraits of Lady Molyneux and Lord Rivers set a standard for Gainsborough's Academy exhibits, and from 1770 to 1772 he sent an important series of paintings including *Captain William Wade* (fig. 75) and *Elizabeth and Mary Linley* (Dulwich Picture Gallery). During his last two years in Bath he did not exhibit at the Academy, but his public exposure in Bath had been enhanced by the display of *Captain William Wade* at the New Assembly Rooms, and the opening of these Rooms must have brought increased numbers of visitors to his own house just round the corner.

Once a portrait was on the wall in the artist's own showroom or at one of the London public exhibitions, it had to fire the imagination of the viewer. Likeness was a principal ingredient, and contemporary comment is peppered with references to artists' ability to catch a likeness, but likeness alone did not satisfy, and it is a fact that Reynolds, the most successful portrait painter of the day, was often said to have failed in this respect. When Gainsborough attempted to define the added ingredient by which a portrait became more than a simple likeness and a good composition, he used the analogy of music. He was writing to William Hoare, who had evidently given or lent him a copy of Reynolds's *Fourth Discourse*, and while expressing admiration for Reynolds's wisdom, he told Hoare that he believed his exhortation to emulate the Italian 'Great style' in modern portraiture was mistaken.[67] 'Fresco would no more do for Portraits than an Organ would please Ladies in the hands of Fischer; there must be Variety of lively touches and surprizing Effects to make the Heart dance . . .'.[68]

Gainsborough used 'surprizing Effects to make the Heart dance' as his principal means of lending a personal stylistic signature to his portraits. Reynolds himself came to fully acknowledge this in his *Fourteenth Discourse* which was dedicated to Gainsborough's memory in the year of his death. Reynolds described the 'chaos' of 'odd scratches and marks' by which Gainsborough built up his pictures, adding,

69 Thomas Gainsborough (1727–1788), *Mary, Countess Howe (1732–1800)* 1763–4, oil on canvas, 96 × 60 inches (244 × 152.5 cm), Iveagh Bequest, English Heritage, Kenwood, London.

70 Thomas Gainsborough (1727–1788), *A Woman with a Rose* 1763–4, chalk on tinted paper, 18¼ × 13 inches (46.4 × 33 cm), British Museum, London.

71 Paul Sandby (1731–1809), *A Woman Walking in a Landscape* date unknown, etching, 8⁵⁄₁₆ × 6⁵⁄₁₆ inches (21.1 × 16.1 cm), Yale Center for British Art, New Haven, Paul Mellon Collection.

That Gainsborough himself considered this peculiarity in his manner and the power it possesses of exciting surprise, as a beauty in his works, I think may be inferred from the eager desire which we know he always expressed, that his pictures, at the Exhibition, should be seen near, as well as at a distance.[69]

The element of surprise created by Gainsborough's painterly manipulation of the surface of his canvases was in part a substitute for the expression of movement as depicted by other artists. Reynolds often caught the attention of his viewers through the physical energy of his figures. His *Commodore Augustus Keppel* strides manfully along a stormy coast and the *Duchess of Marlborough* playfully bounces the little Lady Caroline Spencer on her lap.[70] Gainsborough's attempts to depict figures in action were few and generally unsatisfactory. A notable exception, where gentle movement is expressed, is the portrait of *Mary, Countess Howe* (fig. 69), a portrait that must have been exhibited at Abbey Street, but was not shown in London.[71] Lindsay Stainton has related a number of figure drawings of walking women to the *Mary, Countess Howe* portrait, and it does appear that this portrait was planned in a more detailed manner than was Gainsborough's usual practice.[72] These drawings and the final portrait have a good deal in common with Paul Sandby's etching *Woman Walking* (figs 70 and 71). Sandby's print depicts a very similarly dressed young woman hoisting her skirts to walk in a landscape. There is no way of knowing whether this print anticipates or follows the Gainsborough studies and the *Mary, Countess Howe* painting, but what both artists convey (on quite a different scale) is a new kind of naturalism, a genuine attempt to show women at ease in the countryside rather than posed by an urn or some other symbol of their fathers' or husbands' estates.

Although Gainsborough rarely depicted figures in action, in several portraits of the Bath period he attempted quite complex compositional movement. Robert Wark describes

73 *(above)* Thomas Chambars (c. 1724–1789) after Enoch Seeman (1694–1744), *Self-portrait* 1762 (after a painting of 1726–7), engraving, $6^{11}/_{16} \times 5^{1}/_{4}$ inches (17 × 13.3 cm), published 1762, British Museum, London.

72 *(left)* Thomas Gainsborough (1727–1788), *Mr and Mrs Richard Neave later Sir Richard and Lady Neave* 1765–6, oil on canvas, 87 × 59 inches (221 × 149.9 cm), private collection.

the 'strong diagonal accents and pyramidal organization' of Gainsborough's *Cottage Door* landscape in the Huntington Library and Art Gallery at San Marino.[73] Such compositional devices have an equal part to play in the portraits of Ann Ford and Mr and Mrs Richard Neave. Both pictures are characterised by rapid brushwork, vivid colour and compositional energy. As Michael Kitson observed in his review of the 1980 Gainsborough exhibition at the Tate Gallery, the portrait of Ann Ford is 'a portrait of a dress more than of a woman', with its 'zig-zag surface pattern' and 'shallow composition'.[74] The Neave double portrait contains many of the elements of the *Ann Ford* picture, but taken a stage further. Gainsborough never again attempted such a composition while in Bath, although certain echoes may be found in several of his very latest portraits where distortion and movement are taken to the extreme. For the twisting figure of Richard Neave, Gainsborough appears to have looked to a print after a *Self-portrait* of Enoch Seeman (fig. 73).[75]

Gainsborough's exceptionally lively handling of paint, which set him apart from most of his British contemporaries, caused him to be seen by his admirers as a modern old master. The writer of his obituary observed that he was 'almost the only painter of this country' who approached Van Dyck in his manner of painting.[76] A poem published in 1773, 'On seeing Mr. Gainsborough's Pictures at Bath', chides connoisseurs for blindly favouring ancient art simply because it is old and recognises old-masterly skills in the hand of this modern master,

> Be mine the pleasure, tho' in humble lays,
> True, *modern* merit to admire and praise.
> Yes, *Gainsborough!* yes; thy magic pieces charm,
> And want but age dull connoisseurs to warm.
> Thy vivid colours, elegant design,
> Rich strokes of fancy, chaste and flowing line,
> All nature's beauties in thy tints that glow.[77]

This poem is signed 'D.W.' and seems likely to be the work of Daniel Webb. As will be shown in the context of

Gainsborough's landscape paintings, Daniel Webb and his theoretical writings were important to Bath and English painting as a whole. Mrs Delany was certainly doing as Webb and his publisher hoped when she used his comments on the old masters as a yardstick for appraising Gainsborough's work in Bath in 1760. Two years later an advertisement in the *London Evening Post* appearing in April, at the time of the two public exhibitions, announces, 'This Day was publish'd, Price 2.6d. sew'd (Very proper to be read by those who go to see the Exhibitions of the British Artists). An Enquiry into the Beauties of Painting . . . By Daniel Webb, Esq . . .'.[78]

David Brenneman has traced the relationship between British painting and the old masters in the 1770s and 1780s and the public comment on this relationship as expressed by people who viewed the London exhibitions.[79] The parallels he describes were recognised before the foundation of the Royal Academy and even before the first public exhibitions in London. Discussions on the subject were doubtless taking place within the artistic milieu of Bath by the time Gainsborough settled there, orchestrated by Daniel Webb, William Hoare and their friends. The 'old masterly' qualities that surfaced in Gainsborough's work from 1760 onwards probably owed as much to the local intelligentsia as to the activities of London artists or the examples of old master pictures he saw in the West Country. This will become more evident when the landscape painting of the period is considered in later chapters.

In terms of technique Gainsborough certainly imitated the old masters, but his portrait compositions rarely quoted overtly from earlier Continental models. He did make copies of Van Dyck portraits in several British collections and set his figures in Van Dyckian poses but he did not, as did Reynolds and other contemporary painters, make obvious allusions to famous compositions by Raphael or other Italian painters.[80] Gainsborough was more inclined to reinterpret models that had become standard in England, often with little compositional change. As Marcia Pointon has shown, 'modern-day criteria of originality and individuality need to be set aside . . .' when considering British eighteenth-century portrait-painting practice, and this is especially true in the case of Gainsborough and his approach to composition.[81] Three particular examples of Bath period portraits, *General Honywood* (fig. 74), *Captain William Wade, Master of Ceremonies* (fig. 75) and *John Eld* (fig. 76) illustrate the subtle manner of his reinterpretation of existing conventions.[82]

The portrait of General Honywood, exhibited at the Society of Artists exhibition in 1765, was the painter's most ambitious invention of the Abbey Street period. Its extra-large format reflects the new-found freedom afforded by the spacious painting room and display room at Abbey Street. Its sheer size prompted Honywood to build a new library room on to his house, Marks Hall in Essex, to accommodate it.[83] As with the portrait of *Mary, Countess Howe*, the Honywood composition involved a degree of preparatory work unusual for Gainsborough. This is known, not from the survival of any related drawings, but from undated correspondence with James Unwin in which Gainsborough says that he has just returned 'from Wilton where I have been about a Week, partly for my Amusement, and partly to make a Drawing from a fine Horse of Ld Pembroke's, on which I am going to set General Honeywood, as large as life'.[84]

The first and most obvious source for the composition and painting style of the Honywood portrait is (as was pointed out by Mary Woodall) Van Dyck's *Charles I on Horseback*, now in the National Gallery.[85] The fact that Gainsborough used one of the Earl of Pembroke's horses for the portrait had a profound effect on the final composition of the painting. Compared with other major equestrian portraits of military worthies of the same decade, such as Reynolds's *John, First Earl Ligonier*, Gainsborough's picture has a peculiarly unheroic and two-dimensional quality.[86] Honywood is depicted mounted on a rather small horse with a sharply arched neck, not prancing but progressing in a stately manner through a leafy landscape. There are none of the usual trappings of a military portrait, no background battle scene or smoky skies. All this may be explained by the reference to the Tenth Earl of Pembroke and Wilton. Pembroke had an intense interest in *haute école*, the art of polite horsemanship, a discipline that involved specially bred horses and riders trained to enact a language of movement and gesture as complex as the etiquette of any royal court in Europe.[87] At Wilton Lord Pembroke had a riding school and stables where horses were bred and trained in the manner of the Spanish Riding School in Vienna. What Gainsborough has done in the Honywood portrait is to set the General on a perfectly 'managed' horse of Lord Pembroke's, creating an image that must have been understood by any eighteenth-century viewer versed in the art of horsemanship, but was misunderstood by others. A correspondent signing himself simply 'N', writing to the *Public Advertiser* on 2 May 1765, complained about the depiction of Honywood's sword and scabbard: 'I found a Scabbard to the General's Sword wanting. He is painted in his full Regimentals, with a Broad-Sword in his Hand, and as his Left Side is presented to you fully, any body must be a Judge of this Impropriety'.[88] Others have noted that Gainsborough failed to paint the right foot of Honywood which should logically be seen under the horse's belly.[89] However in *haute école*, the profile created by horse and rider was paramount, as can be seen in a remarkable series of fifty-five gouache paintings still at Wilton of horses performing different routines. As the gouaches show, the manner of carrying the whip was integral to the profile. In the Honywood portrait Gainsborough has completed the 'correct' profile by placing the General's sword vertically as a substitute for the whip. What was unsatisfactory in military terms may be seen as essential in terms of *haute école*. Equally, the deliberate (as it must have been) omission of the General's right foot is mirrored in the small gouache paintings in which the further

74 *(above)* Thomas Gainsborough (1727–1788), *General Philip Honywood* 1764–5, oil on canvas, 124½ × 115½ inches (316.5 × 293.4 cm), Bequest of John Ringling, Collection of the John and Mable Ringling Museum of Art, the State Art Museum of Florida.

75 *(facing page)* Thomas Gainsborough (1727–1788), *Captain William Wade (d. 1809), Master of Ceremonies* 1770–71, oil on canvas, 92¼ × 60¼ inches (234.3 × 153 cm), Victoria Art Gallery, Bath and North East Somerset Council (Assembly Rooms, Bath).

foot of the rider is never shown, presumably because it would detract from the desired profile.

Christopher Brown has noted that Van Dyck's *Charles I on Horseback* deliberately echoes the second-century Roman bronze equestrian sculpture of *Marcus Aurelius* now in the Piazza di Campidoglio.[90] Gainsborough's unusual treatment of Honywood's portrait may also owe something to the presence at Wilton of a copy of this bronze. The *Marcus Aurelius* now crowns Sir William Chambers's triumphal arch near the house, but at the time of Gainsborough's visit it stood on a much lower plinth among trees on a hill in the park.[91] Perhaps Gainsborough sketched the *Marcus Aurelius* as he explored the grounds at Wilton for 'Amusement'. It would not be the only time Gainsborough used sculpture as inspiration: in *The Harvest Waggon* (fig. 160), painted within a few years of *General Honywood*, he referred to the classical sculpture of the *Horse Tamers* in the Piazza del Quirinale, Rome, as has been pointed out by several writers.[92] He also looked to Scheemakers's statue of Shakespeare when painting his full-length portrait of *David Garrick* (formerly Stratford-upon-Avon Town Hall). It is quite likely that he was referring to the Wilton version of the Shakespeare sculpture rather than the Westminster Abbey monument.[93]

The portrait of *General Honywood* is a multi-faceted painting, deriving its composition from a number of sources. Its rather strange iconography lead to misunderstandings and can only have been acceptable to the sitter as a result of a shared interest in the art of *haute école*. Gainsborough may have known Honywood well, since the General and his wife came to Bath every year, and the fact that a new room was built to accommodate the portrait suggests that he was more than pleased with it.[94]

If in *General Honywood* Gainsborough reinvented the equestrian portrait in an original if somewhat esoteric way, his reinterpretation of the two other portrait models to be examined here was more straightforward. For his *Captain William Wade* he looked to existing Master of Ceremony portraits in Bath, and for *John Eld* to other hospital benefactor portraits. The full-length portrait of Captain William Wade was destined for a site above a door in the New or Upper Assembly Rooms in Bath, the rooms being built in response to the shift of population from the lower to the upper town, and opening to the public in autumn 1771.[95] Gainsborough would have been very familiar with the full-length portraits of previous Masters of Ceremonies Beau Nash and Samuel Derrick that hung in the 'old' Lower Assembly Rooms not far from his Abbey Street house. Although it is not entirely clear who painted these, they were probably the work of Van Diest and William Hoare respectively. The full-length of Nash can be seen above a door in Wiltshire's Rooms in more than one contemporary image of the interior of the building (fig. 8). The design of the Octagon card room in the New Rooms incorporated four stucco surrounds for full-length portraits above the doors, echoing the arrangement in the Lower Rooms. Gainsborough's painting of Wade was the first to occupy one of these spaces and it was not until the early nineteenth century that all four were filled with Master of Ceremony portraits. *Captain Wade* appears to have been painted without payment, as a show picture and as an expression of support for the proprietors of the Rooms, several of whom were patrons of the artist. Gainsborough depicted the Master of Ceremonies silhouetted against a bright sky, a powerful and even somewhat stark image that was guaranteed to make a striking effect from a distance. The portrait had to make its presence felt above the hubbub of the Rooms which accommodated several hundred people at a time and were the focal point for Bath's social life from 1771 onwards. As has already been mentioned, the height at which the painting was destined to hang also prompted the artist to adopt a very low viewpoint for the background landscape and probably accounts for the elongated proportion of the figure.

The full-length of *John Eld*, painted in 1774, is one of Gainsborough's most sensitive male portraits of the Bath period (fig. 76). It shows the seventy-year-old Eld, in a red coat trimmed with gold braid, standing in a landscape, holding a plan of the Staffordshire Infirmary. His portrait was commissioned to commemorate his role as the Infirmary's major benefactor. The most obvious model for a full-length portrait of this kind was Thomas Hudson's of Theodore Jacobsen, Governor and designer of the Foundling Hospital, painted in 1746 (fig. 77). Jacobsen is painted in the cross-legged pose often used by Gainsborough, but usually reserved by him for portraits of younger men. Eld is set in a much more solid four-square pose, more reminiscent of the sculpture of Beau Nash in the Pump Room, Bath, the hospital benefactor portrait which would have been most familiar to Gainsborough (fig. 1). Like Eld and Jacobsen, Nash is shown holding a plan of the hospital, leaning on a plinth. The portrait of Nash was carved by the Italian sculptor Giuseppe Plura, working in the studio of William Hoare's brother Prince Hoare. It was set up in the Pump Room in 1752.[96]

Eld's face is beautifully painted, his upward gaze towards the light seeming to signify the wisdom and vision of old age. The portrait has much in common with Gainsborough's earlier full-length of John, Fourth Duke of Argyll (fig. 50), especially in the lighting and modelling of the face, but here the figure and background are perfectly integrated, without any conflict of viewpoint. The nonchalant placing of the sitter's hat at the base of the pillar, next to his elbow, seems to add to the humanity of the portrait. Through his knowledge of the Bath hospital and the balance between self-indulgence and philanthropy that existed in Bath society, Gainsborough understood better than most artists how to create an appropriate image of a hospital benefactor. In Bath itself, William Hoare's position as a governor guaranteed him the lion's share of commissions associated with the Hospital,

76 Thomas Gainsborough (1727–1788), *John Eld (1704–1796)* 1774–5, oil on canvas, 94 × 60¼ inches (238.6 × 153 cm), Special Painting Fund, Courtesy Museum of Fine Arts, Boston.

77 Thomas Hudson (1701–1779), *Theodore Jacobsen (d. 1772)* 1746, oil on canvas, 93 × 54 inches (236.2 × 137.1 cm), Coram Family in the care of the Foundling Museum.

but the Eld commission for a hospital on different territory gave Gainsborough an opportunity to demonstrate his considerable skill in portraying a sitter in such a particular and clearly defined role.

Likeness was always Gainsborough's first consideration, and this was fully appreciated by those who viewed his pictures in Bath and London. According to a poem published in the *Bath and Bristol Chronicle* on 30 November 1769 observers were 'struck' with 'amazement' at Gainsborough's skill in capturing a likeness. He seemed able to represent the innermost character of his sitters as well as their outward appearance. The poem, entitled 'To Mr. Gainsborough, on Mrs. S . . . T . . . D's setting for her Picture', probably refers to the half-length portrait of Mrs Barbara Stratford, later Countess of Aldborough that is thought to have been painted in 1769 but is now lost.[97] Signed only 'A.B.', it begins by describing Mrs Stratford's outward charms and then the artist's extraordinary ability to reveal her 'mind':

> That lovely female see! Her beauteous face,
> Of aspect sweet, to wisdom gives a grace!
> There native virtue in the bosom warms,
> And on the canvas puts forth all her charms.
> Bold was the happy hand, and unconfin'd,
> That shew'd the features of the latent mind,
> Brought it to light, and gave the world to view
> What praise to merit and to worth is due.
> Alien is Art from Nature's genuine laws,
> And only imitates what nature draws,
> But when the subject raises in the mind
> High flights of fancy and of thought refin'd,
> Then do the colours on the canvas glow,
> And living lines in just proportion flow:
> Or, should the Life the Pencil's power excel,
> Thine is the same to imitate so well:
> The picture to th'original so like,
> You all beholders with amazement strike. A. B.

A month earlier the same newspaper published a poem 'On two Ladies consulting on the Choice of a Print of the celebrated General Paoli', an epigram on the subject of likeness:

> Of Paoli, says Betsey, *three* prints have been done,
> Resemblances strong – as the seller will say;
> But tho' the brave chief *may* be like *every one*,
> Each differs from each, as green differs from grey.
>
> If I know where to fix, I'll be hang'd in my garters!
> To my choice your advice will, dear *Dolly*, add strength;
> Shall I purchase him *sideways*, or have his *three quarters*?
> No, says *Dolly*, best take him, my dear, at *full length*.[98]

It is not clear whether the appearance within a few weeks of two anonymous verses addressing the question of likeness was purely coincidental, or whether the writer 'A. B.' was in some way prompted by the Paoli epigram. The Corsican patriot General Pasquale de Paoli (1725–1807) had just visited Bath when the epigram was published and this piece, despite its simple humorous intent, makes a number of interesting points.[99] It shows how keen people were to see and collect images of famous public figures they had seen; it also shows how several very different depictions of one person could all be perceived as satisfactory likenesses, and it implies that the depiction of the full figure contributes to likeness.

In order to sell their work, artists at all levels were anxious to assure the public that their portraits, or their topographical pictures, were accurate likenesses. Artists' advertisements often include the words 'prove' or 'convince' when referring to likeness. Samuel Percy (1750–1820), working from opposite the Guildhall in Bath, advertised miniature likenesses modelled in stained wax, 'To prove what is asserted, numbers of elevated and conspicuous characters are submitted to public inspection'.[100] In other words, Mr Percy took care to exhibit figures who were bound to be generally recognised, in order to 'prove' his ability to take a likeness. A painter of architectural perspective views, Mr Corton, painted Bath streets and exhibited them as close as possible to the actual view. In 1754 he exhibited these pictures in the lower Assembly Rooms (which were sometimes called Long Rooms): 'To convin [sic] the Gentry of his own Works, he has drawn the View of the Grand Parade, and is to be seen at Mr Wiltshire's Long Room'.[101]

Gainsborough was just as keen as these minor artists to convince the public that he took accurate likenesses, memorably telling the Earl of Dartmouth that likeness was 'the principal beauty & intention of a Portrait', although he had no interest in topographical likeness.[102] He did not pretend that likeness was easily achieved and confessed in 1768 (with reference to a portrait that failed to satisfy the family of the sitter), 'I believe nobody can always succeed alike at all times: I can only say it was not for want of either pains or Inclination'.[103] As the writer 'A. B.' recognised, the rapport established between sitter and artist significantly affected the outcome. The opinions of friends and family could also impinge on the final result. The series of letters from Gainsborough's early Bath sitter George Lucy (fig. 78) show how contentious the issue of likeness could be.[104] On 23 February 1760 George Lucy reported, 'I finished sitting for my Phiz yesterday morning, Mr Wise says tis as like as his, but yr. Humble and his Servant Richard, are of a different Opinion, . . . The Painter told Nixon, he feared he had taken somewhat from the likeness, by his Endeavours to finish it as high as possible, A good excuse for Want of likeness'.[105] 'Mr Wise' was Henry Wise, a close friend and neighbour of Lucy, who had already been painted by Gainsborough.[106] Despite the acrimonious tone of Lucy's letter of 23 February, by 2 March he had completely revised his opinion of his portrait, apparently because his friends all told him what a good likeness it was. On the latter date he wrote, 'My Picture, I'm told, is so like, that people who are Unacquainted with me challenges [sic] it, for a person they have seen in the rooms [ie the Assembly Rooms] . . . I like it so well myself, that if the money holds out, I don't know whether I may not sit for another . . .'.[107]

The whole series of George Lucy's letters demonstrates the problem of creating a likeness that satisfied the client while allowing the artist to maintain his integrity. The correspondence also shows how the very public nature of Gainsborough's rooms enabled friends and family of sitters to react to the likeness (or lack of likeness) even before a portrait was finished, and thereby intervene in the relationship between artist and sitter at a very early stage. Another recently discovered letter from Gainsborough himself further underlines the balancing act required in order to please sitter and close family and the wider public. This was written in London in

78 Thomas Gainsborough (1727–1788), *George Lucy (1714–1786)* 1760 or 1761, oil on canvas, 30 × 25 inches (76.2 × 63.5 cm), Charlecote Park, The Fairfax-Lucy Collection (The National Trust).

1778, to the Revd Sir William Lowther, a wealthy Yorkshire clergyman.[108] It shows Gainsborough at the height of his London career preoccupied by the very same problems he encountered at the beginning of his residence in Bath 'I am sorry I have not succeeded in the likeness to the satisfaction of your sons; every body who knows you. that saw the Picture at my House, seem'd struck with the likeness . . .'.

Painters such as Gainsborough and Hoare, working at full-scale, had to fulfil the double obligation of creating a likeness that would satisfy the sitter's immediate circle and the exhibition-going public. Their portraits had to succeed at a distance and at close quarters, not just physically, but psychologically. Miniature painters, who abounded in Bath (several of whom were close friends of Gainsborough), had a simpler task. By the very nature of their work, they had only the immediate friends and family of the sitter to please. An unpublished letter from a Bath visitor Margaret Luttrell illustrates the function of the portrait miniature better than almost any other contemporary document.[109] Mrs Luttrell of Dunster Castle in Somerset was writing from Bath to her husband Henry Fownes Luttrell, in May 1759. Her husband's portrait had recently been painted by Samuel Collins, the Bath-based miniaturist to whom Ozias Humphry was apprenticed.[110] She wrote, 'I waited this morning on Mr Collins where I had ye Pleasure my dear of looking on your

Face, & tomorrow evening I shall have you in my own Possession, & then I can view you as often as I please, & really its a great satisfaction to look at anything so like a Person one Loves.' Collins was known to Gainsborough. Gainsborough gave him as a present a small landscape drawing now in the British Museum and also painted or drew his portrait.[111] That Gainsborough was also friendly with the miniaturists Simon Pine and Ozias Humphry has already been mentioned, and miniaturists Jeremiah Meyer and Samuel Cotes were other long-term friends.[112] It is worth considering Gainsborough's association with the intimate art of miniature-painting since it was in Bath that he created several small-scale portraits, which although not miniatures, are different from his standard-size canvases and from the 'portraits-in-little' of the East Anglian period.

Gainsborough seems to have naturally moved to a smaller than usual format when painting members of his family. In general, after moving to Bath, he never used a canvas smaller than the standard thirty by twenty-five inch 'three-quarter' size for commissioned oil portraits, but there are smaller oils of his niece Susan Gardiner, brother Humphrey Gainsborough and his nephew Gainsborough Dupont (fig. 62).[113] The portrait of Dupont is on a canvas of just over 17 × 14 inches, the others on 24 × 20 inch canvases, a standard size, but not one generally used by Gainsborough. Another small portrait of the Bath period is *The Pitminster Boy* (fig. 111), a youth who is said to have carried the artist's materials when he was painting in the Taunton area near the homes of his friends Coplestone Bampfylde and Goodenough Earle.[114] All these small portraits depict the sitters at less than life size and are clearly private rather than public images, destined to hang in bedrooms or dressing rooms rather than the principal rooms of the house. It was also in Bath that Gainsborough executed several small pastel and chalk portraits. These included portraits of his wife, Gainsborough Dupont and a few of important sitters such as the Duchess of Bedford and Duchess of Buccleuch.[115] William Hoare's great success with pastel made it a favourite medium in Bath, taken up eagerly by the young Ozias Humphry and Thomas Lawrence. Requiring no drying time, it was ideal for a resort town. Despite these advantages, Gainsborough never felt comfortable with pastel and disliked its propensity to smudge, as he told Edward Stratford in a letter of 1771.[116] He seems to have abandoned it altogether after his move to London.

One of the beauties of the miniature or small-scale portrait was that it could capture a moment in the life of the sitter. Large exhibition portraits were required to represent a longer-term public view of the sitter. The nature of this problem for artists is summed up by the Revd John Penrose's reaction on seeing (in the flesh) Pitt the Elder in the Pump Room in Bath. Pitt, he recorded, 'is exactly like his Prints, only his Prints are much younger'.[117] The prints he knew were most probably the several mezzotints after William Hoare's oil portrait which had become a standard image of the great man.[118] The issue of the ageing of sitters and the changing of fashion was also taken up by Ozias Humphry in his discussion of Gainsborough's early Bath portraits. *James Quin* (fig. 164), he noted, was a particularly satisfactory likeness as the actor was painted towards the end of his life and his appearance changed little after the picture was completed.[119]

Rice Charleton, with his plain coat and full-bottomed wig, part of the 'uniform' of his profession, was not subject to the vagaries of fashion and his portrait likewise remained an acceptable likeness. Women, whose dress could change dramatically from one season to the next, presented the greatest difficulty to the artist. Reynolds's approach was sometimes to generalise or classicise the costume of his sitters so that it took on a timeless quality, but Gainsborough declined to paint what he called 'fancied' dress, always preferring to paint the sitter exactly as seen, even if this might lead to requests for repainting in later years.[120] In the portrait of Ann Ford the hair has clearly been repainted, reflecting the fuller hairstyles of around 1770 and the Byams, of course, were redressed within a year or two.

At the conclusion of the epigram about General Paoli, Dolly advises her friend Betsey to buy a full-length print. Arline Meyer has shown how Jonathan Richardson's *Essay on the Theory of Painting*, published in 1715, sets out the aims of portraiture for British artists.[121] Two recurring themes in Richardson's thesis are 'air' and 'attitude'. The term 'air', as used in the eighteenth century, denoted 'the general appearance, or the mien or manner of a person', while the choice of 'attitude' for a figure determined the full expression of character. Richardson discussed only the full-length figure, recognising, as Meyer says, that 'character could not be fully expressed merely by physiognomy'.[122] As we shall see, Gainsborough had certainly read Richardson and it must have been his shared belief in the importance of the whole figure that lead him to take such elaborate steps to 'set' the groundwork of his portraits before he painted the face.[123]

Gainsborough did not send all his best portraits of the Bath period to London exhibitions. Nevertheless most of those that were not sent to London were publicly exhibited in the artist's rooms in Abbey Street and the Circus. Sitters were probably disappointed if their portraits were *not* seen in Gainsborough's rooms and, as George Lucy's correspondence shows, friends and family were quick to voice their reaction to the pictures, even before they were finished. No wonder Gainsborough 'was very familiar and loose in his conversation to his intimate acquaintance; but *knew his own value*; was reserved; and maintained an importance with his sitters . . .'.[124] Ellis Waterhouse was the first to demonstrate how the transition between the portraits of *Ann Ford* and *Lady Molyneux*, via *Mary, Countess Howe* and *Mrs Portman*, expresses the passage of the artist's career in Bath. Waterhouse did not, perhaps, appreciate the extent to which Gainsborough's progress was exposed to the public gaze.[125]

6

Portraits 'for Bread' and Portraits for Friends

The great majority of Gainsborough's Bath sitters were men and women who came to his painting rooms in Abbey Street and the Circus as paying clients, having been made aware of his abilities as a portrait painter either through a visit to one of his showrooms, through seeing paintings in a London exhibition, or through personal recommendation. Of approximately three hundred and eighty portraits painted in Bath, around one third were of titled people, either members of the aristocracy or people with conferred titles. It is often suggested that Gainsborough's practice fell off towards the end, but of the portraits that can with any certainty be assigned to Abbey Street or the Circus, 150 can be dated to Abbey Street (1760–66) and 170 to the Circus (1767–74). This would suggest a fairly consistent rate of work over the whole period. Around seventeen to twenty portraits can be identified with the time the artist spent in lodgings in 1758, 1759 and before June 1760, but this number could well be expanded.[1]

Gainsbrough's attitude to the visiting aristocracy, his most important client group, was ambivalent. In a letter to the Hon. Constantine Phipps, dated Bath, 1772, he wrote,

> By G— You are the only Great Man, except George Pitt, that I care a farthing for, or would wear out a pair of Shoes in seeking after; long-headed cunning people, and rich fools are so plentiful in our country that I don't fear getting now & then a Face to paint for Bread; but a Man of Genius, with truth & simplicity, sense & Good-nature, I think worth his weight in Gold.[2]

On another occasion Gainsborough is supposed to have complained to Garrick that portraiture forced him to 'stew' in 'an elegant carpeted damn'd dungeon, with *two* windows *shut*, and *one half-open*, to paint *fools' heads*!', a remark that might be regarded as merely apocryphal, were not the image conjured up so uncannily like the arrangement of the Abbey Street painting room, with its tripartite window and its proximity to the heat and steam of the public baths.[3]

Whatever his strictures concerning 'rich fools', Gainsborough was in fact on friendly terms with a great many of his moneyed and aristocratic patrons. To the Duke of Bedford he wrote in 1768 appealing for the Duke's support of his friend the musician William Jackson, 'Your Grace knows that I am an <u>Original</u> and therefore I hope will be the more ready to pardon this monstrous freedom'.[4] To the Earl of Dartmouth he confessed himself 'a Wild Goose', unable or unwilling to go along with prevailing taste for clothing female sitters in 'fancied Dresses'.[5] The tenor of these and other letters suggest that the artist was not being entirely honest with Constantine Phipps and did in fact enjoy the company of a number of noble families with whom he came in contact in Bath. He was soon sufficiently confident to dictate terms to these clients, and in this he was not alone; William Hoare was equally at ease in all company and able to set his own parameters. When in 1774 the Duchess of Kingston demanded that her portrait in widow's weeds should include bones scattered at her feet, one contemporary observed approvingly, 'Hoare wd not comply with *that*'.[6] There is evidence that the self-confidence expressed by Hoare and Gainsborough in their dealings with clients was the cause of some bitterness amongst lesser artists. A minor portrait painter John Warren, who came to Bath in 1776, two years after Gainsborough's departure, reported, 'from what I can learn . . . [Gainsborough] was uncommonly rude & uncivil to artists in general, & was even haughty to his employers . . .'.[7] This opinion contrasts strongly with an earlier view that Gainsborough was a model of gentlemanly politeness, but might be partly explained by Thicknesse's assertion in 1773 that, 'though he is a shy man he knows he is one of the first geniuses in Europe'.[8]

As well as his portraits of visitors to Bath, the artist also painted members of the local community. Unlike a number of his fellow artists, Gainsborough does not appear to have had any connections with Freemasonry, but he was linked with several more loosely associated groups including musicians and members of the medical profession. A third area of interest centres on a group that may be termed 'cultural Jacobites', men and women who through family ties were linked with opposition to the Hanoverian succession in the earlier years of the century.

79 Thomas Gainsborough (1727–1788), *Carl Fiedrich Abel (1725–1787)* c. 1765, oil on canvas, 49 × 39 inches (124.5 × 99 cm), The National Portrait Gallery, London.

The two great showpiece portraits that marked the beginning and end of Gainsborough's Bath career are both of musicians, the portrait of Ann Ford exhibited at Abbey Street in 1760 and that of Johann Christian Fischer (fig. 82) shown at the Circus in 1774. Gainsborough probably regarded some of the musicians he encountered in Bath as closer to his ideal of a 'Man of Genius, with truth and simplicity' than many of the 'great men' who also crossed his path. For this reason he may have painted a number of the musicians not 'for Bread', but as gifts, show pictures, or even in order to assist the performer in his or her career. In 1977 Lindsay Stainton analysed the artist's relationship with musicians in the exhibition and accompanying catalogue, *Gainsborough and his Musical Friends*, and in 1988 the exhibition *A Nest of Nightingales* focused on the Linley family, demonstrating their importance to Bath and to Gainsborough in particular.[9] Since that time more has been discovered about Gainsborough's musical life in Bath.

The artist's love of music was established long before he came to the west of England. In Ipswich he had been a member of a musical club and had celebrated his friendship with several musicians such as Joseph Gibbs and the Revd John Chafy by painting their portraits.[10] Bath gave him the opportunity to develop his understanding of music in the company of the great European virtuoso performers of the day, including Carl Friedrich Abel (1725–1787) (fig. 79) and his future son-in-law the oboist Johann Christian Fischer (1733–1800) (fig. 82). Only London or Dublin offered music of a comparable standard. Music was central to the social life of Bath, with the practice of private music-making as important a feature of everyday life as the regular ritual of attending public concerts. When Philip Thicknesse encouraged Gainsborough's move to Bath he must have been fully aware of just how important this aspect of the city's cultural life could be to his protegé: his own brother Ralph Thicknesse had been reckoned 'the best Gentleman Player on the Fiddle in *England*' (and had died while taking part in a concert breakfast in Bath in 1741) and Thicknesse himself was a competent fiddle player and wrote a book on musical theory.[11]

The intensity of music-making, both private and public, is vividly illustrated in contemporary records. As has been mentioned above, Oliver Goldsmith drew attention to the fact that at concert breakfasts 'Persons of rank and fortune who can perform are admitted into the orchestra, and find a pleasure in joining with the performers'.[12] It was not even necessary for amateur musicians to bring instruments to Bath, as these were readily available for hire. The quality of these instruments could be good. Lord Herbert, referring to a cello of his own, wrote, 'It is not an instrument of the first water, & I daresay you may hire a better one at Bath'.[13] Music teachers were on hand to instruct ladies and gentlemen in their own lodgings, one of the best known, Thomas Orpin, being a near neighbour of Gainsborough in Abbey Street.[14] A favourite lodging house for visiting professional musicians was the tailor Thomas Guest's house, just round the corner in Abbey Green, where Fischer lodged in 1769 and 1772 and probably also on other occasions.[15] When Gainsborough lived in Abbey Street, the Linleys were also close to Orpin and the Guests in Abbey Green.[16] Of those professional musicians who were to become Gainsborough's lifelong friends, several visited Bath in the early 1760s and their association with the artist can safely be said to date back to the Abbey Street period of his career. Abel, to whom he was especially close, was in Bath performing at Wiltshire's Assembly Rooms (fig. 8) in February 1760 and again in October and November 1761.[17] The extent to which Abel endeared himself to Bath audiences in the 1760s can be judged from the subscription list to his *Six Sonatas for the Harpsichord*, which includes the names of 'Mr. Gainsborough, Painter' and 'Miss Allen, of Prior Park', 'Miss Bennett of Bath', 'Mr Linley, Organist of Bath', 'Mr Richards, Musician in Bath', 'Mr Townsend, of Bath' and 'Mr Underwood, Musical Instrument-maker, in Bath, 6 Setts'.[18]

When Abel died in 1787 Gainsborough told a friend that he had loved Abel from the moment he first heard him play, commenting that 'If Abel was not so great a man as Handel it was because caprice had ruined music before he ever took up the pen'.[19] It is now known that Gainsborough was associated with Bath's keenest Handelian, the Bath Abbey organist Thomas Chilcot (c. 1707–1766). At the time of Chilcot's sudden death in November 1766 Gainsborough owed him £1.6.0 'for Teaching'.[20] There is no way of telling whether this music tuition was for Gainsborough himself or one of his daughters (Margaret annoyed him with her 'damnd Jangling upon the Harpsicord'), but the link with Chilcot is of great interest.[21] Chilcot was appointed organist of the Abbey Church in January 1726 on the death of Josias Priest, to whom he had been apprenticed since 1721.[22] The post of Abbey organist was the most prestigious musical appointment in Bath at this time, but was not well paid (at £37.12.0 a year), so Chilcot also took pupils, hired out and tuned harpsichords and spinnets, and probably loaned music from his large private library at his house in Wood Street, off Queen Square.[23] Among the treasures in this library were Handel manuscripts including the great composer's own theatre copy of *Muzio Scevola* and a copy of *Deborah*.[24] Chilcot also organised concerts and performed in the Assembly Rooms, the Pump Room (where he was a member of the orchestra), the theatre and at private parties, usually playing the harpsichord. Many of these musical events combined Chilcot's own music with that of Handel and other composers, both English and Continental. One such concert, at Wiltshire's Assembly Rooms in November 1749, featured Chilcot playing a harpsichord concerto and concluded with Handel's *Atalanta*.[25] At another at the Orchard Street Theatre on 30 April 1753 Thomas Chilcot conducted a performance of Handel's *Judas Maccabeus*.[26] Handel himself visited Bath in 1749, when he is said to have stayed with the actor James Quin in Pierrepont Street, and in 1751, when he is believed to have been treated by the Hospital surgeon Jeremiah Peirce.[27] He may, in fact have been a regular visitor, since his patron the Duke of Chandos had substantial property interests in Bath and was one of the first to employ the architect John Wood in the city, between 1727 and 1730.[28] In Keynsham, near Bath, where the Duke's cousin owned land and property, Handel donated an offertory plate engraved 'S. John's Church Keynsham G. F. Handel 1750'.[29] Handel must have met Chilcot in Bath, and he evidently admired the organist's compositions, subscribing to his *Six Suites of Lessons for Harpsichord* in 1734 and his *Twelve English Songs with their Symphonies* in 1744.[30] It must have been Chilcot who introduced Gainsborough to the organist and composer John Stanley (1712–1786) who sat for his portrait, perhaps in 1763, when Gainsborough's bank account shows a payment of £40 by a 'John Stanley'.[31]

One of Chilcot's other published works, his *Six Concertos for Harpsichord* of 1756 (fig. 80) was dedicated to Lady

Six CONCERTOS For the HARPSICHORD

Accompanied with,

Four VIOLINS, VIOLA, VIOLONCELLO, and BASSO-RIPIENO;

Dedicated,

To the Right Honourable

LADY ELIZ: BATHURST,

By

Thomas Chilcot

ORGANIST OF BATH.

Engrav'd by Will: Clark.

London:

Printed for John Johnson, at the Harp & Crown in Cheapside.

1756.

81 *(left)* Thomas Gainsborough (1727–1788), *Thomas Linley senior (1733–1795)* c. 1771, oil on canvas, $29\frac{1}{2} \times 24\frac{1}{2}$ inches (75 × 62.2 cm), Dulwich Picture Gallery, London. Linley is holding his *Elegies for three Voices*, published in 1770.

80 *(facing page)* Title page from Thomas Chilcot's *Six Concertos for Harpsichord* 1756, $12\frac{5}{8} \times 9\frac{1}{16}$ inches (32 × 23 cm), The Bodleian Library, University of Oxford, Tenbury Mus. C. 71 (8).

Elizabeth Bathurst, daughter of Charles, Third Earl of Ailesbury and wife of the Hon. Benjamin Bathurst (1711–1767) of Siddington, near Cirencester in Gloucestershire. Lady Bathurst had promised to pay Chilcot an annuity but died before the arrangement was formalised.[32] The Bathursts were friends and political allies of the Dukes of Beaufort and members of the Bathurst family commissioned two portraits from Gainsborough.[33] The connection between Chilcot and the Bathursts lends some weight to the theory that it was at Badminton that Chilcot first encountered his most famous pupil Thomas Linley (1733–1795) (fig. 81). A report in the *Bath Herald* of 9 June 1798 claims that the boy's musical potential was 'discovered' when Thomas Chilcot paid a visit to Badminton and overheard young Linley singing. It is quite likely that Chilcot, in common with most of his musical contemporaries, would have travelled to great houses in the neighbourhood to perform at private parties, and it is to be expected that one or more of the Bathurst properties and Badminton were among those he visited. It may never be known exactly how Thomas Linley came to be apprenticed to Chilcot, but he was soon earning a living as a performer of harpsichord music, a singer (especially of music by Handel) and a teacher. He quickly became one of the leading figures in Bath's musical life.

Kenneth James has shown in his unpublished dissertation of 1987, 'Concert Life in Eighteenth-Century Bath' (the most complete study to date on this subject) that a power struggle for musical supremacy took place in Bath throughout the 1760s, with Thomas Linley attempting to take control from the Master of Ceremonies Samuel Derrick.[34] Gainsborough did not have a high opinion of Derrick: with reference to an old image of Shakespeare that he was attempting to use as a source for his own Shakespeare portrait, he complained bitterly, 'a Stupider Face I never beheld Except D[erric]k's'.[35] It seems very likely that Gainsborough might have been one of a group who, in 1763, formed a 'Bath Musical Society' which promoted its own concerts in response to Derrick's ineffectual leadership.[36] These Musical Society concerts continued until 1766, and in 1767 Linley was personally promoting a number of independent concerts, including one which featured William Jackson directing performances of his own settings of Milton's *Lycidas* and Wharton's *Ode to Fancy*.[37]

At the beginning of the 1769–70 season, following the death of Derrick, Linley finally found himself in a position

82 Thomas Gainsborough (1727–1788), *Johann Christian Fischer (1733–1800)* 1774, oil on canvas, $89\frac{1}{2} \times 58\frac{3}{4}$ inches (227.3 × 149.2 cm), The Royal Collection © 2001, Her Majesty Queen Elizabeth II.

to dominate Bath's concert life and in 1771 he was made director of music at the new Upper Assembly Rooms, the new focal point for Bath society, where Gainsborough's sitter Captain William Wade presided as Master of Ceremonies. Gainsborough's portrait of Thomas Linley, which can be dated to the early 1770s on the grounds of style, may well have been exhibited in the artist's rooms, just round the corner from the Assembly Rooms, just as the sitter took up his post. Nearly all of Gainsborough's portraits of musicians painted in Bath were of men who were closely associated with Linley and so, at one level, the exhibition of these pictures in his rooms or in London might be interpreted as a gesture of support for the Linley cause. The portrait of the composer William Jackson, whose music Linley played and promoted, was exhibited at the Royal Academy in 1770.[38] A portrait of *Giusto Ferdinando Tenducci* (fig. 83), which exists in two different versions, has been loosely dated to the period 1773–5, and may have been painted and exhibited in Bath. Tenducci was first introduced to Bath by Linley, and became a great favourite with Bath audiences.[39] Whether Gainsborough was commissioned to paint the portraits of members of the Linley family, Jackson, Abel and Tenducci, or painted them as show pictures and then gave them to the sitters, is not on record. His grand full-length of Johann Christian Fischer (fig. 82), now in the Royal collection, was certainly painted without expectation of payment.

The portrait of Fischer is one of Gainsborough's finest male portraits and may be considered the finale to the Bath period of his career.[40] The Fischer we see here is very different from the weasel-faced individual Rowlandson and other caricaturists recorded (fig. 84). Gainsborough's full-length was exhibited at the Royal Academy in 1780, two months after Fischer's marriage to Mary Gainsborough, and is usually dated to 1780, but was in fact painted in Bath in 1774. Martin Postle has revealed how Fischer was painted over the abandoned portrait of Shakespeare, on which the artist was working in the summer of 1768.[41] In a letter of 4 August 1774, Thicknesse mentioned that his wife (the former Ann Ford) saw a portrait of Fischer 'at full length . . . in Scarlet', 'a picture *not to be paid for*', at Gainsborough's house in Bath, and elsewhere Thicknesse expressly says that the Fischer portrait was finished before Gainsborough left Bath.[42] If the portrait of Ann Ford was intended to launch Gainsborough in Bath when it was shown in Abbey Street in 1760, that of Fischer might be regarded as a springboard for the artist's move to London when it was hung at the Circus in 1774.[43]

While Gainsborough's portrait of Thomas Linley may be linked with Linley's appointment to the directorship of music at the new Upper Assembly Rooms, another Linley project was represented in Gainsborough's rooms by the portrait of Revd Dr William Dodd (Prince of Wales Museum, Bombay).[44] It appears that the display of Dodd's portrait in

83 Thomas Gainsborough (1727–1788), *Giusto Ferdinando Tenducci (c. 1734–1790)* c. 1773–5, oil on canvas, 29 × 24½ inches (77.5 × 64 cm), whereabouts unknown.

84 Thomas Rowlandson (1756–1827), *'Two Musicians', here identified as Johann Christian Fischer and Carl Friedrich Abel* c. 1795–1800, pen and ink and watercolour, 7⅛ × 6⅞ inches (18.2 × 17.5 cm), Trustees, Cecil Higgins Art Gallery, Bedford, England. Abel first visited Bath in 1760 and Fischer in 1769. Rowlandson's drawing, which must date from the end of the century, derives from earlier sources including a print of 1773 by James Bretherton entitled *Concerto Spirituale* after a drawing by Henry Bunbury.

85 *(above)* Interior of the Margaret Chapel, Bath, from an advertisement for James Steers' cycle school in the *Bath and County Graphic*, I, no. 7, November 1896.

86 *(right)* Margarets Buildings, Bath, from Brock Street, photograph, 1919. This early twentieth-century view includes a glimpse of the Margaret Chapel, half-way down the street, on the left. A Miss Gainsborough, probably a great-niece of the artist, kept a lodging house in the second or third building on the left from 1789 to 1799.

Gainsborough's rooms in the autumn of 1773 was timed to coincide with the opening of the Margaret Chapel, at which Dodd presided, on 3 October 1773.[45] The Margaret Chapel situated between the Circus and the Royal Crescent, was built by Thomas Linley's father, the Badminton builder William Linley. Thomas Linley was one of its three proprietors and its first organist.[46] This new building (figs 85 and 86) was one of several Church of England proprietary chapels built in Bath in the second half of the eighteenth century in response to a growing need for places of worship for visitors, and it must be to this that Gainsborough referred in his letter to William Dodd when he said, 'I have not neglected the chapel one day, since I took a liking to it, nor don't mean ever to quit it'.[47] The opening of the Margaret Chapel was, no doubt, a grand social occasion, which put Dodd in the spotlight, and Gainsborough's simultaneous exhibition of his portrait, only yards away at the Circus, cannot have been purely coincidental.

Bath musicians seem to have played a large part in Gainsborough's life in the city. From Chilcot he may have gained a special understanding of Handel and through Chilcot and the Linleys he met a number of virtuoso performers who not only inspired his own music-making, but prompted him to paint some of his most sensitive portraits. Thomas Linley's professional progress in Bath followed a similar pattern to Gainsborough's, with the development of the upper town and new Assembly Rooms offering fresh opportunities for him, as they did for the painter. Like Gainsborough, Linley involved himself in property – in his case a proprietary chapel – as a means of securing a secondary income. Both men were creative artists of inexhaustible energy and talent, but also pragmatists, and their common understanding of, and respect for, the workings of Bath society ultimately placed them at the head of their respective professions in the town.

While some of the best musicians in Europe played in Bath at this time, medical men (that second group with which the artist was linked) were the most powerful of the professional classes working and resident in the city. By becoming a friend of several of the leading doctors, Gainsborough placed himself as close as it was possible to be to the seat of local power and influence. The economy of Bath depended on its credibility as a spa and this, in turn, relied on the doctors' interpretation of the efficacy of the waters. They prescribed a regime of either drinking the water, in strictly regulated quantities and at certain times of day, or bathing in it, depending on the nature of people's illnesses. Several local doctors, including Rice Charleton, published treatises on the Bath waters, thereby widely advertising the spa and assuring the public that its benefits could be measured by sound scientific analysis.[48] Cynics held that the doctors wielded far too much power, a view expressed in many satirical prints including *The Knights of the Baythe, or the One Headed Corporation*, attributed to William Hibbart and published in Bath in 1763 (fig. 87). Here, to the left of the composition, a group of doctors, who are also members of the Bath Corporation, are depicted with skull heads, brandishing knives, ready to prey on the sick. The popular perception that doctors reaped huge financial rewards at the expense of the vulnerable was perhaps partly justified, and some Bath doctors did become very wealthy, among them Dr William Oliver who had a country retreat, 'Trevarno', near Shockerwick, three miles from Bath; Dr Abel Moysey who acquired a rural residence at Hinton Charterhouse, outside Bath; and Dr Rice Charleton who developed an estate at Woodhouse, north of Bristol.[49] Nearly every Bath doctor of note of the mid-eighteenth century had his portrait drawn or painted by William Hoare or Gainsborough.[50]

William Hoare, through his early association with the Bath Hospital, was able to use the Hospital as a showcase, placing several of his pictures there in the 1760s, notably his large canvas of *Dr Oliver and Mr Peirce . . . Examining Patients* (fig. 11).[51] Gainsborough, as a newcomer, is unlikely to have tried to compete with Hoare for access to the Hospital walls, but he seems to have been eager to paint members of the medical profession, and to display their portraits in his rooms and in London. As Gainsborough's reputation grew, the doctors were no doubt equally keen to see their likenesses in Gainsborough's prestigious rooms. As with the musical portraits, several of the portraits of doctors were 'not to be paid for'.

In the hierarchy of the medical profession in Bath the Physicians to the Hospital (of which there were generally two at any given time) were at the top of the tree. Their appointment to the Hospital was honorary, but the prestige attached to the post ensured a flourishing private practice. Their position was rather like the one enjoyed by Chilcot as Abbey organist. Surgeons, styled 'Mr' rather than 'Dr', were less well paid, while apothecaries were the most lowly, although

87 Attributed to William Hibbart (1727–1808), *The Knights of the Baythe, or the One Headed Corporation* 1763, etching (trimmed) $7\frac{7}{8} \times 14\frac{1}{2}$ inches (20 × 36.8 cm), published 1763, Victoria Art Gallery, Bath and North East Somerset Council. The print shows Ralph Allen surrounded by members of the Corporation including in the group on the left, doctors with skull heads, and apothecaries with jar heads. On the extreme left is Walter Wiltshire, with a waggon head.

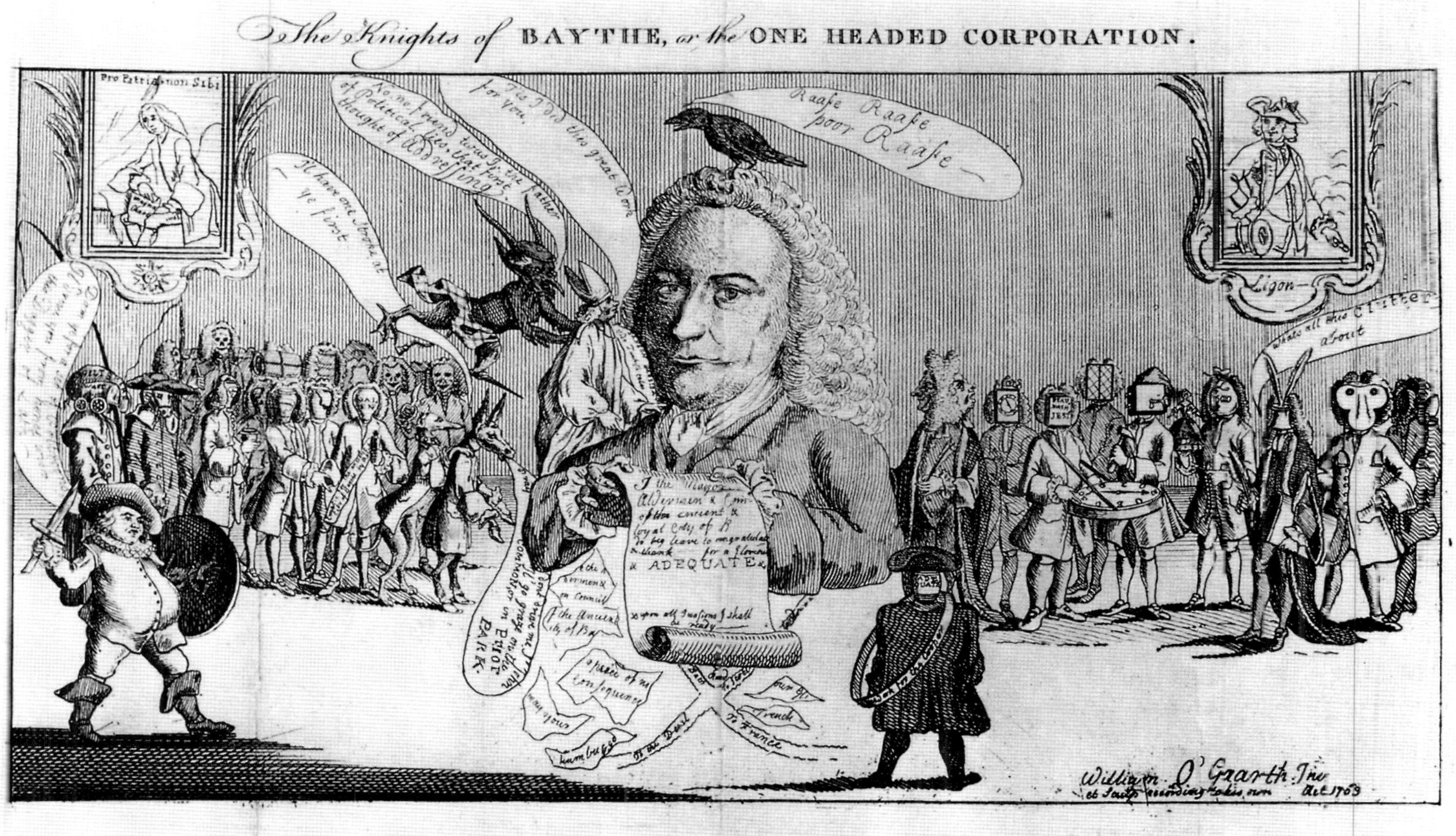

88 *(above)* Thomas Gainsborough (1727–1788), *Doctor Rice Charleton (1710–1789)* 1763–4, oil on canvas, 90 × 60 inches (229 × 152.5 cm), Holburne Museum of Art, Bath.

89 *(right)* William Hoare (1707–1792), *Doctor Rice Charleton (1710–1789)* c. 1755, pencil and red chalk, $7^{1}/_{4}$ × 6 inches (18.5 × 15.2 cm), private collection.

90 Thomas Gainsborough (1727–1788) *Doctor Ralph Schomberg (1714–1792)* c. 1770, oil on canvas, $91^{3}/_{4} \times 60^{1}/_{2}$ inches (233 × 153.6 cm). National Gallery, London.

in Bath the demand for their services was such that they too could make a handsome living. Two of the Physicians to the Hospital, Dr Abel Moysey and Dr Rice Charleton (fig. 88) were Gainsborough's personal doctors, and both were painted by him in 1763–4.[52] Charleton was also well known to William Hoare who drew his likeness more than once in the mid-1750s (fig. 89).[53] Dr Ralph Schomberg (fig. 90) was a Governor, but never succeeded to the coveted post of Physician to the Hospital. Schomberg and Charleton were depicted by Gainsborough out of doors, strolling in a landscape. Both doubtless aspired to the lifestyle their predecessor William Oliver had established for himself earlier in the century. Dr Oliver, the first Physician to the Hospital, took special pleasure in his country residence and its fine views. Looking west, as he described, 'The city crosses the vale about three miles from me, and creeps up Lansdown; and about the same distance beyond it rises Mr. Langton's Park, a knowle of which, well wooded, terminates my view' (figs 37 and 91).[54]

Gainsborough also painted surgeon Philip Ditcher (fig. 92), who was Mayor of Bath in 1774, and one of Bath's most eminent apothecaries Thomas Haviland (fig. 93) and his son, apothecary James Haviland (fig. 94).[55] Of all these pictures connected with the medical profession, two, the portraits of Moysey and Ditcher, are known for certain to have been gifts rather than commissioned works, and it seems likely that others were also painted without payment, either in gratitude for medical care, or as show pictures, the doctors possessing some of the best-known faces in Bath.[56]

Gainsborough's friendship with several of Bath's eminent doctors placed him within one of the most influential sections of Bath society and must have had a beneficial effect on his portrait practice. Rather more unexpectedly, it appears that Gainsborough's technique, and in particular his drawing technique of the late 1760s and early 1770s, was also affected by the medical presence in Bath. The artist was probably encouraged in his technical experiments by a keen amateur apothecary who happened to be a fellow resident in the

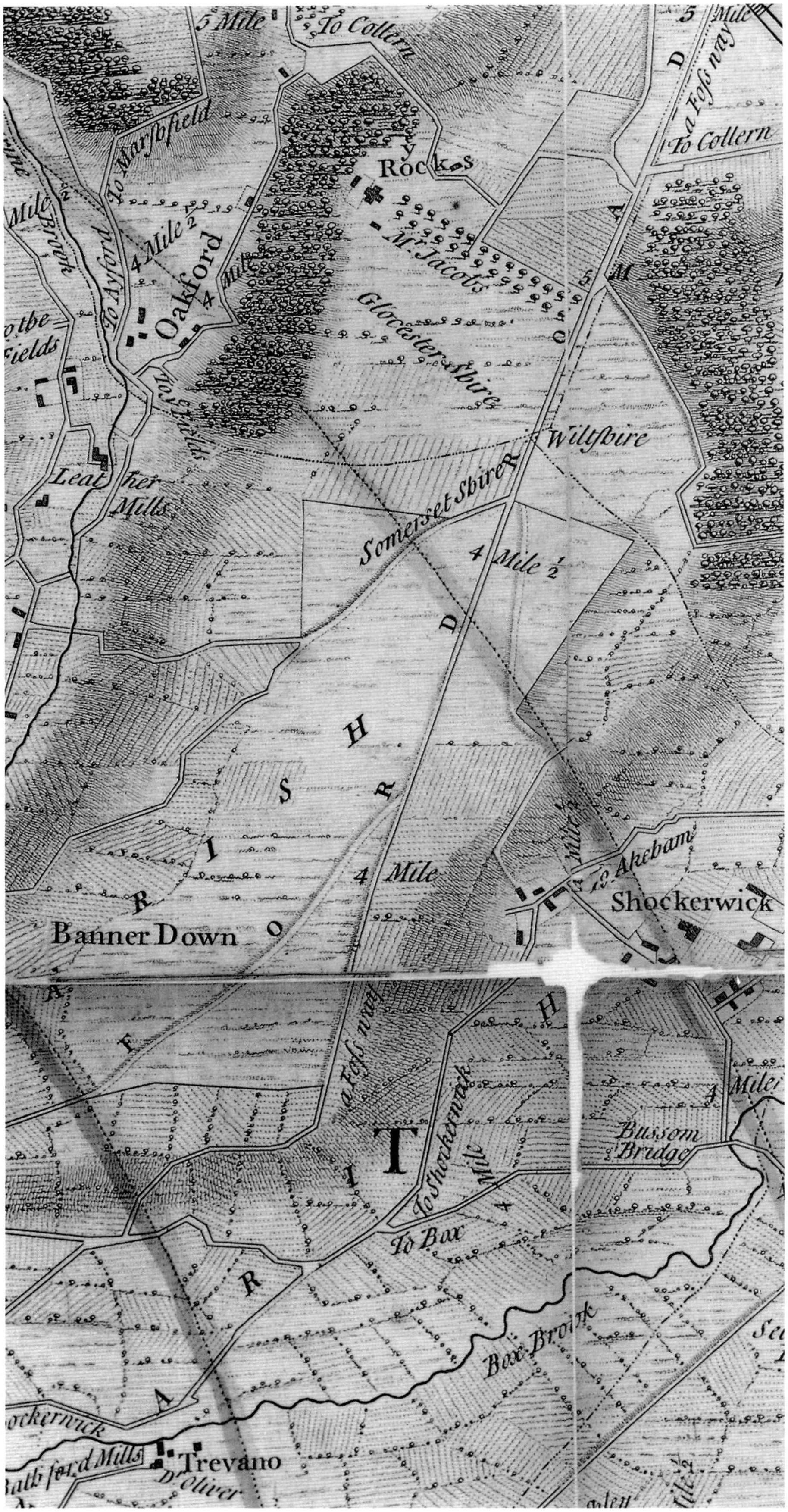

92 *(above)* Thomas Gainsborough (1727–1788), *Philip Ditcher, surgeon (d. 1781), Mayor of Bath in 1774* 1774 (completed later), oil on canvas, 50 × 40 inches (127 × 101.7 cm), private collection.

91 *(left)* Thomas Thorpe, *An Actual Survey of the City of Bath . . . and of Five Miles Round* (detail) 1742, engraving (the whole) $75\frac{5}{8}$ × 77 inches (192.1 × 195.6 cm), published 1742, Bath Record Office, Bath. This actual size detail shows the area to the east of Bath including Trevarno, Dr William Oliver's country residence between Shockerwick and Bath and, further north, The Rocks, John Jacob's country house and garden.

93 *(facing page left)* Thomas Gainsborough (1727–1788), *Thomas Haviland, apothecary (1711–1770)* 1761–3, oil on canvas, 50 × 40 inches (127 × 101.7 cm), Nationalmuseum, Stockholm. Haviland holds a copy of William Lewis's *Experimental History of the Materia Medica*, published in 1761; behind are examples from Haviland's well-known collection of fossils and geological specimens from the Bath region.

94 *(facing page right)* Thomas Gainsborough (1727–1788), *James Haviland, apothecary (1747–1779)* c. 1771, oil on canvas, 30 × 25 inches (76.2 × 63.5 cm), private collection, on loan to Gainsborough's house, Sudbury. James Haviland, son of Thomas Haviland, was probably painted around the time of his marriage which took place in July 1771.

Circus. Benjamin Colborne (d. 1793), described by Thicknesse as 'a gentleman of Bath, of large and independent fortune, of great chymical knowledge' lived at 10, Circus from 1768.[57] Colborne was a proprietor of the new Upper Assembly Rooms and member of its Furnishing Committee at the time Gainsborough gave his portrait of Captain William Wade to the Rooms; he was also a Governor of the Hospital and one of its Treasurers from 1770.[58] He seems to have had a particular interest in the arts and was the inventor of a varnish for use over watercolours. It is not known precisely when Colborne developed this varnish, but an unpublished letter to Ozias Humphry, dated 24 March 1771, instructs Humphry on how to prepare paper for varnished watercolours,

> I will contrive to send you some Vernish in a day or 2; but am afraid it will not be as Clare as I could wish; but if you will put it into a Window where ye Sun Comes it will be clare in a day or two ye reason it is not fine is it was made but yesterday. If you want to paint on Paper you must prepare yr paper first; either with thin Gum Arabic Water; or w.ch is better the Mucilage of Quince Seed; which you may buy one penniworth at ye Herb Shops in your Garden [i.e. Covent Garden] or at ye Drugists; and pour on them a tea cup of hot water & when grown thick squeeze it thro' a clean rag for use & Brush it over yr Paper you intend to paint on. by this means the Paper will bear out the Vernish otherwise the paper will absorb the Vernish & never appear Glossy or fine.
>
> As for mixing your colours with ye Vernish [I] have great reason to think it will not answer. Make yr Picture first & then to secure it Vernish it once twice or as often as you think proper but never do it a second time till the first is quite hard. I could wish it was in my power to give you more light in this affair but at this distance; it is not in my power. I wish it may answer yr expectations and am a well wisher to all artists
> From yr most Humble Servant B. Colborne
>
> Bath March ye 24 1771
>
> PS Since I wrote ye above have found some that has been made some time as such have sent that. the longer all Vernishes are adrying the Better provided you Keep the Dust from it. If it does not dry well let me know & I shall be able to send you other that will dry sooner'[59]

It was while he lived at the Circus that Gainsborough began to use varnish over drawings and watercolours and a letter

he wrote to William Jackson in 1773 describes some of his experiments in considerable detail.[60] It is inconceivable that Colborne's and Gainsborough's experiments with varnish that could be used over works on paper, dating from exactly the same period, are unconnected.

There is no doubt that the physicians Rice Charleton and Abel Moysey and surgeon Philip Ditcher were personal friends of Gainsborough and his family, as well as providers of medical care. Another much more shadowy figure, the surgeon Abraham Bath of Chilcompton, may have provided friendship of a different sort, by offering hospitality to the artist during one or more of his landscape sketching expeditions. A persistent local legend links Gainsborough with a house in the once-picturesque village of Chilcompton, near Radstock, in the coal-mining area of Somerset, to the south-west of Bath.[61] The house is now called '1, Gainsborough' (figs 95 a and b) and although it is impossible to be certain who lived there in the 1760s, its occupier appears to have been Abraham Bath, the apothecary and surgeon who ministered to the local population of gentry, farmers and coal miners.[62]

The medical life of Bath seems, therefore, to have affected Gainsborough and his work in several ways. By hanging portraits of doctors in public places both William Hoare and Gainsborough associated themselves with the important charitable work of the Bath Hospital while, at the same time, advertising their own abilities as portrait painters. Gainsborough and his family seem to have benefited from free medical attention in return for portraits, an important consideration at a time when the artist himself nearly died (in the autumn of 1763) and the first signs of his daughter Mary's descent into mental illness made themselves known. The spirit of scientific inquiry engendered by the concentrated presence of doctors and apothecaries, and even amateur apothecaries, seems to have stimulated Gainsborough's experiments with technique. Lastly, although the facts remain sketchy, an out-of-town member of the medical fraternity may, in some way, have aided the painter's landscape career by inviting him to stay in the heart of the Somerset countryside.

Throughout Gainsborough's stay in Bath, reminders of his wife's connection with Badminton regularly resurface. Since the Dukes of Beaufort and members of their family touched almost every aspect of life in Bath, even the two areas just mentioned – its musical and medical life – this is perhaps not so surprising. As we have seen, Badminton may have played a part in introducing Thomas Linley to Thomas Chilcot; it is also a fact that the Fourth Duke of Beaufort was President of the Bath Hospital in 1748 and the Fifth Duke President in 1766.[63] The ties with Gainsborough go deeper, however, and there is evidence to suggest that Gainsborough received valuable patronage from Tories and former Jacobites who had political links with the Dukes of Beaufort. These patrons were often connected with members of the Price family or Bertie Burgh and James Unwin, the Beaufort agents.

Burgh and Unwin's professional position as employees of the Beauforts inevitably placed them in contact with many former Jacobite sympathisers.[64] Although the Jacobites were a spent force politically by the time Gainsborough came to Bath, the culture P. K. Monod has called 'Jacobite sociability' was surprisingly enduring, a phenomenon 'centred on an image of genteel separation, seclusion or retirement', that lasted well in to the 1760s and beyond.[65] As well as patrons from the Price, Jersey, Mostyn, Bathurst, Tynte, Trevelyan, Prowse and Portman families, a number of Gainsborough's personal friends from his early years in Bath can be identified as members of this old Tory network, from Philip Thicknesse to the Revd Richard Graves.[66] It can thus be argued that Mrs Gainsborough's 'secret' parentage had an unseen, but nevertheless real, effect on her husband's career, an effect that went far beyond the obvious financial benefit of the annuity. This is not to say that Gainsborough necessarily allied himself to any particular political set, and many Whigs sat to him, Robert Craggs Nugent, the subject of his first portrait exhibited in

95 a and b 1, Gainsborough, Chilcompton, Somerset, photographs, 1996. An altered house, of the eighteenth century or earlier, where Gainsborough is thought to have stayed during one or more excursions from Bath.

London, being one of them. His early biographer Fulcher did, however, say that Gainsborough was a Tory and more recently Michael Kitson postulated a common (but possibly accidental) thread of Toryism linking Hogarth, Gainsborough and Constable:

> The fact that Hogarth was a Tory may have been largely because the government of the day was Whig; he was contrary by nature. By the same token, Gainsborough may have been a Tory, in so far as he was taken up by George III, merely because his rival, Reynolds, was a Whig. But Constable's Toryism was not accidental at all. It was expressed in his faith in the time-honoured 'rightness' of the English countryside and its practices, which change and radical agitation could only undermine . . .[67]

Gainsborough, too, had a great respect for the traditions of the English countryside, and this, together with his wife's family connections, may have put him in sympathy with many Tories and former Jacobites. The first indication of the 'Jacobite sociability' of the west of England and West Midlands impinging on Gainsborough's life and career can be traced back to the years before the artist came to Bath. From the 1740s Gainsborough was linked with Burgh and Unwin and in 1755 he borrowed money from Captain Edward Wheeler, the man whose death in 1761 resulted in Unwin's retirement to a life of gentlemanly seclusion in Staffordshire.[68] Captain Wheeler was a nephew of John Wheeler (d. 1746) whose wife Anne was a niece of the first Lord Foley, and it was from this John Wheeler that he inherited Wootton Lodge in Staffordshire.[69] Before purchasing Wootton Lodge the Wheeler family had rented Wollaston Hall, Stourbridge, from the Foleys.[70] The Wheelers, like the Foleys and their West Midland associates the Knights, had made their money in the iron industry in the late seventeenth and early eighteenth centuries.[71] Captain Wheeler's will, in which he determines to leave almost everything he has to his friend James Unwin, makes it clear that he is a staunch Jacobite. This may account for his choice of a naval career, since the navy was a sanctuary for many former Jacobites, and this was another area through which Unwin and Wheeler were connected, since Unwin was also employed by the navy.

At the time Gainsborough was negotiating through Unwin to borrow money from Captain Wheeler, he was also benefiting from the support and encouragement of Philip Thicknesse, with whom he was first acquainted in 1753. Thicknesse was, in his youth, a '*gratis* scholar' at Westminster School, 'by the favour of' Dr Robert Freind, the Jacobite headmaster of the school.[72] From these early beginnings, Thicknesse retained an affection for the Jacobite cause, as is illustrated by the fact that he gave a portrait of Prince Charles Edward Stuart to Sir John Dolben in the 1740s.[73]

One of Gainsborough's first Bath commissions in 1758, the posthumous portrait of Viscount Cornbury (fig. 29), was of a prominent Jacobite sympathiser. Cornbury's visit to Rome in 1731 had resulted in a new restoration plot, and at the time of his death in 1753 he was Tory Member of Parliament for Oxford, a city in which Jacobite loyalty was still a force to be reckoned with in the mid-century.[74] As has been shown, this commission was probably the result of an introduction arranged through one of the Prices of Foxley, who, with the Duke of Beaufort's family, were mutual friends of Lord Cornbury. Within a month or two of painting the *Viscount Cornbury* portrait, in the spring of 1759, Gainsborough was engaged on his portrait of Lady Mostyn (fig. 36), a descendant of Sir Charles Somerset of Troy House, Monmouthshire, a lady of impeccable Tory breeding who had married into the most powerful family in Flintshire, in North Wales.[75] Six months or so later Gainsborough was painting the *Son and Daughter of Benjamin Bathurst*.[76] Benjamin Bathurst of Lydney, Gloucestershire, was described as a 'determined Tory'.[77] Less than a year after he settled in Abbey Street he painted a picture for Sir Charles-Kemeys Tynte (1710–1785), a canvas that is now lost, but may have been a half-length portrait of his wife Lady Anne Tynte (d. 1798) who was a childhood friend of William Lee of Hartwell, one of Gainsborough's first Bath sitters.[78] The only record of the Tynte commission is the payment by Sir Charles-Kemeys Tynte of £33.12.0 to Gainsborough on 2 April 1761.[79] A half-length cost fifteen guineas in 1758: it is not known when Gainsborough increased his price for a picture of this size, but he charged forty guineas by 1763. Sir Charles-Kemeys Tynte lived at Halswell in Somerset (fig. 112) but inherited estates in Wales from his staunchly Jacobite uncle Sir Charles Kemeys. In the 1740s both Sir Charles-Kemeys Tynte and his uncle were members of the Third Duke of Beaufort's 'Loyal Brotherhood' that met at the Cocoa Tree in London and Sir Charles was brought in as Member of Parliament for Monmouth in 1745 by the Duke.[80] Correspondence between John Burgh (Bertie's father) and Sir Charles Kemeys provides evidence of the political networking that linked the Burgh, Kemeys, Tynte and Somerset (Beaufort) families.[81] A fellow Tory and neighbour of Sir Charles-Kemeys Tynte, Sir George Trevelyan of Nettleton, also paid Gainsborough for a picture or pictures early in 1761: the £30.10.6 he paid on 24 February may have been for the half-length of his daughter, *Susanna Trevelyan*.[82] Sir George's father Sir John Trevelyan (?1670–1755) was one of those whose names were included in a list of leading Jacobites sent to the Pretender in 1721.[83] The Trevelyans and Tyntes were close friends of Thomas Prowse (c. 1707–1767) Tory Member for Somerset between 1740 and 1767, another early sitter to Gainsborough.[84] One of the most accomplished and sensitive of Gainsborough's full-length female portraits of the Abbey Street period is that of Mrs Anne Portman (fig. 63). Mrs Portman's husband, Henry William Berkeley Portman (c. 1709–1761), was one of those named on a list of the Pretender's most valuable supporters sent to France before the 1745 Rebellion.[85] Henry William Berkeley Portman was a

96 Wootton Lodge, Wootton, Staffordshire, photograph, 1951. James Unwin inherited Wootton Lodge on the death of Edward Wheeler in 1761. He moved there around 1765 and Gainsborough is believed to have stayed there in the summer of 1771.

fellow Member of Parliament for Somerset with Thomas Prowse from 1741 to 1747 and was related to Norborne Berkeley, uncle and Trustee to the Fourth Duke of Beaufort and the person who uncovered Bertie Burgh's misdeeds.[86]

As Hugh Belsey has pointed out, the great Byam family group portrait may have been painted at the instigation of the Bathurst family, since Mrs Louisa Byam's uncle Benjamin Bathurst had already commissioned a double portrait of his children in 1759–60.[87] The Byams themselves also had West Country roots, however. The eighteenth-century Byams were primarily associated with the West Indies where the George Byam of the portrait was born, but the first family member to travel to Antigua, Lieutenant-General William Byam (1622–1670), haled originally from Somerset.[88] George Byam's first cousin William Byam (1753–1830) married, in 1781, Mary Burgh, a first cousin of Bertie Burgh.[89]

Although Bath drew visitors from all over England it is clear that a great many of Gainsborough's earliest Bath patrons were members of interrelated Tory and former Jacobite families from Somerset, Gloucestershire, Herefordshire and Monmouthshire. How many of these knew of the identity of the artist's wife, or were friends or associates of James Unwin, is less clear. It does appear that Gainsborough's friendship with Unwin strengthened with the artist's move to Bath, and Unwin's periodic presence in Bath was no doubt connected with Beaufort estate business. He was probably in the town early in 1763 since his bank account shows a payment to the Bath bookseller and stationer James Leake on 21 January and a payment the following month of £100 to a Samuel Collins, perhaps a high-risk loan to Samuel Collins the miniaturist who had recently fled Bath to escape scandal and debts.[90] By the beginning of 1765 Margaret Gainsborough told her husband that she considered Unwin 'so much of a Gentleman now', probably because by this date Unwin had inherited a number of Wheeler properties and was in line to take possession of Wootton Lodge (fig. 96).[91] In a letter of July 1770 Gainsborough complained that he could never remember Unwin's address 'these 5 years owing to your removal from Essex', suggesting that the date of the Unwins' move was indeed 1765.[92] Unwin inherited Captain Edward Wheeler's estates in Worcestershire and Staffordshire on Wheeler's death in 1761 and the occupancy of Wootton Lodge on the death of Wheeler's aunt.[93] Wheeler's will stipulates that the Staffordshire properties should be Unwin's, but he must pay an annuity of £300 to Miss Fanny Stephenson. In fact, by marrying Fanny Stephenson himself in 1762, Unwin acquired the estates and all their income and Wootton Lodge still belonged to an Unwin in 1851.[94] Wheeler's will includes an endearing clause commanding his friends to use any spare money left at his death to 'go to a Tavern & play-house or whatever other amusement they may choose', and interestingly, among those named as particular friends are Dr Isaac Schomberg and the naval Captain Alexander Schomberg, brothers of Gainsborough's sitter Dr Ralph Schomberg of Bath.[95]

It appears that Gainsborough's trip to Staffordshire and Derbyshire in the summer of 1771 was made in response to an invitation from James Unwin. In Gainsborough's correspondence with Unwin the artist speaks of visiting Derbyshire, and he addresses his letters to Unwin at Wootton Lodge near Ashbourne in Derbyshire.[96] In fact Wootton Lodge lies in Staffordshire, close to the Staffordshire–Derbyshire border, and not far from Dovedale.

Little has been known of the circumstances in which Gainsborough painted his celebrated landscape, now in Philadelphia, which depicts a scene near King's Bromley in Staffordshire (fig. 97). This *River Landscape* has for some time been recognised as practically unique in Gainsborough's mature oeuvre, since it represents an actual rather than an imagined view. It now appears that Gainsborough must have painted this picture, or at least made studies for it, when he visited Unwin. It has been said that nothing is known of the person for whom it was painted, Samuel Newton of King's Bromley.[97] In fact Newton was an eminent Staffordshire man, Sheriff of the County and grandson of wealthy London merchant Sir Thomas Vernon.[98] King's Bromley lies on the road leading north from Lichfield to Ashbourne, a route Gainsborough would necessarily have taken to reach the Unwins at Wootton Lodge. Sudbury Hall, the seat of Gainsborough's sitter George Venables Vernon (a distant relative of Samuel Newton), lies on the same road.[99]

It may be concluded that the artist must have fulfilled his promise to visit the Unwins in the summer of 1771, enticed out of Bath by the promise of rocks, waterfalls and woodland.[100] The lure of the landscape may have been as strong as the desire to visit one of his oldest friends. In 1782 Joseph Pott, in his *Essay on Landscape Painting*, wrote, 'if the painter should pant for sublime scenes, stupendous mountains, precipices, waterfalls, he will find ample scope to improve his imagination in the Welch counties, or in Derbyshire and the west of England'.[101]

The fact that a number of Gainsborough's portrait patrons also lived in the area may have further encouraged the artist on his Staffordshire excursion, although all of their portraits were probably painted in Bath. George Venables Vernon has already been mentioned, other sitters include: Frances, Lady Littleton, painted in the early 1770s, eldest daughter of Christopher Horton of Catton Hall, Derbyshire and married to Edward Littleton of Pillaton, Staffordshire[102]; the Earl and Countess of Dartmouth, of Patshull, Staffordshire, painted in 1769[103]; Anne Horton, later the Duchess of Cumberland, painted as Mrs Horton in 1766[104] and John Gisborne, of Yoxall, just north of King's Bromley, probably painted in 1761, with a companion portrait of his wife from the same date or earlier.[105] Edward Littleton was one of the few subscribers to John Eld's portrait for the Staffordshire Infirmary in 1774 to contribute two guineas rather than one guinea (fig. 54). It is not known whether the Eld commission had any direct connection with Gainsborough's trip north, since Eld was also a Bath visitor, but one of the other names at the head of the subscription list, Sir John Wrottesley, Member of Parliament for Stafford, was the brother of two of Gainsborough's sitters from the mid-1760s, Miss Elizabeth Wrottesley and Miss Mary Wrottesley.[106]

Before he had the good fortune to inherit Captain Wheeler's estates, James Unwin led a professional life in London. P. K. Monod's characterisation of the eighteenth-century Jacobite gentleman seems designed to fit Unwin, down to the last detail: 'the Jacobite gentleman . . . might have no wider ambition than the peaceful cultivation of his estates. Yet many careers were open to him, from law and medicine to commerce, banking or the navy'.[107] Unwin, who ended his life in peaceful cultivation of an estate, had practised in law (as agent to the Dukes of Beaufort and as an independent attorney), banking (he was Gainsborough's banker until 1762) and the navy. As a Prize Court lawyer for the navy it was his duty to examine the evidence for the legality of seizures made at sea by privateer ships, a thriving business in the eighteenth century.[108] 'Ladies of the first rank' and noblemen had shares in privateer ships.[109] Several of Gainsborough's sitters with a naval connection may have come to the artist through Unwin. Gainsborough's correspondence makes it clear that the portrait he was painting in 1763 of a Mrs Saumarez was for Unwin's naval friend Captain Thomas Saumarez, but more importantly, the commission to paint full-lengths of Richard, Earl Howe, and his wife Mary (figs 52 and 69), two of the major pictures painted in Abbey Street, may owe something to Unwin, or the Unwin–Wheeler association.[110] In 1758 Richard Howe had commanded a squadron which included Captain Edward Wheeler and his ship *Isis* in what were described as 'various desultory expeditions . . . against the coast of France'.[111] One

97 Thomas Gainsborough (1727–1788), *View near King's Bromley, Staffordshire* 1771, oil on canvas, 47 × 66$^{3}/_{16}$ inches (119.4 × 168.1 cm), Philadelphia Museum of Art: The William L. Elkins Collection.

of Wheeler's closest friends, as we know from his will, was Captain Alexander Schomberg, a naval officer whose career ran in parallel with that of Richard Howe and was probably a personal friend of the Howes. The *Bath Chronicle* of 27 September 1764 records, in the same list, the arrival in Bath of Lady Howe and Captain Alexander Schomberg: it seems quite likely that the two families had arranged to meet in Bath. Howe was appointed Treasurer to the Navy in 1765, a post which is most likely to have brought him in contact with the activities of the Prize Courts and the work of James Unwin.[112]

This examination of various groups of people encountered in Bath, from musicians, with whom Gainsborough felt a natural empathy, to doctors who attended to his often fragile state of health, to naval worthies, illustrates the diversity of the support and patronage he enjoyed. It also illustrates the depth of the artist's involvement in the commercial and social life of Bath. That at least some of the support he received from local and visiting patrons may have been connected with Mrs Margaret Gainsborough's 'secret' identity has never before been considered, and while the evidence is fragmentary and sometimes obscure, it does appear convincing. If a significant proportion of the Bath patrons harboured a nostalgia for the Stuart age, Gainsborough's use of Van Dyck as a model for his portraiture was destined to please: it is a moot point as to whether the patrons themselves inspired his love of Van Dyck or whether his personal wish to emulate a sophisticated seventeenth-century style of painting happened by chance to coincide with the taste and desires of this particular set of people.

7

'Nature sat to Mr. Gainsborough'

The place of landscape within Gainsborough's Bath career is difficult to define, although it was in Bath that he completely changed his manner of painting, moving gradually from Dutch-inspired depictions of the countryside, peopled by small figures, to grand, luminous and artificial constructions in which larger-scale fanciful figures play an increasingly important role. During this period he developed what might be termed a landscape of the imagination, a selective vision of nature filtered and channelled by various means in order to focus on composition and to appeal to the emotions.

John Hayes has noted that the artist Thomas Jones recalled that at the outset of his career in 1765, 'there was Lambert, & Wilson, & Zuccarelli, & Gainsborough, & Barret, & Richards, & Marlow in full possession of Landscape business . . .'.[1] As Hayes commented, apart from Zuccarelli, whose Italianate landscapes are unashamedly decorative in intent, Gainsborough was the only one of these artists who chose not to accept any commissions for topographical paintings. Country house and estate views were still, at this date, the mainstay for most English landscape painters and it was only the success of Gainsborough's portrait practice that allowed him to shun this work entirely. It is fair to say that the remarkably rapid progress of his portrait career in Bath is paralleled by an equally rapid development of a new imaginative style of landscape, a style that was seen by Gainsborough's contemporaries as distinctively modern and uniquely expressive of fine feeling and taste. The poem entitled 'On seeing Mr. Gainsborough's Pictures at Bath', published in the *Gentleman's Magazine* in 1773, opens with an appreciation of just these qualities:

> While connoisseurs, with artificial eyes
> Mechanically pore, and fix the prize;
> While, dead to each fine feeling of the heart,
> And every principle of taste and art,
> They center merit in an ancient name,
> And parcel out by *centuries* their fame;
> Be mine the pleasure, tho' in humble lays,
> True, *modern* merit to admire and praise.
> Yes, *Gainsborough!* yes; thy magic pieces charm,
> And want but age dull connoisseurs to warm.[2]

Here, in a reversal of the eighteenth-century norm, the emotive term 'mechanical' is attached to the connoisseurs, as opposed to the professional artist. The artist was usually the one judged incapable of liberal thought or true taste as a result of the 'mechanical' or servile nature of his profession.[3] The fact that in 1773 Gainsborough is presented as liberal-minded, and therefore by implication gentlemanly, indicates the high esteem in which his art was now held; he was quite clearly no longer regarded as simply a portrait painter of Bath. Gainsborough's exclusive focus on imagination, 'feeling', and the formal concerns of composition and chiaroscuro, was recognised by some of his closest allies as an important constituent in the formation of a modern school of English landscape painting.

If the financial success of his portrait painting allowed Gainsborough to pursue a non-topographical form of landscape painting, a number of other external factors also came into play. The first public exhibitions of contemporary art in London placed the art of England on a new footing and acted as a stimulus to artists who wished to demonstrate that English painting could equal that of any other country. A number of enlightened patrons such as Lord Shelburne of Bowood, the banker William Hoare of Stourhead and the St Quintins of Scampston in Yorkshire were ready to buy landscapes by English painters as well as old masters. The passion for landscape gardening, which overtook practically every landowner in the country, also awakened a new interest in landscape art, since there was a common awareness of the interplay between gardening and painting.

Bath was in many ways an ideal base from which Gainsborough could explore the new opportunities on offer to the serious landscape painter. Apart from the presence of a promising clientele, the city was blessed with a number of particular characteristics that appear to have fed his imagination. Firstly, the scenery of the surrounding area was quite different from the Suffolk he had known so intimately as a youth, the nearby hills, woodland and rocky outcrops associ-

98 Thomas Gainsborough (1727–1788), *Sir William St Quintin, Fourth Baronet (1700–1770)* 1760–61, oil on canvas, 50 × 40 inches (127 × 101.7 cm), private collection. Like the Dukes of Beaufort, Sir William St Quintin was a racing enthusiast and had a famous stud at Scampston. In 1746 he gave a horse to Archbishop Thomas Herring; he gave a horse to Gainsborough in the early 1760s.

99 Thomas Gainsborough (1727–1788), *Sir William St Quintin, Fifth Baronet (1729–1795)* c. 1770, oil on canvas, 50 × 40 inches (127 × 101.7 cm), private collection.

ated with local stone-quarrying providing just that *variety* of aspect that was later so enthusiastically admired by the proponents of the Picturesque. Secondly, while the presence of apothecaries, doctors and amateur chemists in Bath probably encouraged Gainsborough to experiment with materials, the medical fraternity may also have stimulated the painter to experiment in other ways. Supporting the doctors were suppliers of medical and optical instruments and the ready availability of the very latest in lens technology may well have been seized upon by the artist as yet another tool in his quest for the ideal landscape composition. Thirdly, the intellectual stimulus provided by those who met in the coffee houses, assembly rooms and Bath's open spaces appears to have had as significant an effect on the artist's development and self-perception as any other factor.

Gainsborough might reasonably have expected that once he had made his name as a portrait painter, which he did within months of arriving in Bath, the patrons who so eagerly sought his portraits might also buy his landscape paintings. It is now very hard to assess how many of the Bath-period landscapes found buyers. Members of the St Quintin family, who commissioned at least five portraits, may have purchased more landscapes than is usually thought.[4] It is established that Sir William St Quintin (1700–1770) (fig. 98) bought the *Wooded Landscape with Country Waggon, Milkmaid and Drover* in 1766 (fig. 100).[5] Sir William seems to have been a thoroughly likeable and kindly man. He gave Gainsborough a horse in order to encourage him outdoors into the fresh air following his severe illness in the autumn of 1763. This horse was apparently not handsome, but 'perfectly sure footed & steady upon the Road', and therefore ideal for exploring the treacherous hills around Bath.[6] Sir William doubtless hoped that the artist would not only recover his health, but revive his interest in landscape painting as a result of being equipped with this reliable mode of transport. At the time of his death Sir William's good-heartedness was acknowledged by Philip Thicknesse in the form of an anecdote supposedly related by an 'arch wag at *Bath*',

100 Thomas Gainsborough (1727–1783), *Wooded Landscape with a Country Waggon, Milkmaid and Drover* 1765–6, oil on canvas, 57 × 47 inches (144.8 × 119.4 cm), private collection.

> Sir William . . . was a polite old gentleman, but he had the manners and breeding rather of the late, than the present age, and though a man deservedly esteemed for his many virtues, was by some thought too ceremonious. Somebody at the round table at *Morgan's* Coffee house [in Bath] happened to say, alas! poor Sir William! he is gone; but he was a good man, and is surely gone to Heaven, and I can tell you what he said when he first entered the holy gates! . . . Why said he, seeing a large concourse of departed souls, and not a soul that he knew, he bowed to the right and left, said he begged pardon, – he feared he was troublesome, and if so, he would instantly retire.[7]

Sir William's son William St Quintin (1729–1795) (fig. 99) apparently lacked some of his father's virtues and ended his days in disgrace, but during the early 1760s he may have been as important a friend to Gainsborough as his father. He appears to have purchased a number of landscapes. In February 1797 the painter Edmund Garvey told Joseph Farington that

> Some of the pictures by Gainsborough in the possession of Gainsborough Dupont were painted for Sir William St Quintin [ie Sir William the Fifth Baronet] – Dupont bought them of Sir William, whose affairs are in a ruinous state. His character is also tainted. He is now abroad and is towards 60 years of age.[8]

Although neither Farington nor Garvey appear to have been aware that Sir William had died, Garvey is likely to have been correct in his remarks about the pictures painted for him, since he knew both Gainsborough and the St Quintins well in the late 1760s. This means that one or two important Bath landscapes that appeared in Dupont's sale in April 1797, such as the *Mountainous Wooded Landscape* (fig. 101) (exhibited at the Society of Artists 1763 exhibition), and the *Wooded landscape with Peasants in a Country Waggon* (fig. 102) may have originally belonged to the younger William St Quintin.[9] It has usually been said that these pictures were unsold, and remained on the artist's hands, passing to Gainsborough Dupont on his death.

101 Thomas Gainsborough (1727–1788), *Mountainous Wooded Landscape* 1762–3, oil on canvas, $57\frac{1}{2} \times 62$ inches (146.1×157.5 cm), Worcester Art Museum, Worcester, Massachusetts.

The St Quintins had a house in Bath and were very much involved in Bath society. They, and one or two other local patrons such as Ralph Allen (fig. 103) (whose encouragement Gainsborough never forgot), seem to have been keen to support Gainsborough's landscape painting which, in general, took second place to portraiture during the early Bath years.[10] The landscapes were not unrecognised, as the poem of 1773, Thomas Jones's recollection and other documents clearly show. The relative lack of sales may in part be due to Gainsborough's own insistence on according landscape an equal if not superior status to portraiture. The figures he charged for landscapes are very hard to come by, but during the first half of the Bath period he appears to have priced them at about the same rate as his portraits. His charge of £43.11.6 to Sir William St Quintin for the *Wooded Landscape with Country Waggon, Milkmaid and Drover* in 1766 compares with a half-length portrait price of forty guineas at that date. This landscape is 7 inches taller and 7 inches wider than a half-length portrait.[11] After moving to the Circus he may have charged rather more for a landscape. In 1773, when

102 Thomas Gainsborough (1727–1788), *Wooded Landscape with Peasants in a Country Waggon* 1760–62, oil on canvas, 56 × 59¾ inches (142.2 × 151.8 cm), Tate Britain, London.

Gainsborough's price for a half-length portrait was sixty guineas, Henry Hoare of Stourhead paid eighty guineas for the slightly larger *Peasants and Colliers going to Market* (fig. 158), but this price may have included a frame and even, in this case, a commission to the painter William Hoare who negotiated the sale.[12] It is worth noting that the same patron, Henry Hoare, had paid Richard Wilson £30 for *The Lake of Nemi or Speculum Dianae* (fig. 122) in 1758 and the elder Sir William St Quintin paid Wilson thirteen guineas for a landscape in 1759.[13] It would appear that Gainsborough's prices were relatively high, and they certainly exceeded those of any other landscape painter in Bath. When Gainsborough charged around forty guineas, his only professional rival in Bath, Edmund Garvey, charged ten guineas.[14] Garvey seems to have scraped a living on landscape and decorative work alone, so it must be assumed that in Bath there was a limited market for landscape, at a price.

Thomas Jones may have been somewhat mistaken when he considered Gainsborough to be one of those who had cornered the landscape *business* by the mid-1760s, but it is

103 Thomas Gainsborough (1727–1788), *Wooded Landscape with Figures, Cottage and Pool* 1760–63, oil on canvas, $11\frac{3}{4} \times 13\frac{1}{2}$ inches (29.8 × 34.3 cm), private collection. This small landscape originally belonged to Ralph Allen of Prior Park, Bath.

clear that the development of Gainsborough's landscape style was not impeded by the lack of financial encouragement. A relatively small number of landscape paintings survive (forty-two in Hayes's *Landscape Paintings* catalogue from the Bath period's fifteen and a half years, compared with seventy-three from the subsequent fourteen years in London), but the evolution of a new style probably owed as much to the activity of drawing as to the production of finished oil paintings.

Apart from an increasingly vigorous handling of paint, which is just as apparent in the Bath landscapes as the portraits, the most marked characteristics of the new landscapes are the larger figures and clearer sense of composition. When, at the end of his life, Gainsborough looked back at one of his earliest landscapes, he perceived its greatest shortcoming was its composition, although he saw its 'touch and closeness to nature' to be equal to anything he produced in his maturity.[15] Increasingly in the Bath paintings the principal features of trees, rocks and hills are massed to create strong areas of light and shade, while the figures, instead of being dotted across the canvas, tend to be fewer and more focused within the composition, as in Dr Charleton's *Wooded landscape with a Woodcutter* (fig. 148) or larger and contained in coherent groups, as in the Earl of Shelburne's *Wooded Landscape with Mounted Peasants* (fig. 104). As John Barrell has put it 'the "general shapes" [Gainsborough's landscapes] assume . . . appear to signify that Gainsborough is aspiring to the more public kind of landscape painted by Claude . . .'.[16] This paring down to the essentials of landscape – which Barrell sees as the elevation of landscape from a private to a public genre, or a movement towards the reinvention of landscape as a genuinely liberal art form – is something that can be traced through the drawings of the period. Using ink washes, watercolour, gouache and densely applied black and white chalks, Gainsborough developed a repertory of landscape compositions in which dark woodlands are pierced by shafts of light, figures and cattle emerge from shadows into sunny glades, travelling along winding paths flanked by jutting rocks, sparkling streams and pools, and branches from fallen trees. Similar arrangements are repeated many times, like musical variations on a single theme. The surviving landscape drawings are not significantly more numerous for Bath than for the earlier and later periods of his career, but the artist seems to have attached a special importance to drawing at this time.[17] Contemporary accounts of his enjoyment of drawing, both in the studio using models, and out of doors in the countryside, nearly all date from the Bath period. The only drawings he ever sent to London exhibitions were a book of drawings shown at the Royal Academy in 1770 and ten landscapes 'in imitation of oil paintings' shown there in 1772.

Between 1761 (when he first exhibited) and 1774 Gainsborough sent thirty-four portraits, seven landscapes, ten landscape drawings and a book of drawings to the London exhibitions held by the Society of Artists, Free Society and Royal Academy. After leaving Bath he exhibited fifty-two portraits, sixteen landscapes and three fancy pictures, but it has to be borne in mind that he did not exhibit at the Academy between 1773 and 1776 or after 1783.[18] There are scattered contemporary references to the Bath landscapes in the press, and in letters and journals. William Hoare's son Prince Hoare reported that the artist was 'so disgusted at the blind preference paid to his powers of portraiture, that, for many years of his residence in Bath, he regularly shut up all his landscapes in the back apartments of his house, to which no common visitors were admitted'.[19] These 'many years' may well have been the years between 1760 and 1766, since there seem to be no references at all to landscapes hanging in the exhibition room in Abbey Street.

Two 'common visitors' to Gainsborough's Circus house, late in the Bath period, did mention landscapes among the pictures hung for public view. Both these visitors were women, and both greatly admired the landscapes they saw, preferring them to the portraits. Mary Hamilton, who came to Bath in May 1774, recorded that the pictures she saw were 'All portraits with the exception of two or three Landscapes. If I might presume to give my opinion, I should prefer him as a Landscape to Portrait Painter, yet they say he pays but little attention to the former'.[20] Mary also visited the home of her great-uncle the Hon. Charles Hamilton (creator of the famous Painshill landscape garden) in the Royal Crescent, where she saw 'some capital Pictures'.[21] Her uncle happened to be away from Bath, but had he been at home, she might have gained a better insight in to Gainsborough's landscapes. Charles Hamilton and Gainsborough were certainly known to one another, since Gainsborough mentions seeing him in Bath just before Mary Hamilton's visit, in February 1774, in a letter to the painter Giovanni Battista Cipriani. Gainsborough wrote,

> I should have done myself the pleasure of writing to you sooner but that I could not 'til yesterday get a sight of Mr Hamilton and his Pictures; I find that he reserved the two Churches you mention'd for his House in The Crescent, and that no Price would tempt him to part with them: They are really very fine Pictures.[22]

Even though Mary Hamilton's informants in Bath may have been mistaken in telling her that Gainsborough paid little attention to landscape, her account of the small but significant presence of landscapes in his rooms is interesting, as is her preference for them. Which pictures she saw cannot be established. Gainsborough did not exhibit landscapes at the Royal Academy or elsewhere in London in 1774, so any unsold paintings might have been on his wall.

The other visitor to record her impression of Gainsborough's landscapes was Dorothy Richardson who visited Bath in May 1770. Her account, written at the back of a 1770 edition of a Bath guidebook was published by Hugh Belsey in 1987 and is the fullest response by any visitor to Gainsborough's rooms at the Circus.[23] Dorothy Richardson noted that she saw pictures both finished and unfinished, in two rooms, including 'A Good Landscape upon an Ezle just finish'd – Another very fine one with Cattle & Horses, – Two very small Landscapes only one of them by Mr. Gainsborough . . .', concluding, 'Gainsborough Paints only in Oil, & excells most in Landscape; his Portraits are painted in a harsh manner, but said to be strong likeness's his Landscapes are very fine'.[24] Once again it is impossible to positively identify the landscapes that Richardson saw at Gainsborough's house. The fact that one was freshly painted is interesting, the month being May, when a good many portrait patrons would still have been in Bath; it is also of interest that she saw a small landscape not by Gainsborough hanging beside one of his own. Might this have been the 'little bit of Tree' that Gainsborough asked Jackson to pursue for him in London in 1768?[25] Of Gainsborough's own landscapes, Richardson lists one with cattle *and* horses, a subject surprisingly rare at this date, but a description that would fit Lord Shelburne's *Wooded Landscape with Mounted Peasants* (fig. 104), a painting that could certainly be described as 'very fine'. Other visitors to Gainsborough's Bath rooms give little indication of what they saw, but simply declared themselves

104 Thomas Gainsborough (1727–1788), *Wooded Landscape with Mounted Peasants returning from Market* 1768–70, oil on canvas, 47 × 66 inches (119.4 × 167.7 cm), Toledo Museum of Art, Ohio, purchased with funds from the Libbey Endowment Gift of Edward Drummond Libbey.

'much pleased' or entertained, giving no clue as to whether they saw landscapes as well as portraits.

Responses to Gainsborough's Bath period landscapes exhibited in London are also generally brief. The commentator who complains in the *Critical Review* of 1765 that Gainsborough's portrait of General Honywood 'wants great correction' nevertheless admitted 'the landscape is very agreeable'.[26] Of the landscape exhibited at the Society of Artists in 1767, generally believed to be the *Harvest Waggon* (fig. 160), an anonymous reviewer said 'The trees are hard, and the sky too blue', while Horace Walpole called it 'very rich, the group of figures delightfully managed, and the horses well drawn, the distant hill one tint too dark'.[27] Walpole referred to the landscape background of the portrait of *Thomas Medlycott* (private collection) exhibited in 1763 as 'tawdry, a fault most of the landscape-painters have caught from Reynolds'.[28] In 1771 he noted that Gainsborough's two Royal Academy landscapes were 'Very good, but too little finished'.[29] By 1777 however, after Gainsborough had left Bath, Walpole was describing his *Watering Place* (National Gallery, London) as 'by far the finest landscape ever painted in England and equal to the great masters'.[30] The most enthusiastic published comments on the Bath landscapes were in fact contained in poems, the one of 1773 quoted above, and another by Richard Graves that was repeated in several different versions, in a variety of publications. These literary offerings, which should realistically be construed as 'puffs' rather than critical responses, are discussed in the next chapter.

While critical reactions to Gainsborough's Bath landscapes are mixed, there is evidence that other painters greatly admired them. Thomas Jones, as we have seen, considered him one of the leading landscape painters of the day by the mid-1760s. Ozias Humphry, in Bath between 1760 and 1764, asked permission to copy one of Gainsborough's pictures and the answer he received makes it clear that such requests had been made before: ' I should be glad to lend you any of my Landskips to copy, did it not affect the sale of new Pictures, to have any copies taken of them. for which reason I have often been obliged to refuse . . .'.[31] If younger artists were anxious to copy Gainsborough's landscapes in the early 1760s, they must either have seen them in the artist's Bath rooms or drawn their inspiration from the few examples they had seen in the London exhibitions. Another, perhaps unexpected artist who apparently admired and wished to support Gainsborough's landscape painting during his stay in Bath was William Hoare. Hoare appears to have negotiated the sale of a major picture, *Peasants and Colliers going to Market* (fig. 158) to Henry Hoare of Stourhead in 1773.[32] Henry Hoare was Gainsborough's London banker and the two men must have been acquainted, but William Hoare was a close family friend of the Stourhead Hoares, and a regular visitor to their Wiltshire estate. His daughter Mary married into the family in 1765.[33] William Hoare did occasionally paint landscape himself, but by the early 1770s he had few professional ambitions, preferring to enjoy the company of his friends and paint fancy and decorative pictures, largely for his own amusement.[34] As elder statesman of the artistic world in Bath, William Hoare seems to have taken pleasure in assisting several younger painters and sculptors including Ozias Humphry, Alexander Cozens and Thomas Lawrence, and the role he played in placing *Peasants and Colliers going to Market* among old masters and major Continental paintings at Stourhead was an important demonstration of his support for Gainsborough.[35]

Another painter who must have valued the landscapes is Ozias Humphry's master Samuel Collins: Gainsborough gave him a small landscape drawing some time between 1760 and 1762.[36] The painter John Hoppner, who closely imitated Gainsborough's landscape drawing style, was clearly referring to the Bath period landscapes when he singled out the productions of the middle of Gainsborough's career as his finest. Hoppner described the painter's earliest landscapes as 'touching by the simplicity of their execution, and choice of scenery'.[37] But he then saw a shift in Gainsborough's art as he came under the influence of Rubens: 'The admirers of cultivated art will find him most varied and beautiful at this period; as his works, strengthened and enriched by the study of Rubens, still possessed a uniformity of character . . .'. Gainsborough's late work was to Hoppner 'greatly inferior'.[38] Interestingly, John Hayes has noted that 'most of the known copies and imitations of Gainsborough's Bath [landscape] style are of works of the early 1760s', indicating again that even if the early Bath landscapes had only limited public exposure, they were well known to other artists.[39]

Gainsborough's own letters give some clues as to his feelings on the subject of landscape at this time. In 1768 he told Unwin he was 'as fond of Landskip as ever' and his curiosity about the rocky and wooded landscape near Unwin's home made him vow in 1770, 'I'll pack up all my Drawing things, and see Derbyshire next summer, if I'm alive'.[40] Also in 1768 he wrote with infectious enthusiasm of the Duke of Montagu's Rubens, the landscape now known as the *Watering Place*, and in the same year he asked Jackson to try to buy for him a 'little bit of Tree' by an unidentified artist that he had seen at a dealer's in London.[41] By 1771 he considered he had produced the best landscapes of his career: the two large canvases he planned to exhibit in London at the Academy in 'handsome frames'.[42] In 1774 he told Cipriani 'I have a tollerable Picture of another rural subject . . .'.[43]

Before considering some of Gainsborough's Bath landscapes in detail it is worth looking at the history of landscape painting in Bath. Statistics show that, in comparison with portrait painters, very few landscape artists worked in Bath.[44] Thomas Ross (*fl.* 1730–57) has already been mentioned as the only landscape artist of any real significance to be associated with the town before Gainsborough's arrival in 1758. Ross is of considerable interest, not least because his path may have crossed with Gainsborough's at an early date, on Gainsborough's home ground in East Anglia. In 1730 Ross wrote to Dr Cox Macro, the Suffolk antiquary, introducing himself as a painter of 'Heads'.[45] Ross subsequently sold several paintings of his own to Macro and probably purchased other works for Macro's collection. Ross also played a part in executing the decorative scheme at Macro's Little Haugh Hall near Bury St Edmunds, a series of paintings begun by Peter Tillemans and completed by Francis Hayman. The staircase at Little Haugh is recorded as '"The History of Archimedes" T. Ross & Hayman, with a figure or two by P. Tillemans. The ceiling entirely by Hayman'.[46] Ross also painted a *Resurrection* altarpiece for a church near Sudbury, a painting which is now lost, as are the wall paintings at Little Haugh Hall.[47]

Ross's earliest association with Bath can be traced back to 1740, the date of John Wiltshire's bookplate which he designed and Jacob Skinner engraved (fig. 163). In January 1743 he was at a Masonic meeting in Bath which was also attended by James Vertue and Skinner.[48] At a meeting of 16 January 1744 Thomas Ross acted as Junior Warden of the Lodge and the small company present included his patron John Wiltshire and one Joshua Ross, presumably the 'Jos. Ross Frame-maker' listed as a subscriber to Thomas Thorpe's 1742 *Survey of . . . Bath* (endpaper). Both Joshua Ross and the landscape and sporting painter J. Ross, generally called James Ross, may have been brothers of Thomas Ross.[49] J. Ross signed a number of sporting landscapes, notably a set of four of *The Duke of Beaufort's Hunt* (figs 21 and 151) that follow in the Tillemans tradition and also have an affinity with the work of John Wootton's master Jan Wyck. Given Thomas Ross's proven connection with John Wiltshire, and the general dearth of landscape painters in Bath in the first half of the century, it may be proposed that the landscapes (often mentioned in guidebooks but never identified) that hung in Wiltshire's Assembly Rooms in Bath might have had something to do with either Thomas or J. Ross.[50] That Gainsborough must have known the Ross landscapes painted for Ralph Allen at Prior Park has already been mentioned above.[51]

Listed next to the framemaker Joshua Ross in the subscriber list to Thomas Thorpe's *Survey* is the quintessentially rococo artist Thomas Robins (1716–1770), who settled in Bath around 1740 and travelled the country recording gentlemen's country houses and gardens using a meticulous watercolour and gouache technique. Robins continued to be based in Bath until his death in 1770 and it must be assumed that he and Gainsborough would have known one another, although no evidence of any friendship has come to light.[52]

The early history of landscape painting in Bath, featuring Ross's gentle Tillemans-inspired style and Robins's decorative topographical work, provides an unlikely backdrop to Gainsborough's rapid personal development. It is also not likely that he gained any direct inspiration from the work

105 Edmund Garvey (*fl.* 1767–1813), *View of Bath* 1769, oil on canvas, 16 × 21 inches (40.6 × 53.4 cm), signed and dated 1769, private collection.

106 Edmund Garvey (*fl.* 1767–1813), *View of Rome* 1769, oil on canvas, 16 × 21 inches (40.6 × 53.4 cm), signed and dated 1769, private collection.

of fellow landscape painters in the area in the 1760s and 1770s. The only professional landscape painter in oils to work in Bath for any length of time during Gainsborough's residence was the Irishman Edmund Garvey (d. 1813), whom Gainsborough described as 'an excellent Landskip Painter and particular Friend of mine'.[53] Incredible as it might seem now, Garvey's and Gainsborough's work was occasionally confused.[54] Garvey settled in Bath by 1768, in which year he submitted a painting of Valentine Morris's famous garden, Piercefield at Chepstow, to the Free Society, giving his address as Bath.[55] A view of Bath and a companion view of Rome dated 1769 entered the St Quintin family collection (figs 105 and 106) and Garvey's *A View of Lake Albano – Morning* exhibited at the Royal Academy in 1771 is inscribed 'E. Garvey/ Bath/ 1770'.[56] As the title of this latter painting suggests, Garvey had been in Italy before settling in Bath and the Italian views he continued to paint are in a loose Wilsonesque style, with a suggestion of the influence of his early Irish master Robert Carver. Garvey's pairing of Bath and Rome for Sir William St Quintin is richly symbolic and suggests that the painter was sensitive to the seriousness of intent underlying the creation of the modern city by John Wood, Ralph Allen and Beau Nash.[57]

Gainsborough's friendship with Garvey was apparently deep rooted. James Northcote, in conversation with painter James Ward, claimed that the only time Gainsborough ever attended a meeting at the Royal Academy was when he went in order to try and secure Garvey's election, 'an unworthy errand' in Northcote's view.[58] A fellow Irish artist in Bath, portraitist John Warren, described Garvey as 'a very sensible friendly fellow' whose pictures 'might be hung up anywhere', but in general he seems not to have been regarded very highly, even suffering the ignominy of being dubbed 'Edmund Garbage' in a contemporary farce.[59] Ellis Waterhouse defined Garvey's landscapes as 'profoundly ordinary and monotonous in colour', a judgement with which it is hard to disagree.[60] Nevertheless Garvey was elected an Associate of the Royal Academy in 1770, the first year in which this designation was used. In the same year he was blackballed when his name came up for election to the Bath Freemasons.[61]

Whatever the merits of his paintings, Garvey remained on friendly terms with Gainsborough and later told Joseph Farington that Gainsborough was 'much affected by any newspaper criticism that remarked unfavourably on any of his works', indicating that at the very least the two artists discussed the London exhibitions together.[62] After Gainsborough's death, Garvey purchased for eight shillings a small landscape with figures by 'Michaud', perhaps the Flemish artist Theobald Michau (1676–1765), together with a copy of it by Gainsborough himself.[63] (Were these the 'Two very small Landscapes only one of them by Mr. Gainsborough' that Dorothy Richardson saw in 1770?) Garvey's mentor Robert Carver spent some time scene painting, and carried out some work for David Garrick, and Garvey too was a decorative painter as well as a producer of easel pictures. While Gainsborough was painting his full-length portrait of *Captain William Wade* to fill the first of the prepared spaces for Master of Ceremonies portraits in the Card Room at the new Assembly Rooms, Garvey was painting decorative blinds for the high-level windows in the adjoining ballroom. Gainsborough was famously standing in the ballroom 'admiring the figures which the ingenious Committee had drawn by Garvey the landscape painter' in October 1771 when he narrowly escaped serious injury as a branch from one of the chandeliers fell to the floor.[64] A visitor to the Rooms in 1794 wrote, 'I was pleased particularly with the manner in which the windows are shut up in the ball-room, the shutters are painted with Herculaneum figures & the mouldings round the windows appear as frames'.[55] According to the *New Bath Guide* the room was lit 'by thirteen windows, to which are blinds painted by a masterly hand with variety [sic] of figures, vases, etc. which rise over the openings of each window from behind a timberwork that supports the column . . .'.[66] A suggestion of the blinds can be made out in old photographs of the ballroom (fig. 107). It is worth noting that the seven-man 'Ingenious Committee' that engaged Garvey, and apparently accepted as a gift Gainsborough's portrait of Wade, included the amateur chemist Benjamin Colborne, the 'well wisher to all artists'.[67] Despite Garvey's popularity as an artist, he could never have been viewed by Gainsborough as a threat to his own career, a factor that may in part account for the good relations that existed between the two. The principal merit of Garvey's work, as far as the picture-buying public was concerned, was that by comparison with Gainsborough's, it was cheap.

Another landscape painter well known to both Gainsborough and Garvey in Bath was the American-born amateur John Taylor (1735–1806). In 1804 Garvey, who was by then living in London, told Joseph Farington that on a recent visit to Bath he had called on 'Mr. Taylor, who was formerly so much celebrated for his painting'.[68] Taylor arrived in Bath from America with his parents in 1762 and settled in the Circus.[69] He quickly established a reputation as a painter specialising in idealised landscapes with ancient ruins (fig. 108). His pictures are a curious amalgamation of the Italian Campagna and the English countryside, dark in tonality with weakly drawn figures. The diarist John Baker encountered Taylor in a coffee house in Bath in 1772 and remarked that he was a 'great genius'.[70] John Warren, however, thought Taylor's landscapes 'pittyful', their shadows being all of 'one dirty, cold, sooty hue' and considered Garvey 'far beyond him both for truth, colour & Effect . . .'.[71] By contrast (and perhaps with a touch of irony), Tobias Smollett's fictional character Matthew Bramble described Taylor as 'the best

107 The Grand Ball Room, Assembly Rooms, Bath, detail of a photograph, c. 1890. This photograph, probably taken in the late nineteenth century by A. Mowbray Green, shows three of Edmund Garvey's window blinds still *in situ* at the east end of the ballroom.

landscape-painter now living', while in 1783 no less a person than Benjamin Franklin lamented, 'Our geniuses all go to Europe. In England at present, the best History Painter West; the best Portrait Painter Copley; and the best Landscape Painter, Taylor, at Bath are all Americans'.[72] Taylor became a close friend of the Revd Richard Graves. Graves must be the 'R.G.' who wrote 'On Viewing Some Pictures of Grecian Ruins, by John Taylor, Esq'. This begins

> Ye Connoisseurs! who vainly thus pursue,
> O'er seas and Alps each species of *vertu*;
> Charm'd with the pomp of antient Greece or Rome,
> Blind to the beauties of your native home;
> See! (vain caprice and prejudice apart)
> With wonder see, these works of *modern* art![73]

These lines closely reflect the opening of the poem about Gainsborough written in 1773 and published in the *Gentleman's Magazine*. While Gainsborough's landscapes could certainly be perceived as truly modern in 1773, the notion of Taylor as modern is hard to swallow and the dismissal by the poet of the 'pomp of antient Greece or Rome' is ironic, given Taylor's lifelong preoccupation with classical ruins. The poems about Gainsborough and Taylor may both have been inspired by a verse that had been pinned to the door of the Society of Artists exhibition in London in 1761, a piece attributed to the sculptor Louis François Roubiliac, extolling the merits of contemporary English art as against a blind preference for anything old.[74] All three verses can be seen as literary equivalents of Hogarth's rather more eloquent engraved tailpiece for the 1761 catalogue of the Society of Artists exhibition catalogue, a monkey connoisseur watering already dead plants representing foreign old masters.

Although Richard Graves may have reflected a fairly widespread admiration for the amateur Taylor, Gainsborough cannot have felt threatened by Taylor any more than he did by Garvey, and again the two painters were probably on good terms. They certainly shared a close friendship with the actors David Garrick and John Henderson and an association with the St Quintin family.[75] Taylor's wealth enabled him to defend his amateur status, even apparently forbidding visitors to his Circus picture room to leave the usual gratuities.[76] He did, however, take pupils, and commission engravings after his own paintings. In the *Bath Chronicle* of 6 May 1776 he announced the publication of two prints with attached remarks on landscape painting, including 'instructions for copying prints, and making drawings in the most easy and pleasing method, calculated principally for young students in that pleasing art, and pointing out the best rules whereby a true judgement may be formed of Landscapes in general'. The painter Thomas Barker was a friend of Richard Taylor, John's son, and apparently gleaned from him tales of the friendship that existed between Gainsborough and his father. One anecdote, so preposterous as to be possibly true, states that Gainsborough and Taylor agreed to each paint a

108 John Taylor (1735–1806), *Wooded Landscape and Classical Ruins* date unknown, oil on canvas, 23 × 19 inches (58.4 × 48.2 cm), private collection.

landscape that was then assessed by a local 'committee' of professional and amateur artists. The verdict was a typically British compromise, with the committee deciding that the foreground of Taylor's picture was better but the background of Gainsborough's superior.[77] If Gainsborough was prepared to indulge in such a parlour game, it can only have been in the safe knowledge that Taylor's peculiarly archaic pictures possessed a certain charm, but would have no lasting significance in the history of British art.

A second local amateur painter who was also keenly supported by Richard Graves, and much admired in his lifetime, probably also numbered among Gainsborough's friends. He was Coplestone Warre Bampfylde (1720–1791) a well-connected gentleman who took great pride both in being the senior officer in charge of the Somerset Militia and in his country estate at Hestercombe near Taunton. In 1774 Edmund Garvey exhibited at the Royal Academy a view of the waterfall at Hestercombe, a well-known sight that was also painted more than once by John Inigo Richards.[78] Bampfylde was a significant member of the artistic community in Bath, regarded by his contemporaries as a man of 'infinite taste and judgement'.[79] He painted oils in the manner of George Lambert and drew competent topographical watercolours (fig. 109). According to Gainsborough's musical

109 Coplestone Warre Bampfylde (1720–1791), *The Grotto at Stourhead* 1753, pen and ink, ink and watercolour washes, 11 × 18½ inches (28 × 47 cm), signed and dated 1753, British Museum, London.

friend William Jackson, Bampfylde was 'thought well of by Artists, and much valued by those whom he honoured with his Friendship'.[80] Two letters in the Somerset Record Office bear witness to the popularity of Bampfylde's paintings among West Country landowners and gentry. In 1759 Henry Fownes Luttrell of Dunster Castle was eagerly awaiting a painting and asked his agent to call at Hestercombe to see whether it was ready. The agent reported home, 'I was at Majr Bampfylds yesterday and Dilivered your Complements your picture is not done yett but ye Major will finish it as fast as possible and send it'.[81] A Bath patron Edward Drax (another member of the Assembly Rooms management committee) was equally keen to see his landscape in 1777:

> We were four days in anxious Expectation of the arrival of your Picture, after Mrs Drax's receiving your letter. When Tuesday arrived, our hopes were more than satisfied by the receipt of one of the most beautiful Landscapes I ever saw for which I return your Ten Thousand Thanks . . .[82]

Bampfylde sat to Gainsborough in Bath for a 'head' portrait in 1759 or 1760, thus forming an early acquaintance with the artist.[83] Like members of the Earl of Jersey's family, Bampfylde may have been introduced to Gainsborough by the Prices. The Prices of Herefordshire were connected by marriage to the Bampfyldes of Devonshire, the name of Uvedale Tomkyns Prices's brother-in-law Bampfylde Rodd reflecting this connection (fig. 126).[84] Unlike Garvey and Taylor, Bampfylde did respond to Gainsborough's landscape style, making several drawings that include images taken directly from Gainsborough.[85] In addition, as Andrew Wilton has noted, Bampfylde sometimes drew in chalk on blue paper in the manner of Gainsborough.[86] Among the pictures sold from Hestercombe in 1872 was a 'Woodman with donkey, 25 by 30 in' by Bampfylde after Gainsborough, and by Gainsborough himself two 'small sketches': a gilt framed watercolour of '3 Donkeys with Shepherd and sheep on the hill' (sic); the portrait *William Jones* and another unidentified portrait.[87] The small oil landscape by Gainsborough that also belonged to Bampfylde is currently on loan to the Tate Gallery (fig. 147).[88] The evidence of the 1872 sale and a number of inventories are in themselves enough to suggest a good deal of interaction between Bampfylde and Gainsborough and a shared love of music may have contributed to their friendship. A Bath sale catalogue of 1878 claims that Bampfylde was a 'great friend' of Gainsborough and if this is true it is very possible that Bampfylde was the source of at least some of the notable collection of Gainsborough drawings from Barton Grange near Taunton published by John Hayes.[89]

Barton Grange, a property that included the advowson of the Church of Pitminster, belonged, as Hayes has pointed out, to Goodenough Earle at the time of Gainsborough's residence in Bath. The well-known oil portrait of a youth known as *The Pitminster Boy* (fig. 111) and the collection of drawings that came from Barton Grange certainly suggest Gainsborough visited the area. It is reasonable to suppose that Bampfylde would have known his neighbour Earle well and that Gainsborough may have combined visits to Hestercombe and Barton Grange. An engraving after Bampfylde's most celebrated landscape, *The Storm*, is dedicated to William Benson Earle, a relative of Henry Hoare of Stourhead, and it seems quite likely that Goodenough Earle and William Benson Earle were connected.[90]

Other neighbours of Bampfylde's certainly known to Gainsborough were the Tyntes of Halswell House who, as we have seen, commissioned one or more portraits in 1761.[91] The artist seems to have been on very cordial terms with the family, since a series of letters embellished with drawings from Gainsborough to Lady Tynte existed until quite recently.[92] Sir Charles-Kemeys Tynte, who was apparently painted by Hogarth in 1753, inherited estates in Wales from his uncle Sir Charles Kemeys, but was mainly resident at Halswell.[93] He owned an important seventeenth-century portrait thought in the 1760s to be by Van Dyck and of Sir Thomas Morgan, a picture that would appear to have been by Lely or Dobson and is now lost, but was copied at Halswell by Bampfylde (fig. 110) and which must have been seen there by Gainsborough.[94] Since Gainsborough's debt to Van Dyck and seventeenth-century portraiture generally during the Bath period has long been acknowledged, it is of interest to be able to add this to the list of pictures he must have seen locally, the examples at Corsham and Wilton being the best known.[95] As well as seeing this impressive seventeenth-century portrait, Gainsborough must have enjoyed the gardens and park at Halswell, which Sir Charles was busy developing in the 1750s and 1760s (fig. 112). A regrettably short diary kept by Sir Charles-Kemeys Tynte between June and August 1756 presents an idyllic picture of country life in Somerset at this date.[96] It charts a regular exchange of visits between Hestercombe and Halswell and equally frequent visits from members of the Prowse and Trevelyan families, all of whom were patrons of Gainsborough in the early 1760s. On 13 July 1756 Tynte recorded 'soon after breakfast went to see my hay makers & was out almost all the morning . . .'. On Saturday 17 July, 'walked with Ly Tynte in the wood till near twelve Mr Prowse came before one walked with him in the wood, Mr Bampfylde & his Lady Miss Bam: Miss Cooper & Lethbridge dined with me the Hestercombe family left me about seven Mr Prowse stay'd with me having no other company . . .'. In mid-August Tynte visited Bristol Hotwells and Valentine Morris's garden at Piercefield.

110 Coplestone Warre Bampfylde (1720–1791), *Copy of a painting said to be a portrait of Sir Thomas Morgan by Van Dyck* date unknown, watercolour, $17\frac{5}{8} \times 10\frac{5}{16}$ inches (44.7 × 26.2 cm), Ashmolean Museum, Oxford.

Whatever the artistic relationship between Coplestone Bampfylde and Gainsborough, the benefit must have been all Bampfylde's. Gainsborough might, though, have enjoyed some of the paintings in Bampfylde's own collection and he would certainly have profited from introductions to Bampfylde's impressive circle of near neighbours and his friends from further afield including the poet William Shenstone and Bampfylde's in-laws, the Knights of Wolverley.[97] Shenstone and Bampfylde's Bath friend Richard Graves mentions Gainsborough and Bampfylde in one breath in his novel *Columella; or the Distressed Anchoret*.[98]

111 Thomas Gainsborough (1727–1788), *Portrait of a Youth, 'The Pitminster Boy'* c. 1767–9, oil on canvas, 24 × 19¾ inches (60.8 × 50.4 cm), private collection, on loan to Gainsborough's House, Sudbury.

112 Lady Elizabeth Harcourt (1739–1811), *Sir Charles-Kemeys Tynte's Wood at Halswell* c. 1760, pen and ink and wash, 10⅞ × 6¾ inches (27.5 × 17.2 cm), British Museum, London.

Finally, Coplestone Bampfylde must be the 'Captain Bonfield' who introduced the German violinist John Malchair to Robert Price of Foxley, thus instigating a chain reaction that ultimately linked Price's drawing methods with those of John Constable at the end of the century. Malchair, who became leader of the Oxford Music Room band and a well-known drawing master in Oxford, learnt from Price the value of always carrying a sketchbook to record landscape and the effects of light and weather, a practice he encouraged among his students. These pupils included Sir George Beaumont and Dr William Crotch, both of whom had an important influence on Constable in the 1790s.[99]

Two further landscape artists who also had strong connections with Bath, although they did not live there before 1774, were Alexander Cozens and his son John Robert Cozens.[100] Alexander Cozens's link with Bath may have been through his father-in-law, the engraver John Pine (1690–1756). Pine engraved the broadsheet publishing the proposed hospital at Bath as early as 1738, at a time when one might have expected John Wood to use the local engraver Jacob Skinner.[101] The print, or perhaps Wood's original drawing, can be seen on the wall in William Hoare's group portrait of *Dr William Oliver and Mr Jeremiah Peirce . . . examining Patients* (fig. 11). John Pine had a good deal in common with Thomas Worlidge, being a like-minded Rembrandt enthusiast (his own portrait was painted in the style of a Rembrandt self-portrait by Hogarth), and it is quite possible that Pine and Worlidge were acquainted with each other in Bath as well as London.[102] Two of Pine's children, Robert and Simon, lived in Bath for parts of their lives.[103] It was Simon Pine who sprung to Gainsborough's defence following the publication of Underwood's derogatory poem in 1767.[104] Robert Edge Pine, the history and portrait painter, lived in Bath between 1772 and 1779, leaving his mark very prominently on the city in the form of the figure of Justice which surmounts the Guildhall.[105] Ten years before he settled in Bath, the public was being invited to subscribe to engravings of his *Surrender of Calais* and *Mrs Pritchard in the Character of Hermione* at Leake's bookshop.[106]

The presence in Bath of so many members of the Pine family might well have encouraged Alexander Cozens to become a regular visitor. His experience as a drawing master at Eton between 1763 and 1768 would also have put him in touch with the affluent young men who enjoyed Bath's social life, many of whom sat to Gainsborough or Hoare when they were in town.[107] It is clear from a series of letters from Alexander Cozens to William Hoare at Bath that Cozens knew both John Taylor and Coplestone Bampfylde.[108] John Robert Cozens etched and hand coloured a set of eight views of Bath 'in the manner of drawings' in 1773, the one depicting the Circus apparently being drawn from inside Gainsborough's sister Mrs Gibbon's house (fig. 113).[109] How John Robert Cozens came to know Richard Payne Knight a few years later, and to accompany him on a trip to Italy, has been regarded as something of a puzzle.[110] This may be explained by the fact that Alexander Cozens knew Bampfylde, as is proved by his letters to Hoare, and thereby gained an introduction to Mrs Bampfylde's first cousin Richard Payne Knight. As I shall show, it also seems very likely that Alexander and John Robert Cozens knew the work of Robert Price, and especially Price's views of the Alps drawn in his grand tour (fig. 137).

Although no definite link between Alexander Cozens and Gainsborough in Bath can be proved, the two artists certainly had much in common in the early 1770s, when John Robert Cozens made his etchings of the city. Both Alexander Cozens and Gainsborough were experimenting with the use of varnish for watercolours. While Gainsborough's Circus neighbour Benjamin Colborne sent advice on this subject to Ozias Humphry in 1771, Alexander Cozens sent recipes for

113 John Robert Cozens (1752–1797), *The Circus* 1773, etching with watercolour wash, 11⅛ × 14¹⁵⁄₁₆ inches (28.2 × 38 cm), published 1773, Victoria Art Gallery Bath and North East Somerset Council. The view appears to have been drawn from inside the house leased at this date by Gainsborough's sister Mrs Mary Gibbon. Gainsborough lived two doors to the east between 1767 and 1774. The southerly view from his house would have been very similar.

varnish to Humphry in 1773.[111] A varnished wash drawing in Gainsborough's style and inscribed 'From Gainsbro' formerly in the A. P. Oppé collection is believed to be by Alexander Cozens (fig. 114).[112] A connection between either Alexander or John Robert Cozens and Gainsborough in Bath is potentially of more interest than the undoubted friendship that existed between the other landscape painters already mentioned, simply because both the Cozens were artists of much greater significance. Any interchange of ideas between Gainsborough and Alexander Cozens could be seen as a genuine two-way process that might positively affect both artists.[113]

The statistics show that landscape painting was always a relatively limited activity in Bath compared with portraiture. It appears that Garvey, Taylor and Bampfylde satisfied a limited market for modestly priced decorative landscapes while Gainsborough, who set his sights higher, was frustrated. Although the few documents that exist show that visitors were impressed by Gainsborough's landscapes, they probably considered them expensive. The paintings Gainsborough succeeded in selling did, however, enter major collections such as Scampston, Bowood and Stourhead, where they hung alongside old masters and played an important role in raising the status of British landscape, setting the scene for what the Earl of Shelburne conceived as 'the *foundation of a school of British landscapes*'.[114]

In order to set Gainsborough's work fully in context it should be pointed out that there also existed in Bath a third tier of landscape painting, well below the standard offered by Gainsborough's friends and associates. In his essay on the genius of the young Thomas Barker, published in 1793, Sir Edward Harington described 'Old Allen', a painter who had

114 Attributed to Alexander Cozens (1717–1786) after Thomas Gainsborough, *Landscape with Figures and Sheep* date unknown, grey wash on varnished tracing paper, $10\frac{7}{8} \times 15\frac{5}{8}$ inches (27.5 × 39.6 cm), Tate Britain, London.

earned a living in Bath for over seventy years painting ridiculously debased versions of Claudean compositions. Although these landscapes were apparently abysmal in quality, they must have found buyers, and the painter managed to maintain some semblance of respectability in Bath society. In old age he clung on to the tradition of wearing a sword 'as a proof of *gentility* and *prowess*', decades after Beau Nash had forbidden all wearing of swords in the city.[115] There were also the 'jobbing painters' such as Joseph Woolley who, in the mid-century was providing 'Landskip Painting, Fruit and Flower Pieces for Chimneys', and a host of other useful decorative work, all evidently at the lowest prices, since his income never allowed him to progress beyond a modest address in Avon Street.[116]

Until the late part of the century relatively few artists recorded the scenery of the area although most visitors (and residents like Dr Oliver) found it attractive. Horace Walpole was an exception: his distaste for Bath even extended to its landscape. 'Mountains', he grumbled, 'are very good frames to a prospect, but here they run against one's nose . . .'.[117] The proximity of the city's encircling hills was the very feature that entranced other visitors. Oliver Goldsmith described how people entertained themselves after noonday Church: 'Some walk in the meadows around the town, winding along the side of the river Avon, and the neighbouring canal; while others are seen scaling some of the romantic precipices that over-hang the city'.[118] These 'precipices' made Bath a very different place from any other that Gainsborough had lived in and there is every indication that he drew inspiration from the wooded and rocky hillsides that characterised the area. He derived great pleasure from riding in the surrounding countryside as a relaxation from portrait painting. Margaret Gainsborough later told the diarist Joseph Farington how 'While he resided at Bath' her father used to 'ride out frequently, after he had recd. his morning sitters'.[119] The artist himself wrote to James Unwin following his illness in 1763, 'I Ride every minute in the Day unless it rains pouring', and both Ozias Humphry and Uvedale Price accompanied him on such rides.[120] Humphry recalled,

> when Summer advanced, and the Luxuriance of Nature invited and admitted it, he [Humphry] accompanied Mr. Gainsborough in his Afternoon Rides on Horseback to the circumjacent Scenery, which was in many Parts, picturesque, and beautiful in a high Degree. To these and succeeding Excursions the Public are indebted, for the greater Part of the Sketches, and more finished Drawings from time to time made public . . .[121]

Gainsborough's ramblings in the countryside were apparently observed by local residents and his association with particular localities was, in the nineteenth century, romantically commemorated by the naming of several natural features after the artist. The hills above Bathampton (fig. 6) were reputed to have been among his favourite haunts and, according to the nineteenth-century antiquary Frederick Shum, 'On the heights above he was often seen sketching, and one of the crags yet bears the name "Gainsborough's Pallett"'.[122] In the nearby man-made landscape of Shockerwick Park, the property of his friend Walter Wiltshire, was a tree known as 'Gainsborough's elm'.[123] A house in the once picturesque village of Chilcompton was named after him, as has already been mentioned.

Ronald Paulson has proposed that 'Gainsborough's landscapes are as much about the art of painting as about the Sudbury or Bath countryside' and he suggests that it might be more appropriate to name the different phases of his career after the painters he imitated than after East Anglia, Bath and London.[124] Thus the artist's early life would be linked with the Dutch painters, and Wijnants in particular, and his Bath period with Rubens and Van Dyck. Michael Rosenthal has recently pointed out that Gainsborough's well-known letter to Lord Hardwicke, in which he declined to paint a '*real View*', may be taken to mean that Gainsborough was 'advocating an elevated, academic, kind of landscape painting, rather than the concentration on actualities implicit in "*real Views*"'.[125] John Barrell, as discussed above, interpreted the shift as from a private to a public art form, and it is significant that the new style of Gainsborough's landscape develops hand-in-hand with the new opportunities afforded by the London public exhibitions. Whatever his new ambitions – and all the evidence is that he was determined never to be shackled by topography – the accounts of Ozias Humphry and others show just how important the observation of nature continued to be. For this reason it is worth looking at some of Bath's 'circumjacent Scenery', as it appeared in the eighteenth century, and to identify those areas that attracted contemporary poets and painters.

Thomas Thorpe's 1742 *Survey of the City of Bath . . . and of Five Miles Round* (figs. 6, 37, 91, 165 and endpapers) gives a good indication of the contours and woodland in the locality, as well as noting the estates and houses with which the artist was linked. The locations most regularly mentioned in contemporary journals, letters, poems and guidebooks are Lansdown, Hampton Rocks (and nearby Warleigh Woods) and Wick Rocks. Lansdown, to the north west of Bath, was the area to which Gainsborough was drawn for its health-giving properties following his illness of 1763. The 'sweetly situated' home he rented was 'about three quarters of a Mile in the Lansdown Road', and it was from here that he intended to ride every day.[126] John Wood said of Lansdown, or *Mons Badonica*, that though it was 'inclosed as possible, [it] nevertheless affords many excellent Parts to ride upon'.[127] It was famous as a place for grazing sheep, and its gipsies were well known. The gipsy children begged from passers-by 'in a strange foreign-sounding idiom'.[128] Gainsborough had painted gipsies before coming to Bath, and it is likely that some of the wayside beggars depicted in his later Bath landscapes may be based on images he saw while riding on Lansdown. Below the slopes of Lansdown was a lane leading to the village of Weston, along which, on occasion, Gainsborough walked to visit his 'good friend' the Rector of Weston, the Revd John Chapman, as he mentioned in a letter to William Dodd in 1773.[129]

The road that crossed the upper slopes of Lansdown lead to the village of Wick, about six miles from the centre of Bath. Wick Rocks, a dramatically deep valley edged by vertical cliffs of up to two hundred feet in height, was a favourite place for excursions in the eighteenth and early nineteenth centuries. The Revd Richard Warner (a one-time assistant to the Revd William Gilpin, writer on the Picturesque) described the place as 'remarkable for its picturesque beauty, as its singular geology. It is a deep rugged glen, about three-quarters of a mile in length, which opens suddenly . . . and presents in its rocky sides and stony bottom a singular contrast to the richness and fertility of the adjacent parts'.[130] In Warner's view the place presented 'the most agreeable studies for the painter; and a rich feast for the admirer of romantic natural scenery'. Pierce Egan, writing in 1819, described Wick Rocks as 'like a wilderness', the glen making 'a pleasing sensation in the mind of the spectator'.[131] Edmund Rack, a nearer contemporary of Gainsborough, visited Wick in 1780 and described the 'bold projections' which 'threaten the traveler below, & look sublimely dreadful when frowning through the Trees'.[132] In the early nineteenth century Benjamin Barker made the place his own in a series of aquatints that record the landscape before it was ruined by a succession of paper, cotton, iron and grist mills that took advantage of the swift-flowing stream (fig. 115). Gainsborough must have visited Wick and several of his studies of rocks and water may have been informed by its geology. Two rapid drawings showing steep quarry or cliff faces dated by John Hayes to 1758–9 may also have been inspired by an early visit to the site (fig. 116).[133]

The rocky outcrops known as Hampton Rocks or Hampton Cliffs in the parish of Bathampton and similar formations at King's Down Hill near Shockerwick were partly man-made, being the result of quarrying for stone. They are marked 'Stone Quarrys' on Thorpe's *Survey* (fig. 165). Large, angular blocks of stone, marked by deep parallel fissures, stood exposed at ground level, many of them having trees and roots growing around and through them. The rock once called 'Gainsborough's Pallett' at Hampton may be the same as the one called 'Gainsborough's table' in the 1840s by Henry Venn Lansdown, author of *Recollections of the Late William Beckford*.[134] Henry Lansdown described 'the hills above Warleigh, with Hampton cliffs and the neighbouring woods, where Gainsborough, Wilson and Barker studied Nature so well, and where is shown the flat rock called Gainsborough's table, on which the first of this picturesque triumvirate so often ate his rustic meal'. Thomas Barker certainly used the vicinity of Hampton Rocks (fig. 117) and was probably inspired to do so by the example of Gainsborough. Several of Gainsborough's friends and patrons, such as Walter Wiltshire and the Revd Richard Graves, lived in this area and Warleigh was the home of Louisa Skrine who was painted in London by Gainsborough as *Louisa, Lady Clarges* (Holburne Museum, Bath) in 1778.[135] The distinctive jutting outcrops of Hampton and King's Down Hill must have been the inspiration for the *Rocky Wooded Landscape with Rustic Lovers, Herdsmen and Cows* (fig. 118) which originally belonged to Walter Wiltshire of Shockerwick, and is believed to be one of the two paintings Gainsborough considered the best he had ever painted in 1771.[136]

John Wood, designer of both Gainsborough's Abbey Street and Circus houses, saw himself as the creator of modern Bath, but acknowledged that the place owed as much to the beauty of its natural setting as it did to his architectural vision. He called it as 'A Region that sets Paradise itself before ones Eyes' and would have thoroughly approved of Edmund Garvey's pairing of paintings of Bath and Rome for Sir William St Quintin.[137] Nearly every eighteenth-century writer with something to say about the Bath landscape comments on its *variety*. It was an area of contrasts, with, at Wick, its own miniature Dovedale and within sight of the city itself the rocks of Bathampton, reminiscent of the much grander rocks and mountains of Wales or Derbyshire. Edmund Rack wrote,

> Even in all the nakedness of winter our prospects are pleasing. The wild irregularity of surface, the extent of varied country, the numbers of objects, and the changes of scene at every step furnishes the spectator with unabated pleasure. Dull indeed must be the soul whose Hours can hang heavy on his Hands at Bath.[138]

Rack's unpublished *Journal* from 1780 already speaks with the language of the Picturesque, discerning pleasure in irregularity and variety. Rack came to Bath in 1775, the year

115 Theodore Fielding (1781–1851) after Benjamin Barker (1776–1838), *Scene above Wick Rocks, near Bath* 1824, aquatint, $8^{15}/_{16} \times 10^{13}/_{16}$ inches (22.7 × 27.5 cm), published 1824, Victoria Art Gallery, Bath and North East Somerset Council.

after Gainsborough left, and it is interesting to consider how significantly Gainsborough's work and influence in Bath affected people's perception of the local landscape. That Gainsborough himself drew inspiration from the particular landscape of the area cannot be doubted. That his choice of landscape features was coloured by the influence of Rubens and by contemporary landscape tastes as expressed by his friends the Prices and Richard Graves, is also undeniable.

The methods by which Gainsborough developed his approach to landscape composition through the activity of drawing are complex and many faceted. Although he never stopped observing nature, his creation of a landscape of the imagination seems on occasion to have involved a deliberate stepping back from the physical landscape by the insertion of some form of model or mechanical device between himself and nature. Samuel Taylor Coleridge's description of a process of distancing or filtering in people's imaginative response to nature seems to sum up what happens in the course of Gainsborough's creation of landscape images. In Coleridge's view,

> It is the nature of thought to be indefinite; – definiteness belongs to external imagery alone. Hence it is that the sense of sublimity arises, not from the sight of an outward object, but from the beholder's reflection upon it; – not from the sensuous impression, but from the imaginative reflex. Few have seen a celebrated waterfall without feeling something akin to disappointment: it is only subsequently that the image comes back full into the mind and brings with it a train of grand or beautiful associations.[139]

Gainsborough was able to stimulate a 'train of grand or beautiful associations' by removing his landscapes from the inhibiting, and even (as Coleridge remarks) disappointing, particularity of topography. The compositions he built as models, and then drew, or possibly viewed through lenses, successfully reduced nature to Coleridge's 'indefinite' forms or what Ronald Paulson has called his 'malleable shapes'.[140]

Just as he experimented with the chemistry of drawing and painting techniques, incorporating new varnishes and other preparations developed with the help of apothecary friends in Bath, so it would appear Gainsborough was ready to harness new technology that came his way. He grew up with an interest in science and discovery. Several members of his family were inventors, including his clergyman brother Humphrey who designed a steam engine that was sufficiently advanced to worry James Watt, who patented his famous engine in 1769.[141] One of the artist's oldest friends was Joshua Kirby, the first professional teacher of the science of perspective in Britain, a man with a keen awareness of the latest knowledge on optics.[142] Bath in the 1760s and 1770s was home to a number of scientists including William Herschel, and lectures on scientific subjects had been popular since the 1720s when Jean-Théophile Desaguliers began his regular series of talks on astronomy and physics that included demonstrations using various optical instruments.[143] In the 1740s Benjamin Martin, author of *A New and Compendious System of Optics*, which contained a chapter on the camera obscura, lived in Bath.[144]

While it appears that Gainsborough may have experimented with lenses and other technology, the first and simplest device he used was the small model. Several witnesses described how the artist composed miniature landscapes on a trestle table, using dried herbs and broccoli for trees; broken mirror glass for water; clay; stones and coal.[145] He also modelled small clay figures, the one that has survived being an old carthorse that at one time was a cherished possession of Gainsborough's great admirer John Constable.[146] The use of models was not a practice unique to Gainsborough. Tintoretto had arranged 'little models of wax and clay' in artificially illuminated 'little houses', sometimes suspending figures on strings in order to formulate compositional ideas.[147] Nicolas Poussin used a complex 'grande machine', a box within which small wax figures were arranged, illuminated through side-slits and then viewed through a small aperture.[148] In eighteenth-century England the portrait painters Bartholomew Dandridge and Arthur Devis used small models to organise figure groups and Paul Sandby used landscape models, like Gainsborough using coal for rocks and even including a miniature cottage in which he lit a small fire so that smoke could curl from the chimney.[149] As Woodall suggested, Gainsborough's use of models may initially have been prompted by Hubert Gravelot who, in common with other French eighteenth-century painters, made regular use of models. Boucher had an entire 'toy' farm including a miniature cart, harrow and wheelbarrow among his studio props.[150] Dandridge's practice might also have had a direct influence on Gainsborough, since he was a member of the St Martin's Lane set of artists known to Gainsborough in his youth and was on several occasions employed by the Price family, the large group portrait of Uvedale Tomkyns Price and his family (fig. 129) being precisely the kind of composition that was constructed with models.[151]

Having built his small models, Gainsborough then drew from them, often in artificial light.[152] It is not clear whether his models were ever arranged within a box-like structure, like Poussin's, but the piercing shafts of side-light in some of his drawings suggest that they might sometimes have been lit in the same way as Poussin's, through slits in the side of a box or through simple barriers which controlled the light. A small number of landscape drawings from Gainsborough's Bath period strongly indicate the influence of a camera obscura, suggesting that he may also have sometimes looked at these models, or perhaps nature itself, through a lens.[153]

116 Thomas Gainsborough (1727–1788), *Study of a Quarry* 1758–60, pencil, $6\frac{1}{6} \times 7\frac{13}{16}$ inches (15.4 × 19.8 cm), British Museum, London.

117 Thomas Barker (1769–1847), *Hampton Rocks, Morning* 1790s, oil on canvas, $29\frac{1}{4} \times 37\frac{1}{2}$ inches (74.3 × 95.2 cm), Victoria Art Gallery, Bath and North East Somerset Council.

118 Thomas Gainsborough (1727–1788), *Rocky Wooded Landscape with Rustic Lovers, Herdsman and Cows* c. 1771, oil on canvas, 47 × 58 inches (119.4 cm × 147.3 cm), National Museum of Wales, Cardiff.

That he was familiar with lens technology is clear from a letter of 1773. Writing about the actor John Henderson, who some said bore a resemblance to the great David Garrick, Gainsborough said, 'He is absolutely a Garrick through a Glass not quite drawn to its focus, a little mist hangs about his outlines, and a little fuzziness in the tone of his voice . . .'.[154] To be able to talk about pulling an image into focus in this way, the artist must have experienced using either a telescope, microscope or camera obscura, or perhaps all three.

Camera obscuras were quite common instruments by the eighteenth century and the fact that Bath was a medical centre might have meant that they were particularly well known there. In Europe generally, optical instruments were manufactured by the men who also made surgical, physical and astronomical instruments.[155] Camera obscuras were used by doctors and anatomists to create medical diagrams and illustrations, one of the clearest images of a camera obscura in use being an engraving showing a man using a very large box-style instrument to draw part of a skeleton for William Cheseldon's *Osteographia, or the Anatomy of Bones* of 1753.[156] Rather sophisticated types of camera obscura were being developed in the 1760s and 1770s, including reflex models that produced an image the right way up (rather than inverted) and ones that could be used indoors. The most advanced British example was Storer's Royal Accurate Delineator, patented in 1778, a device that prompted an excited reaction from Horace Walpole who wrote, 'It is such a perfecting of the camera obscura, that it no longer depends on the sun . . . Sir Joshua Reynolds and West are gone mad with it, and it will be their own faults if they do not excel Rubens in light and shade, and all the Flemish masters in truth. It improves the beauty of trees . . .'.[157] Walpole did not just see the camera obscura as an aid to topographical accuracy, or the drawing of architecture, but as something that could help modern English artists paint as well as the old masters. Historians have generally considered the camera obscura as a tool of the topographer, and of watercolour painters in particular, but Walpole's comments show that it had a much wider application, even stimulating painters such as Reynolds, who had little interest in topography.

What even a simple camera obscura could do was to contain, abstract and harmonise areas of light and shade in the same way as a Claude glass did, but with much greater control and clarity. The Claude glass, an oval, slightly convex reflecting mirror that gave a simple wide-angle view, had been used by both professional and amateur artists throughout the century.[158] A young artist, possibly Gainsborough himself, is shown using one in a woodland setting in a drawing in the collection of the British Museum.[159] The camera obscura, which projected an image through a lens on to a ground glass screen, could be used as a direct drawing aid, in which case prepared paper was placed against the ground glass and the outlines of the view then traced. Indirectly, it was a means of simply observing a reduced 'framed' section of nature, more manageable than the ever-shifting, wide view normally taken in by the eye. Camera obscuras were also used indoors, in a darkened room, to copy drawings and paintings, from the 1720s onwards.[160]

Early camera obscuras tended to distort the viewed image at its edges, leaving trees and other features curved or falling away. This phenomenon, known as 'spherical aberration', results from the use of a single, convex lens, which refracts marginal light rays more strongly than the axial rays, a problem that was only solved with the introduction of the composite lens.[161] It is this characteristic distortion or 'falling away' of the image at the edges that appears in several of Gainsborough's Bath drawings (figs 119 and 120).[162] The two drawings illustrated here are not traced directly from a ground glass screen, since they are not on thin tracing or transfer paper, but they portray the effects of primitive lens distortion.[163] Why Gainsborough should on occasion deliberately imitate the distortion that most artists were at pains to correct, is a puzzling question. It is possible he speculated that the lens of the camera obscura worked like the eye, and that the inclusion of such distortion might add to the veracity of his drawing, particularly in giving an effect of depth.[164]

While it seems highly likely that Gainsborough had an interest in the effects produced by the projection of an image on to a ground glass screen by a lens in a camera obscura, it is known for certain that he used a 'show box' or light box. A show box and a set of landscapes on glass slides, painted by Gainsborough for viewing in the box, survives, and is now in the Victoria and Albert Museum.[165] It is generally agreed that these surviving transparencies date from the 1780s and it is usually supposed that Gainsborough's experiments were prompted by his undoubted excitement at seeing Philippe Jacques de Loutherbourg's *Eidophusikon* and an exhibition of glass paintings by Jervas in London in 1782.[166] It is also the case, however, that light boxes were used for entertainment much earlier than this and Gainsborough could well have begun his experiments in Bath. His baffling remark to Garrick in 1772 about 'the advantage of all our new discoveries of transparent Painting &c &c.' sounds very like a reference to painting on glass.[167] As early as 27 April 1747 an advertisement in the *Bath Journal* described

> the Most Curious Optical Machine, Which contains seven Boxes, completely fitted, with delightful Views, particularly the Beautiful Views, of Lord Cobham's Gardens. – To be Sold, whole, or single Boxes, the lowest Price being fix'd on each Glass. Enquire at Mr. Deverill's, at the Catherine-Wheel, in the Market-Place, Bath.[168]

Another optical device of a different kind, perhaps involving a prism, called 'Sir Isaac Newton's Opticks', or 'Gough's illuminated artificial Wilderness' also entertained Bath visitors in the 1740s, showing fruit trees, 'Busts and Figures of the Ancients standing on Brackets or Trussels, in Roman and Italian Taste'.[169] The boundaries between entertainment and art scarcely existed in Bath in the eighteenth century, with artists' picture rooms providing a diversion for visitors in the mornings in much the same way as 'Gough's Wilderness' or other displays involving the projection of light and illuminated transparencies did. The light boxes with views of Lord Cobham's gardens must have been earlier versions of a device very like Gainsborough's light box and it seems possible that many such instruments existed but, by their very nature, have not survived. Gainsborough's 'transparent Painting', about which he told Garrick in 1772, might have been an enthusiasm shared by Edmund Garvey (who was often associated with painting for the stage) and by John Taylor, his neighbour in the Circus, who is said to have demonstrated a show box in 1766.[170]

While it is clear that there was only a limited commercial demand for landscape painting in Bath in the 1750s, 1760s and 1770s, what emerges is a picture of Gainsborough forging a very personal path, developing new ideas rapidly through drawing, and selling some of his landscapes to a handful of discerning clients. Since most of the other landscape painters present in the city were at best solidly traditional in style, and at worst mere daubers of cheap furnishing pictures, Gainsborough cannot have gained much inspiration from

119 Thomas Gainsborough (1727–1788), *A Hilly Landscape with Figures approaching a Bridge* c. 1763, watercolour and bodycolour, $10\frac{7}{8} \times 14\frac{7}{8}$ inches (27.6 × 37.8 cm), Yale Center for British Art, Yale University Art Collection, James W. and Mary C. Fosburgh Collection. The first owner of this drawing was Dr Rice Charleton.

their efforts, although he appears to have positively enjoyed the company of several of them. Alexander Cozens was the only landscape artist with whom there might have been a genuine exchange of progressive ideas. It must be concluded that Gainsborough's stimulus came more from his contact with people who were not themselves painters, but men who were experimenting in the fields of science and technology, writers, collectors and gardeners. It is to these latter groups, the writers and theorists and people who were busy developing real landscapes at their country estates, that it is necessary to turn in order to gain a deeper insight into the landscapes painted in Bath.

120 *(right)* Thomas Gainsborough (1727–1788), *Wooded Landscape with Drovers and Horses* 1768–70, pencil, grey and brown wash, $7\frac{3}{4} \times 9\frac{3}{4}$ inches (19.7 × 24.8 cm), whereabouts unknown.

8

'Something more elevated': The Intellectual Elite of Bath

Gainsborough has sometimes been cast as a wild, intuitive artist, a pupil of nature rather than any academy of art. The painter himself made a number of self-deprecating remarks to the effect that he had little learning and even little brain, thus contributing to this popular anti-intellectual image, and the comment by William Jackson that he 'detested reading' has been accepted by some as the definitive statement on the subject.[1] As recently as 1995 John Brewer wrote of Gainsborough's 'antipathy . . . to painterly learning'.[2] Marcia Pointon has, however, argued that this notion of Gainsborough as unread or unlearned is false and John Barrell, Michael Rosenthal and others have shown that the artist's work undoubtedly relates to contemporary literary themes.[3] It can also be shown that Gainsborough's life in Bath was closely bound up with a group of men who (like those who were apparently associated with an academy in the early 1740s) were intellectuals with a shared interest in art, aesthetics, landscape and literature. This group included Uvedale Tomkyns Price whose grandson Uvedale formulated Picturesque theory, Daniel Webb, writer on aesthetics, and the clergyman-poet Richard Graves.

Rather than reading, what Gainsborough appears to have hated most of all was intellectual pretentiousness, and any attempt (by the Royal Academy or any other body), to institutionalise him or his art. James Northcote said that Gainsborough never went near the Royal Academy because 'He was too proud and satirical; he was not a person to be managed by such a set'.[4] This does not, however, imply that he was detached from current thinking on art theory, and it can be shown that Gainsborough's presence in Bath in the 1760s had a profound effect on the development of Picturesque theory in the late part of the century. At the same time, those thinkers and writers with whom Gainsborough came into contact in Bath were probably as important to the artist as he was to them, and their broad vision of European culture provided a backdrop to his development of a landscape painting style that was, in J. H. Pott's words, 'something more elevated' than the art of the pre-Bath period.[5]

The Picturesque, as defined by Uvedale Price, William Gilpin and Richard Payne Knight, emerged from Edmund Burke's *A Philosophical Enquiry into the Origin of our Ideas of the Sublime and Beautiful* (of 1757) adding to the sublime and the beautiful a third category of appearances. Burke had described how scenes, objects and words could arouse contrasting passions, the sublime being associated with extremes of form and emotion, while the beautiful embraced all that was smooth, gentle and calm. In terms of landscape, the sublime manifested itself through huge rocks, terrifying ravines, dark storms and windswept trees, the favourite subjects of the painter Salvator Rosa. The beautiful, on the other hand, was to be found in untroubled water, classical architecture and elegantly grouped trees, subjects most effectively portrayed on canvas by Claude Lorrain and in the physical landscape of England by the gardener 'Capability' Brown. The key words for the Picturesque were 'variety' and 'roughness', or what we might today define as 'texture'. The Picturesque was also associated with certain categories of subject matter, generally non-classical in origin, and notions of complexity and playfulness.

The illustrations to Payne Knight's *The Landscape* (of 1794), showing a landscape in the manner of Brown and a Picturesque landscape are, in formal terms, a composition that might have been designed by Richard Wilson contrasted with one in the style of Gainsborough (figs 123 and 124). In this case the illustrations were devised for Payne Knight by the watercolourist Thomas Hearne (1744–1817), but an interesting pair of prints published thirty years earlier exemplifies the contrast through works by Wilson and Gainsborough themselves. They are *The Lake of Nemi, or Speculum Dianae* (fig. 122) after the painting by Richard Wilson then owned by the banker Henry Hoare and *The Gipsies* (fig. 121) by Gainsborough. Their publication was first announced in 1758, just one year after the appearance of Burke's *Philosophical*

121 Thomas Gainsborough (1727–1788), and Joseph Wood (d. 1763) after a painting by Gainsborough, *The Gipsies* (first impressions 1759), engraving, $19\frac{5}{8} \times 17\frac{1}{2}$ inches (49.8×44.5 cm), as published by John Boydell, 1764, private collection. Boydell acquired the plate after Joseph Wood's death.

122 Joseph Wood (d. 1763) after Richard Wilson (1714–1782), *The Lake of Nemi, or Speculum Dianae* (first impressions 1759), engraving, $19\frac{5}{8} \times 17\frac{1}{2}$ inches (49.8 × 44.5 cm), as published by John Boydell, 1764, British Museum, London. As the inscription indicates, the painting by Wilson from which this engraving is taken was originally in the collection of the banker Henry Hoare of Stourhead.

123 Benjamin Thomas Pouncy (d. 1799) after Thomas Hearne (1744–1817), *A Landscape in the Manner of Brown* 1794, etching, 9 × 11¼ inches (22.8 × 28.5 cm), printed as Plate II, inserted between pages 16 and 17 of Richard Payne Knight's *The Landscape, A Didactic Poem, in Three Books. Addressed to Uvedale Price, Esq.*, London 1794.

124 Benjamin Thomas Pouncy (d. 1799) after Thomas Hearne (1744–1817), *A Picturesque Landscape* 1794, etching, 9 × 11¼ inches (22.8 × 28.5 cm), printed as Plate I, inserted between pages 16 and 17 of Richard Payne Knight's *The Landscape, A Didactic Poem, in Three Books. Addressed to Uvedale Price, Esq.*, London 1794. In his text Payne Knight refers to this print as an illustration of an 'undressed' landscape, as opposed to one 'in the modern style'.

Enquiry. These two compositions, which may be considered precursors to Price and Knight's verbal definitions of the beautiful and the Picturesque, were engraved by Gainsborough's mentor Joseph Wood who proposed them as a pair in an advertisement in the *Public Advertiser* of 14 October 1758. The engravings were highly significant for both Wilson and Gainsborough. The *Lake of Nemi* was the first print after a landscape by Wilson, while *The Gipsies* was the first large-scale print attempted by Gainsborough himself.[6] Once he had etched the plate, it was, as the inscription indicates, handed over to Wood, an experienced printmaker, to complete the tonal engraving.[7] It is likely that Joshua Kirby was the instigator of this project. He was one of Gainsborough's earliest friends in the art world and had collaborated with Wood on several projects of his own; he was also Richard Wilson's neighbour in Great Queen Street, just south-west of Holborn.[8] The announcement of the proposed publication of the pair of prints in the press, just as Gainsborough arrived in Bath, must have been carefully timed. It would certainly have been noticed in Bath, where poring over the London newspapers in a coffee shop was a favourite mid-morning pastime for gentlemen, and where, only a week earlier, Gainsborough's arrival in the town was announced in the Bath papers. The pairing of Wilson and Gainsborough's pictures must have been intended to draw attention to the different strengths of the two major emerging landscape artists of the British school. Wilson's picture displays an easy classicism born out of his recent stay in Italy, while Gainsborough adopts a distinctively 'English' approach. In Wilson's composition the goddess Diana and her nymphs are grouped against the glassy sea of Lake Nemi in the Italian Campagna; Gainsborough's tattered gipsies gather with their donkey under an English oak to smoke their pipes and cook a simple meal. Characteristically, Gainsborough has included among his rustic figures a pretty girl who peeps flirtatiously out at the viewer from under a large straw bonnet: she, by accident or design, is the Diana figure of this particular landscape.

Gainsborough's landscapes of the late 1750s and the 1760s, in which rustic figures (peasant labourers as well as gipsies) occupy a richly wooded or rocky countryside, often travelling along deeply rutted winding roads, equate with the Picturesque more closely than those painted earlier or later. The link between Gainsborough and the Picturesque has often been noticed, but scholars

> have not attempted to establish any specific connections between Gainsborough's landscape imagery and Picturesque theory because of a lack of direct textual evidence linking Gainsborough's images to Picturesque literature and because of a widely held view that the artist simply did not read.[9]

Whether or not Gainsborough read is, however, immaterial, since the pictures by him that contain recognisably Picturesque imagery predate the published literature on the subject by two decades or more.[10] What is at issue is whether the evolution of Picturesque theory, long before it was published, involved an intellectual input from the artist, and here important evidence does exist. If it is accepted that Gilpin, Price and Knight are the principal early exponents of Picturesque theory in England, it must be admitted that no direct link between Gilpin and Gainsborough can be found, but it is beyond doubt that a strong connection existed between the artist and Sir Uvedale Price, Price's father and grandfather.[11] Indirect links also existed between Gainsborough and Richard Payne Knight and it should be remembered that that although they subsequently grew apart, Price and Knight initially developed their ideas along very similar lines. Payne Knight's poem *The Landscape* was 'Addressed to Uvedale Price Esq.' on its title page.

In his *Essay on the Picturesque*, Uvedale Price makes a number of direct references to Gainsborough. In a particularly well-known passage he recalls,

> when he lived at Bath, I made frequent excursions with him into the country. He was a man of an eager irritable mind, though warmly attached to those he loved; of a lively and playful imagination, yet at times severe and sarcastic; but I have frequently remarked, that when we came to cottage or village scenes, to groups of children, or to any objects of that kind that struck his fancy, his countenance would take an expression of particular gentleness and complacency.[12]

Price also talks of visiting a collection of paintings with Gainsborough where he and the painter closely scrutinised a portrait by Reynolds which, they concluded, had been drastically overpainted in all but the face.[13] He describes Gainsborough's practice of bringing 'roots, stones and mosses' into his painting room and speaks of the artist's delight in painting small pools and streams of the kind that were created by the abandonment of old gravel pits.[14] He calls the painter 'our own Gainsborough, of whom we have so much reason to be proud'.[15] Not only does Price make these personal references to Gainsborough, but in a number of descriptive passages he appears to be seeing landscape through Gainsborough's eyes. Charlotte Klonk has described how, in Price's writings, 'the picturesque emerges as that category which is capable of representing everyday matters, that is, social reality when seen from an idealised vantage-point, rather than taking exceptional events as its subject-matter, as in the sublime and beautiful'.[16] Klonk draws attention to the fact that the very features Price defines as displaying Picturesque characteristics, 'beggars, gypsies, and all such rough tattered figures . . .' had all been portrayed by Gainsborough in the 1760s.[17] This, of course, was the time Price and Gainsborough were most regularly in each other's company.

Like the sublime and the beautiful, the Picturesque was not only concerned with outward appearances but with layers

125 Thomas Gainsborough (1727–1788), *Beech Trees at Foxley* 1760, pencil, chalk, watercolour and bodycolour, 11¼ × 15$\frac{5}{16}$ inches (28.7 × 38.9 cm), signed and dated 1760, the Whitworth Art Gallery, the University of Manchester. The tower in the distance is a pictorial device: its situation and appearance preclude the possibility that it is any church visible from the Foxley estate, nor is it Ragged Castle, Robert Price's folly.

of meaning. A passage of Uvedale Price's *Essay* on this aspect of Picturesque theory is so redolent of Gainsborough it might almost be an apologia for the artist's work of the late 1750s and the 1760s:

> Picturesqueness when mixed with either of the other characters, corrects the languor of beauty, or the tension of sublimity. But as the nature of every corrective, must be to take off from the peculiar effect of what it is to correct, so does the picturesque when united to either of the others. It is the coquetry of nature; it makes beauty more amusing, more varied, more playful . . . by its partial concealments, it excites that active curiosity which gives play to the mind, loosening those iron bonds, with which astonishment chains up its faculties.[18]

There are also more specific connections between Price's thinking and Gainsborough's practice. Price must have derived from Gainsborough his high regard for the Italian painter Pier Francesco Mola (1612–1666). The name of Mola does not immediately spring to mind in the context of English landscape and it is rather surprising to find Price citing his pictures as 'the most perfect example of the higher stile of picturesqueness'. Price uses the model of Mola and Francesco Albani (1578–1660) to confirm 'the alliance between roughness and picturesqueness, and between smoothness and beauty', adding

> There is hardly any painter whose pictures more immediately catch the eye of a connoisseur than those of Mola, or less attract the notice of a person unused to painting. Salvator has a savage grandeur, often in the highest degree sublime; and sublimity in any shape will command attention: but Mola's scenes and figures, are for the most part neither sublime nor beautiful; they are purely picturesque: his touch is less rough than Salvator's; his colouring has, in general, more richness and variety; and his pictures seem

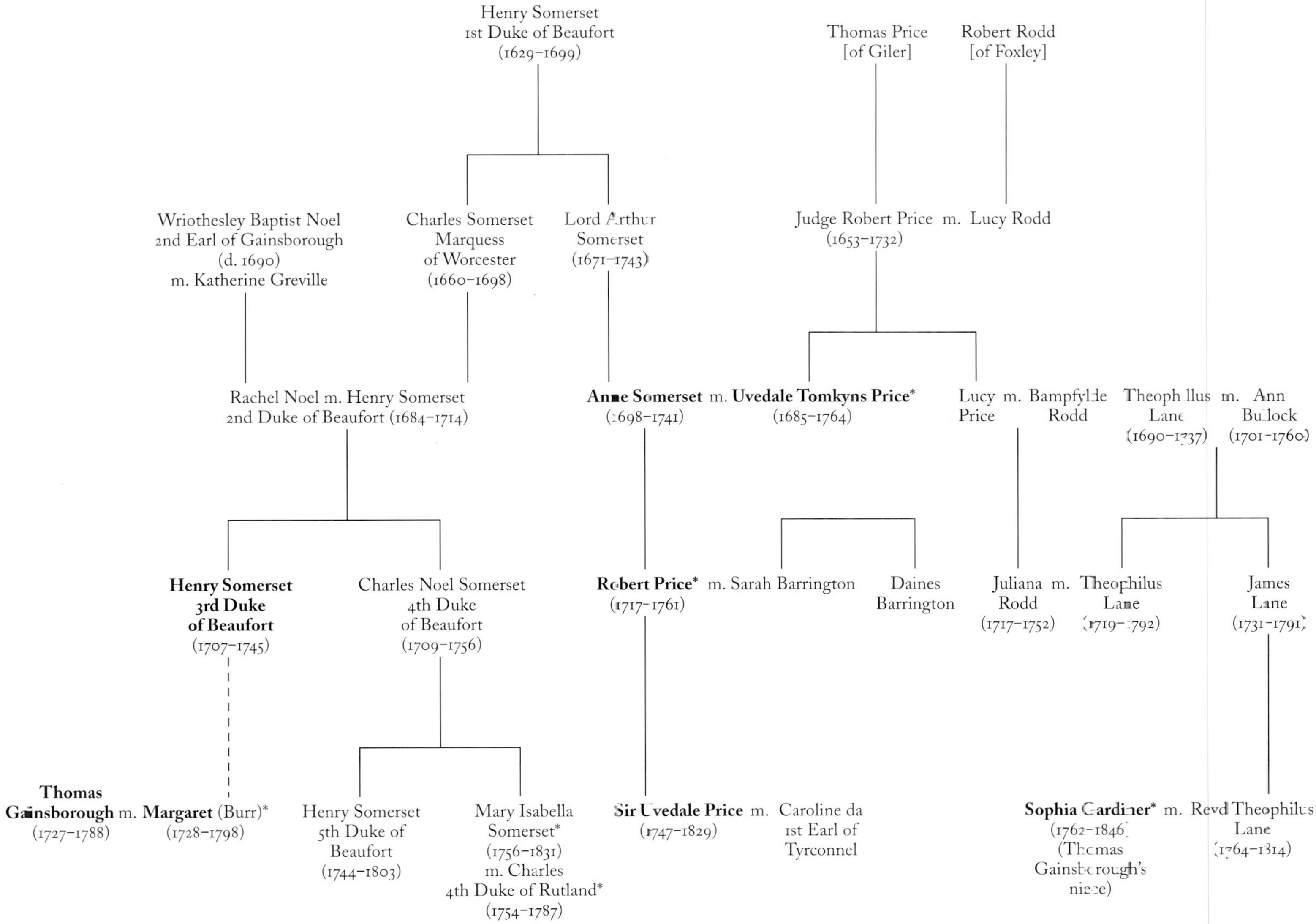

126 The Price family of Foxley in Herefordshire and their relationship with the Dukes of Beaufort, Duke of Rutland and the Noel and Lane families. Asterisks indicate people who sat to Gainsborough.

> to me the most perfect examples of the higher stile of picturesqueness . . .[19]

Mola was an artist ardently admired by Gainsborough. So keen was he to match this painter's colour and 'touch' that he frequently worked with a painting by Mola propped up beside him.[20]

Uvedale Price was only eleven or twelve years old when Gainsborough first visited Bath. He was only thirteen when Gainsborough went to Foxley in the summer of 1760, his first summer in Bath (fig. 125).[21] The artist must have received this early invitation to Herefordshire, probably the first social visit he made anywhere after settling in Bath, from Robert Price. As has already been noted, Robert Price's mother Anne, who had died in 1741, was a cousin of Mrs Margaret Gainsborough's father the Third Duke of Beaufort (fig. 126). The immediate hospitality Gainsborough received from the Prices must have been as a result of this blood tie. Two portraits of Robert Price were painted by Gainsborough before Price's untimely death in 1761, the earlier possibly dating from before Gainsborough's move to Bath and the second from shortly before Price's death (figs 33 and 136). Uvedale Tomkyns Price, who outlived his son, also sat to Gainsborough before his death in Bath in 1764 (fig. 131).[22] Young Uvedale Price's mother had died in 1759, so during the period following Robert Price's death in 1761 responsibility for the boy fell largely to his grandfather in Bath and it was probably at this time that he grew especially close to Gainsborough. The artist was a devoted and protective father to his own two daughters; it is natural that he should have reacted to the plight of the suddenly orphaned Uvedale (three years older that his own daughter Mary), taking him out riding in the countryside and allowing him into his painting room.[23] The landscapes which young Uvedale could have seen being painted at this time, including Dr Charleton's *Landscape with a Woodcutter* (fig. 148) and the large *Mountainous Wooded Landscape*, perhaps painted for William St Quintin

127 George Vertue (1684–1756) after Sir Godfrey Kneller (1648–1723), *Judge Robert Price (1653–1732)* 1717, engraving, 13⅛ × 10¼ inches (33.4 × 26 cm), published by George Vertue, 1717, British Museum, London.

(fig. 101), are those to which the narrative of the *Essay on the Picturesque* most pointedly relates.

The Prices were members of a distinguished Welsh family. Uvedale Tomkyns Price's father, Robert Price, was an eminent judge, Steward to King Charles II's Queen, Catherine of Braganza, from 1685 to 1702 and baron of the Exchequer from 1702 to 1726 (fig. 127).[24] He was a close political ally of the First Duke of Beaufort.[25] A painting by or after Sir Peter Lely at Holkham Hall variously identified as 'Miss Price', Mrs Price or Lady Price, a maid-of-honour to Catherine of Braganza, may represent a member of this Price family.[26] As is remarked in Thomas Pennant's *Tours in Wales*, it was at Giler just south-east of Pentrefoelas in Denbighshire that Judge Robert Price was born in 1653 (fig. 140). Pennant (who sat to Gainsborough in 1776) described Price as 'that upright and able judge . . . [whose] famous speech in the house of commons, against the grant of the great *Welsh* lordships to the earl of *Portland*, will ever testify his love to his country'.[27] Judge Robert Price's attachment to Wales did not prevent him becoming Tory Member of Parliament for Weobley, Herefordshire, after acquiring the estate of Foxley, between Weobley and Hereford. His son Uvedale Tomkyns Price occupied this parliamentary seat from 1713.[28]

Just before becoming a Member of Parliament, Uvedale Tomkyns Price had been in Italy, passing the winter of 1711–12 in Venice, where he acquired a taste for Venetian art, and Tintoretto in particular.[29] His enthusiasm for Venetian painting illuminates his description of the Escorial in his *Account of the Most Remarkable Places and Curiosities in Spain and Portugal* published in 1749.[30] Price described Spain as 'not only the greatest Repository of fine Paintings; but the Face of the Country itself is rich, beautiful, and pittoresque beyond Imagination'.[31] Although Thicknesse scathingly dismissed this book as one written 'over a pipe, in a chimney corner', it does appear to be a first-hand account of places Price had visited.[32] It also includes respectful descriptions of religious ceremony and regalia, indicating that Price, like the Beauforts and many others of this circle, had strong Catholic sympathies. He gave special attention to several pictures that caught his attention in the Escorial, writing of Tintoretto's *Christ washing the Feet of the Disciples*, 'it is so superior . . . that it will ever be esteemed a Miracle in Art', 'You not only see the Air between the Figures; but are apt to think, that you could walk along the Pavement'.[33] He also greatly admired the work of the Spanish painters Velasquez and Murillo. Of the countryside of Granada he wrote that the 'the Hills . . . are so pittoresque, so various and surprising, that the Senses may be said to be ravished than pleased' and the coast north of Alicante he described in the language of the Sublime, 'full of horrid Creeks . . . Frightful Objects . . . to the Timorous and Tasteless; but Luxury and Rapture to the Painter'.[34] Even if it contains some flights of fancy, the elder Price's account of Spain and Portugal is a document to the tastes of a man who appears to have been one of Gainsborough's first supporters in Bath and his feeling for artists who demonstrated the bravura brushwork that characterised the *pittoresco* in Italy is of particular interest.[35] The importance Gainsborough himself attached to brushwork can only have been encouraged by this particular friendship. Gainsborough's fondness for the work of Murillo might also have been inspired by Uvedale Tomkyns Price.[36]

Price's account of the topography of Spain and Portugal also makes it clear that the Price family's interest in landscape did not begin with Sir Uvedale or even Robert Price, but was already well developed in the 1740s. Uvedale Tomkyns Price's use of the word *pittoresque* does not equate with the notion of the Picturesque as expounded by his grandson, but the book does show a particular sensitivity to landscape and a use of language very like Edmund Burke's, but dating from eight years before the first edition of Burke's *Philosophical Enquiry*. The elder Price's fluent literary style suggests that he was the possessor of a fine library, but practically nothing of it survives, only the occasional appearance of his name in subscription lists providing clues as to its contents.[37] In 1747 he was a subscriber to the Revd Joseph

128 Robert Price (1717–1761), *A View of Foxley in Herefordshire* 1753, pen and ink and ink wash, 10 5/16 × 14 3/8 inches (26.4 × 36.5cm), signed and dated 1753, private collection. Uvedale Tomkyns Price built the mansion at Foxley around 1717. After the death of his wife in 1741 he lived mainly in Bath leaving his son Robert to occupy and develop the Foxley estate.

Spence's *Polymetis,* a commentary on ancient literature and art that also contains an important passage championing a 'natural' style of landscape gardening.[38] Later, Gainsborough owned a copy of this book. Did he perhaps acquire it from Price, or on his recommendation?[39]

Like his son and grandson, Uvedale Tomkyns Price applied his interest in landscape to the practicalities of making his own estate pleasing to the eye. An unpublished letter from Anne Somerset, Mrs Price, to her aunt Lady Anne Coventry describes Foxley at the time she and Uvedale Tomkyns Price took it over. At that date (probably 1714), all that was deemed lacking was 'a good House'.[40] Mrs Price declares that the prospect was 'by most allow'd Charming', and she endeavours to picture it for Lady Coventry 'in the best Manner I can'. Mrs Price's short account of 'the Walk' at Foxley is worth recording in full, since it seems to be the earliest description of one of the seminal idealised landscapes in England,

> in the first place you go throw the garden, to a grove that's so shaded with trees that one may in the hotest day, walk without the Least uneaseness, from thence the next is, on the side of a hill, which walk is very plain and from whence one sees all the country, above 16 miles one way, this Last's till, you go into the Mount, which has the advantage of being very Woody, and a vast many pretty walks in it, Mr Price is Resolved to have a Summer House on the top, I intend to work mightily for the Furnishing of our New Grand House . . .

Sir Uvedale Price later described his childhood memory of his grandfather's summer-house, covered with Virginia creeper.[41] Leading up to the summer-house, Uvedale Tomkyns Price created a flight of steps from a terrace featuring Italianate sculpture, fruit trees and exotic shrubs.[42] The furnishing of the 'New Grand House' (now demolished) must certainly have caused Mrs Price to 'work mightily'. It was a substantial nine-bay, three-storey, brick mansion, almost forbidding in its scale and plainness.[43] It is clearly depicted in Robert Price's drawing of 1753 (fig. 128).

129 Bartholomew Dandridge (1691–c. 1754), *The Price Family* c. 1741, oil on canvas 40 × 62 inches (101.6 × 157.4 cm), Metropolitan Museum of Art, New York, Rogers Fund, 1920 (20.40). Uvedale Tomkyns Price helps a lady, almost certainly his wife Anne Somerset, from a boat. His son Robert Price gestures towards the landscape.

Mrs Price, her sister Mary Greville and Frances Scudamore Somerset, Third Duchess of Beaufort (wife of Mrs Gainsborough's father) all became friends and correspondents of the poet Alexander Pope and were regularly in touch with him at the time Pope was helping Ralph Allen to develop the landscape garden at Prior Park at Bath.[44] Mrs Price features prominently in *The Price Family* group portrait by Bartholomew Dandridge (1691–c. 1754) now in the Metropolitan Museum, New York (fig. 129). She is shown being assisted from a punt by her husband Uvedale Price while young Robert Price points towards the landscape and takes the hand of a lady, perhaps his future wife, Sarah Barrington.[45] The picture may date from 1741, the year of Mrs Price's death, and the year in which Robert Price returned from his grand tour, which had kept him away since 1738. It is just possible that Mrs Price's portrait is posthumous, which might account for her rather awkward placing and scale within the composition. The little girl at the centre of the picture is very reminiscent of the children in Dandridge's *The Ladies Noel*, the children of the Fourth Earl of Gainsborough. This is significant, since Rachel Noel, daughter of the Second Earl of Gainsborough became the Second Duchess of Beaufort (fig. 126). It appears

130 *(above right)* William Hoare (1707–1792), *Uvedale Tomkyns Price (1685–1764)* c. 1761–3, lost painting, photograph in the Heinz archive, National Portrait Gallery, London.

131 Thomas Gainsborough (1727–1788), *Uvedale Tomkyns Price (1685–1764)* 1761–3, oil on canvas, 49 × 39 inches (124.5 × 99.1 cm), Bayerische Staatsgemäldesammlungen, Neue Pinakothek, Munich.

132 Jean-Baptiste-Claude Chatelain (1710–1758) after Jacques Courtois (1621–1676), *Classical Landscape* 1744 (after an earlier painting), engraving, 12½ × 15½ inches (31.5 × 39.2 cm), published by Arthur Pond, 1744, British Museum, London.

Dandridge found important patronage within the related Noel, Somerset and Price families. He also painted some of their associates such as Alexander Pope's lifelong friend, the author Nathaniel Hooke.[46] When Mrs Price died in June 1741 Alexander Pope wrote to Ralph Allen, 'Mr Hooke has often shown me the Gratefulness of his Mind to you: his Work goes on well. I expect him & his Daughter for a few days, he is in unfeigned Sorrow for the death of Mrs Price'.[47] This mention of the death of Mrs Price to Allen shows that the Prices and Ralph Allen must also have been well acquainted, perhaps unsurprisingly, given their mutual friendship with Pope and Price's early support for the Bath Hospital.[48] Two years after Mrs Price's death, on 15 June 1743, Bertie Burgh made a payment through Hoare's Bank to Uvedale Tomkyns Price of £700, a substantial sum of money, perhaps associated with Price's retirement to Bath.[49] Payments to various members of the Greville family are also recorded in James Unwin's account, serving as reminders of the close links that existed between Gainsborough's bankers and the Beaufort and Price set long before the artist's move to Bath.[50]

Bartholomew Dandridge's Price family portrait gives us an important glimpse of the people who welcomed Gainsborough on his arrival at Bath. The picture is also notable for another reason. Dandridge's painting style was unlike that of any other English artist of his generation. As has been mentioned before, his use of models may have been known to Gainsborough, but his work is also distinguished by unusually free and fluid brushwork and French-influenced colouring. In fact it has been noted that both the mood and technique of Dandridge's paintings appear to presage the work of Gainsborough.[51] Dandridge's 'full & free pencil' and 'light easy design' may well have struck a chord with Gainsborough when he saw the picture at Foxley or in Uvedale Tomkyns Price's house in Bath.[52]

The elder Uvedale Price emerges as a man of culture and original tastes, a member of a family that employed Kneller,

133 Joseph Wood (d. 1763) after Gaspard Dughet (1615–1675), *Landscape with Bathers* 1743 (after and earlier painting), engraving, 12½ × 15½ inches (31.5 × 39.2 cm), published by Arthur Pond, 1743, British Museum, London.

Lely and Dandridge, and a person with a strong feeling for landscape.[53] He also had a subversive sense of satire that would certainly have appealed to Gainsborough. In 1733 Price published *A New Catechism for the Fine Ladies*, a parody that seems to have been inspired by what Gainsborough later deplored as 'these fine Ladies' and their endless round of 'Tea drinkings, Dancings' and 'Husband huntings' that dominated Bath's social life.[54] The outrageous *Catechism* includes the memorable prayer of 'Miss Coquetilla': 'preserve my Shape, Oh Lord, and keep a continual Watch over my Complexion, . . .'; and her confession, 'I have erred from the Fashion like a *lost Sheep*, and followed the Devices of last Year . . . But I hope to be forgiven . . . and am willing that the *loss* of my *Virginity* should be my *Penance*'.[55]

Despite this evidence of a humorous and even scurrilous side to Price's nature, Gainsborough's portrait of him (fig. 131) has a distinct air of *gravitas* about it. It styles Price as a connoisseur and amateur artist, as does William Hoare's portrait of him, now lost (fig. 130).[56] There is indeed a curious similarity between the two paintings, both showing the sitter's head positioned and illuminated in precisely the same manner. It is possible that, as with the portraits of Thomas Prowse, both paintings may derive from one set of sittings. By contrast, however, Hoare shows Price surrounded by references to classical art, whereas Gainsborough shows him holding a landscape drawing, on which he has evidently been working, seated next to a framed landscape and a stack of portfolios. The framed drawing on the wall, of a tower by an arch or bridge, is of particular interest. The image appears to be a disguised version, in reverse, of an engraving by Jean-Baptiste-Claude Chatelain, one of a series of Italian landscape prints published by Arthur Pond in the 1740s (fig. 132).

Uvedale's son Robert, who was the family member nearest in age to Gainsborough, inherited his father's love of art.[57] Like his father he travelled in Italy and some of the Giovanni Battista Busiri drawings that he smuggled home in his violin

134 Robert Price (1717–1761), *The Castle and Mount at Foxley in Herefordshire* 1744, pen and ink and wash, 11 × 15 inches (28 × 38 cm), signed and dated 1744, Hereford Libraries and Information Service.

case may have prompted Gainsborough to introduce the use of gouache into his own drawings in the early 1760s (figs 119 and 146).[58] Uvedale encouraged Robert's collecting. In December 1741 Robert reported,

> I have shewn my Father my Busiris things, my prints that I bought at Paris, and given him a notion of what he is to expect from my Collection of prints, and Musick, that is coming by the Carrier. He commends me much for having lay'd out my money in so sensible a manner, and not having let slip an opportunity of buying what will be a continual source of pleasure to me.[59]

Although he does not mention it in this letter, Robert Price may also have purchased his large Gaspard Dughet, *Landscape with Bathers*, while abroad. Joseph Wood's engraving of this (published, like the Chatelain, as part of Arthur Pond's Italian landscape series) shows that the picture was in Robert Price's collection by 1743 (fig. 133).[60] Price probably owed his interest in Dughet to Busiri, who perpetuated the Dughet tradition in Italy. Robert Price's Dughet must have been one of the landscapes by that artist that Gainsborough admired in the 1760s.[61] The slender 'feathery' trees silhouetted against the sky are of the type that Gainsborough adopted in Bath in such pictures as *Peasants and Colliers going to Market* (fig. 158). It is clear from Robert Price's drawing *The Castle and Mount at Foxley in Herefordshire* that Price himself also saw the Foxley landscape in Gaspardesque terms (fig. 134).

Robert Price was born at Poston, a Beaufort property in Herefordshire, on 13 May 1717.[62] He was painted as an infant by Arthur Pond, as a boy by Dandridge, again in the Dandridge family group, and twice by Gainsborough. He was said to be much acquainted with Hogarth.[63] A print of Price inscribed as being after Zoffany (fig. 135) is in fact after the second of Gainsborough's portraits (fig. 136).[64] Robert Price had depicted the Alps during his grand tour of 1738–41 (fig. 137) and came back from a tour of Wales in August 1759

136 *(above)* Thomas Gainsborough (1727–1788), *Robert Price (1717–1761)* 1760–61, oil on canvas, 30 × 25 inches (76.2 × 63.5 cm), whereabouts unknown.

135 *(left)* James Basire the younger (1769–1822), inscribed as after Johann Zoffany (1733–1810), *Robert Price (1717–1761)* 1810 (after an earlier painting), engraving, 4¾ × 4 inches (12 × 10.2 cm), published 1810, British Museum, London.

with more than fifty drawings of Welsh scenery (fig. 138), while Benjamin Stillingfleet, who travelled with him, made a study of mountain grasses.[65] As David Solkin has pointed out, the landscape of Wales was relatively unknown to Englishmen in the mid-century, Richard Wilson's Welsh views dating from 1765–7 and William Gilpin's tour of the Wye not taking place until 1770.[66] Price's excursion into Wales in search of landscape scenery (and waterfalls in particular) must have been among the earliest, although John Boydell, a native of North Wales, had engraved and published a view of *Rhaidder Fawr, A great Cataract, three Miles from Penmaen Mawr* in 1750.[67] In attempting to depict the landscape of Wales, Price used the lessons he had learnt from Busiri in Italy, and, perhaps more importantly, from the French painter and engraver Jacques-Phillipe Le Bas, whose practice of carrying a sketchbook at all times he recommended to John Malchair when Malchair visited Foxley in the summer of 1757.[68] Price, like Gainsborough, also learned by imitating Dutch artists such as Anthonie Waterloo (1609/10–1676), the artist whom Payne Knight calls 'humble Waterloe, to nature true': *Wooded Landscape*, a pencil and wash drawing by Price in the British Museum, is inscribed on the back 'After an Etching of Waterlow'.[69] Price's Welsh views, or at least the ones that have survived, are in pencil, pen and wash and depict waterfalls, bridges, lakes and mountains in Merionethshire, Caernarvon and Radnorshire.[70]

Robert Price's depictions of the Alps may have influenced Richard Payne Knight and John Robert Cozens's continental tour of the mid-1770s. As we saw, Alexander Cozens certainly knew Coplestone Bampfylde, whose wife was Payne Knight's cousin, and since Payne Knight and young Uvedale Price were at one time good friends, there would have been plenty of opportunities for Payne Knight to see Robert Price's drawings. There is a distinct sylistic similarity between some of Price's landscapes and John Robert Cozens's watercolours.

137 Francis Vivares (1709–1780) after Robert Price (1717–1761), *View of ye Ice Valley, & Mountains that Surround it, from Mount Anver*, etching, $12\frac{1}{8}$ × $9\frac{1}{2}$ inches (30.8 × 24.2 cm), Witt Collection, Courtauld Institute, London. This print was produced to accompany William Windham's *A Letter from an English Gentleman . . . Giving an Account of a Journey to the Glacieres . . . in Savoy, written in 1741*, London 1744. Robert Price travelled in the Alps in the company of Windham, Benjamin Stillingfleet, the Seventh Earl of Haddington, Richard Pococke and others in 1741.

138 (facing page) Robert Price (1717–1761), *Water-Break-its-Neck, Radnorshire* 1759, pen and ink and ink wash, $9\frac{1}{2} \times 14\frac{1}{2}$ inches (24 × 37 cm), National Library of Wales.

The particular emphasis on waterfalls in Robert Price's Welsh drawings suggests that he may also have played some part in the creative process that led to the building of the elaborately constructed cascade at Coplestone Bampfylde's garden at Hestercombe and, possibly, the cascade at Stourhead, designed by Bampfylde and the painter William Hoare in 1765.[71]

At home in Herefordshire Robert Price combined a keen interest in scientific agricultural practice with the visual improvement of the Foxley estate. In Benjamin Stillingfleet's words, 'he paid particular attention to Agriculture, and rendered his knowledge of art subservient to the improvement of the natural beauties of his demesne, by executing a plan which united novelty, beauty, and profit'.[72] He redesigned the 'walks' around the Foxley estate, creating winding paths through the woods and farmland. The advantages were twofold: 'One was, the walk was lengthened . . . Another was, that by the winding of the path you were constantly enjoying a new prospect; and both these advantages were gained without affectation . . .'.[73] His most remarkable structural creation was 'Ragged Castle', the subject of his own Gaspardesque drawing of Foxley, and one of the earliest Gothick garden buildings in England (figs 139 a and b).[74] Since the drawing is dated 1744 the 'Castle' must have been built soon after Robert Price's return from his grand tour. Although it later became obscured by trees, Ragged Castle was, as Price's drawing shows, a striking landmark in the eighteenth century. It must also have provided excellent views towards the city of Hereford and into Wales. Still standing, though now lacking its Gothick window frames, the Castle is, in plan, a rhomboid.[75] It is built in stone, unlike the house at Foxley, which was of 'English' brick construction. As a result of its singular design the tower appears tall and narrow from one viewpoint and square from another, an optical illusion that must have delighted visitors to Foxley.

A stone external stairway provides access to the upper floor of Ragged Castle. This stairway and the large open arch leading right through the building at ground level (making it rather like a triumphal arch) are clues to its connection with the seventeenth-century gatehouse at Giler, the Price's Denbighshire home (fig. 140).[76] It seems that the rhomboid shape of Ragged Castle, as well as presenting two startlingly different profiles to the spectator, was designed to embody two different cultures. Seen from one aspect its squat pro-

portions make it reminiscent of the Giler gatehouse (symbolising the Price family's Welsh origins); from another viewpoint it appears tall and Italianate, reminding the viewer that the Prices had now broadened their horizons through travel and the activity of collecting. By moving around it, along Robert Price's new winding paths, the visitor could, by a process of association, think himself in Italy one minute and North Wales the next.

In linking Wales and Italy through the symbolism of Ragged Castle and through his Gaspardesque drawings of Wales, Robert Price set the scene for much of the later landscape painting that took place in Wales. The first professional artist to make this sort of connection was Richard Wilson who, in the mid-1760s, painted an upright oil of Lake Nemi entitled *The Lake of Nemi or Speculum Dianae with Dolbadarn Castle*, a picture very similar in design to the one he had sold to Henry Hoare in 1758 (fig. 122). In this later picture, instead of ancient Italian buildings across the lake, he depicted the ruined Dolbadarn Castle which actually stands beside Llanberis Lake in north Wales.[77] Several decades later, following the publication of the literature of the Picturesque, watercolour painters such as Thomas Girtin and John Varley invested the landscape of Wales with a similar kind of grandeur and inspired a host of amateur artists to try to do likewise.

The symbolism of Ragged Castle and the 'Italian' style of Price's Welsh drawings cannot have been lost on Gainsborough, and it is worth reconsidering the framed landscape drawing on the wall in his portrait of *Uvedale Tomkyns Price* in the light of the Prices' creative activities. As we have seen, Robert Price himself depicted the landscape of Foxley as if it was part of the Italian Campagna. Gainsborough's drawing on Uvedale Price's wall shows an Italianate landscape given a distinctively English touch through the introduction of an untidy wooden fence and large trees. Gainsborough's tower in this drawing is not Ragged Castle any more than it is Giler gatehouse, but it is a form of gatehouse, as is the image in Chatelain's print. The framed drawing quietly but pointedly hints at parallels between native and Italian subject matter. As such, it tells us as much about the lessons Gainsborough learnt from the Prices as about the Prices themselves.

Robert Price's admiration of Gaspard Dughet did not prompt him to engage in 'flattening' the Foxley landscape in

139 a and b Ragged Castle, Foxley, photographs, 2001. A folly built by Robert Price in the 1740s, the Castle's rhomboidal plan creates the illusion of a tall tower when viewed from the south-west and a solid, squat building when viewed from the south-east.

the style of Capability Brown, but rather to create a continuous variety of prospects by the careful planning of paths through woodland and productive farmland. His son Uvedale's sympathy for a style of landscape achieved 'without affectation' and his use of painting as a model must grow from Robert's activities at Foxley as well as the influence of Gainsborough. In Uvedale's words,

> There is, indeed, something despotic in the general system of improvement – all must be laid open – all that obstructs levelled to the ground – houses, orchards, gardens, all swept away. *Painting*, on the contrary, tends to humanize the mind: where a despot thinks every person an intruder who enters his domain, and wishes to destroy cottages and pathways, and to reign alone, the lover of painting considers the dwellings, and inhabitants, and the marks of their intercourse as ornaments to the landscape.[78]

Nigel Everett and other commentators have convincingly associated this passage from Uvedale Price's *Essay* with Gainsborough's landscape paintings in which cottages, pathways and the inhabitants of the countryside are certainly perceived as ornaments to the landscape.[79] But in fact, Uvedale's talk of the humanizing power of painting has a very specific source, Reynolds's First Discourse, delivered at the opening of the Royal Academy on 2 January 1769. Reynolds proudly announced that the Academy was 'patronized by a Monarch, who, knowing the value of science and of elegance, thinks every Art worthy of his notice, that tends to soften and humanize the mind'.[80] Uvedale Price appears to have recognised that Gainsborough's art had a particular ability to 'soften and humanize the mind' and was therefore the best available model for a humane landscape. His carefully chosen words demonstrate the extent to which he aligned his landscape theory with current art theory.

What emerges from even a cursory examination of the artist's relationship with the Price family is the impression of a two-way process of support and encouragement. Gainsborough must have learnt much from the elder Uvedale and Robert Price's collections of old master and modern Italian drawings and prints, and their experience of European travel. Robert Price's own drawings of the Alps and the mountains of Wales must have opened Gainsborough's eyes to a new and rugged form of landscape, quite different from the sand dunes and gentle hills of his native East Anglia and of the Dutch pictures by Wijnants and Ruisdael he so admired in his youth. Robert Price's association of the native landscape with the paintings of Gaspard Dughet must have been a major factor in Gainsborough's shift to a 'more elevated' landscape style during the 1760s. The notion of a 'humane' landscape that lacked affectation appears to have been an ideal shared by Gainsborough and Robert Price. It was the essential link between the character of the landscape and the concept of benevolence that was lacking in William Gilpin's Picturesque theory and this is perhaps the reason why there seems to be little meeting of minds between Gainsborough and Gilpin. Everett shows that Gilpin 'sought images of decay, roughness, and age to support aesthetic judgements usually independent of, and often in contrast with, the moral observations that accompanied them': while talking of roughness and other commendable Picturesque qualities, Gilpin still generally recommended Brownian improvements.[81]

140 The Gatehouse at Giler, Cerrig-y-drudion, Denbighshire, photograph Crown Copyright RCAHMW. The gatehouse was built by Judge Robert Price's great-grandfather Thomas Prys in 1623 as an entrance to the house and farm buildings at Giler.

Even Capability Brown's sternest critics had to admit that he was very good at putting his ideas into practice, planning and organising the mechanics of earth-moving, tree-felling and planting. It is of particular interest to note that the first writer to mention Gainsborough's name directly in connection with landscape gardening (as opposed to landscape painting) said 'I could wish therefore that Gainsborough gave the design, and that Brown executed'.[82] The writer was Daines Barrington, brother-in-law of Robert Price and uncle of Sir Uvedale Price, and possibly the author of the comic early account of Gainsborough in Bath published as 'A very extraordinary Journal'. His 'On the Progress of Gardening' was a paper read in 1782 and published in 1785. Dating from a decade before Sir Uvedale's *Essay on the Picturesque*, it is a fascinating document, not only because it proposes Gainsborough's paintings as a model for landscape gardening, but because it seems to indicate that the paintings need to be considered within a literary as well as a painterly context. Barrington traced the history of gardening, believing 'We have indeed allusions to gardens in the present style so early as the time of Tasso, but they existed only in the poet's imagination . . .'.[83] Barrington quotes Spenser's use of Torquato Tasso's Garden of Alcina in *The Faerie Queene*,

> That nature had for wantonness ensu'd
> Art, and that art nature did repine.
> So, thriving each other to undermine,
> Each did the other's works more beautify,
> So differing both in willes, agreed in fine,
> So all agreed through sweet diversity,
> This garden to adorn with all variety.

> It was reserved for Kent to realize these beautiful descriptions, for which he was peculiarly adapted by being a painter; as the true test of perfection in a modern garden is, that a landschape [sic] painter might choose it for a composition.
>
> Kent hath been succeeded by Brown, who hath undoubtedly great merit in laying out pleasure grounds, but I conceive that in some of his plans I see traces of the gardener of Old Stowe, than of Poussin or Claude Lorraine. I could wish, therefore that Gainsborough gave the design, and that Brown executed.[84]

Daines Barrington saw Gainsborough as the natural inheritor of the noble tradition of Claude and Poussin (he probably meant Gaspard Dughet rather than Nicolas Poussin), fearing that Brown was a despoiler of landscape rather like Charles Bridgeman, designer of the old gardens at Stowe at the beginning of the century. Here Barrington may have come close to Gainsborough's own perception of his place within the European tradition of landscape painting. In 1764 in his letter to Lord Hardwicke, Gainsborough wrote that he preferred to paint compositions of his 'own Brain' since 'with regard to <u>real Views</u> from Nature in this Country he has never seen any Place that affords a Subject equal to the poorest imitations of Gaspar or Claude'.[85]

Daines Barrington's paper, with its important conclusion referring to Gainsborough, has been overlooked by writers on Gainsborough and the Picturesque. Barrington was a lawyer, Recorder for Bristol from 1764, a learned, if somewhat eccentric, character who became Vice-President of the Society of Antiquaries.[86] He may have been familiar with Gainsborough's work through his association with Bristol, or through his Price relatives. Only Denis Lambin, writing in 1987 about the development of the Foxley estate, noticed that Daines Barrington pre-empted Price's condemnation of Capability Brown and used Gainsborough's name to recommend a style of landscape that Price subsequently defined and analysed in his *Essay on the Picturesque*.[87]

Barrington's championing of Gainsborough underlines once again the importance of the familial link between the artist and the Prices. There are two postscripts connected with the family tree which should be briefly mentioned here. The tree shows that Mrs Margaret Gainsborough's grandmother, via her natural father the Third Duke of Beaufort, was Rachel Noel, daughter of the Second Earl of Gainsborough (fig. 126). At the time of the artist's death the painting he considered his best, and the one he begged Reynolds to come and see before he died, was the *Woodman*.[88] This picture was purchased by the Fourth Earl of Gainsborough, a sale that must have been extremely gratifying to Margaret Gainsborough since she probably regarded it as ensuring that her husband's greatest achievement remained within the family.[89]

At the opposite end of the family tree are members of the Lane family of Hereford who were related by marriage to the Prices. The Lanes also featured prominently in Mrs Gainsborough's plans after her husband's death. The Gainsboroughs' niece Sophia Gardiner, who had spent part of her childhood in the artist's home, married the Revd Theophilus Lane in Bath in 1796.[90] This niece, rather than any of her other relatives, (such as the Duponts), was chosen by Mrs Gainsborough as executor of her will and members of the Lane family subsequently inherited paintings and drawings as well as other family items. Richard J. Lane, Sophia Gardiner's son, was a lithographer who produced an important set of prints after drawings by Gainsborough and, among his many lithographic portraits, one of Sir Robert Price, son of Sir Uvedale.[91]

Sir Uvedale Price's published references to the artist he calls 'our own Gainsborough' are substantial enough to prove that the great Picturesque theorist grew up knowing the painter well, riding with him in the countryside around Bath and watching him at work. Now that it is known that Mrs Gainsborough was a daughter of Henry Somerset, Third Duke of Beaufort, an explanation can be offered for the friendship between the Prices and the Gainsboroughs. Robert Price was nearest in age to the painter and it would appear that he and his elderly father Uvedale played a supportive role in Gainsborough's early Bath career, introducing him to his most important first patrons, the Earl of Jersey and Viscount Villiers, and probably to other Herefordshire patrons such as their neighbours the Cornewalls of Moccas Court and the Peploes of Garnestone.[92] In turn Sir Uvedale Price was prompted to see Gainsborough in nature and when he came to set down his theory of the Picturesque, to promote those qualities he had first encountered in the Bath paintings of the 1760s. Price's concern for the place of the peasant labourer within the landscape is paralleled in Gainsborough's later Bath landscapes such as the Kenwood *Going to Market*, which Rosenthal identifies as a modern moral subject, illustrating the new peasant hierarchy that emerged from the relentless march of land enclosure.[93] In the light of Gainsborough's strong Tory connections it is worth noting that Sir Uvedale Price's landscape theory was an essentially conservative ideology. In Nigel Everett's analysis Price's clear intention was to link the rise and triumph of improvement with what he took to be a series of alien values – alien in the sense of being contrary to the ideal principles and habits implied by sound constitutional theory, and serving to undermine the authority of landed interest.[94]

Although Sir Uvedale Price is the man remembered as a writer and theorist, his grandfather, as we have seen, was also a writer. All three generations of the family were learned men. In Bath they must have come into contact with Daniel Webb (?1719–1798) who, like the Prices, had spent time in Italy. On his return he settled in Bath to write on painting, music and poetry. If it had been true that Gainsborough never read a book, then the presence of Daniel Webb in Bath throughout the 1760s and 1770s would be of no particular significance. It does appear, however, that Gainsborough had as keen an interest in art theory as any other major painter of his day. Michael Cole has recently shown that Gainsborough had certainly read both Reynolds's third and fourth discourses.[95] A passage in one of the artist's letters also indicates a close knowledge of Jonathan Richardson's *An Essay on the Theory of Painting*, first published in 1715. With reference to the quality of paintings hung at the 1766 Society of Artists exhibition in London, Gainsborough wrote to David Garrick, 'There is certainly a false taste and an impudent stile prevailing, which if Vandyke was living would put him out of countenance; . . . Nature is modest, and the Artist should be so in his addresses to her.'[96] This is a conflation of two passages from Richardson's treatise, dealing with portraiture, painting style and Van Dyck's extraordinary contribution to British art. 'Impudent' painting was, according to Richardson, a form of contrived painterly effect, 'rough' brushwork used for its own sake. In Richardson's words, 'There are two Mistakes very Common; One is because a great many good Pictures are very Rough painted People fancy that is a good Picture that is so. There is *Bold Painting*, but there is also *Impudent Painting*.'[97] The 'false taste' which Gainsborough identified as prevailing in the exhibition was, in Richardson's analysis, the style adopted by a great many English painters who abandoned the example of Van Dyck and fell into the profitable but dishonourable trap of flattery. Richardson believed, 'some Painters possibly finding themselves incapable of succeeding in His [i.e. Van Dyck's] way, and having found their Account in introducing a False Taste, others have follow'd their Example, and forsaking the study of Nature, have prostituted a Noble Art, chusing to exchange the honourable Character of good Painters for that sordid one of the profess'd, mercenary Flatterers . . .'.[98] It is inconceivable that Gainsborough could have written to Garrick about the 'impudent style' and 'false taste' on show in London without a thorough knowledge of Richardson's text. Just as Reynolds was said to have 'imbibed the first delight in his art' from Richardson's writings, so it seems that Gainsborough had them at the forefront of his mind when he came to judge the art of his contemporaries.[99]

If Gainsborough could demonstrate such a close familiarity with one of the great works of art theory of the earlier part of the century, it is likely that he would have taken an interest in a writer of his own generation who lived within the close-knit artistic community of Bath. Daniel Webb's *Inquiry into the Beauties of Painting* was published in February 1760, just in advance of the first of the great public art exhibitions in London. Newspaper advertisements for the book show that it was intended to teach taste to the new exhibition-going public as well as to instruct young travellers setting out on their grand tour.[100] The *Inquiry* proved a success for its author Webb and publisher Robert Dodsley, being reprinted in 1761, 1769, 1777 and in 1802 (after Webb's death) and translated in to French, German and Italian.[101] References to the book appear in contemporary correspondence within a few months of publication. Mrs Delany quoted from Webb when she reported to her sister on her visit to Gainsborough's picture room in October 1760.[102] The painter William Hoare discussed Webb's opinions in a lengthy unpublished letter to Henry Hoare of Stourhead in June 1760, greatly admiring Webb's sustained advocacy of 'a high Idea of the Art of the ancients'.[103] The poet and gardener William Shenstone wrote to the Revd Richard Graves on 7 July 1760, 'I bought Webb instantly; but have not read it'.[104] A month later he evidently had read the book, since he recommended it to Thomas Percy in August 1760.[105]

William Whitehead described his visit to Webb's house in Bath to see pictures in December 1760. He reported to Viscount Nuneham,

> I was much entertained the other morning with a very good copy of the famous Corregio [sic] Picture at Parma. Mr Webb, whom we saw in Italy, is in possession of it. He has likewise a holy family by Julio Romano touched up by Raphael, which is very fine. You must never pass thro' Bath without seeing them.[106]

These pictures were the ones that Webb himself reported buying in Italy, 'two Albani's, a copy of Corregio by Carache, and a small piece by . . . Parmegianino . . . A capital piece by Julio Romano'.[107] From Whitehead's letter it appears that visitors wishing to view paintings were admitted to Webb's house, in the same way they were to artists' picture rooms and grand country houses, Webb perhaps being willing to sacrifice privacy for the purposes of advertising his publications.

The two strongest pointers to an association between Gainsborough and Webb are the poem published in 1773, '*On seeing Mr.* Gainsborough's Pictures *at* Bath', signed 'D.W.', and the presence of Webb's book in a portrait of Gainsborough, now in Santa Barbara, California (fig. 143).[108] The poem, as we have already seen, hails Gainsborough as a modern master in full possession of old masterly skills and taste:

> While connoisseurs, with artificial eyes,
> Mechanically pore, and fix the prize;
> While, dead to each fine feeling of the heart,
> And every principle of taste and art,
> They center merit in an ancient name,
> And parcel out by *centuries* their fame;
> Be mine the pleasure, tho' in humble lays,
> True, *modern* merit to admire and praise.
> Yes, *Gainsborough!* yes; thy magic pieces charm,
> And want but age dull connoisseurs to warm.
> Thy vivid colours, elegant design,
> Rich strokes of fancy, chaste and flowing line,
> All nature's beauties in thy tints that glow,
> At once thy taste and master-judgement show;
> Even beauty's self comes from thy hand improv'd,
> And doubly we are charm'd with what we lov'd.
> The living landscape on thy canvas wears
> New grace, and gay enchantment all appears.
> Oh! To thy charming cottage* let me rove,
> That scene of beauty, and domestic love;
> There could I gaze for ever, and admire
> Thy genius, judgement, elegance, and fire:
> And, were that cottage mine, no lordly peer
> For mercenary gold should enter there;
> In high content the matchless prize I'd hold,
> And rate thy genius far above all gold!
> D.W.
>
> *Alluding to a most elegant painting of Mr. Gainsborough's which has been purchased by a noble Lord.[109]

Although it cannot be proved that 'D.W.' is Webb, the weight of probability seems overwhelming. Webb certainly wrote comparable poetry, publishing some in a slim volume entitled *Literary Amusements in Verse and Prose* in 1787.[110] In a place as small as Bath, Webb and Gainsborough must, at the very least, have been acquainted with one another. Webb was well known to some of Gainsborough's friends such as the Revd Richard Graves. At the end of a letter to Robert Dodsley (publisher of Graves's work as well as Webb's), Graves reported, 'I din'd wth Mr Web. last Saturday . . .'.[111] Webb's reputation in Bath was as a man 'of Great Genius & politeness'.[112]

So it is worth looking at Webb's *Inquiry* and considering why it was so widely read and why it might feature in a portrait of Gainsborough. The book is dedicated to Joseph Spence, author of *Polymetis*. Spence was an old friend of the painter William Hoare, whom he had met in Italy in the 1730s, and copies of *Polymetis*, as we have seen, belonged to Uvedale Tomkyns Price and Gainsborough.[113] The most important aspect of the *Inquiry*, from the point of view of the iconography of the portrait of Gainsborough, is its European, rather than purely English or British, character. Its presence in a portrait of the artist dating from the early 1770s, at precisely the time Thicknesse claimed that Gainsborough knew himself to be 'one of the first geniuses of Europe', must be significant.[114] The *Inquiry* introduced many of the ideas of Johann Joachim Winckelmann and Anton Raphael Mengs to non-German speaking Europe.[115] Diderot was just one of those who knew of Winckelmann's and Mengs's ideas through the *Inquiry* and commended Webb as a man of taste and judgement.[116] Webb's book was written in the form of a dialogue in which a mentor explains to his pupil the principles of painting, using the headings of design, colouring, chiaroscuro (which Webb calls 'the Clear Obscure') and composition. Webb held up as his model of excellence the art of 'the ancients', comparing what was known about their work with examples of 'modern' paintings, and especially those by Raphael, Correggio and Titian. He also compared the work of the moderns with one another, arguing that Titian was the greatest colourist, Correggio the master of chiaroscuro and Raphael the best at composition. In addition he introduced the work of a few north-European painters, believing the brilliant colouring of Rubens, for example, seduced the eye and charmed the viewer but was not based on sound scientific principles, as was Titian's colouring.[117]

Not everyone was convinced by Webb's claims for the 'ancients'. The Gloucestershire poet Richard Owen Cambridge (1717–1802) composed a verse 'On Painting; addressed to Mr. Patch, A Celebrated Picture Cleaner', who was employed at Burleigh House:

> . . . the place where every Muse
> Her favourite elegance may chuse.
> For there the Romans and Venetians
> Display a show, which all the Grecians,
> Whate'er ingenious Webb may say,
> Could ne'er have equall'd in their day.
> Protogenes and famed Apelles –
> The story well enough to tell is,
> How one could colour, t'other draw –
> But were their colours warm or raw?
> Why nothing now remains to show it,
> Except the historian and the poet.[118]

Webb was on surer ground when he discussed the 'moderns' and his remarks about Rubens are of particular interest. His phrase 'the splendid impositions of Rubens', picked up by Mrs Delany with reference to the colouring of Gainsborough's *Ann Ford* portrait, is obscure today and even puzzled some of his contemporaries. Mrs Delany herself said Webb 'unjustly' called Rubens's paintings 'splendid impositions'.[119] The painter Joseph Highmore, writing about Webb's *Inquiry* in the *Gentleman's Magazine* in 1766, found the phrase 'splendid impositions' contradictory, adding that in his view Rubens 'had no equal; and particularly in colouring'.[120] However Webb did not alter this passage in later editions of the book and to some extent his description of Rubens's use of colour seems to have entered the public consciousness. William Jackson (who could not possibly have known of Mrs Delany's private letter to her sister) also turned to Webb when describing Gainsborough's colouring. In *The Four Ages* he wrote,

> Gainsborough once dealt in red shadows; and as he was fond of referring every thing to nature, or where nature was not to be had, to something substituted for it, he contrived a lamp with the sides painted vermillion, which illuminated the shadows of his figures, and made them like the splendid impositions of Rubens.[121]

At this date the word 'imposition' had several meanings in addition to our modern understanding of it, being used by typesetters to mean 'composition' and sometimes meaning 'exhibition': Horace Walpole's personal copy of the catalogue to the 1768 *Free Society* exhibition in London is inscribed by him, 'This was an execrable Imposition, & half the pictures old rubbish'.[122] What is of particular interest is the fact that two quite independent commentators, Mrs Delany and William Jackson, both associated the colouring of Gainsborough's Bath paintings with Rubens, but in both cases their judgement was conditioned by their reading of Webb, which made them wary of Gainsborough's boldness.

Daniel Webb's assessment of Rubens, and in fact many other views expressed in his *Inquiry*, are based on ideas formulated by Mengs in Rome, but not published by Mengs before 1760. Webb was in Italy in 1755–6, during which time he became friendly with both Mengs and Winckelmann.[123] Mengs painted Webb's portrait, which is now lost, and apparently gave Webb a manuscript of his *Gedanken uber die Schonheit und den Geschmack in der Mahlerey* (Thoughts on beauty and taste in painting), which was published anonymously in 1762, and his *Riflessioni sopra i tre gran pittori* (Reflections on the greatest painters), published only in 1780.[124] Some of Webb's *Inquiry* copies Mengs almost word for word. Webb also introduced an English readership to Winckelmann's elevation of Greek art over that of ancient Rome. Winckelmann's famous *Reflections on the Paintings and Sculpture of the Greeks*, originally published in German in 1755, only appeared in an English translation (by Fuseli) in 1765.[125] While Winckelmann fumed at Webb's blatant plagiarism, English readers seem to have been unaware of the sources of the *Inquiry* and Webb, as we have seen, enjoyed respect and celebrity at home.[126]

The *Monthly Review* saw Webb's book as a vital element in the emergence of a British school of art that was, in 1760, 'rising towards perfection' so rapidly, it was 'likely to bear away the palm from our more elegant neighbours'.[127] Webb, in the eyes of the reviewer, deserved 'the approbation and thanks of the public' for his part in the improvement of the art of this country. The writer recognised that Webb's insistence on what William Hoare called 'a high Idea' of ancient art was in itself a means of urging British art onward and upward so that it might compete with the art of any nation on the Continent. Once Webb's *Inquiry* is seen in this light, its symbolic presence in Gainsborough's portrait begins to make sense. It was not that Gainsborough's art was recognisably classical in the way that Mengs's was classical, but it was Gainsborough's claim to be considered a European, a successor to Gaspard Dughet and Claude as well as Rubens and Van Dyck, that set him above and apart from most of his contemporaries.

Gainsborough's espousal of a grander form of art during his residence in Bath was generally recognised by his friends and admirers. In 1770 Philip Thicknesse asserted that although 'Nature was his master . . . with a black lead pencil he is equal to any of the greatest Masters of Antiquity'.[128] J. H. Pott, writing in 1782, felt bound to class Gainsborough above any other English landscape painter and identified a distinct change of aspiration in the artist's middle years. As Pott saw it, 'At his outset in life he appears to have studied and

141 Thomas Gainsborough (1727–1788), *Mary (seated) and Margaret Gainsborough, the Painter's Daughters* c. 1763–64, oil on canvas, 50 × 40 inches (127.2 × 101.7 cm), Worcester Art Museum, Worcester, Massachusetts, Museum purchase.

preferred the Flemish style, and particularly to have imitated Wynants . . .'.[129] Then, 'Upon maturer study and riper judgement, he seems to have aimed at something more elevated; he began to neglect the minuter characters of nature, and to depend more upon the *chiaro oscuro*, and upon the beauty of his figures . . .'.[130] His mature work, Pott concluded, was not equalled 'by any master, antient or modern. His figures are admirable, and . . . beautifully adapted to landscape'.[131]

The move to a 'more elevated' style in Gainsborough's work, with its regard for chiaroscuro and composition seems, therefore, to have been stimulated by Webb as well as Uvedale and Robert Price. The painters William Hoare and Edmund Garvey are also likely to have played a part. It is known from his letter to Hoare that Gainsborough was keen to discuss Reynolds's Fourth Discourse with Hoare 'some Evening over a Glass'.[132] William Hoare's knowledge of European art dated from his own period of study in Italy. His interest was not limited to portraiture or subject pictures: at some unknown date he had etched a landscape after Nicolas Poussin, inscribing his print, 'from A Picture of N. Poussin, which had never been engraved'.[133] In his letter to Henry Hoare he referred to coloured prints after paintings by Italian artists that he owned, and he even purchased a Raphael cartoon, the *Massacre of the Innocents*, which was subsequently bequeathed to the Foundling Hospital in London by Prince Hoare.[134]

Edmund Garvey might seem an unlikely source of inspiration for Gainsborough, but Garvey's experience of Italy immediately before he arrived in Bath may well have been the key to their friendship. After settling in Bath in 1768, Garvey continued to paint Italian subjects, presumably basing them on drawings and sketches he himself had made and perhaps also on prints he brought back to England. In the spring of 1770 Gainsborough sent a 'Book of Drawings' to the second Royal Academy exhibition.[135] This book has never been positively identified but may have been the book of fifty-eight Italian scenes of architecture and landscape by Gainsborough that were still in his studio at his death, and if this is the case, it seems most likely that Garvey provided the source.[136] Another mysterious book of Gainsborough's drawings that he never sold or gave away was a collection of 'imitations from antique vases and sculpture'.[137] It is quite possible that these drawings were connected with Garvey's decorations for the new Assembly Rooms which featured antique vases and sculpture (fig. 107). Gainsborough did involve himself in decorative schemes at other times in his career, producing transparent paintings for the Hanover Square Concert Room in 1774–5 and decorative figures for the Italian Opera House in 1778, and there seems no reason why he might not have helped plan part of the decoration of the interior of the Rooms in Bath.[138] With his own premises just a matter of yards away, the success of the new Rooms was a matter of personal importance to him and a significant number of his own friends and clients had a financial stake in the project.

If Gainsborough did collaborate with Garvey on the production of designs based on classical vases and figures, this would have been one of a handful of occasions on which he demonstrated his familiarity with classical imagery. The double portrait of his daughters, painted around 1763–4, shows the girls as students of art with drawing materials in their hands (fig. 141). In front of them are two casts, one a reduced *Farnese Flora*, a figure that Michael Rysbrack had copied full-size for the gardens at Stourhead; the second another female figure rather indistinctly defined and as yet unidentified, but perhaps the Capitoline *Urania*.[139] A classical motif, the Quirinale *Horse Tamers* was also the source for the leading group of figure and horses in Gainsborough's *Harvest Waggon* of the mid-1760s.[140] The equestrian portrait of *General Honywood* dating from 1765 may, as has been mentioned above, owe something to the *Marcus Aurelius* at Wilton as well as to Van Dyck's portrait *Charles I on Horseback*. An image of the *Three Graces* appeared as a picture on the wall in the background of Gainsborough's first oil portrait of Carl Friedrich Abel when the artist first drafted out his composition on the canvas, although this part of the picture was subsequently painted over.[141] David Solkin has recently shown how Gainsborough's portrait of his wife from the late 1770s takes its pose from the antique sculpture *Pudicita*, an image of fidelity especially suited to a marital portrait.[142]

Gainsborough might have had access to the casts of antique sculpture that had once belonged to the academy of painting that is thought to have existed in Bath, and perhaps still belonged to William Hoare. He might, like many other artists, have had casts in his own painting room. Hoare's portrait of Uvedale Tomkyns Price suggests that Price, too, may have owned casts. The richest collection of classical imagery in Bath was probably associated with the Wicksteeds and their seal-engraving manufactory, which the architect John Wood likened to the sigillarium of ancient Rome. Gainsborough must also have seen the exhibition of classical and modern statuary mounted in October 1765 at a tailor's shop in Bath. A 'Mr. Champione', an Italian sculptor based in Oxford, brought to Bath

> A Large and Curious Collection of Statues modelled from the Antiques of Italy; Busts, and Monumental Ornaments of Kings, Queens, Princes, Poets, Philosophers, Physicians, etc. in fine Paris Plaister Work, after the Italian Manner; being the greatest Ornaments for Halls, Parlours, Stair-Cases, Book-Cases, Dining Rooms, Chimney-Pieces, Summer-Houses, etc. He takes off Faces with the greatest Exactness, and makes Moulds of all Sorts of Figures without any damage to the Originals, bronzes them in different Colours . . .[143]

More significant than the direct quotations from classical sources that occur in some of Gainsborough's Bath paintings is the artist's general movement to a grand style of landscape. As Pott noted, he ceased to focus on the minutiae of nature and concerned himself with broader painterly issues such as chiaroscuro. Readily identifiable British trees are replaced by carefully massed formulaic foliage that is based on the example of Claude and Gaspard Dughet, a Claudean light bathes the landscape in pictures such as *Peasants and Colliers going to Market* (fig. 158) and compositions evidently based on the model of Gaspard Dughet begin to appear (fig. 146). If, in 1773, Daniel Webb could admire Gainsborough's 'genius, judgement, elegance, and fire' in his poem 'On seeing Mr. Gainsborough's Pictures at Bath', it was because he recog-

143 *(left)* Unidentified British artist, *Thomas Gainsborough* c. 1771–2, oil on canvas, 49 × 39¾ inches (124.5 × 101 cm), Santa Barbara Museum of Art, California.

142 *(facing page)* Johan Zoffany (1733–1810), *Thomas Gainsborough* 1771–2, oil on canvas, 7½ × 6¾ inches (19 × 17 cm), Tate Britain, London, on loan to the National Portrait Gallery, London.

nised that by this date the painter had transformed his art through an intelligent assimilation of the art of the past, a process in which Webb himself might have played some part. Webb would surely have been flattered to see his treatise lying on Gainsborough's table in the portrait now in Santa Barbara. It is likely that this portrait dates from within a few years of the publication of the poem, since the likeness of the artist is closely comparable with Zoffany's portrait that was painted in preparation for his Royal Academy group portrait of 1772 (fig. 142).[144] Zoffany probably painted his likeness when he came to Bath some time before February 1772, when Gainsborough took advantage of the visit to ask him to deliver some large drawings to London on his return.[145]

It must be assumed that if visitors to Bath like William Whitehead visited Daniel Webb's house to see his pictures, then Gainsborough, as a permanent resident, must have been familiar with the paintings Webb brought back from Italy, including his own portrait by Mengs and the Correggio copy so admired by Whitehead. The status of Webb's version of Correggio's *Parma Madonna* is not established. In the early eighteenth century there were ten altarpiece copies in Parma alone, some of which were 'very fine'.[146] Many copies by both Italian and English artists found their way into British collections. Gainsborough evidently shared the common enthusiasm for Correggio. When he stayed at Longford Castle he found the Earl of Radnor's chaplain such an extraordinarily comical figure that he felt quite unable to attend chapel, saying that he could not be tempted in 'even if . . . the altarpiece had been painted by Correggio', a telling remark that speaks of his high regard for the Italian master.[147] There is no doubt that some of Gainsborough's 'cottage door' family group scenes are strongly reminiscent of devotional paintings, Hayes noting that the children in the *Woodcutter's Return* (believed to be the picture described in Webb's poem) look 'like putti who have escaped from a Correggio altarpiece' (fig. 157).[148]

Daniel Webb and Richard Graves dined together in May 1763 and, one suspects, on other occasions. Richard Graves (1715–1804), Rector of Claverton, not far from Prior Park (fig. 6), was another Bath writer and thinker who published two important poems about Gainsborough, the first of which appeared as early as 1762. He became a lifelong friend of the artist, who drew his portrait in the 1780s (fig. 144).[149] Graves was an avid collector of pictures which, in his own words, filled his house 'from the parlour into the passages; and thence to the smoky walls of the kitchen'.[150] It would appear that Graves, who was also a regular correspondent of the gardener-poet William Shenstone (1714–1763), was one of those whose interest in literature, gardening and the arts affected the development of Gainsborough's landscape painting. It must have been Graves who prompted Thomas Linley to compose an *Elegy on the Death of Mr Shenstone* in 1763.[151]

Graves's two poems in praise of Gainsborough are better known than the 1773 poem attributed here to Daniel Webb. The first appeared initially in the *London Chronicle* for 24–6 June 1762, where it was headed 'On the Landskips, in Gainsborough's whole-length Portraits of Gentlemen and Ladies, walking in Pairs'. The poem was reprinted in a slightly altered form in *Shenstone's Miscellany 1759–1763* under the changed title, 'On Gainsborough's Landskips with Portraits; full length Figures less than Life, drawn in Pairs as walking thro' woods, etc'; again in Graves's *Festoon* of 1766, and in an expanded version in Graves's *Euphrosyne* of 1776.[152] This final version was boldly entitled 'On Mr. Gainsborough; Equally excellent in Landskip and Portraits':

> Drawn by the magic power of light and shade,
> To Gainsborough's skill be this slight tribute paid.
> To charm the soul with equal force conspire
> The Painter's genius and the Poet's fire.
> When Milton sings of Angels bold in fight,
> Or blooming Cherubs half-dissolv'd in light;
> Or leads his Eve to Adam's longing arms,
> In all the lustre of primaeval charms:
> Fir'd with the song, thro' Eden's blissful groves,
> With the first pair th' enraptur'd fancy roves.
> 'Midst crystal founts or amarinthine bow'rs,
> Ambrosial fruits, and ever-blooming flowers,
> We trace each step by various passions tost,
> And quit with tears the *Paradise* they *lost*.
> Like that blest pair, by Gainsb'rough's pencil drawn,
> Here each fond couple* treads the flow'ry lawn;
> Or sun-burnt heroes shine in mimic arms,
> Or beauties glow in never-fading charms.
> Each eye the animated features strike;
> Even lovers pleas'd, confess the portrait like.
> But when the landskips various charms we trace,
> Where Nature's self appears with heighten'd grace;
> There sylvan scenes present the opening glade,
> Th'enamel'd lawn or cool sequester'd shade;
> The ruddy dawn there gilds the distant tow'r;
> There the smooth lake reflects the purple flow'r.
> In silent wonder fix'd, with joy serene,
> The mind surveys th'imaginary scene;
> And owns the pleasing cheat so well sustain'd;
> Each landskip seems a *Paradise regain'd.*
>
> * Several gentlemen and ladies drawn in that taste.[153]

Graves sees Gainsborough's paintings as reclaiming man's lost paradise on English soil. A reviewer writing about Gainsborough's later 'Cottage Door' picture exhibited at the Royal Academy in 1780 picked up the same theme,

> This beautiful scene where serenity and pleasure dwell in every spot, and the lovely figures composed in the finest rural style, their situation worthy of them, forms a scene of happiness that may truly be called Adam's paradise.[154]

Richard Graves's poem also points to the painter's skill in integrating man and the landscape, as is suggested by

144 Thomas Gainsborough (1727–1788), *Revd Richard Graves (1715–1804), Rector of Claverton* c. 1785, black, white and coloured chalks, 5¼ × 4⅛ inches (13.3 × 10.5 cm), The Pierpont Morgan Library, New York. 1957.12.

the final title he gave to the poem and the position in which it was placed in *Euphrosyne*, between the poem 'To J. T—yl—r, Esq; at Bath; On his admirable Landskips' and one addressed to William Hoare the portrait painter. Graves recognised that Gainsborough's unique contribution was not just creating a new Eden, or a new form of ideal landscape, but in his seamless depiction of man at one with nature. The first version of the poem may have been inspired by Gainsborough's double portrait *Mr and Mrs George Byam* (before the child Selina was added), but the description of 'full length Figures less than Life' used in the title of the second version leaves a lingering doubt as to which pictures Graves had in mind.[155]

Graves's second poem dates from 1784, a decade after Gainsborough left Bath. Its very existence is a testament to the longstanding nature of the two men's friendship. Whereas the earlier poem addresses 'Mr. Gainsborough', this is *To Thomas Gainsborough, Esq. On his Portraits of the Three* Princesses:*

Shall Art with Nature, then, thus boldly vie,
Thus ape the glories of the Orient sky?
How dar'dst thou, mortal, impiously presume,
To imitate, with paint, celestial bloom?
How could'st thou on such radiant beauty gaze,
Uninjur'd by the splendor of its rays?
Some angel, sure, has lent his friendly aid,
To sketch the features of each royal maid.
What sweetness softens their majestic air!
What goodness beams from each distinguish'd fair!
What spirit animates each lovely face!
And in each part what symmetry and grace! –
Such were the forms that bless'd the shepherd's eyes
On Ida's mount, contending for the prize;
Such the three Graces of celestial mold,
That charm'd the sculptors and the bards of old.
Consummate artist! Say, from whence you drew
The precepts of your art, so just, so true?
With freedom thus who bade your pencil flow?
Such force, such sweetness in thy colours glow?
Hast thou, to give perfection to thy piece,
Studied the works of ancient Rome or Greece?
Hast thou survey'd the celebrated* *rule*
Of ancient beauty? Or each modern school
With critic eye compar'd, to store thy mind
With all these wonders of a taste refin'd?
Ah! No; thy matchless skill with scorn disclaims
The fancied merit built on pompous names;
Like great Corregio, *Nature*'s pupil, fraught
With inborn genius, and by practice taught;
Who view'd e'en Raphael's works with conscious pride,
And, "I'm a painter still!" he nobly cried.
O'er seas or alps let other artists roam,
In quest of beauties which you find at home;
Such charms our British nymphs alone can boast,
And he who paints them truest charms us most.

*Princess Royal, Augusta, and Elizabeth
*The canon, or standard of beauty, formed from a number of fine women, by Polycletus. PLIN. 34.8
1784[156]

The subtle shift from 'Mr' to 'Esq' in Graves's title is an indication of the artist's change in status, from Bath portrait painter to painter of members of the Royal family. Graves had addressed the amateur landscape painter John Taylor as 'Esq' since he was a gentleman by virtue of his inherited wealth; Gainsborough had acquired gentlemanly status through his own endeavours. Graves seems to be acknowledging in this later poem that Gainsborough had achieved a form of classical perfection (he compares the Princesses to the Three Graces), not by the slavish following of classical models, but by his own 'inborn genius' and 'by practice'. The poem is a hymn to the triumph of a truly modern painter and as such it mirrors Graves's earlier poem that saw Gainsborough's figures in a landscape as the modern equivalent of Adam and Eve in the Garden of Eden.

In Graves's later poem Gainsborough is likened to 'great Corregio' (sic), '*Nature's* pupil, fraught with inborn genius'.

Elsewhere Graves also coupled Gainsborough's name with that of Claude, an artist particularly admired by the poet. It is possible that Gainsborough's homage to Claude in some of his later Bath landscapes owed something to the influence of Richard Graves. David Brenneman has claimed that 'Bate-Dudley was the only critic to have mentioned Claude's name in the contemporary discussion of Gainsborough's landscapes, and the only occasion in which Claude's name appeared in connection with Gainsborough's was in Bate-Dudley's obituary of the artist'.[157] Graves, however, linked the names of Claude, Gainsborough and Bampfylde in *Columella; or, the Distressed Anchoret* of 1779. Columella's two visitors are sitting having tea in their host's grotto, against a view that Graves describes in terms of a Claudean landscape in an English setting:

> On the brow of one hill appeared the Sybil's temple, ruinated like that at Tivoli; a pediment supported by Ionic columns, rose at the foot of another; the venerable gothic tower of a parish church was discovered amongst the tufted trees; and the whole was terminated by some blue mountains on the horizon, and enlivened by a considerable stream, which ran winding down the valley; over which an old bridge of three arches made a picturesque appearance; and as the sun was now setting behind the western hills, it gave a glowing warmth to the landscape, which would have foiled the pencil of B—f—d, G—b—h, or even of Claud Lorraine himself.[158]

The tribute to Coplestone Bampfylde was necessary since Columella's garden is based on Bampfylde's garden at Hestercombe (where Graves had doubtless enjoyed Bampfylde's hospitality), and Bampfylde had provided the illustration for the frontispiece for *Columella* (fig. 145). In a complicated twist to the Gainsborough–Bampfylde–Claude allusion, Bampfylde's frontispiece and possibly Graves's text may also owe something to the early Bath landscape by Gainsborough that Bampfylde owned (fig. 147), the blazing light, the three-arch bridge, distant hill and village echoing Gainsborough's picture.

Graves's admiration for Claude is expressed throughout his publications. In *The Spiritual Quixote* one of the characters, Mrs Rivers, has a 'sweet smile' which 'like the sun-shine so much admired in the landskapes of Claude Lorraine, diffued [sic] an additional chearfulness over every other object.'[159] While Graves saw Gainsborough as a new Claude, or a new Correggio, recreating Paradise in his landscapes, he did not, like Daines Barrington, feel that Gainsborough's particular vision of landscape was an appropriate model for gardeners. He seems to have been the only person to publish a response to Barrington's recommendation of Gainsborough to gardeners. Writing not long before Gainsborough's death, Graves clung to a Brownian view of man-made landscape:

> The honourable and learned Mr Barrington, in his History of Gardening, had repeated Mr Shenstone's observation 'that a landscape-painter would make the best designer of an English garden in the present taste', and compliments Mr. Gainsborough as the most fit for that purpose. But, though Gainsborough so eminently excels in every branch of art, yet, I think, his style of landscape, though the most pleasing in my eye, is less calculated for the present mode of embellishing the country round our villas, as it is generally confined to mere sylvan scenes and sequestered spots, instead of comprehending that extent of lawn, groups of trees, and distant views, which are usually found near a gentleman's seat, since that good taste has prevailed in England.[160]

Graves's writings about Gainsborough must have been widely read during the artist's lifetime. They certainly seem to have inspired one rather less accomplished local writer

145 Charles Grignion (1716–1810) after Coplestone Warre Bampfylde, *Frontispiece to Volume I of the Revd Richard Graves' novel Columella; or The Distressed Anchoret* 1779, engraving, 5⁵⁄₁₆ × 3⅜ inches (13.4 × 8.5 cm), published 1779.

146 Thomas Gainsborough (1727–1788), *Wooded Landscape with Figures and Distant Mountain* 1763–4, pencil, watercolour and bodycolour, 11 × 14¾ inches (27.9 × 37.5 cm), Ashmolean Museum, Oxford.

147 Thomas Gainsborough (1727–1788), *Wooded Landscape with Figures, Donkeys, a Bridge and Distant Mountain* 1763–4, oil on canvas, 14 × 17½ inches (35.4 × 4.6 cm), signed with initials, private collection. This painting originally belonged to the amateur artist Coplestone Warre Bampfylde of Hestercombe, Somerset.

who, on Gainsborough's death, sent a poem 'The Landscape, To the Memory of Mr. Gainsborough' to the Wiltshire periodical *The County Magazine*. This was signed 'W. de W.' and appeared in August 1788, the month that the artist died. It begins praising Gainsborough's 'breathing-speaking portraits' and goes on, along the lines of both Graves's and Webb's poems, to extol the Britishness of Gainsborough's art, and concludes with the goddess Nature lending him her pencil 'fraught with pow'r divine'. The middle section conjures up images from some of the Bath landscapes:

> The cottage, hedge-row elm, and peaceful glade;
> The hoary rustic on his staff reclin'd,
> The weeping willow waving with the wind;
> The pannier'd ass that bears on either side
> The auburn offspring of the rural bride,
> The blighted trunk, low bending to the ground,
> The creeping ivy fondly clinging round;
> The blossom'd chestnut with its fragrant bloom,
> And the pale poplar glittering through the gloom.
> But most the Druid oak with towering head,
> His genius suited, and his fancy fed;
> The Briton's boast, the source of Gaul's despair,
> The Painter's idol, and the Prince's care.[161]

The publisher of Graves's, Shenstone's and Webb's literary works was Robert Dodsley. Graves was a valued adviser and friend to Robert Dodsley, often acting as a reader of manuscripts for him. Dodsley's publications on art theory, landscape and aesthetics included Joshua Kirby's *Dr Brooke Taylor's Method of Perspective* (1754), Thomas Bardwell's *The Practice of Painting and Perspective made Easy* (1756) and Edmund Burke's *A Philosophical Enquiry into the Origin of our Ideas of the Sublime and the Beautiful* (1757). Robert Dodsley, and then his brother James who took over the firm on Robert's death in 1764, also published several books that related specifically to Bath, such as Dr Rice Charleton's *A Treatise on the Bath Waters* (1754) and Christopher Anstey's comic verses, *The New Bath Guide* (1766).[162]

In 1767 Gainsborough wrote to James Dodsley, since he had noticed that the paper on which the *New Bath Guide* was printed was free of the wire-lines found in standard laid paper, and he wished to purchase some for use as drawing paper.[163] Wirelines presented a problem to artists who used watercolour and ink washes, since the pigment was inclined to 'pool' or settle into an unintentional pattern of parallel lines. Varnishes would also tend to settle in the same manner. At a time when Gainsborough was experimenting with drawing technique and varnishes, paper quality was of the utmost importance. He presumably was aware of the Dodsleys' particular interest in paper and the fact that Robert Dodsley had chaired a Society of Arts committee set up to investigate ways of improving the quality of English paper.[164]

Gainsborough must have known Robert and James Dodsley's brother Isaac, who was Ralph Allen's gardener and a friend of Richard Graves.[165] Isaac Dodsley was at Prior Park from 1741 until 1764 and his significance within the literary and artistic world in Bath has never been recognised. He occupied a rather grand 'cottage' beside the mansion, built for him by Allen, a house that Richard Graves described as a 'comfortable and elegant dwelling', and one that was later rented to 'people of fortune'.[166]

It has never been clear who was responsible for the evolution of the grounds at Prior Park between the early days of Alexander Pope's involvement and the late (and probably very limited) contribution of Capability Brown, just before Allen's death.[167] Isaac Dodsley, whose brothers promoted some of the major landscape theorists of the period, was ideally qualified to lay out as well as care for the gardens and it seems most likely that he is the 'unknown' designer of the 1750s. After 1764 Isaac Dodsley moved to Longleat. The historian John Nichols wrote that Isaac Dodsley 'may justly be named the father of the beautiful plantations at Prior-park and at Long Leate', hardly a description that would be applied to a person who only tended these gardens.[168] He must have been another important figure in the artistic life of Bath and one of the circle of men with a common interest in landscape with whom Gainsborough came into contact in the early 1760s.

It may have been while visiting James Dodsley in London that Richard Graves called on the Gainsboroughs and sat for his portrait in the 1780s, since the Dodsley business was based near Gainsborough's house in Pall Mall. In 1788 or 1789, not long after the artist's death, Graves enclosed a letter or parcel for Mrs Gainsborough within a package he sent to James Dodsley, asking Dodsley to forward it if Mrs Gainsborough had moved from Schomberg House.[169] This gesture reinforces the view that Graves must have enjoyed a close friendship with the Gainsboroughs, since few of the artist's circle attempted to keep in touch with his wife after his death. The tenderness of Gainsborough's portrait of the ageing Graves suggests that the sentiment was mutual.

The elder Prices, Daniel Webb and Richard Graves provided the intellectual backdrop to the development of Gainsborough's landscape painting in Bath. They supplied the foundation for the 'maturer study and riper judgement' that J. H. Pott identified as being at the root of Gainsborough's achievement of 'something more elevated' in this middle period of his life. The Prices took Gainsborough under the family wing, inviting him to Foxley within a year of his move to Bath. Daniel Webb, the author of a book that was acknowledged to be part of the impetus to create a distinctly British school of art, injected a sense of purpose and an international dimension into Bath's artistic milieu. Richard Graves, poet and friend of poets, recognised the lyricism of Gainsborough's vision and was prepared to put pen to paper to promote and encourage what he saw as 'Paradise regain'd' on British soil.

9

'The coquetry of nature'

Sir Uvedale Price called the Picturesque 'the coquetry of nature'.[1] It was, as he believed, an imaginative, playful and multi-layered approach to the natural world. By taking a closer look at several of Gainsborough's Bath-period landscape paintings, and the people who first owned them, it is possible to pick up more of the threads that link the artist with the formulation of Picturesque taste and theory. The paintings selected also illustrate the interaction between his work and local literature and the way in which some of his imagery relates specifically to the local rural economy.

The origins of Picturesque theory seem to lie, at least in part, within the community of Bath visitors of the first half of the 1760s, and Gainsborough's landscapes of this period appear to have influenced the thinking that ultimately led to the publication of Uvedale Price's *Essay on the Picturesque* and Richard Payne Knight's *The Landscape: a Didactic Poem*, and the *Principles of Taste.* It has been shown already that eighteenth-century Bath was a centre for aesthetic debate, a debate that in the 1740s was associated with the General Hospital (and a group of men who apparently formed themselves into an 'Academy of Painting'), and later, in the 1760s, focused on a literary group, most of whom had their writing published by Robert and James Dodsley. A keen interest in landscape and gardening was an underlying factor that bound together many of those who met in the city in the 1760s, whether they were landowners like George Lucy of Charlecote, using their winter leisure time to plan changes to their country estates; practical gardeners like Isaac Dodsley; or theorists like Richard Graves.[2]

As the only serious landscape painter in Bath at this date, Gainsborough was a key figure within this circle. His relationship with the Price family has already been set out: here the connection between certain paintings and Pricean theory will be explored, as will other relationships between the artist and patrons that may have had a bearing on the development of the Picturesque. Although Richard Payne Knight later owned a book of Gainsborough drawings, which he bequeathed to the British Museum, there is no evidence of any direct relationship between him and the artist.[3] Gainsborough did, however, know other members of the Knight family, all of whom had grown rich through the iron industry. He was also a friend of Dr Rice Charleton, John Jacob and Walter Wiltshire, three of the select group who acquired his landscape paintings in the 1760s and early 1770s, and it comes as no surprise to find these same men planning and developing landscapes of their own at the same time. Charleton, owner of the *Landscape with a Woodcutter* (fig. 148) of c. 1762–3 created a landscape in Beaufort Hunt country, overlooking the Severn Estuary; John Jacob, owner of the *Hilly Wooded Landscape with Peasant and Dog crossing a Bridge* (fig. 152) of c. 1763–4, nurtured and developed The Rocks, a dramatic woodland garden near Marshfield; while Walter Wiltshire (condemned by Ronald Paulson as an 'unlettered anticonnoisseur') was enthusiastically engaged in regenerating and redesigning an old parkland near Bath throughout the 1760s and 1770s.[4] A man of considerable social and intellectual ambition, Wiltshire was the proud owner of two of the artist's grandest landscapes of the Bath period, the *Harvest Waggon* (fig. 160) and the *Rocky Wooded Landscape with Rustic Lovers* (fig. 118).

Uvedale Price's theory of the Picturesque appeared in print in the 1790s and in expanded editions which appeared in the first decades of the next century, after a long period of gestation. In the 1760s and 1770s, while Gainsborough was still in Bath, a number of literary offerings inspired by the vogue for 'retirement' were published, several of which are close in spirit to a number of Gainsborough's landscapes of the same period. The interplay between contemporary local literature and Gainsborough's landscape paintings was recognised by Marcia Pointon in her article 'Gainsborough and the Landscape of Retirement' of 1979. A fresh examination of the *Woodcutter's Return* (fig. 157), the first of Gainsborough's 'cottage door' compositions, suggests that this interaction may be even more specific than Pointon realised.

The iconography of the major picture purchased by Henry Hoare, *Peasants and Colliers going to Market* (fig. 158) is complex. It can now be shown that its composition derives from a Dutch model, but it also reflects the reality of rural

148 Thomas Gainsborough (1727–1788), *Wooded Landscape with a Woodcutter* 1762–3, oil on canvas, 39½ × 50 inches (100.3 × 127 cm), Museum of Fine Arts, Houston, Texas.

life in the vicinity of Bath and in this book the word 'colliers' is reintroduced into the title. Some understanding of the local economy helps unravel its meaning.

Henry Hoare's picture dates from the later years of the Bath period. Dr Rice Charleton's *Landscape with a Woodcutter* must belong to the early 1760s. It is precisely the sort of composition that Gainsborough evolved with the use of small models, theatrically lit, in his Abbey Street painting room. It also possesses all the qualities Uvedale Price most admired in landscape paintings, a winding road leading through a hilly countryside flanked by a variety of trees, with the spotlight of the composition being on a ragged peasant wending his way home after a hard day's work. John Hayes describes the dramatic chiaroscuro as the product of painting by candlelight.[5] Ozias Humphry's 'Memoir' certainly states that Gainsborough painted 'several Landscapes of extraordinary merit, that were mostly executed by Candle Light'.[6] Humphry was in Bath from 1760 until August 1764, the period during which Rice Charleton's landscape must have been painted. It seems most probable that the composition, or at least its lighting, was designed with the use of an artificially lit model of the type used by Poussin, or a less formal arrangement of artificial light directed onto a model through apertures in a screen. The lighting may have been provided by a tinted lamp such as William Jackson described, casting a coloured glow onto the model.[7] The artist must at some stage have admitted daylight onto his canvas, even if the models from which he initially worked were lit artificially, since to work solely by artificial light would have resulted in paintings whose colour and tonal balance would subsequently depend on similarly artificial lighting conditions. As discussed above, the chiaroscuro may also owe something to the influence of Daniel Webb.

Every aspect of this picture, from the glow of the light to the humble head-scratching gesture of the tired peasant, is clearly designed to evoke the sympathy of the viewer. The lighting, in particular, ensures that it could never be mistaken for a topographical landscape, but can only be interpreted as an idealised imaginative composition, heavily laden with emotion or sentiment. Richard Payne Knight wrote in his *Analytical Inquiry into the Principles of Taste*, 'That which constitutes the great characteristic difference between liberal and mechanic art; and which gives to the former all its superiority, is feeling or sentiment; a quality that is always easily perceived, but incapable of being described.'[8] This is a truly 'liberal' landscape of the kind Knight defines. Daniel Webb praised Gainsborough's fine feelings and liberality of mind as expressed in the Marquis of Granby's *Woodcutter's Return* of 1773: here, ten years' earlier, the artist produced a painting of a similar intensity, also with a woodcutter as its central character.

If this canvas can be seen to embody the key qualities of 'feeling' and 'sentiment' singled out in Payne Knight's analysis of taste, it is also, down to every last detail, a proto-Picturesque painting in the Pricean sense. Uvedale Price, as we have seen, believed the virtuous cottager to be an ornament to the landscape. His description of the picturesque qualities of a church tower, donkeys and pollarded trees might easily have been inspired by this particular painting. 'The building', Price wrote, 'which gives most consequence to a village . . . is the church. That forms its most conspicuous feature at a distance, and often in the near view a central point, round which the houses are irregularly disposed'. A spire, he believed, 'has its own particular beauty, though of a very inferior kind to that of the tower'.[9] The ass, Price maintained, was 'eminently' picturesque, 'much more than the horse'.[10] Bye-roads with 'sudden and unprepared' turns were, to Price, a source of the richest of visual delights, 'sometimes smooth, and gently but not uniformly sloping; now wildly over-hung with thickets of trees and bushes; now loosely skirted with wood; . . .'.[11] Above all, Price's description of wayside pollarded trees (as distinct from the storm-damaged trees favoured by Salvator Rosa) seems to be informed by this composition and others of the same period, such as the *Wooded Landscape with Peasants in a Country Waggon* (fig. 102) and Ralph Allen's *Wooded Landscape with Figures* (fig. 103):

> there is often a sort of spirit and animation, in the manner in which old neglected pollards stretch out their limbs quite across these hollow roads, in every wild and irregular direction: on some, the large knots and protruberances, add to the ruggedness of their twisted trunks; in others, the deep hollow of the inside, the mosses on the bank, the rich yellow of the touch-wood, with the blackness of the more decayed substance, afford such variety of tints, of brilliant and mellow lights, with deep and particular shades, as the finest timber tree, however beautiful in other respects, with all its health and vigour cannot exhibit.
>
> This careless method of cutting, just as the farmer happened to want a few stakes or poles, gives infinite variety to the general outline of the banks.[12]

The dramatic lighting of Charleton's picture, perhaps inspired by the example of Rubens, also makes it Picturesque in Price's terms: he particularly commended Rubens, with his

> striking contrasts of form, colour, and light and shadow sun-beams bursting through a small opening in a dark wood – a rainbow against a stormy sky – effects of thunder and lightening . . . These sudden gleams, these contrasts of light, these bold oppositions of cloud and darkness, which he has so nobly introduced, would destroy all the beauty and elegance of Claude.[13]

Charleton's picture, painted on a canvas that would normally have been used for a half-length portrait, turned on its side, is one of the first major landscapes Gainsborough painted in Abbey Street. Hayes dates it to around 1762–3, about the time the artist was painting his full-length portrait of the Doctor himself (fig. 88).[14] At this time Charleton was Gainsborough's personal physician and in late 1763, when venereal disease and exhaustion nearly killed him, the artist admitted to James Unwin, 'My life was dispaird of by Doctor Charleton . . .'[15] Dr Charleton may have been related to the Charletons of Ludford, Herefordshire. Sir Francis Charleton of Ludford (d. 1784) did business with a Mr Gainsborough, possibly one of the artist's relatives, in the early 1750s.[16] A good deal of hitherto unnoticed information about Dr Charleton appears in correspondence between the poets William Shenstone and the Revd Richard Graves, and in unpublished Knight family papers.[17]

Charleton's social circle centred on that group of West Midlands industrialists who made fortunes through the iron industry and used their wealth to travel, collect works of art and develop landscape gardens.[18] They also spent a great deal of time visiting one another's homes and gardens. A number of records of such visits show Dr Charleton in the company of the Charletons of Ludford, the Knights and the Foleys, all of whom were connected with one another and with the Wheelers of Wollaston Hall and Wootton Lodge, through various iron industry partnerships.[19] Captain Edward Wheeler, it will be remembered, was the person from whom Gainsborough borrowed money in 1755, through a loan arranged by James Unwin, and the man through whom Unwin inherited Wootton Lodge in Staffordshire.[20] The Knight family controlled a large proportion of the English iron industry, the major ironmaster of the family in the mid-eighteenth century being Edward Knight (1699–1780) of Wolverley near Birmingham. This Edward Knight was the uncle of Richard Payne Knight. Edward Knight's son Edward (d. 1812) was a collector, connoisseur and lover of gardens, and seems to have been particularly close to Dr Charleton and William Shenstone. Young Edward Knight's sister Elizabeth paid a visit to Bath in January 1769, expecting to sit to Gainsborough for her portrait, but found him too busy. In a letter to her brother she wrote, 'I have fulfilled my promise to Gainsborough, in coming to Bath to sit for my Picture, but He's so much engaged that he cannot undertake it'.[21] Elizabeth and Edward Knight's sister Mary was the wife of Coplestone Bampfylde of Hestercombe, and their other sister Sarah was married to Bath's Member of Parliament Sir John Sebright (1725–1794), who sat to Gainsborough in the mid-1760s (fig. 149).[22]

William Shenstone's letters show how close-knit this group, which evidently encompassed Gainsborough on its fringes, was. In a letter of 26 October 1759 Shenstone wrote from his home, The Leasowes, near Birmingham (and close to Wolverley), to Richard Graves, telling him that he planned a visit 'to Lord Foley's, if your friend Dr. Charleton will accompany me . . .'[23] In November 1762 Shenstone again told Graves of a visit to Lord Foley, adding 'I went with young Knight [i.e. Edward Knight]; and the company of the Doctor and Sir Francis Charleton took off all restraint, and made the visit perfectly agreeable'.[24] An account Shenstone sends Graves of eminent visitors to The Leasowes in 1762 includes a significant number of Gainsborough's sitters and associates, including 'Dr. Charleton with Mr. Knight . . . Lord and Lady Vernon of Sudbury . . . Mr. Garrick's brother . . . Miss Wrottesley, Miss Pigott . . . Lord and Lady Dartmouth . . . Colonel Bampfylde, with Mr. Knight's Family etc. etc.'.[25]

Andrew Ballantyne's recent analysis of Richard Payne Knight's contribution to the literature of the Picturesque clearly describes the ways in which Payne Knight relates to (and differs from) Uvedale Price and harks back to Shenstone.[26] Although Price and Knight were initially united in their attack on Capability Brown, their theories diverged in the mid-1790s. While Price offered advice on the arrangement of elements in a landscape to produce agreeable effects, Knight was principally interested in *association*, his *The Landscape: a Didactic Poem* of 1794 suggesting to the viewer of landscape how his imagination might be triggered by particular elements. Shenstone, too, stressed the importance of association, and had placed objects within the landscape at The Leasowes with the intention of prompting specific trains of thought. Ballantyne noted that Shenstone, Payne Knight and Uvedale Price shared a common belief in the power of landscape painting to influence gardening, Shenstone writing in 1764, 'I think the landskip painter is the gardiner's best designer'.[27] It was this passage that Daines Barrington picked up in the 1780s, advocating Gainsborough as the most suitable painter to design gardens.

Dr Rice Charleton's own country house, Woodhouse at Woodhouse Down, was close to the road (now the A38) that Shenstone and the Knights would have taken to visit Hestercombe, and also near to the Aust Passage Severn Crossing that many garden enthusiasts took to see Piercefield, at Chepstow. The same crossing would also have been used by those travelling between Foxley and Bath. Woodhouse was just north of Almondsbury, about eight miles north of Bristol. Charleton's house and grounds commanded a spectacular view across towards the confluence of the Wye and the Severn, a view similar to the one painted by Ross in one of his Beaufort Hunt series (fig. 151). A hint of the view is perhaps indicated by the pointing gesture of young Robert Charleton in Gainsborough's double portrait of the Doctor's children, *Robert and Susanna Charleton* (fig. 150).[28] Just what Woodhouse itself looked like in the eighteenth century is not known. The first Ordnance Survey map of 1882 shows a substantial house with a lodge and outbuildings, a garden, woodland and parkland, but as yet no eighteenth-century descriptions or drawings have been found.[29]

Gainsborough may himself have been to Woodhouse. He writes in 1779 that he had quite forgotten that Charleton had 'a Copy of the little dutch Spire of my Hand', adding, 'hang it in your study at [Wood]house where it may not be compared with the Original . . .'.[30] He might well have visited on his way to or from the Prices or another Herefordshire patron, Lord Bateman, with whom he stayed in 1773.[31] Gainsborough's copy of a 'little dutch spire' was a *Landscape with Figures* after the artists Pieter Bout (1658–1719) and Adriaen Boudewyns (1644–1711): both the original and the copy appeared in a sale at Charleton's death.[32] It is not known when Charleton acquired his Dutch picture, or when Gainsborough copied it, but in 1770 young Edward Knight noted in his pocket book that he saw among 'Mr. Lee's pictures in Belmont Row, Bath' a landscape with small figures by 'Bot & Bodwyn'.[33] Perhaps this was Charleton's picture, then hanging in Belmont Row on Lansdown Road, a short walk from Charleton's Bath town house.

The discovery that Charleton was closely associated with the poets Graves and Shenstone, the Bampfyldes and the ironmasters of the West Midlands, sets him firmly within the context of the wealthy landscape-conscious and literary community, and lends a new significance to Gainsborough's early Bath *Landscape with a Woodcutter*. The woodcutter subject might have held a specific meaning for members of this particular set, since woodcutters played an essential role in the iron industry: an account book for just one of Edward Knight's many iron works documents wages paid to fifty-three named woodcutters.[34] The processes used in the iron industry were in fact undergoing a major change from the mid-century, with coke smelting gradually replacing charcoal smelting, and so if Gainsborough's depictions of agricultural workers on the move can be associated with the progress of land enclosure, by the same reasoning this *Woodcutter* might be seen as representing the close of another chapter in the rural economy of a particular area of England.[35]

149 Thomas Gainsborough (1727–1788), *Sir John Sebright (1725–1794) Member of Parliament for Bath* c. 1766, oil on canvas, 30 × 25 inches (76.2 × 63.5 cm), private collection. In 1766 Sebright married Sarah Knight, sister-in-law of Coplestone Bampfylde and cousin of Richard Payne Knight. This portrait was probably painted around this time.

150 Thomas Gainsborough (1727–1788), *Robert and Susanna Charleton, children of Dr Rice Charleton* c. 1770, oil on canvas, 57 × 46 inches (145 × 117 cm), Virginia Museum of Fine Arts, Richmond, The Adolph D. and Wilkins C. Williams Collection.

151 J. Ross (*fl.* 1733–40), *Full Cry: The Duke of Beaufort's Hunt near the River Severn* c. 1733, oil on canvas, 36 × 57 inches (91.4 × 144.8 cm), private collection.

152 Thomas Gainsborough (1727–1788), *Hilly Wooded Landscape with Peasants and Dog crossing a Bridge* 1763–4, oil on canvas, 25 × 30 inches (63.5 × 76.2 cm), private collection.

153 Thomas Gainsborough (1727–1788), *Hilly Wooded Landscape* 1763–4, oil on canvas, 17 × 24⅛ inches (43.2 × 61.3 cm), private collection, on loan to the Victoria Art Gallery, Bath.

154 Thomas Gainsborough (1727–1788), *Study of a Dog, here identified as a Pug* c. 1760–62, black, red and white chalks on buff paper, $12\frac{7}{16} \times 9\frac{5}{8}$ inches (31.6 × 24.4 cm), Kupferstichkabinett, Staatliche Museen zu Berlin – Preussischer Kulturbesitz.

John Jacob (1723–1776) purchased or was given the *Hilly Wooded Landscape with Peasant and Dog crossing a Bridge* (fig. 152) around the same time that Charleton's picture was painted.[36] Whereas Charleton's picture is the size of a half-length portrait turned sideways, this is painted on a canvas that would normally have been used for a 'head' or 'three-quarters' portrait, turned on its side. It owes a good deal to Rubens, as does a smaller oil study for the composition, currently on loan to the Victoria Art Gallery, Bath (fig. 153).[37]

The landscape is not the only picture that Gainsborough painted for Jacob's family. In the early 1760s Gainsborough painted a portrait of a *Pug Dog* (private collection) that belonged to John Jacob's mother.[38] One of the most expressive of Gainsborough's animal drawings of around the same date is also of a pug, and may well represent a dog belonging to the Jacobs (fig. 154).[39] The artist later gave a copy by his own hand of his portrait of David Garrick to James Clutterbuck, John Jacob's brother-in-law. It was this painting that prompted Clutterbuck to write to Garrick of Gainsborough's 'unbounded liberality' in 1771.[40] John Jacob and his three sisters, Ann, Mary (who married Clutterbuck) and Elizabeth, and three dogs (two of which are pugs) were painted by Francis Hayman around 1743–4, about twenty years before Gainsborough's landscape (fig. 155).[41] Whether Jacob was introduced to Gainsborough by Hayman, or met him in Bath, is not clear.

The Jacobs' pride in their country estates is suggested in the Hayman family group which is set in a landscape with a large haystack prominent in the background. This must be a symbol of the rich pasture that surrounded the Jacob properties of Norton in Wiltshire and The Rocks, just within Gloucestershire. The house and outbuildings at The Rocks incorporated romantic castellated towers (fig. 156). These buildings were surrounded by a landscaped garden which was famous in the first half of the eighteenth century, and is immortalised by a poem, 'To Mrs Jacob, On her Seat call'd The Rocks, in Gloucestershire' in Mary Chandler's *The Description of Bath, A Poem*, of 1738.[42] Chandler describes The Rocks as 'A sweet and cool Retreat', 'At easy distance from the Town' (Bath), where silver streams descend dark, wooded cliffs to 'Elysian Plains' below. The site and situation of The Rocks can be clearly seen on Thomas Thorpe's *Survey* of the vicinity of Bath of 1742 (fig. 91). A recent survey of the site has attempted to identify the various stages of the development of the landscape.[43] Although now much altered, it must have been extremely dramatic in the eighteenth century, with vertical cliffs formed by seventeenth-century quarrying 'topped by grotesquely gnarled and rooty Oak, Beech and Yew' and vistas to Bath from the top.[44] Although much of the landscape was created by John Jacob's mother (the 'Mrs Jacob' of the poem), some features datable to the 1760s show that John Jacob himself continued to develop the site. Like Sir Charles-Kemeys Tynte, Coplestone Bampfylde and others who patronised Gainsborough during the early Bath years, Jacob had a particular interest in landscape and was the owner of an estate notable for its romantic scenery.

While Gainsborough's *Hilly Wooded Landscape* bears no relationship to the topography of Jacob's artificial landscape at The Rocks, the painting has a drama of its own, what Hayes has called a 'Rubensian thrust and counter-thrust' that is especially apparent in the smaller oil study for the composition.[45] The study contains some of the most extraordinary brushwork to be found in any of Gainsborough's Bath-period landscape paintings. It is an essay on the subject of windy weather, the two lightly touched slanting stripes of pink against the dark clouds bringing the stormy sky to life in a manner Payne Knight might have called 'easily perceived but incapable of being described'. Rather disappointingly, the wind has dropped in the finished picture, perhaps because such an air of agitation might not have been acceptable on a larger scale or might have disturbed the peace of Jacob's 'cool Retreat'.

The small oil sketch, which presumably remained a private picture, shows Gainsborough working at speed, applying paint with the same urgency as he applied chalk and washes in his drawings. While in his portraits Gainsborough strove with 'effects to make the Heart dance', here too he seems to be exploring to the full the expensive possibilities of bravura brushwork. The picture may coincide with an outburst of activity following the painter's serious illness in the autumn of 1763, a time when he took stock of his career and determined to let off more of his Abbey Street house as lodgings rather than ruin his health through overwork at portraiture. This study can be associated with the European notion of the unfinished sketch, the type of picture termed *pittoresco* in Italy, and it should be remembered that Uvedale Tomkyns Price, who so admired the Italian masters of bravura brushwork, was still alive at this date, and probably still showing a paternal interest in Gainsborough's career.

Figures play only a minor part in John Jacob's landscape. Ten years later, in the picture normally referred to as the Duke of Rutland's *Woodcutter's Return* (fig. 157), they assume a major role. This picture should more correctly be introduced as the Marquis of Granby's *Woodcutter's Return*, since in 1773, when the picture appears to have been purchased, the 'noble Lord' who bought it had not yet inherited his dukedom.[46] Granby was educated at Eton (at the time Alexander Cozens was drawing master there) and Cambridge, and subsequently became Whig Member of Parliament for Cambridge. In 1775 he married Mary Isabella Somerset, sister of the Fifth Duke of Beaufort and by blood a first cousin of Mrs Margaret Gainsborough (fig. 126). Gainsborough painted the Marquis of Granby's portrait in Bath around 1771–1773 and Mary Isabella's in London in 1782.[47] There is no way of telling whether the payment by the Marquis of £66.10.0 to Gainsborough on 6 August 1773 was for the *Woodcutter's Return* or for his portrait.[48]

Marcia Pointon has asserted that 'it is futile to search for specific texts as sources for the content of Gainsborough's art', but has demonstrated, at the same time, the painter's awareness of contemporary literary themes, notably the idea of 'retreat' and 'retirement'.[49] If the *Woodcutter's Return* is examined in the light of current literature it is possible to associate the picture with a number of texts originating in Bath, some of which, such as Daniel Webb's poem, were inspired by the picture itself, and others which are so close in sentiment as to suggest an exchange of ideas between their authors and the painter.

Webb's poem, as we saw, reverses the usual identification of the artist as one tied to the 'mechanic' aspects of his trade, and styles Gainsborough as the liberal artist and the connoisseurs, blind to the merits of contemporary English art, as those enslaved by the 'mechanic'. The poem particularly praises the colour of the painting, 'All nature's beauties in thy tints that glow', a point of some significance, since Webb considered Titian the finest colourist of modern times, and the warmth of this composition is perhaps closer to Titian than any of Gainsborough's earlier works. Here, what Webb called 'the native and mellow tints of Titian' can indeed be seen to take precedence over what Webb considered the brash colouring of Rubens, something that can be illustrated by a simple comparison with the earlier *Wooded Landscape with Peasants in a Country Waggon* (fig. 102).[50] Although the lighting of the *Woodcutter's Return* is still contrived and artificial, the greens and pinks of the earlier pictures have now mellowed to earthy browns and ochres.

The Duke of Rutland's picture also owes something to Webb's other hero, Correggio, and may have inspired Richard Graves to refer to Gainsborough as 'Like great Correggio,

155 *(left)* Francis Hayman (1708–1776), *John Jacob and his sisters Anne, Mary and Elizabeth* 1743–4, oil on canvas, 38 × 42½ inches (96.5 × 108 cm), private collection.

156 *(below)* The Rocks (formerly Southern Wood Castle), near Marshfield, photograph, 1981.

157 Thomas Gainsborough (1727–1788), *Wooded Landscape with Family grouped outside a Cottage, 'The Woodcutter's Return'* 1773, oil on canvas, 58 × 48½ inches (147.3 × 123.2 cm), The Duke of Rutland, Belvoir Castle.

Nature's pupil, fraught with inborn genius'.[51] John Hayes and others have admitted that 'Gainsborough was more aware of traditional iconography than has usually been suggested', pointing out that the struggling woodman echoes images of Christ carrying his cross and the women and children by the cottage door clearly refer to representations of the Holy Family.[52]

Gainsborough himself, with characteristic informality, called the composition a 'Cottage & ragged family' and the picture is not, of course, a Nativity or Holy Family, but a contemporary idealised vision of English rural life.[53] The cottage around which the figures congregate is built up against an ancient tree, deep in a wood, and, rather improbably, has neatly glazed windows. Notions of retreat and of simple country domesticity were embraced by several of Gainsborough's acquaintances, notably Ann Ford and, as Pointon noted, Richard Graves. William Whitehead was entranced by Ann Ford on meeting her in Bath in the autumn of 1758 and wrote to his former pupil Lord Nuneham, 'You would be desperately in love with her in half an hour .

. . A Cottage with the man she loves is the height of her ambition.'[54] A month later he wrote again, 'She is excellent in music, loves solitude . . . Painting is likewise her most favorite [sic] amusement, & for Poetry she has herself translated most of Metastasio's operas'.[55] Ann Ford's ideal of a cottage and rural solitude found expression later in her life when she wrote in *The School for Fashion* of Felix Cottage, romantically situated near the sea, with its hermitage including a wax model of a hermit, and members of the owner's family dressed as shepherdesses.[56]

Rather nearer in spirit to Gainsborough's cottage and ragged family is a description of a cottage that apparently stood in the parish of Bathampton, one of the areas Gainsborough is known to have frequented. R. Hippisley's *Bath and its Environs: A Descriptive Poem in three Cantos*, published in 1775, includes the passage,

> Near Hampton's Verge, embosom'd in a shade,
> Close to the murmurs of a soft cascade,
> A *Cottage* stands, in which Wood claim'd no part,
> The work of *Nature*, unadorned by art;
> A cottage suited to the owner's state;
> Tho' small, convenient; and, tho' plain, yet neat.
> No fretted cornices; no vaulted room,
> Disguise the *artless neatness* of this dome
> Which sweet *Content* adorns: Within this cell
> A pair, like Baucis and Philemon dwell . . .[57]

Whether such a cottage existed, or was a product of Hippisley's imagination inspired by a picture such as Gainsborough's *Woodcutter's Return*, may never be known. If it did, it was doubtless known to Richard Graves, a keen walker and explorer of the countryside whose Rectory at Claverton was close to the rocky, wooded slopes of Bathampton (fig. 6). Graves notably described the glories and pitfalls of 'retirement' in his comic novel *Columella*, but he also specifically describes an ideal cottage in *The Spiritual Quixote* which was published in 1773, the year of Gainsborough's painting. Under the chapter heading 'An agreeable Solitude. An Holy Family, in the Flemish Style' he describes a cottage encountered by Wildgoose and Tugwell in the Usk Valley in Monmouthshire. The house was 'covered with honey-suckles and sweet-briar: the windows were glazed; and the chimney rose, with truly ancient British magnificence, two feet above the thatch'.[58] 'Wildgoose could not but admire the sequestered situation; and observed, "that, if a true primitive spirit reigned amongst these people, they must be the happiest of mortals"'.[59] In typical fashion, Graves's travellers are quickly disillusioned: the householder turns out not to be a humble cottager living off the land, but an impoverished clergyman surrounded by squabbling children, a 'Holy Family' of quite a different kind. Despite Graves's gentle mockery, there is no doubt that he was keenly attuned to the current quest for spiritual enrichment through solitude and an appreciation of the beauties of nature. Graves, of course, thought Gainsborough's landscapes, with their 'sequestered spots', the most pleasing he knew, although he considered their very intimacy rendered them unsuitable models for landscape gardeners.[60]

The ethereal *Peasants and Colliers going to Market*, purchased by Henry Hoare, was probably painted within the same twelve months as the Marquis of Granby's *Woodcutters Return* and yet two pictures could scarcely be more different. *Peasants and Colliers going to Market* is closer in mood to Claude than many of the painter's earlier Bath landscapes. Gone are the echoes of Rubens's stormy skies and the bold contrasts that, as Uvedale Price observed, made his landscapes the masterpieces they are, but would completely destroy the tranquillity of a composition by Claude. This is not to say that Gainsborough's Bath career can be mapped as a transition from a Rubens-inspired way of depicting landscape to a style based on Claude, since his restless and enquiring nature precluded an orderly progress of this kind. The change is better characterised as an increasingly expansive vision, now able to absorb and adapt the lessons of a whole range of predecessors, including painters of such classical grandeur as Claude. The contrast between the *Woodcutter's Return* and this picture shows how various his mood and intentions could be at every stage of his working life.

As if to prove how adept he was at borrowing and transforming, Gainsborough used as the initial compositional inspiration for this picture a rather unprepossessing image by Philip Wouvermans (1619–1668), a small (approximately thirteen by ten inch) panel from which a same-size engraving was produced by Robert Strange (fig. 159). The Wouvermans painting seems always to have been in Paris during Gainsborough's lifetime. The print, entitled *Le Retour du Marché*, is inscribed as after the picture belonging to Monsieur Le Noir, and since the picture is known to have been sold by Le Noir by 1770, the engraving must have been made before this date.[61] Gainsborough's interpretation of the image is the same way round as the picture, rather than the engraving. It is possible he saw a copy of the painting rather than the print, or, as he did when using Chatelain's print from the Arthur Pond series (fig. 132), he may deliberately have reversed the design in order to disguise its source. Although the Wouvermans features a single horse and cart, rather than a group of mounted figures, the similarities are unmistakable. Wouvermans has a male mounted figure seated sideways on a small horse, looking across at a seated peasant woman suckling a baby at the roadside. In front of the horse, puddles, or patches of marshy water, catch the light, and a dog, walking slightly ahead of the horse, turns towards the nursing woman.

From this humble beginning Gainsborough created a painting of astonishing grandeur, in which English peasants set out (rather than return) and cross the brow of a hill soon after dawn. Apart from the silvery quiet of Gainsborough's picture, the most striking aspect of it is the way in which the

158 Thomas Gainsborough (1727–1788), *Open Landscape with Mounted Peasants going to Market, here identified as 'Peasants and Colliers going to Market; early Morning'* 1772–3, oil on canvas, 48 × 58 inches (121.9 × 147.3 cm), private collection, courtesy of Pyms Gallery, London.

figures dominate the composition. Joseph Pott spoke eloquently of the grace of Gainsborough's figures in the middle period of his life, and the manner in which they are 'beautifully adapted to landscape'.[62] Pott must have had in mind pictures such as *Peasants and Collliers going to Market*, the *Woodcutter's Return* or perhaps the Earl of Shelburne's *Wooded Landscape with Mounted Peasants*, all of which include quite large-scale figures, arranged in coherent groups, occupying a significant proportion of the canvas.

Although quite unlike the most overtly Picturesque of Gainsborough's Bath pictures, such as Dr Charleton's landscape, *Peasants going to Market* can still be identified with Charlotte Klonk's analysis of the Picturesque as 'social reality seen from an idealised vantage-point'.[63] The social reality of the figures in this picture has fascinated many commentators and repays fresh examination.[64] It does appear that it is correct to entitle the picture *Peasants and Colliers going to Market; Early Morning*, as it was called at Stourhead for most of the nineteenth century.[65] The mounted figures, which fall in to two types, can be associated with the two major occupations of the rural poor in north Somerset: agriculture and coal mining. At the front of the group are two figures with baskets of produce; behind are three men, also sitting on saddles designed to support panniers, but not bearing any produce. These men, with distinctly grey faces, appear to be colliers. Agricultural labourers and miners were to be found in almost equal numbers on the hilly roads around Bath in the eighteenth century. A coal pit within three miles of the centre of Bath is marked on Thorpe's *Survey* (fig. 37). Gainsborough must have been fully aware of the important contribution both agricultural labourers and miners made to the local economy, and the ways in which their lives were

159 Robert Strange (1725–1792) after Philip Wouvermans, *Le Retour du Marché* 1760s, engraving, 15 × 10¾ inches (38.2 × 27.5 cm), published before 1770, British Museum, London.

160 Thomas Gainsborough (1727–1788), *Wooded Landscape with Peasants in a Country Waggon, 'The Harvest Waggon'* c. 1766, oil on canvas, $47\frac{1}{2} \times 57$ inches (120.7 × 144.8 cm), Barber Institute of Fine Arts, Birmingham.

being affected by changes in farming. The coal-mining Mendip area was one of the last parts of Somerset to be enclosed, and since many miners were also smallholders, they shared the peasant farmers' distress at the loss of common land. The sense of solidarity between Somerset miners and peasant farmers on the issue of land enclosure in the Mendip region is spelled out in an evocative poem of 1788 in the Salisbury-published *County Magazine*, entitled 'A Letter from a Collier in Somersetshire to his Friend', which includes the lines,

> With gents and jobbers Inglan zwarms,
> And all the land's turn'd to grit farms;
> Thay've tyn'd in all the commin groun,
> And pool'd the cottige houzin doun.[66]

Gainsborough, who frequently rode in the local countryside, must have had plenty of opportunity to observe miners on the road. Coal was transported in panniers carried by single small horses rather than in carts because of the number of steep hills in the area, and the lack of suitable waterways. When not delivering coal, the colliers rode on their horses, using them to travel to and from the pits. Although genteel road users complained of their rudeness and disdain for other travellers, Gainsborough's attitude might have been more in sympathy with that expressed by Edmund Rack, a writer whose concern for the local rural poor was a factor in the establishment of the Bath and West of England Society in 1777. Rack saw in the miners a stoic sense of pride that enabled them to survive the indignities of poverty, instancing the vociferous resistance of a group of miners forced to

161 Unidentified eighteenth-century artist, *Walter Wiltshire's House at Bathford (Shockerwick House)* 1775, pencil and ink wash, $7\frac{3}{8} \times 10\frac{7}{8}$ inches (18.8 × 27.5 cm), British Library, Map Library, King's Topographical Collection, XXXVII, 30c. The carriage in the foreground is initialled 'WW' for Walter Wiltshire; the drawing is inscribed on the back 'July 4 1775'.

162 Samuel Middiman (1750–1831), after Thomas Malton the younger, *View near Bath* 1785, engraving, $5\frac{1}{8} \times 7\frac{1}{4}$ inches (13 × 8.4 cm), published 21 January 1785, Victoria Art Gallery, Bath and North East Somerset Council.

make way for a grand carriage on the road. He concluded that the miners' belief that their wealthy oppressors would 'march directly to the D[evi]l as soon as they die' enabled them to adopt the moral high ground, despite the 'Servitude they are in to the *Rich*'.[67]

It would certainly be going too far to see *Peasants and Colliers going to Market* as a campaigning picture – a wealthy businessman such as Henry Hoare would probably not have purchased it if it was – but it is a composition in which labourers assume a classical dignity that matches the calm of the early morning. The poise of the female mounted peasant, who is associated with the agricultural labourer riding alongside, rather than the following figures, has often been remarked upon. Like the female rider in Lord Shelburne's landscape (fig. 104), she is a beauty, dressed in imitation of a fashionable townswoman. The fact that the women in both pictures are travelling to or from market probably provides the clue to their unexpectedly sophisticated appearance. It is on record that the stalls in the produce market at Newport, Isle of Wight, were, in the eighteenth century, manned by country girls of particular beauty. A contemporary observer noted that these girls 'came on horseback with their baskets . . . have a room where they new dress, and . . . a hairdresser always attends'.[68] There were parallels between the Newport and Bath markets, both being based in fashionable resort towns. In both cases the markets were situated near to luxury-goods shops and were frequented not just by cooks or domestic servants, but by the visiting gentry who generally dined at home in their lodgings and seem to have enjoyed shopping for food as much as they did for clothes or souvenirs.

It seems quite possible that the practice of sending country girls selected for their beauty, to tempt the resort visitors, was a deliberate strategy adopted in the Bath market, just as at Newport. The Bath market, centrally placed beside the Guildhall, only yards from Gainsborough's Abbey Street house, was famous for the variety of its fruit and vegetables, dairy produce, meat and fish.[69] A plentiful supply of local coal from the Somerset and the South Gloucestershire coalfields also contributed significantly to Bath's eighteenth-century prosperity, cheap winter fuel being one of the attractions for people of quality who wished to enjoy comfortable accommodation and have money to spare for theatre- and concert-going, gambling and shopping.[70]

As well as the two groups of mounted figures, here identified as peasants and colliers, there is the nursing figure in Gainsborough's picture, a seated, black-haired woman with two infants, begging at the wayside. Her older child is based on a baby in Raphael's Vatican fresco *The Fire in the Borgo* (which Gainsborough must have known from a print) and she, as well as reflecting Wouvermans's seated peasant woman, might well derive from Gainsborough's observation of the gipsies on Lansdown, who appealed to passers-by in strange, foreign-sounding accents.[71] *Peasants and Colliers going to Market*, for all its classical calm and elegance, may bear a much closer relationship to social reality than has hitherto been appreciated. It also appears to be a picture that is specifically related to Bath and can only be fully understood with reference to the social history of the city at the time of Gainsborough's residence. It is unlikely that he would have painted the same figures after moving to London, and indeed the only other picture in which colliers seem to make an appearance is *Going to Market* (Kenwood, London), acquired by Lord Bateman around 1770.[72]

The last pictures to be considered belonged to Walter Wiltshire. It has long been known that Gainsborough sent pictures to London using Wiltshire's waggon service, and some of Wiltshire's other business enterprises have already been mentioned. Wiltshire is said to have given Gainsborough a grey horse to which the painter had become particularly attached, and which Gainsborough used to ride to London when he left Bath in the autumn of 1774.[73] This horse presumably replaced the one Sir William St Quintin had given him earlier. In return for hospitality, and perhaps other favours, Gainsborough is said to have given Wiltshire *The Harvest Waggon* (fig. 160) and either given or sold him the *Rocky Wooded Landscape with Rustic Lovers* (fig. 118). John Wiltshire, Walter's grandson, later owned *The Gipsies*, whose composition was etched by Gainsborough and engraved by Joseph Wood (fig. 121).[74] It has often been said that one or other of Wiltshire's pictures was painted at his country house, Shockerwick in the parish of Bathford, a few miles outside Bath.[75] As Thomas Thorpe's *Survey* shows, Shockerwick lies only a short distance from the Jacobs' seat at The Rocks, the two estates only being separated by Banner Down or Bannerdown (fig 91 and 165).

The first point that should be made is that it is most unlikely that Gainsborough would have painted large canvases at Shockerwick, since the grand house, which still stands, was only built in the 1770s, just as Gainsborough was leaving Bath. The new house replaced a decaying farmhouse situated nearby. A drawing in the King's Topographical Collection of the British Library shows the new house in 1775, perhaps unfinished, as what appears to be the old farmhouse can be seen behind, still standing to the right of the new building (fig. 161).[76] Throughout most of Gainsborough's residence in Bath Walter Wiltshire's country house was one beside the London road, overlooking the River Avon. A caption to a print of 1785 entitled a *View Near Bath* reads, 'The annexed View, is taken from the great western road, about a mile from *Bath*, in a fine woody country . . . The house seen in the centre belongs to Mr Wiltshire, of *Bath*, who does not reside here, but has lately built an elegant mansion [i.e. Shockerwick] upon an eminence in the neighbourhood of *Box*, about three miles distance' (fig. 162).[77] Walter Wiltshire's elder brother John (1718–1762) had begun acquiring the Shockerwick estate in 1749 and after his death Walter bought the remaining land as it became available in 1768, 1774 and 1778.[78]

163 Jacob Skinner (d. 1754) after Thomas Ross, *John Wiltshire's Bookplate* 1740, etching, image 5 × 3⅞ inches (12.8 × 9.6 cm), inscribed in the plate with the names of both artists and the date 1740, Bath Central Library, Bath, Hunt Collection, V, p. 171.

164 *(right)* Thomas Gainsborough (1727–1788), *James Quin (1693–1766)* 1762–3, oil on canvas, 92 × 60 inches (233.7 × 152.5 cm), National Gallery of Ireland, Dublin.

If proof were needed to refute Ronald Paulson's claim that Walter Wiltshire or any member of his family could be considered an 'unlettered anticonnoisseur', this exists in the form of John Wiltshire's bookplate, designed by Thomas Ross and engraved by Jacob Skinner (fig. 163). Dated 1740, its elaborate design incorporates Shakespeare and Alexander Pope as supporters of the Wiltshire arms, with a bust of the Emperor Augustus on a plinth above. At the feet of the poets are emblems of the arts, including a palette, globe, musical instruments, books and scrolls. That such imagery was adopted by a young man whose family were carriers and Assembly Rooms proprietors, is quite remarkable, and shows that the Wiltshires were tradesmen with their hearts set on gentility, upwardly mobile members of Bath society like Gainsborough himself. When John Wiltshire died in 1762, Walter took over as head of the family and his building of Shockerwick House, to designs by the Bath architect John Palmer, was the greatest outward expression of the wealth he had amassed by the 1770s.[79] Gainsborough's landscapes, and the portrait of James Quin (fig. 164) must have handsomely furnished the new house, and it was there that they were seen by many visitors admitted by Wiltshire, his son John Wiltshire (1762–1842) and grandson John (1786–1866).[80] On this last John Wiltshire's death in 1866, the Gainsborough pictures were sold, along with other paintings including a pair of grand Roman compositions by Panini, described as signed and dated and 'capital'; landscapes by Gaspard Dughet and Wouvermans; a 'White Horse' by Isaac Ostade; 'A Landscape with Nymphs Bathing' by Both and Poelemberg and other foreign and English pictures.[81]

John Wiltshire, who commissioned the bookplate, and his brother Walter were members of the same set of people who,

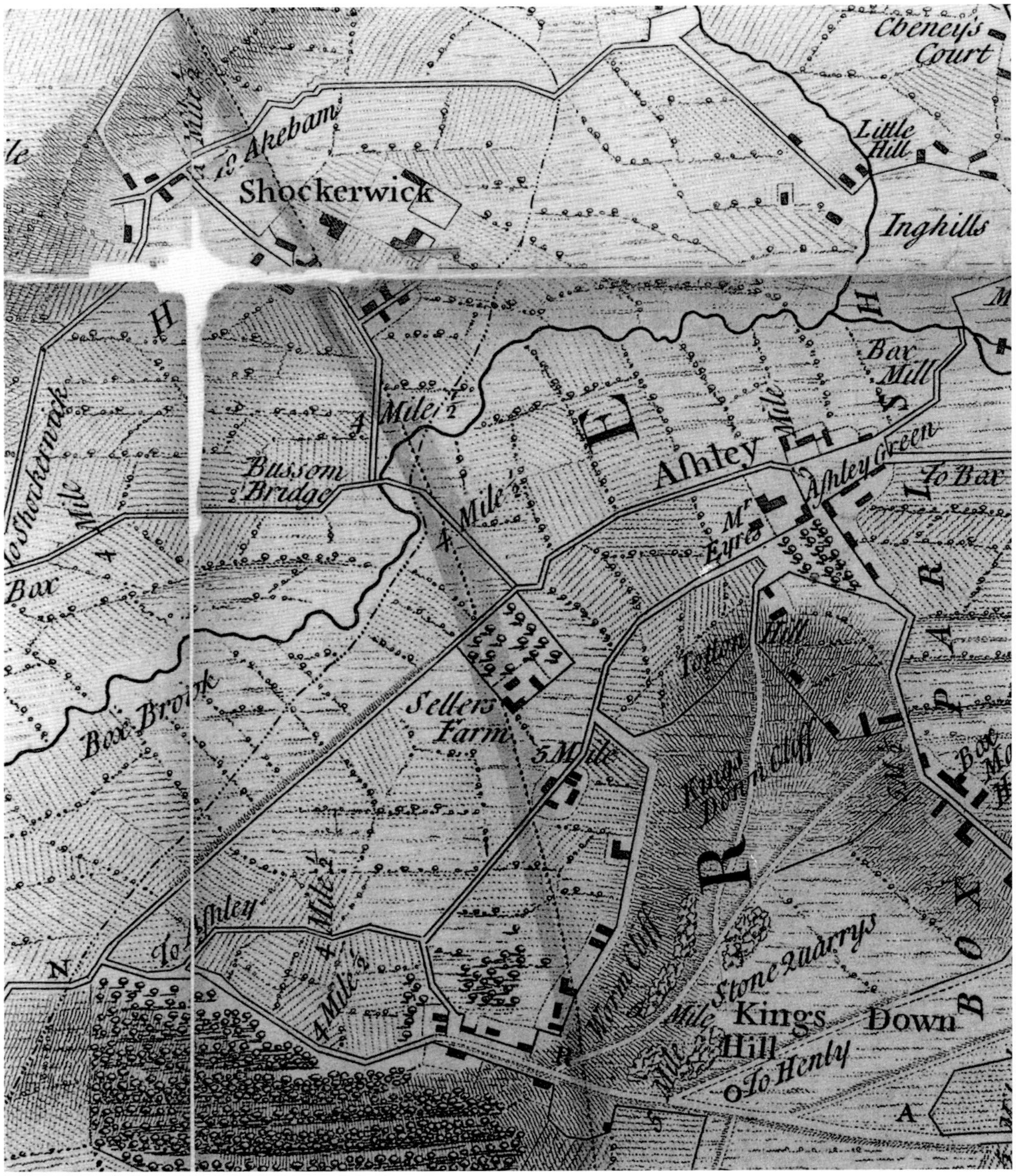

165 Thomas Thorpe, detail from *An Actual Survey of the City of Bath . . . and of Five Miles Round* 1742, engraving (the whole) 75⅝ × 77 inches (192.1 × 195.6 cm), published 1742, Bath Record Office, Bath. This actual size detail of Thorpe's *Survey* shows an area east of Bath with the Wiltshire estate of Shockerwick and King's Down 'Stone Quarrys' such as Gainsborough depicted in Walter Wiltshire's *Rocky Wooded Landscape with Rustic Lovers.*

earlier in the century, had been associated with the Hospital and the circle said by Cleland to have formed an academy of painting. Their names crop up at Masonic meetings (where they met with Thomas Ross and Jacob Skinner, who together produced the bookplate), and through the Assembly Rooms they mixed with musicians and other performers, hosting, among other concerts, Carl Friedrich Abel's first Bath concert in 1760.[82] The Wiltshires evidently knew Richard Graves well, Graves noting in a letter that he attended a performance of Robert Dodsley's *Cleone* with John Wiltshire, the two men standing together in the pit in order to watch the reactions of 'undiguis'd humanity' to the play.[83] According to the local nineteenth-century historian Jerom Murch, 'Walter Wiltshire, like Allen [i.e. Ralph Allen], was a gentleman by nature', and it was he who instigated the 'revival of all that was picturesque and beautiful' in the park at Shockerwick.[84] That Walter Wiltshire considered himself a gentleman we know from the fact that when Mayor of Bath in 1772, he threw a lavish entertainment in the Guildhall, to which tradesmen were not invited, and were thereby greatly offended.[85]

Gainsborough, it will be remembered, was also guilty of offending fellow artists by what was perceived as his arrogance, and it is not hard to see a parallel between Gainsborough's and Wiltshire's progress in Bath society.[86] Lesser artists must have been astonished that Gainsborough, a portrait-painter, occupied a particularly grand house designed for a Duke; the fact that Walter Wiltshire, a carrier and seller of mineral water, built one of the most imposing classical mansions in the vicinity of Bath, must equally have amazed more lowly traders. A love of landscape may have cemented the friendship between the two men. Wiltshire revived a neglected landscape at Shockerwick and evidently cared deeply about trees. When the poet Christopher Anstey's garden behind the Royal Crescent was destined to be destroyed by the new residential development of St James's Square, the mature beech trees, of which Anstey had been particularly fond, were dug up and replanted by Wiltshire in his park at Shockerwick. No effort or expense can have been spared, since the beech trees (and beech are notoriously difficult to establish), were said to be still flourishing in the mid-nineteenth century.[87]

Although Wiltshire's new house was probably only built towards the end of Gainsborough's residence in Bath, it seems quite likely that the artist spent time in the developing park and garden at Shockerwick. The earliest suggestion that this was so seems to be contained in a poem (apparently unpublished) by William Lisle Bowles (1762–1850). The poem is undated, but Bowles was in Bath in 1789 and 1795, and it may well have been written when Walter Wiltshire was still alive.[88] Bowles is said to have composed the verse on retiring to a root-house in the garden at Shockerwick on a beautiful July morning:

> Stirs not a kindred sympathy within,
> When on this tablet thou dost lean
> And gaze upon the selfsame scene
> Beloved, erewhile, by Gainsborough & Quin?
> The summer smiled to them, as now to thee.
> The circling hills, the spreading tree:
> As lovely shone in morning light
> Too soon to sink, like thee, in night. –
> Thou too shalt follow; yet, while all is gay,
> Enjoy the transitory day.
> Tranquil, yet not unmindful of that Power,
> Before whose eye passes this shortening hour
> Enough if Love & Peace, & Harmony,
> Improve some happier moments as they fly.[89]

Unfortunately little is known of what Walter Wiltshire's recreated Shockerwick park looked like. The fact that it included a root-house suggests that it may have contained a number of garden features, but nothing of this sort remains. The drawing of 1775 seems to indicate field divisions and pasture for cattle to the left of the new house. The only other clues as to the style of the park and garden lie in the story of the transplantation of beech trees and in the nineteenth-century memory of a tree named 'Gainsborough's elm'.[90] Bowles's poem simply talks of 'the circling hills, the spreading tree'. Apart from the fantasy of the root-house, the indications are that the emphasis was on trees and views into the existing 'natural' scenery.

Whereas the *Rocky Wooded Landscape with Rustic Lovers* utilises the drama of nearby rocks and woodland (fig. 165), the other major landscape Wiltshire owned, *The Harvest Waggon*, is set in flatter scenery, framed by elegant trees, with the emphasis on a carefully designed figure group and a waggon and horses. Walter Wiltshire's own waggons were not farm carts, but long-distance road waggons, carrying all manner of goods between London and Bath – Richard Graves commended the service as 'the safest and cheapest conveyance' for sending books to Bath – but the very idea of a waggon and horses was central to Wiltshire's life and livelihood.[91] The harvest waggon may be seen as an idealised or romantic version of one of Wiltshire's more prosaic goods waggons. While Wiltshire made his money from being an urban carrier, he may, like the artist, have dreamt of an idealised rural existence in which he could 'walk off to some sweet Village' or lie in a farm cart, 'gazing at Green Trees & Blue Skies'.[92] In fact Gainsborough's musings on rural pleasures, in this famous letter to William Jackson, could easily be inspired by the contrast between Wiltshire's commercial waggons, plying their trade up and down the dusty London Road, with the apparent freedom of a country waggon: 'd—mn it I hate a dust, the kicking up a dust; and being confined in Harness to follow the track, whilst others ride in the Waggon, under cover, stretching their Legs in the straw at Ease, and gazing at Green Trees & Blue Skies . . .'.

Both Wiltshire's paintings may be seen to relate to their owner's personal circumstances, and the parallels between Wiltshire's and Gainsborough's positions in Bath society reinforce the traditionally held view that the two men had much in common. Gainsborough must have encouraged Wiltshire to see beauty in the surrounding landscape and one can picture Wiltshire modelling his park and framing his vistas under Gainsborough's influence. The knowledge that the Wiltshires as a family were not country-bumpkins, but wealthy businessmen intent upon 'improvement', whether self-improvement, or the remodelling of the landscape, suggests that they too may have been part of that intellectual circle from which notions of retirement and the Picturesque evolved during the second half of the eighteenth century

10

Gainsborough of Bath

Gainsborough was never generally known as 'Gainsborough of Bath' in the way that William Hoare was known as 'Hoare of Bath' and Thomas Barker as 'Barker of Bath'. He was too important a figure and was not solely associated with Bath, although it was there that he spent the longest settled period of his adult life. Historically he has been more closely linked with East Anglia, perhaps because Sudbury has done much more to honour its famous son than Bath has done to commemorate one of its most eminent residents. Nevertheless, in 1850 the historian John Britton observed how closely Gainsborough 'identified himself and his works with the scenery and persons of Bath'.[1] This book has set out to explore the extent to which this is true.

By the time Britton was writing, Bath had acquired a cloak of quiet provincial gentility; it was a place of somewhat faded architectural splendour to which people retired in their old age and spent their last days being wheeled between the Pump Room and one of many rest homes and medical establishments. At the end of the nineteenth century a consuming interest in Bath's Roman past resulted in a town centre given over to archaeology and excavation (fig. 167). The Bath that Gainsborough knew was a much more forward-looking city, a place in which an enterprise culture flourished and to which resourceful businessmen were attracted from all over England, setting themselves up in a wide variety of retail and service ventures associated with medicine and leisure. In this period the appearance of the town changed on a daily basis. Modern buildings all but obliterated the seventeenth-century past and spread out beyond the old city boundaries across fields and hills in a bid to accommodate an ever-increasing number of visitors. Those who had the imagination to tap in to this burgeoning economy won friends and influence, and played a delicate game of balancing their business success with philanthropy (usually associated with the Hospital). The handful who rose to the top of the tree called themselves gentlemen rather than tradesmen.

By establishing himself as a successful portrait painter, closely in tune with the mood of Bath's fashionable society, Gainsborough acquired the financial and intellectual freedom he needed in order to develop as an artist. Within a decade he, like Walter Wiltshire, considered himself a gentleman and, as Thicknesse put it, was ready to 'contemn and despise those who treat him in any other light'.[2] Many of Bath's entrepreneurs were women, and Gainsborough's predominantly female household was ideally placed to provide the support he needed as a background to his career. His sister's millinery undoubtedly complemented his portrait practice and her rapid success in the lodging house business must have spared the artist some of the burden of responsibility associated with renting out his own Abbey Street property.

If Gainsborough's sister played a key part in his Bath career, so too did his wife. Margaret Gainsborough, we know, had to remind the artist to charge customers for packing cases (and probably other incidental expenses) but more important than her dabbling in the minutiae of the portrait business was her link with the Dukes of Beaufort which gave her a special place in Bath society. As the architect John Wood recognised in his *Essay towards a Description of Bath*, published in 1749, one of the most important contributory factors to Bath's eighteenth-century economic growth was the Avon navigation scheme, initiated in 1711, which opened the city to the movement of goods to and from the whole of Britain and beyond.[3] As Wood also acknowledged, the Avon navigation owed everything to Henry, Second Duke of Beaufort, who personally lobbied for and paid for the Act of Parliament necessary to set the scheme in motion. Beaufort's Buildings was named in recognition of the Duke's generosity, and successive Dukes of Beaufort continued to be honoured in various ways throughout the century, the Fourth Duke, for example, being President of the Hospital in 1748 and the Fifth Duke President in 1766.[4] The artist James Vertue dedicated his large print of Bath Abbey, one of the most enduring images of eighteenth-century Bath, to the Fourth Duke (fig 4).

Gainsborough's marriage to the Third Duke of Beaufort's illegitimate daughter in 1746 paved the way for his move to Bath in the late 1750s, assuring him of a support network on his arrival in the city. Members of the Price family and James Unwin, Gainsborough's banker, were key figures in this

166 Detail of fig. 101.

167 The Roman Baths, Bath, with Gainsborough's Abbey Street house on the right, photograph, c. 1892, Bath Central Library. Two men can be seen looking out of Gainsborough's house from one of the south-facing first floor windows above what was originally the passage to the King's and Queen's Baths. By this date the passage arcade had been blocked in. The eighteenth-century ground level is 5 or 6 feet above the heads of the people assembled by the newly excavated Roman Baths.

network, the Prices being related by bonds of marriage and friendship to the Beauforts and James Unwin being a long-standing employee of successive Dukes. The received wisdom that Gainsborough began his Bath career by painting the portraits of the prosperous middle classes, and progressed to painting the aristocracy as he developed an elegant and distinctive style, is now turned on its head.[5] The evidence of the artist's first winter season of 1758–9 shows that on arrival in Bath he was immediately employed by members of the Earl of Jersey's family, some of the most fashionable and 'well-bred' men in the land, and that these commissions almost certainly came about as a result of an introduction arranged by one of the Prices. The self-confidence engendered by these first commissions allowed the artist to develop a bold personal style that found early expression in the portrait of the Earl of Jersey's idol, Ann Ford, the future Mrs Thicknesse. The portrait of Ann Ford was the first of many sumptuous show pictures that advertised Gainsborough's ability to capture a likeness and astonished those who stepped in to the artist's elegant rooms on their way to the Pump Room or Assembly Rooms. Well-informed viewers such as Daniel Webb and Revd Richard Graves recognised the skill with which the painter combined old-masterly technique and colour with an understanding of modern concepts of taste, 'politeness' and 'ease', and the most discerning of the Bath audience also recognised the painter's potential to create a modern style of landscape painting.

The majority of Gainsborough's portrait sitters came to Bath as pleasure-seekers, wanting, in R. S. Neale's words, a temporary respite from 'the competitive reality of the economic life of property and wealth'.[6] These people were, of course, sustained by their business interests, and there is every indication that Gainsborough was aware of the underlying significance of coalfields, stone-quarrying, the iron industry and modern farming in the economy of the west of England and, by implication, in his own career. While Joseph Wright of Derby painted overtly industrial and scientific images, and displayed some of these in Bath shortly after Gainsborough moved to London, Gainsborough too made good use of modern science and technology, but in a very different way. It is likely that he experimented with optical instruments, which would have been readily available in the shops of those who supplied medical equipment. It is also probable that the material development of his technique was aided by Benjamin Colborne, a highly respected amateur apothecary who happened to be a fellow resident in the Circus. It can also be shown that his landscape paintings include references to stone quarries and coalminers, for example, although the changing landscape of Bath and hazy memory of local coalfields have meant that these references have not been recognised in recent times. Gainsborough's work in Bath was, in fact, closely enmeshed with the beginnings of the industrial revolution.

If the local coal industry provided imagery for at least two of the artist's landscape paintings, the iron industry of the West Midlands provides a link between various aspects of Gainsborough's life and art in East Anglia and Bath. In 1755, while living in Ipswich, Gainsborough borrowed the considerable sum of £300 from Captain Edward Wheeler, a member of the Wheeler family of Stourbridge and Staffordshire whose wealth derived from various iron industry partnerships. The iron works with which the Wheelers were associated were dominated by the Knight and Foley families of Worcestershire and Herefordshire, families well known to Gainsborough's physician and friend Dr Rice Charleton. It can be argued that the woodman in Charleton's landscape (fig. 148), and similar figures in other landscapes painted in Bath, are labourers associated with the iron industry. In 1769 a young woman of the Knight family came to Bath to fulfil a promise to sit to Gainsborough, only to find the artist too busy to undertake her portrait.

At around this time, or perhaps shortly before he left Bath, Gainsborough appears to have given one of his most remarkable portraits, *The Blue Boy* to one of the Buttalls, ironmongers from Wrexham, north Wales, who also traded in Greek Street, Soho. The Buttalls represented the retail end of the iron industry, selling the pots, pans, nails and other products that began life in the furnaces belonging to the Foleys, Wheelers and Knights. How Gainsborough came to know the Buttalls is unclear, but records show that members of this family visited Bath from time to time. Since they, like the Prices of Foxley, came from the county of Denbighshire, it is possible their shared Welsh heritage lead to friendship and that Uvedale Tomkyns Price introduced them to the artist.

The importance of Gainsborough's connection with the Prices during the time he lived in Bath cannot be overstated. Not only do some of Gainsborough's major landscape paintings of the period, such as the *Mountainous Wooded Landscape* (fig. 101) seem to be coloured with the red Herefordshire soil, but his visual vocabulary was absorbed by the young Uvedale Price and later translated into the *Essay on the Picturesque*. The painting of *The Gipsies* (now only known from the print) dating from immediately before Gainsborough's move to Bath, and shortly after the publication of Edmund Burke's *A Philosophical Enquiry into the Origin of our Ideas of the Sublime and the Beautiful*, can be identified as a seminal model for the Picturesque. It was an image that was widely dispersed through Wood's engraving which had an effect on artists from Francis Wheatley to John Constable. Wheatley, as is now well known, based his *Harvest Waggon* (fig. 168) of 1774 on Gainsborough's picture of the same subject which belonged to Walter Wiltshire (fig. 160), but he also looked to *The Gipsies* for inspiration.[7] The overall composition of Wheatley's large canvas is based on *The Gipsies* and details, including the burdock leaves and the figures of the standing young woman and the gesturing man beside the cart also derive from Gainsborough's print. Eleven years later, in 1785,

168 *(right)* Francis Wheatley (1747–1801), *The Harvest Waggon* 1774, oil on canvas, 50¼ × 40 inches (128.3 × 101.6 cm), signed and dated 1774, City of Nottingham Museums, Castle Museum and Art Gallery.

169 *(facing page top)* Thomas Gainsborough (1727–1788), *Wooded landscape with Peasants and Donkey round a Camp Fire, 'The Gipsy Encampment'* c. 1778–80, oil on canvas, 47½ × 59 inches (120.7 × 149.8 cm), Tate Britain, London.

170 *(facing page bottom)* Francis Wheatley (1747–1801), *Gipsies cooking their Kettle* 1785, etching, 7⅝ × 10 inches (19.4 × 25.5 cm), Signed and dated 1785, British Museum, London. Edward Edwards called this etching 'Gypsies cooking their Kettle'.

Wheatley etched a scene of gipsies round a fire, again using Gainsborough's *Gipsies* as his model (fig. 170). Constable, too, owned a copy of the engraving of *The Gipsies* and its composition finds an echo in several of his greatest pictures, including *The Cornfield* (National Gallery, London) and *Dedham Vale* (National Galleries of Scotland, Edinburgh).[8] Both these upright landscapes by Constable feature tall groups of trees to one side, a winding path leading towards a church tower on the horizon and powerfully 'structural' clouds. *Dedham Vale* even includes a gipsy mother and child by a fire in the foreground.

The Gipsies and landscapes of the Bath period were the pictures by Gainsborough that Sir Uvedale Price knew best (and he probably watched some of them being painted), but Price also seems also to have been familiar with later canvases including one that rekindles the gipsy theme, the *Wooded Landscape with Peasants and Donkey round a Camp Fire* (fig. 169). In this painting of the later 1770s a group of gipsies gather round a fire under dark trees. Once again a zig-zagging path separates the larger mass of woodland from a smaller balancing group of trees, and a church tower forms a focal point near the horizon.[9] Uvedale Price included in one of the later editions of his *Essay* an imaginary 'Dialogue on the Distinct Characters of the Picturesque and the Beautiful' which is closely based on Gainsborough's gipsy pictures and one or other of the 'cottage door' compositions, perhaps the Marquis of Granby's *Woodcutter's Return* (fig. 157). According to Price's narrative three friends, two of whom are lovers of paintings, are taking a walk when they lose their way and come to 'a wild unfrequented part of the country'. Then:

> suddenly, they came to a ruinous hovel on the outskirts of a healthy common. In a dark corner of it, some gypsies were sitting over a half-extinguished fire, which every now and then, as one of them stooped down to blow it, feebly blazed up for an instant, and shewed their sooty faces, and black tangled locks. An old male gypsy stood at the entrance with a countenance that well expressed his three-fold occupation, of beggar, thief, and fortune-teller; and by him a few worn-out asses; one loaded with rusty panniers, the other with tattered cloaths and furniture. The hovel was propt and over-hung by a blighted oak; its bare roots staring through the crumbling bank on which it stood. A gleam of light from under a dark cloud, glanced on the most prominent parts: the rest was buried in deep shadow: except where the dying embers
>
> 'Taught light to counterfeit a gloom'
>
> The three friends stood a long while contemplating this singular scene; but the two lovers of painting could hardly

Wheatly 1785
Designd & etchd by F Wheatly

171 Thomas Gainsborough (1727–1788), *Wooded Landscape with Peasants and Horses outside a Shed* c. 1775–79, soft ground etching, $11\frac{1}{8} \times 13\frac{3}{4}$ inches (28.3 × 34.9 cm), Witt Collection, Courtauld Institute of Art.

> quit it: they talked in raptures of every part; of the old hovel, the broken ground, the blasted oak, gypsies, asses, panniers, the catching lights, the deep shadows, the rich mellow tints, the grouping, the composition, the effect of the whole; and the words beautiful, and picturesque, were a hundred times repeated.[10]

If proof were needed that Gainsborough's art was the catalyst for the Picturesque, it is surely contained in this passage.

When Gainsborough's earlier *Gipsies* was paired with Wilson's *The Lake of Nemi* the juxtaposition emphasised the Englishness of Gainsborough's art. The Englishness of his landscapes was also lauded by Daniel Webb, Richard Graves and Uvedale Price. Richard Payne Knight may also have had Gainsborough's landscapes in mind when he contrasted the deceptive beauty of Italian landscape with the pure beauty of England. The 'pearly hue' of the Italian Campagna as depicted by Claude Lorrain was, Knight recognised, captivating, but Claude's artistic skills masked the reality of the place itself, where 'vapours' and insects were known to rise from the swamps. Anyone lying down to sleep in this terrain risked contracting some deadly disease. The native landscape, by contrast, presented no such threat, and the English peasant could enjoy the freedom of untroubled sleep in the field,

> Secure at noon, he snores beneath the brake,
> Nor fears, diseas'd, with fevrous pulse to wake[11]

Unavoidably this passage brings to mind the drawings, paintings and etching by Gainsborough in which peasants sleep without a care in a farm cart or on the ground (fig. 171). The sleeping peasant, when seen in this context, becomes a symbol of the honest beauty of the native countryside.

Gainsborough's particular achievement during the Bath years was, as we have seen, to unite an Italianate grandeur of conception with his observation of the scenery of England. The architect John Wood's concept of the modern city of Bath had at its heart a desire to demonstrate that the city was not 'a City standing in a Hole, and built on a Quagmire', but a place of natural beauty which in pre-Roman times was occupied by a race of Britons who were a 'Civilised People' with a distinctive culture and architecture of marble.[12] In designing Bath's new architecture he set about recreating this ancient ideal, planning buildings and open spaces that would be civilising in their influence, and were classical but distinctively British, rather than slavishly imitative of Roman models. Gainsborough's life in Bath, lived out in two houses designed by John Wood, is in many respects a fulfilment of Wood's ideal. He absorbed from the people he met in Wood's buildings, parades and squares a profound knowledge of the art and culture of the past, but he spoke in a modern idiom, using his new-found intellectual freedom to build an art form that his friend Richard Graves defined as 'Paradise regain'd' on English soil.

The all-important middle period of Gainsborough's life can now be viewed in a clearer light, with the artist's personal development seen not in isolation, but as part of the life of a city that was, fleetingly, one of the cultural centres of Europe. Being at a distance from London, but enjoying the benefits of patronage of 'quality', the artist worked at his own pace to create a distinctive and increasingly idealised or public style of portrait and landscape painting. By sending paintings to the new London exhibitions he was able to set his work against that of every other leading painter of the day, regularly reminding the widest possible audience of his abilities. That Gainsborough could achieve a commanding position within the eighteenth-century art world from the distance of Bath is indeed remarkable, but may now be a little better understood.

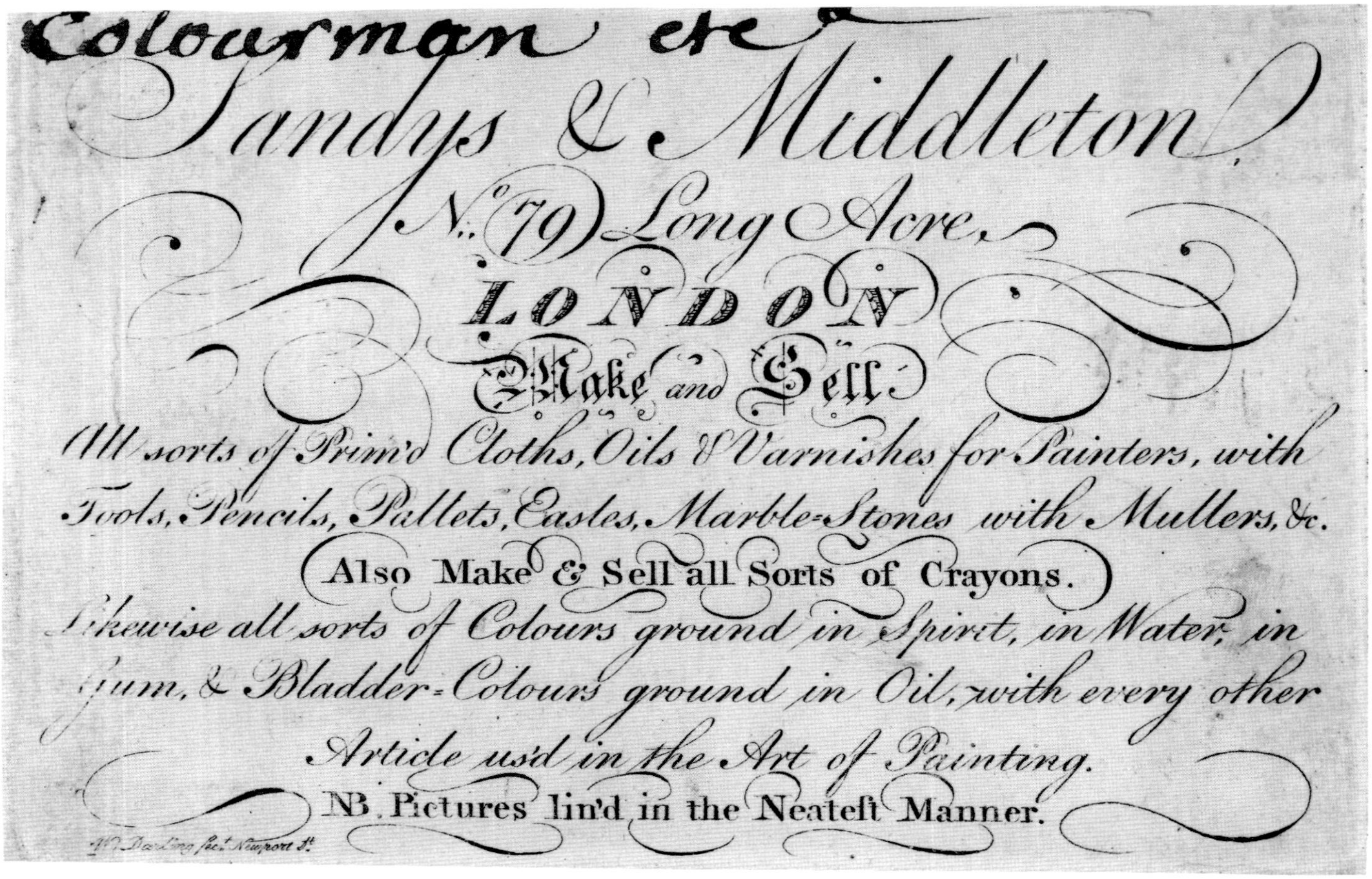

172 W. Darling (*fl.* 1780–90), trade card for Sandys and Middleton, colourmen, 1780s, engraving, 3⅛ × 5 inches (8 × 12.8 cm), British Museum, London, Heal trade card collection.

Appendix I

Artists in Bath in the Eighteenth Century

Categories of work

A amateur painter
C caricaturist
F flower or fruit painter
Fa fan painter
H history painter
I illustrator
L landscape or topographical painter
M miniature painter
P portrait painter
Pr printmaker
S silhouette or profile painter
T teacher of drawing and/or painting

Dates

These do not signify the artist's continuous presence in Bath, but refer to records of him or her between the given dates

Sources

BBJ	*Boddely's Bath Journal*
BJ	*Bath Journal*
BRB	Bath City Rates Books, Bath Record Office
Chron	*Bath Chronicle*
EE	Edward Edwards, *Anecdotes of Painters who have resided or been born in England*, London 1808
Fo	Daphne Foskett, *Miniatures, Dictionary and Guide*, Woodbridge 1987
Harris	John Harris, *Gardens of Delight: The Rococo English Landscape of Thomas Robins the Elder*, 2 vols, London 1978
Humphry	Ozias Humphry papers, RA, London
Lewis Walpole	Charles Hanbury Williams Correspondence, Lewis Walpole Library, 31-11375, 11338 (papers transcribed for me by Hugh Belsey)
NBG	*The New Bath Guide* (Bath guidebooks not Christopher Anstey's verses of the same name)
Turner	A. J. Turner, *Science and Music in Eighteenth Century Bath* (exh. cat., Holburne Museum, Bath), Bath 1977
VAG	Victoria Art Gallery, Bath, collections or archive files
Wa	Ellis Waterhouse, *Dictionary of British Eighteenth-Century Painters*, Woodbridge 1981
White	Philip White, *A Gentleman of Fine Taste: The Watercolours of Coplestone Warre Bampfylde* (exh. cat., Christie's, London), London 1995
Whitley	William T. Whitley, *Thomas Gainsborough*, London 1915
Wr	Reginald Wright, 'Index of Artists resident and working in Bath', undated typescript, copies at Victoria Art Gallery and Bath Central Library

This list excludes artists such as Benjamin West, Sir Joshua Reynolds and Johan Zoffany who visited Bath for social or health reasons and are unlikely to have produced any commissioned work while in the city.

Name	Category	Dates of Visits or Residency in Bath	Source
Alcock, Edward (*fl.* 1757–8)	M P	1757	Wa
Allen, George (*fl.* 1711–58)	P	1758	Lewis Walpole
Ames, Mrs	S	c. 1785	Wr
Arnold, R	M P	1790	Wr
Bampfylde, Coplestone (1720–1791)	A L Pr	c. 1750–90	White
Barber, Rupert (*fl.* 1736–72)	M	1736–52	Fo; Wa; Wr
Barker, Thomas (1769–1847)	H L P Pr	1782–1847	Wa; Wr
Barry, John	M	1796	Chron
Beach, Thomas (1738–1806)	P	1772–1803	Chron; Wa
Beauclerk, Lady Diana (1734–1808)	A H P	1776–7	Wr
Beauvais, John (*fl.* 1757–73)	M	not recorded	Fo
Becker, Ferdinand (d. 1825)	L Pr	1794–1812	Chron; Wr
Bell, Mrs Catherine	H	1797	Wr
Bell, John Hay (*fl.* 1798–1808)	H P M	1798–1808	VAG; Wr
Benazech, Peter Paul (c. 1744–1798)	Pr	1779–98	Chron; Wr
Benwell, J. Hodges (1762–1785)	I T	not recorded	Wa
Blackamore, James	L	1780s	VAG
Blackamore, William	L	1780s	VAG
Bonner, George William (d. 1836)	Pr	1782	Wr
Bonner, Thomas (*fl.* 1763–1807)	L	1792	Wr
Bradshaw, Mrs	T	1772	Chron
Braham	Pr	1791–2	Chron
Branston, Allen Robert	Pr	not recorded	Wr
Brockmer (*fl.* 1758–76)	M	1758–72	BBJ; Fo; Wr
Bunbury, William Henry (1750–1811)	C	1782–1804	Chron; Wr
Burke	P	1772	Wa
Carpentiers, Adriaen (*fl.* 1739–78)	P	1743	VAG
Collins, Mrs R.	M S	1777–9	Chron; Fo
Collins, Samuel (c. 1735–1768)	M	c. 1758–62	Fo
Cooke, John	M P T	not recorded	Fo; Wr
Cooper, Richard (*fl.* 1793–9)	M	not recorded	Fo
Corton	L	1754	BJ
Cossley, Elizabeth Claybourne	A L Pr	1759	VAG
Cotes, Samuel (1734–1818)	M	?1763	Fo; Wr
Cozens, John Robert (1752–1797)	L Pr	1773, 1779–83	Chron; BRB
Cranch, John (1751–1821)	A H L P	not recorded	Fo; Wa
Crook, H.		1790	Wr
Cruikshank, Isaac (1756/7–1810/11)	C	1789–99	Wr
Dalton, Richard (?1715–91)	L Pr	1755	Wr
Dance, George (1740–1825)	P	1793–95/6	Wr
Daniel, Abraham (d. 1806)	M	not recorded	Fo
Daniel, Joseph (c. 1760–1803)	M	1786–1803	Fo; Wr
Darly, Matthew	C Pr	1778–80	Chron
De Barde	M	not recorded	Wr
Dixon, Samuel	F	1757, 1768	BBJ; Wr; Whitley
Dupont, Gainsborough (1754–1797)	L P	1772–4	Wa
Dusign, Dederick (d. 1770)	P	before 1770	Wa
Eccles, Revd (*fl.* 1777)	F	1777	Wa
Edwards, Edward (1738–1806)	H L P	1782	EE
Ehrman	M	1772	Wr
Farrer, Nicholas		1778	Wr
Faucigny	M	1798	Wr

Finney, Samuel (1718/19–1798)	M	1748	BJ
Ford, John (*fl.* 1764–76)	M	not recorded	Fo
Gainsborough, Thomas (1727–88)	L P Pr	1758, 1759–74	
Garvey, Edmund (*fl.* 1767–1813)	L	1768–78	Wa; Whitley; Wr
Gerrard, Revd J.	T	1784	Wr
Gilchrist	M	1796	Wr
Gill, Charles (*fl.* 1769–c. 1828)	P	1775–87	Wa; Wr; NBG
Gingell (d. 1819)	Pr	1783–1802	Wr
Green, Amos (1735–1807)	F L	from c. 1767	Wr
Grimm, Samuel Hieronymous (1734–1794)	L	1788–90	VAG; Wr
Grist, Mrs	S	1778	Wr
Groombridge, William	L M	1792–5	Wr
Guest, T.	P	1789	Wr
Hackert, Johann Gottlieb (1744–1773)	L	1773	EE; Wr
Hall	P T	1774	Chron; Wr
Hamlet, T. (1779–1815)	S	not recorded	Fo
Hamlin (or Hamlyn), N. (*fl.* 1773–1793)	M	1773–86	Chron; Fo; Wr
Hamlyn, Augusta (*fl.* 1779–1830)	M	not recorded	Fo
Hancock, Richard	Pr	1793–1800	Wr
Harrington, Mrs	S	1778–81	Chron; Wr
Harris, Thomas (*fl.* 1773–5)	M	1773	Chron; Fo; Wr
Harris, William	P	1791	Chron; Wr
Hay, W. (*fl.* 1776–97)	M P	1787–90	Chron; Fo; Wa; Wr
Hearne, Thomas (1744–1817)	L	1791	Chron; VAG; Wr
Heins, D. (1697–1756)	P Pr	1751	Wr
Hewlett, James (1768–1836)	F T	1794–1804	Fo; Wr
Hewson	P	1796	Wr
Hibbart, Charles (1765–1819)	Pr	1790–1819	Wr
Hibbart, John (1768–1848)	Pr	c. 1790–1848	Wr
Hibbart, William (1725–1808)	P Pr T	1738–1808	Wr
Hickey, Thomas (1741–1824)	P	1776–80	BRB; Wr
Hoare, William (1707–1792)	P Pr	1738–92	Newby 1990
Hobday, William Armfield (1771–1831)	M P	not recorded	Fo; Wr
Hollway (d. 1805)	P	not recorded	Wr
Hulley, Henry (*fl.* 1783–1800)	L	1787	Wa
Hulley, Thomas	L T	1797–1817	Wr
Humphry, Ozias (1742–1810)	M P	1760–64	Wa
Huquier, Jacques Gabriel (1725–1805)	P Pr	1780	Turner
Hutchisson, Joseph (1747–1830)	M P	1797–1804	VAG; Wr
Jackson, William (1730–1803)	A L	1760s	Wa
Jagger, J. (*fl.* 1774–84)	L	1774–9	Wr
James, George (d. 1795)	P	1780–92	Wa; Wr; NBG
Jones	M S T	1782	Chron; Wr
Jones, William (*fl.* 1764–77)	F	1768–74	Chron; Wa; Wr
Keenan, John (c. 1785–c. 1819)	M P	1792–8	Wa; Wr
King, Miss	P T	1799–1805	Wr
Laine, Francis (1721–1810)	M	1764	Chron; Wr
Lambert, George (1700–1765)	L	1760	Wr
Laroon, Marcellus (1697–1772)	C P	1732	Wr
Lawrence, Thomas (1769–1830)	P	1779/80–1785/6	BRB; Chron; Wr
Leake, Henry (*fl.* 1760–66)	P	1760	BJ; Wa; Wr
Lens, Bernard (1659–1725)	L	1718–19	Wr
Lens, Bernard (1682–1740)	L	1727	VAG
Lens, Peter	L	1747	Wr

Lesley	L	1792	Chron; Wr
Lightfoot, Mary	M	1787	Wr
Loggan, Thomas	Fa	1752–3	BJ; Wr
Malden, Lady Sarah (c. 1761–1838)	A M	1788	Wr
Malton, Thomas (1748–1804)	L T	1769–84	Chron; VAG
Martin, Elias (1739–1818)	L P	1785–90	Wa; Wr
Mawbrye, Edward (*fl.* 1775–82)	P	1775	Wr
Mayo, William	P	1746–55	Chron; Wr
Millington, Henry (c. 1735–1764)	M	1757	Fo
Morris, Benjamin (1722–1807)	P T	1784–1807	Chron; Wr
Mussard, Andreas	M P	1765	Chron; Wr
Myles	M	c. 1770	Fo
Nicholson, Francis (1753–1844)	L	1795	Wr
Ogier, Peter (1769 – after 1800)	M P	1795–9	Chron; Fo; Wr
O'Keefe, Daniel (1740–1787)	M	1777	Chron; Fo; Wr
Pack, Faithful Christopher (1759–1840)	M P T	1797	Chron; Wr
Parker, G. G.	L P	1787–1837	VAG; Wr
Payne, William (*fl.* 1776–1830)	L P T	1788	VAG; Wr
Pine, Robert Edge (c. 1730–1788)	H P	1772–9	BRB; Chron; Wa; Wr
Pine, Simon (Simonneau) (d. 1772)	M	1765–72	BRB; EE; Wr
Redmond, Thomas (c. 1745–1785)	M	1769–85	Chron; Wr
Robins, Thomas (1716–1770)	Fa F L	1742–70	Chron; Harris; Whitley; Wr
Robins, Thomas (1742–1806)	F	1770–1806	Chron; Harris; Wr
Robinson, John (1715–1745)	P	1740s	Wr
Roche, Samuel Twogood (1757–1847)	M S	1792–1822	Wr
Rosenberg, Charles Christian (1745–?1844)	M S	from 1787	Wr
Ross, J.	L	1744	see Chapter 7
Ross, Thomas (*fl.* 1730–57)	L	1740–44	see Chapter 7
Roth, George (*fl.* 1768–86)	M P	1776–86	Wa; NBG
Rymsdyk, Andreas van (1754–1786)	M P	1784–6	Chron; Wa
Saunders, John (1750–1825)	P	1790 – after 1800	Wa
Scott, Samuel (c. 1702–1772)	L	1771	Wa
Seton, John Thomas (*fl.* 1758–1806)	P	1766	Wa
Serres, Dominic (1722–1793)	L	not recorded	Humphry
Sharples, James (c. 1751–1811)	P	1783–1803	Chron; Wa; Wr
Sheldon, Joseph (*fl.* 1781–1821)	L P T	from 1781	Chron; Wr
Shirreff, Charles (*fl.* 1773–1800)	M	1791–4	Chron; Wr
Simmons, Miss S.	T	1787	Wr
Skinner, Jacob (d. 1754)	Pr	1738/9–54	Wr
Smith, William (1707–1764)	F L P	1764	Wr
Spornberg, Jacob (d. 1840)	L M S	1785–1827	Chron; VAG: Wr
Stranover, Tobias (1784–1756)	F	1756	BJ
Stennet, Ralph	L P T	before 1809	Chron; VAG
Stuart	Pr T	1796	Wr
Sullivan, Luke (c. 1725–1771)	L M Pr	1750s	VAG
Taylor, John (1735–1806)	A L	1762–1806	Wa; Wr; see Chapter 17
Taylor, John 'Old' (1739–1838)	M P T	1775–1805	Chron; Wr
Turner, Joseph Mallord William (1775–1851)	L	1793	VAG
Van Diest, Johann (*fl.* 1695–1757)	H P	1728 – c. 1745	VAG
Vandyke, Peter (1729 – after 1795)	P	1784	Wr
Vaslet, Lewis (1742–1808)	F M P	1775–1805	Chron; Wa; Wr
Vertue, James (*fl.* 1744–60)	L T	1744–60	BBJ; Wr; see Chapter 1
Walmesley, Thomas (1763–1806)	L	1794–1805	EE; Wa; Wr
Warren, John (*fl.* 1764–88)	P	1776–95	see Chapter 7

West, John (1772–1836)	M T	1795–1801	Wr
Weston	M	1794	Wr
Williams, Solomon (1757–1824)	H P	1785–1806	Chron; Wr
Woolley, Joseph	F L	1754	BJ
Worlidge, Thomas (1700–1766)	M P Pr	c. 1744–65	see Chapter 1
Wright, Joseph (1734–1797)	H L P	1775–7	BRB

Appendix II

Thomas Gainsborough's Account at Hoare's Bank, Fleet Street

Transcribed by kind permission of C. Hoare & Co.

Hoare's Bank was established in 1672 at the sign of the Golden Bottle in Cheapside. At the time Gainsborough used the bank (between 1762 and 1785) it was at 37 Fleet Street. Prior to 1762 Gainsborough used Bertie Burgh and James Unwin, attorneys at Castle Yard, Holborn, agents to the Dukes of Beaufort, as bankers. Burgh and Unwin had a long association with Hoare & Co, Bertie Burgh's grandfather Ulysses Burgh, Bishop of Ardagh having used the bank, as well as several other members of both families. From 1785 until his death in 1788 the artist banked with Drummond's. The account with Hoare & Co was used mainly for the banking of Mrs Gainsborough's annuity from the Dukes of Beaufort; very few other credits are recorded. It must be assumed that the artist used the services of businessmen in Bath for the majority of his financial transactions. He was also still occasionally using James Unwin after 1762 (see Hayes 2001, no. 9, p. 18). The opening of Gainsborough's Hoare's account was partly necessitated by James Unwin's change of circumstances (following Bertie Burgh's bankruptcy and his own substantial inheritance from Captain Edward Wheeler), but it also coincides with the move to Bath of the artist's sister Mary Gibbon. Mrs Gibbon, an astute businesswoman, shared the painter's Abbey Street premises from March or April 1762: the account was opened in May 1762.

A running number has here been given to each entry. An explanation in the form of a key is provided at the end. For the sake of clarity, debits and credits are amalgamated into one table: in the original ledgers they occupy facing pages. Superscript letters are indicated by a full stop before the raised letter. The spelling of names is verbatim, even if clearly inconsistent or inaccurate.

Ledger 66/423

	Year	Date		Debits			Credits		
1	1762	29 May	By John Sutton				16	16	
2		13 July	By Rect. To Duke of Beaufort's Trus.s				100		
3		30 July	To R.d Gardiner	12					
4		21 Aug	To Mary Gibbon	32					
5		14 Sep	To Isaac Gossett	15					
6		12 Oct	To Richd. Harford	20					
7	1763	4 Jan	By bill on H. Hoare & Co.				100		
8		21 Jan	To Cha.s Sandys	50					
9		5 Feb	To Ann Christian	23					
10		7 Feb	To Bennett & Co.	15					
11		25 Feb	To Mary Gibbon	20					
12		5 Mar	To D.o.	10					
13		29 Apr	By John Stanley				40		
14		15 June	To John Oldfield	10	10				
15		30 June	By the Duke of Beauforts's Trus.s for ½ Year's Anny to Mids.r last				100		
16		21 July	By Lord Howe				32	11	
17		12 Aug	To Mr Standish	10					

No.	Year	Date	Entry	£	s	d	£	s	d
18		19 Aug	To Fra.s Bennett	20					
19		13 Sep	To Isaac Gossett	39	4				
20		2 Dec	To Mary Gibbon	30					
21	1764	7 Jan	By Himself				100		
				306	14		489	7	

Ledger 69/300

No.	Year	Date	Entry	£	s	d	£	s	d
	1764		To mony p.d & bro.t from L.r 66 fol. 423	306	14				
			By mony rec.d & bro.t from L.r 66 fol. 423				489	7	
22		21 Jan	To Richard Whatley	150					
23		3 Feb	To Sam.l Kilderbee	21					
24		24 July	By the Duke of Beaufort's Trus.s				100		
25		26 July	To Rich.d Harford	50					
26		21 Aug	To rec.t	10	10				
27		28 Aug	By Lord Hardwicke				21		
28		31 Aug	To Rich.d Gardiner	20					
29		8 Oct	To Rec.t	21	3				
30		22 Oct	To Griffith Davies	31					
31	1765	1 Jan	By the Duke of Beaufort's Trus.s				100		
32		18 Jan	To William Kirby	18	18				
33		26 Jan	To Rich.d Whatley	66					
34		7 Feb	By Adam Brodrick				10	14	
35		20 Feb	To Rec.t	25	16				
36		27 June	By Rec.t to Duke of Beauforts Trus.s				100		
37		11 July	To W.m Yescombe	100					
38	1766	2 Jan	By Rec.t to Duke of Beauforts Trus.s				100		
39		7 Jan	By Mrs Langston				11		
40		15 Jan	To R.d Whatley	100					
41		7 Feb	By Thomas Nobbs & Cha.s Lowth Ex.rs Mr. Quin for a Legacy				50		
42		18 Feb	To John Gainsborough	10					
43		20 Feb	To W.m Kirby	51					
				982	1		982	1	
44	1766	10 July	By the Duke of Beaufort's Trus.s for ½ y.rs Ann.y to Mids.r				100		
45		29 July	To Mary Gibbon	30					
46		23 Aug	To R. Harford	30					
47		26 Aug	To Alex Munn	10					
48		6 Sep	To Wm Townsend	30					
49	1767	2 Jan	By the Duke of Beaufort's Trus.s for ½ year to Christmas last				100		
50		19 Mar	To Rich.d Whatley	100					
51		8 Aug	By the Duke of Beaufort's Trus.s for ½ year to Mid.r				100		
52		19 Aug	To Edw.d Parker	100					
53		1 Dec	By Mr Hart				2[illegible]		
54	1768	16 Mar	By Duke of Beaufort's Trus.s for ½ years Anny due at Christmas				100		
55		29 Mar	To Richard Gardiner	50					
56		5 Apr	To Sus.a Newton	10					
57		15 Apr	To Edw.d Parker	40					
58		14 May	To Mary Gibbon	20					
59		19 July	By Duke of Beaufort's Trus.s for ½ year to Mids.r				100		
60		24 Sep	To Cha.s Sandys	37					
61		30 Sep	To Mary Gibbon	10					

				£	s	d	£	s	d
				467			521		
							467		
			Balance				54		

Ledger 76/31

				£	s	d	£	s	d
			By balance br.t from L.r 69 fol. 300				54		
62		1 Oct	To Mary Gibbon	45	2				
63		2 Nov	To Mary Gibbon	25					
64	1769	21 Feb	By the Duke of Beaufort's Trus.s for ½ Years Anny to Christmas last				100		
65		8 Mar	To Francis Hayman	21					
66		9 Mar	To Mileson Hingeston	20					
67		29 Mar	To Edward Parker	30					
68		29 Jul	To R.d Whatly	60					
69		15 Sep	By the Duke of Beaufort's Trus.s ½ year to Mids.r				100		
70		27 Sep	To Sus.a Gardiner	28					
71	1770	2 Jan	By the Duke of Beaufort's Trus.s ½ year to Xmas last				100		
72		2 Jan	To James Burnes	9	9				
73		22 Jan	To Hugh Penny	30					
74		30 Apr	To James Burns	20					
75		11 Jun	To Rect.	65	9				
76		18 Sep	By Cash				100		
77		25 Oct	To Ja.s Burns	8	15				
78		3 Nov	To Edw.d Parker	25					
79		14 Dec	To Will Ewill	35					
80	1771	23 Apr	By Rec.t to the Duke of Beaufort's Trustees				100		
81		14 May	To Tho.s King	18	18				
82		22 May	To John Deare	48	6				
83		11 June	To Edward Parker	50					
84		11 Jul	By Cash				100		
				539	19		654		
							539	19	
			Bal.ce				114	1	

Ledger 84/323

				£	s	d	£	s	d
			By mony due & bro.t from L.r 76 fol. 31				114	1	
85		16 Jul	To Ja.s Burns	17					
86		20 Jul	To Edw.d Parker	20					
87		30 Jul	By Lord Ligonier pr Oliver Farrer				105		
88		13 Aug	To Nich.s Tucker	31	10				
89		17 Aug	To Edward Parker	45					
90	1772	17 Jan	By Duke of Beauforts Trus.s for ½ y.r to Christ.s				100		
91		25 Jan	To Edward Parker	50					
92		28 Jan	To Bennett & Co.	50					
93		3 Mar	To James Burns	20					
94		7 Apr	To Hugh Penny	40					
95		3 Aug	To Tho.s Lawrence	30					
96		4 Aug	To W.m Plees	32	18				
97		27 Aug	To Sandys & Co.	20					
98		18 Sep	By Duke of Beaufort's Trus.s for ½ y.rto Mid.r				100		
99		24 Sep	To Ja.s Burns	10					
100		24 Nov	To W.m Cross	20					
101		8 Dec	To Wal. Wiltshire	20					

102		26 Dec	By Duke of Beaufort's Trus.s for ½ y.r to Xtmas			100	
103	1773	19 Jan	To Edw.d Parker	100			
104		10 Jul	By Duke of Beaufort's Trus.s for ½ y.r to Mids.r			100	
105		19 Jul	To H Penny	54	10		
106		20 Jul	To Nich.s Bacon	26	5		
107		6 Aug	By Marquis of Granby			66	10
108		27 Oct	To Ja.s Burns	18			
109	1774	5 Jan	By Rec.t to Duke of Beaufort's Trus.s			100	
110		6 Jan	To J.C. Fisher	52	10		
111		19 Jan	To Ja.s Goddard	10			
112		25 Jan	To W.m Sparrow	20			
113		10 Feb	To Mary Gibbon	50			
114		8 Mar	To Mary Gibbon	50			
115		5 Jul	To John Kempson	7			
116		9 Jul	To Edw.d Parker	50			
117		17 Jul	By Rec.t to Duke of Beaufort's Trus.s			100	
118		19 Jul	To Bennett & Co.	40	18		
119		21 Sep	By Lord Radnor pr R.t Sanxay			252	
				885	11	1137	11
						885	11
			Balance			252	

Ledger 92/235

			By mony due & bro.t from L.r 84 fol.323			252	
120		15 Oct	To Danvers & Co	100			
121		18 Oct	To Hen.y Fisher	18			
122		25 Oct	Ro Rec.t	4			
123		18 Nov	To Edw.d Ireland	50			
124		6 Dec	To John Middleton	52			
125		31 Dec	To G. Dupont	30			
126	1775	19 Jan	By Rec.t to the Duke of Beaufort			100	
127		19 Jan	To Mr. Whitcomb	46			
128		21 Jan	To Ja.s Bevans	24	13		
129		11 Feb	To Gainsb: Dupont	31	10		
130		1 July	To Ja.s Bradburn	50			
131		3 July	By Rec.t to the Duke of Beaufort			100	
132		24 July	To G Dupont	45	17		
133		30 Dec	By Rec.t to the Duke of Beaufort			100	
134	1776	9 Feb	To John Bradborne	100			
135		31 July	By Rec.t to the Duke of Beaufort			100	
136		31 July	To Mr Dupont	50			
137		17 Aug	To P.r Toms	21			
138		9 Nov	To Mr Dupont	29			
139		26 Dec	By Rec.t to the Duke of Beaufort			100	
140	1777	15 May	To Mr Dupont	100			
141		30 June	By Rec.t to the Duke of Beaufort			100	
142		1 July	By cash			54	6
143		19 July	To 200 Cons.d 3 p C.ts at 77 p C.t & ⅛ p C.t Brok.a	154	5		
144		6 Oct	To Gainsborough Dupont	20			
145		20 Dec	By cash			20	
146	1778	6 Jan	By cash			100	
147		6 Jan	To G. Dupont	100			
148		10 Aug	By cash			130	
149		11 Aug	To £200 Cons.d 3 p.Cts at 63 p C.ts & ⅛ p C.t Brok.a	126	5		

				£	s	d	£	s	d
				1152	10		1156	6	
							1152	10	
			Bal.ce				3	16	

Ledger 3/154

				£	s	d	£	s	d
			By Money due & bro.t from L.r 92 f.o 235				3	16	
150		25 Aug	To R Strobe	21					
151		6 Oct	By Cash				21		
152	1779	6 Aug	To C.F. Abel	41	3	6			
153		25 Aug	By Cash				7	7	
154		26 Aug	By bill on Hanbury & Co				14		
155		26 Aug	on Page & Co				20		
156	1781	28 July	To J. Burns	50					
157		30 July	By Cash				100		
158		Sep 4	To Bearer	10	10				
159		Sep 10	By Cash				10	10	
160		Sep 18	To G. Dupont	50					
161		Dec 27	To S. Cooper	50					
162	1782	Jan 24	By Cash				100		
163		Apr 19	To S. Cooper	50					
				272	13	6	276	13	
							272	13	6
			Bal.e C.r				3	19	6

Ledger 15/382

				£	s	d	£	s	d
			By money due & bro.t from L.r 3 fol 154				3	19	6
164	1783	11 Jan	To Mr Merlin	10	10				
165		20 Jan	By Cash				100		
166		20 Jan	To G. Dupont	50					
167		1 Mar	To Mr Dupont	43					
168	1785	4 July	By Cash				10		
169		4 July	By Cash				52	10	
170		4 July	To Mr Newton	62	10				
				166			166	9	6
							166		
			Bal.ce					9	6

The final sum of £0.9.6 moved to Transfer Ledger, fol. 21.

Key to Entries

1 Robert Sutton (1726–1775) of Scofton, Nottinghamshire, sat to Gainsborough for a half-length portrait in the early 1760s: the picture was sold at Christie's, London, on 11 July 1986 (lot 71) and was with Leger Galleries, London, in 1988. This payment by John Sutton may be a part-payment or even a full payment for this picture: it is not known what Gainsborough's charge for a half-length was in 1762.

2 Mrs Margaret Gainsborough's annuity, the half-yearly payment due on 25 June. At this time the annuity was paid by trustees acting for the Fifth Duke of Beaufort who had not come of age.

3 Richard Gardiner (1725–1779), the artist's brother-in-law, married to his sister Susan (b. 1726) often known as Susanna, see Belsey 1988, pp. 20–22 and table VI.

4 Mary Gibbon (1713–1791) the artist's sister, a milliner who moved to Bath in March or April 1762 and became one of Bath's principal lodging house keepers, see Bensusan-Butt 1993, pp. 24–5 and Sloman 1992, pp. 35–7. On her arrival in Bath she apparently took the 'shop' within Gainsborough's Abbey Street house for her millinery: this and other payments made by the artist to Mrs Gibbon may be associated with their shared responsibility for the building.

5 Isaac Gosset, often spelled Gossett (1713–1799), framemaker of Poland Street, London, see Lippincott 1983, pp. 180–81, n. 16.

6 A Richard Harford was a woollen draper in Bath in the 1720s and 1730s, see Neale 1981, p. 111.

7 Almost certainly a half-yearly payment of Mrs Gainsborough's annuity due on 25 December.

8 Charles Sandys, colourman, of Long Acre, London, see Whitley 1928, I, p. 332. Several people by name of Sandys are recorded in Hatton Garden (where

Gainsborough lived between c. 1743 and 1749). A Mrs Sandys, a maiden lady of Hatton Garden 'worth 60,000 l.' died on 2 July 1739, see the *Gentleman's Magazine*, IX, part I, p. 383. See also fig. 172.

9 Hayes suggests Ann Christian may be the wife of Revd Humphry Christian (d. 1773) an East Anglian clergyman, see Hayes 2001, no. 116, p. 179 and no. 126, p. 183.

10 Francis Bennett, a linen and woollen draper, was Mayor of Bath in 1773 and 1781. One of Francis Bennett's advertisements from 1744 for his shop at The Star, Abbey Churchyard, is printed in Trevor Fawcett, *Voices of Eighteenth-Century Bath*, Bath 1995, p. 28. In addition to fabrics he sold tea, coffee and snuff.

11 Mary Gibbon, as no. 4 above.

12 The same.

13 Probably John Stanley (1712–1786) the well-known blind composer and organist, see Stainton 1977, no. 19. Stainton judged that Gainsborough's 'head' of Stanley, now only known from a mezzotint of 1781, dated from the 1760s. In 1762 Gainsborough charged ten guineas for a 'head' and by January 1765 he charged twenty; his price between these dates is not known, but he seems always to have charged in guineas rather than pounds. It is possible the mezzotint is based on a half-length portrait. Gainsborough's price for a half-length in 1765 was forty guineas; before that his price is unclear. Stanley was organist of the Inner Temple from 1734 and well known for his organ voluntaries; he must have been known to the Abbey organist Thomas Chilcot who gave music lessons to Gainsborough or his daughters.

14 John Oldfield of Tufton Street, Westminster, owned four landscapes by Gainsborough and employed the artist to repair a Dutch landscape that he owned, Hayes 1982, II, p. 64. It is possible he was a picture dealer, and that Gainsborough's payment to him was for a painting.

15 Mrs Margaret Gainsborough's half-yearly annuity payment due on 25 June.

16 Perhaps a completion half-payment for the full-length portrait *The Countess Howe* or *Richard, First Earl Howe* (Waterhouse 1966, nos 386 and 387, p. 75).

17 Mr Standish has not been identified.

18 Francis Bennett, as no. 10 above.

19 Isaac Gosset, as no. 5 above.

20 Mary Gibbon, as no. 4 above.

21 Almost certainly Mrs Gainsborough's half-yearly annuity payment, due 25 December.

22 Richard Whatley was the Bradford-on-Avon based agent to Evelyn, Second Duke of Kingston (1711–1773), owner of the house in Abbey Street, Bath, which Gainsborough rented between 1760 and 1774 at £150 per year, see Sloman 1992, pp. 32–3. Whatley may have been related to George Whatley, landlord of the Black Bear Inn, Devizes (see the *Bath Chronicle*, 27 February 1766, for an announcement of his marriage). Thomas Lawrence, father of the painter Thomas Lawrence, was subsequently landlord of the Black Bear (see no. 95 below).

23 Samuel Kilderbee (1725–1813), an attorney and Town Clerk of Ipswich, painted by Gainsborough in the 1750s (Waterhouse 1966, nos 407 and 408, p. 76). A lifelong friend of the artist.

24 Mrs Gainsborough's half-yearly annuity payment due on 25 June.

25 Richard Harford, as no. 6 above.

26 Unidentified.

27 Philip Yorke, Second Earl of Hardwicke (1720–1796) succeeded his father as Earl of Hardwicke just five months before this payment. In 1764 twenty guineas was probably the artist's price for a 'head' portrait, but this may have been a half-payment for a forty-guinea half-length portrait (Waterhouse 1966, no. 350, p. 73). The Yorkes were friends of Ralph Allen of Bath and, like Allen and the Prices of Foxley, regular clients of Arthur Pond, see Lippincott 1983, pp. 28, 46, 59–60, 90.

28 Richard Gardiner, as no. 3 above.

29 Unidentified.

30 Griffith Davies has not been identified. There seems no good reason to associate him with the G. Davies who was a Newfoundland merchant in Prescot Street, London in 1768 (Baldwin 1768, p. 111).

31 Mrs Gainsborough's half-yearly annuity payment due on 25 December.

32 William Kirby (1719–1791) brother of the Suffolk painter and architect Joshua Kirby. William visited Bath in 1756 (SURO HA 21/B1/1). Joshua Kirby also had a son William who was briefly (in 1759) a pupil of Gainsborough, see Owen 1996, pp. 61–75.

33 Richard Whatley, as no. 22 above.

34 Adam Brodrick may be connected with Vice Admiral Brodrick (1705–1769) who sat for a 'head' 30 × 25 inch portrait in the mid-1760s. The portrait was with Raphael Valls, London, in 1994 (Hugh Belsey kindly supplied this information). Gainsborough's price for a 'head' in 1765 was twenty guineas.

35 Unidentified.

36 Mrs Margaret Gainsborough's half-yearly annuity payment due on 25 June.

37 William Yescombe (1738/9–1774) was an attorney in Bath from 1760. He also acted as an agent for selling and letting properties. He was responsible for letting Dr Rice Charleton's house in Kingsmead Square, Bath, in November 1764 and Gainsborough's house in Lansdown Road in 1767 (information kindly provided by Edward Yescombe).

38 Mrs Margaret Gainsborough's half-yearly annuity payment due on 25 December.

39 Mrs Langston may be the wife of John Langston whose full-length portrait by Gainsborough was finished in 1787. Waterhouse records Mrs John Langston's 'head' portrait, which he dates to the 1770s (Waterhouse 1966, nos 425 and 425a, p. 77) Mrs Langston's payment of £11 might be a part-payment for a 'head' portrait which in 1766 would have cost twenty guineas.

40 Richard Whatley, as no. 22 above.

41 James Quin (1693–1766), the eminent actor, sat for a full-length portrait in 1762–3 (Waterhouse 1966, no. 567, p. 86). Quin retired to Bath and was one of the city's best-known residents: Handel is said to have stayed at Quin's Pierrepont Street house during his visit to Bath in 1749 (James 1987, IV, p. 646).

42 Probably John Gainsborough (1711–1789), the artist's brother, but possibly his cousin John Gainsborough (1752–1791), see Belsey 1988, table II and table III. The artist is known to have given financial support to his brother John. An 'eccentric and unfortunate man' according to Thicknesse, he was continuously in financial difficulties (Belsey 1988, pp. 17–18).

43 William Kirby, as no. 32 above.

44 Mrs Margaret Gainsborough's half-yearly annuity payment due on 25 June.

45 Mary Gibbon, as no. 4 above.

46 Richard Harford, as no. 6 above.

47 Alex Munn has not been identified. The watercolour painter Paul Sandby Munn (1773–1845) was the son of a carriage and decorative painter James Munn of Greenwich.

48 A William Townsend was a hardware and toyman at 73 Fleet Street, London (the same street as Hoare's Bank), in 1768 (Baldwin 1768, p. 166). A William Townsend, plateworker of Walcot Street, Bath, entered his mark at Goldsmiths' Hall, London, on 7 September 1774 and a John Townsend, plateworker of Walcot Street entered his on 10 September 1783 (BCL, Clippings File, under Goldsmiths, R 185/1). A Thomas Townsend is listed as a jeweller in High Street, Bath, in 1784 (*Bailey's British Directory for the Year 1784*. London 1784, p. 340).

49 Mrs Margaret Gainsborough's half-yearly annuity payment due on 25 December.

50 Richard Whatley, as no. 22 above.

51 Mrs Margaret Gainsborough's half-yearly annuity due on 25 June.

52 Edward Parker (d. 1785/6) was a wine and brandy merchant of Westgate Street, Bath. He was a wealthy man, leaving

£3,000 and £2,000 to his nephews Henry Edward Howse and Samuel Howse in his will (BRO, Accession 72, Probate of will of Edward Parker, dated 19 January 1786). He also left £100 to his godson William Makepeace Thackeray, either William Makepeace Thackeray (1749–1813) of the East India Company, or William Makepeace Thackeray (1770–1849) who became an eminent physician in Chester. Colin Johnston kindly drew my attention to this information. The sums paid to Parker may not all have been payments for wine or brandy. It is possible that he (like Bath wine merchant Isaac de Vic before him) offered banking services.

53 Mr Hart has not been identified. In 1767 twenty guineas was the artist's price for a 'head' portrait.

54 Mrs Margaret Gainsborough's half-yearly annuity payment due on 25 December (paid nearly three months late).

55 Richard Gardiner, as no. 3 above.

56 Susanna Newton has not been identified. A Mr Newton also receives a payment in 1785 (no. 170 below). A Thomas Newton was a laceman at 40 Lombard Street and a John Newton a woollen draper at Minories, London (Baldwin 1768, p. 145). Francis Milner Newton (1720–1794) was first Secretary to the Royal Academy in 1768 and a cousin of Goodenough Earle of Barton Grange near Taunton, see John Hayes, 'The Gainsborough drawings from Barton Grange', *Connoisseur*, CLXI, no. 648, February 1966, pp. 86–93. Gainsborough also painted a landscape for Samuel Newton (see Chapter 6, pp. 115–6) and portraits of Mr and Mrs Newton (Hayes 1982, II, no. 94, p. 438).

57 Edward Parker, as no. 52 above.

58 Mary Gibbon, as no. 4 above.

59 Mrs Margaret Gainsborough's half-yearly annuity payment due on 25 June.

60 Charles Sandys, as no. 8 above.

61 Mary Gibbon, as no. 4 above.

62 The same.

63 The same. These payments are likely to be connected with the artist's Abbey Street house, which was by this date let as lodgings. Mary Gibbon, who became one of Bath's leading lodging house keepers, probably managed this side of Gainsborough's business, see Sloman 1992, pp. 23–44.

64 Mrs Margaret Gainsborough's half-yearly annuity payment due on 25 December (nearly two months late).

65 Francis Hayman (1708–1776), painter and teacher at the St Martin's Lane Academy in London when Gainsborough studied there in the early 1740s. This twenty-guinea payment to Hayman may have been for a painting, or it might have been a gift or a loan. Business was especially good at this stage of Gainsborough's career and Hayman was unwell in the spring of 1769: three months after this payment he asked to be excused from teaching at the recently founded Royal Academy as he was suffering from gout, see Allen 1987, p. 9.The *Bath and Bristol Chronicle* of 17 May 1770 records the arrival of 'Mr Hayman' in Bath.

66 Mileson Hingeston was a bookseller in the Strand who was later employed at the Ordnance Office. His mother, who lived in Hatton Garden, died in her eighty-seventh year on 30 March 1793 (*Gentleman's Magazine*, LXIII, part I, p. 377). The Revd Robert Hingeston (1699–1766), Master of Ipswich School, was the first owner of Gainsborough's double portrait *The Painter's Daughters Chasing a Butterfly* (Judy Egerton, *The British School*, London 1998, no. NG1811, p. 92 and p. 97, nn. 8 and 10). The name Mileson must derive from the Mileson family of Norton, Suffolk. William Kirby, brother of Gainsborough's close friend Joshua Kirby (see no. 32 above), mentions a Mileson Edgar in his will (SURO, IC/AA/211/41 (i–ii). The Edgar family were important Ipswich patrons of Gainsborough (Waterhouse 1966, nos. 231–4, pp. 65–6).

67 Edward Parker, as no. 52 above.

68 Richard Whatley, as no. 22 above.

69 Mrs Margaret Gainsborough's half-yearly annuity payment due on 25 June (nearly three months late).

70 Susan Gardiner (b. 1726), the artist's sister, see Belsey 1988, pp. 20–22. Her daughter Sophia, born in 1762, spent much of her childhood in the Gainsboroughs' home in Bath.

71 Mrs Margaret Gainsborough's half-yearly annuity payment due on 25 December.

72 James Burnes or Burns has not been identified. A James Burn, merchant, was trading at 23 Threadneedle Street, in the City of London, in 1785 (Kent 1785, p. 31). It is just possible James Burns might have been one of Mrs Gainsborough's relatives, but so far no one of this name has been linked with her. In 1783 the artist appealed to the architect Sir William Chambers on behalf of an unnamed Scottish joiner of about thirty years of age, one of his wife's relations who had been forced to London in search of employment (Hayes 2001, no. 91, p. 151).

73 Hugh Penny is probably the Mr Penny whose name appears in the margin in Bath City Rates Books (BRO) against the entries for payments for 17 Circus, which Gainsborough rented from late 1766 until 1774. Penny is likely to have been the owner or leaseholder of the property. It is not known whether he is connected with the 'Mr Penny, an eminent goldsmith' whose death at Wells on 6 June 1789 is noted in the *Gentleman's Magazine*, LIX, part I, p. 577.

74 James Burns, as no. 72 above.

75 Unidentified.

76 Almost certainly a cash payment of Mrs Margaret Gainsborough's half-yearly annuity, due 25 June, paid, as in the previous year, nearly three months late.

77 James Burns, as no. 72 above.

78 Edward Parker, as no. 52 above.

79 William Ewill is almost certainly William Evill who by 1759 was trading in the Marketplace, Bath, at the sign of the 'Golden Knife-and-Fork and Stocking-Legs', that is, in cutlery and hosiery. He was soon selling a more general range of 'toys' and in 1771–2 supplied Richard Brinsley Sheridan with a toothpick case and a pair of swords among other goods, see Fawcett 1990, pp. 68–70.

80 Mrs Margaret Gainsborough's half-yearly annuity payment, due 25 December, paid four months late. At this time the Beaufort Trustees faced financial difficulties which lead to the selling of property, including the hunting estate at Netheravon, Wiltshire, the source of the annuity. In March 1773 the source of the annuity was transferred to Skenfrith, Monmouthshire, see Sloman 1996a, p. 48 and Appendix II, pp. 57–8.

81 Thomas King the Elder (1741–1804), sculptor of Bath, was also a carver of picture frames and it is most likely that this payment is for a frame or frames, perhaps the 'handsome frames' Gainsborough planned for his two large landscapes exhibited at the Royal Academy in April 1771 (Hayes 2001, no. 49, p. 83).

82 John Deare was a carver, guilder and picture framer at Kingsmead Street, Bath from 1766. He was still there, trading as Deare & Son in the 1790s (this information was kindly supplied by Trevor Fawcett). John Deare (1759–1798), a Liverpool-born sculptor who was something of a childhood prodigy, may have been a relative. Like the preceding payment to Thomas King, this may have been connected with one or both of the two handsome frames Gainsborough planned for his two landscapes exhibited at the Royal Academy in April 1771 (Hayes 2001, no. 49, p. 83).

83 Edward Parker, as no. 52 above.

84 Almost certainly a cash payment of Mrs Margaret Gainsborough's half-yearly annuity, due 25 June, paid only two weeks after the due date.

85 James Burns, as no. 72 above.

86 Edward Parker, as no. 52 above.

87 A payment of 100 guineas, presumably for the full-length portrait of *Viscount Ligonier* (Waterhouse 1966, no. 443, p. 78), or that of his wife (ibid., no. 444, p. 78), both apparently painted in 1770 (see Hayes 2001, no. 46, pp. 78–9). Alternatively, this may be the second of two half-payments for the pair. Although painted in 1770 the pictures were exhibited at the Royal Academy in April–May 1771 and the final payment may not have been due until both were returned after the Exhibition.

88 'Mr Nicholas Tucker' was a subscriber to Thomas Thorpe's *Survey* of 1742 (see endpaper) and a Nicholas Tucker was apprenticed to the Bath printmaker Jacob Skinner in 1737 (information kindly supplied by David Alexander). A notice in the Bath Chronicle of 29 April 1779 asks those indebted to the late Nicholas Tucker 'Painter' to contact his executors Thomas Paty and Thomas King (see entry 81 above).

89 Edward Parker, as no. 52 above.

90 Mrs Margaret Gainsborough's half-yearly annuity payment due on 25 December.

91 Edward Parker, as no. 52 above.

92 Bennett & Co, as no. 10 above.

93 James Burns, as no. 72 above.

94 Hugh Penny, as no. 73 above.

95 Thomas Lawrence (1725–1797), father of the artist Thomas Lawrence (1769–1830) was landlord of the Black Bear Inn, Devizes, between 1772 and 1779, where he was reckoned 'the only man upon the road for warm rooms, soft beds and for reading Milton' (Richard Graves, *Columella*, 2 vols, London 1779, I, pp. 95–6). If this payment was to this Thomas Lawrence it is not clear what it was for: £30 is too large a sum to be associated with accommodation. ThomasLawrence senior was known to people within Gainsborough's circle including David Garrick (see Susan Sloman and Andrew Wyld, 'The actor Thomas Grist: A portrait by Lawrence', *British Art Journal*, II, no. 1, autumn 2000, pp. 81–2).

96 William Plees, probably the W. Plees, weaver, at 1 Old Artillery Ground, Spitalfields, London. A Richard Plees, weaver, is also listed at Red Lion Street, Spitalfields (Baldwin 1768, p. 150).

97 Sandys & Co, as no. 8 above.

98 Mrs Margaret Gainsborough's half-yearly annuity payment due on 25 June.

99 James Burns, as no. 72 above.

100 A William Cross traded as an 'Upholder, Auctioneer and Undertaker' in Milsom Street, Bath in the 1770s and 1780s (see BRO, Bath City Rates Books, in which Cross is recorded paying for two adjoining properties in Milsom Street, and *Bailey's British Directory for the Year 1784*, London 1784, p. 337).

101 Walter Wiltshire (1719–1799) the carrier who transported Gainsborough's pictures to London and became a friend of the painter (see Chapters 4 and 9).

102 Mrs Margaret Gainsborough's half-yearly annuity payment due on 25 December.

103 Edward Parker, as no. 52 above.

104 Mrs Margaret Gainsborough's half-yearly annuity payment due on 25 June.

105 Hugh Penny, as no. 73 above.

106 Nicholas Bacon is perhaps the Revd Nicholas Bacon of Suffolk for whom Gainsborough purchased a 'Fruit-piece' in 1769, see Hayes 2001, no. 139, p. 190.

107 The Marquis of Granby, later Fourth Duke of Rutland (1754–1787), sat to Gainsborough for a half-length portrait and purchased the landscape usually known as *The Woodcutter's Return*, see Chapter 9, pp. 179–81. This payment may relate to either picture.

108 James Burns, as no. 72 above.

109 Mrs Gainsborough's half-yearly annuity payment due on 25 December.

110 Johann Christian Fischer (1733–1800), oboist, was a particular favourite with Bath audiences and in 1780 married Gainsborough's daughter Mary. Gainsborough may have been painting his full-length portrait at the time this payment (perhaps for an instrument) was made, see Chapter 5 p. 85 and Chapter 6, p. 105.

111 James Goddard has not been identified. A Richard Goddard, son of Ambrose Goddard of Box, Wiltshire (just near Shockerwick, the estate of Walter Wiltshire) matriculated at New College, Oxford, on 30 August 1746, aged 18 (Joseph Foster, *Alumni Oxonienses, the members of the University of Oxford, 1715–1886*, 8 vols, Oxford 1887–91, II, p. 532).

112 A William Sparrow, mercer, is recorded in Bath in 1718 (Benjamin Boyce, *The Benevolent Man, A Life of Ralph Allen*, Harvard 1967, p. 20) and a Sparrow & Co., silk dyers, are listed at 73 Snowhill, Holborn London in 1768 (Baldwin 1768, p. 161). James Sparrow (d. 1774) was Rector of Walcot, Bath: he subscribed to Thomas Thorpe's *Survey* in 1742 (see endpaper). Gainsborough painted a half-length portrait of John Sparrowe (1689/90–1762) of Ipswich in the mid-1750s (Waterhouse 1966, no. 627, p. 90, illustrated above, fig. 25), and *Miss Sparrow* in the later 1770s (Waterhouse 1966, no. 626, p. 90).

113 Mary Gibbon, as no. 4 above.

114 The same.

115 John Kempson was a druggist at 77 Snowhill, Holborn, London (a few doors from Sparrow & Co., silk dyers, see no. 112 above) in 1768 (Baldwin 1768, p. 133).

116 Edward Parker, as no. 52 above.

117 Mrs Margaret Gainsborough's half-yearly annuity payment due 25 June.

118 Bennett & Co., as no. 10 above.

119 William, First Earl of Radnor (1725–1776), of Longford Castle near Salisbury, Wiltshire, commissioned several family portraits, see Waterhouse 1966, no. 572, p. 86 and Appendix III, p. 21 and p. 251, n. 1.

120 Daniel Danvers (d. 1780) was a partner in the firm of Cam, Clutterbuck, Whitehead, Danvers & Phillott which traded as The Bath Bank in Trim Street, Bath, from 1768 (Clews 1994, p. 113). His portrait was painted by William Hoare (Newby 1990, no. 40, p. 54). This payment, dated 15 October 1774 and that to Henry Fisher, on 18 October, may be the last the artist made from Bath.

121 Henry Fisher was a Bath stonemason, a partner in the well-known firm of Jelly and Fisher which probably built Gainsborough's Abbey Street House (Sloman 1992, p. 26). This payment, made at about the time Gainsborough left Bath for London, may be for reversing some alteration Gainsborough had made to either of his Bath houses.

122 Unidentified.

123 Edward Ireland may be connected with John Ireland, the early supporter of the actor John Henderson who became a friend of Gainsborough in Bath. Whitley says John Ireland 'was intimate with Gainsborough' (Whitley 1915, p. 85). The artist gave his portrait of Henderson to John Ireland. A Samuel Ireland was a Spitalfields weaver (Baldwin 1768, p. 133). A John Ireland (*fl.* 1754) was a musician in London and in 1759 a Thomas Ireland, proprietor of Lambeth Wells, London, staged a one-night performance at the Haymarket Theatre of Robert Dodsley's play *Cleone* using all child actors: the cast included his son in a leading role (Philip H. Highfill Jr., Kalman A. Burnim and Edward A. Langhans, *A Biographical Dictionary of Actors, Actresses, Musicians, Dancers, Managers and other Stage Personnel in London, 1660–1800*, 16 vols, Carbondale and Edwardsville, 1973–1993, VIII, p. 102).

124 John Middleton, artists' colourman of St Martin's Lane (see Chapter 4, p. 70). In the 1780s he and Charles Sandys (see no. 8 above) went into partnership as Sandys & Middleton at 79 Long Acre (fig. 172).

125 Gainsborough Dupont (1754–1797), Gainsborough's nephew, apparently lived with the artist from an early age. He was apprenticed to Gainsborough in 1772.

Thereafter he assisted Gainsborough in his portrait practice. Dupont also worked as an independent painter of portraits and landscapes, often, like his uncle, working by artificial light (Whitley 1915, pp. 395–6).

126 Mrs Margaret Gainsborough's half-yearly annuity payment due 25 December.

127 Mr Whitcomb has not been identified.

128 'Mr. James Bevan' was a subscriber to Thomas Thorpe's *Survey* in 1742 (see endpapers): he has not been identified.

129 Gainsborough Dupont, as no. 125 above.

130 James Bradburn has not been identified.

131 Mrs Margaret Gainsborough's half-yearly annuity payment due 25 June.

132 Gainsborough Dupont, as no. 125 above.

133 Mrs Margaret Gainsborough's half-yearly annuity payment due 25 December.

134 John Bradborne (or possibly Bradburn, as no. 130 above) has not been identified.

135 Mrs Margaret Gainsborough's half-yearly annuity payment due 25 June.

136 Gainsborough Dupont, as no. 125 above.

137 Peter Toms (d. 1777) was an expert drapery painter who worked for Joshua Reynolds and Francis Cotes after training as a pupil of Thomas Hudson in the 1740s (see Chapter 4, pp. 70–71).

138 Gainsborough Dupont, as no. 125 above.

139 Mrs Margaret Gainsborough's half-yearly annuity payment due 25 December.

140 Gainsborough Dupont, as no. 125 above.

141 Mrs Margaret Gainsborough's half-yearly annuity payment due 25 June.

142 Unidentified.

143 An investment purchase.

144 Gainsborough Dupont, as no. 125 above.

145 Unidentified.

146 A cash payment of Mrs Margaret Gainsborough's half-yearly annuity due 25 December.

147 Gainsborough Dupont, as no. 125 above.

148 An unidentified cash payment, perhaps Mrs Margaret Gainsborough's half-yearly annuity due 25 June plus a further £30.

149 An investment purchase.

150 R. Strobe is unidentified. A Samuel Strode was an oil and colourman at 126 High Holborn between 1768 and 1785 (Baldwin 1768, p. 163; Kent 1785, p. 156). By the latter date he was trading as 'S. Strode & Son'.

151 Unidentified.

152 The musician Carl Friedrich Abel (1725–1787) was one of Gainsborough's dearest friends (see Chapter 6, pp. 100–01). This payment may have been for an instrument.

153 Unidentified.

154 Hanbury & Co. were merchants of 34 Tower Street, London in 1768 (Baldwin 1768, p. 124).

155 Page & Co. may have been Page & Gates, ironmongers of Great Queen Street, London in 1768 (Baldwin 1768, p. 147), or Page & Basin, insurance brokers of 26 Queen Street, Cheapside, London at the same date (Baldwin 1768, p. 147).

156 James Burns, as no. 72 above.

157 A cash payment of Mrs Margaret Gainsborough's half-yearly annuity due 25 June.

158 Unidentified.

159 This unidentified ten-guinea credit presumably relates to the previous entry.

160 Gainsborough Dupont, as no. 125 above.

161 S. Cooper has not been identified.

162 A cash payment of Mrs Margaret Gainsborough's half-yearly annuity due 25 December.

163 S. Cooper, as no. 161 above.

164 John Joseph Merlin (1735–1803), mechanic and inventor, was painted by Gainsborough around 1780, see Anne French, Michael Wright and Frances Palmer, *John Joseph Merlin, The Ingenious Mechanick* (exh. cat., Iveagh Bequest, Kenwood), London 1985. Gainsborough's portrait of J. C. Fischer shows him leaning on a Merlin harpsichord (fig. 82).

165 A cash payment of Mrs Margaret Gainsborough's half-yearly annuity due 25 December.

166 Gainsborough Dupont, as no. 125 above.

167 The same.

168 Unidentified.

169 Unidentified.

170 A Henry Newton, wine and brandy merchant, was at 47 Aldgate Without in 1785 (Kent 1785, p. 120).

Appendix III

Gainsborough's Portrait Prices

'Heads' or 'three-quarters' portraits (30 × 25 inches)

October 1758	5 gns		(Thicknesse 1788, pp. 16–17)
April 17599	8 gns		(NG, (P) NC 340 LEE, receipt)
February 1760	8 gns		(Sloman 1997, p. 326)
April 1760	8 gns		(ibid.)
April 1762	10 gns		(Hayes 2001, no. 130, p. 185)
January 1765	20 gns		(Waterhouse 1966, no. 54, p. 54)
February 1765	£10.14.0	[perhaps a part-payment]	(Appendix II, entry 34)
April 1766	£20	[20 gns meant?]	(Sloman 1992, p. 39, n. 19)
January 1766	£11	[perhaps a part-payment]	(Appendix II, entry 39)
March 1767	20 gns		(Hayes 1983, pp. 98–100)
April 1767	20 gns		(Hayes 1983, pp. 98–100)
April 1768	20 gns		(Waterhouse 1966, no. 57, p. 54)
July 1773	£70.16.0	[for 2 portraits including frames and case]	(SRO, Tudway receipt DD/TD Box 2/1/52)
September 1774	30 gns		(Appendix II, entry 119[1])

Half-length portraits (50 × 40 inches)

August 1758	15 gns		(Waterhouse 1966, no. 715, p. 95)
February 1761	£30.10.6	[perhaps for a half-length]	(SRO, DD/WO 54/2/27, Trevelyan receipt[2])
April 1761	£33.12.0	[perhaps for a half-length]	(paid by Sir Charles-Kemeys Tynte, 2 April, C. Hoare & Co, Ledger 64/222)
May 1762	16 gns	[perhaps a part-payment for a half-length]	(Appendix II, entry 1)
November 1765	40 gns		(paid by the Earl of Warwick, 15 November, C. Hoare & Co, Ledger c/454)
April 1766	£40	[40 gns meant ?]	(Sloman 1992, p. 39, n. 19)
May 1769	£126	[for two half-length portraits, presumably including expensive frames]	(Hayes 2001, no. 138, p. 189)
November 1769	40 gns		(Waterhouse 1966, no. 55, p. 54)
August 1773	£66.10		(paid by the Marquis of Granby for a portrait or landscape, Appendix II, entry 107)

Whole lengths (generally 94 × 58 inches)

July 1763	£32.11.0	[possibly a part-payment for a full-length]	(Appendix II, entry 16)
April 1766	£60	[60 gns meant ?]	(Sloman 1992, p. 39, n. 19)
1768	60 gns		(Hayes 2001, no. 35, p. 58)
November 1768	60 gns		(Waterhouse 1966, no. 53, p. 54)
1769	60 gns		(Hayes 2001, no. 137, p. 189)
July 1771	100 gns		(Appendix II, entry 87)
1774–6	100 gns	[Eld portrait, see Chapter 4 above]	

Appendix IV

Gainsborough's Exhibited Portraits

The exhibits between 1761 and 1768 were shown at the Society of Artists exhibition in the Great Room, Spring Gardens, Charing Cross; those of 1769–72 at the Royal Academy in its first exhibition room in Richard Dalton's print warehouse on the south side of Pall Mall. Gainsborough's single portrait exhibit at the Free Society of Artists exhibition of 1774 was shown in Mr Christie's Great Room, next to Cumberland House in Pall Mall. The appearance of the 1771 Royal Academy exhibition (including two or three of Gainsborough's exhibits) is recorded by Michel Vincent (Charles) Brandoin, see Sloman 1994, p. 54, fig. 19. Catalogue numbers (preceded by 'w') refer to Waterhouse 1966. The titles of pictures are quoted as in the original exhibition catalogues but omitting the use of 'ditto' for 'a portrait of' or 'a whole length'.

Society of Artists

1761	From 9 May	no. 34	*Whole length of a Gentleman* (*Robert Craggs Nugent*, w523)
1762	From 17 May	no. 30	*A whole length of a gentleman with a gun* (*William Poyntz*, w554)
1763	14 May – 9 June	no. 41	*Mr. Quin, whole length* (*James Quin*, w567)
1764	9 April – 7 May	no. 37	*A gentleman, three quarters* (? *Joshua Kirby*, w419)
		no. 42	*A gentleman, whole length* (*Thomas Medlycott*, w477)
1765	23 April – 21 May	no. 33	*A general officer on horseback* (*General Honywood*, w375)
		no. 34	*An officer, whole length* (*Edmund Craggs Nugent*, w524)
1766	21 April – 19 May	no. 50	*A gentleman whole length* (*David Garrick*, w304)
		no. 51	*A gentleman, whole length* (*Dr Rice Charleton*, w136)
		no. 52	*A lady and gentleman, whole length* (probably *Mr and Mrs Richard Neave*, w513)
1767	23 April – 20 May	no. 58	*A lady, whole length* (*Lady Henrietta Grosvenor*, w332)
		no. 59	*A nobleman, whole length* (*John, Fourth Duke of Argyll*, w19)
		no. 60	*A gentleman, whole length* (*George Vernon*, w693)
1768	28 April – 27 May	no. 59	*An officer, whole length* (*Thomas Needham*, w514)
		no. 60	*A sea officer, whole length* (*Captain Augustus Hervey*, w82)
1768	Second exhibition opening 30 September	no. 46	*An officer, whole length* (*Thomas Needham*, w514 again ?)

Royal Academy

1769	26 April – 27 May	no. 35	*Portrait of a lady; whole length* (*Viscountess Molyneux*, w606)
		no. 36	*A portrait of a gentleman* (*George, First Lord Rivers*, w577)
		no. 38	*A boy's head* (the *Pitminster Boy*, w779 ?)
1770	24 April – 26 May	no. 83	*Portraits of a lady and child; whole length* (*Lady Maria Eardley with her Daughter Maria*, w228)
		no. 84	*A portrait of a gentleman; whole length* (*Dr Ralph Schomberg*, w614, or *Arthur, First Marquis of Donegal*, w199)
		no. 85	*A portrait of a young gentleman* (*The Blue Boy*, w106)
		no. 86	*A portrait of a gentleman; three-quarters* (*David Garrick*, w305)
		no. 87	*A portrait of a gentleman; three-quarters* (*William Jackson*, w398)

1771	24 April – 28 May	no. 74	*Portraits of a lady and child; whole length* (*Countess of Sussex and Lady Barbara Yelverton*, w644)
		no. 75	*A portrait of a lady in a fancied dress; whole length* (*Penelope, Viscountess Ligonier*, w444)
		no. 76	*A portrait of a nobleman with a horse; whole length* (*Edward, Second Viscount Ligonier*, w443)
		no. 77	*A portrait of a gentleman; whole length* (probably *Mr Nuthall*, w525)
		no. 78	*A portrait of Captain Wade, Master of the Ceremonies at Bath* (*Captain William Wade*, w697)
1772	24 April – 29 May	no. 94	*A portrait of a lady; whole length* (*Lady Margaret Fordyce*, w266)
		no. 95	*A portrait of two young ladies; whole length* (*Elizabeth and Mary Linley*, w450)
		no. 96	*A portrait of a gentleman; whole length* (probably *Sir William Pulteney*, w565)
		no. 97	*A portrait of a gentleman; three-quarters* (unidentified)

Gainsborough did not exhibit at the Royal Academy in 1773 or 1774.

Free Society of Artists

1774	4 May – 8 June	no. 347	*The portrait of a nobleman* (unidentified)

173 Thomas Gainsborough (1727–1788), *A Spaniel belonging to Henry Portman* c. 1764–5, oil on canvas, $24\frac{1}{4} \times 29\frac{1}{2}$ inches (61.5 × 75 cm), Trustees of the Portman Settled Estates. The owner of this dog was presumably Henry William Portman, son of Mrs Henry William Berkeley Portman, whose portrait (fig. 66) was painted around 1764–5.

Abbreviations

BadM	Badminton Muniments, Badminton
BCL	Bath Central Library, Bath
BL	British Library, London
BM	British Museum, London
BMT	Bath Masonic Trust, Old Orchard Street, Bath
BRO	Bath Record Office, Bath
CWA	City of Westminster Archives, London
DRO	Denbighshire Record Office, Ruthin, Denbighshire
GH	Gainsborough's House, Sudbury
GRO	Gloucestershire Record Office, Gloucester
HRO	Herefordshire Record Office, Hereford
NG	National Gallery Archive, London
NPG	National Portrait Gallery, Heinz Archive and Library, London
PMC	Paul Mellon Centre for Studies in British Art
PRO	Public Record Office, London
RA	Royal Academy Library, Burlington House, London
SHM	Stanton Harcourt Manor, Oxfordshire
SRO	Somerset Record Office, Taunton
StRO	Staffordshire Record Office, Stafford
SuRO	Suffolk Record Office, Ipswich
W&SRO	Wiltshire and Swindon Record Office, Trowbridge
WoRO	Worcestershire Record Office, Worcester
WRO	Warwickshire Record Office, Warwick

Notes

Introduction

1 Michael Rosenthal, *The Art of Thomas Gainsborough,* New Haven and London 1999.

2 Pointon 1979, pp. 441–55; Pointon 1984, pp. 187–205.

3 Michael Rosenthal, 'The Rough and the Smooth: Rural Subjects in Later Eighteenth-Century British Art', *Eighteenth-Century Life*, XVIII, May 1994, pp. 36–58.

4 Michael Kitson, 'Gainsborough Observed', *Apollo*, CXII, no. 225, November 1980, pp. 351–2.

5 Mary Woodall, *An Exhibition of Paintings: Thomas Gainsborough* (exh. cat., Victoria Art Gallery, Bath etc.), London 1949; Mary Woodall, *An Exhibition of Paintings and Drawings by Thomas Gainsborough, 1727–1788* (exh. cat., Victoria Art Gallery), Bath 1951.

6 Ann Sumner and Philippa Bishop, *Gainsborough in Bath* (exh. cat., Holburne Museum), Bath 1988.

1 Bath

1 Herbert 1950, p. 262, Lord Herbert to Revd W. Coxe, from Wilton, 25 October 1784.

2 William Kirby (1719–1791) kept a notebook recording his 'Journey to Bath' on which he set out on 19 September 1756 (SURO, HA 21/B1/1). His expenses for this trip amounted to £25. He noted that there were then twenty or more physicians at Bath and thirty-three apothecaries, statistics that must have been of personal interest to him as his own son-in-law James Lynn was a surgeon, as is revealed by his will, also in the SURO (IC/AA1/211/41 (i–ii)). Kirby also includes a sketched plan of the city of Bath, which he had some difficulty drawing, showing two possible locations for the projected Circus. Joshua Kirby's son, also named William, became Gainsborough's pupil in the summer of 1759, when the artist briefly returned to Ipswich before settling in Bath (Owen 1996, pp. 61–75).

3 For an account of the development of the road, see Brenda Buchanan, 'The Great Bath Road, 1700–1830', *Bath History*, IV, 1992, pp. 71–94.

4 Mcintyre 1981, p. 210.

5 Ibid., p. 211.

6 Llanover 1861, III, p. 606, Mrs Delany to her sister Mrs Dewes, 28 October 1760.

7 Peter Borsay (ed.), *The Eighteenth-Century Town, A Reader in English Urban History 1688–1820*, London and New York 1990, p. 223.

8 SRO, Luttrell MSS, DDL 2/44/9, Margaret Fownes Luttrell to her husband Henry Fownes Luttrell, from Bath 23 May [1759].

9 Hayes 2001, no. 29, p. 50.

10 Neale 1981, p. 297.

11 Ibid., p. 235.

12 Mcintyre 1981, p. 217.

13 Neale 1981, p. 235.

14 Sloman 1992, pp. 23–44.

15 Mcintyre 1981, p. 214; Neale 1981, p. 44.

16 Wood 1749, II, p. 351.

17 Neale 1981, p. 46; Mcintyre 1981, p. 208.

18 BCL, Edmund Rack, 'A Disultory Journal of Events etc at Bath 1779–1780', MS III, 9 January 1780.

19 Mcintyre 1981, p. 208.

20 Tyte 1903, pp. 28–9.

21 BCL, Rack, 'A Disultory Journal of Events etc at Bath', 3 January 1780.

22 Johanna Schopenhauer, *A Lady Travels: Journeys in England and Scotland from the Diaries of Johanna Schopenhauer*, trans. and ed. Ruth Michaelis-Jena and Willy Merson, London 1988, p. 120. The traveller was the mother of the philosopher.

23 Hayes 2001, no. 40, p. 68.

24 Ibid., no. 90, p. 165.

25 Vertue 1934, p. 158.

26 Hayes 1970, I, p. 30; Hayes 2001, no. 9, pp. 17–18.

27 Hayes 2001, no. 27, p. 67; no. 70, p. 131; no. 50, pp. 99–101; no. 91, pp. 167–9; no. 32, p. 73; no. 45, pp. 93–5.

28 Ibid., no. 91, p. 169.

29 Elise S. Beach, *Thomas Beach, A Dorset Portrait Painter*, London 1934, pp. 35–47.

30 BCL, 'Diary of a Tour undertaken by Three Students, 1725', MS 38.43, p. 115: '[the Pump Room] is shutt up about ten every morning'. Goldsmith 1762, pp. 44–8 describes the daily routine.

31 Goldsmith 1762, p. 47.

32 Hayes 1980, p. 28. The writer of the 'Very extraordinary Journal' discussed in Chapter 3 below, apparently recording a visit to Gainsborough's first Bath lodgings in 1758, found the artist already occupied with a sitter when he called at ten a.m.

33 Hayes 2001, no. 50, p. 84.

34 Penny 1986, p. 60.

35 William Hickey, *Memoirs of William Hickey*, ed. Alfred Spencer, 4 vols, London n.d., I, p. 283.

36 Philip Dormer Stanhope, *The Letters of Philip Dormer Stanhope, 4th Earl of Chesterfield*, ed. Bonamy Dobrée, 6 vols, London 1932, V, p. 2264.

37 In 1758 the Earl of Jersey's family hoped to take a portrait away from Bath less than two months after it was painted, see below, Chapter 3, p. 38. A more normal delivery time from the date of a first sitting was five to six months, see Pointon 1984, p. 197.

38 David Garrick, *The Letters of David Garrick*, ed. David M. Little and George Kahrl, 3 vols, Oxford 1963, III, no. 907, p. 1005, David Garrick to Hannah More, Bath 4 May 1775.

39 Walter Sichel, *Bolingbroke and his Times*, London 1901, p. 126.

40 Neale 1981, p. 38.

41 Schopenhauer, *A Lady Travels*, London 1988, p. 22. Schopenhauer noted that

the hilly character of the town, which rendered private carriages superfluous, contributed to the inexpensive lifestyle. Plentiful cheap coal from the nearby Somerset coalfield also cut down household bills.

42 Lewis and Smith 1937–83, x, p. 231, Horace Walpole to George Montagu, Bath 18 October 1766.

43 Tobias Smollett, *The Expedition of Humphry Clinker*, ed. Lewis M. Knapp, Oxford 1984 (first edition 1771), p. 57.

44 Newby 1990, p. 12.

45 Hayes 2001, no. 17, p. 33.

46 Ibid., no. 18, pp. 34–5; no. 84, pp. 149–151; no. 87, p. 157.

47 Dack 1907, p. 11; Vertue 1934, p. 157. For Hackert, see Edwards 1808, p. 41.

48 Whitley 1915, p. 79.

49 A daughter Mary was buried on 1 March 1748, less than two years after Thomas and Margaret Gainsborough were married, see David Tyler, 'The Gainsborough family: Births, Marriages, and Deaths Re-examined', *Gainsborough's House Review 1992/93*, 1993, p. 41.

50 I am extremely grateful to Trevor Fawcett who first alerted me to the fact that there appears to have been an academy linked to the Hospital in Bath and pointed me to the Cleland source. For other academies see Ilaria Bignamini and Martin Postle, *The Artist's Model: Its Role in British Art from Lely to Etty* (exh. cat., University Art Gallery, Nottingham and Iveagh Bequest, Kenwood), Nottingham and London 1991, pp. 8–9.

51 Rolls 1988, pp. 63–5 summarises the 'Cleland affair'.

52 Anon, *An Appeal to the Public: or Plain Narrative of the Facts, Relating to the Proceedings of a Party of the Governors of the New General-Hospital at Bath, against Mr Archibald Cleland*, London and Bath 1743, p. 18, and Cleland 1744, pp. 13–14.

53 Cleland 1744, p. 14.

54 Ibid., unnumbered note on p. 37.

55 Newby 1990, p. 10.

56 SRO, Walcot Churchwarden's Accounts 1721–1757, D/P/Wal, SW 4/1/1. For rates payments in 1742, next to an entry for 'Mr Bartrand' in Barton Street is 'Mr Grs [Gratious] Stride 1 House [crossed out] Mr Hoare'. In 1743 the entries read in order 'Mr Bartrand', 'Mr Stride', 'Mr Hoore'. A group of five ratepayers, including these three, consistently pay a uniform higher rate than others in Barton Street. There are five houses in the terrace making the east side of Queen Square. Early maps show Barton Street extending north and south of Queen Square on the east side of the Square. An advertisement in the *Bath Journal* of 10 November 1755 for the sale after Bertrand's death refers to 'his late Dwelling House in Queen Square'.

57 Jeremiah Peirce is one of the two doctors in Hoare's group portrait that was presented to the Hospital in 1762 but painted earlier, see Newby 1990, p. 37 and Mary Holbrook, 'Painters in Bath in the Eighteenth century', *Apollo*, XCVIII, no. 141, November 1973, p. 375 and p. 384, n. 4.

58 Bertrand is however mentioned in Fawcett 1990, pp. 49–75. This article provides the best recent account of retailing in Bath and includes details of the sort of business that was transacted by toymen and milliners, for example. It is not clear whether the painter Mary Bertrand, who exhibited at the Royal Academy between 1772 and 1776, was a relative of Paul Bertrand. A Mary Bertrand was buried in Bath Abbey on 20 April 1784 'Under Dr Wall's monument' (BRO, Bath Abbey Registers of Baptisms, Marriages and Burials, transcripts).

59 Sir Ambrose Heal, *The London Goldsmiths 1200–1800*, Cambridge 1935, p. 107. Clayton 1997, p. 12 states that Bertrand was selling prints in his Bath toy shop in 1733. Attending the same Masonic meeting as Bertrand in 1737 was the eminent scientist and designer Jean-Théophile Desaguliers (later the leader of British Freemasonry) and James Leake, see Anon 1917, p. 310. Paul Bertrand had an account with Hoare's Bank in Fleet Street: numerous transactions are listed in, for example, C. Hoare & Co, Ledgers 40 (for 1739–40) and Ledger 47 (for 1747).

60 The largest single donation made in a collection on Sunday 23 October 1748 was 'Lady Betty Jermain, by Mr Bertrand £10.10.0' (*Bath Journal*, 31 October 1748). Bertrand also played an active part in the life of St Swithin's, the parish church of Walcot, the largest parish in Bath. His signature records his presence at Vestry Meetings on 2 April 1746 and 23 April 1747 (SRO, Walcot Churchwardens' Accounts). He was buried in St Swithin's in 1755 (ibid., under list of burials in St Swithin's, 'Mr Bertrand in the Vault 0.6.8').

61 *Bath Journal*, 10 November 1755. No copy of the sale catalogue is known.

62 Lewis and Smith 1937–83, IX, p. 83. Walpole calls Mrs Bertrand's sister Mrs Daniel Chevenix. R. A. Austin-Leigh, 'Chevenix's Toyshop', *Notes and Queries*, CLXVI, 20 January 1934, p. 46 corrects the name to Chenevix, and notes that Daniel Chenevix (d. 1742) was, like Bertrand, a goldsmith in St Martin-in-the-Fields. Further information about Chenevix's toy shop is given by Tessa Murdoch in *The Quiet Conquest, The Huguenots 1685 to 1985* (exh. cat., Museum of London) London 1985, pp. 258–9, nn 381, 382.

63 Lewis and Smith 1937–83, XIII–XIV, p. 103, n. 11.

64 Ibid., IX, p. 83.

65 Fawcett 1990, fig. 5, p. 66.

66 *Boddely's Bath Journal*, 23 June 1760.

67 Neale 1981, pp. 24–5.

68 Aleyn Lyell Reade, 'Samuel Richardson and his Family Circle, II', *Notes and Queries*, XI, 16 September 1922, p. 225.

69 Ibid. Leake quickly became Baths 'official' bookseller and stationer. There are numerous payments to him in BRO, City of Bath Chamberlain's Accounts (Shickle transcripts, III, 1725–1772), and he is described as stationer to the Hospital and bookseller to Ralph Allen by Archibald Cleland (Cleland 1744, p. 13).

70 *Boddely's Bath Journal*, 27 September 1762.

71 Earl of Orrery, *The Orrery Papers*, ed. Countess of Cork and Orrery, 2 vols, London 1903, I, p. 99. The Earl of Orrery, writing on 16 October 1731 notes that Leake 'speaks not to a Marquis whilst a Duke is in the Room. As yet he is ignorant that my Earldom lies in Ireland, and to keep him so, I have borrowed the only Book of Heraldry he had in his Shop by this method I shall be served many degrees above my Place . . .'.

72 Reade, 'Samuel Richardson and his Family Circle, II', p. 225.

73 Neale 1981, pp. 23–4.

74 Rolls 1988, p. 145. When appointed in 1742 Morris was paid £60 a year and given board and lodging. In 1744 this was reduced to £40.

75 Ibid., pp. 44 and 46 mention the work of Benjamin Morris in the Hospital but does not suggest a relationship with the Apothecary. However a Benjamin Morris, son of John Morris, was baptised in Bath Abbey on 10 May 1722 (BRO Bath Abbey Registers, transcripts).

76 Benjamin Boyce, *The Benevolent Man, A life of Ralph Allen*, Harvard 1967, pp. 3, 25, 31, 45, 71. When Allen was decorating Prior Park he commissioned a copy of a painting in possession of 'Mr Morrice' (ibid., p. 104, n. 15). Was this in fact a picture belonging to John Morris?

77 Lippincott 1983, p. 47. Lippincott also notes (pp. 28, 47) that Bishop William Warburton (who married Allen's niece, the inheritor of Prior Park) was a frequent buyer of prints from Pond. Pond's collection of prints was acquired by Sir Edward Astley, Thomas Worlidge's most important patron. An oil portrait of Allen attributed to Pond now hangs in the Pump Room, Bath (Anon 1991, p. 85).

78 Cleland 1744, p. 14.

79 Graves 1806, p. 67.

80 Rolls 1988, p. 159.
81 Norman 1920, p. 136. Also present was John Wiltshire; either John Wiltshire senior, assembly rooms proprietor and carrier, or his son John Wiltshire junior. They were father and brother of Gainsborough's friend Walter Wiltshire.
82 Vertue 1934, p. 158.
83 Tyte 1903, p. 100. Tyte says that Robinson was born in Bath. Waterhouse 1981, p. 315 says Robinson was apprenticed to Vanderbank and had a bright future, but died young.
84 Newby 1990, p. 9.
85 Allen 1987, p. 4.
86 Ibid., no. 7, p. 89. An account of the Jacob family's association with Gainsborough in the 1760s follows below, Chapter 9.
87 Michael Kitson, 'Hogarth's Apology for Painters', *Walpole Society*, XLI, 1968, pp. 47, 55–66, and Allen 1987, p. 4. Kitson shows that the St Martin's Lane Academy was run by Vanderbank and Cheron for a few years from 1720 and then, after a break, by Hogarth from 1735.
88 *Bath Journal*, 18 March 1754, carries an advertisement for the remaining contents of Vertue's shop including 'several curious Drawings and Prints' and 'all Sorts of Rappee and other Snuffs'. After this date he concentrated on teaching drawing and painting.
89 Sloman 1992, p. 29.
90 Josiah Wedgwood, *The Selected Letters of Josiah Wedgwood*, ed. Ann Finer and George Savage, London 1965, p. 124.
91 Neale 1981, p. 295.
92 Appendix 1, pp. 200–03.
93 BCL, 'Diary of a Tour undertaken by Three Students, 1725', p. 114.
94 Wood 1749, II, p. 423.
95 Ibid.
96 BRO, 'List of Honorary Freemen extracted from Council Books 1632–1775' (Shickle transcripts), 'John Wicksted' paid £10.10.0 for his freedom on 17 July 1733. A signboard for Wicksteed's shop on the new Pulteney Bridge can be seen in Thomas Malton's watercolour of the bridge dated 1777 in the collection of the Victoria Art Gallery (Accession no. PD 1993.15). Trevor Fawcett has kindly given me a copy of his typescript notes on the Wicksteeds and their businesses in Bath.
97 Tyte 1903, pp. 48–9.
98 *Bath Journal*, 1 October 1744; *Boddely's Bath Journal*, 9 January 1758. The *Bath Journal* was known as *Boddely's Bath Journal* from 1756 to 1773.
99 Sherburn 1956, IV, p. 469, 'Mr Arbuthnot is heartily yours and begs you would send to Wicksted the Seal Cutter for a Seal of his, that he may take it with him from your house'. Sherburn dates this letter to 1743.
100 *Bath Journal*, 22 April 1745. BRO, Bath City Council Minutes (transcripts), 19 February 1738/9, 'Mr Jacob Skinner made a freeman of this City, in consideration of his engraving the boxes of Gold and Silver for the Prince [Frederick, Prince of Wales] and his attendants, the fees of his freedom to be paid by the Chamber of this City'.
101 See n. 65 above.
102 The elder Mrs Wicksteed, Sarah, was still advertising 'her old established Toy and China Shop, in the Orange Grove' in *Boddely's Bath Journal*, 1 December 1760 and *Boddely's Bath Journal*, 12 September 1763.
103 Still the fullest record of Worlidge's career is Dack 1907. This, however, takes little account of Worlidge's activity in Bath. An undated typescript of a lecture in the collection of BCL, by Reginald Wright, 'Thomas Worlidge', seems to contain fantasy as well as fact. The present author has (1998) written a new entry on the artist for the *New Dictionary of National Biography*.
104 The drawing of Nash, signed and dated 1736, is in the Royal Collection and another metalpoint on vellum miniature signed and dated 1743 is in the collection of the Victoria Art Gallery, Bath. Worlidge's marriage to Mary Wicksteed took place at the church of St Thomas à Becket, Widcombe, Bath (BRO, St Thomas à Becket Parish Registers, microfiche). I am most grateful to Trevor Fawcett for this information.
105 BRO, Bath Abbey Registers (transcripts).
106 Christopher White, David Alexander, Ellen D'Oench, *Rembrandt in Eighteenth-Century England* (exh. cat., Yale Center for British Art), New Haven 1983, pp. 93–4.
107 Dack 1907, no. 188, p. 28; no. 2, p. 19.
108 Yale Center for British Art, New Haven, accession no. B 1977.14.5190.
109 Norman 1920, p. 158.
110 *Bath Journal*, 16 September 1754.
111 *Bath Journal*, 16 December 1754.
112 *Bath Journal*, 10 November 1755.
113 *Bath Advertiser*, 14 April 1759.
114 BL, 'Travels of Dr Richard Pocock, Bishop of Ossory in 1764', Additional Manuscript 14260, fol. 211.
115 Horace Walpole, *The Works of Horatio Walpole, Earl of Orford*, 5 vols, London 1798, III, opposite p. 481. A new entry on William Hibbart for the *New Dictionary of National Biography* has recently (1998) been written by the present author.
116 SRO, DD/GC/103, correspondence between Coplestone Warre Bampfylde and Christopher Anstey dated between 6 March 1776 and 5 January 1777. Anstey must have brought in William Hoare to bring Hibbart's plates up to a standard that would satisfy Bampfylde. Anstey reported (5 January 1777) 'Mr Hoare has taken a great deal of pains and has corrected many parts of them . . .'.
117 *Boddely's Bath Journal*, 5 April 1762. Desmond Shawe-Taylor, *The Georgians, Eighteenth-Century Portraiture and Society*, London 1990, p. 18 says, 'Hogarth was unique in having a tradesman-like shop-sign outside his studio, illustrating Van Dyck's head'. However, in Bath (and possibly in London too) it seems to have been normal practice to advertise with a signboard, see Sloman 1996b, p. 143. The Golden Head sign was regularly used by printmakers and printsellers in London.
118 Worlidge is not mentioned in Mary Holbrook, 'Painters in Bath in the Eighteenth century', *Apollo*, XCVIII, no. 141, November 1973, pp. 375–84, but Evelyn Newby has subsequently expressed the view (verbally, 1995) that Worlidge might have taught Hoare to etch.
119 Rolls 1988, p. 46. The portrait appears close in style to certain Worlidge portraits.
120 Newby 1990, p. 11 notes that several of Hoare's most influential patrons were Freemasons, as was Ralph Allen. Beau Nash is mentioned as a member of the earliest Bath Masonic Lodge which met at the Queen's Head, although he does not seem to have gone on to become a member of the subsequent Bear Inn Lodge (Anon 1917, p. 285).
121 Hugh Belsey, 'Two Works by Gainsborough', *National Art Collections Fund Review for the year ended 31 December 1992*, 1992, pp. 8–11.
122 Michael Rosenthal, 'Testing the Water: Gainsborough in Bath in 1758', *Apollo*, CXLII, no. 403, September 1995, p. 50.
123 Ibid.
124 Desmond Shawe-Taylor, *The Georgians, Eighteenth-Century Portraiture and Society*, London 1990, p. 14.
125 Wright spent two seasons in Bath with little success, see Sloman 1996b, pp. 137–8.
126 [Nigel Surry], *George Beare* (exh. cat., Pallant House, Chichester), Chichester 1989 (published anonymously), provides a useful insight into the life of an unremarkable but apparently successful provincial portrait painter. Gainsborough wrote from Bath to the musician William Jackson, a native of Exeter, 'Exeter is no more a place for a Jackson, than Sudbury in Suffolk is for a G—' (Hayes 2001, no. 24, p. 43).
127 Newby 1990, no. 13, p. 28.
128 Ibid., p. 11.
129 For example, Ann Ford, later Mrs Philip Thicknesse; Philip Thicknesse; George

Villiers, later Fourth Earl of Jersey; Charles Pratt, First Earl Camden; Thomas Prowse; Uvedale Tomkyns Price and Philip, Fourth Earl of Chesterfield.

130 Sloman 1992, p. 39, n. 19. For Gainsborough's prices, see Appendix III, p. 213. It is not known what he charged for a full-length in 1764, but it was certainly not more than sixty guineas, the price he is known to have charged between 1766 and 1769.

131 Ibid. See also Anon 1991, p. 55.

132 RA, Humphry papers, HU/1/20–40.

133 Waterhouse 1981, p. 386.

134 Benjamin Boyce, *The Benevolent Man: A life of Ralph Allen,* Harvard 1967, pp. 104–12.

135 Ibid., pp. 104–05.

136 Eight of Van Diest's portraits of Bath councillors and his portrait of Wade survive and remain in the present Guildhall, see Anon 1991, p. 109. A note in the City Chamberlain's Accounts for 13 February 1750 records, 'Paid for Cleansing the Pictures £5.10.0' (BRO, City of Bath Chamberlain's Accounts (Shickle transcripts, III, 1725–72)).

137 [W. C. Borlase], *The Descent, Name and Arms of Borlase of Borlase in the County of Cornwall,* London 1888, p. 182. Borlase was later drawn by William Hoare, see Newby 1990, no. 43, p. 55. Newby does not suggest that the arrival of Hoare put Van Diest out of business, but the timing of this letter, a year after Hoare is first recorded in Bath, certainly suggests this may have happened.

138 The pair of portraits now attributed to Enoch Seeman hangs in the present Guildhall, (Anon 1991, p. 34, catalogued as by Jeremiah Davison) as does Van Diest's full-length of General Wade (ibid., p. 109). Those of the original set of three-quarter length portraits of Councillors that survive now hang in the present Council Chamber (ibid., p. 109).

139 Ibid., p. 55. This portrait of Nash now hangs in the Pump Room, Bath.

140 Anon, *New Bath Guide,* Bath n.d. (inscribed 1762 on the spine of the BCL copy), pp. 28–9.

141 The painting can be seen in Pinchbeck's fan leaf, illustrated here and in drawings by Thomas Robins and James Vertue, see Sloman 1994, p. 57, n. 32.

142 Anon, *Bath and Bristol Guide,* Bath 1755 (Kingsmead facsimile reprint, Bath 1969), p. 21. Only later in the century were pictures shown in the Pump Room. See for example, BCL, Rack, 'A Disultory Journal of Events etc at Bath', 5 January 1780.

143 Anon, *Catalogue of the Rich Houshold [sic] Furniture etc of the late Ralph Allen Esq.,* 17 August 1769 and eight following days, lots 6–9 (copy of the sale catalogue in BCL). The sale catalogue lists lot 9 as 'A view of the brass mill and one arch bridge at Tiverton by Ross'. This is almost certainly a misspelling for Twerton, Bath (where there was a brass mill and bridge), which was often called Twiverton or Twyverton.

144 Anon 1991, p. 97.

145 Marjorie Williams, *Lady Luxborough goes to Bath,* Oxford 1945, p. 6. Lady Luxborough wrote to the poet Shenstone in 1752, '[Nash] is new hanging his Collection of Beauties, so as to have space to hang up as many future Belles. His Apelles is Howard [Hoare] (in crayons; his Praxiteles is Howard's Brother [Prince Hoare] . . .'.

146 [Thicknesse] 1778, p. 18 says the 'Beauties' were 'chiefly' by Hoare.

147 Rolls 1988, pp. 9, 44–6, 48, 145, 156.

148 Newby 1990, no. 17, p. 37.

149 Rolls 1988, p. 46.

150 For the Abbey altarpiece see Susan Legouix Sloman, 'General Wade's altarpiece for Bath Abbey: a reconstruction', *Burlington Magazine,* CXXXIII, no. 1061, August 1991, pp. 507–10. The two paintings still in the present St Michael's church in Bath are thought to have been painted for the previous church on the same site, c. 1742. The Robinson painting of Moses is by far the more accomplished of the two. Revd G. N. Wright, *Historic Guide to Bath,* Bath 1864, p. 220 says that the *Christ Bearing the Cross* is the work of Thomas Lawrence at the age of sixteen. There was, however, a painting fitting the description of the present *Christ* in the church before Lawrence's birth. It is possible (but unlikely) that the present picture is a copy by Lawrence of one by Hoare, now lost. Lawrence did paint this subject, but his painting is said to have been taken to London (Kenneth Garlick, *Sir Thomas Lawrence: A Complete Catalogue of the Oil Paintings,* Oxford 1989, no. 886, p. 294). Garlick was not aware of Wright's claim concerning the picture in St Michael's church. Newby 1990, p. 12 assumes Hoare's *Christ* lost.

151 Anon, *New Bath Guide,* Bath n.d. (inscribed 1762 on the spine of the BCL copy), p. 15. Mitchell and Penrose 1983, p. 115.

152 Newby 1990, p. 154.

153 David Solkin, *Painting for Money: The Visual Arts and the Public Sphere in Eighteenth-Century England,* New Haven and London 1993, fig. 57, p. 164 and fig. 58, p. 166.

154 *Bath Journal,* 26 November 1744.

155 *Bath Journal,* 15 April 1754.

156 *Boddely's Bath Journal,* 31 October 1757; *Boddely's Bath Journal,* 30 October 1758.

157 *Bath Journal,* 14 March 1748.

158 *Boddely's Bath Journal,* 24 December 1759, this was their first showing in England, the exhibition having been brought from Berlin; *Boddely's Bath Journal,* 26 April 1762.

159 See Chapter 8, p. 165.

160 *Bath Advertiser,* 7 October 1758.

161 SHM, William Whitehead, untitled 3-volume collection of MS letters, I, Whitehead to Lord Nuneham from Bath, 9 December 1760.

162 BCL, Rack, 'A Disultory Journal of Events etc at Bath', 11 February 1780: Rack called Webb 'a man of Great Genius & politeness'. Webb published *An Inquiry into the Beauties of Painting,* London 1760; *Remarks on the Beauty of Poetry,* London 1762; *Observations on the Correspondence between Poetry and Music,* London 1769, and *Literary Amusements,* London 1787. Webb's writings are discussed below in Chapter 8

163 Llanover 1861, III, p. 605. Mrs Delany was referring to Webb's criticism of the colouring of Rubens's paintings, which he considered inferior to the mellow colouring of Titian.

164 *Bath and Bristol Chronicle,* 31 December 1772. Whitley 1915, p. 92, describes Jones's activities as a dealer and suggests he may have been the source of some of Gainsborough's collection.

165 *Bath and Bristol Chronicle,* 19 October 1769.

166 Waterloo is named in Jones's advertisement in the *Bath and Bristol Chronicle,* 19 December 1769, Teniers in the same newspaper for 7 December 1769, and Snyders in the same newspaper for 31 December 1772. John Hayes mentions these three artists as at various times inspiring Gainsborough's landscapes, in, for example, Hayes 1982, I, p. 115 (Teniers), p. 130 (Snyders) and Hayes 1970, I, pp. 15, 31, 57, 59.

167 This paragraph on artists' picture rooms is a brief summary of Sloman 1996b, pp 132–54.

168 Horace Walpole, *Anecdotes of Painting in England: 1760–1795,* ed. F. W. Hilles and P. B. Daghlian, New Haven and London 1937, pp. 20–22.

169 Trevor Fawcett, 'Ambiguous Monarchs: Authority and Function of the Masters of Ceremonies', *Studies on Voltaire and the Eighteenth Century,* no. 303, 1992, pp. 180–83.

170 [Sir Richard Steele], *The Tunbridge and Bath Miscellany for the Year 1714,* London 1714 (published anonymously), pp. 19–20.

171 Goldsmith 1762, p. 46.

172 Pointon 1984, p. 187.

173 A draft conveyance of 1771 between William and H. P. Hoare and Benjamin

Colborne, concerning a plot of land near the new Upper Assembly Rooms names William Hoare, 'Gentleman', although his late brother Prince Hoare is referred to as a 'Statuary' (BRO, Bryant Catalogue, Draft Conveyance between William and H. J. Hoare and Benjamin Colborne, 24 July 1771).

174 Quoted in Lindsay 1982, p. 100.

175 Webb 1760, p. 18. This passage from Webb is discussed in Iain Pears, *The Discovery of Painting*, New Haven and London 1988, pp. 192–3.

176 Pointon 1984, p. 198, Pointon observes that Gainsborough 'enjoyed a degree of autonomy unusual for the period' as early as 1765.

2 *Mrs Margaret Gainsborough*

1 Farington 1978–98, IV, 1979, p. 1152.

2 This chapter is an expansion, with additional information, of an article by the present writer, published under the same title in *Gainsborough's House Review 1995/96*, 1996, pp. 47–55. Full transcriptions of Mrs Gainsborough's annuity documents are given as Appendices to that article.

3 Harrison 1922a, p. 5 and Harrison 1922b, pp. 87–91. Harrison believed the annuity probably came from Charles Noel Somerset, Fourth Duke of Beaufort. James Unwin is usually said to have died in 1776, but David Tyler has found that his will was proved on 26 May 1774 (PRO, PROB 11/998/207). I am most grateful to him for this information.

4 Sloman 1996a, Appendix I, p. 56. I am most grateful to his Grace the Duke of Beaufort for allowing me to study Badminton muniments and to Mrs Margaret Richards, archivist, whose work at Badminton brought the annuity documents to light. Information about the Duke's marriage is given in H. A. Doubleday, the Hon. Vicary Gibbs, Duncan Warrand and Lord Howard de Walden (eds), *The Complete Peerage*, 13 vols, London 1910–40, II, p. 54. The separation took place in June 1740.

5 *Boddely's Bath Journal*, 25 February 1744/5, 'Yesterday, about 5 o'Clock in the Afternoon, died here, the Most Noble Henry Somerset Scudamore, Duke of Beaufort, in the 38th Year of his Age: He is succeeded in Honour and Estate by his Brother, Lord Noel Somerset, Member of Parliament for Monmouth, now Duke of Beaufort'. The Third Duke had added the name Scudamore to his own on his marriage.

6 Peter Townend (ed.), *Burke's Genealogical and Heraldic History of the Peerage, Baronetage and Knightage*, London 1970, p. 725.

7 Mr John D'Arcy kindly informs me (by letter 8 September 1995) that he knows of no connection between his and the Duke of Beaufort's family. Seals on documents do not in themselves possess any legal status and it is not unknown for them to have been used in an arbitrary fashion in the eighteenth century. Patrick Darcy is noted in Rome in 1729 and Venice in 1733, according to Ingamells 1997, p. 276. He and his wife Anne gave hospitality to visiting English Jacobites at the Casa de Gesuiti, Rome (ibid., p. 242). One of his most eminent guests in November 1730 was the Jacobite Lord Cornbury, whose posthumous portrait was painted by Gainsborough in 1758 or 1759.

8 Kingsmill Evans was a member of a prominent Herefordshire family which was also associated with Lydart, a mile from the Beaufort property of Troy in Monmouthshire, see C. J. Robinson, *A History of the Mansions and Manors of Herefordshire*, London and Hereford 1873, p. 279 and Charles Heath, *Monmouthshire Tracts: Historical and Descriptive Accounts of the Ancient and Present state of the Town of Monmouth*, Monmouth 1804, no printed page numbers, but numbered p. 673 in the author's copy.

9 *Hawking Party at Netheravon: The Third Duke and Party* (photograph in the Witt Library, Courtauld Institute of Art).

10 Nikolaus Pevsner, *The Buildings of Wiltshire* (revised edition by Bridget Cherry), Harmondsworth 1975, p. 354. Pevsner believed Netheravon House to be late eighteenth century, but the essential five-bay design which can be seen in Wootton's paintings seems to survive as the skeleton of the present house. The stable block, now disfigured by later accretions, may well be late eighteenth century and a replacement of the Duke of Beaufort's stables. Netheravon was purchased by the Third Duke of Beaufort in 1734, see Margaret Richards' introduction to the 'Catalogue of Badminton Muniments', p. xiii (GRO, undated typescript). The Netheravon Estate was sold for £29,500, see GRO, Badminton Muniments, PB 2/1, an undated manuscript list of 'The Duke of Beaufort's Estates Sold and to be Sold'.

11 Sloman 1996a, Appendix II, pp. 57–8.

12 GRO, Badminton Muniments, QA 4/16. Edmund Estcourt (1752–1814) was steward of the Duke of Beaufort's Welsh estates at this date. The *Bath Chronicle* of 25 December 1766 records the marriage at Malmesbury of William Earle, the King's receiver-general for North Wiltshire, to the only daughter of the late Edmund Estcourt, a young lady with a fortune of thirty thousand pounds. She was perhaps a relative of the Duke of Beaufort's steward.

13 Sloman 1996a, Appendix III, p. 58.

14 Fulcher 1856, p. 34.

15 Cunningham 1829–32, I, pp. 323–4. Cunningham's source was the artist's niece Sophia Lane, see Colonel Francis Cunningham's extra-illustrated copy of Cunningham 1829–32, in the National Art Library, Victoria and Albert Museum, London.

16 Lucy Abel Smith, 'The Duke of Beaufort's Marble Room', *Burlington Magazine*, CXXXVIII, no. 1114, January 1996, p. 25.

17 CWA, Parish of St George, Hanover Square, Poor Rate Collecting Books, c 274. The lists of payments for Duke Street from 1742 to 1745 were examined. The name Burr does not occur.

18 Thicknesse 1788, p. 8; Hayes 2001, no. 91, p. 151; Fulcher 1856, pp. 4, 33.

19 Tyler's research into the Aikman–Burr family relationship is ongoing, but he can show that Mrs Margaret Gainsborough had a nephew, James Burr of Bells Mills, Edinburgh and a niece, Mary Burr. This would suggest that she was the half-sister of Isaak Burr (b. 1719) and Alexander Burr (b. 1720) and daughter of Margaret Burr (née Aikman) who married William Burr (b. c. 1690) around 1718. The fact that the Christian name 'Gainsborgh' was given to a grandson of Alexander Burr may be significant. I am most grateful to David Tyler for this information.

20 Osbert Sitwell, 'The Red Folder, II', *Burlington Magazine*, LXXX, no. 470, May 1942, p. 118. Lucy Abel Smith ('The Duke of Beaufort's marble room') mistranscribes Aikman as 'Lihmann' in her version of the text of the letter quoted by Sitwell. Information on the Aikman business in Leghorn (now Livorno) is to be found in the Brinsley Ford Archive at the PMC. The Aikmans' role in shipping the Third Duke's grand tour purchases was noticed by the present writer after David Tyler suggested an Aikman connection in the Burr family tree.

21 Information conveyed verbally by Mrs Margaret Richards, 1995.

22 No record of Margaret Burr's birth date has been found. Her name does not appear amongst those baptised at St George's, Hanover Square in 1728 or 1729 (CWA).

23 Andrew Wilton and Ilaria Bignamini (eds), *The Grand Tour: The Lure of Italy in the Eighteenth Century* (exh. cat., Tate Gallery, London and Palazzo delle

Esposizioni, Rome), London 1996, no. 11, p. 53. The catalogue entry by Brian Allen gives a concise account of the Duke's grand tour.

24 The profile drawing was sold at Sotheby's, London, 11 November 1993, lot 25, and is now in a private collection. A copy of the etching is in the BM, Department of Prints and Drawings. Other profile portrait etchings by Hoare, executed in the manner of Jonathan Richardson, are also in the same collection. Hoare also portrayed Charles Noel, Fourth Duke of Beaufort, in pastel (photograph in the Witt Library, Courtauld Institute of Art).

25 Horatia Durant, *The Somerset Sequence*, 1951, pp. 156–8, and Osbert Sitwell, 'The Red Folder, I', *Burlington Magazine*, LXXX, no. 469, April 1942, pp. 85–90. Andrew Graham-Dixon, writing in the *Independent* of 26 February 1991 under the heading 'Moving furniture – the biggest sideboard in the world or a treasury of cultural significance?' made some interesting observations on the subject of the Badminton Cabinet, which is, in his words,

> an object fit for a king – or, at least, for a king-maker. This may be the last key to unlock its meaning . . . The Beauforts, who had lost much of their wealth in a disastrous attempt to support Charles I, had always been particularly devoted to the Stuarts . . . Perhaps the Duke dreamed of playing a major part in some future Stuart restoration. His cabinet certainly suggests that he saw himself as a man of destiny.

26 Osbert Sitwell, 'The Red Folder, I', *Burlington Magazine*, LXXX, no. 469, April 1942, p. 89.

27 Horatia Durant, *The Somerset Sequence*, London 1951, pp. 157–8.

28 The two are also depicted together in another of Wootton's Badminton canvases, *Racing at Newmarket* (photograph in the Witt Library, Courtauld Institute of Art).

29 Eveline Cruickshanks (ed.), *Ideology and Conspiracy: Aspects of Jacobitism, 1689–1759*, Edinburgh 1982, pp. 56–7.

30 Girouard 1959, p. 599.

31 Gainsborough also knew Unwin's brother, since he mentions visiting him when in London (Hayes 2001, no. 9, pp. 17–19; no. 12, pp. 23–5). This may have been the Charles Unwin whose name crops up periodically in Bertie Burgh's account with Hoare's Bank and would appear to have been a member of the firm, or business associate.

32 Hayes 2001, no. 13, p. 26.

33 Ibid., no. 18, p. 35.

34 The portrait is now untraced and only known from an engraving in William Cowper, *The Works of William Cowper, Esq.*, ed. Robert Southey, 15 vols, London 1835–7, III, opposite p. 301. The engraving by H. Robinson, after a drawing from the original portrait by W. Harvey, is inscribed 'By Gainsborough 1764', but this date cannot be correct. William Cawthorne Unwin was only ordained deacon in 1767 and priest in 1769, and he is wearing clerical dress in the print. The date 1764 appears on a paper held by the sitter in the engraving: this was probably intended to represent the Chancellor's Classical Medal and Degree awarded to Unwin at Cambridge University in 1764 (William Cowper, *The Letters and Prose Writings of William Cowper*, ed. James King and Charles Ryskamp, 3 vols, Oxford 1979–82, I, p. xli.). One of the Castle Hedingham Unwins was, like James Unwin, connected with the legal profession: George, son of Joseph Unwin of Castle Hedingham was apprenticed in 1723 to Richard Arnold, clerk of the King's Bench Court (PRO, Apprentice Records I.R.17).

35 It may be significant that a George Unwin, son of John Unwin of Coggeshall, Essex, was apprenticed to cordwainer Edward Gardiner of Coggeshall in 1718 (PRO, Apprentice Records I.R.17). The artist's sister Susanna married a Richard Gardiner at Tollesbury, Essex in 1750.

36 Sir Joseph Alfred Bradney, *History of Monmouthshire*, 2 vols, 1904–11, II, part 2, pp. 163–8. Mrs Margaret Richards kindly drew my attention to this source which includes a Burgh family tree.

37 Charles Heath, *Monmouthshire Tracts: Historical and Descriptive Accounts of the Ancient and Present State of the Town of Monmouth*, Monmouth 1804, no printed page numbers, but numbered in the author's copy pp. 770, 779.

38 Sir Joseph Alfred Bradney, *History of Monmouthshire*, 2 vols, 1904–11, II, part 2, pp. 166–8. John Burgh's own properties were inherited by his eldest surviving son the Revd Henry Burgh, but Bertie inherited the stewardship. The Hon. James Bertie of Stanwell, Middlesex, was Tory Member of Parliament for Woodstock from 1695 to 1705 and for Middlesex from 1710 to 1734.

39 C. Hoare & Co., Ledger 38/29: James Burgh's account shows payments of five guineas to James Unwin on 11 October 1737 and three guineas on 26 October 1737; Ledger 39/146 shows a payment by James Burgh of £10.11.0 to James Unwin on 3 January 1738/39. Ledger 39/300 documents a payment by Bertie Burgh of £10 to a 'Mr Unwin' on 26 March 1738/39. Bertie Burgh's account for 1740 lists three payments of £10 to a Mr Unwin, named in one entry as James Unwin (Ledger 40/239). A Charles Unwin is also named at various times in Bertie Burgh's account. At this time accounts with Hoare & Co were also held by the Bath toyman Paul Bertrand and the ironmonger Jonathan Buttall whose family later owned Gainsborough's portrait known as *The Blue Boy*. Buttall's account was held between 1739 and 1751 but very few entries are recorded and payments in and out of the account appear to have been in cash, since no names are given (Ledger 40/163; Ledger 47/195; Ledger 48/415).

40 C. Hoare & Co, Ledger 47/131.

41 David Tyler, 'Thomas Gainsborough's days in Hatton Garden', *Gainsborough's House Review 1992/93*, 1993, pp. 30–31 and 32, n. 28. Tyler notes that the Gainsboroughs left Hatton Garden for Sudbury early in 1749, perhaps around the time of this payment by Burgh.

42 C. Hoare & Co., Ledger 61/5, the precise sum is £85,473.4.11. Bertie Burgh's account for 1749 to 1750 shows total credits of £42,773.17.4 (Ledger 50/166).

43 See Margaret Richards, 'Catalogue of Badminton Muniments', p. xiii (GRO, undated typescipt). Norborne Berkeley (1718–1770) created Fourth Baron Botetourt in 1764, was a member of the Society of Dilettanti who in 1768 became Governor of Virginia. He was a popular Governor, and a statue to him was erected in Williamsburg, see Anna Wells Routledge, 'Portraits of American Interest in British Collections', *Connoisseur*, CXLI, May 1958, pp. 267–8.

44 GRO, Badminton Muniments PB 1/3, a letter from Unwin not bearing the name of the addressee (sheet torn), but almost certainly to Norborne Berkeley, dated 19 February 1764. In the same letter Unwin attributed his spell of extreme ill-health to his anxiety over the non-repayment of his loan. Gainsborough also referred to this illness of Unwin's in a letter of 21 January 1765 (Hayes 2001 no. 18, pp. 34–5). Unwin's own scheme for paying off the Duke of Beaufort's estate's debts is summarised in the GRO, Badminton Muniments PB 2/1. In a letter in the same collection of archives dated 4 March 1762 to Norborne Berkeley (PB 1/3) Unwin says 'I wd. not take a Draft on Mr. Burgh for Twenty five shillings, much less for Twenty five Hundred pounds'. The Beaufort Trustees account with Hoare's Bank confirms that Unwin did indeed

lend £4,000: a payment of £80 interest on this loan was made to Unwin on 19 May 1759 (Ledger 62/1).

45 GRO, Badminton Muniments PB 1/3 includes two copies of the will of Captain Edward Wheeler. The will is dated 31 May 1760 and was proved 7 May 1761. Wheeler was killed on 1 April 1761 in an engagement with a French vessel, the *Oriflamme*, in the Mediterranean, see Charnock 1794–8, VI, p. 96.

46 GRO, Badminton Muniments PB 1/3. Wheeler took care to explain the nature of his will, since 'many curious people may think I have by this will taken a good deal of pains to Bastardize (as they may wittily term it) my Estate . . .'. Girouard 1959, pp. 598–9 quotes from Wheeler's will and says that Wheeler married Fanny Stephenson immediately after making his will, and that she married Unwin in 1762. Girouard does not mention any connection between James Unwin and Gainsborough.

47 The portrait was exhibited in 1991, see Ian G. Lumsden, *Gainsborough in Canada* (exh. cat., Beaverbrook Art Gallery), Fredericton 1991, cat. no. 5.

48 Harrison 1922a, pp. 5, 7. On 30 June 1757, 'By Cash to Edwd. Wheeler Esqr. for princ: on Bond . . . 300'.

49 Hayes 2001, no. 2, p. 6.

50 C. Hoare & Co., Ledger 47/131, 17 February 1748/9, 'To Tho. Gainsborough' £145.16.0; Ledger 50/359, 16 February 1749/50, 'To Mr Ganesborough' £20, and 19 March 1749/50, 'To Thos Ganesborough' £20; Ledger 51/126, 19 May 1750 'To Thos Gainsborough' £80; Ledger 53/29, 13 December 1751 'To Mr. Gainsborough' £100 and 2 January 1752 'To Thos. Gainsborough's bill' £260.

51 C. Hoare & Co., Ledger 56/277, 22 May 1755, 'To Thos Gainsborough' £100 and 30 May 1755, 'To Mr. Gainsborough' £26; Ledger 61/387, 3 August 1759, 'To Thos Gainsborough's bill' £50.

52 GRO, Badminton Muniments, PB 1/3. A letter from Unwin dated 2 November 1763 to Norborne Berkeley begs for the repayment of the £4,000 he had personally lent the Fourth Duke of Beaufort. An angry reply is drafted on the same sheet (apparently by Norborne Berkeley) and another on a separate sheet: 'I never act from resentment but it would be very improper for me to distress the Duke of Beaufort <u>upon your account</u> as he has already <u>sufficiently</u> [above the line 'exceedingly'] suffered from the Partnership in which you also was so powerful an Actor'.

53 A detailed Price family tree is to be found in HRO, Phillips genealogical MSS, B56/2, fol. 86 verso – fol. 87.

54 Hayes 1971, no. 1, p. 35, and plates 26–32.

55 Bensusan-Butt 1993, p. 66 lists Joseph Wood's engravings.

56 Castle Yard was on the site of the present Furnival Street. Castle Yard and Cursitor's Alley are marked on John Pine and John Tinney's large-scale map, *London from a survey by John Rocque*, of 1746 (BM, Department of Prints and Drawings). Bensusan-Butt 1993, pp. 50–51 outlines Joseph Wood's association with Kirby and Gainsborough. Bensusan-Butt noted that Wood was in Cursitor's Alley but was not aware of its proximity to Unwin's office.

57 Bensusan-Butt 1993, pp. 45–6.

58 Owen 1996, pp. 61–75.

59 Hayes 1971, no. 2, p. 41, and plates 33–6. Wood produced impressions of the print dated March 1759, when Gainsborough was almost certainly in Bath. It was published by John Boydell in 1764, after Wood's death. This print is discussed further in Chapter 8, pp. 141–45.

60 Black 1911, p. 5.

61 GRO, Badminton Muniments, PB 3/1.

62 Susan Legouix Sloman, 'The Rediscovery of Luke Sullivan c. 1725/30–1771', *Watercolours and Drawings*, V, no. 1, 1990, pp. 30–33.

63 Clayton 1997, p. 13, notes that Sullivan was a pupil of Baron in 1748. In 1727 Baron had engraved a set of four hunting pictures after Wootton (ibid., p. 82). Given Wootton's close association with Badminton, it may be that he arranged for Sullivan to become Baron's pupil.

64 Bensusan-Butt 1993, p. 46.

65 Katharine Eustace, *Michael Rysbrack, Sculptor 1694–1770* (exh. cat., City of Bristol Museum and Art Gallery), Bristol 1982, no. 1, pp. 62–3, illus., p. 63.

66 Ibid., nos. 62–71, pp. 148–59.

67 Ibid., nos. 40–41, pp. 120–23.

68 Rolls 1988, p. 11.

69 Clews 1994, pp. 104–24.

70 Paul Bertrand's account shows large numbers of transactions in the 1740s (C. Hoare & Co, Ledger 47/362 for example); John Wiltshire's account includes payments to Mary Bertrand and Hanbury Pettingall, both in 1761 (Ledger 64/449); Walter Wiltshire's account includes a payment to Paul Bertrand in 1747 (Ledger 48/68); Jonathan Buttall's account has entries between 21 November 1739 and 31 August 1751, but no names of debtors or creditors are listed (Ledgers 40/163, 47/195, 48/415); Rice Charleton's account of 1759 is not enlightening (Ledger 61/429); Sir Charles-Kemeys Tynte held an account between 1751 and 1778, including a payment to Gainsborough of £33.12.0 on 2 April 1761 (Ledger 64/222). This is not an exhaustive list.

71 Appendix II, entries 51, 52, pp. 209–10.

72 BRO, Accession 72, Probate of Will of Edward Parker, dated 19 January 1786. Parker also left £100 to his godson William Makepeace Thackeray, see Appendix II, entry 52, p. 205.

73 Waterhouse 1966, no. 5, p. 51. Willoughby Bertie's unfinished portrait is discussed in Stainton 1977, no. 8 (no page numbers).

3 Bath, 1758–1759

1 The first part of this chapter is a revised and expanded version of the author's notice 'Gainsborough in Bath 1758–59', *Burlington Magazine*, CXXXVII, no. 1109, August 1995, pp. 509–12.

2 The late John Bensusan-Butt, Hugh Belsey and David Tyler have done most in recent years to unravel fact from fiction. I am grateful to all three for sharing their findings, both through their publications and, more informally, through conversation and correspondence.

3 Appendix II, entry 66, p. 206.

4 Susan Foister, Rica Jones and Olivier Meslay, *Young Gainsborough* (exh. cat., National Gallery), London 1997, p. 19.

5 David Tyler, 'Thomas Gainsborough's Days in Hatton Garden', *Gainsborough's House Review 1992/93*, 1993, p. 27, and p. 31, n. 1.

6 Quoted in Judy Egerton, *The British School, National Gallery Catalogues*, London 1998, p. 95.

7 Hayes 2001, no. 10, p. 21.

8 Hayes 1982, I, p. 92.

9 Hayes 1980, p. 22; Lindsay 1982, p. 46; [Lloyd] 1994, p. 10.

10 Edwards 1808, p. 130.

11 Cunningham 1829–32, I, p. 326. The sentence quoted continues (mistakenly), 'and took lodgings in the Circus, at the rate of fifty pounds annually'. The section of the Circus in which Gainsborough lived was not built at this date. He only moved there at the end of 1766.

12 Tunstall 1847, p. 287.

13 Fulcher 1856, p. 58.

14 Wright was Curator from 1919 to 1954. Although his research is not always accurately set down, he did uncover much valuable material about the eighteenth-century art world in Bath through his exhaustive reading of the contemporary press.

15 The newspaper reference in *Boddely's Bath Journal* was first noted, without comment, in Wright [n.d.], under Gainsborough.

16 *Bath Advertiser*, Saturday 7 October 1758, 'Last Tuesday arrived Mr. Nash in good Health, and the same Evening the Balls

began for the Season, at Mr. Simpson's, the Ball was opened by Mr. Heywood and Miss Fane'.

17 Mitchell and Penrose 1983, p. 36, letter dated 15 April 1766. Not all those listed could strictly be termed 'Gentry'. The names regularly included doctors, apothecaries, actors, musicians and tradesmen as well as the nobility and gentry.

18 Whitley 1915, p. 28.

19 Arthur B. Chamberlain, *Thomas Gainsborough*, London n.d. [1903], p. 53 and A. E. Fletcher, *Thomas Gainsborough R.A.*, London and New York 1904, p. 71.

20 Edward William Harcourt (ed.), *The Harcourt Papers*, 14 vols, Oxford 1880–1905, III, p. 65.

21 The present Middleton Park is a house of 1938 which replaced a Georgian house built c. 1753, described by Pevsner as 'large and undistinguished' (Nikolaus Pevsner and Jennifer Sherwood, *The Buildings of Oxfordshire*, Harmondsworth 1974, p. 703).

22 The letter is transcribed by kind permission of the Hon. Mrs C. Gascoigne, Stanton Harcourt Manor, near Oxford. It is bound into the first of three volumes of Whitehead correspondence arranged in date order, here referred to as SHM, Whitehead letters.

23 *Boddely's Bath Journal*, 24 August 1761. The poem is introduced, 'Sir, By making Room in your next for the enclosed Verses, you will much oblige one who for many Years has been your constant Reader'.

24 *Bath Advertiser*, 11 November 1758; *Boddely's Bath Journal*, 13 November 1758. The *Advertiser* was published on Saturdays, the *Journal* on Mondays.

25 SHM, Whitehead letters, I, Whitehead to Viscount Nuneham, 28 December 1758, 'We arrived last night in the cool climate of Middleton . . .'.

26 Bruce Robertson, *The Art of Paul Sandby* (exh. cat., Yale Center for British Art) New Haven 1985, no. 14, p. 21; H. A. Doubleday, the Hon Vicary Gibbs, Duncan Warrand and Lord Howard de Walden (eds.), *The Complete Peerage*, 13 vols, London 1910–40, VI, p. 301.

27 William Whitehead, *Plays and Poems*, 3 vols, London and York 1774–88, III, p. 78. A 'Memoir of the Life and Writings of Mr. William Whitehead' by the poet William Mason introduces vol. III.

28 Luke Herrman, *Paul and Thomas Sandby*, London 1986, pp. 23–4. One of Paul Sandby's oils, *A view of Lord Harcourt's Seat at Newnham* is illustrated, fig. 7, p. 24.

29 Pevsner and Sherwood, *The Buildings of Oxfordshire*, p. 726. Nuneham Park, originally called Newnham, was built 1756–1758 by Stiff Leadbetter.

30 A Sandby drawing of Lady Elizabeth Harcourt is illustrated in Aileen Ribeiro, *A Visual History of Costume, The Eighteenth Century*, London 1983, p. 75, fig. 79.

31 Robertson, *The Art of Paul Sandby*, no. 14, p. 21. One of the etchings, a romanticised view of Windsor Castle, is dated 1758.

32 SHM, Whitehead letters, I, Whitehead to Viscount Nuneham from Middleton Park, 29 September 1761, 'My friend Mr Wright . . . wants your advice about Prints etc . . .'.

33 The portrait, now in a private collection, is an oval, 73.5 × 61 cm (photograph, Witt Library, Courtauld Institute of Art, London). He reported to Nuneham on 4 November 1758, 'I likewise called in upon Wilson; what he has done to the picture I cannot tell, but the likeness is considerably lessened' (Edward William Harcourt (ed.), *The Harcourt Papers*, 14 vols, Oxford 1880–1905, III, p. 251).

34 SHM, Whitehead letters, I, Whitehead to Viscount Nuneham 16 November 1758.

35 Ibid., Whitehead to Viscount Nuneham 16 December 1758. In 1761 Ann Ford published *A Letter from Miss F—d, addressed to a Person of Distinction* in which she claimed her father urged her to accept £800 from the Earl of Jersey (Lindsay 1982, p. 54). In a letter to George Montagu dated 7 February 1761 Horace Walpole wrote, 'Have you seen a scandalous letter in print from Miss Ford to Lord Jersey?' (Lewis and Smith 1937–83, IX, pp. 338–9).

36 From Miss Ford, Whitehead proceeds to the subject of the stage, one of Viscount Nuneham's abiding interests. The identity of the play he hopes to see is not clear. Mrs Frances Sheridan, mother of Richard Brinsley Sheridan, wrote a comedy entitled *A Journey to Bath* which was sometimes mistakenly called *A Trip to Bath*, but this is thought not to have been written until 1763. The play still had not opened at the theatre on 16 December and no advertisements for it can be found in the local press. Following the paragraph about Gainsborough, Whitehead again turns to the stage and enquires about Robert Dodsley's play *Cleone*. This was first performed at Covent Garden on 2 December 1758 and was soon to be seen in Bath in March 1759. Whitehead's letters to Viscount Nuneham make frequent reference to the Pritchards. Mrs Hannah Pritchard (1711–1768) was apparently the poet's favourite actress. She regularly played opposite Garrick and was accepted as the greatest Lady Macbeth of her day. She was to die in Bath in 1768. The *Busy Body* dating from 1709 and written by Susannah Centlivre played throughout December 1758 at Drury Lane. When Whitehead says he is unlikely to reach 'Grosvenorshire' before Christmas he is referring to the Jersey town residence in Grosvenor Square. The Captain Stephens (later General Stephens) who sent regards via Whitehead was a family friend who had shared Whitehead as a tutor with Lord Villiers.

37 This picture was last recorded with Howard Young, New York, 1936.

38 Anonymous contribution signed X.Y.Z., headed 'A very extraordinary Journal', *The Town and Country Magazine; or, Universal Repository of Knowledge, Instruction and Entertainment*, IV, September 1772, pp. 482–6.

39 Whitley 1915, pp. 29–30; Hayes 1982, I p. 300.

40 The magazine's notorious 'Tête-à-Tête' series chronicled the love affairs of well-known figures of the day, illustrating the protagonists with portrait prints.

41 Wark 1958, p. 3:2. The letter from Thicknesse to John Cooke, dated 22 December 1773, refers to a trip made by Gainsborough and Thicknesse to Lord Bateman's seat at Shobdon, Herefordshire, '. . . nor ought he [Lord Bateman] to have urged Gainsbro to stay beyond his time as every five days was a loss to him of at least an hundred pound: & this I told him, & that I had promised Mrs Gainsbro to return in the time agreed to . . .'.

42 Michael Rosenthal, 'Testing the Water: Gainsborough in Bath in 1758', *Apollo*, CXLII, no. 403, September 1995, pp. 49–54.

43 Michael Levey, *Sir Thomas Lawrence 1769–1830* (exh. cat., National Portrait Gallery), London 1979, p. 14 and no. 31 p. 65 discusses Barrington's early reference to Lawrence and the artist's subsequent portrait, *The Hon. Shute Barrington, Bishop of Durham*, this sitter being Daines Barrington's brother.

44 Thicknesse 1788, p. 11.

45 Clayton 1997, p. 115. Clayton illustrates Major's 1754 broadsheet catalogue that lists the print, priced at three shillings.

46 Thicknesse 1788, p. 15.

47 Sloman 1992, pp. 23–43.

48 Thicknesse 1788, pp. 15–17.

49 D. E. Williams, *The Life and Correspondence of Sir Thomas Lawrence, Kt.*, 2 vols, London 1831, I, p. 75.

50 Meehan 1901, p. 16.

51 Villiers's arrival is not listed in the Bath press, but Whitehead says he had already left Bath by 6 December.

52 The Earl of Jersey was in Bath again, between November 1759 and January 1760 and could have been painted then, but this is most unlikely since he was so

severely afflicted with gout that the family were confined to their lodgings (*Boddely's Bath Journal*, 19 November 1759, for Lord Jersey's arrival; SHM, Whitehead letters, I, Whitehead to Viscount Nuneham, 25 December 1759 and 10 January 1760, from Bath).

53 Robin Gibson, *Catalogue of Portraits in the Collection of the Earl of Clarendon*, London 1977 (privately published), no. 52, p. 48. Both portraits remain in the family collection. Henry, Viscount Cornbury's niece Charlotte married Thomas Villiers, brother of William, Third Earl of Jersey, the subject of Gainsborough's portrait. Viscount Cornbury predeceased his father by six months in 1753, leaving his title 'Earl of Clarendon and Rochester' extinct. Thomas Villiers became the new First Earl of Clarendon in a second creation of the title. Gibson convincingly suggests that the portrait of Viscount Cornbury is based on an oval oil by Van Loo (no. 51, p. 47 in the same catalogue). The Van Loo would certainly have been small enough (27 × 21 inches) to have been brought or sent to Bath by a member of Lord Jersey's entourage.

54 Basil Duke Henning, *The History of Parliament: The House of Commons 1660–1690*, 3 vols, London 1983, III, p. 286. Jenkins 1983, pp. 145, 165 and elsewhere, describes the role of Judge Robert Price as political supporter of the First Duke of Beaufort.

55 Mrs Price was much affected by the scandal of her cousin's marital problems, see Sherburn 1956, IV, p. 266. Martha Blount, writing to Mrs Anne Price, 8 September 1740 says in a note at the end of the letter, 'They have given over talking of the Duchess of B. I don't hear her named now: I was sensible of the grief that affair gave you'.

56 Beryl Hartley, 'Naturalism and Sketching: Robert Price at Foxley and on Tour', in Stephen Daniels and Charles Watkins (eds.), *The Picturesque Landscape: Visions of Georgian Herefordshire* (exh. cat., City Art Gallery, Hereford and University Art Gallery, Nottingham), Nottingham 1994, p. 35. Uvedale Tomkyns Price seems often to have been associated with Bath rather than Herefordshire: a copy of [Price] 1733 in the BL is inscribed in the front 'The Gift of the Author Uvedale Price Esq. of Bath'.

57 Sir Bernard Burke, *A Genealogical and Heraldic Dictionary of the Peerage and Baronetage of the British Empire*, London 1856, pp. 818–19; Wood 1749, II, p. 276. Wood publishes a list of those who contributed to a collection made for the Hospital in the autumn of 1723 by William King. This includes 'Uvedale Price, Esq; [£]0.11.6'.

58 Sherburn 1956, p. 266. Alexander Pope's letter to Mrs Anne Price at Spa opens, 'Pray, Madam, tell my Lord Cornbury, I am not worse than when he left me . . .'. A letter dated 8 September 1740 from Martha Blount to Mrs Price, probably sent by the same post, also makes several references to Lord Cornbury (ibid., p. 265). Lord Cornbury was Tory Member of Parliament for Oxford University between 1732 and 1750. Lord Clarendon, father of Lord Cornbury, was also associated with the early history of the Bath hospital: his donation in 1738 is recorded in the BRO, Royal National Hospital for Rheumatic Diseases Archive, General Hospital Committee Minute Book I, p. 25, and his admission as a Trustee on p. 78.

59 Both Uvedale Tomkyns Price's father and Lord Cornbury's grandfather had been closely linked with the Court of Charles II. Judge Robert Price, Uvedale Tomkyns Price's father, was Steward to Queen Catherine of Braganza, wife of Charles II from 1685 to 1702. Edward Hyde, First Earl of Clarendon, was a minister to Charles II. For Viscount Cornbury's political activities see Eveline Cruickshanks, 'Lord Cornbury, Bolingbroke and a Plan to Restore the Stuarts 1731–1735', *Royal Stuart Papers*, XXVII, 1986, pp. 1–12.

60 *Bath Advertiser*, 25 September 1756 lists 'Mr. U. Price', which is clearly a reference to Uvedale Tomkyns Price of Foxley. Many other listings of the name 'Mr. Price' exist, but without qualification.

61 Waterhouse 1966, no. 434 and no. 435, p. 78.

62 A few years later, in 1763, William Lee's first cousin Sir William Lee married Lady Elizabeth Harcourt, Lord Nuneham's sister (John Burke and John Bernard Burke, *A Genealogical and Heraldic History of the Extinct and Dormant Baronetcies of England, Ireland and Scotland*, London 1841, p. 305).

63 Lord Chief Justice Lee (1688–1754) is recorded among visitors arrived in Bath in the *Bath Journal*, 15 September 1746, 'Lord Chief Justice Lee, and Lady'; *Bath Journal*, 12 September 1748, 'Lord Chief Justice Lee'; and Lady Lee in the *Bath Journal*, 1 February 1747/48, 'Lady Lee'.

64 The Hoare bust-length pastel of Lord Lee wearing his chain of office was sold at Phillips, London, 15 April 1985 (lot 71).

65 The Hoare pastel of Sir William Lee, Fourth Baronet (d. 1799) was sold at Phillips, London, 15 April 1985 (lot 65) and Miss Sarah Lee, daughter of Sir Thomas Lee, Second Baronet, in the same sale (lot 69).

66 Lee arrivals in the Bath press include, *Bath Advertiser*, 2 December 1758, 'Mr. and Mrs. Lee'; 23 December 1758, 'Mr. and Mrs. Lee'; 17 March 1759, 'Mr. and Mrs. Lee'; *Boddely's Bath Journal*, 4 December 1758, 'Mr. and Mrs. Lee'; 25 December 1758, 'Mr. and Mrs. Lee'; 19 March 1759, 'Mr. and Mrs. Lee'; 16 April 1759, 'Mr. Lee'. It is by no means certain that all these listings refer to the Lees who sat to Gainsborough. The actor John Lee (1725–1781) and his wife Mrs Anna Sophia Lee were in Bath for the 1758–1759 season at the Orchard Street Theatre and so at least one of the listings might be for them (Arnold Hare (ed.), *Theatre Royal, Bath: A Calendar of Performances at the Orchard Street Theatre 1750–1805*, Bath 1977, pp. 15–16). The Lees who arrived in mid-March cannot be the actors, however, since they were already in the town at that date.

67 NG, (P) NC 340 LEE. On the outer face of the folded sheet is an added note, 'This bill/was found at Totteridge Park. 1830/J.L.'.

68 David Mannings, 'Notes on Some Eighteenth-Century Portrait Prices in Britain', *British Journal for Eighteenth-Century Studies*, VI, 1983, p. 189, and Smart 1999, p. 419, 'Ramsay's Prices', showing that in June 1759 Ramsay was paid fifteen guineas each for the Earl and Countess of Seafield's portraits which were three-quarters or 30 × 25 inches in size.

69 Vertue 1934, p. 85.

70 Samuel Finney (1718/19–1798) advertised in the *Bath Journal*, 2 May 1748 and Henry Millington (c. 1735–1764) in *Boddely's Bath Journal*, 21 March 1757.

71 Waterhouse 1966, no. 328, p. 71. This picture was sold at Sotheby's, London on 4 July 2001 (lot 39).

72 Waterhouse 1966, nos 329 and 330, pp. 71–2. Both portraits are now at Scampston Hall, Yorkshire, see John Cornforth, 'Scampston Hall, Yorkshire, II, The Seat of Sir Charles Legard, Bt', *Country Life*, CXCIV, no. 5, 3 February 2000, p. 66.

73 *Boddely's Bath Journal*, 8 January 1759, 'Mr. Griffith'. However an actor by name of Griffith was also in Bath: a benefit performance was given for him at the Orchard Street Theatre on 10 January 1759 (*Bath Advertiser*, 6 January 1759).

74 Hayes 2001, no. 10, p. 21; Hayes 1982, II, no. 87, pp. 426–7.

75 Farington 1978–98, III, p. 764. This point is discussed further in Chapter 7 below.

76 Rebecca St Quintin died in April 1758 and if this portrait does represent her it must have been painted in Ipswich. Waterhouse 1966, no. 597, p. 88 calls the portrait *Lady St Quintin*, the daughter-in-law of Sir William St Quintin, Fourth Baronet,

but notes that the painting is labelled *Rebecca St Quintin*. Hayes 1980, no. 67, p. 84 reverts to calling the picture *Rebecca St Quintin*. A further portrait (Waterhouse 1966, no. 597a, p. 88) apparently of the same sitter, differently dressed, was with Sabin Galleries in 1957 (cutting, Witt Library, Courtauld Institute of Art, London). This latter portrait remained in the collection of the Fane family until 1956 suggesting it may represent Lady St Quintin, formerly Miss Charlotte Fane (d. 1762), niece of Thomas, Eighth Earl of Westmorland who also sat to Gainsborough (Waterhouse 1966, no. 716, p. 95; L. G. Pine (ed.), *Burke's Genealogical and Heraldic History of the Landed Gentry*, London 1952, pp. 2228–9; Peter Townend (ed.), *Burke's Genealogical and Heraldic History of the Peerage, Baronetage and Knightage*, London 1970, p. 2799). A cutting in the NPG illustrating the portrait catalogued as Waterhouse 1966, no. 597, p. 88 has been annotated in pencil to suggest that the sitter is Miss Mary St Quintin.

77 *Bath Advertiser*, 9 December 1758, 'Miss St Quintin'; *Boddely's Bath Journal*, 11 December 1758, 'Miss St Quintin'; *Bath Advertiser*, 23 September 1758, 'Miss Fane'; *Boddely's Bath Journal*, 25 September 1758, 'Miss Fane'.

78 *Boddely's Bath Journal*, 25 September 1758; *Bath Advertiser*, 3 March 1759; 10 March 1759; 17 March 1759.

79 Waterhouse 1966, no. 501, p. 82. Very similar dress is depicted in Gainsborough's portraits *Elizabeth Cochrane*, *Mrs Thomas Murdoch* (not catalogued by Waterhouse), sold Sotheby's, London, 15 March 1967, lot 91; *Mrs Elizabeth Uvedale* (not catalogued by Waterhouse), sold Christie's, London, 22 June 1979, lot 128; *Lady in Blue* (not catalogued by Waterhouse), private collection, USA, on loan to the Santa Barbara Museum of Art, California (photograph, Witt Library, Courtauld Institute of Art, London). Although the formality of the dress might be argued to point to Bath, where fashion was taken very seriously, there is no concrete evidence to link these four sitters to Bath. Gainsborough's portrait of Elizabeth Uvedale's father-in-law *Revd Samuel Uvedale* (Waterhouse 1966, no. 689, p. 94) was painted in Bath.

80 John Burke and John Bernard Burke, *The Royal Families of England, Scotland, and Wales*, 2 vols, London 1848, I, Pedigree LXXI (no page numbers in this section).

81 Graham Davis, *The Langtons at Newton Park*, Bath n.d. [1976], pp. 8–9 and p. 27, n. 6. See also Chapter 5, p. 74 for the relationship between Gainsborough's *Ann Ford* and Lely's *Barbara Villiers* portraits.

82 Daines Barrington, *Miscellanies*, London 1781, opposite p. 232, table IV, a family tree of the Wynn family (here styled Wynne), showing the relationship between the Williams Wynns and Mostyns.

83 Waterhouse 1966, nos 426 and 427, p. 77. The last of the Gore-Langtons, Algernon, Fifth Earl Temple died in 1940. The Newton Park estate was then sold to the Duchy of Cornwall (Graham Davis, *The Langtons at Newton Park*, Bath n.d. [1976], p. 26). Waterhouse records the loss of the paintings in an air raid. They were possibly awaiting a local sale in Bath. As yet I have found no evidence of their appearance, nor any further details of their fate.

84 The portrait is not catalogued by Waterhouse. The portrait of Skipwith's son Thomas George Skipwith (d. 1790), later Sir Thomas George Skipwith may also have been painted in March 1759: it too is not catalogued by Waterhouse. It was with Sabin Galleries, London in 1979 (photograph in NPG).

85 Penny 1986, p. 58. M. Kirby Talley Jr., in an account of Reynolds's technique, describes the five standard sizes of portrait canvases used by Reynolds and his contemporaries. He describes the thirty by twenty-five inch as bust-length and including one or both hands. The size was called 'three-quarters' because it measured three quarters of a yard.

86 Waterhouse 1966, no. 395, p. 75; no. 387, p. 75.

87 John Hayes, 'Some Unknown Early Gainsborough Portraits', *Burlington Magazine*, CVII, no. 743, February 1965, pp. 65–6.

88 Hayes 2001, no. 52, pp. 87–8. In a letter to the Earl of Dartmouth dated Bath, 8 April 1771, Gainsborough makes it clear that he will not alter his portrait of Lady Dartmouth (which has been sent to Bath for the purpose), 'unless from the Life'.

89 Tobias Smollett, *The Expedition of Humphry Clinker*, ed. Lewis M. Knapp, Oxford 1984, (first edition 1771) pp. 48–9, Jery Melford to Sir Watkin Phillips, dated Bath, 30 April. Smollett was a regular Bath visitor. He arrived in Bath the same week as Gainsborough in 1758, *Boddely's Bath Journal*, 9 October 1758.

90 Hayes 2001, no. 103, p. 168.

91 Sloman 1992, pp. 23–43. Gainsborough's largest Bath period canvases were the *Byam Family* (Waterhouse 1966, no. 108, p. 57) and *General Honywood* (ibid., no. 375, p. 74), both produced at Abbey Street where the artist had a painting room that was slightly larger than his subsequent room at the Circus.

92 Thicknesse 1788, p. 15.

93 *Boddely's Bath Journal*, 3 September 1759 lists a 'Mr. Wollaston' and 'Miss Wollaston'. The name Woolaston and Woollaston occurs in the same newspaper in October and December 1758 and March 1759. Since there are a number of verifiable instances of the misspelling of names in the published lists, any of these listings might refer to Gainsborough's sitter.

94 The name Rustat is misspelled Russat in *Boddely's Bath Journal*, 25 December 1758. The style of Mrs Rustat's portrait is quite consistent with others of the period such as *Lady Mostyn*, and it is possible her portrait was painted in Bath rather than Suffolk. For the Rustat family and the two portraits see P. I. Lewin, 'The Revd Tobias Rustat of Stutton and his family', *Gainsborough's House Society Annual Report 1989/90*, 1990, pp. 35–9. The portrait of *Mrs Rustat* is illustrated, fig. 10, p. 36. Mr Tobias and Mrs Rustat were subscribers to Thicknesse's *Memoirs and Anecdotes Philip Thicknesse*, 3 vols [London] 1788–91, their names being noted in a list included at the front of the first volume.

95 The 'Mr Muilman' could equally have been Peter Darnell Muilman's uncle Peter Muilman, see Chapter 4, pp. 68.

96 Waterhouse 1966, no. 41, p. 53.

97 [Lloyd] 1994, p. 10.

98 Hayes 2001, no. 39, pp. 64–6; no 46, pp. 78–80.

99 The document was purchased by Gainsborough's House, Sudbury, in 2001 (accession no 2001.021). It reads 'May 9th 1759/Thompson Scott Esq./To T Gainsborough/To one Painting/Love at the Well 35.00/Frame etc etc 5.00/40.00/Settled T Gainsborough/No 17 [or possibly 12] Hatton Garden'.

100 Walter Thornbury, *The Life of J. M. W. Turner, R.A.*, 2 vols, London 1862, II, p. 64.

101 Hayes 2001, no. 139, p. 190.

4 'Your Likeness Man'

The chapter-title quotation is taken from a letter of 1772 from Gainsborough to the Hon. Constantine Phipps, which Gainsborough signed with these words. Hayes 2001, no. 56, p. 94.

1 Sloman 1992, pp. 23–44 identifies Gainsborough's first house in Bath and documents the activities of members of Gainsborough's family as lodging house keepers in Bath between 1760 and 1800.

2 *Boddely's Bath Journal*, 1 November 1762.

3 Clews 1994, pp. 104–5; *Bath Journal*, 3 November 1746.

4 A payment of £100 to the Bath attorney William Yescombe on 11 July 1765 may

well be a loan. The preceding entry in the painter's bank account is the payment of Mrs Gainsborough's annuity of £100 (Appendix II, entries 35, 36, p. 205). If the artist had no immediate need of cash at the time the annuity was paid, he might well have used the money in this way. Yescombe acted as agent for the reletting of the artist's Lansdown house in 1767, but the £100 is too large a sum to be associated with this property. Edward Yescombe, a descendant of the attorney, has reasonably suggested this might have been a loan (by letter 14 May 2001).

5 Hayes 2001, no. 48, p. 82.

6 Sloman 1992, p. 44.

7 Hayes 2001, no. 80, p. 134.

8 Sloman 1992, p. 44.

9 Anon, 'A very extraordinary Journal', *The Town and Country Magazine, or, Universal Repository of Knowledge, Instruction and Entertainment* IV, September 1772, p. 485.

10 Fulcher 1856, p. 36 says that Gainsborough's rent in Ipswich was £6 a year, but a receipt dated April 1760, for rent due 'at Lady Last' is for a half-year payment of £5.10.0, Woodall 1963, no. 105, p. 179.

11 Harrison 1922a, p. 5.

12 It is also possible that this £70 was the repayment of a loan or some other form of monetary transaction: it has been noted that certain drapers were associated with banking (Clews 1994, p. 105).

13 Hanbury Pettingal father and son advertised regularly in the Bath press. The younger Hanbury Pettingal took over the business in 1785 and finally retired in 1790. An advertisement in *Boddely's Bath Journal* for 22 October 1759 shows the Pettingals in Pierrepont Street at that date, selling silks 'warranted of the newest fashion', together with 'Norwich Crapes and Bombazines' and a 'Great Variety of Bath Laces'. An advertisement in the *Bath Chronicle* for 4 April 1771 describes the location of the shop at that date as the 'second door' in Pierrepont Street. Black 1911, pp. 14–17 discusses the sites of the Linley's houses. They moved from Abbey Green (where they were in 1759) to Pierrepont Place some time in the early or mid-1760s. It is possible that Gainsborough's large payment to Pettingal was the repayment of a loan. In the absence of any dedicated bank in Bath at this date many retailers must have provided financial services.

14 RA, Humphry papers, HU/6/147, an undated letter to Mr Horton of Bath. The younger Hanbury and Winifred Pettingal had seven children baptised at St James's Church in Bath between 1770 and 1779 (BRO, St James's Parish Registers of Baptisms, Marriages and Burials, transcripts). Trevor Fawcett discusses the role of the Pumper in 'Custodians of the Pump', *Guidelines*, no. 58, June 1999, pp. 12–16. Mrs Winifred Pettingal was Pumper from 1807 to 1810. I am grateful to Trevor Fawcett for this information.

15 Sloman 1992, p. 23.

16 Anon. 1917, p. 317.

17 Sloman 1992, fig. 5, p. 27 and fig. 9, p. 24. Llanover 1861, III, p. 624, Mrs Delany to her sister Mrs Dewes, from Bath, 28 December 1760.

18 Sloman 1996b, p. 139.

19 Lewis and Smith 1937–83, x, p. 228.

20 Hayes 2001, no. 12, p. 23. As well as smoke, steam rose from the baths immediately behind the house, and the artist might have been referring to this in addition to the coal smoke that hung over the centre of the town.

21 Hayes 2001, no. 12, pp. 23–4.

22 Ibid.

23 R. W. M. Wright first identified Gainsborough's Bath country residence as Lansdown Lodge (R. W. M. Wright, 'Gainsborough's Residences in Bath: Proof of Evidence', 1960, lecture typescript, copy in Bath central Library, A 609080). The house was advertised in the *Bath Journal* on 16 March 1767 and the *Bath Chronicle*, 6 August 1767 until 17 September 1767. In the advertisement for the house in the *Bath Chronicle* the rent is given as thirty shillings a year. Gainsborough quoted a figure of £30 a year in his letter to Unwin, Hayes 2001 no. 12, p. 23. The discrepancy may be explained by differences in the type of lease on offer.

24 Tunstall 1847, p. 218, 'proceeding down the road [from Lansdown Grove] we come to Bellevue house, where Gainsborough resided'.

25 Wood 1749, II, p. 440.

26 *Boddely's Bath Journal*, 17 October 1763, 'The same Day [ie Friday last] died Mr. Gainsborough, an eminent Painter, of this City'. The following week, 24 October 1763, 'Mr. Gainsborough (an eminent Limner of this City) is not dead, as mention'd in our last'.

27 Sloman 1992, p. 29. Mrs Gibbon's activities were first charted by John Bensusan-Butt.

28 Christopher Anstey, *The New Bath Guide*, Cambridge 1766, p. 25.

29 Sloman 1992, n. 24, pp. 39–40.

30 Ibid.

31 For Miss Roach, see *Boddely's Bath Journal*, 5 January 1761; Elizabeth Broderip, *Boddely's Bath Journal*, 17 October 1763; Janetta Cooke, *Boddely's Bath Journal*, 6 November 1758; Mrs Parkes, *Boddely's Bath Journal*, 28 January 1760.

32 All advertised in *Boddely's Bath Journal*, Mrs Tucker, 24 December 1759; Thornton's, 5 February 1759; Francis Bennett, 5 February 1759; Marmaduke Webb, 19 January 1761; James Wall, 1 October 1759; Thomas Creaser, 25 October 1762; W. Rogers, 13 December 1762; W. Taylor, 4 October 1762; Mr Grandi, 21 February 1763. Gainsborough's payments to Francis Bennett are recorded in his Hoare's Bank account, Appendix II, entries 10, 18, 92, 118, pp. 204–7. The same account shows a payment to a Nicholas Tucker (Appendix II, entry 88, p. 206), perhaps an associate of Mrs Tucker of the China shop.

33 *Boddely's Bath Journal*, 29 October 1759.

34 Ibid., 4 January 1762.

35 Ibid., 3 January 1763.

36 Ibid., 17 October 1763.

37 Ibid., 22 April 1745; 5 April 1762. For an account of the different symbols traditionally used by particular tradesmen, see Sir Ambrose Heal, *Sign Boards of Old London Shops*, London 1988, pp. 8–10.

38 *Bath Journal*, 16 September 1754.

39 [Thicknesse] 1778, p. 49.

40 In Bristol in 1760 a Doctor Speakman advertised 'his Name in large Letters over the Door' according to his advertisement in *Boddely's Bath Journal*, 10 November 1760.

41 Herbert 1950, pp. 77, 79.

42 Hayes 2001 no. 77, pp. 130–31. A reference to 'Penny's Money' must be to Gainsborough's landlord. The name Penny appears in the margin next to Gainsborough's in BRO, Bath City Rates Books from 1766. R. W. M. Wright correctly identified Gainsborough's house as 17 Circus, 'Gainsborough's Residences in Bath', 1960, lecture typescript, BCL, A 609080. A Thomas Penny 'gent.' is mentioned in BRO, Bath City Council Minutes (transcripts), 1 April 1745, and a person of the same name subscribed to Thomas Thorpe's *Survey . . . of Bath*, of 1742, but Gainsborough's payments to a Hugh Penny on 22 January 1770, 7 April 1772 and 19 July 1773 are perhaps part-payments for rent (Appendix II, entries 73, 94, 105, pp. 206–7). A goldsmith by name of Penny died at Wells in 1789 (*Gentleman's Magazine*, LIX, part I, 1789, 6 June 1789 'At Wells, Mr. Penny, an eminent goldsmith').

43 Mitchell and Penrose 1983, p. 67, 'No House in the Circus, less than £100 per ann.'.

44 Sloman 1992, p. 38, n. 5; Hayes 2001, no. 12, pp. 23–5. Gainsborough's Lansdown Road house was advertised in the *Bath Journal*,

16 March 1767, 'For particulars, enquire of Mr. Gainsborough, in the Circus', and the *Bath Chronicle*, 6 August 1767.

45 Sloman 1992, p. 23.

46 Sloman 1996b, p. 147 and p. 152, n. 48.

47 Neale 1981, p. 221.

48 J. Timbs, *Anecdote Biography*, London 1860, p. 232. The Lawrences were at 2 Alfred Street. Editions of the *New Bath Guide* published between 1784 and 1788 include, under regularly printed lists of artists resident in Bath, 'Laurence [sic], portrait-painter in crayons' at Alfred Street.

49 Sloman 1996b, p. 147 and p. 152, n. 45.

50 BRO, City Rate Book commencing 24 June 1772 has a Michael Hickey in Abbey Churchyard. [Thicknesse] 1778, p. 49 says the painter Thomas Hickey was near the Pump Room (which would probably mean Abbey Churchyard). The Mr Hickey at Bellmont noted by George Breeze, 'Thomas Hickey's Stay in Bath', *Somerset Archaeological and Natural History Society*, CXXVIII, 1984, pp. 83–4, may be a different person. A Benjamin Hickey was a well-known bookseller in Bristol, see *Bath Journal*, 4 March 1744/45 and 21 November 1748. Thomas Malton advertised in the *Bath Chronicle*, 18 February 1779.

51 Sloman 1996b, pp. 137–9 and p. 151, n. 22.

52 WRO, Lucy papers, L6/1462, George Lucy to Phillipa Hayes, 5 April 1761. The water-colour painter Michael Angelo Rooker exhibited a *View of the Court of Claims, or Painted Chamber* at the 1767 Society of Artists exhibition.

53 The pediment stones were preserved when the house was demolished in 1892 but lay forgotten, thought to be part of the Melfort Cross from the Cross Bath, until 1992 when they were identified by the present writer, Sloman 1992, p. 32.

54 BL, Kingston estate papers, Egerton Charter 6060 dated 30 May 1760, a lease agreement between Evelyn, Duke of Kingston and Thomas Gainsborough, 'Portrait Painter'.

55 BL, Kingston estate papers, Egerton MS 3657, p. 67. Arthur Trimmell was paid this sum for 'papering Rooms etc' when Mrs Gibbon left the house in 1776.

56 Sloman 1996b, p. 139 and p. 151, n. 26.

57 Hayes 2001 no. 12, pp. 23–4.

58 Walkley 1994, p. 10.

59 Sloman 1992, p. 23; p. 38, n. 8. Distances in Bath guidebooks were given from the Pump Room, considered the focal point of the town. In 1760 Gainsborough's house was the newest property of any substance close to the Pump Room.

60 George Romney took over Francis Cotes's house, see Walkley 1994, p. 23. Walkley also cites other examples.

61 George Roth (*fl.* 1768–86) is listed in Abbey Churchyard in 1785 and 1786 editions of the *New Bath Guide*; Charles Gill (*fl.* 1769–1828), a former pupil of Reynolds, and son of the pastry-shop owner Gill, is noted in the Circus in the 1782, 1783 and 1784 editions of the same *Guide*.

62 John Hayes, *Gainsborough: Paintings and Drawings*, London 1975, p. 23; Hayes 1980, p. 33.

63 Sloman 1992, p. 40, n. 30.

64 Nigel Surry, 'James Northcote at Portsmouth', *Burlington Magazine*, CXXXVI, no. 1093, April 1994, p. 235, n. 7.

65 A print of 1816 shows matching windows (and no Venetian window) on the north side of Gainsborough's house, James Lees-Milne and David Ford, *Images of Bath*, Richmond-upon-Thames 1982, fig. 83 (no page numbers in plates section). The north façade of the house may have been rationalised during Abbey Church Yard improvements of 1810. At this date alterations were made to all the north-facing shops between Gainsborough's house and the Pump Room.

66 BL, Egerton MS 3648.

67 Walkley 1994, p. 8.

68 Walkley 1994, fig. 23, p. 30.

69 RA, Humphry papers HU/1/20–40. The passage on Gainsborough commences on an unnumbered sheet between fols. 36 and 37.

70 [Lloyd] 1994, p. 50.

71 Olivier Meslay, Arlette Serullaz, Barthelemy Jobert (eds.), *D'outre-Manche, l'Art Britannique dans les Collections Publiques Françaises*, (exh. cat., Louvre), Paris 1994, no. 16, pp. 50–51; Waterhouse 1966, no. 13, p. 51; Hayes 1981, no. 25, pp. 108–9. Waterhouse dated Lady Alston's portrait to the mid-1760s and Hayes to the early 1760s. An earlier date seems more likely, but it is rather surprising that Humphry does not mention this picture.

72 RA, Humphry papers HU/1/33, fol. 33 verso, indicates that the MS was written in 1803. HU/1/37, unnumbered fol. between 37 and 38, states that Humphry left Bath on 5 August 1764.

73 Waterhouse 1966, no. 556, p. 85; no. 108, p. 57; no. 513, p. 63.

74 Whitley 1915, p. 96.

75 Hayes 2001, no. 63, p. 108.

76 Sloman 1994, p. 52.

77 [William Jackson], *Thirty Letters on Various Subjects*, 2 vols, London 1783 (published anonymously) II, pp. 32–40, letter XXI, 'A False Principle in Painting Exposed'.

78 Ibid., p. 39.

79 Waterhouse 1966, no. 577, p. 87; no. 606, p. 89; no. 506, p. 82; no. 697, p. 94.

80 Beechey 1988, p. 24.

81 Waterhouse 1966, no. 19, p. 52.

82 Beechey 1988, p. 22.

83 Anon., obituary, *Gentleman's Magazine*, LVIII, part 2, August 1788, p. 754.

84 Whitley 1915, p. 109.

85 Two drawings for the portrait of Ann Ford are known: Hayes 1970, I, no 16, p. 114 and a drawing sold at Christie's, London, 8 November 1994 (lot 13), not catalogued by Hayes. Another portrait study drawing of this period is that for *Carl Friedrich Abel* (Hayes 1970, I, no. 27, p. 117).

86 Waterhouse 1966, no. 386, p. 75; no. 82, p. 56.

87 Penny 1986, p. 15; Alastair Smart, *Allan Ramsay, 1713–1784* (exh. cat., Scottish National Portrait Gallery), Edinburgh 1992, pp. 11–12.

88 Anon., obituary, *Gentleman's Magazine*, LVIII, part 2, August 1783, p. 754.

89 Wark 1958, p. 332.

90 Appendix III, p. 213.

91 Sloman 1994, pp. 46, 49–50.

92 Waterhouse 1966, no. 482, p. 81.

93 RA, Humphry papers, HU/1/20–40; Waterhouse 1966, p. 24.

94 Tancred Borenius, *A Catalogue of the Pictures at Corsham Court*, London 1939, no. 178, p. 106; no. 184, p. 109; no. 213 p. 122; no. 214, p. 123. It appears that Gainsborough was originally asked to paint Mrs Matilda Methuen as well as her husband Paul Cobb Methuen. The artist's cut-down portrait of her is now in the collection of the National Gallery of Art, Washington, see John Hayes, *British Paintings of the Sixteenth through Nineteenth Centuries: The Collections of the National Gallery of Art Systemic Catalogue*, Cambridge 1992, pp. 87–90. The couple were married on 20 April 1776.

95 W&SRO, Methuen papers, 'Paul Methuen's Daybook', MS 1742/8113.

96 Pippa Mason of Hazlitt, Gooden and Fox in a contribution to a symposium 'Picture Framing in Britain and the Framing of British Pictures' at the National Portrait Gallery, London, 1 February 1997, pointed out that Thomas Allwood was Romney's framer and was probably introduced to Paul Methuen by Romney. She also referred to the fact that Sir Paul Methuen's pictures were put in frames of his choice, and pictures which were not strictly pairs were put in matching frames

97 A receipt dated 17 February 1773 now in the GH collection, accession no. 1990.042, is for a half-payment for three portraits of the Miss Harleys (Hayes 2001, no. 143, p. 192). Malcolm Cormack refers to a payment to Gainsborough of £32.10.0 in July 1763 by Lord Howe, and suggests that

this may have been a part-payment for one of the full-lengths of Richard, First Earl Howe and Mary, Countess Howe (Malcolm Cormack, *The Paintings of Thomas Gainsborough*, Cambridge 1991, no. 27, p. 84). If this figure, which is half of sixty guineas, is a half-payment for a full-length, it is an important indicator that the artist charged sixty guineas as early as 1763. See Appendix II, entry 16, p. 204.

98 Waterhouse 1966, p. 19 believed he raised his price to 100 guineas some time between 1770 and 1772.

99 Appendix II, entry 87, p. 206.

100 Waterhouse 1966, no. 237, p. 66.

101 STRO, Royal Infirmary Account Book, MS D685/1/1, for the account between John Stephenson and the Trustees of the Stafford Royal Infirmary. The subscription list is in the front of the volume. There are no further references to the portrait. Jean Guiffrey, 'The Portrait of John Eld by Gainsborough', *Museum of Fine Arts Bulletin*, [Boston], X, no. 59, October 1912, p. 34, gives the date as 1772, as does Waterhouse 1966, no. 237, p. 66.

102 The second page of the subscription list, not illustrated here, shows that a total amount of £101.17.0 was given to Eld on 9 January 1776. The Hospital Treasurer's account shows that Eld submitted two receipts from Gainsborough for £52.10.0 on 16 February and 25 March 1775 (STRO, D685/ 7/1, f. 1–2). I am most grateful to Hugh Belsey for transcribing this information for me.

103 Appendix III, p. 213; Newby 1990, no. 20a, p. 41.

104 Anon., *Catalogue of Paintings at Guildhall, The Assembly Rooms and Pump Room, Bath*, Bath 1985, p. 7.

105 Ibid.

106 Newby 1990, no. 34, p. 50, n. 3. Henry Hoare of Stourhead paid William Hoare this figure for '4 boys after Rubens'. The same patron paid Gainsborough £84 for his landscape *Peasants going to Market* in 1773 (Hayes 1995, p. 15, n. 1).

107 Smart 1999, p. 419; Penny 1986, p. 58; Ellis Waterhouse, *Reynolds*, London 1941, p. 13.

108 Penny 1986, p. 58; Smart 1999, p. 419.

109 Sloman 1997, p. 327, n. 20.

110 Ibid., p. 327.

111 Hayes 2001, no. 130, p. 185.

112 Whitley 1915, p. 67.

113 Hayes 2001, no. 34, p. 57.

114 Whitley 1928, II, p. 246. Three Gossets were active in London: James, a wax-modeller and framer of Berwick Street, Soho, and Isaac and Gideon who were in the same business in Poland Street. Gideon made frames for Hogarth, Hoare and Gainsborough (Lippincott 1983, pp. 180–81, n. 16; Newby 1990, no. 20a, p. 41).

115 Hayes 2001, no. 6, p. 13; Appendix II, entry 5, p. 204. Another payment to Isaac Gosset of £39.4.0 occurs on 13 September 1763 (Appendix II, entry 19, p. 205).

116 Sir Charles-Kemeys Tynte's account with Hoare's Bank shows him paying Gainsborough £33.12.0 on 2 April 1761 (C. Hoare & Co, Ledger 64/222) and Isaac Gosset £12.0.0 on 10 June 1761 (Ledger 65/47). Tynte also paid Isaac Gosset £14.14.0 on 3 May 1762 (Ledger 65/48).

117 Whitley 1915, p. 309.

118 All three advertised in *Boddely's Bath Journal*, Frime and Joy, 23 January 1764; Thomas Smith, 27 April 1761 and Charles Davis, 30 April 1764.

119 Hayes 2001, no. 29, p. 50.

120 James Paty advertised as a carver and gilder of frames in the *Bath Chronicle*, 11 October 1770. Gunnis [n.d.], pp. 294–5 describes the activities of several members of the Paty family.

121 Eileen Harris, 'Architect of Rococo Landscapes, Thomas Wright, III', *Country Life*, CL, no. 3874, 9 September 1971, pp. 612–15.

122 Appendix II, entry 81, p. 206.

123 Information about King is given in Gunnis [n.d.], p. 229. King or one of his sons also supplied the monuments to Poole Bathurst in Lydney, Gloucestershire in 1792 and Thomas Linley in Wells Cathedral in 1795.

124 Gunnis gives the date of the Debden memorial to Peter Muilman as 1785, but Peter Muilman of Kirby Hall, Essex was born in 1706 (in Amsterdam) and died in 1790. I am grateful to David Tyler for identifying the two Peter Muilmans. Thomas King also carved a memorial to Richard Chiswell in Debden in 1772: he was perhaps the Richard Chiswell of Debden Hall whose sister Mary married the elder Peter Muilman in 1733.

125 Appendix II, entry 82, p. 206.

126 Hayes 2001, no. 49, p. 83.

127 Whitley 1915, p. 213.

128 Hayes 2001, no. 7, p. 14.

129 Thicknesse 1788, p. 19; Hayes 2001, no. 98, pp. 160–61.

130 STRO, D685/2/3, Staffordshire General Infirmary Minutes, Weekly Board, Friday 24 November 1775, 'Ordered that Joseph Smith ye joyner be desired to work up the Case which came with Mr Elds Picture into Partitions for the Beds in the Uper Wards . . . And also that he do make a Cratch in the Kitchen for the purpose of drying Cloths on'. I am most grateful to Hugh Belsey for this reference. It is not clear who made the crates for Gainsborough's pictures.

131 John Wiltshire, Walter's brother, commissioned a bookplate from Thomas Ross in 1740, illustrated in Chapter 9 above, fig. 163. Ross, Skinner and Wiltshire were members of the same Freemasons' Lodge, [Anon] 1917, pp. 298–9.

132 BRO, Bath City Council Minutes (transcripts), 7 July 1746; Neale 1981, p. 257.

133 Whitley 1915, p. 40.

134 BRO, Bath City Council Minutes (transcripts), 27 June 1743, 28 June 1762.

135 BRO, Bath City Rate Book commencing 24 June 1766. This was most probably Walter Wiltshire since his elder brother John had died by this date.

136 C. Hoare & Co, entries for Walter Wiltshire's account, Ledger 81/434, 10 July 1770 (£100 to Sir William St Quintin); Ledger 81/435, 17 July 1770 (£200 to Sir William St Quintin); Ledger 81/435, 27 July 1770 (£100 to Sir William St Quintin).

137 C. Hoare & Co, Walter Wiltshire's account, Ledger 83/264, 18 June 1771 (£100 to Dr Rice Charleton); Ledger 83/270, 27 November 1771 (£600 to Dr Rice Charleton), Ledger 83/264, 9 July 1771 (£100 to Philip Ditcher); Ledger 70/316, 30 November 1764 (£500 to Edward Parker). These are samples only: other payments to each of these men are noted elsewhere.

138 C. Hoare & Co, Ledger 70/312–70/321.

139 Anon, *New Bath Guide*, Bath 1766, p. 36. As well as balls and musical entertainments, the Rooms hosted lectures such as 'A New and Compleat Course of Experimental Philosophy. By Benj. Martin. The Subscription One Guinea. To begin at Eleven in the Morning' (*Bath Journal*, 23 September 1745).

140 Trevor Fawcett, *Bath Entertain'd*, Bath 1998, p. 10.

141 *Bath Journal*, 27 January 1745/46.

142 One payment of £20 to Walter Wiltshire is recorded in the artist's Hoare's Bank account, Appendix II, entry 101, p. 206.

143 Woodall 1963, plate 13, opposite p. 89. The apprenticeship indenture is now in the GH collection.

144 The three versions and their provenance have been identified by Hugh Belsey. I am most grateful to him for showing me his preliminary catalogue notes on these. A summary, compiled by Belsey, appears in the notes in Christie's (London) sale catalogue of 1 December 2000, when one set was sold (lot 32).

145 Hugh Belsey has shown that Gainsborough probably used Hoare's portrait at Berkley House. This picture is illustrated in Giles Worsley 'Berkley House, Somerset, the House of Mr. Michael Philips', *Country Life*, CLXXXII, 19 May 1988, fig. 6, p. 170.

146 Appendix III. See also Chapter 6, p. 113. I am most grateful to Elizabeth Einberg

who drew my attention to the Tynte payment to Gainsborough.

147 Sloman 1997, p. 326.
148 Hayes 2001, no. 62, p. 105.
149 Ibid., no. 51, p. 85.
150 Waterhouse 1966, no. 54, p. 54.
151 Woodall 1963, no. 6, p. 35.
152 Waterhouse 1966, no. 54, p. 54.
153 Woodall 1963, no. 6, p. 35.
154 Sloman 1997, p. 327.
155 Whitley 1915, p. 72.
156 *Boddely's Bath Journal*, 14 November 1763.
157 W&SRO, 'Paul Methuen's Daybook', MS 1742/8113.
158 Ibid.; Hayes 2001, no. 44, pp. 74–5.
159 Whitley 1915, p. 71.
160 *Boddely's Bath Journal*, 20 October 1760, 'Francis Woolley, Painter, at St Luke's Head, in North-gate-street, near the Market-Place, Bath' advertised house painting at five pence a yard as well the sale of materials, prints and paintings. Whitley 1915, pp. 92–3 mentions Francis Woolley, Charles Davis and Joseph Granger, all suppliers of painting materials in Bath.
161 The Bath painter and writer William Williams warns of the dangers of using improperly prepared materials, William Williams, *Essay on the Mechanics of Oil Colours*, Bath 1787, p. 24.
162 BM, Department of Prints and Drawings, Heal Collection of Trade Cards, 89.137. Notes by Ambrose Heal accompanying the card indicate that this firm's records were destroyed during World War II. The firm became Brodie and Middleton in the 1840s. A portrait *John Middleton and his Family* is in the collection of the Museum of London; it is illustrated in Kit Wedd, Lucy Peltz and Cathy Ross, *Creative Quarters: The Art World in London 1700–2000*, London 2001, pl. 39, p. 47.
163 Appendix II, entries 6, 60, 124, pp. 204, 205, 207.
164 *Bath Chronicle*, 16 November 1786, 'The lovers of art will be sorry to hear, that Middleton, the pencil maker who first brought that valuable and useful little article into esteem . . . [is] reduced to great distress . . .'. It is not entirely clear what these 'little articles' were. The term pencil commonly applied to artists' brushes in the eighteenth century, but Middleton may have been an early supplier of graphite pencils. Whitley 1928, I, pp. 334–5 points out that Taylor and Norrie of Edinburgh may have been agents for one or more London colourmen: it seems quite likely that the major London colourmen would have supplied the Bath market through a local retailer.
165 Whitley 1928, I, pp. 333–4. Whitley states that John Middleton sold black lead pencils at sixpence each and camel hair brushes at a penny. James Ayres also points out that Middleton discussed the preparation of colours for use in watercolour drawings with Paul Sandby, one of the first great exponents of watercolour in England, and an artist known to and admired by Gainsborough, see James Ayres, *The Artist's Craft*, London 1985, pp. 108 and 130.
166 Whitley 1928, II, p. 362 and Whitley 1915, p. 248. Whitley's assertion that Gainsborough may have used Scott comes from Walter Thornbury, Turner's biographer, whose information came from the Revd Kirby Trimmer. Trimmer reported that Gainsborough had, in his later years, obtained cremona white from Scott in the Strand (Walter Thornbury, *The Life of J. M. W. Turner, R.A.*, 2 vols, London 1862, II, p. 64). Gainsborough's receipt for the picture that he bought from Thompson Scott in 1759 is referred to in Chapter 3, p. 47.
167 Appendix II, entry 48, p. 205.
168 *Bath Chronicle*, 7 January 1813. The notice says that Townsend was 'known among his large circle of friends by the appellation "Beau Townsend"'. A 'Mr Townsend' was among the Bath subscribers to Abel's *Six Sonatas for the Harpsichord*, see Chapter 6, p. 101.
169 Hayes 2001, no. 64, p. 110.
170 John Gage, 'A Romantic Colourman: George Field and British Art', *Walpole Society*, LXIII, 2001, pp. 5–6 discusses the early nineteenth-century production of artists' colours in Conham, Bristol, but these were apparently not manufactured locally at an earlier date.
171 Thicknesse 1788, p. 45.
172 Appendix II, entries 125, 129, 132, p. 207.
173 Appendix II, entries 136, 138, 140, 144, 147, 160, 166, 167, pp. 207–8.
174 Penny 1986, p. 180.
175 Hayes 1982, I, p. 188; Appendix II, entry 137, p. 207. Reynolds is said to have paid Toms fifteen guineas for a full-length portrait, see Richard Wendorf, *Sir Joshua Reynolds: The Painter in Society*, Harvard and London 1996, p. 60. It is tempting to suggest that the two payments of £50 to an unidentified S. Cooper in 1781 and 1782 (Appendix II, entries 161 and 163, p. 208) may also have been for studio assistance. No artist by the name of S. Cooper fits the bill, but a Richard Cooper was a successful landscape painter in Edinburgh and London in the 1780s and 1790s. He was a one-time pupil of Robert Edge Pine.
176 Whitley 1915, p. 82. Clutterbuck was the brother-in-law of one of Gainsborough's landscape patrons, John Jacob, see Chapter 9, p. 178.

5 *Show Pictures and Exhibitions*

For the chapter-title quotation see Hayes 2001, no. 49, p. 83, Gainsborough to Edward Stratford, 21 March 1771.

1 Thicknesse 1788, p. 19.
2 Hayes 2001, no. 62, p. 105.
3 Lindsay 1982, p. 57.
4 Hayes 2001, no. 62, p. 105.
5 Sloman 1994, pp. 53–4.
6 Sloman 1996b, p. 137.
7 Quoted in Clifford 1978, p. 31.
8 Ibid., p. 41.
9 Llanover 1861, III, p. 605.
10 Catherine MacLeod and Julia Marciari Alexander, *Painted Ladies: Women at the Court of Charles II* (exh. cat., National Portrait Gallery and Yale Center for British Art), London and New Haven 2001, no. 33, pp. 118–20. Lely's portrait was painted c. 1662 and was at Knole, Kent by 1706, where it has remained. Gainsborough could easily have seen one of the many studio copies. *Ann Ford* was originally conceived with a landscape in the background, as in Lely's portrait. Barbara Villiers (1641–1709) was the daughter of William Villiers, Second Viscount Grandison, and ancestor of William, Third Earl of Jersey.
11 Hayes 1982, I, pp. 114–15.
12 Horace Walpole, *The Letters of Horace Walpole*, ed. Lord Dover, 6 vols, 1846, VI, additional note, pp. 2–3. This information was communicated to Lord Dover by the sitter's grandson. I am most grateful to Hugh Belsey for telling me about this reference to the Johnston portrait. The picture is generally dated to 1763–4, but an earlier date, when Gainsborough was especially eager to make his mark on Bath society, seems possible.
13 Ibid., pp. 2–3. The Johnstons were close to Field Marshal Conway who employed Gainsborough's brother Humphrey on various engineering projects in Henley-on-Thames.
14 Wark 1958, p. 333.
15 Quoted by Robert R. Wark, *Gainsborough's The Blue Boy*, San Marino 1963, p. 6. Wark's clear account of the early history of the picture is restated with some additions, in Wark 1971, pp. 29–41.
16 Edwards 1808, p. 140.
17 Jonathan Spilsbury's mezzotint of Reynolds's portrait of *Giuseppe Marchi* was included in the London Museum's exhibition *Creative Quarters: The Art World in London 1700–2000* from 30 March–15 July 2001. A book rather than a catalogue accompanied this exhibition, but the label text for this exhibit read 'During Reynolds' lifetime, the oil

portrait of Marchi hung in Reynolds' Leicester Square studio where it was called *The Turkish Boy* and used to advertise the artist's skills'.

18 Penny 1986, no. 18, p. 180.

19 Chaloner Smith 1883, III, no. 31, p. 1333.

20 Ibid., III, no. 35, p. 1334. The *Monks* is listed by Chaloner Smith (p. 1335) but not catalogued. The painting was seen at Gainsborough's house at the Circus by Dorothy Richardson in 1770 (Hugh Belsey, 'A visit to the Studios of Gainsborough and Hoare', *Burlington Magazine*, CXXIX, no. 1007, February 1987, p. 108). Spilsbury seems to have been a regular visitor to Bath. In 1766 he made a mezzotint of William Hoare's *Charles, Lord Camden* (Chaloner Smith 1883, III, no. 8, p. 1326). In 1765 he subscribed to a locally published collection of poems written by a Bath carpenter: William Brimble, *Poems, Attempted on various Occasions, by William Brimble, of Twerton, near Bath, Carpenter*, Bath 1765. I am very grateful to Piers Davies who told me about this obscure publication and Spilsbury's subscription to it.

21 Quoted by Wark 1971, p. 39.

22 *Boddely's Bath Journal*, 16 April 1764; *Bath Chronicle*, 3 February 1774; *Bath Chronicle*, 30 June 1774. The 3 February 1774 entry for 'Mr. and Mrs. Buttalls' may just possibly mean two couples by name of Buttall arriving together.

23 Hayes 1970, nos 73–6, p. 132. Boydell acquired *The Gipsies* after the printmaker Joseph Wood died in 1763.

24 DRO, Glyndwr MSS DD/G/1604. For the death date of the elder Jonathan Buttall I am indebted to David Tyler who found that he died on 8 October 1768 and was buried at St Anne's, Soho.

25 There appear to have been two James Buttalls as well as two Jonathans. A James Buttall who, as David Tyler found, married Hannah Slade on 14 June 1768 cannot be the James Buttall (1718/19–1793) who was married to an Elizabeth Pain (DRO, Glyndwr MSS DCC/G/1604).

26 David Tyler has found that it was a 'Mr Buttall' who was reported at the artist's funeral, not Jonathan Buttall as in Whitley 1915, p. 309. Those present were listed in the *General Evening Post*, 12 August 1788.

27 Andrew Wilton, *The Swagger Portrait* (exh. cat., Tate Gallery), London 1992, p. 11.

28 [Thicknesse] 1778, p. 37.

29 In tracing the response to Gainsborough's exhibits in London I have been greatly aided by the compilation of press cuttings relating to London public exhibitions from the London newspapers at the Paul Mellon Centre, London. I am grateful to Emma Lauze and Emma Floyd for access to this material. The source will be subsequently referred to as 'PMC cuttings'.

30 *London Chronicle*, 6–8 May 1760 (PMC cuttings).

31 Waterhouse 1966, no. 523, p. 83.

32 *Public Advertiser*, 17 April 1761 (PMC cuttings).

33 Sidney C. Hutchison, *The History of the Royal Academy 1768–1968*, London 1968, p. 53. Hoare was not strictly a foundation member of the Academy as was Gainsborough. His name, together with that of Zoffany, was added to the original list towards the end of 1769 at the request of George III. See Appendix IV, pp. 214–15 for Gainsborough's exhibits.

34 Seaton exhibited three portraits from Bath at the Society of Artists exhibition in 1766, nos 150, 151, 152 and one (no. 138) in 1767 (Graves 1907, p. 229). Anon 1766, commenting on no. 151, says, 'In this picture the right arm is too short the sattin is green, the execution tame, and the whole is void of taste'.

35 Smith's model of the Duke of Newcastle in coloured wax was no. 214 in the 1766 exhibition; he also showed two other portraits, a gentleman (no. 216) and a lady (no. 217) and a model of a young lady 'for a ring' (no. 215) (Graves 1907, p. 239). Anon 1766, says of no. 214, 'The action is stiff, but the whole neatly finished'. The Miss Smith who exhibited paintings of an auricula and butterflies in 1766 (nos 300, 301) may not be the same person as the Miss Sophia Smith who exhibited miniature portraits in 1767 (nos 147, 148), but both Miss Smiths are listed as of Bath (Graves 1907, p. 241).

36 Simon Pine exhibited a miniature of a lady in 1768 (no. 127) and two of ladies (nos 98, 99) in 1770 (Graves 1907, p. 200). Thomas Redmond showed two miniatures (nos 143, 144) in 1769 (the second being a portrait of Bath's Master of Ceremonies Samuel Derrick) and two (nos 107, 108) in 1770 (ibid., p. 210). Redmond produced miniatures of Gainsborough's landlord the Duke of Kingston, after the Duke's death: a payment 'To Mr Thomas Redmond of Bath for 6 copies of the late Duke of Kingston's Picture in miniature per her Grace's order £25.4.0' is recorded in BL, Egerton MS 3657, under the heading Miscellaneous Payments, not dated. Jones showed 'A Fruit piece' (no. 71) and 'A bunch of grapes' (no. 72) (Graves 1907, p. 133).

37 *Public Advertiser*, 12 May 1766 (PMC cuttings).

38 At the Free Society exhibition of 1764, no. 50, 'Mr Ford, at Bath. A busto of young Mr Worlidge, in white marble' (Graves 1907, p. 94). Thomas Worlidge the painter made an etched portrait of Ford (Dack 1907, no. 76, p. 24).

39 At the Free Society exhibition of 1768, no. 100, by Garvey at Bath, 'A study from Purcefield [ie Persfield or Piercefield, Chepstow], the seat of Val. Morris, Esq.' (Graves 1907, p. 100).

40 Brenneman 1995. I am most grateful to David Brenneman for allowing me to read and quote from this unpublished thesis.

41 Anon, *Critical Review of the Pictures, Sculptures, Designs in Architecture, Drawings, Prints etc Exhibited at the Great-Room in Spring Gardens, Charing Cross*, London 1765, says in full of Honywood (no. 33 in the exhibition), 'It may be reproach'd to the author, that the intire piece wants great correction, the whole being too heavy, and the performance too large; the landscape is very agreeable'.

42 Horace Walpole, 'Notes by Horace Walpole, First Earl of Orford, on the Exhibitions of the Society of Artists and Free Society of Artists', *Walpole Society*, XXVII, 1939, p. 66. Fulcher 1856, p. 65 says George III 'wished to become the possessor' of the Honywood portrait.

43 Anon, *Critical Review of the Pictures, Sculptures, Designs in Architecture, Drawings, Prints etc Exhibited at the Great-Room in Spring Gardens, Charing Cross*, London 1767, of the portrait of the Duke of Argyll, no. 59 in the Society of Artists exhibition. In the same exhibition, no. 61, 'A Landscape and Figures. The trees are hard, and the sky too blue'. This has been identified as the *Harvest Waggon*, see Spencer-Longhurst 1995, p. 10.

44 *Middlesex Journal*, 23–26 April 1772 (PMC cuttings).

45 Hayes 2001, no. 58, p. 99.

46 Philip Thicknesse, *Sketches and Characters of the most Eminent and most Singular Pesons now Living*, Bristol 1770, pp. 124, 132.

47 Rice Charleton (1710–1789) was Physician to the General Hospital from 1757 to 1781. Physicians 'regarded themselves as the intelligentsia of the profession, distinguished themselves by having a university degree and were allowed to call themselves *Doctor*' (Rolls 1988, p. 151).

48 T. Underwood, 'An Epistle, To a Friend in Town, sent from Bath', *Satyric Poems, Epigrams, Poetic Epistles, etc*, Bath 1768, p. 223. The end of the extract quoted is marked by an asterisk which refers to a footnote, 'Intended for the Spring-Garden Exhibition'. In the same publication, pp. 80–82, is 'A Poetic Epistle, Addressed to Mr. Gainsborough, Painter,

at Bath; in which the Author reminds him of his Promise made last April, to present him with a whole length Picture'. This latter poem was clearly written *after* the former, but is confusingly printed first in the book.

49 Whitley 1915, pp. 51–5.

50 Christopher Lennox-Boyd, Guy Shaw, Sarah Halliwell, *Theatre: The Age of Garrick* (exh. cat., Courtauld Institute Galleries), London 1994, no. 30, p. 71.

51 Hayes 2001, no. 13, pp. 25–8.

52 John Hayes, *British Paintings of the Sixteenth through Nineteenth Centuries, in the Collection of the National Gallery of Art, Systematic Catalogue*, Washington 1992, p. 86. [Lloyd] 1994, no. 12, p. 42, says the portrait of Fischer was 'in all likelihood painted either in Bath or London in 1774'; Thicknesse 1788, pp. 36–7 says 'Mr. Fischer' was one of the portraits 'finished *before* he left Bath'.

53 See, for example, *Boddely's Bath Journal*, 16 October 1758, 'Mrs. Byam'; *Boddely's Bath Journal*, 19 April 1762, 'Mr. Byam'; *Boddely's Bath Journal*, 7 May 1764, 'Mr. and Mrs. Byham'; *Bath Chronicle*, 31 July 1766, 'Mr. and Mrs. Byam'; *Bath Chronicle*, 6 November 1766, 'Mr. and Mrs. Byam'; *Bath Chronicle*, 15 October 1767, 'Mr. and Mrs. Byam'; *Bath and Bristol Chronicle*, 14 December 1769, 'Mr. and Mrs. Byam and family'; *Bath and Bristol Chronicle*, 5 April 1770, 'Mr. and Mrs. Byam'.

54 Waterhouse 1966, p. 21.

55 Belsey 2001, pp. 19–21.

56 Mitchell and Penrose 1983, pp. 40, 41.

57 Ibid., pp. 24–5, 30.

58 Waterhouse 1966, no. 192, p. 63. Waterhouse simply calls the Dehany portrait 'Bath period'. In the sale catalogue Sotheby's, London, 16 November 1988 (lot 59) little Mary Dehany's birth was given as June 1759. The picture was subsequently exhibited by Leger Galleries, Old Bond Street, London in 1989. A Mr and/or Mrs Dehany's and Miss Dehany's arrival in Bath is listed in *Boddely's Bath Journal* for 18 May 1761, 28 December 1761, 19 April 1762, 12 July 1762, 31 January 1763 and 11 March 1765. A Mr and Mrs Dehany's arrival at Bristol Hotwells is also announced in the same newspaper for 23 May 1763.

59 Anon 1766, no. 52, p. 6 reads in full, 'A lady and gentleman ditto [ie whole length] There is so much confusion in this picture, owing to the ill distribution of light and shadow, that I think it does the artist no credit'. Hugh Belsey has independently reached the same conclusion that the double portrait exhibited in 1766 is most likely to be the Neave picture (verbal discussion, 1995).

60 I am most grateful to the staff of the Government Art Collection for permission to study the Neave portrait while it was on loan to 11 Downing Street.

61 The Neave portrait appears to have influenced Francis Cotes's *Mr and Mrs Thomas Crawthorne* of 1767 which has been remarked on for its 'noticeable exploitation of highlights . . .' (Edward Mead Johnson, *Francis Cotes*, Oxford 1976, no. 216, p. 85 and fig. 89). A further double portrait apparently influenced by the Neave painting is George James's *Revd Martin Madan and C. R. de Coetlogon*, of 1774 (photograph, Witt Library, Courtauld Institute of Art, London). James became a Bath resident in 1780. Zoffany used a pose related to that of Gainsborough's Richard Neave in his small full-length of *Lady Elizabeth Noel* (Sotheby's, London, 10 November 1993, lot 53).

62 Whitley 1915, p. 43 says Gainsborough's exhibit of that year was a portrait of Joshua Kirby.

63 Hayes 2001, no. 13, pp. 25–8. In a letter to Unwin of July 1770 Gainsborough discribes George Pitt as 'a staunch Friend' (Hayes 2001, no. 46, p. 78).

64 Hayes 1998, no. 13, p. 88.

65 Waterhouse 1966, p. 21.

66 Hayes 2001, no. 56, p. 94.

67 Ibid., no. 65, p. 112.

68 Ibid., no. 65, p. 113.

69 Reynolds 1959, pp. 257–8. Brenneman 1995, pp. 195–7 believes this passage in Reynolds's *Fourteenth Discourse* to be double-edged in meaning. Michael Rosenthal, '*In my view* . . . Titian's reputation: The Limitations of History', *Apollo*, CXXXIX, no. 382, December 1993, pp. 397–8, points out that Reynolds's account of Gainsborough's technique is based on Vasari's description of Titian's late style.

70 Penny 1986, no. 19, pp. 181–2; no. 59, pp. 226–7.

71 Waterhouse 1966, no. 387, p. 75.

72 Hayes 1998, no. 55, p. 172.

73 Wark 1971, p. 106.

74 Michael Kitson, 'Gainsborough Observed', *Apollo*, CXII, no. 225, November 1980, p. 351.

75 The Seeman *Self-portrait* was engraved in mezzotint by John Faber the Younger, published in 1727 (Chaloner Smith 1883, I, no. 321, p. 422) as well as the line engraving by Thomas Chambars illustrated (fig. 67).

76 The comment occurs in the anonymous obituary in the *Morning Chronicle* of 8 August 1788 and is repeated in the *Gentleman's Magazine*, LVIII, part 2, August 1788, p. 754. Brenneman 1995, pp. 31–53 points out that the use of Van Dyckian models for portraiture was nothing unusual, with Reynolds and Ramsay regularly doing the same. What was unusual was a *technique* that approached Van Dyck.

77 *Gentleman's Magazine*, XLIII, 1773, p. 614. For the full poem see below, Chapter 8, p. 161.

78 *London Evening Post*, 22–4 April 1762 (PMC cuttings).

79 Brenneman 1995, pp. 54–84.

80 Deborah Cherry and Jennifer Harris, 'Eighteenth-Century Portraiture and the Seventeenth-Century Past: Gainsborough and Van Dyck', *Art History*, V, no. 3, September 1982, pp. 287–309, shows how Gainsborough adapted Van Dyck to his own ends. Ellis Waterhouse, 'Gainsborough in Park Lane, Exhibition at Sir Philip Sassoon's', *Connoisseur*, XCVII, March 1936, p. 128, observed, 'Not the least interesting thing about Gainsborough is to observe how – unlike Reynolds, who took most of his poses from Italian Renaissance or Baroque models – he always seems to have worked and developed his inventions within the prescribed orbit of the purest English tradition', citing Van Dyck and Kneller as Gainsborough's immediate models.

81 Pointon 1984, p. 195.

82 Waterhouse 1966, no. 375, p. 74; no. 697, p. 94 (now in the collection of the Victoria Art Gallery, Bath); no. 237, p. 66.

83 William B. Boulton, *Thomas Gainsborough, his Life, Work, Friends and Sitters*, London 1905, p. 89. Philip Honywood unexpectedly succeeded to the estates of Downe, Kent and Marks Hall, Essex in 1758 on the death of his ten-year-old nephew (Edward Hasted, *The History and Topographical Survey of the County of Kent*, 4 vols, London 1778–1801, II, 1782, pp. 449–50).

84 Hayes 2001, no. 14, p. 28.

85 Woodall 1939, pp. 16–17.

86 The portrait of Ligonier was exhibited at the Society of Artists exhibition in 1761, see Ellis K. Waterhouse *Reynolds* London 1941, p. 61.

87 The Tenth Earl of Pembroke travelled extensively in Europe and wrote about the theory of equitation as well as building a riding school at Wilton. Mary Hoare, daughter of William Hoare, and her husband Henry Hoare (whom she married in July 1765) were close friends of the Tenth Earl, see Newby 1990, p. 16.

88 *Public Advertiser*, 2 May 1765 (PMC cuttings).

89 Mary Woodall, *Thomas Gainsborough: His Life and Work*, London 1949, p. 57.

90 Christopher Brown, *Van Dyck*, Oxford 1982, p. 168.

91 *An Exact Plan of the Gardens and Park at Wilton* . . . , surveyed and drawn by J. Rocque, engraved by R. White, 1746 (copy of the plan on display at Wilton House, 1996).
92 Spencer-Longhurst 1995, p. 18.
93 Waterhouse catalogues the now lost Garrick portrait, Waterhouse 1966, no. 304, p. 70. It is usually said to be influenced by the Westminster Abbey monument. The Wilton Shakespeare was supplied by Peter Scheemakers in 1743, two years after the Westminster Abbey version. Scheemakers was working for Paul Methuen at Corsham Court near Bath between 1763 and 1765, see Frederick J. Ladd, *Architects at Corsham Court*, Bradford-on-Avon 1978, pp. 32, 61–2, 64.
94 General Honywood and his wife are recorded in the arrivals lists in *Boddely's Bath Journal* for 17 August 1761, 14 September 1761, 17 May 1762 and 18 June 1764. The same newspaper for 24 May 1762 records the General's gift to the General Hospital of 2 guineas 'by Mr Leake' the bookseller.
95 For a full discussion of the portrait of Captain Wade see Sloman 1994.
96 John Fleming, 'The Pluras of Turin and Bath', *Connoisseur*, CXXXVIII, November 1956, p. 180.
97 Waterhouse 1966, no. 11, p. 51.
98 *Bath and Bristol Chronicle*, 26 October 1769.
99 After holding out for a year against the French, Paoli was forced to capitulate in 1768. He was treated to a hero's welcome on fleeing from Corsica to England that year. His arrival in Bath and the dinner arranged in his honour by the Bath Corporation in the Guildhall are recorded in the *Bath and Bristol Chronicle* of 19 October 1769 and 26 October 1769.
100 *Bath Chronicle*, 30 November 1786.
101 *Bath Journal*, 15 April 1754, Corton described himself as 'Painter in Perspective Views in large and small, of Architecture and Sea-Pieces'. He adds that he would personally be in attendance at the Assembly Rooms from 12 until 3 o'clock daily and at other times of day could be found at Moses Roubel's jewellery shop.
102 Hayes 2001, no. 53, p. 90; no. 15, pp. 30–31.
103 Ibid., no. 29, p. 50.
104 Sloman 1997, p. 325–8.
105 Ibid., p. 326.
106 Waterhouse 1966, no. 727, p. 96.
107 Sloman 1997, p. 326.
108 Alex Kidson, 'Thomas Gainsborough and the Revd Sir William Lowther: An Unpublished Letter', *Gainsborough's House Review 1995/96*, 1996, p. 60.
109 SRO, Luttrell papers, DDL 2/44/9. The letter is one from a bundle all dating from 1759. This particular letter is only dated 23 May, but can be safely assumed to be from 1759.
110 Humphry's relationship with Collins, whose 'eccentric Gallantries would furnish chapters for a romance', according to Humphry, is described in RA, Humphry papers, HU/1/20–40. Humphry's apprenticeship indenture is dated August 1760 (HU/1/69), but on 30 August 1762 Humphry applied to the City of Bath to be freed of the indenture as Collins had fled to Dublin to escape either debt or scandal (HU/1/70).
111 Clifford 1978, no. 26, pp. 13–14. As the catalogue authors point out, Collins was also responsible for introducing Gainsborough to the musician William Jackson, who became, for a time a close friend. The evidence for Gainsborough painting Collins is contained in an entry in the Ozias Humphry sale of 29 June 1810 at Christie's, London, lot 50, which was a portrait by Gainsborough of Samuel Collins which sold for twelve shillings, see Algernon Graves, *Art Sales from early in the Eighteenth Century to early in the Twentieth Century*, London 1918, I, p. 312.
112 Whitley 1915, p. 309. Gainsborough probably first met Samuel Cotes in Bath.
113 Waterhouse 1966, no. 301, p. 70 (now in the Yale Center for British Art, New Haven); no. 274, p. 68 (now in the Yale Center for British Art); no. 221, p. 65 (now in the Tate Gallery, London). For his family portraits in general see Belsey 1988.
114 Waterhouse 1966, no. 779, p. 101 (currently on loan to GH). See also Hayes 1966, pp. 86–93. The provenance of the Barton Grange drawings is not fully resolved and it is suggested in Chapter 7 below that one of Gainsborough's reasons for visiting the Taunton area was his friendship with Coplestone Warre Bampfylde and Sir Charles-Kemeys and Lady Tynte.
115 A pastel drawing of Mrs Margaret Gainsborough was sold as a *Portrait of a Lady*, Sotheby's, London, 9 November 1995, lot 25; Hayes 1970, I, no. 49, p. 123; no. 44, p. 122; no. 43, p. 121 (subsequently sold at Sotheby's, London 16 July 1992, lot 56).
116 Hayes 2001, no. 49, pp. 82–3.
117 Mitchell and Penrose 1983, p. 98.
118 Newby 1990, nos 13–13e, pp. 28–31.
119 Chapter 4, p. 57.
120 Hayes 2001, no. 52, pp. 87–8.
121 Arline Meyer, 'Re-dressing Classical Statuary: The Eighteenth-Century "Hand-in-Waistcoat" Portrait', *Art Bulletin*, LXXVII, no. 1, March 1995, pp. 45–7.
122 Ibid., p. 45, n. 7.
123 Gainsborough's reading of Richardson is discussed in Chapter 8, p. 160.
124 Farington reported these words about Gainsborough, as spoken by Sir Francis Bourgeois: they are quoted by Michael Rosenthal, *The Art of Thomas Gainsborough*, New Haven and London 1999, p. 77.
125 Ellis Waterhouse, 'Bath and Gainsborough', *Apollo*, XCVIII, no. 141, November 1973, pp. 360–65.

6 *Portraits 'for Bread' and Portraits for Friends*

The chapter-title quotation comes from a letter of 1 March 1764 to James Unwin in which Gainsborough speaks of teaching his daughters to paint landscape, so that 'in case of an Accident' they 'may do something for Bread' (Hayes 2001, no. 13, p. 26).

1 A list of portraits of the Bath period compiled from Waterhouse's catalogue (Waterhouse 1966) together with works that have appeared since, either in private collections or the salerooms, can be divided up using any available dates together with stylistic and costume evidence. The great majority of portraits are either 'head' or half-length, only sixty-three (just over one in six) being full-length pictures.
2 Hayes 2001, no. 56, p. 94. Constantine Phipps, later Baron Mulgrave (1744–1792) was closely associated with Bath: he became a member of the Bath Philosophical Society founded by Edmund Rack and Thomas Curtis in 1779, see A. J. Turner, *Science and Music in Eighteenth Century Bath* (exh. cat., Holburne Museum), Bath 1977, pp. 82–3.
3 Ephraim Hardcastle [William Henry Pyne], *Wine and Walnuts, or, After Dinner Chit-Chat*, 2 vols, London 1823, II, p. 223. Many contemporary accounts of the spa at Bath refer to visitors 'stewing' in the waters.
4 Hayes 2001, no. 32, p. 54.
5 Ibid. no. 54, p. 91 ; no. 53, p. 90.
6 M. Elwin, *The Noels and the Milbankes*, London 1967, p. 37.
7 McEvansoneya 1999, pp. 153–4, 165. I am most grateful to Philip McEvansoneya for sending me the text of this letter in advance of the publication of his article. A similar view of Gainsborough's relationship with sitters is given in Jerom Murch, *Biographical Sketches of Bath Celebrities*, London and Bath 1893, p. 186, where he is described as 'brusque and independent' in his dealing with sitters. The source of this opinion is not given, but Jerom Murch was a Bath writer.

8 Fulcher 1856, pp. 40–41, Sarah Kirby advised her brother, who was briefly a pupil of Gainsborough, to imitate the painter's politeness; Wark 1958, p. 332.

9 Stainton 1977; Beechey 1988.

10 *Joseph Gibbs* (Waterhouse 1966, no. 313, p. 70); *Revd John Chafy* (ibid., no. 127, p. 59) shows the sitter in a landscape playing a cello; in the *Muilman Conversation Piece* (ibid., no. 747, p. 98) Peter Darnell Muilman, Charles Crockatt and William Keable are shown with woodwind instruments. Gainsborough's painting *The Ipswich Musical Club* (ibid., no. 748, p. 98) is lost.

11 James 1987, I, p. 42; Philip Thicknesse, *A Treatise in the Art of Decyphering and of writing in Cypher with a Harmonic Alphabet*, London 1772. Ralph Thicknesse was buried in Bath Abbey on 18 May 1741 (BRO, Bath Abbey Registers of Baptisms, Marriages and Burials, transcripts).

12 James 1987, I, p. 42 points out that a 1757 production of Handel's *Acis and Galatea* included 'several Ladies and Gentlemen of the first Distinction' among the performers.

13 Herbert 1950, p. 78, letter dated 27 December 1780.

14 Several members of the Orpin family of Bradford-on-Avon were musicians. The *Bath Chronicle*, 16 November 1786, announces the death of Mrs Elizabeth Orpin, spinster, organist of Bradford-on-Avon for 'near thirty years'. An earlier notice in the *Boddely's Bath Journal*, 23 May 1763, advertising a benefit concert for the organist Mr Orpin at Devizes Town Hall may refer to the same Thomas Orpin, or another family member. The portrait of Thomas Orpin's father, Bradford-on-Avon Parish Clerk Edward Orpin (d. 1781), once in the collection of the Wiltshire family and long attributed to Gainsborough (in the Tate Gallery), is now given to Nathaniel Hone.

15 *Bath and Bristol Chronicle*, 7 December 1769, an advertisement for a benefit concert for Fischer, tickets five shillings from the Rooms and 'of Mr Fisher [sic], at Mr Guest's, in the Abbey-Green'. Fischer was also with the Guests in December 1772, see James 1987, IV, p. 601. Thomas Guest's daughter Mary-Jane, afterwards Mrs Miles, became a famous keyboard performer and teacher and was one of those who played in the musical entertainment in Thomas Beach's rooms (Chapter I, p. 20).

16 Black 1911, p. 14.

17 *Bath Advertiser*, 2 February 1760, announcing a benefit for Abel. Abel and Giardini's arrival is noted in the *Bath Chronicle* of 29 October 1761. *Boddely's Bath Journal* of 9 November 1761 announces a concert of vocal and instrumental music on 11 November at which Abel, Giardini (first violin) and other European musicians, including Giovanni Battista Noferi and Angiola Calori, were to perform.

18 A copy of the *Six Sonatas* in the Bodleian Library, Oxford, includes the subscription list (Bodleian Tenbury Mus. c.75(5)). I am most grateful to Warwick Cole who drew my attention to this. The library catalogue dates the music to 1760, but no date of publication is printed on the sheets, and a slightly later date seems more probable. Gainsborough probably knew all these people who subscribed. 'Miss Bennett' may have been a relative of the Abbey Churchyard draper Francis Bennett who was patronised by the artist (Appendix II, entries 8, 18, etc); Gainsborough painted a portrait of David Richards's wife (Waterhouse 1966, no. 575, p. 87); 'Mr Townsend' may be one of the jewellers or goldsmiths by name of Townsend whom Gainsborough patronised (Appendix II, entry 48, p. 205).

19 Hayes 2001, no. 101, p. 164.

20 I am extremely grateful to Edward Yescombe for giving me this information. His ancestor William Yescombe, a Bath attorney, was Chilcot's executor and trustee. Yescombe noted that he received 'of Mr Gainsborough for Teaching [£]1 6[s]' (PRO C/12/1929/32, Court of Chancery, *Walker v Yescombe*, answer by William Yescombe of 25 July 1770, Second Schedule, moneys received for the Chilcot estate).

21 Hayes 2001, no. 31, p. 53.

22 James 1987, I, pp. 95–100; II, p. 140 and III, pp. 537–40. Tim Rishton, 'Thomas Chilcot' in *The New Grove Dictionary of Music and Musicians*, ed. Stanley Sadie, 29 vols, London 2001 (second edition), V, p. 607. What follows about Chilcot is taken from these two sources and information given to me by Edward Yescombe.

23 Trevor Fawcett, *Bath Administer'd: Corporation Affairs at the Eighteenth-Century Spa*, Bath 2001, pp. 84–5. The organist was employed by the Corporation, as was the organ blower, who, as Fawcett notes, was paid only £2 a year.

24 These both contained Chilcot's bookplate. The manuscript of *Deborah* is now BL, Additional Manuscript 34006.

25 Otto Erich Deutsch, *Handel: A Documentary Biography*, London 1955, p. 676.

26 Ibid., pp. 763–4.

27 James 1987, IV, p. 646.

28 Walter Ison, *The Georgian Buildings of Bath*, Bath 1980, pp. 4–5.

29 James 1987, IV, p. 647–8.

30 Ibid, p. 646.

31 Appendix II, entry 13, p. 204.

32 Edward Yescombe's researches into William Yescombe's handling of the Chilcot estate yielded this information. Lady Elizabeth Bathurst's husband the Hon. Benjamin Bathurst was the son of Allen, the First Earl Bathurst.

33 Belsey 2001, p. 18. Belsey points out that Mrs Byam was born Louisa Bathurst, the daughter of Peter Bathurst (1687–1748) of Clarendon Park, near Salisbury, brother of Allen, First Earl Bathurst. Peter Bathurst's brother Benjamin Bathurst (?1691–1767) of Lydney, Gloucestershire, commissioned a double portrait of his two children in 1759–60, ibid., no. 7, p. 41.

34 James 1987, II, pp. 173–82.

35 Hayes 2001, no. 35, p. 58.

36 James 1987, II, p. 173.

37 Ibid., p. 182.

38 Waterhouse 1966, no. 398, p. 76.

39 James 1987, V, pp. 1002–7. Hayes 1998, pp. 94–5 catalogues the version of the Tenducci portrait at the Barber Institute of Fine Arts, Birmingham.

40 Waterhouse 1966, no. 252, p. 67. [Lloyd] 1994, no. 12, p. 42.

41 Martin Postle, 'Gainsborough's 'lost' picture of Shakespeare', *Apollo*, CXXXIV, no. 358, December 1991, pp. 372–9.

42 Wark 1958, p. 333; Thicknesse 1788, pp 36–7.

43 A curious entry in the *Bath Chronicle* of 13 October 1774 may (as Kenneth James believes) refer to Mary Gainsborough's already acknowledged attachment to Fischer. Entitled 'Verses written on Mr. Fischer, by a young Lady, on her taking leave of him, after having heard him play on the Hautboy', this was followed up by a response in the *Bath Chronicle* of 27 October 1774, and may suggest that the Gainsborough family had moved to London by 13 October 1774.

44 Waterhouse 1966, no. 198, p. 63. The portrait of Dodd is illustrated in Hayes 2001, p. 121.

45 Gainsborough's letter to Dodd, dated 22 November 1773 (Hayes 2001, no. 71, pp. 120–22) refers to Dodd's portrait, then hanging in his show room at the Circus, and to the artist's amusement at listening through the keyhole to visitors discussing it. The chapel opening is announced in the *Bath Chronicle* of 16 September 1773.

46 Various notices in the *Bath Chronicle* (25 March 1772; 15 July 1773) invite subscriptions for pews, applicants being directed to William Linley's home in Market Place, Bath. The organ is described in Anon, *New Bath Guide*, Bath 1774, p. 31. It was 'exceeding fine-toned' and built by John Snetzler. It has been suggested that

Linley's Margaret Chapel was built in response to William Herschel's appointment as organist of the new Octagon Chapel in 1766, Herschel's move to Bath being seen as a threat to Linley's domination of concert life in the city (Beechey 1988, p. 49).

47 Hayes 2001, no. 71, p. 121. I am grateful to Trevor Fawcett, who first pointed out (verbally) that the Margaret Chapel must be the one mentioned in the artist's letter to Dodd.

48 Rice Charleton, *A Treatise on the Bath Waters*, London 1754. Charleton was one of the first to attempt a statistical analysis of the treatments given to patients at the Bath Hospital. He was also the first to associate lead-poisoning from cider barrels with paralysis. In Somerset, an area well known for its cider, this was a widespread problem.

49 Dr Oliver's country house was named after his birthplace in Cornwall. Moysey's country residence is mentioned in BCL, Boodle Collection of cuttings and MSS relating to Bath and Somerset, undated, XXXV, p. 163. A note says that Moysey purchased the estate of Charterhouse Hinton, now Hinton Charterhouse. Rice Charleton's country estate is discussed in Chapter 9, p. 174.

50 Hoare painted Dr Oliver (one of three Physicians to the Hospital appointed at its opening in 1740) together with surgeon Peirce, the first surgeon to the Hospital, in the group portrait illustrated (fig. 11); he also painted Henry Wright, surgeon to the Hospital 1742–94 (Rolls 1988, p. 156, illustrated) and made two drawings of Dr Rice Charleton, see n. 53 below.

51 Chapter 1, p. 17–19.

52 Waterhouse 1966, no. 505, p. 82; no. 136, p. 59. The Charleton portrait was exhibited in 1766, but painted by early 1764.

53 One of the drawings, in the Witt Collection at the Courtauld Institute of Art (no. 733) is dated 1755; the other (fig. 89) appears closely similar in date.

54 [W. C. Borlase], *The Descent, Name and Arms of Borlase of Borlase in the County of Cornwall*, London 1888, p. 181. Mr Langton, of Newton St Loe, west of Bath, was the father of Gainsborough's sitter Joseph Langton (Waterhouse 1966, no. 426, p. 77).

55 Gainsborough also appears to have painted eight portraits for the wealthy Royal doctor Sir Caesar Hawkins who retired to Kelston near Bath in 1759. All are now lost, see Sloman 1994, p. 58, n. 39.

56 A great deal of information about Dr Abel Moysey and Gainsborough's portraits of him and his son Abel Moysey MP is given in the catalogue by Hugh Belsey, *The Moysey Family* (exh. cat., Gainsborough's House), Sudbury 1984. After he left Bath Gainsborough wrote to Mrs Ditcher, making it clear that he had declined payment for the portrait, adding that he considered himself 'overpaid abundantly by my worthy friend's attention to my family while we lived in Bath' (Hayes 2001, no. 85, p. 141).

57 Philip Thicknesse, *Memoirs and Anecdotes of Philip Thicknesse Late Governor of Land Guard Fort and Unfortunately Father to George Touchet Baron Audley*, 3 vols [London] 1788–91, 1, pp. 232–3; BRO, City Rates Books, book commencing 24 June 1768 and following books. William Colborne, Benjamin's brother, lived at 3, Circus at the same time. Benjamin Colborne's daughter and heir Sarah Colborne (d. 1806) married in 1777 Sir Matthew White Ridley (1745–1813); her second son took the name of Colborne and became Sir Nicholas William Ridley-Colborne. An album of drawings by George Frost, John Constable and other members of the Constable family descended in the Ridley-Colborne collection and was sold in 1971 (Ian Fleming-Williams and Leslie Parris, *The Discovery of Constable*, London 1984, p. 233, unnumbered note).

58 BRO, Proceedings of the Committee for Managing the New Assembly Rooms at Bath, 3 June 1771 – 16 December 1775; and New Assembly Rooms, Minutes of the Furnishing Committee, 27 March 1771 – 17 May 1772. BRO, Royal National Hospital for Rheumatic Diseases Archive, General Hospital Annual Reports 1738–1842.

59 RA, Humphry Papers HU/1/113. The letter is addressed to Humphry at King Street, Covent Garden, and is inscribed on the outside, 'An eminent Dilettante Chemist, who invented a water colour varnish'.

60 Hayes 2001, no. 64, pp. 110–11. J. P. Derow, 'Gainsborough's Varnished Watercolour Technique', *Master Drawings*, 26, August 1988, pp. 259–71 discusses Gainsborough's experiments and points out that the use of varnish in combination with watercolour was extremely unusual in the 1770s.

61 David Strawbridge, *Meandering through Chilcompton*, Chilcompton 1990, pp. 77–8.

62 The late Mrs G. Thwaites, former owner of 1, Gainsborough, kindly allowed me to see the house and garden. Dr Kate Harris, Librarian and Archivist to the Marquess of Bath, Longleat, provided the information that surgeon James Flower occupied the house in 1784. The *Bath Chronicle*, 2 October 1777 reports that following his recent accident, surgeon Abraham Bath of Chilcompton is to be assisted in his practice by Mr Flower, his partner and former apprentice. Whether Flower took over Bath's house as well as his practice is not established, but an unusually spacious and well-lit upper room in the house might well have been designed for professional purposes. P. J. and R. V. Wallis, *Eighteenth-Century Medics (Subscriptions, Licences, Apprenticeships)*, Newcastle upon Tyne 1988, pp. 37–8 records a surgeon Abraham Bath in Chilcompton from before 1755 to after 1781, and p. 204 a surgeon James Flower at Chilcompton from before 1760 to after 1808.

63 Rolls 1988, p. 169.

64 Unwin's Christian name, James, and his brother's, Charles, suggest that they were born into a Jacobite family. James Unwin named his own two sons James William and Edward. I am most grateful to David Tyler, who looked at a number of Unwin family wills in the Public Record Office and let me have copies of his findings. Mrs Frances Unwin's will (PRO, PROB 11/1552/99, dated 17 May 1807) shows that by 1807 she was living in Bath, but asked to be buried in the family vault at Ellastone in Staffordshire. Her will was proved on 14 February 1814.

65 Monod 1989, p. 305.

66 Ibid., p. 153. Monod says that the evidence of Graves's Jacobitism is 'slight but compelling'. There is further evidence: Graves, as a young man, was domestic chaplain to William Fitzherbert of Tissington in Derbyshire, a Jacobite who was involved with a 'Tory Club' at Ashbourne and the 'Bowling Green Club' at Uttoxeter, see BCL, letter from Richard Graves to Samuel Jackson Pratt, dated 1799, AL 2051. J. H. Overton, *The Nonjurors, their Lives, Principles, and Writings*, London 1902, pp. 339–40 shows that Ashbourne was one of the last strongholds of Jacobitism.

67 Fulcher 1856, p. 153; Michael Kitson, Felicity Owen and Hugh Belsey, *From Gainsborough to Constable* (exh. cat., Gainsborough's House, Sudbury and The Leger Galleries, London), Sudbury 1991, p. 12.

68 Harrison 1922a, pp. 5, 7.

69 Girouard 1959, p. 598.

70 In his will (PRO, PROB 11/1552/99) Captain Edward Wheeler asked to be buried in the family vault at Old Swinford if he should die in England. In WORO, BA 3762/6-12, reference 6899:31, Foley Scrapbook, 1, p. 356 is a sketch of a map of Old Swinford Parish in 1699. This includes a crude representation of Wollaston Hall as it appeared at that date, a handsome half-timbered building with a triple gable.

71 B. L. C. Johnson, 'The Foley Partnerships: The Iron Industry at the end of the

Charcoal Era', *Economic History Review*, second series, IV, no. 3, 1952, pp. 322–40.

72 Philip Thicknesse, *Memoirs and Anecdotes of Philip Thicknesse Late Governor of Land Guard Fort and Unfortunately Father to George Touchet Baron Audley*, 3 vols [London] 1788–91, I, p. 14.

73 Monod 1989, p. 151.

74 Eveline Cruickshanks, 'Lord Cornbury, Bolingbroke and a Plan to restore the Stuarts 1731–1735', *Royal Stuart Papers*, XXVII, 1986, pp. 1–2.

75 See Chapter 3, pp. 44–6.

76 Belsey 2001, no. 7, p. 41.

77 Sedgwick 1970, I, p. 445.

78 Gervase Jackson-Stops records the childhood friendship between Lady Tynte and William Lee in his article 'Arcadia under the Plough, The Garden at Halswell, Somerset', *Country Life*, CLXXXIII, no. 6, 9 February 1989, p. 86.

79 The payment is recorded in Sir Charles-Kemeys Tynte's account, C. Hoare & Co., Ledger 64/222. I am most grateful to Elizabeth Einberg who told me of this. Lady Tynte's arrival in Bath is recorded in *Boddely's Bath Journal* of 7 July 1760 and 10 November 1760. The portrait or portraits were presumably painted between July 1760 and April 1761, when her husband paid Gainsborough. Sir Charles-Kemeys and Lady Tynte were in Bath again in November 1761 (*Boddely's Bath Journal*, 30 November 1761). Inventories of Sir Charles-Kemeys Tynte's possessions at Halswell, made around the time of his death in 1785, are in the SRO, but none identifies a painting by Gainsborough. One inventory dated 14 October 1785 includes '1 Picture of Lady Tynte half length' in the Library (SRO DD/S/WH 267).

80 Jenkins 1983, pp. 131, 165–7, 171, 175, describes the friendship between the Dukes of Beaufort and the Kemeys and Tynte families.

81 Sir Joseph Alfred Bradney, *History of Monmouthshire*, 2 vols, 1904–11, II, part 2, pp. 166–7.

82 Appendix III, p. 213.

83 Sedgwick 1970, II, p. 482.

84 See Chapter 4, p. 69.

85 Sedgwick 1970, II, p. 362.

86 John Burke, *Genealogical and Heraldic History of the Commoners*, 2 vols, London 1836, I, pp. 62–4.

87 Belsey 2001, p. 18.

88 John Burke and John Bernard Burke, *The Royal Families of England, Scotland, and Wales, with their Descendants*, 2 vols, London 1848–51, I, Pedigree CXCVI, 'W. Byam Esq. and Rev. R. Burgh Byam'. Burke says that Byam was from Luckham, Somerset, presumably Luccombe, west of Minehead.

89 Ibid. Mary was the daughter of the Revd Richard Burgh of Mount Bruis, County Tipperaray, grandson of Ulysses Burgh, Bishop of Ardagh.

90 C. Hoare & Co, James Unwin's account, Ledger 67/241, a payment of £25 to 'Mr Leake' on 21 January 1763 and £100 to Samuel Collins on 1 February 1763. Collins had left Bath by August 1762. See also Chapter 5, nn. 109, 110.

91 Hayes 2001, no. 18, p. 35. Pevsner called Wootton Lodge 'monumental', one of a group of houses by or close to Robert Smythson (Niklaus Pevsner, *The Buildings of Staffordshire*, Harmondsworth 1974, pp. 327–9).

92 Hayes 2001, no. 46, p. 78. Unwin is however still described as 'of Great Baddoe' on a document of 3 October 1765 in WORO, (deeds etc relating to members of the Unwin and other families, BA 4000/366 reference 705.260), concerning the letting of buildings in High Street, Stourbridge to a Mr William Winnall, the document prepared by Price and Harward, Solicitors of Stourbridge. These buildings must have been part of Unwin's inheritance from Captain Wheeler. Further documents in the same collection show that members of the Unwin family still owned properties and land in Stourbridge in the mid-nineteenth century. The name of Harward is significant: in 1796 Gainsborough's nephew Edward Richard Gardiner married Susanna Harward of Worcestershire (Janet Harris, 'The Harward family and the 1923 sale', *Gainsborough's House Society Annual Report 1991/92*, 1992, pp. 45–9).

93 The will of Edward Wheeler, PRO, PROB 11/1552/99. It is signed on 31 May 1760 and proved on 7 May 1761. He states,

> And whereas I am entitled to the reversion after the death of Mrs Ann Wheeler, my uncle John's widow (being in jointure to her for life) of an estate lying in the several parishes of Wootton Ramshorn and Ellastone in the county of Stafford I do hereby give the said estate and all my manors tenements etc in the said county to the before named worthy Mr James Unwin for his natural life . . .

James Unwin's eldest son James William Edward Wheeler Unwin (c. 1763–1818/19) is described in his will dated 12 February 1816 as 'of Wootton Lodge' (PRO, PROB 11/1613/98).

94 In 1851 Wootton Lodge was unoccupied but owned by a Miss Unwin (information kindly provided by Miss E. Street, Staffordshire Archive Service, Stafford). An Edward Unwin, presumably James Unwin's second son the Revd Edward Unwin, was a subscriber to Stebbing Shaw's *History and Antiquities of Staffordshire*, 2 vols, London 1798–1801, when he was described as of Wootton Lodge.

95 PRO, PROB 11/1552/99.

96 Hayes 2001, no. 46, pp. 78–80; no 48, pp. 81–2.

97 Richard Dorment, *British Painting in the Philadelphia Museum of Art*, Philadelphia and London 1986, pp. 116–18. Dorment mentions the artist's possible visit to the Unwins but concludes, 'until we have more information about Gainsborough's movements and patrons in these years, the mystery [as to how or why Gainsborough should be in Staffordshire] must remain unsolved'. See also Hayes 1982, II, no. 94, pp. 437–8.

98 Sampson Erdeswick, *A Survey of Staffordshire*, ed. Revd Thomas Harwood, London 1844, pp. 234–5. Samuel Newton (d. 1771) succeeded to his father John Newton's King's Bromley manor and estate in 1706, John Newton having died at the age of only thirty-nine. This John Newton was married to Mary, daughter of Sir Thomas Vernon of London. Samuel Newton's eldest son, another John, died in 1783: it is possible it was he who commissioned the landscape rather than his father. His estate, including (presumably) the Gainsborough landscape, passing to his sister Elizabeth (d. 1794) who in turn passed it to her cousins John and Thomas Lane. According to Dorment, *Philadelphia Museum*, p. 118, the painting belonged to a John Newton Lane in 1854.

99 Gainsborough's sitter George Venables Vernon (1735–1813) became the Second Lord Vernon on the death of his father in 1780 (Waterhouse 1966, no. 693, p. 94). George Venables Vernon's grandfather (d. 1702) was married to Catherine, daughter of Sir Thomas Vernon of London. Thus the Newtons and the Sudbury Hall Vernons were related by marriage.

100 Hayes 2001, no. 31, pp. 52–4; no. 46, pp. 78–80.

101 Quoted by Malcolm Andrews in *The Search for the Picturesque*, London 1990, p. 35.

102 Waterhouse 1966, no. 451, p. 79.

103 Ibid., nos 185, 186, p. 62. Ann Horton was first married to Christopher Horton of Catton Hall, Derbyshire.

104 Ibid., no. 179, p. 62.

105 Ibid., nos 314, 315, pp. 70–71. *Boddely's Bath Journal* 27 April 1761 records the arrival of a Mr Gisborne and the same newspaper dated 4 May 1761 the arrival of Mrs Gisborne. The Gisbornes may well have visited Bath earlier, although their arrival

is not noted. A MS authentication by Charles Holmes attached to the painting of John Gisborne when it was sold at Parke-Bernet, New York, 15 November 1945 (lot 56) pointed out that the style of the portrait reflected the influence of William Hoare and proposed a date of 1760 rather than 1758, the year of the Gisbornes' marriage.

106 Sir John Wrottesley (1744–1787) was the brother of Mary (1740–1769) (Waterhouse 1966, no. 739, p. 97) and Elizabeth, later Duchess of Grafton (1745–1822) (ibid., nos 737, 738, p. 97). Sir John was MP for Stafford from 1768–1787, a good enough reason for his name to be second on the Eld portrait subscription list, with a donation of two guineas. Fourth on the list is Lord Pigot, brother-in-law of Frances Wrottesley, another sister of Sir John's. The first name on the Eld subscription list is Sir William Bagot. His father Sir Walter Bagot (1723–1792) visited Bath in 1762 (*Boddely's Bath Journal*, 12 April 1762) and his mother was a daughter of the First Earl of Dartmouth. Sir Walter Bagot was also a Governor of the Foundling Hospital and was painted by Reynolds (the portrait sold at Sotheby's, London, 9 April 1997, lot 30).

107 Monod 1989, p. 283.

108 The activities of the Prize Courts are described in David J. Starkey's *British Privateering Enterprise in the Eighteenth Century*, Exeter 1990.

109 Ibid., p. 67.

110 Captain Thomas Saumarez (d. 1766) was in command of a ship he had captured, the *Belliqueux*, off the West Indes in 1761, but apparently returned to England as a result of ill-health (Charnock 1794–8, VI, pp. 91–2). The portrait of Mrs Saumarez is mentioned in Gainsborough's letter to Unwin of 24 July 1763 (Hayes 2001, no. 9, pp. 17–19), and on 1 March 1764 (ibid., no. 85, p. 155), although it is possible the later reference is to a portrait of Captain Saumarez himself, rather than that of his wife. The portrait of Mrs Saumarez was still apparently unfinished in July 1770, when Gainsborough promised to begin a new one (ibid., no. 91, p. 169). *Mrs Saumarez* is catalogued in Waterhouse 1966, no. 601, p. 88.

111 Charnock 1794–8, VI, p. 95.

112 Ibid., V, pp. 457–73. Howe also served under Vice Admiral Edward Boscawen (d. 1761), whose daughter Elizabeth Boscawen married in 1766 Henry, Fifth Duke of Beaufort.

7 *'Nature sat to* Mr. Gainsborough'

For the chapter-title quotation see Thicknesse 1788, p. 38.

1 Hayes 1980, p. 27.

2 *Gentleman's Magazine*, XLIII, December 1773, p. 614. The full text is given in Chapter 8, p. 161.

3 Chapter 1, p. 21. The extent to which landscape was regarded as a liberal art by Sir Joshua Reynolds and others in the eighteenth century is considered in Barrell 1986, pp. 15–19 and pp. 120–23.

4 The portraits are discussed in Chapter 3 above and catalogued in Waterhouse 1966, nos 595–7a, p. 88, and no. 330, p. 71.

5 The landscape owned by Sir William the Fourth Baronet is catalogued in Hayes 1982, II, no. 87, pp. 426–7.

6 Hayes 2001, no. 10, p. 21.

7 Philip Thicknesse, *A Year's Journey through France and Part of Spain*, 2 vols, Dublin 1777, II, p. 42.

8 Farington 1978–98, III, p. 764, entry for 7 February 1797.

9 Hayes 1982, II, no. 80, p. 419; no. 75, pp. 412–14.

10 See Chapter 8, n. 165.

11 For portrait prices see Appendix III, p. 213. The price for the landscape may have included carriage, packing, or a frame: Hayes 1982, II, no. 87, pp. 426–7.

12 Hayes 1995, p. 15, n. 1. *Peasants and Colliers going to Market* is 8 inches larger than a half-length portrait canvas in both dimensions.

13 Solkin 1982, no. 77, p. 192 and no. 78, p. 193. The *Lake of Nemi* purchased by Henry Hoare seems not to be the picture catalogued by Solkin (no. 77) but the upright composition engraved by Joseph Wood in 1758–9 and illustrated here as fig. 122

14 Gainsborough's *Wooded Landscape with Country Waggon, Milkmaid and Drover* sold to Sir William St Quintin in 1766 is believed to be the picture exhibited at the Society of Artists exhibition that year (Hayes 1982, II, no. 87, pp. 426–7). Garvey's *A View of the lake of Nemea, towards Larissa* was priced at ten guineas in the catalogue to the same exhibition, Graves 1907, p. 100. It is not on record what size this view was, but his exhibited Italian landscapes seem to have measured 40 × 50 inches or larger. His *Lake Albano and Castel Gandolfo* sold at Christie's, London, 11 April 1997 (lot 21) was 40½ × 51 inches and another Italianate landscape attributed to Garvey that sold at Christie's, South Kensington on 17 July 1998 (lot 200) measured 44½ × 57¾ inches.

15 Hayes 2001, no. 104, p. 168.

16 Barrell 1986, p. 121.

17 Hayes 1970, I, catalogues 157 drawings for the period up to 1758–9; 212 for the Bath period and 440 for the following London period.

18 The figures are from Graves 1907, p. 98 and Graves 1905–6, III, pp. 191–2. In addition to the fifty-two portraits from the post-1776 period was the group of eight small Royal Family portraits exhibited as a close-hung set in 1783.

19 Prince Hoare, *Epochs of the Arts: Including hints on the Use and Progress of Painting and Sculpture in Great Britain*, London 1813, pp. 76–7. A list of known records of visitors to Gainsborough's Bath picture rooms is given in Sloman 1996b, p. 153. To this should be added a diary entry in Robin Gard (ed.), *The Observant Traveller*, London 1989, p. 23, from the diary of Elizabeth Giffard, 26 December 1766: 'we afterwards took a walk to the Circus to see Mr Gainsborough's paintings with which we were much pleased'. This reference, which was kindly pointed out to me by Dr Philip McEvansoneya, is most important as it shows Gainsborough was already resident at the Circus by Christmas 1766. It is not possible to tell from the BRO Bath City Rates Books the precise date at which Gainsborough moved to the Circus.

20 Elizabeth and Florence Anson (eds), *Mary Hamilton*, London 1925, p. 26.

21 Ibid., p. 27.

22 Hayes 2001, no. 72, p. 123. Mary Woodall, in her edition of Gainsborough's letters (Woodall 1963, no. 13, pp. 44–5), identified 'Mr Hamilton' as Colonel James Hamilton, but the person visited by Gainsborough must have been the Hon. Charles Hamilton whose house, 14 Royal Crescent, was well known to Bath visitors and whose collection was known to, among others, the young Thomas Lawrence, who made copies of some of the pictures in the following decade.

23 Hugh Belsey, 'A Visit to the Studios of Gainsborough and Hoare', *Burlington Magazine*, CXXIX, no. 1007, February 1987, pp. 107–9. Belsey has confused the Anon, *New Bath Guide*, a guidebook published in Bath by Richard Cruttwell with Christopher Anstey's satirical verses, *The New Bath Guide*. Richardson's notes are at the back of a Cruttwell guidebook and include page references to the preceding printed text. At the time of Dorothy Richardson's visit Gainsborough was probably away from Bath at George Pitt's country house painting Lord and Lady Ligonier. On 9 June 1770 the artist was back in Bath and told William Jackson he had just been at Mr Pitt's for three months. On 10 July 1770 he told James Unwin he had been taken prisoner by Mr Pitt for a month's work, Hayes 2001, no. 45, pp. 75–6 and no. 46, pp. 78–80. Dorothy Richardson also recorded a visit

to Benjamin West's gallery and adjoining painting room in 1785, see Kit Wedd, Lucy Peltz and Cathy Ross, *Creative Quarters: The Art World in London 1700–2000*, London 2001, p. 70.

24 Her comment that Gainsborough 'Paints only in Oil' was prompted by the visit she made to William Hoare's rooms in Edgar Buildings immediately on leaving the Circus. There she greatly admired Hoare's pastel portraits and fancy pictures, thinking them the best she had ever seen in that medium.

25 Hayes 2001, no. 30, p. 51. Gainsborough had been 'struck with the leaving and touch of a little bit of Tree; the whole Picture not above 8 or 10 Inches high & about a foot long' at a dealer's premises near Hanover Square and asked Jackson to find out how much was being asked for it. Gainsborough might also have hung together the small Dutch landscape that later belonged to Dr Rice Charleton, and his own copy of this (Chapter 9, p. 174). The small landscape by Michaud and the copy of it by Gainsborough, both of which were later purchased by Edmund Garvey, could equally have dated from the Bath period and be the pair of pictures seen by Dorothy Richardson (see p. 126 and n. 63).

26 Anon, *Critical Review of the Pictures, Sculptures, Designs in Architecture, Drawings, Prints etc Exhibited at the Great-Room in Spring Gardens, Charing Cross*, London 1765, p. 33.

27 Hayes 1982, II, no. 88, p. 430.

28 Horace Walpole, 'Notes by Horace Walpole, Fourth Earl of Orford, on the exhibitions of the Society of Artists and Free Society of Artists' (transcribed and edited by Hugh Gatty), *Walpole Society*, XXVII, 1939, p. 66. The portrait is catalogued in Waterhouse 1966, no. 477, p. 80.

29 Graves 1905–6, III, p. 191.

30 Ibid.

31 Hayes 2001, no. 16, p. 32.

32 Hayes 1995, p. 15, n. 1. Hayes notes that the payment for the picture was made not to Gainsborough, but to William Hoare. This must indicate either that Hoare was acting as an agent or that he had previously acquired the picture from Gainsborough and was selling it on. The former seems the more likely possibility.

33 Newby 1990, p. 16.

34 W&SRO, Stourhead papers, an inventory of pictures at Stourhead dated 1784, 383/714 (II), fol. 77, in the Damask Bed Chamber, 'A view of the Gardens at Stourhead By Mr Hoare of Bath'. This may have been the picture Hoare exhibited at the Royal Academy in 1770, Newby, 1990, p. 14, n. 36.

35 Sloman 1998, p. 47 and p. 52, nn. 3–7.

36 Clifford 1978, no. 26, pp. 13–14.

37 Fulcher 1856, p. 248.

38 Ibid.

39 Hayes 1982, I, p. 280.

40 Hayes 2001, no. 31, p. 53; no. 46, p. 80.

41 Rubens's *Watering Place* is now in the National Gallery, London; Hayes 2001, no. 35, p. 58; no. 30, p. 51.

42 Ibid, no. 49, p. 83.

43 Ibid, no. 72, p. 124.

44 Appendix 1, pp. 199–203.

45 Edward Croft Murray, *Decorative Painting in England 1537–1837*, 2 vols, London 1970, II, pp. 271–2.

46 Allen 1987, p. 79, n. 32.

47 Murray, *Decorative Painting in England*, II, p. 272; Allen 1987, pp. 52–3.

48 BMT, Subscription Book 2, consulted by kind permission of Mr Ken Hall and the Trustees of the Masonic Hall.

49 Norman 1920, p. 136.

50 Chapter 1 above, p. 17.

51 One further indirect link between Gainsborough and Thomas Ross can be traced through the illustrators who worked on the well-known engraved English town panoramas produced in the 1720s, 1730s and 1740s by Samuel and Nathaniel Buck. Thomas Ross produced several of the studies which were used as foreground staffage for the Buck prints, including the figures for the prospects of Bath, printed in 1734, King's Lynn of 1741 and Portsmouth of 1749. Gainsborough's early master Hubert Gravelot was another major contributor to this project.

52 [John Harris], *Gardens of Delight: The Art of Thomas Robins* (exh. cat., RIBA, Heinz Gallery), London 1975 (published anonymously, no page numbers), includes a list of Robins's Bath views and a chronology of his life. His son Thomas continued as a flower painter and drawing master in Bath and was associated with Edmund Rack and the Bath and West Society (mentioned in Chapter 9 in connection with Gainsborough's *Peasants and Colliers going to Market*).

53 Hayes 2001, no. 84, p. 140.

54 BM, Department of Prints and Drawings, Anderdon Royal Academy catalogues, I, fol. 128, a MS note about the 1770 exhibition lists Thos Gainsborough, RA Bath here are 3 views of Italy. NB I remember no others'. The works listed were Garvey's, nos 90–93 in the exhibition.

55 Graves 1907, p. 100.

56 The picture exhibited at the Academy is probably the one sold at Christie's, London, 11 April 1997, lot 21.

57 Tim Mowl and Brian Earnshaw, *John Wood: Architect of Obsession*, Bath 1988, pp. 135–47.

58 Ernest Fletcher (ed.), *Conversations of James Northcote R.A. with James Ward on Art and Artists*, London 1901, p. 160.

59 McEvansoneya 1999, p. 156; BM, Department of Prints and Drawings, Anderdon Royal Academy catalogues, I, fol. 397.

60 Waterhouse 1981, p. 143.

61 Wright [n.d.], under Garvey. Garvey went on to be elected RA in 1783.

62 Farington 1978–98, V, p. 1784.

63 M. H. Spielmann, A Note on Thomas Gainsborough and Gainsborough Dupont, Comprising a complete list of the works of both artists formerly in the possession of the Gainsborough Dupont Family, and Disposed of in the Years 1797, 1874 and 1892', *Walpole Society*, V, 1917, p. 105.

64 Whitley 1915, pp. 79–80.

65 Ellen Wilson, 'A Shropshire Lady in Bath, 1794–1807', *Bath History*, IV, 1992, p. 100. Two fancy figure pictures by William Hoare, a *Spring* and a *Summer*, were also called 'Herculaneum Nymphs' and both Garvey and Hoare must have been reflecting the enthusiasm for the antiquities of Herculaneum following the excavations of the 1730s and 1740s. Both artists had been to Italy, but local knowledge is not necessarily implied, since images from the site were well known throughout Europe from the eight illustrated volumes *Le Antichita di Ercolano* published in Naples between 1757 and 1796. Volumes I, II, III, IV and VII published in 1757, 1760, 1762, 1765 and 1769 respectively, illustrated the wall paintings discovered at Herculaneum.

66 Anon, *New Bath Guide*, Bath n.d. (dated 1771 on spine of the BCL copy), p. 22.

67 BRO, New Assembly Rooms, Minutes of Furnishing Committee, 27 March 1771 – 17 May 1772; BRO, Proceedings of the Committee for Managing the New Assembly Rooms at Bath 3 June 1771 – 16 December 1775.

68 Farington 1978–98, VI, p. 2244.

69 The best account of Taylor's career is Arthur S. Marks, 'An Eighteenth-Century American Landscape Painter Rediscovered: John Taylor of Bath', *American Art Journal*, X, no. 2, November 1978, pp. 81–96.

70 John Baker, *The Diary of John Baker*, ed. Philip C. Yorke, London 1931, pp. 248–9. On 11 November 1772 Baker wrote, 'At Coho talked with Mrs Clive's husband – la [i.e. there] Melmoth the author, who lives at Bath Mr Taylor the painter here (North American and great genius) . . .'.

71 McEvansoneya 1999, p. 161.

72 Marks, 'John Taylor of Bath', pp. 81–2.

73 The poem was published in the *Gentleman's Magazine*, LX, part II, 1790, p. 938

Marks included it in his article of 1978 (p. 96), but was unaware of the identity of the author. In Graves 1806, pp. 93–5 is a poem of which Marks was apparently unaware, 'Mercury and the Woodman, A Fable, To John Taylor Esq, of Bath, who presented the Author with a gold-headed Cane; on seeing him greatly concerned for the loss of a gilt-headed one, which he had used for forty years'.

74 David Solkin, *Painting for Money: The Visual Arts and the Public Sphere in Eighteenth-Century England*, New Haven and London 1993, pp. 251–3. The verse was published in the *St James's Chronicle* in 1761 (ibid., p. 299, n. 12) and so could easily have been known to Graves and the author of the poem about Gainsborough, identified here as Daniel Webb.

75 The St Quintins were related by marriage to John Taylor. Taylor enhanced his already considerable wealth by marrying the heiress Rebecca Luther, sister of the Duchess of Westmorland. Her niece, the Duke and Duchess's daughter Charlotte married Sir William St Quintin, the Fifth Baronet.

76 Wright [n.d.], under Taylor.

77 Ibid.

78 Garvey's picture was exhibited at the Royal Academy in 1774; Richards exhibited 'A Cascade at Hestercombe' at the Royal Academy in 1769, and another version signed and dated 1770 is at Stourhead (Waterhouse 1981, p. 309, illustrated). Richards's view of Halswell was exhibited at the Society of Artists 1764 exhibition.

79 [Sir Edward Harington], *A Schizzo on the Genius of Man: in which . . . the Merit of Mr. Thomas Barker . . . is particularly considered*, Bath 1793 (published anonymously), note on p. 52.

80 Amal Asfour and Paul Williamson, 'William Jackson of Exeter: New Documents', *Gainsborough's House Review 1996/97*, 1997, p. 69.

81 SRO, Luttrell papers, DDL/2/44/9, Henry Rowselle to Henry Fownes Luttrell, from Taunton, 19 May 1759.

82 SRO, Coplestone Warre Bampfylde correspondence, DD/GC 103. The Drax family was from Charborough, Dorset. From 1770 to 1772 Bampfylde and Edward Drax both occupied houses in Queen's Parade, Bath (BRO, Bath City Rates Books, books commencing 25 December 1770 and 25 December 1771).

83 The portrait, a standard 30 × 25 inch 'head', is now in a private collection. It is substantially overpainted in nearly all but some parts of the face and the lace cuff. This may have been done by Bampfylde himself to reflect his elevation to the rank of Colonel of the Somerset Militia in 1767. The painting of the epaulette is particularly weak and quite unrelated to Gainsborough's style. I am most grateful to the owner of the painting for allowing me to examine it.

84 Like the Prices and the Beauforts, the Bampfyldes had been Jacobite sympathisers earlier in the century, the artist's namesake Sir Coplestone Bampfylde of Poltimore, Devon, instructing his family to remain loyal to the cause after his death (Monod 1989, pp. 306–07).

85 Philip White, *A Gentleman of Fine Taste: The Watercolours of Coplestone Warre Bampfylde* (exh. cat., Christie's), London 1995, fig. 61, p. 49; fig. 62, p. 50.

86 Wilton 1980, no. 145, p. 53.

87 Anon, *Furniture, Paintings, Drawings . . . etc, late the Property of Miss Warre, deceased, Hestercombe*, 8–11 October 1872 (copy of the catalogue in the Local History Library, Taunton), lots 380, 236 and 199. Also, lot 166, 'Portrait, 50 × 50 in, gilt frame *Gainsborough*'. The size given for this lot was almost certainly incorrect, unless the picture was a full-length cut down. The portrait of William Jones (lot 199) has been identified by Hugh Belsey, using enhanced old photographs of the interiors of Hestercombe House, as the picture catalogued as Waterhouse 1966, no. 762, pp. 99–100. I am most grateful to Hugh Belsey for this information.

88 Hayes 1982, II, no. 83, pp. 422–3. This was lot 208 in the 1872 Hestercombe Sale.

89 Anon, *Catalogue of a Portion of the Collection . . . of Mr. Robert Walker*, Bath 4–5 December 1878 (copy of the catalogue in BCL), lot 80, Gainsborough: 'A Landscape with a Winding Lane, Donkeys and Figures, a Village in the Distance, from the Hestercombe Sale. Colonel Bampfielde [sic] the owner of Hestercombe was a great friend of the Artist'. This is the picture catalogued as lot 208 in the Hestercombe Sale. John Hayes, 'The Gainsborough drawings from Barton Grange', *Connoisseur*, CLXI, no. 648, February 1966, pp. 86–93 describes the Barton Grange collection. Hayes notes (p. 87) that an oil belonging to Francis Wheat Newton at Barton Grange in 1895 was said to have come from a Warre sale in 1766. Coplestone Warre Bampfylde's mother was a Margaret Warre and Hestercombe had belonged to the Warre family since 1391. I have not been able to trace a Warre family sale of 1766 but the Hestercombe estate and Coplestone Bampfylde's effects were inherited by his nephew John Tyndale Warre. At his death in 1819 there was a sale that included 'The valuable and original Paintings, Prints and Drawings' from Hestercombe. The sale was announced in the *Taunton Courier* of 16 September 1819 and the pictures were sold on 5 October. No copy of this sale catalogue has been found. I am most grateful to Philip White and Audrey Mead for providing me with the details that are known of this sale.

90 Bampfylde's *The Storm* was exhibited at the Royal Academy in 1774. The engraving by Peter Benazech was published in 1779. An impression is in the BM, Department of Prints and Drawings, 1917–12–8–2917. William Benson Earle (1740–1796) was named after the architect William Benson of Wilbury, near Salisbury, Henry Hoare's uncle. William Benson Earle's name appears on an Indenture concerning the marriage settlement of Richard Colt Hoare dated 27 January 1784 (W&SRO, Stourhead papers 383/714, II, fol. 51). Prince Hoare engraved a profile portrait of William Benson Earle in 1769. Some details of the Earle family are given in A. W. Vivian-Neale, 'Barton Grange', *Proceedings of the Somerset Archaeological and Natural History Society*, LXXVII, pp. 108–11. The Barton Grange Earles descended from the Earles of West Harptree, Somerset.

91 Chapter 6, p. 113.

92 Hayes 1970, I, p. 37.

93 John Burke and John Bernard Burke, *A Genealogical and Heraldic Dictionary of the Landed Gentry*, 2 vols, London 1848, II, pp. 1449–50. In the collection of the National Museum of Wales at Cardiff is a copy by a Bristol artist Henry S. Parkman (*fl.* 1840–60) of a portrait of Sir Charles-Kemeys Tynte, said to be after an original by Hogarth, see [John Steegman and Philip J. Barlow] *National Museum of Wales, Catalogue of Oil Paintings*, Cardiff 1955, p. 41. Sir Charles-Kemeys Tynte paid Hogarth £42 in June 1753, see Gervase Jackson-Stops, 'Arcadia under the Plough: The Garden at Halswell, Somerset', *Country Life*, CLXXXIII, no. 6, 9 February 1989, p. 85.

94 If the portrait was by Van Dyck it could not have represented Sir Thomas Morgan at the siege of Dunkirk (as Bampfylde asserts in his caption), as this took place in 1657, fifteen years after Van Dyck's death. Sir Thomas Morgan (d. c. 1679) had connections with South Wales, the area with which the Kemeys family was associated, and Herefordshire.

95 Deborah Cherry and Jennifer Harris, 'Eighteenth-Century Portraiture and the Seventeenth-Century Past: Gainsborough and Van Dyck', *Art History*, V, no. 3, September 1982, pp. 287–309.

96 SRO, DD/S/WH/320.

97 Coplestone Bampfylde married Mary Knight, daughter of Edward Knight of Wolverley, in 1755 (White, *Bampfylde*, 1995, p. 5). Correspondence linking the Knights, Shenstone, Dr Rice Charleton and others is discussed below, Chapter 9.

98 Revd Richard Graves, *Columella; or, The Distressed Anchoret*, 2 vols, London 1779, I, p. 48. The full passage is quoted in Chapter 8, p. 168.

99 Colin Harrison, Susan Wollenberg and Julian Munby, *John Malchair of Oxford, Artist and Musician* (exh. cat., Ashmolean Museum), Oxford 1988, p. 10 and p. 30, n. 7. Harrison mentions that it had already been established that no 'Captain Bonfield' could be identified, and that the name of Bampfylde had been suggested as a possible explanation by A. P. Oppé: he does not, however, make the connection with Coplestone Bampfylde.

100 Woodall 1939, p. 80 says that Alexander Cozens settled in Bath in 1765, taught drawing and worked out his system of *blottings* there, but provides no evidence to verify this. The Bath drawing master Ferdinand Becker (d. 1825) certainly perpetuated Cozens's system of *blottings* in the city.

101 The print is illustrated in Rolls 1988, p. 16. John Wood described how 'By the 9th of February [1737/38] I not only perfected my Designs for the Hospital, but made a fair Plan and Elevation of it, which the Trustees desired Mr. Nash to take to London, to the End that the Draught might be laid before his Majesty and the rest of the Royal Family, and then be immediately convey'd to Mr. Pine in Order to be Engraved' (Wood 1749, II, p. 290).

102 Robert G. Stewart, *Robert Edge Pine: A British Portrait Painter in America 1784–1788*, Washington 1979, fig. 1, p. 14, illustrates Pine's portrait by Hogarth. John Pine was a Governor of the Foundling Hospital in London and may have had some connection with the A. Pyne whose name appears regularly in the earliest minute books of the Bath General Hospital. The notice of Pine's death in the *Gentleman's Magazine*, XXVI, 1756, p. 262, which calls him 'Engraver to the King's Signet and Stamp Office'.

103 Edwards 1808, p. 172: 'In the year 1772, upon the death of his brother Simon, he [Robert] went to Bath, and staid there till 1779'. These dates are supported by the appearance of his name in BRO, City Rates Books. Simon Pine had been living in Milsom Street, Bath and after his death Lucy Pine's name continues to appear in Milsom Street in the Rates Books until 1779. For Robert Edge Pine in Bath see Sloman 1996b, p. 148. The same article (p. 149) gives some information about John Robert Cozens in Bath: he rented a house in Westgate Buildings, Bath between 1779 and 1783. The 'Mr. and Mrs. Cozens' whose arrival in Bath is recorded in the *Boddely's Bath Journal*, 8 April 1765 could be Alexander Cozens and his wife.

104 Whitley 1915, p. 54.

105 The figure was scullpted by John Cheere, BRO, City General Committee Memorandum Book, 13 December 1774 – 13 March 1779, entry for 27 July 1776.

106 *Boddely's Bath Journal*, 15 March 1762.

107 It is also the case that Alexander Cozens's first private pupils were George Simon, Viscount Nuneham and his sister Elizabeth. The letter from William Whitehead to Viscount Nuneham that establishes the date for Gainsborough's first stay in Bath in 1758 is discussed in Chapter 3, pp. 38–9.

108 Wilton 1980, p. 36. In one letter Alexander Cozens asks William Hoare to send 'Compliments to Mr. Taylor' and in another he tells Hoare, 'What you write of Mr. Bamfylde has given me great joy & satisfaction. I return him my' [end of fragment].

109 *Bath Chronicle*, 17 March 1774.

110 Wilton 1980, pp. 38–40.

111 Kim Sloan, *Alexander and John Robert Cozens: The Poetry of Landscape*, New Haven and London 1986, p. 166.

112 Wilton 1980, no. 154, p. 56. Wilton doubts that the drawing is in fact by Cozens, although he concedes that there are marked similarities between Gainsborough and Cozens: 'Gainsborough's approach to the making of landscape drawings was similar to that of Alexander Cozens not only in his use of standard elements which he arranged and rearranged but in his methods and techniques' (ibid., no. 153, p. 56).

113 Several of Alexander Cozens's oils that have only come to light in recent years suggest that there are some common interests in both artists' approach to oil landscapes as well as drawings.

114 Hayes 1982, II, no. 89, p. 431.

115 [Sir Edward Harington], *A Schizzo on the Genius of Man: in which . . . the Merit of Mr. Thomas Barker . . . is particularly considered*, Bath 1793, (published anonymously), pp. 59–68. Apparently Allen's speciality was 'a miserable building, which he called a temple, with wretchedly proportioned columns, a man and a woman ascending a flight of steps . . . a turn-spit dog . . . lifting one of his hind legs against a tree . . .'. Allen called the composition 'a beautiful . . . imitation of Claude Lorraine'. A naïve etching is inserted in Harington's text, showing the interior of the Grove Coffee House in Bath with two of Allen's paintings propped up for discussion on chairs (ibid., opposite p. 59).

116 *Bath Journal*, 16 September 1754.

117 Lewis and Smith 1937–83, X, p. 231, Walpole to George Montagu, from Bath, 18 October 1766.

118 Goldsmith 1762, p. 47.

119 Farington 1978–98, IV, p. 1149.

120 Hayes 2001, no. 12, p. 24, from Bath 30 December 1763.

121 RA, Humphry papers, HU 1/20–40, unnumbered sheet between fols 36 and 37. The full passage is quoted in Chapter 4, p. 57.

122 Frederick Shum, 'Some notes on Gainsborough and his connection with Bradford', *Wiltshire Archaeological and Natural History Magazine*, XX, 1882, p. 62.

123 Meehan 1901, p. 47.

124 Paulson 1989, p. 275.

125 Michael Rosenthal, 'Gainsborough and St Martin's Lane', *Gainsborough's House Review 1997/98*, 1998, p. 43.

126 Hayes 2001, no. 12, p. 23.

127 Wood 1749, II, p. 440.

128 Tunstall 1847, p. 224.

129 Hayes 2001, no. 71, p. 121. The *Bath Chronicle* of 18 February 1772 records the marriage of the Revd John Chapman (1742–1816) to Miss Phillott, daughter of the late landlord of the famous Bear Inn, the meeting place for Bath Freemasons earlier in the century. In the same newspaper of 5 December 1771 is a note that John Chapman had been appointed Domestic Chaplain to the Earl of Westmorland. This must be the Ninth Earl, son of Gainsborough's sitter Thomas, Eighth Earl (Waterhouse 1966, no. 716, p. 95).

130 Revd Richard Warner, *A New Guide through Bath, and its Environs*, Bath 1811, pp. 183–4.

131 Pierce Egan, *Walks through Bath*, Bath 1819, p. 244.

132 BCL, Edmund Rack, 'A Disultory Journal of Events etc at Bath 1779–1780', MS III entry for 7 January 1780.

133 Hayes 1970, I, nos 244, 245, p. 165.

134 Henry Venn Lansdown, *Recollections of the Late William Beckford*, Kingsmead facsimile reprint, Bath [n.d.], p. 23 The original memoir is dated 1838 in the text.

135 Ann Sumner, 'Gainsborough's "Portrait of Lady Clarges"', *Burlington Magazine*, CXXX, no. 1027, October 1988, pp. 761–3.

136 Hayes 1982, II, no. 113, pp. 459–60.

137 Wood 1749, II, p. 440.

138 BCL, Rack, 'A Disultory Journal of Events etc at Bath', entry for 9 February 1780.

139 Samuel Taylor Coleridge, *Coleridge's Essays and Lectures on Shakespeare*, quoted by John Whale, 'Romantics, explorers and Picturesque travellers', in Stephen Copley and Peter Garside (eds), *The Politics of the Picturesque*, Cambridge 1994, pp. 179–80.

140 Paulson 1989, p. 275.

141 Belsey 1988, p. 22.

142 Kemp 1990, pp. 152–3.

143 Trevor Fawcett, 'Science Lecturing at Bath, 1724–1800', *Bath History*, VII, 1998, pp. 55–77.

144 Ibid., pp. 58–61.

145 Jackson 1798, pp. 167–8 (note); Reynolds 1959, p. 250; Edwards 1808, p. 139.

146 Mary Woodall, 'Gainsborough's Use of Models', *Antiques*, October 1956, pp. 363–5; William T. Whitley, 'Art Notes', *The Collector (formerly Old Furniture)*, IX, no. 34, March 1930, pp. 148–52. The latter article illustrates Gainsborough's model of a woodman, then in the possession of Alfred Hill (p. 148).

147 Tomas Nichols, 'Jacopo Tintoretto', in ed. Jane Turner, *Dictionary of Art*, 34 vols, London 1996, XXXI, p. 14, quotes Ridolfi's report of Tintoretto's use of models.

148 Oskar Batschmann, *Nicolas Poussin: Dialectics of Painting*, London 1990, pp. 27–9. Batschmann includes diagrams to show how Poussin's device, which is known from contemporary written descriptions, might have functioned.

149 Elizabeth Einberg, *Manners and Morals: Hogarth and British Painting 1700–1760* (exh. cat., Tate Gallery), London 1987, p. 113; Malcolm Andrews, *The Search for the Picturesque*, London 1990, pp. 34, 113.

150 Mary Woodall, 'Gainsborough's Use of Models', *Antiques*, October 1956, p. 364.

151 Ibid., p. 365. Woodall's article illustrated this portrait and referred to the use of models but did not make the connection between the sitters and Gainsborough.

152 Gainsborough is said to have entertained himself by drawing in the long winter evenings (Fulcher 1856, p. 163) and he is also said to have 'contrived a lamp with the sides painted with vermillion' in order to give a Rubensian glow to his subject (ibid., p. 166).

153 The only suggestion I have found that Gainsborough did use a camera obscura is in Michael Clarke, *The Tempting Prospect: A Social History of English Water-colours*, London 1981, p. 18. He says 'Smaller and more portable versions of the camera obscura were produced in the eighteenth century and a number of artists are known to have had recourse to one. The great Italian view-painter Canaletto, the Daniells, active in India, Thomas Sandby and Thomas Gainsborough are but a few of the artists who can be cited in this respect.' Was he perhaps confusing Gainsborough's 'show box' with a camera obscura?

154 Hayes 2001, no. 66, pp. 114–15.

155 J. H. Hammond, *The Camera Obscura: A Chronicle*, Bristol 1981, p. 74.

156 Ibid., p. 56.

157 Ibid., p. 79. Storer's Royal Accurate Delineator was demonstrated by William Storer in Bath in 1781 (Sloman 1996b, p. 148).

158 Kemp 1990, p. 199. Kemp believes the Claude Glass is probably so-called because of its harmonising effects, rather than because such a device was used or invented by Claude Lorrain.

159 Hayes 1970, I, no. 10, p. 112.

160 J. H. Hammond, *The Camera Obscura: A Chronicle*, Bristol 1981, fig. 47, p. 73. This copy-stand type of camera obscura dating from 1727 used a shaft of light in a darkened room, the light entering through a hole cut in a shutter. Gainsborough himself apparently had a shutter with a small circular aperture cut in it (Whitley 1915, pp. 247–8), perhaps another indication that he experimented with camera obscuras or similar optical instruments.

161 I am most grateful to Mike Gray, Curator of the Fox Talbot Museum at Lacock, for discussing with me the development of the camera obscura and its use by artists. He generously pointed me to published sources of information on the subject and showed me some of his own research, as yet unpublished. The characteristics of spherical aberration are illustrated in diagrammatic form in Otto Lummer, *Contributions to Photographic Optics* (translated by Silvanus P. Thompson), London 1900, pp. 33–5.

162 Hayes 1970, I, no. 264, p. 170 and no. 321, p. 183. Amal Asfour and Paul Williamson have also drawn attention to the curving compositions of many of Gainsborough's landscapes and suggested the influence of a Claude glass (Amal Asfour and Paul Williamson, *Gainsborough's Vision*, Liverpool, 1999, pp. 163–70).

163 Tracing paper or the paper used for transferring designs onto ceramics were the papers commonly used against the ground glass. Often the paper was oiled or varnished to give a better image. I am grateful to Mike Gray for this information. Another explanation for the distortion in these particular drawings by Gainsborough might be that he had in mind a notion of curvilinear perspective, something that Turner recognised and expressed in his well-known oil of *Petworth Park* of c. 1828 (Tate Gallery, London). Martin Kemp has pointed out that Gainsborough's friend Joshua Kirby was 'alert to the latest debates on problems of perception, and, as a result, steered a middle course between absolute obedience to rule and reliance upon 'our common Judgement and Estimation of the Appearance of objects from Custom and Experience' (Kemp 1990, pp. 152–3). Kemp proposes that Kirby's flexibility might allow for a recognition of curvilinear perspective.

164 Both Lawrence Binyon and Mary Woodall noted that among Gainsborough's drawings there are some in which the main outlines of the design appear to be transferred to the paper surface rather than drawn directly on to it. Binyon suggested the lines themselves were drawn in oil colour (Woodall 1939, p. 102). Technical analysis has failed to prove whether or not a process of offsetting is involved (John Hayes, 'Gainsborough Drawings: A Supplement to the Catalogue Raisonné', *Master Drawings*, XXI, winter 1983, pp. 369–70). If it is, these drawings might have been traced from a ground glass and then transferred from the back of the tracing paper. No direct offsetting from the ground glass is used, since the normal direction of Gainsborough's shading is maintained (it would be reversed in a direct offset). Since the images themselves are idealised rather than topographical, Gainsborough may have been viewing a model through a camera obscura, or copying another drawing using a copy-stand type of instrument.

165 Hayes 1982, II, no. 132, p. 497; no. 133, pp. 497–8; no. 134, pp. 498–9; no. 139, pp. 505–6; no. 140, p. 506; nos 154, 155, p. 527; no. 172, p. 553; no. 173, p. 555; no. 177, p. 560.

166 Fulcher 1856, pp. 123–4. The *Eidophusikon* and Jervas's glass were both also shown in Bath in 1781 and 1782, see Sloman 1966b, pp. 148–9.

167 Hayes 2001, no. 63, p. 108. Another form of transparency was the transparent window blind, examples of which survive from the 1780s. These were oiled cloths on which were painted decorations, see James Ayres, *Building the Georgian City*, New Haven and London 1998, pp. 224–5.

168 Lord Cobham's gardens were those at Stowe in Buckinghamshire.

169 *Bath Journal*, 26 November 1744. The 'Wilderness' was open from 10am until 9pm, at the upper end of Grand Parade. Entry was six pence. It is not clear what the 'Wilderness' was, but following Sir Isaac Newton's death in 1727 there was a huge popular interest in his writings on light and the prism (Marjorie Nicolson and G. S. Rousseau, *'This Long Disease,*

My Life': Alexander Pope and the Sciences, Princeton 1968, pp. 267–9).

170 Horace Walpole, *Anecdotes of Painting in England, 1760–1795*, ed. F. W. Hilles and P. B. Daghlian, 5 vols, New Haven and London 1937, v, p. 89, describes Robert Carver and Garvey's paintings for *The Touchstone* in 1779, with 'transparent figures . . . by Mr. Rigaud of Titchfield-street'. Taylor is said to have shown Thomas Sandby a show box in 1766, something claimed to be a new invention (Wright [n.d.], under Taylor), but as the newspaper advertisement cited in the main text above shows, such devices were in use by the 1740s.

8 *The Intellectual Elite of Bath*

1 Hayes 2001, no. 39, pp. 64–5, in a letter to William Jackson, from Bath, Gainsborough observed that a Mr John Dunning, whose formidable intelligence he greatly admired, had a jutting forehead, quite opposite to his own receding brow. When asked to advise on the subject of a disputed painting by Poussin in a court of law, Gainsborough opened his statement by saying that 'having had no opportunity for the study, he was no judge of the hands of the Masters', but then proceeded to give a firm view on the lack of quality in the painting (Whitley 1915, p. 297). Jackson 1798, p. 160 says the artist 'detested reading', but some of Jackson's sweeping statements about Gainsborough in *The Four Ages* are over-simplified. It should be noted that some of Gainsborough's contemporaries believed Jackson to be unreliable, Sir George Beaumont for example, wondered why Jackson should have apparently 'intended to make him ridiculous as a man'? (Woodall 1963, no. 107, p. 181). John Hayes's interpretation of Gainsborough as an intuitive artist has occasionally prompted criticism, see for example David Solkin's review 'The Battle of the Books; or, the Gentleman Provok'd – Different Views on the History of British Art', *Art Bulletin*, lxvii, no. 3, September 1985, pp. 507–15.

2 John Brewer, 'Cultural Production, Consumption, and the Place of the Artist in Eighteenth-Century England', in ed. Brian Allen, *Towards a Modern Art World: Studies in British Art 1*, New Haven and London 1995, p. 18.

3 Pointon 1979, pp. 441–55. Michael Rosenthal, 'The Rough and the Smooth: Rural Subjects in Late Eighteenth-Century British Art', *Eighteenth-Century Life*, xviii, May 1994, pp. 36–58 and Michael Rosenthal, 'Landscape as High Art', in ed. Katharine Baetjer, *Glorious Nature: British Landscape Painting 1750–1850* (exh. cat., Denver Art Museum), Denver, Colorado, 1993, pp. 22–5.

4 Ernest Fletcher (ed.), *Conversations of James Northcote R.A. with James Ward on Art and Artists*, London 1901, p. 160.

5 [Pott] 1782, p. 73

6 Solkin 1982, no. 77, p. 192 identifies the *Lake of Nemi* landscape by Wilson that Henry Hoare purchased in 1758 with a different picture, but he does not mention the engraving with its inscription stating that this upright composition belonged to Hoare.

7 Clayton 1997, p. 182 and p. 301, n. 7, refers to Wood's advertisement in the *Public Advertiser*. Early impressions of *The Gipsies* dating from 1759 are known (Hayes 1971, no. 2, pp. 37–41), but most impressions of the print date from Boydell's publication of it in 1764 following Wood's death in March 1763 (Bensusan-Butt 1993, pp. 50–51). It is not correct to say, as Bensusan-Butt does, that Boydell's edition lacks any reference to Wood as engraver. A painting formerly in a collection in Eastbourne that appeared on the market in 2001 (Sotheby's, London, 4 July 2001, lot 70), said in the sale catalogue to be the original painting by Gainsborough of *The Gipsies*, lacks all the refinement of the print, and Hayes would seem to be correct in suggesting it is a copy of the original (Hayes 1982, ii, no. 44, p. 376). Hayes proposes a date of 1753–4 for the original painting. A later date, nearer to 1758, seems more likely to this author, since the supposed study or preliminary version of the picture of c. 1753–4 (Hayes 1982, ii, no. 43, pp. 375–6) is quite different in concept. It also seems likely Joseph Wood would have engraved a more recently painted picture.

8 Owen 1996, p. 65.

9 David A. Brenneman, 'Thomas Gainsborough and the Picturesque Sketch', *Word & Image*, xiii, no. 4, October–December 1997, p. 393.

10 William Gilpin's domestic tours were written and privately circulated in the 1770s but the first to be published was his *Observations on the River Wye* that appeared in 1782, see Stephen Copley, 'Gilpin on the Wye: Tourists, Tintern Abbey, and the Picturesque', in Michael Rosenthal, Christiana Payne and Scott Wilcox (eds), *Prospects for the Nation: Recent Essays in British Landscape, 1750–1880, Studies in British Art 4*, New Haven and London 1997, pp. 133–55.

11 Gilpin himself said, 'With Gainsborough's pictures I am little acquainted' (Brenneman, 'Thomas Gainsborough and the Picturesque Sketch', p. 398).

12 Price 1796–8, ii, pp. 429–30.

13 Price 1794, p. 10.

14 Price 1796–8, ii, p. 90; pp. 96–7.

15 Ibid., p. 97.

16 Charlotte Klonk, *Science and the Perception of Nature: British Landscape Art in the Late Eighteenth and Early Nineteenth Centuries*, New Haven and London 1996, p. 28.

17 Ibid., p. 27.

18 Price 1810, i, p. 89.

19 Ibid., pp. 66–7.

20 Whitley 1915, p. 396 and Hayes 1982, i, p. 130. Gainsborough's Mola was presumably the painting described as by 'F. Mili' in the Schomberg House Sale of 1789. Numbered 44 in the catalogue, it sold for ten guineas to J. Barwell, see Ellis Waterhouse, 'The Sale at Schomberg House, 1789', *Burlington Magazine*, lxxxvi, no. 504, March 1945, p. 77.

21 Hayes 1970, i, no. 248, p. 166. Hayes notes the labels on the back of the drawing which indicate that it dates from a visit made by Gainsborough to Foxley in 1760 but calls Robert Price 'Sir Robert Price', perhaps confusing Robert Price with his grandson Robert who was a Baronet. The signature 'Tho: Gainsborough/del 1760' is on a fragment of paper now attached to the back.

22 Uvedale Tomkyns Price is buried in Bath Abbey. There is a memorial to him on the wall at low level near the north west entrance to the church. The inscription reads,

> Here lies the Body of Uvedale Price of Geelar in the County of Denbigh Esq. Son of Robert Price Baron of the Exchequer who died in this City the 17th of March 1764 aged 79 Years. He Marry'd Anne daughter and co-heiress of Lord Arthur Somerset fifth son of Henry Duke of Beaufort and by Her was father of Robert Price of Foxley in the County of Hereford Esq. Who died before him leaving by Sarah his Wife, daughter of John Lord Viscount Barrington, several children of whom Uvedale the eldest hath succeeded to the antient family Estates of Geelar and Foxley'.

23 Uvedale Price was born in 1747, Mary Gainsborough, the artist's elder daughter, early in 1750. The correct birth dates of the artist's daughters are established in David Tyler's article 'Thomas Gainsborough's daughters', *Gainsborough's House Society Annual Report 1991/92*, 1992, pp. 50–64.

24 Basil Duke Henning, *The History of Parliament: The House of Commons 1660–1690*,

3 vols, London 1983, iii, p. 286. Robert Price had acquired Foxley from his wife's family by buying out the Rodd coheirs in 1681.

25 Jenkins 1983, pp. 145, 165 *passim*.

26 Freeman O'Donoghue and Henry M. Hake, *Catalogue of Engraved British Portraits in the Department of Prints and Drawings* . . . , 6 vols, London 1912–25, iii, pp. 514–15 lists various Price family prints including a small stipple engraving of 'Miss Price' of 1819. Also the npg provides the information that at Holkham the painting is called 'Mrs Price'. The appellation 'Lady Price' might actually indicate that the picture represents Lucy Price (née Rodd), Uvedale's mother, since Robert Price, baron of the Exchequer was often called Baron Price or Lord Baron Price. Lucy caused a family scandal by running away with Thomas Neale, see Lord Rennell of Rodd, *Valley on the March: A History of a Group of Manors on the Hereford March of Wales*, London 1958, pp. 268–70.

27 Thomas Pennant, *Tours in Wales*, 3 vols, Caernarvon 1883 (first published 1773–84), ii, p. 213. Gainsborough's portrait of Pennant, which shows him holding a volume of his *Tours*, is in the National Museum of Wales, Cardiff (Waterhouse 1966, no. 540, p. 84).

28 Sedgwick 1970, ii, p. 369.

29 Ingamells 1997, p. 787. Uvedale Tomkyns Price was in Padua on 16 September 1711 and in Venice by 18 September when it was reported that 'the eldest son of Lord Baron Price is to come to pass the winter here'. Edward Hyde, Lord Cornbury, father of the Lord Cornbury painted by Gainsborough, was also in Italy in 1711 and included Venice in his itinerary. It is not known whether the two men's paths crossed on this occasion (ibid., p. 242).

30 Udal ap Rhys [Uvedale Tomkyns Price], *An Account of the Most Remarkable Places and Curiosoties in Spain and Portugal*, London 1749. The title page indicates this book was for sale via booksellers including James Leake of Bath. Price's interest in this part of Europe was presumably prompted by his father's close contact with the Portuguese Catherine of Braganza.

31 Ibid., introduction, p. iii.

32 Philip Thicknesse, *A Year's Journey through France, and Part of Spain*, 2 vols, Dublin 1777, i, p. 282.

33 [Price], *An Account of the Most Remarkable Places*, pp. 67–8.

34 Ibid., pp. 127 and 156.

35 Philip Sohm, *Pittoresco: Marco Boschini, his Critics, and their Critiques of Painterly Brushwork in Seventeenth- and Eighteenth-Century Italy*, Cambridge 1991, shows how painterly brushwork was associated with inspired creativity unrestrained by academic learning and how the word *pittoresco* came to be linked with brushwork. He quotes a letter from Salvator Rosa of 1652 in which the painter describes two pictures of his own as 'two small canvases with flowers painted *alla pittoresca*, that is, *di furia*, . . .' (p. 93).

36 Waterhouse 1966, p. 36 goes as far as to suggest that 'Murillo seems in fact to have been (perhaps after Van Dyck) Gainsborough's favourite painter'.

37 Reid 1980, p. 57 refers to Uvedale Tomkyns Price's copy of *Vitruvius Britannicus* (1715) in which, against the plate of Stoke Edith, the Herefordshire home of the Foley family, Price wrote 'invented by Mr Davies a carpenter'.

38 Revd Joseph Spence, *Polymetis: or, An Enquiry concerning the Agreement Between the Works of the Roman Poets and the Remains of the Antient Artists*, London 1747, p. 2. Uvedale Tomkyns Price's name is listed among subscribers on p. xi. Daniel Webb also subscribed (p. xii), as did Ralph Allen (p. vii), Nathaniel Hooke (p. ix), the Late Duke of Beaufort (p. vii) and Lord Barrington, Robert Price's father-in-law (p. xii) who subscribed to three copies. Spence uses this book to advocate a style of landscape gardening in which there exists a seamless link between the 'garden' and the surrounding scenery. Polymetis, surveying the gardens below his villa, explains to his friends, 'Their general air, I hope, has nothing stiff or unnatural in it; and the lower part, in particular, joins in with the view of the country, as if made a part of it' (ibid., p. 2).

39 Whitley 1915, p. 352. Gainsborough also owned a copy of *Vitruvius Britannicus*, again, a book owned by Uvedale Tomkyns Price.

40 BadM, Somerset family papers fm t/b 1/2/23. The letter is one of several between Mrs Anne Price and her aunt Lady Anne Coventry, sister to Lord Arthur Somerset, Mrs Price's father. It is dated 18 June. The house building at Foxley was planned by May 1715, as another letter in the same bundle dated 20 May 1715 shows. The complicated history of how Foxley came into the possession of the Price family is set out in Lambin 1987, pp. 244–70. See also Stephen Daniels, Susanne Seymour and Charles Watkins, 'Border Country: The Politics of the Picturesque in the Middle Wye Valley', in Rosenthal, Payne and Wilcox (eds.), *Prospects for the Nation*, p. 163.

41 Price 1810, ii, pp. 123–4.

42 Ibid., pp. 120–24. Uvedale Price pulled down his grandfather's summer-house, an action he lived to regret. He admitted that during a period of his youth he came under the influence of the Brownian 'improvers' and swept aside his grandfather's rococo garden. He later realised he could have rearranged the sculptures and other garden features in a Picturesque manner rather than destroy them. From this it appears that Price's theory of the Picturesque was the result of a mature reflection on the lessons he had learnt from Gainsborough. It was only after he himself had, for a time, been swayed by the fashion for 'flattening' that he came to appreciate the importance of landscape painting to garden design.

43 Reid 1980, p. 26. Reid points out that Foxley was in the style of the Smith family of architects of Warwick. It remained in the Price family until 1856, after which date numerous alterations were made and extensions built. It was demolished in 1948 following damage during army occupation during World War ii.

44 Michael Brennan, 'Alexander Pope and the Somerset Family', *Review of English Studies*, xlv, 1994, pp. 357–69. I am grateful to Michael Brennan for pointing me to this article.

45 The picture was sold at Christie's, London, 6 May 1893, lot 49, at which time it was attributed to Hogarth, perhaps partly because Sir Uvedale Price recorded that his father was much acquainted with Hogarth (Price 1796–8, ii, pp. 269–70). The picture was convincingly attributed to Dandridge by C. H. Collins Baker in 'The Price Family by Bartholomew Dandridge', *Burlington Magazine*, lxxii, no. 420, March 1938, pp. 132–9. Collins Baker took the seated boy to be Robert Price and therefore dated the picture to c. 1728, but the standing young man has very distinctive features that entirely accord with Gainsborough's portraits of Robert Price and the picture is close in style to Dandridge's *The Ladies Noel* of c. 1739–40, now in Manchester City Art Gallery. In a letter to the *Burlington Magazine*, lxxii, no. 424, July 1938, pp. 38–9, Michael F. J. McDonnell pointed out that Dandridge and Uvedale Tomkyns Price were both pupils of St Paul's School, London and so could well have known each other as children.

46 The portrait is now in the National Portrait Gallery, London. It should also be noted that Dandridge's portrait of Frederick, Prince of Wales was apparently painted for Lord Barrington (Collins Baker, 'The Price Family by Bartholomew Dandridge', p. 136).

47 Sherburn 1956, IV, p. 350, Pope to Ralph Allen, 14 (?July) 1741. A letter from Lady Anne Coventry to Lord Noel Somerset of 15 June 1741 reports Mrs Price's death: 'Tho the death of my poor Neice [sic] Price must greatly affect all her friends it will to her, be a happy release' (BadM, Somerset family papers, FM J 2/24 (30)). As early as 18 October 1737 Mrs Price herself had written to Lord Noel Somerset thanking him for a present of wine, 'I beg pardon for the many defects of this Letter; but tis the product of an unsteady hand, and more than ordinarily confus'd Head' (BadM, Somerset family papers, FM J 2/15 (12)).

48 See Chapter 3, p. 43 and n. 57.

49 C. Hoare & Co., Ledger 41/197.

50 For example, C. Hoare & Co., Ledger 57/182, the entry in Unwin's account for 5 April 1756 notes a payment of £315 'To Hester Grevile'. Other payments to Fulke Greville or Grevile and 'Mrs Grevile' occur in Burgh's and Unwin's accounts.

51 Elizabeth Einberg, *Manners and Morals: Hogarth and British Painting 1700–1760* (exh. cat., Tate Gallery), London 1987, no. 108, p. 126 and no. 95, p. 113, *The Ladies Noel*.

52 Ibid., p. 126, quoting George Vertue.

53 In the Christie's sale catalogue cited above, n. 45, were Price family pictures, including Gainsborough's portrait of Uvedale Tomkyns Price now in Munich (lot 46); a picture that must have been one of Gainsborough's 'heads' of Robert Price (lot 48), and a portrait of Mrs Anne Price (lot 47) listed as Gainsborough, but since Mrs Price died in 1741 this cannot have been by him, unless it was a posthumous portrait. Also listed was a portrait of Lord Arthur Somerset, Mrs Price's father, by Kneller (lot 51) and a portrait of Robert Price's wife Sarah by Arthur Pond (lot 58). In family correspondence Lady Anne Coventry refers to sending to Foxley a copy of Kneller's portrait of her son by Thomas Gibson, with the costume altered by Wootton (BadM, Somerset family papers FM T/B 1/2/23).

54 [Price] 1733. Gainsborough made this complaint in a letter from Bath to William Jackson dated only 4 June (Hayes 2001, no. 40, p. 68).

55 [Price] 1733, pp. 15 and 31.

56 Hoare's portrait is known only through a photograph in the NPG entitled Sir Uvedale Price, Bart by Robert Edge Pine. It can be identified as Hoare's by a record drawing by Hoare in the BM, Department of Prints and Drawings, see Newby 1990, nos 27 and 27a, p. 45.

57 Hayes noted that some of the old master drawings that belonged to the Price family may have had an influence on Gainsborough's drawing style (Hayes 1970, I, pp. 58–9). Hayes believed these drawings to have been purchased by the young Sir Uvedale Price on his grand tour in 1767–8, but the elder Uvedale and his son Robert were also keen collectors, and many of their drawings were acquired from Pond rather than abroad, as Lippincott shows.

58 Francis W. Hawcroft, 'The "Cabinet" at Felbrigg', *Connoisseur*, CXLI, May 1958, pp. 216–19. For Price's grand tour and Busiri see also R. W. Ketton-Cremer, *Felbrigg: The Story of a House*, Ipswich 1962, pp. 113–16.

59 Hawcroft, 'The "Cabinet" at Felbrigg', p. 216.

60 Marie-Nicole Boisclair, *Gaspard Dughet (1615–1675)*, Paris 1986, p. 350, catalogue no. G. 22, *Paysage*, inscribed: 'Gaspar Possin pinx. – I.Wood Sculp./ In the Collection of Rob.t Price Esq.r/ Publish'd by Ar. Pond July 6th 1743 – 3 feet 3 Inch. Wide/ 2 feet 5 Inch high.' Boisclair mistakenly describes this and other prints after Dughet inscribed I. Wood and published by Pond as by 'John' Wood, but they are in fact by Joseph Wood (d. 1763).

61 The artist's admiration for Dughet is expressed in his letter to Lord Hardwicke (Hayes 2001, no. 15, p. 30) as well as through his work. See John Hayes, 'Gainsborough and the Gaspardesque', *Burlington Magazine*, CXII, no. 806, May 1970, pp. 308–11. Hayes notes that 'Gainsborough first became aware of Gaspard at the time of his moving to Bath in 1759 . . .', but does not suggest how or where he saw any paintings by the artist.

62 F. I. McCarthy, 'Some Newly Discovered Drawings by Robert Price of Foxley', *National Library of Wales Journal*, XIII, no. 3, summer 1964, p. 289.

63 Price 1796–8, II, pp. 269–70.

64 The ascription to Zoffany may have come about as a result of the fact that Zoffany did paint a portrait of Price's close friend *Benjamin Stillingfleet* (National Portrait Gallery). The print by James Basire was made to illustrate Coxe 1811, II, pp. 169–82, Stillingfleet's 'Recollection' of Robert Price.

65 Lambin 1987, p. 252, and Beryl Hartley, 'Naturalism and Sketching: Robert Price at Foxley and on Tour', Stephen Daniels and Charles Watkins (eds), *The Picturesque Landscape: Visions of Georgian Herefordshire* (exh. cat., Hereford City Art Gallery and University Art Gallery, Nottingham), Nottingham 1994, pp. 34–7.

66 Solkin 1982, p. 103.

67 Boydell's print is illustrated in Clayton 1997, fig. 131, p. 115. For early depictions of Wales in general see Peter Lord, *The Visual Culture of Wales: Imaging the Nation*, Cardiff 2000.

68 Chapter 7, p. 132 and n. 99. It was thanks to the patronage of Shute Barrington, Robert Price's brother-in-law, that Malchair became leader of the Oxford Music Room orchestra in 1759. Price's monochrome drawings such as his *View up the River Wye near Bridge Sollars in Herefordshire* (BM, Department of Prints and Drawings, 1983-5-21-36) had a profound influence on Malchair's drawing style.

69 Knight 1794, p. 25; BM, Department of Prints and Drawings, Robert Price, *Wooded Landscape after A. Waterloo*, pencil and brown ink wash, 20.1 × 25 cm, 1983-5-21-35.

70 A collection of eighteen drawings is in the National Library of Wales, Aberystwyth, see McCarthy, 'Some Newly Discovered Drawings by Robert Price of Foxley', pp. 289–94, and plates 9–10.

71 Sloman 1998, p. 47 and p. 52, n. 8.

72 Stillingfleet's recollection of Robert Price in Coxe 1811, II, p. 174.

73 Ibid., pp. 174–5.

74 Reid 1980, p. 26.

75 Jack Calow, 'The Ragged Castle, An Architectural Feature on the Foxley Estate, Herefordshire', *The Picturesque*, no. 34, spring 2001, pp. 1–14. Jack Calow seems to be the first person to have made a serious study of the Castle. His article describes the optical trickery involved in the plan of the structure and suggests the involvement of Sanderson Miller (1716–1780) in its creation. He also illustrates the original Gothic form of the windows (now altered to Georgian sash-style). I am most grateful to Jack Calow for discussing his ideas about the Castle with me. He does not connect Ragged Castle with Giler. Neither Reid or Calow comment on the name, or when the structure was first called 'Ragged Castle'. A later folly at Badminton, built by Thomas Wright between 1748 and 1756 is also called 'Ragged Castle', see Eileen Harris, 'Architect of Rococo Landscapes, Thomas Wright – III', *Country Life*, CL, no. 3874, 9 September 1971, fig. 7, p. 614.

76 I am most grateful to the staff of the Royal Commission on the Ancient and Historical Monuments of Wales, Aberystwyth, for information about the Giler gatehouse which is dated 1623 in a plaster panel over the fireplace in the upper floor room. The history of Giler is described in Douglas B. Hague, 'Giler, Cerrig-y-drudion, Denbighshire', *Denbighshire Historical Society Transactions*, VII, 1958, pp. 67–85.

77 Solkin 1982, no. 106, pp. 216–17. Wilson's *The Lake of Nemi or Speculum Dianae with Dolbadarn Castle* was one of four canvases painted for Henry Blundell of Ince Hall. Blundell was married to Elizabeth Mostyn, a relative of Gainsborough's sitter Lady Mostyn. The picture is now in the collection of Bristol City Museum and Art Gallery.

78 Price 1796–8, I, pp. 378–9.

79 Everett 1994, p. 113.

80 Reynolds 1959, p. 14.

81 Everett 1994, p. 127.

82 Daines Barrington, 'On the Progress of Gardening', a paper read on 13 June 1782, published in *Archaeologia: or Miscellaneous Tracts relating to Antiquity*, VII, 1785, p. 130.

83 Ibid., p. 129.

84 Ibid., p. 130. By 'the gardener of Old Stowe' Barrington must have meant Charles Bridgeman. Bridgeman was regarded by some as a spoiler of landscape (Everett 1994, p. 46). For Bridgeman and the 'starkness of geometry', see Tom Williamson, *Polite Landscapes: Gardens and Society in Eighteenth-Century England*, Baltimore 1995, p. 52. The passage from *The Faerie Queene* is from book 2, canto 12, verse 59, transcribed in Edmund Spenser, *Edmund Spenser: The Fairy Queen*, ed. Douglas Brooks-Davies, London 1996 (first published 1590–96), as,

> One would have thought (so cunningly the rude
> And scorned parts were mingled with the fine)
> That Nature had, for wantonness, ensued
> Art, and that Art at Nature did repine:
> So striving each the other to undermine,
> Each did the other's work more beautify;
> So, differing both in wills, agreed in fine;
> So all agreed through sweet diversity
> This garden to adorn with all variety.

85 Hayes 2001, no. 15, p. 30. Whether Gainsborough ever 'gave the design' for a landscape garden in a direct practical sense is not on record. It is worth noting that in 1763 the artist's brother Humphrey Gainsborough built an extraordinary bridge, 'composed of rocks that appear to have been tumbled together', as part of the improvements to Park Place at Henley in Berkshire, a scheme that also included a 'very pretty' cottage (George H. Peters, *Humphry Gainsborough, Engineer, Inventor*, Henley 1948, pp. 14–15). The bridge may be seen as one of the earliest expressions of Picturesque style in England, built over thirty years before Sir Uvedale Price's *Essay* was published, and since Humphrey Gainsborough's principal talent was for engineering, it seems more than likely that Thomas Gainsborough was the inspiration for its design.

86 Daines Barrington's mother was the daughter of Sir William Daines, sheriff of Bristol, who died in 1763.

87 Lambin 1987, p. 257.

88 Fulcher 1856, pp. 140 and 193; Whitley 1915, p. 307.

89 The *Woodman* sold for five hundred guineas to the Earl of Gainsborough. It was no. 82 in the exhibition at Schomberg House in 1789, see Ellis Waterhouse, 'The Sale at Schomberg House, 1789', *Burlington Magazine*, LXXXVI, no. 504, March 1945, p. 77. The painting was destroyed by fire at Eaton Park (Fulcher 1856, p. 140).

90 Belsey 1988, p. 40. Whitley 1915, p. 310 says that Sophia Lane had lived with the Gainsboroughs and helped care for the artist in his final illness. Sophia's husband Theophilus Lane was the son of James Lane of Hereford, Treasurer for the County of Herefordshire, Auditor of the Cathedral, Bailiff and Chief Steward to the Dean and Chapter (Revd Francis T. Havergal, *Monumental Inscriptions in the Cathedral Church of Hereford*, London 1881, p. 45). I am most grateful to Janet Harris for sharing information on the Lane family with me.

91 NPG, among a collection of Richard J. Lane Letters, L.O.i, an unsigned letter of 1828, numbered 9, from Sir Robert Price, son of Sir Uvedale, to Richard J. Lane, regarding the lithograph after a drawing by J. Slater. Price thanks Lane for 'the trouble and interest Mr. Lane has taken in the work'. Elsewhere in the same collection is a letter from C. R. Leslie, numbered 6, dated 1827, in which Leslie says, 'If you think Don Quixote's head worth ten guineas without my robbing you of any Gainsboroughs & can oblige me with it, it will be very useful to me'. In letter no. 13 Lord Cawdor thanks Lane for 'the admirable copy from Gainsborough'. Letter no. 214, dated 1851, from F. R. Lee asks Lane to look at a painting in the collection of Mr Bransley Cooper, an eminent surgeon, which Lee believes to be by Gainsborough.

92 Waterhouse 1966, no. 17, p. 52, *Claudius Amyand* and nos 164–6, p. 61, portraits of Charles, Frederick and Thomas Cornewall. The Amyands and Cornewalls were both of Moccas, which bordered Foxley on the west. On the death of Velters Cornewall of Moccas in 1768 the estate passed to his daughter Catherine, the wife of Sir George Amyand. In 1771 Amyand took the name and arms of Cornewall (C. J. Robinson, *A History of the Mansions and Manors of Herefordshire*, London and Hereford 1873, p. 209). Garnestone borders Foxley to the east. I am most grateful to Rupert Peploe who drew my attention to an engraving by James Thomson inscribed as after a portrait by Gainsborough of the Revd Samuel Peploe. The engraving appears in Samuel Hibbert-Ware, *History of the Foundations in Manchester*, 3 vols, London and Manchester 1834–48, II, opposite p. 82. The family also believes that Gainsborough painted Samuel Peploe's son, John Peploe.

93 Rosenthal, 'Landscape as High Art', pp. 22–5.

94 Everett 1994, p. 91.

95 Michael Cole, 'Gainsborough's Diversions', *Word & Image*, XIII, no. 4, October–December 1997, pp. 369–70.

96 Hayes 2001, no. 21, p. 38.

97 Richardson 1715, p. 159.

98 Ibid., pp. 41–2. Other writers such as Shaftesbury also refer to 'a false Taste of Pleasure' (Barrell, 1986, p. 11), but it is the coupling of 'false taste' and 'impudent taste' and their link with the exemplar of Van Dyck that points to Richardson as the specific source.

99 Prince Hoare, 'Introduction: Dangers to which the Progress of the Arts in England has been exposed . . .', essay dated 14 March 1807, in Prince Hoare (ed.), *The Artist: A Collection of Essays*, 2 vols, London 1810, I, p. 8. Gainsborough's assimilation of Richardson's treatise may have had a profound effect, not only on his judgement of the art of his contemporaries, but in his own deeper understanding of Van Dyck. This text may even have prompted some of his own experiments in portraiture. Richardson describes how Van Dyck enhanced likeness by depicting implied movement in the features of his sitters, these 'Moving Features . . . are as much part of the Man as the Fix'd ones . . . And contribute more to a Surprizing Likeness than any thing else. Van-Dyck, in a Picture I have of him, has given a brisk Touch upon the Under-Lip which makes the Form, and Set of the Mouth very particular . . .' (Richardson 1715, p. 98). This is precisely the effect Gainsborough experimented with in portraits such as *Johann Christian Bach* of 1776 (Waterhouse 1966, no. 31, p. 52).

100 *London Evening Post*, 22–4 April 1762 (PMC cuttings).

101 Johannes Dobai, *Die Kunstlerliteratur des Klassizismus und der Romantic in England*, 4 vols, Bern c. 1974 – c. 1984, III, pp. 718–34. The various editions are listed on p. 734.

102 Llanover 1861, III, p. 605, letter from Bath dated 23 October 1760.

103 W&SRO, Stourhead papers 383/907, a letter dated Bath 5 June 1760. Hoare wrote, 'As for Elegance Simplicity and Grace, the Antients will ever bear the preeminence & I join with Mr Webb there & in many other things, & I like his keeping up throughout his Book a high Idea of the Art, whether it be true or no that the Exemplars reached that pitch of perfection'. Henry Hoare's own copy of the *Inquiry* is now in the Victoria and Albert Museum, see Roettgen 1993, no. 55, p. 150.

104 Shenstone 1768–73 III, p. 318, no. CII, letter from The Leasowes, dated 7 July 1760.

105 Hans Hecht, *Daniel Webb: Ein Beitrag zur Englischen Asthetik des Achtzehnten Jahrhunderts*, Hamburg 1920, p. 1. This is the only book on Webb. I am most grateful to Jeremy Key-Pugh for translating essential passages for me.

106 SHM, Whitehead letters, Whitehead to Lord Nuneham, from Bath, 9 December 1760.

107 Ingamells 1997, p. 983.

108 John Hayes included an illustration of a detail of the portrait in his, *Gainsborough, Paintings and Drawings*, London 1975, fig. 3, p. 20, but apparently later ceased to believe that it could represent Gainsborough when he noticed that the book on the table is titled 'WEBB on Painting'. In an annotation on an illustration of the portrait in the NPG Hayes suggests the portrait might rather represent Webb himself. However the man depicted is clearly an artist or amateur artist (holding a porte-crayon and a drawing), which Webb was not, and the likeness accords very well with the Zoffany's portrait that must be closely similar in date. I am also grateful to Hugh Belsey, who has examined the portrait in Santa Barbara and believes it does represent Gainsborough. Victor Chan, 'A Portrait of Thomas Gainsborough', *Archivero 1: Research Papers on Works in the Collection of the Santa Barbara Museum of Art*, Santa Barbara 1973, pp. 93–114 describes the portrait and attributes it to Hoare but does not identify the book on the table as Webb's. The article contains a number of errors, including dating Zoffany's portrait to 'three years before Gainsborough's death' (p. 94), rather than to 1771–2 as is generally accepted.

109 *Gentleman's Magazine*, XLIII, December 1773, p. 614.

110 Published in London by James Dodsley. In one verse, on p. 13, he mentions the famous Dr Monro, admirer of Gainsborough, curing a madman. The castrato singer Tenducci, the subject of two Gainsborough portraits, is also named (p. 12).

111 Tierney 1988, p. 475, a letter dated Bath 21 May 1763 to Robert Dodsley in London.

112 BCL, Edmund Rack, 'A Disultory Journal of Events etc at Bath 1779–1780', MS III, 11 February 1780.

113 Newby 1990, p. 10.

114 Wark 1958, p. 332.

115 Roettgen 1993, p. 18 and no. 55, p. 150.

116 Denis Diderot, *Diderot on Art II*, trans. John Goodman, New Haven and London 1995, pp. 294–6.

117 Webb 1760, p. 94: 'Rubens has painted in imitation of the rainbow; all the colours cooperate; the effect is good but accidental; but, in Titian and Correggio, this arrangement is the result of science . . .'.

118 A. Chalmers, *English Poets*, 21 vols, London 1810, XVIII, pp. 295–6. Cambridge's poem is not dated. The same poet also addressed a poem to Ozias Humphry, in 1777, ibid., pp. 294–5.

119 Llanover 1861, III, p. 605.

120 [Joseph Highmore], 'Remarks on some Passages in Mr Webb's "Enquiry into the Beauties of Painting" etc', *Gentleman's Magazine*, XXXVI, August 1766, p. 353.

121 Jackson 1798, pp. 167–8.

122 Walpole's catalogue is now in the Library of the Yale Center for British Art, New Haven.

123 Ingamells 1997, p. 983.

124 Roettgen 1993, no. 55, p. 150.

125 Johann Joachim Winckleman, *Reflections on the Painting and Sculpture of the Greeks*, trans. Henry Fusseli, London 1765.

126 Reviewers seem to have been unaware of Webb's sources. In addition to Highmore's in the *Gentleman's Magazine*, anonymous reviews were printed in *The Monthly Review, or Literary Journal*, XXII, 1760, pp. 305–14; *The Critical Review: or, Annals of Literature*, IX, 1760, pp. 197–205 and *The Annual Register, or a View of the History, Politics, and Literature For the Year 1760*, (seventh edition 1789), part 2, pp. 249–53. This last review was published by James Dodsley, brother of Robert Dodsley and Webb's own publisher after the death of Robert and so a favorable notice is to be expected. Nevertheless, the reviewer criticises Webb for unnecessarily translating 'chiaroscuro' into the clumsy 'clear obscure' and asks why Webb should introduce the term *nud* in place of the perfectly good English word 'naked' (p. 249).

127 *Monthly Review, or Literary Journal*, XXII, 1760, p. 306. The anonymous writer does not use the words 'British school' but clearly distinguishes British art from that of other European countries. For a discussion of terminology associated with the ascendancy of British painting see John Gage, '*The British School* and the British School', in Brian Allen (ed.), *Towards a Modern Art World: Studies in British Art 1*, New Haven and London 1995, pp. 109–20.

128 Philip Thicknesse, *Sketches and Characters of the most Eminent and most Singular Persons now Living*, Bristol 1770, p. 95.

129 [Pott] 1782, p. 71.

130 Ibid., p. 73.

131 Ibid., p. 74.

132 Hayes 2001, no. 65, p. 113.

133 BM, Department of Prints and Drawings, *Honorary Engravers vol. 1, Men*, fol. 234, no. 250.

134 R. H. Nichols and F. A. Wray, *The History of the Foundling Hospital*, London 1935, p. 263. William Hoare urged 'an opulent friend' to buy this with him, subsequently securing full ownership of the cartoon in exchange for portraits of members of his friend's family.

135 Graves 1905–6, III, p. 191: '89 A book of drawings (*Very good* – Walpole)'.

136 Hayes 1970, I, p. 31; Woodall, 1939, p. 10.

137 Hayes 1970, I, p. 31 and no. 8, pp. 111–12. There is, however, no evidence that the single drawing of an urn catalogued here is from the book of drawings of 'imitations from antique vases and sculpture' by Gainsborough.

138 Stainton 1977, no page numbers, introduction.

139 Belsey 1988, no. 20, pp. 88–90. Belsey identifies the *Flora*, but does not suggest what the second shadowy cast might be. The *Urania* appears with a group of casts in W. van Haecht's painting *The Picture Gallery of Cornelis van der Geest*, reproduced in Francis Haskell and Nicholas Penny, *Taste and the Antique*, New Haven and London 1981, fig. 18, p. 34.

140 Spencer-Longhurst 1995, p. 18.

141 Ann Sumner and Philippa Bishop, *Gainsborough in Bath*, (exh. cat., Holburne Museum), Bath 1988, no. 18, p. 33.

142 David H. Solkin, 'Gainsborough's Classically Virtuous Wife', *The British Art Journal*, II, no. 2, winter 2000/01, pp. 75–7. See also Hilary S. Brown, 'Gainsborough's Classically Ambivalent Wife', *The British Art Journal*, III, no. 1, autumn 2001, pp. 78–9.

143 *Bath Chronicle*, 10 October 1765. Champione gives his Oxford address as 'the Golden Head, next Door to Mr. Nourse, Surgeon, in Oxford'. His advertisement goes on to list prints from Italy

and France, medals and frames for prints. It concludes 'His Stay in Bath will be very short', a common ploy by seasonal advertisers to drum up business. Like Gainsborough before him, Mr Champione is arriving at the beginning of the Bath autumn season.

144 Mary Webster, *Johann Zoffany 1733–1810* (exh. cat., National Portrait Gallery), London 1976, nos 73 and 74, pp. 56–8. In the event Gainsborough was not included in the Royal Academy group portrait.

145 Hayes 2001, no. 94, p. 56. Gainsborough wrote to the Hon. Constantine Phipps on 13 February 1772, 'I have been trying a large Cartoon Landskip in the way of the Drawings I sent by Zaffani . . .'.

146 Cecil Gould, *The Paintings of Correggio*, London 1976, p. 262. The painting was engraved by Agostino Carracci in 1586.

147 Lindsay 1982, p. 112.

148 Hayes 1982, II, no. 105, p. 450.

149 Hayes 1970, I, no. 55, pp. 124–5. Graves gave the portrait to his daughter in 1786.

150 Graves 1806, p. 39.

151 James 1987, I, p. 104.

152 Pointon 1979, p. 450 prints and discusses the version that appeared in *Shenstone's Miscellany*. Pointon does not seem to be aware of the other versions of the poem. Clarence Tracy, *A Portrait of Richard Graves*, London and Toronto 1987, p. 158 lists the versions except the one in *Shenstone's Miscellany*.

153 Revd Richard Graves, *Euphrosyne; or, Amusements on the Road of Life*, 3 vols, London 1783 (first edition 1776), I, pp. 131–2.

154 Whitley 1915, p. 170.

155 See Belsey 2001, pp. 9–10.

156 [Revd Richard Graves] The Late Peter of Pontefract, *Lucubrations: consisting of Essays, Reveries etc.*, London 1786, pp. 140–42.

157 David Brenneman, 'Thomas Gainsborough's *Wooded Landscape with Cattle by a Pool*, Art Criticism and the Royal Academy', *Gainsborough's House Review 1995/96*, 1996, p. 42.

158 Revd Richard Graves, *Columella; or, the Distressed Anchoret*, 2 vols, London 1779, I, pp. 47–8.

159 [Revd Richard Graves], *The Spiritual Quixote: or, the Summer's Ramble of Mr. Geoffrey Wildgoose, a Comic Romance*, 2 vols, London 1808 (first published 1773), I, p. 212.

160 [Revd Richard Graves], *Recollections of Some Particulars in the Life of the Late William Shenstone, Esq.*, London 1788 (published anonymously), pp. 67–8.

161 *The County Magazine for August 1788*, II, no. 32 (published Salisbury), August 1788, p. 123. The 'pannier'd ass' bearing auburn-headed children sounds surprisingly like the drawing *Peasants going to Market* of the early 1770s purchased by Gainsborough's House in 1993 (1993.001), but the 'Druid oak' could well refer to *The Gipsies* engraving, which also includes a baby in a pannier.

162 Dodsley did not publish the first, but did publish the subsequent editions of Anstey's very popular *New Bath Guide*.

163 Hayes 2001, no. 25, pp. 44–5. Dodsley failed to send him the right paper. The artist's disappointment is clear in his reply (ibid., no. 26, pp. 45–6).

164 Tierney 1988, pp. 49–50.

165 Ibid., pp. 484–5, a letter from Richard Graves to Robert Dodsley dated Claverton, 30 Mar[ch 1764] ends with a note, 'P.S. Since I wrote this your Brother has been here, with Mr Allen's Compliments to know whether Mr Shenstone's works are yet publish'd or not. He has sent 2 or 3 times to Mr Leake – & I find is very impatient – chiefly, yr Brother says, as he hears there are some sentiments upon Gardening . . .'. It should be remembered that Gainsborough looked back on Allen 'with a degree of veneration' later in life, presumably at least in part because of Allen's support of an intellectual circle that included Graves, Isaac Dodsley and William Hoare (Anon, 'Obituary of Considerable Persons; with Biographical Anecdotes' [Thomas Gainsborough], *Gentleman's Magazine*, LVIII, part 2, August 1788, p. 755).

166 Graves 1806, p. 65. The 'cottage' still stands, and is now a boarding house for girls, part of Prior Park College.

167 For the date of Brown's involvement at Prior Park see Sloman 1997, p. 325.

168 John Nichols, *Minor Lives: A Collection of Biographies by John Nichols*, E. L. Hart (ed.), Cambridge, Mass. 1971, pp. 250–51.

169 SRO, Revd Richard Graves correspondence, DD/SK 28/1 no. 58, a fragment of a letter from Graves to James Dodsley which includes a postscript, 'As I am not certain whether Mrs Gainsborough continues in the same house, I will beg you to send it if she should be remov'd.' The letter is dateable to 1788–9 on the grounds that it concerns Graves's translation of *The Heir Apparent; or, the Life of Commodus . . . from . . . Herodian*, a book Dodsley published in 1789.

9 *'The coquetry of nature'*

1 Price 1810, I, p. 89. The full passage is quoted in Chapter 8, p. 146.

2 Sloman 1997, p. 325, n. 2. Lucy, at the time he sat to Gainsborough, was also arranging to meet Capability Brown in Bath to discuss plans for Charlecote. Brown was in Bath to make plans for Prior Park and Newton Park, for Gainsborough's sitter Joseph Langton.

3 Hayes 1970, I, p. 96.

4 Paulson 1989, p. 274.

5 Hayes 1982, II, no. 77, pp. 415–16.

6 Chapter 4, p. 57.

7 Chapter 7, n. 145.

8 Richard Payne Knight, *An Analytical Inquiry into the Principles of Taste*, London 1805 (second edition, first edition also 1805), p. 241.

9 Price 1796–8, II, pp. 419 and 422.

10 Ibid., I, p. 71.

11 Ibid., I, p. 29.

12 Price 1810, I, pp. 26–7.

13 Price 1796–8, I, pp. 153–4.

14 Although the portrait of Rice Charleton was exhibited at the Society of Artists London exhibition in 1766, it was completed by March 1764, see Hayes 2001, no. 13, pp. 25–8.

15 Ibid., no. 11, p. 22.

16 Adrienne Corri, *The Search for Gainsborough*, London 1984, pp. 206–8. Corri believes the payments she transcribes from Bank of England ledgers are to Thomas Gainsborough the artist, but several merchants by name of Gainsborough were active at this time.

17 Charleton is mentioned on numerous occasions in the Knight family papers at the WORO, especially the papers grouped under Accession no. BA 10470. In WORO, Knight papers BA 10470/2/108 is a letter from Shenstone to the Knights at Wolverley, dated 31 October 1762, in which Shenstone writes, 'My Lord [Foley] repeated the Invitation he had formerly given me to come to Whitley, & I told him ye agreement I had made with Dr Charleton to pay our respects to him as soon as ye Dr. came from Buxton. He replied, the Dr would come from his Brother's to Whitley, about ye middle of this week'. Charleton is also mentioned in two letters from Sarah Sebright (née Knight), wife of Sir John Sebright to her mother at Wolverley, (WORO, Knight papers BA 10470/20, nos 1405 and 1408). In one of Edward Knight's Pocket Books (WORO, Knight papers BA 10470/2/285) is a record dated 1 February 1766 of a payment of £1.8.0 to Dr Charleton for 'Walps [Walpole's] Anecdotes'. In another Pocket Book (in the same collection) entries for 27 June 1768 and 23 July 1768 record payments of one shilling at or for 'Dr Charltons', possibly gratuities paid to servants at the Doctor's house (WORO, Knight papers, BA 10470/2/287). On 22 July 1772 Edward Knight paid Gosset £2.14.0 for a picture frame for Dr

Charleton, a sum that was repaid by Charleton on 24 July (WORO, Knight papers, BA 10470/2/288).

18 It is not yet known where Charleton came from, or was born, but his home county may have been Worcestershire. In an unpublished letter from Revd Richard Graves to Shenstone, Graves writes, 'Dr Charlton was to send me a Pupil an orphen [sic] & ward of his [illegible word] of Worcestershire' (SRO, Revd Richard Graves correspondence, DD/SK 28/1/3). Graves ran a school at Claverton.

19 B. C. L. Johnson, 'The Foley Partnerships: The Iron Industry at the end of the Charcoal Era', *Economic History Review*, second series, IV, no. 3, 1952, pp. 322–40. Johnson describes the elaborate web of partnerships in the ownership and management of furnaces, mills and forges of the West Midlands and South Wales areas.

20 Chapter 2, p. 28.

21 WORO, Knight papers BA 10470/2/127, letter from Elizabeth Palmer from Bath to her brother Edward Knight, then in London, dated 4 January 1769. This reference to Gainsborough was kindly given to me by Philip White, who found it when researching the life of Coplestone Warre Bampfylde. Another letter (same collection, no. 124) dated 27 September 1769, again from Elizabeth to her brother, staying at Hestercombe, refers to a completed portrait of herself, painted for her brother. It is not clear whether the portrait is by Gainsborough or Mason Chamberlin, who is referred to in the letter.

22 Waterhouse 1966, no. 605, p. 89.

23 Shenstone 1768–73, III, no. XCVIII, p. 302.

24 Ibid., no. CVII, p. 342, Shenstone to Graves from The Leasowes, 20 November 1762. Sir Francis Charlton or Charleton (d. 1784) was the son of Sir Blundel Charlton or Charleton and his wife Mary, the sister of Lord Foley. Shenstone regularly couples the names of Sir Francis and Dr Rice Charleton.

25 Ibid., no. CVII, p. 340, Shenstone to Graves from The Leasowes, 20 November 1762. The Vernons, Dartmouths, Pigotts and Wrottesleys all had portraits painted by Gainsborough (Waterhouse 1966, nos 693 and 694, p. 94; nos 185–7, p. 62; no. 544, p. 84; nos 737 and 739, p. 97). In the same collection of Shenstone's letters is one from Shenstone to Sherrington Davenport (Shenstone 1768–73, no. CIX, p. 348) dated 4 January 1763 in which the poet says 'and does not my friend G – [Graves] reside at Claverton . . . and have you not Mr. Webb, and now Mr. Melmoth, to make Bath enviable for the residence of Literature?'. Sherrington Davenport was married to Gratiana Rodd, the sister of Juliana Rodd who married Theophilus Lane (see Price family tree, fig. 124).

26 Andrew Ballantyne, *Architecture, Landscape and Liberty: Richard Payne Knight and the Picturesque*, Cambridge 1997.

27 Ibid. p. 211, quoting from Shenstone's *Unconnected Thoughts on Landscape Gardening*.

28 In his letter to Charleton of 1779 Gainsborough jokingly refers to young Robert Charleton using his gun to protect his father's property in the event of a French invasion via the Severn estuary, Hayes 2001, no. 83, pp. 138–9.

29 Nicholas Kingsley, Archivist at Birmingham Record Office, author of *The Country Houses of Gloucestershire 1660–1830*, Chichester 1992, has no knowledge of the property or its grounds and there is no information at the GRO. I am grateful to Nicholas Kingsley for discussing this with me.

30 Hayes 2001, no. 83, p. 139.

31 Wark 1958, p. 332.

32 Christie's, 5–6 March 1790, *A Catalogue of the Valuable and Well-Chosen Collection of . . . Pictures . . . of the late Doctor Charlton, of Bath* . . . , lots 16 (the original) and 17 (Gainsborough's copy). An annotated copy of the catalogue in Christie's Library shows that both pictures sold to the same buyer, the original fetching £0.18.0 and Gainsborough's copy £2.19.0. The *Landscape with a Woodcutter* under discussion here fetched £72.9.0, by far the highest price in the sale.

33 WORO, Knight papers BA 10470/2/287, pocket book covering the period September 1767–January 1771. It is not clear whether Mr Lee of Belmont Row had anything to do with Baptist Lee of Little Livermere Hall, Suffolk, whose gardens Edward Knight visited.

34 WORO, Knight papers, BA 10470/2/000160, ref. 899:31C, 'Stour General Accounts, ladyday 1770 – Ladyday 1771'. The inventory for this works, within the same account book, includes twelve charcoal waggons.

35 Arthur Raistrick, *Dynasty of Iron Founders: The Darbys and Coalbrookdale*, London, New York and Toronto 1953, pp. 68–9 shows that Edward Knight was one of the first and largest customers for the new pig iron developed by Abraham Darby. Another major customer was Lord Foley.

36 Hayes 1982, II, no. 82, pp. 420–1. Hayes dates the picture to 1763–4.

37 Ibid., no. 81, p. 420.

38 Waterhouse 1966, no. 818, p. 106 describes the *Pug Dog* as a 'Dog belonging to Mrs Downes', and shows that the picture descended in the family of John Jacob's sister Elizabeth, who married a John Buxton. Mrs Downes was John Jacob's mother, Mary, née Smith, who married George Downes of Sion Orchard, Isleworth, Middlesex, after the death of John Jacob senior (d. 1728). In John Jacob junior's will, dated 15 January 1749/50 (W&SRO, 212B, 6664), he refers to 'Mary Downes my mother'. Mrs Downes's death is recorded in the *Boddely's Bath Journal* of 25 January 1762, 'On Thursday the 14th Inst. Died at her House call'd the Rocks, in the parish of Marshfield, in the county of Gloucestershire, Mrs Downes, in the 78th year of her Age . . .'. If the picture of the pug dog was painted for Mrs Downes it must therefore date from before January 1762. There may have been yet another Gainsborough painting associated with The Rocks. A picture entitled 'Gamekeeper at the Rocks' by Gainsborough, 'Formerly property of Dr. Herlock Lent by J. Scullthorpe, Esq' was exhibited in 1906: Anon., *Spring Loan Exhibition of Works by British Artists of the Eighteenth and Nineteenth Centuries and of Old Miniatures* (exh. cat., Victoria Art Gallery), Bath n.d. [1906], no. 87. The Rocks was inherited by Isaac Webb Horlock on the death of John Jacob's sister Ann in 1787, so Herlock must be a slip for Horlock.

39 Hayes 1970, I, no. 372, p. 312. Hayes dates the drawing to the late 1750s and calls it 'Study of a Bull-terrier' in the text, but captions the illustration (ibid., II, pl. 71) 'Study of a bulldog', indicating that he was in some doubt about the breed of dog. Comparison with the painting of the dog that belonged to Mrs Downes (identified as a pug in Hayes 1980, no 94, p. 109) and other eighteenth-century paintings of pugs shows that the drawing undoubtedly represents a pug.

40 Whitley 1915, p. 82.

41 Allen 1987, no. 7, pp. 89–90.

42 Mary Chandler, *The Description of Bath. A Poem. Humbly Inscribed To Her Royal Highness the Princess Amelia*, London 1738, pp. 73–5. The book was published for James Leake, the Bath bookseller, and also contains the earliest description of Ralph Allen's garden at Prior Park.

43 Mike Chapman, David Lambert, Alister Rankine, 'An Historic Landscape Survey of the Rocks Historic Garden, The Rocks East Woodland, Marshfield, Avon', 1994. I am most grateful to Mike Chapman for discussing the landscape with me and giving me a copy of this report that was funded by The Countryside Commission and Avon County Council.

44 Ibid., p. 3.
45 Hayes 1982, II, no. 81, p. 420.
46 The Fourth Duke of Rutland (1754–1787) was styled Marquis of Granby between 1770 and 1779. The picture is believed to be the one referred to in the poem of 1773 attributed in this book to Daniel Webb, see Hayes 1982, II, no. 105, pp. 449–50. The full text of the poem and its footnote are given in Chapter 8, p. 161.
47 Waterhouse 1966, no. 590, p. 88 and no. 591, p. 88.
48 Appendix II, entry 107, p. 207.
49 Pointon 1979, pp. 444 and 448.
50 Webb 1760, p. 14, comparing the 'splendid impositions of Rubens' with 'the native and mellow tints of Titian'.
51 Chapter 8, p. 167.
52 John Hayes, 'Gainsborough's Drawings: A Supplement to the Catalogue Raisonné', *Master Drawings*, XXI, winter 1983, p. 379, quoting Lindsay Stainton; Hayes 1982, II, no. 105, p. 450. It may be possible to go even further and suggest that the central image of a bundle of sticks has an iconographic significance. In the Revd J. Fleetwood's *The Christian's Dictionary*, London 1775 (no page numbers), unity, and in particular family unity, is expressed through a parable in which a bundle of twigs is shown to be unbreakable, whereas a single twig is easily destroyed.
53 Hayes 2001, no. 72, p. 124. The letter refers to the second, almost identical version of this composition.
54 SHM, Whitehead Letters, I, a letter dated 16 November 1758.
55 Ibid., I, letter from Whitehead to Lord Nuneham, from Bath, dated 16 December 1758.
56 Ann Thicknesse, *The School for Fashion*, 2 vols, London 1800, II, pp. 35–44. Elsewhere in this publication (I, pp. 69–70), the author describes the visit of 'a large party of the very first fashion' to Mr Allen of Prior Park, where 'they were all entertained with that hospitality and magnificence which every one must have experienced who had the pleasure of being introduced to that worthy and truly respectable master of the place'. Since Allen had died in 1764, nearly forty years before this book was published, this passage proves how enduring was Allen's and Prior Park's reputation. Prior Park of course had its own 'cottage' that was built by Allen to house the gardener Isaac Dodsley. Felix Cottage must be based on Philip Thicknesse's cottage at Felixstowe.
57 R. Hippisley, *Bath and Its Environs: A Descriptive Poem in three Cantos*, Bath 1775, pp. 22–3. Line 3 refers to John Wood, the architect.
58 [Revd Richard Graves], *The Spiritual Quixote: or, the Summer's Ramble of Mr. Geoffrey Wildgoose, a Comic Romance*, 2 vols, London 1808 (first published 1773), II, p. 15.
59 Ibid.
60 Chapter 8, p. 168. Uvedale Price also described a cottage that seems to be inspired by Gainsborough (Price 1810, III, pp. 279–80), but the description is closer to the artist's later *Cottage Door* compositions and a number of works by Francis Wheatley than to the Rutland picture.
61 The Wouvermans oil on panel appeared in the sale of the Holford Collection at Christie's, London, on 17–18 May 1928, lot 77 (photograph, Witt Library). The picture had moved from the Le Noir to the La Live de Jully collection, Paris, by 1770.
62 [Pott] 1782, p. 74.
63 Charlotte Klonk, *Science and the Perception of Nature: British Landscape Art in the Late Eighteenth and Early Nineteenth Centuries*, New Haven and London 1996, p. 28.
64 The ensuing passage derives from the present author's article, 'The Holloway Gainsborough: Its Subject Re-examined', in *Gainsborough's House Review 1997/98*, 1998, pp. 47–54, with significant additions.
65 Ibid., pp. 48–9. Interestingly Mary Woodall in *An Exhibition of Paintings: Thomas Gainsborough* (exh. cat., Victoria Art Gallery, Bath etc), London 1949, no. 12, p. 11, entitled the picture 'Going to Market, Early Morning, Peasants and Colliers'. She seems to be the only writer in relatively recent times to include a reference to colliers.
66 Anon., 'A Letter from a Collier in Somersetshire to his Friend', *County Magazine for April 1788* (published Salisbury), April 1788, p. 62.
67 Sloman 1998, p. 50.
68 Ibid., p. 51.
69 GH, Dorothy Richardson MS 'Description of Bath', written on blank pages at the back of a copy of Anon, *New Bath Guide*, Bath [1770], p. 31, describes over forty varieties of fish on sale, from 'Fresh Sturgeon' to 'Smelts & Sprats'.
70 One visitor noted that in 1779 coal in Bath cost ten pence a bushel when it was five shillings a bushel in London, Sloman 1998, p. 53, n. 27.
71 Tunstall 1847, p. 224.
72 Hayes 1982, II, no. 95, pp. 438–40. A further picture of a similar date of peasants travelling on a road may also include colliers, although the figures are rather less specific, ibid., no. 98, pp. 442–3.
73 Ibid., pp. 17–18.
74 Christie's, 25 May 1867, a mixed sale that included pictures from the collection of the late John Wiltshire (Walter's grandson), includes as lot 131, by Gainsborough, 'A Landscape: the gipsies' repast. Etched by the artist.' Waterhouse 1966, no. 887, p. 112 notes the picture in the Wiltshire sale and gives a possible earlier provenance, all or parts of which, he says, may refer to the painting. Hayes 1982, I, no. 44, p. 376 gives the same provenance, noting that Fulcher referred to the picture being in John Wiltshire's collection (Fulcher 1856, p. 234).
75 The sale catalogue for the Christie's Sale that included the Wiltshire pictures (25 May 1867) described the *Harvest Waggon* (lot 126) and *A Grand Landscape* (i.e. the *Rocky Wooded Landscape with Rustic Lovers*) (lot 127) as 'Painted at Shockerwick'. However the same was said of the portrait of *Orpin, Parish Clerk of Bradford-on-Avon* (lot 129), a picture not even by Gainsborough.
76 I am most grateful to Godfrey Laurence for sharing his considerable knowledge of the history of Bathford with me and drawing my attention to the drawing in the BL, Map Library.
77 A copy of the print in BCL, Hunt Collection, Accession no. 18–1567. I am grateful to Christopher Woodward who first alerted me to this print and its relevance for the dating of Shockerwick. I am also grateful to Timothy Mowl, who has confirmed Shockerwick could not possibly be designed by John Wood or date from as early as 1750, as has sometimes been claimed.
78 BRO, notes by Cdr A. S. Craig on 'The Manor and Tithing of Shockerwick' for a lecture given to the Bathford Society, 13 April 1987.
79 BCL, Chapman Collection, II, p. 88, accession no. 00.437, an elevation drawing inscribed 'Palmer Architect' illustrates Shockerwick as built, without later alterations and additions. In the same collection are two watercolours by W. Walton (probably William Walton Senior, d. 1846), no. 00.438, *Shockerwick from near the Lodge* and no. 00.439, *Shockerwick from the Brook in front of the Bridge*, p. 89.
80 The portrait of Quin was bequeathed to Wiltshire by Gainsborough, according to the Christie's sale catalogue of 25 May 1867 (lot 128). Also in the sale was a portrait called 'Portrait of Foote, The Comedian' (lot 130). It is not known when the Wiltshires acquired this picture, or exactly what it was. Waterhouse 1966, no. 777, p. 101 catalogues it as 'Unknown man', and gives no provenance earlier than the 1867 Wiltshire sale. As recently as the 1950s a portrait by Gainsborough of one of Walter Wiltshire's daughters

was said to hang in a house in Bathampton (BCL, Bath Chronicle Notes and Queries (transcripts), in answer to Query 1585). A Miss May J. Wiltshire wrote on 14 March 1953, 'Mrs Price-Davis of Bathampton . . . told me she had a portrait of Miss Wiltshire by Gainsborough and invited me to go to see her when I returned to England'. (The meeting never took place, as Mrs Price-Davis died soon after.) Two other miniature portraits of members of the Wiltshire family, said to be by Gainsborough, were shown to the present writer in 1991. The portraits, in pencil and watercolour on paper, ovals, measuring $5^{1}/_{8} \times 4$ inches (12.9×10.1 cm), are inscribed on the backing paper 'John Wiltshire/ By / T. Gainsborough' and 'Miss Wiltshire/ By / T. Gainsborough'. They are certainly not by Gainsborough, but could well have represented Walter Wiltshire's son and one of his daughters. The female portrait was additionally inscribed 'This young lady is Represented / in the Market Waggon'.

81 Christie's 25 May 1867, lots 136, 137 (Panini); 142 (Gaspard Poussin); 140 (Wouvermans); 145 (Ostade) and 144 (Both and Poelemberg). If the last picture had been known to Gainsborough, (and there is no way of telling which member of the Wiltshire family purchased it) it might have lingered in his mind and been one of the sources of inspiration for his late *Diana and Actaeon* canvas, now in the Royal Collection.

82 John Collinson, *History and Antiquities of Somerset*, 3 vols, Bath 1791, I, p. 49. Collinson's remarks about Walter Wiltshire, written during Wiltshire's lifetime, include a mention of him being a Governor and supporter of the Hospital. Abel's concert is advertised in the *Bath Advertiser*, 2 February 1760.

83 SRO, Graves correspondence, DD/SK 28/1, letter 75, dated only 27 March.

84 Jerom Murch, *Biographical Sketches of Bath Celebrities*, London and Bath 1893, p. 187; p. 186.

85 Whitley 1915, pp. 39–40.

86 McEvansoneya 1999, p. 165.

87 Tunstall 1847, p. 219. The trees were said by Tunstall to be still flourishing. The development of St James's Square, by the architect of Shockerwick, John Palmer, commenced in 1790.

88 In 1789 the Bath publisher Cruttwell printed Bowles's *Fourteen Sonnets written chiefly on Picturesque Spots during a Journey*. Bowles's 'Elegiac Stanzas written during Sickness at Bath' are dated December 1795, see William Lisle Bowles, *The Poetical Works of William Lisle Bowles*, ed. Revd George Gilfillan, Edinburgh, London and Dublin, 2 vols, 1855, I, pp. 73–6.

89 BM, Department of Prints and Drawings, Anderdon Royal Academy Catalogues, I, fol. 60, 'Thomas Gainsborough RA, Sonnet'. The sonnet is not one of the fourteen published by Cruttwell, but might have been originally intended as part of this set.

90 Meehan 1901, p. 47.

91 An unpublished letter dated 12 October 1769 from Graves to James Dodsley (SRO, Graves correspondence DD/SK 28/1, letter no. 20). In another letter in the same collection from Graves to Robert Dodsley, dated 25 April 1763 (letter no. 14) he asks Dodsley to send him 'a volume or two', either by the hand of a friend or 'in a Packet by Wiltshire's Waggon, directed for me at Mr Frederick's [i.e. the bookseller] in the Grove'.

92 Hayes 2001, no. 40, p. 68.

10 Gainsborough of Bath

1 John Britton, *Auto-Biography*, London 1850, p. 225.

2 Quoted in Lindsay 1982, p. 100.

3 Wood 1749, II, p. 341.

4 Rolls 1988, p. 169.

5 This perfectly reasonable thesis has been set out by many writers, including Evelyn Newby in 'Bath: Art Life and Organization', in Jane Turner (ed.), *The Dictionary of Art*, 34 vols, London 1996, III, p. 372.

6 Neale 1981, p. 38.

7 Spencer-Longhurst 1995, no. 15, p. 49. Spencer-Longhurst describes the influence of Gainsborough's *Harvest Waggon* on Wheatley's picture, but does not refer to *The Gipsies*.

8 Michael Kitson, Felicity Owen and Hugh Belsey, *From Gainsborough to Constable* (exh. cat., Gainsborough's House, Sudbury and The Leger Galleries, London), Sudbury 1991, no. 6, p. 40.

9 The first state of Gainsborough's print of *The Gipsies* does not include the smaller group of trees, neither does the oil copy of the original, sold at Sotheby's on 4 July 2001 (lot 70).

10 Price 1810, III, pp. 262–3.

11 Knight 1794, pp. 64–5.

12 Wood 1749, I, pp. 4–5.

Appendix III

1 A sum of £252.0.0 is credited to Gainsborough's Hoare's Bank account on 21 September 1774 (Appendix II, entry 119, p. 207). Hugh Belsey has convincingly proposed (verbally, 1996) that this is for eight 30×25 inch portraits costing thirty guineas each and not for six portraits as has previously been suggested. Of the eight, one is now untraced.

2 The receipt in the SRO dated 24 February 1761 refers to a payment made by Sir George Trevelyan to Thomas Hudson (presumably the painter Thomas Hudson) for Gainsborough. This very interesting document, apparently shows Hudson acting as agent for Gainsborough, just as William Hoare did in 1773 for the sale of Gainsborough's landscape *Peasants and Colliers going to Market* to Henry Hoare of Stourhead. The Trevelyan reference, which probably relates to the half-length portrait of Susanna Trevelyan (Waterhouse 1966, no. 673, p. 93) was very kindly given to me by Philip McEvansoneya.

Bibliography

Allen 1987 — Brian Allen, *Francis Hayman* (exh. cat., Yale Center for British Art, New Haven and Iveagh Bequest, Kenwood), New Haven and London 1987

Anon 1766 — Anon, *Critical Review of the Pictures, Sculptures, Designs in Architecture, Drawings, etc Exhibited at the Great-Room in Spring Gardens, Charing Cross*, London 1766

Anon 1917 — Anon, 'The Masonic Lodges of Bath', *Transactions of the Somerset Masters Lodge*, no. 3746, I, part 3, 1917, pp. 285–321

Anon 1991 — Anon, *Victoria Art Gallery, Bath: Concise Catalogue of Paintings and Drawings*, Bath 1991

Baldwin 1768 — R. Baldwin, *New Complete Guide to London*, London 1768

Barrell 1986 — John Barrell, *The Political Theory of Painting from Reynolds to Hazlitt: 'The Body of the Public'*, New Haven and London 1986

Beechey 1988 — Gwilym Beechey, Helen Glanville and Giles Waterfield, *A Nest of Nightingales* (exh. cat., Dulwich Picture Gallery), London 1988

Belsey 1988 — Hugh Belsey, *Gainsborough's Family* (exh. cat., Gainsborough's House), Sudbury 1988

Belsey 2001 — Hugh Belsey, *Love's Prospect: Gainsborough's Byam Family and the Eighteenth-Century Marriage Portrait* (exh. cat., Holburne Museum of Art), Bath 2001

Bensusan-Butt 1993 — John Bensusan-Butt, *Gainsborough in his Twenties*, Colchester 1993 (second edition, first edition 1989, privately published)

Black 1911 — Clementina Black, *The Linleys of Bath*, London 1911

Brenneman 1995 — David Andrew Brenneman, 'The Critical Response to Thomas Gainsborough's Painting: A Study of the Contemporary Perception and Materiality of Gainsborough's Art', unpublished Ph.D. thesis, Brown University 1995

Chaloner Smith 1883 — John Chaloner Smith, *British Mezzotinto Portraits*, 4 vols, London 1883

Charnock 1794–8 — John Charnock, *Biographia Navalis*, 6 vols, London 1794–8

Clayton 1997 — Timothy Clayton, *The English Print, 1688–1802*, New Haven and London 1997

Cleland 1744 — Archibald Cleland, *A Full Vindication of Mr Cleland's Appeal to the Public*, Bath 1744

Clews 1994 — Stephen Clews, 'Banking in Bath in the Reign of George III', *Bath History*, V, 1994, pp. 105–24

Clifford 1978 — Timothy Clifford, Anthony Griffiths and Martin Royalton-Kisch, *Gainsborough and Reynolds in the British Museum* (exh. cat., British Museum), London 1978

Coxe 1811 — W. Coxe, *Literary Life and Select Works of Benjamin Stillingfleet*, 2 vols, London 1811

Cunningham 1829–32 — Allan Cunningham, *The Lives of the Most Eminent British Painters, Sculptors, and Architects*, 5 vols, London 1829–32

Dack 1907 — Charles Dack, *Sketch of the Life of Thomas Worlidge, Etcher and Painter, with a Catalogue of his Works*, Peterborough 1907

Edwards 1808 — Edward Edwards, *Anecdotes of Painters who have resided or been born in England*, London 1808

Everett 1994 — Nigel Everett, *The Tory View of Landscape*, New Haven and London 1994

Farington 1978–98 — Joseph Farington, *Diary of Joseph Farington RA*, ed. Catherine Cave, Kenneth Garlick, Angus Macintyre and Evelyn Newby, 17 vols, New Haven and London 1978–98

Fawcett 1990 — Trevor Fawcett, 'Eighteenth-Century Shops and the Luxury Trade', *Bath History*, III, 1990, pp. 49–75

Fulcher 1856 — George Williams Fulcher, *Life of Thomas Gainsborough, R.A.*, London 1856 (second edition, first edition also 1856)

Girouard 1959 — Mark Girouard, 'Wootton Lodge, Staffordshire, II: The Home of Major Alan Rook', *Country Life*, CXXV, no. 3244, 19 March 1959, pp. 596–9

Goldsmith 1762 — Oliver Goldsmith, *The Life of Richard Nash of Bath, Esq.*, London 1762

Graves 1806 — Revd Richard Graves, *The Triflers*, London 1806

Graves 1905–6 — Algernon Graves, *The Royal Academy of Arts, A Complete Dictionary of Contributors and their work from its foundation in 1769–1904*, 8 vols, London 1905–6

Graves 1907 — Algernon Graves, *The Society of Artists of Great Britain 1760–1791, The Free Society of Artists 1761–1783. A Complete Dictionary of Contributors and their Work from the Foundation of the Societies to 1791*, London 1907

Gunnis [n.d.] — Rupert Gunnis, *Dictionary of British Sculptors*, London n.d.

Harrison 1922a — Sydney E. Harrison, 'New Light on a Gainsborough Mystery: Important Discovery of Original Documents', *Connoisseur*, LXII, no. 245, January 1922, pp. 3–10

Harrison 1922b — Sydney E. Harrison, 'New Light on a Gainsborough Mystery: The Unwin Correspondence, Part II', *Connoisseur*, LXII, no. 246, February 1922, pp. 87–91

Hayes 1970 — John Hayes, *The Drawings of Thomas Gainsborough*, 2 vols, London 1970 (the two volumes are not numbered, but here the text volume is called I and the plates volume II)

Hayes 1971 — John Hayes, *Gainsborough as Printmaker*, London 1971

Hayes 1980 — John Hayes, *Thomas Gainsborough* (exh. cat., Tate Gallery), London 1980

Hayes 1982 — John Hayes, *The Landscape Paintings of Thomas Gainsborough*, 2 vols, London 1982

Hayes 1983 — John Hayes, 'Four Gainsboroughs for the Nation', *National Art-Collections Fund Review*, 1983, pp. 98–100

Hayes 1995 — John Hayes, *The Holloway Gainsborough*, London 1995

Hayes 1998 — John Hayes, *Thomas Gainsborough* (exh. cat., Palazzo dei Diamanti), Ferrara 1998

Hayes 2001 — Thomas Gainsborough, *The Letters of Thomas Gainsborough*, ed. John Hayes, London and New Haven 2001

Herbert 1950 — Henry Tenth Earl of Pembroke, *Pembroke Papers (1780–1794): Letters and Diaries of Henry Tenth Earl of Pembroke and his Circle*, ed. Lord Herbert, London 1950

Ingamells 1997 — John Ingamells, *A Dictionary of British and Irish Travellers in Italy 1701–1800*, New Haven and London 1997

Jackson 1798 — William Jackson, *The Four Ages; together with essays on various subjects*, London 1798

James 1987 — Kenneth E. James, 'Concert Life in Eighteenth-Century Bath', unpublished Ph.D. thesis, University of London, 5 vols, 1987

Jenkins 1983 — Philip Jenkins, *The Making of a Ruling Class. The Glamorgan Gentry 1640–1790*, Cambridge 1983

Kemp 1990 — Martin Kemp, *The Science of Art*, New Haven and London 1990

Kent 1785 — Anon, *Kent's Directory for the Year 1785*, London 1785

Knight 1794 — Richard Payne Knight, *The Landscape, A Didactic Poem, in Three Books, Addressed to Uvedale Price Esq.*, London 1794

Lambin 1987 — Denis A. Lambin, 'Foxley: The Prices' Estate in Herefordshire', *Journal of Garden History*, VII, no. 3, 1987, pp. 244–70

Lewis and Smith 1937–83 — Horace Walpole, *Yale Edition of Horace Walpole's Correspondence*, ed. W. S. Lewis and W. H. Smith, 48 vols, New Haven 1937–83

Lindsay 1982 — Jack Lindsay, *Thomas Gainsborough: His Life and Art*, London 1982 (second edition, first edition 1981)

Lippincott 1983 — Louise Lippincott, *Selling Art in Georgian London, The Rise of Arthur Pond*, New Haven and London 1983

Llanover 1861 — Mary Delany, *The Autobiography and Correspondence of Mary Granville, Mrs Delany*, ed. Lady A. Llanover, 3 vols, London 1861

[Lloyd] 1994 — [Christopher Lloyd], *Gainsborough and Reynolds: Contrasts in Royal Patronage* (exh. cat., The Queen's Gallery, Buckingham Palace), London 1994 (published anonymously)

McEvansoneya 1999 — Philip McEvansoneya, 'An Irish Artist goes to Bath: Letters from John Warren to Andrew Caldwell, 1776–1784', *Irish Architectural and Decorative Studies: The Journal of the Irish Georgian Society*, II, 1999, pp. 146–73

Mcintyre 1981 — Sylvia Mcintyre, 'Bath: The Rise of a Resort Town, 1660–1800', in Peter Clark (ed.), *Country Towns in pre-industrial England*, Leicester 1981, pp. 198–249

Meehan 1901 — J. F. Meehan, *Famous Houses of Bath and District*, Bath 1901

Mitchell and Penrose 1983 — Revd John Penrose, *Letters from Bath 1766–1767 by the Rev. John Penrose*, ed. Brigitte Mitchell and Hubert Penrose, Gloucester 1983

Monod 1989 — Paul Kleber Monod, *Jacobitism and the English People, 1688–1788*, Cambridge 1989

Neale 1981 — R. S. Neale, *Bath 1680–1850: A Social History or the Valley of Pleasure, Yet a Sink of Iniquity*, London 1981

Newby 1990 — Evelyn Newby, *William Hoare of Bath R.A., 1707–1792* (exh. cat., Victoria Art Gallery), Bath 1990

Norman 1920 — George Norman, 'The Masonic Lodges of Bath', *Transactions of the Somerset Masters Lodge no. 3746*, 1920, pp. 136–71

Owen 1996 — Felicity Owen, 'Joshua Kirby (1716–1774) A Biographical Sketch', *Gainsborough's House review 1995/96*, 1996, pp. 61–75

Paulson 1989 — Ronald Paulson, *Breaking and Remaking: Aesthetic Practice in England, 1700–1820*, New Brunswick and London 1989

Penny 1986 — Nicholas Penny (ed.), *Reynolds* (exh. cat., Royal Academy of Arts), London 1986

Pointon 1979 — Marcia Pointon, 'Gainsborough and the Landscape of Retirement', *Art History*, II, no. 4, December 1979, pp. 441–55

Pointon 1984 — Marcia Pointon, 'Portrait-Painting as a Business Enterprise in London in the 1780s', *Art History*, VII, no. 2, June 1984, pp. 187–205

[Pott] 1782 — [J. H. Pott], *An Essay on Landscape Painting, with Remarks General and Critical, on the Different Schools and Masters, ancient and modern*, London 1782 (published anonymously)

[Price] 1733 — [Uvedale Tomkyns Price], *A New Catechism for the Fine Ladies*, Paris 1733 (published anonymously)

Price 1796–8 — Uvedale Price, *Essay on the Picturesque*, 2 vols, London 1796–8

Price 1810 — Uvedale Price, *Essays on the Picturesque*, 3 vols, London 1810

Reid 1980 — Peter Reid, *Burke's and Savills Guide to Country Houses, II: Herefordshire, Shropshire, Warwickshire, Worcestershire*, London 1980

Reynolds 1959 — Sir Joshua Reynolds, *Sir Joshua Reynolds: Discourses on Art*, ed. Robert R. Wark, San Marino 1959

Richardson 1715 — Jonathan Richardson, *An Essay on the Theory of Painting*, London 1715

Roettgen 1993 — Steffi Roettgen, *Anton Raphael Mengs 1728–1779 and his British Patrons* (exh. cat., Iveagh Bequest, Kenwood), London 1993

Rolls 1988 — Roger Rolls, *The Hospital of the Nation, the Story of Spa Medicine and the Mineral Water Hospital at Bath*, Bath 1988

Sedgwick 1970 — Romney Sedgwick, *The History of Parliament, The House of Commons 1715–1754*, 2 vols, London 1970

Shenstone 1768–73 — William Shenstone, *The Works, in Verse and Prose of William Shenstone, Esq.*, 3 vols, 1768–73 (third edition, first edition 1764–9)

Sherburn 1956 — Alexander Pope, *The Correspondence of Alexander Pope*, ed. George Sherburn, 5 vols, Oxford 1956

Sloman 1992 — Susan Legouix Sloman, 'Gainsborough and "the lodging-house way"', *Gainsborough's House Society Annual Report 1991/92*, 1992, pp. 23–44

Sloman 1994 — Susan Legouix Sloman, '"The Immaculate Capt. Wade": "Arbiter Elegantiae"', *Gainsborough's House Review 1993/94*, 1994, pp. 46–61

Sloman 1996a — Susan Legouix Sloman, 'Mrs Margaret Gainsborough, "A Prince's Daughter"', *Gainsborough's House Review 1995/96*, 1996, pp. 47–58

Sloman 1996b — Susan Legouix Sloman, 'Artists' Picture Rooms in Eighteenth-Century Bath', *Bath History*, VI, 1996, pp. 133–54

Sloman 1997 — Susan Legouix Sloman, 'Sitting to Gainsborough at Bath in 1760', *Burlington Magazine*, CXXXIX, no. 1130, May 1997, pp. 325–8

Sloman 1998 — Susan Legouix Sloman, 'The Holloway Gainsborough: Its Subject Re-examined', *Gainsborough's House Review 1997/98*, 1998, pp. 47–54

Smart 1999 — Alastair Smart, *Allan Ramsay: A Complete Catalogue of his Paintings*, ed. John Ingamells, New Haven and London 1999

Solkin 1982 — David H. Solkin, *Richard Wilson: The Landscape of Reaction* (exh. cat., Tate Gallery), London 1982

Spencer-Longhurst 1995 — Paul Spencer-Longhurst and Janet M. Brooke, *Thomas Gainsborough: The Harvest Wagon* (exh. cat., Birmingham Museum and Art Gallery and Art Gallery of Ontario), Birmingham and Toronto 1995

Stainton 1977 — Lindsay Stainton, *Gainsborough and his Musical Friends* (exh. cat., Iveagh Bequest, Kenwood), London 1977

[Thicknesse] 1778 — [Philip Thicknesse], *The New Prose Bath Guide for the Year 1778, Dedicated to Lord N—*, London 1778 (published anonymously)

Thicknesse 1788 — Philip Thicknesse, *A Sketch of the Life and Paintings of Thomas Gainsborough*, London 1788

Tierney 1988 — Robert Dodsley, *The Correspondence of Robert Dodsley 1733–1764*, ed. James E. Tierney, Cambridge 1988

Tunstall 1847 — James Tunstall, *Rambles about Bath, and its Neighbourhood*, London and Bath 1847

Tyte 1903 — William Tyte, *Bath in the Eighteenth Century: Its Progress and Life Described*, Bath 1903

Vertue 1934 — George Vertue, 'Vertue Note Books, Volume III', *Walpole Society*, XXII, 1934, pp. 1–162

Walkley 1994 — Giles Walkley, *Artists' Houses in London 1764–1914*, London 1994

Wark 1958 — Robert R. Wark, 'Thicknesse and Gainsborough: Some New Documents', *Art Bulletin*, XL, December 1958, pp. 331–4

Wark 1971 — Robert R. Wark, *Ten British Pictures 1740–1840*, San Marino 1971

Waterhouse 1966 — Ellis Waterhouse, *Gainsborough*, London 1966 (second edition, first edition 1958, same catalogue numbers)

Waterhouse 1981 — Ellis Waterhouse, *The Dictionary of Eighteenth-Century Painters*, Woodbridge 1981

Webb 1760 — Daniel Webb, *An Inquiry into the Beauties of Painting*, London 1760

Whitley 1915 — William T. Whitley, *Thomas Gainsborough*, London 1915

Whitley 1928 — William T. Whitley, *Artists and their Friends in England 1700–1799*, 2 vols, London 1928

Wilton 1980 — Andrew Wilton, *The Art of Alexander and John Robert Cozens* (exh. cat., Yale Center for British Art), New Haven 1980

Wood 1749 — John Wood, *An Essay towards a Description of Bath*, 2 vols, London 1749

Woodall 1939 — Mary Woodall, *Gainsborough's Landscape Drawings*, London 1939

Woodall 1963 — Thomas Gainsborough, *The Letters of Thomas Gainsborough*, ed. Mary Woodall, London 1963 (second edition, first edition 1961)

Wright [n.d.] — R. W. M. Wright, 'Index of artists resident and working in Bath', unpublished, undated typescript, 2 copies, one at Bath Central Library, one at the Victoria Art Gallery, Bath

Photograph Credits

Numbers refer to figure references

Albany Institute of History and Art, 36
Ashmolean Museum, Oxford, 14, 56, 110, 146
By permission of the Auckland Art Gallery Toi o Tamaki, 25
Barber Institute of Fine Arts, University of Birmingham / Bridgeman Art Library, 160
Bath and North East Somerset Council / Fotek (Bath Central Library), 145, 167; (Bath Record Office) endpapers, 6, 37, 91, 165; (Victoria Art Gallery) frontispiece, 1, 2, 4, 5, 10, 39, 45, 75, 87, 107, 113, 115, 162
Bayerische Staatsgemäldesammlungen, Neue Pinakothek, Munich, 131
Beaverbrook Art Gallery, Fredericton, 22
Belvoir Estate, 157
Bildarchiv preussischer kulturbesitz Berlin, Jörg P. Anders, 15, 154
The Bodleian Library, University of Oxford, 80
© British Library (Map Library), 161
© The British Museum, 7, 61, 70, 73, 109, 112, 116, 122, 123, 124, 127, 132, 133, 135, 159, 170, 172
Andrew Brownsword Arts Foundation / The Holburne Museum, 65
Trustees, Cecil Higgins Art Gallery, Bedford, England, 84
© Christie's Images Ltd, 21, 149, 151
Cincinnati Art Museum, 58
© Cleveland Museum of Art, 2001, Gift of the John Huntington Art and Polytechnic Trust, 1971.2, 49
A. C. Cooper (Colour) Ltd, 117
Coram Family in the Care of the Foundling Museum, 77
Dr P. M. J. Crook, 28
Photography by Prudence Cuming Associates Limited, 64
Simon C. Dickinson Ltd., 72
By permission of the Trustees of Dulwich Picture Gallery, 81
© English Heritage Photo Library, 52, 69
Reproduced by permission of English Heritage, © Crown copyright NMR, 86, 96, 128, 156
Gainsborough's House, Sudbury, Suffolk, 26, 68, 111
Herefordshire Libraries and Information Service, 134
Holburne Museum of Art, Bath, 88
Courtesy of the Huntington Library, Art Collections, and Botanical Gardens, San Marino, California, 60
Leger Galleries Ltd., London, 34
Jonathan Lynch, 103
The Trustees, Masonic Hall, Old Orchard Street, Bath, 13
Metropolitan Museum of Art, New York, 129
The Morgan Library, New York, 144
Courtesy, Museum of Fine Arts, Boston. Reproduced with permission. © 2002 Museum of Fine Arts, Boston, 76
Museum of Fine Arts, Houston, All Rights Reserved, 148
© National Gallery, London, reproduced by courtesy of the Trustees, The National Gallery, London, 27, 51, 90
Courtesy of the National Gallery of Ireland, 59, 164
By permission of the National Library of Wales, 138
National Museum and Gallery of Wales, Cardiff, 118
Nationalmuseum, Stockholm, 93
The Board of Trustees of the National Museums and Galleries on Merseyside (Walker Art Gallery), 48
By courtesy of the National Portrait Gallery, London, 9, 47, 79, 130
© Charlecote Park, The Fairfax-Lucy Collection (The National Trust) NTPL / Angelo Hornak, 78
© Ickworth, The Bristol Collection (The National Trust) NTPL / John Hammond, 53
City of Nottingham Museums, 168
The Paul Mellon Centre for Studies in British Art, London, 11, 98, 99, 105, 108, 152, 173
Philadelphia Museum of Art, 97
Trustees of the Portman Settled Estates / Christie's, 66
Courtesy Pyms Gallery, London, 158
British Architectural Library, RIBA, London / A. C. Cooper (Colour) Ltd., 42
The John and Mable Ringling Museum of Art, The State Art Museum of Florida, 74
The Royal Collection © 2001 Her Majesty Queen Elizabeth II, 82
Copyright reserved. © Crown copyright: Royal Commission on the Ancient and Historical Monuments of Wales, 140
Royal National Hospital for Rheumatic Diseases, NHS Trust, Bath, 12
Santa Barbara Museum of Art, Gift of Mrs H. Chase, 143
Scottish National Portrait Gallery, 50, 55
Ron Sloman, Bath, 19, 29, 41, 44, 46, 89, 139
Sotheby's Picture Library 16
Staffordshire Record Office, 54
© Tate, London 2001, 26, 62, 102, 114, 142, 147, 169
Rodney Todd-White and Son, 24, 121
Toledo Museum of Art, 104
© Virginia Museum of Fine Arts, photo Katherine Wetzel, 150
The Whitworth Art Gallery, The University of Manchester, 125
Witt Library, Courtauld Institute of Art, 17, 20, 30, 137, 171
Worcester Art Museum, Worcester, Massachusetts, 101, 141 166
Yale Center for British Art, New Haven, 67, 71, (photograph by Richard Caspole) 119

Index

Numbers in *italic* refer to illustrations

K

Mr Hugh Kennedy

L

Sr Thos Lowther Bart 4
Joseph Langton Esq
Henry Leaves
Mr John Lansdown
Mr James Leake Bookseller 200
Mr Thomas Lloyd
Mr Edwd Lluellin
Mr George Longman
Mr Wm Lydard
Mr Lookup

M

Sr John Moore Knt
Nicholas Man Esqr
John Macie Esqr
Richd Monger Esqr
Mr Hugh Meare
Richd Marchant Esqr 3
Mr Charles Morgan
Mr Richd Millord
Mr Charles Milsom
Mr Daniel Milsom
Mr John Morley
Mr John Morris
Mr Thomas Mullins 2
Mr John Mullins
Mr Thomas Mitchel
Mr Walter Masters

N

Duke of Norfolk 2
Richard Naish Esqr 16
The Rev. Mr Needham
Mr John Normand

O

Doctor Oliver 4

P

Alexander Pope Esqr
Willm Perkins Esqr 2
William Paston Esqr
Mr Jer. Peirce Surgeon 5
Mr Tho Palmer Surgeon
Mr Thomas Penny
Mr Saml Partenent 2
Mr Michael Payne
Mr James Perryman
Mr John Perry
Mr Perry
Mr Isaac Pillston
Mr Thos Shrine Pritchard
Mr Pritchard
Mr John Pritchard
Mr Thomas Pryn
Mr Samuel Pryn
Mr Robt Parsons Carver
Mr Tho Paulin
Mr Paston
Mr Joseph Phillott
Mr John Parsons

R

Richard Roberts Esq
Doctor Rayner 4
Doctor Roberts
Mr Willm Ring Senr
Mr Willm Ring Junr
Thos Rowland Esqr
Mr John Richards
Mr Johnson Robbinson
Mr Thos Rayner
Mr Wm Ralphs
Mr John Roogue 2
Mr Thos Robbins
Mr Jos. Ross Framemaker
Mr Roger Rogers
Mr Charles Rotten

S

The Honble John Stanup
Sr John Swinbourn Kt
Sim Adolphus Sloper Esq
Robert Smith Esqr
Bryan Salvin Esqr
Revd Mr John Shergold
Revd Mr Sparrow
Rev. Mr Stevenson
Mr Tho Scudamore D.M.
Mr Tho Scudamore Attor
Mr Charles Stone Alderm
Mr Willm Sainsbury 2
Mr Thos Swinbourn
Mr Nath Sellen
Mr John Shurmer
Mr John Sherborne
Mr Joseph Shenring
Mr Jacob Skinner
Mr Nath Skrine
Mr Robert Smith
Mr Willm Spurrell
Mr Willm Smith
Mr James Smith
Mr Hen Smith
Mr Willm Strong
Madam Skrine
Mr Willm Stamps
Mr Gratious Stride 4
Mr Saml Shering
Mrs Eliz. Swallow
Mr Stapylton

T

Sr Robt Throcmorton Bt
John Talbot Esqr Senr
John Talbot Esqr Junr
Thos Tyndal Esqr
Lady Throcmorton
Revd Mr Tho Talbot
Revd Mr Taylor Salwarp
Revd Mr Taylor Leycoch
Revd Mr Taylor Bath
Mr Jno Taylor Watchmaker
Mr Jno Taylor Jeweller
Mr Evan Thomas
Mr John Thomas
Mr William Toll
Mr William Tucker
Mr Nicholas Tucker
Mr Abraham Taylor

V

Revd Mr Vincent
Mr Isaac De Vice
Mr Will Underwood
Widdow Underwood

W

Henry Walters Esqr
John Wood Esqr 10
Hanbury Williams Esq
Francis Woodhouse Esq
John Whittington Esqr 2
Mr Worgan
John Wood Esqr
Mrs Wood
Miss Maria Wood
Mr Jno Wiltshire Senr
Mr John Wiltshire Junr
Mr Walter Wiltshire
Mr Henry Wright Surgn
Mr John Walton
Mr John Wickstead 6
Mr Joseph Williams
Mrs Eliz. Walton
Mr Robt White Innholder
Mr Wooley
Mr John Waters
Mr Walter Wise
Mr Mathias Walter
Mr Willou[illegible]

Y

Mr William York 6
Mr Yerbury

Mr Philip Dutcher Surgeon
Mr Philip Gardner
Mr Jobe Gardner
Mr John Pike
Mr John Thorp
Mr Tho Thorp
Mr Tho Heath
Mr John Sear